CONSUMER SOURCEBOOK

A Directory and Guide to Government Organizations;
Associations, Centers and Institutes; Media Services; Company
and Trademark Information; and Bibliographic Material
Relating to Consumer Topics, Sources of Recourse,
and Advisory Information

Paul Wasserman
Managing Editor

Jean Morgan
Associate Editor

SECOND EDITION

Volume 2
Companies and Trade Names (I-Z)
Selected Bibliography
Indexes

GALE RESEARCH COMPANY • BOOK TOWER • DETROIT, MICHIGAN 48226 • 1978

Editorial Staff Manager: Effie Knight
Editorial Assistants: Elzbieta Danecka-Kaszubski, Steven R. Wasserman

Copyright © 1978 by Paul Wasserman
Library of Congress Catalog Card Number 77-279
ISBN 0-8103-0382-5

TABLE OF CONTENTS

Volume 1

INTRODUCTION v
ORGANIZATION OF THE VOLUME vii
HOW TO USE THIS BOOK ix

SECTION I

GOVERNMENT ORGANIZATIONS

    United States Government 1
    State, County, and City Government Consumer Offices 34
    State Public Utility Commissions 67
    Metropolitan Washington, D.C., Government Offices 72

SECTION II

ASSOCIATIONS, CENTERS, INSTITUTES, ETC.

    Consumer Affairs Organizations 81
    State and Local Voluntary Consumer Organizations 95
    Environment Organizations 121
    Health Organizations 136
    Safety Organizations 180
    Social Welfare Organizations 192
    Legal Organizations 231
    Trade and Professional Organizations 240

SECTION III

MEDIA SERVICES

    Syndicated Newspaper Columns 269
    Newspapers 271
    Radio Network Programs 296
    Radio Stations 297
    Television Network Programs 308
    Television Stations 309

SECTION IV

COMPANIES AND TRADE NAMES (A-H) 319

Volume 2

SECTION IV (continued)

COMPANIES AND TRADE NAMES (I-Z) 801

SECTION V

SELECTED BIBLIOGRAPHY

    Directories, Bibliographies, Abstracts and Indexes 1449
    Books and Pamphlets 1457
    Periodicals and Newsletters 1488
    Continuing Publications Series 1496
    Audiovisual Materials 1502

SECTION VI

INDEXES

    Organization Index 1523
    Personnel Index 1547
    Publication Index 1604

I

I.A.C. INC.
11 West 25th Street
New York, New York 10010
(212) 243-8020

IBC (homes)
See Reasor Corporation

IBM CORPORATION
See International Business Machines Corporation

IBR INC.
462 Penn Street
Yeadon, Pennsylvania 19050

I.C. (men's coats)
See Isaac Cohen & Son Clothes Company Inc.

I.C. (processed foods)
See Marion Foods Corporation

I.D.A. FOOD PRODUCTS INC.
710 West Girard
Philadelphia, Pennsylvania 19123
(215) 925-2490

I.D. COMPANY
230 Fifth Avenue
New York, New York 10001
(212) 683-5600

IDL MANUFACTURING & SALES CORPORATION
730 Garden Street
Carlstadt, New Jersey 07072
(201) 933-5774

I.D.U. PRODUCTS COMPANY
626 North Third Avenue
Wausau, Wisconsin 54401

IGA (groceries)
See Independent Grocers' Alliance Distributing Company

IH (motor vehicles)
See International Harvester Company

I.H.B. INDUSTRIES
57 Willoughby
Brooklyn, New York 11201
(212) 522-2122

IKS IMPORTS INC.
Box 1604
Aspen, Colorado 81611

IML FREIGHT, INC.
(Subsidiary of Gates Rubber Company)
2175 South 3270 West
Salt Lake City, Utah 84110
A.T. Bozich, President
(801) 321-2211

I. M. P. (food products)
See Allied Foods, Inc.

I.M.R. PRODUCTS INC.
8020 West 47th Street
Lyons, Illinois 60534

IMS CORPORATION
3825 Edith Boulevard N.E.
Albuquerque, New Mexico 87107
(505) 345-3644

I. MILLER & SONS COMPANY
See Genesco Inc.

I-P-C (tea bags, instant coffee)
See International Provision Company, Ltd.

IPC INDUSTRIAL PRODUCTS CORPORATION
5 Beekman
New York, New York 10038
(212) 344-4847

ISC WORLDWIDE COMPANY
30 West 26th Street
New York, New York 10010
(212) 675-7400

ITT AETNA CORPORATION
(Subsidiary of ITT Corporation)
7400 South Alton Court
Ingewood, Colorado 80110
David R. Corwin, Chairman of the Board
(303) 773-6774

ITT COMMUNITY DEVELOPMENT CORPORATION
(Subsidiary of ITT Corporation)
430 Park Avenue
New York, New York 10022
Dr. Norman Young, Chairman
(212) 751-7800

ITT CONSUMER SERVICES CORPORATION
320 Park Avenue
New York, New York 10022
James V. Lester, President
(212) 752-6000

ITT CONTINENTAL BAKING COMPANY, INC.
Post Office Box 731
Halstead Avenue
Rye, New York 10580
M. Cabell Woodward, Jr., President
(914) 967-4747
See also Morton Frozen Foods; and Pearson Candy Company

ITT CORPORATION
320 Park Avenue
New York, New York 10022
Harold S. Geneen, President
(212) 752-6000
See also Avis Rent-A-Car System, Inc.; and Scott & Son Company, O.M.

Companies and Trade Names

ITT DECCA MARINE INC.
40 West 57th Street
New York, New York 10016
(212) 397-9500

ITT EXPORT CORPORATION
75 Varick Street
New York, New York 10013
(212) 334-0020

ITT GRINNELL CORPORATION
260 West Exchange
Providence, Rhode Island 02901
(401) 831-7000

ITT GWALTNEY, INC.
Smithfield, Virginia 23430
George A. Brown, President
(804) 357-3131

ITT JABSCO PRODUCTS
1485 Dale Way
Costa Mesa, California 92626
Otto L. Eriksen, President
(714) 545-8251

ITT LAMP
330 Lynnway
Lynn, Massachusetts 01901
Ronald G. Timlin, President
(617) 599-7500

ITT LEVITT & SONS, INC.
Lake Success, New York 11040
Louis E. Fischer, President
(516) 574-4000

ITT LIGHTING FIXTURE
(Division of ITT Corporation)
850 West River Road
Vermillon, Ohio 44089
(216) 967-3131

ITT MARLOW
Box 200
445 Godwin Avenue
Midland Park, New Jersey 07432
Scott R. Schleicher, General
    Manager
(201) 444-6900

ITT ROYAL ELECTRIC
95 Grand Avenue
Pawtucket, Rhode Island 02862
William W. Crossman,
    President
(401) 722-8600

ITT THORP CORPORATION
Thorp, Wisconsin 54771
Robert E. Laws, Chairman of the
    Board
(715) 669-5551

ITT WORLD COMMUNICATIONS,
INC.
67 Broad Street
New York, New York 10004
James R. McNitt, President
(212) 797-3300

IVC (vitamins)
    See Ives Laboratories

I. W. HARPER (whiskey)
    See Schenley Industries, Inc.

I Z INDUSTRIES
Box 735
Acton, Massachusetts 01720

IAVA (cigarettes)
    See G.A. Georgopulo &
    Company, Inc.

IBERIA (Spanish food products)
    See Joseph Victori & Company,
    Inc.

IBERIA AIR LINES OF SPAIN
97-77 Queens Boulevard
Rego Park, New York 11374
Alfredo Fuchs, General Manager
(212) 793-5000

IBIS EXPORT IMPORT COMPANY
800 West End Avenue
New York, New York 10025
(212) 663-0654

IBOLD CIGAR COMPANY, M.
825 Central Avenue
Cincinnati, Ohio 45202
Eugene B. Wilger, President
(513) 721-3135

ICE (menswear)
    See Blye International Ltd.

ICE CAP (seafoods)
    See Danland Seafood Corporation

ICE CASTLE (canned foods)
    See J.W. Windsor Company Ltd.

ICE-MASTER (ice makers, water
chillers)
    See Morris & Associates

ICE 'N WATER (refrigerator)
    See Amana Refrigeration Inc.

ICE-O-DERM (skin-care products)
    See Shulton, Inc.

ICE PAK (reusable ice substitute)
    See Stanbel Inc.

ICEBERG (cigarettes)
    See American Tobacco Company

ICEBERG (food products)
    See Western Dressing Inc.

ICELANDIC (seafood)
    See Coldwater Seafood
    Corporation

ICELANDIC AIRLINES, INC.
630 Fifth Avenue
New York, New York 10020
Sigurdur Helgason, President
(212) 974-2900

Companies and Trade Names

ICELANDIC IMPORTS INC.
1407 Broadway
Room 1914
New York, New York 10018
(212) 239-7235

ICER-ETTES (ice maker)
See Raritan Engineering Company

ICETTE (insulated ice bucket)
See Kromex

ICEWOOL (sports apparel)
See Icelandic Imports Inc.

ICE BAY (seafood)
See Gorton, Slade & Company, Inc.

ICY POINT (canned seafoods)
See New England Fish Company

ICY WATERS (seafoods)
See Ivar Wendt Inc.

ICYCLE (seafood)
See Seward Fisheries

IDAHO CANDY COMPANY
Post Office Box 1217
500 South Eighth Street
Boise, Idaho 83701
(208) 342-5505

IDAHO FIRST NATIONAL BANK
10th and Idaho Streets
Boise, Idaho 83727
Thomas C. Frye, President
(208) 384-7000

IDAHO FRESH-PAK INC.
Post Office Box 302
Lewisville, Idaho 83431

IDAHO FROZEN FOODS
Post Office Box FF
Twin Falls, Idaho 83301

IDAHO FRUIT SALES, INC.
131 Evans Avenue
Caldwell, Idaho 83605

IDAHO-OREGON FRUIT GROWERS INC.
Fruitland, Idaho 83619

IDAHO POWER COMPANY
1220 Idaho Street
Boise, Idaho 83721
Albert Carlsen, President
(208) 345-7210

IDAHO TROUT PROCESSORS COMPANY
1340 Vista Avenue
Boise, Idaho 83705

IDEA DEVELOPMENT COMPANY
113 West Houghton Avenue
Houghton, Michigan 49931

IDEA GROUP, THE
108 Chatsworth Avenue
Larchmont, New York 10538

IDEAL (alarm clocks)
See Acsons Import Company

IDEAL (canned vegetables)
See David Lord, Ltd.

IDEAL (household products)
See Classic Products

IDEAL (processed foods)
See Acme Markets, Inc.

IDEAL (shears, scissors, garden shears, etc.)
See J. Wiss & Sons Company

IDEAL (tools)
See Leisure Group, Inc., Lyman Products

IDEAL BRUSHES INC.
6925 Tujunga Avenue
North Hollywood, California 91609
William G. Van Beckum, President
(213) 877-0401

IDEAL CORPORATION
1000 Pennsylvania Avenue
Brooklyn, New York 11207
John Wenzel, President
(212) 498-4000

IDEAL LADIES UNDERGARMENT COMPANY, INC.
1350 Broadway
New York, New York 10018
(212) 564-6840

IDEAL MACARONI COMPANY
26001 Richmond Road
Bedford Heights, Ohio 44146

IDEAL MUSICAL MERCHANDISE COMPANY
149 Fifth Avenue
New York, New York 10010
(212) 675-5050

IDEAL ORIGINALS
241 Concord Street
Glendale, California 91203

IDEAL RECREATIONAL PRODUCTS
184-10 Jamaica Avenue
Hollis, New York 11423
(212) 454-5000

IDEAL SCHOOL SUPPLY COMPANY
11000 South Lavergne Avenue
Oak Lawn, Illinois 60453
Donald H. McGannon, Chairman
(312) 425-0800

IDEAL STENCIL MACHINE COMPANY
102 Iowa Avenue
Belleville, Illinois 62222
(618) 233-0162

Companies and Trade Names

IDEAL SYSTEM COMPANY
Post Office Box 1030
Berkeley, California 94701
(415) 654-7272

IDEAL TEA PACKING COMPANY, INC.
147 Clinton Road
West Caldwell, New Jersey 07006
(201) 575-0228

IDEAL TOY CORPORATION
200 Fifth Avenue
New York, New York 10010
Lionel Weintraub, President
(212) 675-6100

IDEALS PUBLISHING COMPANY
11315 Watertown Plank
Milwaukee, Wisconsin 53226
James F. Cape, Jr., President
(414) 771-2700

IDEAS INC.
118 Grand Avenue
Laramie, Wyoming 82070

IDEASINC COMPANY
103 Baker Street
Maplewood, New Jersey 07040

IDEAWEST CREATIONS INC.
Post Office Box 2182
Redwood City, California 94064

IDENTICAL FORM, INC.
17 West 60th Street
New York, New York 10023
(212) 586-3708

IDENTICASE (luggage)
See United States Luggage Corporation

IDENTICON CORPORATION
300 Second Avenue
Waltham, Massachusetts 02154
Harvey White, Chairman, President and Treasurer
(617) 890-6600

IDLE HOUR (shoes, rubber footwear, slippers)
See Lidi Trading Corporation

IGLOO CORPORATION
Post Office Box 19322
1001 West Belt Drive
Houston, Texas 77024
James F. Hutchinson, President
(713) 465-2571

IGMOR CRYSTAL LITE CORPORATION
45 West 25th Street
New York, New York 10010
(212) 243-2400

IGNIS USA CORPORATION
1700 Broadway
New York, New York 10019
(212) 586-8860

IITTALA USA LTD.
225 Fifth Avenue
New York, New York 10010
(212) 689-7430

IKE'S CANDY COMPANY
125 West 2700 South
Salt Lake City, Utah 84115
(801) 467-1743

IKON OF AMERICA, INC.
Post Office Box 14
Ann Arbor, Michigan 48107

IL FLORENTINO (wine)
See Joseph E. Seagram & Sons Inc.

IL MIGLIORE (food products)
See NCC Food Corporation

ILCO CORPORATION
35 Daniels Street
Fitchburg, Massachusetts 01420
Aaron M. Fish, President
(617) 343-3011

ILEX OPTICAL COMPANY INC.
690 Portland Avenue
Rochester, New York 14621
Irving Gerb, President and Chief Executive Officer
(716) 342-3200

ILLES COMPANY
5527 Redfield Street
Box 35412
Dallas, Texas 75235
(214) 631-8350

ILLINOIS (window shades)
See Graber Company

ILLINOIS BAKING COMPANY
(Division of Keebler Company)
10839 South Langley Street
Chicago, Illinois 60628
(312) 995-7200

ILLINOIS BELL TELEPHONE COMPANY
(Subsidiary of American Telephone & Telegraph Company)
225 West Randolph Street
Chicago, Illinois 60606
James E. Olson, President
(312) 727-9411

ILLINOIS BRONZE POWDER & PAINT COMPANY
300 East Main Street
Lake Zurich, Illinois 60047
Robert S. Rothschild, President
(312) 438-8201

ILLINOIS-CALIFORNIA EXPRESS, INC.
510 East 51st Avenue
Denver, Colorado 80216
(303) 825-7011

Companies and Trade Names

ILLINOIS CENTRAL GULF
  RAILROAD COMPANY
(Subsidiary of Illinois Central
  Industries Inc.)
233 North Michigan Avenue
Chicago, Illinois 60601
Glen P. Brock, Chairman of the
  Board
(312) 565-1600
  See also Midas-International
    Corporation

ILLINOIS CEREAL MILLS INC.
613 South Jefferson Avenue
Paris, Illinois 61944
W. Frank Wiggins, President and
  Treasurer
(217) 465-5331

ILLINOIS LOCK COMPANY
(Subsidiary of The Eastern Company)
301 West Hintz Road
Wheeling, Illinois 60090
(312) 537-1800

ILLINOIS MOULDING COMPANY
2330 South Western Avenue
Chicago, Illinois 60608
Milton J. Stone, President, Sales
  and Advertising Manager
(312) 847-6240

ILLINOIS POWER COMPANY
500 South 27th Street
Decatur, Illinois 62525
Wendell J. Kelley, President
(217) 428-7711

ILLINOIS SYRUP COMPANY
1301 Estes
Elk Grove Village, Illinois 60007
(312) 593-5700

ILLINOIS TOOL WORKS, INC.
8501 West Higgins Road
Chicago, Illinois 60631
Harold Byron Smith, Jr., President
(312) 693-3040

ILWACO FISH COMPANY
Box 216
Ilwaco, Washington 98624

IMAGE O'YOUTH FOUNDATIONS
  See Milady

IMAGE PRODUCTIONS
Post Office Box 394
Brookline, Massachusetts 02147

IMAGE 3 (decorative clocks)
  See Rodman-Transeuropa, Inc.

IMAGE II (shirts)
  See Cluett, Peabody &
    Company Inc.

IMAGINEERING INC.
510 South 52nd Street
Phoenix, Arizona
(602) 968-7761

IMAGING SYSTEMS
  CORPORATION
1233 Walnut Street
Latrobe, Pennsylvania 15650
(412) 539-8592

IMITATION EDIBLES INC.
1721 Raymond Avenue
Anaheim, California 92801

IMMERSE-A-MATIC (electric fry
pan)
  See Westinghouse Electric
    Corporation

IMP BOATS
Box 321
Iola, Kansas 66749

IMP ORIGINALS INC.
112 West 34th
New York, New York 10001
(212) 563-5510

IMP PRESS
213 Church Street
White Plains, New York 10603

IMPACT (seat belts and safety
products)
  See American Safety Equipment
    Corporation

IMPALA (cigars)
  See Gesty Trading &
    Manufacturing Corporation

IMPECCO LTD.
310 Cedar Lane
Teaneck, New Jersey 07666

IMPERIA FOODS, INC.
24 Harrison
New York, New York 10013
(212) 966-2338

IMPERIAL (band instruments)
  See Boosey & Hawkes Ltd.

IMPERIAL (blended whiskey)
  See Hiram Walker, Inc.

IMPERIAL (electric piano)
  See Castiglione Accordion &
    Distributing Company

IMPERIAL (food products)
  See C.H.B. Foods Inc.

IMPERIAL (freezers)
  See Revco Inc.

IMPERIAL (margarine)
  See Lever Brothers Company

IMPERIAL (scales)
  See Triner Scale &
    Manufacturing Company

IMPERIAL (tobacco)
  See Peterson's Ltd., Inc.

805

Companies and Trade Names

IMPERIAL (tools, hardware, lawn and garden supplies)
See Hardware Supply Company Inc.

IMPERIAL CAMERA CORPORATION
(Subsidiary of Cenco Inc.)
421 North Western Avenue
Chicago, Illinois 60612
Maurice Fischberg, President
(312) 829-2424

IMPERIAL CHEMICAL COMPANY
2412 Eads
Los Angeles, California 90031
(213) 222-6500

IMPERIAL CLOCK COMPANY
616 13th Street
Highland, Illinois 62249

IMPERIAL COMMODITIES CORPORATION
110 Wall Street
New York, New York 10005
Stephen H. Gluck, President
(212) 943-5131

IMPERIAL CRAYON COMPANY
649 Lexington Avenue
Brooklyn, New York 11221
(212) 491-4000

IMPERIAL CRYSTALS & CHINA COMPANY
16 West 23rd Street
New York, New York 10010
(212) 255-5087

IMPERIAL DAX COMPANY
23 Vreeland Street
Lodi, New Jersey 07664

IMPERIAL 500 (dishwashers)
See Whirlpool Corporation

IMPERIAL FOODS
505 Woodland Avenue
Cleveland, Ohio 44115
(216) 241-5324

IMPERIAL '400' NATIONAL INC.
375 Sylvan Avenue
Englewood Cliffs,
New Jersey 07632

IMPERIAL GLASS CORPORATION
Box 250
29th and Belmont Streets
Bellaire, Ohio 43906
(614) 676-3511

IMPERIAL HARDWARE COMPANY
345 Olive Street
El Centro, California 92243
John E. Kearney, President
(714) 353-1120

IMPERIAL HARDWARE CORPORATION
190 Leonia Avenue
Bogota, New Jersey 07603

IMPERIAL HARVEST (canned and frozen vegetables)
See Delta Food Processing Corporation

IMPERIAL HOUSE MOTELS INC.
90 Compark Road
Centerville, Ohio 45459

IMPERIAL INTERNATIONAL CORPORATION
1776 Broadway
New York, New York 10019
(212) 757-1814

IMPERIAL INTERNATIONAL LEARNING CORPORATION
Box 548
Kankakee, Illinois 60901

IMPERIAL K (rechargeable flashlights)
See Garrity Industries, Dynatron Division

IMPERIAL KNIFE ASSOCIATED COMPANIES INC.
1776 Broadway
New York, New York 10019
(212) 757-1814
See also Cutlers International Ltd.

IMPERIAL LEATHER FURNITURE COMPANY
315 West 47th Street
New York, New York 10019
(212) 246-1150

IMPERIAL LINENS INC.
302 Fifth Avenue
New York, New York 10001
(212) 594-0740

IMPERIAL MARINE EQUIPMENT INC.
7601 N.W. 66th Street
Miami, Florida 33166
(305) 592-0073

IMPERIAL METHODS COMPANY
750 South Circle Avenue
Forest Park, Illinois 60130
(312) 366-0835

IMPERIAL MIXTURE (tobacco)
See Comoy's of London

IMPERIAL OIL & GREASE COMPANY
(Division of Beatrice Foods)
10960 Wilshire Boulevard
Los Angeles, California 90024
Robert L. McVicar, President
(213) 478-3577

IMPERIAL 120 (cigarettes)
See G.A. Georgopulo & Company

IMPERIAL PEARL SYNDICATE INC.
600 West Jackson Boulevard
Chicago, Illinois 60606
(312) 332-2005

Companies and Trade Names

IMPERIAL POLISH COMPANY, INC.
State Street
Millersburg, Pennsylvania 17061
Samuel G. Shoop, President
(717) 692-3559

IMPERIAL PRODUCTS, INC.
See K-Tel International, Inc.

IMPERIAL READING COMPANY
1290 Avenue of the Americas
New York, New York 10019
R.M. Kelly, Chairman of the Board
(212) 581-9600

IMPERIAL SKYLOUNGE (campers)
See Gladding-Del-Rey

IMPERIAL STAR (wind and other musical instruments)
See Elger Company

IMPERIAL SUGAR COMPANY
Post Office Box Nine
Sugar Land, Texas 77478
H.L. Williams, President
(713) 494-9181

IMPERIAL TOY COMPANY
2060 East Seventh Street
Los Angeles, California 90021
(213) 489-2100

IMPERIAL UNDERGARMENT COMPANY
16 West 30th Street
New York, New York 10001
(212) 684-3833

IMPETUOUS (cologne, dusting powder, perfume)
See Admiracion (Division of Turner Hall Corporation)

IMPEX (watches)
See Delta Impex Watch Corporation

IMPEX ENTERPRISES LTD.
Post Office Box 445
Reading, Pennsylvania 19603

IMPORT ASSOCIATES
(Division of United States Industries)
212 Fifth Avenue
New York, New York 10016
(212) 532-2851

IMPORT PRODUCT SALES COMPANY
1140 Broadway
New York, New York 10001
(212) 685-4115

IMPORTA LTD.
10 West 33rd Street
New York, New York 10001
(212) 695-0370

IMPORTED FINE PRODUCTS
Post Office Box 6103
Burbank, California 91505

IMPORTED RUG ASSOCIATES, LTD.
919 Third Avenue
New York, New York 10022
(212) 838-1500

IMPORTERS SHOWROOM, INC.
1-D World Trade Center
Houston, Texas 77002

IMPORTS BY PENCO, INC.
810-812 South First Street
New Bedford, Massachusetts 02744

IMPORTS DIRECT
712 South Olive Street
Los Angeles, California 90014
(213) 622-5555

IMPORTS-EXPORTS INTERNATIONAL
Post Office Box 3183
Daly City, California 94015

IMPORTS INTERNATIONAL INC.
1635 17th Street
Denver, Colorado 80202
(303) 573-9474

IMPRESSIONS (shoes)
See Oomphies, Inc.

IMPREVU (perfume, talc, bath oil, etc.)
See Coty (Division of Pfizer, Inc.)

IMPRINT ART PRODUCTS, INC.
14-01 Maple Avenue
Fairlawn, New Jersey 07410
Ted Scarlet, President
(201) 797-2500

IMPTEX INTERNATIONAL CORPORATION
15 Park Row
New York, New York 10038
(212) 233-8020

IMPULSE (shoes)
See Genesco Inc.

IMTRA CORPORATION
151 Mystic Avenue
Medford, Massachusetts 02155
(617) 391-5660

IN-MAC
(Invention Manufacturing Company Inc.)
757 109th Street
Arlington, Texas 76011

IN-SINK-ERATOR
(Division of Emerson Electric Company)
4700 21st Street
Racine, Wisconsin 53406

INCA GOLD (bath oil, hand and body lotion, tanning aid)
See Scruggs Pharmacal Company, Inc.

Companies and Trade Names

INCABLOC CORPORATION
730 Fifth Avenue
New York, New York 10019
(212) 245-7715

INCLINATOR COMPANY OF
   AMERICA
Post Office Box 1557
2200 Paxton Street
Harrisburg, Pennsylvania 17105
(717) 234-8065

INCOTAX SYSTEMS INC.
Guaranty Building
West Palm Beach, Florida 33401

INCREDIBLE SHRINKING TABLE
(folding table)
   See L.E. Mason Company

INDECOR INC.
Post Office Box 4449
9 Depot Street
Milford, Connecticut 06460
(203) 878-8546

INDELICATO FOOD DISTRIBUTORS
107-05 51st Avenue
Corona, New York 11368

INDEPENDENCE CHEMICAL
   COMPANY
North Railroad and Essex Streets
Gloucester City, New Jersey 08030
(609) 456-6100

INDEPENDENT (fruit)
   See Washington Fruit & Produce
   Company

INDEPENDENT CHEMICAL
   CORPORATION
70-30 79th Place
Glendale, New York 11227

INDEPENDENT CORDAGE
   COMPANY INC.
38 Laight Street
New York, New York 10013
(212) 925-4240

INDEPENDENT FUR BROKERS INC.
131 West 30th Street
New York, New York 10001
(212) 594-4737

INDEPENDENT GROCERS ALLI-
   ANCE DISTRIBUTING
   COMPANY
5725 East River
Chicago, Illinois 60631
(312) 693-4520

INDEPENDENT LIFE & ACCIDENT
   INSURANCE COMPANY
233 West Duval Street
Jacksonville, Florida 32202
J.F. Bryan, III, President
(904) 358-5151

INDEPENDENT PRODUCTS
   COMPANY INC.
911 Levick
Philadelphia, Pennsylvania 19111
(215) 722-8616

INDEPENDENT WHOLESALE
   GROCERS
Northern Pacific Industrial Site
Billings, Montana 59101

INDERA MILLS COMPANY
400 South Marshall Street
Winston-Salem,
   North Carolina 27101
F.F. Willingham, President
(919) 723-7311

INDEX MATIC (tape cassette)
   See Memocord

INDEX SALES CORPORATION
350 La Londe Avenue
Addison, Illinois 60101
Donald L. Keenan, President
(312) 543-9144

INDIA (tea)
   See Tea Association of the
   U.S.A.

INDIA CHINA TRADING COMPANY
849 Folsom Street
San Francisco, California 94107
(415) 986-2408

INDIA EMPORIUM INC.
236 Fifth Avenue
New York, New York 10016
(212) 689-9088

INDIA IMPORTS OF RHODE
   ISLAND INC.
Box 1026
Providence, Rhode Island 02901

INDIA JEWELRY & GIFTS, INC.
18 West 45th Street
New York, New York 10036
(212) 867-8559

INDIA NEPAL INC.
233 Fifth Avenue
New York, New York 10016
(212) 481-1315

INDIA ZEPHYR (men's furnishings)
   See Knothe Brothers Company
   Inc.

INDIACRAFTS
Post Office Box 853
1038 Polk
San Francisco, California 94101
(415) 776-8228

INDIAN (motor homes and campers)
   See Winnebago Industries Inc.

INDIAN DEER (fruit)
   See Deerfield Groves Company

INDIAN GEM (groceries)
   See Sales Producers Associates,
   Inc.

INDIAN GRILL (food products)
   See Bluhill-American Products

Companies and Trade Names

INDIAN HEAD (canned fruits and vegetables)
See F.C. Tripi Company Inc.

INDIAN HEAD, INC.
1211 Avenue of the Americas
New York, New York 10036
Richard J. Powers, Chairman of the Board
(212) 764-3100
See also Campax Corporation; and Laurens Glass Company

INDIAN HEAD YARN & THREAD
(Division of Indian Head, Inc.)
Blue Mountain, Alabama 36201
William J. Davis, President
(205) 237-9461

INDIAN INDUSTRIES, INC.
817 Maxwell Avenue
Evansville, Indiana 47717
Robert E. Griffin, President
(812) 426-2281

INDIAN INSTITUTE, INC.
Post Office Box 1911
Williamsburg, Virginia 23185

INDIAN RIDGE CANNING COMPANY, INC.
416 East Park Avenue
Houma, Louisiana 70360
(504) 876-3720

INDIAN SUMMER (enamel cookware)
See Herman Dodge & Son

INDIAN SUMMER INC.
631 East Walnut
Evansville, Indiana 47713
(812) 424-7991

INDIAN TEPEE (tent)
See National Canvas Products Corporation

INDIAN TRAIL CRANBERRY COMPANY
(Division of Green Bay Food Company)
Post Office Box 460
Green Bay, Wisconsin 54305

INDIANA & MICHIGAN ELECTRIC COMPANY
2101 Spy Run Avenue
Fort Wayne, Indiana 46801
(219) 422-3456

INDIANA BELL TELEPHONE COMPANY
(Subsidiary of American Telephone & Telegraph Company)
240 North Meridian Street
Indianapolis, Indiana 46204
John W. Arbuckle, President
(317) 265-2266

INDIANA CASH DRAWER COMPANY
Box 236 T
Shelbyville, Indiana 46176
(317) 398-6643

INDIANA DESK COMPANY
1226 Mill Street
Jasper, Indiana 47546
L. G. Bohnert, President
(812) 482-5727

INDIANA GENERAL CORPORATION
(Division of Electronic Memories & Magnetics Corporation)
405 Elm Street
Valparaiso, Indiana 46383
(219) 462-3131

INDIANA GLASS COMPANY
(Subsidiary of Lancaster Colony Corporation)
717 E Street
Dunkirk, Indiana 47336
J.E. Hooffstetter, President
(317) 768-6789

INDIANA HANDLE COMPANY INC.
Paoli, Indiana 47454
(812) 723-3159

INDIANA KING (food products)
See Ray Brothers and Noble Canning Company Inc.

INDIANA MAID (household products)
See Standard Brush & Broom Company

INDIANA MILLS & MANUFACTURING INC.
120 West Main Street
Carmel, Indiana 46032
(317) 844-1191

INDIANA NATIONAL BANK
1 Indiana Street
Indianapolis, Indiana 46266
J. Fred Risk, Chairman of the Board
(317) 266-6000

INDIANA POPCORN COMPANY
3105 East Jackson
Muncie, Indiana 47303

INDIANAPOLIS MEAT COMPANY, INC.
1725 South East
Indianapolis, Indiana 46225
(317) 632-9388

INDIANAPOLIS POWER & LIGHT COMPANY
25 Monument Circle
Indianapolis, Indiana 46206
Zane G. Todd, President
(317) 635-6868

INDIANA'S FAVORITE (canned foods)
See Eaton Foods Inc.

INDIANA'S FINEST (canned foods)
See Red Gold, Inc.

Companies and Trade Names

INDIRAN, INC.
East Halsey Road
Parsippany, New Jersey 07054

INDIVIDUALITY (carpets)
See Lees Carpets

INDONESIAN TRADING &
TRANSPORT COMPANY (USA)
LTD.
15 Park Row
New York, New York 10038
(212) 349-0590

INDOOR/OUTDOOR (suntan lotion)
See Sea & Ski Corporation

INDUSSA CORPORATION
1212 Avenue of the Americas
New York, New York 10016
Victor Shick, President
(212) 764-0880

INDUSTRIAL BOLT & NUT
COMPANY
191 Fabyan Place
Newark, New Jersey 07112
(201) 374-4300
See also Handi-Man Industries Inc.

INDUSTRIAL COMMERCE
CORPORATION
105-07 Metropolitan Avenue
Forest Hills, New York 11375
(212) 268-5277

INDUSTRIAL DRUG SUPPLIES, INC.
92-61 165th Street
Jamaica, New York 11433
(212) 291-2206

INDUSTRIAL FORMULATIONS
CORPORATION
637 West Montauk Highway
Lindenhurst, New York 11757

INDUSTRIAL GLOVES COMPANY
See Steel Grip Safety Apparel
Company Inc.

INDUSTRIAL MARKETING
(Division of A.E. Staley
Manufacturing Company)
2200 East Eldorado Street
Decatur, Illinois 62525

INDUSTRIAL NATIONAL BANK
OF RHODE ISLAND
111 Westminster Street
Providence, Rhode Island 02903
John J. Cummings, Jr., President
(401) 278-6000

INDUSTRIAL VALLEY BANK &
TRUST COMPANY
IVB Building
Philadelphia, Pennsylvania 19103
Joseph A. Gallagher, President
(215) 561-3000

INDUSTRIES OF THE BLIND INC.
Box 3544
914 West Lee Street
Greensboro, North Carolina 27403
Oliver D. Nelson, President
(919) 274-1591

INDUSTRILINE COMPANY
Lewis Street
Maine, New York 13802

INEXAMER COMMERCIAL
CORPORATION
605 Third Avenue
New York, New York 10036
(212) 986-4240

INFA-LAB INC.
3922 14th Avenue
Brooklyn, New York 11218
(212) 854-6462

INFANETTE (nursery equipment)
See American Hospital Supply
Corporation

INFANSEAT COMPANY
(Division of Questor Corporation)
1709 15th Avenue
Eldora, Iowa 50627

INFANT ITEMS INC.
513 Wayne Place
Fremont, Ohio 43420

INFERNO (men's toiletries)
See Mark II Company

INFINI (women's toiletries)
See Caron Corporation

INFLATABLES (inflatable furniture)
See Modern Air Decor

INFORMATION CONTROL
SYSTEMS, INC.
Post Office Box 281
313 North First
Ann Arbor, Michigan 48107
Ben J. Staal, President
(313) 761-1600

INFRARUB (analgesic ointment)
See Whitehall Laboratories

INGENUE (shoes)
See Genesco, Inc.

INGERSOLL-RAND
200 Chestnut Ridge Road
Woodcliff Lakes, New Jersey 07675
Thomas A. Holmes, President
(201) 573-0123
See also Millers Falls Company;
and Pendleton Tool
Industries, Inc.

INGLEHEART OPERATIONS
General Foods Corporation
1600 First Avenue
Evansville, Indiana 47710

INGLIS FROZEN FOODS
COMPANY, JOHN
(Subsidiary of United Foods Inc.)
305 South Daly
Modesto, California 95351

Companies and Trade Names

INGRAHAM INDUSTRIES
112 Redstone Hill Road
Bristol, Connecticut 06010

INGRAM MANUFACTURING
COMPANY
Post Office Box 2020 TR
San Antonio, Texas 78297
(512) 733-8141

INGRAM PHARMACEUTICAL
COMPANY
202 Green Street
San Francisco, California 94111
(415) 362-1700

INGRAM'S FOOD PRODUCTS
COMPANY
1421 92nd Avenue
Oakland, California 94603

INITIAL-IT, INC.
500 North Dearborn
Chicago, Illinois 60610
(312) 644-2438

INJECTOR (razor blades)
See Schick Safety Razor Company

INK SPECIALTIES COMPANY INC.
1436 East Davis Street
Arlington Heights, Illinois 60005
(312) 394-5494

INLAND
(Division of General Motors
Corporation)
Box 1224
Dayton, Ohio 45401
T.O. Mathues, General Manager
(513) 445-5000

INLAND ALKALOID COMPANY
4200 Laclede Street
Saint Louis, Missouri 63108
(314) 533-9600

INLAND MARINE COMPANY
79 East Jackson
Wilkes-Barre, Pennsylvania 18701

INLAND MILLS COMPANY
Post Office Box 1857
1925 East Grand Avenue
Des Moines, Iowa 50316
Gregory H. Johnson, General
Manager
(515) 266-3121

INLAND STEEL COMPANY
30 West Monroe Street
Chicago, Illinois 60603
(312) 346-0300
See also Scholz Homes, Inc.;
and Schult Mobile Home
Corporation

INLAND VALLEY (food products)
See Rogers Walla Walla Inc.

INLINE PRODUCTS INC.
208 North Lee Street
Alexandria, Virginia 22314

INMONT CORPORATION
1133 Avenue of the Americas
New York, New York 10036
William R. Barrett, Sr., President
and Chief Executive Officer
(212) 765-1100

INN-KEEPER (appliance and
lighting timer)
See AMF/Paragon Electric
Company, Inc.

INN SUPPLIER CORPORATION
265 Wyndcliff Road
Scarsdale, New York 10583

INNER CIRCLE (skin-care products,
makeup)
See Admiracion (Division of
Turner Hall Corporation)

INNERCLEAN COMPANY
500 Egan Avenue
Beaumont, California 92223

INNES CORPORATION, O.G.
10 East 40th Street
New York, New York 10016

INNOGRAPHIC INDUSTRIES, INC.
34-21 56th Street
Woodside, New York 11377

INNOVATION (wall storage
cabinets)
See Continental Imports

INNOVATIVE LEARNING
INTERNATIONAL
Box 1084
Worcester, Massachusetts 01601

INNOVATOR (men's slacks)
See Michaels/Stern & Company
Inc.

INNOVATORS (alarm clocks)
See General Electric Company

INNSBRAU (beer)
See Fuhrmann & Schmidt
Brewing Company

INNSBRUCK (sports apparel)
See Allen-A Company

INSECT-O-CUTOR, INC.
1531 Stone Ridge Drive
Stone Mountain, Georgia 30083
(404) 939-2835

INSIGHTS (men's underwear)
See Hanes Knitwear

INSILCO CORPORATION
1000 Research Parkway
Meriden, Connecticut 06450
Durand B. Blatz, President
(203) 634-2000
See also Enterprise Paint
Manufacturing Company

Companies and Trade Names

INSKIP, INC., J.S.
120 Commerce Road
Carlstadt, New Jersey 07072

INSTA-COM (intercom system)
See Fasco Industries Inc.

INSTA-FOCUS (binoculars)
See Bushnell Optical Company

INSTA-MEDIC (first-aid spray)
See Approved Pharmaceutical Corporation

INSTAMATIC (cameras, projectors, film)
See Eastman Kodak Company

INSTANT BREAKFAST (breakfast drink)
See Carnation Company

INSTANT DO (frozen instant foods)
See Unique Pure Foods Corporation

INSTANT LEARNING (foreign language records)
See Pickwick International Inc.

INSTANT REPLAY (powdered high-energy beverage mix)
See General Foods Corporation

INSTAPIANO (electric pianos)
See J.M. Greene Music Company Ltd.

INSTI-PAK (canned foods)
See Fall River Canning Company

INSTITUTIONAL MART
38 South Broadway
Red Hook, New York 12571

INSTITUTIONAL WHOLESALERS, INC.
Highway 247 North and Liberty Church Road
Macon, Georgia 31206

INSTRUMENT CITY PAD PRODUCTS INC.
3412 California Road
Elkhart, Indiana 46514

INSTRUMENT SYSTEMS CORPORATION
789 Park Avenue
Huntington, New York 11743
B.R. Garrett, President
(516) 549-8200
See also Lightron Corporation; and Lyncoach & Truck Company Inc.

INSTY-PRINTS INC.
417 North Fifth Street
Minneapolis, Minnesota 55401
(612) 335-9573

INSURANCE COMPANY OF NORTH AMERICA
1600 Arch Street
Philadelphia, Pennsylvania 19101
John G. Paine, President
(215) 241-4000

INTECH INC.
1220 Coleman Avenue
Santa Clara, California 95050
Leroy M. Bucker, Chairman, President and Treasurer
(408) 244-0500

INTEGRITY TEXTILES INC.
2460 Coral Street
Philadelphia, Pennsylvania 19125
Otto Gardner, President
(215) 634-3343

INTENSIVE CARE (baby products, skin-care products)
See Chesebrough-Pond's, Inc.

INTER-ATLANTIC FRAME CORPORATION
85 Highland Avenue
Passaic, New Jersey 07055

INTER-COMMUNICATION SYSTEM OF AMERICA
1303 South Michigan Street
Chicago, Illinois 60605
(312) 922-2936

INTER-CONTINENTAL HOTELS
(Subsidiary of Pan American World Airways)
PanAm Building
New York, New York 10017
Paul C. Sheeline, Chairman of the Board
(212) 973-2500

INTER-TECHNICAL GROUP INC., THE
Box 23
Irvington, New York 10533

INTERAMERICAN FRUIT & PRODUCE CORPORATION
19 Rector Street
New York, New York 10009
(212) 344-1062

INTERCHEMICAL CORPORATION
See Inmont Corporation

INTERCO, INC.
See Big Yank Corporation; Florsheim Shoe Company, The; International Shoe Company; and Shainberg Company, Sam

INTERCONTINENTAL INDUSTRIES, INC.
3530 Forest Lane
Dallas, Texas 75234
(214) 358-3326

INTERCONTINENTAL WINES & SPIRITS LTD.
3000 Marcus Avenue
Lake Success, New York 11040

Companies and Trade Names

INTERCRAFT INDUSTRIES
CORPORATION
10 South Riverside Plaza
Chicago, Illinois 60606
Philip Spertus, President
(312) 454-0770

INTERDESIGN CRAFT INC.
Post Office Box 22128
Cleveland, Ohio 44122

INTERGLOBE IMPORTS LTD.
1407 Broadway
New York, New York 10018
(212) 279-1625

INTERIORS & SOUND INC.
1307 Second Avenue
New York, New York 10021
(212) 288-7705

INTERLUX (adhesives, coatings, paints and painting accessories)
See International Paint Company Inc.

INTERMATIC INC.
Intermatic Plaza
Spring Grove, Illinois 60081
James C. Miller, President
(815) 675-2321

INTERMEDIA INC.
20 Grant Avenue
Dumont, New Jersey 07623

INTERNATIONAL (cigarettes)
See Philip Morris Inc.

INTERNATIONAL (cigars)
See Yorkana Cigar Company

INTERNATIONAL (electric heaters, air conditioners, furnaces)
See Intertherm Inc.

INTERNATIONAL (furniture)
See Schnadig Corporation

INTERNATIONAL (luggage)
See Hartmann Luggage Company, Inc.

INTERNATIONAL (trumpets, trombones)
See Boosey & Hawkes Ltd.

INTERNATIONAL AFFILIATES COMPANY
147 West 35th
New York, New York 10001
(212) 868-2025

INTERNATIONAL AIRPORT HOTEL SYSTEM INC.
6225 West Century Boulevard
Los Angeles, California 90045
William Ash, President
(213) 670-9000

INTERNATIONAL APPLIANCE CORPORATION
918-940 Stanley Avenue
Brooklyn, New York 11208
W. Litner, President
(212) 649-8900

INTERNATIONAL ARTWARE CORPORATION
1999 Enterprise Parkway
Cleveland, Ohio 44135
(216) 425-4271

INTERNATIONAL BADGER CORPORATION
730 Clifton Avenue
Clifton, New Jersey 07013
(201) 778-8600

INTERNATIONAL BAKERS SERVICES INC.
52245 United States 31 North
South Bend, Indiana 46637

INTERNATIONAL BENT GLASS INC.
1825 North 19th Street
Saint Louis, Missouri 63106
(314) 621-0600

INTERNATIONAL BOAT COMPANY
1217 Hyde Park Avenue
Hyde Park, Massachusetts 02136

INTERNATIONAL BRANDS
60 Park Place
Newark, New Jersey 07102
(201) 642-3437

INTERNATIONAL BUSINESS MACHINES CORPORATION
Old Orchard Road
Armonk, New York 10504
Frank T. Cary, Chairman
(914) 765-1900

INTERNATIONAL CAMERA CORPORATION
844 West Adams Street
Chicago, Illinois 60607
(312) 421-3230

INTERNATIONAL CANDLE
349 Congress Street
Boston, Massachusetts 02110
(617) 542-7749

INTERNATIONAL CARBON & RIBBON COMPANY INC.
Logan, Ohio 43148

INTERNATIONAL CHEMICAL CORPORATION
720 Fifth Avenue
New York, New York 10019
(212) 397-3300

INTERNATIONAL CHEMICAL LABORATORIES
185 Park Drive
Eastchester, New York 10707

INTERNATIONAL CHINA CORPORATION
41 Madison Avenue
New York, New York 10010
(212) 481-5200

Companies and Trade Names

INTERNATIONAL CLUB (men's toiletries)
See Bishop Industries Inc.

INTERNATIONAL DAIRY QUEEN, INC.
5701 Green Valley Drive
Minneapolis, Minnesota 55437
Harris Cooper, President
(612) 835-3700
See also American Dairy Queen

INTERNATIONAL DESIGNERS GROUP
See IDG-International Designers Group

INTERNATIONAL DESIGNS
70 North Second Street
Philadelphia, Pennsylvania 19106

INTERNATIONAL DIOXCIDE, INC.
7-11 East 44th Street
New York, New York 10017
(212) 987-7460

INTERNATIONAL DISPLAY EQUIPMENT ASSOCIATES
138 Brookline Avenue
Boston, Massachusetts 02215
(617) 266-4332

INTERNATIONAL DUNES COMPAN COMPANY
3395 S.W. Garden View Avenue
Portland, Oregon 97225
(503) 297-1811

INTERNATIONAL EDGE TOOL COMPANY
Post Office Box P
565 Eagle Rock Avenue
Roseland, New Jersey 07068
(201) 228-5300

INTERNATIONAL EDITIONS INC.
See Pace Editions Inc.

INTERNATIONAL FABRICATORS, INC.
941 Oak
Elkhart, Indiana 46514
Richard N. Paulson, President and Chief Executive Officer
(219) 264-1101

INTERNATIONAL FIBER OPTICS
2644 Buckaroo Avenue
Oxnard, California 93030

INTERNATIONAL FOOD PRODUCTS COMPANY
4705 South Christiana Avenue
Chicago, Illinois 60632

INTERNATIONAL FRENCH CAFES INC.
Randhurst Center
Mount Prospect, Illinois 60056

INTERNATIONAL HARVESTER COMPANY
401 North Michigan Avenue
Chicago, Illinois 60611
Brooks McCormick, President
(312) 670-2000

INTERNATIONAL HEATER COMPANY
2007 Teechgrove Place
Utica, New York 13501
Everett S. Glines, President
(315) 724-7111

INTERNATIONAL HOUSE OF PANCAKES
(Division of International Industries)
6837 Lankersham Boulevard
North Hollywood, California 91605
Rod MacPherson, President
(213) 875-0444

INTERNATIONAL IMPORTS COMPANY
152 West 42nd Street
New York, New York 10036
(212) 221-6964

INTERNATIONAL INDUSTRIES, INC.
6464 Sunset Boulevard
Los Angeles, California 90028
Walter McBee, President
(213) 466-8251

INTERNATIONAL LABORATORIES
3000 Bronx Park East
Bronx, New York 10467
(212) 882-2005

INTERNATIONAL LABORATORIES
18 Harvard Street
Rochester, New York 14607
(716) 244-2402

INTERNATIONAL LIGHTING FIXTURES, INC.
86 North Sixth Street
Brooklyn, New York 11211
(212) 388-4260

INTERNATIONAL MANUFACTURING COMPANY
2500 Washington Street
Roxbury, Massachusetts 02119
Morris J. Goldberg, President and Treasurer
(617) 442-9700

INTERNATIONAL MARINE SERVICES
Box 1136
Marina del Rey, California 90291

INTERNATIONAL MARKETING & MANUFACTURING CORPORATION
105 North Columbia Street
Suites 12-13
Chapel Hill, North Carolina 27514

INTERNATIONAL MARKETING SERVICES, INC.
147 East 50th Street
New York, New York 10022
(212) 688-3930

Companies and Trade Names

INTERNATIONAL METAL POLISH
COMPANY
2000 North Meridian
Indianapolis, Indiana 46203
(317) 925-1431

INTERNATIONAL METAL PRODUCTS
(Division of McGraw-Edison
  Company)
500 South 15th Street
Phoenix, Arizona 85034
V.A. Rydberg, President
(602) 254-7101

INTERNATIONAL MILL & TIMBER
COMPANY
1905 South Wenona Avenue
Bay City, Michigan 48706

INTERNATIONAL MILLING
COMPANY
1200 Multifoods Building
Minneapolis, Minnesota 55402
(612) 340-3300
   See also Midland Flour Mills

INTERNATIONAL MINERALS &
CHEMICAL CORPORATION
IMC Plaza
Libertyville, Illinois 60048
Richard A. Lenon, President
(312) 362-8100

INTERNATIONAL MOTEL
CORPORATION N.V.
170 Forbes Road
Braintree, Massachusetts 02184

INTERNATIONAL MULTIFOODS
CORPORATION
1200 Multifoods Building
Minneapolis, Minnesota 55402
Darrell M. Runke, President
(612) 340-3300
   See also Kretschmer Wheat Germ
   Products; and Mister Donut
   of America Inc.

INTERNATIONAL NEEDLE
CORPORATION
1841 Broadway
New York, New York 10023
(212) 582-0080

INTERNATIONAL NICKEL
COMPANY, INC., THE
1 New York Plaza
New York, New York 10004
John H. Page, President and Chief
  Executive Officer
(212) 742-4000

INTERNATIONAL OF
SCHAFFHAUSEN (watches)
   See Henri Stern Watch Agency,
   Inc.

INTERNATIONAL OIL BURNER
COMPANY
   See Intertherm, Inc.

INTERNATIONAL PAINT
COMPANY
17 Battery Place North
New York, New York 10004
Thomas M. Reinhardt, President
(212) 825-0800

INTERNATIONAL PAPER
COMPANY
220 East 42nd Street
New York, New York 10017
Judson Hannigan, President
(212) 490-6000

INTERNATIONAL PAPER
COMPANY
Facelle Company Division
Box 866
Oxnard, California 93030

INTERNATIONAL PAPER
COMPANY
Nonwoven Products Division
40 Ford Road
Denville, New Jersey 07834

INTERNATIONAL PARTS
CORPORATION
4101 West 42nd Place
Chicago, Illinois 60632
(312) 254-4500

INTERNATIONAL PHARMACEUTICAL
CORPORATION
400 Valley Road
Warrington, Pennsylvania 18976

INTERNATIONAL PLAYTEX
CORPORATION
888 Seventh Avenue
New York, New York 10019
Joel E. Smilow, President
(212) 957-3000

INTERNATIONAL PLUMBING
PRODUCTS INC.
195 East Merrick Road
Freeport, New York 11520
(516) 546-1100

INTERNATIONAL POLYGONICS
LTD.
200 East 27th Street
New York, New York 10016
(212) 683-2914

INTERNATIONAL REGISTER
COMPANY
Intermatic Plaza
Spring Grove, Illinois 60081

INTERNATIONAL RUG COMPANY
360 Amsterdam Avenue
New York, New York 10024
(212) 787-9300

INTERNATIONAL SALT COMPANY
(Subsidiary of Akzona, Inc.)
Clarks Summit, Pennsylvania 18411
John L. Ryon, President
(717) 587-5131
   See also Pfeiffer's Foods, Inc.

Companies and Trade Names

INTERNATIONAL SEAWAY
    TRADING CORPORATION
1382 West Ninth Street
Cleveland, Ohio 44113
Eugene Zychick, President
(216) 696-7800

INTERNATIONAL SHOE COMPANY
(Division of Interco Inc.)
1509 Washington Avenue
Saint Louis, Missouri 63166
J. Carl Powers, President
(314) 342-7000

INTERNATIONAL SILVER
    COMPANY
    See Insilco Corporation

INTERNATIONAL SPORTSWEAR
    INC.
1545 Commercial Street
East Weymouth, Massachusetts 02189

INTERNATIONAL TELEPHONE AND
TELEGRAPH
    See ITT Corporation

INTERNATIONAL THREAD COMPANY
    COMPANY INC.
15 West 17th Street
New York, New York 10011
(212) 255-6866

INTERNATIONAL TRADE
    SERVICES INC.
Post Office Box 344-T
Willingboro, New Jersey 08046
(609) 387-3099

INTERNATIONAL VINTAGE WINES
(Division of United Vintners, Inc.)
14 Commerce Drive
Cranford, New Jersey 07016

INTERNATIONAL WAX REFINING
    COMPANY INC.
99 East Hawthorne Avenue
Valley Stream, New York 11580
(516) 561-2500

INTERNATIONAL YOGURT
    COMPANY
628 North Doheny
Los Angeles, California 90069
(213) 274-9917

INTEROCEAN CHEMICAL &
    MINERALS CORPORATION
500 Fifth Avenue
New York, New York 10036
(212) 564-5645

INTERPACE CORPORATION
260 Cherry Hill Road
Parsipanny, New Jersey 07054
William R. Hartman, President
(201) 335-1111
    See also Shenango China; and
        Tiffin Glass Company Inc.

INTERPHOTO CORPORATION
23-20 Jackson Avenue
Long Island City, New York 11101
Daniel A. Porco, President
(212) 392-7600

INTERROYAL CORPORATION
1 Park Avenue
New York, New York 10016
Alexander A. Dadourian, President
(212) 686-3500
    See also Croydon Furniture Inc.

INTERSIL INC.
10900 North Tantau Avenue
Cupertino, California 95014
Frederick R. Adler, Chairman and
    President
(408) 257-5450

INTERSTATE (frozen foods)
    See Chef Reddy Foods
        Corporation

INTERSTATE (hosiery)
    See Burlington Industries Inc.

INTERSTATE
(Division of Royal Industries)
14777 Don Julian Road
City of Industry, California 91744
(213) 968-1443

INTERSTATE BRANDS
    CORPORATION
Post Office Box 1627
12 East Armour Boulevard
Kansas City, Missouri 64141
B.J. Hinkle, President
(816) 561-6600

INTERSTATE DRUG EXCHANGE
Engineers Hill
Plainview, New York 11803

INTERSTATE FOLDING BOX
    COMPANY
South Verity Parkway
Middletown, Ohio 45042
Frank D. Bergstein   President
(513) 422-5434

INTERSTATE FOODS
    CORPORATION
(Division of CFS Continental, Inc.)
3800 South Morgan Street
Chicago, Illinois 60609
Kenneth J. Smargon, President
(312) 254-9400

INTERSTATE GROCER COMPANY,
    INC.
207 Walnut
Helena, Arkansas 72342

INTERSTATE INNS
(Division of Rite-A-Way Industries
    Inc.)
Kimball, Nebraska 69145

INTERSTATE LIFE & ACCIDENT
    INSURANCE COMPANY
(Subsidiary of The Interstate
    Corporation)
Interstate Life Building
Chattanooga, Tennessee 37402
H. Clay Evans Johnson, Chairman
    of the Board
(615) 267-5681

816

Companies and Trade Names

INTERSTATE MILLING COMPANY
620 West Tenth Street
Charlotte, North Carolina 28201
(704) 332-3163

INTERSTATE MOTOR FREIGHT
 SYSTEM
(Subsidiary of Fuqua Industries, Inc.)
134 Grandville Avenue, S.W.
Grand Rapids, Michigan 49502
J.T. Hite, President
(616) 456-5351

INTERSTATE MOTOR INNS
2002 Glenwood Drive
West Monroe, Louisiana 71291

INTERSTATE POWER COMPANY
1000 Main Street
Dubuque, Iowa 52001
M.L. Kapp, Chairman of the Board
(319) 582-5421

INTERSTATE STORES, INC.
111 Eighth Avenue
New York, New York 10011
Herbert B. Siegel, President
(212) 620-4100

INTERTHERM, INC.
3800 Park Avenue
Saint Louis, Missouri 63110
Jordan Heiman, President
(314) 771-2410

INTERTYPE COMPANY
(Division of Harris-Intertype
 Corporation)
215 United States Highway 22
Watchung, New Jersey 07060

INTERWORLD INC.
Post Office Box 2924
Hialeah, Florida 33012

INTERWOVEN ESQUIRE (socks)
 See Kayser-Roth Hosiery
  Company, Inc.

INTIMATE (women's toiletries)
 See Revlon Inc.

INTRADE COMPANY, INC., THE
5 West 31st Street
New York, New York 10001
(212) 244-0660

INTREPID (clothing)
 See Manhattan Shirt Company

INTREPID INC.
Post Office Box 2060
South Bend, Indiana 46615

INTSEL CORPORATION
825 Third Avenue
New York, New York 10022
Walter Wimer, President and Chief
 Operations Officer
(212) 758-5880

INVADER (men's footwear)
 See L.B. Evans' Son Company

INVAL-AID (chairs, traction
equipment, etc. for invalids)
 See Simmons Company, Hausted
  Division

INVENTEX CORPORATION
1901 South 12th Street
Allentown, Pennsylvania 18103

INVENTO PRODUCTS
 CORPORATION
145 East 57th Street
New York, New York 10022
(212) 355-6543

INVENTORS PRODUCTS COMPANY
 See IPCO

INVENTORY GROUP (shelves and
brackets)
 See Shelves Unlimited

INVER HOUSE (Scotch)
 See Continental Distilling
  Corporation

INVESTMENTWEEDS (clothing)
 See Davidow, Inc.

INVICTA PLASTICS
200 Fifth Avenue
New York, New York 10010
(212) 691-0666

INVINCIBLE METAL FURNITURE
 COMPANY
842 South 26th Street
Manitowoc, Wisconsin 54220
John H. Schuette, President
(414) 682-4601

INVITATION (thermal ware)
 See Flambeau Production
  Corporation

IODENT CHEMICAL COMPANY
24901 Northwestern Highway
Suite 314-B
Southfield, Michigan 48075
L. Weisberg, President
(313) 358-1170

IOMEC INC.
3300 Scott Boulevard
Santa Clara, California 94050
Harold E. Eden, President
(408) 246-2950

ION COMPANY, INC., THE
225 East Baker Avenue
Costa Mesa, California 92626
(714) 546-2507

IONA (grocery products)
 See Great Atlantic & Pacific
  Tea Company, Inc.,
  Ann Page Division

Companies and Trade Names

IONA MANUFACTURING
  COMPANY, THE
Regent Street
Manchester, Connecticut 06040
William S. Sleith, President
(203) 643-2111

IONIC INDUSTRIES INC.
128 James Street
Morristown, New Jersey 07960

IORIO (accordions)
  See Syn-Cordion Musical
    Instrument Corporation

IOWA BEEF PROCESSORS, INC.
Dakota City, Nebraska 68731
J. Fred Haigler, President
(402) 494-2061

IOWA ELECTRIC LIGHT & POWER
  COMPANY
Post Office Box 351
Cedar Rapids, Iowa 52406
Duane Arnold, President
(319) 398-4411

IOWA-ILLINOIS GAS & ELECTRIC
  COMPANY
206 East Second Street
Davenport, Iowa 52801
Charles H. Whitmore, Chairman of
  the Board
(319) 326-7111

IOWA PAINT MANUFACTURING
  COMPANY, INC.
17th Street and Grand Avenue
Des Moines, Iowa 50309
Harold Goldman, President
(515) 283-1501

IOWA POWER & LIGHT COMPANY
823 Walnut Street
Des Moines, Iowa 50303
Dwight H. Swanson, President
(515) 281-2800

IOWA PUBLIC SERVICE COMPANY
Orpheum-Electric Building
Sioux City, Iowa 51102
F.W. Griffith, President
(712) 277-7500

IRELAND'S (food products)
  See Great Western Foods
    Company

IRIL (sports apparel)
  See Free Trade Center Inc.

IRIS (food products)
  See Smart & Final Iris Company

IRIS CORPORATION, JOAN
135 Madison Avenue
New York, New York 10016
(212) 683-2300

IRISH CREAM (ale)
  See F. & M. Schaefer
    Brewing Company

IRISH INTERNATIONAL AIRLINES
564 Fifth Avenue
New York, New York 10036
Cathal Mullan, Vice President
(212) 575-8400

IRISH MIST (liqueur)
  See Heublein, Inc.

IRISH SPRING (soap)
  See Colgate-Palmolive Company

IRMA SHORELL, Inc.
509 Madison Avenue
New York, New York 10022
Irma Shorell, President
(212) 355-6747

IRMISCHER COMPANY, A. & P.
939 West North Avenue
Chicago, Illinois 60622
Paul Irmischer, Chairman and
  President
(312) 642-8960

IRON ART COMPANY
Post Office Box 187
Phillipsburg, New Jersey 08865

IRON CITY (beer)
  See Pittsburgh Brewing Company

IRON MOUNTAIN STONEWARE,
  INC.
Laurel Bloomery, Tennessee 37680

IRONEES COMPANY
Front and Venango Streets
Philadelphia, Pennsylvania 19134
David Lehrman, President
(215) 634-6760

IRONMASTER (dry irons)
  See Sunbeam Appliance Company

IRONMASTER (pumps)
  See LFE Corporation, Eastern
    Industries Division

IROQUOIS CHINA COMPANY,
  INC.
Post Office Box 1246
Syracuse, New York 13201

IROQUOIS GAS CORPORATION
(Subsidiary of National Fuel Gas
  Company)
10 Lafayette Square
Buffalo, New York 14203
Louis R. Reif, President
(716) 824-2500

IROQUOIS INDUSTRIES, INC.
41 West Putman
Greenwich, Connecticut 06830
Douglas H. Bradley, Chairman
  of the Board
(203) 661-1490
  See also A-W Brands, Inc.

IRRESISTIBLE (makeup products)
  See Nestle-LeMur Company

Companies and Trade Names

IRVIN INDUSTRIES, INC.
51 Weaver Street
Greenwich, Connecticut 06830
Eugene P. Conese, President
(203) 661-1600

IRVING DREW CORPORATION
Forest Rose and Mulberry
Lancaster, Ohio 43130
George R. Utley, President
(614) 653-4271

IRVING TEXTILE PRODUCTS INC.
Valley Avenue
Atglen, Pennsylvania 19310
(215) 593-5145

IRVING TRUST COMPANY
1 Wall Street
New York, New York 10015
Gordon T. Wallis, Chairman of the Board
(212) 553-1212

IRVINGTON INDUSTRIES, INC.
1407 Broadway
New York, New York 10018
Irving Rothman, President
(212) 675-4500

IRVINWARE COMPANY
24-60 47th Street
Long Island City, New York 11103
(212) 721-7700

IRWIN AUGER BIT COMPANY
92 Grant
Wilmington, Ohio 45177
Ray C. Fischer, President
(513) 382-3811

IRWIN-HODSON COMPANY
2838 S.E. Ninth Avenue
Portland, Oregon 97202
(503) 236-1161

IRWIN-WILLERT COMPANY
4044 Park Avenue
Saint Louis, Missouri 63110
A.W. Willert, Jr., President
(314) 772-2822

IRWIN YACHT & MARINE CORPORATION
13055 49th Street North
Saint Petersburg, Florida 33732

ISAACSON-CARRICO MANUFACTURING COMPANY
Post Office Box 1060
El Campo, Texas 77437

ISBA (sports apparel and accessories)
See Regina Imports

ISCO (cameras)
See Camera Specialty Company Inc.

ISELIN JEFFERSON-WOODSIDE
(Division of Dan River, Inc.)
260 South Pleasantburg Drive
Greenville, South Carolina 29607
(803) 242-5950

ISLAND (seafood)
See Royal River Packing Company

ISLAND CLUB (seafood)
See Continental Seafoods Inc.

ISLAND CREEK COAL COMPANY
(Subsidiary of Occidental Petroleum Corporation)
2355 Harrodsburg Road
Lexington, Kentucky 40511
Stonie Becker, Jr., President
(606) 276-1525

ISLAND EQUIPMENT CORPORATION
1080 East 31st
Hialeah, Florida 33013

ISLAND FARM (canned and frozen vegetables)
See Draper Canning Company

ISLAND HOLIDAYS, LTD.
(Subsidiary of AMFAC, Inc.)
Post Office Box 8519
Honolulu, Hawaii 96815
Myrtle Lee, President
(808) 923-1111

ISLAND SUN COMPANY, INC.
100 Bush
San Francisco, California 94105
(415) 781-1662

ISLANDER YACHTS INC.
777 West 17th Street
Costa Mesa, California 92627
See also Yachtcraft

ISLE OF ALOE, INC.
907 North Winchester Avenue
Chicago, Illinois 60622
(312) 486-2504

ISLE OF GOLD (food products)
See Hawaiian Sun Products Inc.

ISLE O'GOLD (dairy products)
See Eastern Retailer-Owned Grocers Cooperative Inc.

ISMERT-HINCKE MILLING COMPANY
1550 West 28th Street
Kansas City, Missouri 64108
(816) 561-7880

ISO-SEAL (scales)
See John Chatillon & Sons

ISRAEL COCOA INC., A.C.
110 Wall Street
New York, New York 10005
(212) 943-8700

ISRAEL COFFEE COMPANY, INC., A.C.
110 Wall Street
New York, New York 10005
(212) 943-8700

Companies and Trade Names

ISRAEL DESIGNS
70-72 North Second Street
Philadelphia, Pennsylvania 19106
(215) 925-1000

ISRAEL HANDCRAFT
See Handcraft Importing Company

ISRAEL WINES LTD.
745 Fifth Avenue
New York, New York 10022
(212) 421-7866

ISRAELI ART-CRAFT IMPORTING
COMPANY, INC.
527 North Eighth
Philadelphia, Pennsylvania 19123
(215) 925-8121

ISRAELI HANDICRAFTS IMPORTING
COMPANY
94 Canal Street
New York, New York 10002
(212) 966-1319

ISRAELI ORIGINALS
2 Hawthorne Drive
Livingston, New Jersey 07039

ITABIRA INTERNATIONAL
COMPANY LTD.
650 Fifth Avenue
New York, New York 10019
(212) 265-1480

ITALIAN BALM (hand lotion)
See Campana Corporation

ITALIAN CHEF (Italian sauces,
frozen Italian foods)
See Pastorelli Food Products, Inc.

ITALIAN FASHION IMPORTS
(menswear)
See Irving Greenberg

ITALIAN LINE
1 Whitehall Street
New York, New York 10004
Tomaso Busso, General Manager
(212) 797-7000

ITALIAN SWISS COLONY (wine)
See United Vintners, Inc.

ITALIANO (dressing)
See Henri's Food Products
Company Inc.

ITALICS (women's dress shoes)
See Johansen Brothers Shoe
Company, Inc.

ITALWINE IMPORT COMPANY
53-26 211th Street
Bayside, New York 11364

ITALY SPORTSWEAR INC.
1261 Broadway
New York, New York 10001
(212) 684-3283

ITEK BUSINESS PRODUCTS
(Division of Itek Corporation)
1001 Jefferson Road
Rochester, New York 14603
Robert Wolf, President
(716) 244-5600

ITEK CORPORATION
10 Maguire Road
Lexington, Massachusetts 02173
Franklin A. Lindsey, Chairman of
the Board
(617) 276-2000
See also Univis, Inc.

ITHACA GUN COMPANY, INC.
Terrace Hill
Ithaca, New York 14850
John W. Park, President
(607) 273-0200

ITKIN (carriages)
See Carriage Corner Ltd.

ITOH & COMPANY (AMERICA)
INC., C.
270 Park Avenue
New York, New York 10017
Tai Mizuki, President
(212) 953-5200

ITOMAN (U.S.A.) INC.
1211 Avenue of the Americas
New York, New York 10036
(212) 869-1700

IVALDI COMPANY, INC., B.
68 Jay Street
Brooklyn, New York 11201
(212) 858-7333

IVANHOE (lighting fixtures)
See Miller Company

IVANHOE (tobacco)
See American Tobacco Company

IVERS & POND (pianos)
See Aeolian Corporation

IVERSEN BAKING COMPANY
1753 North Tripp Avenue
Chicago, Illinois 60639
(312) 489-1330

IVERSON CYCLE CORPORATION
Yaphank and Patchogue Roads
Medford, New York 11763
(516) 924-4000

IVES LABORATORIES, INC.
(Subsidiary of American Home
Products Corporation)
685 Third Avenue
New York, New York 10017
Sidney Elston, President
(212) 986-1000

IVO COMPANY
7340 Washington Avenue South
Minneapolis, Minnesota 55435
(612) 941-1432

IVORY (soap)
See Procter & Gamble Company

IVY CORPORATION
23 Fairfield Place
West Caldwell, New Jersey 07006

IVY INTERNATIONAL LTD.
119 West 40th Street
New York, New York 10018
(212) 354-1300

IZOD (men's sportswear)
See David Crystal, Inc.

Companies and Trade Names

J

J. & C. FISCHER (pianos)
See Aeolian Corporation

J & F (men's suits)
See The Joseph & Feiss Company

J. & G. MEAKIN
41 Madison Avenue
New York, New York 10010
(212) 532-5950

J & M (shoes for men)
See Genesco, Inc.

J A (cigars)
See Parodi Cigar Corporation

JAF MOTORS, INC.
1371-73 Lower Broadway
Schenectady, New York 12306

J-B (watchbands)
See Jacoby-Bender, Inc.

J.B. & W. MANUFACTURING
CORPORATION
240 Madison Avenue
New York, New York 10016
(212) 686-4268

JBI INC.
Benson Manor G-Four
Jenkintown, Pennsylvania 19046

JBL (stereo equipment)
See James B. Lansing Sound Inc.

JBL
3249 Casitas Avenue
Los Angeles, California 90039
Arnold Wolf, President
(213) 665-4101

J-BIRD (frozen poultry)
See J.D. Jewell Inc.

JB'S BIG BOY FAMILY
RESTAURANTS, INC.
1010 West 2610 South
Salt Lake City, Utah 84119
Jack M. Broberg, President
(801) 487-4211

J.E.K. INDUSTRIES INC.
811 East Maple
Mora, Minnesota 55051
(612) 679-3811

JFD ELECTRONICS CORPORATION
(Subsidiary of Riker-Maxson
Corporation)
15th Avenue at 62nd Street
Brooklyn, New York 11219
Albert Finkel, President
(212) 331-1000

JFG COFFEE COMPANY
(Subsidiary of William B. Reily &
Company)
200 West Jackson Avenue, N.W.
Knoxville, Tennessee 37901
Ed L. Johnson, President
(615) 546-2120

J5 (portable typewriter)
See Adler Business Machines Inc.

JHC (menswear)
See Joseph H. Cohen & Sons
(Division of Rapid-American
Corporation)

J.I. (frozen foods)
See John Inglis Frozen Foods
Company

JI (jute carpet backing, yarn,
specialty products, twine, flax,
and cotton goods)
See Jute Industries, Ltd. of
New York

JIB LABORATORY
1437 South 49th Avenue
Cicero, Illinois 60650

J.J.J. MERCHANDISE
CORPORATION
15 West 26th Street
New York, New York 10010
(212) 686-6416

J. M. (automobile clocks and fire
extinguishers)
See Johns-Manville Corporation

JMR ENTERPRISES, INC.
1026 Main Street
Worcester, Massachusetts 01603

J. M. RUBIN & SONS
51 East Fulton Street
Gloversville, New York 12078

JP (coffee, tea, soup, and hot-
chocolate products)
See Rudd-Melikian, Inc.

JPM (groceries)
See J.P. Michael Company

JP'S (cigar)
See Joseph P. Manning
Company, Inc.

J S & A NATIONAL SALES GROUP
(Subsidiary of The J S & A Group
Inc.)
4200 Dundee Road
Northbrook, Illinois 60062

J.S. RESEARCH LABORATORY
14 South Street
Westboro, Massachusetts 01581

J.S.T. ENTERPRISES, LTD.
230 Fifth Avenue
New York, New York 10001
(212) 473-1350

Companies and Trade Names

JVC AMERICA, INC.
50-35 56th Road
Maspeth, New York 11378
M. Furuta, President
(212) 392-7100

J.W. DANT (whiskey)
   See Schenley Industries, Inc.

JA-RU SALES COMPANY INC.
2950 Powers Avenue
Jacksonville, Florida 32207

JABBERWOCKS (shoes)
   See Curtis-Stephens-Embry
       Company

JABERT PHARMACAL COMPANY
69 Hampton Place
Freeport, New York 11520

JABSCO (marine equipment)
   See ITT Jabsco Products

JAC-O-NET (hair accessories)
   See Hairnet Corporation of
       America

JACAMAN GIFT COMPANY, INC.
1212 San Eduardo Avenue
Laredo, Texas 78040

JACARANDA FASHIONS LTD.
389 Fifth Avenue
New York, New York 10016
(212) 725-8550

JACK & JILL TOGS, INC.
112 West 34th Street
New York, New York 10001
Irving Tucker, President
(212) 594-9500

JACK AND THE BEAN STALK
(canned foods)
   See Agripac, Inc.

JACK AUGUST ENTERPRISES INC.
2155 Columbus Avenue
Springfield, Massachusetts 01104

JACK DANIEL DISTILLERY
(Subsidiary of Brown-Forman
   Distillers Corporation)
Lynchburg, Tennessee 37352
Winton E. Smith, Chairman of the
   Board
(615) 759-7142

JACK FROST (sugar)
   See National Sugar Refining
       Company

JACK-IN-THE-BOX (fast-food
service)
   See Foodmaker, Inc.

JACK NICKLAUS (golf shoes)
   See Kayser-Roth Shoes, Inc.

JACK NICKLAUS (menswear)
   See Hart Schaffner & Marx

JACK-O-LANTERN (canned foods)
   See Joan of Arc Company

JACK SPRAT (groceries)
   See Sales Producers Associates,
       Inc.

JACK SPRATT WOODWIND SHOP
199 South Beach Avenue
Old Greenwich, Connecticut 06870

JACK WINTER, INC.
8100 North Teutonia Avenue
Milwaukee, Wisconsin 53223
Jack A. Winter, President
(414) 354-4100

JACKEL FARMS & COLD STORAGE
Post Office Box Eight
La Grangeville, New York 12540

JACKES-EVANS MANUFACTURING
   COMPANY
11737 Administration Drive
Saint Louis, Missouri 63141
A.M. Cornwell, President
(314) 567-4600

JACKS BEAN COMPANY
Fort Morgan, Colorado 80701

JACKSON & CHURCH COMPANY
Post Office Box 73
Au Gres, Michigan 48703
(517) 876-2191

JACKSON & PERKINS COMPANY
Medford, Oregon 97501
David H. Holmes, Chairman of the
   Board
(503) 779-2121

JACKSON BREWING COMPANY
620 Decatur
New Orleans, Louisiana 70130
(504) 523-7461

JACKSON-EDWARDS BAG
   CORPORATION
Bonwood Industrial Park
Jackson, Tennessee 38301

JACKSON ELECTRONIC
   CORPORATION
(Subsidiary of IEA Corporation)
1515 S.E. 16th Street
Fort Lauderdale, Florida 33316

JACKSON FURNITURE
   CORPORATION
600 Mobile Avenue
Jackson, Tennessee 38301

JACKSON MANUFACTURING
   COMPANY
Department T
South Cameron and Lochiel Road
Harrisburg, Pennsylvania 17105
(717) 234-6291

Companies and Trade Names

JACKSON-MITCHELL
PHARMACEUTICALS
Box 4787
Santa Barbara, California 93103

JACKSON RECREATION PRODUCTS
1100 Hamon Avenue
Winter Park, Florida 32789

JACKSON ROPE CORPORATION
Ninth and Oley Streets
Reading, Pennsylvania 19604
John C. Sauer, President
(215) 376-7671

JACKSON VITRIFIED CHINA
COMPANY
1132 Kane Concourse
Miami Beach, Florida 33154
Philip R. Distillator, President
(305) 865-0377

JACLO INC.
162 Carlton Avenue
Brooklyn, New York 11205
(212) 852-3906

JACLYN, INC.
635 59th Street
West New York, New Jersey 07093
Abe Ginsburg, President
(201) 868-9400

JACOB ASSOCIATES, INC.
West Chester, Pennsylvania 19380
(215) 686-1502

JACOBI ASSOCIATES INC.
1385 York Avenue
New York, New York 10021
(212) 861-8851

JACOBS (scales)
See Detecto Scales, Inc.

JACOBS CIGAR COMPANY
Red Lion, Pennsylvania 17356

JACOBS COMPANY INC., PHIL
1331 Oak
Kansas City, Missouri 64106
(816) 471-6377

JACOBS CORPORATION, THE
5735 Arapahoe Avenue
Boulder, Colorado 80303

JACOBS, MALCOLM & BURTT
2001 Jerrold Avenue
San Francisco, California 94124
(415) 285-0400

JACOBS MANUFACTURING
COMPANY
(Subsidiary of The Chicago
Pneumatic Tool Company)
1 Jacobs Road
West Hartford, Connecticut 06110
F. W. Mohney, President
(203) 233-4411

JACOBSEN MANUFACTURING
COMPANY
(Subsidiary of Allegheny Ludlum
Industries, Inc.)
1721 Packard Avenue
Racine, Wisconsin 53403
Neal D. Crane, President
(414) 637-6711

JACOBSON (sports accessories and
equipment)
See Silva Company

JACOBSON CANDY COMPANY
Box 842
1640 East Court
Des Moines, Iowa 50304
(515) 266-5746

JACOBSON STORES, INC.
1200 North West Avenue
Jackson, Michigan 49202
Nathan Rosenfeld, Chairman of the
Board
(517) 787-3600

JACOBY-BENDER, INC.
62-10 Northern Boulevard
Woodside, New York 11377
Bernard Kanter, Vice President
(212) 335-2000

JACQUELINE (shoes)
See Wohl Shoe Company

JACQUELINE COCHRAN, INC.
630 Fifth Avenue
New York, New York 10020
(212) 489-2430

JACQUELINE LEIGH (skin- and
hair-care products, deodorant, etc.)
See Pharmaceutics Company

JACQUES RENEE (cosmetics and
accessories)
See International Cosmetic
Company

JACQUES RICHE (menswear)
See Barney Sampson Company,
Ltd.

JACQUIN ET CIE, INC., CHARLES
2633 Trenton Avenue
Philadelphia, Pennsylvania 19125
Elsie Cooper, President
(215) 323-8100

JACUZZI BROTHERS, INC.
11511 New Benton Highway
Little Rock, Arkansas 72203
Raymond E. Horan, President
(501) 562-1234

JACUZZI RESEARCH, INC.
1440 San Pablo Avenue
Berkeley, California 94702
Peter L. Kosta, President
(415) 526-0334

JADE EAST (men's toiletries)
See Swank Inc.

Companies and Trade Names

JADEE (guitars)
　See White Eagle Rawhide Manufacturing

JADOW AND SONS INC., B.
53 West 23rd Street
New York, New York 10010
(212) 741-9500

JAEGER-LE COULTRE WATCHES, INC.
(Division of Longines-Wittnauer Watch Company)
Box 2500
New Rochelle, New York 10810
Leonard Solomon, Vice President
(914) 576-1000

JAFFA QUEEN (food products)
　See Prince Edward Food Products Ltd.

JAGENBURG, INC., E.R.
130 Cuttermill Road
Great Neck, New York 11022

JAGUAR (cigarettes)
　See Stephano Brothers

JAGUAR (men's toiletries)
　See Yardley of London, Inc.

JAK-PAK INC.
Box 374
236 North Water Street
Milwaukee, Wisconsin 53202
(414) 272-1461

JAKA HAM COMPANY, INC.
350 Campus Drive
Somerset, New Jersey 08873
J. Blom-Jensec, President
(201) 469-4444

JAKL, VICTOR
130-138 South Central Avenue
Elmsford, New York 10523

JAMAICA (cigars)
　See Faber, Coe & Gregg, Inc.

JAMAR DRUGS INC.
910 26th Avenue E
Tuscaloosa, Alabama 35401

JAMBOREE (food products)
　See Fruitcrest Corporation

JAMCO COMPANY
158 Carroll Street
Brooklyn, New York 11231

JAMECO METAL PRODUCTS COMPANY
94-34 158th Street
Jamaica, New York 11433
(212) 297-2056

JAMES (bicycles)
　See AMF, Inc.

JAMES & GEORGE STODART LTD.
(Scotch whiskey)
　See Hiram Walker, Inc.

JAMES E. PEPPER SCOTTISH
(whiskey)
　See Schenley Industries, Inc.

JAMES FOXE (Canadian whiskey)
　See Seagram Distillers Company

JAMES INDUSTRIES INC.
Post Office Box 230
Beaver Street Extension
Hollidaysburg, Pennsylvania 16648
(814) 695-5681

JAMES METAL PRODUCTS COMPANY INC.
2905-29 North Oakley Avenue
Chicago, Illinois 60618
Marshall J. Hollander, President
(312) 472-2611

JAMES RIVER PAPER COMPANY
Post Office Box 2218
Tredegar Street East
Richmond, Virginia 23219
(804) 644-5411

JAMES RIVER SMITHFIELD (meat products, etc.)
　See Smithfield Ham & Products Company, Inc.

JAMESTOWN LOUNGE COMPANY
40 Winsor Street
Jamestown, New York 14701
(716) 485-1154

JAMESTOWN PAINT & VARNISH COMPANY
108 Main Street
Jamestown, Pennsylvania 16134
(415) 932-3101

JAMESWAY
(Division of Butler Manufacturing Company)
104 West Milwaukee Avenue
Fort Atkinson, Wisconsin 53538

JAMESWAY CORPORATION
40 Hartz Way
Secaucus, New Jersey 07094
Herbert Fischer, President
(201) 348-8200

JAMIE '08 (Scotch)
　See Twenty One Brands, Inc.

JAMIESON-MCKAMES, INC.
3227 Morganford Road
Saint Louis, Missouri 63116
(314) 776-3434

JAMIESON PHARMACAL COMPANY, INC.
640 Palisade Avenue
Englewood Cliffs, New Jersey 07632

825

Companies and Trade Names

JAMISON BEDDING, INC.
Nashville Highway
Franklin, Tennessee 37064
(615) 794-6611

JAMOL LABORATORIES, INC.
13 Ackeman Avenue
Emerson, New Jersey 07630

JAMY INC.
1 Jamy Lane
Kingston, Pennsylvania 18704
Robert M. Prashker, President
(717) 287-9647

JAN KRIML (violins, violas, basses)
See Targ & Dinner Inc.

JAN-MAR INDUSTRIES INC.
Post Office Box 314
Hillsdale, New Jersey 07642

JAN OPTICAL COMPANY INC.
351 Scally Place
Westbury, New York 11590
(516) 334-5002

JAN-U-WINE FOODS, INC.
Box 2121
Los Angeles, California 90051
Jaisohn Hyan, President
(213) 773-1311

JANALYN LABORATORIES INC.
85 East Worcester Street
Worcester, Massachusetts 01604

JANBRA INC.
7325 Radford Avenue
North Hollywood, California 91605
(213) 765-2068

JANCO (groceries)
See Janney-Marshall Company, Inc.

JANCYN MANUFACTURING CORPORATION
155 Oval Drive
Central Islip, New York 11722
(516) 231-5000

JANDALS (outdoor shoes)
See Jantzen, Inc.

JANE COLBY, INC.
1411 Broadway
New York, New York 10018
Hy Dubin, President
(212) 279-2858

JANE LOGAN (ice cream)
See Abbotts Dairies, Inc.

JANE PARKER (baked goods)
See The Great Atlantic & Pacific Tea Company

JANEL MANUFACTURING COMPANY
3402 N.E. 12th Avenue
Fort Lauderdale, Florida 33307

JANEX CORPORATION
65 Chestnut Street
Red Bank, New Jersey 07701

JANITOR IN A DRUM (industrial-strength cleaner)
See Texize Chemicals, Inc.

JANITROL (space-heating equipment, etc.)
See Midland-Ross Corporation

JANNEY-MARSHALL COMPANY
401 Princess Ann Street
Fredericksburg, Virginia 22401

JANPE (footwear)
See Otto Gmeiner

JANSZEN (stereo equipment)
See Electronic Industries Inc.

JANTIMATE, INC.
360 Park Avenue
Worcester, Massachusetts 01610

JANTZEN, INC.
Post Office Box 3001
Portland, Oregon 97208
Robert Roth, President
(503) 238-5000

JANTZEN INC.
Intimate Apparel Division
666 Fifth Avenue
New York, New York 10019
(212) 221-2740

JANUARY & WOOD COMPANY
237 West Second Street
Maysville, Kentucky 41056
W.C. Adair, President
(606) 564-3301

JANUS PLASTICS COMPANY, INC.
Box 3335
Inglewood, California 90304

JAPAN AIR LINES/AMERICAN REGION
655 Fifth Avenue
JAL Building
New York, New York 10022
Kichi Ito, Vice President
(212) 758-8850

JAPAN FOOD CORPORATION
11-31 31st Avenue
Long Island City, New York 11106
(212) 721-6820

JAQUET (cosmetics)
See Houbigant, Inc.

JAR-IT DRILL COMPANY
(Division of Pic Corporation)
30 Canfield Street
Orange, New Jersey 07050

JARD ENGINEERING COMPANY
Elm and Center Streets
North Wales, Pennsylvania 19454

Companies and Trade Names

JARDE (oboes and English horns)
See Ardsley Musical Instrument Corporation

JARED HOLT PLYMOUTH
(Division of Emhart Corporation)
107 Broad
Albany, New York 12202
(518) 463-1101

JARET'S MANUFACTURING COMPANY, INC.
640 Broadway
New York, New York 10012
(212) 777-6174

JARI CORPORATION
733 First Street N.E.
Little Falls, Minnesota 56345

JARNOW & COMPANY, INC.
27-02 41st Avenue
Long Island City, New York 11101
(212) 784-4315

JARU ART PRODUCTS INC.
10117 West Jefferson Boulevard
Culver City, California 90230

JARVINEN (sports accessories and equipment)
See Trak Inc.

JARVIS COMPANY, JANE
2452 N.W. 78th Street
Miami, Florida 33147
(305) 691-0142

JASCO CHEMICAL CORPORATION
Post Office Drawer J
Mountain View, California 94040
(415) 968-6005

JASCO PRODUCTS INC.
50 Webster Avenue
New Rochelle, New York 10801

JASON (scissors and shears)
See John Ahlbin & Sons Inc.

JASON ART SERVICE
342 Madison Avenue
New York, New York 10017
(212) 986-5484

JASON DAIRY PRODUCTS COMPANY
9204 Ditmas Avenue
Brooklyn, New York 11236
(212) 498-1881

JASON EMPIRE INC.
9200 Cody
Overland Park, Kansas 66214
Richard M. Levin, President
(913) 888-0220

JASPER CORPORATION
Box 360
Jasper, Indiana 47546
Thomas L. Habig, President
(812) 482-1600

JASPER ENGINE & TRANSMISSION EXCHANGE
Highway 231 South
Jasper, Indiana 47546

JASPER TABLE COMPANY INC.
East 15th Street
Jasper, Indiana 47546
Omer Sturm, President
(812) 482-6121

JASPER WARE (urns, vases, bowls, etc.)
See Josiah Wedgwood & Sons Inc.

JATO (all-purpose spray cleaner)
See Lehn & Fink Products Company

JAVELINS (cigars)
See House of Windsor, Inc.

JAX (beer)
See Pearl Brewing Company

JAXWAY WHOLESALE SUPPLY COMPANY INC.
9309 North Major
Morton Grove, Illinois 60053

JAY-ARR SLIMWEAR, INC.
3 Quincy Street
Norwalk, Connecticut 06851

JAY-CEE COMPANY
Main Street S.W.
Lancaster, Massachusetts 01523

JAY COMPANY, THE
167-23 Union Turnpike
Flushing, New York 11366

JAY-DEE PRODUCTS INC.
Box 997
Stamford, Connecticut 06904

JAY DRUG COMPANY
See Cook-United, Jay Drug Division

JAY FOOD LABORATORIES INC.
713 Jefferson Avenue
Kenilworth, New Jersey 07033

JAY GARMENT COMPANY, INC.
Fifth and South Meridian Street
Portland, Indiana 47371
R. Dwight Young, Chairman of the Board
(317) 726-7151

JAY INC., EDWIN
20 Cooper Square
New York, New York 10003
(212) 674-8300

JAY PRODUCTS, D.
Post Office Box 797
55 Clifton
Newark, New Jersey 07101
(201) 243-6886

Companies and Trade Names

JAY SHOE MANUFACTURING
COMPANY
179 Lincoln
Boston, Massachusetts 02111
(617) 426-1303

JAYEM SALES CORPORATION
5214 First Avenue
Brooklyn, New York 11232
(212) 492-3232

JAYMAR-RUBY, INC.
5000 South Ohio Street
Michigan City, Indiana 46360
Burton B. Ruby, President
(219) 879-7341

JAYS FOODS, INC.
825 East 99th Street
Chicago, Illinois 60628
Leonard Japp, Sr., President
(312) 731-8400

JAYVEE BRAND INC.
113 Foothills Road
Lake Oswego, Oregon 97034

JE REVIENS (cologne, perfume, toiletries, etc.)
See Parfums Worth Corporation

JEALOUSY (colognes, perfumes, bath oil etc.)
See Del Laboratories, Inc.

JEAN CARTIER (band instruments)
See Targ & Dinner Inc.

JEAN CASANAVE (men's furnishings)
See Varsity Pajamas

JEAN D'ALBRET (toiletries)
See Morton Norwich Products, Inc.

JEAN NATE, INC.
40 West 57th Street
New York, New York 10019
(212) 489-4500

JEAN PATOU, INC.
(Subsidiary of Borden, Inc.)
680 Fifth Avenue
New York, New York 10019
Richard Lockman, President

JEAN PIERRE PRODUCTS, INC.
19750 Magellan Drive
Los Angeles, California
(213) 770-2367

JEAN SHRIMPTON (cosmetics)
See Yardley of London, Inc.

JEAN VERNON, INC.
South Sterley and Catherine Streets
Shillington, Pennsylvania 19607

JEANIE (sportswear)
See Blue Bell, Inc.

JEANMARIE GALLERY
896 Third Avenue
New York, New York 10022
(212) 355-3620

JEANNE DURRELL (dresses)
See Lorch-Westway Corporation

JEANNE LANVIN (hosiery)
See Picturesque Hosiery Company

JEANNE WEST (dresses)
See Smoler Brothers, Inc.

JEANNETTE (canned vegetables)
See David Lord, Ltd.

JEANNETTE CORPORATION
Bullitt Avenue
Jeannette, Pennsylvania 15644
Mark B. Silverberg, President
(412) 523-6501
See also Brookpark-Royalon Inc.; Royal China, Inc.; and Royal Imports Inc.

JEBAVY-SORENSON ORCHARD
COMPANY
Box 280
Manistee, Michigan 49660

JEEP CORPORATION
(Subsidiary of American Motors Corporation)
Box 903
Toledo, Ohio 43610
(419) 244-2861

JEFF EASE (menswear)
See Lord Jeff Knitting Company Inc.

JEFFERSON (tools, hardware, paints, etc.)
See Moore-Handley Inc.

JEFFERSON (whiskey)
See National Distillers & Chemical Corporation

JEFFERSON ELECTRIC COMPANY
910 25th Avenue
Bellwood, Illinois 60104
William C. Anderson, President
(312) 626-7700

JEFFERSON GLASS, INC.
Post Office Box 395
Ceredo, West Virginia 25507

JEFFERSON INDUSTRIES INC.
2100 South Marshall Boulevard
Chicago, Illinois 60623
(312) 277-6100

JEFFERSON MANUFACTURING
COMPANY
2433 North Orianna Street
Philadelphia, Pennsylvania 19133
(215) 425-0595

JEFFERSON SCREW CORPORATION
691 Broadway
New York, New York 10012
(212) 777-8400

Companies and Trade Names

JEFFERSON STANDARD LIFE
  INSURANCE COMPANY
Post Office Box 21008
Greensboro, North Carolina 27420
Howard Holderness, Chairman of
  the Board
(919) 378-2011

JEFFERSON STORES, INC.
15800 N.W. 13th Avenue
Miami, Florida 33169
Harry Mufson, Chairman of the
  Board
(305) 625-7541

JEFFORDS INDUSTRIES INC.
3143 East Roosevelt
Phoenix, Arizona 85008
(602) 275-1311

JEFFREY MARTIN, INC.
1020 Commerce Avenue
Union, New Jersey 07083
Martin Himmel, President
(201) 687-4000

JEFSTEEL BUSINESS EQUIPMENT
  CORPORATION
1345 Halsey Street
Ridgewood, New York 11227
(212) 497-4004

JEL SERT COMPANY, THE
Post Office Box 261
59th and Conde Streets
West Chicago, Illinois 60185
(312) 921-8477

JELINEK (wines and brandy)
  See Imported Brands, Inc.

JELL-A-TEEN (desserts)
  See McCormick & Company,
    Schilling Division

JELL-O (desserts)
  See General Foods Corporation

JELLIFF CORPORATION
345 Pequot Road
Southport, Connecticut 06490
Halsted W. Wheeler, President and
  Treasurer
(203) 259-1615

JEM CORPORATION
Post Office Box 554
Marion, Virginia 24354

JEN MUSICAL PRODUCTS
  COMPANY
Box 282, South Station
Yonkers, New York 10705

JEN PRODUCTS COMPANY
Bethel, Vermont 05032
Myron Jenner, President
(802) 234-9409

JENCO (dairy products)
  See Carthage Creamery Company

JENISON & COMPANY, H.S.
Wenatchee, Washington 98816

JENKINS LABORATORIES, INC.
17-19 Wall Street
Auburn, New York 13021
(315) 252-3561

JENKINS SPIRITS CORPORATION,
  LTD.
Manchester, New Hampshire 03101

JENKINTOWN METAL PRODUCTS
  INC.
Box 185
Jenkintown, Pennsylvania 19046

JENN-AIR CORPORATION
3030 Shadeland
Indianapolis, Indiana 46226
Louis J. Jenn, Chairman of the
  Board
(317) 545-2271
  See also Connor Engineering &
    Manufacturing Inc.

JENNIE-O FOODS, INC.
2505 Willmar Avenue, S.W.
Willmar, Minnesota 56201
Charles B. Olson, President
(612) 235-2622

JENNISON COMPANY, W.J.
Box D
Mankato, Minnesota 56001

JENNISON-WRIGHT CORPORATION
Post Office Box 691
Toledo, Ohio 43694
Carleton G. Carver, President
(419) 382-3411

JENNY JUG (coolers)
  See Dillon Beck Manufacturing
    Company

JENNY LEE INC.
115 West Plato Boulevard
Saint Paul, Minnesota 55107
(612) 227-8277

JENO'S INC.
525 Lake Avenue, South
Duluth, Minnesota 55802
Donald G. Wirtanen, President
(218) 727-8871

JENSEN AUTO CONSOLES
300 Fay Avenue
Addison, Illinois 60101

JENSEN CANDY, INC., W.F.
33 North Main Street
Logan, Utah 84321

JENSEN-FISCHER INC.
524 Cypress Avenue
Hermosa Beach, California 90254

JENSEN INC., GEORGE
(Subsidiary of Kenton Corporation)
601 Madison Avenue
New York, New York 10022
(212) 935-2800

Companies and Trade Names

JENSEN MANUFACTURING
   COMPANY INC.
700 Arlington Avenue
Jeannette, Pennsylvania 15644
(412) 523-8281

JENSEN MARINE
235 Fischer
Costa Mesa, California 92626
(714) 540-3440

JENSEN OF DENMARK INC.,
   SVEND
1010 Boston Post Road
Rye, New York 10580

JENSEN SOUND LABORATORIES
4310 Trans World Road
Schiller Park, Illinois 60176
Jerry Kalov, General Manager
(312) 671-5680

JEPPSON GALLERIES INC.
9004 Honeybee Lane
Bethesda Maryland 20034
(301) 365-7400

JER MARAI, INC.
18625 East Railroad Avenue
City of Industry, California 91745

JERANT COMPANY, INC., THE
2345 Alaska Avenue
El Segundo, California 90245

JERED INDUSTRIES INC.
1300 South Coolidge Road
Birmingham, Michigan 48008
E.R. Davies, President
(313) 647-1200

JERGENS COMPANY, THE
   ANDREW
(Subsidiary of American Brands,
   Inc.)
2535 Spring Grove
Cincinnati, Ohio 45214
K.C. Schuster, President
(513) 421-1400

JERI-JO KNITWEAR INC.
234 West 39th Street
New York, New York 10018
(212) 354-0660

JERIE & COMPANY
1001 Avenue of the Americas
New York, New York 10018
(212) 279-0550

JERO (canned food)
   See Queensway Canning
   Company

JERO-BLACK PRODUCTS
   COMPANY
(Subsidiary of Sunstar Foods, Inc.)
118 Iowa Avenue
Streator, Illinois 61364
George Keister, Chairman of the
   Board
(815) 672-3127

JERRELL COMPANY, S.T.
2511 Second
West Birmingham, Alabama 35204

JERRICO, INC.
1949 Nicholasville Road
Lexington, Kentucky 40503
Warren W. Rosenthal, President
(606) 276-2525

JERROLD ELECTRONICS
   CORPORATION
200 Witmar Road
Horsham, Pennsylvania 19044
John Malone, President
(215) 925-9870

JERRY COOLER (insulated cooler/
   chest)
   See Dillon-Beck Manufacturing
   Company

JERRY JOLLY'S TIMESAVERS
788 West Eighth Avenue
Denver, Colorado 80204
(303) 893-3000

JERRY'S (meat products)
   See Indianapolis Meat Company,
   Inc.

JERRY'S DRIVE-IN RESTAURANTS
   See Jerrico Inc.

JERRY'S HICKORY PRODUCTS
1800 Washington
Paducah, Kentucky 42001

JERRY'S PIZZA KING INC.
507 Avenue R, S.E.
Winter Haven, Florida 33880

JERSEY CENTRAL POWER &
   LIGHT COMPANY
Madison at Punchbowl
Morristown, New Jersey 07960
S. Bartnoff, President
(201) 539-6111

JERSEY GOLD (ice cream, milk)
   See National Dairy Products
   Corporation

JERSEY'S BEST (seafood)
   See Riggin & Robbins Inc.

JESPERSEN SCANDINAVIAN
   IMPORTS, EJNER
527 West Seventh Street
Los Angeles, California 90014
(213) 622-7272

JESSE FRENCH (pianos)
   See Selmer (Division of the
   Maganavox Company)

JESSICA (food products)
   See M. Polaner & Son Inc.

JESSO (canned foods)
   See Viking Foods Inc.

JESSON COMPANY, H.L.
507 South Spring Street
Los Angeles, California 90013

830

Companies and Trade Names

JET (cigar, cigarette, and pipe lighters)
See Beattie Jet Products Inc.

JET (snowmobiles)
See Sno Jet

JET (sports accessories and equipment)
See Free Trade Center Inc.

JET-AER CORPORATION
100 Sixth Avenue
Paterson, New Jersey 07524
Henry Friedman President
(201) 278-8300

JET AERATOR (faucet attachment)
See Melard Manufacturing Company

JET-AIR (tires)
See The General Tire & Rubber Company

JET-AWAY (handbags)
See Rockland Leather Goods Corporation

JET-DRI (paint)
See Luminall Paints, Inc.

JET-LITE (flashlights)
See Bantam-Lite, Inc.

JET SET (wine)
See United Vintners, Inc.

JET SPRAY CORPORATION
195 Bear Hill Road
Waltham, Massachusetts 02154
Richard C. Jacobs, Vice President
(617) 890-7700

JET-X CORPORATION
2550 West Second Avenue
Denver, Colorado 80217
Anthony R. Tyrone, Chairman of the Board
(303) 936-2347

JETAWAY (luggage)
See Platt Luggage Inc.

JETCO, INC.
1133 Barranca Drive
El Paso, Texas 79935
John E. Turner, President
(915) 591-6661

JETSTAR (typewriters)
See Royal Typewriter Company

JETSTREAM (lawn and garden sprinklers, nozzles, and other accessories)
See Melnor Industries

JETTACHE (luggage)
See Stebco Products Corporation

JEUNET (bicycle)
See Beacon Cycle & Supply Company

JEWEL (salad oil)
See Swift Edible Oil Company (Division of Swift & Company)

JEWEL COMPANIES, INC.
5725 East River Road
Chicago, Illinois 60631
Weston R. Christopherson, President
(312) 693-6000
See also Brigham's; and Star Market Company

JEWEL-TONE (handbags and wastebaskets)
See General Crafts Corporation

JEWELITE SIGN COMPANY
13 East 31st Street
New York, New York 10016
(212) 683-4474

JEWELL, INC., J.D.
311 North Green
Gainesville, Georgia 30501
R. Carl Chandler, President
(404) 534-3511

JEWETT & SHERMAN COMPANY
Post Office Box 218
500 South Prairee Avenue
Waukesha, Wisconsin 53186
Robert C. Brunner, President

JEZEBEL (cigarettes)
See G.A. Georgopulo & Company, Inc.

JEZEBEL (foundation garments)
See Renee of Hollywood

JIANAS BROTHERS PACKING COMPANY
2533 Southwest Boulevard
Kansas City, Missouri 64108
(816) 421-2880

JIB LABORATORY
1437 South 49th Avenue
Cicero, Illinois 60650

JICO (venetian glass)
See Jordans Importing Company, Inc.

JIF (peanut butter)
See Procter & Gamble Company

JIFFCO (frozen vegetables)
See John Inglis Frozen Foods Company

JIFFIES (plastic garbage bags)
See Flex-O-Glass Inc.

Companies and Trade Names

JIFFIES (slippers)
See Kayser Roth Hosiery Company, Inc.

JIFFY (baking mixes)
See Chelsea Milling Company

JIFFY (toothache drops)
See Block Drug Company, Inc.

JIFFY DRYER (dryer)
See Alger Creations, Inc.

JIFFY ENTERPRISES, INC.
3100 Admiral Wilson Boulevard
Pennsauken, New Jersey 08109
(609) 665-9292

JIFFY FOODS CORPORATION
Route 286
Saltsburg, Pennsylvania 15681
Bernard J. Erenstein, President
(412) 639-3551

JIFFY FRY/FOREMOST FOODS
Crookston, Minnesota 56716

JIFFY MANUFACTURING COMPANY, INC.
360 Florence Avenue
Hillside, New Jersey 07205
(201) 688-9200

JIFFY PLASTICS MANUFACTURING COMPANY
810 South Maumee Street
Tecumseh, Michigan 49286
(313) 423-8311

JIFFY POP (popcorn)
See American Home Foods

JIFFY PRODUCTS
100 United States Highway Number 22
Green Brook, New Jersey 08812
(201) 968-4060

JIFFY-WRAP (plastic wrap)
See Flex-O-Glass Inc.

JIFOAM (cleaner)
See Clorox Company

JILL'S (food products)
See Yakima Valley Grape Producers

JIM BEAM (bourbon)
See James B. Beam Distilling Company

JIM DANDY (tractors)
See Engineering Products Company

JIM DANDY COMPANY, THE
(Subsidiary of Savannah Foods & Industries, Inc.)
Post Office Box 10687
Birmingham, Alabama 35202
Robert E. Rogers, President
(205) 322-4461

JIM DANT (Kentucky bourbon)
See Schenley Industries, Inc.

JIM DUNLOP COMPANY
Post Office Box 821
Benicia, California 94510

JIM GRIFFITH COMPANY
Box 99188
132 Clement
San Francisco, California 94109
(415) 668-8586

JIM WALTER CORPORATION
1500 North Dale Mabry Highway
Tampa, Florida 33607
Joe B. Cordell, President
(813) 876-4811

JIMBLL'S (restaurant franchise)
See Mister Softee Inc.

JIMBO (canned and frozen foods)
See Village Kitchen Foods, Inc.

JIMBO'S JUMBOS, INC.
Edenton, North Carolina 27932

JIMMY DEAN MEAT COMPANY, INC.
1341 Mockingbird Lane
Dallas, Texas 75247
Jimmy Dean, President
(214) 638-1190

JIM'S BOATYARD
144 Ocean Avenue
Amityville, New York 11701

JO-AN IMPORTS
17530 Ventura Boulevard
Encino, California 91316

JO ANN (wines)
See Schenley Industries, Inc.

JO-BI FARMS (canned and frozen foods)
See Blue Star Foods, Inc. (Iowa)

JO-HAN MODELS INC.
17255 Moran Avenue
Detroit, Michigan 48212
(313) 366-2230

JO JUNIOR (dresses)
See Parkland of Dallas, Inc.

JO MAR PRODUCTS INC.
12702 N.E. 124th Street
Kirkland, Washington 98033

JOAN CANDY COMPANY
Box 160 B
Bush, Louisiana 70431

JOAN IRIS CORPORATION
135 Madison Avenue
New York, New York 10016
(212) 683-2300

Companies and Trade Names

JOAN OF ARC
2231 West Altorfer Drive
Peoria, Illinois 61614
Robert H. Truitt, President and
  Chief Executive Officer
(309) 692-1020

JOANNA WESTERN MILLS
  COMPANY
2141 South Jefferson Street
Chicago, Illinois 60616
William F. Uecker, President and
  Chief Executive Officer
(312) 226-3232

JOANNE LINGERIE COMPANY,
  INC.
38 East 32 Street
New York, New York 10016
(212) 689-8555

JOBBERS CANDY COMPANY, INC.
203 Washington Street
Bristol, Virginia 24201
(703) 669-2721

JOBLOT AUTOMOTIVE INC.
98-11 211th Street
Queens Village, New York 11429

JOCKEY CLUB (cigarettes)
  See G.A. Georgopulo &
    Company

JOCKEY CLUB (whiskey)
  See National Distillers &
    Chemical Corporation

JOCKEY INTERNATIONAL, INC.
2300 60th Street
Kenosha, Wisconsin 53140
R.V. Jensen, President
(414) 658-8111

JODEE BRA COMPANY
200 Madison Avenue
New York, New York 10016
(212) 689-3005

JODI'S PRIDE (groceries)
  See Leon Supply Company

JODY (boys' wear)
  See Elder Manufacturing
    Company

JOEL MANUFACTURING
  COMPANY
2249 San Gabriel Boulevard
Rosemead, California 91770

JOEL PRODUCTS
4722 Woodman Avenue
Sherman Oaks, California 91403

JOELEE IMPORTING COMPANY,
  INC.
7201 Adam Street
North Bergen, New Jersey 07049

JOELI WINE DISTRIBUTORS, INC.
560 Bercik Street
Elizabeth New Jersey 07201

JOFFE CANDY COMPANY, INC.
206 South 13th Avenue
Mount Vernon New York 10550
(914) 668-3236

JOGS (men's footwear)
  See Kayser-Roth Shoes Inc.

JOHANN WINTER (violins, violas,
bass viols, cellos)
  See Maxwell Meyers Inc.

JOHANSEN BROTHERS SHOE
  COMPANY, INC.
1136 Washington Boulevard
Saint Louis, Missouri 63101
Paul E. Johansen, Sr., President
(314) 231-0700

JOHN ALDEN (groceries)
  See Laurans-Standard Grocery
    Company, Inc.

JOHN BEGG (Scotch whiskey)
  See Somerset Importers, Ltd.

JOHN C. ROBERTS (shoes)
  See International Shoe Company

JOHN COLLINS (gin)
  See Gooderham & Worts, Ltd.

JOHN COMPANY, ROBERT
King Manor Drive
King of Prussia, Pennsylvania 19406

JOHN DAVID COMPANY, INC.
360 Park Avenue
Worcester, Massachusetts 01610

JOHN DEERE (power mowers,
tractors, snowmobiles, etc.)
  See Deere & Company

JOHN DORY BOAT WORKS INC.
14 West Meadow Lane
Stony Brook, New York 11790

JOHN E. LUCEY (shoes)
  See George E. Keith Company

JOHN-EE-SEAT CORPORATION
47-25 27th Street
Long Island City, New York 11101
(212) 392-6868

JOHN FURNITURE CORPORATION,
  B.P.
(Division of Consolidated Foods
  Corporation)
5200 S.W. Macadam Avenue
Portland, Oregon 97201
R.H. Nyssen, President
(503) 223-6263

JOHN HANCOCK MUTUAL LIFE
  INSURANCE COMPANY
200 Berkeley Street
Boston, Massachusetts 02116
Gerhard D. Bleicken, Chairman
  of the Board
(617) 421-6000

Companies and Trade Names

JOHN HENRY COMPANY, THE
Post Office Box 1410
Lansing, Michigan 48904

JOHN MEYER APPAREL
(Division of Hatco Group)
1 Connecticut Avenue
Norwich, Connecticut 06360
John Meyer, President
(203) 889-3801

JOHN POWER (Irish whiskey)
See McKesson Liquor Company

JOHN ROLFE (tobacco)
See House of Edgeworth

JOHN SEYMOUR LTD. (silver-plate holloware)
See Eisenberg-Lozano, Inc.

JOHN WARD (shoes)
See Genesco Inc.

JOHNNY CARSON (footwear)
See Kayser-Roth Shoes, Inc.

JOHNNY CARSON (men's apparel)
See Van Baalen, Heilbrun & Company

JOHNNY CARSON (men's neckwear)
See Superba Cravats Inc.

JOHNNY CARSON APPAREL, INC.
(Subsidiary of M. Wile & Company)
77 Goodell Street
Buffalo, New York 14203
Johnny Carson, President
(716) 252-8280

JOHNNY HARRIS FAMOUS BAR-B-CUE SAUCE COMPANY
2802 Wicklow
Savannah, Georgia 31404

JOHNNY WALKER (Scotch)
See Somerset Importers, Ltd.

JOHN'S CHILI PARLOR
37 West Columbia Street
Logansport, Indiana 46947

JOHNS ENTERPRISES, ROBERT A.
4929 Lighthouse Drive
Racine, Wisconsin 53402

JOHNS-MANVILLE CORPORATION
Post Office Box 5108
Greenwood Plaza
Denver, Colorado 80217
W. Richard Goodwin, President
(303) 770-1000

JOHNS-MANVILLE FIBER GLASS, INC.
(Division of Johns-Manville Corporation)
Ken Caryl Ranch
Denver, Colorado 80217
H.P. Hahn, General Manager
(303) 979-1000

JOHNSON
(Division of Peter Paul, Inc.)
4500 West Belmont
Chicago, Illinois 60641

JOHNSON & JOHNSON
501 George Street
New Brunswick, New Jersey 08901
Joan Stanley, Director, Consumer Services
(201) 524-6768
   See also Cellulose Products Corporation; Chicopee Mills, Inc.; Codman & Shurtleff Inc.; Graham Manufacturing Company; Ortho Pharmaceutical Corporation; Permacel; Personal Products Company; and Pitman-Moore Inc.

JOHNSON & SON, INC., S.C.
1525 Howe Street
Racine, Wisconsin 53403
William K. Eastham, President
(414) 554-2000
   See also Northern Laboratories

JOHNSON BOAT WORKS
White Bear, Minnesota 55110
(612) 429-7229

JOHNSON BROTHERS
107-13 171st Street
Jamaica, New York 11433
(212) 526-7544

JOHNSON CANDY COMPANY
Kenton, Ohio 43326

JOHNSON CANDY CORPORATION
42 Jaques Street
Somerville, Massachusetts 02145
(617) 776-6255

JOHNSON-CARPER FURNITURE COMPANY
Hollins Road
Roanoke, Virginia 24012

JOHNSON CHAIR COMPANY, THE
Lackawanna Street
Wayland, New York 14572

JOHNSON COMPANY, C.J.
Post Office Box 379
East Main and Durkee Streets
Bradford, Pennsylvania 16701
(814) 368-7515

JOHNSON COMPANY, E.F.
299 Tenth Avenue, S.W.
Waseca, Minnesota 56093
Richard E. Horner, President
(507) 835-2050

JOHNSON COMPANY, H.A.
155 North Beacon Street
Boston, Massachusetts 02135
(617) 254-1400

JOHNSON COMPANY, H.T.
6 Glenville Terrace
Boston, Massachusetts 02134
(617) 783-1397

Companies and Trade Names

JOHNSON COMPANY, HOWARD
222 Forbes Road
Braintree, Massachusetts 02184

JOHNSON COMPANY INC.,
C. SHERMAN
Main Street
Middle Haddam, Connecticut 06456

JOHNSON COMPANY, L.H.
649 South Olive Street
Los Angeles, California 90014
(213) 458-8994

JOHNSON COMPANY, MATT
1114 Fourth Street
Devils Lake, North Dakota 58301

JOHNSON COMPANY, S.T.
940 Arlington
Oakland, California 94608
(415) 652-6000

JOHNSON INC., PALMER
61 Michigan Street
Sturgeon Bay, Wisconsin 54235

JOHNSON MACHINE COMPANY,
THE CARLYLE
52 Main
Manchester, Connecticut 06040
(203) 643-1531

JOHNSON MANUFACTURING
COMPANY, NESTOR
(Division of Servotronics, Inc.)
1900 North Springfield Avenue
Chicago, Illinois 60647
(312) 252-1120

JOHNSON MANUFACTURING
COMPANY, PAT
Post Office Box 4210-T
700 South Ewing
Dallas, Texas 75203
(214) 943-7494

JOHNSON-MARCH
CORPORATION, THE
3018 Market
Philadelphia, Pennsylvania 19104
(215) 222-1411
See also Waverly Mineral
Products Company

JOHNSON MOTOR LINES, INC.
2426 North Graham Street
Charlotte, North Carolina 28206
William L. Nahrgang, President
(704) 376-1561

JOHNSON NUT COMPANY
1515 South Fifth Street
Hopkins, Minnesota 55343
(612) 938-3511

JOHNSON OUTBOARDS
(Division of Outboard Marine
Corporation)
Sea-Horse Drive
Waukegan, Illinois 60085
Carl Ruesch, General Manager
(312) 689-6200

JOHNSON PET-DOR INC.
Post Office Box 643
Northridge, California 91324

JOHNSON PRODUCTS COMPANY
531 North Front
Memphis, Tennessee 38101
(901) 525-7497

JOHNSON PRODUCTS COMPANY,
INC.
8522 South LaFayette Avenue
Chicago, Illinois 60620
George E. Johnson, President
(312) 483-4100

JOHNSON PUBLISHING
COMPANY
820 South Michigan Avenue
Chicago, Illinois 60605
(312) 786-7600

JOHNSON REELS COMPANY
1531 Madison Avenue
Mankato, Minnesota 56001
Paul A. Mulready, General Manager
(507) 345-4623

JOHNSON STEEL & WIRE
COMPANY INC.
(Subsidiary of Wheeling-Pittsburgh
Steel Corporation)
53 Wiser Avenue
Worcester, Massachusetts 01607
R.E. Lauterbach, President
(617) 756-8301

JOHNSON, STEPHENS &
SHINKLE COMPANY
11710 Administration Drive
Saint Louis, Missouri 63141
(314) 567-4720

JOHNSONIAN GUIDE-STEPS
(men's shoes)
See Endicott-Johnson Company

JOHNSON'S (foot soap, spray)
See Combe, Inc.

JOHNSON'S GROCERY PRODUCTS,
HOWARD
97-20 Springfield Boulevard
Queens Village New York 11429

JOHNSTON & MURPHY (shoes)
See Genesco Inc.

JOHNSTON COMPANY, INC.,
ROBERT A.
(Subsidiary of Ward Foods Company)
4023 West National Avenue
Milwaukee, Wisconsin 53201
(414) 645-3780

JOHNSTON CORPORATION,
GASTON
24-64 45th Street
Long Island City, New York 11103
(212) 932-0200

Companies and Trade Names

JOHNSTON LAWN MOWER (power lawn mowers)
See Jacobsen Manufacturing Company

JOHNSTON PIE COMPANY
4201 Long Beach Boulevard
Long Beach, California 90807

JOHNSTON'S SNOW WHITE PRODUCTS
Post Office Box 644
Glen Echo, Maryland 20768

JOHNSVILLE (electric clocks)
See Franklin Instrument Company

JOKINEN, TEPPO K.
Post Office Box 4163
Stamford, Connecticut 06907

JOLEN, INC.
25 Walls Drive
Fairfield, Connecticut 06430

JOLENE (fashion shoes)
See Tober-Saifer Shoe Manufacturing Company, Inc.

JOLI GREETING CARD COMPANY
2520 West Irving Park
Chicago, Illinois 60618
(312) 588-3770

JOLLY FOAM (jugs, coolers)
See Hamilton-Skotch Corporation

JOLLY GOOD (canned foods)
See Krier Preserving Company

JOLLY GOOD (food products)
See Crown Food Products Inc.

JOLLY JOAN (grain products--flour, cereal, etc.)
See Sam Wylde Flour Company

JOLLY KING (restaurants)
See Royal Inns of America Inc.

JOLLY RANCHER CANDIES, INC.
5060 Ward Road
Wheatridge, Colorado 80033

JOMAC INC.
863 Easton Road
Warrington, Pennsylvania 18976
H. Howard Colehower, President
(215) 343-0800

JON MCCAULEY (dresses)
See R. Lowenbaum Manufacturing Company

JONAS BROTHERS, INC.
1037 Broadway
Denver, Colorado 80203
(303) 255-4813

JONATHAN HAAGER (leather goods)
See Hagerstown Leather Goods Company

JONATHAN LOGAN INC.
3901 Liberty Avenue
North Bergen, New Jersey 07047
Richard J. Schwartz, President and Chief Executive Officer
(212) 695-4440

JONATHAN RICHARDS KNITTING MILLS
719 Walnut
Bolder, Colorado 80302

JONES & LAUGHLIN STEEL CORPORATION
3 Gateway Center
Pittsburgh, Pennsylvania 15230
Thomas C. Graham, President
(412) 565-4224

JONES BOX CORPORATION, JESSE
Post Office Box 5120
2250 Butler
Philadelphia, Pennsylvania 19141
(215) 744-7900

JONES BROTHERS CANNING COMPANY
Box 401
Greer, South Carolina 29651

JONES CHEMICALS, INC.
4151 Sunny Sol Boulevard
Caledonia New York 14423
(716) 538-2311

JONES CORSETS, STANLEY
See Figureplane

JONES DAIRY FARM
Fort Atkinson, Wisconsin 53538
E.C. Jones, President
(414) 563-2431

JONES ENTERPRISES, PARNELLI
20555 Earl Street
Torrance, California 90503

JONES FARMS INC., S.M.
Box 421
Bayboro, North Carolina 28515

JONES, INC., HAROLD W.
25 Broadway
New York, New York 10004
(212) 943-3252

JONES LEISURE PRODUCTS LTD.
2731 South Broadway
Los Angeles, California 90007
(213) 749-3231

JONES MOTOR COMPANY
Spring City, Pennsylvania 19475
C.B. Hoffberger, President
(215) 948-7900

Companies and Trade Names

JONES NEW YORK
1411 Broadway
New York, New York 10018
(212) 221-4660

JONES PUBLISHING COMPANY
Post Office Box 568
Dyersburg, Tennessee 38024

JONES TRUCK LINES, INC.
610 East Emma Avenue
Springdale, Arkansas 72764
Harvey Jones, Chairman of the
  Board
(501) 751-4806

JONES-ZYLON, INC.
Box 158
Center and Woods Streets
West Lafayette, Ohio 43845
(614) 545-6341

JONFISHER (boats)
  See Sears, Roebuck & Company

JONKERS (diamonds)
  See Harry Winston, Inc.

JONNA INDUSTRIES, INC.
320 Fifth Avenue
New York, New York 10001
(212) 947-8778

JONNY (cigarettes)
  See G.A. Georgopulo &
    Company, Inc.

JONTEEL (toiletries)
  See Dart Industries

JORDAN (canned and frozen
vegetables)
  See Sherman Brothers Canning
    Company

JORDAN COMPANY, W.A.
Galesburg, Illinois 61401

JORDAN INDUSTRIES, INC.
3030 N.W. 75th
Miami, Florida 33147
(305) 691-5172

JORDAN LABORATORIES, INC.
15490 N.W. Seventh Avenue
Miami, Florida 33169
(305) 685-5001

JORDAN MARSH COMPANY
1501 Biscayne Boulevard
Miami, Florida 33139
W.S. Rubin, President
(305) 377-1911

JORDAN'S (bread and cake)
  See American Bakeries Company

JORDON MARSH COMPANY
450 Washington Street
Boston, Massachusetts 02158
Robert G. Hoye, President
(617) 426-9000

JOSAM MANUFACTURING
  COMPANY
Corymbo Road
Michigan City, Indiana 46360
Lewis H. Polster, President
(219) 872-5531

JOSE CUERVO (tequila)
  See Heublein, Inc.

JOSEPH & FEISS COMPANY, THE
(Division of Phillips Van Heusen)
2149 West 53rd
Cleveland, Ohio 44113
Bert G. Cox, President
(216) 961-6000
  See also Cricketeer, Inc.

JOSEPH GARNEAU COMPANY,
INC., THE
  See Brown-Forman Distillers
    Corporation

JOSEPH, GEORGE F.
5201 Orchard Drive
Yakima, Washington 98901

JOSEPH'S (cheese, horseradish,
pickles)
  See Keller Food Company

JOSHUAS KOSHER (processed foods)
  See Blue Ridge Farms

JOSKE'S OF TEXAS
(Affiliation of Allied Stores
  Corporation)
Alamo Plaza
San Antonio, Texas 78206
William W. McCormick, President
(512) 227-4343

JOSLIN MANUFACTURING
  COMPANY, A.D.
123 Lake Drive
Manistee, Michigan 49660
(616) 723-3581

JOSTENS, INC.
5501 Norman Center Drive
Minneapolis, Minnesota 55437
H. William Lurton, President
(612) 830-3300

JOURDAN & SONS, B.G.S.
Star Route Box 61
Darlington, Maryland 21034

JOURNAL COMPANY, THE
333 West State Street
Milwaukee, Wisconsin 53203
Donald B. Albert, President
(414) 224-2000

JOUVET (French wine)
  See Munson Shaw Company

JOVAN, INC.
875 North Michigan Avenue
Chicago, Illinois 60611
Richard E. Meyer, President
(312) 787-2929

Companies and Trade Names

JOY (cat and dog food)
See Best Feeds & Farm Supplies, Inc.

JOY (liquid detergent)
See Procter & Gamble Company

JOY OPTICAL COMPANY
Department DRG
73 Fifth Avenue
New York, New York 10003
(212) 929-5807

JOYCE (shoes)
See United States Shoe Corporation

JOYCE FILING COMPANY, EDWARD J.
2100 West Grand Avenue
Chicago, Illinois 60612
(312) 829-5466

JOYCE RECORD SYSTEMS INC.
142 Boardman-Poland Road
Youngstown, Ohio 44512

JOYCRAFTERS
234 Laurel Grove
San Rafael, California 94904
(415) 479-6860

JOYVA CORPORATION
53 Varick Avenue
Brooklyn, New York 11237
Alex Radutzky, President
(212) 497-0170

JR.
See Junior

JU-C-ORANGE OF AMERICA
406 Broad Street
Lebanon, Pennsylvania 17042

JUANITA'S (canned foods)
See Harbor Canning Company, Inc.

JUBILEE (chord organ)
See Emenee Audion

JUBILEE (dairy products)
See Challenge Cream & Butter Association

JUBILEE (kitchen wax)
See S.C. Johnson & Son Inc.

JUBILEE BRASSIERE COMPANY
200 Madison Avenue
New York, New York 10016
(212) 686-1332

JUBILEE MANUFACTURING COMPANY
1929 South 20th Street
Omaha, Nebraska 68108
(402) 341-7544

JUBILEE PRODUCTS INC.
1014 Vine
Cincinnati, Ohio 45210
(513) 621-1180

JUDGE ASSOCIATES, INC., JEAN
125 Prospect Avenue
Hackensack, New Jersey 07601
(201) 342-2643

JUDSON & ASSOCIATES INC.
15-106 Merchandise Mart
Chicago, Illinois 60654
(312) 644-4416

JUDSON CANDIES, INC.
(Division of Southdown, Inc.)
831 South Flores
San Antonio, Texas 78204
Louis G. Fritz, President
(512) 227-5201

JUDSON RESEARCH & MANUFACTURING COMPANY
541 East Hector Street
Conshohocken, Pennsylvania 19428
(215) 828-3011

JUDY-ANN (salads, spreads, meat items)
See Wine & Schultz Inc.

JUDY BOND, INC.
1375 Broadway
New York, New York 10018
Jack Rothenberg, President
(212) 695-4560

JUG (fruit-flavored wines)
See Mogen David Wine Corporation

JUGEAT INC., JACQUES
225 Fifth Avenue
New York, New York 10010
(212) 684-6760

JUICE BOWL PRODUCTS INC.
Post Office Box 1048
Lakeland, Florida 33802

JUICE KING (juicer)
See National Die Casting Company

JUICE-O-MAT (juicer)
See Rival Manufacturing Company

JUICY FRUIT (gum)
See William Wrigley Jr. Company

JULEP COMPANY
5664 West Raymond Street
Indianapolis, Indiana 46241
(317) 243-3521

JULIAN & KOKENGE COMPANY, THE
(Division of Amadac Industries, Inc.)
280 South Front
Columbus, Ohio 43215
Robert E. Gerwin, President
(614) 224-9164

Companies and Trade Names

JULIE ANNE (smoked meats and sausages)
See H. Trenkle Company, Inc.

JULIE MARIE, INC.
456 West Frontage Drive
Northfield, Illinois 60093

JULIET (alarm clock)
See Robertshaw Controls Company

JULIETTE (electronic products)
See Topp Electronics, Inc.

JULIUS KAYSER (wines)
See Browne Vintners Company Inc.

JUMBO (peanut butter)
See Frank Foods Company

JUMBO FOOD STORES INC.
1906 Allison N.E.
Washington, D.C. 20018
(202) 832-8700

JUMBO FOURSOME (luggage)
See Hartmann Luggage Company Inc.

JUMBO JUG (insulated containers)
See Thermos (Division of King-Seeley Thermos Company)

JUMPING JACKS (shoes)
See United States Shoe Corporation

JUNE TAILOR INC.
Box 125
Hartland, Wisconsin 53029

JUNEX (menswear)
See Barney Sampson Company, Ltd.

JUNG PRODUCTS, INC.
311 East Central Parkway
Cincinnati, Ohio 45202
Robert A. Conway, President
(513) 421-1215

JUNGLE JUICE (food products)
See National Flavors, Inc.

JUNIOR (tricycles)
See AMF Inc.

JUNIOR CLIQUE (dresses)
See Barmon Brothers Company, Inc.

JUNIOR HOST (juvenile furniture)
See R & D/Avant

JR. HOT SHOPPES (restaurants)
See Marriott Corporation

JUNIOR HOUSE, INC.
710 South Third Street
Milwaukee, Wisconsin 53204
Kenneth Ross, President
(414) 671-2500

JUNIOR LANE (coats and suits for women)
See Brand and Puritz

JUNIOR MISS (dresses)
See R. Lowenbaum Manufacturing Company

JUNIORFLEX (girdles, bras, garter belts)
See S. Sunkin and Son, Inc.

JUNIORITE, INC.
1407 Broadway
New York, New York 10018
Herb Karp, President
(212) 947-3480

JUNIUS FOOD PRODUCTS CORPORATION
800 West N.W. Highway
Palatine, Illinois 60067
(312) 359-9393

JUNKET (desserts, mixes)
See Salada Foods, Inc., United States Division

JUNKUNC BROTHERS AMERICAN LOCK COMPANY
Exchange Road and Kedzie Avenue
Crete, Illinois 60417
(312) 534-2000

JUNO BRA (bras)
See Q-T Foundations

JUPITER (cigars)
See Yorkana Cigar Company

JUPITER STORES
See S.S. Kresge Company

JURO NOVELTY COMPANY INC.
18 East 18th Street
New York, New York 10003
(212) 242-0429

JUST BORN, INC.
1300 Stefko Boulevard
Bethlehem, Pennsylvania 18017
Ira B. Born, President
(215) 867-7568
See also Marlon Confections

JUST FOR KICKS (junior sportswear)
See Aladdin Blouse & Sportswear, Inc.

JUST-RITE (canned meats, flour, meal)
See Southern Style Foods, Inc.

JUST SUITS (vegetables and meats)
See Purdie Brothers

JUSTIN BOOT COMPANY
Hemphill and Daggett
Fort Worth, Texas 76101
John S. Justin, President
(817) 332-4385

JUSTMAN (menswear)
   See Barney Sampson Company, Ltd.

JUSTRITE MANUFACTURING
   COMPANY
2061 North Southport Avenue
Chicago, Illinois 60614
Charles Barancik, Chairman and
   President
(312) 348-2111

JUTE INDUSTRIES, LTD. OF
   NEW YORK
202 Mamaroneck Avenue
White Plains, New York 10601

JUVA-TEX INC.
311 North Desplaines Street
Chicago, Illinois 60606
(312) 332-7130

JUVENIA WATCH DISTRIBUTORS
(Division of Berman Watch Company,
   Inc.)
580 Fifth Avenue
New York, New York 10036
Milton Berman, President
(212) 265-8088

JUVENILE SHOE CORPORATION
   OF AMERICA, THE
Carnation Drive
Aurora, Missouri 65605
Gale Pate, President
(417) 678-2181

K

K & B MANUFACTURING
(Division of Aurora Plastics Corporation)
12152 South Woodruff Avenue
Downey, California 90241
(213) 923-5493

K & C FOOD SALES
656 South Alameda
Los Angeles, California 90021
(213) 627-3781

K & K LABORATORIES, INC.
121 Express Street
Plainview, New York 11803
(516) 433-6262

K. & L. (whiskey and gin)
  See Standard Distillers Products, Inc.

K & M COMPANY
525 Maple Avenue
Torrance, California 90503

K & T INTERNATIONAL INDUSTRIES
127 West 25th Street
New York, New York 10001
(212) 989-8343

K & W PRODUCTS INC.
(Subsidiary of Berkshire Hathaway, Inc.)
8319 South Allport Avenue
Santa Fe Springs, California 90670
R.M. Cate, President
(213) 693-8229

K & Z (food products)
  See Kaplan & Zubrin Inc.

KBF (canned goods)
  See Kling Brothers & Fischer Inc.

K C FOODS
(Affiliation of Hulman & Company)
Post Office Box 704
3401 East Broadway
North Little Rock, Arkansas 72115
(501) 945-1456

KCS INDUSTRIES INC.
5111 South Ninth Street
Milwaukee, Wisconsin 53221
(414) 744-5111

KDI CORPORATION
5721 Dragon Way
Cincinnati, Ohio 45227
Louis W. Matthey, President
(513) 272-1421

K-D MANUFACTURING COMPANY
3575 Hempland Road
Lancaster, Pennsylvania 17604
C. Paul Myers, President
(717) 285-4581

KFC CORPORATION
(Subsidiary of Heublein, Inc.)
Post Office Box 1331
Louisville, Kentucky 40213
James H. Wille, President
(502) 459-8600

K.I.K. COMPANY
Box 256
Bethlehem, Pennsylvania 18016

KK CORPORATION
Railroad Number Four
Celina, Ohio 45822

KLH RESEARCH & DEVELOPMENT CORPORATION
30 Cross Street
Cambridge, Massachusetts 02139
(617) 491-5060

KLM COSMETICS COMPANY, INC.
218 North Long Beach Road
Rockville Centre, New York 11570

K.L.M. ROYAL DUTCH AIRLINES
North American Division
609 Fifth Avenue
New York, New York 10017
S. van der Orliandini, President
(212) 759-2400

K.M. (canned goods)
  See Kling Brothers & Fischer Inc.

K-M (electric table appliances)
  See Knapp-Monarch (Division of The Hoover Company)

K MART (chain stores)
  See S.S. Kresge Company

K-P MANUFACTURING COMPANY
415 Royalston Avenue
Minneapolis, Minnesota 55405
(612) 336-5811

K S M
(Division of Omark Industries, Inc.)
301 New Albany Road
Moorestown, New Jersey 08057
W.J. Thompson, President
(609) 235-6900

K-TEE MANUFACTURING COMPANY, INC.
1228 Oakwood
Toledo, Ohio 43607

K-TEL INTERNATIONAL INC.
11311 K-tel Drive
Minneapolis, Minnesota 55343
Philip Kives, Chairman and President
(612) 932-4000

K-2 CORPORATION
Vashon Island, Washington 98070

K2R (spot remover)
  See Texize Chemicals, Inc.

K2 SILICONE (spray lubricant)
  See Marson Corporation

841

Companies and Trade Names

K.W. (grocery products)
See Kar Wah Trading Company, Ltd.

K-WAY (sports apparel)
See Gondola Internationale Inc.

KAAG TROPHIES INC.
2040 Artesia Boulevard
Torrance, California 90504

KABAR (knives)
See Cole National Corporation

KABAT COMPANY, ALOIS
3156 West 26th Street
Chicago, Illinois 60623
(312) 247-7550

KABNICK, DR. STUART
Broad Locust Building
Philadelphia, Pennsylvania 19102
(215) 735-8830

KABRO (groceries)
See Kay-Bee Food Products Inc.

KABUKI (bowls, lighters, canisters, etc.)
See Albert Kessler & Company

KABUKI (canned foods)
See C. Itoh & Company, Inc.

KACKI (toiletries)
See Avon Products, Inc.

KADEE QUALITY PRODUCTS
720 South Grape Street
Medford, Oregon 97501
(503) 772-9890

KADIN BROTHERS, INC.
20 West 33rd
New York, New York 10001
(212) 244-1144

KAFFEE-HAG (instant and regular coffee)
See General Foods Corporation

KAHANER & BROTHER INC., SOL
55 West 38th Street
New York, New York 10018
(212) 391-9755

KAHLENBERG LABORATORIES
(Division of T.E. Watson Company)
Box 3829
Sarasota, Florida 33578
(813) 959-3889

KAHLUA (coffee liqueur)
See Jules Berman & Associates, Inc.

KAHN, INC., DAVID
Deer Lake, Pennsylvania 17961
Julius M. Kahn, President
(717) 366-1011

KAHNAY ENTERPRISES
Post Office Box 722
Kendall, Florida 33578

KAHN'S SONS COMPANY, THE E.
(Division of Consolidated Foods Corporation)
3241 Spring Grove Avenue
Cincinnati, Ohio 45225
Milton J. Schloss, President
(513) 541-4000

KAIER FIBERGLASS PRODUCTS INC., WILLIAM
Box 12-D
Lakehurst, New Jersey 08733
(201) 657-8401

KAISER AGRICULTURAL CHEMICALS
214 North Cherry Street
Dothan, Alabama 36301
Arthur A. Morris, Jr., General Manager

KAISER ASSOCIATES INC., JOHN
Box 3982
Wilmington, Delaware 19807

KAISER INDUSTRIES CORPORATION
300 Lakeside Drive
Oakland, California 94612
Edgar F. Kaiser, Chairman of the Board
(415) 271-2211

KAKOVER (teakettles)
See Kromex

KAL KAN FOODS, INC.
(Subsidiary of Mars, Inc.)
3386 East 44th Street
Los Angeles, California 90058
Frank Ryan, Chairman of the Board
(213) 583-4111

KALAMAZOO (cigarette lighters)
See Bowers Lighter Company

KALAMAZOO (musical instruments)
See Norlin Music, Inc.

KALAMAZOO LABEL COMPANY
321 West Ransom Street
Kalamazoo, Michigan 49006
Jack L. Page, President
(616) 381-5820

KALAN, INC.
7002 Woodbine Avenue
Philadelphia, Pennsylvania 19151
(215) 477-1946

KALART VICTOR CORPORATION
Hultenius Street
Plainville, Connecticut 06062
Morris Schwartz, Chairman
(203) 747-1663

KALEIDOSCOPE ENTERPRISES
2340 Stanwell Circle
Concord, California 94520

Companies and Trade Names

KALFUS COMPANY, INC., I.
303 Powell
Brooklyn, New York 11212
(212) 346-9898

KALIMAR, INC.
2644 Michigan Avenue
Saint Louis, Missouri 63118
Robert J. Lipsitz, President
(314) 771-0747

KALINSKY & SON INC., SAM
156 Fifth Avenue
New York, New York 10010
(212) 929-4700

KALMAN DEVELOPMENT CORPORATION
See Welcome World Creations

KALMAR DESIGNS COMPANY
3303 Merrick Road
Wantagh, New York 11793

KALO COMPANY, THE
2620 Ellington Road
Quincy, Illinois 62301
(217) 222-0194

KALTON (watches)
See United States Time Corporation

KALVA CORPORATION
3940 Porett Drive
Gurnee, Illinois 60031
(312) 336-1200

KALVEX, INC.
425 Park Avenue
New York, New York 10022
Emanuel L. Wolf, President
(212) 752-3000

KAMAN CORPORATION
Old Windsor Road
Bloomfield, Connecticut 06002
Charles H. Kaman, President
(203) 243-8311
See also Aviation Instrument Inc.; Coast Wholesale Music Company of Los Angeles; Currier Piano Company, Inc.; and National Musical String Company

KAMAR, INC.
2020 West 139th Street
Gardena, California 90249
(213) 321-2911

KAMEYAMA CANDLE COMPANY, U.S.A. LTD.
(Division of Block Importing Company)
525 Byrd Street
Richmond, Virginia 23219
(804) 643-8619

KAMINSKY & SONS, INC., H.R.
North Dixie Highway
Fitgerald, Georgia 31750
H.R. Kaminsky, President
(912) 423-4396

KAMLOOPER (fishing supplies)
See Acme Tackle Company

KAMP TOGS, INC.
(Subsidiary of Modern Textile Company)
897 Fee Fee Road
Maryland Heights, Missouri 63043
Jack Koplow, President
(314) 878-9300

KAMPGROUND OF AMERICA, INC.
Mutual Benefit Life Building
Billings, Montana 59103
Darrell R. Booth, President
(406) 248-7444

KAMPIT (sportsmen's clothing)
See Utica-Duxbak Corporation

KANAWHA GLASS COMPANY
Post Office Box 280
Dunbar, West Virginia 25064

KANE IMPORT CORPORATION
123 Chatsworth Avenue
Larchmont, New York 10538
(212) 792-4566

KANE LINES INC., MILTON
1301 Superior Building
Cleveland, Ohio 44114
(216) 621-2105

KANE-MILLER CORPORATION
See Delsaco Foods Corporation; Fox Foods Inc.; Monarch Wine Company of Georgia; and Webster Company, G.L.

KANEMATSU-GOSHO (U.S.A.)
1 World Trade Center
New York, New York 10048
(212) 432-0900

KANGAROO (shorts)
See Munsingwear

KANGOL (men's caps)
See E. Stern & Company

KANNER IMPORTS, LESLIE
613 Pershing Drive
Silver Spring, Maryland 20901
(301) 588-5481

KANO LABORATORIES INC.
1000 South Thompson Lane
Nashville, Tennessee 37211
(615) 833-4101

KANON (men's toiletries)
See Scannon Ltd.

Companies and Trade Names

KANOX COMPANY
Box 244
Garden Grove, California 92640

KANSAS CITY POWER & LIGHT COMPANY
1330 Baltimore Avenue
Kansas City, Missouri 64141
Robert K. Zimmerman, President
(816) 471-7000

KANSAS CITY SOUTHERN LINES
114 West 11th Street
Kansas City, Missouri 64105
J.S. Carter, President
(816) 842-0077

KANSAS CITY STAR COMPANY
1729 Grand Avenue
Kansas City, Missouri 64108
W.W. Baker, President
(816) 421-1200

KANSAS CITY VACCINE COMPANY
1611 Genesee Street
Kansas City, Missouri 64102
(816) 842-5966

KANSAS GAS & ELECTRIC COMPANY
Post Office Box 208
Wichita, Kansas 67201
Ralph P. Fiebach, President
(316) 264-1111

KANSAS POWER & LIGHT COMPANY
818 Kansas Avenue
Topeka, Kansas 66612
Balfour S. Jeffrey, Chairman of the Board
(913) 233-1351

KANT-MISS (canned foods)
See Marshfield Canning Company

KANTOR, APOTHECARIES, IRVING
1494 Saint Nicholas Avenue
New York, New York 10033
(212) 923-0164

KANTWET COMPANY
See Questor Juvenile Furniture (Division of Questor Corporation)

KAOLA (vegetable oil)
See Durkee Industrial Foods Group

KAOPECTATE (diarrhea remedy)
See Upjohn Company

KAP-GO IMPORT COMPANY
48 Irving Avenue
Englewood Cliffs, New Jersey 07632

KAPER KRAFTS
(Division of Southern Machinery Company)
Box Ten
Greer, South Carolina 29651

KAPLAN & SONS, INC., JOSEPH A.
137 Saw Mill River Road
Yonkers, New York 10701
Harold M. Kaplan, President
(914) 476-4000

KAPLAN & ZUBRIN INC.
Second and Kaighns Avenue
Camden, New Jersey 08103
Ronald Kaplan, President
(609) 964-1083

KAPLAN FURNITURE COMPANY
574 Boston Avenue
Medford, Massachusetts 02155
Simon Kaplan, President and Treasurer
(617) 395-7350

KAPLAN MUSICAL STRING COMPANY
Post Office Box 427
104 Highland Avenue
South Norwalk, Connecticut 06856
(203) 866-3455

KAPLAN PRODUCTS & TEXTILES
29 West 35th Street
New York, New York 10001
(212) 736-8200

KAPTAIN KIDD (seafood)
See H. Morgan Daniel Seafoods Inc.

KAR-KARE CORPORATION
Post Office Box 36
Charlotte, North Carolina 28134

KAR PRODUCTS COMPANY
Post Office Box 10334
6016 North Greeley
Portland, Oregon 97210
(503) 285-0809

KARAM NEGLIGEE COMPANY INC.
31 East 32nd Street
New York, New York 10016
(212) 532-4940

KARASTAN RUG MILLS
919 Third Avenue
New York, New York 10003
(212) 980-3434

KARAY COMPANY, E.A.
10 Columbus Circle
New York, New York 10019
(212) 765-0500

KARE, INC.
8310 Wilshire Boulevard
Beverly Hills, California 90211

KARE PHARMACAL COMPANY, INC.
999 Asylum Avenue
Hartford, Connecticut 06105

Companies and Trade Names

KARIBE SERIES (broadloom carpeting)
See Duraloom Carpet Mills Inc.

KARIKA (food products)
See National Papaya Company

KARISMA (housewares and appliances)
See Charisma Trading Company

KARL BECK (violins and accessories)
See Pacific Music Supply Company

KARL KNILLING (violins, violas, cellos, basses)
See Saint Louis Music Supply Company

KARL MANUFACTURING COMPANY
Box 7243
Grand Rapids, Michigan 49510

KARL ZIESS (brass musical instruments)
See DeKalb Musicians Supply Company Inc.

KARLA FASHIONS, INC.
1350 Broadway
New York, New York 10018
(212) 431-5825

KARL'S SHOES
(Division of Hartfield-Zody's)
431 South Fairfax
Los Angeles, California 90036
Edward Solomon, President
(213) 937-2430

KARMELKORN CORPORATION
709 Phillip Avenue
Norfolk, Nebraska 68701
Wes Fleming, President
(402) 371-9221

KARO (syrups)
See Best Foods

KAROL WESTERN CORPORATION
5207 Downey Road
Los Angeles, California 90058
(213) 588-5266

KAROLTON ENVELOPE
(Division of Kimberly-Clark Corporation)
2063 Frontage Road
Des Plaines, Illinois 60018
Richard W. Kohl, General Manager
(312) 296-8104

KARP & SONS, INC., L.
1301 Estes Boulevard
Elk Grove Village, Illinois 60007
J.L. Karp, Executive Vice President
(312) 593-5700

KARPEK ACCORDION MANUFACTURING COMPANY
820 South 16th Street
Milwaukee, Wisconsin 53204
(414) 383-3500

KARPET-SQUARES (cotton carpeting)
See Allen Industries, Inc.

KARPETEX (carpeting)
See Forest City Products Inc.

KARPETWALL (movable partitions)
See Modern Partitions Inc.

KARTELL (plastic furniture)
See Beylerian Ltd.

KAS-KEL ELECTRIC COMPANY INC.
5 Union Square
New York, New York 10003
Edward Kaskel, President
(212) 255-9090

KASAR LABORATORIES
7313 North Harlem Avenue
Niles, Illinois 60648

KASCO (tools)
See Coleman Systems

KASDENOL CORPORATION, THE
50 Elm Street
Huntington, New York 11743

KASEN INDUSTRIES
Circle K Tape Division
850 Wilson Avenue
Newark, New Jersey 07105
(201) 589-8941

KASHINS, HERMAN
41 Madison Avenue
New York, New York 10010
(212) 532-4724

KASHOH U.S.A. INC.
7 Lakeside Drive
Larchmont, New York 10538

KASITSNA BAY (canned seafood)
See Ekren Packing Company

KASS CHINA COMPANY
909-911 Vine Street
East Liverpool, Ohio 43920

KASSER DISTILLERS PRODUCTS CORPORATION
Third and Luzerne
Philadelphia, Pennsylvania 19140
Raymond H. Kasser, President
(215) 223-3100

KASSER IMPORTS
8510 Dixon Avenue
Silver Spring, Maryland 20910
(301) 585-0334

KASSOY INC., I.
30 West 47th Street
New York, New York 10036
(212) 582-3260

KASTINGER (sports accessories and equipment)
See A & T Ski Company

845

Companies and Trade Names

KASTLE (sports accessories and equipment)
See Beconta Inc.

KASTMASTER (fishing equipment)
See Acme Tackle Company

KASUGA (guitars)
See Rocky Mountain Music Distributors

KASUGA SALES LTD.
212 Fifth Avenue
New York, New York 10010
(212) 532-2840

KATE GREENWAY INDUSTRIES, INC.
1333 Broadway
New York, New York 10018
Irving L. Goldberger, President
(212) 594-7200
See also Wohl & Company, L.

KATEN & COMPANY, INC., K.
244 Fifth Avenue
New York, New York 10001
(212) 683-5257

KATHARINE BEECHER, INC.
Manchester, Pennsylvania 17345

KATHARINE GIBBS SCHOOL, INC.
(Subsidiary of Macmillian, Inc.)
200 Park Avenue
New York, New York 10017
Edith L. Gardner, President
(212) 867-9300

KATHERINE GRAY INC.
Box BD
Riverton, Wyoming 82501

KATT ASSOCIATES, ELLIOT M.
10945 Bluffside Drive
Number 122
Studio City, California 91604

KATTEN LTD., WALTER
10 East 33rd Street
New York, New York 10016
(212) 679-7898

KATZ & BESTHOFF, INC.
1 K & B Plaza
New Orleans, Louisiana 70130
S.J. Besthoff, Chairman of the Board
(504) 586-1234

KATZ & COMPANY, EMIL
1001 Avenue of the Americas
New York, New York 10018
(212) 947-2889

KATZ INC., A.
225 Fifth Avenue
New York, New York 10010
(212) 685-3493

KATZ UNDERWEAR COMPANY
Sixth Street
Honesdale, Pennsylvania 18431
Edward L. Freeman, President
(717) 253-2544

KATZINGER (kitchen tools)
See Ekco Products Inc.

KAUFFMAN, JACOB
1020 New Market Street
Philadelphia, Pennsylvania 19123
(215) 925-8085

KAUFMAN CARPET COMPANY
1800 Boston Road
Bronx, New York 10460
Samuel Fox, Chairman of the Board
(212) 991-0700

KAUFMAN GLASS COMPANY
1301-03 Northeast Boulevard
Wilmington, Delaware 19899
(302) 654-9937

KAUFMANN, R. & M.
(Division of Russ Togs, Inc.)
1601 East Mountain Street
Aurora, Illinois 60507
Lester M. Kaufmann, President
(312) 898-6700

KAUFMANN'S
(Division of The May Company)
400 Fifth Avenue
Pittsburgh, Pennsylvania 15219
C. Hal Silver, President
(412) 281-1000

KAUKAUNA KLUB CHEESE
(Division of International Multifoods Corporation)
Box 229
Kaukauna, Wisconsin 54130

KAUMAGRAPH COMPANY
14th and Poplar
Wilmington, Delaware 19899
Frederick T. Marston, President
(302) 575-1500

KAUTENBERG COMPANY, W.E.
1235 South Adams Avenue
Freeport, Illinois 61032
(815) 233-1914

KAVA (coffee)
See Borden Foods

KAWAI PIANO (AMERICAN) CORPORATION
24200 South Vermont Avenue
Harbor City, California 90710
Tadao Nakamichi, General Manager
(213) 534-2350

KAWASAKI MOTOR CORPORATION
1062 McGaw Avenue
Santa Ana, California 92705
Y. Hamawaki, President
(714) 540-9980

Companies and Trade Names

KAWECKI BERYLCO INDUSTRIES, INC.
Box 1462
Reading, Pennsylvania 19603
Walter R. Lowry, President
(215) 929-0781

KAWNEER COMPANY, THE
(Subsidiary of American Metal Climax)
1105 North Front Street
Niles, Michigan 49120
V.B. Evans, President
(616) 683-0200

KAY-BEE FOOD PRODUCTS, INC.
94-10 92nd Street
Ozone Park, New York 11416

KAY CORPORATION
320 King Street
Alexandria, Virginia 22314
Anthonie C. van Ekris, President
(703) 683-3800

KAY-DEE MANUFACTURING COMPANY, THE
Walton, Nebraska 68461

KAY DUNHILL (dresses)
See Korell Company

KAY FINCH CERAMICS
3901 East Coast Highway
Corona Del Mar, California 92014

KAY INSTRUMENT SALES COMPANY
3057 North Rockwell
Chicago, Illinois 60618
(312) 267-2318

KAY PHARMACAL COMPANY, INC.
Box 50375
Tulsa, Oklahoma 74150

KAY PREPARATIONS COMPANY, INC.
345 West 58th Street
New York, New York 10019
(212) 245-0030

KAY-TOWNES INC.
Box 593
Rome, Georgia 30161
(404) 235-0141

KAY WHITNEY (dresses)
See Huntington Industries, Inc.

KAY WINDSOR, INC.
(Subsidiary of V.F. Corporation)
1400 Broadway
New York, New York 10018
Carl Shapiro, Chairman of the Board
(212) 736-3900

KAYANEE CORPORATION OF AMERICA
200 Fifth Avenue
New York, New York 10010
(212) 243-0964

KAYDETTE MANUFACTURING CORPORATION
152 Madison Avenue
New York, New York 10016
(212) 684-1235

KAYE COMPANY, INC., S.L.
230 Fifth Avenue
New York, New York 10001
(212) 683-5600

KAYLON (spray paint)
See Borden Chemical Company

KAYOT INC.
1301-E 14th Street
Indianola, Iowa 50125

KAYOT, INC.
Marine Division
Post Office Box 789
500 Industrial Road, North
Mankato, Minnesota 56001
Denis Daly, President
(507) 387-3401

KAYSER RHINE (wine)
See Browne-Vintners Company

KAYSER-ROTH CORPORATION
640 Fifth Avenue
New York, New York 10019
Norman M. Hinerfield, President
(212) 757-9600
See also Catalina; Century Mills; Champion Pants Manufacturing Company Inc.; Cole of California, Inc.; Excello; Lawrence Clothes Inc.; Mercury Slippers; Paris Accessories For Men; and Scandcastle Swimwear

KAYSER-ROTH HOSIERY COMPANY, INC.
(Division of Kayser-Roth Corporation)
1221 Avenue of the Americas
New York, New York 10020
Merwin J. Joseph, President
(212) 764-4000

KAYSER-ROTH INTIMATE APPAREL COMPANY, INC.
(Division of Kayser-Roth Corporation)
640 Fifth Avenue
New York, New York 10019
Philip Simon, President
(212) 757-9600

KAYSER-ROTH SHOES, INC.
(Division of Kayser-Roth Corporation)
9 Marble Street
Whitman, Massachusetts 02382
William Sheskey, President
(617) 447-4422

Companies and Trade Names

KAYSER-WISPESE COMPANY
(Division of Kayser-Roth Corporation)
640 Fifth Avenue
New York, New York 10019
(212) 757-9600

KAYSONS INTERNATIONAL
CORPORATION
531 Central Park Avenue
Scarsdale, New York 10583

KAYSTAN PAGEANT DOLL
COMPANY, THE
Post Office Box 19
Bangor, Maine 04401

KAYTEE IMPORTS, INC.
28 West 27th Street
New York, New York 10001
(212) 679-6250

KAYWOODIE PRODUCTS, INC.
(Division of S.M. Frank & Company, Inc.)
745 Fifth Avenue
New York, New York 10022
Morris Gartenlaub, Vice President
(516) 924-6900

KAZ, INC.
614 West 49th Street
New York, New York 10019
Lawrence Katzman, President
(212) 586-1630

KAZOO COMPANY INC.
8703 South Main Street
Eden, New York 14057
(716) 992-3960

KEARNEY & TRECKER
CORPORATION
11000 Theodore Trecker Way
Milwaukee, Wisconsin 53214
Russell A. Hedden, President and Chief Executive Officer
(414) 476-8300

KEBOW, INC., DUDLEY
2631 Southwest Drive
Los Angeles, California 90043
(213) 753-2181

KEDS (shoes)
See Uniroyal, Inc.

KEE LOX MANUFACTURING
COMPANY
(Subsidiary of Parchment Paper Company)
Post Office Box 137
100 Kee Lox Place
Rochester, New York 14608
R.A. Stanford, President
(716) 235-1550

KEEBLER COMPANY
677 Larch Avenue
Elmhurst, Illinois 60126
Arthur E. Larkin, Jr., President
(312) 833-2900
See Illinois Baking Company

KEEN-EDGE (shears, scissors, etc.)
See J. Wiss & Sons Company

KEEN KUTTER (tools, hardware, housewares, appliances, etc.)
See Val-Test Distributors Inc.

KEENE COIN HANDLING
(Division of Keene Corporation)
4619 North Ravenswood
Chicago, Illinois 60640

KEENE PHARMACEUTICALS, INC.
333 South Mockingbird
Keene, Texas 76059

KEEP N TOUCH GREETING
CARDS, INC.
Box 912
Framingham, Massachusetts 01701

KEEPSAKE (diamond rings)
See A.H. Pond Company, Inc.

KEES MANUFACTURING COMPANY, F.D.
21 High Street
Beatrice, Nebraska 68310
(402) 223-2391

KEEVER STARCH COMPANY
324 Dering Avenue
Columbus, Ohio 43207
(614) 444-1158

KEEZER MANUFACTURING
COMPANY, INC.
Chadwick Street
Plaistow, New Hampshire 03865
(603) 382-8509

KEG (pipe tobacco)
See House of Edgeworth

KEGLET (beer)
See Rheingold Breweries, Inc.

KEIL LOCK COMPANY
See Ilco Corporation

KEITH (clocks, barometers, and lamps)
See Soriano Ltd.

KEITH CHEMICALS, INC., WALLING
Post Office Box 2112
Birmingham, Alabama 35201

KEITH COMPANY, GEORGE E.
Perkins Avenue
Brockton, Massachusetts 02403
Paul I. Kleven, President
(617) 583-5000
See also Klev Brothers Shoe Manufacturing Company

KEITH, INC., NANCY
(Division of Mrs. Arnold's)
155 Park Avenue
Bersenville, Illinois 60100

848

Companies and Trade Names

KEL RAY MILLS, INC.
148 Madison Avenue
New York, New York 10016

KELCO COMPANY
Post Office Box 23076
8355 Aero Drive
San Diego, California 92123
(714) 292-4900

KELITE CHEMICAL CORPORATION
(Division of the Richardson Company)
1250 North Main Street
Los Angeles, California 90012
J.W. Bruce, Jr., President
(213) 222-0201

KELL-MOR LECTERN COMPANY
1283 North Main Street
Rockford, Illinois 61103

KELLER-CHARLES OF PHILADELPHIA
2413-27 Federal Street
Philadelphia, Pennsylvania 19146
(215) 732-2614

KELLER COMPANY, THE
South Main Street
Mechanicsburg, Ohio 43044

KELLER FOOD COMPANY
2917 Brooklyn Avenue
Kansas City, Missouri 64109
(816) 921-3500

KELLER FOOD PRODUCTS
COMPANY
2631 West Hagert
Philadelphia, Pennsylvania 19132
(215) 229-2414

KELLER INDUSTRIES, INC.
18000 State Road Nine
Miami, Florida 33162
H.A. Keller, President
(305) 945-3511

KELLER MANUFACTURING
COMPANY
Corydon, Indiana 47112
Charles A. Keller, Chairman of
the Board
(812) 738-2222

KELLER-SCROLL INC.
(Subsidiary of Keller Industries Inc.)
800 N.W. 166th
Miami, Florida 33164
(305) 625-1331

KELLERMAN MANUFACTURING
COMPANY, INC.
320 Driggs Avenue
Brooklyn, New York 11222
(212) 389-7610

KELLEY & COMPANY INC., H.E.
Box 128
New Church, Virginia 23415

KELLEY CANNERY INC., R.O.
Box 235
Midville, Georgia 30441

KELLEY CANNING COMPANY
INC.
Box Ten
Prairie Grove, Arkansas 72753

KELLEY, FARQUHAR & COMPANY
Box 1737
Tacoma, Washington 98401
Robert C. Farguhar, President
(206) 572-4455

KELLEY INDUSTRIES, INC.
Post Office Box 1317
Houston, Texas 77001
Edward W. Kelley, Jr., President
(713) 526-8461

KELLOGG-AMERICAN, INC.
565 Cedar Way
Oakmont, Pennsylvania 15139
R.S. Candee, President
(412) 828-7700

KELLOGG BRUSH MANUFACTURING
COMPANY
122 Pleasant Street
Easthampton, Massachusetts 01027
Thomas M. Futter, President,
Clerk and Sales Manager
(413) 527-2450

KELLOGG COMPANY
235 Porter Street
Battle Creek, Michigan 49016
J.E. Lonning, President
(616) 962-5151
See also Fearn International Inc.;
and Salada Foods, Inc.

KELLOGG INDUSTRIES, INC.
159-163 West Pearl Street
Jackson, Michigan 49201
Robert Williams, President and
General Manager
(517) 782-0579

KELLOGG VINEGAR COMPANY,
PAUL
165 South Broadway
Lowell, Michigan 49331

KELLOGG'S INSECTICIDE
COMPANY
213 Agostino Road
San Gabriel, California 91776

KELLOGG'S PROFESSIONAL
PRODUCTS INC.
Box 1201
Sandusky, Ohio 44870

KELLS CORPORATION
109 Howe Street
Fall River, Massachusetts 02724

KELLWOOD COMPANY
600 Kellwood Parkway
Saint Louis, Missouri 63017
Fred W. Wenzel, President
(314) 576-3100

Companies and Trade Names

KELLY ARDEN
(Division of Bobbie Brooks Inc.)
1400 Broadway
New York, New York 10018

KELLY COMPANY, F.
(Division of Cornwall & Patterson Company)
1155 Railroad Avenue
Bridgeport, Connecticut 06605
(203) 366-4911

KELLY DANT (tractor tires)
See Goodyear Tire & Rubber Company

KELLY FOODS INC.
(Division of Krey Packing Company)
Box 548
Jackson, Tennessee 38301

KELLY INC., GEORGE J.
56 Sanderson Avenue
Lynn, Massachusetts 01903

KELLY-MOORE PAINT COMPANY
1015 Commercial Street
San Carlos, California 94070
William E. Moore, President
(415) 592-8337

KELLY SERVICES, INC.
16130 Northland Drive
Southfield, Michigan 48075
William R. Kelly, Chairman of the Board
(313) 352-4000

KELLY-SPRINGFIELD TIRE COMPANY, THE
(Subsidiary of Goodyear Tire & Rubber Company)
Kelly Boulevard
Cumberland, Maryland 21502
R.E. Mercer, President
(301) 724-2850

KELLY, WEBER & COMPANY, INC.
415 Ann
Lake Charles, Louisiana 70601

KELTON (watches)
See United States Time Corporation

KELTY MOUNTAINEERING-BACKPACKING
Box 3645
Glendale, California 91201

KELVIN SAVELL
9819 Hawley Road
El Cajon, California 92021

KELVINATOR APPLIANCE COMPANY
(Division of White Consolidated Industries, Inc.)
1545 Clyde Park, S.W.
Grand Rapids, Michigan 49509
C.C. Rieger, President
(616) 241-6501

KEM COMPANY
1404 First Avenue N.E.
Cedar Rapids, Iowa 52402

KEM GLO (paint)
See Sherwin-Williams Company

KEM INTERNATIONAL COMPANY
233 Broadway
New York, New York 10007
(212) 267-2239

KEM MARINE
21215 West Bluemont
Waukesha, Wisconsin 53186

KEM PLASTIC PLAYING CARDS INC.
745 Fifth Avenue
New York, New York 10022
(212) 688-8650

KEM-TONE (paint)
See Sherwin-Williams Company

KEMAK (glass cleaner, furniture polish, room fresheners, etc.)
See Gem Inc.

KEMIKO, INC.
2443 North Naomi Street
Burbank, California 91504

KEMP & BEATLEY INC.
10 East 34th Street
New York, New York 10016
(212) 689-4610

KEMP COMPANY LTD., W.H.
515 Homestead Avenue
Mount Vernon, New York 10550
(914) 664-5900

KEMP CORPORATION, E.F.
Department CB
110 Walnut Street
Somerville, Massachusetts 02143
(617) 666-3300

KEMP FURNITURE INDUSTRIES, INC.
Box 1678
Goldsboro, North Carolina 27530
William P. Kemp, Jr., President
(919) 735-2801

KEMP SHREDDER COMPANY
800 Kemp Building
Erie, Pennsylvania 16512
(814) 838-4526

KEMPER COMPANY CABINETS
See The Tappan Company

KEMPER INSURANCE COMPANIES
Long Grove, Illinois 60049
James S. Kemper, Jr., President
(312) 540-2000
See also American Motorist Insurance Company

KEMPS (dairy products)
See Ward Foods, Inc.

Companies and Trade Names

KEMPS
(Division of Marigold Foods, Inc.)
2929 University Avenue, S.E.
Minneapolis, Minnesota 55414
David Ramsay, President
(612) 331-3775

KEN-L RATION (dog foods)
See Quaker Oats Company

KENAI PACKERS
1455 North Northlake Place
Seattle, Washington 98103

KENBERRY
(Division of Etamco Industries)
1 Montgomery Street
Belleville, New Jersey 07109

KENBURY GLASS WORKS
154 West 14th Street
New York, New York 10011
(212) 924-3186

KENDALL (food products)
See Parman Kendall Corporation

KENDALL COMPANY, THE
(Division of Colgate-Palmolive Company)
225 Franklin Street
Boston, Massachusetts 02110
Willard M. Bright, President
(617) 482-3030
See also Davies Rose Hoyt Pharmaceutical

KENDALL, DR. B.J.
(Division of J.H. Guild Company, Inc.)
Rupert, Vermont 05768
(802) 394-7733

KENDALL HALL (men's furnishings)
See Varsity Pajamas

KENDALL REFINING COMPANY
See Witco Chemical Corporation

KENDREGAN COMPANY, H.
166 Valley Road
River Edge, New Jersey 07661

KENDRICK COMPANY, INC., JAMES R.
6139 Germantown Avenue
Philadelphia, Pennsylvania 19144
Warren R. Kendrick, President and Secretary
(215) 438-1122

KENMORE (major appliances)
See Sears, Roebuck and Company

KENMORE INDUSTRIES
Post Office Box 155
Woodbine Road
Belmont, Massachusetts 02178
(617) 484-7480

KENNAMETAL INC.
1 Lloyd Avenue
Latrobe, Pennsylvania 15650
Alex G. McKenna, President and Chief Executive Officer
(412) 537-3311

KENNAN MANUFACTURING COMPANY
820 Minor Avenue North
Seattle, Washington 98109
(206) 624-5580

KENNECOTT COPPER CORPORATION
161 East 42nd Street
New York, New York 10017
Frank R. Milliken, President
(212) 687-5800

KENNEDY MANUFACTURING COMPANY
Post Office Box 151
Van Wert, Ohio 45891
Roger K. Thompson, President and Chairman
(419) 238-2442

KENNEDY MAYONNAISE PRODUCTS
415 17th Avenue North
Hopkins, Minnesota 55343
(612) 935-2187

KENNEDY'S (Irish whiskey)
See M.S. Walker, Inc.

KENNEDY'S, INC.
(Subsidiary of Phillips-Van Heusen Corporation)
30 Summer Street
Boston, Massachusetts 02110
Allan J. Knopf, President
(617) 482-4200

KENNER MANUFACTURING COMPANY, INC.
Box 100
Knoxville, Arkansas 72845
(501) 885-4131

KENNER PRODUCTS
(Division of General Mills Fun Group, Inc.)
912 Sycamore Street
Cincinnati, Ohio 45202
Bernard Loomis, President
(513) 579-4000

KENNETT CANNING COMPANY
(Division of S.S. Pierce Company)
Box K
Kennett Square, Pennsylvania 19348

KENNY-K (sports apparel)
See Gondola Internationale Inc.

KENRO CORPORATION
Fredonia, Wisconsin 53021
K.B. Welch, President
(414) 692-2411

KENROSE MANUFACTURING COMPANY
(Division of Genesco, Inc.)
1350 Broadway
New York, New York 10018
Arthur Rosenstein, President
(212) 524-2001

Companies and Trade Names

KEN'S FOODS INC.
110 Alexander Street
Framingham, Massachusetts 01701

KENSINGTON (furniture)
See Aluminum Company of America

KENSINGTON RUBBER WORKS
8804 Third Avenue
Brooklyn, New York 11209
(212) 238-0910

KENSKILL (travel trailers)
See Redman Industries, Inc.

KENT (cigarettes)
See Lorillard Corporation

KENT (flashlights, batteries)
See Bright Star Industries, Inc.

KENT (meat products)
See North American Foods (Division of Deltec International Ltd.)

KENT CANNING COMPANY
Gibson, Georgia 30810

KENT INTERNATIONAL
200 Fifth Avenue
New York, New York 10010
(212) 242-6700

KENTILE FLOORS, INC.
58 Second Avenue
Brooklyn, New York 11215
David O'D. Kennedy, President
(212) 768-9500

KENTON PHARMACAL COMPANY, INC., THE
Box 232
Covington, Kentucky 41012

KENTUCK (food products)
See Standard Foods Inc.

KENTUCKY (whiskey)
See Four Roses Distillers Company

KENTUCKY BEAU (Bourbon whiskey)
See Renfield Importers, Ltd.

KENTUCKY BEAUTY (canned foods)
See Owensboro Canning Company Inc.

KENTUCKY CENTRAL LIFE INSURANCE COMPANY
Kentucky Central Building
Lexington, Kentucky 40507
David L. Brain, President
(606) 254-5561

KENTUCKY COLONEL (whiskey)
See National Distillers & Chemical Corporation

KENTUCKY CREST (whiskey)
See Schenley Industries Inc.

KENTUCKY FRIED CHICKEN CORPORATION
(Subsidiary of Heublein, Inc.)
Post Office Box 13331
Louisville, Kentucky 40213
James Wille, President
(502) 459-8600

KENTUCKY GENTLEMEN (whiskey)
See Barton Brands, Ltd.

KENTUCKY KANDIES COMPANY
735 North Maple Avenue
Danville, Kentucky 40422

KENTUCKY KINGS (cigarettes)
See Brown & Williamson Tobacco Corporation

KENTUCKY UTILITIES COMPANY
120 South Limestone
Lexington, Kentucky 40507
William A. Duncan, President
(606) 255-1461

KENTWOOD DRUG COMPANY
Corryton, Tennessee 37721

KENWOOD ELECTRONICS INC.
15777 South Broadway
Gardena, California 90247
(213) 323-1400

KENWOOD LABORATORIES, INC.
39 Lawton Street
New Rochelle, New York 10801

KENWORTH TRUCK COMPANY
8801 East Marginal Way South
Seattle, Washington 98108
H.N. Gross, General Manager
(206) 764-5400

KENYON & THOMAS COMPANY
28 Grove Street
Adams, New York 13605

KENYON MARINE
Department BOBG 128
Guilford, Connecticut 06437
(203) 453-4374

KEPPEL'S INC.
323 North Queen Street
Lancaster, Pennsylvania 17604
Robert F. Keppel, Jr., Chairman, President and Chief Executive Officer
(717) 397-8214

KERALA (housewares and appliances)
See Koffler Sales Corporation

KERMCO PRODUCTS
Route One
Monroe, Iowa 50170

KERN FOODS, INC.
13000 East Temple Avenue
City of Industry, California 91746
Charles Kern, President
(213) 962-5111
See also Fruit Nectars Inc. & Caroline Foods Inc.

Companies and Trade Names

KERNEL-FRESH (salted nuts)
See General Foods Corporation

KERNS COMPANY, E.L.
302 North Broad Street
Trenton, New Jersey 08608
(609) 695-6151

KERR-CHANGEPOINT
8166 East 44th Street
Tulsa, Oklahoma 74145
(918) 622-0610

KERR CHEMICALS, INC.
500 Vista Avenue
Addison, Illinois 60101
(312) 543-2020

KERR GLASS MANUFACTURING CORPORATION
611 South Shatto Place
Los Angeles, California 90005
William A. Kerr, President
(213) 387-8243

KERR GLASS MANUFACTURING CORPORATION
Packaging Products Division
Lancaster, Pennsylvania 17604

KERR-MCGEE CORPORATION
Kerr-McGee Center
Oklahoma City, Oklahoma 73125
James J. Kelly, President and Chief Operations Officer
(405) 236-1313

KERRIGAN'S (whiskey)
See Four Roses Distillers Company

KERX (lawn and garden supplies)
See Lawn & Garden Supply Company

KESSELER COMPANY, D.E.
23 Leonard Street
New York, New York 10013
(212) 431-4700

KESSLER (whiskies and gin)
See Four Roses Distillers Company

KESSLER & COMPANY, ALBERT
1355 Market Street
San Francisco, California 94103
(415) 621-4000

KESSLER, INC., WILLIAM B.
1290 Avenue of the Americas
New York, New York 10019
Chester Kessler, President
(212) 581-1730

KESSLING THERMOMETER COMPANY, E.
682 Jamaica
Brooklyn, New York 11208
(212) 827-7730

KESTELL FURNITURE COMPANY, INC.
1311 Milwaukee Drive
New Holstein, Wisconsin 53061

KESTENMAN BROTHERS MANUFACTURING COMPANY
280 Kinsley Avenue
Providence, Rhode Island 02903

KESTER SOLDIER COMPANY
(Division of Litton Industries, Inc.)
4201 Wrightwood Avenue
Chicago, Illinois 60639
L.D. Kramer, President
(312) 235-1600

KETCHAM & MCDOUGALL, INC.
465 Eagle Rock Avenue
Roseland, New Jersey 07068
(201) 226-6060
See also Aqua Meter Instrument Corporation; Park Sherman; and Pat Products

KETCHIAN PHOTOGRAPHERS
259 Westview Avenue
Fort Lee, New Jersey 07024

KETCHUM & COMPANY
16 East 40 Street
New York, New York 10016
Harold M. Altshul, President
(212) 679-7930
See also Bio Products, Inc.

KETCHUM LABORATORIES, INC.
16 East 40th Street
New York, New York 10016
(212) 679-7930

KETTENBURG MARINE, INC.
(Division of Whittaker Corporation)
2810 Carleton Street
San Diego, California 92106
Paul A. Kettenburg, President
(714) 224-8211

KETTERING BAKING COMPANY
1823 Morgantown Avenue
Fairmont, West Virginia 26654

KETTLER OF AMERICA INC.
380 Franklin Turnpike
Mahwah, New Jersey 07430

KEUFFEL & ESSER COMPANY
20 Whippany Road
Morristown, New Jersey 07960
Thomas R. Nye, President
(201) 285-5000

KEW ELECTRONICS OF AMERICA
1A Ramapo Avenue
Suffern, New York 10901

KEW GARDENS (rattan furniture)
See Decorative Imports

KEW HILLS IMPORTS
77-03-05 Jamaica Avenue
Woodhaven, New York 11421

KEWAUNEE EQUIPMENT COMPANY
Post Office Box 186
401 Park Street
Kewaunee, Wisconsin 54216
(414) 388-3232

Companies and Trade Names

KEWPIE (canned foods)
See Mammoth Spring Canning Corporation

KEY (wines)
See Mogen David Wine Corporation

KEY CONTROL SYSTEMS, INC.
Post Office Box 96A
Bechtelsville, Pennsylvania 19505
(215) 845-7585

KEY INDUSTRIES, INC.
523 West Wall Street
Fort Scott, Kansas 66701
Kenneth W. Pollack, President
(316) 223-2000

KEY KOOL (food products)
See Keystone Co-operative Grape Association

KEY-MEN (shoes)
See Musebeck Shoe Company, Inc.

KEY NOVELTY MANUFACTURING COMPANY
309 North Third Street
Philadelphia, Pennsylvania 19106
(215) 925-3650

KEY PHARMACEUTICALS, INC.
Box 3670
50 N.W. 176th Street
Miami, Florida 33169
Michael Jaharis, Jr., President and Chief Executive Officer
(305) 652-2276
See also American Urologicals, Inc.

KEYES-DAVIS COMPANY
74 14th Street
Battle Creek, Michigan 49016
(616) 962-7505

KEYES FIBRE COMPANY
160 Summit Avenue
Montvale, New Jersey 07645
Wilson W. Cross, President and Chief Executive Officer
(201) 573-0200

KEYS ARCH SUPPORT COMPANY
90-32 51st Avenue
Elmhurst, New York 11373

KEYSTONE (kitchen cabinets)
See United Cabinet Corporation

KEYSTONE (photographic equipment, calculators)
See Berkey Keystone (Division of Berkey Photo Inc.)

KEYSTONE
(Division of Pennwalt Corporation)
21 and Lippincott Streets
Philadelphia, Pennsylvania 19132
(215) 225-7473

KEYSTONE BRONZE PAINT CORPORATION
See Keystone Paint & Varnish Corporation

KEYSTONE CANE & CRUTCH COMPANY
510 Abbott Drive
Broomall, Pennsylvania 19008
(215) 544-1020

KEYSTONE CO-OPERATIVE GRAPE ASSOCIATION
63 Wall
North East, Pennsylvania 16428

KEYSTONE CONSOLIDATED INDUSTRIES INC.
411 Hamilton Boulevard
Peoria, Illinois 61602
John R. Sommez, Chairman
(309) 676-8000
See also National Lock Hardware

KEYSTONE LABORATORIES, INC.
1103 Kansas Street
Memphis, Tennessee 38106
(901) 744-8860

KEYSTONE LAMP MANUFACTURING CORPORATION
(Subsidiary of LCA Corporation)
Slatington, Pennsylvania 18080
Walter Glover, President
(215) 767-3821

KEYSTONE ROOFING MANUFACTURING COMPANY
Windsor Park
York, Pennsylvania 17043
(717) 854-3894

KEYSTONE STEEL & WIRE
(Division of Keystone Consolidated Industries, Inc.)
7000 South Adams Street
Peoria, Illinois 61641
(309) 697-7020

KEYWOUND (alarm clocks)
See Westclox

KHATTAR, ANTOINE
47 West 34th Street
New York, New York 10001

KICKAPOO JOY JUICE (beverage)
See Moxie-Monarch-Nugrape Company

KIDD & COMPANY, INC.
308 North Martin Street
Ligonier, Indiana 46767
(219) 894-3131

KIDDE & COMPANY, INC., WALTER
9 Brighton Road
Clifton, New Jersey 07012
Fred R. Sullivan, President
(201) 777-6500
See also Grove Manufacturing Company; LCA Corporation; and Lefebure Corporation

Companies and Trade Names

KIDDIE BOUNCER (juvenile product)
See Hedstrom Company

KIDDIE CHAIRS (juvenile furniture)
See Century Products Inc.

KIDDIE PRODUCTS, INC.
1 Kiddie Drive
Avon, Massachusetts 02322
J.M. Karp, President
(617) 588-1220

KIDDIE WALKER (infants' product)
See Hedstrom Company

KIDIBUK (infants' auto seats)
See Century Products Inc.

KIDSTUFF (juvenile furniture)
See Group 7 Inc.

KIEHL PHARMACY
109 Third Avenue
New York, New York 10003
(212) 475-3400

KIEKHAEFER AEROMARINE
MOTORS INC.
Post Office Box 1458
1970 Aeromarine Drive
Fond du Lac, Wisconsin 54935
(414) 921-5330

KIEKHAEFER MERCURY
See Mercury Marine

KIENZLE TIME CORPORATION
INC.
436 Frontage Road
Northfield, Illinois 60693

KIERULFF ELECTRONICS INC.
(Subsidiary of Ducommun, Inc.)
2585 Commerce Way
Los Angeles, California 90040
John F. Darcy, President
(213) 685-5511

KIJAFA (Danish wines)
See General Wine & Spirits
Company

KIK-STEP (stools)
See Cramer Industries Inc.

KIKKOMAN (wines)
See Imported Brands, Inc.

KIKKOMAN INTERNATIONAL,
INC.
1581 Webster Street
San Francisco, California 94115
S. Suzuki, Vice President
(415) 563-8700

KIKO (pipes)
See Riesco Manufacturing &
Import Company

KIKU (women's toiletries)
See Faberge, Inc.

KILBOURN MACHINE COMPANY
INC.
Box 238
Stand Rock Road
Wisconsin Dells, Wisconsin 53965
(608) 254-2100

KILBURN CHEMICAL COMPANY
19615 Lake Road
Cleveland, Ohio 44116
(216) 333-3153

KILDEW (mildew preventive)
See John Clarke & Company,
Inc.

KILGORE CORPORATION
(Subsidiary of Conwood Corporation)
Toone, Tennessee 38381
D.K. Griffin, President
(901) 658-5231

KILIM (rugs)
See Cepelia Corporation

KILKENNY (men's sportswear)
See Alps Sportswear
Manufacturing Company Inc.

KILLASHUN SALES
Post Office Box 1252
Dothan, Alabama 36301

KILLINGER COMPANY, THE
Post Office Box 488
Marion, Virginia 24354

KILLINGTON MANUFACTURING
COMPANY
173 West Street
Rutland, Vermont 05701
Bernard Montant, President and
General Manager
(802) 773-3336

KILTIE (groceries)
See Alfred Lowry & Brother

KIM (cigarettes)
See Brown & Williamson
Tobacco Corporation

KIM CRAFTSMEN LTD.
16 West 36th Street
New York, New York 10018
(212) 244-1400

KIM PRODUCTS COMPANY INC.
Box 528
Clarksville, Arkansas 72830

KIMBALL PIANO & ORGAN
COMPANY, INC.
15th and Cherry Streets
Jasper, Indiana 47546
Thomas L. Habig, President
(812) 482-1600

KIMBALL PRODUCTS COMPANY
INC.
60 Union Avenue
Sudbury, Massachusetts 01776

Companies and Trade Names

KIMBALL-SCHMIDT INC.
Box 8158
Stockton, California 95204
Loren C. Belcher, President
(209) 466-1486

KIMBALL SYSTEMS
(Division of Litton Business Systems Inc.)
151 Cortlandt Street
Belleville, New Jersey 07109
H. Swett, Executive Vice President
(201) 759-6500

KIMBELL CANDY COMPANY
6546-56 West Belmont Avenue
Chicago, Illinois 60634
Jack G. Kimbell, President and Treasurer
(312) 777-2770

KIMBELL FOODS INC.
(Division of Kimbell Inc.)
Box 1540
920 Avenue R
Fort Worth, Texas 76101
(817) 647-1771

KIMBELL-HOT SPRINGS COMPANY
Hot Springs National Park, Arkansas 71901

KIMBELL, INC.
1929 South Main Street
Fort Worth, Texas 76101
Bob F. Scott, President
(817) 924-3271

KIMBERLY-CLARK CORPORATION
128 North Lake Street
Neenah, Wisconsin 54956
Harry J. Sheerin, President
(414) 729-1212
See also Karolton Envelope; Nylonge Corporation; and One-Way

KIMBERLY KNITWEAR
1411 Broadway
New York, New York 10018
(212) 221-7373

KIMBERRY CREATIONS, LTD.
79-76 Cooper Avenue
Glendale, New York 11227

KIMBIES (contour disposable diaper)
See Kimberly-Clark Corporation

KIMBLE
(Division of Owens-Illinois Inc.)
Box 1035
Toledo, Ohio 43601

KINCAID (pianos)
See Grand Piano Company Inc.

KINCAID FURNITURE COMPANY
Box 605
Hudson, North Carolina 28638
J. Wade Kincaid, President
(704) 728-3261

KINDL PRODUCTS, INC.
Box 228
Ridgewood, New Jersey 07451

KINDNESS (hair-care products)
See Clairol, Inc.

KINFOLKS (food products)
See Athens Canning Company

KING (minibike)
See King O'Lawn, Inc.

KING (rubber products)
See Ace Lite Step Company, Inc.

KING (syrup, starch, ammonia, bleach, fabric softener)
See Mangels, Herold Company

KING (whiskey)
See Brown-Forman Distillers Corporation

KING & CHOIE YACHTS
3333 West Coast Highway
Newport Beach, California 92660

KING ATHLETIC GOODS CORPORATION
2615 West Hunting Park Avenue
Philadelphia, Pennsylvania 19129
Harold Rosenbaum, President
(215) 223-8181

KING BROADCASTING COMPANY
320 Aurora Avenue, North
Seattle, Washington 98109
Ancil Payne, President
(206) 223-5000

KING CANDY COMPANY
Box 2080
813 East Ninth Street
Fort Worth, Texas 76102
Lonnie Oakes, President
(817) 332-6161

KING CARTER (seafood)
See Virginia Seafoods Inc.

KING COLE (groceries)
See Barbour Foods Ltd.

KING COLE (processed foods)
See Draper Canning Company

KING COMPANY, THE
Post Office Box 287
Travis Street
Owatonna, Minnesota 55060
(507) 451-3770

KING COMPANY, THE K.
307 North Camino Real
San Clemente, California 92672

KING COTTON (wine)
See Monarch Wine Company of Georgia

Companies and Trade Names

KING CRUISER ENGINE
 CORPORATION
2950 Ravenswood Road
Fort Lauderdale, Florida 33312
(305) 583-6171

KING EDWARD (cigars)
 See Jno. H. Swisher & Son Inc.

KING FILING SUPPLY
 CORPORATION
37 West 20th Street
New York, New York 10011
(212) 929-1565

KING FOODS, INC.
Post Office Box 26
Saint Paul, Minnesota 55075
(612) 459-5566

KING FROST FOODS, INC.
1900 Alfred
Detroit, Michigan 48207
(313) 965-1387

KING GEORGE IV (Scotch whiskey)
 See Munson Shaw Company

KING JAMES (Scotch whiskey)
 See American Distilling Company

KING KOIL (mattresses)
 See United States Bedding
  Company

KING KORN (food products)
 See Big Stone Canning Company

KING KORN STAMP COMPANY
6001 North Clark
Chicago, Illinois 60626
Ira Kaplan, President
(312) 274-7338

KING KULLEN (beer)
 See Horlacher Brewing Company

KING KULLEN GROCERY
 COMPANY
1194 Prospect Avenue
Westbury, New York 11590
Walter H. Miller, President
(516) 333-7100

KING KUP-SCHOENER CANDIES,
 INC.
Eighth and Reading Avenues
West Reading, Pennsylvania 19602

KING LABORATORIES
Plant 333 Kirby
Garland, Texas 75040

KING MANUFACTURING
 COMPANY
2601 Davison
Flint, Michigan 48506

KING MUSICAL INSTRUMENTS
(Division of Seeburg Corporation)
33999 Curtis Boulevard
Eastlake, Ohio 44094
Nate Dolin, President
(216) 946-6100
 See also Deford Inc., E.L.

KING NEPTUNE COMPANY
1445 N.W. 56th Street
Seattle, Washington 98107
(206) 783-9143

KING O'LAWN, INC.
10127 Adella Avenue
South Gate, California 90280
Leonard A. Faas, Sr., Chairman
(213) 567-2103

KING OF SPUDS, INC.
Post Office Box 191
East Grand Forks, Minnesota 56721
T.G. Light, President
(218) 773-9761

KING PHARMACEUTICAL
 COMPANY
26 North 77th Street
Birmingham, Alabama 35206
 See also Riddle Laboratories

KING PHARR CANNING
 OPERATIONS, INC.
Box 130
Cullman, Alabama 35055
(205) 734-5520

KING RADIO CORPORATION
400 North Rogers Road
Olathe, Kansas 66061
Edward J. King., Jr., President
(913) 782-0400

KING RESEARCH, INC.
114 12th Street
Brooklyn, New York 11215
(212) 788-0122

KING SALES & ENGINEERING
 COMPANY
870 Harrison Street
San Francisco, California 94107
(415) 392-7664

KING SANO (cigarettes)
 See United States Tobacco
  Company

KING-SEELY THERMOS COMPANY
(Subsidiary of Household Finance
 Corporation)
3989 Research Park Drive
Ann Arbor, Michigan 48104
Robert C. Trow, President
(313) 769-4200
 See also Halsey Taylor; Queen
  Products; Rochester Paper;
  and Structo

KING SHRIMP COMPANY, INC.
Post Office Box 899
Brunswick, Georgia 31520
J. Roy Duggan, President
(912) 265-5155

KING STOVE & RANGE COMPANY
Sheffield, Alabama 35660
William H. Martin, III, President
(205) 383-2421

Companies and Trade Names

KING TEXTILES, INC., NANCY
Post Office Box 848
North Wilkesboro,
 North Carolina 28659

KING TOPPER (canned foods)
 See Philip Olender & Company

KING WILLIAM IV (Scotch whiskey)
 See Renfield Importers, Ltd.

KINGMAN MANUFACTURING
 COMPANY, INC.
Cunningham, Kansas 67035
(316) 298-2811

KINGPIN (tobacco and cigarettes)
 See Liggett & Myers Inc.

KING'S CHOICE (seafood)
 See K & C Food Sales

KINGS CRAFT CORPORATION
Post Office Box 2306
Florence, Alabama 35630
(205) 764-5512

KINGS CREEK CANNING
 COMPANY, INC.
Post Office Box 206
Princess Anne, Maryland 28153
(301) 651-1717

KING'S DEPARTMENT STORES,
 INC.
150 California Street
Newton, Massachusetts 02158
Paul Kwasnick, President
(617) 969-6600

KING'S FOOD PRODUCTS INC.
12 North 35th Street
Belleville, Illinois 62223

KING'S HOUSE (frozen foods)
 See A.J. Pietrus & Sons Company

KING'S RANSOM (Scotch)
 See International Brands

KING'S SPECIALTY COMPANY
Post Office Box 207
Fort Wayne, Indiana 46801
(219) 742-7231

KINGS SPECIALTY COMPANY
482 Baltic
Brooklyn, New York 11217
(212) 624-7510

KINGSBURY (beer)
 See G. Heileman Brewing
 Company

KINGSDOWN INC.
Third and Holt Streets
Mebane, North Carolina 27302
(919) 563-3531

KINGSFORD COMPANY
Post Office Box 1033
940 Commonwealth Building
Louisville, Kentucky 40201
Owen Pyle, President
(502) 583-2801

KINGSLEY (sportswear)
 See Lampl Fashions

KINGSLEY COMPANY, L.J.
Box 726
Binghamton, New York 13902

KINGSLEY FURNITURE COMPANY,
 INC.
101 Park Street
La Porte, Indiana 46350
Louis E. Kottler, President
(219) 362-3105

KINGSRIDGE (menswear)
 See J. Schoeneman Inc.

KINGSTON (cigars)
 See Stephano Brothers

KINGSTON (vacuum cleaner)
 See Scott & Fetzer Company,
 Douglas Division

KINGSTON (watches)
 See World Wide Watch
 Company, Inc.

KINGSTON INDUSTRIES
 CORPORATION
205-A Lexington Avenue
New York, New York 10016
(212) 889-0190

KINGSTON KNITTING MILLS,
 INC.
139 Cornell Street
Kingston, New York 12401
Richard H. Pauker, President
(914) 331-1600

KINGSWAY (shoes)
 See International Shoe Company

KINGWOOD CERAMICS
Box 30
East Palestine, Ohio 44413

KINKEAD INDUSTRIES, INC.
(Subsidiary of United States
 Gypsum Company)
5860 North Pulaski Road
Chicago, Illinois 60646
William S. Kinkead, Chairman
(312) 463-7800

KINNEAR CORPORATION, THE
1191 Fields Avenue
Columbus, Ohio 43201
Gordon Hildreth, President
(614) 294-4451

KINNEY & COMPANY, INC.
1307 12th Street
Columbus, Indiana 47201

KINNEY RENT A CAR
170 Broadway
New York, New York 10018
(212) 962-6772

858

Companies and Trade Names

KINNEY SHOE CORPORATION
(Subsidiary of F.W. Woolworth Company)
233 Broadway
New York, New York 10007
R.L. Anderson, President
(212) 349-8300

KINNEY'S CANDIES
Post Office Box 1609
Big Spring, Texas 79720

KINRECO PRODUCTS COMPANY, INC.
324 Broadway
Valley Falls, Kansas 66088

KIP (burn ointment, first-aid cream, etc.)
See BBC Laboratories

KIP PHARMACEUTICAL
134-02 Liberty Avenue
Richmond Hill, New York 11419

KIPPER YACHTS
928 West 17th Street
Costa Mesa, California 92627

KIPPY KIT COMPANY
Box 149
Circleville, Ohio 43113

KIRBY COMPANY
(Division of Scott & Fetzer Company)
1920 West 114th Street
Cleveland, Ohio 44102
Adrian E. Budlong, Jr., President
(216) 228-2400

KIRBY'S (shoes)
See Cannon Shoe Company

KIRCHHEIMER, WALTER A.
67-66 108th Street
Forest Hills, New York 11375
(212) 544-0535

KIRIN BREWERY COMPANY LTD.
700 South Flower Street
Los Angeles, California 90017
(213) 628-5374

KIRK & MATZ LTD.
Post Office Box 221
Danbury, Connecticut 06810

KIRK & SON, INC., SAMUEL
Kirk Avenue and 25th Street
Baltimore, Maryland 21218
Samuel Kirk Millspaugh, President
(301) 243-2960

KIRK CORPORATION
International Division
11 East 26th Street
New York, New York 10010
(212) 889-6033

KIRK LABORATORIES INC., C.F.
655 Madison Avenue
New York, New York 10021
Raymond Spector, Chairman and President
(212) 838-2285

KIRK PLASTIC COMPANY, INC.
170 East Jefferson Boulevard
Los Angeles, California 90011
(213) 231-9288

KIRKLAND CUSTOM CANNERY
640 Eighth Avenue
Kirkland, Washington 98033

KIRKMAN (soap products)
See Colgate-Palmolive Company

KIRKMAN LABORATORIES, INC.
934 N.E. 25th Avenue
Portland, Oregon 97208
Stanley N. Bachman, Chairman of the Board
(503) 233-4444

KIRKPATRICK'S (food products)
See Mark 7 Seafood & Industries

KIRKWOOD (mobile homes)
See Redman Industries Inc.

KIRSCH BEVERAGES, INC.
112-02 15th Avenue
College Point, New York 11356
Lee Kirsch, President
(212) 358-2000

KIRSCH COMPANY
309 North Prospect Street
Sturgis, Michigan 49091
John W. Kirsch, Chairman of the Board
(616) 651-2311

KIRSCH CORPORATION, J.A.
299 Broadway
New York, New York 10007
(212) 233-3800

KIRSCH IMPORTS INC., H.
22-03 Parsons Boulevard
Whitestone, New York 11357

KIRSTEN PIPE COMPANY, INC.
Post Office Box 70526
1807 N.W. Dock Place
Seattle, Washington 98107
(206) 783-0700

KISSELINCHEV, INC., L.
261 Broadway
New York, New York 10007
(212) 267-3559

KISSLING COMPANY, A.C.
140 East Richmond Street
Philadelphia, Pennsylvania 19125
A.C. Kissling, President
(215) 423-4700

KIST (beverages)
See Monarch-Nugrape Company

KIT (floor wax)
See S.C. Johnson & Son, Inc.

859

Companies and Trade Names

KIT MANUFACTURING COMPANY
1700 Santa Fe Avenue
Long Beach, California 90813
Dan Pocapalia, President
(213) 436-5264

KITCHEN GRAND (food products)
See Loyal Canning Corporation

KITCHEN HOLIDAY (frozen prepared foods)
See Morton Frozen Foods (Division of ITT Continental Baking Company)

KITCHEN KING (jams and jellies)
See J.M. Smucker Company

KITCHEN KOMPACT, INC.
811 East 11th Street
Jeffersonville, Indiana 47130
W. Dwight Gahm, President
(812) 282-6681

KITCHEN-KRISPER (electric tray)
See Phinney-Hale Inc.

KITCHEN MASTER (housewares)
See Gemini International Corporation

KITCHEN QUEEN (food products)
See Aunt Nellie's Foods Inc.

KITCHEN-QUIP, INC.
405 East Marion Street
Waterloo, Indiana 46793
Francis M. Metrailer, President
(219) 837-8311

KITCHEN READY (seafood)
See Carnation Seafoods

KITCHEN TREAT (canned and frozen foods)
See Blue Star Foods, Inc. (Iowa)

KITCHENAID
(Division of The Hobart Manufacturing Company)
Troy, Ohio 45373
David B. Meeker, President
(513) 335-7171

KITCHENS OF SARA LEE
(Subsidiary of Consolidated Foods Corporation)
500 Waukegan Road
Deerfield, Illinois 60015
Thomas F. Barum, President
(312) 945-2525

KITCHING (percussion musical instruments)
See Coast Wholesale Music Company of Los Angeles

KITTAY & BLITZ INC.
104 West 29th Street
New York, New York 10001
(212) 594-7900

KITTEN (children's clothing)
See Jayvee Brand, Inc.

KITTENETTES (shoes)
See Brauer Brothers Shoe Company

KITTEN'S (shoes)
See Brauer Brothers Shoe Company

KITTINGER COMPANY, INC.
(Division of General Interiors Corporation)
1893 Elmwood Avenue
Buffalo, New York 14207
Fred J. Batson, Chairman of the Board
(716) 876-3010

KITTY (cat food)
See New England Fish Company

KITZBUHEL (men's sportswear)
See Alps Sportswear Manufacturing Company Inc.

KIWI POLISH COMPANY, THE
Pottstown, Pennsylvania 19464
Lawrence Emley, President
(215) 326-5800

KLARER OF KENTUCKY, INC.
(Subsidiary of Armour, Inc.)
Post Office Box 1200
1200 Story Avenue
Louisville, Kentucky 40201
(502) 582-0011

KLASSIC MANUFACTURING COMPANY
Box 557
Sedalia, Missouri 65301

KLAUBER BROTHERS, INC.
114 East 32nd Street
New York, New York 10016
Roger Klauber, President
(212) 686-2531

KLAUBER WANGENHEIM COMPANY
611 Island Avenue
San Diego, California 92112
Howard Gardner, President and Treasurer
(714) 234-0201

KLEAN 'N KLING (kitchen carpet tiles)
See Ozite Corporation

KLEAN STRIP
Post Office Box 1879
Memphis, Tennessee 38101
G.E. Conaway, President
(901) 775-0100

KLEAR (wax)
See S.C. Johnson & Son Inc.

Companies and Trade Names

KLEECO PUBLISHING INC.
834 North Church Road
Elmhurst, Illinois 60126
(312) 833-1990

KLEEN CHEMICAL
  MANUFACTURING COMPANY
2511 North Sheffield Avenue
Chicago, Illinois 60614
Robert G. Edison, President
(312) 472-7312

KLEEN GUARD (furniture polish)
  See Alberto-Culver Company

KLEEN TEST PRODUCTS INC.
Post Office Box 574
102 East Keefe Avenue
Milwaukee, Wisconsin 53212
Bruce L. Milligan, President
(414) 372-2090

KLEENETTE MANUFACTURING
  COMPANY
2215 South Michigan
Chicago, Illinois 60616
(312) 326-3800

KLEENEX (table napkins, tissues, towels)
  See Kimberly-Clark Corporation

KLEENITE (denture cleanser)
  See Vick Chemical Company

KLEER FLO COMPANY, THE
(Division of Practical Manufacturing
  Company)
250 West 57th
New York, New York 10019
(212) 246-5941

KLEER-VU INDUSTRIES INC.
666 Third Avenue
New York, New York 10017
Benjamin Osher, Chairman, President and Chief Executive
  Officer
(212) 697-6900

KLEERPAK MANUFACTURING
  COMPANY
13051 Saticoy Street
North Hollywood, California
Sidney Yedlin, President and
  Purchasing Agent
(213) 875-0951

KLEID NAUTICAL INSTRUMENTS,
  ROBERT E.
24 Lee Drive
Fairfield, Connecticut 06430

KLEIN & COMPANY
29-10 Thomson Avenue
Long Island City, New York 11101
Jesse L. Salwen, Chairman and
  President
(212) 937-4010

KLEIN CHOCOLATE COMPANY
Brown Street
Elizabethtown, Pennsylvania 17022

KLEIN INC., MAX
715 Lynn Avenue
Baraboo, Wisconsin 53913
(608) 356-6626

KLEIN INC., RICHARD A.
349 Lenox Street
Norwood, Massachusetts 02062
M.H. Brodrick, President
(617) 762-3520

KLEIN, SAMUEL
70 Jay Street
Brooklyn, New York 11201
(212) 858-7333

KLEIN STEEL COMPANY
432 North Buckeye Street
Bellevue, Ohio 44811
Edgar A. Klein, President and
  Secretary
(419) 483-3840

KLEINERT'S, INC.
350 Fifth Avenue
New York, New York 10001
Jack Brier, President
(212) 946-1933

KLEINFELD INC., LEONARD T.
59-08 Woodside Avenue
Woodside, New York 11377

KLEPA ART INTERNATIONAL INC.
6739 Odessa Avenue
Van Nuys, California 91406

KLEV BROTHERS SHOE
  MANUFACTURING COMPANY
(Division of George E. Keith
  Company)
Manchester Road
Derry, New Hampshire 03038
Paul I. Kleven, President
(603) 432-3341

KLING (furniture)
  See Ethan Allen, Inc.

KLING PHOTO CORPORATION
25-20 Brooklyn-Queens Expressway
  West
Woodside, New York 11377

KLIPSCH & ASSOCIATES, INC.
Post Office Box 688
Hope, Arkansas 71801
Paul W. Klipsch, President
(501) 777-6751

KLIX CHEMICAL COMPANY
551 Railroad Avenue
South San Francisco,
  California 94080
M.R. Takata, President and
  General Manager
(415) 761-0622

KLOPP ENGINEERING INC.
Post Office Box 2098
35551 Schoolcraft Street
Livonia, Michigan 48151
(313) 421-4000

Companies and Trade Names

KLUG
See Galen Laboratories

KLUGHARTT THORNHILL
MACHINERY COMPANY
1205 Woodswether Road
Kansas City, Missouri 64105
(816) 421-6296

KLUGMANN & SON, MORITZ
99 Nassau Street
New York, New York 10038
(212) 962-5484

KLUGMANN INC., ALFRED
43 West 16th Street
New York, New York 10011
(212) 924-5886

KLUTCH COMPANY
403 Lake Street
Elmira, New York 14902

KLUXEN WINES, HERMAN A.
Post Office Box 154
Spring Lake, New Jersey 07762
(201) 449-4774

KNABE (pianos)
See Aeolian Corporation

KNACK (safety razor)
See Gillette Company, Safety Razor Division

KNACKS (men's slacks)
See Ratner Clothes for Men

KNAPE & VOGT MANUFACTURING
COMPANY
2700 Oak Industrial Drive N.E.
Grand Rapids, Michigan 49505
Donald J. Knope, President
(616) 459-3311

KNAPP KING-SIZE CORPORATION
1 Knapp Centre
Brockton, Massachusetts 02401
Winthrop A. Short, President
(617) 588-9000

KNAPP-SHERRILL COMPANY
Drawer E
Eighth and Silver Streets
Donna, Texas 78537
(512) 464-3382

KNEIP INC., E.W.
(Subsidiary of Peter Eckrich & Sons Inc.)
Box 161
7501 Brown Avenue
Forest Park, Illinois 60130
John C. Stamm, President
(312) 379-8200

KNEISSL (sports accessories and equipment)
See Saska Sports Industries

KNICKERBOCKER CASE
CORPORATION
2950 West Chicago Avenue
Chicago, Illinois 60622
Chester W. Buchsbaum, President
(312) 489-489-4038

KNICKERBOCKER FEATHER
CORPORATION
233 Norman Avenue
Brooklyn, New York 11222
(212) 389-6464

KNICKERBOCKER GUILD INC.
687 Broadway
New York, New York 10012
(212) 673-9000

KNICKERBOCKER MILLS
COMPANY
Box Nine, Totowa Bridge
Totowa, New Jersey 07511
(201) 256-7700

KNICKERBOCKER TOY COMPANY,
INC.
1107 Broadway
New York, New York 10010
Leo L. White, President
(212) 924-6810

KNIGHT COMPANY, THE CHARLES
Box 3613
Birmingham, Alabama 35211

KNIGHT CORPORATION, STANLEY
1600 East Birchwood Avenue
Des Plaines, Illinois 60018

KNIGHT PHARMACAL COMPANY
705 West Kirk Place
San Antonio, Texas 78226

KNIGHT-RIDDER NEWSPAPER,
INC.
1 Herald Plaza
Miami, Florida 33101
Alva H. Chapman, President
(305) 350-2082

KNIGHT TOY & NOVELTY
CORPORATION
57 Hanse Avenue
Freeport, New York 11520

KNIT-MATES, INC.
32 33rd Street
Brooklyn, New York 11232
Bernard Schwartz, President
(212) 768-2800

KNOBLER & COMPANY, INC.,
ALFRED E.
200 Moonachie Avenue
Moonachie, New Jersey 07074

KNOCABOUTS (luggage)
See Hartmann Luggage Company, Inc.

862

Companies and Trade Names

KNOEPFLER BROTHERS
200 Fifth Avenue
Suite 636
New York, New York 10010
(212) 924-0673

KNOLL & COMPANY, INC., H.G.
99 Tracy Place
Hewlett, New York 11557

KNOLL PHARMACEUTICAL COMPANY
30 North Jefferson Road
Whippany, New Jersey 07981
(201) 887-8300

KNOMARK, INC.
(Division of A Papercraft Company)
132-20 Merrick Boulevard
Jamaica, New York 11434
Jack F. Kofoed, Vice President
(212) 276-3400

KNOPF, INC., ALFRED A.
(Affiliation of Random House, Inc.)
201 East 50th Street
New York, New York 10022
Robert Gottlieb, President
(212) 751-2600

KNORR (soups)
See CPC International Inc., Best Foods Division

KNORR BEESWAX PRODUCTS, INC.
Box 109
Del Mark, California 92014

KNOTHE BROTHERS COMPANY INC.
24 West 40th Street
New York, New York 10018
Harold Cohen, President
(212) 391-0550
See also Varsity Pajamas

KNOTT HOTELS CORPORATION
575 Madison Avenue
New York, New York 10022
James Knott, Chairman of the Board
(212) 759-6100

KNOTT'S BERRY FARM
Preserving Department
8039 Beach Boulevard
Buena Park, California 90620

KNOUSE FOODS, INC.
Peach Glen, Pennsylvania 17306
Dean L. Carey, President
(717) 677-8181

KNOX (gelatine)
See Thomas J. Lipton, Inc.

KNOX (men's hats)
See Byer-Rolnick (Division of Koracorp Industries Inc.)

KNOX FIBERGLASS PRODUCTS INC.
Box 12126
Knoxville, Tennessee 37912

KNOX LABORATORIES
2335 South Michigan Avenue
Chicago, Illinois 60616
Mitchell Knox, Sales Manager
(312) 326-2828

KNOX STOVE WORKS
Post Office Box 751
Knoxville, Tennessee 37901
James W. McNutt, President
(615) 524-4113

KNOXALL (hand tools and furniture)
See O. Ames Company

KNOXVILLE UTILITIES BOARD
626 Gay Street, S.W.
Knoxville, Tennessee 37901
Thomas J. Stephenson, Jr., Chairman of the Board
(615) 524-2911

KNUDSEN CORPORATION
231 East 23rd Street
Los Angeles, California 90011
J.R. Vaughan, President
(213) 747-6471

KNUT AND KNUT LTD.
487 Fullerton Avenue
Elmhurst, Illinois 60126

KO-WE-BA (groceries)
See Kothe, Wells & Bauer Company, Inc.

KOALA INN (hotel/motel chain)
See International Motel Corporation N.V.

KOBRAND CORPORATION
134 East 40th Street
New York, New York 10016
John Bush, President
(212) 686-3322

KOCH RECORDER
Haverhill, New Hampshire 03765

KOCH SONS INC., GEORGE
Post Office Box 358
10 South 11th Avenue
Evansville, Indiana 47744
Robert L. Koch, President and Treasurer
(812) 425-1321

KOCKUMS (enamel cookware)
See RMH International, Inc.

KODACHROME (photographic film, etc.)
See Eastman Kodak Company

KODAK (photographic products-- film, cameras, projectors)
See Eastman Kodak Company

KODEMASTER (door chimes, freezer alarms)
See Faraday, Inc.

863

Companies and Trade Names

KODIAK (seafood)
See Washington Fish & Oyster Company, Inc.

KOEHLER ASSOCIATES, KARL
Box 144
Coopersburg, Pennsylvania 18036

KOEHLER-DAYTON INC.
(Division of Litton Industries)
Box 309
South Street
New Britain, Connecticut 06050
Frank Bogusz, President and General Manager
(203) 225-3501

KOEHLER'S (beer, etc.)
See Erie Brewing Company

KOEHRING COMPANY
780 North Water Street
Milwaukee, Wisconsin 53202
Richard J. Lindgren, Chairman and President
(414) 273-2300

KOENIG & COMPANY, HARRY D.
7 Main Street
East Rockaway, New York 11518

KOERNER & COMPANY, INC., JOHN E.
218 Airline Highway
Metairie, Louisiana 70001

KOFF MUSIC COMPANY
Box 1442
Studio City, California 91604

KOFFLER SALES CORPORATION
4501 Lincoln Avenue
Chicago, Illinois 60625
(312) 334-5200

KOH-I-NOOR RAPIDOGRAPH, INC.
100 North Street
Bloomsbury, New Jersey 08804
William E. Danjczek, President
(201) 479-4124

KOHINOOR DIAMOND CORPORATION
City National Bank Building
Birmingham, Alabama 35203

KOHL & COMPANY
407 Seventh Street
Rock Falls, Illinois 61071

KOHL CORPORATION
11100 West Burleigh Street
Milwaukee, Wisconsin 53201
Herbert Kohl, President
(414) 771-8000

KOHLER & CAMPBELL, INC.
Box 448
Highway 321A, North
Granite Falls,
   North Carolina 28630
Charles L. Clayton, President
(704) 396-3376

KOHLER COMPANY
High Street
Kohler, Wisconsin 53044
Herbert V. Kohler, Jr., President
(414) 457-4441

KOHLERT (bassoons and other woodwind instruments)
See Sorkin Music Company Inc.

KOHL'S FOOD STORES
5940 West Touhy
Niles, Illinois 60648

KOHMAN, H.A.
6533 Wilkins Avenue
Pittsburgh, Pennsylvania 15217
(412) 521-1716

KOHNER BROTHERS, INC.
(Subsidiary of General Foods Corporation)
Box 294
1 Paul Kohner Place
East Paterson, New Jersey 07407
Oran G. Kirkpatrick, President
(201) 797-9500

KOHNSTAMM & COMPANY, INC., H.
161 Avenue of the Americas
New York, New York 10013
Paul L. Kohnstamm, President and Treasurer
(212) 929-7000

KOHNSTAMM INC., V. & E.
Third Avenue and 33rd Street
Brooklyn, New York 11232
(212) 788-6320

KOK IMPORTS, JAC
1359 River Avenue
Lakewood, New Jersey 08701

KOKEN MANUFACTURING COMPANY INC.
1932 North Broadway
Saint Louis, Missouri 63102
Tak Yoshikawa, President
(314) 231-7383

KOKOMO OPALESCENT GLASS COMPANY, INC.
Box 809
State and Market Streets
Kokomo, Indiana 46901
Lawrence G. Coles, President
(317) 457-8136

KOL-PAK (seafood)
See Quality Col-Pak Inc.

KOLB & SON LTD., ANDREW
112 Madison Avenue
New York, New York 10016
(212) 684-2980

KOLB-LENA CHEESE COMPANY
Lena, Illinois 61048

KOLCRAFT PRODUCTS INC.
1511 West 38th Street
Chicago, Illinois 60609
Sanfred Koltun, Chairman and President
(312) 247-4494

Companies and Trade Names

KOLD-GUARD (air-cooling units)
See Frick Company

KOLD-HOLD
(Division of Tranter Manufacturing Inc.)
735 East Hazel
Lansing, Michigan 48909
(517) 372-8410

KOLD KIST, INC.
5329 East Washington Boulevard
Los Angeles, California 90022
Edwin H. Jarvis, President
(213) 261-0331

KOLDWAVE MARINE
(Division of Heat Exchangers Inc.)
8100 North Monticello
Skokie, Illinois 60076

KOLE ENTERPRISES, INC.
Post Office Box 520152
3553 N.W. 50th Street
Miami, Florida 33142
(305) 633-2556

KOLLER & SMITH COMPANY INC.
532 Fifth Avenue
Pelham, New York 10803
(914) 738-1303

KOLLMORGEN CORPORATION
60 Washington Street
Hartford, Connecticut 06106
Robert L. Swiggett, President
(203) 547-0600

KOLLSMAN INSTRUMENT CORPORATION
(Subsidiary of Standard Kollsman Industries, Inc.)
575 Underhill Boulevard
Syosset, New York 11791

KOLMAR LABORATORIES, INC.
Skyline Drive
Port Jervis, New York 12771
Richard L. Kole, Chairman of the Board
(914) 856-5311

KOLOR KOTER CORPORATION
85 Brookside Avenue
Amsterdam, New York 12010

KOLTER BUCKEYE COMPANY
460 South Elizabeth Street
Lima, Ohio 45802

KOLVET (cameras)
See Camera Specialty Company Inc.

KOMAR & SONS, INC., CHARLES
180 Madison Avenue
New York, New York 10016
(212) 725-1500

KOMBI LTD.
114 Manhattan Street
Stamford, Connecticut 06902

KOMISAR & SON INC., DAVID
560 Hempstead Avenue
West Hempstead, New York 11552
(212) 347-6330

KOMMEL & SONS, A.
65 West 36th Street
New York, New York 10018
(212) 524-7317

KONA KAI (menswear)
See Jantzen Inc.

KONDON MANUFACTURING COMPANY
(Division of Wonderful Dream Salve Company)
Box 223
Croswell, Michigan 48422

KONEL CORPORATION
(Subsidiary of Narco Scientific Industries, Inc.)
271 Harbor Way
South San Francisco, California 94080
Aldo De Francesco, President
(415) 873-9393

KONGO CHEMICAL COMPANY, INC.
456 Charlotte Avenue
Detroit, Michigan 48201
(313) 833-0086

KONICA CAMERA COMPANY
(Division of Berkey Photo, Inc.)
25-20 Brooklyn-Queens Expressway, West
Woodside, New York 11377
Henry Froehlich, President
(212) 932-4040

KONKOTE (paints and paint sundries)
See Gable-Tite Products Company Inc.

KONTAK (food freezer)
See Frick Company

KONTRELL INDUSTRIES INC.
Jeanne Drive
Newburgh, New York 12550

KONZ WOOD PRODUCTS COMPANY
616 North Perkins
Appleton, Wisconsin 54911
R.L. Konz, President
(414) 734-7770

KOOL (cigarettes)
See Brown & Williamson Tobacco Corporation

KOOL-AID (soft-drink mixes)
See General Foods Corporation

KOOL-SHADE (awnings)
See Borg-Warner Corporation

KOOLY KUPP, INC.
Box 373
360 King Street
Pottstown, Pennsylvania 19464
Albert P. Castello, President
(215) 326-7900

Companies and Trade Names

KOPPER KETTLE (food)
See C.H.B. Foods Inc.

KOPPEREX (anodized aluminum kitchen ware, canister sets)
See Kromex

KOPPER'S CHOCOLATE SPECIALTY COMPANY
18 Waverly Place
New York, New York 10003
(212) 254-5827

KOPPERS COMPANY INC.
Koppers Building
Pittsburgh, Pennsylvania 15219
Douglas Grymes, President
(412) 391-3300

KOPPERS COMPANY, INC.
Metal Products Division
Box 298
Baltimore, Maryland 21203
(301) 727-2500

KOPY KAT INSTANT PRINTING CENTERS
Executive Plaza
Fort Washington, Pennsylvania 19034

KORACORP INDUSTRIES, INC.
617 Mission Street
San Francisco, California 94105
William K. Warnock, President
(415) 957-2000
See also Capri Sportswear, Inc.; Koret of California, Inc.; Oxford Clothes Inc.; and Rainfair, Inc.

KORAL LABORATORIES, INC.
188 Casino Drive
Farmingdale, New Jersey 07727

KORALLE SAILBOAT COMPANY
4140 Lincoln Boulevard
Marina del Rey, California 90291

KORBEL & BROTHERS, INC., F.
Guerneville, California 95446

KORBRO OIL CORPORATION
129-19 89th Avenue
Richmond Hill, New York 11419
(212) 849-1600

KORD MANUFACTURING COMPANY, INC.
4510 White Plains Road
Bronx, New York 10470
Sidney Unger, President
(212) 325-7700

KOREA SILK COMPANY, INC.
480 Seventh Avenue
New York, New York 10001
(212) 594-9741

KORES MANUFACTURING CORPORATION
11 Clearbrook Road
Elmsford, New York 10523
(914) 593-3310

KORET, INC.
(Subsidiary of Gordon International, Ltd.)
33 East 33rd Street
New York, New York 10016
Michael Gordon, President
(212) 683-8544

KORET OF CALIFORNIA, INC.
(Division of Koracorp Industries Inc.)
611 Mission
San Francisco, California 94105
(415) 957-2000

KORETZ COMPANY, PAUL
128 Central Park South
New York, New York 10019
(212) 246-6639

KOREX INDUSTRIES
821 Malcolm Road
Burlingame, California 94010

KORNLAND (meats)
See Rath Packing Company

KORODY COMPANY, INC., ALEXANDER
118 East 25th Street
New York, New York 10010
(212) 674-8787

KORRECT-WAY (wood and metal furniture)
See American Fixture Inc.

KORRIGAN CORPORATION
1410 Broadway
New York, New York 10018
P.J. Ancellin, Vice President
(212) 244-5482

KORVETTES
(Division of Arlen Realty & Development Corporation)
450 West 33rd Street
New York, New York 10001
Marshall Rose, Chairman of the Board
(212) 560-6500

KORVYN, INC., T.G.
66 Broad
Carlstadt, New Jersey 07072
(212) 564-1252

KOSCHERAK BROTHERS, INC.
225 Fifth Avenue
New York, New York 10010
(212) 684-4545

KOSHER DESSERTS, INC.
8 West 28th Street
New York, New York 10001
(212) 685-4672

KOSS CORPORATION
4129 North Port Washington Avenue
Milwaukee, Wisconsin 53212
John C. Koss, Chairman of the Board
(414) 964-5000

KOSTER KEUNEN INC.
Bourne Boulevard
Sayville, New York 11782
(516) 589-0400

Companies and Trade Names

KOSTO FOOD PRODUCTS
COMPANY
430 South Wheeling Road
Wheeling, Illinois 60090

KOTEX (feminine-hygiene products)
See Kimberly-Clark Corporation

KOTHE, WELLS & BAUER
COMPANY, INC.
50 South Ko-We-Ba Lane
Indianapolis, Indiana 46201
Albert C. Gisler, Chairman and
President
(317) 636-4507

KOTON (house paint)
See Embree Manufacturing
Company

KOUNTRY KITCHEN (cast-iron ware)
See National Silver Company

KOUNTY KIST (vegetables)
See Green Giant Company

KOURY COMPANY, INC. W.
633 Chatham Street
Sanford, North Carolina 27330
Joseph D. Koury, President
(919) 775-5415

KOWA AMERICAN CORPORATION
45 West 34th Street
New York, New York 10001
(212) 868-9450

KOWALSKI SAUSAGE COMPANY,
INC.
2270 Holbrook Avenue
Hamtramck, Michigan 48212
Stephen Z. Kowalski, President
(313) 873-8200

KOYLON-CRESTAIRE (mattresses)
See Uniroyal, Inc.

KOZY (radiant-heat pad)
See Radiant Products (Department
of The Bouligny Company)

KRACO ENTERPRISES, INC.
2411 North Santa Fe Avenue
Compton, California 90224
Lawrence M. Kraines, President
(213) 774-2550

KRACOR INC.
1045 13th Avenue
Grafton, Wisconsin 53024
(414) 377-3355

KRAEMER MERCANTILE
CORPORATION
500 Fifth Avenue
New York, New York 10036
Harris E. Baer, President
(212) 564-5665

KRAEUTER (hand tools)
See Dresser Industries, SK Tools
Hand Tool Division

KRAFFT'S CANDIES, INC.
2204 San Pablo Avenue
Berkeley, California 94702

KRAFT FOODS
(Division of Kraftco Corporation)
500 Peshtigo Court
Chicago, Illinois 60690
O. Everett Swain, President
(312) 222-4600

KRAFT PHARMACEUTICAL
COMPANY
1442 Klosterman Avenue
Oreland, Pennsylvania 19075

KRAFTCO CORPORATION
Kraftco Court
Glenview, Illinois 60025
William O. Beers, Chairman of the
Board
(312) 998-2000
See also Breakstone Sugar Creek
Foods; Humko Products;
and Sealtest Foods

KRAFTWARE CORPORATION
225 Fifth Avenue
Suite 312-316
New York, New York 10010
(212) 679-8186

KRAK-TITE (paints and paint
sundries)
See Gable-Tite Products
Company Inc.

KRAKAUER BROTHERS
115 East 138th Street
Bronx, New York 10451
Robert K. Bretzfelder, President
(212) 292-0573

KRAKOW (food products)
See Marietta Canning Company

KRAKUS (Polish ham)
See United States Food Products,
Inc.

KRAMER & COMPANY, WILLIAM C.
26th and Parrish Streets
Philadelphia, Pennsylvania 19130
(215) 765-1688

KRAMER-AZIF TEXTILE COMPANY
180 Madison Avenue
New York, New York 10016
(212) 532-3120

KRAMER YACHTS
21 Colorado Avenue
Bridgeport, Connecticut 06605
(203) 384-8000

KRANE MANUFACTURING
COMPANY
(Division of Northwestern Bottle
Company)
2222 North Second Street
Saint Louis, Missouri 63160
(314) 231-5959

Companies and Trade Names

KRANICH & BACH
(Division of Aeolian Corporation)
33 West 57th Street
New York, New York 10019
W.G. Heller, Chairman of the
  Board
(212) 751-0050

KRASKIN BATON COMPANY
Post Office Box 23022
219 Master
Minneapolis, Minnesota 55423
(612) 890-5153

KRASS-JOSEPH, INC.
401 Hackensack Avenue
Hackensack, New Jersey 07601

KRATEN (food products)
  See Kraft Foods

KRATT COMPANY, WILLIAM
988 Johnson Place
Union, New Jersey 07083
(201) 688-8600

KRAUS COMPANY LTD., FRANK
92 North Avenue
New Rochelle, New York 10802

KRAUSE MILLING COMPANY
Post Office Box 1156
611 East Wisconsin Avenue
Milwaukee, Wisconsin 53201
Charles A. Krause, President
(414) 272-6200

KRAUSE PLOW CORPORATION
Hutchinson, Kansas 67501
(316) 663-6161

KRAUSS, INC., JOHN
144-27 94th Avenue
Jamaica, New York 11435
Donald Timmons, President
(212) 523-7600

KRAUTH & BENNINGHOFEN INC.
3001 Symmes Road
Hamilton, Ohio 45015
Frederick B. Diesbach, President
(513) 874-4400

KRAZY GLUE INC.
53 West 23rd Street
New York, New York 10010
(212) 741-9544

KRAZY KANDLES INC.
Post Office Box 1137
Santa Cruz, California 95061

KREIS LABORATORIES
158 South Rodeo Drive
Beverly Hills, California 90212

KREISLER MANUFACTURING
  CORPORATION
9015 Bergenline Avenue
North Bergen, New Jersey 07047
Edward L. Stern, President
(201) 869-0131

KREISS, INC., SIDNEY J.
350 Fifth Avenue
New York, New York 10001
Sidney J. Kreiss, President
(212) 564-4340

KREMENTZ & COMPANY
49 Chestnut Street
Newark, New Jersey 07101
Richard Krementz, Jr., President
(201) 621-8300

KREMERS-URBAN COMPANY
Box 2038
5600 West County Line Road
Milwaukee, Wisconsin 53201
Ray A. Johns, President
(414) 354-4300

KREML (hair-care products)
  See J.B. Williams Company

KRESGE COMPANY, S.S.
3100 West Big Beaver Road
Troy, Michigan 48084
Ervine Wardlow, President
(313) 643-1000

KRESGE FARM FOOD PACKERS
R.F.D. Number Two
Lehighton, Pennsylvania 18235

KRESO DIP NO. 1 (disinfectant)
  See Parke, Davis and Company

KRESS & COMPANY, S.H.
(Division of Genesco, Inc.)
114 Fifth Avenue
New York, New York 10011
A.L. Walker, President
(212) 929-2700

KRESS & OWEN COMPANY
Box 198
Oceanport, New Jersey 07757

KRETSCHMER WHEAT GERM
  PRODUCTS
(Division of International
  Multifoods Corporation)
126 Maple Ridge
Carrollton, Michigan 48724

KREY PACKING COMPANY
3607 North Florissant
Saint Louis, Missouri 63107
John F. Krey, President
(314) 231-2925
  See also Kelly Foods Inc.

KRIBKINS (juvenile furniture)
  See Lullabye Company

KRIER PRESERVING COMPANY
Belgium, Wisconsin 53004
Ray D. Krier, President and
  Treasurer
(414) 285-3411

Companies and Trade Names

KRISCHER METAL PRODUCTS
COMPANY
111 Moonachie Avenue
Moonachie, New Jersey 07074
Max Gelfman, President
(201) 935-4040

KRISPY (saltines)
See Sunshine Biscuits, Inc.

KRISPY KITCHENS (frozen foods)
See Tyson Foods Inc.

KRISTAL KRAFT INC.
900 Fourth Street
Palmetto, Florida 33561
(813) 722-3206

KRISTIN ELLIOTT INC.
Box 23
Beverly, Massachusetts 01915

KRISTIN INTERNATIONAL (sports apparel)
See Jacobs Corporation

KRISWILL (tobacco)
See Sutliff Tobacco Company

KROEHLER MANUFACTURING
COMPANY
222 East Fifth Avenue
Naperville, Illinois 60540
Richard E. Burow, President
(312) 420-6789

KROGER COMPANY, THE
1014 Vine Street
Cincinnati, Ohio 45202
James P. Herring, Chairman
(513) 381-8000

KROMEX
(Division of Atapco)
880 East 72nd Street
Cleveland, Ohio 44103
(216) 361-2922

KRONA-CHROME (razor blades)
See Schick Safety Razor
Company

KRONE MANUFACTURING INC.
3670 North Milwaukee Avenue
Chicago, Illinois 60641
(312) 282-1670

KRONE-ROYALE PRODUCTS
COMPANY
17115 Sherfield Place
Southfield, Michigan 48075

KRONENBOURG (beer)
See Original Beer Importing &
Distributing Company, Inc.

KROULEE CORPORATION
250 East Hartsdale Avenue
Hartsdale, New York 10530
(914) 725-5867

KROUPA'S INC.
11586 Center Road
Traverse City, Michigan 49684

KROWN FOODS
415 Madison Avenue
New York, New York 10017

KROYSEN (beer)
See Joseph Schlitz Brewing
Company

KRU-KUT COMPANY
Box 445
San Clemente, California 92672

KRUEGER (beer and ale)
See Narragansett Brewing
Company

KRUEGER COMPANY, RUDOLPH E.
883-G West 16th Street
Newport Beach, California 92660

KRUM & COMPANY, S.S.
90 West Broadway
New York, New York 10007
(212) 964-4497

KRUMRINE & SONS
R.F.D. Two
Westminster, Maryland 21157

KRYSTAL COMPANY
701 Cherry Street
Chattanooga, Tennessee 37402
R.B. Davenport, III, President
(615) 266-3643

KRYSTAL SKIS INC.
1942 East 11th Street
Tacoma, Washington 98401

KUBLA KHAN FOOD COMPANY
3617 East 17th Avenue
Portland, Oregon 97202
Percy W. Loy, President
(503) 234-7494

KUEHN COMPANY, OTTO L.
4065 North 35th
Milwaukee, Wisconsin 53216
(414) 873-9100

KUEHNERT & COMPANY,
INC., A.
150 Madison Avenue
New York, New York 10016
(212) 684-5448

KUEPPER FAVOR COMPANY, INC.
Post Office Box 428
206 North Cass Street
Peru, Indiana 46970
George C. Kuepper, President
(317) 473-5586

KUGEL, L.J.
16A4B Atlanta Merchandise Mart
Atlanta, Georgia 30303

Companies and Trade Names

KUHN'S BIG K STORES
CORPORATION
3040 Sidco Drive
Nashville, Tennessee 37204
Jack W. Kuhn, President
(615) 242-6321

KULICKE/CONTRACT
636 Broadway
New York, New York 10012
(212) 254-0140

KULMBACHER IMPORT COMPANY,
INC.
61-20 71st Avenue
Glendale, New York 11227

KUNDO (clocks)
See Cuckoo Clock Manufacturing
Company, Inc.

KUNER-EMPSON COMPANY
(Division of Stokely Van Camp,
Inc.)
Box 329
Brighton, Colorado 80601
Maynard K. Tescher, President
(303) 659-1710

KUNST FORUM, LTD.
350 Warren Street
Jersey City, New Jersey 07302

KUNTZENDORF & COMPANY, C.
436 South Wabash Avenue
Chicago, Illinois 60605
(312) 427-6688

KUPFER INC., JULIUS
79-10 Albion Avenue
Elmhurst, New York 11373
(212) 898-0700

KUPPENHEIMER & COMPANY,
INC., B.
3040 West Lake Street
Chicago, Illinois 60612
Harry Roth, Chairman of the Board
(312) 632-2727

KUPPER INC., HERMAN C.
11 East 26th Street
New York, New York 10010
(212) 684-2952

KURL-OFF (paint and varnish
remover)
See Hillyard Chemical Company

KURLASH COMPANY, INC., THE
(Subsidiary of House of Westmore)
128 South Avenue
Rochester, New York 14604
Irving L. Smith, President
(716) 232-7860

KURLY KATE CORPORATION
2215 South Michigan
Chicago, Illinois 60616
Edward Matz, Jr., President
(312) 842-2327

KURTZ BROTHERS INC.
Post Office Box 392
Fourth and Reed Streets
Clearfield, Pennsylvania 16830
Robert M. Kurtz, Jr., President
(814) 765-6561

KURTZ COMPANY, INC., DAVID
350 Fifth Avenue
New York, New York 10001
(212) 594-2540

KURZ-HASTINGS, INC.
Dutton and Darnell Roads
Philadelphia, Pennsylvania 19154
(215) 632-2300

KUSAN, INC.
(Subsidiary of Bethlehem Steel
Corporation)
3206 Belmont Boulevard
Nashville, Tennessee 37212
R.L. Chickey, President
(615) 385-1560
See also Nichols-Kusan, Inc.;
and Schaper Manufacturing
Company

KUSAN INC.
J. Halpern Division
810 Penn Avenue
Pittsburgh, Pennsylvania 15222
(412) 462-2171

KUSH-N-ARCH (shoes)
See Musebeck Shoe Company,
Inc.

KUSTOM ELECTRONICS INC.
1010 West Chestnut
Chanute, Kansas 66720
Wayne A. McMurtney, President
(316) 431-4380

KUTCHINS KITCHEN (bread)
See New Process Baking Company

KUTZ-KWIK, INC.
19 West 269 Lake Street
Addison, Illinois 60101

KUTZIT (liquid paint remover)
See Savogran Company

KWAL PAINTS INC.
3900 Joliet Street
Denver, Colorado 80217
Harold Weinberg, President
(303) 371-5600

KWIK-BILT INC.
3114 Benton Street
Garland, Texas 75042
(214) 494-1164

KWIK CHEK STORES
See Winn-Dixie Stores, Inc.

KWIK-KOLD, INC.
Post Office Box 696
Moberly, Missouri 65270

KWIK-KOPY CORPORATION
3308-K Ella Boulevard
Houston, Texas 77018
(713) 688-2571

Companies and Trade Names

KWIK STEAK (frozen meat)
See Meal Time Foods, Inc.

KWIKSET
(Division of Emhart Corporation)
516 East Santa Ana Street
Anaheim, California 92803
C.B. Mortensen, President
(714) 535-8111

KWIP INDUSTRIES
Post Office Box 5188
Santa Monica, California 90405

KYANIZE PAINTS INC.
Second and Boston
Everett, Massachusetts 02149
Harry A. Hall, III, President and
 Treasurer
(617) 387-5000

KYLE COSMETIC COMPANY
1800 North Highland Avenue
Hollywood, California 90028
(213) 463-3504

KYSOR INDUSTRIAL CORPORATION
1 Madison Avenue
Cadillac, Michigan 49601
Raymond A. Weigel, President and
 Chief Executive Officer
(616) 775-4646
   See also Warren-Sherer

L

L & B (food products)
See Roberts Food Corporation

L & B PRODUCTS CORPORATION
Post Office Box 53
3232 Lurting Avenue
Bronx, New York 10469
(212) 882-5400

L & D PRODUCTS INTERNATIONAL
1112A West Ninth Street
Upland, California 91786

L & J (wine)
See California Wine Association

L & L SPECIALTIES COMPANY
1133 Arch Street
Philadelphia, Pennsylvania 19107
(215) 563-0644

L & M (cigarettes)
See Liggett & Myers Inc.

L & R MANUFACTURING
COMPANY
577 Elm Street
Kearny, New Jersey 07032
James J. Lazarus, President
(201) 991-5330

L & S BAIT COMPANY, INC.
148 South Kennedy Avenue
Bradley, Illinois 60915
(815) 932-5733

L & S BEARING COMPANY
Post Office Box 1537
6 South Pennsylvania Avenue
Oklahoma City, Oklahoma 73101
(405) 236-5501

L.A.L. PRODUCTS
Eighth and Randolph Streets
Radford, Virginia 24141

L.A.T. DESIGNS
504 South Oak Park Avenue
Oak Park, Illinois 60302

LB LABS. INC.
1605 South Central Avenue
Glendale, California 91204

LCA CORPORATION
(Subsidiary of Walter Kidde & Company)
2 Decker Square
Cynwyd, Pennsylvania 19004
Jerome H. Feig, President
(215) 839-0450
See also Farber, S.W.; Keystone Lamp Manufacturing Corporation; and Rexair Inc.

LCA CORPORATION
Weltron Division
260 Bethpage Spagnolia Road
Melville, New York 11746

L.C. GOOD CANDY COMPANY
1825 East Tremont Street
Allentown, Pennsylvania 18103

LFE CORPORATION
1601 Trapelo Road
Waltham, Massachusetts 02154
Herbert Roth, Jr., President and Chief Executive Officer
(617) 890-2000

LFE CORPORATION
Eastern Industries Division
100 Skiff Street
Hamden, Connecticut 06514
(203) 248-3841

L-K ENTERPRISES
1125 Ellen Kay Drive
Marion, Ohio 43302

L.M.G. CORPORATION
8915 Northend
Ferndale, Michigan 48220

LP (percussion instruments)
See Latin Percussion

LPS RESEARCH LABORATORIES INC.
2050 Cotner
Los Angeles, California 90025
Thomas M. Cavanagh, President
(213) 478-0095

L Q MOTOR INNS INC.
Century Building, Suite 300-E
San Antonio, Texas 78216

LTV CORPORATION, THE
Post Office Box 5003
Dallas, Texas 75222
W. Paul Thayer, Chairman of the Board
(214) 742-9555
See also Wilson & Company, Inc.

LXX (tires)
See Firestone Tire & Rubber Company

LA BELLE INDUSTRIES INC.
Oconomowoc, Wisconsin 53066

LA BOHEME (wine)
See Schenley Industries, Inc.

LA CHOY FOOD PRODUCTS
(Division of Beatrice Foods Company)
Post Office Box 220
Stryker Street
Archbold, Ohio 43502
J.J. McRobbie, General Manager
(419) 445-8015

LA CONGA (rum)
See Continental Distilling Corporation

Companies and Trade Names

LA CORONA (cigars)
　See American Cigar

LA COSTA (food products)
　See Heublein Inc.

LA CREPE (restaurant franchise)
　See General Franchising Corporation

LA CROSSE PHARMACEUTICAL COMPANY
1502 Miller Drive
La Crosse, Wisconsin 54601

LA DAINTY (hair-care products, bleaching ointment, etc.)
　See Tyson-White Labs.

LA FAMOSA (juices, nectars, tomato sauce)
　See Frozen Fruit Concentrates, Inc.

LA FAVORITA (groceries)
　See Tosi & Company

LA FEMME (shoes)
　See Bristol Manufacturing Corporation

LA FLEUR (handbags)
　See Fancy Industries Inc.

LA FLEUR IMPORTING CORPORATION
Brooklyn Navy Yard, Building 5
Brooklyn, New York 11205
(212) 834-8100

LA FRANCE (laundry products)
　See General Foods Corporation

LA GUSTOSA (food products)
　See Tillie Lewis Foods Inc.

LA HUERTA (food products)
　See C-100 Corporation

LA JOLLA (fine china)
　See Sascha Brastoff of California Inc.

LA LAME INC.
1170 Broadway
New York, New York 10001
(212) 532-7324

LA LANNE COMPANY, THE JACK
621 Allen Avenue
Glendale, California 91201
Jack La Lanne, President
(213) 843-8010

LA LICORNE (sports apparel)
　See Gondola Internationale Inc.

LA MANCHA (cigars)
　See Consolidated Cigar Corporation

LA MANCHA (guitars, mandolins)
　See Sorkin Music Company Inc.

LA MAR TOY COMPANY INC.
148 39th Street
Brooklyn, New York 11232
(212) 788-2537

LA MARCHE MANUFACTURING COMPANY
106 Bradrock Drive
Des Plaines, Illinois 60018
(312) 299-1195

LA MAUR, INC.
Post Office Box 1221
5601 East River Road
Minneapolis, Minnesota 55440
Richard G. Spiegel, President
(612) 566-1234
　See also House of Style, The

LA MERE INDUSTRIES, INC.
227 North Main Street
Walworth, Wisconsin 53184
(414) 275-2171

LA MESA (food products)
　See Heublein Inc.

LA MONICA (seafood)
　See Cape May Canners Inc.

LA PALINA (cigars)
　See Consolidated Cigar Corporation

LA PALOMA (spaghetti, macaroni, noodles)
　See Anthony Macaroni Company

LA PAREE (brass musical instruments)
　See David Wexler & Company

LA PINA (flour)
　See General Mills, Inc.

LA PINE SCIENTIFIC COMPANY
6001 South Knox Avenue
Chicago, Illinois 60629
(312) 735-4700

LA PRIMADORA (cigars)
　See Universal Cigar Corporation

LA QUINTA (hotel/motel chain)
　See L Q Motor Inns Inc.

LA REGINA (macaroni and noodle products)
　See Long Island Macaroni Company

LA REINE (women's boots)
　See Torch Rubber Company

LA REYNA (food products)
　See C-100 Corporation

Companies and Trade Names

LA ROSA & SONS, INC.
1495 Greenleaf
Elk Grove Village, Illinois 60007
(312) 437-8935

LA SALLE EXTENSION UNIVERSITY
(Subsidiary of Macmillan, Inc.)
417 South Dearborn Street
Chicago, Illinois 60605
Warren B. Smith, President
(312) 427-4181

LA SOLANA POTTERIES, INC.
Box 613
Scottsdale, Arizona 85252
(602) 945-6123

LA TOURAINE-BICKFORD'S
 FOODS, INC.
1 Gateway Center
Newton, Massachusetts 02158
John C. Harding, President
(617) 969-4050

LA TOURAINE COFFEE COMPANY
(Division of La Touraine-Bickford's
 Foods, Inc.)
1 Gateway Center
Newton, Massachusetts 02158
(617) 969-4050

LA TRIQUE BRASSIERES
171 Madison Avenue
New York, New York 10016
(212) 685-1653

LA VICTORIA FOODS INC.
Box 309
Rosemead, California 91770

LA VIE (champagne)
 See Cucamonga Vineyard
 Company

LA VOZ CORPORATION
8484 San Fernando Road
Sun Valley, California 91352

LA-Z-BOY CHAIR COMPANY
1284 North Telegraph
Monroe, Michigan 48161
C.T. Knabasch, President
(312) 242-1444

LAACKE & JOYS COMPANY
1433 North Water Street
Milwaukee, Wisconsin 53202
H.C. Woehr, President
(414) 271-7878

LABATT IMPORTERS, INC.
3980 Sheridan Drive
Buffalo, New York 14226
(716) 839-5440

LABCO PRODUCTS COMPANY
285 Washington Street
Somerville, Massachusetts 02143
(617) 625-3100

LABEL GUN INC.
2115 Colorado Avenue
Santa Monica, California 90406

LA BELLE INDUSTRIES, INC.
Oconomowoc, Wisconsin 53066
W.M. Ivie, Manager
(414) 567-5527

LABELON CORPORATION
10 Chapin Street
Canandaigua, New York 14424
E. Billings Brewster, President and
 Treasurer
(315) 394-6220
 See also Philips Ribbon & Carbon
 Company

LABORATORY DATA CONTROLS
Interstate Industrial Park
Riviera Beach, Florida 33404
(305) 844-5241

LABORATORY DIAGNOSTICS
 COMPANY
1116 Walnut Street
Roselle, New Jersey 07203

LABORATORY FOR ELECTRONICS,
 INC.
 See LFE CORPORATION

LABROT & GRAHAM (whiskey)
 See Brown-Forman Distillers
 Corporation

LAC-O-NAML (paint)
 See Gard Industries, Inc.

LACAGNINA & SONS, L.
83 Jay Street
Rochester, New York 14608
(716) 546-7042

LACE OF FRANCE, INC.
989 Avenue of the Americas
New York, New York 10018
(212) 947-6333

LACEY MILLING COMPANY
Post Office Box 1193
Hanford, California 93230
(209) 584-6634

LACKAWANNA LEATHER COMPANY
Richard Mine Road
Wharton, New Jersey 07885
(201) 361-5600

LACKAWANNA PANTS MANU-
 FACTURING COMPANY
3000 Brooks
Scranton, Pennsylvania 18502
Theodore Koppelman, President
(717) 342-9221

LACLEDE STEEL COMPANY
10 South Broadway
Saint Louis, Missouri 63102
Paul B. Akin, President
(314) 621-5800

LACO PRODUCTS, INC.
4201 Pulaski Highway
Baltimore, Maryland 21224
(301) 327-5010

874

Companies and Trade Names

LACOLITE INDUSTRIES
936 North Michigan Avenue
Chicago, Illinois 60611
(312) 664-4700

LACONIA SHOE COMPANY
(Subsidiary of Morton's Shoe Stores, Inc.)
59 Water Street
Laconia, New Hampshire 03246
Robert J. Selig, President
(603) 524-2000

LACOSTE (toiletries)
See Jean Patou Inc.

LACROSSE RUBBER MILLS COMPANY
Indian Hill
LaCrosse, Wisconsin 54602
Albert P. Funk, Jr., President
(608) 782-3020

LACSA AIRLINES
238 Biscayne Boulevard
Miami, Florida 33132
Roberto Carrillo, General Manager
(305) 377-4793

LACTONA CORPORATION
(Division of Warner-Lambert Pharmaceutical Company)
201 Tabor Avenue
Morris Plains, New Jersey 07950
(201) 540-2470

LACTOPINE (men's and women's toiletries)
See Swiss Pine Importing Company, Inc.

LACY MANUFACTURING COMPANY, INC.
901 Adele Street
Martinsville, Virginia 24112
W.J. Lester, President
(703) 638-2437

LADCO LABORATORIES, INC.
3821 West Jefferson Boulevard
Los Angeles, California 90016
(213) 734-9141

LADD IMPORTING COMPANY INC.
11 West 37th Street
New York, New York 10018

LADDERLITE (aluminum ladders)
See Lawnlite Company

LADDS-NESSLER COMPANY, INC.
Water Street
Chester, Connecticut 06412

LADIES CHOICE (food products)
See R & S Pickle Company Inc.

LAD'N DAD SLACKS, INC.
(Subsidiary of Pacesetter Industries)
Post Office Box 246
Cumming, Georgia 30130
Joe Cohen, President
(404) 887-2353

LADY ALDEN (groceries)
See Laurans-Standard Grocery Company, Inc.

LADY ALICE (grocery products)
See Piggly Wiggly Corporation

LADY ARISTETTE (home hair dryers)
See Metal Ware Corporation

LADY ARNOLD (plastic housewares, furniture, dinnerware)
See Arnoldware-Rogers Inc.

LADY ARROW
(Division of Cluett Peabody & Company Inc.)
1001 Sixth Avenue
New York, New York 10009
(212) 279-8500

LADY BALTIMORE (luggage and leather goods)
See Baltimore Luggage Company

LADY BERKLEIGH (pajamas)
See Michael Berkowitz Company, Inc.

LADY BERKSHIRE (dresser sets)
See National Silver Company

LADY BETTY (grocery products)
See Shedd-Bartush Foods Inc.

LADY BOSCA (leather goods and gifts)
See Hugo Bosca Company, Inc.

LADY BOSTONIAN (women's shoes)
See Kayser-Roth Shoes, Inc.

LADY CHESTERFIELD (robes)
See H. Hanchrow & Company

LADY CLARK (ironing tables, platform ladders)
See J.R. Clark Company

LADY EMILY
(Division of Glamorise Foundations, Inc.)
135 Madison Avenue
New York, New York 10016
(212) 684-5025

LADY ESTER LINGERIE CORPORATION
152 Madison Avenue
New York, New York 10016
Sam W. Sadock, President
(212) 684-1235

LADY ESTHER (face powder, cream)
See Cooper Labs.

LADY EVERSHARP (razors)
See Schick Safety Razor Company

LADY FASHION (shoes)
See International Shoe Company

LADY GODIVA COSMETICS
Box 536
Sonora, California 95370

Companies and Trade Names

LADY KENMORE (major appliances)
See Sears, Roebuck and Company

LADY LORA COMPANY, INC.
8340 South Birkhoff Avenue
Chicago, Illinois 60620
Eric Otten, President
(312) 487-9191

LADY LYNNE LINGERIE
105 Madison Avenue
New York, New York 10016
(212) 686-6655

LADY MAC CORSET COMPANY, INC.
700 Main Street
Buffalo, New York 14202
(716) 854-1034

LADY MANHATTAN COMPANY, THE
(Division of Manhattan Industries, Inc.)
1407 Broadway
New York, New York 10018
Richard J. Cole, President
(212) 765-1250

LADY MARLENE BRASSIERE CORPORATION
20 West 33rd Street
New York, New York 10001
S. Gerstein, President

LADY NELSON (watches)
See M.Z. Berger & Company Inc.

LADY OF PARIS (hosiery)
See Virginia Maid Hosiery Mills, Inc.

LADY PEPPERELL (bed and bathroom furnishings)
See West Point Pepperell

LADY PETITE (housewares and appliances)
See Allied Hardware Services Inc.

LADY PRESCO (ironing boards and covers, laundry aids)
See Pressing Supply of California

LADY ROMANCE INC.
31 East 32nd Street
New York, New York 10016
(212) 685-4062

LADY ROSE (food products)
See Food Specialties Company Inc.

LADY ROSE
(Division of Masters, Inc.)
725 Summa Avenue
Westbury, New York 11590
Louis Biblowitz, Chairman of the Board
(516) 997-8000

LADY SHAVEX (electric razors)
See Electro Engineering Products Company, Inc.

LADY SUZANNE FOUNDATIONS INC.
2615 West 13th Street
Brooklyn, New York 11223
(212) 373-7700

LADY TECHMATIC (razors)
See Gillette Safety Razor Company

LADY VANITY (hair dryer)
See Atlas Corporation, Merit Division

LADY WEBCOR (home appliances)
See Consolidated Merchandising Company

LADY WINSTED (small appliances)
See Capitol Products Company (Connecticut)

LADY WRANGLER (sportswear)
See Blue Bell, Inc.

LADYBUG (high-intensity lamp)
See Tensor Corporation

LADYBUG (women's apparel)
See Villager Industries, Inc.

LADYFINGER PRODUCTS
(William Thomas & Sons, Inc.)
Slocum Avenue
Ridgefield, New Jersey 07657

LAFAYETTE COMPANY
253 West 16th Street
New York, New York 10011
(212) 242-0850

LAFAYETTE PHARMACAL, INC.
522-26 North Earl Avenue
Lafayette, Indiana 47904
(317) 447-3129

LAFAYETTE PRODUCTS COMPANY, INC.
203 East Third Street
Mount Vernon, New York 10550

LAFAYETTE RADIO ELECTRONICS CORPORATION
111 Jericho Turnpike
Syosset, New York 11791
Leonard D. Pearlman, President
(516) 921-7700

LAFF MASTERS STUDIOS INC.
Post Office Box T
Merrick, New York 11566

LAFRANCE (hosiery)
See Bachelor's Friend Hosiery Company

LAGOSTA (rose wine)
See Austin, Nichols & Company, Inc.

LAGRANGE (cognac)
See Park, Benziger & Company, Inc.

Companies and Trade Names

LAGRANGE INC.
13209 Saticoy
North Hollywood, California 91605
(213) 875-0061

LAGUNA COSMETIC COMPANY
465 Forest Avenue
Laguna Beach, California 92652

LAHCO (sports apparel)
See Free Trade Center Inc.

LAHER SPRING & ELECTRIC CAR CORPORATION
2615 Magnolia Street
Oakland, California 94607
T.J. Laher, President
(415) 444-1350
See also Lasco Brake Products Corporation, Ltd.

LAIDLAW CORPORATION
200 N.E. Adams
Peoria, Illinois 61602
(309) 673-9021

L'AIGLON (pipes)
See Peterson's Ltd.

L'AIGLON APPAREL, INC.
1400 Broadway
New York, New York 10018
Louis Epstein, President
(212) 594-0800

L'AIMANT (perfume, hand and body lotion, etc.)
See Coty

L'AIR DU TEMPS (bath oil, perfume, etc.)
See Nina Ricci

LAIRD & COMPANY
Laird Road
Scobeyville, New Jersey 07724
L.W. Laird, President
(201) 542-0312

LAIRD O'LOGAN (Scotch whiskey)
See Four Roses Distillers Company

LAITRAM CORPORATION
Post Office Box 50699
New Orleans, Louisiana 70150
(504) 581-9521

LAKE CHARLEVOIX (canned and frozen vegetables)
See Sherman Brothers Canning Company

LAKE CHELAN GROWERS UNION
Chelan, Washington 98816

LAKE CHEMICAL COMPANY
250 North Washtenaw Avenue
Chicago, Illinois 60612
E. Cooper, President
(312) 826-1700

LAKE COUNTY FRUIT EXCHANGE
Post Office Box 365
Kelseyville, California 95451

LAKE GOLD (fruit juices)
See Golden Gem Growers Inc.

LAKE HAMILTON CITRUS, INC.
Box 351
Bartow, Florida 33830

LAKE PLACID (sports accessories and equipment)
See Silva Company

LAKE PRODUCTS COMPANY
1254 Grover Road
Saint Louis, Missouri 63125
(314) 892-3600

LAKE REGION (canned foods)
See Durand Canning Company

LAKE SHORE (food products)
See W.F. Straub & Company

LAKE TO LAKE DAIRY COOPERATIVE
2000 South Tenth Street
Manitowoc, Wisconsin 54220
Russell Gash, President
(414) 684-3343

LAKELAND (dairy products)
See Carthage Creamery

LAKELAND MANUFACTURING COMPANY
Sheboygan, Wisconsin 53081
George Holman, President
(414) 457-7759

LAKE'S MANUFACTURING INC.
Box 382
Ypsilanti, Michigan 48197
(313) 483-0257

LAKESHORE ARTISANS
Post Office Box 160
Belgium, Wisconsin 53004

LAKESIDE CANDY COMPANY, INC.
3200 16th Street
Zion, Illinois 60099

LAKESIDE CENTRAL COMPANY
2945 West 31st Street
Chicago, Illinois 60623
W.A. Jaicks, Jr.
(312) 254-5000

LAKESIDE INDUSTRIES
See Leisure Dynamics, Inc.

LAKESIDE LABORATORIES
(Subsidiary of Colgate-Palmolive Company)
1707 East North Avenue
Milwaukee, Wisconsin 53201

LAKESIDE METALCRAFT COMPANY
339 West Hovey Avenue
Muskegon Heights, Michigan 49444

Companies and Trade Names

LAKESIDE PACKING COMPANY
Box 186
Manitowoc, Wisconsin 54220
(414) 684-3356

LAKEVIEW (food products)
See Wilson & Company Inc.

LALANI (pineapple)
See Safeway Stores, Inc.

LAMA COMPANY, TONY
1137 Tony Lama Street
El Paso, Texas 79915
Joseph H. Lama, President
(915) 778-8311

LAMALLE, CHARLES F.
1123 Broadway
New York, New York 10010
(212) 924-2348

LAMB-WESTON, INC.
(Subsidiary of Amfac, Inc.)
Post Office Box 23507
6600 S.W. Hampton Street
Portland, Oregon 97223
John E. Gomena, President
(503) 639-8612

LAMBA-FI (men's sportswear)
See Alps Sportswear Manufacturing Company, Inc.

LAMBDA PHARMACAL
LABORATORIES
1 Fairchild Court
Plainview, New York 11803

LAMBERT CORPORATION
519 Hunter Avenue
Dayton, Ohio 45404
W.B. Lambert, President
(513) 223-7295

LAMBERT-KAY
(Division of Carter-Wallace, Inc.)
32 Lake Street
Winsted, Connecticut 06098
(203) 379-8559

LAMBERTI (wines)
See Renfield Importers, Ltd.

LAMBOOY-UNIQUE CORPORATION
2222 North 13th Street
Terre Haute, Indiana 47904
(812) 232-9561

LAMINATED & COATED PRODUCTS
(Division of Saint Regis Paper Company)
55 Starkey Avenue
Attleboro, Massachusetts 02703
Kermit Greene, Vice President and
  Division General Manager
(617) 222-3500

LAMINEX INC.
Post Office Box 368
Matthews, North Carolina 28105

LAMOTT (oboes, English horns,
clarinets, etc.)
See Jack Spratt Woodwind Shop

LAMOUR HAIR PRODUCTS, INC.
88 North Highland Avenue
Ossining, New York 10562
Charles C. Lamour, President
(914) 762-4540

LAMPARIELLO & SON, D.
210-12 Grand Street
New York, New York 10013
(212) 226-3441

LAMPCRAFT INDUSTRIES INC.
3320 South Normal Avenue
Chicago, Illinois 60616
William Field, Vice President
(312) 548-5222

LAMPL FASHIONS
(Bobbie Brooks Inc.)
30600 Carter
Solon, Ohio 44139

LAMPLIGHT PRODUCTS INC.
3625 North 126th Street
Brookfield, Wisconsin 53005
(414) 781-6300

LAMPLIGHTER (gin)
See McKesson Liquor Company

LAMPLIGHTER (sportswear)
See Revere Knitting Mills Inc.

LAMPS OF BEAUTY (table lamps)
See Mario Sales Inc.

LAMSON & GOODNOW
MANUFACTURING COMPANY
45 Conway
Shelburne Falls, Massachusetts 01370
Lucius Nims, President
(413) 625-6331

LAMSTON, INC., M.H.
212 Fifth Avenue
New York, New York 10010
Burton Adelman, President
(212) 689-3260

LAN-CHILE AIRLINES
150 S.E. Second Avenue
Miami, Florida 33131
Rolando Duque, General Manager
(305) 377-4721

LAN-O-SHEEN, INC.
1 West Water
Saint Paul, Minnesota 55107
(612) 224-5681

LAN-O-TONE PRODUCTS
65 Wooster Street
New York, New York 10012

LANA LOBELL (ladies' apparel)
See Hanover House Industries,
  Inc.

LANACANE (medicated skin cream)
See Combe, Inc.

LANAKILA CRAFTS INC.
1809 Bachelot Street
Honolulu, Hawaii 96817
(808) 531-0555

Companies and Trade Names

LANARK (men's coats)
See Edward Makransky Company, Inc.

LANCASTER COLONY CORPORATION
37 West Broad Street
Columbus, Ohio 43215
J.B. Gerlach, President
(614) 224-7141
See also Barr, Inc.; Brody Company, E.O.; Colony Cookware Corporation; Enterprise Aluminum Company; Indiana Glass Company; Pitman-Dreitzer; and Pretty Products Inc.

LANCASTER GLASS CORPORATION
220 West Main Street
Lancaster, Ohio 43130
Robert K. Fox, President
(614) 653-0311

LANCASTER, INC.
6700 11th Avenue
Los Angeles, California 90043
(213) 758-1134

LANCASTER SALTED NUT COMPANY
Lancaster, Pennsylvania 17604
(717) 392-7381

LANCASTER TOY COMPANY
535 East Mifflin Street
Lancaster, Pennsylvania 17602
(717) 397-2791

LANCE, INC.
Post Office Box 2389
Pineville Road
Charlotte, North Carolina 28234
A.F. Sloan, President
(704) 525-1421

LANCE INDUSTRIES
(Subsidiary of Hoffman Electronic's Corporation)
13001 Bradley Avenue
Sylmar, California 91342
Milton Mann, President
(213) 367-1811

LANCER INDUSTRIES INC.
6315 East Coast Highway
Carpinteria, California 93013

LANCER MOBILE HOMES, INC.
(Subsidiary of Shelter Resources Corporation)
1660 Magnolia
Corona, California 91720
Ken Moore, President
(714) 757-91720

LANCES CORPORATION, EDITH
31 East 31st Street
New York, New York 10016
(212) 683-1990

LANCET ASSOCIATES INC., A. LINCOLN
7365 Melrose Avenue
Los Angeles, California 90046
(213) 653-3053

LANCHART INDUSTRIES, INC.
425 Hamilton Building
Wichita Falls, Texas 76307
Ben D. Woody, President
(817) 322-5474

LANCOME
(Division of Cosmair, Inc.)
530 Fifth Avenue
New York, New York 10036
(212) 697-5115

LANCRAFT MARINE
526 East Alton Avenue
Santa Ana, California 92702

LAND (camera)
See Polaroid Corporation

LAND-N-LAKES (men's sportswear)
See Gordon & Ferguson Company

LAND-O-LAKES (canned vegetables)
See Oconomowoc Canning Company

LAND O'GOSHEN (poultry products)
See Polo Food Products Company

LAND O'LAKES, INC.
614 McKinley Place
Minneapolis, Minnesota 55413
Ralph Hofstad, President
(612) 331-6330

LAND-ROVER (motor vehicles)
See British Leyland Motors, Inc.

LANDAU (motor homes)
See RV Industries Inc.

LANDAU & COMPANY, INC., MAX
8-10 West 37th Street
New York, New York 10018
(212) 736-2444

LANDAU STORES, INC., M.N.
(Subsidiary of Cook United, Inc.)
16501 Rockside Road
Cleveland, Ohio 44137
William Landau, President
(216) 475-1000

LANDCRUISER (automobile)
See Toyota Motor Sales, U.S.A., Inc.

LANDER COMPANY, INC.
25 West 39th Street
New York, New York 10018
Alvin L. Burack, President
(212) 565-0110

LANDER'S LABORATORIES
10244 East Rosecrans
Bellflower, California 90706

LANDERS-SEGAL COLOR COMPANY
78 Delavan Street
Brooklyn, New York 11231
(212) 625-1041

LANDFALL, THE
859 Mamoroneck Avenue
Mamoroneck, New York 10543

Companies and Trade Names

LANDIS & GYR, INC.
4 Westchester Plaza
Elmsford, New York 10523
(914) 592-4400

LANDLUBBER (jeans)
See M. Hoffman & Company, Inc.

LANDMASTER (rotary tillers)
See Krause Plow Corporation

LANDON COMPANY, INC.
Delavan, Wisconsin 53115

LANDORF & COMPANY, INC., SAM
112 West 34th Street
New York, New York 10001
William Glottstein, President
(212) 244-3077

LANDRETH SEED COMPANY, D.
2700 Wilmarco Avenue
Baltimore, Maryland 21223
(301) 233-6804

LAND'S END YACHT STORES INC.
2241 North Elston Avenue
Chicago, Illinois 60614
(312) 384-4170

LANDSBERGER INC., LEOPOLD F.
48 West 27th Street
New York, New York 10001
(212) 679-0498

LANDSEM (sports accessories and equipment)
See Gerry

LANDSMAN PACKING COMPANY INC.
Box B
Red Hook, New York 12571

LANE & SON, E.F.
744 Kevin Court
Oakland, California 94621

LANE & SONS INC., M.R.
2717 Haverford Road
Ardmore, Pennsylvania 19003

LANE & YOUNG, INC.
128 Mallory Avenue
Jersey City, New Jersey 07304

LANE BRYANT, INC.
1501 Broadway
New York, New York 10036
Arthur Malsin, President
(212) 532-0200
See also Coward Shoe, Inc.

LANE CANDY COMPANY INC., LETTY
Box 67
Westville, New Jersey 08093

LANE COMPANY, INC.
Altavista, Virginia 24517
Hamptom O. Powell, President
(703) 396-5641
See also Hickory Chair Company

LANE LIMITED
419 Park Avenue South
New York, New York 10016
(212) 686-1032

LANE MAGAZINE & BOOK COMPANY
Middlefield and Willow Roads
Menlo Park, California 94025
L.W. Lane, Jr., Chairman of the Board
(415) 321-3600

LANE WOOD, INC.
Davis Building
Dallas, Texas 75202
Charles P. Aberg, President
(214) 748-0411

LANG, EDMOND J.
10 Cottage Place
New Rochelle, New York 10802

LANG FEED COMPANY, INC.
17018 Inkster Road
Romulus, Michigan 48174

LANG, WILLIAM W.
20 Vesey Street
New York, New York 10007
(212) 227-1743

LANGE COMPANY
(Subsidiary of Garcia Company)
3400 Industrial Lane
Bloomfield, Colorado 80020
Robert B. Lange, President
(303) 469-2111

LANGE MEDICAL PUBLICATIONS
Los Altos, California 94022

LANGENBACH (wines)
See Frederick Wildman & Sons, Ltd.

LANGFELDER, HOMMA, & CARROLL INC.
163 Fifth Avenue
New York, New York 10010
(212) 473-3195

LANGHORNE (clocks)
See Franklin Instrument Company

LANGNER INDUSTRIES CORPORATION
200 60th Street
Brooklyn, New York 11220
(212) 492-7033

LANGNICKEL INC., A.
251 West 19th Street
New York, New York 10011
(212) 255-8340

Companies and Trade Names

LANGS (Scotch whiskey)
See Carillon Importers, Ltd.

LANGSAM-BILLIG COMPANY
1035 Pacific Street
Brooklyn, New York 11238
(212) 783-7900

LANIER BUSINESS PRODUCTS
(Division of Oxford Industries Inc.)
1700 Chantilly Drive N.E.
Atlanta, Georgia 30324
Gene W. Milner, President
(404) 321-9011

LANMAN & KEMP-BARCLAY &
COMPANY, INC.
15 Grand
Palisades Park, New Jersey 07650
Milton G. Johnson, President
(201) 943-3100

LANNETT COMPANY, INC.
9000 State Road
Philadelphia, Pennsylvania 19136
Samuel Gratz, Chairman and
President
(215) 333-9000

LANNOM MANUFACTURING
COMPANY
West Lincoln Street
Tullahoma, Tennessee 37388
Charles E. Parish, President
(615) 455-0691
See also Worth Bat Company

LANOLIN PLUS (hair-care products)
See Bishop Industries, Inc.

LANPAR COMPANY
2727 West Mockingbird Lane
Dallas, Texas 75235
O. Parmeter, Chairman and
President
(214) 357-2836

LANSDALE PRODUCTS
CORPORATION
Post Office Box 568
Lansdale, Pennsylvania 19446

LANSDOWNE (whiskey)
See Schenley Industries, Inc.

LANSING SOUND, INC., JAMES B.
3249 Casitas Avenue
Los Angeles, California 90039
Sterling Sander, President
(213) 665-4101

LANSMITH CHERRY & FRUIT
COMPANY
116 West Main
Ripley, New York 14775

LANVIN-CHARLES OF THE RITZ, INC.
(Subsidiary of Squibb Corporation)
40 West 57th Street
New York, New York 10019
Frank W. Green, President
(212) 489-4500
See also Charles of the Ritz

LANZ OF CALIFORNIA, INC.
6150 Wilshire Boulevard
Los Angeles, California 90048
Kurt H. Scharff, President
(213) 937-1400

LANZA, BOSTON EAST INC.
145 Border Street
East Boston, Massachusetts 02128
Benjamin Linden, President and
Treasurer
(617) 569-2600

LANZI CANDY COMPANY
1135 West Chicago Avenue
Chicago, Illinois 60622
(312) 666-0403

LAREDO (cigars by Villiger A.G.)
See Gesty Trading &
Manufacturing Corporation

LAREDO (tobacco, cigarettes,
cigarette-making kits)
See Brown & Williamson Tobacco
Corporation

LARGE-CHARGE, INC.
Box 1777
Clearwater, Florida 33517

L'ARGENE PRODUCTS COMPANY,
INC.
23 Meadow
Brooklyn, New York 11206
(212) 456-9155

LARGO (cigars)
See General Cigar Company

LARK (cigarettes)
See Liggett & Myers Inc.

LARK
See Bi-Flex International Inc.

LARK LUGGAGE CORPORATION
350 Fifth Avenue
New York, New York 10001
Joseph Y. Pelavin, President
(212) 563-7830

LARKOTEX COMPANY
1002 Olive Street
Texarkana, Texas 75501
(214) 793-4647

LARKS (shoes)
See Wohl Shoe Company

LARROQUE DRUG COMPANY
1305 Main Street
Jeanerette, Louisiana 70544

LARROWE MILLS
(Division of the Birkett Mills)
Penn Yan, New York 14527
(315) 536-3786

Companies and Trade Names

LARRY MATHEWS (health, beauty, and personal-care products)
See Dynamic Classics Ltd.

LARSEN COMPANY, THE
520 North Broadway
Green Bay, Wisconsin 54303
Mark H. Mitchell, Chairman
(414) 435-5301

LARSEN INC., JACK LENOR
41 East 11th Street
New York, New York 10003
(212) 674-3993

LARSON COMPANY, CHARLES O.
Post Office Box E
Sterling, Illinois 61081
Charles O. Larson, President
(815) 625-0503

LARSON INDUSTRIES, INC.
2850 Metro Drive
Minneapolis, Minnesota 55420
Sumner S. Young, President
(612) 854-4020

LARSON LABORATORIES, INC.
1320 Irwin Drive
Erie, Pennsylvania 16505
(814) 452-6815

LARSON LADDER COMPANY
651 Martin Avenue
Santa Clara, California 95050
Louis C. Larson, President
(408) 241-3300

LARSON'S ANIMAL HOSPITAL, DR.
Box 344
Fergus Falls, Minnesota 56537

LARSONS OF SWEDEN INC.
2710 North Avenue
Bridgeport, Connecticut 06604

LARUS & BROTHER COMPANY, INC.
18 South 22nd
Richmond, Virginia 23217
J. A. Gauntley, President
(804) 644-1877

LAS FLORISTAS (cookware)
See National Silver Company

LAS-STIK MANUFACTURING COMPANY
B & Wayne Avenue
Hamilton, Ohio 45013
Neil L. Sohngen, II, President and General Manager
(513) 893-4781
See also Ohio-Buckeye

LASALLE & KOCH COMPANY
(Division of R. H. Macy Company, Inc.)
Adams and Huron Streets
Toledo, Ohio 43604
John H. Griffin, President
(419) 243-8811

LASCO (groceries)
See Allen•Foods, Inc.

LASCO BRAKE PRODUCTS CORPORATION, LTD.
(Subsidiary of Laher Spring & Electric Car Corporation)
2615 Magnolia Street
Oakland, California 94607
P. J. Laher, President
(415) 444-1350

LASER, INC.
2000 North Main Street
Crown Point, Indiana 46307

LASER LABORATORIES, INC.
Box 123
Excelsior, Minnesota 55331

LASSIE MAID (junior and misses coats)
See Barkin, Levin & Company, Inc.

LAST INC., ALVIN
Box 152
Yonkers, New York 10710

LAST WORD ENTERPRISES
Rural Route 3, Box 43E
Rio Piedras, Puerto Rico 00928

LATAMA, INC.
67 Putmam Street
Mount Vernon, New York 10551

LATEX FIBER INDUSTRIES INC.
(Subsidiary of Uniroyal Inc.)
100 Main Street
Beaver Falls, New York 13305
(315) 346-6111

LATEX FOUNDATIONS COMPANY INC.
48 East 21st Street
New York, New York 10010
(212) 254-0924

LATHAN MANUFACTURING COMPANY
1400 Industrial Way
Redwood City, California 94063

LATIN AMERICAN IMPORTS
12125 South Prairie Avenue
Hawthorne, California 90250

LATIN PERCUSSION
454 Commercial Avenue
Palisades Park, New Jersey 07650

LATINUS TRADING CORPORATION
370 Seventh Avenue
New York, New York 10001
(212) 564-8221

LATOJA
Box 125
Kendall Park, New Jersey 08824

Companies and Trade Names

LATROBE BREWING COMPANY
Labrobe, Pennsylvania 15650
(412) 537-5545

LAU INDUSTRIES
2027 Home Avenue
Dayton, Ohio 45047
(513) 263-3591

LAUDER INC., ESTEE
767 Fifth Avenue
New York, New York 10022
(212) 826-3600

LAUDERDALE MARINA INC.
1900 S.E. 15th Street
Fort Lauderdale, Florida 33316

LAUDER'S (Scotch whiskey)
See Gooderham & Worts, Ltd.

LAUFFER COMPANY, INC., H. E.
Belmont Drive
Somerset, New Jersey 08873
H. E. Lauffer, President
(201) 356-7676

LAUGH & PLAY GAME COMPANY
Post Office Box 689
Madera, California 93637

LAUGHLIN CHINA COMPANY,
  THE HOMER
Newell, West Virginia 26050

LAUGHLIN HOSIERY MILLS, INC.
Box 517
Randleman, North Carolina 27317
Theron L. Laughlin, President
(919) 498-2678

LAUNDRY SOIL & STAIN REMOVER
(laundry products)
See Miracle White Company

LAURA LEE CANDIES
(Division of Francois Jacquemoux, Inc.)
3670 N.W. 79th Street
Miami, Florida 33147
(305) 698-9693

LAURA MAE LIFE (blouses)
See M. Serman & Company, Inc.

LAURA SCUDDER'S SNACK FOODS
(Division of Pet, Inc.)
1525 North Raymond Avenue
Anaheim, California 92805
George A. Jeppsson, President
(714) 772-5151

LAURANS-STANDARD GROCERY
  COMPANY
55 Brook
New Bedford, Massachusetts 02746

LAUREL (electric heating pads)
See Walgreen Company

LAUREL LAMP MANUFACTURING
  COMPANY INC.
Rome and Magazine
Newark, New York 07105
Harold J. Weiss, President
(201) 589-1148

LAUREL RIDGE (food products)
See Musselman

LAURELCREST (carpets)
See Fieldcrest Mills, Inc.

LAURENS (cigarettes)
See G. A. Georgopulo & Company

LAURENS GLASS COMPANY
(Division of Indian Head, Inc.)
Catherine Street
Laurens, South Carolina 29360
C. W. Bussey, Jr., President
(803) 984-2541

LAURI ENTERPRISES MANUFACTURERS
Phillips-Avon, Maine 04966

LAURITZEN & COMPANY, INC.
1197 Willis Avenue
Wheeling, Illinois 60090

LAUTIER FILS, INC.
300 Webro Road
Parsippany, New Jersey 07046

LAVA (soap)
See Procter & Gamble Company

LAVA-SIMPLEX INTERNATIONALE,
  INC.
1650 West Irving Road
Chicago, Illinois 60603
Edward E. Sheldon, President and
  Secretary
(312) 528-6000

LAVALLEE & IDE, INC.
Grape Street
Chicopee, Massachusetts 01013
John A. Lavallee, President and
  Treasurer
(413) 592-4115

LAVANTE (guitars)
See York Musical Instrument
  Company Inc.

LAVELLE RUBBER COMPANY
424 North Wood
Chicago, Illinois 60622
(312) 733-2410

LAVENO ITALIAN CERAMICS INC.
See Ceramar

LAVINA-VILLERT (watches)
See Henri Stern Watch Agency,
  Inc.

Companies and Trade Names

LAVOPTIK COMPANY
661 Western Avenue North
Saint Paul, Minnesota 55103
(612) 489-1351

LAVORIS (breath spray, mouthwash)
See Vick Chemical Company)

LAW, JONATHAN
Kennebunkport, Maine 04046

LAW (auto alarms)
See Alertronics Inc.

LAWCO (canned foods)
See Lawtons Canning Company, Inc.

LAWN & GARDEN SUPPLY
COMPANY
2222 North 27th Avenue
Phoenix, Arizona 85009

LAWN BOY (outdoor power equipment)
See Cushman (Division of Outboard Marine Corporation)

LAWN CHAMP (lawn mowers)
See Sunbeam Outdoor Company

LAWNCOMB (lawn and garden tools)
See Etamco Industries

LAWNFLITE (power mowers, garden tools)
See MTD Products, Inc.

LAWNLITE COMPANY
3789 N.W. 46th Street
Miami, Florida 33142
Victor Reiter, President
(305) 635-0665

LAWNMATE (tools for home use)
See McGraw-Edison Company, Portable Electric Tools Division

LAWRENCE & COMPANY, INC.
88 Commercial
Lewiston, Maine 04240

LAWRENCE CLOTHES INC.
(Division of Kayser-Roth Corporation)
2200 Arch Street
Philadelphia, Pennsylvania 19103
(215) 564-5340

LAWRENCE COMPANY, STEPHEN
41 Mount Vernon Street
Ridgefield Park, New Jersey 07660

LAWRENCE FOODS INC.
2200 Lunt Avenue
Elk Grove Village, Illinois 60007
Major Lawrence, President
(312) 437-2400

LAWRENCE IMPORTS
119 West Hubbard Street
Chicago, Illinois 60610
(312) 943-1151

LAWRENCE PACKAGING SUPPLY
CORPORATION
113 North 13th Street
Newark, New Jersey 07107

LAWRY'S FOODS, INC.
568 San Fernando Road
Los Angeles, California 90065
Richard N. Frank, President
(213) 225-2491

LAWSON (gas and electric water heaters)
See Bradford-White Corporation

LAWSON & LAWSON
MANUFACTURING COMPANY
Post Office Box 651
Danville, California 94526

LAWSON COMPANY, THE F. H.
801 Evans Street
Cincinnati, Ohio 45204
(513) 251-2400

LAWSON MILK COMPANY
(Division of Consolidated Foods Corporation)
210 Broadway, East
Cuyahoga Falls, Ohio 44222
J. E. Rasteter, President
(216) 923-0421

LAWTER CHEMICALS, INC.
990 Skokie Boulevard
Northbrook, Illinois 60062
Daniel J. Terra, Chairman and President
(312) 498-4700

LAWTEX CORPORATION
Brickyard Road
Dalton, Georgia 30720
Donald Lorberbaum, President
(404) 226-1500

LAWTON'S CANNING COMPANY, INC.
Lawtons, New York 14091
(716) 337-2567

LAWYERS & JUDGES PUBLISHING
COMPANY
4156 East Grant Road
Tucson, Arizona 85716

LAYLA (nail-care products, depilatory, etc.)
See Cosmetics Distributors, Inc.

LAYMON CANDY COMPANY
444 Colton Avenue
Colton, California 92324

LAY'S (snack foods)
See Frito-Lay, Inc.

LAYTON INDUSTRIES INC.
542 East Squantum Street
North Quincy, Massachusetts 02171
(617) 328-9690

LAYTON LABORATORIES
4 Claremont Road
Bernardsville, New Jersey 07924

Companies and Trade Names

LAYTON'S (food products)
See Douglas Food Corporation

LAZABOUT (men's furnishings)
See Varsity Pajamas

LAZARUS & COMPANY, F. & R.
(Division of Federated Department Stores, Inc.)
Town and High Streets
Columbus, Ohio 43215
Charles Y. Lazarus, Chairman of the Board
(614) 463-2121

LAZIO FISH COMPANY, INC., TOM
1 Commercial Street
Eureka, California 95501
Tom Lazio, President
(707) 442-2981

LAZURUS DIVISION
See Federated Department Stores, Inc.

LAZY-BONES (shoes)
See Juvenile Shoe Corporation of America

LAZY DAY SLO-COOKER (cookware)
See Dart Industries

LAZY DAYS MANUFACTURING COMPANY, INC.
Holiday Road
Buford, Georgia 30518
(404) 945-7517

LAZY IKE CORPORATION
Box 1177
Fort Dodge, Iowa 50501
(515) 576-4118

LAZY JOE (men's shoes)
See International Shoe Company

LE BARON CLOTHES
2801 South Main Street
Los Angeles, California 90007
(213) 747-9461

LE BARON HOTELS INC.
250 Hotel Circle North
San Diego, California 92108

LE COMTE & COMPANY INC.
147 41st Street
Brooklyn, New York 11232
Douglas K. Le Comte, President
(212) 788-2366

LE GALION (perfumes)
See Parfums Le Galion, Inc.

LE GEAR
(Division of O'Neal, Jones & Feldman, Inc.)
1304 Ashby Road
Saint Louis, Missouri 63132
(314) 997-6650

LE GUI (cologne, perfume, toilet water)
See Parfums Duvelle, Inc.

LE JOUR (watches)
See Continental Time Corporation

LE KHEDIVE (cigarettes)
See G. A. Georgopulo & Company, Inc.

LE KITCHEN (frozen fish entrees)
See Libby, McNeill & Libby

LE LIPSTICK (cosmetics)
See Helena Rubinstein

LE MART (groceries)
See Institutional Mart

LE MONDE CORSET COMPANY
See Kellogg Industries Inc.

LE MUGUET DU BONHEUR (eau de cologne, spray powder, etc.)
See Caron Corporation

LE PAGE'S, INC.
(Subsidiary of Papercraft Corporation)
Papercraft Park
Pittsburgh, Pennsylvania 15238
Joseph M. Katz, President
(412) 362-8000

LE SEMEUR (vegetables)
See A. Sargenti Company Inc.

LE SUEUR (processed foods)
See Green Giant Company

LE TOURNEAU INC., R. G.
See Marathon Le Tourneau Company, Longview Division

LE TREFLE (copper cookware)
See Milnor Sales Agency

LEA & FEBIGER
600 Washington Square
Philadelphia, Pennsylvania 19106
(215) 922-1330

LEA & PERRINS, INC.
Pollitt Drive
Fair Lawn, New Jersey 07410
James F. Lunn, President
(201) 791-1600

LEA ENTERPRISES
Post Office Box 43
Dover, Delaware 19901

LEA INDUSTRIES, INC.
(Subsidiary of Sperry & Hutchinson Company)
Post Office Box 25476
Richmond, Virginia 23260
E. Angus Powell, Chairman of the Board
(804) 232-3471

Companies and Trade Names

LEACH INC., SYD
4036 Monroe Street
Toledo, Ohio 43606

LEACOCK (Madeira)
See Julius Wile Sons & Company, Inc.

LEACOCK & COMPANY INC.
1040 Avenue of the Americas
New York, New York 10018
(212) 736-5252

LEADER (canned foods)
See Hayward Food Products

LEADER (wood desks, tables)
See Hoosier Desk Company

LEADER CANDIES, INC.
132 Harrison Place
Brooklyn, New York 11237
Jack J. Kastin, President and Sales Manager
(212) 366-6900

LEADING LADY FOUNDATIONS INC.
3748 East 91st Street
Cleveland, Ohio 44105
(216) 641-2370

LEADWAY (grocery products)
See Thiemann Brothers Inc.

LEAF BRANDS
(Division of W. R. Grace & Company)
1155 North Cicero Avenue
Chicago, Illinois 60651
Sam Shankman, President
(312) 378-6000

LEAF OIL LABORATORIES
Post Office Box 461
Sutton, Nebraska 68979

LEAFSAVER CORPORATION
(Division of Magic Marker Corporation)
1 Magic Marker Lane
Cherry Hill, New Jersey 08003

LEAR (cigarettes)
See Brown & Williamson Tobacco Corporation

LEAR SIEGLER, INC.
3171 South Bundy Drive
Santa Monica, California 90406
Robert T. Campion, Chairman, President and Chief Executive Officer
(213) 391-7211
See also Borroughs; Hypro; and No-Sag Spring

LEAR SIEGLER, INC.
Home-Siegler Division
900 Brooks Avenue
Holland, Michigan 49423
Clarence J. Becker, President
(616) 396-1481

LEARN & PLAY (children's books)
See McGraw-Hill Book Company Educational Games & Aids Division

LEARNING GAMES INC.
34 South Broadway
White Plains, New York 10601

LEARNING PRODUCTS INC.
11632 Fairgrove Industrial Boulevard
Saint Louis, Missouri 63043
(314) 432-5823

LEART COMPANY, S. A.
50 Jefferson Street
Newark, New Jersey 07105

LEARY CARTOONS
1227 East King Street
Lancaster, Pennsylvania 17602

LEATH & COMPANY
7111 North Lincoln Avenue
Chicago, Illinois 60646
I. H. Hartman, Jr., Chairman of the Board
(312) 675-1980

LEATHER 'N LYME (aftershave, cologne)
See Davlyn Laboratories, Inc.

LEATHER SHOP INC., THE
330 Fifth Avenue
New York, New York 10001

LEATHER SPECIALTY COMPANY
10570 Chester Road
Cincinnati, Ohio 45215
(513) 771-0200

LEATHER-TONE (table and floor lamps)
See Georgian Lighting Studios Inc.

LEATHERFOAM, INC.
236 South Michigan Street
South Bend, Indiana 46601

LEATHERS' SONS, L. M.
675 Pulaski Street
Athens, Georgia 30601

LEATHERSMITH OF LONDON LTD.
3 East 48th Street
New York, New York 10017
(212) 752-2690

LEAVENWORTH FRUIT COMPANY, THE
Leavenworth, Washington 98826

LEAVITT CORPORATION, THE
100 Santilli Highway
Everett, Massachusetts 02149
James T. Hintlian, President
(617) 389-2600

Companies and Trade Names

LEAVITT PRODUCTS COMPANY, K. D.
208 Griggs Street
Department MAC
Urbana, Illinois 61801

LEBANON WOOLEN MILLS
Lebanon, Tennessee 37087
Henry Counts, President
(615) 444-3842

LEBLANC CORPORATION G.
7019 30th Avenue
Kenosha, Wisconsin 53140
Vito Pascucci, President
(414) 658-1644

LEBOW (men's suits)
See After Six Inc.

LEBOW BROTHERS, INC.
(Division of After Six, Inc.)
310 East Oliver
Baltimore, Maryland 21202
Harry Lebow, President
(301) 685-7444

LECHLER-HOLIDAY
554 Broadway
New York, New York 10012
(212) 226-0388

LECHNER PULP & PAPER COMPANY
13 Arcadia Road
Old Greenwich, Connecticut 06870

LECO CORPORATION
3000 Lakeview Avenue
Saint Joseph, Michigan 49085
George J. Krasl, President
(616) 983-5533

LECROY & SON INC., JOHN
Palm, Pennsylvania 18070
(215) 679-6206

LECTRIC SHAVE (shaving products)
See J. B. Williams Company

LECTRO-STIK CORPORATION
3721 Broadway
Chicago, Illinois 60613
(312) 528-8860

LECTROJOG COMPANY, THE
Box 68
Defiance, Missouri 63341

LEDERLE LABORATORIES
(Division of American Cyanamid Company)
Pearl River, New York 10965
R. A. Schoelhorn, President
(914) 735-5000

LEE (batteries)
See Battery Systems, Inc.

LEE (men's hats)
See Stetson Hat Company, Inc.

LEE & COMPANY, INC., WILLIAM W.
1007 24th Street
Watervliet, New York 12189
(518) 273-6222

LEE & SHUFORD COMPANY
Post Office Box 98
Lawndale, North Carolina 28090

LEE ALUMINUM FOUNDRY & MANUFACTURING COMPANY
5800 Hosch Street
New Albin, Iowa 52160
(319) 544-4255

LEE-BERT, INC.
7 Rust Lane
Saginaw, Michigan 48602
(517) 754-8332

LEE COMPANY, INC., H. D.
(Subsidiary of VF Corporation)
Johnson Drive
Shawnee Mission, Kansas 66201
William J. McKenna, President
(913) 236-9933

LEE COMPANY, RICHARD T.
7201 Adams Street
North Bergen, New Jersey 07047

LEE DRUG COMPANY
5203 Leavenworth Street
Omaha, Nebraska 68106

LEE FILTER
(Division of Filter Dynamics, International)
191 Talmadge Road
Edison, New Jersey 08817
Richard J. Roberts, General Manager
(201) 287-2700

LEE GIFTIQUES
Atlanta Merchandise Mart, Suite 830
Atlanta, Georgia 30303

LEE HY (juvenile furniture)
See Min-Dee Distributors Inc.

LEE PHARMACEUTICALS
1444 Santa Anita Avenue
South El Monte, California 91733
Henry L. Lee, Jr., Chairman and President
(213) 442-3141

LEE PRODUCTS COMPANY
800 East 80th Street
Minneapolis, Minnesota 55420
(612) 854-3544

LEE-RICK (foods)
See Brown Derby

LEE-ROWAN COMPANY
6301 Etzel Avenue
Saint Louis, Missouri 63133
E. Desmond Lee, President
(314) 781-3363

LEE TREVINO (sportswear)
See Blue Bell, Inc.

Companies and Trade Names

LEE WAY MOTOR FREIGHT
COMPANY
3000 West Reno
Oklahoma City, Oklahoma 73108
R. E. Lee, Chairman of the Board
(405) 236-3001

LEECH PRODUCTS, INC.
Box 391
Hutchinson, Kansas 67501
(316) 665-7961

LEEDALL PRODUCTS MANUFAC-
TURING COMPANY INC.
130 Van Liew Avenue
Milltown, New Jersey 08850
Eugene DiLuco, President and
Treasurer
(201) 828-1045

LEEDS (shoes)
See Edison Brothers Stores, Inc.

LEEDS OF CALIFORNIA
654 Venice Boulevard
Venice, California 90291

LEEDS PHARMACAL CORPORATION
147 Frederick Street
Garfield, New Jersey 07026

LEEDS TRAVELWEAR
(Division of Rapid-American
Corporation)
888 Seventh Avenue
New York, New York 10019
John F. Maisano, President

LEEMING/PACQUIN
(Division of Pfizer, Inc.)
New York, New York 10017
Bill B. Scott, President
(212) 573-3131

LEES CARPET
(Division of Burlington Industries, Inc.)
1000 Adams Avenue
Norristown, Pennsylvania 19401
Joseph Quirk, President
(215) 666-7770

LEE'S TACKLE INC.
2185 N.W. 34th Avenue
Miami, Florida 33142
(305) 634-7695

LEETONIA TOOL COMPANY, THE
142 Main Street
Leetonia, Ohio 44431
(216) 427-6944

LEFAX PUBLISHING COMPANY
2867 East Allegheny Avenue
Philadelphia, Pennsylvania 19134
(215) 426-9710

LEFEBURE CORPORATION
(Division of Walter Kidde &
Company, Inc.)
308 29th Street, N.E.
Cedar Rapids, Iowa 52406
(319) 366-2771

LEFFINGWELL CHEMICAL
COMPANY
111 South Berry
Brea, California 92621
(714) 529-3973

LEFKOWITZ & BROTHERS, LOUIS
50 Washington Avenue
Milltown, New Jersey 08850
Bernard Brindis, President
(201) 545-6565

LEFT BANK (lotion, cologne,
foundation for men)
See Yardley of London, Inc.

LEFTON COMPANY, GEORGE
ZOLTAN
3622 South Morgan Street
Chicago, Illinois 60609
George L. Lefton, President
(312) 254-4344

LEGACY (Scotch)
See Sazerac Company, Inc.

LEGGETT & PLATT, INC.
600 West Mound Street
Carthage, Missouri 64836
Harry M. Cornell, Jr., President
and Chief Executive Officer
(417) 358-8131

L'EGGS PRODUCTS INC.
(Subsidiary of Hanes Corporation)
Post Office Box 2495
Winston-Salem, North Carolina 27102

LEGION (canned foods)
See Charles G. Summers, Jr., Inc.

LEGION EXPORT & IMPORT
COMPANY
479 Washington Street
New York, New York 10013
(212) 925-8989

LEGO SYSTEMS INC.
Brookfield, Connecticut 06804

LEGRANDE (food products)
See Western Dressing Inc.

LEGULO COMPANY
5618 West Eddy Street
Chicago, Illinois 60634
(312) 685-3694

LEHIGH ANIMAL SUPPLY
COMPANY
104 Union
Allentown, Pennsylvania 18105

LEHIGH-LEOPOLD FURNITURE
COMPANY
(Division of Litton Industries)
2825 Mount Pleasant Street
Burlington, Iowa 52601
Richard Tierney, President
(319) 753-2271

LEHIGH PORTLAND (cement)
See Lehigh Portland Cement
Company

Companies and Trade Names

LEHIGH PORTLAND CEMENT
COMPANY
718 Hamilton Street
Allentown, Pennsylvania 18105
W. J. Young, President
(215) 434-6171

LEHIGH SAFETY SHOE COMPANY
(Subsidiary of Endicott Johnson
Corporation)
1100 East Main Street
Endicott, New York 13760
Raymond Codrea, President
(607) 754-7980

LEHIGH SALES & PRODUCTS INC.
3027 Highland Street
Allentown, Pennsylvania 18104

LEHIGH VALLEY (frozen foods)
See Vita Frost Foods Inc.

LEHIGH VELLEY COOPERATIVE
FARMERS
1000 North Seventh Street
Allentown, Pennsylvania 18001
Alpheus L. Ruth, President
(215) 433-5115

LEHIGH WHOLESALE GROCERY
COMPANY
1135 North Plymouth
Allentown, Pennsylvania 18103

LEHMAN BROTHERS SILVERWARE
CORPORATION
1250 Brunswick Avenue
Far Rockaway, New York 11691

LEHMAN COMPANY, A. J.
317 East Eighth Street
Cincinnati, Ohio 45202
(513) 241-1676

LEHMAN MANUFACTURING
COMPANY INC.
800 East Elizabeth Avenue
Linden, New Jersey 07036
(201) 486-5700

LEHMANN INC., WILLIAM F.
Box 7601
11490 Hudson Boulevard
Saint Paul, Minnesota 55119
(612) 739-0686

LEHN & FINK PRODUCTS
COMPANY
(Division of Sterling Drug, Inc.)
225 Summit Avenue
Montvale, New Jersey 07645
Arthur D. Juceam, President
(201) 391-8500

LEHRMAN & SON, INC., LOUIS
Box 2261
Harrisburg, Pennsylvania 17105

LEIBER INC., JUDITH
14 East 32nd Street
New York, New York 10016
(212) 683-6684

LEICA (cameras, microscopes, etc.)
See E. Leitz, Inc.

LEICY'S INC.
1531-33 West Market Street
Steubenville, Ohio 43952

LEIGHTON IMPORTS LTD., FRED
214 Sullivan Street
New York, New York 10012
(212) 533-9090

LEININGER KNITTING COMPANY,
WILLIAM G.
Mohnton, Pennsylvania 19540
William L. Ruth, President and
Treasurer
(215) 777-1365

LEIPZIG & LIPPE, INC.
1 Haynes Street
Elmsford, New York 10523

LEISTER GAME COMPANY, INC.
511 Summer Street
Toledo, Ohio 43609
(419) 248-4449

LEISTERS FURNITURE INC.
433 Ridge Avenue
Hanover, Pennsylv nia 17331

LEISURE DYNAMICS, INC.
4400 West 78th Street
Minneapolis, Minnesota 55435
Louis F. Polk, Jr., President
(612) 920-1330

LEISURE GROUP, INC.
445 South Figueros Street
Los Angeles, California 90017
Merle H. Banta, President
(213) 624-2621
See also High Standard Sporting
Firearms

LEISURE GROUP, THE
(Lyman Products)
Middlefield, Connecticut 06455

LEISURE IMPORTS INC.
(Subsidiary of Harrison-Hoge
Industries, Inc.)
104 Arlington Avenue
Saint James, New York 11780

LEISURE KING (reclining chair)
See Cleveland Chair Company

LEISURE LOVERS, INC.
110 East Ninth Street
Los Angeles, California 90015
(213) 927-1273

LEISURE-O (seafood)
See Stein Fish Company

LEISURE TIME (phonograph records)
See Shelby Singleton Corporation

LEISURE TIME PRODUCTS INC.
Box 232
Highway 6
Nappanee, Indiana 46550
(219) 773-7761

Companies and Trade Names

LEISUREDYNE INC.
166 Ridgedale Avenue
Morristown, New Jersey 07960

LEISUREST (upholstered couches)
  See Imperial Leather Furniture
     Company

LEITZ, INC., E.
Link Drive
Rockleigh, New Jersey 07647
William H. Mann, President
(201) 767-1100

LEK MANUFACTURING COMPANY
4040 West 123rd Street
Alsip, Illinois 60658

LEKAS CANDY MANUFACTURING
   COMPANY
979 Seventh Street
Oakland, California 94607

LEKTRO BLADE (electric shavers)
  See Remington Electric Shaver

LEMBERGER FOOD COMPANY,
   INC.
129 Fair Street
Palisades Park, New Jersey 07650

LEMMON PHARMACAL COMPANY
Post Office Box 30
Sellersville, Pennsylvania 18960
Harris N. Hollin, Chairman and
   President
(215) 723-5544

LEMON PRODUCTS
(Division of Sunkist Growers Inc.)
Box 640
310 North Joy Street
Corona, California 91720
W. A. Delaney, Jr., Division
   Manager
(714) 737-2420

LEMON TREE
118 Forest Drive
Jericho, New York 11753

LEMON TREE INNS OF AMERICA
3905 Oleander Drive
Wilmington, North Carolina 28401

LEMON UP (antiblemish lotion,
facial cleanser, shampoo)
  See Gillette Company

LEMON VELVET (toiletries)
  See Avon Products, Inc.

LENAL WOOD PRODUCTS
97-45 Queens Boulevard
Forest Hills, New York 11374

LENK (tools)
  See Wall-Lenk Manufacturing
     Company

LENKOTEX COMPANY, INC.
333 West 52nd Street
New York, New York 10019
(212) 247-3388

LENMAN INDUSTRIES INC.
Box 689
Cape Coral, Florida 33904

LENNERT COMPANY, H. B.
88-11 Elmhurst Avenue
Elmhurst, New York 11373

LENNOX INDUSTRIES, INC.
200 South 12th Avenue
Marshalltown, Iowa 50158
Ray C. Robbins, President
(515) 754-4011

LENOIR HOSIERY MILLS
237 Realty Street
Lenoir, North Carolina 28645
William B. Schey, President
(704) 754-3443

LENOIR HOUSE (furniture)
  See Broyhill Industries

LENORKA INC.
Main Street
Chester, New Jersey 07930

LENOX
(Division of Hoover Ball & Bearing
   Company)
Box 148
Lenox, Iowa 50851

LENOX CANDLES, INC.
Post Office Box 890
627 Bay Shore Drive
Oshkosh, Wisconsin 54901
(414) 231-9620

LENOX CRYSTAL, INC.
(Subsidiary of Lenox, Inc.)
Lenox Road
Mount Pleasant, Pennsylvania 15666
(412) 547-4541

LENOX, INC.
Prince & Meade Streets
Trenton, New Jersey 08605
John M. Tassie, President
(609) 392-5141
  See also Wood, Inc., J.R.

LENOX SYRUP COMPANY
89 Heath
Boston, Massachusetts 02152
(617) 440-7777

LENS COMPANY CHEMICALS,
   INC.
1314 North Front Street
Philadelphia, Pennsylvania 19122
(215) 634-3700

LENS WICK COMPANY, INC.,
   THE
5565 Halsey Drive
Baton Rouge, Louisiana 70811

Companies and Trade Names

LENTON IMPORTERS
1118 Constantinople Street
Laredo, Texas 78040

LENTZ NOVELTY COMPANY
235 Fairfield Avenue
Upper Darby, Pennsylvania 19082

LENZO COMPANY
1314 North Front Street
Philadelphia, Pennsylvania 19122
(215) 634-3700

LEON PRODUCTS, INC.
Box 16537
3733 University Boulevard, West
Jacksonville, Florida 32217
(904) 733-0221

LEON SUPPLY COMPANY
84 Winter
Worcester, Massachusetts 01604

LEONARD IMPORTERS, INC.
1170 Broadway
New York, New York 10001
(212) 889-1360

LEONARD INC., CHARLES
79-11 Cooper Avenue
Glendale, New York 11227

LEONARD INTERNATIONAL
1545 Clyde Park S.W.
Grand Rapids, Michigan 49509

LEONARD, JOHN
19400 Pruneridge Avenue
Cupertino, California 95014

LEONARD PUBLISHING
  CORPORATION, HAL
64 East Second Street
Winona, Minnesota 55987

LEONARD SILVER INTERNATIONAL, INC.
144 Addison Street
Boston, Massachusetts 02128
Leonard Florence, President
(617) 569-7600

LEONARDO STRASSI LTD.
20 West 33rd Street
New York, New York 10001
(212) 594-2287

LEONARD'S INC.
200 Houston Street
Fort Worth, Texas 76102
Harlan Swain, President
(817) 336-9111

LEONE & SONS, N.
30660 Plymouth Road
Livonia, Michigan 48150

LEONHARDT CANDY COMPANY, HENRY
8020 South King Drive
Chicago, Illinois 60619
(312) 874-3233

LEONORA, INC.
148 Madison Avenue
New York, New York 10016
Bertram H. Rosenbloom, President
(212) 684-2487

LEONORE DOSKOW INC.
Route 9A
Montrose, New York 10548

LEOPOLD F. LANDSBERGER INC.
48 West 27th Street
New York, New York 10001
(212) 679-0498

LEOPOLD INC., ARTHUR M.
150 Commerce Road
Carlstadt, New Jersey 07072

LEPAGE'S INC.
(Subsidiary of Papercraft Corporation)
Papercraft Park
Pittsburgh, Pennsylvania 15238
Joseph M. Katz, Chairman and
  President
(412) 362-8000

LEPLER LABORATORIES, INC.
83 Lafayette Road
Salisbury, Massachusetts 01950

LERCH INC., EMIL
Penn Street
Hatfield, Pennsylvania 19440

LERMER PACKAGING CORPORATION
502 South Avenue
Garwood, New Jersey 07027
J. D. Proctor, President
(201) 789-0900

LERNER STORES CORPORATION
(Subsidiary of McCrory Corporation)
460 West 33rd Street
New York, New York 10001
Harold M. Lane, Jr., President
(212) 736-1222

LEROUX (liqueurs and brandies)
  See General Wine & Spirits
  Company

LERRO'S CANDIES
601 Columbia Avenue
Darby, Pennsylvania 19023

LES PARFUMS DE DANA, INC.
625 Madison Avenue
New York, New York 10022
(212) 751-3700

LESCH CORPORATION
414 West Lenox Avenue
Oak Park, Illinois

Companies and Trade Names

LESCHEN WIRE ROPE COMPANY
(Subsidiary of Wire Rope Corporation of America Inc.)
Post Office Box 407
609 North Second Street
Saint Joseph, Missouri 64502
(816) 233-2563

LESHER (band instruments)
See Selmer (Division of Magnavox Company)

LESLIE FAY, INC.
1400 Broadway
New York, New York 10018
John Pomerantz, President
(212) 594-9000

LESLIE FOODS INC.
Box 364
Newark, California 94560
See also Orrell's Food Products Inc.

LESLIE SALT COMPANY
7200 Central Avenue
Newark, California 94560
John M. Lillie, President
(415) 797-1820

LESNEY PRODUCTS CORPORATION
141 West Commercial Avenue
Monnachie, New Jersey 07074
Elliot Harrowe, President
(201) 935-3800

LESSER COMPANY, INC., MURRAY
20 West 38th Street
New York, New York 10018
(212) 947-0026

LESTOIL (cleaning agent)
See Noxell Corporation

LETRASET U.S.A. INC.
33 New Bridge Road
Bergenfield, New Jersey 07621

LETTERA 36 (typewriter)
See Olivetti Corporation of America

LETTUCE COMPANY
(Division of Dover American Corporation)
516 Northtown Office Building
Spokane, Washington 99207

LETTY LANE CANDY COMPANY, INC.
Box 67
Westville, New Jersey 08093

LEUPOLD & STEVENS, INC.
Post Office Box 688
Beaverton, Oregon 97005
Norbert Leupold, Chairman of the Board
(503) 646-9171

LEVEDAG & COMPANY, INC.
42 Broadway
New York, New York 10004
(212) 425-6666

LEVEEN & COMPANY, INC., E. F.
111 West 40th Street
New York, New York 10018
(212) 345-7788

LEVEL-AIRE INC.
Box L
Plymouth, Indiana 46563

LEVENSON, MONTY H.
Hilltop Drive
Willits, California 95490

LEVER BROTHERS COMPANY
390 Park Avenue
New York, New York 10022
Thomas S. Carroll, President
(212) 688-6000
See also Glamorene Products Corporation

LEVERENZ SHOE COMPANY
828 Alabama Avenue
Sheboygan, Wisconsin 53081
(414) 458-8771

LEVEY INC., HERMAN M.
418 Broom Street
New York, New York 10013
(212) 226-3682

LEVIN (guitars)
See C. F. Martin Organisation

LEVINE DEPARTMENT STORE
(Division of Zale Corporation)
3000 Diamond Park
Dallas, Texas 75247
Norman Crohn, President
(214) 634-4011

LEVI'S (jeans and sportswear)
See Levi Strauss & Company

LEVITON MANUFACTURING COMPANY
236 Greenpoint Avenue
Brooklyn, New York 11222
Harold Leviton, President
(212) 383-4500

LEVITZ FURNITURE CORPORATION
1400 N.W. 167th Street
Miami, Florida 33169
Robert M. Elliot, President
(305) 625-6421

LEVOLOR LORENTZEN, INC.
720 Monroe Street
Hoboken, New Jersey 07030
Maurice Schaller, President
(201) 792-2600

LEVON PRODUCTS, INC.
4424 16th Avenue
Brooklyn, New York 11204
(212) 436-3732

Companies and Trade Names

LEVY & SON, INC., HENRY S.
115 Thames Street
Brooklyn, New York 11237
Samuel Rubin, President
(212) 497-2700

LEVY, INC. HERBERT
325 West Jackson Boulevard
Chicago, Illinois 60606
Herbert Levy, President
(312) 939-5915

LEW MANUFACTURING COMPANY
See Garland Industries Inc.

LEWAL INDUSTRIES, INC.
65 Plain Avenue
New Rochelle, New York 10801
Harry N. Wessel, Jr., President
(914) 235-1200

LEWBILL INDUSTRIES INC.
Post Office Box 221-A
Scottdale, Pennsylvania 15683
(412) 887-7710

LEWIS (stringed musical instruments)
See Chicago Musical Instrument Company

LEWIS & SONS, INC., EDGAR P.
200 Commercial Street
Malden, Massachusetts 02148
Richard S. Lewis, President
(617) 324-3300

LEWIS FOOD COMPANY
(Division of National Pet Foods Corporation)
6700 Cherry Avenue
Long Beach, California 90805
O. J. Draguesku, General Manager
(213) 531-1110

LEWIS FOODS INC., TILLIE
(Subsidiary of Ogden Corporation)
Fresno and Charter Way
Stockton, California 95201

LEWIS GROCER COMPANY
Highway 49
Indianola, Mississippi 38751
Celian M. Lewis, President

LEWIS-HOWE COMPANY
319 South Fourth Street
Saint Louis, Missouri 63102
(314) 621-2304

LEWIS INC., J. H.
287 East Sixth Street
Saint Paul, Minnesota 55101
(612) 224-1028

LEWIS PURSES INC.
135 Madison Avenue
New York, New York 10016

LEWIS RESEARCH LABORATORIES
75 Oak Street
Norwood, New Jersey 07648
(201) 767-0300

LEWIS RICHARD PRODUCTS COMPANY
Box 6 E
Brooklyn, New York 11226

LEWMAR MARINE INC.
203 Front Street
Greenport, New York 11944

LEXINGTON (cigarettes)
See House of Edgeworth

LEXINGTON CHEMICAL COMPANY, INC.
Box 609
Waltham, Massachusetts 02154

LEXINGTON LEATHER GOODS COMPANY
4300 West Lake
Chicago, Illinois 60624
(312) 379-9190

LEXINGTON SPECIALTY FOODS INC.
(Subsidiary of Colonial Stores Inc.)
205 Walltown Road
Lexington, North Carolina 27292

LEXINGTON TYPEWRITER & TRADING COMPANY
109 East 23rd Street
New York, New York 10010
(212) 674-8584

LEXITRON CORPORATION
9600 DeSoto Avenue
Chatsworth, California 91311
Richard O. Baily, President and Chief Executive Officer
(213) 882-5040

LEXOL CORPORATION, THE
810 Passaic Avenue
West Caldwell, New Jersey 07006
Mary C. Gencher, President
(201) 226-7303

LEYLAND MOTOR SALES
See British Leyland Motors, Inc.

LEYSE ALUMINUM COMPANY
203 Ellis Street
Kewaunee, Wisconsin 54216
Paul J. Mutchow, President
(414) 388-3111

LI'L GENERAL STORES
(Division of General Host Corporation)
5303 South MacDill Street
Tampa, Florida 33611
Lowell Caldwell, President

LIAN BROTHERS INC.
319 Fifth Avenue
New York, New York 10016
(212) 684-7387

LIANA HAWAIIAN PERFUMES, INC.
419 Waiakamilo Road
Honolulu, Hawaii 96817
(808) 847-4202

Companies and Trade Names

LIBBEY GLASS
(Division of Owens-Illinois Inc.)
Post Office Box 919
Toledo, Ohio 43601
(419) 242-6543

LIBBEY-OWENS-FORD COMPANY
811 Madison Avenue
Toledo, Ohio 43695
Robert G. Wingerter, Chairman
   of the Board
(419) 242-5781
   See also Aeroquip Corporation;
      and Woodall Industries, Inc.

**LIBBY-MAJORETTE DOLL
CORPORATION**
31 West 21st Street
New York, New York 10010
(212) 675-5448

LIBBY, MCNEILL & LIBBY
200 South Michigan Avenue
Chicago, Illinois 60604
Douglas B. Wells, President
(312) 341-4111

LIBER & COMPANY, INC., JOHN
Alliance, Ohio 44601

LIBERAL MARKET, INC.
230 Concord Street
Dayton, Ohio 45408
Hyman Schear, President
(513) 224-1271

LIBERTY BELL CHRISTMAS INC.
910 South Oyster Bay Road
Hicksville, New York 11808

**LIBERTY BELL WHOLESALE
   GROCERY COMPANY**
490 Main
Charlestown, Massachusetts 02129

**LIBERTY CHERRY & FRUIT
   COMPANY, INC.**
227 West Southern
Covington, Kentucky 41015
(606) 431-3470

LIBERTY DISTRIBUTORS GROUP
2570 Devon Avenue
Des Plaines, Illinois 60018

LIBERTY FABRICS OF NEW YORK
295 Fifth Avenue
New York, New York 10016
Michael Gottlieb, President
(212) 686-1484

LIBERTY GLASS COMPANY
Collins Building
Sapulpa, Oklahoma 74066
George F. Collins, Jr.
(918) 224-1440

LIBERTY HOMES, INC.
Post Office Box 35
Goshen, Indiana 46526
Edward J. Hussey, President
(219) 457-3121

LIBERTY HOUSE AND RHODES
1501 Broadway
Oakland, California 94612
H. Vernon Elder, President
(415) 835-4321

LIBERTY HOUSE-HAWAII
(Subsidiary of Amfac, Inc.)
Post Office Box 2690
Honolulu, Hawaii 96803
Donald C. Onasch, President
(808) 941-2345

LIBERTY IMPORT CORPORATION
66 Broad
Carlstadt, New Jersey 07072
(201) 935-4500

**LIBERTY LIFE INSURANCE
   COMPANY**
Liberty Life Building
Greenville, South Carolina 29602
Francis M. Hipp, Chairman of the
   Board
(803) 268-8111

LIBERTY LOAN CORPORATION
7711 Bonhomme Avenue
Saint Louis, Missouri 63105
David B. Lichtenstein, Chairman
   of the Board
(314) 726-5800

**LIBERTY MUTUAL INSURANCE
   COMPANY**
175 Berkeley Street
Boston, Massachusetts 02117
Frank L. Farwell, Chairman of the
   Board
(617) 357-9500

**LIBERTY NATIONAL BANK &
   TRUST COMPANY**
Main, Court and Pearl Streets
Buffalo, New York 14202
Avery H. Fonda, President
(716) 854-4520

**LIBERTY NATIONAL LIFE
   INSURANCE COMPANY**
301 South 20th Street
Birmingham, Alabama 35202
Frank P. Samford, Chairman of the
   Board
(205) 325-2722

LIBERTY/UA, INC.
6920 Sunset Boulevard
Los Angeles, California 90028
Alvin S. Bennett, President
(213) 461-9141

LIBERTY OF LONDON (men's
neckties)
   See Berkley Cravats Inc.

**LIBERTY ORCHARDS COMPANY,
   INC.**
117-123 Mission
Cashmere, Washington 98815
(509) 782-2191

LIBERTY TREE COLLECTION (pine
furniture)
   See Leisters Furniture Inc.

Companies and Trade Names

LIBERTY VITAMIN CORPORATION
520 South Dean Street
Englewood, New Jersey 07631

LICEK POTATO CHIP COMPANY
618 East Cerro Gordo
Decatur, Illinois 62523

LIDA TRADING CORPORATION
122-124 Duane Street
New York, New York 10007
(212) 962-5446

LIDCO, INC.
1325 Nichols Road
Central Islip, New York 11722
(516) 234-1110

LIDE LABORATORIES, INC.
515 Timberwyck Drive
Saint Louis, Missouri 63131
(314) 965-1210

LIDO (frozen produce)
See United Foods, Inc.

LIDO (hosiery)
See Kayser-Roth Hosiery Company

LIDO FOUNDATIONS
  INTERNATIONAL INC.
26 West 17th Street
New York, New York 10011
(212) 255-4767

LIDO OF CALIFORNIA
22926 Mariposa Avenue
Torrance, California 90502

LIDO TOY INC.
7 East 17th Street
New York, New York 10003
(212) 255-9292

LIDZ BROTHERS
250 West 36th Street
New York, New York 10018
Edward Lidz, President
(212) 524-3100

LIEBOTSCHANER (beer)
See Stegmaier Brewing Company

LIEDERKRANZ (cheese)
See Borden Foods

LIEHMANN, R. H.
15 West 37th Street
New York, New York 10018

LIETHEN CORPORATION
113 North Badger Avenue
Appleton, Wisconsin 54911

LIEVENSE, LTD., C.
255 West End Avenue
New York, New York 10023
(212) 595-9370

LIF-O-GEN INC.
Post Office Box 149
Woods Road
Cambridge, Maryland 21613
(301) 228-6400

LIFE (cereal)
See Quaker Oats Company

LIFE (cigarettes)
See Brown & Williamson
  Tobacco Corporation

LIFE & CASUALTY INSURANCE
  COMPANY OF TENNESSEE
(Subsidiary of American General
  Insurance Company)
Life and Casualty Tower
Nashville, Tennessee 37219
Allen M. Steele, President
(615) 254-1511

LIFE INDUSTRIES INC.
381 Congress Street
Boston, Massachusetts 02210
(617) 542-5764

LIFE INSURANCE COMPANY OF
  GEORGIA
600 West Peachtree Street, N.E.
Atlanta, Georgia 30308
John M. Bragg, President
(404) 881-8800

LIFE INSURANCE COMPANY OF
  NORTH AMERICA
(Subsidiary of INA Corporation)
1600 Arch Street
Philadelphia, Pennsylvania 19103
Donald G. Heth, President
(215) 241-4000

LIFE INSURANCE COMPANY OF
  VIRGINIA
914 Capitol Street
Richmond, Virginia 23219
Warren M. Pace, Chairman of the
  Board
(804) 644-8561

LIFE-LIKE PRODUCTS INC.
1600 Union Avenue
Baltimore, Maryland 21211
(301) 889-1023

LIFE LITE (rechargeable flashlights)
See Gulton Industries Inc.

LIFE MANUFACTURING COMPANY
  INC.
20 Meridian Street
East Boston, Massachusetts 02128
(617) 569-1200

LIFE O'EASE (men's slacks)
See Hart Schaffner & Marx

LIFE SAVERS CONFECTIONS &
  GUM
40 West 57th Street
New York, New York 10019
William Morris, President
(212) 489-3100

LIFE SAVERS INC.
(Subsidiary of Squibb Corporation)
40 West 57th Street
New York, New York 10019
(212) 489-2000

895

Companies and Trade Names

LIFE STRIDE (shoes)
See Brown Group, Inc.

LIFEBUOY (soap)
See Lever Brothers Company

LIFEGUARD (food products)
See Silver Springs Citrus Cooperatives

LIFELINE (seat belts)
See American Safety Equipment Corporation

LIFELINER PREMIUM (tires)
See Cooper Tire and Rubber Company

LIFELONG (canister vacuum cleaner)
See SCM Corporation

LIFEMASTER (paint)
See Glidden-Durkee

LIFESPAN PRODUCTS COMPANY
126 Quality Plaza
Hicksville, New York 11801

LIFESTYLE (casual furniture)
See Syroco

LIFETIME (motor homes)
See Bendix Home Systems Inc. Recreational Vehicle Division

LIFETIME (seat belts and safety products)
See American Safety Equipment Corporation

LIFETIME CAREER SCHOOLS
2251 Barry Avenue
Los Angeles, California 90064
Norman A. Morris, Director
(213) 478-0617

LIFETIME CUTLERY CORPORATION
241 41st Street
Brooklyn, New York 11232
Milton L. Cohen, President
(212) 499-9500

LIFETIME DISTRIBUTORS, INC.
26943 Westwood Road
Westlake, Ohio 44091
Fritz H. Zepht, Jr., President
(216) 871-7000

LIFOAM (plastic-foam ice chests, swim goods, etc.)
See Life-Like Products Inc.

LIFT-ALL COMPANY INC.
102 South Heintzelman Street
Manheim, Pennsylvania 17545
(717) 665-6821

LIFT-LOK (adjustable chairs and stools)
See Garrett Tubular Products Inc.

LIFTON MANUFACTURING CORPORATION, THE
84-40 101st Street
Richmond Hill, New York 11418

LIGGETT & MYERS, INC.
4100 Roxboro Road
Durham, North Carolina 27702
Raymond J. Mulligan, President
(919) 471-7511
See also Allen Products Company, Inc.; Austin Nichols & Company, Inc.; Brite Industries, Inc.; Carillon Importers, Ltd.; National Oats Company, Inc.; Paddington, Corporation, The; and Perk Foods Company

LIGGETT DRUG COMPANY
See Dart Industries, Inc.

LIGHT & SON, M.
611 Broadway S.W.
Knoxville, Tennessee 37901

LIGHT FANTASTIC (menswear)
See J. Schoeneman Inc.

LIGHT N' LIVELY (fat-free dairy products)
See Sealtest Foods (Division of Kraftco Corporation)

LIGHTCRAFT OF CALIFORNIA, INC.
(Division of Scovill Manufacturing Company)
1600 West Slausan Avenue
Los Angeles, California 90047
Everett Cook, General Manager
(213) 971-2170

LIGHTHOUSE OYSTER COMPANY INC.
826 S.E. Belmont Street
Portland, Oregon 97214

LIGHTOLIER, INC.
346 Claremont Avenue
Jersey City, New Jersey 07305
William F. Blitzer, President
(201) 333-5120

LIGHTRON CORPORATION
(Subsidiary of Instrument Systems Corporation)
789 Park Avenue
Huntington, New York 11743
Martin Gindoff, President
(516) 549-8200

LIGHTRONICS (lighting fixtures)
See Guth Lighting (Division of Sola Basic Industries)

LIGHTS FANTASTIC (plexiglas lamps)
See Dixson Inc. (Creative Decor Group)

LIGNUM-VITAE PRODUCTS CORPORATION
993 Belleville Turnpike
Kearny, New Jersey 07032

Companies and Trade Names

LIKE FRESH (food products)
See General Grocer Company

LIL' ALICE (dresses)
See Alice of California

LIL' DUFFER OF AMERICA INC.
105 East Tenth Street
Topeka, Kansas 66612

LI'L GENERAL STORES
5303 South MacDill Avenue
Tampa, Florida 33611

LILAC HEDGES CORPORATION
203 Chapala Street
Santa Barbara, California 93101

LILIENFELD, MOLLYE
30 Irving Place
New York, New York 10003
(212) 473-1350

LILIENTHAL & COMPANY,
RICHARD S.
180 Madison Avenue
New York, New York 10016
(212) 684-3234

LILLI-ANN CORPORATION
2701 16th Street
San Francisco, California 94103
Adolph P. Schuman, President
(415) 863-2720

LILLY AND COMPANY, ELI
Post Office Box 618
307 East McCarty Street
Indianapolis, Indiana 42606
Thomas H. Lake, President
(317) 636-2211

LILLY COMPANY, CHARLES H.
7737 N.E. Killingsworth Street
Portland, Oregon 97218
Fred C. Trullinger, President
(503) 256-4600

LILT (home permanents)
See Procter & Gamble Company

LILY (groceries)
See Kothe, Wells & Bauer
Company, Inc.

LILY
(Division of Owens-Illinois)
Post Office Box 1035
Toledo, Ohio 43666
(419) 242-6543

LILY CREAM COMPANY
2 Fourth Street
Wheeling, West Virginia 26003

LILY LAKE CHEESE COMPANY,
INC.
347 Greenwich Street
New York, New York 10013
(212) 925-3620

LILY LYNN, INC.
1400 Broadway
New York, New York 10018
Robert Giddins, President
(212) 565-4900

LILY MILLS COMPANY
(Subsidiary of Belding Hemingway
Company Inc.)
Shelby, North Carolina 28150
Robert R. Forney, President
(704) 487-6361

LILY OF FRANCE, INC.
90 Park Avenue
New York, New York 10016
Marvin Bienenfeld, President
(212) 392-2200

LILY-TULIP
(Division of Owens-Illinois, Inc.)
Post Office Box 1035
Toledo, Ohio 43601
C. D. "Doc" Pawlicki, Vice
President
(419) 242-6543

LILYETTE BRASSIERE COMPANY
105 Madison Avenue
New York, New York 10016
(212) 683-5000

LIMINALL PAINTS, INC.
2750 South Garfield Avenue
Los Angeles, California 90040
Charles F. Farrell, Jr., President
(213) 724-0500

LIMITED STORES, INC.
4661 East Main Street
Columbus, Ohio 43213
Leslie H. Wexner, President
(614) 861-3000

LIMPERT BROTHERS INC.
N.W. Boulevard and Plum Street
Vineland, New Jersey 08360
(609) 691-1353

LIN BROADCASTING CORPORATION
1370 Avenue of the Americas
New York, New York 10019
Donald A. Pels, Chairman,
President and Chief Executive
Officer
(212) 765-1902

LIN-N-LOOK COMPANY INC.
555 West Goodale Boulevard
Columbus, Ohio 43216
(614) 228-5781

LINCOLN (homes)
See Swift Industries, Inc.

LINCOLN BAG COMPANY, INC.
1010 North Kolmar Avenue
Chicago, Illinois 60651
(312) 252-4200

LINCOLN CAVENDISH (tobacco)
See House of Edgeworth

Companies and Trade Names

LINCOLN CRAWFORD PHARMACY, INC.
6770 North Lincoln Avenue
Lincolnwood, Illinois 60646

LINCOLN ELECTRIC COMPANY
22801 Saint Clair Avenue
Cleveland, Ohio 44117
George Willis, President
(216) 481-8100

LINCOLN FIBERGLASS INC.
Route 62
Glasondale Industrial Park
Stow, Massachusetts 01775
(617) 562-9555

LINCOLN FIRST BANK OF ROCHESTER
1 Lincoln First Square
Rochester, New York 14643
Alexander D. Hargrave, President
(716) 262-2000

LINCOLN FOODS, INC.
1 Newbury
Lawrence, Massachusetts 01840
Daniel Issenberg, President
(617) 685-9151
  See also Bessey Foods Corporation

LINCOLN INCOME LIFE INSURANCE COMPANY
6100 Dutchman's Lane
Louisville, Kentucky 40205
John T. Acree, III, President
(502) 459-5650

LINCOLN LABORATORIES, INC.
Box 1139
Decatur, Illinois 62525
Gary L. Hein, Chairman and President
(217) 877-2531

LINCOLN LACE & BRAID MANUFACTURING COMPANY
61 Ponogansett Avenue
Providence, Rhode Island 02909
Benjamin Gittleman, President and Treasurer
(401) 351-4400

LINCOLN MANUFACTURING COMPANY INC.
909 Baltimore Boulevard
Westminster, Maryland 21157
Roger I. Bair, Sr., President
(301) 876-2100

LINCOLN-MERCURY
(Division of Ford Motor Company)
3000 Schaefer Road
Dearborn, Michigan 48126
Walter S. Walla, General Manager
(313) 322-3000

LINCOLN METAL PRODUCTS CORPORATION
225 42nd Street
Brooklyn, New York 11232
Darwin Sussberg, President
(212) 499-8100

LINCOLN NATIONAL LIFE INSURANCE COMPANY
1301 South Harrison Street
Fort Wayne, Indiana 46802
Thomas A. Watson, Chairman of the Board
(219) 742-5421
  See also American States Insurance Company

LINCOLN PAPER COMPANY
6800 McCormick Road
Chicago, Illinois 60645
(312) 539-7300

LINCOLN TELEPHONE & TELEGRAPH COMPANY
1440 M Street
Lincoln, Nebraska 68508
Thomas C. Woods, Jr., President
(402) 435-4321

LINDAL CEDAR HOMES, INC.
10411 Empire Way, South
Seattle, Washington 98178
Robert M. McLennaghm, President
(206) 725-0900

LINDALE (hosiery)
  See Bulluck Hosiery Company, Inc.

LINDBERG PRODUCTS, INC.
8050 North Monticello
Skokie, Illinois 60076
Kenneth E. Rathke, President
(312) 677-6800

LINDELL (band instruments)
  See Saint Louis Music Supply Company, Inc.

LINDEN (alarm, wall, and mantle clocks)
  See Cuckoo Clock Manufacturing Company, Inc.

LINDEN FARMS (meat and dairy products)
  See Lobaw Ind.

LINDEN HOUSE (groceries)
  See Twin County Grovers Inc.

LINDER BROTHERS, INC.
1043 Capouse Avenue
Scranton, Pennsylvania 18509
Bertram N. Linder, President
(717) 342-3291

LINDIG MANUFACTURING CORPORATION
1881 West County Road C
Saint Paul, Minnesota 55113
(612) 633-3072

LINDMART JEWELRY MANUFACTURING COMPANY
122 West 27th Street
New York, New York 10001
(212) 675-2620

LINDSAY COMPANY
(Division of Ecodyne Corporation)
455 Woodlane Drive
Saint Paul, Minnesota 55165
Gerald T. Shannon, President
(612) 739-5330

Companies and Trade Names

LINDSAY INTERNATIONAL
(Division of Lindsay Olive Growers)
155 Bovet Road
San Mateo, California 94402
Earl S. Fox, President
(415) 574-2661

LINDSAY OLIVE GROWERS
Post Office Box 278
Lindsay, California 93247
Earl S. Fox, President
(209) 562-5151

LINDSEY COMPANY
(Division of Ecodyne Corporation)
445 Wood Lane Drive
Saint Paul, Minnesota 55119
Gerald T. Shannon, President
(612) 739-5330

LINDY PEN COMPANY
7250 Laurel Canyon Boulevard
North Hollywood, California 91605
Sidney Linden, President
(213) 875-1500

LINDY PRODUCTS COMPANY
(Division of Fecor Industries, Ltd.)
1656 East 233rd Street
Bronx, New York 10466
E. R. McDonald, Chairman and
  President
(212) 994-8800

LINE-FOLD (shirts, suits)
  See New Era Shirt Company

LINEA 88 (typewriters)
  See Olivetti Corporation of
    America

LINEAR SYSTEMS INC.
220 Airport Boulevard
Watsonville, California 95076
(408) 722-4177

LINEN SUPPLY ASSOCIATION
  OF AMERICA
Box 2427
975 Arthur Godfrey Road
Miami Beach, Florida 33140
(305) 532-6371

LINENS BY VERA, INC.
417 Fifth Avenue
New York, New York 10016
(212) 532-8000

LINETTE INC., JAMES P.
Front and Washington Streets
Reading, Pennsylvania 19601

LINEX (cameras)
  See Lionel Corporation

LING-EEZ (food products)
  See Columbia Products Inc.
    (Washington)

LINHOF (photo equipment)
  See Kling Photo Corporation

LINIT (laundry starch)
  See CPC International Inc.

LINK-BELT SPEEDER
(Division of FMC Corporation)
1201 Sixth Street S.W.
Cedar Rapids, Iowa 52406

LINK COMPANY, O. E.
(Division of Walco-Link Corporation)
1234 State Highway 46
Clifton, New Jersey 07015

LINK INC., OTTO
121 S.W. Fifth Street
Pompano Beach, Florida 33060

LINK 'N LEATHER (watchbands)
  See Vogue Watch Strap Creations,
    Inc.

LINK-TAYLOR CORPORATION
Cotton Grove Road
Lexington, North Carolina 27292
Henry T. Link, Chairman of the
  Board
(704) 352-2121

LINOTILE (floor covering)
  See Armstrong Cork Company

LINZ JEWELERS, THE
1608 Main
Dallas, Texas 75201
Albert Linz Hirsch, President
(214) 742-4391

LINZER & SONS INC., D.
440 Lafayette Street
New York, New York 10003
(212) 674-5350

LION (food products)
  See California-Omega Foods

LION (phonograph records)
  See Metro-Goldwyn-Mayer

LION BRAND (shirts)
  See M. Nirenberg Monsanto
    Company

LION, INC.
Gibbons Brewery
700 North Pennsylvania Avenue
Wilkes-Barre, Pennsylvania 18705
William J. Smulowitz, President
(717) 823-8801

LION KNITTING MILLS COMPANY
3256 West 25th Street
Cleveland, Ohio 44109
James R. Hibschman, President
(216) 351-5137

Companies and Trade Names

LION MATCH CORPORATION OF
   AMERICA
680 Fifth Avenue
New York, New York 10019
Frank J. Prince, Chairman of the
   Board
(212) 582-7770

LION OIL COMPANY
(Subsidiary of The Oil Shale
   Corporation)
Lion Oil Building
El Dorado, Arkansas 71730
J. A. Bierbaum, General Manager
(501) 863-3111

LION PACKAGING PRODUCTS
   COMPANY, INC.
(Affiliate of Eagle Beef Cloth
   Company)
15 East Bethpage Road
Plainview, New York 11803
Nathan Levine, President
(516) 249-1400

LION RIBBON COMPANY, INC.
385 Gerard Avenue
Bronx, New York 10451
(212) 585-1900

LION UNIFORM, INC.
2735 Kearns Avenue
Dayton, Ohio 45414
Clarence Lapedes, President
(513) 278-6531

LIONEL (model electric trains and
accessories)
   See Fundimensions

LIONEL CORPORATION
9 West 57th Street
New York, New York 10019
Ronald D. Saypol, President
(212) 371-2100
   See also Bernardi Brothers, Inc.

LIONEL LEISURE, INC.
2951 Grant Avenue
Philadelphia, Pennsylvania 19114
Leonard Wasserman, President
(215) 677-4800

LIP-STAE COMPANY
Box 1059
Flushing, New York 11351

LIP-TEX, INC.
146 West 12th Avenue
Denver, Colorado 80204

LIPETZ TRADING COMPANY
79 Madison Avenue
New York, New York 10016
(212) 683-3534

LIPIC PEN COMPANY, JOSEPH
2200 Gravois Street
Saint Louis, Missouri 63104
Leonard G. Lipic, President and
   Treasurer
(314) 664-2111

LIPITZ COMPANY, BENJAMIN
2700 East Lehigh Avenue
Philadelphia, Pennsylvania 19125
(215) 426-2151

LIPMAN'S IMPORTS INC.
Wyandanch Avenue
Wyandanch, New York 11798

LIPPER INTERNATIONAL, INC.
225 Fifth Avenue
New York, New York 10010
(212) 686-6076

LIPPINCOTT BOAT WORKS
Canal Avenue
Riverton, New Jersey 08077

LIPPINCOTT, COMPANY, J. B.
East Washington Square
Philadelphia, Pennsylvania 19105
J. W. Lippincott, President
(215) 925-4100

LIPTON, INC., THOMAS J.
800 Sylvan Avenue
Englewood Cliffs, New Jersey 07632
H. M. Tibbetts, President
(201) 567-8000
   See also Good Humor Corporation,
The; and Morton House
   Kitchen Inc.

LIPTON MARINE INDUSTRIES, INC.
Rock Ridge
Mamaroneck, New York 10543

LIPTON PET FOODS, INC.
(Division of Thomas J. Lipton, Inc.)
800 Sylvan Avenue
Englewood Cliffs, New Jersey 07632

LIQUID CARBONIC CORPORATION
135 South La Salle
Chicago, Illinois 60603
J. A. Edwards, President
(312) 855-2500

LIQUID CRYSTAL INDUSTRIES, INC.
Post Office Box 8124
6638 Woodwell Avenue
Pittsburgh, Pennsylvania 15217
(412) 421-0800

LIQUID GLAZE, INC.
735 May Street
Lansing, Michigan 55950
(517) 484-5495

LIQUID-LITE (enamel)
   See O'Brien Corporation

LIQUID MARBLE (paint)
   See Luminall Paints, Inc.

LIQUID PAPER CORPORATION
Box 31067
9130 Markville Drive
Dallas, Texas 75231
(214) 234-3211

LIQUID-PLUMR (drain cleaner
and germicide)
   See Clorox Company

LISANNE, INC.
152 Madison Avenue
New York, New York 10016
(212) 686-1780

Companies and Trade Names

LISETTE HANDBAGS LTD.
14 East 33rd Street
New York, New York 10016
(212) 684-6272

LISK-SAVORY CORPORATION
901 Fuhrmann Boulevard
Buffalo, New York 14240
S. Shephard Wilson, President
(716) 856-1818

LISNER & COMPANY, D.
393 Fifth Avenue
New York, New York 10016
Victor W. Ganz, President
(212) 689-8080

LISS & COMPANY, M. C.
1413 Palisade Avenue
Teaneck, New Jersey 07666

LISSY (swimwear)
See Elizabeth Stewart Swimwear

LISTERINE (antiseptic, breath fresheners, cold remedy, toothpaste, etc.)
See Warner-Lambert Company

LISTO PENCIL CORPORATION
Post Office Drawer J
1925 Union Street
Alameda, California 94501
D. G. Stuart, President
(415) 522-2910

LIT DRUG COMPANY
2530 Polk Street
Union, New Jersey 07083

LIT-NING PRODUCTS COMPANY
2496 South Cherry Avenue
Fresno, California 93706
Kirk C. Kirkorian, Jr., President
(209) 237-4771

LITE BEAMS (lamps)
See Clover Lamp Company

LITE-LINE (low-fat dairy products)
See Borden Inc. Dairy & Services Division

LITE LINER (motor homes)
See Ute Liner Inc.

LITE-PANELS (lights)
See Drake Manufacturing Company

LITE-TREND (lighting)
See Halo Lighting (Division of McGraw-Edison Company)

LITE-WELL PRODUCTS
1832 North Lockwood Avenue
Chicago, Illinois 60639
(312) 622-4777

LITERARY GUILD OF AMERICA, INC.
501 Franklin Avenue
Garden City, New York 11531
John T. Sargent, President
(516) 294-4561

LITH O SKETCH
31 Commercial Street
Gloucester, Massachusetts 01930

LITHO-ART PRODUCTS INC.
204 West Carpenter Road
Wheeling, Illinois 60090
(312) 459-1123

LITRONIX INC.
19000 Homestead Road
Cupertino, California 95014
Bruce Blakkan, Chairman and President
(408) 257-7910

LITTER GREEN (cat-box litter)
See Clorox Company

LITTLE ADMIRAL (cigars)
See American Tobacco Company

LITTLE BOY (canned foods)
See A. T. Hipke & Sons Inc.

LITTLE BOY BLUE (liquid bluing)
See Purex Corporation, Ltd.

LITTLE BRIDE (canned foods)
See Growers & Packers Coop, Canning Company Inc.

LITTLE, BROWN, & COMPANY, INC.
34 Beacon Street
Boston, Massachusetts 02108
Arthur H. Thornhill, Jr., President
(617) 227-0730

LITTLE CHEF (food products)
See Morgan Packing Company Inc.

LITTLE CHIEF (food products)
See Southern Shell Fish Company

LITTLE CROW MILLING COMPANY
Warsaw, Indiana 46580
(219) 267-7141

LITTLE FOLKS (juvenile furniture)
See Simmons Company

LITTLE GIANT CORPORATION
3810 North Tulsa Street
Oklahoma City, Oklahoma 73112
M. G. McKool, President
(405) 947-2511

LITTLE GRIDDLE CORPORATION
1249 Washington Boulevard, 7th Floor
Detroit, Michigan 48226

LITTLE-JONES COMPANY, INC., THE
225 Fifth Avenue
New York, New York 10001
(212) 689-1950

Companies and Trade Names

LITTLE KENNY PUBLICATIONS INC.
1315 West Belmont Avenue
Chicago, Illinois 60657
(312) 281-7633

LITTLE LADY (shoes for children)
See Brown Group Inc.

LITTLE MILL (food products)
See Steele Canning Company Inc.

LITTLE ORGANIZER (watchbands)
See Brite Industries Inc.

LITTLE PROFESSOR BOOK CENTERS OF AMERICA INC.
11900 Mayfield
Livonia, Michigan 48150

LITTLE ROCK FURNITURE MANUFACTURING COMPANY
1498 East Second
Little Rock, Arkansas 72203
R. G. Morrow, Jr., President
(501) 372-5491

LITTLE SAILOR (canned foods)
See Chilton Canning Company

LITTLE SANO (cigars)
See United States Tobacco Company

LITTLE STAR FROCKS, INC.
Orchard and Walnut
Bridgeton, New Jersey 08302
Morris H. Seibel, President
(609) 451-4200

LITTLE TIKES BY ROTADYNE INC.
8705 Freeway Drive
Macedonia, Ohio 44056

LITTLE WONDER
(Division of Schiller-Pfeiffer)
1028 Streed Street
Southampton, Pennsylvania 18966
(215) 357-5110

LITTLEFIELD, ADAMS & COMPANY
81 Adams Drive
Totowa, New Jersey 07512
Gilbert Raff, President
(201) 256-8600

LITTON INDUSTRIES, INC.
360 North Crescent Drive
Beverly Hills, California 90210
John H. Martin, President
(213) 273-7860
See also Adler Business Machines Inc.; Airtron; Allis Company, The Louis; Cole; Eureka Company; Fitchburg Coated Products Inc.; Hewitt-Robins; Kester Solder Company; Koehler-Dayton Inc.; Lehigh-Leopold Furniture Company; McBee Loose Leaf Bindery Products; Monroe Calculator Company; Pronto File; Royal Typewriter Company; Royfax; Streater Store Fixtures, Inc.; and Sweda International

LITTON MICROWAVE COOKING PRODUCTS
400 Shelard Plaza South
Minneapolis, Minnesota 55426
William W. George, President
(612) 553-2000

LIV-A-SNAPS, INC.
4251 Fernwood-Arden Hills
Saint Paul, Minnesota 55105
(612) 636-1144

LIVE AISLE (mobile storage system)
See Dexion Inc.

LIVE WIRE (guitars and strings)
See York Musical Instrument Company Inc.

LIVELYAIRE (fans)
See Westinghouse Electric Corporation

LIVERMORE SHOE COMPANY
19 Bennett Street
Lynn, Massachusetts 01905
Ted Poland, President
(617) 598-5300

LIVINGSTON INDUSTRIES
136 North Ash Street
Inglewood, California 90301
(213) 674-3081

LIVINGSTONE EVANS ENTERPRISES
916 North La Cienega Boulevard
Los Angeles, California 90069
(213) 474-4009

LLOYD ASSOCIATES LTD.
322 Center Avenue
Mamaroneck, New York 10534

LLOYD MANUFACTURING COMPANY, THE
3010 Tenth Street
Menominee, Michigan 49858
John H. Heywood, President
(906) 863-2661

LLOYDS BANK OF CALIFORNIA
548 Spring Street
Los Angeles, California 90013
Robert W. Brown, President
(213) 629-4381

LLOYD'S ELECTRONICS, INC.
18601 South Susana Road
Compton, California 90221
Paul Chudnow, President
(213) 774-4270

LLOYD'S LONDON (dry gin and rum)
See Julius Wile Sons & Company, Inc.

LLOYDS OF CALIFORNIA
527 West Seventh Street
Los Angeles, California 90014
(213) 622-1754

Companies and Trade Names

LO-BEL COMPANY, THE
112 West 34th Street
New York, New York 10001
(212) 565-0040

LO BELLO COMPANY, ANNETTE
2314 San Jacinto
Dallas, Texas 75201

LO DUCA BROTHERS MUSICAL
INSTRUMENTS, INC.
400 North Broadway
Milwaukee, Wisconsin 53202
(414) 347-0700

LO TONES (shoes)
See Jay Shoe Manufacturing
Company

LOBEL CHEMICAL CORPORATION
100 Church Street
New York, New York 10007
(212) 267-4265

LOBICA-DEBRUILLE, INC.
195 East Main Street
Brewster, New York 10509

LOBLAW, INC.
678 Bailey Avenue
Buffalo, New York 13240
W. Galen Weston, President
(716) 825-111
See also Better Foods, Inc.

LOBOB LABORATORIES
1020 Chestnut
San Jose, California 95110
(408) 295-4683

LOCALITE (desk and table lamps)
See Fostoria-Fannon Inc.

LOCHAN ORA (Scotch liqueur)
See General Wine & Spirits
Company

LOCKE (shoes)
See Julian & Kokenge Company

LOCKE STOVE COMPANY
114 West 11th Street
Kansas City, Missouri 64105
Edward M. Douthat, President
(816) 421-1650

LOCKHEED AIRCRAFT
CORPORATION
2555 Hollywood Way
Burbank, California 91503
Daniel J. Haughton, Chairman of
the Board
(213) 847-6121

LOCKHEED ELECTRONICS
COMPANY, INC.
(Subsidiary of Lockheed Aircraft
Corporation)
U.S. Highway 22
Plainfield, New Jersey 07061

LOCKHEED-GEORGIA COMPANY
(Division of Lockheed Aircraft
Corporation)
Marietta, Georgia 30061

LOCKLEY MANUFACTURING
COMPANY, INC.
310 Grove Street
New Castle, Pennsylvania 16103
(412) 658-1551

LOCKLIN PRODUCTS INC.
4647 Lown Street North
Saint Petersburgh, Florida 33714
(815) 525-1473

LOCKPORT CANNING COMPANY
Lake Avenue
Lockport, New·York 14094

LOCKPORT NONFERROUS
CASTINGS INC.
Box 100
Lockport, New York 14094

LOCTITE CORPORATION
705 North Mountain Road
Newington, Connecticut 06111
E. R. Eggers, President
(203) 278-1280

LODI CANNING COMPANY INC.
Box 303
Lodi, Wisconsin 53555
(608) 592-4236

LODI WINERY, INC.
Lodi, California 95240

LOEB (clothing)
See Oxford Industries, Inc.

LOEB & COMPANY INC., MARCEL
919 Third Avenue
New York, New York 10017
(212) 752-7350

LOEB CORPORATION, M.
Elk Grove Village, Illinois 60007

LOEHMANN'S, INC.
3450 Baychester Avenue
Bronx, New York 10469
Charles C. Loehmann, Chairman of
the Board
(212) 654-4000

LOEWENSTEIN INC., HANK
3105 S.W. Second Avenue
Fort Lauderdale, Florida 33315

LOEWY MACHINERY SUPPLIES
COMPANY
305 East 47th Street
New York, New York 10017
(212) 758-0744

LOFT CANDY CORPORATION
See Barricini, Inc.

LOG CABIN (syrups)
See General Foods Corporation

LOG CABIN (whiskey)
See National Distillers &
Chemical Corporation

903

Companies and Trade Names

LOGAN & COMPANY, S. B.
122 North Mill Street
Genoa City, Wisconsin 53128

LOGAN COMPANY
200 Cabel
Louisville, Kentucky 40206
Joseph M. Hammond, President
(502) 587-1361

LOGAN CONCESSION SUPPLY
330 East First Street
Tulsa, Oklahoma 74120

LOGAN ELECTRIC SPECIALTY
   MANUFACTURING COMPANY
1431 West Hubbard Street
Chicago, Illinois 60622
(312) 226-5888

LOGAN INC.
16952 Milliken Avenue
Irvine, California 92705
(714) 556-6441

LOGAN INC., JONATHAN
3901 Liberty Avenue
North Bergen, New Jersey 07047
(201) 864-7200
   See also Alice Stuart; Bleeker
      Street Apparel Corporation;
      Misty Harbor; and R. & K.
      Originals

LOHALL ENTERPRISES, INC.
Post Office Box 3746
Milwaukee, Wisconsin 53217
(414) 351-1270

LOHMANN FOODS
(Division of Pfeiffer's Foods Inc.)
4651 Dewey Avenue
Gorham, New York 14461
(315) 596-6341

LOKATO COMPANY
25-09 Broadway
Fair Lawn, New Jersey 07410

LOKTUFT (carpet backing)
   See Phillips Fibers Corporation

LOLITA (processed foods)
   See Butcher Boy Food Products

LOMA CORPORATION
Post Office Box 40350
9651 Highway 81, South
Fort Worth, Texas 76140
Irving N. Levine, President
(817) 293-2551

LOMA LINDA FOODS
11503 Pierce Street
Riverside, California 92505
L. Delmer Wood, President
(714) 785-2444

LOMBARDI FOOD COMPANY
605 East Ten Mile Road
Royal Oak, Michigan 48067

LOMMA BILLARD CORPORATION
Lomma Building
Wyoming Avenue and Spruce Street
Scranton, Pennsylvania 18503
(717) 343-4741

LONDON (dry gin and vodka)
   See Schenley Industries, Inc.

LONDON CANDIES, HARRY
1281 South Main Street
North Canton, Ohio 44720

LONDON CHOP HOUSE (food
products)
   See Macgowan Coffee Company

LONDON DOCK (tobacco)
   See Whitehall Products, Inc.

LONDON DRY LTD.
407 South Pine Street
Spartanburg, South Carolina 29302

LONDON FOG (raincoats)
   See Londontown Corporation

LONDON HILL (gin)
   See H. Stone & Company Ltd.

LONDON LODGE (food products)
   See Hamilton & Sons Canning
      Company

LONDON LOOK (toiletries)
   See Yardley of London, Inc.

LONDON MIST (perfume, dusting
powder, cologne)
   See Herb Farm Shop, Ltd.

LONDON RECORDS INC.
539 West 25th Street
New York, New York 10001
(212) 675-6060

LONDONER (men's coats)
   See Isaac Cohen & Son Clothes
      Company Inc.

LONDON'S CHOCOLATES
Rural Delivery 3, Box 123
Punxsutawney, Pennsylvania 15767

LONDONTOWN CORPORATION
3600 Clipper Mill Road
Baltimore, Maryland 21211
Jonathan Myers, President
(301) 366-6200

LONE PINE (canned foods)
   See Fort Lupton Canning Company

LONE STAR (ladders)
   See Pat Johnson Manufacturing
      Company

Companies and Trade Names

LONE STAR BREWING COMPANY
600 Lone Star Boulevard
San Antonio, Texas 78204
Harry D. Jersig, Chairman of the
  Board
(512) 226-8301

LONE STAR FOODS COMPANY
Post Office Box 10546
Dallas, Texas 75207

LONE STAR GAS COMPANY
301 South Harwood Street
Dallas, Texas 75201
Roy E. Pitts, Chairman of the Board
(214) 741-3711

LONE STAR INDUSTRIES, INC.
1 Greenwich Plaza
Greenwich, Connecticut 06830
Robert W. Hutton, President and
  Chief Executive Officer
(203) 661-3100

LONE STAR INDUSTRIES, INC.
Northwest Division
901 Fairview North
Seattle, Washington 98109
(206) 622-2900

LONE STAR INSTITUTIONAL GROCERS
2666 Manana
Dallas, Texas 75220

LONE TOY TREE INC., THE
Box 4746
Carmal, California 93921

LONG BEACH SALT COMPANY
Post Office Box 149
San Diego, California 92112

LONG COMPANY, F. A.
Box 277
Benton Harbor, Michigan 49022
(616) 925-0011

LONG ISLAND IMPORT CENTER
90 Porter Avenue
Brooklyn, New York 11237
(212) 456-2658

LONG ISLAND LIGHTING
  COMPANY
250 Old Country Road
Mineola, New York 11501
John J. Tuohy, President
(516) 747-1000

LONG ISLAND MACARONI
  COMPANY
325 Marcus Boulevard
Deer Park, New York 11729

LONG ISLAND RAILROAD
  COMPANY, THE
(Subsidiary of Metropolitan Transit
  Authority (MTA))
Archer Avenue and Sutphin
  Boulevard
Jamaica, New York 11435
Walter L. Schlager, Jr., President
(212) 526-0900

LONG JOHN (Scotch)
  See Schenley Industries, Inc.

LONG LIFE (food products)
  See Greenville Dairy Company

LONG MANUFACTURING
  COMPANY
280 Hegenberger Road
Oakland, California 94621

LONG MANUFACTURING NORTH
  CAROLINA INC.
Box 1139-V
Torboro, North Carolina 27886
(919) 823-4151

LONGCHAMP'S INC.
230 Park Avenue
New York, New York 10017
Lawrence Ellman, President
(212) 889-5100
  See also Steak & Brew, Inc.

LONGHORN (sporting firearms)
  See High Standard Manufacturing
    Corporation

LONGINES-WITTNAUER WATCH
  COMPANY, INC.
(Subsidiary of Westinghouse Electric
  Corporation)
145 Huguenot
New Rochelle, New York 10801
Robert Pliskin, President
(914) 576-1000
  See also Jaeger-Le Coultre
    Watches, Inc.

LONGO COMPANY
1205 Broadway
Camden, New Jersey 08104

LONGS DRUG STORES, INC.
141 North Civic Drive
Walnut Creek, California 94596
Joseph M. Long, Chairman
(415) 937-1193

LONGSHORE (seafood)
  See J. R. Hardee Shrimp Company

LONGSTREET PHARMACAL
  CORPORATION
5001 New Utrecht Avenue
Brooklyn, New York 11219
(212) 436-9200

LOOART PRESS, INC.
3525 North Stone
Colorado Springs, Colorado 80901

LOOK (cigarettes)
  See Brown & Williamson Tobacco
    Corporation

LOOK CANNING COMPANY,
  A. M.
East Machias, Maine 04630

LOOK INC., H.W.
Box 504
Rockland, Maine 04841

Companies and Trade Names

LOOPING (clocks)
See Heuer Time Corporation

LOOS & COMPANY
3074 Cable Road
Pomfret, Connecticut 06258
Augus W. Loos, Chairman and President
(203) 928-7981

LOOSE LEAF HOUSE
156 West 31st Street
Los Angeles, California 90007
(213) 749-9291

LORA LABORATORIES, INC.
2542 North Elston
Chicago, Illinois 60647
(312) 772-4770

LORANN OILS
2130 Hamilton Road
Okemos, Michigan 48864

LORCA INC.
1410 Broadway
New York, New York 10018
(212) 279-8418

LORCH-WESTWAY CORPORATION
4949 Beeman Street
Dallas, Texas 75223
A. Lorch Folz, President
(214) 826-7500

LORD & BURNHAM
(Division of Burnham Corporation)
Main Street
Irvington, New York 10533
Burnham Bowden, President
(914) 591-8800

LORD & TAYLOR
(Division of Associated Dry Goods Corporation)
424 Fifth Avenue
New York, New York 10018
Joseph E. Brooks, Chairman of the Board
(212) 947-3300

LORD CALVERT (whiskies)
See Calvert Distillers Company

LORD CHESTERFIELD (canned foods)
See McCall Farms, Inc.

LORD ELGIN (watches, jewelry)
See Elgin Watch Company Inc.

LORD HORATIO (cigars)
See S. Frieder & Sons Company

LORD JEFF KNITTING COMPANY INC.
10 Maple Street
Norwood, New Jersey 07648

LORD-MOTT (frozen fruit)
See Duffy-Mott Company, Inc.

LORD NELSON (watches)
See M. Z. Berger & Company Inc.

LORD'S (cigarettes)
See House of Edgeworth

L'OREAL OF PARIS (hair- and nail-care products, etc.)
See Cosmair, Inc.

LORETTO FOODS INC.
Box 353
Olean, New York 14760

LORI (toiletries)
See Freeda Pharmaceuticals

LORIET FASHIONS INC.
330 Fifth Avenue
New York, New York 10001
(212) 736-6677

L'ORIGAN (perfume, dusting powder, talc, etc.)
See Coty (Division of Pfizer, Inc.)

LORILLARD (snuff)
See Whitehall Products, Inc.

LORILLARD COMPANY, P.
(Division of Loews Theatres, Inc.)
200 East 42nd Street
New York, New York 10017
Curtis H. Judge, President
(212) 983-4400

LORING RESEARCH, INC.
Box 151
Greenwich, Connecticut 06830

LORLINK (menswear)
See Lord Jeff Knitting Company Inc.

LOROMAN COMPANY, INC.
230 Fifth Avenue
New York, New York 10001
(212) 683-2511

LORRAINE INDUSTRIES, INC.
450 Hancock Avenue
Bridgeport, Connecticut 06605
Robert Smolian, President
(203) 333-5148

LORRAINE LINGERIE
261 Madison Avenue
New York, New York 10016
(212) 661-8180

LORTOGS, INC.
112 West 34th Street
New York, New York 10001
Arthur Flachs, President
(212) 564-0830

LORVIC CORPORATION, THE
8810 Frost Avenue
Saint Louis, Missouri 63134
(314) 524-7444

LOS ANGELES AIRWAYS, INC.
5901 West Imperial Highway
Los Angeles, California 90045
Clarence M. Belinn, President
(213) 646-4730

Companies and Trade Names

LOS ANGELES NUT HOUSE
722 Market Court
Los Angeles, California 90021
William Gendel, President
(213) 623-2541

LOS ANGELES SOAP COMPANY
617 East First Street
Los Angeles, California 90054
De Witt A. Barton, President
(213) 627-5011
See also White King, Inc.

LOS ANGELES TIMES
(Division of The Times Mirror Company)
Times Mirror Square
Los Angeles, California 90053
Otis Chandler, Publisher
(213) 625-2345

LOS ANGELES WHOLESALE ELECTRIC COMPANY INC.
214-216 East Third
Los Angeles, California 90013
(213) 625-5181

LOSITO MUSHROOM CORPORATION
Toughkenamon, Pennsylvania 19374

LOSURDO FOODS INC.
20 Owens Road
Hackensack, New Jersey 07601

LOTTA COLA COMPANY
7500 Melrose Street
Pittsburgh, Pennsylvania 15218

LOTUS (cosmetics)
See Yardley of London, Inc.

LOTUS (guitars)
See Midwest Musical Instrument Company

LOTUS (porcelain-on-steel cookware and bakeware)
See Club Products Company

LOTUS (sewing machines)
See White Dewing Machine Company

LOTUS/EAST, INC.
Box 394
Salisbury, Connecticut 06068

LOTUS GLASS COMPANY, THE
Post Office Box 191
Barnesville, Ohio 43713
(614) 425-1996

LOTUS MANUFACTURING COMPANY
529 San Pedro
San Antonio, Texas 78212

LOTUS PRODUCTS, INC.
1510 Hess Street
Columbus, Ohio 43212

LOU MAR COMPANY, INC.
Rural Delivery 2
Girard, Pennsylvania 16417

LOU-RAN HANDBAG INC.
162 Madison Avenue
New York, New York 10016
(212) 684-5686

LOU-ROD CANDY, INC.
1047 Sabattus Street
Lewiston, Maine 04240

LOUIE GLASS COMPANY INC.
631 East Third Street
Weston, West Virginia 26452
Michael R. Strum, General Manager
(304) 269-4700

LOUIS JADOT (wines)
See Kobrand Corporation

LOUIS MARTINI (wines)
See Twenty One Brands, Inc.

LOUIS SHERRY, INC.
18 West Putnam Avenue
Greenwich, Connecticut 06830
James P. McCaffrey, Chairman
(203) 661-3131

LOUISIANA (canned foods)
See Bruce Foods Corporation

LOUISIANA POWER & LIGHT COMPANY
142 Delaronde Street
New Orleans, Louisiana 70114
E. A. Rodrigue, President
(504) 366-2345

LOUISVILLE & NASHVILLE, RAILROAD COMPANY
908 West Broadway
Louisville, Kentucky 40203
Prime F. Osborn, President
(502) 587-5000

LOUISVILLE BEDDING COMPANY
10400 Bunsen Way
Louisville, Kentucky 40299
James R. Hartstock, Chairman of the Board
(502) 491-3370

LOUISVILLE, CEMENT COMPANY
501 South Second Street
Louisville, Kentucky 40202
Gene P. Gardner, President

LOUISVILLE CYCLE & SUPPLY COMPANY
4700 Allmond Avenue
Louisville, Kentucky 40221

LOUISVILLE GAS & ELECTRIC COMPANY
311 West Chestnut Street
Louisville, Kentucky 40201
G. R. Armstrong, Chairman of the Board
(502) 582-3511

Companies and Trade Names

LOUISVILLE STONEWARE COMPANY, INC.
731 Brent Street
Louisville, Kentucky 40204
John M. Robertson, President and General Manager
(502) 637-2543

LOUISVILLE TIN & STOVE COMPANY
Box 1079
737 South 13th Street
Louisville, Kentucky 40201
(502) 589-5380

LOUMAR TEXTILE BY-PRODUCTS, INC.
320 Central Park West
New York, New York 10025
(212) 874-1794

LOUNGE-RITE (reclining chair)
See National of Evansville

LOUNGEES, INC.
505 Court Street
Brooklyn, New York 11231
Henry Farah, President
(212) 855-4416

LOVABLE COMPANY
3050 Jones Ferri Road
Norcross, Georgia 30071
Dan Garson, President
(404) 448-1980

LOVE (cosmetics)
See Menley & James Laboratories

LOVE, JOSEPH, INC.
1333 Broadway
New York, New York 10018
Stanley Love, President
(212) 524-8117

LOVE NOTES COLONY INC.
10218 South Shore Drive
Minneapolis, Minnesota 55427

LOVEKIN (gas and electric water heaters)
See Bradford-White Corporation

LOVELACE CANDY MANUFACTURING COMPANY INC.
Post Office Box 310
Greenbrier, Tennessee 37073

LOVELAND BROOM COMPANY
Post Office Box 395
Loveland, Colorado 80537

LOVELY LADY (canned and frozen seafood)
See Bay View Foods

LOVEMAN, JOSEPH & LOEB
(Division of City Stores Company)
212-224 North 19th Street
Birmingham, Alabama 35203
Clifford D. Hoehne, President
(205) 323-6511

LOVERA (cigars)
See Consolidated Cigar Corporation

LOVE'S RESTAURANTS
See International House of Pancakes

LOVIBOND OF AMERICA, INC.
870 Willis Avenue
Albertson, New York 11507

LOVING CARE (hair coloring)
See Clairol, Inc.

LOWE & FLETCHER INC.
30 Lincoln
Boston, Massachusetts 02111
(617) 787-3421

LOWE COMPANY, SAMUEL
1324 52nd Street
Kenosha, Wisconsin 53140

LOWE, INC., E. S.
(Division of Milton Bradley Company)
39-34 43rd Street
Long Island City, New York 11104
Robert O'Konski, General Manager
(212) 729-4000

LOWE INDUSTRIES INC.
Post Office Box 989
Lebanon, Missouri 65536
(417) 532-9101

LOWE SEED COMPANY
217 South West Avenue
Kankakee, Illinois 60901
Edward J. Strasma, President
(815) 933-4471

LOWELL PACKING COMPANY
Dixie Highway
Fitzgerald, Georgia 31750
L. M. Downing, President
(912) 423-2051

LOWENBAUM, MANUFACTURING COMPANY, R.
5236 Oakland Avenue
Saint Louis, Missouri 63110
Ralph Lowenbaum, President
(314) 533-2311

LOWENSTEIN & SONS, INC., M.
1430 Broadway
New York, New York 10018
Joseph Anderer, President
(212) 560-5000
See also Wamsutta Mills

Companies and Trade Names

LOWE'S COMPANIES, INC.
Post Office Box 1111
North Wilkesboro, North Carolina 28659
Edwin Duncan, Sr., Chairman
(919) 677-3111

LOWES CORPORATION
666 Fifth Avenue
New York, New York 10019
Laurence Tisch, Chairman of the Board
(212) 586-4400

LOWE'S FOOD STORES, INC.
Highway 268 West
Wilkesboro, North Carolina 28697
J. C. Fan, President
(919) 838-3187

LOWE'S, INC.
North Edward
Cassopolis, Michigan 49031
(616) 445-3881

LOWESTOFT (china)
See Spode, Inc.

LOWETH-NATIONAL BUYING SERVICE CORPORATION
469 Seventh Avenue
New York, New York 10018
(212) 244-4900

LOWNDES PRODUCTS
Post Office Box 606
Easley, South Carolina 29640

LOWRANCE ELECTRONICS MANUFACTURING COMPANY
12000 East Skelly Drive
Tulsa, Oklahoma 74128
Darrel Lowrance, President
(918) 437-6881

LOWRY & BROTHERS, ALFRED
1200 Ferry Avenue
Camden, New Jersey 08104

LOXON (paint, floor enamel, and concrete)
See Sherwin-Williams Company

LOYAL (luggage, leather goods)
See Luxor Leathercraft Corporation

LOYAL CANNING CORPORATION
Box 278
Loyal, Wisconsin 54446
(715) 255-8521

LOYAL GIFT PRODUCTS, INC.
11 East 26th Street
New York, New York 10010
(212) 689-9240

LOYAL PACKING COMPANY
3327 West 47th
Chicago, Illinois 60632
(312) 847-0705

LOZIER STORE FIXTURES INC.
Post Office Box 249
Omaha, Nebraska 68101
See also American Fixture Inc.

L'QUALITAIRE LINGERIE MILLS
See Superba Mills

LU WANE PRODUCTS COMPANY
Post Office Box 321
Wayne, New Jersey 07470
Edward C. Hunter, President
(201) 696-2100

LU-WOW (food products)
See Morton-Norwich Products Inc.

LUAU (food products)
See Hawaiian Sun Products Inc.

LUBRIPLATE
(Division of Fiske Brothers Refining Company)
129 Lockwood Street
Newark, New Jersey 07105
(201) 589-9150

LUCARELLI (men's toiletries)
See Frances Denney

LUCAS & COMPANY, JOHN
(Division of Sherwin Williams)
101 Prospect Avenue, N.W.
Cleveland, Ohio 44115
(216) 566-2650

LUCAS, INC., CAMILLA
981 Second Avenue
New York, New York 10022
(212) 752-1516

LUCAS MANUFACTURING COMPANY
420 Walnut Street
Columbia, Pennsylvania 17512
Janet S. Varian, President
(717) 684-6911

LUCAS PRODUCTS CORPORATION
3839 Seiss Avenue
Toledo, Ohio 43612

LUCAS STUDIO CREATIONS
17 North State Street
Chicago, Illinois 60202
(312) 726-0538

LUCCA PACKING COMPANY OF CALIFORNIA, INC.
360 Harbor Way
South San Francisco, California 94080
John Stanghellini, President
(415) 589-0221

LUCCI MARINE
(Division of Mechtron International)
2140 West Washington Street
Orlando, Florida 32809

Companies and Trade Names

LUCE CANDY COMPANY
1560 Murchison Street
Los Angeles, California 90033
(213) 221-4646

LUCE CORPORATION, THE
18 Marshall
South Norwalk, Connecticut 06856
(203) 866-2529

LUCERNE (watches)
See Windert Watch Company

LUCIEN LELONG PARFUMS CORPORATION
(Division of General Beauty Products Inc.)
529 Fifth Avenue
New York, New York 10036
(212) 867-8900

LUCIEN PICCARD INDUSTRIES, INC.
580 Fifth Avenue
New York, New York 10036
Stanley Blumstein, President
(212) 757-4360

LUCIKON (cameras)
See M. P. Goodkin Company

LUCILLE BOUCHARD
Route 9
Wilton, New York 12866

LUCITE (paints)
See E. I. DuPont de Nemours, & Company, Inc.

LUCKIDAY (vacuum cleaner)
See Sunbeam Appliance Company

LUCK'S (vegetables)
See American Home Foods

LUCKS COMPANY, OSCAR
3434 Socond Avenue South
Seattle, Washington 98134
(206) 622-4608

LUCKY BOY (boy's shirts)
See Charles Greenberg & Sons, Inc.

LUCKY BREWERIES, INC.
2601 Newhall Street
San Francisco, California 94124
R. F. Lewarne, Chairman of the Board
(415) 467-2211

LUCKY CLUB COMPANY
3224 South Kinghighway Boulevard
Saint Louis, Missouri 63139
(314) 772-5254

LUCKY DUCK ENTERPRISES INC.
16 Shelley Terrace
West Orange, New Jersey 07052

LUCKY HEART COSMETICS
388 Mulberry Street
Memphis, Tennessee 38103
B. M. Spears, President
(901) 526-7658

LUCKY INTERNATIONAL COMPANY
1240 Broadway
New York, New York 10001
(212) 594-6946

LUCKY LADY (canned and packaged foods)
See C. B. Ragland Company

LUCKY LEAF (canned foods)
See Knouse Foods, Inc.

LUCKY STAR UNDERGARMENTS, INC.
85 DeKalb Avenue
Brooklyn, New York 11201
(212) 625-1840

LUCKY STORES, INC.
6300 Clark Avenue
Dublin, California 94566
Wayne H. Fisher, Chairman of the Board
(415) 828-1000

LUCKY STRIKE (canned meats)
See Loyal Packing Company

LUCKY STRIKE (cigarettes)
See American Tobacco Company

LUCKY WHIP (whipped topping mix)
See Lever Brothers Company

LUDEN'S, INC.
200 North Eighth Street
Reading, Pennsylvania 19601
H. Richard Dietrich, Jr., President
(215) 376-2981

LUDFORD FRUIT PRODUCTS, INC.
1411-21 Western Avenue
Los Angeles, California 90006
(213) 737-8212

LUDLOW CORPORATION
145 Rosemary Street
Needham Heights, Massachusetts 02194
Austin B. Mason, President
(617) 444-4900
See also Walter Carpet Mills

LUDWIG (pianos)
See Cunningham Piano Company

LUDWIG CANDY COMPANY
South Route 54
Manteno, Illinois 60950

LUDWIG INDUSTRIES CORPORATION
1728 North Damen Avenue
Chicago, Illinois 60647
William F. Ludwig, Jr., President
(312) 276-3360

Companies and Trade Names

LUDWIG MANUFACTURING
COMPANY INC.
1405 16th Street
Racine, Wisconsin 53403
(414) 632-5720

LUDWIG MOTOR CORPORATION
421 East 91st Street
New York, New York 10028
(212) 876-7015

LUFT-TANGEE, INC.
(Subsidiary of A. R. Winarick, Inc.)
400 Gotham Parkway
Carlstadt, New Jersey 07072
Jules Winarick, President
(201) 935-1700

LUFTHANSA GERMAN AIRLINES
1640 Hempstead Turnpike
East Meadow, New York 11554
Frank Ebbinghausen, Manager,
  Customer Relations
(516) 489-2020

LUG (shoe heels and soles)
  See Goodyear Tire & Rubber
     Company

LUGER INDUSTRIES, INC.
3800 West Highway 13
Burnsville, Minnesota 55337
R. J. Luger, President
(612) 890-3000

LUHRS COMPANY
Boundary Road
Marlboro, New Jersey 07746
(201) 462-8900

LUIS COMPANY, INC., M. S.
15 Park Row
New York, New York 10038

LULL-A-BABY (infants' bedding)
  See Fine Art Pillow & Specialties
     Corporation

LULLABY (disposable diapers)
  See Diana Manufacturing
     Company

LULLABYE FURNITURE COMPANY
(Division of Questor Corporation)
1017 Third Street
Stevens Point, Wisconsin 54481
H. W. Mower, General Manager
(715) 344-6900

LUMATECH INC.
4789 N.E. Tenth Terrace
Fort Lauderdale, Florida 33308

LUMBERJACK (bakery products)
  See Grocers Baking Company

LUMBERMENS MUTUAL CASUALTY
COMPANIES
  See Kemper Insurance Company

LUMEX INC.
100 Spence Street
Bay Shore, New York 11706
Charles Mourcott, President
(516) 273-2200

LUMIN JEWELRY COMPANY
12 Edgeboro Road
East Brunswick, New Jersey 08816
(212) 243-7884

LUMINALL PAINTS, INC.
2750 South Garfield Avenue
Los Angeles, California 90040
Charles F. Farrell, Jr., President
  and Chief Executive Officer
(213) 724-0500
  See also Great Lakes Paint &
     Varnish Company

LUMINIERE CORPORATION
4269 Park Avenue
Bronx, New York 10457
Herbert Lagin, President
(212) 295-5450

LUMINOUS CEILINGS, INC.
(Subsidiary of Jim Walter Corporation)
3701 North Ravenswood Avenue
Chicago, Illinois 60613
Arthur W. Segil, President
(312) 935-8900

LUMITIME (watches and clocks)
  See Ricoh Time Corporation

LUMMIS & COMPANY
(Division of U.S. Tobacco Company)
444 East Washington Street
Suffolk, Virginia 23434
(804) 539-7452

LUMMUS SUPPLY COMPANY, INC.,
  THE S. P.
1917 Market
Philadelphia, Pennsylvania 19103
(215) 563-7550

LUMNITE (interior cold-water
paint)
  See Bondex International, Inc.

LUMURED PLASTICS CORPORATION
330 Fifth Avenue
New York, New York 10001
(212) 695-0001

LUNA (food products)
  See Ancona Brothers Wholesale
     Grocery Company

LUNA GLO (fluorescent paint and
paper products)
  See IMS Corporation

LUND AMERICAN INC.
Box 248
Highway 10W
New York Mills, Minnesota 56567
Gordon H. Lund, President
(218) 385-2235

Companies and Trade Names

LUNDELL MANUFACTURING
  COMPANY, INC.
Cherokee, Iowa 51012
Vernon J. Lundell, President
(712) 225-5181

LUNDIA, MYERS INDUSTRIES INC.
Capitol Way
Jacksonville, Illinois 62650
William J. Hunt, President and
  Chief Executive Officer
(217) 245-9646

LUNDSTROM LABORATORIES, INC.
Densiwood Products Division
Frankfort Industrial Park
Frankfort, New York 13340
(315) 894-2420

LUNT SILVERSMITHS (sterling-silver tableware)
  See Rogers, Lunt & Bowlen Company

LUSK CANDY COMPANY
Post Office Box 3973
2371 Boies Avenue
Davenport, Iowa 52802
(319) 324-3243

LUSTER LEAF PRODUCTS, INC.
Box 13971
Atlanta, Georgia 30324

LUSTOL COMPANY
675 Madison Avenue
New York, New York 10021
(212) 838-6450

LUSTRA LIGHTING
ITT Lamp Division
East Rutherford, New Jersey 07073
(201) 935-3700

LUSTRASILK CORPORATION
Box 334
Minneapolis, Minnesota 55440

LUSTRE (toiletries)
  See Colgate-Palmolive Company

LUSTRE-CREME (hair-care products)
  See Colgate-Palmolive Company

LUSTRE LINE (tools, general hardware)
  See Noblit Brothers & Company

LUSTRO-WARE
(Division of Borden, Inc.)
1625 West Mound
Columbus, Ohio 43223
Paul B. Nelson, General Manager
(614) 274-8475

LUSTRON (hair products)
  See Zotos International, Inc.

LUSTRWAX-BEST PRODUCTS
  COMPANY
2100 Harrison
Kansas City, Missouri 64108
(816) 842-3940

LUST'S HEALTH FOODS
Box 368
Beaumont, California 92223

LUTHERAN BROTHERHOOD
  INSURANCE SOCIETY
701 Second Avenue South
Minneapolis, Minnesota 55402
Monroe A. Lee, Assistant Vice
  President, Customer Relations
(612) 332-0211

LUTRON ELECTRONICS COMPANY
  INC.
Post Office Box 205
Sutter Road
Coopersburg, Pennsylvania 18036
Joel S. Spira, President
(215) 282-3800

LUTZ & SCHRAMM, INC.
Post Office Box 307
904 South Lee
Ayden, North Carolina 28513
(919) 746-6191

LUX (soap)
  See Lever Brothers Company

LUX TIME
(Division of Robertshaw Controls
  Company)
400 Captain Neville Drive
Waterbury, Connecticut 06720

LUXAIRE, INC.
West of Filbert Street
Elyria, Ohio 44035
W. R. Davies, Jr., Chairman of
  the Board
(216) 323-5561

LUXDOR (room dividers)
  See Plastic Products, Inc.

LUXEMBURG (tobacco)
  See Lorillard (Division of Loew's
    Theatres, Inc.)

LUXO LAMP CORPORATION
1976 Purdy Avenue
Port Chester, New York 10573
(914) 937-4433

LUXOR LEATHERCRAFT
  CORPORATION
11 East 26th Street
New York, New York 10010
(212) 689-9240

LUXOR TRADING COMPANY, INC.
261 Broadway
New York, New York 10007
(212) 233-4881

Companies and Trade Names

LUXURAY
(Division of Beaunit Corporation)
261 Madison Avenue
New York, New York 10016
(212) 972-2500

LUXURIA COSMETICS LTD.
(Division of Harriet Hubbard Ayer, Inc.)
730 Fifth Avenue
New York, New York 10019
(212) 489-0060

LUXURY (appliances)
See Dart Industries

LUXURY (tobacco)
See House of Edgeworth

LUYTIES PHARMACAL COMPANY
4200 Laclede Avenue
Saint Louis, Missouri 63108
(314) 533-9600

LUZCO IMPORT EXPORT DISTRIBUTORS
Post Office Box 837
Belvedere, California 94920

LUZIANNE COFFEE COMPANY
(Division of William B. Reily & Company, Inc.)
Box 60296
640 Magazine Street
New Orleans, Louisiana 70130
Carl Henley, President
(504) 524-6131

LUZIER, INC.
(Subsidiary of Bristol-Myers Company)
Box 496
3216 Gillham Plaza
Kansas City, Missouri 64141
Carol Cook, President
(913) 384-1000

LYDIA E. PINKHAM MEDICINE COMPANY
See Cooper Laboratories, Inc.

LYKES FOOD PRODUCTS INC.
(Subsidiary of Lykes Brothers Inc.)
Box K
Tampa, Florida 33605

LYKES PASCO PACKING COMPANY
(Subsidiary of Lykes Brothers Inc.)
Box 97
Dade City, Florida 33525
(904) 567-5211

LYKES YOUNGSTOWN CORPORATION
See Youngstown Sheet and Tube Company

LYLE (guitars)
See Norlin Music, Inc.

LYMAN INC.
1615 First Street
Sandusky, Ohio 44870

LYME (cigarettes)
See Brown & Williamson Tobacco Corporation

LYN-CRAFT BOAT COMPANY
Box 10744
Tampa, Florida 33609

LYNCH-JAMENTZ COMPANY
1109 North Virgil Avenue
Los Angeles, California 90029
(213) 663-1189

LYNCHBURG HOSIERY MILLS INC.
Lynchburg, Virginia 24504

LYNCOACH & TRUCK COMPANY INC.
(Division of Instrument Systems Corporation)
Post Office Drawer 446
Troy, Alabama 36081

LYNDEN (canned foods)
See Western Farmers Association

LYNDONVILLE CANNING COMPANY
151 West Avenue
Lyndonville, New York 14098
George M. Smith, President
(716) 765-2231

LYNE LABORATORIES
750 Main Street
Winchester, Massachusetts 01890
(617) 729-8877

LYNN-EDWARDS CORPORATION
Post Office Box 15737
Sacramento, California 95813

LYNN FOODS CORPORATION
910 East 70th
Cleveland, Ohio 44103

LYNN HAVEN (mobile homes)
See Redman Industries Inc.

LYNN MAR COMPANY
4702 Laurie Lane
Richmond, Virginia 23223

LYNN PRODUCTS, INC.
200 West Spangler
Elmhurst, Illinois 60126

LYNWOOD PHARMACAL COMPANY
1359 Copley Road
Akron, Ohio 44320

LYON & SONS, R. H.
320 Carisle
Harrisburg, Pennsylvania 17104
(717) 238-8381

LYON COMPANY INC., RENE D.
135-06 101st Avenue
Richmond Hill, New York 11419

LYON FOOD PRODUCTS INC.
2301 Nevada Avenue North
Minneapolis, Minnesota 55427

LYON METAL PRODUCTS, INC.
25 Madison Street
Aurora, Illinois 60505
T. R. Conklin, President
(312) 897-8421

LYON MOVING & STORAGE
 COMPANY
(Subsidiary of Transamerica
 Corporation)
1950 South Vermont Avenue
Los Angeles, California 90007
Dana G. Levitt, President
(213) 742-5150

LYONS (toothpaste)
 See Glenbrook Laboratories

LYONS BAND INSTRUMENT
 COMPANY, INC.
 See Selmer

LYONS CANNING COMPANY
 INC.
Box 231
Clyde, New York 14433

LYONS COMPANY INC., R. H.
270 Denton Avenue
New Hyde Park, New York 11040

LYON'S IMPORT EXPORT
 COMPANY INC.
558 Fifth Avenue
New York, New York 10001
(212) 695-1098

LYONS-MAGNUS, INC.
3789 East Alluvial
Clovis, California 93612
Robert E. Smittcamp, President
(209) 299-2183

LYONS TRANSPORTATION LINES,
 INC.
(Subsidiary of New Erie Corporation)
136 East 26th Street
Erie, Pennsylvania 16512
John M. Cochran, Chairman
(814) 456-8551

LYPHO-MED, INC.
4122 West Grand Avenue
Chicago, Illinois 60651
(312) 342-6170

LYSOL (disinfectant)
 See Lehn & Fink Consumer
 Products

LYT-ALL (paint and varnish)
 See Pratt & Lambert, Inc.

LYTTON & COMPANY, HENRY C.
(Division of Cluett, Peabody &
 Company, Inc.)
235 South State Street
Chicago, Illinois 60604
John W. Cole, President
(312) 922-3500

Companies and Trade Names

M

M & C ENTERPRISES
431 Isis Avenue
Inglewood, California 90301
(213) 641-3680

M & D (canned foods)
See M & D Foods, Inc.

M & E (unit coolers and heaters, etc.)
See Merchant & Evans Company

M & G (meat stew)
See Mask & Gay Food Products, Inc.

M & H LABORATORIES
2705 Archer Avenue
Chicago, Illinois 60608
(312) 842-2132

M. & H. TIRE COMPANY
Watertown, Massachusetts 02172

M & M (candy)
See Mars, Inc.

M & M KNITTING MILLS, INC.
Seventh and Grange Streets
Philadelphia, Pennsylvania 19120
Sam H. Batt, President
(215) 549-2442

M & M LUGGAGE COMPANY INC.
205 Tenth
Jersey City, New Jersey 07302
(201) 656-1230

M & M - MARS
(Division of Mars, Inc.)
High Street
Wackettstown, New Jersey 67840
Eleanor C. Trautwein, Customer Service Manager
(201) 852-1000

M & M STATIONERY CORPORATION
See Micke Rellim

M & M TRANSPORTATION COMPANY
186 Alewife Brook Parkway
Cambridge, Massachusetts 02138
Sidney Marks, Chairman
(617) 491-6000

M & N CIGAR MANUFACTURERS, INC.
2701 16th Street
Tampa, Florida 36601
(813) 248-2124

M & R FOOD SERVICE COMPANY
1215 West Mound Street
Columbus, Ohio 43223
(614) 228-5876

M & R SEAL PRESS COMPANY, INC.
305 Cox Street
Roselle, New Jersey 07203
(201) 245-7325

M & S TOYS INC.
50 East 11th Street
New York, New York 10003
Saul Maisel, President and Treasurer
(212) 473-0382

M & W GEAR COMPANY
Route 47 South
Gibson City, Illinois 60936
William B. Ertel, President
(217) 784-4261

M & W MANUFACTURING COMPANY
547 East 63rd Street
Chicago, Illinois 60637

M.A.B. (paint)
See M.A. Bruder & Sons, Inc.

M-B HARD CANDIES, INC.
5625 West Cemak Road
Cicero, Illinois 60650
(312) 652-6422

MB SPORTCYCLES
See American Marine Industries, Inc.

MBT (instant broths)
See Riviana Foods, Inc.

MCA, INC.
100 Universal City Plaza
Universal City, California 91608
S.J. Sheinberg, President
(213) 985-4321

M.C. LISS & COMPANY
1413 Palisade Avenue
Teaneck, New Jersey 07666

M C P FOODS, INC.
Post Office Box 3633
Anaheim, California 92803
(714) 535-2871

M.D. (eyedrops, vitamins, nasal spray, etc.)
See Medical Drug Products

ME-90 (electronic air cleaner)
See Master Appliance Corporation

MFA MUTUAL INSURANCE COMPANY
1871 West Broadway
Columbia, Missouri 65201
A.D. Sappington, President
(314) 445-8441

915

Companies and Trade Names

M.F. ATHLETIC COMPANY
Post Office Box 6632
Providence, Rhode Island 02904
(401) 942-9363

MFG BOAT COMPANY
44 Fourth Avenue
Union City, Pennsylvania 16438
(814) 438-3841

MG (motor vehicles)
See British Leyland Motors, Inc.

MGA (canned and frozen foods)
See Mushroom Co-Operative Canning Company

MGA (electronic appliances, televisions)
See Mitsubishi International Corporation

M. G. ART INC.
63 Tiffany Place
Brooklyn, New York 11231
(212) 858-0621

MGM RECORDS INC.
(Subsidiary of Polygram Corporation)
7165 Sunset Boulevard
Los Angeles, California 90046
John Fruin, President
(213) 466-9574

M. I. HUMMEL (figurines)
See Hummelwerk

M-J (frozen poultry)
See Mar-Jac, Inc.

M J B COMPANY
665 Third Street
San Francisco, California 94107
Edward Branstein, President
(415) 421-7311

M. J. LABORATORIES
Box 432
Little River Station
Miami, Florida 33138
(305) 754-2247

M.K.M. HOSIERY MILLS, INC.
Rochdale, Massachusetts 01542
Barnett D. Gordon, President
(617) 895-5711

M. MARTIN (saxophones, clairnets, flutes)
See Maxwell Meyers Inc.

MPC (models)
See Fundimensions

M.P.L. LABORATORIES, INC.
1506 Hennepin Avenue
Minneapolis, Minnesota 55403
(612) 338-2035

M. R. D. & ASSOCIATES INC.
151 East Prospect Avenue
Danville, California 94526
(415) 837-1441

MSA (steel guitars)
See Chicago Musical Instrument Company

MTD PRODUCTS INC.
Post Office Box 2741
5389 West 130th Street
Cleveland, Ohio 44111
Curtis E. Moll, President
(216) 267-2600
See also Columbia Manufacturing Company Inc., The; and Midwest Industries, Inc.

MTI CORPORATION
11 East 26th Street
New York, New York 10010
(212) 683-0860

MT/ST (magnetic-tape typewriter)
See International Business Machines Corporation

MT-10 (sports accessories)
See Trak Inc.

MVP (men's slacks)
See Barrow Manufacturing Company

MA GRIFFE (bath products, hair spray, perfume, etc.)
See Carven Parfums

MA-LECK INDUSTRIES INC.
Post Office Box 24T
Wingate, North Carolina 28174
J. Ben Helms, President
(704) 233-4031

MAALOX (antacid)
See William H. Rorer, Inc.

MAC ALLEN COMPANY, INC., THE
Bay Road
Newmarket, New Hampshire 03857
(603) 659-5555

MAC GILLIS & GIBBS COMPANY
4278 North Teutonia Avenue
Milwaukee, Wisconsin 53209
A.J. Bumby, President
(414) 871-1100

MAC GREGOR YACHTS (boats)
1631 Placentia
Costa Mesa, California 92626
(714) 642-6830

MAC INTOSH (Scotch whiskey)
See Twenty One Brands, Inc.

MAC 'N RICE (macaroni and rice products)
See V. LaRosa & Sons, Inc.

MAC-O-LAC PAINTS INC.
(Division of RPM Inc.)
5400 East Nevada
Detroit, Michigan 48234
(313) 892-1900

Companies and Trade Names

MAC-TACS (self-adhesive products)
See Carr Adhesive Products Inc.

MACANDREWS & FORBES COMPANY
Third Street and Jefferson Avenue
Camden, New Jersey 08104
(609) 964-8840

MACAULAY'S (Canadian whiskey)
See Sazerac Company, Inc.

MACBESS FOUNDATIONS
44 West 28th Street
New York, New York 10001
(212) 689-1411

MACCO (coatings and resins)
See Glidden-Durkee (Division of SCM Corporation)

MACDIL ENTERPRISES, INC.
15 Park Row
New York, New York 10038
(212) 895-2617

MACDONALD SHOPPING BAG FOOD STORES INC., E.F.
1702 South DelMar Avenue
San Gabriel, California 91776
(213) 282-7603

MACDONALD STAMP COMPANY, E.F.
115 South Ludlow
Dayton, Ohio 45402
George C. Gilfillen, Jr., Chairman
(513) 461-4500

MACFARLANE'S CANDIES
See Pangburn Company

MACGOWAN COFFEE COMPANY
218 Yerger Street
Jackson, Mississippi 39205
Clifford Macgowan, President and Treasurer
(601) 948-3545

MACGREGOR/BRUNSWICK
(Division of Brunswick Corporation)
I-75 and Jimson Road
Cincinnati, Ohio 45215
G.J. O'Keefe, President
(513) 733-2000

MACH (motorcycles)
See Kawasaki Motors Corporation

MACINTOSH (men's raincoats)
See The Majer Company/Diversified

MACINTOSH COMPANY, INC., THE
48 Butternut Street
Lyons, New York 14489
(315) 946-6531

MACK PRINTING COMPANY
20th and Northampton Streets
Easton, Pennsylvania 18042
John Wilbur Mack, Chairman, President and Chief Executive Officer
(215) 258-9111

MACK SHIRT CORPORATION
333 West Seymour Avenue
Cincinnati, Ohio 45216
Alan R. Mack, President
(513) 761-6060

MACK TRUCKS, INC.
(Subsidiary of Signal Company, Inc.)
2100 Mack Boulevard
Allentown, Pennsylvania 18105
H.J. Nave, Chairman
(215) 439-3011

MACKENZIE (Scotch)
See Glenmore Distilleries Company

MACKLANBURG-DUNCAN COMPANY
Post Office Box 25188
Oklahoma City, Oklahoma 73125
(405) 528-4411

MACK'S (nose clips, earplugs, eyeshades)
See McKeon Products Company

MACK'S MEDICAL COMPANY, INC.
Box 295
Waltham, Massachusetts 02154
(617) 894-0710

MACKWIN COMPANY
Box 108
25 McConner Drive
Winona, Minnesota 55987
(507) 452-2910

MACLEAN-FOGG LOCK NUT COMPANY
1000 Allanson Road
Mundelein, Illinois 60060
Barry L. MacLean, President
(312) 566-0010

MACLEANS (toothpaste)
See Beecham Products Inc.

MACMILLAN (spices and extracts)
See Asmus Products

MACMILLAN COMPANY
60 Fifth Avenue
New York, New York 10011
(212) 935-2000

MACMILLAN PUBLISHING COMPANY, INC.
866 Third Avenue
New York, New York 10022
Raymond C. Hagel, Chairman of the Board
(212) 935-2000

MACMILLAN RING-FREE OIL COMPANY, INC.
90 Park Avenue
New York, New York 10016
Robert A. Collier, Chairman of the Board
(212) 867-0250

Companies and Trade Names

MACNAIR'S (Scotch whiskey)
See Gooderham & Worts, Ltd.

MACNAUGHTON (Canadian whiskey)
See Schenley Industries Inc.

MACO TAG & LABEL PRODUCTS INC.
110 West 19th Street
New York, New York 10011
(212) 929-0357

MACON ELECTRIC SPECIALTY CORPORATION
337 Kings Highway
Brooklyn, New York 11223
(212) 339-2330

MACPANEL COMPANY
Box 5027
High Point, North Carolina 27262
(919) 882-8138

MACRODYNE-CHATILLON CORPORATION
See Chatillan & Sons, John

MAC'S (coatings and resins)
See Glidden-Durkee (Division of SCM Corporation)

MAC'S FAMOUS FOODS INC.
1415 East Maryland
Evansville, Indiana 47711
(812) 425-1301

MACSIL, INC.
A Street and Lehigh Avenue
Philadelphia, Pennsylvania 19125
(215) 423-5566

MACTAC (pressure-sensitive materials)
See Morgan Adhesives Company

MACTAVISH (tobacco)
See Sutliff Tobacco Company

MACWHYTE COMPANY
(Subsidiary of Amsted Industries Inc.)
2906 14th Avenue
Kenosha, Wisconsin 53140
John E. Kaiser, President
(414) 654-5381

MACY & COMPANY, INC., R.H.
151 West 34th Street
New York, New York 10001
Donald B. Smiley, Chairman of the Board
(212) 695-4400
See also Bamberger & Company, L.; Davison-Paxon Company; and Lasalle & Koch Company

MACY'S CALIFORNIA
(Division of R.H. Macy & Company)
Post Office Box 7888
170 O'Farrell
San Francisco, California 94120
Edward Finkelstein, President
(415) 397-3333

MACY'S MISSOURI-KANSAS
(Division of R.H. Macy & Company)
1030 Main Street
Kansas City, Missouri 64105
Harold S. Olsen, President
(816) 221-3737

MACY'S NEW YORK
(Division of R.H. Macy & Company)
Herald Square
New York, New York 10001
Ronald Seltzer, Chairman of the Board
(212) 695-4400

MAD INFLATABLES (inflatable furniture)
See Modern Air Decor

MAD MAGAZINE
See Warner Communications, Inc.

MADAME ADRIENNE, INC.
See Mardi-Bra Creations Corporation

MADAME ALEXANDER DOLLS
See Alexander Doll Company Inc.

MADAME C.J. WALKER MANUFACTURING COMPANY, THE
617 Indiana Avenue
Indianapolis, Indiana 46202
(317) 631-7143

MADAME OLGA (skin-care products, cosmetics)
See Madame Olga Pataky

MADAME ROCHAS (fragrance)
See Parfums Rochas Inc.

MADDUX OF CALIFORNIA
3030 Fletcher Drive
Los Angeles, California 90065
(213) 255-1561

MADE IN AMERICA (farm and garden tools)
See Union Fork & Hoe Company

MADEIRA (guitars)
See Guild Musical Instruments

MADEIRA (tobacco)
See R.J. Reynolds Tobacco Company

MADELAINE CHOCOLATE NOVELTIES INC.
96-03 Beach Channel Drive
Rockaway Beach, New York 11693
(212) 945-1500

MADEMOISELLE (luggage)
See Hartmann Luggage Company, Inc.

MADEMOISELLE (magazine)
See Conde Nast Publications, Inc.

Companies and Trade Names

MADEMOISELLE FURS, INC.
350 Seventh Avenue
New York, New York 10001
(212) 736-8620

MADEMOISELLE LIBERTE
152 Madison Avenue
New York, New York 10016
(212) 683-7370

MADEST MANUFACTURING
  CORPORATION
38 East 32nd Street
New York, New York 10016
(212) 689-8555

MADISON (food products)
  See Worthington Foods, Inc.

MADISON COMPANY, THE H.W.
(Division of The J.M. Smucker
  Company)
200 North State Road
Medina, Ohio 44256
(216) 723-3281

MADISON FOODS COMPANY
830 South Bond Street
Baltimore, Maryland 21231
(301) 675-8804

MADISON INDUSTRIES INC.,
  DOLLY
Lafayette Building
Philadelphia, Pennsylvania 19106
(215) 923-5850

MADISON-KIPP CORPORATION
222 Waubesa Street
Madison, Wisconsin 53704
(608) 244-3511

MADISON LABORATORIES
(Division of Ciba-Geigy Corporation)
556 Morris Avenue
Summit, New Jersey 07901
(201) 277-5900

MADISON SQUARE GARDEN
  CORPORATION
2 Pennsylvania Plaza
New York, New York 10001
Alan N. Cohen, President
(212) 563-8100

MADLAND LABORATORIES
152 West Wisconsin Avenue
Milwaukee, Wisconsin 53203
(414) 271-6866

MADMAR QUALITY INC.
2150 Erie Street
Utica, New York 13501

MADOLENE (food products)
  See Vlasic Food Products
    Company

MADONNA (food products)
  See Contadina Foods

MADRIGAL (German wines)
  See Kobrand Corporation

MADRILUME (aluminum holloware)
  See Tri-M, Inc.

MADYE'S, INC.
385 Fifth Avenue
New York, New York 10016
(212) 532-0431

MAES INC.
Box 1010-T
Holland, Michigan 49423
(616) 392-8545

MAESTRO (musical instruments)
  See Norlin Music, Inc.

MAG BAT (sporting goods)
  See Hillerich & Bradsby
    Company, Inc.

MAG-NIF INC.
8820 East Avenue
Mentor, Ohio 44060
(216) 255-9366

MAG RACK (magnetic toolholder)
  See Apex Specialties Company

MAGEE CARPET COMPANY, THE
919 Third Avenue
New York, New York 10022
James A. Magee, President

MAGGI (food products)
  See Nestle Company, Inc.

MAGGIE MAGNETIC
(Division of Selfix Inc.)
313 West Superior Street
Chicago, Illinois 60610
(312) 337-7190

MAGGIE MUFFETS COUNTRY
  KITCHENS (restaurant franchise)
  See Eugene L. Mauro Industries
    Inc.

MAGGIONI & COMPANY, L.P.
Plaza Industrial Park
Savannah, Georgia 31402
(912) 236-3396

MAGI-PAT (patent-leather cleaner)
  See Oil-Kraft, Inc.

MAGIC (liquid bleach)
  See Purex Corporation, Ltd.

MAGIC (paint rollers)
  See Wooster Brush Company

MAGIC (repair products)
  See Magic American Chemical
    Corporation

MAGIC (shaving products)
  See Carson Chemical Company

Companies and Trade Names

MAGIC AMERICAN CHEMICAL CORPORATION
23700 Mercantile Road
Cleveland, Ohio 44122
James M. Reich, President and Treasurer
(216) 464-2353

MAGIC BRAND (stationery items)
See Majestic Penn State Inc.

MAGIC BRUSH (lint brush)
See Reeve & Mitchell Company, Inc.

MAGIC CHEF (cutlery)
See Lifetime Cutlery Corporation

MAGIC CHEF (meat products)
See Acme Packing Company

MAGIC CHEF, INC.
740 King Edward Avenue
Cleveland, Tennessee 37311
S.B. Rymer, Jr., President
(615) 472-3371
See also Gaffers & Sattler, Inc.

MAGIC CIRCLE (animal repellent)
See J.C. Ehrlich Chemical Company, Inc.

MAGIC CLIP (magnetic clips)
See Wescosa Inc.

MAGIC-COLOR (antennas)
See GC Electronics

MAGIC COLOR (hair coloring)
See Dorothy Gray-Tussy, Ltd.

MAGIC-CREME (furniture polish)
See Golden Star Polish Manufacturing Company, Inc.

MAGIC CRYSTALS (instant dry milk)
See Carnation Company

MAGIC DESSERT MAKER (condensed milk)
See Borden Inc.

MAGIC 8 BALL (fortune-telling ball)
See Alabe Products Inc.

MAGIC FINISH (spray starch)
See Armour & Company

MAGIC GARDEN (plants that grow without soil)
See NTS Company

MAGIC HANDS (latex gloves)
See Seiberling Latex Products

MAGIC HOSTESS (housewares)
See Rival Manufacturing Company

MAGIC LADY
(Division of Exquisite Form Industries Inc.)
385 Fifth Avenue
New York, New York 10016
(212) 532-8160

MAGIC LEAF (silver cleaner)
See Paul-Reed, Inc.

MAGIC MAGNETS (metal magnets)
See Magnet Sales Company

MAGIC MAID (appliances)
See Son-Chief Electrics, Inc.

MAGIC MARKER CORPORATION
1 Magic Marker Lane
Cherry Hill, New Jersey 08003
Ira Ingerman, President
(609) 424-5880

MAGIC MENDING TAPE
See 3M Company

MAGIC MOLD INC.
10 Taylor Street
Freeport, New York 11520
(516) 868-0800

MAGIC MOMENT (hair coloring)
See Gillette Company

MAGIC MOTION LAMPS (scenes-in-motion lamps)
See Creative Light Products Company

MAGIC MOUNTS (wall hangers)
See Miller Studio Inc.

MAGIC NEEDLE (men's furnishings)
See Varsity Pajamas

MAGIC NOVELTY COMPANY INC.
95 Morton Street
New York, New York 10014
(212) 243-6333

MAGIC PAGE (self-stick photo albums)
See P. Nielsen Imports

MAGIC SECRET (wrinkle cream)
See Helene Curtis Industries, Inc.

MAGIC SPRAY (fabric sizing)
See Armour & Company

MAGIC STICK (scrapbooks)
See Holes-Webway

MAGIC TOUCH (ice-cube trays)
See Inland Manufacturing (Division of General Motors Corporation)

MAGIC TOUCH (makeup)
See Campana Corporation

Companies and Trade Names

MAGIC TURBAN (hair protector)
See Lu Wane Products Company

MAGIC VALLEY FOODS, INC.
Box 475
Rupert, Idaho 83350
(208) 436-3126

MAGICARE (stainless-steel polish)
See Glamour Care Inc.

MAGICOATS (uniforms)
See Morris & Company, Inc.

MAGICOLOR (paints)
See Enterprise Paint
Manufacturing Company

MAGICUBE (flashbulbs)
See G. E. Lamp (Department of
General Electric Company)

MAGIE (cologne, perfume)
See Lancome

MAGIK BRUSH (lint brushes)
See Helmac Products Corporation

MAGIKITCHEN EQUIPMENT
CORPORATION
Post Office Box 342
Quakertown, Pennsylvania 18951
(215) 536-8140

MAGIKOTER (paint rollers)
See Wooster Brush Company

MAGIX (pressure-sensitive letters
and numbers)
See Keyes-Davis Company

MAGLA PRODUCTS
1066 Clinton Avenue
Irvington, New Jersey 07111
(201) 399-1500

MAGMA ALBA (ointment)
See Durel Pharmaceutical, Inc.

MAGNA AMERICAN
CORPORATION
(Subsidiary of Magna Corporation)
Post Office Box 90
Raymond, Mississippi 39154
W.A. Caldwell, Jr., President
(601) 857-5211

MAGNA-BEAM (flashlights)
See Piano Molding Company

MAGNA, INC.
Box 473
South River Road
Leitchfield, Kentucky 42754
(502) 259-4021

MAGNA LUX LIGHTER COMPANY
143 East 60th Street
New York, New York 10022
(212) 759-9765

MAGNAFLUX CORPORATION
(Subsidiary of Champion Spark Plug
Company)
7300 West Lawrence Avenue
Chicago, Illinois 60656
R.G. Strother, President
(312) 867-8000

MAGNAFOLD (magnetic billfolds)
See Hugo Bosca Company Inc.

MAGNALITE (cast aluminumware)
See General Housewares
Corporation, Cookware
Group

MAGNAMUSIC-BATON INC.
6390 Delmar Boulevard
Saint Louis, Missouri 63130
(314) 427-5660

MAGNANO & SONS INC., A.
1502 Fourth South
Seattle, Washington 98134
(206) 622-3021

MAGNATAG PRODUCTS
Post Office Box 411
Mendon, New York 14506

MAGNAVOX COMPANY, THE
345 Park Avenue
New York, New York 10022
Pieter C. Vink, President
(212) 758-6600
See also Baker Furniture; and
Selmer

MAGNE BELL (bell instruments)
See Schulmerich Carillons Inc.

MAGNET MILLS, INC.
308 Cullom Street
Clinton, Tennessee 37716
Samuel I. Burd, Chairman of the
Board
(615) 457-1212

MAGNET SALES COMPANY
3935 South Vermont Avenue
Los Angeles, California 90037
(213) 829-4471

MAGNETIC AIDS, INC.
488 Madison Avenue
New York, New York 10022
(212) 371-2250

MAGNETIC-FOAM (brooms)
See Master Manufacturing
Company

MAGNIFIQUE (tarnish-resistant
silver plate)
See Bisco, Inc.

MAGNILITE (illuminated magnifiers)
See O.C. White Company

MAGNIN & COMPANY, I.
(Division of Federated Department
Stores, Inc.)
Union Square
San Francisco, California 94108
Norman V. Wechsler, President
(415) 362-2100

Companies and Trade Names

MAGNIN COMPANY, INC.,
JOSEPH
(Division of Amfac, Inc.)
59 Harrison Street
San Francisco, California 94105
Harvey L. Lowenthal, President
(415) 433-4224

MAGNOLIA (toilet seats and other custom molded plastic items)
See Beneke Corporation

MAGNUM (stainless-steel flatwear)
See H.E. Lauffer Company, Inc.

MAGNUM MARINE
2900 N.E. 188th Street
North Miami Beach, Florida 33160
(305) 931-4292

MAGNUS
(Division of Economics Laboratory Inc.)
Osborn Building
Saint Paul, Minnesota 55102
(612) 224-4678

MAGNUS ORGAN CORPORATION
(Subsidiary of Magnus International Inc.)
1600 Edgar Road West
Linden, New Jersey 07036
Peter M. Bobley, President
(201) 862-8700

MAH CHENA CORPORATION
4600 South Packers Avenue
Chicago, Illinois 60609
(312) 847-7464

MAHAN COMPANY
8501 Moller Road
Indianapolis, Indiana 46268
John R. Williams, President
(317) 297-4800

MAHARAJAH (linens and domestics)
See Hostess Creations, Inc.

MAHARAJAH INTERNATIONAL
ENTERPRISES LTD.
13 East 30th Street
New York, New York 10016
(212) 279-8810

MAHARAM FABRIC CORPORATION
Rasons Court
Hauppauge, New York 11787
Donald H. Maharam, President
(516) 582-3434

MAHATMA (rice)
See Riviana Foods Inc.

MAHDEEN LABORATORIES
Post Office Box 34630
Dallas, Texas 75234
(214) 233-6857

MAHEU (food products)
See J.A. Ferland et Fils

MAHLERS, INC.
3124 Pawtucket Avenue
Department NR5
East Providence, Rhode Island 02915
(401) 438-5438

MAH'S (Chinese foods)
See Mah Chena Corporation

MAI-LAN (Vietnamese art, ceramic ceramics, handicrafts)
See House of Mai-Lan, Inc.

MAI TAI (power-boat kit)
See Glen-L Marine Designs

MAICO HEARING INSTRUMENTS
(Subsidiary of Textron, Inc.)
7375 Bush Lake Road
Minneapolis, Minnesota 55435
John J. Kojis, President
(612) 941-3900

MAID-RITE (appliances)
See A.F. Dormeyer
Manufacturing Company Inc.

MAIDENFORM, INC.
90 Park Avenue
New York, New York 10016
Beatrice Coleman, President
(212) 953-1400

MAIER BREWING COMPANY
500 East Commercial
Los Angeles, California 90012
(213) 622-1061

MAIER PRODUCTS COMPANY LTD.
(Division of Ed and Don's Candies and Ice Cream)
1202 Waimanu Street
Honolulu, Hawaii 96814
(808) 536-1811

MAIL-O-GRAMS (airmail envelopes, letterheads)
See Whitehall Inc.

MAIL POUCH (chewing tobacco)
See Whitehall Products, Inc.

MAIL POUCH (tobacco)
See Bloch Brothers Tobacco Company

MAIL-WELL ENVELOPE COMPANY
2515 Mailwell Drive
Portland, Oregon 97222
Willett R. Lake, Jr., President
(503) 654-3141

MAILGRAM (letter service)
See Western Union Telegraph Company

MAILLARD CORPORATION
Box 1066
1300 Stefko Boulevard
Bethlehem, Pennsylvania 18018
(215) 867-7568

MAINE AIRES (shoes)
See Penobscot Shoe Company

Companies and Trade Names

MAINE DELIGHT (canned foods)
See Port Clyde Packing Company

MAINE LINE (wines and liquors)
See Lawrence & Company, Inc.

MAINE MANUFACTURING
COMPANY, THE
46 Bridge Street
Nashua, New Hampshire 03060
John B. Stevens, President
(603) 882-5142

MAINE SUGAR INDUSTRIES INC.
Easton, Maine 04740
John C. Farley, President
(207) 488-2061

MAINLY FOR MEN (bath
accessories)
See Holt-Howard

MAINSAIL (men's sportswear)
See Alps Sportswear Manufacturing Company

MAINTENANCE, INC.
(Division of Premier Industrial
Corporation)
West Liberty Street, Extension
Wooster, Ohio 44691
(216) 264-6262

MAINZER INC., ALFRED
39-33 29th Street
Long Island City, New York 11101
Alfred Mainzer, President
(212) 786-6840

MAISEL COMPANY
510 Central S.W.
Albuquerque, New Mexico 87102
(505) 243-6781

MAISON INTERNATIONAL LTD.
40 Oak Street
Norwood, New Jersey 07648
(201) 768-6200

MAISON ROCHER (clocks and
watches)
See Roxhall Time Corporation

MAJA (perfumes, soaps)
See Myrurgia Perfumes, Inc.

MAJER COMPANY/DIVERSIFIED,
THE
1290 Avenue of the Americas
Room 1575
New York, New York 10019
(212) 581-3920

MAJESTIC (dust cloths, cleaners)
See Majestic Wax Company

MAJESTIC (flatware, cutlery)
See Regal Specialty Manufacturing Company

MAJESTIC CARPET MILLS
See Jim Walter Corporation

MAJESTIC COMPANY, THE
(Division of American Standard,
Inc.)
733 Erie
Huntington, Indiana 46750
Don A. Purviance, President
(219) 356-8000

MAJESTIC DRUG COMPANY, INC.
711 East 134th Street
Bronx, New York 10454
(212) 292-1310

MAJESTIC PENN STATE INC.
Comly and Caroline Roads
Philadelphia, Pennsylvania 19154
Benjamin Levy, President
(215) 676-7600

MAJESTIC SILVER COMPANY
241 Wolcott Street
New Haven, Connecticut 06513
Milton Baker, President
(203) 562-5171

MAJESTIC TOOL MANUFACTURING
COMPANY
2000 West Fulton
Chicago, Illinois 60612
(312) 421-2244

MAJESTIC WAX COMPANY
1600 Wynkoop
Denver, Colorado 80202
(303) 534-2826

MAJIC MARKETS (food-store
franchise)
See Munford Inc.

MAJOR ELECTRONICS
CORPORATION
5802 Third Avenue
Brooklyn, New York 11220
Stephen L. Lane, President
(212) 680-7000

MAJOR METALFAB INC.
370 Alice Street
Wheeling, Illinois 60090
(312) 537-7890

MAJOR POOL EQUIPMENT
CORPORATION
200 Entin Road
Clifton, New Jersey 07014
Richard W. Cohen, Chairman of
the Board
(201) 472-1100

MAKADO (food products)
See PVO International Inc.

MAKE-A-BETTER BURGER (soy meat
extender)
See Thomas J. Lipton Inc.

MAKE OVER (cosmetics)
See Clairol, Inc.

MAKELITE (food products)
See PVO International Inc.

Companies and Trade Names

MAKEPEACE COLONY PRESS INC., THE
Box 111
Stevens Point, Wisconsin 54481
(715) 344-2636

MAKEWELL (leather goods)
See Charisma by Makewell

MAKO MARINE INC.
4355 128th Street
Miami, Florida 33054
(305) 685-6591

MAKOTO IMPORTS INC.
3001 N.W. Industrial
Portland, Oregon 97210
(503) 226-2482

MALARKEY (plywood products)
See Simpson Timber Company

MALATESTA, F.
15 Victoria
Everett, Massachusetts 02149

MALATHION (insecticides)
See American Cyanamid Company

MALAY MODERN (furniture)
See Ficks Reed Company

MALCO PRODUCTS INC.
361 Fairview Avenue
Barberton, Ohio 44203
Abe Glauberman, President
(216) 753-0361

MALCOLM KENNETH (men's overcoats, outerwear, rainwear)
See After Six Inc.

MALCUS TOOLS CORPORATION
195 Armstrong
Garden City Park, New York 11040
(516) 248-5515

MALE CALL (young men's clothing)
See Santone Industries, Inc.

MALE CHAUVINIST (men's cosmetics)
See Cosmetco

MALERNE (woodwind instruments)
See Peate Musical Supplies Ltd.

MALIBU (canned foods)
See Case-Swayne Company, Inc.

MALIBU (water skis and accessories)
See Medalist Water Sports

MALIBU OUTRIGGER ASSOCIATION
Box 1007
Topanga, California 90290

MALIN-HALL
510 South 52nd
Philadelphia, Pennsylvania 19143
(215) 472-3411

MALING BROTHERS, INC.
(Subsidiary of Zale Corporation)
1400 Wrightwood Avenue
Chicago, Illinois 60614
I.D. Shapiro, President
(312) 348-8310

MALING DESIGN, JOHN
Post Office Box 1113
Menlo Park, California 94025

MALKIN'S (canned foods)
See Westfair Foods Ltd.

MALLARD, INC.
3021 Wabash Avenue
Detroit, Michigan 48216
Karl Mallard, President
(313) 831-8330

MALLARD PEN & PENCIL COMPANY, INC.
Bourbon Street and Chambers Avenue
Georgetown, Kentucky 40324
(502) 863-0954

MALLEABLE IRON RANGE COMPANY
715 North Spring Street
Beaver Dam, Wisconsin 53916
Michael J. Maier, President
(414) 885-3311
See also Monarch Kitchen Appliances

MALLEM & SON, INC., EZRA
295 Fifth Avenue
New York, New York 10016
(212) 684-4674

MALLET & COMPANY
Box 474
Carnegie, Pennsylvania 15106
Dorothy M. Mallet, Chairman and President
(412) 923-2900
See also Max-Ams Company

MALLINCKRODT INC.
3600 North Second Street
Saint Louis, Missouri 63147
Stanley H. Anonsen, President
(314) 231-8980

MALLORCA (furniture)
See Ficks Reed Company

MALLORY & COMPANY, INC., P.R.
3029 East Washington
Indianapolis, Indiana 46206
A. Clark Daughtery, President
(317) 636-5353

MALLORY BATTERY COMPANY
(Division of P.R. Mallory & Company, Inc.)
South Broadway
Tarrytown, New York 10591
(914) 591-7000

Companies and Trade Names

MALLORY PLASTICS
See Krone Manufacturing Inc.

MALLORY RANDALL CORPORATION
122 East 42nd Street
New York, New York 10017
David B. Rosenbloom, President
(212) 661-8164

MALMSTROM CHEMICAL
  CORPORATION
Box 587
1501 West Elizabeth Avenue
Linden, New Jersey 07036
(201) 862-7500

MALONE INC., MINDY
1400 Broadway
New York, New York 10018
(212) 354-5770

MALOW CORPORATION
Post Office Box 464
Des Plaines, Illinois 60018
(312) 956-0200

MALT-O-MEAL COMPANY
1115 Northstar Center
Minneapolis, Minnesota 55402
Glenn S. Brooks, President
(612) 332-8894

MAMA COOKIE BAKERIES, INC.
7200 South Kostner Avenue
Chicago, Illinois 60629
(312) 767-8200

MAMA K (food products)
See M & K Foods Inc.

MAMARY SLEEPWEAR, INC.
135 Madison Avenue
New York, New York 10002
(212) 683-3866

MAMIYA (photographic equipment)
See Ponder & Best

MAMIYE BROTHERS INC.
112 West 34th Street
New York, New York 10001
(212) 279-4150

MAMMOTH MART, INC.
321 Manley Street
West Bridgewater,
  Massachusetts 02379
Max Coffman, Chairman of the
  Board
(617) 583-6800

MAMMOTH SPRING CANNING
  CORPORATION
219 Main Street
Sussex, Wisconsin 53089
(414) 246-3515

MAN ALIVE (medicated skin-care
product for men)
See Colgate-Palmolive Company

MAN-KNITS (menswear)
See The Manhattan Shirt
  Company

MAN-POWER (deodorant, shaving
cream)
See Shulton, Inc.

MAN SPRAY (men's hair spray)
See LB Laboratories Inc.

MANATEE BOAT
Box Six
12th Avenue
Palmetto, Florida 33561
(813) 722-6112

MANBECK BREAD COMPANY
Hagerstown, Maryland 21740
(301) 739-2570

MANCHARD TRADING
  CORPORATION
2315 Broadway
New York, New York 10024
(212) 787-4833

MANCHESTER HOSIERY MILLS
(Division of Hampshire-Designers,
  Inc.)
540 North Commercial Street
Manchester, New Hampshire 03101
Melvin J. Gordon, President
(603) 625-6911

MANCHESTER KNITTED FASHIONS,
  INC.
McGregor and Bridge
Manchester, New Hampshire 03102
Herman S. Werner, President
(603) 669-5370

MANCO (enamel cookware)
See Seymour Mann, Inc.

MAND CARPET MILLS
2310 East 52nd
Vernon, California 90058
Emery M. Mand, President
(213) 589-6901

MANDALAY (cookware)
See National Silver Company

MANDALAY (dinnerware)
See Wallace Silversmiths

MANDALAY (rattan furniture)
See Ficks Reed Company

MANE TAME (men's hair spray)
See Ernst Inc.

MANETTA MILLS, INC.
Lando, South Carolina 29724
G.A. Heath, President
(803) 789-5111

MANGEL STORES CORPORATION
115 West 18th Street
New York, New York 10011
Joseph H. Lamm, President
(212) 924-9200

Companies and Trade Names

MANGELS HEROLD COMPANY, INC.
Key Highway and Boyle
Baltimore, Maryland 21230
Roger N. Mangels, President
(301) 752-5550

MANGELSDORF & BROTHER, INC., EDWARD F.
1020 South Fourth Street
Saint Louis, Missouri 63166
(314) 621-0500

MANGINI & ASSOCIATES
4850 West Belmont Avenue
Chicago, Illinois 60641
(312) 282-8181

MANGROVE FEATHER COMPANY INC.
468 Greenwich Street
New York, New York 10013
(212) 431-5806

MANHATTAN COFFEE COMPANY
301 South Eighth
Saint Louis, Missouri 63102
(314) 241-8660

MANHATTAN DRUG COMPANY, INC.
201 Route 22
Hillside, New Jersey 07205
(201) 926-0816

MANHATTAN EYE SALVE COMPANY
Post Office Box 4202
1863 Arlington Avenue
Louisville, Kentucky 40204
(502) 895-4482

MANHATTAN FEATHER & DOWN COMPANY
121 Percheron Lane
Roslyn Heights, New York 11577
(516) 621-1456

MANHATTAN GREETING CARD PUBLISHING COMPANY INC.
657 Broadway
New York, New York 10012
(212) 254-2596

MANHATTAN INDUSTRIES, INC.
1271 Avenue of the Americas
New York, New York 10020
Laurence C. Leads, Jr., Chairman
(212) 265-3700
See also Berkley Cravats Inc.; Blouses by Vera, Inc.; Lady Manhattan Company; and Manhattan Shirt Company

MANHATTAN NOVELTY CORPORATION
263 Canal Street
New York, New York 10013
(212) 255-9000

MANHATTAN SHIRT COMPANY, THE
(Division of Manhattan Industries, Inc.)
1271 Avenue of the Americas
New York, New York 10020
Henry Grethel, President
(212) 265-3700

MANHATTAN TRADING COMPANY
1261 Broadway
New York, New York 10001
(212) 683-6120

MANISCHEWITZ (kosher wine)
See Monarch Wine Company Inc.

MANISCHEWITZ COMPANY, THE B.
9 Clinton Street
Newark, New Jersey 07102
Bernard Manischewitz, President
(201) 624-1134

MANITOWOC EQUIPMENT WORKS
(Division of the Manitowoc Company, Inc.)
500 South 16th Street
Manitowoc, Wisconsin 54220
(414) 684-6621

MANLEY, INC.
1920 Wyandotte
Kansas City, Missouri 64108
Charles G. Manley, President and Treasurer
(816) 421-6155

MANLY (shoes)
See United States Shoe Corporation

MANN & BROTHERS, INC.
20 West 37th Street
New York, New York 10018
(212) 868-3535

MANN CHEMICAL CORPORATION
520 West Main Street
Louisville, Kentucky 40202
(502) 585-2001

MANN, ELWIN R.
2838 Freedom Boulevard
Watsonville, California 95076

MANN MANUFACTURING, INC.
Post Office Box 10339
El Paso, Texas 79994
Gary I. Mann, President
(915) 778-9941

MANNE COMPANY, KENNETH A.
Box 8649
Canton, Ohio 44711
(216) 455-5717

MANNEQUIN (women's shoes)
See Genesco Inc.

MANNIE GELBAND (lamps, lighting fixtures, wooden candles)
See Artistic Candles by Gelband

Companies and Trade Names

MANNING-BOWMAN
(Division of McGraw-Edison
    Company)
Vine and Second Street
Boonville, Missouri 65233
J.R. McDermott, President
(816) 882-2762

MANNING COMPANY,
    JOSEPH P.
4 Alger
South Boston, Massachusetts 02127
Edward F. Goggin, President and
    Treasurer
(617) 269-4200

MANNING COMPANY, MARTHA
701 West Main Street
Collinsville, Illinois 62234
(618) 344-7131

MANNING INC., MRS. M.
803 South Clinton Street
Baltimore, Maryland 21224
(301) 732-4450

MANNING'S FAMOUS FOODS,
INC.
    See Chef Francisco

MANNING'S, INC.
(Division of John Labatt, Ltd.)
901 Battery Street
San Francisco, California 94111
Roland Austin, President
(415) 981-0525

MANNINGTON MILLS, INC.
Salem, New Jersey 08079
Arthur Williams, President
(609) 935-3000

MANON (canned vegetables)
    See Girard Inc.

MANOR (bakery products)
    See Campbell-Taggart Inc.

MANOR HOUSE (frozen turkeys)
    See Safeway Stores Inc.

MANOR HOUSE (mobile homes)
    See Marshfield Homes

MANPOWER, INC.
5301 North Ironwood Road
Milwaukee, Wisconsin 53217
Elmer L. Winter, President
(414) 961-1000

MANSFIELD (guitars, basses,
banjos)
    See Peate Musical Supplies Ltd.

MANSFIELD INDUSTRIES (furniture)
    See Renson of Mountain View

MANSFIELD SANITARY INC.
150 First Street
Perrysville, Ohio 44864
Luis J. Ott, President
(419) 938-5211

MANSFIELD TIRE & RUBBER
    COMPANY, THE
515 Newman Street
Mansfield, Ohio 44902
J.H. Hoffman, President
(419) 522-4111

MANSFIELDS (shoes)
    See Kayser-Roth Shoes, Inc.

MANSID COMPANY, INC., THE
1483 East 32nd Street
Brooklyn, New York 11234
(212) 253-6611

MANSON INDUSTRIES INC.
Route Eight
Topeka, Kansas 66604
(913) 478-4662

MANTELL EXPORT COMPANY
1414 Avenue of the Americas
New York, New York 10019
(212) 755-5454

MANUAL ARTS FURNITURE
    COMPANY
3472 Beekman Street
Cincinnati, Ohio 45223
(513) 681-5821

MANUFACTURERS & TRADERS
    TRUST COMPANY
(Subsidiary of First Empire State
    Corporation)
1 M and T Plaza
Buffalo, New York 14240
Maude F. Schuchter, Chairman
(716) 842-4200

MANUFACTURERS BRUSH COMPANY
12501 Elmwood Avenue
Cleveland, Ohio 44111
Walter Brandschutz, President and
    Chief Executive Officer
(216) 252-4330

MANUFACTURERS HANOVER
    TRUST COMPANY
350 Park Street
New York, New York 10022
Gabriel Hauge, Chairman of the
    Board
(212) 350-3300

MANUFACTURERS MARKETING
COMPANY USA, INC., THE
    See Vigilant Products Company,
        Inc.

MANUFACTURERS NATIONAL
    BANK OF DETROIT
151 West Fort Street
Detroit, Michigan 48226
Dean E. Richardson, Chairman of
    the Board
(313) 222-4000

MANWELL FOODS INC.
Box 336
Sweetser, Indiana 46987

Companies and Trade Names

MANWICH (sandwich sauce)
See Hunt-Wesson Foods, Inc.

MANZANA PRODUCTS COMPANY
9141 Green Valley Road
Sebastopol, California 95472
Constance N. Sandborn, President
(707) 823-5313

MANZANITA RANCH
Box 684
Julian, California 92036
(714) 765-0102

MAPCO INC.
1437 South Boulder
Tulsa, Oklahoma 74119
See also Thermogas, Inc.

MAPES INDUSTRIES INC.
130 Cutter Mill Road
Great Neck, New York 11022
Luis B. Moss, President
(516) 487-7995

MAPES PIANO STRING COMPANY
408 North Pine Street
Elizabethton, Tennessee 37643

MAPLE CITY RUBBER COMPANY
55 Newton Street
Norwalk, Ohio 44857
(419) 663-7711

MAPLE FLOORING
  MANUFACTURERS ASSOCIATION
424 Washington Avenue
Oshkosh, Wisconsin 54901
(414) 233-1920

MAPLE GROVE
167 Portland Street
Saint Johnsbury, Vermont 05819
Stephen R. Astle, President
(802) 748-2611

MAPLE ISLAND INC.
2815 Blaisdell Avenue South
Minneapolis, Minnesota 55408
D.W. O'Brien, President and
  Secretary
(612) 827-2974

MAPLE LEAF (dairy products)
See Breakstone Sugar Creek
  Foods (New York)

MAPLE LEAF (sports apparel and
accessories)
See Sportco Inc.

MAPLE LEAF-NOLTE
CORPORATION
507 Elk
Buffalo, New York 14210
(716) 825-4900

MAPLETON (tobacco, cigarettes,
and pipe cleaners)
See United States Tobacco
  Company

MAPLEWOOD (canned foods)
See Friend Brothers, Inc.

MAQUEDA (Spanish sherries)
See Park, Benziger & Company

MAR-JAC POULTRY, INC.
Airport Circle
Gainesville, Georgia 30501
Max F. Ward, President
(404) 532-8448

MAR-KES (Mexican foods)
See Riviana Foods Inc.

MAR-QUIPT INC.
232 S.W. Fifth Street
Pompano Beach, Florida 33060
(305) 942-0440

MARA LYNNE (hair-care products)
See Penntest Pharmacal
  Corporation

MARACA (rum)
See W.A. Taylor & Company

MARAILCO
Box 20065
Saint Petersburg, Florida 33742
(813) 577-0591

MARANTZ COMPANY INC.
8460 San Fernando Road
Sun Valley, California 91352

MARATHON (guitars and accessories)
See Southland Musical
  Merchandise Corporation

MARATHON BATTERY COMPANY
8301 Imperial Drive
Waco, Texas 76710
(817) 776-0650

MARATHON CAREY-MCFALL
COMPANY
2156 East Dauphin Street
Philadelphia, Pennsylvania 19125
(215) 634-5000

MARATHON COMPANY
Attleboro, Massachusetts 02703
(617) 222-5444

MARATHON LE TOURNEAU
COMPANY
Longview Division
Post Office Box 2307
600 Jefferson
Longview, Texas 75657
Gene M. Woodfin, Chairman,
  President and Chief Executive
  Officer
(214) 753-4411

MARATHON OIL COMPANY
539 South Main Street
Findlay, Ohio 45840
H.D. Hoopman, President
(419) 422-2121

Companies and Trade Names

MARATHON RUBBER PRODUCTS
  COMPANY
510 Sherman
Wausau, Wisconsin 54401
(715) 845-6255

MARBELLA (occasional furniture)
  See Loroman Company, Inc.

MARBERT, INC.
6600 Whitestone Road
Baltimore, Maryland 21207
(301) 944-9410

MARBLE ARMS CORPORATION
Glandston Industrial Park
Gladstone, Michigan 49837
Clarence M. Goodman, President
(906) 425-2841

MARBLE-CRAFT (marble tables,
desk accessories, ashtrays, and lamp
parts)
  See E. & S. Sales

MARBLE FURNITURE COMPANY
(Division of W.H. Furniture
  Group, Inc.)
89 Willis Street
Bedford, Ohio 44146
William P. McQuinn, President
(216) 232-0100

MARBLE KING, INC.
First Avenue
Paden City, West Virginia 26159
(304) 337-2264
  See also Pink Berry Industries

MARBLETONE (paneling)
  See Masonite Corporation

MARBORO BOOKS INC.
205 Moonachie Road
Moonachie, New Jersey 07074
(201) 440-3800

MARC NICOLET (watches)
  See Berman Watch Company,
    Inc.

MARCAL PAPER MILLS, INC.
1 Market Street
East Paterson, New Jersey 07407
Robert L. Marcalus, President
(201) 796-4000

MARCEL FRANCE (atomizers)
  See Germaine Monteil
    Cosmetiques Corporation

MARCH PRODUCTS INC.
611 Manhattan Avenue
Brooklyn, New York 11222
(212) 383-3328

MARCHI & FIGLI (religious articles)
  See Schmid Brothers, Inc.

MARCIA CERAMICS OF
  CALIFORNIA, INC.
(Subsidiary of Federal Filter
  Company)
2311 East 16th Street
Los Angeles, California 90021
(213) 627-1532

MARCIA'S PRIDE (produce)
  See Jackel Farms & Cold
    Storage

MARCO (ceramics and glassware)
  See Mark Ross & Company

MARCO (lighting fixtures)
  See Marvin Electric Manu-
    facturing Company (MARCO)

MARCO (men's shoes)
  See Arthur M. Leopold Inc.

MARCO CASUALS (handbags)
  See Ethan Industries Inc.

MARCO, INC.
619 West Chicago Avenue
Chicago, Illinois 60607
Leo H. Schoenhofen, Chairman
  of the Board
(312) 467-8800

MARCOE & SON'S CANDIES
4100 South M Street
Tacoma, Washington 98408
(206) 472-5172

MARCREST (lamps and accessories)
  See J.F. Marr Company, Inc.

MARCUS WIESEN, INC.
26 East 14th Street
New York, New York 10003
(212) 255-6933

MARCUS DISPLAY INDUSTRIES,
  INC.
114 Lincoln Street
Boston, Massachusetts 02111
(617) 542-1405

MARDI BRA CREATIONS
  CORPORATION
135 Madison Avenue
New York, New York 10016
Aaron Sokol, President
(212) 684-4088

MARDI GRAS (carpet)
  See West Point Pepperell
    Carpet & Rug

MARDI GRAS ENTERPRISES
Lower Simms Street
Simmesport, Louisiana 71369

MAREMONT (auto parts)
  See Rayco International, Inc.

MAREMONT CORPORATION
168 North Michigan Avenue
Chicago, Illinois 60601
Richard B. Black, President and
  Chief Operations Officer
(312) 263-7676

MAREZINE (motion-sickness remedy,
nausea remedy)
  See Burroughs Wellcome Company

Companies and Trade Names

MARGA-RITA (food products)
   See Real Fresh Inc.

MARGARET HOLMES (canned foods)
   See Holmes Canning Company, Inc.

MARGIE LOWE (dresses)
   See R. Lowenbaum Manufacturing Company

MARGLO PRODUCTS CORPORATION
32 Gansevoort Street
New York, New York 10014
(212) 243-6855

MARGO (food products)
   See Tillie Lewis Foods Inc.

MARGOLIN & COMPANY, H.
380 River Street
Fitchburg, Massachusetts 01422
Jay Rome, Vice President
(617) 345-4336

MARGO'S LA MODE, INC.
2909 Live Oak
Dallas, Texas 75204
Joe Glickman, President
(214) 521-3183

MARGUISE (ovenproof glassware)
   See Jet Enterprises Ltd.

MARHILL INC.
466 Broad Street
Central Falls, Rhode Island 02863
(401) 728-2040

MARICOM (marine instruments)
   See Maritime Communications Inc.

MARIE ANTOINETTE (imported foods)
   See William H. Singer

MARIE BRIZARD (liqueur)
   See Schieffelin & Company

MARIE THUMAS (canned vegetables)
   See Euro-Foods Inc.

MARIETTA CANNING COMPANY
58-15 57th Road
Maspeth, New York 11378
(212) 894-3070

MARIETTA INSTITUTIONAL WHOLESALERS
161 Marble Mill Road
Marietta, Georgia 30060

MARIGOLD (food products)
   See Ward Foods, Inc.

MARIGOLD FOODS INC.
2929 University Avenue S.E.
Minneapolis, Minnesota 55411
(612) 331-3775
   See also Kemps

MARINAIRE CORPORATION
3904 North 29th Avenue
Hollywood, Florida 33020
(305) 921-5800

MARINE (weather and scientific instruments)
   See Danforth (Division of Eastern Company)

MARINE BAND (harmonicas)
   See M. Hohner Inc.

MARINE BANK & TRUST COMPANY
Box 3303
Tampa, Florida 33601
A. Clewis Howell, President
(813) 224-2121

MARINE COLLOIDS, INC.
Post Office Box 308
Rockland, Maine 04841
Harris J. Bixler, President
(207) 594-4436

MARINE CRAFTS INTERNATIONAL
The Breakwater
Santa Barbara, California 93109

MARINE DEVELOPMENT & RESEARCH CORPORATION
116 Church Street
Freeport, New York 11520
(516) 546-1162

MARINE DEVELOPMENT CORPORATION
Post Office Box 8570
Richmond, Virginia 23226
(804) 746-1313

MARINE FASHION INC.
314 South Main Street
Deep River, Connecticut 06417

MARINE FIRE WATCH (flame detection and suppression system)
   See Pyrotector Inc.

MARINE IMPORTS COMPANY OF AMERICA INC.
85 Saint John Street
New Haven, Connecticut 06501
(203) 865-0163

MARINE LIFE (music boxes, wall decor, lamps, etc.)
   See House International

MARINE MEDIC
11800 Woodruff
Downey, California 90241

MARINE METAL PRODUCTS
1222 Range Road
Clearwater, Florida 33515
(813) 445-8001

Companies and Trade Names

MARINE MIDLAND BANK-NEW YORK
(Subsidiary of Marine Midland Banks, Inc.)
140 Broadway
New York, New York 10015
Charles F. Mansfield, President
(212) 797-4000

MARINE MIDLAND BANKS, INC.
1 Marine Midland Center
Buffalo, New York 14203
Edward W. Duffy, President
(716) 843-2424

MARINE MUFFLERS INC.
400 S.W. 12th Avenue
Pompano Beach, Florida 33061
(305) 781-9190

MARINE STRIP (paint and varnish remover)
See James B. Day Company

MARINE TRADING INTERNATIONAL INC.
571 West Lake Avenue
Bay Head, New Jersey 08742
(201) 899-6800

MARINE WATER SYSTEMS
6400 Marina Drive
Long Beach, California 90803
(213) 598-9000

MARINER (houseboat)
See Cron Houseboats

MARINER COMPANY
1714 17th Street
Santa Monica, California 90404

MARINETTE (dresses)
See Martin Manufacturing Company

MARION (canned and frozen foods)
See Agripac, Inc.

MARION FOODS CORPORATION
(Subsidiary of Seneca Foods Corporation)
60 South Main Street
Marion, New York 14503
(315) 926-4284

MARION-KAY (extracts, teas, coffees, and spices)
See Marion-Kay Company, Inc.

MARION-KAY COMPANY, INC.
Brownstown, Indiana 47220
(812) 358-3000

MARION LABORATORIES, INC.
10236 Bunker Ridge Road
Kansas City, Missouri 64137
Ewing M. Kauffman, President
(816) 761-2500
See also Derm-Arts Laboratories

MARION MANUFACTURING COMPANY INC.
174 Chester Avenue
Atlanta, Georgia 30316
T.L. Waxelbaum, President
(404) 523-6475

MARIPAC (canned seafoods)
See Maritime Packers

MARITIME COMMUNICATIONS INC.
766 Washington Street
Marina del Rey, California 90291

MARITIME PRODUCTS COMPANY
15427 Woodrow Wilson
Detroit, Michigan 48238
(313) 883-6464

MARITIMER (seafood)
See Caribou Fisheries

MARK (seafood)
See Crest Importing Company

MARK CRAIG LTD. (men's slacks)
See Paxton Sportswear Inc.

MARK CROSS, INC.
711 Fifth Avenue
New York, New York 10022
Edward Wasserberger, President
(212) 421-3000

MARK VIII (fishing gear)
See Sportsmen's Industries, Inc.

MARK V (recreational vehicle)
See Kit Manufacturing Company

MARK IV (car air conditioners)
See John E. Mitchell Company

MARK-FOUR GAME
See Molor Products Company

MARK IV HOMES, INC.
Hampton Industrial Park
Taylor, Pennsylvania 18504
Sal H. Alfiero, Chairman of the Board
(717) 562-3690

MARK KNITTING MILLS
26 Palisade Avenue
Bergenfield, New Jersey 07621
(201) 384-1111

MARK LABORATORIES, INC.
Box 18091
San Francisco, California 94118
(415) 668-1542

MARK ONE HOSPITAL PRODUCTS, INC.
2700 Roberts Avenue
Philadelphia, Pennsylvania 19129
(215) 455-6400

MARK I, INC.
1700 West Irving Park Road
Chicago, Illinois 60613
(312) 281-1111

Companies and Trade Names

MARK 7 SEAFOOD INDUSTRIES INC.
Mill and Pine
Houston, Delaware 19954
Mark R. Prudent, Chairman and President
(302) 422-9631

MARK SPITZ (swimming and diving products)
See Elton Corporation

MARK TEN B (ignition system)
See Delta Products Inc.

MARK XII (shoes)
See Craddock-Terry Shoe Corporation

MARK 11 (portable typewriters)
See Remington Rand Office Machines (Division of Sperry Rand Corporation)

MARKAL COMPANY
270 North Washtenaw Avenue
Chicago, Illinois 60612
(312) 826-1700

MARKAY BAGS INC.
15 East 32nd Street
New York, New York 10016
(212) 689-6910

MARKEE (patio port)
See Acosta Awning Corporation

MARKEL ELECTRIC PRODUCTS INC.
593 Amherst
Buffalo, New York 14207
(716) 875-7660

MARKER (sports accessories and equipment)
See K-2 Corporation

MARKET BASKET (groceries)
See Ritchie Grocer Company

MARKET CONFECTIONS, INC.
4375 Bandini
Los Angeles, California 90023
Roger K. Duerr, Executive Vice President and General Manager
(213) 264-1221

MARKET WHOLESALE GROCERY COMPANY
815 Thompson Avenue
Glendale, California 91201
H. Edward Moore, President
(213) 245-9571

MARKETEER (musical instruments)
See Chicago Musical Instrument Company

MARKETS INC.
1701 Marina Boulevard
San Leandro, California 94577
(415) 357-2000

MARKOV (vodka)
See L. Hirsch & Son

MARKSMAN PRODUCTS
Post Office Box 2983
Torrance, California 90509

MARKWELL MANUFACTURING COMPANY INC.
424 West 33rd Street
New York, New York 10001
Mort Newburg, President
(212) 695-6969

MARLA (plastic cleaner)
See Santa Pharmaceuticals, Inc.

MARLBORO (cigarettes)
See Philip Morris, Inc.

MARLEN MARBLE LTD.
34-46 Vernon Boulevard
Long Island City, New York 11106
(212) 626-1372

MARLEN MARINE PRODUCTS COMPANY
5150 Richmond Road
Bedford, Ohio 44146
(216) 292-7060

MARLENE INDUSTRIES CORPORATION
1370 Broadway
New York, New York 10018
Charles Meltzer, President
(212) 279-0877
See also Mademoiselle-Town & Country

MARLENN CORPORATION
1801 Byrd Street
Baltimore, Maryland 21230
(301) 837-7731

MARLETTE HOMES, INC.
Marlette, Michigan 48453
Earl W. Swett, President
(517) 635-7521

MARLIN (outboard motors)
See Jetco Inc.

MARLIN (radiotelephones)
See Unimetrics Inc.

MARLIN FIBERGLASS COMPANY
2429 South Birch Street
Santa Ana, California 92707
(714) 546-5837

MARLIN FIREARMS COMPANY, THE
100 Kenna Drive
North Haven, Connecticut 06473
Frank Kenna, President
(203) 239-5621

MARLIN LINE (metal furniture)
See Harrison Steel Desk & File Company

Companies and Trade Names

MARLIN PRODUCTS INC.
1695 West 32nd Place
Hialeah, Florida 33013
(305) 821-3848

MARLIN-ROCKWELL
(Division of TRW Inc.)
402 Chandler
Jamestown, New York 14701
Earl F. Myerholtz, Vice President
 and General Manager
(716) 661-2600

MARLIN TOY PRODUCTS INC.
304 Ellison Street
Horicon, Wisconsin 53032
(414) 485-4463

MARLITE
(Division of Masonite Corporation)
Dover, Ohio 44622
D.D. Gould, General Manager
(216) 343-6621

MARLON CONFECTIONS
(Subsidiary of Just Born, Inc.)
1300 Stefko Boulevard
Bethlehem, Pennsylvania 18018
Ira B. Born, President
(215) 867-7568

MARLON CREATIONS
29-04 37th Avenue
Long Island City, New York 11101
(212) 361-2088

MARLOW (stainless-steel flatware)
 See W.M.F. of America, Inc.

MARLY (woodwind instruments)
 See J.M. Greene Music
  Company Ltd.

MARLYLE SWIMWEAR
 CORPORATION
650 Catiague Road
Jericho, New York 11753
Milton Fox, President
(516) 333-9800

MARMAC PRODUCTS INC.
Post Office Box 22039
Cleveland, Ohio 44122
(216) 292-6525

MARMON GROUP
Detroit Steel Products Division
6000 Caniff Avenue
Detroit, Michigan 48212
Gene W. Brown, General Manager
(313) 891-4000

MARMOREK & SON, HERBERT
2153 78th Street
Brooklyn, New York 11214
(212) 256-8080

MARNAT PACKING COMPANY
Box 80
Bennettsville, South Carolina 29572
(803) 479-3811

MARNAY SALES & MANU-
 FACTURING COMPANY INC.
41 East 42nd Street
New York, New York 10017
(212) 682-0920

MARNAY-SIGNORE (chairs, desks,
files)
 See Signore Inc./Marnay Sales

MARON FAMOUS CANDIES, INC.
510 South 52nd Street
Philadelphia, Pennsylvania 19143
(215) 472-3411

MARPLEX COMPANY
1930 West 139th Street
Gardena, California 90249

MARQUESA COSMETICS, INC.
4878 Fountain Avenue
Hollywood, California 90029
(213) 666-2844

MARQUETTE CORPORATION
First American Center
Nashville, Tennessee 37238
James E. Poole, Chairman and
 President
(615) 259-4000

MARQUETTE PETROLEUM
 PRODUCTS INC.
7270 South Chicago Avenue
Chicago, Illinois 60619
(312) 643-2000

MARQUIS (guitars)
 See Harmony Company

MARQUIS (portable televisions)
 See Philco-Ford Corporation

MARQUISE (shoes)
 See Wohl Shoe Company

MARR COMPANY, INC., J.F.
Dixon Avenue
Woodstock, New York 12498
(914) 679-2040

MARR DUPLICATOR COMPANY
 INC.
66 West Broadway
New York, New York 10004
(212) 227-1680

MARRIOTT (processed foods)
 See Fairfield Farm Kitchens

MARRIOTT CORPORATION
5161 River Road, N.W.
Washington, D.C. 20016
J. Willard Marriott, Jr., President
(301) 986-5000
 See also Fairfield Farm Kitchens;
  Rogers Family Restaurant

MARS FUDGE & FRUIT COMPANY,
 INC.
811 Lexington Avenue
Brooklyn, New York 11221
(212) 491-6750

Companies and Trade Names

MARS, INC.
1651 Old Meadow Road
McLean, Virginia 22101
A.C.C. Baxter, President
(703) 893-2210
   See also Kal Kan Foods, Inc.;
   and Uncle Ben's Foods

MARS-LUMOGRAPH (drawing
pencils, erasers, leads)
   See J.S. Staedtler Inc.

MARSALA (olive oil and wine
grapes)
   See Nick Sciabica & Sons

MARSCH CHEMICAL COMPANY
9649 North Tripp Avenue
Skokie, Illinois 60076
(312) 679-1616

MARSH & SON, M.
915 Market Street
Wheeling, West Virginia 26003
Robert E. Michener, President and
   Treasurer
(304) 232-0770

MARSH CHALKBOARD COMPANY
(Division of Marsh Lumber Company
   Inc.)
Post Office Box 467
524 River Street
Dover, Ohio 44622
(216) 343-8825

MARSH COMPANY, JORDAN
(Subsidiary of Allied Stores
   Corporation)
450 Washington Street
Boston, Massachusetts 02107

MARSH-EMORY LABORATORIES
Box 8027
Albuquerque, New Mexico 87108
(505) 268-5888

MARSH INC., J.L.
7600 Wayzata Boulevard
Minneapolis, Minnesota 55426
(612) 544-4201

MARSH INDUSTRIES
1224 East 28th Street
Los Angeles, California 90011
(213) 233-4394

MARSH SUPERMARKETS, INC.
Yorktown, Indiana 47396
Estel V. Marsh, Chairman
(317) 759-8101

MARSHALL (groceries)
   See Sales Producers Associates

MARSHALL BOAT COMPANY
1232 East Pomona Street
Santa Ana, California 92707
(714) 558-0722

MARSHALL COSMETICS LTD.,
   EVELYN
14 East 38th
New York, New York 10016
(212) 532-6400

MARSHALL FIELD & COMPANY
25 East Washington Street
Chicago, Illinois 60690
Joseph A. Burnham, President
(312) 236-7272
   See also Halle Brothers Com-
      pany; and Spokane Dry
      Goods Company

MARSHALL IMPORTS INC., R.A.
1319 Hickory
Kansas City, Missouri 64101
(816) 221-4166

MARSHALL INTERNATIONAL INC.,
   J.D.
Box 59446
7440 North Long Avenue
Skokie, Illinois 60076
Joel D. Honigberg, President and
   Treasurer
(312) 583-6060

MARSHALL PRODUCE COMPANY
Box 1088
Marshall, Minnesota 56258
(507) 532-4426

MARSHALL RAY CORPORATION
701 River Street
Troy, New York 12180
Clyde W. Rea, President
(518) 272-6700

MARSHALL SMOKED FISH
   COMPANY, INC.
23 Anthony
Brooklyn, New York 11222
(212) 384-7621

MARSHALLAN MANUFACTURING
   COMPANY
1971 West 85th Street
Cleveland, Ohio 44102
Alan P. Bedol, President
(216) 631-2400

MARSHALLS, INC.
83 Commerce Way
Woburn, Massachusetts 01801
Alfred Marshall, Chairman
(617) 935-8200

MARSHBURN FARMS INC.
Box 529
Santa Fe Springs, California 90670

MARSHFIELD CANNING COMPANY
1616 South Central Avenue
Marshfield, Wisconsin 54449
(715) 384-3195

MARSHFIELD HOMES
(Division of Wick Building Systems)
2301 East Fourth Street
Marshfield, Wisconsin 54449
(715) 387-2551

MARSHMALLOW FLUFF (dessert)
   See Durkee-Mower, Inc.

MARSHMALLOW PRODUCTS INC.
9 West Mitchell Avenue
Cincinnati, Ohio 45217
(513) 641-2345

Companies and Trade Names

MARSON CORPORATION
(Subsidiary of Swingline, Inc.)
143 Crescent Avenue
Chelsea, Massachusetts 02150
John H. Behr, President
(617) 884-7760

MARSON FASTENER CORPORATION
143 Crescent Avenue
Chelsea, Massachusetts 02150
(617) 884-7760

MARSTEN LABORATORIES
Box 3547
Beverly Hills, California 90212
(213) 274-0659

MARSTON BROOM-MOPS FACTORY
Marston, North Carolina 28363
(919) 582-3713

MARTA (canned foods)
See Martinez Food Canners, Ltd.

MARTELL (cognac)
See Brown-Forman Distillers Corporation

MARTELLO (food products)
See Barbour Foods Ltd.

MARTEX (bedroom and bathroom furnishings)
See West Point Pepperell

MARTHA MAID MANUFACTURING COMPANY
220 South State Street
Chicago, Illinois 60604
Joseph W. Horwitch, Chairman and President
(312) 939-3131

MARTHA MANNING COMPANY
1700 Saint Louis Road
Collinsville, Illinois 62234
M. Henry Hess, President
(618) 344-7131

MARTHA MAY (candy)
See Thurman's Inc.

MARTHA WHITE FOODS, INC.
110 21st Avenue, South
Nashville, Tennessee 37203
Robert V. Dale, President
(615) 327-4961
See also Byron's Inc.

MARTHA'S VINEYARD SHIPYARD, INC.
Beach Road
Vineyard Haven, Massachusetts 02568
(617) 693-6400

MARTIL CLOTHING COMPANY
2701 North Broad Street
Philadelphia, Pennsylvania 19132
(215) 226-3500

MARTIN (air conditioners)
See Martin Stamping & Stove Company

MARTIN (food products)
See Foster Canning Inc.

MARTIN (food products)
See Saint Jacobs Canning Company Ltd.

MARTIN & COMPANY, C.F.
510 Sycamore Street
Nazareth, Pennsylvania 18064
Frank H. Martin, President
(215) 759-2837

MARTIN & GRAFTON LTD.
(English jams, marmalades, and candy)
See Grace Rush

MARTIN BUSINE (band instruments)
See Targ & Dinner Inc.

MARTIN COMPANY
620 Andrews Avenue
Kewanee, Illinois 61443

MARTIN COMPANY, C.J.
Post Office Box 1089
606 West Main Street
Nacogdoches, Texas 75961
(713) 564-1413

MARTIN COMPANY, JACK
9731 Factorial Way
South El Monte, California 91733

MARTIN COMPANY, THE
(automobile accessories)
1150 West Third
Cleveland, Ohio 44113
(216) 621-9381

MARTIN DRUG COMPANY
1212 Buchanan
Jackson, Mississippi 39209
(601) 353-2781

MARTIN-FRERES (woodwind instruments)
See Buegeleisen & Jacobson Ltd.

MARTIN MANUFACTURING COMPANY
315 East Eighth Street
Los Angeles, California 90014
(213) 627-6691

MARTIN MARINE COMPANY
Pepperrell Road
Kittery Point, Maine 03905
(207) 439-1507

MARTIN ORGANISATION, C.F.
510 Sycamore Street
Nazareth, Pennsylvania 18064
(215) 759-2837

MARTIN PACKING COMPANY
49 University Avenue
Newark, New Jersey 07102
(201) 621-9100

Companies and Trade Names

MARTIN PAINT STORES, INC.
153-22 Jamaica Avenue
Jamaica, New York 11432
Samuel Glick, Chairman of the
 Board
(212) 526-1796

MARTIN-PHILLIPS LABORATORIES
8604 Verree
Philadelphia, Pennsylvania 19115
(215) 568-1541

MARTIN REEL COMPANY, INC.
30 East Main
Mohawk, New York 13407
C.M. Lyon, President
(315) 866-1690

MARTIN SALES
(Division of American Laundry
 Machinery Industries)
2005 Ross Avenue
Cincinnati, Ohio 45212
(513) 731-5500

MARTIN-SENOUR COMPANY
(Division of Sherwin-Williams
 Company)
2500 South Senour Avenue
Chicago, Illinois 60608
M.W. Hurdlebrink, President
(312) 842-5000

MARTIN'S V.O. SCOTCH
 See McKesson Liquor Company

MARTIN STAMPING & STOVE
 COMPANY
3414 Governors Drive, West
Huntsville, Alabama 35805
W.H. Martin, Jr., Chairman of
 the Board
(205) 539-9434

MARTIN THEATRE COMPANIES
(Subsidiary of Fuqua Industries, Inc.)
1308 Broadway
Columbus, Georgia 31902
Frank L. Brady, President
(404) 323-7365

MARTINDALE ELECTRIC COMPANY
1375 Hird Avenue
Cleveland, Ohio 44107
Robert H. Martindale, Chairman,
 President, Chief Engineer and
 Works Manager
(216) 521-8567

MARTINEAVY (band instruments)
 See Targ & Dinner Inc.

MARTINELLI (wines)
 See Italwine Import Company

MARTINELLI & COMPANY, S.
Watsonville, California 95076

MARTINI (automobile products)
 See Thexton Manufacturing
  Company

MARTINI & ROSSI (vermouth)
 See Renfield Importers Ltd.

MARTINO (food products)
 See Foster Canning Inc.

MARTIN'S HEREND IMPORTS INC.
735 Lamont Street N.W.
Washington, D.C. 20010
(202) 882-2490

MARTIN'S VVO (Scotch whiskey)
 See McKesson Liquor Company

MARTINSON COFFEE
(Division of Tetley, Inc.)
190 Franklin
New York, New York 10013
David Graham, Vice President
(212) 593-6742

MARTINSON'S (canned foods)
 See Beech-Nut, Inc.

MARTRUDE SALES CORPORATION
56-45 58th Street
Maspeth, New York 11378
(212) 894-3166

MARUEM (lightweight luggage and
 leather goods)
 See Meitetsu Inc.

MARUMAN PRODUCTS
 See Allied Products (Division of
  Consolidated Cigar
  Corporation)

MARVEL (amplifiers, electric
 guitars and basses)
 See Sorkin Music Company Inc.

MARVEL (saws)
 See Armstrong-Blum Manufacturing
  Company

MARVEL METAL PRODUCTS
 COMPANY
3843 West 43rd Street
Chicago, Illinois 60632
(312) 523-4804

MARVEL OIL COMPANY, INC.
331 North Main
Port Chester, New York 10573
John P. Gardell, President
(914) 937-4000

MARVEL SCHEBLER-TILLOTSON
(Division of Borg-Warner Corporation)
761 Berdon Avenue
Toledo, Ohio 43612
W.S. Blalock, President and
 General Manager
(419) 255-2050

MARVEL WORKER (vegetable slicers)
 See M.E. Heuck Company

MARVELLA, INC.
385 Fifth Avenue
New York, New York 10016
Richard E. Weinreich, President
(212) 685-9671

Companies and Trade Names

MARVELLE UNDERWEAR COMPANY
561 Broadway
New York, New York 10012
(212) 226-5760

MARVELLO TOILETRIES, INC.
7723 South Western Avenue
Chicago, Illinois 60620
(312) 737-0304

MARVELOUS (seafood)
See Reuther's Sea Food Company, Inc.

MARVELVET (upholstered furniture)
See Marble/Imperial Furniture

MARVELWOOD (mirrors, frames, etc.)
See Etco Industries

MARVIN ACCESSORIES, INC.
48-50 West 38th Street
New York, New York 10018
(212) 244-5532

MARVIN COMPANY, THE W.H.
Urbana, Ohio 43078
(513) 653-7131

MARVIN ELECTRIC MANUFAC-
TURING COMPANY (MARCO)
(Division of ICA)
6100 South Wilmington Avenue
Los Angeles, California 90021
(213) 583-6557

MARVIN ENVELOPE & PAPER
COMPANY
2040 West North Avenue
Chicago, Illinois 60647
(312) 489-3300

MARWIN ROBY LTD. (occasional tables)
See Cadmian Crafts Inc.

MARX & COMPANY INC., LOUIS
(Subsidiary of The Quaker Oats Company)
45 Church Street
Stamford, Connecticut 06906
Jach Asthalter, President
(203) 357-1000

MARX & NEWMAN COMPANY, INC.
(Division of United States Shoe Corporation)
9 West 57th Street
New York, New York 10019
(212) 371-1600

MARX-HAAS CLOTHING COMPANY
1717 Olive
Saint Louis, Missouri 63103
Irvin Bettman, Jr., President
(314) 421-2900

MARX PURE FOODS, INC.
East Kemper Road
Loveland, Ohio 45140
(513) 683-6000

MARX TOYS
See Marx & Company Inc., Louis

MARXMAN PIPES, INC.
(Division of Mastercraft Pipes, Inc.)
25 West 32nd Street
New York, New York 10001
(212) 736-7990

MARY ANN (kitchen tools)
See Ekco Products Inc.

MARY BAKER (cake mixes and cookies)
See Fleming Company

MARY CARTER INDUSTRIES, INC.
Gunn Highway and Henderson
Tampa, Florida 33615
Joseph A. Affronti, President
(813) 920-6611

MARY CHESS, LTD.
(Division of Profit Centers Inc.)
Pratt Oval
Glen Cove, New York 11542
Anthony Cangemi, President
(516) 676-2140

MARY ELLEN (dressings, eggs)
See Spartan Stores Inc.

MARY ELLEN (jams and jellies)
See J.M. Smucker Company

MARY GREY HOSIERY MILLS INC.
Bristol, Virginia 24201

MARY JANE (candy)
See Charles N. Miller Company

MARY JANE COMPANY
5510 Cleon Avenue
North Hollywood, California 91601
Maurice A. Cattani, President
(213) 877-7166

MARY JANE, INC.
152 Madison Avenue
New York, New York 10016

MARY KAY COSMETICS, INC.
8900 Carpenter Freeway
Dallas, Texas 75247
Mary Kay Ash, Chairman of the Board
(214) 631-3942
See also Cosmetic Creations, Inc.

Companies and Trade Names

MARY KITCHEN (canned and frozen foods)
See George A. Hormel & Company

MARY LANE (coats and suits for women)
See Brand and Puritz

MARY LEE (groceries)
See Ellenbee Foods Inc.

MARY LEE TAYLOR (ice milk and dips)
See Pet Inc., Dairy Division

MARY LOUISE & ASSOCIATES
1801 South Michigan Avenue
Chicago, Illinois 60616
(312) 225-6044

MARY MAXIM INC.
2001 Holland Avenue
Port Huron, Michigan 48060

MARY MEYER MANUFACTURING COMPANY INC.
Townshend, Vermont 05353
(802) 365-7793

MARY MILES (canned foods)
See F.W. Fearman Company, Ltd.

MARY PROCTOR (electrical appliances)
See Proctor-Silex Inc.

MARYDEL (processed foods)
See H.P. Cannon & Sons Inc.

MARYLAND (cigarettes)
See American Tobacco Company

MARYLAND CASUALTY COMPANY
(Subsidiary of American General Insurance Company)
3910 Keswick Road
Baltimore, Maryland 21203
Roy C. McCollough, President
(301) 366-1000

MARYLAND CHIEF (canned foods)
See J. Langrall & Brother, Inc.

MARYLAND CUP CORPORATION
10100 Reisterstown Road
Ownings Mills, Maryland 21117
Arthur H. Shapiro, President
(301) 363-1111
See also Gulf Cone Company, Inc.; Maryland Match Corporation; and Sweetheart Corporation

MARYLAND MATCH CORPORATION
(Division of Maryland Cup Corporation)
1100 South Eutaw Street
Baltimore, Maryland 21230
Martin P. Gerbery, Executive Vice President
(301) 363-1111

MARYLAND NATIONAL BANK
10 Light Street
Baltimore, Maryland 21203
Robert D. H. Harvey, Chairman of the Board
(301) 962-6111

MARYLAND 100s (cigarettes)
See American Brands Inc.

MARYLAND PLASTICS DIVISION
251 East Central Avenue
Federalsburg, Maryland 21632
E. Donegan, Division President
(301) 754-5566

MARY'S CHOICE (tomato products)
See Fettig Canning Corporation

MARZANO (canned tomato products)
See Ralph L. Mason Canning Company

MARZETTI COMPANY, T.
Box 29163
1120 Morse Road
Columbus, Ohio 43229
Gansey R. Johnston, President
(614) 846-2232

MA'S OLD FASHION INC.
Laird Street and Route 315
Wilkes-Barre, Pennsylvania 18702
(717) 829-3471

MASA HARINA (tortilla flour mix)
See Quaker Oats Company

MASADA (guitars and accessories)
See Southland Musical Merchandise Corporation

MASAL COMPANY, INC., THE
11 Park Place
New York, New York 10007
(212) 267-9158

MASBACK HARDWARE COMPANY
330 Hudson Street
New York, New York 10013
(212) 255-1300

MASCO CORPORATION
21001 Van Born Road
Taylor, Michigan 48180
Alex Manoogian, Chairman of the Board
(313) 274-7400
See also Delta Faucet Company

MASCOTT (fire protection equipment)
See American LaFrance Consumer (Division of American LaFrance, Inc.)

MASCULINI (men's jackets)
See La Jolla Clothes

Companies and Trade Names

MASELTOV (Israeli foods)
See Strohmeyer & Arpe Company

MASK & GAY FOOD PRODUCTS, INC.
Box Eight
Brooks, Georgia 30205

MASKETEERS OF WEST VIRGINIA INC.
Industrial Park
Belington, West Virginia 26250
S.L. Yeager, President
(304) 823-1600

MASKEY'S CANDIES
700 West Pacific Coast Highway
Long Beach, California 90806
(213) 437-2737

MASKIN DRUG COMPANY
2456 Keyworth Avenue
Baltimore, Maryland 21215

MASLAND & SONS, C.H.
Spring Road
Carlisle, Pennsylvania 17013
William S. Masland, President
(717) 249-1866

MASLAND DURALEATHER COMPANY, THE
(Division of Uniroyal)
3236-90 Amber
Philadelphia, Pennsylvania 19134
A.C. McKoy, President
(215) 425-3050

MASON (candies)
See Tootsie Roll Industries, Inc.

MASON (jars)
See Ball Corporation

MASON & HAMLIN (pianos)
See Aeolian Corporation

MASON & MASON COMPANY
550 Frontage Road
Northfield, Illinois 60093
Ralph E. Mason, President
(312) 441-6336

MASON & RISCH (pianos)
See Aeolian Corporation

MASON BOX COMPANY
521 Mount Hope Street
Attleboro Falls, Massachusetts 02763
Robert P. Mason, President and Treasurer
(617) 695-9381

MASON CANDY COMPANY
411 Market Street
Trinidad, Colorado 81082
(303) 846-2112

MASON CANNING COMPANY, RALPH L.
Post Office Box 34
Newark, Maryland 21841
(301) 957-3030

MASON COMPANY, L.E.
100 Business Street
Boston, Massachusetts 02136
(617) 361-1710

MASON-DIXON IMPORTS, THE
225 West King Street
Saint Paul, Minnesota 55117
(612) 224-5364

MASON-DIXON LINES, INC., THE
Eastman Road
Kingsport, Tennessee 37664
E. William King, Chairman of the Board
(615) 246-4121

MASON MARKING SYSTEMS CORPORATION
925 West 21st Street
Norfolk, Virginia 23517
(804) 627-7702

MASON SHOE MANUFACTURING COMPANY
Chippewa Falls, Wisconsin 54729
J. Owen Mason, President
(715) 723-4491

MASON STATIONERY PRODUCTS INC.
(Division of Master Woodcraft Inc.)
80 39th Street
Brooklyn, New York 11232
(212) 499-8998

MASONITE CORPORATION
29 North Wacker Drive
Chicago, Illinois 60606
Samuel S. Greeley, President
(312) 372-5642
See also Marlite

MASPETH (music boxes and door chimes)
See Coehler-Coptex Company

MASSACHUSETTS ELECTRIC COMPANY
(Subsidiary of New England Electric System)
20 Turnpike Road
Westborough, Massachusetts 01581
John I. Ahern, Chairman of the Board
(617) 366-9011

MASSACHUSETTS ENVELOPE COMPANY
30 Cobble Hill Road
Somerville, Massachusetts 02143
Steven Grossman, President
(617) 623-8000

MASSACHUSETTS MUTUAL LIFE INSURANCE COMPANY
1295 State Street
Springfield, Massachusetts 01111
William J. Clark, President
(413) 788-8411

MASSASOIT COMPANY
3500 Parkdale Avenue
Baltimore, Maryland 21211
(301) 462-4400

Companies and Trade Names

MASSEGNEZ (French fruit brandy)
See Dreyfus, Ashby & Company

MASSENGILL (feminine-hygiene products, baby products)
See Beecham Products Inc.

MASSEY-FERGUSON, INC.
1901 Bell Avenue
Des Moines, Iowa 50315
J.E. Mitchell, President
(515) 284-2011

MASSILLON WIRE BASKET COMPANY
Post Office Box 516
Massillon, Ohio 44646
(216) 833-7641

MASSO (fillets of anchovy, other fish products)
See March Company Inc.

MASSON VINEYARDS, PAUL
Post Office Box 97
Saratoga, California 95070
A. Huneeus, President
(408) 257-7800

MASTACUT (menswear)
See Barney Sampson Company, Ltd.

MASTEPS CORPORATION
4018 Bennett Valley Road
Santa Rosa, California 95404

MASTER (bread, rolls, doughnuts, toast)
See Zinsmaster Baking Company

MASTER (can openers)
See Vaughan Manufacturing Company Inc.

MASTER (foods)
See Europa Foods Ltd.

MASTER (peanut products)
See Stevens Industries, Inc.

MASTER (wood and aluminum ladders)
See Watling Ladder Company

MASTER ADDRESSER COMPANY
7506 West 27th Street
Minneapolis, Minnesota 55426
(612) 929-2681

MASTER APPLIANCE CORPORATION
2512 18th Street
Racine, Wisconsin 53403
Henry Meltzer, President
(414) 633-7791

MASTER APPLIANCES, INC.
1600 Factory Avenue
Marion, Indiana 46952

MASTER CASTER COMPANY
(Division of Master Manufacturing Company)
9200 Inman Avenue
Cleveland, Ohio 44105
(216) 641-0500

MASTER CHARGE (credit cards)
See First National City Corporation

MASTER-CRAFT CORPORATION
(Subsidiary of Shaw-Walker Company)
831 Cobb Avenue
Kalamazoo, Michigan 49001
(616) 345-2131

MASTER ELECTRONICS CORPORATION
2410 High Road
Huntingdon Valley, Pennsylvania 19006
(215) 997-6030

MASTER FENCE FITTINGS INC.
700 East Lambert Road
La Habra, California 90631
(213) 691-0815

MASTER HOSTS INTERNATIONAL
See Copper Penny Family Restaurants

MASTER LOCK COMPANY
(Subsidiary of American Brands, Inc.)
2600 North 32nd Street
Milwaukee, Wisconsin 53245
Hyland J. Barnes, President
(414) 444-2800

MASTER MANUFACTURING COMPANY
9200 Inman Avenue
Cleveland, Ohio 44105
(216) 641-0500

MASTER MOLDERS INC.
Box 815
McCoy Road
Clarksville, Texas 75426
(214) 427-2926

MASTER PRODUCTS MANUFACTURING COMPANY
3481 East 14th Street
Los Angeles, California 90023
Hal J. Webb, President and Treasurer
(213) 269-3107

MASTER SLICER (fishing equipment)
See Fishmaster Products Inc.

MASTER TROUSER CORPORATION
350 Fifth Avenue
New York, New York 10001
Emanuel G. Rosenblatt, President
(212) 564-8700

MASTER WAX (automobile cleaner/wax)
See Simoniz Company

Companies and Trade Names

MASTER WOODCRAFT INC.
80 39th Street
Brooklyn, New York 11232
Luis B. Moss, Chairman and
  President
(212) 965-2800
    See also American Visual Aids;
      and Mason Stationery
      Products Inc.

MASTERBILT FOUNDATIONS INC.
105 Temple Avenue
Hackensack, New Jersey 07601
(201) 342-0682

MASTERCRAFT (tools, hardware,
paints, sporting goods, etc.)
    See Coast to Coast Stores
      (Central Organization)

MASTERCRAFT MEDICAL &
INDUSTRIAL CORPORATION
    See Thermalene 73 (Division of
      Mastercraft Plastics, Inc.)
    See also Curvlite Surgical Products; and M.M.I. Products

MASTERCRAFT PEN COMPANY
31284 San Antonio Street
Hayward, California 94544

MASTERCRAFT PIPES, INC.
25 West 32nd Street
New York, New York 10001
Bernard Hochstein, President
(212) 736-7990
    See also Marxman Pipes Inc.

MASTERFLETCHER (archery
equipment)
    See Miller Ski Company

MASTERGLAS (plastic products)
    See Gisholt Machine Company

MASTERGUILD (housewares)
    See Stanley Roberts Inc.

MASTERIAN CHAMOIS (chamois,
sponges)
    See Schroeder & Tremayne Inc.

MASTERLINE (stacking chairs)
    See Peabody Seating Company
      Inc.

MASTERLINE (tools)
    See Gisholt Machine Company

MASTERMAT (floor mats)
    See Master Woodcraft Inc.

MASTERMATIC (deep-fat fryer)
    See J.C. Pitman & Sons, Inc.

MASTERPIECE (tobacco)
    See Liggett & Myers, Inc.

MASTERPIECE STUDIOS, INC.
3450 South 54th Avenue
Cicero, Illinois 60650
Edward I. Horwich, President
(312) 656-4000

MASTERPOINT (carpeting)
    See Bigelow-Sanford Inc.

MASTERS (tires)
    See Uniroyal, Inc.

MASTER'S, INC.
725 Summa Avenue
Westbury, New York 11590
Louis Biblowitz, Chairman of the
  Board
(516) 997-8000
    See also Lady Rose

MASTERSET BRUSHES, INC.
(Subsidiary of EZ Painter
  Corporation)
2525 East Norwich Street
Milwaukee, Wisconsin 53207
John L. Touchoff, President
(414) 481-4500

MASTERTONE (band instruments)
    See Peate Musical Supplies Ltd.

MASTERWORK (paint)
    See Harris Paint Company

MASTERWORKS (phonograph records)
    See CBS Records

MASTERY (carpeting)
    See Bigelow-Sanford Inc.

MASTI-KURE PRODUCTS COMPANY
166 Yantic Street
Norwich, Connecticut 06360
(203) 887-1663

MASTIC CORPORATION
131 South Taylor Street
South Bend, Indiana 46601
C.C. Hinds, President
(219) 288-4621

MASTIK (automotive accessories)
    See Allen Products Corporation

MASTIPAVE (floor covering)
    See Fibreboard Corporation

MASTRIPPOLITO & SONS INC., P.
Box 445
Coatesville, Pennsylvania 19320
(215) 486-0880

MASURY-COLUMBIA COMPANY
(Subsidiary of Alberto-Culver
  Company)
2525 Armitage Avenue
Melrose Park, Illinois 60160
Lawrence Zalusky, President
(312) 279-2800

MAT-O-BEL (nonreflecting flat
glass)
    See Glaverbel, Inc.

MATADOR (mobile homes)
    See Nashua Homes

Companies and Trade Names

MATADOR (tequila)
See Heublein, Inc.

MATCH MATES (shoes)
See Bristol Manufacturing Corporation

MATCHBOX MODELS OF YESTERYEAR (miniature authentic models of antique cars)
See Lesney Products Corporation

MATCHLESS (tomato products)
See Acme Preserve Company

MATCHLINE (modular furniture)
See Jasper Table Company Inc.

MATCHSTICK (draperies and blinds)
See Otto Gerdau Company

MATCO COMPANY
832 South Cooper Street
Memphis, Tennessee 38104

MATERNA-LINE, INC.
See Flexnit Company

MATEUS (Portuguese wines)
See Dreyfus, Ashby & Company

MATFER (French molds and whisks)
See B.I.A. Cordon Bleu Inc.

MATLAWS (clams)
See Codman Trading Company

MATNEY COMPANY, INC., ARTHUR
117 32nd Street
Brooklyn, New York 11232
(212) 965-4110

MATO-MIX (food products)
See Tillie Lewis Foods Inc.

MATON (acoustic and electric guitars and basses)
See Garden State Music Supply

MATSON FRUIT COMPANY
Post Office Box 307
Selah, Washington 98942
(509) 697-7100

MATSON MANUFACTURING COMPANY, INC.
347 Fifth Avenue
New York, New York 10016
(212) 725-5474

MATSUSHITA ELECTRIC CORPORATION OF AMERICA
1 Panasonic Way
Secaucus, New Jersey 07094
Akira Harada, President
(201) 348-7000
See also Quasar Electronics Corporation

MATTEL, INC.
5150 Rosecrans Avenue
Hawthorne, California 90250
Spencer Boise, Vice President, Corporate Affairs
(213) 644-0411
See also Metaframe Corporation; and Monogram Models, Inc.

MATTERHORN (men's neckwear)
See Superba Cravats Inc.

MATTHEWS & COMPANY, JAMES H.
Marking Systems Division
6688 Pennsylvania Avenue
Pittsburgh, Pennsylvania 15206
Thomas F. Purner, Jr., President
(412) 363-2500

MATTHEWS COMPANY, THE
Box M
Port Clinton, Ohio 43452
(419) 732-3154

MATTINGLY & MOORE (Bourbon whiskey)
See Calvert Distillers Company

MATTOX & MOORE INC.
1503 East Riverside Drive
Indianapolis, Indiana 46202
(317) 632-7534

MATTRESS FRESH (mildew preventive)
See Cardinal Products Corporation

MATTS (beer)
See West End Brewing Company

MAUER-NEUER (meat products)
See John Morrell & Company

MAUI PINEAPPLE COMPANY
1 California Street
San Francisco, California 94111
(415) 392-4150

MAULL COMPANY, LOUIS
215-19 North Market Street
Saint Louis, Missouri 63102
Louis T. Maull, President and Treasurer
(314) 241-8410

MAURICE CERAMICS OF CALIFORNIA
6626 Tenth Avenue
Los Angeles, California 90043
(213) 753-1771

MAURO INDUSTRIES INC., EUGENE L.
1 Pinewood Road
Poughkeepsie, New York 12603

MAURRY BIOLOGICAL COMPANY, INC.
6109 South Western Avenue
Los Angeles, California 90047
(213) 759-1127

MAUTHE (clocks)
See Coehler-Coptex Company

Companies and Trade Names

MAVAR SHRIMP & OYSTER COMPANY, LTD.
Post Office Box 208
Biloxi, Mississippi 39533
(601) 374-1373

MAVERICK (western wear)
See Blue Bell, Inc.

MAVEST INC.
1290 Avenue of the Americas
Suite 1437
New York, New York 10019
(212) 581-5710

MAVIS (bath oil, dusting powder, cologne, talcum)
See Nestle-Le Mur Company

MAVIS (hosiery)
See Rudin & Roth, Inc.

MAVRO-DAPHNE ACHAIA CLAUSS (wine)
See Carillon Importers, Ltd.

MAX (hair dryer)
See Gillette Company, Personal Care Division

MAX-AMS COMPANY
(Division of Mallet & Company, Inc.)
Carnegie, Pennsylvania 15106

MAX FACTOR & COMPANY
(Subsidiary of Norton Simon, Inc.)
1655 North McCadden Place
Hollywood, California 90028
Chester Firestein, President
(213) 462-6131
See also Denver Chemical Manufacturing Company, Inc.

MAX FROST (sports apparel)
See American Ski Corporation

MAX GERMAN MEAT COMPANY
3836 Aldine Street
Saint Louis, Missouri 63113
(314) 533-1100

MAX HATTER (hair dryer)
See Gillette Company, Personal Care Division

MAX HURNI IMPORTER INC.
Box 67
Newbury, Massachusetts 01950
(617) 462-7722

MAX-PAX (premeasured ground coffee)
See General Foods Corporation

MAXAFIL (sun-screening agent)
See Texas Pharmacal Company

MAXFIELD CANDY COMPANY
Post Office Box 554
Salt Lake City, Utah 84110
(801) 355-5321

MAXIM (cigars)
See Havatampa Cigar Corporation

MAXIM (freeze-dried coffee)
See Maxwell House

MAXIM (snails and tomatoes)
See Louis Ender Inc.

MAXIM CHEMICAL COMPANY, INC.
45 John Street
New York, New York 10038
(212) 964-8630

MAXIM CHEMICALS, LTD.
116 Bellingham Street
Chelsea, Massachusetts 02150

MAXIM COMPANY, LTD., THE
45 John Street
New York, New York 10038
(212) 964-8630

MAXIM, INC., MARY
2001 Holland Avenue
Port Huron, Michigan 48060

MAXIM LTD. (men's formal shirts)
See Merrill-Sharpe Ltd.

MAXIM MARINE COMPANY, INC.
2431 Frankford Avenue
Philadelphia, Pennsylvania 19125
(215) 425-2650

MAXIMILLIAN LUGGAGE CORPORATION
171 Madison Avenue
New York, New York 10016

MAXIMUM, INC.
8 Sterling Drive
Dover, Massachusetts 02030
(617) 785-0113

MAXON IMPORT COMPANY
710 Indiana Avenue
West Bend, Wisconsin 53095

MAXTAN (bras)
See Do-All Brassiere, Inc.

MAXWELL HOUSE
203 Kuller Road
Clifton, New Jersey 07015
(201) 271-5100

MAY-BELLA (natural cheese)
See Purity Cheese Company

MAY COMPANY, J.R.
Box 147
Friendswood, Texas 77546

Companies and Trade Names

MAY DEPARTMENT STORES
COMPANY
Sixth and Olive Streets
Saint Louis, Missouri 63101
David C. Farrell, President
(314) 436-3300
See also Famous Barr Company;
Hecht Company; and O'Neil
Company, M.

MAY HOSIERY MILLS
(Division of Wayne Gossard
Corporation)
425 Chestnut Street
Nashville, Tennessee 37202
Shepard Schwartz, President
(615) 242-1611

MAY FRESH (groceries)
See Detroit City Dairy, Inc.

MAY-LO-NAISE (food products)
See Tillie Lewis Foods Inc.

MAY-RAIN (hair-care products)
See All Brands, Inc.

MAY TAG & LABEL CORPORATION
111 West 19th Street
New York, New York 10011
Frank May, President
(212) 929-0357

MAYA (guitars)
See Rokkoman Inc.

MAYA (stainless-steel flatware)
See Georg Jensen Inc.

MAYBELLINE COMPANY
(Subsidiary of Plough Inc.)
12900 South Crawford Avenue
Chicago, Illinois 60658
H.B. Solmson, President
(312) 585-0800

MAYER & COMPANY INC., R.J.
1382 Lexington Avenue
New York, New York 10005
(212) 369-7821

MAYER & COMPANY, OSCAR
Post Office Box 1409
910 Mayer Avenue
Madison, Wisconsin 53701
Robert M. Bolz, President
(608) 241-3311

MAYER CHINA-INTERPACE
CORPORATION
Box 561
Beaver Falls, Pennsylvania 15010

MAYER COMPANY, INC.,
ERWIN W.
111 West 57th Street
New York, New York 10019
(212) 757-8840

MAYER IMPORT COMPANY, INC.
25 West 37th Street
New York, New York 10018
(212) 947-5372

MAYER LABORATORY INC.
701 Bridgeway
Sausalito, California 94965

MAYER MANUFACTURING
CORPORATION
303 State Street
Chicago Heights, Illinois 60411
(312) 757-7100

MAYER, MARTIN E.
118-09 83rd Avenue
Kew Gardens, New York 11415

MAYER, MOR L.
1133 Broadway
New York, New York 10010
(212) 243-8444

MAYFAIR (luggage)
See Hartmann Luggage Company,
Inc.

MAYFAIR (melamine products)
See Brookpark-Royalon

MAYFAIR (men's slacks)
See Corman & Wasserman, Inc.

MAYFAIR INDUSTRIES INC.
Depot Plaza
South Tarrytown, New York 10591

MAYFAIR MOLDED PRODUCTS
CORPORATION
3700 North Rose Street
Schiller Park, Illinois 60176
R.E. Theis, President and General
Manager
(312) 678-5440

MAYFIELD (menswear)
See Merit Clothing Company

MAYFIELD (whiskey)
See National Distillers &
Chemical Corporation

MAYFIELD COMPANY, H.
303 Grand Street
New York, New York 10002
(212) 226-6627

MAYFLOWER (doughnuts)
See DCA Food Industries, Inc.

MAYFLOWER (groceries)
See Sales Producers Associates

MAYFLOWER (whiskey)
See Schenley Industries, Inc.

MAYFLOWER GLASS WORKS
Post Office Box 43
Mayflower Building
Route 30 East
Latrobe, Pennsylvania 15650
(412) 539-8508

MAYFLOWER HOUSEHOLD MOVERS
See Aero Mayflower Transit
Company

Companies and Trade Names

MAYFLOWER SUPER FOODS
See Kohl's Food Stores

MAYLINE COMPANY
619 North Commerce Street
Sheboygan, Wisconsin 53081
Charles Barancik, Chairman,
    President and Treasurer
(414) 457-5538

MAYNARD (sports equipment)
See MacGregor/Brunswick

MAYNARD ENTERPRISES
Box 62
Felicity, Ohio 45120

MAYNARD INC.
2341 Milwaukee Avenue
Chicago, Illinois 60647
(312) 235-5225

MAYON CERAMICS (ironstone)
See Crown Lynn Ceramics (USA) Ltd.

MAYON FOODS OF CALIFORNIA
Box 565
Colton, California 92324
(714) 825-4014

MAYONETTE GOLD (imitation mayonnaise)
See Carter-Wallace, Inc.

MAYORK CORPORATION
1133 Broadway
New York, New York 10010
(212) 243-8159

MAYOR'S (hair coloring)
See Mayor Company

MAYO'S CUT PLUG (tobacco)
See American Tobacco Company

MAYPO (maple-flavored oatmeal)
See Standard Milling Company

MAYRAND, INC.
Box 20246
Greensboro, North Carolina 27420
(919) 275-9601

MAYROSE (meats)
See Swift & Company

MAYS, INC., J.W.
510 Fulton Street
Brooklyn, New York 11201
M.L. Shulman, President
(212) 624-7400

MAYTAG COMPANY, THE
403 West Fourth Street, North
Newton, Iowa 50208
Daniel J. Krumm, President
(515) 792-7000

MAYWOOD PACKING COMPANY
Box 588
Corning, California 96021

MAZDA MOTORS OF AMERICA, INC.
3040 East Ana Street
Compton, California 90221
Jiro Morikawa, President
(213) 537-2332

MAZE NAILS
(Division of W.H. Maze Company)
Post Office Box 449
Peru, Illinois 61354

MAZER COMPANY INC., JOSEPH J.
29 West 36th Street
New York, New York 10018
A. Lincoln Mazer, President
(212) 947-2660

MAZOLA (cooking oil)
See Best Foods (Division of CPC International Inc.)

MAZURKA (canned and pickled foods)
See San-Del Packing Company

MAZZINI (imported and domestic foods)
See Di Santo & Company

MAZZOLI COFFEE INC.
236 Avenue U
Brooklyn, New York 11223
(212) 449-0909

MCANDREWS (apparel)
See Koracorp Industries, Inc.

MCARDS MANUFACTURERS' AGENCIES
Box 163
Plainview, New York 11803

MCARTHUR-MAYFAIR (aluminum folding chairs)
See Mayfair Industries Inc.

MCATEER COMPANY, R.C.
Box 80
Ripley, New York 14775
(716) 736-4752

MCBEE LOOSE LEAF BINDER PRODUCTS
(Division of Litton Industries)
424 North Cedarbrook Avenue
Springfield, Missouri 65801
Carl D'Angelo, Vice President and
    General Manager
(417) 866-0822

MCCALL FARMS INC.
Effingham, South Carolina 29541

MCCALL PATTERN COMPANY, THE
230 Park Avenue
New York, New York 10017
Earle K. Angstandt, Jr., President
(212) 983-3200

MCCALLUM-LEGAZ FISH COMPANY INC.
Pier 66
Seattle, Washington 91821
(206) 623-5125

Companies and Trade Names

MCCANN-ERICKSON, INC.
485 Lexington Avenue
New York, New York 10017
Eugene H. Kummel, Chairman of
 the Board
(212) 697-6000

MCCARTHY SALES COMPANY
1114 Carondelet Building
New Orleans, Louisiana 70130
(504) 523-5814

MCCARTY'S SACRO-EASE
3320 Piedmont Avenue
Oakland, California 94611

MCCLANCY COMPANY, GEORGE
Southland Industrial Park
Charlotte, North Carolina 28212

MCCLEARY INDUSTRIES, INC.
South Beloit, Illinois 61080

MCCLINTOCK & COMPANY, J.M.
Box 335
Ingomar, Pennsylvania 15127

MCCLINTOCK-TRUNKEY COMPANY
East 11016 Jackson
Spokane, Washington 99206
(509) 928-7700

MCCLOSKEY VARNISH COMPANY
7600 State Road
Philadelphia, Pennsylvania 19136
Howard W. Hecht
(215) 624-4400

MCCOLLUM LABORATORIES
435 West Alondra Boulevard
Gardena, California 90247
(213) 770-2340

MCCONNON & COMPANY
25 McConnon Road
Winona, Minnesota 55987
Ben A. Miller, Chairman and
 President
(507) 452-2910

MCCORD CORPORATION
2850 West Grand Boulevard
Detroit, Michigan 48202
E. Paul Casey, President
(313) 875-7000

MCCORMICK (nuts)
 See Azar Brothers

MCCORMICK & COMPANY,
 INC.
McCormick Building
Baltimore, Maryland 21202
Harry K. Wells, President
(301) 667-7300

MCCORMICK & COMPANY, INC.
Schilling Division
1311 Schilling Place
Salinas, California 93901
 See also Baker Extract Company

MCCORMICK DISTILLING
 COMPANY
Box 38
Weston, Missouri 64098
Richard B. Cray, President
(816) 386-2276

MCCORMICK'S (whiskey)
 See Schenley Industries, Inc.

MCCOY POTTERY COMPANY,
 THE NELSON
Gordon Street
Roseville, Ohio 43777
Nelson McCoy, President
(614) 697-7331
 See also Sun-Rise Clocks

MCCOY'S PRODUCTS, INC.
101 Park Avenue
New York, New York 10017
(212) 689-2484

MCCRACKIN INDUSTRIES, INC.
Spilene Drive
Conley, Georgia 30027
Helen Steinman, President
(404) 366-9600

MCCREARY TIRE & RUBBER
 COMPANY
Box 749
Indiana, Pennsylvania 15701
Harry C. McCreary, President
(412) 357-6600

MCCRORY CORPORATION
(Subsidiary of Rapid American
 Corporation)
888 Seventh Avenue
New York, New York 10019
Meshulam Riklis, Chairman of the
 Board
(212) 889-8500
 See also Lerner Stores Corpora-
  tion; and Newberry
  Company, J.J.

MCCUBBIN HOSIERY, INC.
Post Office Box 24047
Oklahoma City, Oklahoma 73124

MCCULLOCH CORPORATION
5400 Alla Road
Los Angeles, California 90066
R.V. Dempster, President
(213) 390-8711

MCCURDY & COMPANY, INC.
285 East Main Street
Rochester, New York 14604
Gilbert J.C. McCurdy, Chairman
 of the Board
(716) 232-1000

MCDONALD & SONS, J.A.
Rogersville, Tennessee 57857
(615) 456-7621

MCDONALD CHOCOLATE
 COMPANY, MRS. J.G.
2250 South Third East
Salt Lake City, Utah 84115
(801) 487-3201

946

Companies and Trade Names

MCDONALD COMPANY, J.M.
(Division of Gamble-Skogmo, Inc.)
2635 West Second Street
Hastings, Nebraska 68901
Charles E. Trussell, President
(402) 462-5111

MCDONALD CO-OPERATIVE
   DAIRY COMPANY
Post Office Box 469
Flint, Michigan 48501
Garfield Wagner, President
(313) 232-9193

MCDONALD PRODUCTS
   CORPORATION
721 Seneca Street
Buffalo, New York 14210
Frank V. Herr, President
(911) 853-7200

MCDONALD'S CORPORATION
McDonald's Plaza
Oak Brook, Illinois 60521
Fred L. Turner, President
(312) 887-3200

MCDONOUGH POWER
   EQUIPMENT, INC.
(Subsidiary of Fuqua Industries, Inc.)
McDonough, Georgia 30253
A.A. Malizia, President
(404) 957-9141

MCDOUGALL-BUTLER
(Division of Bisonite Company, Inc.)
2250 Military Road
Tonawanda, New York 14150

MCDOWELL-CRAIG
13146 Firestone Boulevard
Norwalk, California 90650
(213) 773-3451

MCELWAIN COMPANY, J.F.
(Division of Melville Shoe
   Corporation)
12 Murphy Drive
Nashua, New Hampshire 03060
Richard E. West, President
(603) 889-6102

MCFADDEN-BARTELL
   CORPORATION
205 East 42nd Street
New York, New York 10017
Edward R. Downe, Jr., President
(212) 983-5600

MCFISHERIES, INC.
235 Northern Avenue
Boston, Massachusetts 02210
(617) 542-4135

MCGARVEY COFFEE COMPANY
1129 Currie Avenue North
Minneapolis, Minnesota 55403
Robert M. McGarvey, Jr., President
(612) 336-3611

MCGILL METAL PRODUCTS
   COMPANY
142 East Prairie Street
Marengo, Illinois 60152
S.C. Wernham, President
(815) 568-7244

MCGRAW-EDISON COMPANY
333 West River Road
Elgin, Illinois 60120
Edward J. Williams, President
(312) 741-8900
   See also Air Comfort; American
   Laundry Machinery; Bersted
   Manufacturing; Bussman
   Manufacturing; Edison Battery; Halo Lighting; International Metal Products;
   Manning-Bowman; Modern
   Maid Inc.; Portable
   Electric Tools; Speed
   Queen; and Village Blacksmith

MCGRAW-EDISON COMPANY
Air Comfort Division
704 North Clark
Albion, Michigan 49224
John Henning, President
(517) 629-2101

MCGRAW-EDISON COMPANY
Bussmann Manufacturing Division
University at Jefferson
Saint Louis, Missouri 63107
Joseph A. Bussmann, Jr., President
(314) 421-1740

MCGRAW-EDISON COMPANY
International Metal Products Division
500 South 15th Street
Phoenix, Arizona 85034
V.A. Rydberg, President
(602) 254-7101

MCGRAW-EDISON COMPANY
Portable Electric Tools Division
1200 East State
Geneva, Illinois 60134
Robert Schultz, President
(312) 232-2500

MCGRAW-EDISON COMPANY
Time Products Division
333 West River Road
Elgin, Illinois 60120
E.J. Williams, President
(312) 741-8900

MCGRAW-HILL BOOK COMPANY
1221 Avenue of the Americas
New York, New York 10020
Harold W. McGraw, President
(212) 997-1221

MCGRAW-HILL, INC.
1221 Avenue of the Americas
New York, New York 10020
Harold W. McGraw, Jr., President
   and Chief Executive Officer
(212) 997-1221
   See also American Heritage
   Publishing Company, Inc.;
   and Standard & Poor's
   Corporation

MCGREGOR & COMPANY
18063 James Couzens Highway
Detroit, Michigan 48235
(313) 342-7040

Companies and Trade Names

MCGREGOR-DONIGER, INC.
666 Fifth Avenue
New York, New York 10019
Stanley C. Gillette, President
(212) 245-0800

MCHUTCHISON & COMPANY, INC.
695 Grand Avenue
Ridgefield, New Jersey 07657
(201) 943-2230

MCKEE & COMPANY, LANNESS K.
Box 207
404 Sandy Street
Fairmont, North Carolina 28340
(919) 628-7940

MCILHENNY COMPANY
Avery Island, Louisiana 70513
Walter S. McIlhenny, President
(318) 365-8173

MCKEE BAKING COMPANY
Post Office Box 750
Apison Pike
Collegedale, Tennessee 37315
O.D. McKee, Chairman of the Board
(615) 396-2151

MCKEE CITY DISTRIBUTORS INC.
406 English Creek Avenue
McKee City, New Jersey 08232

MCKENZIE (frozen foods)
See Southern Frozen Foods Inc.

MCKENZIE BOAT MANUFACTURING COMPANY
Box Ten
121 North Highland Drive
McKenzie, Tennessee 38201
(901) 352-3392

MCKEON PRODUCTS COMPANY
23220 Ithaca Street
Oak Park, Michigan 48237

MCKESSON & ROBBINS DRUG COMPANY
Crocker Plaza
San Francisco, California 95111
George M. Keller, President
(415) 983-8300
See also Norcliff Laboratories

MCKESSON LABORATORIES
Box 548
Bridgeport, Connecticut 06602

MCKESSON LIQUOR COMPANY
(Division of Foremost-McKesson, Inc.)
155 East 44th Street
New York, New York 10017
Raymond R. Herrmann, Jr., President
(212) 557-0300

MCKINNEY SAILBOAT SALES
10239 Prospect Avenue
Santee, California 92071

MCLAUGHLIN GORMLEY KING COMPANY
8810 Tenth Avenue North
Minneapolis, Minnesota 55427
William D. Gullickson, President
(612) 544-0341

MCLEAN TRUCKING COMPANY
Post Office Box 213
Winston-Salem,
   North Carolina 27102
Amory Mellen, Jr., President
(919) 724-6341

MCMILLAN BOOK COMPANY INC.
128 Spencer Street
Syracuse, New York 13201
(315) 472-4385

MCMILLAN MUSIC COMPANY
2815 Philmont Avenue
Huntingdon Valley,
   Pennsylvania 19006

MCMILLIN FOLEY PUBLISHING COMPANY
6126 Broadway
Cleveland, Ohio 44128
(216) 641-2119

MCMULLEN FOOD BANK INC.
205 Houston Avenue S.W.
Live Oak, Florida 32060

MCNAIR MARINE INC.
Box 3770
Higganum, Connecticut 06441

MCNAUGHTON'S (liquor)
See Schenley Industries, Inc.

MCNEIL LABORATORIES, INC.
Camp Hill Road
Fort Washington,
   Pennsylvania 19034
John H. Kip, President
(215) 836-4500

MCQUAY NORRIS MANUFACTURING COMPANY
See Eaton Corporation, Aftermarket Division

MCQUEEN'S PURE MUTTON TALLOW
Route One
Nunnelly, Tennessee 37137

ME (apparel)
See Puritan Fashions Corporation

MEAD CORPORATION, THE
118 West First Street
Dayton, Ohio 45401
James W. McSwiney, Chairman of the Board
(513) 222-9561
See also Gilbert Paper Company; Montag; and Vernon Company, S.E.&M.

Companies and Trade Names

MEAD-HATCHER ASSOCIATES
752 Military Road
Buffalo, New York 14216
(716) 877-1185

MEAD JOHNSON & COMPANY
(Subsidiary of Bristol-Myers
    Company)
2400 West Pennsylvania Street
Evansville, Indiana 47712
James M. Tuholski, M.D., President
(812) 426-6000

MEAD PAPERS
Talbott Tower
Dayton, Ohio 45402
(513) 222-9561

MEAD-RAYMOND CORPORATION
25005 S.W. 193rd Avenue
Homestead, Florida 33030

MEADOW GOLD (ice cream, butter, and milk)
    See Beatrice Foods Company

MEADOW QUEEN (diary products)
    See Mid-West Producers
        Creameries, Inc.

MEADOWBROOK (dairy products)
    See Sommer Maid Creamery, Inc.

MEADOWCRAFT (wrought-iron furniture)
    See Birmingham Ornamental
        Iron Company Inc.

MEADOWDALE (grocery products)
    See Allied Supermarkets, Inc.

MEADWOOD (whiskey)
    See American Distilling Company,
        Inc.)

MEAKINS MCKINNON, INC.
378 Niagara Street
Lockport, New York 14094

MEANS ENTERPRISES, INC.
Post Office Box 8310
Phoenix, Arizona 85066

MEARL CORPORATION, THE
217 North Highland Avenue
Ossining, New York 10562

MEASUREMADE (shoes)
    See E.T. Wright & Company,
        Inc.

MEAT SEASONINGS, INC.
West 406 Third Avenue
Spokane, Washington 99204
(509) 624-6155

MEAT TRADING COMPANY, INC.
325 Spring Street
New York, New York 10013
(212) 924-2933

MECHANICAL ENTERPRISES INC.
8000 Forbes Place
Springfield, Virginia 22154
R.H. Twyford, President
(703) 321-8282

MECHANICAL METHODS
COMPANY
3400 South Federal Highway
Fort Lauderdale, Florida 33316

MECHANICAL MIRROR WORKS
Post Office Box 220
New York, New York 10032
(212) 795-2100

MED-A-SAFE
(Division of Hayes-Albion
    Corporation)
437 Fern
Jackson, Michigan 49202

MEDA-PEDIC (juvenile bedding)
    See Nurserytyme Products Inc.

MEDAGLIA D'ORO (espresso)
    See S.A. Schonbrunn &
        Company, Inc.

MEDAL DISTRIBUTING COMPANY
330 Vine Avenue
Sharon, Pennsylvania 16146

MEDALIE MANUFACTURING
COMPANY
5211 Lakeland Avenue
Minneapolis, Minnesota 55429
(612) 535-1286

MEDALIST (cigars)
    See Bayuk Cigars, Inc.

MEDALIST (skates)
    See Chicago Roller Skate
        Company

MEDALIST INDUSTRIES INC.
735 North Fifth Street
Milwaukee, Wisconsin 53203
Reimer A. Perkins, President
(414) 271-8186
    See also Can-Pro; Cut'n Jump
        Ski Corporation; Medalist
        Ripon Industries; Medalist
        Water Sports; and Ripon
        Industries, Inc.

MEDALIST RIPON INDUSTRIES
(Division of Medalist Industries Inc.)
107 East Mullet Street
Portage, Wisconsin 53901
W.R. Murphy, President and
    General Manager
(608) 742-5535

MEDALIST WATER SPORTS
(Subsidiary of Medalist Industries Inc.)
11525 Sorrento Valley Road
San Diego, California 92121

MEDALLION (melamine products)
    See Boonton Molding Company,
        Inc.

Companies and Trade Names

MEDALLION INSTRUMENTS INC.
917 West Savidge Street
Spring Lake, Michigan 49456
(616) 842-0650

MEDALLION POOL CORPORATION
3 Sidney Court
Lindenhurst, New York 11757
(212) 893-2500

MEDANA WATCH CORPORATION
14 East 32nd Street
New York, New York 10016
(212) 889-3564

MEDCO SUPPLY COMPANY
2410 Kilgore Avenue
Muncie, Indiana 47304

MEDCOVA, INC.
Box 722
Harrisonburg, Virginia 22801

MEDDOLAND (canned foods)
See Stanislaus Food Products Company

MEDEX CORPORATION
323 Niagara Street
Buffalo, New York 14201
(716) 853-6380

MEDI-BAND (spray-on bandage)
See Purepac Corporation

MEDI-CHRON (timepiece for taking medicine)
See General Time Corporation

MEDI, INC.
27 Maple Avenue
Holbrook, Massachusetts 02343
Roger E. Travis, President
(617) 767-1232

MEDI-KIT (first-aid kits)
See Acme Cotton Products Company, Inc.

MEDI-QUIK (first-aid spray)
See Lehn & Fink Consumer Products

MEDIATRIC (steroids, dietary supplement, antidepressant)
See Ayerst Laboratories

MEDIC-AIR (room vaporizer spray)
See Halsey Drug Company, Inc.

MEDICAL ARTS LABORATORIES, INC.
1106 13th Street
Tuscaloosa, Alabama 35401

MEDICAL CHEMICALS CORPORATION
2137 North 15th Avenue
Melrose Park, Illinois 60160

MEDICAL DRUG PRODUCTS
2312 West Main Street
Evanston, Illinois 60202

MEDICAL ECONOMICS COMPANY
(Division of Litton Publications)
550 Kinderkamack Road
Oradell, New Jersey 07649
Charles P. Daly, President
(201) 262-3030

MEDICAL PRODUCTS PANAMERICANA, INC.
Box 771
Coral Gables, Florida 33134

MEDICAL PROFESSIONALS INC.
Box 126
Monterey, Tennessee 38574

MEDICAL SERVICES INC.
Box 1185
Tulsa, Oklahoma 74101
(918) 589-5247

MEDICAL SUPPLY COMPANY
3703 North Main Street
Rockford, Illinois 61101

MEDICAL WORLD, INC.
2301 Main Street
Evanston, Illinois 60202

MEDICO (sports apparel)
See Sport-Obermeyer Ltd.

MEDICONE COMPANY
225 Varick Street
New York, New York 10014
(212) 924-5166

MEDICS PHARMACEUTICAL CORPORATION
203 Rio Circle
Decatur, Georgia 30030

MEDIPROD LABORATORIES, INC.
Box 686
Selma, Alabama 36701

MEDIQUE LABORATORIES
2312 Main Street
Evanston, Illinois 60202

MEDISCO, INC.
520 Broadway
New York, New York 10012
(212) 925-1474

MEDLEY BROTHERS (whiskey)
See Renfield Importers, Ltd.

MEDLIN (mildew preventive)
See Noble Pine Products Company

MEDOMAK CANNING COMPANY
Box 100
Winslow's Mills, Maine 04577

MEDS (tampons)
See Personal Products Company

Companies and Trade Names

MEDUSA CORPORATION
Box 5668
Monticello and Lee
Cleveland, Ohio 44101
Robert W. Fort, President and
 Chief Executive Officer
(216) 371-4000

MEDUSA PORTLAND CEMENT
COMPANY
See Medusa Corporation

MEEHANITE METAL CORPORATION
New King Street
White Plains, New York 10604

MEEKER COMPANY
Seventh and School Streets
Joplin, Missouri 64801
(417) 623-8500

MEER CORPORATION
9500 Railroad Avenue
North Bergen, New Jersey 07047
George Meer, Jr., President
(201) 861-9500

MEERGANS COMPANY INC.,
 GUENTHER
South Main Street
Route 114
Middleton, Massachusetts 01949

MEETER BROTHERS & COMPANY
Union Grove, Wisconsin 53182
(414) 878-1231

MEGA INDUSTRIES CORPORATION
64A Brook Avenue
Deer Park, New York 11729
(516) 586-7029

MEGO CORPORATION
41 Madison Avenue
New York, New York 10010
(212) 689-8600

MEGUIAR'S MIRROR GLAZE
(chrome and metal polish)
See Mirror Bright Polish Company

MEHER ENTERPRISES INC.
115 West 30th Street
New York, New York 10001
(212) 594-9055

MEHLER-ZARIN CORPORATION
99 West Hawthorne
Valley Stream, New York 11582

MEHRON, INC.
325 West 37th Street
New York, New York 10036
(212) 564-3466

MEHTA INTERNATIONAL
Box 523
Hatboro, Pennsylvania 19040

MEIER & FRANK DEPARTMENT
STORES
See May Department Stores
 Company

MEIER, JOSHUA
(Division of W.R. Grace &
 Company)
7401 West Side Avenue
North Bergen, New Jersey 07047
Jack Mintzer, President
(201) 869-8200
See also Banov-Bernsley &
 Company

MEIER'S WINE CELLARS, INC.
6955 Plainfield Pike
Cincinnati, Ohio 45236
Charles Safran, President
(513) 891-2900

MEIJER, INC.
2727 Walker Avenue
Grand Rapids, Michigan 49504
Frederick Meijer, President
(616) 451-2801

MEIJI (food products)
See L.J. Rench & Company

MEILINK STEEL SAFE COMPANY
Post Office Box 2847
1672 Oakwood Avenue
Toledo, Ohio 43607
James J. Akers, President
(419) 536-4641

MEISEL MUSIC COMPANY INC., C.
6451 San Fernando Road
Glendale, California 91201

MEISTER BRAU, INC.
1000 West North Avenue
Chicago, Illinois 60622
J.W. Howard, President
(312) 664-6300

MEISTER KNIT (sports apparel)
See Hagemeister-Lert Inc.

MEITETSU, INC.
24 California
San Francisco, California 94111
(415) 362-2557

MEL BAY PUBLICATIONS INC.
107 Jefferson
Kirkwood, Missouri 63122

MEL-L-KOTE (paints)
See Adelphi Paint & Color
 Works, Inc.

MEL-O-GOLD COMPANY
327 East Edison Avenue
Des Moines, Iowa 50315
(515) 283-2553

MELADUR (melamine dinnerware)
See Stetson Corporation

MELAN MANUFACTURING
 COMPANY
Post Office Box 22074
243 Jefferson Avenue
Memphis, Tennessee 38122
(901) 522-8250

Companies and Trade Names

MELARD MANUFACTURING
   CORPORATION
153 Linden Street
Passaic, New Jersey 07055
Sidney J. Shames, President
(212) 881-4444

MELBOURNE CANNING COMPANY
Drawer 879
Melbourne, Florida 32901

MELCO FOUNDRY &
   MANUFACTURING COMPANY
820 North Wolcott Avenue
Chicago, Illinois 60622
(312) 772-4470

MELCOR ELECTRONICS
   CORPORATION
(Subsidiary of Newton Electronics
   Systems Inc.)
1750 New Highway
Farmingdale, New York 11735
Edward Helfer, President
(516) 694-5570

MELCORT, INC. (direct mail
footwear)
   See Melville Shoe Company

MELDONA, INC.
13-15 Industrial Avenue
Fairview, New Jersey 07022

MELE LOKE PUBLISHING
   COMPANY
Box 7142
Honolulu, Hawaii 96821
(808) 734-8611

MELE MANUFACTURING
   COMPANY INC.
10 East 34th Street
New York, New York 10016
(212) 689-4421

MELGES BOAT WORKS INC.
Box 1-BG
Zenda, Wisconsin 53195

MELHADO & COMPANY, LOUIS
1641 Hyde Park Avenue
Boston, Massachusetts 02136
(617) 364-3400

MELIND COMPANY
3524 North Clark Street
Chicago, Illinois 60657
(312) 477-4200

MELINI (Italian wine)
   See Renfield Importers, Ltd.

MELITTA INC.
1401 Berlin Road
Cherry Hill, New Jersey 08034

MELLO (food products)
   See Blue Banner Foods Inc.

MELLO-GLO PRODUCTS
30 Corwood Drive
Weston, Massachusetts 02193

MELLODY LANE FOODS
(Division of Hawthorn Mellody,
   Inc.)
4201 West Chicago Avenue
Chicago, Illinois 60651
John P. Ryan, President
(312) 638-7800

MELLON NATIONAL BANK &
   TRUST COMPANY
Mellon Square
Pittsburgh, Pennsylvania 15230
James H. Higgins, Chairman of
   the Board
(412) 232-4100

MELLOWEVE (men's furnishings)
   See Knothe Brothers Company
      Inc.

MELLOWOOD (kitchen cabinets)
   See Kitchen Kompact, Inc.

MELMAC (melamine dinnerware)
   See American Cyanamid Company

MELNOR INDUSTRIES
1 Carol Place
Moonachie, New Jersey 07074
Joseph E. Testa, President
(201) 641-5000
   See also Walton Laboratories

MELO ENVELOPE COMPANY INC.
665 Broadway
New York, New York 10012
(212) 777-3271

MELODIE (fabric brightener and
spray starch)
   See Shulton, Inc.

MELODIGRAND (pianos)
   See Aeolian Corporation

MELODY HOMES MANUFACTURING
   COMPANY
Box 1227
Fort Worth, Texas 76101
Lee Paulsel, Chairman of the Board
(817) 232-0350

MELOSKY CUT GLASSWARE
20 West Northampton Street
Wilkes-Barre, Pennsylvania 18701

MELOTI (piano accordions)
   See Coast Wholesale Music
      Company of Los Angeles

MELOTONE (accordions)
   See Massimino Music Studio

MELROE
(Division of Clark Equipment
   Company)
Gwinner, North Dakota 58040

MELROSE DISTILLERS, INC.
   See Schenley Industries, Inc.

Companies and Trade Names

MELROSE LAMP & SHADE
   COMPANY, INC.
11 Canal Place
Bronx, New York 10451
(212) 635-8800

MELSTER CANDIES INC.
Box 47
Madison Street
Cambridge, Wisconsin 53523
Raymond G. Wheeler, Chairman
   and President
(608) 423-3221

MELTZ ICE (ice- and snow-melting
compound)
   See Empire Chemical Products
   Company

MELVILLE CONFECTIONS, INC.
   See Curtiss Candy Company

MELVILLE SHOE CORPORATION
3000 Westchester Avenue
Harrison, New York 10528
Ward Melville, Chairman of the
   Board
(914) 253-8000
   See also McElwain Company,
   J.F.; and Metro Pants
   Company, Inc.

MEM COMPANY, INC.
Union Street
Northvale, New Jersey 07647
Gay H. Meyer, President
(201) 767-0100
   See also Fields Ltd., Tom

MEMENTO (watches)
   See Windert Watch Company

MEMINDEX INC.
149 Carter
Rochester, New York 14621
(716) 342-7740

MEMOCORD
78 East Palisade Avenue
Englewood, New Jersey 07631
(201) 567-5200

MEMPHIS FURNITURE
   MANUFACTURING COMPANY
715 South Camilla
Memphis, Tennessee 38101
S.R. Leatherman, Jr., President
(901) 527-1401

MEMPHIS LIGHT GAS & WATER
   DIVISION
220 South Main Street
Memphis, Tennessee 38101
Calvin R. Henze, President
(901) 528-4011

MEN PREFER (men's toiletries)
   See Swank, Inc.

MENDELL COMPANY INC.,
   EDWARD
185 Ashburton Avenue
Yonkers, New York 10702

MENDORA (rattan furniture)
   See Ficks Reed Company

MENLEY & JAMES LABORATORIES
(Subsidiary of Smith, Kline &
   French Laboratories)
1500 Spring Garden Street
Philadelphia, Pennsylvania 19101
Peter Godfrey, President
(215) 854-5000

MENLO PARK (old-fashioned lamps
and light bulbs)
   See American Jubilee Company

MENNEL MILLING COMPANY
128 West Crocker Street
Fostoria, Ohio 44830
Donald M. Mennel, President and
   Treasurer
(419) 435-8151

MENNEN COMPANY, THE
Box 1000
Hanover Avenue
Morristown, New Jersey 07960
John P. Kennedy, President
(201) 538-7100

MEN'S CLASSIC, INC.
120 Broadway
Suite 3013
New York, New York 10005
(212) 267-1900

MEN'S LIFTS (support hose)
   See Modern Globe Sales, Inc.

MENSE, INC.
8004 California Avenue
Fair Oaks, California 95628

MENTHOLATUM COMPANY, THE
1360 Niagara Street
Buffalo, New York 14213
George T. Hyde, President
(716) 882-7660

MENTOS PRODUCTS COMPANY
6010 Haverford Avenue
Philadelphia, Pennsylvania 19151
(215) 472-5934

MENTOSAN COMPANY, THE
78-63 76th Street
Glendale, New York 11227

MENU-MAKER (frozen vegetables)
   See Stokely-Van Camp Inc.

MENU MASTER (microwave oven)
   See Litton Industries Inc.,
   Atherton Division

MENU-PAK (canned meats)
   See Wilson & Company, Inc.

MENULISTO (frozen and canned
meats)
   See Caribtrade Corporation

MEPHISTO TOOL COMPANY INC.
Post Office Box 16
Hudson, New York 12534
(518) 828-1563

Companies and Trade Names

MERANO (guitars, accordions, concertinas)
See J.M. Sahlein Music Company

MERCANTILE MANUFACTURING COMPANY INC.
314 Dennis Drive
Minden, Louisiana 71055
(318) 377-0844

MERCANTILE STORES COMPANY
7 South Orchard
Boise, Idaho 83707
Henry C. Flenor, President
(208) 343-0581

MERCANTILE STORES COMPANY, INC.
100 West Tenth Street
Wilmington, Delaware 19801
James C. Lovell, President
(302) 658-7581

MERCANTILE TRUST COMPANY, N.A.
721 Locust Street
Saint Louis, Missouri 63101
Donald E. Lasater, Chairman of the Board
(314) 231-3500

MERCANTUM TRADING COMPANY
225 Broadway
New York, New York 10007
(212) 233-0412

MERCEDES (musical instruments)
See Selmer (Division of Magnavox Company)

MERCEDES-BENZ OF NORTH AMERICA, INC.
1 Mercedes Drive
Montvale, New Jersey 07645
Karlfried Nordmann, President
(201) 573-0600

MERCER CONSOLIDATED CORPORATION
216 Lake Avenue
Yonkers, New York 10701

MERCER GLASS WORKS, INC.
725 Broadway
New York, New York 10003
(212) 673-5620

MERCER MILLING COMPANY
Baldwinsville, New York 13027

MERCHANDISING CONCEPTS INC.
(Subsidiary of CTP Industries Inc.)
1019 East 46 Street
Brooklyn, New York 11203
(212) 469-1300

MERCHANT & EVANS COMPANY
100 Connecticut Drive
Burlington, New Jersey 08016
James M. O'Donnell, President and Chief Executive Officer
(609) 287-3033

MERCHANT PRINCE CORPORATION
2305 Rhode Island Avenue N.E.
Washington, D.C. 20018
(202) 635-0200

MERCHANTS & MANUFACTURERS SUPPLY INC.
2100 East Bessemer
Greensboro, North Carolina 27405

MERCHANTS BOX COMPANY
230 Fifth Avenue
New York, New York 10001

MERCHANTS COFFEE COMPANY, INC.
800 Magazine
New Orleans, Louisiana 70150
(504) 581-7515

MERCHANTS IMPORTING INC.
65 West 36th Street
New York, New York 10018
(212) 947-8646

MERCHANTS NATIONAL BANK & TRUST COMPANY
11 South Meridian Street
Indianapolis, Indiana 46204
Donald W. Tanselle, President
(317) 638-2461

MERCHANTS TRADING COMPANY, INC.
105 Hudson Street
New York, New York 10013

MERCIER (bicycle)
See Beacon Cycle & Supply Company

MERCK & COMPANY, INC.
126 East Lincoln Avenue
Rahway, New Jersey 07065
John J. Horan, President
(201) 574-4000
See also Animal Health Products; Calgon Consumer Products Company; and Calgon Corporation

MERCUROCHROME (medical preparation)
See Hynson, Westcott & Dunning, Inc.

MERCURY (motor vehicles)
See Lincoln-Mercury (Division of Ford Motor Company)

MERCURY (water skis and accessories)
See Nash Manufacturing, Inc.

MERCURY CASUALS (menswear)
See Cross Country Clothes

MERCURY MARINE
(Division of Brunswick Corporation)
Fond du Lac, Wisconsin 54935
J.F. Reichert, President
(414) 921-8220

Companies and Trade Names

MERCURY RECORD PRODUCTIONS, INC.
35 East Wacker Drive
Chicago, Illinois 60601
Irwin H. Steinberg, President
(312) 332-5788

MERCURY SAILBOATS
6355 Hollis Street
Emeryville, California 94608

MERCURY SLIPPERS
(Division of Kayser-Roth Corporation)
1221 Avenue of the Americas
New York, New York 10020
Jay Greenblatt, President
(212) 764-4050

MERDEL GAME MANUFACTURING COMPANY
Ludington, Michigan 49431

MEREDITH CORPORATION
1716 Locust Street
Des Moines, Iowa 50336
Robert A. Burnett, President
(515) 284-9011

MERICON INDUSTRIES
420 S.W. Washington
Peoria, Illinois 61602

MERIDIAN FOODS INC.
Box 155
Eaton, Indiana 47338

MERINO WOOL COMPANY, INC.
1140 Broadway
New York, New York 10001
(212) 686-0050

MERIT CLOTHING COMPANY, INC.
South Fifth
Mayfield, Kentucky 42066
Howard Hawes, President
(502) 247-3510

MERIT ENTERPRISES, INC.
(Division of Atlas Corporation)
577 Wortman Avenue
Brooklyn, New York 11208
Paul Fine, President
(212) 649-1800

MERIT FOUNDATIONS
27 Harrison Street
Bridgeport, Connecticut 06603

MERIT INDUSTRIES INC.
3103 Executive Parkway
Toledo, Ohio 43694

MERIT LINGERIE COMPANY
483 Broadway
New York, New York 10013
(212) 226-5095

MERIT PHARMACAL COMPANY
Main Street
Somers, Connecticut 06071

MERIT PHARMACEUTICAL COMPANY, INC.
Box 12625
8243 Telephone Street
Houston, Texas 77017
(713) 644-5474

MERIT WATCH COMPANY, INC.
630 Fifth Avenue
New York, New York 10020
(212) 247-3118

MERKIN (paints)
See Baltimore Paint & Chemical Corporation

MERLE COMPANY, AMY
64 Lakeview Avenue
Clifton, New Jersey 07015

MERLE NORMAN COSMETICS
9130 Bellanca Avenue
Los Angeles, California 90045
Robert Nethercutt, President
(213) 641-3000

MERLITE INDUSTRIES INC.
116 Fifth Avenue
New York, New York 10016
(212) 924-6440

MERMAID (canned seafood)
See L.P. Maggioni & Company

MEROLA, INC., C.J.
82 Beaver Street
New York, New York 10005
(212) 422-4970

MERRELL-NATIONAL LABORATORIES
(Division of Richardson-Merrell, Inc.)
110 East Amity Road
Cincinnati, Ohio 45215
Ivan S. Husonsky, President
(513) 948-9111

MERRELL-SOULE (food products)
See Borden Inc.

MERRIAM COMPANY, G. & C.
(Subsidiary of Encyclopedia Britannica, Inc.)
47 Federal Street
Springfield, Massachusetts 01101
William A. Llewellyn, President
(413) 734-3134

MERRIAM MANUFACTURING COMPANY
100 Main Street
Durham, Connecticut 06422
(203) 349-3436

MERRIBEE COMPANY
(Subsidiary of Tandy Corporation)
2904 West Lancaster Street
Fort Worth, Texas 76107
(817) 335-9414

MERRICK MEDICINE COMPANY, INC.
Post Office Box 1489
501 South Eighth Street
Waco, Texas 76703
(817) 753-3461

Companies and Trade Names

MERRIE ENGLAND, INC.
220 Ferris Avenue
White Plains, New York 10603

MERRILL BLUEBERRY FARMS INC.
Box 149
Ellsworth, Maine 04605

MERRILL LYNCH, PIERCE,
    FENNER & SMITH, INC.
1 Liberty Plaza
New York, New York 10006
Donald T. Regan, Chairman of the
    Board
(212) 766-1212

MERRILL-SHARPE LTD.
181 Madison Avenue
New York, New York 10016
(212) 679-0750

MERRIMAID MANUFACTURING
    COMPANY, INC.
22 Amherst Street
Manchester, New Hampshire 03101

MERRIMAN HOLBROOK INC.
301 River Street
Grand River, Ohio 44065
(216) 352-8988

MERRY (mops, brooms, paint rollers)
    See Corcoran Manufacturing
        Company, Inc.

MERRY GO ROUND (bars)
    See Park Industries, Inc.

MERRY MAID (canned foods,
clothespins)
    See Rex Sales, Inc.

MERRY MANUFACTURING
    COMPANY (farm and garden
    equipment)
Edmonds, Washington 98020

MERRY MITES (children's apparel)
    See Villager Industries, Inc.

MERRY TUNE ANIMALS (musical
toys)
    See Gund Manufacturing
        Company

MERRY'S CANDIES
Post Office Box 764
Oak Park, Illinois 60303

MERSMAN BROTHERS
(Division of Congoleum Industries,
    Inc.)
Celina, Ohio 45822
R.H. Clapp, President
(419) 586-2351

MERWOOD SPECIALTY COMPANY
Box 3987
Anaheim, California 92803

MESPO UMBRELLA COMPANY,
    INC.
22 West 32nd Street
New York, New York 10001
(212) 279-9631

MESSAGE CENTER (telephone-
answering device)
    See Dictaphone Corporation

MESSENGER (radiotelephone)
    See E.F. Johnson Company

MESSER IMPORT CORPORATION
38 West 32nd Street
New York, New York 10001
(212) 947-5525

MESSER IMPORTS, SONIA
527 West Seventh Street
Suite 404
Los Angeles, California 90014
(213) 622-5068

MESSIRE (men's toiletries)
    See Norwich Pharmacal
        Company, Jean D'Albert
        Division

METABOLIC PRODUCTS
    CORPORATION
37 Hurley Street
Cambridge, Massachusetts 02141

METAFORA COMPANY, INC.,
    LOUIS
148 State
Boston, Massachusetts 02109
(617) 742-0544

METAFRAME CORPORATION
(Division of Mattel, Inc.)
87 Route 17
Maywood, New Jersey 07607
Harding W. Willinger, President
(201) 845-4900

METAL GLOW (polish)
    See Continental Chemical
        Corporation

METAL KLEAN (metal cleaner)
    See Sunbeam Corporation

METAL KLEENER
    See H.A. Calahan

METAL MARINE PILOT INC.
2219 Mildred Street West
Tacoma, Washington 98466
(206) 564-5902

METAL PRODUCTS ENGINEERING
    INC.
3864 Santa Fe
Los Angeles, California 90058
(213) 581-8121

METAL TEXTILE COMPANY
(Division of General Cable
    Corporation)
Box 315
South Bound Brook,
    New Jersey 08880

Companies and Trade Names

METAL WARE CORPORATION, THE
1700 Monroe
Two Rivers, Wisconsin 54241
W.C. Drumm, President
(414) 793-1368

METALART COMPANY
(Division of Crownmark Corporation)
166 Valley Street
Providence, Rhode Island 02909
(401) 521-6410

METALCRAFT (furniture, gifts, and accessories)
See George Koch Sons Inc.

METALCRAFT ENGINEERING COMPANY
3625 North 48th Street
Lincoln, Nebraska 68504

METALCRAFT INC.
149 Fourth Street S.W.
Mason City, Iowa 50401
(515) 423-9460

METALCRETE MANUFACTURING COMPANY
10330 Brecksville
Cleveland, Ohio 44131
(216) 526-5600

METALIZED CERAMICS CORPORATION
100 Niantic Avenue
Providence, Rhode Island 02907
Harold Ottobrini, President and Secretary
(401) 943-2200

METALMAST MARINE
Box 471-Y
Putnam, Connecticut 06260

METALSTAND COMPANY
11200 Roosevelt Boulevard
Philadelphia, Pennsylvania 19115
Joel H. Golden, President
(215) 673-5300

METALTEX INC.
70 Avenue A
Bayonne, New Jersey 07002
(201) 436-4734

METAMUCIL (laxative, reducing aid)
See Searle Laboratories

METASCO, INC.
401 Fifth Avenue
New York, New York 10016
Leonard C. Smith, President
(212) 764-2345

METAWEB (nonwoven fabrics)
See Kendall Company

METAXA (brandy)
See Austin, Nichols & Company, Inc.

METCALF CHARCOAL COMPANY
Mount Vernon, Illinois 62864

METEOR INC.
135 East Railroad Avenue
Monrovia, California 91016
(213) 357-2211

METHODS RESEARCH CORPORATION
Department OP
46 Asbury Avenue
Farmingdale, New Jersey 07727
(201) 988-6000

METHOW (produce)
See Floyd Dahn Fruits, Inc.

METHOW-PATEROS GROWERS, INC.
Pateros, Washington 98846

METLOX POTTERIES
1200 Morningside Drive
Manhattan Beach, California 90266
(213) 545-4516
See also Vernonware

METRECAL (reducing aid)
See Drackett Company

METRO (food products)
See Globe Products Company Inc.

METRO EQUIPMENT CORPORATION
Box 187
Agnew Station
Santa Clara, California 95054
(408) 247-8787

METRO-FLOR, INC.
137 Commercial Street
Plainview, New York 11803

METRO GAME MANUFACTURING CORPORATION
145-55 226th Street
Jamaica, New York 11413
(212) 525-8500

METRO-GOLDWYN-MAYER, INC.
10202 West Washington Boulevard
Culver City, California 90230
Fred Benninger, Chairman of the Board
(213) 836-3000

METRO MED., INC.
2502-06 South Boulevard
Houston, Texas 77006

METRO MOSAICS, INC.
137 Commercial Street
Plainview, New York 11803

METRO PANTS COMPANY, INC.
(Division of Melville Shoe Corporation)
390 Fifth Avenue
New York, New York 10018
Milton M. Winograd, Chairman of the Board
(212) 695-9380

Companies and Trade Names

METRO-TEL CORPORATION
409 Railroad Avenue
Westbury, New York 11590
Venerando J. Indelicato, President
(516) 333-7650

METROMEDIA, INC.
277 Park Avenue
New York, New York 10017
John W. Kluge, President
(212) 682-9100

METROPOLITAN (pianos)
See Grand Piano Company Inc.

METROPOLITAN (women's shoes)
See Craddock-Terry Shoe
Corporation

METROPOLITAN CUTLERY
COMPANY
25-27 West 36th Street
New York, New York 10018
(212) 947-5322

METROPOLITAN EDISON
COMPANY
Post Office Box 542
Reading, Pennsylvania 19603
W.M. Creitz, President
(215) 929-3601

METROPOLITAN GREETINGS INC.
215 First Street
Cambridge, Massachusetts 02142
Joan Sann, Chairman and President
(617) 661-0050

METROPOLITAN HOUSEWARES
CORPORATION
101-04 Liberty Avenue
Ozone Park, New York 11417

METROPOLITAN LIFE INSURANCE
COMPANY
1 Madison Avenue
New York, New York 10010
Richard R. Shinn, President
(212) 578-2211

METROPOLITAN TRANSIT
AUTHORITY (MTA)
1700 Broadway
New York, New York 10019
William T. Ronan, Chairman
(212) 262-6900
See also Long Island Railroad
Company, The

METROPOLITAN UTILITIES DISTRICT
1723 Harney Street
Omaha, Nebraska 68102
Frank L. Frost, Chairman of the
Board
(402) 341-5760

METROPOLITAN VACUUM
CLEANER COMPANY INC.
19 Wayne Avenue
Suffern, New York 10901

METROPOLITAN WIRE GOODS
CORPORATION
North Washington Street and
George Avenue
Wilkes-Barre, Pennsylvania 18705

METZ BAKING COMPANY
1500 United States Highway 75
North
Sioux City, Iowa 51108
Dale C. Putman, President
(712) 255-7611

METZ OLD HOME BAKERY OF
RAPID CITY
601 12th Street
Rapid City, South Dakota 57701

MEULIEN-PIGNERET (French wines)
See Park, Benziger & Company

MEXENE (food products)
See Austex Foods (Division of
Riviana Foods Inc.)

MEXICAN FOOD PRODUCTS
COMPANY
59051 Havenridge
New Haven, Michigan 48048

MEXSANA (medicated powder,
skin cream)
See Plough Inc.

MEYENBERG MILK PRODUCTS
COMPANY
(Subsidiary of Vorado Inc.)
339 Industrial Avenue
Ripon, California 95366
John D. Mordoff, President

MEYER (clarinets, oboes, bassoons,
piccolos)
See Ideal Musical Merchandise
Company

MEYER & COMPANY, WILSON &
GEORGE
270 Lawrence Avenue
South San Francisco,
California 94080
(415) 929-1600

MEYER APPAREL, JOHN
(Division of Hatco Group of W.R.
Grace & Company)
1 Connecticut Avenue
Norwich, Connecticut 06360

MEYER BROTHERS DRUG COMPANY
1201 Macklind Avenue
Saint Louis, Missouri 63110
C.F.G. Meyer, III, President
(314) 647-8000

MEYER FURNACE COMPANY
1300 South Washington Street
Peoria, Illinois 61601
Frank Meyer, President
(309) 673-6351

MEYER, INC., FRED
3800 S.E. 22nd
Portland, Oregon 97202
Fred G. Meyer, Chairman of the
Board
(503) 235-8844

Companies and Trade Names

MEYER INC., THEODORE
922 Callowhill
Philadelphia, Pennsylvania 19123
(215) 629-1850

MEYER LABORATORIES
1900 West Commercial Boulevard
Fort Lauderdale, Florida 33309

MEYER MANUFACTURING
COMPANY INC., MARY
Townshend, Vermont 05353

MEYER PACKING COMPANY,
H.H.
(Subsidiary of John Morrell &
Company)
2115 Partridge Place
Cincinnati, Ohio 45214
H. Harold Meyer, Chairman
(513) 621-3200

MEYER THREAD COMPANY,
JOHN C.
62 Freemont Street
Worcester, Massachusetts 01603

MEYERCORD COMPANY
365 East North Avenue
Carol Stream
Wheaton, Illinois 60187
L.A. Knopf, President
(312) 682-6200

MEYERS & ROSSER
1711 Pacific
Dallas, Texas 75201
(214) 747-8784

MEYERS COMPANY, H.C.
225 Fifth Avenue
New York, New York 10010
(212) 532-5020

MEYERS INC., MAXWELL
4040 Black Gold
Dallas, Texas 75247
(214) 634-2270

MEYERS INDUSTRIES INC.
Tecumseh-Clinton Road
Tecumseh, Michigan 49286
Wayne Seagraves, Vice President
(313) 423-2151

MEYERS MANUFACTURING
COMPANY
330 Fifth Avenue
New York, New York 10001
(212) 736-2586

MI-TOT (bottle and nipple brushes,
pacifiers)
See Woltra Company, Inc.

MIA (cosmetics)
See Faberge, Inc.

MIACK CHEMICAL COMPANY
48 West 33rd Street
New York, New York 10001
(212) 695-6366

MIAHATI, INC.
27 West Fourth Street
New York, New York 10012
(212) 254-7860

MIAMI CAREY
(Division of Jim Walter Corporation)
203 Garver Road
Monroe, Ohio 45050
Gordon Loftin, President
(513) 539-8441

MIAMI MARGARINE COMPANY,
THE
5226 Vine
Cincinnati, Ohio 45217
James K. Heidrich, Sr., President
(513) 242-2310

MIAMI PRODUCTS & CHEMICAL
COMPANY
520 Lonoke
Dayton, Ohio 45401
(513) 253-7461

MIAMI PROPELLER SERVICE INC.
2057 N.W. 11th Street
Miami, Florida 33125
(305) 643-1313

MIAMI SYSTEMS CORPORATION
Robertson at 34th Avenue
Cincinnati, Ohio 45209
(513) 351-4941

MIAMI VALLEY MILK PRODUCERS
ASSOCIATION
135 South Perry Street
Dayton, Ohio 45402
(513) 223-6273

MICARTA (plastics)
See Champion International
Corporation

MICHAEL & COMPANY, INC.,
DAVID
10801 Decatur Road
Philadelphia, Pennsylvania 19154
(215) 632-3100

MICHAEL & SON, C. F.
Post Office Box 181
Berkeley Springs,
West Virginia 25411

MICHAEL BUSINESS MACHINES
CORPORATION
145 West 45th Street
New York, New York 10036
(212) 582-2900

MICHAELS ART BRONZE COMPANY
Kenton Lands Road
Erlanger, Kentucky 41018
Robert L. Michaels, President and
Advertising Manager
(606) 341-5400

MICHAELS STERN & COMPANY,
INC.
87 Clinton Avenue, North
Rochester, New York 14602
Lester E. Frankenstein, President
(716) 454-5260

Companies and Trade Names

MICHEL & PELTON COMPANY
5713 Landregan
Emeryville, California 94608
(415) 652-1610

MICHELE MARTIN (hypoallergenic cosmetics)
See Revlon, Inc.

MICHELIN TIRE CORPORATION
2500 Marcus Avenue
Lake Success, New York 11040
J.H. Gillies, Vice President
(516) 488-3500

MICHELOB (beer)
See Anheuser-Busch, Inc.

MICHI-CRAFT CORPORATION
19995 19 Mile Road
Big Rapids, Michigan 49307
(616) 796-2675

MICHIGAN APPLE COMMITTEE
2726 East Michigan Avenue
Lansing, Michigan 48912

MICHIGAN BELL TELEPHONE COMPANY
(Subsidiary of American Telephone & Telegraph Company)
444 Michigan Avenue
Detroit, Michigan 48226
Kenneth J. Whalen, President
(313) 223-8181

MICHIGAN BLUEBERRY GROWERS ASSOCIATION
Box B
Grand Junction, Michigan 49056

MICHIGAN CHEMICAL CORPORATION
(Subsidiary of Northwest Industries, Inc.)
351 East Ohio Street
Chicago, Illinois 60611
Theodore A. Girard, President
(312) 454-7900

MICHIGAN CONSOLIDATED GAS COMPANY
1 Woodward Avenue
Detroit, Michigan 48226
Charles R. Montgomery, President
(313) 965-2430

MICHIGAN DYNAMICS
32400 Ford Road
Garden City, Michigan 48135
Ray Okonski, President
(312) 522-4000

MICHIGAN FARM CHEESE DAIRY, INC.
Millerton Road
Fountain, Michigan 49410

MICHIGAN FROSTED FOODS COMPANY
903 East John Street
Bay City, Michigan 48706

MICHIGAN FRUIT CANNERS, INC.
(Subsidiary of Consolidated Foods Corporation)
Benton Harbor, Michigan 49022
R.L. Hutchinson, President
(616) 927-4411

MICHIGAN GLASSLINE PRODUCTS COMPANY
199 West Ann Arbor Trail
Plymouth, Michigan 48170

MICHIGAN MADE (food products)
See Packers Canning Company Inc.

MICHIGAN MANUFACTURING COMPANY
Stephenson and Fifth Streets
Iron Mountain, Michigan 49801
(906) 774-4050

MICHIGAN NATIONAL BANK
Lansing, Michigan 48904
Stanford C. Stoddard, Chairman
(517) 485-3241

MICHIGAN NATIONAL BANK OF DETROIT
500 Griswold Street
Detroit, Michigan 48226
Lee T. Knutson, President
(313) 961-5300

MICHIGAN QUEEN (canned foods)
See Traverse City Canning Company

MICHIGAN WINERIES, INC.
(Affiliation of Paw Paw Grape Juice Company)
706 South Kalamazoo Street
Paw Paw, Michigan 49079

MICHLIN CHEMICAL CORPORATION
9045 Vincent
Detroit, Michigan 48211

MICKE RELLIM
320 Bridge Street
Brooklyn, New York 11201
(212) 855-3244

MICKELBERRY'S CORPORATION
405 Park Avenue
New York, New York 10022
James C. Marlas, President
(212) 832-0303

MICKEY BIKE (lawn equipment)
See King O'Lawn Inc.

MICKEY MOUSE (skates)
See Kusan Inc.

MICO DEVELOPMENT COMPANY INC.
4300 48th Street
Bladensburg, Maryland 20710
(301) 277-6760

MICON PRODUCTS
(Division of Medical Supply Company)
Rockford, Illinois 61103

960

Companies and Trade Names

MICOSA INC.
510 North Dearborn
Chicago, Illinois 60610
(312) 642-3520

MICRIN (mouthwash)
See Johnson & Johnson Company

MICRO-FRETS CORPORATION
100 Grove Road
Frederick, Maryland 21701

MICRO MUSICAL PRODUCTS
CORPORATION
10 West 19th Street
New York, New York 10011

MICRO OHM CORPORATION
4900 Double Drive
El Monte, California 91731

MICRO OPTICS COMPANY
28165 Greenfield Road
Southfield, Michigan 48076

MICRO-THERAPEUTICS, INC.
330 West 58th Street
New York, New York 10019
Peter W.H. Burgard, President
(212) 582-6833

MICROFILM PRODUCTS INC.
40 West 15th Street
New York, New York 10011
(212) 691-7954

MICROPOINT, INC.
620 East Taylor Avenue
Sunnyvale, California 94086
Rodney T. Geiman, President and
  Treasurer
(408) 736-5409

MID-AMERICA DAIRYMEN, INC.
Post Office Box 1837
S.S. Station
Springfield, Missouri 65805
William A. Powell, President
(417) 865-9641

MID-AMERICAN LINES, INC.
127 West Tenth Street
Kansas City, Missouri 64105
Wayne E. Hollowell, President
(816) 842-1355

MID-CONTINENT METAL
PRODUCTS COMPANY
2717 North Greenview
Chicago, Illinois 60614
(312) 549-3900

MID-CONTINENT SALES
COMPANY
See Micosa, Inc.

MID-ISLAND MEDICAL SUPPLY
COMPANY
2093 Wantagh
Wantagh, New York 11793

MID SOUTH PACKERS INC.
Drawer 829
Tupelo, Mississippi 38801

MID-VALLEY PRODUCTS
CORPORATION
Box 337
Roslyn Heights, New York 11577

MID-WEST FOOD PACKERS INC.
Box 152
Fowlerton, Indiana 46930
(317) 948-4134

MID-WEST PRODUCERS'
CREAMERIES INC.
224 West Jefferson Boulevard
South Bend, Indiana 46601

MID-WEST TOBACCO COMPANY,
INC.
1000 Evans
Cincinnati, Ohio 45204
(513) 921-4436

MIDAS-INTERNATIONAL
CORPORATION
(Subsidiary of Illinois Central
  Industries, Inc.)
222 South Riverside Plaza
Chicago, Illinois 60606
Ralph J. Weiger, President
(312) 648-5600

MIDDENDORF ENTERPRISES INC.
152 Madison Avenue
New York, New York 10016
(212) 684-4121

MIDDLE BAY (food products)
See Marine/Land Resources Inc.

MIDDLE EARTH COMPANY
809 Harrison Street
Kalamazoo, Michigan 49007

MIDDLEBROOKE LANCASTER,
INC.
304 Hewes Street
Brooklyn, New York 11211
Mitchel Miller, President
(212) 387-9644

MIDDLEBY, JR., INC.,
JOSEPH
327-347 Summer Street
Boston, Massachusetts 02210
Frank E. Sands, III, President
(617) 542-1534

MIDDLESEX (canned foods,
household products)
See Middlesex Foods Inc.
  (New Jersey)

MIDDLESEX (fruits, relishes,
preserves)
See Whipple Company

MIDDLESEX FOODS, INC.
Box 336
Meriden, Connecticut 06450

Companies and Trade Names

MIDDLESEX FOODS, INC.
425 Cleveland Avenue
Highland Park, New Jersey 08903

MIDDLETON, INC., JOHN
Church Road
King of Prussia, Pennsylvania 19406
H.H. Middleton, Jr., President
(215) 265-1400

MIDDLETOWN LEATHER COMPANY
200 Valentine Street
Hackettstown, New Jersey 07840

MIDDLING (food products)
See Whipple Company

MIDDY MARINE PRODUCTS INC.
1151 N.W. 46th Street
Seattle, Washington 98107
(206) 784-6707

MIDGET LOUVER COMPANY
800 Main Avenue
Norwalk, Connecticut 06852
(203) 866-2342

MIDLAND COOPERATIVES, INC.
2021 East Hennepin Avenue
Minneapolis, Minnesota 55413
C.S. Nelson, Chairman of the Board
(612) 331-6030

MIDLAND
(Division of The Dexter Corporation)
East Water Street
Waukegan, Illinois 60085
George E. Batrel, President
(312) 623-4200

MIDLAND ENTERPRISES INC.
580 Building
Cincinnati, Ohio 45202
John D. Geary, President
(513) 721-4000

MIDLAND FLOUR MILLS
(Division of International Milling Company)
Minneapolis, Minnesota 55402
(612) 340-3363

MIDLAND GLASS COMPANY
Cliffwood Avenue
Cliffwood, New Jersey 07721
Emanuel M. Terner, Chairman, President and Chief Executive Officer
(201) 566-4000

MIDLAND GROCERY COMPANY
405 North High Street
Columbus, Ohio 43216
John A. Hammond, President and Sales Manager
(614) 224-3181

MIDLAND INDUSTRIES INC.
Post Office Box 1627
Cedar Rapids, Iowa 52406

MIDLAND LABORATORIES
210 Jones Street
Dubuque, Iowa 52001
(319) 583-1787

MIDLAND-ROSS CORPORATION
55 Public Square
Cleveland, Ohio 44113
Harry J. Bolwell, President
(216) 771-4800
See also Ross Engineering Machinery

MIDNIGHT (carbon paper, ribbons, fountain-pen inks)
See Carter's Ink Company

MIDNIGHT SUN (hair lightener)
See Clairol, Inc.

MIDNITE (drinkware)
See Lotus Glass Company

MIDOL (menstrual-discomfort relief, feminine deodorant spray)
See Glenbrook Laboratories

MIDSHIP YACHT COMPANY
15051 Goden West Circle
Westminster, California 92683

MIDWAY MEDICAL COMPANY, INC.
415 Samson Street
Glasgow, Kentucky 42141
See also Vanguard Laboratories

MIDWAY MOTOR LODGE
North Six West 23673 Bluemound Road
Waukesha, Wisconsin 53186

MIDWEST (food products)
See Perry Canning Company

MIDWEST BEAN COMPANY, INC.
Box 296
Gering, Nebraska 69341

MIDWEST BUILDING PRODUCTS COMPANY
Post Office Box 2964
21010 Center Ridge
Cleveland, Ohio 44116
(216) 333-0818

MIDWEST CARD COMPANY
1113 Washington Avenue
Saint Louis, Missouri 63101
Mrs. Doris Harrington, President
(314) 231-2720

MIDWEST EMERY FREIGHT SYSTEM, INC.
7100 West Center Road
Omaha, Nebraska 68106
Milton D. Ratner, Chairman of the Board
(402) 391-8010

Companies and Trade Names

MIDWEST FOLDING PRODUCTS
1414 South Western Avenue
Chicago, Illinois 60608
Lester D. Speyer, President
(312) 666-3366

MIDWEST FOOTWEAR COMPANY, INC.
328 Manion Street
Sullivan, Missouri 68010
J.K. Endervelt, Chairman and President
(314) 468-4136

MIDWEST HANGER COMPANY
339 South Leonard
Liberty, Missouri 64068
Carl O. Jones, Chairman, President and Sales Manager
(816) 781-4737

MIDWEST HEALTH AIDS
612 North Michigan
Chicago, Illinois 60611
(312) 787-6505

MIDWEST INDUSTRIES, INC.
(Division of MTD Products, Inc.)
979 Conwell Avenue
Willard, Ohio 44890
S.E. Watterworth, President
(419) 935-6611

MIDWEST INTERNATIONAL INC.
101 High Street
Kellogg, Iowa 50135
Frederick G. Perkins, III, President
(515) 526-8211

MIDWEST MANUFACTURING COMPANY (blackboards, easels, etc.)
South and Cherry Streets
Lebanon, Ohio 45036

MIDWEST MANUFACTURING COMPANY (cleaning agents, polishes)
17126 Schaefer Highway
Detroit, Michigan 48235
(313) 861-4466

MIDWEST MUSICAL INSTRUMENT COMPANY
908 West Fayette Avenue
Effingham, Illinois 64201

MIDWEST NORTH
(Division of Ron Pair Enterprises Inc.)
Charlevoix, Michigan 49720

MIDWEST OUTERWEAR INC.
603 North Moore Road
Port Washington, Wisconsin 53074
(414) 284-2621

MIDWEST PLASTICS INC.
956 Prosperity Avenue
Saint Paul, Minnesota 55106
(612) 771-8891

MIDWEST ROTARY MANIFORMS COMPANY
1065 East Caro Road
Caro, Michigan 48723

MIDWEST SPORTING GOODS MANUFACTURING COMPANY
2200 North 11th Street
Milwaukee, Wisconsin 53205
(414) 264-3017

MIDWESTERN INDUSTRIES CORPORATION
Post Office Box 185
Harlan, Indiana 46743

MIETH MANUFACTURING COMPANY INC., P.J.
2129 Bridge Avenue
Point Pleasant, New Jersey 08742

MIFFLIN MCCAMBRIDGE COMPANY
6400 Rhode Island Avenue
Riverdale, Maryland 20840
Leonard Brown, President
(301) 277-7064

MIGHTY DOG (dog food)
See Carnation Company

MIGHTY-MAC
Emerson Avenue
Gloucester, Massachusetts 01930
Richard S. Bell, President
(617) 283-6200

MIGHTY MAX (portable hair dryer)
See Gillette Company

MIGHTY MITE (styler/dryer)
See North American Philips Corporation

MIGHTY-TONKA (scale-model steel cars and trucks)
See Tonka Toy (Division of Tonka Corporation)

MIJLA (groceries)
See Aljim Wholesale Grocery Company

MIJON COMPANY INC.
1105 Redondo Boulevard
Inglewood, California 90302

MIKASKA COMPANY
(Subsidiary of American Commercial, Inc.)
25 Enterprise Avenue
Secaucus, New Jersey 07094
A. Funabashi, President
(201) 867-9210

MIKE MATTHEWS FREEDOM (amplifiers)
See Electro-Harmonix Inc.

MIKE ROBERTS COLOR PRODUCTIONS
2023 Eighth Street
Berkeley, California 94710

MIKE'S BOAT SHOP
Box 421
Gloucester Point, Virginia 23062

Companies and Trade Names

MIKHAEL, INC., DAVID
500 Fifth Avenue
New York, New York 10036
(212) 391-2177

MIKO (beef and sausage products)
See Hilo Meat Company, Ltd.

MILADY BRASSIERE & CORSET
 COMPANY, INC.
6 East 32nd Street
New York, New York 10016
Hyman Bernstein, President
(212) 679-8060
 See also Roxane Swim Suits
 Company Inc.

MILADY'S (bath accessories)
See Specialty Items Company Inc.

MILADY'S (frozen blintzers,
dumplings, potato pancakes)
See Pet, Inc.

MILANI FOODS, INC.
(Subsidiary of Alberto-Culver
 Company)
2525 Armitage
Chicago, Illinois 60647
(312) 531-2000

MILANO (spaghetti, macaroni,
noodles)
See Tamico Foods, Inc.

MILBREW INC.
6101 North Teutonia Avenue
Milwaukee, Wisconsin 53209
(414) 462-3700
 See also Amber Laboratories

MILBURN COMPANY
3246 East Woodbridge Street
Detroit, Michigan 48207
(313) 259-3410

MILCO INDUSTRIES, INC.
550 East Fifth Street
Bloomsburg, Pennsylvania 17815
Marco Mitrani, President
(717) 784-0400

MILE HI (meats)
See Sigman Meat Company,
 Inc.

MILE HIGH (canned fruits and
vegetables)
See Kuner-Empson Company

MILE ROCK (canned seafood)
See Tom Lazio Fish Company
 Inc.

MILES (shoes)
See Melville Shoe Corporation

MILES COMPANY INC., E.E.
South Lancaster,
 Massachusetts 01561

MILES INSTRUMENT COMPANY
1431 Underwood Avenue
Milwaukee, Wisconsin 53213
(414) 258-5830

MILES KIMBALL COMPANY
Kimball Building
Oshkosh, Wisconsin 54901
Alberta S. Kimball, Chairman of
 the Board
(414) 231-3800

MILES LABORATORIES, INC.
Consumer Products Group
1127 Myrtle Street
Elkhart, Indiana 46514
Robert J. Wallace, Consultant,
 Consumer Affairs
(219) 264-8111
 See also Ames Company; Dome
 Laboratories; and Worthing-
 ton Foods, Inc.

MILES LABORATORIES INC.
Household Products Division
7123 West 65th
Bedford Park, Illinois 60411

MILES RIVER (food products)
See Harrison & Jarboe

MILESMASTER INC. OF AMERICA
1 East Wacker Drive
Chicago, Illinois 60601
(312) 751-0422

MILESTONE (percussion instruments)
See Arc Musical Instruments

MILEX, INC.
1 Plymouth Meeting
Plymouth Meeting,
 Pennsylvania 19462
Louis Alfierie, President
(215) 825-4300

MILEX PRODUCTS, INC.
5915 Northwest Highway
Chicago, Illinois 60631
(312) 631-6484

MILFORD CANNING COMPANY
Box 27
Milford, Illinois 60953
(815) 889-4115

MILFORD ENGINEERING
1507 Harding
Ames, Iowa 50010

MILGRAM FOOD STORES, INC.
Post Office Box Five
4231 Clary Boulevard
Kansas City, Missouri 64130
Lester Milgram, Chairman of the
 Board
(816) 861-5280

MILIUM (fabrics)
See Deering, Milliken Inc.

Companies and Trade Names

MILK-BONE (dog biscuit)
See Nabisco Inc.

MILK OF MAGNESIA (antacid and laxative)
See Charles H. Phillips Chemical Company

MILK SPECIALTIES COMPANY
Water and Illinois
Dundee, Illinois 60118
Vincent W. Nielsen, President
(312) 426-3411

MILKMAID (cosmetics)
See Minnetonka Laboratories, Inc.

MILL FARM (bourbon)
See Gooderham & Worts, Ltd.

MILL-MARK PHARMACEUTICALS INC.
236 Zimmerman Street
North Tonawanda, New York 14120

MILL-ROSE COMPANY, INC.
7995 Tyler
Mentor, Ohio 44060
(216) 255-9171

MILLAR & COMPANY INC., GEORGE W.
284 Lafayette Street
New York, New York 10012
T.P. Greenman, President
(212) 226-0880

MILLAR COFFEE COMPANY, E.B.
Box 5147 T A
Denver, Colorado 80217
(303) 292-1880

MILLARD-NORMAN COMPANY, THE
See Milnor Sales Agency

MILLBROOK (bread and cakes)
See Interstate Brands Corporation

MILLBURN PEAT COMPANY INC.
Post Office Box 297
Otterbein, Indiana 47970

MILLCREEK (food products)
See Albro Packing Company

MILLE LACS MAPLE PRODUCTS CORPORATION
308 Prince
Saint Paul, Minnesota 55101

MILLE LACS WILD RICE COMPANY
Aitken, Minnesota 56431

MILLEN CARDS INC.
230-03 Linden Boulevard
Jamaica, New York 11411
(212) 525-9100

MILLER (cookies)
See Banner Biscuit Company, Inc.

MILLER (tires)
See B.F. Goodrich Company

MILLER & COMPANY, INC., ROBERT E.
50 Broadway
Room 1103
New York, New York 10004
(212) 943-5114

MILLER & RHOADS
(Division of Garfinkel, Brooks Brothers, Miller & Rhoads, Inc.)
Sixth and Broad Street
Richmond, Virginia 23127
Edwin Hyde, Chairman
(804) 648-3111

MILLER & SONS COMPANY, I.
See Genesco, Inc.

MILLER & SONS, FRANK
13831 South Emerald Avenue
Chicago, Illinois 60627
(312) 468-3500

MILLER ASSOCIATES LTD., ARTHUR M.
225 Fifth Avenue
New York, New York 10010
(212) 725-4844

MILLER BARBER LOUISVILLE (golf equipment)
See Hillerich & Bradsby Company Inc.

MILLER BREWING COMPANY
(Subsidiary of Philip Morris, Inc.)
4000 West State Street
Milwaukee, Wisconsin 53201
John A. Murphy, President
(414) 931-2000

MILLER BROTHERS COMPANY
(Affiliation of Frederick Atkins, Inc.)
Seventh and Broad
Chattanooga, Tennessee 37401
George Blackwell Smith, Chairman of the Board
(615) 265-4211

MILLER BROTHERS INDUSTRIES, INC.
2700 Canton Street
Dallas, Texas 75226
I. Benjamin Parrill, President
(214) 748-5131

MILLER CLOCK COMPANY, HOWARD
860 East Main Street
Zeeland, Michigan 49464

MILLER COMPANY, CHARLES N.
Post Office Box Eight
10 Bridge Wat.
Boston, Massachusetts 02101
(617) 926-5880

MILLER COMPANY, S.J.
Post Office Box 3522
Boulder, Colorado 80303

Companies and Trade Names

MILLER COMPANY, THE
99 Center Street
Meriden, Connecticut 06451
B.G. Tremaine, Jr., President
(203) 235-4474

MILLER CURTAIN COMPANY
1602 Centennial Avenue
San Antonio, Texas 78211
Fred Miller, President
(512) 923-4587

MILLER ELECTRIC
    MANUFACTURING COMPANY
718 South Bounds Street
Appleton, Wisconsin 54911
Elizabeth Miller, President
(414) 734-9821

MILLER HESS & COMPANY
Seventh and Main
Akron, Pennsylvania 17501
Orie O. Miller, Chairman of the
    Board
(717) 859-1161

MILLER IMPORT CORPORATION
370 19th Street
Brooklyn, New York 11215
(212) 499-9200

MILLER, INC., HERMAN
140 West McKinley Street
Zeeland, Michigan 49464
Hugh De Pree, President
(616) 772-2161

MILLER-JONES (shoes)
    See Cannon Shoe Company

MILLER LITTLE GIANT COMPANY
    INC.
494 Villaume Avenue
South Saint Paul, Minnesota 55075
(612) 451-1761

MILLER MANUFACTURING
    COMPANY
1105 South Ayers
Fort Worth, Texas 76105
(817) 536-7355

MILLER MANUFACTURING
    COMPANY INC.
Seventh and Stockton Streets
Richmond, Virginia 23211
J.R. Buckle, President
(804) 232-4551

MILLER-MORTON COMPANY
(Subsidiary of A.H. Robins Company,
    Inc.)
2007 North Hamilton
Richmond, Virginia 23230
DeWitt F. Helm, Jr., President
(804) 257-2000

MILLER PACKING COMPANY
206 Second
Oakland, California 94604
(415) 451-7200

MILLER PRODUCTS COMPANY,
    INC.
29 Warren Street
New York, New York 10007
(212) 267-5334

MILLER SKI COMPANY
Post Office Box 396
Orem, Utah 84057
Earl A. Miller, President
(801) 225-1100

MILLER STUDIO INC.
734 Fair Avenue N.W.
New Philadelphia, Ohio 44663

MILLER SUPPLY CORPORATION
151 South Fulton Street
White Plains, New York 10606

MILLERKINS (women's shoes)
    See Genesco Inc.

MILLERS FALLS COMPANY
(Subsidiary of Ingersoll-Rand
    Company)
57 Wells Street
Greenfield, Massachusetts 01301
R.F. Garvey, Jr., President
(413) 773-5426

MILLERS FALLS PAPER COMPANY
Mill Road
Millers Falls, Massachusetts 01349
Walker J. Hosmer, President and
    General Manager
(413) 659-3911

MILLERS FORGE MANUFACTURING
    CORPORATION
80 Pearl Street
Keene, New Hampshire 03431
Jack Brown Miller, President and
    Treasurer
(603) 352-6911

MILLER'S HONEY COMPANY
Post Office Drawer 500
Colton, California 92324

MILLER'S, INC.
(Subsidiary of Garfinckel, Brooks
    Brothers, Miller & Rhoads, Inc.)
Henley Street
Knoxville, Tennessee 37902
Willard O. Bent, Chairman of the
    Board
(615) 524-4040

MILLER'S QUALITY HONEY
609 North Broadway
Blackfoot, Idaho 83221

MILLER'S ROSY COMPANY
170 Louiselle Street
Mobile, Alabama 36607

MILLET (sports accessories)
    See Eiger Mountain Sports

MILLICENT LINGERIE INC.
38 East 32nd Street
New York, New York 10016
(212) 684-4924

MILLIKEN (fabrics and woolens)
    See Deering, Milliken &
    Company

Companies and Trade Names

MILLIONS DAILY (pins, staples, clips, thumbtacks)
　See Noesting Pin Ticket Company Inc.

MILLS & COMPANY, INC., A.J.
1 Pennsylvania Plaza
New York, New York 10017
(212) 594-3250

MILLS & COMPANY, WILLIAM J.
125 Main Street
Greenport, New York 11944
(516) 477-1500

MILLS & SON INC., WILLIAM
21 Park Place
New York, New York 10007

MILLS COMPANY
965 Wayside Road
Cleveland, Ohio 44110
Osborne Mills, President and Chief Executive Officer
(216) 531-1100

MILLS PHARMACEUTICALS, INC.
11715 Westline Industrial Drive
Saint Louis, Missouri 63141

MILLS PRODUCTS CORPORATION
707 Summit Avenue
Union City New Jersey 07087

MILLS PRODUCTS INC.
33106 West Eight Mile Road
Farmington, Michigan 48024
George T. Mash, Chairman and President
(313) 476-4550

MILLS SALES & MANUFACTURING COMPANY
Post Office Box 391
San Gabriel, California 91778

MILNE MANUFACTURING COMPANY
1641 Blake Street
Denver, Colorado 80202
(303) 893-3715

MILNER HOTELS & INNS
1526 Centre Street
Detroit, Michigan 48226
(313) 962-5400

MILNOT COMPANY
120 West Saint John Street
Litchfield, Illinois 62056
Martin Hauser, President
(217) 324-2146

MILO (flour and grits)
　See Krause Milling Company

MILROY LABORATORIES, INC.
Post Drawer 188
Tallevast, Florida 33588
(813) 355-3405

MILSHIRE (gin)
　See Heublein, Inc.

MILSHIRE INTERNATIONAL CORPORATION
102 Franklin Street
New York, New York 10013
(212) 226-2642

MILSMITH INDUSTRIES INC.
　See El-Mar Boat Company

MILSTAR (carpet)
　See Deering Milliken, Inc.

MILSTEEL PRODUCTS COMPANY
　See Atco Steel Products Company

MILTENBERG & SAMTON, INC.
101 Park Avenue
New York, New York 10017
(212) 686-5822

MILTENBERG, INC., E.
300 Park Avenue South
New York, New York 10010
(212) 777-0620

MILTON BRADLEY COMPANY
1500 Main Street
Springfield, Massachusetts 01115
James J. Shea, Jr., President
(413) 525-6411
　See also Amsco Industries; Lowe, Inc., E.S.; Playskool, Inc.; and South Bend Toy Manufacturing Company

MILTON SHOE MANUFACTURING COMPANY, INC.
700 Hepburn Street
Milton, Pennsylvania 17847
Saul Putterman, President
(717) 742-9621

MILTOWN (tranquilizer)
　See Wallace Pharmaceuticals

MILWAUKEE (machine tools)
　See Kearney & Trecker Corporation

MILWAUKEE CHAIR COMPANY
4383 Fruitland Avenue
Los Angeles, California 90058
(213) 583-4211

MILWAUKEE CHEESE COMPANY
770 North Springdale Road
Waukesha, Wisconsin 53187

MILWAUKEE DUSTLESS BRUSH COMPANY
10930 West Lapham
Milwaukee, Wisconsin 53214
(414) 476-1147

MILWAUKEE ELECTRIC TOOL CORPORATION
13135 West Lisbon Road
Brookfield, Wisconsin 53005
Jack R. Jaeger, President
(414) 781-3600

Companies and Trade Names

MILWAUKEE METAL STAMPING CORPORATION
800 South 72nd Street
Milwaukee, Wisconsin 53214
Ralph Robinson, President
(414) 476-2400

MILWAUKEE VALVE COMPANY
2375 South Burrell
Milwaukee, Wisconsin 53207
Herschel L. Seder, Chairman and President
(414) 744-5420

MILWAUKEE'S BEST (beer)
See Miller Brewing Company

MIMEO MANUFACTURING COMPANY INC.
45 Werman Court
Plainview, New York 11803

MIMEOGRAPH (duplicator)
See A.B. Dick Company

MIMI COSMETIQUE
(Division of Bevee Cosmetics Company, Inc.)
153 Chestnut Avenue
Irvington, New Jersey 07111

MIN-DEE DISTRIBUTORS INC.
Post Office Box 130
Syosset, New York 11791
See also Supreme Enterprises Ltd.

MINCING TRADING CORPORATION
25 Broadway
New York, New York 10004
(212) 425-1100

MINDY MALONE INC.
1400 Broadway
New York, New York 10018
(212) 354-5770

MINELECTRIC (typewriters)
See Olivetti Corporation of America

MINER INDUSTRIES, INC.
125 Walnut Avenue
Bronx, New York 10454
Eugene A. Swee, President
(212) 993-1700

MINERVA WAX PAPER COMPANY
310 Grant Street
Minerva, Ohio 44657
Rodney E. Bauer, President
(216) 868-4126

MINETTE PHARMACEUTICAL CORPORATION
3024 Genesee
Buffalo, New York 14225
(716) 896-7791

MING (teas)
See Heublein Inc.

MINI-GALLEY (stove)
See Fores Manufacturing Corporation

MINI HOME (motor homes)
See Motor Homes Inc.

MINI-LABS (educational science kits)
See Educational Resources (Division of Educational Design Inc.)

MINI MEAL (food product)
See George A. Hormel & Company

MINI-MIST (dry shampoo)
See Block Drug Company, Inc.

MINI MOTOR HOME
See Gladding-Del-Rey

MINI-POT (marine toilets)
See Thetford Corporation

MINI-TONKA (scale-model steel cars and trucks)
See Tonka Toy (Division of Tonka Corporation

MINIAC (computer)
See Electronic Associates Inc.

MINICRAFT MODELS INC.
1510 West 228th Street
Torrance, California 90501

MINIGRIP INC.
Route 303
Orangeburg, New York 10962
Steven Ausnit, President
(212) 365-6900

MINIPOO (dry shampoo)
See Block Drug Company, Inc.

MINIT-RUB (analgesic balm)
See Bristol-Myers Company

MINIT-SPRAY (aerosol paints and sundries)
See Kerr Chemicals Inc.

MINIVEIL CORPORATION
303 Washington
New Castle, Pennsylvania 16105
(412) 658-3551

MINK & PEARLS (bath oil, dusting powder, eau de cologne, perfume, etc.)
See Jovan, Inc.

MINK'S CANDIES
See L.C. Good Candy Company

MINN-KOTA MANUFACTURING COMPANY
201 North 17th Street
Moorhead, Minnesota 56560
(218) 233-1316

Companies and Trade Names

MINNESOTA FABRICS, INC.
5600 North County Road 18
New Hope, Minnesota 55428
C. Wilbur Peters, President
(612) 535-3505

MINNESOTA GAS COMPANY
733 Marquette Avenue
Minneapolis, Minnesota 55402
Paul R. Doelz, Chairman of the Board
(612) 372-4664

MINNESOTA MINING & MANUFACTURING COMPANY
See 3 M Inc.

MINNESOTA MUTUAL LIFE INSURANCE COMPANY
345 Cedar Street
Saint Paul, Minnesota 55101
Franklin Briese, Chairman of the Board
(612) 298-3500

MINNESOTA PAINTS, INC.
1101 Third Street
Minneapolis, Minnesota 55415
(612) 332-7371

MINNESOTA POWER & LIGHT COMPANY
30 West Superior Street
Duluth, Minnesota 55802
J.F. Rowe, President
(218) 722-2641

MINNETONKA LABORATORIES INC.
Frontier Center
Chanhassen, Minnesota 55317
Robert R. Taylor, President
(612) 474-4181

MINOR & SON, INC., P.W.
3 Treadeasy Avenue
Batavia, New York 14020
Henry H. Minor, Jr., President
(716) 343-1500

MINOT FOOD PACKERS INC.
Penn and Bank Streets
Bridgeton, New Jersey 08360
John B. Morello, President and Treasurer
(609) 451-2035

MINSTER CANNING COMPANY
South Ohio Street
Minster, Ohio 45865
Luke F. Beckman, President
(419) 628-2315

MINT PACK (skin-care products)
See Aditi, Inc.

MINTER'S CANDIES INC.
Fourth and Coates Streets
Bridgeport, Pennsylvania 19405

MINTON, INC.
See Doulton and Company, Inc.

MINUET (controlled-label grocery products)
See Staff Supermarkets Associates

MINUTE FRESH (prepared frozen seafood)
See Eat-All Frozen Food Company, Inc.

MINUTE MAID (frozen juices, fruits)
See Cocoa-Cola Company, Foods Division

MINUTE MAN (frozen foods, meats)
See Colonial Beef Company Inc. (Pennsylvania)

MINUTE MASTER (microwave ovens)
See Litton Industries, Atherton Division

MINUTE MINDERS (electric timers)
See Robertshaw Controls Company, Lux Time Division

MINUTE RICE (precooked rice)
See General Foods Corporation

MINUTE TAPIOCA (quick-cooking tapioca)
See General Foods Corporation

MINUTEMAN (lawn and garden supplies, plumbing and heating supplies)
See Sentry Hardware Corporation

MINX MODES (dresses)
See R. Lowenbaum Manufacturing Company

MIO TRADING CORPORATION
1123 Broadway
New York, New York 10010
(212) 255-0639

MIONE MANUFACTURING COMPANY
Collingdale, Pennsylvania 19023

MIR-O-LITE (electric makeup mirrors)
See Heritage Workshops

MIRA-PLATE (paint)
See O'Brien Corporation

MIRABELLA CONTINENTAL (shoes)
See George E. Keith Company

MIRACL-EDGE (knives)
See W.R. Case & Sons Cutlery Company

MIRACLE (beaters and can openers)
See Ekco Housewares Company

MIRACLE (grass seed)
See Cargill, Inc.

Companies and Trade Names

MIRACLE (sandwich spread, margarine, etc.)
See Kraft Foods

MIRACLE (vegetable slicers)
See M.E. Heuck Company

MIRACLE ADHESIVES CORPORATION
250 Pettit Avenue
Bellmore, New York 11710
Timothy R. Cutler, President
(516) 221-0950

MIRACLE AID (soft-drink bases)
See Standard Brands Inc.

MIRACLE DRUG PRODUCTS INC.
1061 Ponce de Leon Avenue N.E.
Atlanta, Georgia 30306
(404) 876-0381

MIRACLE-GRO (plant food)
See Stern's Nurseries

MIRACLE MAIZE (food products)
See Little Crow Milling Company

MIRACLE MART
1609 Fourth Avenue N.W.
Minot, North Dakota 58701

MIRACLE POWER PRODUCTS CORPORATION
1101 Belt Line
Cleveland, Ohio 44109
(216) 741-1388

MIRACLE RECREATION EQUIPMENT COMPANY
Post Office Box 275
Grinnell, Iowa 50112
Paul Ahrens, President and Production Manager
(515) 236-7536

MIRACLE TREAD (shoes)
See Craddock-Terry Shoe Corporation

MIRACLE WHIP (salad dressing and margarine)
See Kraft Foods

MIRACLE WHITE COMPANY
(Division of Beatrice Foods, Company)
4000 West 40th Street
Chicago, Illinois 60632
Leo Singer, President
(312) 847-5900

MIRANDA (cameras and photographic equipment)
See AIC Photo, Inc.

MIRACORD (record-playing units)
See Benjamin Electronic Sound Corporation

MIRAFLORE (wine)
See Paterno Imports Ltd.

MIRAFONE CORPORATION
8484 San Fernando Road
Sun Valley, California 91352

MIRAMAR OF CALIFORNIA, INC.
603 North Ford Boulevard
Los Angeles, California 90022
(213) 269-8117

MIRANDA (photo equipment)
See Allied Impex Corporation

MIRAPLAS TILE COMPANY
980 Parsons Avenue
Columbus, Ohio 43206
Frederick B. Hill, III, President
(614) 443-9701

MIRO-FLEX COMPANY
3050 North Saint Francis
Wichita, Kansas 67219
James E. Hadley, Vice President and Secretary
(316) 838-0881

MIRRA-COAT (veterinary product)
See Borden Company, Chemical Division/Smith-Douglass

MIRRA-COTE COMPANY
120 Standard Street
El Segundo, California 90245
Robert B. Webster, President and Treasurer
(213) 772-2191

MIRRO ALUMINUM COMPANY
1512 Washington Street
Manitowoc, Wisconsin 54220
C.W. Ziemer, President
(414) 684-4421

MIRROLAC (enamels)
See Celanese Corporation

MIRROPANE (mirrors)
See Libbey-Owens-Ford

MIRROR BRIGHT POLISH COMPANY
Irvine Industrial Complex
Box C-T
Irvine, California 92664
(714) 557-9200

MIRSA ITALIAN KNITWEAR, LTD.
1410 Broadway
New York, New York 10018
(212) 354-0768

MISEMER PHARMACEUTICALS, INC.
Box 3177
Springfield, Missouri 65804

MISHAN & SONS INC., E.
1170 Broadway
New York, New York 10001
(212) 689-9094

MISHAWAKA RUBBER COMPANY, INC.
(Subsidiary of Uniroyal, Inc.)
312 North Hill Street
Mishawaka, Indiana 46544
M.B. Barrick, President
(219) 255-2181

Companies and Trade Names

MISS AMERICA (canned foods)
See King Pharr Canning
Operations, Inc.

MISS AMERICA (shoes)
See Brown Shoe Company Inc.

MISS AMERICAN TEEN-AGER, INC.
331 Webster Drive
New Milford, New Jersey 07646
Sol Abrams, President
(201) 262-4111

MISS BRECK (hair-care products)
See John H. Breck Inc.

MISS BUXTON (billfolds)
See Buxton, Inc.

MISS CALIFORNIA (food products)
See NCC Food Corporation

MISS CLAIROL (hair-care products)
See Clairol, Inc.

MISS DIOR (bath oil, eau de
cologne, perfume, etc.)
See Christian Dior

MISS ELAINE LINGERIE
1717 Olive
Saint Louis, Missouri 63103
(314) 421-3312

MISS FASHIONALITY
(Division of David Peet Inc.)
1370 Broadway
New York, New York 10018
(212) 244-5222

MISS FRESH (dairy, bakery, and
snack foods)
See Florida Retail Owned
Grocers, Inc.

MISS GEORGIA (canned foods)
See King Pharr Canning
Operations, Inc.

MISS HOLLYWOOD UNDER-
GARMENT CORPORATION
152 Madison Avenue
New York, New York 10016
(212) 684-0757

MISS LOLLYPOP (soap, colognes,
and powders)
See Avon Products, Inc.

MISS LOU (canned fruits and
vegetables)
See King Pharr Canning
Operations, Inc.

MISS MUFFET FOODS, INC.
500 Wall Street
Suite 410
Seattle, Washington 98121
(206) 622-1061

MISS PAT
1515 Santee Street
Los Angeles, California 90015
Morton I. Abbott, President
(213) 748-2222

MISS PLASTICS INC.
Post Office Box 83
Raleigh, Mississippi 39153

MISS SPRAY NET (hair spray)
See Helene Curtis Industries

MISS VIRGINIA (groceries)
See Virginia Foods, Inc.

MISS WINSTED (small appliances)
See Capitol Products Company
(Connecticut)

MISS WONDERFUL (shoes)
See International Shoe Company

MISS YOUTHFORM CREATIONS
CORPORATION
38 East 30th Street
New York, New York 10016

MISSION FOODS CORPORATION
7 31st Street
San Diego, California 92102

MISSION-HARLINGEN CANNING
COMPANY
Box 31
Harlingen, Texas 78550
(512) 423-5190

MISSION INDUSTRIES
Post Office Box 1087
Escondido, California 92026

MISSION MACARONI
(Division of Golden Grain Company)
4715 Sixth Avenue, South
Seattle, Washington 98108
Paskey DeMonenico, President
(206) 623-2038

MISSION OF CALIFORNIA, INC.
(Subsidiary of Cott Corporation)
197 Chatham
New Haven, Connectituct 06513
George Martin, President
(203) 562-5142

MISSION PHARMACAL COMPANY
Box 1676
San Antonio, Texas 78296
(512) 533-7118

MISSISSIPPI POWER & LIGHT
COMPANY
Electric Building
Jackson, Mississippi 39101
D.C. Lutkin, President
(601) 969-2311

MISSISSIPPI POWER COMPANY
Gulfport, Mississippi 39501
V.J. Daniel, Jr., President
(601) 864-1211

MISSOURI BRUSH & CRAYON
COMPANY
2726 Brentwood Boulevard
Saint Louis, Missouri 63144
(314) 961-5916

Companies and Trade Names

MISSOURI FARMERS ASSOCIATION, INC.
201 South Seventh Street
Columbia, Missouri 65201
Fred V. Heinkel, President
(314) 443-1661

MISSOURI HICKORY CORPORATION
2209 Portrero Avenue
South El Monte, California 91733

MISSOURI MEERSCHAUM COMPANY
Front and Cedar
Washington, Missouri 63090
Carl J. Otto, President
(314) 239-2109

MISSOURI PACIFIC RAILROAD COMPANY
Missouri Pacific Building
Saint Louis, Missouri 63103
Downing B. Jenks, Chairman of the Board
(314) 622-0123
See also Texas & Pacific Railway

MISSOURI PUBLIC SERVICE COMPANY
10700 East 50th Highway
Kansas City, Missouri 64138
Richard C. Green, President
(816) 353-5000

MISSOURI ROLLING MILL CORPORATION
6800 Manchester Avenue
Saint Louis, Missouri 63143
Carl Bauer, President and Treasurer
(314) 645-3500

MISSY PETITES (dresses)
See Ginsburg & Abelson, Inc.

MIST 'N CURL (steam hair curlers)
See Associated Mills, Inc.

MIST-STICK (electric curler/styler)
See Sunbeam Appliance Company

MISTEE LINGERIE, INC.
417 Fifth Avenue
New York, New York 10016
(212) 685-8625

MR. AND MRS. "T" PRODUCTS
(Division of Taylor Food Products Inc.)
El Segundo, California 90245

MISTER B GREETING CARD COMPANY
3500 N.W. 52nd Street
Miami, Florida 33142
(305) 633-1556

MR. BARTENDER PRODUCTS, INC.
7450 Industrial Road
Florence, Kentucky 41042

MR. BLACKWELL (dresses)
See R.L. Spencer, Inc.

MR. BOSTON DISTILLER, INC.
955 N.E. 125th Street
North Miami, Florida 33161
Paul Berkowitz, President
(305) 891-8750

MR. BOSTON SEAFOODS CORPORATION
Fish Pier
Boston, Massachusetts 02210
(617) 542-3566

MR. BOXMAN OF AMERICA
1401 S.W. Second Street
Pompano Beach, Florida 33060

MR. CHRISTMAS, INC.
212 Fifth Avenue
New York, New York 10010
Jerry Hermanson, President and Treasurer
(212) 889-7220

MR. CLEAN (household cleaner)
See Procter & Gamble Company

MR. COFFEE (drip coffee maker)
See North American Systems Inc.

MR. COLOR (spray paint)
See Gard Industries Inc.

MR. D. FASHIONS (sports apparel)
See M. R. D. & Associates Inc.

MR. DENTURE (denture cleanser)
See Brown Pharmaceutical Company Inc. (New York)

MISTER DONUT OF AMERICA, INC.
(Subsidiary of International Multifoods Corporation)
89 Providence Highway
Westwood, Massachusetts 02090
Richard A. Niglio, President
(617) 326-8000

MR. DOWN-UNDER (frozen seafood products)
See Gilman International, Inc.

MR. DUNDERBAKS CHEESE AND SAUSAGE SHOPS
744 Cherry Hill Mall
Cherry Hill, New Jersey 08034

MR. FIX (repair products)
See Marson Corporation

MR. FROLIC (playground equipment)
See Gym Dandy Inc.

MR. FROSTY SEAFOODS, INC.
800 Jefferson
Newport News, Virginia 23607

MR. G (food products)
See Ore-Ida Foods Inc.

MR. HOCKEY
Box 63
Madison, New Jersey 07940

Companies and Trade Names

MR. INSIDE (carpet-to-rubber mats)
   See Akro Corporation

MR. JAC
148 Madison Avenue
New York, New York 10016
(212) 889-3150

MISTER KILLER (insecticides)
   See Chemical Specialties
      Company, Inc.

MR. LEISURE INC.
200 Fifth Avenue
Room 620
New York, New York 10010
(212) 242-2427

MR. MUSCLE (oven cleaner)
   See Drackett Company

MISTER MUSTARD (mustard)
   See Frank Tea & Spice Company

MR. NEAT (yard and garbage bags, trash-can and wastebasket liners)
   See Strout Plastics, Inc.

MISTER PANTS, INC.
1441 Broadway Avenue
New York, New York 10018
(212) 730-1270

MR. PIZZA
560 Sylvan Avenue
Englewood Cliffs,
   New Jersey 07632

MR. POTATO HEAD (plaything)
   See Hasbro Industries Inc.

MR. QUICK INC.
3760 41st
Moline, Illinois 61265

MR. QUILL INC.
18744 Parthenia Street
Building 10
Northridge, California 91324

MR. REX (insect repellent, tanning aids)
   See Sunshine State Cosmetics, Inc.

MR. SANDWICH U.S.A. INC.
2 West 45th Street
New York, New York 10036
(212) 867-5750

MR. SIMMS (syrups, juices, cherries)
   See Castle Products Company

MR. SIMON (dresses)
   See Martha Manning Company

MISTER SOFTEE, INC.
901 East Clements Bridge Road
Runnemede, New Jersey 08078
William A. Conway, President
(609) 931-0200

MR. STEAK, INC.
5100 Race Court
Denver, Colorado 80216
James A. Mather, Chairman of
   the Board
(303) 292-3070

MR. SUN (sun/health lamp)
   See North American Phillips
      Corporation

MR. TOPPS FROZEN FOODS
Box 1415
Columbus, Georgia 31907

MR. TRANSMISSION
2319 Crestmoor Road
Nashville, Tennessee 37215

MR. WIZARD (educational toys)
   See Owens-Illinois Inc.

MR. WONDERFUL (men's ties)
   See Beau Brummell Ties

MR. WRANGLER (sportswear)
   See Blue Bell, Inc.

MISTI (hair-care products)
   See Research Specialties
      Company

MISTLETOE (pickles, olives, preserves, jellies)
   See Bishop Company, Inc.

MISTOL (decongestant, nasal mist, nose drops)
   See Plough Inc.

MRS. ALISON'S COOKIE COMPANY
1780 Burns Avenue
Saint Louis, Missouri 63132
Jack C. Elliott, President
(314) 429-2111

MRS. BAIRD'S BAKERIES, INC.
Post Office Box 937
Fort Worth, Texas 76101
H. Vernon Baird, President
(817) 293-6230

MRS. BELL'S (condiments, jellies, etc.)
   See Atlantic Preserving Company

Companies and Trade Names

MRS. BUTTERWORTH'S (maple syrup)
See Lever Brothers Company

MRS. DAY'S IDEAL BABY SHOE COMPANY
20 Locust Street
Danvers, Massachusetts 01923
James R. McGinnity, President
(617) 774-0161

MRS. FILBERT'S (margarine)
See J.H. Filbert, Inc.

MRS. GILES COUNTRY KITCHENS, INC.
Box 1297
Lynchburg, Virginia 24505

MRS. GRASS
(Division of Hygrade Food Products Corporation)
725 South 25th Avenue
Bellwood, Illinois 60104

MRS. HALFIN'S (pet foods)
See National Pet Supply Company

MRS. J.G. MCDONALDS CHOCOLATE COMPANY
2250 South Third East
Salt Lake City, Utah 84115
Roderick N. McDonald, President
(801) 487-3201

MRS. KARLS (bread)
See Interstate Brands Corporation

MRS. PAUL'S KITCHENS, INC.
5830 Henry Avenue
Philadelphia, Pennsylvania 19128
E.J. Piszek, President
(215) 483-4000

MRS. SCHLORER'S, INC.
Scotts Lane
Philadelphia, Pennsylvania 19129
(215) 839-6400

MRS. STITLER'S CANDIES, INC.
5130 West 26th Street
Cicero, Illinois 60650

MRS. SMITH'S PIE COMPANY
South and Charlotte Streets
Pottsdown, Pennsylvania 19464
Robert P. Smith, Chairman of the Board
(215) 326-2600
See also Harriss Pie Company, Lloyd J.

MRS. TUCKER'S (salad oil, shortening)
See Anderson Clayton Foods

MRS. WAGNER'S (pies)
See also Lynn Foods Corporation

MISTY HARBOR (coats)
See Jonathan Logan

MISTYVALE (canned foods)
See National Fruit Canning Company

MIT-SHEL COMPANY
(Division of Brower Manufacturing Company)
640 South Fifth
Quincy, Illinois 62301

MITCHE, INC.
7730 Herschel Avenue
La Jolla, California 92037

MITCHEL (guitars)
See J.L. Marsh Inc.

MITCHELL (fans, heaters, etc.)
See Cory Corporation

MITCHELL & BROTHER INC., F.O.
1719 Perryman Road
Perryman, Maryland 21130
Parker Mitchell, Jr., President
(301) 272-3636

MITCHELL COMPANY, C.H.
Electronic Tools Division
14614 Raymer Street
Van Nuys, California 91405
(213) 781-0351

MITCHELL COMPANY, JOHN E.
3800 Commerce
Dallas, Texas 75226
G.R. Hollingsworth, President
(214) 921-5161

MITCHELL FOODS, INC.
152 West Main Street
Fredonia, New York 14063
Frank Mitchell, President
(716) 672-2138

MITCHELL LURIE (reed instruments and accessories)
See La Voz Corporation

MITCHELL MANUFACTURING COMPANY
2740 South 34th
Milwaukee, Wisconsin 53215
(414) 645-8140

MITCHELLACE INC.
1740 Eighth Street
Portsmouth, Ohio 45662
Kerry Keating, President
(614) 353-2158

MITCHELL'S IRISH (whiskey)
See Seagram Distillers Company

MITCHUM-THAYER, INC.
(Subsidiary of Revlon, Inc.)
1 Scarsdale Road
Tuckahoe, New York 10707
(914) 779-6300

MITE CORPORATION
446 Blake Street
New Haven, Connecticut 06515
Leo J. Brangato, President
(203) 387-2572
See also Stromberg Products

Companies and Trade Names

MITIN (mothproofing product)
See Ciba-Geigy Corporation

MITSUBISHI INTERNATIONAL
CORPORATION
277 Park Avenue
New York, New York 10017
Shunkichi Nishada, President
(212) 922-3700
See also Onkyo; and Pilot Radio Sales

MITSUBISH RAYON COMPANY
LTD.
227 Park Avenue
New York, New York 10017
(212) 759-5605

MITTELDORFER STRAUS, INC.
41 Madison Avenue
New York, New York 10010
(212) 683-1494

MITY FRESH (food products)
See Watsonville Canning & Frozen Food Company

MITY NICE (canned foods)
See A.T. Hipke & Sons Inc.

MITZI (emery boards, eyebrow pencils, pumice stones)
See Eagle Druggists Supply Company, Inc.

MIX-ME-NOT (ready-to-bake cake)
See Campbell-Taggart Inc.

MIX-O-MATIC (electric mixers)
See Rival Manufacturing Company

MIXERS (sportswear)
See Phillips Van Heusen Corporation

MIXING EQUIPMENT COMPANY, INC.
135 Mount Read Boulevard
Rochester, New York 14611
Richard D. Boutros, President
(716) 436-5550

MIXMASTER (food mixers)
See Sunbeam Appliance Company

MIZZY, INC.
Cliftondale Park
Clifton Forge, Virginia 24422
(703) 862-4151

MOBAY CHEMICAL COMPANY
(Division of Boychem Corporation)
Penn Lincoln Parkway West
Pittsburgh, Pennsylvania 15205
K.M. Weis, President
(412) 923-2700

MOBI CORPORATION
4800 Flat Rock Road
Philadelphia, Pennsylvania 19127
(215) 487-0700

MOBI PRODUCTS
725 East University
Bloomington, Indiana 47401

MOBIL CHEMICAL COMPANY
3327 Broadview
Cleveland, Ohio 44128
(216) 252-4050

MOBIL CHEMICAL COMPANY
Plastics Division
3848 Richard
Macedon, New York 14502

MOBIL OIL CORPORATION
150 East 42nd Street
New York, New York 10017
Rawleigh Warner, Jr., Chairman of the Board
(212) 883-4242

MOBILAIRE (fans)
See Westinghouse Electric Corporation

MOBILE BAY (seafoods)
See Aughinbaugh Canning Company

MOBILE MAID (dishwasher)
See General Electric Company

MOBILUX CORPORATION
Rural Street
Evergreen, Alabama 36401

MOC ABOUTS (footwear)
See Nashua Footwear Corporation

MOCC-STOMPERS (footwear)
See Dunham

MOCHA MIX (food products)
See Presto Food Products, Inc.

MOCK SEED COMPANY
13th and Smallman
Pittsburgh, Pennsylvania 15230
(412) 281-3193

MOCKEL GALLERY, HENRY R.
Box 726
Twentynine Palms, California 92277

MOD-DECOR (plastic furniture)
See Republic Molding Corporation

MOD-ROD (decorative traverse rod)
See Kirsch Company

MODAR ELECTRONICS INC.
1301 East Algonquin Road
Schaumburg, Illinois 60172

Companies and Trade Names

MODE CRAFT COMPANY
(Division of Village Industries, Inc.)
500 Seventh Avenue
New York, New York 10018
Fred P. Greenberg, President
(212) 279-1250

MODE-MAKER (desks and tables)
See General Fireproofing
Company

MODECRAFT (wearing apparel)
See Villager Industries, Inc.

MODEL (tobacco)
See United States Tobacco
Company

MODEL DIE CASTING INC.
3811 West Rosecrans
Hawthorne, California 90250
(213) 678-3131

MODEL RECTIFIER CORPORATION
2500 Woodbridge Avenue
Edison, New Jersey 08817
Roy C. Gelber, President
(201) 985-7800

MODELL, HENRY & COMPANY, INC.
280 Broadway
New York, New York 10007
William Modell, President
(212) 962-6200

MODELS COAT, INC.
(Division of Swirl, Inc.)
1411 Broadway
New York, New York 10018
Jack Nachman, President
(212) 564-8890

MODERA (mobile homes)
See Marshfield Homes

MODERN AGE (shoes)
See Curtis-Stephens-Embry
Company

MODERN AIR DECOR
Post Office Box 194
Beacon Falls, Connecticut 06403

MODERN ART (lamps and fixtures)
See DeSoto Inc., Home
Accessories Division

MODERN BRASS (tarnish-resistant brassware)
See Philcraft Imports Inc.

MODERN BRIDAL AND FORMAL SHOPS
1 Cherry Hill
Cherry Hill, New Jersey 08034

MODERN CRAFTS COMPANY
6301 Etzel Avenue
Saint Louis, Missouri 63133
(314) 721-3363

MODERN DUST BAG COMPANY, INC.
Box 637
Joliet, Illinois 60434

MODERN FORGE MANUFACTURING COMPANY
2136 North Wayne Avenue
Chicago, Illinois 60614
(312) 327-9890

MODERN GLOBE SALES, INC.
90 Park Avenue
New York, New York 10016
Ovide E. de Saint Aubin, President
(212) 972-1590

MODERN HEAT CORPORATION
Box 754
Kingsport, Tennessee 37662

MODERN IMAGE, INC.
418 54th Street
West New York, New Jersey 07093

MODERN MAID FOOD PRODUCTS, INC.
200 Garden City Plaza
Garden City, New York 11530
Jack Silverman, President
(516) 877-1000

MODERN MAID, INC.
(Subsidiary of McGraw-Edison Company)
East 14th Street
Chattanooga, Tennessee 37401
Oliver Benton, Jr., President
(615) 624-2661

MODERN MATERIALS CORPORATION
(Subsidiary of American Forest Products Corporation)
16000 West Nine Mile Road
Detroit, Michigan 48220
Lucien Lamoureux, President and Treasurer
(313) 841-4422

MODERN MEDICAL METHODS LABORATORY
2842 Delaware
Kenmore, New York 14217

MODERN MILTEX CORPORATION
280 East 134th Street
New York, New York 10454
Albert Schnitt, President
(212) 585-6000

MODERN OFFICE DEVICES INC.
731 Hempstead Turnpike
Franklin Square, New York 11010
(516) 483-9436

MODERN PACKAGINGS, INC.
1341 Conant Street
Dallas, Texas 75207
(214) 638-7470

MODERN PARTITIONS INC.
545 East 32nd Street
Holland, Michigan 49423

Companies and Trade Names

MODERN PRODUCTS, INC.
3015 West Vera
Milwaukee, Wisconsin 53209
(414) 352-3333

MODERN SILVER (tarnish-resistant silver)
See Philcraft Imports Inc.

MODERN SPECIALTIES COMPANY, THE
4301 Ogden Avenue
Chicago, Illinois 60623
(312) 762-8000

MODERN TEA-BALL SERVICE INC.
386 West Broadway
New York, New York 10012
(212) 966-2722

MODERN TEXTILE COMPANY
See Kamp Togs, Inc.

MODERNE CARD COMPANY, INC.
3855 Lincoln Avenue
Chicago, Illinois 60613
(312) 248-4600

MODERNFOLD INDUSTRIES
Box 310
New Castle, Indiana 47362

MODERNPHONE (telephone equipment)
See Paul C. Roche Company, Inc.

MODESS (feminine-hygiene products)
See Personal Products Corporation

MODESTO OLIVE OIL COMPANY
4813 McHenry Avenue
Modesto, California 93550

MODGLIN MAID INC.
Post Office Box 30
Hazlehurst, Mississippi 39083

MODILAC (baby formula)
See Gerber Products Company

MODOC (produce)
See George F. Joseph

MODU/BASE (cushioned carpet baseboards)
See Commercial Carpet Corporation

MODU-FLOAT (houseboat)
See Marine Structures

MODULAIRE GROUP (upholstered furniture)
See Monarch Furniture Corporation

MODULAR SYSTEMS INC.
169 West Park Street
Fruitport, Michigan 49415

MODULINE (bookcases)
See Modular Systems Inc.

MODULINE INTERNATIONAL, INC.
Post Office Box 209
Chehalis, Washington 98532
Leonard C. Merta, President
(206) 748-6626

MOELLER INSTRUMENT COMPANY
(Subsidiary of Viking Instruments, Inc.)
3366 Union Road
Buffalo, New York 14225
Robert W. Danielson, President and Treasurer
(716) 685-4000

MOELLER MANUFACTURING COMPANY
Pickett Street
Greenville, Mississippi 38701
(601) 335-2326

MOEN
(Division of Stanadyne)
377 Woodland Avenue
Elyria, Ohio 44035

MOEN & PATTON METAL PRODUCTS INC.
Lancaster, Pennsylvania 17603
(717) 392-8220

MOENNING MUSIC COMPANY
Oak and Las Tunas Drive
Temple City, California 91780

MOET & CHANDON (champagne)
See Schieffelin & Company

MOFFETT MEDICINE COMPANY, C.J.
1 West 37th Street
New York, New York 10018
(212) 244-3398

MOFFITT INC., LUCIAN Q.
Box 1415
Akron, Ohio 44309

MOGEN DAVID WINE CORPORATION
(Division of Coca-Cola Bottling Company of New York, Inc.)
3737 South Sacramento Avenue
Chicago, Illinois 60632
J. Myron Bay, President
(312) 254-6300

MOHASCO CORPORATION
57 Lyon Street
Amsterdam, New York 12010
Herbert L. Shuttleworth, II, President
(518) 841-2111
See also Chromcraft Corporation Futorian Manufacturing Company; and Monarch Furniture Corporation

MOHAWK (carpets)
See Mohasco Corporation

Companies and Trade Names

MOHAWK (men's apparel)
See Utica-Duxbak Corporation

MOHAWK (sheets and pillowcases)
See J.P. Stevens & Company Inc.

MOHAWK AIRLINES
See Allegheny Airlines, Inc.

MOHAWK BRUSH COMPANY
(Subsidiary of Fuller Brush Company)
37 Fuller Road
Albany, New York 12201
Richard F. Sonneborn, President
(518) 438-6226

MOHAWK GLOVES INC.
1015 Dewey Street
Freeland, Pennsylvania 18224

MOHAWK LIQUEUR CORPORATION
1965 Porter
Detroit, Michigan 48216
(313) 962-4545

MOHAWK RUBBER COMPANY
50 Executive Parkway
Hudson, Ohio 44236
Henry M. Fawcett, President
(216) 653-3111

MOHERTUS TRADING COMPANY
45 West 38th Street
New York, New York 10018
(212) 563-5533

MOHLER, A.
Onamia, Minnesota 56359
(612) 532-3144

MOIST & EASY (cake mix)
See Procter & Gamble Company

MOIST MEALS (cat food)
See Quaker Oats Company

MOISTAIRE (humidifiers)
See Mutz Corporation

MOISTURE PETALS (cosmetics, skin-care products)
See DuBarry

MOISTURELLE (women's toiletries)
See Bristol-Myers Company

MOJAVE FOODS COMPANY
5335 Valley Boulevard
Los Angeles, California 90032
(213) 225-2211

MOJUD (hosiery)
See Kayser-Roth Hosiery Company, Inc.

MOLDED FIBER GLASS BOAT COMPANY
55 Fourth Avenue
Union City, Pennsylvania 16438
Richard S. Morrison, President
(814) 438-3841

MOLDED FRUIT BALL COMPANY
Post Office Box 448
North East, Pennsylvania 16428

MOLDED MAGIC (lingerie)
See Wonder Maid Inc.

MOLDED PRODUCTS COMPANY
Post Office Box 267
Dowagiac, Michigan 49047

MOLDED RUBBER COMPANY
Main and Rector Streets
Philadelphia, Pennsylvania 19127
(215) 482-3455

MOLECUDYNE INC.
72 Second Street
Cambridge, Massachusetts 02141

MOLEX INC.
2222 Wellington Court
Lisle, Illinois 60532
John H. Krehbiel, Sr., Chairman and President
(312) 969-4550

MOLINA DESIGNS, INC., EDWARD
940 Glenview
Ridgewood, New Jersey 07450

MOLINE MALLEABLE IRON COMPANY
Saint Charles, Illinois 60174

MOLITOR, INC.
(Subsidiary of Stainless Equipment Company)
2829 South Santa Fe
Englewood, Colorado 80110
(303) 789-2231

MOLLA, INC.
110 State Street
Westbury, New York 11590
Otto W. Molla, President
(516) 334-2885

MOLLE (shaving cream)
See Glenbrook Laboratories

MOLLER, INC., M.P.
403 North Prospect Street
Hagerstown, Maryland 21740
W. Riley Daniels, President
(301) 733-9000

MOLOR PRODUCTS COMPANY
151 Einsenhower Lane
Lombard, Illinois 60148

MOLZAHN & COMPANY, INC., WALTER
2330 Lincoln Avenue
Chicago, Illinois 60614
(312) 528-0550

MONARCA (mobile kitchen cabinets)
See Monarch Industries, Inc.

Companies and Trade Names

MONARCH (hosiery and socks)
See Dwight S. Williams & Company, Inc.

MONARCH (knives)
See Cole National Corporation

MONARCH (scissors and shears)
See Acme United Corporation

MONARCH CARPET MILLS
5025 New Peachtree Road
Chamblee, Georgia 30341
E.T. Barwick, President
(404) 451-4761

MONARCH FURNITURE CORPORATION
(Subsidiary of Mohasco Industries)
Post Office Drawer 1351
600 Scientific Street
High Point, North Carolina 27261
Harold M. Gutterman, President
(919) 454-1131

MONARCH INDUSTRIES, INC.
Post Office Box One
Goshen, Indiana 46540
Richard C. Mynsberge, President
(219) 533-9581

MONARCH INSTITUTIONAL FOODS
(Division of Consolidated Foods Corporation)
White Horse Road
Greenville, South Carolina 29605

MONARCH KITCHEN APPLIANCES
(Division of Malleable Iron Range Company)
Department NR 73
Beaver Dam, Wisconsin 53916
M.J. Maier, President
(414) 885-3311

MONARCH LUGGAGE COMPANY, INC.
5 Delevan Street
Brooklyn, New York 11231
Jerome Fried, President
(212) 858-6900

MONARCH MARKING SYSTEMS INC.
Post Office Box 608
Dayton, Ohio 45401
Thomas R. Loemker, President
(513) 866-7401

MONARCH-NUGRAPE COMPANY
3742 Northeast Freeway
Doraville, Georgia 30340
(404) 451-6133

MONARCH PHARMACEUTICALS
1956 N.E. 151st Street
North Miami Beach, Florida 33160

MONARCH RUBBER COMPANY
3500 Pulaski Highway
Baltimore, Maryland 21224
Joseph Schwaber, Jr., President
(301) 342-8510

MONARCH WINE COMPANY, INC.
4500 Second Avenue
Brooklyn, New York 11232
Leo Starr, President
(212) 788-3500

MONARCH WINE COMPANY OF GEORGIA
(Division of Kane-Miller Corporation)
451 Sawtell Avenue S.E.
Atlanta, Georgia 30315
(404) 622-4496

MONARK BOAT COMPANY
Patton Street
Monticello, Alaska 71655
Zach McClendon, Jr., President
(501) 367-5361

MONARK EGG CORPORATION
601 East Third Street
Kansas City, Missouri 64106
(816) 421-1970

MONASTERY (wines and cordials)
See Consolidated Distilled Products, Inc.

MONAX (glass products)
See Corning Glass Works

MONCRIEF (furnaces and air conditioning)
See Luxaire, Inc.

MONECO COMPANY
Post Office Box 944
New Haven, Connecticut 06504
Bertram Frankenberger, President, Treasurer and Purchasing Agent
(203) 624-3889

MONFORT OF COLORADO, INC.
Post Office Box G
Greeley, Colorado 80631
Kenneth W. Monfort, President
(303) 353-8200

MONGOL (pencils)
See Eberhard Faber, Inc.

MONIQUE (toiletries, hair-care products, etc.)
See Quality Cosmetics Corporation

MONIQUE BRASSIERE COMPANY
7422 New Utrecht Avenue
Brooklyn, New York 11204
(212) 256-8500

MONIQUE LINGERIE
44 East 32nd Street
New York, New York 10016
(212) 889-5030

MONIQUE ORIGINALS (bath and boudoir accessories)
See Tanyana of California

MONITOR (tape recorder-reproducer)
See SoundScriber Corporation

Companies and Trade Names

MONITOR COACH COMPANY
(Subsidiary of The Wickes Corporation)
State Road Number 19 North
Wakarusa, Indiana 46573
Lawrence D. Poskas, General Manager
(219) 862-4521

MONITOR SUGAR COMPANY
2600 South Euclid Avenue
Bay City, Michigan 48706

MONKIEWICZ, INC., K.
50 Winnisimmet
Chelsea, Massachusetts 02150

MONKS' BREAD
Abbey of the Genesee
Piffard, New York 14533

MONNET (cognac)
See Munson Shaw Company

MONNET (sports apparel)
See Eiger Mountain Sports

MONNIG DRY GOODS COMPANY
500 Houston Street
Fort Worth, Texas 76102
Oscar E. Monnig, President
(817) 332-7211

MONO-KOTE (fireproofing)
See W.R. Grace & Company, Construction Products Division

MONO MANUFACTURING COMPANY
Post Office Box 2787
CSS
Springfield, Missouri 65803
Denton H. Smith, Chairman and President
(417) 862-9324

MONOGRAM (initialed grooming products for men)
See Ellen Kaye Laboratories, Inc.

MONOGRAM COMPANY OF CALIFORNIA
500 Hampshire Street
San Francisco, California 94110
Stephen Barker, President
(415) 863-3600

MONOGRAM INDUSTRIES INC.
100 Wilshire Boulevard
Santa Monica, California 90401
William R. Zimmerman, President
(213) 870-9661

MONOGRAM MODELS, INC.
(Subsidiary of Mattel, Inc.)
8601 Waukegan Road
Morton Grove, Illinois 60053
Thomas A. Gannon, Jr., President
(312) 966-3500

MONONGAH (hand tools and furniture)
See O. Ames Company

MONONGAHELA POWER COMPANY
(Subsidiary of Alleghany Power System, Inc.)
Monongahela Power Building
Fairmont, West Virginia 26554
C. B. Finch, President
(304) 366-3000

MONONGAHELA VALLEY CUT GLASS COMPANY
See Valcraft, Inc.

MONOPOLY (real-estate trading game)
See Parker Brothers

MONOPOXY (enamels and undercoats)
See Andrew Brown Company

MONROE (canned foods)
See C-B Foods

MONROE AUTO EQUIPMENT COMPANY
International Drive
Monroe, Michigan 48161
Charles S. McIntyre, III, President
(313) 241-8000

MONROE FROZEN FOODS INC.
(Subsidiary of Quality Brands Inc.)
111 Kelly Avenue
Middleport, New York 14105

MONROE TABLE COMPANY, THE
300 North Walnut Street
Colfax, Iowa 50054
Robert K. Underwood, General Manager
(515) 674-3511

MONROE, THE CALCULATOR COMPANY
(Division of Litton Industries)
550 Central Avenue
Orange, New Jersey 07051
Robert F. Kane, President
(201) 673-6600

MONSANTO COMPANY
800 North Lindbergh Boulevard
Saint Louis, Missouri 63166
John W. Hanley, President
(314) 694-1000

MONSANTO TEXTILES COMPANY
(Division of Monsanto Company)
1114 Avenue of the Americas
New York, New York 10036
(212) 764-5000

MONSEY PRODUCTS COMPANY
Coldstream Road
Kimberton, Pennsylvania 19442
(215) 933-8888

MONSIEUR HENRI WINES, LTD.
(Division of PepsiCo, Inc.)
Purchase, New York 10577
James P. Schadt, General Manager
(914) 253-2000

Companies and Trade Names

MONT BLANC (sports apparel)
See United Knitwear Company Inc.

MONT ROYALE CRYSTAL
1123 Broadway
New York, New York 10010
(212) 675-3232

MONTAG
(Division of The Mead Corporation)
245 North Highland Avenue N.E.
Atlanta, Georgia 30307
(404) 525-5311

MONTAKNIT COMPANY INC.
112 West 34th Street
New York, New York 10010
(212) 279-6512

MONTANA (sports accessories)
See Beconta Inc.

MONTANA FLOUR MILLS COMPANY
900 16th Street, North
Great Falls, Montana 59401
J.A. Mactier, President
(406) 453-4321

MONTANA PETROLEUM ASSOCIATION
(Division of Rocky Mountain Oil and Gas Association)
Post Office Box 1398
311 Petroleum Building
Billings, Montana 59103
Don L. Allen, Executive Director
(406) 252-3871

MONTANA POWER COMPANY
40 East Broadway
Butte, Montana 59701
John E. Corette, Chairman of the Board
(406) 723-5421

MONTANA-DAKOTA UTILITIES COMPANY
400 North Fourth Street
Bismarck, North Dakota 58501
Cecil W. Smith, Chairman of the Board
(701) 224-3000

MONTANT (sports apparel and accessories)
See Killington Manufacturing Company

MONTCLAIR (cigarettes)
See American Tobacco Company

MONTCLAIR IMPORTS, INC.
35 Bethpage Road
Hicksville, New York 11802

MONTEATH COMPANY, J.H.
2500 Park Avenue
Bronx, New York 10451
Douglas M. Dayton, President
(212) 292-9333

MONTEBELLO LIQUORS, INC.
Bank Street and Central Avenue
Baltimore, Maryland 21202
Samuel J. Bernstein, President
(301) 539-3727

MONTEGO (men's toiletries)
See Shulton, Inc.

MONTEGO (menswear)
See J. Schoeneman Inc.

MONTEIL COSMETIQUES CORPORATION, GERMAINE
(Subsidiary of British American Tobacco)
40 West 57th Street
New York, New York 10019
(212) 582-3010

MONTELLO PRODUCTS COMPANY
33 West Street
Montello, Wisconsin 53949
(414) 297-2166

MONTENE MORRIS (food products)
See McCall Farms Inc.

MONTEREY (foundation garments, lingerie)
See Youthcraft/Charmfit

MONTEREY (guitars)
See Harmony Company

MONTEREY (kitchens)
See Youngstown Kitchens (Division of Mullins Manufacturing Corporation)

MONTEREY HOUSE
3310 South Richey
Houston, Texas 77017
David Garza, Jr., President
(713) 944-1431

MONTEREY UNDERGARMENT COMPANY
118 Madison Avenue
New York, New York 10016
(212) 684-0520

MONTESSORI TOYS INC.
376 Wyandanch Avenue North
Babylon, New York 11704

MONTGOMERY MARINE PRODUCTS
959 West 17th Street
Costa Mesa, California 92627

MONTGOMERY WARD & COMPANY, INC.
(Subsidiary of Marcor, Inc.)
619 West Chicago Avenue
Chicago, Illinois 60607
Edward S. Donnell, President
(312) 467-2000

Companies and Trade Names

MONTGOMERY WARD CREDIT CORPORATION
(Subsidiary of Montgomery Ward & Company)
Edgemart Building
4 Denny Road
Wilmington, Delaware 19809
James C. Morton, President
(302) 762-5252

MONTICELLO (whiskey)
See Schenley Industries, Inc.

MONTICELLO CANNING COMPANY, INC.
Box 487
Crossville, Tennessee 38555

MONTICELLO DRUG COMPANY
45 Broad Street Viaduct
Jacksonville, Florida 32202
T.S. Roberts, Jr., President
(904) 355-3666

MONTICELLO MANUFACTURING COMPANY, INC.
Post Office Box 436
Monticello, Kentucky 42633
Noel Zinman, President
(606) 348-4311

MONTINI (canned foods)
See Tillie Lewis Foods, Inc.

MONTMORENCY (canned foods)
See Duffy-Mott Company, Inc.

MONTROSE (clocks)
See P.R. Myers & Company

MONUMENTAL LIFE INSURANCE COMPANY
Charles and Chase Streets
Baltimore, Maryland 21202
Donald H. Wilson, Jr., President
(301) 685-2900

MONY
See Mutual of New York

MONY-X, INC.
Post Office Box 45040
Tulsa, Oklahoma 74145

MONZA MARINE INC.
5731 S.W. 23rd Street
Hollywood, Florida 33023

MOODY TOOLS INC.
42 Dudley Street
Providence, Rhode Island 02905

MOODY'S INVESTORS SERVICE, INC.
(Subsidiary of Dun & Bradstreet, Inc.)
99 Church Street
New York, New York 10007
Richard D. Simmons, President
(212) 267-8800

MOOG (ski equipment)
See Collins Ski Products Inc.

MOOG AUTOMOTIVE, INC.
6565 Wells Avenue
Saint Louis, Missouri 63133
Hubert C. Moog, President
(314) 385-3400

MOOG MUSIC INC.
Box 131
Academy Street
Williamsville, New York 14221
(716) 633-2280

MOON DROPS (cosmetics, skin-care products, etc.)
See Revlon Inc.

MOON FLOWER (melamine products)
See Boonton Molding Company, Inc.

MOON PENCIL COMPANY INC., J.R.
Fifth Avenue North
Lewisburg, Tennessee 37091

MOONGLO (foundation garments, lingerie)
See Teenform, Inc.

MOONKIST (canned vegetables)
See Desoto Canning Company

MOONLITERS (battery-operated cordless patio lites)
See Meteor (Division of Nu-Rod Inc.)

MOORE & CLARK
1095 North Seventh
San Jose, California 95112

MOORE & COMPANY, A.F.
538 Franklin
Worcester, Massachusetts 01604

MOORE & COMPANY, BENJAMIN
51 Chestnut Ridge Road
Montvale, New Jersey 07645
(201) 573-9600

MOORE & COMPANY SOUPS INC.
166 Abington Avenue
Newark, New Jersey 07107
(201) 484-4111

MOORE COMPANY, E.R.
(Division of Beatrice Foods Company)
7230 North Caldwell Avenue
Niles, Illinois 60648
Edwin R. Moore, President
(312) 774-6600

MOORE COMPANY, GEORGE C.
Beach Street
Westerly, Rhode Island 02891
Thomas F. Moore, Jr., President
(401) 596-2816

MOORE CORPORATION
653 New Circle Road N.E.
Lexington, Kentucky 40501

Companies and Trade Names

MOORE CORPORATION, JOHN C.
67 Stone Street
Rochester, New York 14604
(716) 442-8860

MOORE DRUG EXCHANGE, INC., H.L.
610 Arch Street
New Britain, Connecticut 06050

MOORE-HANDLEY INC.
Post Office Box 2607
Birmingham, Alabama 35202
W.W. French, III, President
(205) 663-8011

MOORE, INC., GOODLOE E.
2811 North Vermillion
Danville, Illinois 61832

MOORE KIRK LABORATORIES INC.
(Division of Zemmer Company)
231 Hulton Road
Oakmont, Pennsylvania 15139

MOORE-MCCORMACK LINES, INC.
1 Landmark Square
Stamford, Connecticut 06901
James R. Barker, Chairman of the Board
(203) 357-1100

MOORE PUSH PIN COMPANY
113-125 Berkley
Philadelphia, Pennsylvania 19144
(215) 842-3116

MOORE SONS, INC., EDWARD J.
46 11th Street
Long Island City, New York 11101
(212) 729-7557

MOORE SPECIAL TOOL COMPANY, INC.
800 Union Avenue
Bridgeport, Connecticut 06607
Wayne R. Moore, President
(203) 366-3224

MOORES (baked goods)
See Blue Bird Baking Company Inc.

MOORE'S (gas heaters)
See Locke Stove Company

MOORE'S EDGEMONTE CANDIES
3004 Pinewood
Baltimore, Maryland 21214

MOORE'S FOOD PRODUCTS, INC.
Post Office Box 128
Fort Atkinson, Wisconsin 53538
Scott Moore, President
(414) 563-6625

MOORGUARD (paints)
See Benjamin Moore & Company

MOORHEAD & COMPANY, INC.
Box 2728
Van Nuys, California 91404

MOORMAN MANUFACTURING COMPANY
1000 North 30th Street
Quincy, Illinois 62301
Robert B. Hulsen, President
(217) 222-7100

MOORS (menswear)
See Lord Jeff Knitting Company Inc.

MOOTZ CANDY COMPANY
152 Summit Street
Toledo, Ohio 43604

MOP & GLO (floor-care products)
See Lehn & Fink Products Company

MOP RENEW (dustmop treatment)
See Continental Chemical Corporation

MOPAR (automotive parts)
See Chrysler Corporation

MOPARD (dust-cloth treatment)
See Frank Miller & Sons

MOR (food products)
See Wilson & Company, Inc.

MOR-FLO INDUSTRIES, INC.
18450 South Miles Road
Cleveland, Ohio 44128
Walter L. Abt, President
(216) 663-7300

MORAN STUDIOS, MALCOLM
Post Office Box 310
Monterey, California 93940

MORE CANDY COMPANY, INC.
54 Brown Street
Rochester, New York 14608
(716) 546-5771

MOREBA PHARMACEUTICAL CORPORATION
(Division of Stiefel Laboratories, Inc.)
15418 South Broadway
Gardena, California 90247
(213) 323-7012

MOREDDI (contemporary furniture)
See Richards Morganthau Company

MOREL (vermouth)
See Distillerie Stock U.S.A. Ltd.

MORETZ CANDY COMPANY, INC.
1139 Wagner Road
Bristol, Virginia 24201

MORGAN (food products)
See Burnette Farms Packing Company

983

Companies and Trade Names

MORGAN & COMPANY, INC.
300 A Street
Boston, Massachusetts 02210
(617) 482-6666

MORGAN ADHESIVES COMPANY
4560 Darrow Road
Stow, Ohio 44224
Blake H. Hooper, President and
  Chief Executive Officer
(216) 688-1111

MORGAN-BOCKIUS STUDIOS INC.
1412 Old York Road
Warminster, Pennsylvania 18974

MORGAN CITY FREEZER & COLD
  STORAGE INC.
115 Second Street
Morgan City, Louisiana 70380

MORGAN CONSTRUCTION
  COMPANY
15 Belmont Street
Worcester, Massachusetts 01605
Paul S. Morgan, President
(617) 755-6111

MORGAN GUARANTY TRUST
  COMPANY OF NEW YORK
23 Wall Street
New York, New York 10015
Walter H. Page, President
(212) 483-2323

MORGAN JONES (sheets)
  See Springs Mills, Inc.

MORGAN MILLS
25 North Cedar
Lititz, Pennsylvania 17543

MORGAN PACKING COMPANY
Austin, Indiana 47102
Ivan H. Morgan, President
(812) 794-1170

MORGAN PRESS INC.
145 Palisade Street
Dobbs Ferry, New York 10522

MORGAN QUINN (shoes)
  See Leverenz Shoe Company

MORGAN SIGN MACHINE
  COMPANY, THE
4510 North Ravenswood Avenue
Chicago, Illinois 60640
(312) 561-5926

MORGAN YACHT CORPORATION
Post Office Box 11598
Saint Petersburg, Florida 33733

MORGANTON HOSIERY MILLS,
  INC.
(Subsidiary of Dan River, Inc.)
101 Lenoir Street
Morganton, North Carolina 28655
Stephen A. Bundy, President
(704) 437-0661
  See also Flatterknit by Dan
    River, Inc.

MORGENSTERN & COMPANY,
  CHARLES
200 East Sunrise Highway
Freeport, New York 11520

MORGRO (garden products)
  See Wasatch Chemical (Division
    of Entrada Industries Inc.)

MORHAND (hardware, lawn and
garden supplies, paints, etc.)
  See Moore-Handley Inc.

MORILLA COMPANY, THE
43-01 21st Street
Long Island City, New York 11101
(212) 361-1303

MORNING GLORY (mattress)
  See Taylor Bedding
    Manufacturing Company

MORNING JOY (coffee)
  See American Coffee Company,
    Inc.

MORNING TREAT COFFEE
  COMPANY INC.
4535 Choctaw Road
Baton Rouge, Louisiana 70806

MORO CIGAR COMPANY
(Division of Consolidated Cigar
  Corporation, A Gulf & Western
  Company)
2161 N.W. 25th Avenue
Miami, Florida 33142
(305) 634-2295

MOROCCO LEATHER GOODS INC.
1141 Broadway
New York, New York 10001
(212) 684-7714

MOROLINE (hairdressing, petroleum
jelly)
  See Plough Inc.

MORONEY, INC., JAMES
243 North 63rd
Philadelphia, Pennsylvania 19139
(215) 748-6200

MOROSCO (sporting goods)
  See Morris Rosenbloom &
    Company Inc.

MORPAC INC.
4215 21st Avenue, West
Seattle, Washington 98199
Robert F. Morgan, Chairman and
  President
(206) 284-2940

MORPHY-RICHARDS INC.
128 Ludlow Avenue
Northvale, New Jersey 07647

MORRELL & COMPANY, JOHN
(Subsidiary of United Brands
  Company)
208 South LaSalle Street
Chicago, Illinois 60604
Elias Paul, President
(312) 443-3000
  See also Golden Sun Feeds Inc.;
    Greenebaum Inc., M.H.; and
    Meyer Packing Company, H.H.

Companies and Trade Names

MORRIS & ASSOCIATES
801 Fayetteville Street
Raleigh, North Carolina 27602

MORRIS & COMPANY INC.,
  OWEN
39 West 32nd Street
New York, New York 10001
(212) 689-4943

MORRIS ASSOCIATED FACTORIES
  INC., RALPH
37 West Fall Creek Parkway
Indianapolis, Indiana 46208
(216) 923-3388

MORRIS COMPANY, BERT M.
11612 West Olympic Boulevard
Los Angeles, California 90064
(213) 272-4186

MORRIS COMPANY, I.T.
427 South Main Street
Canandaigua, New York 14424

MORRIS COMPANY, J. II.
394 Elm Street
Southbridge, Massachusetts 01550
J. Iiwin Morris, President and
  Treasurer
(617) 764-4394

MORRIS CORPORATION,
  NORMAN M.
301 East 57th Street
New York, New York 10022
Norman M. Morris, President
(212) 753-3000

MORRIS-FLAMINGO INC.
80 Eastgate Drive
Danville, Illinois 61832
Bob A. Wilson, President
(217) 442-6860

MORRIS, INC., JOYCE
264 Fifth Avenue
New York, New York 10001

MORRIS, INC., PHILIP
100 Park Avenue
New York, New York 10017
(212) 679-1800

MORRISON BOOK COMPANY
Princeton, Illinois 61356

MORRISON CANDY COMPANY
252 Pillow Street
Butler, Pennsylvania 16001

MORRISON COMPANY, THE
110 Tasker
Philadelphia, Pennsylvania 19148
(215) 467-9600

MORRISON FOOD PRODUCTS OF
  MISSISSIPPI INC.
Box 10627
Jackson, Mississippi 39209

MORRISON, INC.
Post Office Box 2608
Mobile, Alabama 36601
D.R. Cowart, President
(205) 432-9711

MORRISON MILLING COMPANY
319 East Prairie
Denton, Texas 76201
Edward W. Morrison Jr., President
(817) 387-6111

MORRO CASTLE (cigars)
    See Perfecto Garcia & Brothers,
    Inc.

MORROWS INC.
Post Office Box 2281
Wichita Falls, Texas 76307

MORROW & COMPANY, WILLIAM
105 Madison Avenue
New York, New York 10016
J. Lawrence Hughes, President
(212) 889-3050

MORSE CONTROLS
(Division of Rockwell International)
21 Clinton Street
Hudson, Ohio 44236
A.J. O'Neil, Vice President and
  General Manager
(216) 653-9161

MORSE ELECTRO PRODUCTS
  CORPORATION
101-10 Foster Avenue
Brooklyn, New York 11236
Philip S. Morse, President
(212) 272-4343

MORSE SHOE, INC.
555 Turnpike Street
Canton, Massachusetts 02021
Alfred L. Morse, Chairman of the
  Board
(617) 828-9300

MORSE-STARRETT PRODUCTS
  COMPANY
1204 49th Avenue
Oakland, California 94601
(415) 534-7571

MORSE'S FOODMARTS, INC.
1364 Blue Hill Avenue
Mattapan, Massachusetts 02126

MORTELL COMPANY
550 North Hobbie Avenue
Kankakee, Illinois 60901
Donald Mortel, President
(815) 933-5514

MORTON FOODS OPERATIONS
(Division of W.R. Grace &
  Company)
6333 Denton Drive
Dallas, Texas 75235
Dan Neal, President
(214) 351-3291

Companies and Trade Names

MORTON FROZEN FOODS
(Division of ITT Continental Baking
    Company)
Post Office Box 731
Rye, New York 10580
George E. Mrdeze, President
(914) 967-4747

MORTON HOUSE KITCHENS, INC.
(Subsidiary of Thomas J. Lipton,
    Inc.)
Tenth Street Seventh Corso
Nebraska City, Nebraska 68410
W.G. Barker, President
(402) 873-6671

MORTON, INC., JERI
14 East 32nd Street
New York, New York 10016
(212) 686-3257

MORTON-NORWICH PRODUCTS,
    INC.
110 North Wacker Drive
Chicago, Illinois 60606
William D. Davies, Jr., President
(312) 621-5200
    See also Norwich Pharmacal
        Company

MORTON PHARMACEUTICALS
1625 North Highland
Memphis, Tennessee 38108
(901) 386-8840

MORTON SALT COMPANY
(Division of Morton-Norwich
    Products)
110 North Wacker Drive
Chicago, Illinois 60606
Kline Weatherford, President
(312) 621-5200

MORTON'S SHOE STORES, INC.
647 Summer Street
Boston, Massachusetts 02210
Louis Narva, Chairman of the Board
(617) 269-6100
    See also Lacomia Shoe Company

MORU CANDY COMPANY
1112 Walnut Street
Roselle, New Jersey 07203

MOSBY COMPANY, C.V.
11830 Westline Industrial Drive
Saint Louis, Missouri 63141
Robert C. Strain, President
(314) 872-8370

MOSCAHLADES BROTHERS, INC.
28-30 North Moore Street
New York, New York 10013
(212) 226-5410

MOSEMAN COMPANY, H.B.
27 North Prince Street
Lancaster, Pennsylvania 17603

MOSER, INC., EDGAR
315 Fifth Avenue
New York, New York 10016
(212) 684-3521

MOSHY BROTHERS, INC.
89 Chambers Street
New York, New York 10007
(212) 227-6267

MOSINEE PAPER CORPORATION
Mosinee, Wisconsin 54455
C. Sholtens, President
(715) 693-2111
    See also Bay West Paper
        Company

MOSKOWITZ CORPORATION,
    MORRIS
1 East 33rd Street
New York, New York 10016
(212) 679-3340

MOSKOWITZ LACE CORPORATION
15 West 38th Street
New York, New York 10018
(212) 354-1805

MOSLER SAFE COMPANY
(Division of American-Standard Inc.)
1561 Grand Boulevard
Hamilton, Ohio 45012
(513) 867-4000

MOSRITE (guitars and accessories)
    See Pacific Music Supply
        Company

MOSS CHEMICAL COMPANY, INC.
183 Saint Paul Street
Rochester, New York 14604
(716) 546-6187

MOSS, CHEMIST, BELLE
19114 Saint Marys
Detroit, Michigan 48235
(313) 272-4240

MOSS LABORATORIES
500 Clements Bridge Road
Barrington, New Jersey 08007

MOSS SHIRTMAKERS INC.
10 West 33rd Street
New York, New York 10001
(212) 239-8786

MOSS-SIMCO (cutlery)
    See S.I. Moss Company, Inc.

MOSSBERG & SONS, INC., O.F.
7 Grasso Avenue
North Haven, Connecticut 06473
Alan Mossberg, President
(203) 288-6491

MOSSE ENTERPRISES LTD.
3115 Arlington Avenue
Riverdale, New York 10463

MOSSMAN COMPANY INC., S.L.
Strother Field
Winfield, Kansas 67156

Companies and Trade Names

MOTA-NU INC.
3109 Bryan
Fort Worth, Texas 76101
(817) 921-0209

MOTALOY MANUFACTURING
CORPORATION
8603 North New Braunfels Avenue
San Antonio, Texas 78209

MOTEL 6 INC.
1888 Century Park East
Los Angeles, California 90067
Daniel R. Shaughnessy, President
(213) 277-6666

MOTHER EARTH (canned and frozen foods)
See Mushroom Co-Operative Canning Company

MOTHER MURPHY'S LABORATORIES
2826 South Elm
Greensboro, North Carolina 27405

MOTHER NATURE'S NUTRITION
CENTERS INC.
76 Garth Road
Scarsdale, New York 10583

MOTHER'S (food products)
See Vita Food Products Inc.

MOTHER'S CAKE & COOKIE
COMPANY
810 81st Avenue
Oakland, California 94621
George F. Kinst, President
(415) 569-2323

MOTHER'S COOKIE COMPANY
(Division of Beatrice Foods)
2287 Ralph Avenue
Louisville, Kentucky 40216
Robert O. Denham, President
(502) 448-1730

MOTHERS PRIDE (flour, feed, meal, etc.)
See Shawnee Milling Company

MOTION-MATIC SYSTEMS
(Division of C. M. Smillie & Company)
1100 Woodward Heights
Ferndale, Michigan 48220

MOTIONETICS INC.
2320 Lewis Street
Endicott, New York 13760

MOTOMCO, INC.
89 Terminal Avenue
Clark, New Jersey 07066
(201) 381-3033

MOTOR CLUB OF AMERICA
484 Central Avenue
Newark, New Jersey 07107
William Green, Chairman of the Board
(201) 733-4114

MOTOR-GUIDE
Box 551
Starkville, Mississippi 39759

MOTOR HOMES INC.
(Subsidiary of PRF Industries Inc.)
3709 West Erie Avenue
Lorain, Ohio 44053

MOTOR INN (motor homes)
See Winnebago Industries Inc.

MOTOR TITE (automotive accessories)
See Nationwide Industries Inc.

MOTOR-TOTER (safety car seats for children)
See Century Products Inc.

MOTOR WHEEL CORPORATION
(Subsidiary of Goodyear Tire & Rubber Company)
1600 North Larch Street
Lansing, Michigan 48914
Robert J. Derleth, President
(517) 485-4000

MOTORCRAFT (batteries, oil filters, and parts)
See Ford Motor Company

MOTOROLA, INC.
5725 North East River Road
Chicago, Illinois 60631
William J. Weisz, President
(312) 399-2100

MOTORS INSURANCE
CORPORATION
(Subsidiary of General Motors Acceptance Corporation)
767 Fifth Avenue
New York, New York 10022
Frank A. Mingle, President
(212) 486-5000

MOTOVATOR (motor home)
See Cayo RV Corporation

MOTTAHEDEH & COMPANY INC.
225 Fifth Avenue
New York, New York 10010
(212) 685-3050

MOTT'S (canned foods)
See Duffy-Mott Company, Inc.

MOTT'S SUPER MARKETS, INC.
59-63 Leggett Street
East Hartford, Connecticut 06108
Stanford Cohen, President
(203) 289-3301

MOULDED PRODUCTS INC.
Maple Plain, Minnesota 55359
Donald L. Pipal, President
(612) 479-1911

MOUNDS (candy)
See Peter Paul, Inc

MOUNT CLEMENS POTTERY
COMPANY
261 Church Street
Mount Clemens, Michigan 48043
Ernest Paul, President
(313) 468-4558

Companies and Trade Names

MOUNT HOOD CHEMICAL
CORPORATION
4444 N.W. Yeon Avenue
Portland, Oregon 97210

MOUNT LAUREL CANNING
CORPORATION
1108 Beaumont Avenue
Temple, Pennsylvania 19560

MOUNT MAURICE (food products)
See Big Stone Canning Company

MOUNT MESA (food products)
See Skyland Food Corporation

MOUNT OLIVE PICKLE COMPANY
Box 390
Mount Olive, North Carolina 28365
John N. Walker, President and
  Treasurer
(919) 658-2535

MOUNT ROSE CANNING
COMPANY INC.
King George Virginia 22485

MOUNT STEWART (food products)
See C.M. McLean Ltd.

MOUNT VERNON (whiskey)
See National Distillers &
  Chemical Corporation

MOUNT ZION (kosher wines)
See Madera Bonded Wine &
  Liquor Company

MOUNTAIN CREST (food products)
See S. & G. Products Inc.

MOUNTAIN DEW (soft drink)
See Pepsi-Cola Company

MOUNTAIN FARM PRODUCTS INC.
1570 DeKalb Avenue N.E.
Atlanta, Georgia 30307
(404) 377-4267

MOUNTAIN HERITAGE (fruit
products)
See Ranson Fruit Company Inc.

MOUNTAIN HOME (food products)
See Old Virginia Inc.

MOUNTAIN HOUSE (freeze-dried
foods)
See Oregon Freeze-Dry Foods,
  Inc.

MOUNTAIN LID, THE
Box 3802
Aspen, Colorado 81611

MOUNTAIN MADE (canned foods)
See Perry Canning Company

MOUNTAIN MAID (frozen poultry)
See Rockingham Poultry
  Marketing Cooperative

MOUNTAIN MARINE INC.
1146 South Kalamath
Denver, Colorado 80223

MOUNTAIN MIST (frozen foods)
See Symons Frozen Foods Inc.

MOUNTAIN MIST (quilting cotton)
See Stearns & Foster Company

MOUNTAIN PASS CANNING
COMPANY
(Subsidiary of Pet, Inc.)
Post Office Box 220
Anthony, Texas 88021
W.E. Dyer, President
(915) 886-3951

MOUNTAIN PRODUCTS
CORPORATION
Box 1846
123 South Wenatchee Avenue
Wenatchee, Washington 98801
(509) 663-1196

MOUNTAIN STATES BEAN
COMPANY
4401 East 46th Avenue
Denver, Colorado 80216
Grant W. Hartman, President
(303) 355-3545

MOUNTAIN STATES TELEPHONE &
TELEGRAPH COMPANY
(Subsidiary of American Telephone &
  Telegraph Company)
931 14th Street
Denver, Colorado 80202
R.K. Timothy, President
(303) 624-2424

MOUNTAIN TROUT (fish)
See Virginia Trout Company, Inc.

MOUNTAIN VALLEY SPRING
COMPANY
150 Central Avenue
Hot Springs, Arkansas 71901
John G. Scott, President
(501) 623-6671

MOUNTIE (produce)
See Pacific Fruit & Produce
  Company

MOUQUIN (brandy)
See Austin, Nichols & Company,
  Inc.

MOVADO (watches)
See Zenith Movado Time
  Corporation

MOVIE STAR, INC.
392 Fifth Avenue
New York, New York 10018
Irwin Goldberger, President
(212) 563-3000

MOXIE (beverages)
See Monarch-Nugrape Company

Companies and Trade Names

MOYER BROTHERS
Post Office Box 667
Luray, Virginia 22835
(703) 743-6298

MOYERS (food products)
See Gordon Pickle Company

MOZART (canned vegetables)
See W.J. Weaver & Son

MOZART (cigars)
See Consolidated Cigar Corporation

MR.
See Mister

MRS.
See Mistress

MT.
See Mount

MUEHLEBACH (lager beer)
See Joseph Schlitz Brewery Company

MUEHLSTEIN & COMPANY, INC., H.
475 Steamboat Road
Greenwich, Connecticut 06830
(203) 661-3300

MUELLER & COMPANY, R.L.
Post Office Box 843
Pasadena, California 91102

MUELLER BROTHERS FISH COMPANY
11430 West Burleigh Street
Milwaukee, Wisconsin 53222
(414) 771-8600

MUELLER CLIMATROL CORPORATION
255 Old Brunswick Road
Piscataway, New Jersey 08854
(201) 981-0300

MUELLER COMPANY
500 West Eldorado Street
Decatur, Illinois 62522
Harlan A. White, President
(217) 423-4471

MUELLER COMPANY, C.F.
180 Baldwin Avenue
Jersey City, New Jersey 07306
Lester R. Thurston Jr., President
(201) 653-3800

MUELLER COMPANY, INC., LUDWIG
21 West Street
New York, New York 10006
(212) 344-4670

MUELLER COMPANY, PAUL
Post Office Box 828
Springfield, Missouri 65801
Paul Mueller, President, Chief Executive Officer and Product Development Manager
(417) 865-2831

MUELLER'S RX PHARMACY
2129 University Avenue
Berkeley, California 94704

MUENCH-KREUZER CANDLE COMPANY
(Division of Rust Craft Greeting Cards, Inc.)
4577 Buckley Road
Liverpool, New York 13088
Robert Levine, General Manager
(315) 652-6520
See also Emkay Candles

MUENCHENER (beer)
See Anheuser-Busch, Inc.

MUGUET (cologne, talc, bath powder)
See April Showers, Inc.

MUGUET DES BOIS (perfume, talc, bubble bath etc.)
See Coty

MUIRHEAD'S (Scotch whiskey)
See McKesson Liquor Company

MUKAMAL & SON COMPANY
61 Broadway
New York, New York 10006
(212) 269-4583

MULCO PRODUCTS, INC.
Marshall Street
Milford, Delaware 19963

MULLANE TAFFY COMPANY INC.
4108 Spring Grove Avenue
Cincinnati, Ohio 45223
(513) 542-5373

MULLINS MANUFACTURING CORPORATION
605 South Ellsworth Avenue
Salem, Ohio 44460
Harry D. Hirsch, Chairman of the Board
(216) 337-8771
See also Youngstown Kitchens

MULTI-CLEAN PRODUCTS
2277 Ford Parkway
Saint Paul, Minnesota 55116
(612) 698-8833

MULTI-MATO (food products)
See Tillie Lewis Foods Inc.

MULTI PRODUCTS INC.
824 West 36th Street
Chicago, Illinois 60609
(312) 523-3568

MULTI-PUMP (multi-purpose pump)
See Zoeller Company

Companies and Trade Names

MULTI-PURPOSE (fire extinguishers)
See Badger-Powhatan

MULTIBLITZ (cameras)
See Camera Specialty Company Inc.

MULTIFILTER (cigarettes)
See Philip Morris, Inc.

MULTILITH (office equipment)
See Addressograph-Multigraph Corporation

MULTIPLATE GLASS CORPORATION
100 Schmitt Boulevard East
Farmingdale, New York 11735

MULTIPLE TOYMAKERS
125 Walnut Avenue
New York, New York 10454
(212) 989-4422

MULTIPLEX DISPLAY FIXTURE COMPANY
1555 Larkin Williams Road
Fenton, Missouri 63026
Louis C. Meyer, President
(314) 343-5700

MULTISCRUB (cleansing scrub, medicated lathering lotion)
See Clinton (Division of Bristol-Myers Company)

MULTISTAMP COMPANY, THE
527-529 West 21st
Norfolk, Virginia 23517
(703) 622-2351

MULTITINT (paints)
See Colony Paints

MULTIVOX (electronic pianos, organs)
See Sorkin Music Company Inc.

MUM (deodorant)
See Clinton (Division of Bristol-Myers Company)

MUMM'S (champagne)
See Browne Vintners Company

MUMSEY CANDY COMPANY
1801-05 Federal Street
Camden, New Jersey 08105

MUNCHKINS (bite-size donut snack)
See Dunkin' Donuts of America

MUNCHOS (potato-crisp snack)
See Frito-Lay, Inc.

MUNCIE METAL SPINNING INC.
1012 East 20th
Muncie, Indiana 47302
(317) 288-1937

MUNDUS (wine)
See James B. Bean Distilling Company

MUNFORD, INC.
68 Brookwood Drive, N.E.
Atlanta, Georgia 30309
Dillard Munford, Chairman of the Board
(404) 873-6641

MUNRO GAMES, INC.
(Subsidiary of Servotronics, Inc.)
3901 Union Road
Buffalo, New York 14225
Robert G. Trbovich, President
(716) 633-9600

MUNSEY PRODUCTS INC.
8507 New Benton Highway
Little Rock, Arkansas 72209

MUNSINGWEAR, INC.
718 Glenwood Avenue
Minneapolis, Minnesota 55405
A. Byron Reed, President
(612) 340-4700
See also Vassarette

MUNSON MINIATURES
93 Winslow Park
Forest, Illinois 60466

MUNSON SHAW COMPANY
(Division of National Distillers & Chemical Corporation)
99 Park Avenue
New York, New York 10016
Kresten Hvass, President
(212) 697-0700

MUNTZ (televisions)
See TV Manufacturers of America

MURAI LABORATORIES, INC.
301 Almeria
Coral Gables, Florida 33134
See also Serum & Vaccines of America

MURATA CORPORATION OF AMERICA
2 Westchester Plaza
Elmsford, New York 10523

MURCH COMPANY, A.F.
Rural Free Delivery 4
Paw Paw, Michigan 49079
Robert W. McLean, President
(616) 657-3171

MURD COMPANY
2322 North American Street
Philadelphia, Pennsylvania 19123
(215) 739-6116

MURDOCK, INC.
15800 South Avalon
Compton, California 90220
Harold G. Murdock, Jr., President and Treasurer
(213) 770-0220

MURIEL (cigars)
See Consolidated Cigar Corporation

Companies and Trade Names

MURIEL GREETING CARDS
Mariposa, California 95338

MURINE COMPANY
(Division of Abbott Laboratories)
660 North Wabash
Chicago, Illinois 60611
(312) 944-0660

MURMAC IMPORTING
 CORPORATION
226 Fifth Avenue
New York, New York 10001
(212) 532-3744

MURO PHARMACAL LABORATORIES
121 Liberty Street
Quincy, Massachusetts 02169

MURPHY & NYE INC.
2243 North Elston Avenue
Chicago, Illinois 60614
(312) 384-2828

MURPHY BED & KITCHEN
 COMPANY, INC.
40 East 34th Street
New York, New York 10016
(212) 682-8936

MURPHY COMPANY, G.C.
531 Fifth Avenue
McKeesport, Pennsylvania 15132
S. Warne Robinson, Chairman of
 the Board
(412) 664-4441

MURPHY GRAIN & MILLING
 COMPANY
108 Crittendon Street
Owensboro, Kentucky 42302
F.X. Murphy, President
(502) 684-5211

MURPHY MANUFACTURING
 COMPANY INC.
600 Bergman Street
Louisville, Kentucky 40203
(502) 636-5178

MURPHY-MILLER INC.
931 Wing Avenue
Owensboro, Kentucky 42301
John M. Farish, President
(502) 684-4221

MURPHY MOTOR FREIGHT LINES,
 INC.
2323 Terminal Road
Saint Paul, Minnesota 55113
Edward L. Murphy, Jr., President
(612) 633-7911

MURPHY OIL CORPORATION
200 Jefferson Avenue
El Dorado, Arkansas 71730
Robert J. Sweeney, President
(501) 862-6411

MURPHY-PHOENIX
9505 Cassius Avenue
Cleveland, Ohio 44105
Murlan J. Murphy, Sr.
(216) 341-2211

MURPHY SUPPLY COMPANY
4087 Dry Ridge Road
Cincinnati, Ohio 45239
(513) 385-7738

MURPHY'S (Irish whiskey)
 See Austin, Nichols &
  Company, Inc.

MURRAY (food products)
 See H.A. Johnson Company

MURRAY-ALLEN IMPORTS, INC.
30 Pine Street
New Rochelle, New York 10801
Alan D. Caston, President
(914) 235-6000

MURRAY AMERICAN
 CORPORATION
15 Commerce Street
Chatham, New Jersey 07928

MURRAY OHIO MANUFACTURING
 COMPANY
Post Office Box 606
Brentwood, Tennessee 37027
William M. Hannon, President
(615) 373-4500

MURRAY OIL PRODUCTS
 COMPANY
17 Battery Place
New York, New York 10004
(212) 425-8790

MURRAY'S SUPERIOR PRODUCTS
 COMPANY
456 Charlotte
Detroit, Michigan 48201
(303) 833-0085

MUS-L-ON COMPANY
2034 American Avenue
Hayward, California 94545

MUSCATINE PEARL WORKS
Post Office Box 731
Muscatine, Iowa 52761
(319) 263-8411

MUSCO OLIVE PRODUCTS INC.
Fifth and Swift Streets
Orland, California 95963

MUSEBECK SHOE COMPANY, INC.
605 East Forest and Westover Street
Oconomowoc, Wisconsin 53066
W.W. Gallaher, President
(414) 567-5564

MUSETTE (pianos)
 See Aeolian Corporation

MUSEUM PIECES INC.
15 West 27th Street
New York, New York 10001
(212) 686-4796

Companies and Trade Names

MUSGRAVE PENCIL COMPANY
Post Office Box 290
Shelbyville, Tennessee 37160
G.H. Hulan, Jr., President
(615) 684-3611

MUSHROOM CO-OPERATIVE
 CANNING COMPANY
Post Office Box 389
Kennett Square, Pennsylvania 19348
C. James Yeatman, President
(215) 444-1400

MUSHROOM GROWERS
 ASSOCIATION SALES COMPANY
18 Water Market
Chicago, Illinois 60608
(312) 421-7088

MUSIC BOX KING (music boxes)
 See John Goodman Company,
  Inc.

MUSIC EXCHANGE
1619 Broadway
New York, New York 10019
(212) 245-8860

MUSIC GUILD (phonograph records)
 See Westminster Recording
  Company, Inc.

MUSIC PRINT CORPORATION
828 Pearl Street
Boulder, Colorado 80302

MUSICAL RESEARCH LABORATORIES
Post Office Box 146
Golden Bridge, New York 10526

MUSICARO (foods)
 See Caruso Foods Inc.

MUSKIE (outboard motors)
 See Jetco Inc.

MUSKIN CORPORATION
(Subsidiary of Amcord, Inc.)
225 Acacia Street
Colton, California 92324
B.G. Ramos, President
(714) 825-8200

MUSONIC INC.
1271 Rand Road
Des Plaines, Illinois 60016

MUSSELMAN FRUIT PRODUCTS
(Division of Pet, Inc.)
Biglerville, Pennsylvania 17307
Robert Lincoln, President
(717) 677-7111

MUSSER (musical instruments)
 See Coast Wholesale Music
  Company of Los Angeles

MUSTANG (badminton sets)
 See National Sporting Goods
  Corporation

MUSTANG (cameras)
 See Camera Specialty Company
  Inc.

MUSTANG (water skis and
accessories)
 See Cypress Gardens Skis, Inc.

MUSTEE & SONS INC., E.L.
6911 Lorain Avenue
Cleveland, Ohio 44102
(216) 281-1155

MUSTEROLE (analgesic ointment)
 See Plough Inc.

MUTCHLER CHEMICAL COMPANY
258 Broadway
New York, New York 10007
(212) 349-4735

MUTSCHLER DIVISION
302 South Madison
Nappanee, Indiana 46550
Dick E. Shoemaker, President
(219) 773-3111

MUTTERPERL COMPANY, SOL
330 Fifth Avenue
New York, New York 10001
(212) 239-0345

MUTUAL BENEFIT LIFE
 INSURANCE COMPANY
520 Broad Street
Newark, New Jersey 07101
W. Paul Stillman, Chairman of the
 Board
(201) 624-6600

MUTUAL BISCUIT COMPANY, INC.
65 Cedar Street
New Rochelle, New York 10801

MUTUAL BRIEF CASE COMPANY
 INC.
133 Kossuth Street
Newark, New Jersey 07105
(201) 589-7790

MUTUAL BROADCASTING
 SYSTEM, INC.
918 16th Street, N.W.
Washington, D.C. 20006
John A. Hardin, Chairman of the
 Board
(202) 785-6300

MUTUAL FISH COMPANY INC.
2335 Rainier Avenue South
Seattle, Washington 98108
(206) 322-4368

MUTUAL METAL STAMPING &
 MANUFACTURING INC.
1135 North McKinley Avenue
Los Angeles, California 90059
(213) 321-8750

Companies and Trade Names

MUTUAL OF NEW YORK
1740 Broadway
New York, New York 10019
James S. Bingay, President
(212) 586-4000

MUTUAL OF OMAHA INSURANCE
 COMPANY
Dodge at 33rd Street
Omaha, Nebraska 68131
V.J. Skutt, Chairman of the Board
(402) 342-7600

MUTUAL PRODUCTS COMPANY
509 North Fourth Street
Minneapolis, Minnesota 55401
Joseph C. Winslow, Chairman,
 President and Treasurer
(612) 335-5112

MUTUAL PRODUCTS COMPANY
 INC.
110 Barber Avenue
Worcester, Massachusetts 01606
O. Eric Peterson, President
(617) 853-6012

MUTUAL SUNSET LAMP
 MANUFACTURING COMPANY
230 Fifth Avenue
New York, New York 10001
Morris Thau, President
(212) 684-7438

MUTZ CORPORATION
1853 Ludlow Avenue
Indianapolis, Indiana 46201
(317) 634-3400

MUZAK CORPORATION
100 Park Avenue
New York, New York 10017
U.V. Muscio, President
(212) 889-1330

MY-KO LABORATORIES
70 East Stewart Avenue
Lansdowne, Pennsylvania 19050

MY SIN (perfume, bath oil,
dusting powder, soap, etc.)
 See Lanvin Parfums, Inc.

MY-T-FINE (desserts and pie-crust
mix)
 See RJR Foods, Inc.

MY-T-GOOD (food products)
 See Southern Style Foods Inc.

MY-T-GOOD (processed foods)
 See DeJean Packing Company

MY-T-TUFF (socks)
 See William G. Leininger
  Knitting Company

MY-TE-FINE (processed foods)
 See Roundup Company

MY TOY COMPANY, INC.
140 43rd Street
Brooklyn, New York 11232
Harold Hills, President
(212) 788-0060

MYAKKA PROCESSORS INC.
Box 387
Arcadia, Florida 33821

MYCRAFT PRODUCTS
303 Fifth Avenue
New York, New York 10016
(212) 689-6689

MYER'S (rum)
 See Park Avenue Imports

MYERS & COMPANY, P.R.
132 Larchmont Avenue
Larchmont, New York 10538

MYERS CANDY COMPANY
1028 44th Avenue
Oakland, California 94601

MYERS CANNING COMPANY
Box 276
Temple, Pennsylvania 19560

MYERS-CARTER LABORATORIES
5160 West Bethany Home Road
Glendale, Arizona 85301
(602) 939-1426

MYERS FOODS INC.
Kellers Church Road
Plumsteadville, Pennsylvania 18949
Joseph P. Monaghan, President
(215) 766-8832

MYERS LABORATORIES, INC.
121 Central Avenue
Warren, Pennsylvania 16365

MYERS PRODUCTS, CARMEL
332 Main Street
Madison, New Jersey 07940

MYERS, W.H.
Box 874
Cathedral City, California 92234

MYERSON CANDY COMPANY,
 BEN
928 Towne Avenue
Los Angeles, California 90021
(213) 623-6266

MYLANTA (antacid)
 See Stuart Pharmaceuticals

MYLEN COMPANY
7 West 22nd Street
New York, New York 10010
(212) 242-1992

MYLES CORPORATION, LEE
54-24 Maurice Avenue
Maspeth, New York 11378
Charles George, President
(212) 386-0100

MYNETTE (ladies' dresses)
    See Florian Fashions, Inc.

MYRNA SHOE, INC.
(Division of Shaer Shoe Corporation)
Canal and Dow
Manchester, New Hampshire 03105
David L. Shaer, President
(603) 625-8566

MYRTLE DESK COMPANY
Taylor and Millis
High Point, North Carolina 27261
T.R. Pitts, President
(919) 885-4021

MYRURGIA PERFUMES, INC.
730 Fifth Avenue
New York, New York 10019
Pablo Medina, Vice President
(212) 541-5410

MYSAN LABORATORIES
Post Office Box 2111
Macon, Georgia 31203

MYSTIC (foam rug cleaner)
    See American Cyanamid,
        Household Products
        Department

MYSTIC TAPE
(Division of Borden, Inc.)
1700 Winnetka Avenue
Notthfield, Illinois 60093
Howard E. Pendergast, General
    Manager
(312) 446-4000

Companies and Trade Names

N

N & S (food products)
See Nicholson & Stetler Ltd.

N & W INDUSTRIES, INC.
(Subsidiary of Nunnally & McCrea Company)
1415 Kemper Street
Lynchburg, Virginia 24501
C. Dickie Williamson, Chairman of the Board
(703) 847-7761

N.B. (plumbing and heating supplies)
See International Plumbing Products Inc.

NBC (bread, etc.)
See Nabisco, Inc.

NBC
See National Broadcasting Company, Inc.

NCC FOOD CORPORATION
(Subsidiary of National Can Corporation)
Box 5040
San Jose, California 95150

NCC INDUSTRIES, INC.
105 Madison Avenue
New York, New York 10016
Sol Heyman, President
(212) 532-6100

NCK ENTERPRISES
Box 48
Cold Spring Harbor, New York 11724

NCR COMPANY
Main and K Streets
Dayton, Ohio 45409
William S. Anderson, President
(513) 449-2000
See also Appleton Papers

N.D.K. COMPANY, THE
440 Charles Street
New Iberia, Louisiana 70561

N. F. C. ENGINEERING COMPANY
2939 Sixth Avenue North
Anoka, Minnesota 55303

NFC INDUSTRIES, INC.
80 Hartford Avenue
Mount Vernon, New York 10553

N.K.R. PRECISION MANUFACTURING CORPORATION
Post Office Box 333
Harriman, New York 10926
(914) 782-8562

N-L (concentrate cleaner)
See Lehn & Fink Products Company

NL INDUSTRIES, INC.
111 Broadway
New York, New York 10006
Edward R. Rowley, Chairman of the Board
(212) 732-9400
See also Bunting Brass & Bronze Company

N-R (lawn and garden supplies)
See Nelson-Roanoke Corporation

N-RICH (nondairy coffee creamer)
See Beatrice Foods Company

NS (steel shelving)
See Neiman Steel Equipment Company Inc.

NTZ (antihistamine)
See Winthrop Laboratories

NVF COMPANY
Post Office Box 68
Yorklyn, Delaware 19736
Walter E. Gregg, President
(302) 239-5281

NW CONTROLS INC.
Shelly Road
Harleysville, Pennsylvania 19438
(215) 287-7871

N.Y.C.-BOMBAY TEXTILES, INC.
15 Park Row
New York, New York 10038
(212) 233-8020

NA-CHURS PLANT FOOD COMPANY
421 Leader Street
Marion, Ohio 43302
(614) 382-5701

NAAS FOODS, INC.
Box 1029
Portland, Indiana 47371

NABISCO, INC.
425 Park Avenue
New York, New York 10022
Robert M. Schaeberle, President
(212) 751-5000
See also Amend Company, Fred W.; Associated Products, Inc.; Freezer Queen Foods, Inc.; and Williams Company, Inc., J.B.

NABISCO, INC.
Candy Division
810 Main
Cambridge, Massachusetts 02139
James O. Welch, Jr., President
(617) 491-2500

NABOB (grocery products)
See Douglas Kelly & Company, Ltd.

Companies and Trade Names

NACEYS (groceries)
See C.H.B. Foods Inc.

NACHI AMERICAN COMPANY LTD.
23 Brook Avenue
Maywood, New Jersey 07607

NACHMAN CORPORATION
(Subsidiary of Korf Industries, Inc.)
2600 River Road
Des Plaines, Illinois 60018
Sanford E. Strickland, President
(312) 694-4040

NACOR MEDICINE COMPANY, THE
125 West 22nd
Indianapolis, Indiana 40602
Alfred B. Maschke, President
(317) 925-8782

NADEL & SONS TOY CORPORATION
900 Broadway
New York, New York 10003
(212) 254-1677

NADEX INDUSTRIES, INC.
220 Delaware Avenue
Suite 515
Buffalo, New York 14202
(716) 853-7030

NADIN COMPANY
1815 Flower Street
Glendale, California 91201
(213) 245-3687

NADINE FORMALS, INC.
1717 Olive Street
Saint Louis, Missouri 63103
Vincent Nania, Jr., President
(314) 436-0070

NADINOLA (cleansing cream, facial soap, vanishing cream, etc.)
See National Toiletries Company

NAFCO (fence products)
See National Fence Manufacturing Company Inc.

NAFCO (floor covering)
See National Floor Products Company

NAGEL INC.
11-02 Bridge Plaza South
Long Island City, New York 11101
Margaret A. Nagel, President
(212) 361-1300

NAHIGIAN, INC., M.H.
295 Fifth Avenue
New York, New York 10016
(212) 685-1761

NAHON IMPORT CORPORATION, JACK
155 West 23rd Street
New York, New York 10011
(212) 691-8720

NAIR (depilatory)
See Carter-Wallace, Inc.

NALAD CORPORATION, THE
4203 Ponce de Leon Boulevard
Coral Gables, Florida 33146

NALCO (enamels)
See NL Industries, Inc.

NALCO (lamps)
See North American Electric Lamp Company

NALCO CHEMICAL COMPANY
2901 Butterfield Road
Oak Brook, Illinois 60521
Robert T. Powers, Chairman, President and Chief Executive Officer
(312) 887-7500

NALLE PLASTICS INC.
108 West Second Street
Austin, Texas 78701
George S. Nalle, Jr., President
(512) 477-6168

NALLEY'S FINE FOODS
(Division of W.R. Grace & Company)
3303 South 35th Street
Tacoma, Washington 98411
David J. McDonald, President
(206) 383-1621

NAMAN PHARMACAL COMPANY
361 Canal Street
Lawrence, Massachusetts 01842

NAME-MAKER CORPORATION
30 Irving Place
New York, New York 10003

NAMETH ENTERPRISES
3627 Farquhar Avenue
Los Alamitos, California 90720

NAMPA CUSTOM CANNERY
Nampa, Idaho 83651

NAMSCO INC.
333 31st Avenue
Bellwood, Illinois 60104
(312) 544-4460

NAN FLOWER LINGERIE
152 Madison Avenue
New York, New York 10016
(212) 725-5870

NANCRAFT INC.
Pumpkin Hook Road
Jordanville, New York 13361

NANCY VALENTINE (dresses and suits)
See Puritan Fashions Corporation

Companies and Trade Names

NANNETTE MANUFACTURING
COMPANY, INC.
3800 Frankford Avenue
Philadelphia, Pennsylvania 19124
Robert J. Rosenau, President
(215) 289-1000

NANNETTE UNDIES COMPANY,
INC.
476 Jefferson Street
Brooklyn, New York 12210
(212) 456-1100

NANKEE (paints and paint sundries)
See Cantor Brothers Inc.

NANTUCKET INDUSTRIES INC.
105 Madison Avenue
New York, New York 10016
(212) 889-5656

NAOMI (food products)
See Hayward Food Products

NAPCO (pet foods)
See National Pet Supply
Company

NAPIER COMPANY, THE
Napier Park
Meriden, Connecticut 06450
John A. Shulga, President
(203) 237-5522

NAPLES SABOT ASSOCIATION
5267 Castle Hills Drive
San Diego, California 92019

NAPOLEON (brandy)
See Carillon Importers, Ltd.

NAPOLEON (olive oil and vinegar)
See A. Magnano & Sons

NAPOLEONS (cigars)
See Garcia y Vega, Inc.
(Division of Bayuk Cigars
Inc.)

NAPOLI'S ITALIAN FOODS INC.
2139 West Broad
Athens, Georgia 30601

NAPPE-SMITH MANUFACTURING
COMPANY
(Subsidiary of Dart Industries, Inc.)
Southard Avenue
Farmingdale, New Jersey 07727
M.B. Chernoff, President
(201) 938-6221

NAPSAK (baby carriers)
See Happy Family Products

NARCO SCIENTIFIC INDUSTRIES
Commerce Drive
Fort Washington,
    Pennsylvania 19034
Aldo J. DeFrancesco, President
(215) 643-2050
    See also Konel Corporation

NARDIS OF DALLAS, INC.
1300 Corinth Street
Dallas, Texas 75215
Allen J. Gold, President
(214) 426-5671

NAREN INDUSTRIES INC.
1214-22 West Madison Street
Chicago, Illinois 60607
(312) 243-1766

NARON CANDY COMPANY, INC.
651 South Monroe Street
Baltimore, Maryland 21223
(301) 945-0800

NARRAGANSETT (men's outerwear)
See Jacob Finkelstein & Sons,
    Inc.

NARRAGANSETT BOAT COMPANY
INC.
801 Pontiac Avenue
Cranston, Rhode Island 02910

NARRANGANSETT BREWING
COMPANY
(Subsidiary of Falstaff Brewing
Corporation)
New Depot Avenue
Cranston, Rhode Island 02920
Fred J. Gutting, President
(401) 942-7000

NARRANGANSETT ELECTRIC
COMPANY
(Subsidiary of New England
Electric System)
280 Melrose Street
Providence, Rhode Island 02901
Edward E. Mulligan, President
(401) 781-0100

NARROW FABRIC COMPANY
(Division of Wyomissing Corporation)
Post Office Box 742
Reading, Pennsylvania 19603
(215) 376-2891

NARVIK (Rya rugs)
See Imported Rug Associates,
    Ltd.

NASCO (giftware and housewares)
See National Silver Company

NASCO INTERNATIONAL, INC.
901 Janesville Avenue
Fort Atkinson, Wisconsin 53538
Arthur W. Nesbitt, President and
    Chief Executive Officer
(414) 563-2446

NASCO DOLL INC.
80 Grove Street
Paterson, New Jersey 07503
(201) 279-4300

NASCO WEST
Post Office Box 3837
Modesto, California 95352

Companies and Trade Names

NASH-FINCH COMPANY
3381 Gorham Avenue
Minneapolis, Minnesota 55426
Thomas A. Riley, President
(612) 929-0371

NASH MANUFACTURING INC.
315 West Ripy
Fort Worth, Texas 76110
(817) 926-5223

NASHARR FRERES
925 Merchandise Mart
Chicago, Illinois 60654
(312) 644-0490

NASHMARINE
32906 Avenida Descanso
San Juan Capistrano,
  California 92675

NASHUA (mobile homes)
  See Conchemco Inc., Homes
  Group

NASHUA CORPORATION
44 Franklin
Nashua, New Hampshire 03060
William E. Conway, President and
  Chief Executive Officer
(603) 880-2323

NASHUA FOOTWEAR
  CORPORATION
300 Canal Street
Lawrence, Massachusetts 01840
Paul N. Chedekel, President
(617) 685-5131

NASHVILLE DRUG
  MANUFACTURING COMPANY
Stahlman Building
Nashville, Tennessee 37201

NASON (paints)
  See Fuller-O'Brien Corporation

NASON & MORETTI (colored
glassware)
  See Ceramar

NASON TRADING COMPANY,
  INC.
230 Fifth Avenue
New York, New York 10001
(212) 686-3307

NASSAU ROYALE (liquor)
  See Schenley Industries, Inc.

NASSAU SPONGE COMPANY
325 West Huron Street
Chicago, Illinois 60610
(312) 644-1928

NAST INC., NAT
(Division of Beatrice Foods)
Box 415
Bonner Springs, Kansas 66012

NATBEFCO INC.
3490 Sunrise Highway
Wantagh, New York 11793

NATCON CHEMICAL COMPANY
  INC.
1 Fairchild Court
Plainview, New York 11803
(516) 931-3300

NATHAN'S FAMOUS, INC.
1515 Broadway
New York, New York 10036
Murray Handwerker, President
(212) 869-0600

NATHANSON-SYLVESTER
  ASSOCIATES
2608 Valleybrook
Toledo, Ohio 43615

NATION WIDE (fruits, vegetables,
etc.)
  See Cummings Brothers

NATIONAL (freezers)
  See Revco, Inc.

NATIONAL AIRLINES, INC.
Post Office Box 592055
Miami, Florida 33159
Lewis B. Maytag, Chairman of the
  Board
(305) 874-4111

NATIONAL ALLIED PRODUCTS
(Division of Aidex Corporation)
I-29 and Highway 370 Council
  Bluffs
Omaha, Nebraska 68112
(402) 366-2424

NATIONAL APPAREL
  CORPORATION
130 Hamilton Street
New Haven, Connecticut 06506
Seymour Shapiro, President
(203) 772-3030

NATIONAL ARTCRAFTS, INC.
(Subsidiary of Rust Craft Greeting
  Cards)
3000 West Fort Street
Detroit, Michigan 48216
Donald Taub, President
(313) 825-4172

NATIONAL AUTO WAX SYSTEMS
  INC.
908 West Hall Street
Melbourne, Florida 32901

NATIONAL BAKERS SERVICES,
  INC.
1747 Van Buren
Hollywood, Florida 33020
(305) 920-7666

NATIONAL BAND & TAG
  COMPANY
721 York
Newport, Kentucky 41071

Companies and Trade Names

NATIONAL BANK OF COMMERCE
OF SEATTLE
(Affiliation of Marine Bancorporation)
Second Avenue and Spring Street
Seattle, Washington 98101
Andrew Price, Jr., Chairman of
the Board
(206) 587-2111

NATIONAL BANK OF DETROIT
611 Woodward
Detroit, Michigan 48232
Robert M. Surdam, Chairman of the
Board
(313) 225-1000

NATIONAL BANK OF NORTH
AMERICA
(Subsidiary of C.I.T. Financial
Corporation)
44 Wall Street
New York, New York 10005
John H. Vogel, President
(212) 623-4000

NATIONAL BANKAMERICARD
Post Office Box 26673
San Francisco, California 94126
John R. McKinney, Director,
Operations Support
(415) 397-5755

NATIONAL BELLAS HESS, INC.
715 Armour Road
North Kansas City, Missouri 64116
(816) 471-3080

NATIONAL BISCUIT COMPANY
See Nabisco, Inc.

NATIONAL BLANK BOOK
COMPANY INC.
Water Street
Holyoke, Massachusetts 01040
Louis F. Oldershaw, President
(413) 539-9811
See also All-Matic Corporation

NATIONAL BOAT CORPORATION
Anclote Road
Tarpon Springs, Florida 33589
(813) 934-5761

NATIONAL BOAT WORKS, INC.
Box 1527
Greenville, North Carolina 27834
(919) 752-2111

NATIONAL BREWING COMPANY
7 East Redwood Street
Baltimore, Maryland 21202
Jerold C. Hoffberger, President
(301) 276-1100

NATIONAL BRIAR PIPE COMPANY
108 Railroad Avenue
Jersey City, New Jersey 07302
(201) 435-6880

NATIONAL BROADCASTING
COMPANY, INC.
(Subsidiary of RCA Corporation)
30 Rockefeller Plaza
New York, New York 10020
Jack G. Thayer, President, Radio
Division
Robert T. Howard, President, TV
Network
(212) 247-8300

NATIONAL BRUSH COMPANY
101 West Illinois Avenue
Aurora, Illinois 60506
Charles R. Parr, President
(312) 897-9133

NATIONAL CAN CORPORATION
8101 Higgins Road
Chicago, Illinois 60631
Robert Stuart, Chairman of the
Board
(312) 399-3000
See also NCC Food Corporation

NATIONAL CANVAS PRODUCTS
CORPORATION
Camping and Sporting Goods
Post Office Box 955
Toledo, Ohio 43695
(419) 246-3643

NATIONAL CAR RENTAL SYSTEM,
INC.
(Division of Household Finance
Corporation)
5501 Green Valley Drive
Minneapolis, Minnesota 55437
J.W. James, President
(612) 830-2121

NATIONAL CARATERIA SYSTEMS
INC.
1821 University Avenue
Saint Paul, Minnesota 55113

NATIONAL CARD, MAT & BOARD
COMPANY
4318 West Carroll Avenue
Chicago, Illinois 60624
(312) 261-7611

NATIONAL CASH REGISTER
COMPANY, THE
See NCR Corporation

NATIONAL CASKET COMPANY
(Division of Walco National
Corporation)
355 Commonwealth Avenue
Boston, Massachusetts 02115
Paul D. Schurgot, Jr., President
(617) 266-2670

NATIONAL CENTRAL BANK
23 East King Street
Lancaster, Pennsylvania 17604
Wilson D. McElhinny, President
(717) 397-7411

NATIONAL CHEMICAL LABS OF
PENNSYLVANIA INC.
Tenth and Callowhill Streets
Philadelphia, Pennsylvania 19123
(215) 922-1200

NATIONAL CIGAR COMPANY
407 North Main Street
Frankfort, Indiana 46041

Companies and Trade Names

NATIONAL CITY BANK
623 Euclid Avenue
Cleveland, Ohio 44114
Claude M. Blair, Chairman of the Board
(216) 861-4900

NATIONAL CITY LINES, INC.
5 Denver Technological Center
Denver, Colorado 80217
D.M. Pratt, President
(303) 770-5681

NATIONAL CLEANERS CHEMICAL MANUFACTURING COMPANY
2807-19 West Lake
Chicago, Illinois 60612
(312) 638-5100

NATIONAL CLOTHESPIN COMPANY COMPANY, INC.
Post Office Box 427
Granite Street
Montpelier, Vermont 05602
W.A. Crowell, President
(802) 223-7332

NATIONAL COMMERCIAL BANK & TRUST COMPANY
60 State Street
Albany, New York 12207
Lester W. Herzog, Jr., President
(518) 478-8888

NATIONAL CONVENIENCE STORES, INC.
3200 Travis Street
Houston, Texas 77006
F.J. Dyke, Jr., President
(713) 529-5711

NATIONAL COOPERATIVES, INC.
See Universal Cooperatives, Inc.

NATIONAL CRAFT & HOBBY COMPANY INC.
11300 K-Tel Drive
Minnetonka
Minneapolis, Minnesota 55420
(612) 935-2100

NATIONAL CRAYON COMPANY
117 Main Street
Easton, Pennsylvania 18042
(215) 253-0531

NATIONAL DECALCOMANIA CORPORATION
5548-54 Chestnut Street
Philadelphia, Pennsylvania 19139
(215) 472-1122

NATIONAL DIE CASTING COMPANY
3635 West Touhy Avenue
Chicago, Illinois 60645
(312) 465-6000

NATIONAL DISTILLERS AND CHEMICAL CORPORATION
99 Park Avenue
New York, New York 10016
Drummond C. Bell, President
(212) 949-5000
    See also Almaden Vineyards, Inc.; Bridgeport Brass Company; Holland House Brands Company; Munson Shaw Company; and United States Industrial Chemicals Company

NATIONAL DISTILLERS PRODUCTS COMPANY
(Affiliation of National Distillers and Chemical Corporation)
99 Park Avenue
New York, New York 10016
(212) 697-0700

NATIONAL DRUG COMPANY
(Division of Richardson-Merrell, Inc.)
4663 Stanton Avenue
Philadelphia, Pennsylvania 19144
J.P. Dodd, President and General Manager
(215) 455-8800

NATIONAL DYNAMICS CORPORATION
145 East 32nd Street
New York, New York 10010
(212) 689-0160

NATIONAL ENGRAVING COMPANY
Box 2311
Highway 280 at Valley Dale Road
Birmingham, Alabama 35201
James W. Dewberry, President
(205) 967-4232

NATIONAL EQUIPMENT CORPORATION
322 Bruckner Boulevard
Bronx, New York 10454
Richard Greenberg, Vice President
(212) 585-0200

NATIONAL FENCE CORPORATION
3449 Tchoupitonlas
New Orleans, Louisiana 70115
(504) 899-8255

NATIONAL FENCE MANUFACTURING COMPANY
4301 46th Street
Bladensburg, Maryland 20710
Henry F. Long, Jr., President
(301) 779-8300

NATIONAL FIBERSTOK CORPORATION
2801 Grant Avenue
Philadelphia, Pennsylvania 19114
Edward L. Howard, President
(215) 464-8700

NATIONAL FLAVORS, INC.
26 Garden Street
Bensenville, Illinois 60106

NATIONAL FLOOR PRODUCTS COMPANY
Post Office Box 354-A
Florence, Alabama 35630
(205) 766-0234

NATIONAL FLOOR PRODUCTS COMPANY
532 Plaster Avenue, N.E.
Atlanta, Georgia 30324
(404) 874-3661

Companies and Trade Names

NATIONAL FOAM SYSTEM, INC.
Union and Adams Streets
West Chester, Pennsylvania 19380

NATIONAL FOOD PRODUCTS
412 East Avenue
Lewiston, Maine 04240

NATIONAL FOOD STORES, INC.
(Subsidiary of National Tea
    Company)
Excelsior and Interlachen
Hopkins, Minnesota 55343
Norman A. Stepelton, President
(612) 938-3521

NATIONAL FRUIT CANNING
    COMPANY
2371 East Lake Avenue East
Seattle, Washington 98102
(206) 322-8900

NATIONAL FRUIT FLAVOR
    COMPANY
421 Girod Street
New Orleans, Louisiana 70130
(504) 529-1122

NATIONAL FRUIT PRODUCT
    COMPANY, INC.
Post Office Box 609
Winchester, Virginia 22601
Frank Armstrong, III, President
(703) 662-3401

NATIONAL FURNITURE COMPANY
215 Factory Street
Mount Airy, North Carolina 27030
J.R. Smith, President
(919) 786-6121

NATIONAL FUEL GAS COMPANY
    See Iroquois Gas Corporation

NATIONAL GENERAL
    CORPORATION
    See Bantam Books, Inc.

NATIONAL GRANGE MUTUAL
    INSURANCE COMPANY
Custom Service Department
55 West Street
Keene, New Hampshire 03431
Magnus Nodtvedt, President
(603) 352-4000

NATIONAL GROCERY COMPANY
702 North First Avenue
Yakima, Washington 98902

NATIONAL GYPSUM COMPANY
325 Delaware Avenue
Buffalo, New York 14202
Colon Brown, Chairman of the
    Board
(716) 852-5880
    See also DMH Company

NATIONAL HOMES CORPORATION
Earl and Wallace
Lafayette, Indiana 47902
James J. Shaw, President
(317) 447-3131

NATIONAL HYGIENIC PRODUCTS
    CORPORATION
10 East 53rd Street
New York, New York 10022
(212) 421-5650

NATIONAL INDUSTRIES, INC.
510 West Broadway
Louisville, Kentucky 40202
Joseph A. Gammon, President
(502) 583-7602
    See also Hawthorn Mellody,
        Inc.; and National
        Recreation Products Inc.

NATIONAL INDEPENDENT
    DISTRIBUTORS ASSOCIATES INC.
437 N.E. Harding
Minneapolis, Minnesota 55413
(612) 331-3733

NATIONAL INSTRUMENT
    CORPORATION
53 State Street
Boston, Massachusetts 02109
(617) 523-5365

NATIONAL KINNEY CORPORATION
75 Rockefeller Plaza
New York, New York 10010
Andrew J. Frankel, President
(212) 484-6050

NATIONAL LATEX PRODUCTS
    COMPANY
246 East Fourth Street
Ashland, Ohio 44805
Harry R. Gill, II, Chairman,
    President and Treasurer
(419) 323-1541

NATIONAL LEAD COMPANY
    See N L Industries Inc.

NATIONAL LIBERTY CORPORATION
Office of Consumer Affairs
Valley Forge, Pennsylvania 19481
Arthur S. DeMoss, President
(215) 648-5616

NATIONAL LIBERTY MARKETING,
    INC.
(Subsididary of the National
    Liberty Corporation)
Valley Forge, Pennsylvania 19481

NATIONAL LICORICE COMPANY
    See Y & S Candies, Inc.

NATIONAL LIFE & ACCIDENT
    INSURANCE COMPANY
Secretary's Department
National Life Center
Nashville, Tennessee 37250
C.H. Berson Sr., Vice President
    and Secretary
(615) 749-1333

NATIONAL LIFE INSURANCE
    COMPANY
National Life Drive
Montpelier, Vermont 05602
Norman L. Campbell, President
(802) 223-3431

Companies and Trade Names

NATIONAL LOCK HARDWARE
(Division of Keystone Consolidated Industries, Inc.)
1902 Seventh Street
Rockford, Illinois 61101
Charles W. Holtzworth, President
(815) 962-4455

NATIONAL MAGNESIA COMPANY, INC.
83rd Street and Cooper Avenue
Brooklyn, New York 11227
(212) 326-1500

NATIONAL MANIFOLDING COMPANY
514 Wayne Avenue
Dayton, Ohio 45410
(513) 222-1041

NATIONAL MANUFACTURING COMPANY
1218 North 22nd Street
Lincoln, Nebraska 68503
W.C. Ferris, President
(402) 432-4603

NATIONAL MANUFACTURING COMPANY INC
12 River Road
Chatham, New Jersey 07928
(201) 635-8846

NATIONAL MANUFACTURING CORPORATION (paints, coatings)
Box 189
Tonawanda, New York 14150

NATIONAL MATTRESS COMPANY
Post Office Box 1450
Huntington, West Virginia 25716
Carter W. Wild, President
(304) 522-7334

NATIONAL METAL INDUSTRIES
203 Circuit Avenue
West Springfield, Massachusetts 01089
Patrick J. O'Toole, President
(413) 785-5861

NATIONAL MOLASSES COMPANY
(Subsidiary of C. Brewer & Company Ltd.)
708 Blair Mill Road
Willow Grove, Pennsylvania 19090

NATIONAL MOWER COMPANY
702 Raymond Avenue
Saint Paul, Minnesota 55114
(612) 646-4079

NATIONAL MUSICAL STRING COMPANY
(Subsidiary of Kaman Corporation)
120 Georges Road
New Brunswick, New Jersey 08903
Herbert N. Hagel, President
(201) 545-0038

NATIONAL NU-GRAPE COMPANY
See Monarch-Nugrape Company

NATIONAL OATS COMPANY, INC.
(Subsidiary of Liggett & Myers, Inc.)
1515 H Avenue, N.E.
Cedar Rapids, Iowa 52402
Richard Proctor, President
(319) 364-9161

NATIONAL OF EVANSVILLE
1501 Keller Street
Evansville, Indiana 47705
R.G. Altman, General Manager
(812) 423-4228

NATIONAL OFFICE FURNITURE COMPANY
Box 1799
11th and Filbert Streets
Philadelphia, Pennsylvania 19107
(215) 922-1760

NATIONAL PAINT & VARNISH COMPANY
2835 East Washington Boulevard
Los Angeles, California 90023
Melvin Spellens, President
(213) 268-2823

NATIONAL PAPAYA COMPANY
4701-99 West South Avenue
Tampa, Florida 33614

NATIONAL PENCIL COMPANY
Shelbyville, Tennessee 37160
(615) 684-3198

NATIONAL PET FOODS CORPORATION
617 South D Street
Monmouth, Illinois 61462
W.A. Hart, Vice President
(309) 734-3121

NATIONAL PET FOODS CORPORATION
Lewis Food Division
6700 Cherry Avenue
Long Beach, California 90805
O.J. Draguesku, General Manager
(213) 531-1110

NATIONAL POLYCHEMICALS, INC.
(Subsidiary of Stepan Chemical Company)
51 Eames Street
Wilmington, Massachusetts 01887

NATIONAL POTTERIES
26201 Richmond Road
Bedford Heights, Ohio 44146
William F. Rein, President
(216) 292-6161

NATIONAL PREMIUM (beer)
See National Brewing Company

NATIONAL PRESERVE COMPANY
Box 5391
San Jose, California 95150
(408) 259-4800

NATIONAL PRESTO INDUSTRIES, INC.
1515 Ball
Eau Claire, Wisconsin 54701
LaVern G. Soper, President
(715) 832-1611

Companies and Trade Names

NATIONAL PRIDE (food products)
See Henderson's Portion Pak

NATIONAL PRODUCTS COMPANY
1206 East Crosstown Parkway
Kalamazoo, Michigan 49003

NATIONAL PRODUCTS INC.
(wall coverings, mirrors, cabinets, etc.)
900 Baxter Avenue
Louisville, Kentucky 40204
(502) 583-0206

NATIONAL PROPANE CORPORATION
768 Fifth Avenue
New York, New York 10019
Victor Posner, President
(212) 343-8300

NATIONAL PULP & PAPER COMPANY
342 Madison Avenue
New York, New York 10017
(212) 687-3810

NATIONAL PURITY SOAP & CHEMICAL COMPANY
110 Fifth Avenue S.E.
Minneapolis, Minnesota 55414
(612) 378-1465

NATIONAL RADIO INSTITUTE
3939 Wisconsin Avenue, N.W.
Washington, D.C. 20016
Edward E. Booher, Chairman of the Board
(202) 244-1600

NATIONAL RAILROAD PASSENGER CORPORATION (AMTRAK)
Consumer Services
955 L'Enfant Plaza North, S.W.
Washington, D.C. 20024
Bruce O. Pike, Director of Government Affairs
(202) 484-7679

NATIONAL RAILROAD PASSENGER CORPORATION (AMTRAK)
Public Relations
955 L'Enfant Plaza North, S.W.
Washington, D.C. 20024
Edwin E. Edel, Vice President, Public Affairs
(202) 484-7220

NATIONAL RECREATION PRODUCTS, INC.
(Subsidiary of National Industries, Inc.)
510 West Broadway
Louisville, Kentucky 40202
Jack Segell, President
(502) 584-6373

NATIONAL SCENT COMPANY
10660 Stanford Avenue
Garden Grove, California 92640

NATIONAL SCHOOL SLATE COMPANY
Seventh and Church Streets
Slatington, Pennsylvania 18080
Michael P. Papay, President
(215) 767-2022

NATIONAL SCOOP & METAL MANUFACTURING COMPANY
225 Brown Street
Philadelphia, Pennsylvania 19123
(215) 923-3717

NATIONAL SEA PRODUCTS (UNITED STATES) CORPORATION
Box 23027
Tampa, Florida 33622

NATIONAL SEMICONDUCTOR CORPORATION
2900 Semiconductor Drive
Santa Clara, California 95051
Charles E. Sporck, President
(408) 732-5000

NATIONAL SHOES, INC.
595 Gerard Avenue
Bronx, New York 10451
Sherman N. Baker, President
(212) 665-9000

NATIONAL SILVER INDUSTRIES, INC.
241 Fifth Avenue
New York, New York 10016
Milton Bernstein, President
(212) 689-7300
See also Rogers Silver Company, Inc., F.B.

NATIONAL SODA STRAW COMPANY
2323 South Halsted
Chicago, Illinois 60608
Sidney G. Graham, President
(312) 243-9400

NATIONAL SPINNING COMPANY
183 Madison Avenue
New York, New York 10016
Joseph Leff, President
(212) 889-3800

NATIONAL SPORTING GOODS CORPORATION
1107 Broadway
New York, New York 12204
(212) 741-9400

NATIONAL STARCH & CHEMICAL CORPORATION
10 Finderne Avenue
Bridgewater, New Jersey 08876
Carlyle G. Caldwell, President and Chief Executive Officer
(201) 526-6300

NATIONAL STATE BANK OF ELIZABETH
68 Broad Street
Elizabeth, New Jersey 07207
W. Emlen Roosevelt, President
(201) 354-3400

Companies and Trade Names

NATIONAL STEEL CONSTRUCTION
COMPANY
Customer Service Department
Post Office Box 524
Newark, California 94560
Darrel Johnson, Manager, Customer
Service
(415) 792-1345

NATIONAL STEEL CORPORATION
2800 Grant Building
Pittsburgh, Pennsylvania 15219
Howard M. Love, President
(412) 471-5600
   See also Granite City Steel
   Company

NATIONAL SUGAR REFINING
COMPANY, THE
1037 North Delaware Avenue
Philadelphia, Pennsylvania 19125
Nathan Bilger, President
(215) 627-7300
   See also Bireley's Inc.

NATIONAL SYSTEMS
CORPORATION
4361 Birch Street
Newport Beach, California 96220
John Jay Corley, President
(714) 546-7360

NATIONAL TEA COMPANY
100 North Crosby Street
Chicago, Illinois 60610
James A. Watson, President
(312) 664-1800
   See also National Food Stores,
   Inc.

NATIONAL TECHNICAL SCHOOLS
4000 South Figueroa
Los Angeles, California 90037
L.J. Rosenkranz, President
(213) 234-9061

NATIONAL TINSEL
MANUFACTURING COMPANY
1133 South 16th Street
Manitowoc, Wisconsin 54220
(414) 684-4448

NATIONAL TOILETRIES COMPANY
(Division of Chattem Drug &
Chemical Company)
1715 West 38th Street
Chattanooga, Tennessee 37409
(615) 265-4521

NATIONAL TRAILWAYS BUS
SYSTEM
400 Trailways Building
1200 Eye Street, N.W.
Washington, D.C. 20005
M.E. Walsh, President
(202) 628-6534

NATIONAL UNION ELECTRIC
CORPORATION
66 Field Point Road
Greenwich, Connecticut 06830
Joseph V. McKee, President
(203) 661-1900
   See also Eureka Company; and
   Pilot Radio Corporation

NATIONAL UNION FIRE
INSURANCE COMPANIES
102 Maiden Lane
New York, New York 10005
Elmer N. Dickinson, President
(212) 791-7000

NATIONAL VAN LINES, INC.
2800 Roosevelt Road
National Plaza
Broadview, Illinois 60153
F.L. McKee, Sr., President
(312) 345-2900

NATIONAL VINEGAR COMPANY
Box 2761
4115 Gillespie Street
Houston, Texas 77001
(713) 223-4214

NATIONAL VITAMIN PRODUCTS
COMPANY
3401 Hiawatha Avenue
Minneapolis, Minnesota 55406
(612) 722-6681

NATIONAL WASHBOARD
COMPANY
1217 Florida Street
Memphis, Tennessee 38109
(901) 946-1671

NATIONWIDE INDUSTRIES INC.
1603 Orrington Avenue
Evanston, Illinois 60201
Edward W. Ross, President
(312) 866-6050

NATIONWIDE INSURANCE
COMPANY
Customer Relations Department
246 North High Street
Columbus, Ohio 43216
John E. Fisher, President
(614) 227-7111

NATIONWIDE MARKETING INC.
1819 South Central
Kent, Washington 98031

NATOWITZ, BERNARD
650 West End Avenue
New York, New York 10025
(212) 362-9919

NATRIPHENE COMPANY
Post Office Box 1126
Midland, Michigan 48641

NATURA STUDIOS INC.
Post Office Box 298
Calais, Maine 04619

NATURAL BEAUTY FENCE
   See Natbefco Inc.

NATURAL BRIDGE (shoes)
   See Craddock-Terry Shoe
   Corporation

NATURAL COLOR CARDS
COMPANY
26 Overpeck Avenue
Ridgefield Park, New Jersey 07660

Companies and Trade Names

NATURAL DECORATIONS INC.
Post Office Box 268
Evergreen, Alabama 36401

NATURAL HERB CREAMGEL (skin cleanser)
See Revlon, Inc.

NATURAL HONEY (moisture lotion)
See Revlon, Inc.

NATURAL SCIENCE INDUSTRIES LTD.
51-17 Rockaway Beach Boulevard
Far Rockaway, New York 11691
See also Butterfly Company

NATURAL WONDER (medicated makeup)
See Revlon, Inc.

NATURALIZER (shoes for women)
See Brown Group, Inc.

NATURALLY FEMININE (feminine deodorant spray)
See Johnson & Johnson

NATURE FOOD CENTRES
292 Main Street
Cambridge, Massachusetts 02142
(617) 661-8480

NATURE PRODUCTS
Box A
Palm Springs, California 92262

NATURE VALLEY (granola cereal)
See General Mills, Inc.

NATURE'S BOUNTY, INC.
55 North Mall
Plainview, New York 11803

NATURE'S REMEDY (laxative)
See Lewis-Howe Company

NATURIPE BERRY GROWERS
Box 6390
San Jose, California 95150
(408) 998-9220

NAUGAHYDE (vinyl fabric)
See Uniroyal Inc., Coated Fabrics & Koylon Seating

NAUS TRIMMING COMPANY INC.
1369 Broadway
New York, New York 10018
(212) 947-7415

NAUTA-LINE INC.
1 Nauta-Line Drive
Hendersonville, Tennessee 37075

NAUTI-KNOTS
2921 Cassia Street
Department 18
Newport Beach, California 92660

NAUTICA CORPORATION
Box 26
Paramus, New Jersey 07652

NAUTICAL BOATS LTD.
2644 Barrett Street
Virginia Beach, Virginia 23452

NAUTICAL DEVELOPMENT COMPANY INC.
25 Matinecock Avenue
Port Washington, New York 11050

NAUTICAL FABRIC DEVICES
Box 2254
Hialeah, Florida 33012

NAUTILUS INDUSTRIES
Post Office Box 159
Hartford, Wisconsin 53027

NAUTRON CORPORATION
587 Granite Street
Braintree, Massachusetts 02184

NAUVOO MILK PRODUCTS COMPANY
Nauvoo, Illinois 62354
(217) 453-2213

NAV-AIDS INC.
Box 293
McLean, Virginia 22101

NAVAJO FREIGHT LINES, INC.
1205 South Platte River Drive
Denver, Colorado 80223
Carl B. Tauffer, President
(303) 778-1892

NAVAL JELLY COMPANY INC.
(Division of Link Laboratories)
310 West Ninth Street
Kansas City, Missouri 64105
(816) 221-3562

NAVIS MERCHANDISE COMPANY, INC.
41 Union Square
New York, New York 10003
(212) 242-5481

NAVTEC INC.
146 Main Street
Maynard Industrial Park
Maynard, Massachusetts 01754
(617) 897-5373

NAYLOR COMPANY, H.W.
14 Main Street
Morris, New York 13808
A. Naylor Elliott, President
(607) 263-5145

NE PLUS ULTRA (whiskey)
See Schenley Industries, Inc.

NEAL PHARMACAL COMPANY
125 Kraus Street
Saint Louis, Missouri 63111
(314) 352-7330

NEALE MUSIC
Box 3294
San Bernardino, California 92404

Companies and Trade Names

NEALEY LABORATORIES, INC.
3908 Kilbourne Road
Columbia, South Carolina 29205

NEAR EAST FOOD PRODUCTS, INC.
95 Prescott Street
Worcester, Massachusetts 01605

NEBRASKA (meat products, pet foods)
See Central Nebraska Packing Company

NEBRASKA CONSOLIDATED MILLS COMPANY
See Conagra Inc.

NECCO (candy)
See New England Confectionery Company

NECCO (canned foods)
See New Era Canning Company

NECTA SWEET (sweetener)
See Norwich Pharmacal Company

NECTAROSE (Rosé wine)
See Browne Vintners Company, Inc.

NEDICK'S STORES, INC.
(Subsidiary of Ogden Foods, Inc.)
513 West 166th Street
New York, New York 10032
Lewis Phillips, President
(212) 795-4200

NEEDHAM HARPER & STEERS, INC.
909 Third Avenue
New York, New York 10022
Paul C. Harper, Jr., Chairman of the Board
(212) 758-7600

NEEDLE PAINTERS GUILD LTD.
Box 695
Weaverville, North Carolina 28787

NEEDLEPOINT USA INC.
37 West 57th Street
New York City, New York 10019

NEENAH PAPER COMPANY
(Division of Kimberly-Clark Corporation)
Post Office Box 211
Neenah, Wisconsin 54956

NEET (depilatory)
See Whitehall Laboratories

NEFCO (seafood)
See New England Fish Company

NEFF & COMPANY, INC., H.L.
Mason and Charles Streets
Red Lion, Pennsylvania 17356
Harold L. Neff, President, Sales Manager and Purchasing Agent
(717) 244-7351

NEFF & SONS, LLOYD L.
201 East 12th Street
Kansas City, Missouri 64106
(816) 842-5111

NEHI ROYAL CROWN CORPORATION
2849 West 47th Street
Chicago, Illinois 66632
Myron F. Weil, President
(312) 376-7000

NEIMAN-MARCUS COMPANY
(Subsidiary of Broadway-Hale Stores, Inc.)
Main and Ervay
Dallas, Texas 75201
Richard C. Marcus, President
(214) 741-6911

NEIMAN STEEL EQUIPMENT COMPANY INC.
Balfour and Venango Streets
Philadelphia, Pennsylvania 19134
(215) 425-7900

NEISNER BROTHERS, INC.
49 East Avenue
Rochester, New York 14604
F.S. Silverstein, President
(716) 232-4200

NEKOOSA-EDWARDS PAPER COMPANY
(Subsidiary of Great Northern-Nekoosa Corporation)
Port Edwards, Wisconsin 54469
Gerard E. Veneman, President
(715) 887-5111

NELAND PHARMACEUTICAL, INC.
20 Farmington Avenue
Hartford, Connecticut 06105

NELCO CORPORATION
164 West 25th Street
New York, New York 10001
(212) 924-7604

NELLY DON, INC.
1600 Swift Avenue
North Kansas City, Missouri 64116
Hal S. Hardin, President
(816) 421-5500

NELSON & SONS, THOMAS
407 Seventh Avenue South
Nashville, Tennessee 37206

NELSON CORPORATION, L.R.
7719 North Pioneer Lane
Peoria, Illinois 61614
David P. Ransburg, President
(309) 692-2200

NELSON CRAB INC.
Tokeland, Washington 98590

NELSON-DYKES COMPANY
4071 Shilling Way
Dallas, Texas 75237
(214) 331-4395

NELSON INC., J.G.
412 East Franklin Street
El Segundo, California 90245

Companies and Trade Names

NELSON, INC., PUBLISHERS, THOMAS
405 Seventh Avenue, South
Nashville, Tennessee 37203
Sam Moore, President
(615) 244-3733

NELSON MACHINE & MANUFACTURING COMPANY
Box 340
Ashtabula, Ohio 44004
(216) 992-3139

NELSON MANUFACTURING COMPANY INC., L.R.
7719 North Pioneer Parkway
Peoria, Illinois 61614
(309) 692-2200

NELSON McCOY POTTERY COMPANY, THE
Gordon Street
Roseville, Ohio 43777

NELSON MUFFLER CORPORATION
Box 308
Stoughton, Wisconsin 53589
Edwin E. Bryant, President
(608) 873-6641

NELSON-RICKS CREAMERY COMPANY
314 West Third South Street
Salt Lake City, Utah 84101
Calvin L. Nelson, President
(801) 364-3607

NELSON-ROANOKE CORPORATION
Box 2827
Roanoke, Virginia 24001
Robert W. Woody, Chairman and President
(703) 343-2481

NEMBUTAL (sedative)
See Abbott Laboratories

NEMO (foundation garments, lingerie)
See Kops Brothers

NEMO CORPORATION
29001 Cedar
Cleveland, Ohio 44124
(216) 442-9080

NEO-PHARMACAL COMPANY
45-46 202nd Street
Bayside, New York 11361

NEO-SYNEPHRINE (cold remedies)
See Winthrop Laboratories

NEOCO CORPORATION
1000 North Highland Avenue
Los Angeles, California 90038
Elvirita Lewis, Chairman, President and Treasurer
(213) 465-8187

NEOLITE (shoe products)
See Goodyear Tire & Rubber Company

NEOSHO PAPER PRODUCTS
Post Office Box 578
Chanute, Kansas 66720

NEPHRON CORPORATION
3319 Pacific Avenue
Tacoma, Washington 98408
(206) 475-3452

NEPTUNE METER COMPANY
30 Perimeter Park
Atlanta, Georgia 30341
(404) 458-8111

NERVINE (mild tranquilizer)
See Consumer Products Group of Miles Laboratories, Inc.

NESBITT FOOD PRODUCTS, INC.
(Subsidiary of The Clorox Company)
2946 East 11th
Los Angeles, California 90023
Lee H. Grayson, President
(213) 263-7143

NESCAFE (coffee)
See Nestle Company, Inc.

NESCO-KNAPP-MONARCH
(Division of The Hoover Company)
101 East Maple Street
North Canton, Ohio 44720
G.G. Bettis, Vice President
(216) 499-9200

NESSLER PRODUCTS, INC., CHARLES
Box 27
Avon, Connecticut 06001

NESTEA (tea)
See Nestle Company, Inc.

NESTLE COMPANY, INC., THE
100 Bloomingdale Road
White Plains, New York 10605
David E. Guerrant, President
(914) 946-6400
See also Crosse & Blackwell Vintage Cellars; and Gerber Cheese Company, Inc.

NESTLE-LEMUR COMPANY
902 Broadway
New York, New York 10010
Murray C. Becker, President
(212) 777-8200
See also Marchand Company, Charles; and Seaforth Corporation

NETHERLANDS-AMERICAN YACHTS INC.
1199 S.E. 17th Street
Fort Lauderdale, Florida 33316

NETTIE'S HOME PRESERVING COMPANY
1710 Howard
Indianapolis, Indiana 46221
(317) 632-6112

Companies and Trade Names

NETTLETON COMPANY, A.E.
(Subsidiary of Endicott Johnson
  Corporation)
313 East Willow Street
Syracuse, New York 13203
L.W. Affolter, President
(315) 422-1248

NEUBAUER MANUFACTURING
  COMPANY
525 Lowry Avenue N.E.
Minneapolis, Minnesota 55418
(612) 789-5841

NEUHOFF BROTHERS, PACKERS
2821 Alamo Street
Dallas, Texas 75201
Henry Neuhoff, III, President
(214) 741-5531

NEUMANN'S CONFECTIONS
235 South Roosevelt
Green Bay, Wisconsin 54301

NEUSE RIVER (seafood)
  See Sound Packing Company

NEUSHAFFER, HELEN
(Division of Supronics Corporation)
101 New Era Drive
South Plainfield, New Jersey 07080
Lester G. Kaufman, President
(201) 561-6300

NEUTRO-STAT (antistatic sprays
  for rugs)
  See Simco Company, Inc.

NEUTROGENA CORPORATION
5755 West 96th Street
Los Angeles, California 90045
Lloyd E. Cotsen, President
(213) 776-5223

NEUWIRTH COMPANY, INC.
225 Fifth Avenue
New York, New York 10010
(212) 685-6420

NEVA-CLOG PRODUCTS, INC.
506 Logan
Bridgeport, Connecticut 06601
(203) 333-4148

NEVADA POWER COMPANY
Fourth and Stewart Streets
Las Vegas, Nevada 89151
Harry Allen, President
(702) 385-5011

NEVAMAR (laminated plastic)
  See Exxon Chemical Company
    U.S.A.

NEVCO PRODUCTS COMPANY
500 Nepperhan Avenue
Yonkers, New York 10701

NEVER SLIP (can openers)
  See Vaughan Manufacturing
    Company

NEW AMERICAN LIBRARY, INC.
(Subsidiary of The Times Mirror
  Company)
1301 Avenue of the Americas
New York, New York 10019
Herbert K. Schnall, President
(212) 956-3800

NEW AMSTERDAM IMPORT
  COMPANY
470 Mamaroneck
White Plains, New York 10605

NEW BEDFORD GAS & EDISON
  LIGHT COMPANY
693 Purchase Street
New Bedford, Massachusetts 02740
G.E. Anderson, President
(617) 996-8211

NEW CASTLE PRODUCTS INC.
  See Modernfold Industries, Inc.

NEW DAWN (hair coloring)
  See Alberto-Culver Company

NEW DESIGN SAILBOATS
Box 279-S
Benbrook Lakeview Drive
Fort Worth, Texas 76126
(817) 249-0166

NEW DIAMOND
(Division of Ketcham & McDougall
  Inc.)
465 Eagle Rock Avenue
Roseland, New Jersey 07068
(201) 226-6060

NEW DIRECTIONS
1629 K Street, N.W.
Washington, D.C. 20006
(202) 872-1996

NEW ENGLAND APPLE PRODUCTS
  COMPANY, INC.
Harward Road
Littleton, Massachusetts 01460
David R. Rowse, President
(617) 486-3522

NEW ENGLAND CLOCK COMPANY
Farmington Industrial Park
Spring Lane
Farmington, Connecticut 06010
(203) 677-4253

NEW ENGLAND CONFECTIONERY
  COMPANY
254 Massachusetts Avenue
Cambridge, Massachusetts 02139
Joseph A. Dancewicz, President
(617) 876-4700

NEW ENGLAND ELECTRIC SYSTEM
20 Turnpike Road
Westboro, Massachusetts 05181
Robert F. Krause, Chairman of the
  Board
(617) 366-9011
  See also Massachusetts Electric
    Company; and Narrangansett
    Electric Company

NEW ENGLAND FENCE MANU-
  FACTURING COMPANY INC.
Box 37
Montville, Connecticut 06353

Companies and Trade Names

NEW ENGLAND FISH COMPANY
Pier 89
Seattle, Washington 98119
Richard D. Saunders, President
(206) 284-2750

NEW ENGLAND GAS & ELECTRIC
  ASSOCIATION
130 Austin Street
Cambridge, Massachusetts 02139
Gerald E. Anderson, President
(617) 864-3100

NEW ENGLAND GROCER SUPPLY
  COMPANY
(Subsidiary of Springfield Sugar &
  Products Company)
Post Office Box 638
Northborough, Massachusetts 01532
David Ginsberg, Vice President
(617) 393-6711

NEW ENGLAND MERCHANTS
  NATIONAL BANK OF BOSTON
Prudential Center
Boston, Massachusetts 02199
Roderick M. MacDougall, President
(617) 742-4000

NEW ENGLAND MUTUAL LIFE
  INSURANCE COMPANY
501 Boylston Street
Boston, Massachusetts 02117
Gordon D. MacKay, Vice President,
  Public Affairs
(617) 266-3700

NEW ENGLAND POWER COMPANY
20 Turnpike Road
Westborough, Massachusetts 01581
Robert F. Krause, Chairman of the
  Board
(617) 366-9011

NEW ENGLAND PROVISION
  COMPANY, INC.
(Subsidiary of Wilson & Company,
  Inc.)
960 Massachusetts Avenue
Boston, Massachusetts 02118
Max Berger, President
(617) 442-8400

NEW ENGLAND ROPES INC.
Popes Island
New Bedford, Massachusetts 02740
(617) 999-2351

NEW ENGLAND SAILBOAT
  COMPANY
2218 Ramsey Road
Monroeville, Pennsylvania 15146

NEW ENGLAND SERUM
  COMPANY
239 Newburyport Turnpike
Topsfield, Massachusetts 01983

NEW ENGLAND SHRIMP
  COMPANY
212 Maplewood
Boston, Massachusetts 02149
(617) 321-5820

NEW ENGLAND STATIONERY
  COMPANY
77 North Washington Street
Boston, Massachusetts 02114
Warren Abrams, President and Sales
  Manager
(617) 523-0770

NEW ENGLAND TELEPHONE &
  TELEGRAPH COMPANY
185 Franklin Street
Boston, Massachusetts 02107
William C. Mercer, President
(617) 743-9800

NEW ENGLAND TOY COMPANY
410 E Street
Boston Massachusetts 02127
(617) 269-6190

NEW ENGLAND TOY MANU-
  FACTURING COMPANY INC.
Post Office Box 188
474 Barnum Avenue
Bridgeport, Connecticut 06608
(203) 333-0315

NEW ENGLAND TWINE &
  CORDAGE COMPANY
67 Walker Street
Lincoln, Rhode Island 02865
Earl Percelay, President, Treasu
  and National Sales Manager
(401) 722-3737

NEW ERA (educational musical
instruments)
  See Selmer (Division of
    Magnavox Company)

NEW ERA CANNING COMPANY
United States 31
New Era, Michigan 49446
(616) 861-2151

NEW ERA MILLING COMPANY
615 West Chestnut
Arkansas City, Kansas 67005
A. James Sowden, President
(316) 442-5500

NEW ERA OPTICAL COMPANY
17 North Wabash Avenue
Chicago, Illinois 60690
Ralph Levin, President and Sales
  Manager
(312) 782-8000

NEW FASHION JEWELRY
  COMPANY
45 Glen Cove Road
Greenvale, New York 11548

NEW FREEDOM (adhesive-backed
feminine napkins)
  See Kimberly-Clark Corporation

NEW HAMPSHIRE INSURANCE
  COMPANY
1750 Elm Street
Manchester, New Hampshire 03104
Carl P. Barton, President
(603) 669-6300

Companies and Trade Names

NEW HAVEN WATER COMPANY
100 Crown Street
New Haven, Connecticut 06510
John J. Crawford, Corporate
 Secretary
(203) 281-3011

NEW HOLLAND
(Division of Sperry Rand Corporation)
Franklin and Roberts Streets
New Holland, Pennsylvania 17557
Kenneth F. Thompson, President
(717) 354-1121

NEW HOME SEWING MACHINE
 COMPANY, THE
171 Commerce Road
Carlstadt, New Jersey 07072

NEW HOPE MILLS
R.F.D. Number Two
Moravia, New York 13118

NEW HORIZON (foods)
 See General Foods Corporation

NEW IDEA CHEMICAL COMPANY
Box 67
Kingston, Massachusetts 02364

NEW JERSEY BANK, N.A.
1 Garret Mountain Plaza
West Paterson, New Jersey 07509
Maurice J. Brick, President
(201) 881-5000

NEW JERSEY BELL TELEPHONE
 COMPANY
(Subsidiary of American Telephone &
 Telegraph Company)
540 Broad Street
Newark, New Jersey 07101
Robert W. Kleinert, President
(201) 649-9900

NEW JERSEY MANUFACTURERS
 INSURANCE COMPANY
Sullivan Way
Trenton, New Jersey 08607
Vincent E. Hoyer, President
(609) 883-1300

NEW JERSEY NATIONAL BANK
1 West State Street
Trenton, New Jersey 08603
John H. Walther, President
(609) 989-7700

NEW JERSEY NATURAL GAS
 COMPANY
601 Bangs Avenue
Asbury Park, New Jersey 07712
W.D. Williams, President
(201) 988-2800

NEW JERSEY PLANT PRESERVERS
85 Newman Street
Hackensack, New Jersey 07601

NEW LIFE (coffee and tea)
 See Thomas Coffee Company

NEW LIFE (hair preparation)
 See Johnson Publishing Company

NEW METHOD MANUFACTURING
 COMPANY
Box 175
Bradford, Pennsylvania 16701
(814) 362-6611

NEW MOON (mobile homes)
 See Redman Industries, Inc.

NEW ORLEANS CUISINE, INC.
1700 Baronne Street
New Orleans, Louisiana 70113
(504) 588-9131

NEW ORLEANS MACARONI
 MANUFACTURING COMPANY,
 INC.
1107 Dauphine Street
New Orleans, Louisiana 70116
(504) 523-5419

NEW ORLEANS PUBLIC SERVICE,
 INC.
(Subsidiary of Middle South Utilities,
 Inc.)
317 Baronne Street
New Orleans, Louisiana 70160
William McCollam, Jr., President
(504) 586-2121

NEW PLANT LIFE
(Division of Charles O. Finley &
 Company, Inc.)
Box 45
LaPorte, Indiana 46350

NEW PROCESS BAKING COMPANY
2883 South Hillock
Chicago, Illinois 60608
Longin Kutchins, President
(312) 376-7700

NEW PROCESS COMPANY
220 Hickory Street
Warren, Pennsylvania 16365
John L. Blair, President
(814) 723-3600

NEW RICHMOND (canned
vegetables)
 See Friday Canning Corporation

NEW RICHMOND FARMS
(Division of Domain Industries)
Faribault, Minnesota 55021

NEW WOMAN (bath oil, dusting
powder, toilet soap)
 See Pfizer Inc.

NEW YORK AIRWAYS, INC.
Box 426
LaGuardia Airport Station
Flushing, New York 11371
Warren A. Fucigna, President
(212) 476-5656

NEW YORK AMERICAN BEVERAGE
 COMPANY, INC.
 See American Beverage
  Corporation

Companies and Trade Names

NEW YORK GIRL COAT
COMPANY, INC.
520 Eighth Avenue
New York, New York 10018
(212) 564-8920

NEW YORK IMPERIAL
FOUNDATIONS
87 34th Street
Brooklyn, New York 11232
(212) 788-8010

NEW YORK INSTITUTE OF
PHOTOGRAPHY
112 West 31st Street
New York, New York 10001
Lawrence Esmond, President
(212) 244-3462

NEW YORK INTERNATIONAL
SALES CORPORATION
1393 Palisade Avenue
Teaneck, New Jersey 07666

NEW YORK LABEL & BOX
CORPORATION
275 Seventh Avenue
New York, New York 10001
(212) 929-7339

NEW YORK LIFE INSURANCE
COMPANY
51 Madison Avenue
New York, New York 10010
Marshall P. Bissell, President
(212) 576-7000

NEW YORK MERCHANDISE
COMPANY, INC.
32 West 23rd Street
New York, New York 10010
Milton M. Shaw, President
(212) 675-3500

NEW YORK NEWS, INC.
(Subsidiary of Tribune Company)
220 East 42nd Street
New York, New York 10017
W.H. James, President
(212) 682-1234

NEW YORK PENCIL COMPANY
Nu-Masca Division
46-14 Astoria Boulevard
Long Island City, New York 11103
(212) 721-2000
See also Pretty Naturally

NEW YORK STATE ELECTRIC &
GAS CORPORATION
Post Office Box 287
Ithaca, New York 14850
Lloyd A. Kelly, President
(607) 347-4131

NEW YORK STOCK EXCHANGE
11 Wall Street
New York, New York 10005
James J. Needham, Chairman of
the Board
(212) 623-3000

NEW YORK SYRUP CORPORATION
54-18 Third
Maspeth, New York 11378

NEW YORK TELEPHONE
COMPANY
(Subsidiary of American Telephone &
Telegraph Company)
1095 Avenue of the Americas
New York, New York 10036
William M. Ellinghaus, President
(212) 395-2121

NEW YORK TIMES COMPANY
229 West 43rd Street
New York, New York 10036
Arthur Ochs Sulzberger, President
(212) 556-1234

NEW YORK TOY CORPORATION
200 Fifth Avenue
New York, New York 10010
(212) 924-0240

NEW YORK VON COMPANY
Box 215
Tuckahoe, New York 10707

NEW YORK WIRE COMPANY
441 East Market
York, Pennsylvania 17403
(717) 854-9571

NEWARK FELT NOVELTY COMPANY
50 Jelliff Avenue
Newark, New Jersey 07108
(201) 243-2525

NEWARK PARAFFINE PAPER
COMPANY
70 Blanchard Street
Newark, New Jersey 07105
(201) 589-4200

NEWARK SPECIALTY COMPANY
20 Prince Street
Newark, New Jersey 07103
(201) 623-7135

NEWAY BRUSH COMPANY
390 Capitol Avenue
Hartford, Connecticut 06106

NEWBERG & COMPANY, INC., A.
209 Little East Neck Road
Babylon, New York 11702

NEWBERRY COMPANY, J.J.
(Subsidiary of McCrory Corporation)
888 Seventh Avenue
New York, New York 10019
Stanley H. Kunsberg, President
(212) 889-8500

NEWCOMB AUDIO PRODUCTS
COMPANY
12881 Bradley Avenue
Sylmar, California 91342
Robert Newcomb, President

NEWELL COMPANIES, INC.
916 South Arcade Avenue
Freeport, Illinois 61032
Daniel C. Ferguson, President
(815) 235-4171

1011

Companies and Trade Names

NEWLAND, SCHNEELOCH & PIEK, INC.
See N.S.P., Inc.

NEWLY WEDS FOODS, INC.
4140 West Fullerton
Chicago, Illinois 60639
Paul M. Angell, President
(312) 489-7000

NEWMAN BROTHERS INC.
5609 Center Hill
Cincinnati, Ohio 45216
(513) 242-0011

NEWMAN INDUSTRIES INC.
Post Office Box 1208
300 Newman Road
Miami, Oklahoma 74354
(918) 542-4474

NEWMAN, JARVIS
Southwest Harbor,
    Massachusetts 04679

NEWMAN PHARMACAL COMPANY
Box 10066
Louisville, Kentucky 40210

NEWORG CERAMIC SPECIALTIES
1260 Logan Avenue
Costa Mesa, California 92626

NEWPORT (cigarettes)
See Lorillard Corporation

NEWPORT (food products)
See Stokely-Van Camp Inc.

NEWPORT (vodka)
See McKesson Liquor Company

NEWPORT CATAMARAN INC.
1355 Logan Street
Costa Mesa, California 92626

NEWPORT CREAMERY, INC.
West Main Road
Newport, Rhode Island 02842
Peter W. Rector, President
(401) 847-0390

NEWPORT DESIGN
202 Stevens
Santa Ana, California 92707

NEWPORT SUPPLY COMPANY
17421 Daimler Street
Irvine, California 92705

NEWS (heavy-duty detergent)
See Purex Corporation, Ltd.

NEWSDAY, INC.
(Subsidiary of Times Mirror Company)
550 Stewart Avenue
Garden City, New York 11530
William Attwood, President
(516) 294-3527

NEWSPAPER INSTITUTE OF
    AMERICA, INC.
2 Park Avenue
New York, New York 10016
Lois Stuart
(212) 685-9690

NEWSWEEK, INC.
444 Madison Avenue
New York, New York 10022
Robert D. Campbell, President
(212) 350-2000

NEWTON FOODS INC.
81 Ingell Street
Taunton, Massachusetts 02780

NEWTON GLOVE, INC.
North Main Avenue
Newton, North Carolina 28658
Robert M. Yount, President
(704) 464-4771

NEYPACO PAPER CORPORATION
185-01 Hillside Avenue
Jamaica, New York 11432
(212) 657-9085

NIAGARA (indoor-outdoor carpeting)
See General Felt Industries

NIAGARA ENVELOPE COMPANY
701 Seneca Street
Buffalo, New York 14210
Frederick S. Pierce, President
(716) 854-8251

NIAGARA FRONTIER SERVICES
(TOPS Supermarkets)
60 Dingens Street
Buffalo, New York 14206
Savino P. Nanula, President
(716) 823-3712

NIAGARA FRONTIER TRANSIT
    SYSTEM, INC.
855 Main Street
Buffalo, New York 14203
Alex D. Trumble, President
(716) 884-6800

NIAGARA MOHAWK POWER
    CORPORATION
300 Erie Boulevard, West
Syracuse, New York 13202
John G. Haehl, Jr., President
(315) 474-1511

NIAGARA THERAPY MANU-
    FACTURING CORPORATION
Adamsville, Pennsylvania 16110
Charles E. Murphy, President
(412) 932-3171

NIBLACK COMPANY, K.G.
395 Linwood Avenue
Buffalo, New York 14209
(716) 886-3482

NIBLACK FOODS, INC.
20 Magnolia Street
Rochester, New York 14608
(716) 328-5745

Companies and Trade Names

NIBLETS (corn)
　See Green Giant Company

NIC-L-SILVER BATTERY COMPANY
　See Battery Systems, Inc.

NICE 'N EASY (hair coloring)
　See Clairol, Inc.

NICE-PAK PRODUCTS, INC.
150 North MacQuesten
Mount Vernon, New York 10550
(914) 664-7800

NICHOLL BROTHERS INC.
1204 West 27th Street
Kansas City, Missouri 64108
(816) 753-7343

NICHOLS (whiskey)
　See Austin, Nichols & Company, Inc.

NICHOLS-HOMESHIELD INC.
188 Industrial Drive
Elmhurst, Illinois 60126
J.M. Morris, President
(312) 833-4000

NICHOLS-KUSAN, INC.
(Subsidiary of Kusan, Inc.)
Post Office Box 1191
Jacksonville, Texas 75766
Billy E. Michie, President
(214) 586-9831

NICHOLS PRODUCTS COMPANY
325 West Main Street
Moorestown, New Jersey 08057

NICHOLS, S.E., INC.
500 Eighth Avenue
New York, New York 10018
Manfred Brecker, President
(212) 695-5120

NICHOLSON (men's overcoats, raincoats)
　See Chester Barrie, Ltd.

NICHOLSON COMPANY, H.R.
Kenshaw and Oakleaf Avenues
Baltimore, Maryland 21215
(301) 764-2323

NICHOLSON FILE COMPANY
667 Waterman Avenue
East Providence, Rhode Island 02914
　See also Danco

NICHOLSON, INC.
Post Office Box 1081
Burlington, North Carolina 27215

NICHOLSON RUG COMPANY, INC.
Nicholson, Pennsylvania 18446

NICHOLSON SEED COMPANY, ROBERT
Post Office Box 15487
2700 Logan Street
Dallas, Texas 75215
(214) 421-7181

NICHOLSON'S LAMPLIGHTER (gin)
　See McKesson Liquor Company

NICKELL BROTHERS (produce)
　See Floyd Dahn Fruits, Inc.

NICKERSON BOAT WORKS
East Moriches, New York 11940

NICOLAU (Greek wines)
　See Austin, Nichols & Company, Inc.

NICROMETAL MARINE HARDWARE COMPANY
2065 West Avenue 140th
San Leandro, California 94577

NIDAY LATCH COMPANY
4858 Brightview Drive
Covina, California 91722

NIELSEN (pipes)
　See S. Brandt Imports Inc.

NIELSEN IMPORTS, P.
850 Ramona Avenue
Albany, California 94706

NIEMANN & COMPANY, WILLIAM H.
55 Paramus Road
Paramus, New Jersey 07652

NIEMEYER INC., THEODORUS
803 South 12th Street
Louisville, Kentucky 40201

NIFDA (teas, coffees, and spices)
　See Ekelunds' Inc.

NIGHT-EYE CORPORATION, THE
503 Iowa State Bank Building
Iowa City, Iowa 52240

NIGHT HAWK RESTAURANTS, INC.
Frozen Food Division
512 East Riverside Drive
Austin, Texas 78704

NIGHT OWL (cigars)
　See General Cigar Company Inc.

NIGHTINGALE (lamps)
　See Adjustable Fixture Company

NIKKO CERAMICS, INC.
222 Fifth Avenue
New York, New York 10001
(212) 889-2590

NIKOBAN (smoking deterrent)
　See J.B. Williams Company, Inc.

NIKOLAI (vodka)
　See Four Roses Distillers Company

Companies and Trade Names

NIKON, INC.
(Subsidiary of Ehrenreich Photo
   Optical Industries, Inc.)
623 Stewart Avenue
Garden City, New York 11530
Herbert Sax, Vice President
(516) 248-5200

NILE-THERM (insulated glassware)
   See Federal Tool & Plastic

NILODOR COMPANY, INC.
60 East 42nd Street
New York, New York 10017
(212) 697-5280

NIMROD, INC.
500 Ford Boulevard
Hamilton, Ohio 45011
James D. Tucker, Chairman of the
   Board
(513) 863-2200

NINA RICCI PARFUMS
630 Fifth Avenue
New York, New York 10020
(212) 489-2430

NINETY-SIX CANNING COMPANY
109 South Cambridge Street
Ninety-Six, South Carolina 29666

NION CORPORATION
11581 Federal Drive
El Monte, California 91734
Elvirita Lewis, Chairman, President
   and Treasurer
(213) 686-2105

NIP-CO MANUFACTURING INC.
Route 28
Glenford, New York 12433
(914) 657-8100

NIPKOW & KOBELT INC.
468 Park Avenue South
New York, New York 10016
(212) 689-8840

NIPPON (steel and classical
   guitars)
   See European Crafts Inc.

NIPPY MANUFACTURING
   COMPANY, INC.
Box 428
Jamaica, New York 11431
(212) 739-4644

NISHIMOTO TRADING COMPANY,
   LTD.
2734 New Jersey
Los Angeles, California 90030
(213) 265-2897

NISONGER CORPORATION
35 Bartels Place
New Rochelle, New York 10801

NISSAN MOTOR CORPORATION,
   U.S.A.
18501 South Figueroa Street
Carson, California 90744
Y. Katayama, Chairman of the
   Board
(213) 639-7860

NISSEN CORPORATION
930 27th Avenue, S.W.
Cedar Rapids, Iowa 52404
George P. Nissen, President
(319) 365-7561

NITINE, INC.
(Subsidiary of Shulton, Inc.)
697 Route 46
Clifton, New Jersey 07015

NIX (deodorant)
   See Plough Inc.

NIX COMPANY
633 North Main Street
Brockton, Massachusetts 02401

NO.
   See Number

NO BUGS M'LADY (treated shelf
and drawer paper)
   See Paper Products Inc.

NO BURN (urn ring)
   See Seiling Urn & Bag
      Company

NO-CAL (diet beverages)
   See No-Cal Corporation

NO-CAL CORPORATION
112-02 15th Avenue
College Point, New York 11356
David A. Kirsch, President
(212) 358-2000

NO MORE TANGLES (hair-care
products)
   See Johnson & Johnson Company

NO-NAIL HANGER COMPANY
Post Office Box 3127
Flint, Michigan 48502

NO-NOX (gasoline)
   See Gulf Oil Corporation

NO RINSE LABORATORIES
20 Compark Road
Centerville, Ohio 45459

NO-RUB (floor wax, shoe
cleaner, and polish)
   See Wilbert Products Company,
      Inc.

NO-SAG SPRING
(Division of Lear Siegler, Inc.)
3500 West 11 Mile Road
Berkley, Michigan 48072
Harold W. Inman, President
(313) 547-5600

NO-SHOK SAFETY LOCK (switch
plates, extension cords, etc.)
   See Bell Electric Company

1014

Companies and Trade Names

NO-STAT (antistatic rinse)
See Robert Smith Manufacturing Company, Inc.

NO TRUMPETS-NO DRUMS
5 Ledge Road
Ogunquit, Maine 03907

NO-VENT (gas heaters)
See Suburban Manufacturing Company

NO-WASH (paint remover)
See Wilson-Imperial Company

NO-WORK (oven cleaner)
See Wilbert Products Company, Inc.

NOB-HILL (tobacco)
See House of Edgeworth

NOBIL SHOE COMPANY
(Subsidiary of Endicott Johnson Corporation)
750 East Tallmadge Avenue
Akron, Ohio 44330
George Kettlewell, President
(216) 633-6610

NOBILITY HOMES, INC.
3741 S.W. Seventh Street
Ocala, Florida 32670
Terry E. Trexler, President
(904) 732-8161

NOBLE (accordions)
See Harris-Teller Inc.

NOBLE & WESTBROOK
(Division of The Bristol Brass Corporation)
20 Westbrook Street
East Hartford, Connecticut 06108
George A. Reed, General Manager
(203) 289-2717

NOBLE INC., BENJAMIN
105 Madison Avenue
New York, New York 10016
(212) 532-6100

NOBLE PINE PRODUCTS COMPANY
Box 41
Centuck Station
Yonkers, New York 10710
(914) 968-3034

NOBLIT BROTHERS & COMPANY
Richmond and Norris
Philadelphia, Pennsylvania 19125
(215) 634-7700

NOCONA BOOT COMPANY, INC., THE
East Highway 82
Nocona, Texas 76255
Enid Justin, President
(817) 285-3321

NOESTING PIN TICKET COMPANY INC.
728 East 136th Street
New York, New York 10454
G.F. Griffiths, Jr., President
(212) 669-6465

NOILLY PRAT (vermouth)
See Brown-Forman Distillers Corporation

NOLAN BROOM WORKS
Princeton, Florida 33171

NOLAND TANK & GALVANIZING COMPANY
705 Merritt Avenue
Nashville, Tennessee 37202
Henry Leonard Glymp, President
(615) 256-0135

NOLDE BROTHERS, INC.
2520 East Broad Street
Richmond, Virginia 23223
George F. Nolde, Jr., President
(703) 643-3456

NOMA-WORLDWIDE, INC.
7400 West Industrial Drive
Forest Park, Illinois 60130
Albert V. Sadacca, President
(312) 771-9400

NOMIS (canned foods)
See Furman Canning Company

NON-SCUFF (floor wax)
See Simoniz Company

NON-STOP PEN & PENCIL COMPANY
22-01 120th Street
College Point, New York 11356

NONESUCH RECORDS
See Warner Brothers Records, Inc.

NOODLE RONI (packaged noodle dish)
See Golden Grain Macaroni Company

NOODY PRODUCTS COMPANY
2278 Tremainsville
Toledo, Ohio 43613

NOON HOUR FOOD PRODUCTS, INC.
652 West Randolph Street
Chicago, Illinois 60606
Paul Buhl, President
(312) 782-1177

NOONE SHOE COMPANY, FRANK
Taunton, Massachusetts 02780
T. Francis Noone, President
(617) 822-5356

NOPEL CORPORATION
112 East 19th Street
New York, New York 10003
(212) 982-5841

Companies and Trade Names

NOR-AM AGRICULTURAL PRODUCTS
PRODUCTS INC.
20 North Wacker Drive
Chicago, Illinois 60606
(312) 346-8182

NOR-EAST (men's suits)
See L. Greif & Brother

NORAMEX COMPANY, INC.
61-71 Alderton Street
Rego Park, New York 11374

NORBEST, INC.
1224 First Security Building
Salt Lake City, Utah 84111
J.W. Tallman, President
(801) 328-1655

NORCA CORPORATION
350 Fifth Avenue
New York, New York 10001
(212) 760-1776

NORCLIFF LABORATORIES
(Division of McKesson & Robbins
   Drug Company)
Post Office Box 471
Fairfield, Connecticut 06430
C.A. Pergola, General Manager
(203) 259-1654

NORCO (aspirin, hydrogen peroxide, mouthwash, saccharin, etc.)
See Norton Products Company

NORCO METAL PRODUCTS
   COMPANY
2300 Wyandotte Road
Willow Grove, Pennsylvania 19090
(215) 657-3084

NORCOLD, INC.
1501 Michigan Street
Sidney, Ohio 45365
R.J. Riedl, President
(513) 492-1111

NORCREST CHINA COMPANY
55 West Burnside Street
Portland, Oregon 97209
(503) 288-7404

NORCROSS, INC.
260 Madison Avenue
New York, New York 10016
Mary Calvo, President
(212) 689-1700

NORD-NEW YORK, INC.
Box 467
Westport, New York 12993

NORD YACHTS
(Division of Recreational Equipment
   Company)
11892 Cardinal Circle
Garden Grove, California 90640

NORDAM TRADING
   CORPORATION
234 Hampton
Southhampton, New York 11968

NORDEN LABORATORIES, INC.
(Subsidiary of Smith Kline & French
   Laboratories)
601 West Cornhusker Highway
Lincoln, Nebraska 68501
R.D. Andersen, President
(402) 475-4541

NORDEX BOATS
Box JJ
Venice, Florida 33595

NORDIC SKI IMPORTS INC.
250 East Fifth Street
Saint Paul, Minnesota 55101

NORDIC WARE (aluminum products)
See Northland Aluminum
   Products Inc.

NORDICA (sports accessories and equipment)
See Beconta Inc.

NORDLIE, INC.
262 East Montcalm Street
Detroit, Michigan 48201
(313) 963-2454

NORDSTROM, INC.
1501 Fifth Avenue
Seattle, Washington 98101
John A. Nordstrom, President
(206) 628-2111

NOREEN (hair coloring)
See Lehn & Fink Consumer
   Products

NORELCO (electric appliances, shavers, tape recorders)
See North American Philips
   Corporation

NORELCO KIT
(Division of Herman H. Smith Inc.)
812 Snediker Avenue
Brooklyn, New York 11207
(212) 272-9400

NORELL (cologne, perfume)
See Revlon, Inc.

NORFELL INC.
14 Alpha Road
Chelmsford, Massachusetts 01824

NORFOLK & WESTERN RAILWAY
8 North Jefferson Street
Roanoke, Virginia 24042
John P. Fishwick, President
(703) 981-4000

NORFOLK PACKING COMPANY,
   INC.
620 East Olney Road
Norfolk, Virginia 23510

NORFORMS (feminine-hygiene products)
See Norwich Pharmacal Company

1016

Companies and Trade Names

NORGE (sports accessories and equipment)
See Eiger Mountain Sports

NORGE
(Division of Fedders Corporation)
Woodbridge Avenue
Edison, New Jersey 08817
Salvatore Giordeno, Chairman and President
(201) 549-7200

NORGINE LABORATORIES, INC.
207 East 37th Street
New York, New York 10016
(212) 697-1513

NORIS (photo equipment)
See Graflex, Inc.

NORITAKE COMPANY, INC.
41 Madison Avenue
New York, New York 10010
Susumu Saegi, President
(212) 481-3300

NORLIN MUSIC, INC.
7373 North Cicero Avenue
Lincolnwood, Illinois 60646
Arnold M. Berlin, President
(312) 675-2000
See also Gibson, Inc.

NORMA-FEND COMPANY
143 East 60th Street
New York, New York 10022
(212) 759-9765

NORMAL (shoes)
See Dunn & McCarthy, Inc.

NORMAL PHARMACAL COMPANY
1101 Broadway
Oakland, California 94607

NORMAN COSMETICS, MERLE
9130 Bellanca Avenue
Los Angeles, California 90045
Robert Nethercutt, President
(213) 641-3000

NORMAN, FOX & COMPANY
5611 South Boyle Avenue
Vernon, California 90058

NORMAN WIATT (women's dresses)
See Norman Wiatt Company, Inc.

NORMAN WIATT COMPANY, INC.
3221 South Hill Street
Los Angeles, California 90007
Harold Sonners, President
(213) 748-6303

NORMANDIE PRESS
41-10 22nd Street
Long Island City, New York 11101
(212) 392-7200

NORMANDY HALL INDUSTRIES
11731 South Austin Avenue
Worth, Illinois 60482

NORMANDY MANUFACTURING CORPORATION
126 West 22nd Street
New York, New York 10011
(212) 691-8590

NORMARK CORPORATION
1710 East 78th Street
Minneapolis, Minnesota 55423
(612) 869-3228

NORMATT INC.
3275 Country Drive
Saint Paul, Minnesota 55117

NORMY ENTERPRISES
865 East Wood
Decatur, Illinois 62521

NORPAC (food products)
See United Flav-R-Pac Growers, Inc.

NORPAC GROWERS, INC.
Box 203
Dundee, Oregon 97115

NORPLAC, INC.
2415 Pilot Knob Road
Saint Paul, Minnesota 55118

NORREN MANUFACTURING INC.
778 North Georgia Avenue
Azusa, California 91702
(213) 334-7416

NORRIS INDUSTRIES
5215 South Boyle Avenue
Los Angeles, California 90058
Kenneth T. Norris, Jr., Chairman of the Board
(213) 588-7111
See also Pressed Steel Tank Company Inc.; Thermador; and Waste King

NORRIS LABORATORIES
Forrest Avenue and Elm Street
Norristown, Pennsylvania 19401

NORSE CHEMICAL CORPORATION
2121 Norse Avenue
Cudahy, Wisconsin 53110

NORSE COMPANY
Box 49
White Plains, New York 10602

NORSK MARINE INC.
Villa Industrial Park
Villa Rica, Georgia 30180

NORSTAR ENTERPRISES
12th and Wolf Streets
Philadelphia, Pennsylvania 19148
(215) 389-5533

NORSTAR SKI CORPORATION LTD.
37 Industrial Drive
Londonderry, New Hampshire 03053

NORTECH LABORATORIES
2468 North Jerusalem Road
North Bellmore, New York 11710

Companies and Trade Names

NORTH & JUDD MANUFACTURING COMPANY
(Subsidiary of Gulf & Western Industries, Inc.)
699 Middle Street
Middletown, Connecticut 06457
R.T. McLaurin, Chief Executive Officer
(203) 632-2600

NORTH AMERICA WINES CORPORATION
57-02 48th Street
Maspeth, New York 11378

NORTH AMERICAN ASBESTOS CORPORATION
150 North Wacker Drive
Chicago, Illinois 60606
C.G. Morgan, President and Treasurer
(312) 726-8515

NORTH AMERICAN BOAT CORPORATION
3355 S.W. Second Avenue
Fort Lauderdale, Florida 33315
(305) 524-6952

NORTH AMERICAN CORRESPONDENCE SCHOOLS
See National Systems Corporation

NORTH AMERICAN EQUIPMENT CORPORATION
179 Michigan Avenue
Kenilworth, New Jersey 07033
William F. Van Loan, President
(201) 241-3600

NORTH AMERICAN FOODS
(Division of Deltec International)
2801 Ponce de Leon Boulevard
Coral Gables, Florida 33134
(305) 443-2351

NORTH AMERICAN LIFE & CASUALTY COMPANY
1750 Hennepin Avenue
Minneapolis, Minnesota 55403
Howard E. Barnhill, President
(612) 377-5511

NORTH AMERICAN LIFE INSURANCE COMPANY OF CHICAGO
Policy Service Department
35 East Wacker Drive
Chicago, Illinois 60601
Forrest D. Guynn, President
(312) 236-4700

NORTH AMERICAN MANUFACTURING COMPANY
4455 East 71st Street
Cleveland, Ohio 44105
Robert J. Neville, President and Treasurer
(216) 271-6000

NORTH AMERICAN MUSHROOM COMPANY
Oak Forest and Ridgeland Avenues
Tinley Park, Illinois 60477

NORTH AMERICAN PHARMACAL, INC.
6851 Chase Road
Dearborn, Michigan 48121

NORTH AMERICAN PHILIPS CORPORATION
100 East 42nd Street
New York, New York 10017
Pieter C. Vink, President
(212) 697-3600
See also Anchor Brush Company; Frederick Controls; Philips Business System Inc.; and Thompson-Hayward Phillips Company

NORTH AMERICAN PHILIPS LIGHTING CORPORATION
Bank Street
Hightstown, New Jersey 08520
Stephen C. Tumminello, President
(609) 448-4000

NORTH AMERICAN PLAQUE CORPORATION
10 Wilshire Drive
Syosset, New York 11791

NORTH AMERICAN PLYWOOD CORPORATION
800 Third Avenue
New York, New York 10017
(212) 751-3236

NORTH AMERICAN POLISH CORPORATION
9517 Cumberland Avenue
Cleveland, Ohio 44104
(216) 231-2843

NORTH AMERICAN ROCKWELL CORPORATION
See Rockwell International

NORTH AMERICAN SYSTEMS INC.
Shaker and Warrensville Center
Shaker Heights, Ohio 44120

NORTH AMERICAN VAN LINES, INC.
(Subsidiary of PepsiCo., Inc.)
Lincoln and Meyer
Fort Wayne, Indiana 46801
Richard J. Caley, Chairman of the Board
(219) 422-2511

NORTH AMERICAN WATCH CORPORATION
1345 Avenue of the Americas
New York, New York 10019
G. Grinberg, President
(212) 586-6569

NORTH CAPE (seafood)
See Frionor Kitchens Inc.

NORTH CAPE (sports apparel)
See Knut and Knut Ltd.

NORTH CAROLINA NATIONAL BANK
1 NCNB Plaza
Charlotte, North Carolina 28255
Luther H. Hodges, Chairman of the Board
(704) 374-5000

Companies and Trade Names

NORTH CENTRAL AIRLINES
7500 Northliner Drive
Minneapolis, Minnesota 55450
Hal N. Carr, Chairman of the Board
(612) 726-7411

NORTH CENTRAL PLASTICS INC.
136 Main Street
Ellendale, Minnesota 56026
(507) 684-3721

NORTH COAST (fruit)
   See Manzana Products Company, Inc.

NORTH COAST CHEMICAL
   COMPANY
6300 17th Avenue South
Seattle, Washington 98108
(206) 763-1340

NORTH COLLINS (canned foods)
   See Growers & Packers Coop, Canning Company Inc.

NORTH COUNTRY (sports apparel)
   See Nordic Ski Imports Inc.

NORTH DAKOTA MILL & ELEVATOR
Mill Road
Grand Forks, North Dakota 58201
(701) 772-4841

NORTH EAST AND SOUTHERN
   YACHT SALES
132 Cushing Highway
Route Three A
Cohasset, Massachusetts 02025

NORTH EAST PACKING
   CORPORATION
Box 407
North East, Pennsylvania 16428

NORTH GEORGIA WOOD
   PRODUCTS COMPANY
Box 54503
478 Peachtree N.E.
Atlanta, Georgia 30308
(404) 525-7277

NORTH LUBEC MANUFACTURING
   & CANNING COMPANY
North Lubec, Maine 04663
Eugene L. Bailey, President,
   Treasurer and Sales Manager
(207) 733-5524

NORTH PACIFIC CANNERS &
   PACKERS, INC.
5200 S.E. McLaughlin Boulevard
Portland, Oregon 97202
(503) 234-7241

NORTH PACIFIC PROCESSORS INC.
1455 North Northlake Place
Seattle Washington 98103
(206) 632-5979

NORTH PACIFIC PRODUCTS INC.
Post Office Box 871
Bend, Oregon 97701
(503) 382-3231

NORTH RIVER INSURANCE
   COMPANY
Box 2387
Morristown, New Jersey 07960
Bobby P. Russell, Chairman
(212) 233-1100

NORTH SHORE BOTTLING
   COMPANY
97-40 91st Street
Ozone Park, New York 11416

NORTH SHORE GAS COMPANY
(Subsidiary of Peoples Gas Company)
3001 Grand Avenue
Waukegan, Illinois 60085
George L. Morrow, President
(312) 431-4000

NORTH SHORE MANUFACTURING
   COMPANY
500 South 59th Avenue, West
Duluth, Minnesota 55807

NORTH SIDE PACKING COMPANY
2200 Spring Garden Avenue
Pittsburgh, Pennsylvania 15212
(412) 231-7300

NORTH STAR DAIRY
625 New York Building
Saint Paul, Minnesota 55101

NORTH STAR ICE EQUIPMENT
   COMPANY INC.
Box 70668
Seattle, Washington 98107
(206) 784-4500

NORTH STATE CANNING
   COMPANY
Boone, North Carolina 28607
(704) 264-3045

NORTH STATE TELEPHONE
   COMPANY
111 North Main Street
High Point, North Carolina 27260
Robbins Tilden, President
(919) 885-5121

NORTH STATES INDUSTRIES INC.
Post Office Box 11037
3650 Fermont Avenue
Highland Station
Minneapolis, Minnesota 55411
(612) 522-6505

NORTHBROOK PLASTIC PLAYING
CARD COMPANY
   See Arrco Playing Card Company

NORTHCOOL (men's apparel)
   See Sagner, Inc.

NORTHEAST AIRCRAFT
   CORPORATION
964 Crescent Avenue
Bridgeport, Connecticut 06607
(203) 335-8146

NORTHEAST AIRLINES, INC.
   See Delta Air Lines, Inc.

Companies and Trade Names

NORTHEAST DAIRY COOPERATIVE
  FEDERATION, INC.
Box 491
Oneida, New York 13421

NORTHERN DYEING COMPANY
(Division of Castle Creek Fabrics)
Washington, New Jersey 07882

NORTHERN ELECTRIC COMPANY
(Subsidiary of Sunbeam Corporation)
5224 North Kedzie Avenue
Chicago, Illinois 60625
W.A. Crews, President
(312) 267-5100

NORTHERN FRUIT COMPANY
Post Office Box 1486
Wenatchee, Washington 98801

NORTHERN ILLINOIS GAS
  COMPANY
Post Office Box 190
Aurora, Illinois 60507
C.J. Gauthier, President
(312) 355-8000

NORTHERN INSTRUMENTS
4599 North Chatsworth
Saint Paul, Minnesota 55112

NORTHERN LABORATORIES
(Subsidiary of S.C. Johnson & Son
  Inc.)
Post Office Box 808
Manitowoc, Wisconsin 54220

NORTHERN LIGHT (whiskey)
  See Hiram Walker Inc.

NORTHERN NATURAL GAS
  COMPANY
2223 Dodge Street
Omaha, Nebraska 68102
Willis A. Strauss, Chairman of the
  Board
(402) 348-4000
  See also Northern Petrochemical
  Company

NORTHERN OHIO TELEPHONE
  COMPANY
100 Executive Drive
Marion, Ohio 43302
Robert M. Wopat, President
(419) 483-8241

NORTHERN PETROCHEMICAL
  COMPANY
(Subsidiary of Northern Natural
  Gas Company)
2350 East Devon Avenue
Des Plaines, Illinois 60018
H.M. Sampson, President
(312) 297-2400

NORTHERN PRODUCTS
  CORPORATION
705 Terminal Sales Building
Seattle, Washington 98101
(206) 622-6677

NORTHERN QUEEN (seafood)
  See Pelican Sales Company

NORTHERN SHOE COMPANY
(Division of Brierwood Shoe
  Corporation)
Pulaski, Wisconsin 54162
John H. Coppens, President
(414) 822-3255

NORTHERN STAR COMPANY
3171 S.E. Fifth Street
Minneapolis, Minnesota 55414
(612) 339-8981

NORTHERN STAR INDUSTRIES INC.
690 Muncy Avenue
Lindenhurst, New York 11757
Jack I. Green, President and
  Production Manager
(516) 587-1515

NORTHERN STATES POWER
  COMPANY
Consumer Affairs Department
414 Nicollet Avenue
Minneapolis, Minnesota 55401
Donald W. McCarthy, President
(612) 330-5500

NORTHERN STATES POWER
  COMPANY - WISCONSIN
100 North Barstow Street
Eau Claire, Wisconsin 54701
John L. Carroll, President
(715) 839-2424

NORTHFIELD SPECIALTIES
  COMPANY
215 Madison Street
Northfield, Minnesota 55057

NORTHLAND (groceries)
  See M.A. Gedney Company

NORTHLAND (recreational
  equipment)
  See Larson Industries, Inc.

NORTHLAND ALUMINUM
  PRODUCTS INC.
Highway Seven and Belt Line
Minneapolis, Minnesota 55416
H. David Dalquist, President
(612) 920-2888

NORTHLAND CANNING
  COMPANY
Cokato, Minnesota 55321
(612) 286-2166

NORTHLAND CHEMICAL
  COMPANY
East Grand Forks, Minnesota 56721

NORTHLAND MILK & ICE
  CREAM COMPANY
128 University Avenue, S.E.
Minneapolis, Minnesota 55414
L.H. Heller, Sr., President
(612) 339-5211

NORTHLAND PHARMACAL
  COMPANY
218 West Washington Street
Brainerd, Minnesota 56401

NORTHRIDGE (men's suits)
  See Jacobson Stores Inc.

1020

Companies and Trade Names

NORTHRUP & ASSOCIATES
2218 Ramsey Road
Monroeville, Pennsylvania 15146

NORTHRUP, KING & COMPANY
1500 Jackson Street, N.E.
Minneapolis, Minnesota 55413
D. Kenneth Christensen, Chairman
   of the Board
(612) 781-8011

NORTHVILLE LABORATORIES, INC.
1 Vanilla Lane
Northville, Michigan 48167

NORTHWEAVE (men's apparel)
   See Sagner, Inc.

NORTHWEST AIRLINES, INC.
Minneapolis/Saint Paul International
   Airport
Saint Paul, Minnesota 55111
Donald W. Nyrop, President
(612) 726-3333

NORTHWEST BERRY PACKERS INC.
Bainbridge Island, Washington 98110

NORTHWEST COLD PACK
   COMPANY
Box 396
Bainbridge Island, Washington 98110

NORTHWEST CONE COMPANY
7575 South Kostner
Chicago, Illinois 60652
Henry Shapiro, President
(312) 767-3300

NORTHWEST GROCERY COMPANY
6433 S.E. Lake Road
Portland, Oregon 97222
(503) 654-6501

NORTHWEST INDUSTRIES, INC.
6300 Sears Tower
Chicago, Illinois 60606
Ben W. Heineman, President
(312) 876-4000
   See also Acme Boot Company

Inc.; Buckingham Corporation; Fruit of the Loom, Inc.; Michigan Chemical Corporation; Union Underwear Company; and Velsicol Chemical Corporation

NORTHWEST MARINE PRODUCTS
   INC.
8764 S.W. Burnham Road
Portland, Oregon 97223

NORTHWEST METAL PRODUCTS
   COMPANY
1337 East Mason Street
Department Ten E
Green Bay, Wisconsin 54301
(414) 432-5865

NORTHWEST NATURAL GAS
   COMPANY
735 Southwest Market Street
Portland, Oregon 97201
Francis F. Hill, President
(503) 226-4211

NORTHWEST ORIENT AIRLINES
   See Northwest Airlines, Inc.

NORTHWEST PACKING COMPANY
440 North Columbia Boulevard
Portland, Oregon 97211
Alan Macdonald, President
(503) 285-3686

NORTHWEST PAPER COMPANY,
   THE
(Subsidiary of Potlatch Forests, Inc.)
Cloquet, Minnesota 55720
Richard C. Nordham, Vice President
(218) 879-6784

NORTHWEST PEA & BEAN
   COMPANY, INC.
Box 5202
Spokane, Washington 99205
(509) 328-8227

NORTHWEST PHARMACY
20 Fourth Avenue S.W.
Minot, North Dakota 58701

NORTHWEST SANITATION
   PRODUCTS INC.
Post Office Box 728
150 North Main
Fort Bragg, California 95437
(707) 964-4647

NORTHWEST SYSTEMS
   CORPORATION
5922 Excelsior Boulevard
Minneapolis, Minnesota 55416
Gerald B. Frederick, President
(612) 929-7839

NORTHWEST WHOLESALE, INC.
Post Office Box 1649
Wenatchee, Washington 98801

NORTHWESTERN BELL TELEPHONE
   COMPANY
(Subsidiary of American Telephone &
   Telegraph Company)
100 South 19th Street
Omaha, Nebraska 68102
Thomas S. Nurnberger, President
(402) 422-2000

NORTHWESTERN BOTTLE COMPANY
2222 North Second Street
Saint Louis, Missouri 63102
(314) 231-5959
   See also Krane Manufacturing
   Company

NORTHWESTERN EXTRACT
   COMPANY
3590 North 126th
Milwaukee, Wisconsin 53202
(414) 781-6670

NORTHWESTERN MUTUAL LIFE
   INSURANCE COMPANY
720 East Wisconsin Avenue
Milwaukee, Wisconsin 53202
Francis E. Ferguson, President
(414) 271-1444

1021

Companies and Trade Names

NORTHWESTERN NATIONAL BANK OF MINNEAPOLIS
Seventh and Marquette
Minneapolis, Minnesota 55480
Philip B. Harris, President
(612) 372-8123

NORTHWESTERN NATIONAL LIFE INSURANCE COMPANY
20 Washington Avenue South
Minneapolis, Minnesota 55440
John E. Pearson, President
(612) 372-5432

NORTHWESTERN PUBLIC SERVICE COMPANY
Huron, South Dakota 57350
A.D. Schmidt, President
(605) 352-8411

NORTHWESTERN STEEL & WIRE COMPANY
121 Wallace Street
Sterling, Illinois 61081
W.M. Dillon, President and Treasurer
(815) 625-2500

NORTHWOOD FRUIT BLUE GOOSE GROWERS INC.
3578 Alpine N.W.
Grand Rapids, Michigan 49504

NORTIC PRODUCTS (photo frames, vanity trays, clocks)
See J.H. Citron & Son Inc.

NORTON & COMPANY, INC., W.W.
500 Fifth Avenue
New York, New York 10036
George P. Brockway, President
(212) 354-5500

NORTON COATED ABRASIVE & TAPE
(Division of Norton Company)
Department 7040
Troy, New York 12181

NORTON PRODUCTS
12-14 Warren Street
New York, New York 10007
(212) 732-5658

NORTON SIMON, INC.
277 Park Avenue
New York, New York 10017
David J. Mahoney, Chairman of the Board
(212) 832-1000
See also Canada Dry Corporation; Factor & Company, Max; Hunt-Wesson Foods, Inc.; Max Factor & Company, Inc.; Old Fitzgerald Distillery; Somerset Importers, Ltd.; and Southern Shell Fish Company

NORVAL COMPANY
Box 10222
Santa Ana, California 92711

NORWALK FURNITURE CORPORATION
Post Office Box 410
Norwalk, Ohio 44857
J.R. Gerken, Jr., President
(419) 668-4461

NORWALK LABORATORIES
909 Third Avenue
New York, New York 10022
(212) 758-3600

NORWAY CO-OP CANNING ASSOCIATION, INC.
Box 162
Norway, Michigan 49870

NORWEGIAN SILVER CORPORATION
114 East 57th Street
New York, New York 10022
(212) 752-3111

NORWICH MILLS
(Division of Champion Products Inc.)
96 East Main Street
Norwich, New York 13815
Edward H. O'Hara, President
(607) 334-3206

NORWICH PACKING CORPORATION
North Norwich, New York 13814
See also Rea-D-Pack Foods Inc.

NORWICH PHARMACAL COMPANY
(Subsidiary of Morton-Norwich Products, Inc.)
17 Eaton Avenue
Norwich, New York 13815
George W. Bengert, Chairman of the Board
See also Eaton Laboratories

NORWICH SHOE COMPANY, INC.
Norwich, New York 13815
J.K. Weinman, President
(607) 334-3261

NORWOOD (Bourbon)
See Standard Distillers Products Inc.

NOSECT (insecticides)
See Chemical Specialties Company, Inc.

NOTABLES (shoes)
See Viner Brothers, Inc.

NOTT MANUFACTURING COMPANY, INC.
Pleasant View Road
Pleasant Valley, New York 12569
(914) 635-3243

NOTTINGHAM CANNING COMPANY INC.
Box 45
Nottingham, Pennsylvania 19362

Companies and Trade Names

NOUVEAU ENTERPRISES, INC.
2965 Winchester Pike
Columbus, Ohio 43227

NOVA (canned and frozen foods)
See M.W. Graves & Company Ltd.

NOVA EXPORT CORPORATION
8484 San Fernando Road
Sun Valley, California 91352

NOVA SALES COMPANY
(Subsidiary of Homasote Company)
Post Office Box 240
West Trenton, New Jersey 08628

NOVACHORD (musical instruments)
See Hammond Organ Company

NOVASPORT (sports apparel and accessories)
See Regina Imports

NOVEL SPORTING GOODS COMPANY
6911 Corline Drive
Fort Wayne, Indiana 46807

NOVELETTE INDUSTRIES INC.
204 Monmouth Road
Oakhurst, New Jersey 07753

NOVELTY MANUFACTURING COMPANY INC.
480 Washington Street
Newark, New Jersey 07102
(201) 623-1010

NOVIK & COMPANY INC.
41 West 38th Street
New York, New York 10018
(212) 564-7740

NOVO CARD PUBLISHERS INC.
3855 Lincoln Avenue
Chicago, Illinois 60613
(312) 248-4600

NOVOCOL CHEMICAL MANUFACTURING COMPANY INC.
2911 Atlantic
Brooklyn, New York 11207
(212) 277-5400

NOVOFLEX (lenses and accessories)
See Burleigh Brooks Optics Inc.

NOVUS
(Division of National Semiconductor Corporation)
2900 Semiconductor Drive
Santa Clara, California 95051
Charles E. Sporck, President
(408) 732-5000

NOW (dresses and suits)
See Puritan Fashions Corporation

NOW! DESIGNS
540 Hampshire Street
San Francisco, California 94110
(415) 626-6150

NOWAK & WILLIAMS COMPANY
37 Gooding Avenue
Bristol, Rhode Island 02809

NOXELL CORPORATION
Consumer Services Department
11050 York Road
Baltimore, Maryland 21203
George L. Bunting, Jr., President
(301) 666-2662

NOXIDE (paint and varnish)
See Pratt & Lambert, Inc.

NOXZEMA (skin-care products, shaving products, etc.)
See Noxell Corporation

NOYES COMPANY, THE P.J.
101 Main Street
Lancaster, New Hampshire 03584
(603) 788-4952

NOYMER MANUFACTURING COMPANY
430 Summer Street
Boston, Massachusetts 02210
Fritz S. Noymer, President and Treasurer
(617) 426-6383

NOZAKI ASSOCIATES INC.
1 World Trade Center
Suite 3441
New York, New York 10048
(212) 466-1222

NOZZOLE CHIANTI CLASSICO (wine)
See Kobrand Corporation

NU-ART INC.
6247 West 74th Street
Bedford Park, Illinois 60638
(312) 496-4940

NU-CRAFT METAL PRODUCTS INC.
321 Clarkson Avenue
Brooklyn, New York 11226
(212) 284-2253

NU HOUSE (canned fruit)
See Snokist Growers

NU-LIFT MATERNITY COMPANY
See Flexnit Company, Inc.

NU-LINE INDUSTRIES
Post Office Box 217
Suring, Wisconsin 54174
(414) 842-2141

NU MADE (grocery products)
See Safeway Stores, Inc.

NU-MASCA COSMETICS
46-14 Astoria Boulevard
Long Island City, New York 11103
(212) 721-2000

Companies and Trade Names

NU-MATIC (shoes)
See Wisconsin Shoe Company

NU-MIST LABORATORIES
Box 269
Dixon, Illinois 61021

NU-MODE CORSET COMPANY INC.
2 Cortland Street
Marathon, New York 13803

NU-NAILS
5249 West Harrison Street
Chicago, Illinois 60644
(312) 287-5255

NU-PAK (canned foods)
See Hungerford Packing Company, Inc.

NU-PAK, INC.
(Division of Round Tubes & Cores Company)
900 West Cullerton Street
Chicago, Illinois 60608
(312) 243-5300

NU-SASH (replacement windows)
See Georgia-Pacific Corporation

NU-TILE (epoxy spray)
See Illinois Bronze Powder & Paint Company

NU-TONE PRODUCTS CORPORATION
49 East 21st Street
New York, New York 10010
(212) 475-7091

NU-VITA FOODS
7524 S.W. Macadam Avenue
Portland, Oregon 97219
(503) 246-5433

NU WAY DISTRIBUTORS
1101 North Rolling Road
Baltimore, Maryland 21228

NU-WAY MOBILEHOME MANUFACTURING COMPANY, INC.
8701 Harmon Road
Fort Worth, Texas 76106
Allen Blair, President
(817) 232-1350

NUACE ART COMPANY
See Ace Art Company

NUANCE (fragrance)
See Coty

NUBREST
770 Madison Avenue
New York, New York 10021
(212) 535-4035

NUCOA (margarine)
See Best Foods (Division of CPC International, Inc.)

NUCREST (canned goods)
See Omaha Institutional Service

NUEVO MUNDO
Box 182
Suffern, New York 10901

NUGGET (frozen and canned foods)
See City Ice Company

NUGGET (groceries)
See Ellenbee Foods, Inc.

NUGGET (groceries)
See Pieri Distributing Company, Inc.

NUGGET (groceries, nonfoods)
See Davis-Le Grand Company

NUGGET (seafood)
See Sea Pass Corporation

NUGRAPE (beverage)
See Monarch-Nugrape Company

NUIT DE NOEL (bath oil, cologne, dusting powder, etc.)
See Caron Corporation

NUM SPECIALTY INC.
Post Office Box 326
Murrysville, Pennsylvania 15668

NUM-ZIT (teething lotion and gel)
See Purepac Corporation

NUMERO UNO (men's toiletries)
See Clairol, Inc.

NUMERO UNO (Tequila)
See Fleischmann Distilling Corporation

NUMERO UNO (water skis and accessories)
See Cut 'N Jump Ski Corporation

NUNN & SONS MILLING COMPANY, CHARLES
4700 New Harmony Road
Evansville, Indiana 47712

NUNN-BUSH SHOE COMPANY
(Division of Weyenberg Shoe Manufacturing Company)
Post Office Box 2044
2822 North Fifth
Milwaukee, Wisconsin 53201
Peter Grossman, President
(414) 374-8900

NUNNALLY & MCCREA COMPANY
See N & W Industries, Inc.

NUNNALLY'S CANDIES
(Division of Fine Products Company, Inc.)
827 Telfair
Augusta, Georgia 30903

NUPLA CORPORATION
11912 Sheldon Street
Sun Valley, California 91352
(213) 875-2750

Companies and Trade Names

NURISH (lawn and garden product)
See W.R. Grace & Company, Agricultural Chemicals Group

NURSE BRAND (rectal ointment, suppositories, thermometers)
See De Pree Company

NURSERY ORIGINALS INC.
112 West 34th Street
New York, New York 10001
(212) 695-1886

NURSERYTYME PRODUCTS INC.
649 39th Street
Brooklyn, New York 11232
(212) 853-7000

NUSSBAUM, ERIK B.
381 Park Avenue South
New York, New York 10016
(212) 684-3072

NUSTEEL COMPANY
1714 South Ashland Avenue
Chicago, Illinois 60608
(312) 421-5760

NUTEX (shortening)
See Procter & Gamble Company

NUTONE
(Division of Scoville Manufacturing Company)
Madison and Red Bank Roads
Cincinnati, Ohio 45227
E. Herbert Bladh, Vice President
(513) 527-5100

NUTRAMENT (dietary supplement)
See Drackett Company

NUTRILAB, INC.
725 County Line Road
Deerfield, Illinois 60015

NUTRILITE PRODUCTS, INC.
5600 Beach Boulevard
Buena Park, California 90621
Richard De Vos, President
(714) 521-3900

NUTRINE LTD.
See Middlebrooke Lancaster, Inc.

NUTRITION CONTROL PRODUCTS
Post Office Box 151
Hollywood, Florida 33022

NUTRITION ENTERPRISES
325 West Huron Street
Chicago, Illinois 60610
(312) 787-8705

NUTRITIONAL BIOCHEMICALS CORPORATION
26201 Miles
Cleveland, Ohio 44128
(216) 831-3000

NUTRITIONAL RESEARCH ASSOCIATES
Box 353
South Whitley, Indiana 46787
(219) 723-4931

NUTS & BOLTS (men's toiletries)
See Colton Company

NUVO (sportswear)
See Levi Strauss & Company

NUWEAVE (socks)
See Archer Mills, Inc.

NYE INC., WILLIAM F.
Post Office Box G-927
New Bedford, Massachusetts 02742

NYE SILVER SHOP, STUART
Post Office Box 9068
Asheville, North Carolina 28805

NYKO (dental-plate container, denture adherent, cleanser, brush)
See Dark-Eyes Company, Inc.

NYLAST (hosiery wash)
See Lewal Industries, Inc.

NYLON-BRITE (detergent)
See Household Research Corporation

NYLONGE CORPORATION
(Subsidiary of Kimberly-Clark Corporation)
Station Plaza E
Great Neck, New York 11021
William T. Carney, President and Treasurer
(516) 829-6666

NYMAN & SON INC., AL
665 Mokena Drive
Miami Springs, Florida 33166
(305) 885-8121

NYMAN MANUFACTURING COMPANY
275 Ferris Avenue
East Providence, Rhode Island 02916
(401) 438-3410

NYQUIL (cold remedy)
See Vick Chemical Company

NYTEX CORPORATION
220 Fifth Avenue
New York, New York 10001
(212) 683-4890

NYTOL (sleeping aid)
See Block Drug Company, Inc.

Companies and Trade Names

O

O-AT-KA MILK PRODUCTS CO-OP INC.
Cedar and Ellicott Streets
Batavia, New York 14020

O-CEDAR (cleaning products)
See Drackett Company

O-CEL-O (sponges)
See General Mills, Inc.

OEM MEDICAL INC.
29 Meridian Road
Edison, New Jersey 08817
(201) 494-2330

O. F. C. (whiskies)
See Schenley Industries Inc.

O-JIB-WA MEDICINE COMPANY
2901 East Court Street
Flint, Michigan 48506
(313) 232-5839

O.K. (seafood)
See Otto L. Kuehn Company

OK CORRAL (restaurant franchise)
See National Carateria Systems Inc.

OMC-LINCOLN
(Division of Outboard Marine Corporation)
Post Office Box 82409
Lincoln, Nebraska 68501
Daniel L. Hedglin, Service Manager
(402) 435-2995

OMC PARTS ACCESSORIES
(Division of Outboard Marine Corporation)
McClure Street
Galesburg, Illinois 61401
S.C. Spink, Vice President and Division Manager
(309) 343-0141

OMC STERN DRIVE
(Division of Outboard Marine Corporation)
3145 Central Avenue
Waukegan, Illinois 60085

O.N.C. FREIGHT SYSTEMS
(Subsidiary of Recor International)
2800 West Bayshore Road
Palo Alto, California 94303
David P. Roush, President
(415) 326-7000

O. N. T. (thread)
See Coats & Clark's Sales Corporation

007 (men's toiletries)
See Colgate-Palmolive Company

006 (aftershave lotion)
See Bonne Bell, Inc.

O S R CORPORATION
88 Hazel Street
Glen Cove New York 11542
Leonard Osrow President
(516) 671-5300

O-SO BEVERAGES, INC.
(Division of Hurty-Peck & Company, Inc.)
5600 West Raymond Street
Indianapolis, Indiana 46241
(317) 243-3521

O SO GOOD (processed foods)
See Diamond Fruit Growers, Inc.

OTC
(Division of Surgical Appliance Industries)
Erie Avenue
Cincinnati, Ohio 45209
(513) 271-4594

O-U SPORTS INC.
208 Third Avenue South
Seattle, Washington 98104
(206) 624-6948

OAHU PUBLISHING COMPANY, THE
10333 Coggins Drive
Sun City, Arizona 85351

OAK CREEK KILNS
119 Oak Creek Boulevard
Sedona, Arizona 86336

OAK CREST (mobile home)
See Kit Manufacturing Company

OAK GROVE (canned foods)
See Roberts Brothers Inc.

OAK RUBBER COMPANY, THE
219 South Sycamore
Ravenna, Ohio 44266
W.R. Collette, President
(216) 296-3416

OAKITE PRODUCTS, INC.
50 Valley Road
Berkeley Heights, New Jersey 07922
Fred A. Schnitzler, Director of Public Relations
(201) 464-6900

OAKLAND CORPORATION
1754 Maplelawn
Troy, Michigan 48084

OAKVILLE
(Division of Scovill Manufacturing Company)
Main Street
Oakville, Connecticut 06779

Companies and Trade Names

OASIS (batteries)
See The Prestolite Company

OASIS (cigarettes)
See Liggett & Myers, Inc.

OASIS (electric dehumidifiers, water coolers)
See Ebco Manufacturing Company

OASIS (figs, peaches, apricots)
See Santa Clara Packing Company

OASIS (self-watering planter)
See Saxon Agencies Ltd.

OASIS (skin-care products)
See Luxuria Cosmetics Ltd.

OASIS HOT'N COLD (coolers)
See Ebco Manufacturing Company

OBEE INSTITUTIONAL FOOD SERVICE COMPANY
10700 West Waveland
Franklin Park, Illinois 60131

OBENDORFERS, THE
225 Fifth Avenue
New York, New York 10010

OBERMEYER (sports apparel, accessories, and equipment)
See Sport-Obermeyer Ltd.

OBETROL PHARMACEUTICALS
(Division of Rexar Pharmaceutical Corporation)
396 Rockaway Avenue
Valley Stream, New York 11581

O'BOYLE COMPANY, PATRICK
61-33 Fresh Meadow Lane
Fresh Meadows, New York 11365

O'BRIEN CORPORATION, THE
Post Office Box 4037
2001 West Washington Avenue
South Bend, Indiana 44634
Jerome J. Crowley, President
(219) 233-9361

O'BRIEN, SPOTORNO, MITCHELL
(Subsidiary of Del Monte Corporation)
2455 Mason Street
San Francisco, California 94133
Walter Zolezzi, President
(415) 771-2300

O'BRYAN BROTHERS, INC.
4220 West Belmont Avenue
Chicago, Illinois 60641
Michael L. O'Bryan, President
(312) 283-3000

OBTUNDIA (calamine lotion, first-aid cream, surgical dressing, etc.)
See Otis Clapp & Son, Inc.

OCCIDENTAL LIFE INSURANCE COMPANY OF CALIFORNIA
(Subsidiary of Transamerica Corporation)
Hill and Olive at 12th Street
Los Angeles, California 90015
Earl Clark, President
(213) 742-2111

OCCIDENTAL PETROLEUM CORPORATION
10889 Wilshire Boulevard
Los Angeles, California 90024
Dr. Armand Hammer, Chairman of the Board
(213) 879-1700
See also Hooker Chemical Corporation; and Island Creek Coal Company

OCE'-INDUSTRIES INC.
6500 North Lincoln Avenue
Chicago, Illinois 60645
Paul Grevendick, President
(312) 338-1700

OCEAN (seafood)
See R. B. & C. G. Stevens Company

OCEAN BEAUTY (seafood)
See Portland Fish Company

OCEAN COFFEE COMPANY, INC.
430 Davis
Shreveport, Louisiana 71107

OCEAN DELIGHT (canned foods)
See Port Clyde Packing Company, Inc.

OCEAN FOAM INC.
3001 New
Oceanside, New York 11572

OCEAN GARDEN PRODUCTS, INC.
2260 Columbia
San Diego, California 92101

OCEAN GLEN (seafood)
See New England Fish Company

OCEAN LABS, INC.
Box BL
Irvine, California 92664

OCEAN PRIDE (seafood)
See Rubenstein Foods Inc.

OCEAN SPRAY CRANBERRIES, INC.
Main Street
Hanson, Massachusetts 02341
Harold Thorkilsen, President
(617) 293-6311

OCEANA CANNING COMPANY
Post Office Box 156
Shelby, Michigan 49455
Howard C. McDonald, President
(616) 861-2141

Companies and Trade Names

OCEANIC SALES COMPANY
1726 Smith Tower
Seattle, Washington 98104
(206) 622-6870

OCEANS OF THE WORLD, INC.
10889 Wilshire Boulevard
Los Angeles, California 90024
(213) 477-9011

OCEANWAY (seafood)
See King Shrimp Company, Inc.

O'CEDAR (furniture polish)
See The Drackett Company

O'CLAIR (food products)
See Eau Claire Packing Company

OCONOMOWOC CANNING COMPANY
Post Office Box 248
626 East Wisconsin Avenue
Oconomowoc, Wisconsin 53066
(414) 567-9151

OCTAGON (detergent and soap)
See Colgate-Palmolive Company

OCTOGEN PHARMACAL COMPANY
3024 Genesee Street
Buffalo, New York 14225
(716) 896-7791

OCUSOL (eyedrops, lotion)
See Norwich Pharmacal Company

ODALISQUE (perfume)
See Nettie Rosenstein, Inc.

O'DAY COMPANY
(Division of Bangor Punta Inc.)
168 Stephens Street
Fall River, Massachusetts 02722
Robert Saltenstall, Jr., President
(617) 678-5291

ODDS & ENDS & THINGS
8 North Church Street
Wesh Chester, Pennsylvania 19380

ODE (phonograph records)
See A & M Records

ODELL (processed foods)
See Diamond Fruit Growers, Inc.

ODLO (sports apparel)
See Gerry

ODOL CHEMICAL CORPORATION
207 Lodi Street
Hackensack, New Jersey 07602
(201) 489-3740

ODOMASTER (odor-control system)
See Surco Products, Inc.

O'DONNELL INDUSTRIES
Broadmeadow Road
Marlboro, Massachusetts 01752

O'DONNELL-USEN FISHERIES CORPORATION
1 Fish Pier
Boston, Massachusetts 02110
Irving Usen, President
(617) 542-2700

ODOR EATER (refrigerator deodorizer)
See Gold Seal Company

ODOR-MASTER (electric deodorizer)
See Edco International Corporation

ODYSSEY CREATIONS INC.
Post Office Box 31774
World Trade Center
Dallas, Texas 75231
(214) 748-1890

OELWEIN CHEMICAL COMPANY, INC.
Occo Drive
Oelwein, Iowa 50662
(319) 283-1142

OFF (insect repellent)
See S.C. Johnson & Son, Inc.

OFFICE PRODUCTS INC.
26029 West Eight Mile Road
Detroit, Michigan 48240
(313) 537-5700

OFFICE-RITER (typewriter)
See Remington Rand Office Machines (Division of Sperry Rand Corporation)

OFFICIAL BOY SCOUT (shoes)
See Brown Group, Inc.

OFFICIAL GIRL SCOUT (shoes)
See Brown Group, Inc.

OFFRAY & SON INC., C.M.
261 Madison Avenue
New York, New York 10016
(212) 682-8010

OFFSHORE YACHTS
Harbormaster's Office
Pacific Marina
Alameda, California 94501

OGAN COMPANY, INC., THE
59 Revere Beach Parkway
Revere, Massachusetts 02151

OGILVY & MATHER, INC.
2 East 28th Street
New York, New York 10017
Andrew G. Kerstaw, Chairman of the Board
(212) 688-6100

OGLALA SIOUX MOCCASINS
See Sunbell Corporation

Companies and Trade Names

OH BOY CORPORATION
1516 First Street
San Fernando, California 91340
Pietro Vitale, President
(213) 361-1128

OH DE LONDON (women's toiletries)
See Yardley of London, Inc.

OH-DEAR LABORATORIES
661 Western Avenue North
Saint Paul, Minnesota 55103

O'HARA & SONS INC., F.J.
Tillson Avenue
Rockland, Maine 04841

O'HARA, LEVY & MAHON, INC.
295 Fifth Avenue
New York, New York 10016
(212) 683-5696

OHAUS SCALE CORPORATION
1650 Commerce Avenue
Union, New Jersey 07083

OHIO ART COMPANY, THE
Post Office Box 111
East High Street
Bryan, Ohio 43506
W.C. Killgallon, President
(419) 636-3141
See also Fli-Back Company Inc.

OHIO BELL TELEPHONE COMPANY, THE
(Subsidiary of American Telephone & Telegraph Company)
100 Erieview Plaza
Cleveland, Ohio 44114
Charles E. Hugel, President
(216) 822-9900

OHIO-BUCKEYE
(Division of The Las-Stik Manufacturing Company)
B and Wayne Streets
Hamilton, Ohio 45012

OHIO CARBON COMPANY
12508 Berea Road
Cleveland, Ohio 44111
I.L. Harvey, President
(216) 252-6100

OHIO CASUALTY INSURANCE COMPANY
136 North Third Street
Hamilton, Ohio 45025
Howard L. Slonecker, Jr., Chairman of the Board
(513) 867-3000

OHIO CHAIR COMPANY
(Division of Corry Jamestown)
4021 Mahoning Avenue
Youngstown, Ohio 44509

OHIO EDISON COMPANY
47 North Main Street
Akron, Ohio 44308
John R. White, President
(216) 762-9661
See also Pennsylvania Power Company

OHIO FLOCK-COTE COMPANY
14500 Industrial North
Cleveland, Ohio 44137
(216) 663-3700

OHIO MATCH COMPANY
(Division of Hunt-Wesson Foods, Inc.)
254 Main Street
Wadsworth, Ohio 44281
Arthur A. Kattan, President
(216) 335-1531

OHIO NATIONAL BANK
51 North High Street
Columbus, Ohio 43216
Walter C. Mercer, President
(614) 462-2100

OHIO NATIONAL LIFE INSURANCE COMPANY
237 William Howard Taft Road
Cincinnati, Ohio 45219
Paul E. Martin, Chairman of the Board
(513) 861-3600

OHIO POWER COMPANY
(Subsidiary of American Electric Power)
301-305 Cleveland Avenue, S.W.
Canton, Ohio 44702
Donald Cook, President
(216) 455-8931

OHIO THERMOMETER SIGN COMPANY
33 Walnut Street
Springfield, Ohio 44501
Charles L. Wappner, President and Treasurer
(513) 324-5786

OHIO VALLEY DRUG COMPANY
2 Fourth Street
Wheeling, West Virginia 26003

OHRBACH'S
5 West 34th Street
New York, New York 10001
Kermit G. Claster, President
(212) 695-4000

OIL-DRI CORPORATION OF AMERICA
520 North Michigan
Chicago, Illinois 60611
Richard M. Jaffee, President and Treasurer
(312) 321-1515

OIL-KRAFT, INC.
3330 Beekman Street
Cincinnati, Ohio 45223
(513) 541-2225

OK-COR-IN (canned foods)
See Oklahoma Correctional Industries

Companies and Trade Names

O'KEEFE & MERRITT COMPANY
(Division of Tappan Company)
3700 East Olympic Boulevard
Los Angeles, California 90023
A.S. Fernandez, President
(213) 268-8231

OKLA HOMER SMITH FURNITURE
MANUFACTURING COMPANY
416 South Fifth Street
Fort Smith, Arkansas 72901
Okla Bennett Smith, President
(501) 783-6191

OKLAHOMA CORRECTIONAL
INDUSTRIES
Oklahoma State Prison
Box 97
McAlester, Oklahoma 74501

OKLAHOMA GAS & ELECTRIC
COMPANY
Third and Harvey Avenue
Oklahoma City, Oklahoma 73101
Donald S. Kennedy, Chairman of
the Board
(405) 272-3000

OKONITE COMPANY, THE
(Subsidiary of Omega-Alpha, Inc.)
Post Office Box 340
Ramsey, New Jersey 07446
Victor Viggiano, Chairman, President and Chief Executive Officer
(201) 825-0300

OKRAY'S LTD.
3000 Welsby
Stevens Point, Wisconsin 54481

OL' SOUTH (food products)
See Piknik Products Company

OL' TEXAS (food products)
See Stegner Food Products
Company

OLA/RAG (sports apparel)
See Halstead Imports Inc.

OLAFSEN (diaper-rash and prickly-heat remedy)
See Walgreen Company

OLBAS (cough syrup, throat lozenges, skin-care products, etc.)
See Heidi E. Ritter

OLD AMERICAN (frozen foods)
See Tyson Foods Inc.

OLD AMERICAN (whiskey)
See American Distilling
Company, Inc.

OLD ANGUS (Scotch whiskey)
See Carillon Importers Ltd.

OLD BAY (seasonings)
See The Baltimore Spice
Company

OLD BLUE RIBBON (whiskey)
See Schenley Industries, Inc.

OLD BOHEMIAN (beer)
See Eastern Brewing Corporation

OLD BOONE DISTILLERY
COMPANY
Post Office Box 72010
Valley Station
Louisville, Kentucky 40272
J. Barret Buse, President
(502) 937-1400
See also Fairfield Distillery
Company

OLD BOURBON HOLLOW
(whiskey)
See Barton Brands, Ltd.

OLD BRIAR (tobacco)
See United States Tobacco
Company

OLD BRIARWOOD (whiskey)
See J.T.S. Brown Distillers
Company

OLD BUSHMILLS (Irish whiskey)
See Brown-Forman Distillers
Corporation

OLD CARAVAN (whiskey)
See James Barclay & Company,
Ltd.

OLD CHARTER (whiskey)
See Schenley Industries, Inc.

OLD CLASSIC (whiskey and gin)
See Continental Distilling
Corporation

OLD COLONY (furniture)
See Kaplan Furniture Company

OLD COLONY (gin)
See American Distilling
Company, Inc.

OLD COLONY (soft drinks)
See Crush International Inc.

OLD COLONY SHOE COMPANY
See Alden Shoe Company, Inc.

OLD COMISKEY (whiskey)
See James B. Beam Distilling
Company

OLD CORN PATCH (whiskey)
See J.T.S. Brown Distillers
Company

OLD CROW (whiskey)
See National Distillers &
Chemical Corporation

OLD DOMINION CANDIES, INC.
850 East Main Street
Salem, Virginia 24153

Companies and Trade Names

OLD DOMINION PEANUT
CORPORATION
23rd Street and Omohundro Avenue
Norfolk, Virginia 23517
(804) 622-1633

OLD DOVER (whiskey)
See National Distillers &
Chemical Corporation

OLD DUTCH (paints and paint
sundries)
See A. Flohr Company Inc.

OLD DUTCH CLEANSER
See Purex Corporation, Ltd.

OLD DUTCH COMPANY
Box 2540
Daytona Beach, Florida 32015

OLD DUTCH FOODS, INC.
2375 Terminal Road
Saint Paul, Minnesota 55113
Vernon O. Aanenson, President
(612) 633-8810

OLD DUTCH INTERNATIONAL
LTD.
376 Railroad Avenue
Hackensack, New Jersey 07601

OLD DUTCH MUSTARD COMPANY
80 Metropolitan Avenue
Brooklyn, New York 11211
Uriel Asscoff, President
(212) 387-9155

OLD EL PASO (Mexican foods)
See Pet Inc.

OLD ENGLISH (canned foods)
See Fort Lupton Canning
Company

OLD ENGLISH (cheddar cheese)
See Kraft Foods

OLD ENGLISH (furniture polish)
See Boyle-Midway, Inc.

OLD FARMERS ALMANAC
See Yankee Inc.

OLD FASHION (canned foods)
See Wisconsin Foods, Inc.

OLD FASHIONED KITCHEN, INC.
1045 Towbin Avenue
Lakewood, New Jersey 08701
(212) 388-1132

OLD FASHIONED MILLERS, INC.
899 Randolph
Saint Paul, Minnesota 55102

OLD FITZGERALD DISTILLERY,
INC.
(Subsidiary of Norton Simon, Inc.)
Station D
Louisville, Kentucky 40210
Ralph W. Burnside, President
(502) 448-2860

OLD FLORIDA RUM COMPANY
Post Office Drawer 510
Winter Haven, Florida 33880

OLD FORESTER (Bourbon)
See Brown-Forman Distillers
Corporation

OLD FORGE (hand tools)
See Quality Tools Corporation

OLD FORMAN (whiskey)
See Brown-Forman Distillers
Corporation

OLD GOLD (cigarettes)
See Lorillard Corporation

OLD GRAND DAD (whiskey)
See National Distillers &
Chemical Corporation

OLD GRAND-DAD CAVENDISH
(pipe tobacco)
See Consolidated Cigar
Corporation

OLD GREENWICH BOAT COMPANY
Box 125
Old Greenwich, Connecticut 06870

OLD GRIMES (canned beans and
fruit drinks)
See Beaver Valley Canning
Company

OLD HARBOR CANDLE COMPANY
Post Office Box 486
Scudder Avenue
Hyannis Port, Massachusetts 02647
Harold Perkins, President
(617) 775-1341

OLD HARDESTY (Bourbon)
See Old Boone Distillery
Company

OLD HERMITAGE (whiskey)
See National Distillers &
Chemical Corporation

OLD HICKORY (Bourbon)
See Continental Distilling
Corporation

OLD HICKORY (knives and cutlery)
See Ontario Knife Company

OLD HOME (bakery products)
See Metz Old Home Bakery of
Rapid City

OLD HOMESTEAD (wines)
See Southland Wine Company

OLD HONESTY (food products)
See H.A. Johnson Company

Companies and Trade Names

OLD JUDGE COFFEE COMPANY
4410 Hunt Avenue
Saint Louis, Missouri 63110
Seymour Mindel, President
(314) 652-4200

OLD KEG (soft drinks)
See S. Twitchell Company

OLD KENTUCKY TAVERN (whiskey)
See Glenmore Distilleries Company, Inc.

OLD KETTLE (apple butter, applesauce)
See Roanoke Apple Products Company

OLD LOG CABIN (whiskey)
See National Distillers & Chemical Corporation

OLD LONDON FOODS, INC.
1776 Eastchester Road
Bronx, New York 10461
(212) 597-6400

OLD MAMMY'S (food products)
See Morgan Packing Company Inc.

OLD MANSION INC.
330 South Tenth
Richmond, Virginia 23208
(804) 648-0193

OLD MILL (snuff)
See United States Tobacco Company

OLD MILL STORAGE
2024 Valley Avenue
Winchester, Virginia 22601

OLD MILWAUKEE (beer)
See Joseph Schlitz Brewing Company

OLD MOTHER HUBBARD DOG FOOD COMPANY
Box 1411
Lowell, Massachusetts 01853

OLD NIAGARA (whiskey)
See James Barclay & Company, Ltd.

OLD 95 (whiskey)
See Schenley Industries, Inc.

OLD 97 COMPANY
Box 5207
Tampa, Florida 33675
(813) 248-5761

OLD OVERHOLT (whiskey)
See National Distillers & Chemical Corporation

OLD PAL (fishing equipment)
See Woodstream Corporation

OLD PHILADELPHIA (colonial paint colors)
See Turco's Colour Cupboard

OLD POINDEXTER (whiskey)
See Schenley Industries, Inc.

OLD QUAKER (whiskey)
See Schenley Industries, Inc.

OLD RANCHERS COMPANY
Box 117
Upland, California 91786

OLD RANGER (groceries)
See J.C. Wright Sales Company

OLD RARITY (12-year-old Scotch)
See Park, Benziger & Company, Inc.

OLD RECIPE (food products)
See Roberts Food Corporation

OLD SALEM (varnishes, coatings)
See Pettit Paint Company Inc.

OLD SALT SEAFOODS INC.
Box 439
Easton, Maryland 21601

OLD SAN GABRIEL (wines, brandies, champagnes, and vermouth)
See Cucamonga Vineyard Company

OLD SOUTH (frozen concentrated juices)
See Lykes Pasco Packing Company

OLD SPICE (men's toiletries)
See Shulton, Inc.

OLD TANKARD (ale)
See Pabst Brewing Company

OLD TAVERN FOOD PRODUCTS, INC.
Waukesha, Wisconsin 53218

OLD TAYLOR (whiskey)
See National Distillers & Chemical Corporation

OLD THOMPSON (whiskey)
See Glenmore Distilleries Company

OLD TIME (groceries)
See Roundy's Inc.

OLD TIME (whiskey)
See Jack Daniel Distillery

OLD TIMER (food products)
See Mrs. Giles Country Kitchens Inc.

Companies and Trade Names

OLD TOWN CANOE COMPANY
58 Middle Street
Old Town, Maine 04468
Deane B. Gray, President
(207) 827-5513

OLD TOWN CORPORATION
750 Pacific Street
Brooklyn, New York 11238
Lawrence I. Weisman, Chairman
and President
(212) 622-2600

OLD TOWN SHOE COMPANY
(Division of Penobscot Shoe Company)
Old Town, Maine 04468

OLD TUB (whiskey)
See James B. Beam Distilling
Company

OLD VIRGINIA, INC.
Front Royal, Virginia 22630
J.N. Major, Jr., President
(703) 635-3141

OLD VIRGINIA VILLAGE STORE
INC.
Box 479
Williamsburg, Virginia 22185

OLD WORLD (mobile homes)
See Marshfield Homes

OLD WORLD COFFEES (flavored
coffees)
See Carnation Company

OLD WORLD TREASURES
1212 Halifax Court
Tallahassee, Florida 32303

OLDE BOURBON
See Schenley Industries, Inc.

OLDE HEIRLOOM (Bourbon)
See Fleischmann Distilling
Corporation

OLDE MARYLAND (canned foods)
See J. Langrall & Brother, Inc.

OLDE THOMPSON
6041 Variel Avenue
Woodland Hills, California 91364

OLDE WINDJAMMER
Little Clear Pond
R.F.D. Three
Plymouth, Massachusetts 02360

OLDMAINE TROTTERS (women's
shoes)
See Old Town Shoe Company

OLDS (musical instruments)
See Norlin Music, Inc.

OLDSMOBILE
(Division of General Motors
Corporation)
920 Townsend Street
Lansing, Michigan 48921
H.H. Kehrl, General Manager
(517) 373-5000

OLE SMOKY CANDY KITCHEN
Post Office Box 232
Gatlinburg, Tennessee 37738

OLE TEQUILA
See Schenley Industries, Inc.

OLE WYE (canned foods)
See S.E.W. Friel

O'LEARY INC., LYDIA
575 Madison Avenue
New York, New York 10022
(212) 753-4600

OLEG CASSINI (men's sportswear,
neckwear)
See Burma-Bibas Inc.

OLEG CASSINI, INC.
445 Park Avenue
New York, New York 10022
Oleg Cassini, President
(212) 759-9270

OLEIDE PRODUCTS COMPANY
455A Albany Avenue
Amityville, New York 11701

OLENDER & COMPANY, PHILIP
5800 Vincent Ham
Detroit, Michigan 48211
(313) 921-3310

OLFACTORY CORPORATION, THE
2217 Pontius Avenue West
Los Angeles, California 90064
(213) 272-6523

OLFISCO INC.
815 North Fifth
Minneapolis, Minnesota 55401
(612) 332-3531

OLGA COMPANY
7900 Haskell Avenue
Van Nuys, California 91406
Jan J. Erteszek, President
(213) 782-7568

OLIN CORPORATION
120 Long Ridge Road
Stamford, Connecticut 06904
James F. Towey, President
(203) 356-2000
See also Turner Company

OLIN SKI COMPANY INC.
(Division of Olin Corporation)
475 Smith Street
Middletown, Connecticut 06457

OLINER FIBRE COMPANY, INC.
170 North Fifth Street
Brooklyn, New York 11211
(212) 782-9370

Companies and Trade Names

OLIVE HEIGHTS CITRUS
ASSOCIATION
16381 Main Street
Olive, California 92665

OLIVE PRODUCTS COMPANY
(Division of Beatrice Foods Company)
Box 191
1795 Mitchel Avenue
Oroville, California 95965
(916) 533-3303

OLIVER & SON, FRANK S.
Box 926
Watsonville, California 95076

OLIVER MACHINERY COMPANY
445 Sixth Street N.W.
Grand Rapids, Michigan 49504
Ralph B. Baldwin, President
(616) 456-1591

OLIVER TIRE & RUBBER COMPANY
4345 San Pablo Avenue
Oakland, California 94608

OLIVES INC.
Third and North Streets
Corning, California 96021
(916) 824-5447

OLIVETTI CORPORATION OF
AMERICA
500 Park Avenue
New York, New York 10022
Guido Lorenzotti, President
(212) 371-5500

OLIVIA CANNING COMPANY
Olivia, Minnesota 56277
(612) 523-1702

OLLA INDUSTRIES
1250 Broadway
New York, New York 10001
(212) 695-5070

OLOFDAUGHTERS
350 Fifth Avenue
New York, New York 10001
(212) 239-8408

OLSEN'S (canned and frozen seafoods)
See Olfisco, Inc.

OLSON COMPANY, INC.,
ROBERT E.
8526 North New Braunfels Avenue
San Antonio, Texas 78212
(512) 824-7474

OLSON COMPANY, J.A.
Post Office Box 629
Winona, Mississippi 38967
(601) 283-4431

OLSON CONTROLLED
MAINTENANCE
Box 2067
Stuart, Florida 33494

OLSON ELECTRONICS, INC.
260 South Forge
Akron, Ohio 44308
Lawrence L. LeKashman, President
(216) 535-9191

OLSON RUG COMPANY
4805 West Fullerton Avenue
Chicago, Illinois 60639
Raphael Musicus, President
(312) 889-3000

OLSONITE CORPORATION
8801 Conant
Hamtramck, Michigan 48211
Oscar L. Olson, President and
General Manager
(313) 875-5831

OLSSON TRADING COMPANY,
A.V.
1 Pondfield Road
Bronxville, New York 10708

OLSTEN CORPORATION
Merrick Avenue
Westbury, New York 11590
William Olsten, Chairman of the
Board
(516) 997-7200

OLT COMPANY, PHILIP S.
Post Office Box 550
Pekin, Illinois 61554
(309) 348-3633

OLYMPIA (playing cards)
See Arrco Playing Card Company

OLYMPIA (seafood)
See Norwegian Fish Importers,
Inc.

OLYMPIA BREWING COMPANY
Post Office Box 947
Olympia, Washington 98507
Robert A. Schmidt, President
(206) 352-4811
See Hamm Company, Theodore

OLYMPIA SPORTS COMPANY INC.
95 Fourth Street
Garden City Park, New York 10040
Fred J. Heumann, President
(516) 747-3380

OLYMPIA TILE CORPORATION
40 Robert Pitt Drive
Spring Valley, New York 10977

OLYMPIA USA INC.
Post Office Box 22
Somerville, New Jersey 08876

OLYMPIAN (band instruments)
See Targ & Dinner Inc.

OLYMPIAN (water skis and accessories)
See Medalist Water Sports

Companies and Trade Names

OLYMPIC (carpeting)
See Stephen-Leedom Carpet Company Inc.

OLYMPIC AIRWAYS
888 Seventh Avenue
New York, New York 10019
M. Hamid, Manager, Customer Relations
(212) 956-8400

OLYMPIC INTERNATIONAL, LTD.
89-89 Union Turnpike
Glendale, New York 11227
Herbert Kabat, President
(221) 261-9300

OLYMPIC PLASTICS COMPANY
5800 West Jefferson Boulevard
Los Angeles, California 90016
Carl Goldman, President
(213) 837-5321

OLYMPUS (carpeting)
See Sequoyah Industries Inc.

OLYMPUS (food products)
See Ostrom Mushroom Farms (Division of The Ostrom Company)

OLYMPUS (photographic equipment)
See Ponder & Best

OMAHA INSTITUTIONAL SERVICE
724 North 16th
Omaha, Nebraska 68102

OMAHA PUBLIC POWER DISTRICT
1623 Harney Street
Omaha, Nebraska 68102
Richard T. Dugdale, President
(402) 536-4000

OMAHA STEAKS INTERNATIONAL
4400 South 96th
Omaha, Nebraska 68127
(402) 331-1010

O'MALLEY VALVE COMPANY, EDWARD
4228 Eighth Avenue
Saint Petersburg, Florida 33711

OMALON (carpet underlay)
See Olin Corporation

OMAR (wallpaper, cleaner)
See Clean Products Company

OMARK INDUSTRIES
2100 S.E. Milport Road
Portland, Oregon 97222
Edward S. Smith, President
(503) 654-6531
See also KSM

OMEGA (cigars)
See Lorillard Company

OMEGA (food products)
See California-Omega Foods

OMEGA (photographic supplies)
See Simmon Omega

OMEGA
(Division of Berkey Marketing Companies)
2520 Brooklyn Queens Expressway
Woodside, New York 11377
Leonard P. Strauss, National Service Manager
(212) 932-4040

OMEGA IMPORT COMPANY
156 Fifth Avenue
New York, New York 10016
(212) 929-6486

OMEGA OIL (analgesic liquid)
See Block Drug Company, Inc.

OMEGA WATCH COMPANY
Omega Building
301 East 57th Street
New York, New York 10022
Norman M. Morris, President
(212) 753-3000
See also Tissot Watch Company

OMNI
(Division of Hoover Ball and Bearing Company)
604 West Seminary Street
Charlotte, Michigan 48813

OMNIBOOK COMPANY
Post Office Box 3782
Milwaukee, Wisconsin 53217
(414) 781-2866

ON-GUARD CORPORATION OF AMERICA
350 Gotham Parkway
Carlstadt, New Jersey 07072
Stanley Geller, President and Treasurer
(201) 939-5822

ON THE ROCKS (liquid cocktail mix)
See Borden, Inc.

ONAN CORPORATION
(Subsidiary of Studebaker-Worthington, Inc.)
1400 73rd Avenue, N.E.
Minneapolis, Minnesota 55432
Thomas G. Valenty, President
(612) 786-6322

ONCE (lawn food)
See Swift & Company

ONDINE (food products)
See NCC Food Corporation

ONDINE (foundation garments, lingerie)
See Teenform, Inc.

Companies and Trade Names

ONDINE (perfumes)
See Mem Company, Inc.

ONE-A-DAY (vitamins)
See Miles Laboratories, Inc.

ONE DESIGN SPECIALTIES INC.
123 Tollgate Trail
Longwood, Florida 32750

ONE HOUR MARTINIZING (dry-cleaning franchise)
See Martin Sales (Division of American Laundry Machinery Industries)

100 PIPERS (Scotch)
See Seagram Distillers Company

ONE-OF-A-KIND WORKSHOP
24 Pine Mountain Road
Ridgefield, Connecticut 06877

ONE STAR (groceries)
See S.E. Rykoff & Company

ONE STEP (floor-care product)
See Penn-Champ

ONE-TIME PACKAGE PRODUCTS, INC.
(Subsidiary of Acme United Corporation)
100 Hicks Street
Bridgeport, Connecticut 06609
James F. Farrington, Vice President
(203) 384-1371

ONE-WAY (disposable linens)
See Service Products (Division of Kimberly-Clark Corporation)

O'NEAL, JONES & FELDMAN INC.
1304 Ashby Road
Saint Louis, Missouri 63132
Jim O'Neil, Chairman, President and Chief Executive Officer
(314) 997-6650
See also Durst Drug; and Le Gear

ONEIDA, LTD.
Kenwood Station
Oneida, New York 13421
Pierrepont T. Noyes, President
(315) 361-3000

O'NEIL COMPANY, M.
(Division of May Department Stores Company)
Customer Relations
226 South Main Street
Akron, Ohio 44308
John W. Christian, Jr., President
(216) 375-5000

ONEITA KNITTING MILLS
350 Fifth Avenue
New York, New York 10001
Robert D. Devereux, President
(803) 264-5225

ONEPIE (food products)
See Medomak Canning Company

ONION RINGS (snack food)
See Holland-American Wafer Company

ONKOR (detergent)
See Pacific Soap Company

ONKYO
(Division of Mitsubishi International Corporation)
25-19 43rd Avenue
Long Island, New York 11101
(212) 729-2323

ONOX, INC.
240 Hamilton Avenue
Palo Alto, California 94301

ONTARIO KNIFE COMPANY
(Subsidiary of Servotronics Inc.)
Box 145
Franklinville, New York 14737

ONTRA (cafeterias)
See John R. Thompson Company

ONTRA (canned vegetables)
See Seymour Canning Company

ONYUMS (snack product)
See General Mills, Inc.

ONYX (stainless-steel flatware)
See H.E. Lauffer Company, Inc.

OO-LA-LA! (foundation garments, lingerie)
See Teenform, Inc.

OOMPHIES, INC.
(Division of United States Industries, Inc.)
5 Franklin Street
Lawrence, Massachusetts 01840
Charles H. Gessner, President
(617) 682-5268

OPAL (canned vegetables)
See David Lord, Ltd.

OPALAX (glass products)
See Corning Glass Works

OPALO (glassware)
See Gillinder Brothers

OPEL (motor vehicles)
See Buick Motors (Division of General Motors Corporation)

OPELIKA MANUFACTURING CORPORATION
361 West Chestnut Street
Chicago, Illinois 60610
Donald P. Cohen, President
(312) 664-8300
See also Whitehouse Manufacturing Corporation

OPEN DOOR COMPANY, THE
1249 Dell Avenue
Campbell, California 95008

Companies and Trade Names

OPEN HOUSE (food products)
See M & K Foods Inc.

OPEN KETTLE (pickled foods)
See Paisley Farm

OPEN PANTRY FOOD MARTS INC.
75 East Wacker Drive
Chicago, Illinois 60601
(312) 372-1976

OPEN PIT (barbecue sauce)
See General Foods Corporation

OPERATION DEEP FREEZE (underwear)
See Duofold Inc.

OPPENHEIMER & COMPANY, A.
(Division of Cadogan Investments, Ltd. of America)
435 North Midland Avenue
Saddle Brook, New Jersey 07662
(201) 791-8480

OPTICAID (clip-on optical products)
See Edroy Products Company

OPTICAL SCIENCES GROUP INC.
24 Tiburon Street
San Rafael, California 94901
(415) 453-8980

OPTIK-AIDS, INC.
2046 Broadway
Santa Monica, California 90404

OPTIMA (typewriter)
See Continental Typewriter Trading Corporation

OPTIMA EXPORT COMPANY
855 Avenue of the Americas
New York, New York 10001
(212) 594-2830

OPTIMO (cigars)
See Universal Cigar Corporation

OPTIMUS
646 East Commonwealth
Fullerton, California 92631

OPTIMUS PHARMACEUTICALS COMPANY, INC.
Box 97
Taylors, South Carolina 29687

OPTION (toiletries, soap, and shampoo)
See Clairol, Inc.

OPTIQUE INC.
4507 Third Avenue
Bronx, New York 10457
(212) 365-0001

OPTOMETICS, INC.
140 East Duarte Road
Monrovia, California 91016

ORA-JEL (toothache remedy)
See Commerce Drug Company, Inc.

ORACIN (throat lozenges)
See Vick Chemical Company

ORAFIX (denture adhesive)
See Norcliff Laboratories

ORAL B
(Division of Cooper Laboratories)
546 Bedford Road
Bedford Hills, New York 10507

ORAL PROPHYLACTIC ASSOCIATION, INC.
1915 East Eighth Street
Duluth, Minnesota 55812

ORANGE & ROCKLAND UTILITIES, INC.
75 West Route 59
Spring Valley, New York 10977
Dean B. Seifried, President
(914) 352-6000

ORANGE COMPANY, INC.
2011 Riverside Drive
Columbus, Ohio 43221
S. Robert Davis, President
(614) 481-8126

ORANGE JULIUS OF AMERICA
6464 West Sunset Boulevard
Hollywood, California 90028
(213) 462-7879

ORANGE PACKING COMPANY
245 West Hermosa
Lindsay, California 93247

ORANGE PHARMACEUTICALS, INC.
1812 Merritt Park Drive
Orlando, Florida 32803

ORANGE PLUS (frozen orange-juice concentrate)
See General Foods Corporation

ORANGE PRODUCTS INC.
Passaic Avenue
Chatham, New Jersey 07928

ORAPHYLL
(Division of Eastwood Laboratories)
Box 116
Oyster Bay, New York 11771

ORBAN COMPANY INC., KURT
Orban Way
Wayne, New Jersey 07470

ORBAR INTERNATIONAL LTD.
711 South Sleight Street
Naperville, Illinois 60540

ORBISIL (hand cream)
See Winsale Drug Company

ORBIT PHARMACEUTICAL COMPANY, INC.
1304 North Fifth Street
Kansas City, Kansas 66101
(913) 321-0410

Companies and Trade Names

ORBITOR 4000 (razor)
See Gillette Company

ORCHARD BOY (apple products)
See Shenandoah Apple Co-Operative, Inc.

ORCHARD CORPORATION OF AMERICA, THE
1154 Reco Avenue
Saint Louis, Missouri 63126
Robert H. Orchard, President
(314) 822-3880

ORCHARD GEM (fruit)
See Fruit Growers Marketing Association

ORCHARD KING (groceries)
See Steinberg's, Ltd.

ORCHARD PRIDE (canned foods)
See Wisconsin Foods, Inc.

ORCHARD YARN & THREAD COMPANY
524 West 23rd Street
New York, New York 10011
(212) 243-8995

ORCHID (shoes)
See Tober-Saifer Shoe Manufacturing Company, Inc.

ORCHIDS OF HAWAII INTERNATIONAL INC.
305 Seventh Avenue
New York, New York 10001
(212) 675-6500

ORCO (rubber products)
See Oliver Tire & Rubber Company

ORDER OF MERIT (brandy)
See Schenley Industries, Inc.

ORDIBEL COLLATORS INC.
205 Hudson
New York, New York 10013
(212) 966-2191

ORDWAY & COMPANY, INC., A.P.
82 Beaver
New York, New York 10018
(212) 425-3384

ORE-CAL CORPORATION
634 Crocker Avenue
Los Angeles, California 90021
(213) 680-9540

ORE-IDA FOODS, INC.
(Subsidiary of H.J. Heinz Company)
Post Office Box Ten
Boise, Idaho 83707
Robert K. Pederson, President
(208) 343-7941

OREGON CHIEF (meats)
See Portland Provision Company

OREGON FREEZE DRY FOODS, INC.
770 West 29th Avenue
Albany, Oregon 97321
Ellis M. Byer, President
(503) 926-6001

OREGON FRUIT PRODUCTS COMPANY
Box 526
Salem, Oregon 97308
(503) 581-6211

OREGON PRUNE EXCHANGE
1840 B Street
Forest Grove, Oregon 97116

OREGON TRAIL (food products)
See Northwest Packing Company

OREGON'S FINEST (canned and frozen foods)
See Agripac, Inc.

OREMET CHEMICAL CORPORATION
65 Hudson Street
Hackensack, New Jersey 07601

OREO (cookies)
See Nabisco, Inc.

ORETETIC (canned foods)
See Oregon Fruit Products Company

ORGANAIRE INC.
1153 West Fayette Street
Syracuse, New York 13201
(315) 475-3712

ORGANICOLOR (hair care products)
See La Maur, Inc.

ORGANO (lawn and garden supplies)
See Lawn & Garden Supply Company

ORGANON, INC.
375 Mount Pleasant Avenue
West Orange, New Jersey 07052
Joseph J. Ruvance, Jr., President
(201) 731-6000

ORGATRON (electronic organs)
See GTR Products Inc.

ORGILL BROTHERS & COMPANY
2100 Latham Street
Memphis, Tennessee 38109
(901) 948-3381

ORICA (seafood)
See K. & C. Food Sales

ORIENTAL (Oriental-style foods)
See La Choy Food Products

ORIENTAL E. & I. COMPANY INC.
West-53 Century Road
Paramus, New Jersey 07652

Companies and Trade Names

ORIENTAL EXPORTERS, INC.
2 Pennsylvania Plaza
New York, New York 10001
(212) 594-7800

ORIGINAL BEER IMPORTING &
  DISTRIBUTING COMPANY INC.
21-55 51st Avenue
Long Island City, New York 11101
(212) 361-7616

ORIGINAL CUCAMONGA WINERY
Post Office Box 696
Cucamonga, California 91730

ORIGINAL NOTES & COMPANY
384 Mulberry Road
Guilford, Connecticut 06437

ORIGINAL TOY CORPORATION
86 34th Street
Brooklyn, New York 11232
(212) 788-7373

ORIGINALA, INC.
512 Seventh Avenue
New York, New York 10018
Nathan Bader, Chairman of the
  Board
(212) 695-5100

ORIGINALS INTERNATIONAL INC.
2995 44th Avenue North
Saint Petersburg, Florida 33714

ORINGER MANUFACTURING
  COMPANY INC.
22 Liberty Street
Quincy, Massachusetts 02169

ORION (guitars)
  See Pacific Music Supply
    Company

ORION ELECTRONICS
  CORPORATION
3547 Webster Avenue
Bronx, New York 10467
(212) 231-7700

ORION INDUSTRIES, INC.
101 Continental Boulevard
El Segundo, California 90245
Philip W. Colburn, President
(213) 640-0850

ORJENE NATURAL COSMETICS
5-43 48th Avenue
Long Island City, New York 11101

ORKIDEER (produce)
  See Deerfield Groves Company

ORLANDO (guitars and accessories)
  See Pacific Music Supply
    Company

ORLANDO BOAT COMPANY, INC.
Box 15770
Orlando, Florida 32808

ORLANDO FOODS INC.
4667 East Date Avenue
Fresno, California 93725

ORLEANS SEAFOOD COMPANY
(Division of Southland Canning &
  Packing Company, Inc.)
800 Edwards Avenue
Jefferson Parish, Louisiana 70123

ORLEANS SILVER COMPANY
(Division of United China & Glass
  Company)
Post Office Box 51510
4500 Tchoupitoulas
New Orleans, Louisiana 70151
(504) 891-5881

ORLON (acrylic fiber)
  See E.I. du Pont de Nemours &
    Company, Inc., Textile
    Fibers Department

ORMONT DRUG & CHEMICAL
  COMPANY
520 South Dean Street
Englewood, New Jersey 07631
(201) 567-0820
  See also Panray; and Parlam

ORNA-METAL INC.
7129 Olive Boulevard
Saint Louis, Missouri 63130
(314) 862-5030

ORO MANUFACTURING COMPANY
Post Office Box 479
Monroe, North Carolina 28110
(704) 283-2186

OROSI FOOTHILL CITRUS
  ASSOCIATION
Orosi, California 93647

OROVILLE UNITED GROWERS
Post Office Box 128
Oroville, Washington 98844

OROWAN, CHARLES E.
2211 Broadway
New York, New York 10024
(212) 873-2472

ORR & COMPANY, ROBERT
901 Sixth Avenue North
Nashville, Tennessee 37202
Glen Nelson, Jr., President
(615) 255-8333

ORR & SEMBOWER, INC.
(Subsidiary of Rayburner Company)
Post Office Box 231
Middletown, Pennsylvania 17057
R.C. Westover, Jr., President
(717) 944-4631

ORREFORS (Swedish crystal)
  See Fisher, Bruce & Company

ORRELL'S FOOD PRODUCTS, INC.
(Subsidiary of Leslie Foods Inc.)
575 Independent Road
Oakland, California 94621

ORTEGA (sauces, pimientos, etc.)
  See Heublein, Inc.

Companies and Trade Names

ORTEGA PHARMACEUTICAL
COMPANY
Box 6212
586 South Edgewood Avenue
Jacksonville, Florida 32205
(904) 387-0536

ORTEX INDUSTRIES INC.
100 Pulaski Street
West Warwick, Rhode Island 02983
(401) 821-0100

ORTH COMPANY, PHILIP
7350 South Tenth Street
Oak Creek, Wisconsin 53154

ORTHO (agricultural and garden chemicals)
See Chevron Chemical Company

ORTHO-GRO (insecticides and plant foods)
See Standard Oil of California

ORTHO INDUSTRIES
49 Lawton Street
New Rochelle, New York 10801

ORTHO PHARMACEUTICAL
CORPORATION
Raritan, New Jersey 08869
Wilfred H. Norman, Chairman of the Board
(201) 524-0400

ORTHOCIDE (agricultural and garden chemicals)
See Chevron Chemical Company

ORTHOPEDIC EQUIPMENT
COMPANY INC.
Bourbon, Indiana 46504
(219) 342-3415

ORTHWINE MERCHANDISING
ASSOCIATION INC.
1301 Avenue of the Americas
New York, New York 10019
(212) 765-6666

ORTOFON
9 East 38th Street
New York, New York 10016
(212) 889-9114

ORVIN INNS
Post Office Box 482
Charleston, South Carolina 29402

ORVIS COMPANY, INC., THE
Manchester, Vermont 05254
L.H. Perkins, President
(802) 362-1300

OSAGE PECAN COMPANY, INC.
Box 270
Butler, Missouri 64730

OSBORN MANUFACTURING
CORPORATION
Post Office Box 271
961 North Lake Street
Warsaw, Indiana 46580
(219) 267-6156

OSCAR DE LA RENTA (men's suits)
See After Six, Inc.

OSCAR MAYER & COMPANY
910 Mayer Avenue
Madison, Wisconsin 53701
Robert M. Bolz, President
(608) 241-3311

OSCARSSON SALES COMPANY
INC.
16 Parkway
Katonah, New York 10536

OSCEOLA FRUIT DISTRIBUTORS
Box 430
Kissimmee, Florida 32741

OSCILLOTRON (tools)
See Coleman Systems

OSCO MOTORS CORPORATION
Souderton, Pennsylvania 18964
(215) 855-8268

OSHKOSH B'GOSH, INC.
112 Otter Avenue
Oshkosh, Wisconsin 54901
C.F. Hyde, Jr., President
(414) 231-8800

OSHKOSH TRUCK CORPORATION
2307 Oregon Street
Oshkosh, Wisconsin 54901
John P. Mosling, President
(414) 235-9150

OSHUN (hair-care products)
See Summit Laboratories, Inc.

OSLO (stainless-steel flatware)
See H.E. Lauffer Company Inc.

OSLO (stemware)
See Susquehanna Glass Company

OSHMAN'S SPORTING GOODS,
INC.
2302 Maxwell Lane
Houston, Texas 77023
Alvin N. Lubetkin, President
(713) 928-3171

OSMOSE WOOD PRESERVING
COMPANY OF AMERICA, INC.
980 Ellicott
Buffalo, New York 14209
John L. Surdam, President
(716) 882-5905

OSOGUD CANDIES, INC.
1211 Azusa Canyon Road
West Covina, California 91790

OSROW PRODUCTS COMPANY,
INC.
Hazel Street
Glen Cove, New York 11542
Harold Osrow, Chairman of the Board
(516) 671-5300

OSSA (motorcycles)
See Yankee Motor Company

Companies and Trade Names

OSSIAN CANNING COMPANY INC.
Box 37
Ossian, Indiana 46777

OSSOLA COMPANY, INC., J.
Taft Road
Totowa, New Jersey 07512

OSTER CORPORATION
(Subsidiary of Sunbeam Corporation)
5055 North Lydell Avenue
Milwaukee, Wisconsin 53217
G.W. Orr, President
(414) 332-8300

OSTERMOOR & COMPANY INC.
348 George
Bridgeport, Connecticut 06604
David K. Lebowitz, Vice President
(203) 367-6634

OSTI PRODUCTS COMPANY, INC.
(Subsidiary of Whitestone Products Corporation)
595 Broad Hollow Road
Farmingdale, New York 11735

OSTROM MUSHROOM FARMS
(Division of The Ostrom Company)
Route Steilacoom Road
Olympia, Washington 98125

OSTROWSKY, INC., S.
1133 Broadway
New York, New York 10010
(212) 929-4860

O'SULLIVAN RUBBER CORPORATION
Post Office Box 603
Winchester, Virginia 22601
John J. Armstrong, President
(703) 662-0311

OSWEGO CANDY COMPANY, INC.
275 West First Street
Oswego, New York 13126

OTAGIRI MERCANTILE COMPANY, INC.
20 Hanes Drive
Wayne, New Jersey 07470
(212) 239-8400

OTARION ELECTRONICS, INC.
Box 711
Ossining, New York 10562
Leland E. Rosemond, President
(914) 941-6700

OTASCO
(Division of McCrory Corporation)
11333 East Pine Street
Tulsa, Oklahoma 74116
Abe Brand, President
(918) 437-7171

OTHER MOTHER COMPANY
23-36 38th Street
Astoria, New York 11105

OTHINE (deodorant, hormone cream, skin bleach)
See J. Strickland & Company

OTIS (underwear)
See E-Z Mills, Inc.

OTIS ELEVATOR COMPANY
245 Park Avenue
New York, New York 10017
Ralph A. Weller, Chairman of the Board
(212) 557-5700

OTTAWA CHIEF (canned foods)
See Silver Fleece Inc.

OTTENS MANUFACTURING COMPANY, HENRY H.
1234 Hamilton
Philadelphia, Pennsylvania 19123
(215) 627-5030

OTTER TAIL POWER COMPANY
215 South Cascade Street
Fergus Falls, Minnesota 56537
Albert V. Hartl, Chairman of the Board
(218) 736-5411

OUACHITA MARINE AND INDUSTRIAL CORPORATION
721 Main Street
Little Rock, Arkansas 72201

OUIJA (board game)
See Parker Brothers

OUR BABY'S FIRST SEVEN YEARS
(Subsidiary of Mothers Aid)
5841 Maryland Avenue
Chicago, Illinois 60637
(312) 667-5184

OUR BEST CANNING COMPANY INC.
323 Third Avenue
Pulaski, Wisconsin 54162

OUR DARLING (food products)
See Joan of Arc Company

OUR FAMILY (canned goods)
See Nash-Finch Company

OUR OWN HARDWARE COMPANY
2300 West Highway 13
Burnsville, Minnesota 55378

OUR SPECIAL (groceries)
See B G Wholesale Inc.

OUR VALUE (groceries)
See S.M. Flickinger Company, Inc.

OUR VALUE (groceries and cleaning needs)
See Tyler & Simpson Company

Companies and Trade Names

OUTBOARD MARINE CORPORATION
100 Sea Horse Drive
Waukegan, Illinois 60085
Ralph S. Evinrude, Chairman of the Board
(312) 689-6200
See also Cushman Motors; Evinrude Motors; Gale Products; Johnson Outboards; OMC-Lincoln; OMC Parts Accessories; and OMC Stern Drive

OUTDOOR GIRL (cosmetics)
See Marshall Field & Company

OUTDOOR GIT (dog repellent)
See Animal Repellents, Inc.

OUTDOOR LEISURE PRODUCTS
Post Office Box 27424
5433 Westheimer Street
Houston, Texas 77027
(713) 626-9710

OUTDOOR POWER EQUIPMENT
(Division of FMC Corporation)
215 South Park Street
Port Washington, Wisconsin 53074
David L. Hill, Division Manager
(414) 284-5521

OUTDOOR SPORTS INDUSTRIES, INC.
518 17th Street
Denver, Colorado 80202
Richard H. Olson, President
(303) 825-6266
See also Gerry

OUTDOORSMAN (insect repellent)
See Pet Chemicals, Inc.

OUTDOORSMAN (work shoes)
See International Shoe Company

OUTGRO (ingrown-nail treatment)
See Whitehall Laboratories

OUTLET COMPANY
176 Weybosset Street
Providence, Rhode Island 02902
Kenneth Logowitz, President
(401) 331-8700

OVAL (water softener)
See International Salt Company

OVALTINE PRODUCTS
1 Ovaltine Court
Villa Park, Illinois 60181
Carl K. Glickman, President
(312) 832-4800

OVATION INSTRUMENTS INC.
(Subsidiary of Kaman Corporation)
Greenwoods Road
New Hartford, Connecticut 06057

OVELMO COMPANY
3707 Villa Nova Road
Baltimore, Maryland 21207
(301) 484-2020

OVEN CRISP (food products)
See Ore-Ida Foods Inc.

OVEN-FRESH (bakery products)
See Grocers Baking Company

OVEN FRESH (cookies and crackers)
See Southern Biscuit Company

OVEN FRESH (fresh and frozen pies)
See Puritan Pie Company

OVEN-GARD (spray)
See Drackett Company

OVEN KING (porcelain oven-to-table ware)
See Europa Commerce Inc.

OVER & UNDER (cleaning products)
See S.C. Johnson & Son

OVERHEAD DOOR CORPORATION
6250 LBJ Freeway
Dallas, Texas 75240
Robert C. Haugh, President
(214) 233-6611

OVERMYER-PERRAM GLASS COMPANY
Box 2477
Tulsa, Oklahoma 74101
(918) 587-7462

OVERNITE TRANSPORTATION COMPANY
1100 Commerce Road
Richmond, Virginia 23224
Kenneth G. Gentil, President
(804) 231-6211

OVEROCEAN CLOCK COMPANY INC.
23 West 18th Street
New York, New York 10011
(212) 242-2254

OVERSEAS LEATHER IMPORTING COMPANY
510 Madison
New York, New York 10022
(212) 752-4668

OVERSEAS MAILMAN, INC.
Palisades Boulevard and Grand Avenue
Palisades Park, New Jersey 07650

OVERSEAS MOTORS, INC.
32400 Plymouth Road
Livonia, Michigan 48150

OVERSEAS NATIONAL AIRWAYS, INC.
Kennedy International Airport
Jamaica, New York 11430
G.F. Steedman Hinckley, Chairman of the Board
(212) 632-8200

Companies and Trade Names

OVERSEAS PRODUCE CORPORATION
Number One Depot Plaza
Mamaroneck, New York 10543

OVERSEAS PUBLISHERS' REPRESENTATIVES
424 Madison Avenue
New York, New York 10014
(212) 421-1329

OVERTIME (disinfectant and deodorizer)
See Chesebrough-Pond's Inc.

OVERTON COMPANY, S.E.
Indiana and Elkenburg
South Haven, Michigan 49090
Frank W. Overton, President
(616) 637-1194

OVIMPEX INC.
2 Pennsylvania Plaza
New York, New York 10001
(212) 868-7215

OWATONNA CANNING COMPANY
Post Office Box 447
Owatonna, Minnesota 55060
Steve J. Lange, President
(507) 451-7670

OWATONNA MANUFACTURING COMPANY INC.
Box 547
Owatonna, Minnesota 55060
Eugene F. Diedrich, President
(507) 451-2860

OWEN DRUG COMPANY
115 B Avenue
Salisbury, North Carolina 28144
(704) 636-0951

OWEN LABORATORIES, INC.
Box 34630
3737 Belt Line Road
Dallas, Texas 75234
Dougles Owen Brown, Chairman and President
(214) 233-6621

OWENS BRUSH COMPANY
(Division of Cooper Laboratories, Inc.)
Post Office Box 552
Iowa City, Iowa 52240
(319) 338-5411

OWENS-CORNING FIBERGLASS CORPORATION
Fiberglass Tower
Toledo, Ohio 43604
William W. Boeschenstein, President
(419) 259-3000

OWENS-ILLINOIS, INC.
Post Office Box 1035
Toledo, Ohio 43601
Edwin D. Dodd, President
(419) 242-6543
See also Lily

OWENS-ILLINOIS LIBBEY
See Libbey (Division of Owens-Illinois Inc.)

OWENSBORO CANNING COMPANY INC.
Box 734
Owensboro, Kentucky 42301

OWL (produce)
See Watsonville Exchange Inc.

OXCO BRUSH
221 Pine Street
Florence, Massachusetts 01060
(413) 584-1780

OXEQUIP HEALTH INDUSTRIES
12601 South Springfield Avenue
Chicago, Illinois 60658
(312) 371-3500

OXFORD (apparel)
See Koracorp Industries, Inc.

OXFORD (electric clocks)
See Gibraltar Manufacturing Company Inc.

OXFORD BONE CHINA
See Lenox, Inc.

OXFORD CHEMICALS
(Division of Consolidated Foods Corporation)
5001 Peachtree Industrial Boulevard
Chamblee, Georgia 30005
Dave Center, Chairman of the Board
(404) 451-4311

OXFORD CLUB (gin)
See Schenley Industries, Inc.

OXFORD CORPORATION, THE
135 North Fifth
Oxford, Pennsylvania 19363

OXFORD HALL SILVERSMITHS LTD.
95 State Street
New Cassel, New York 11590

OXFORD INDUSTRIES, INC.
222 Piedmont Avenue, N.E.
Atlanta, Georgia 30312
Carl J. Reith, President
(404) 659-2424
See also Lanier Business Products

OXFORD LABORATORIES, INC.
Dayton, Virginia 22821

Companies and Trade Names

OXFORD PENDAFLEX
     CORPORATION
35 Clinton Road
Garden City, New York 11530
William I. Thompson, President
(516) 741-3200

OXFORD PICKLES
(Division of John E. Cain Company)
15 Jewett Avenue
South Deerfield,
     Massachusetts 01373

OXFORD ROYAL MUSHROOM
     PRODUCTS, INC.
Kelton, Pennsylvania 19346
Alfred Fortugno, President
(215) 869-2404

OXFORD SPEAKER COMPANY
4647 West 47th Street
Chicago, Illinois 60632
(312) 585-4491

OXFORD UNIVERSITY PRESS INC.
200 Madison Avenue
New York, New York 10016
James Y. Huws-Davies
(212) 679-7300

OXIPOR VHC (psoriasis treatment)
     See Whitehall Laboratories

OXNARD FROZEN FOODS
     CORPORATION
711 Diaz Avenue
Oxnard, California 93030
George H. Rees, President
(805) 486-1623

OXWALL TOOL COMPANY
(Division of Consolidated Foods
     Corporation)
133-10 32nd Avenue
Flushing, New York 11354
Melvin L. Merians, Vice President
(212) 539-5000

OXXFORD CLOTHES, INC.
(Subsidiary of Koracorp Industries,
     Inc.)
1220 West Van Buren Street
Chicago, Illinois 60607
Jack McDonald, President
(312) 829-3600

OXYCLEAN DISTRIBUTING
     CORPORATION
141 Brookdale
Williamsville, New York 14221

OXYDOL (detergent)
     See Procter & Gamble Company

OYSTER BAR (restaurants)
     See Ward Foods, Inc.

OYSTERETTES (crackers)
     See Nabisco Inc.

OZ FOOD CORPORATION
4551 South Racine Avenue
Chicago, Illinois 60609
(312) 927-1240

OZARK AIR LINES, INC.
Post Office Box 10007
Lambert Field
Saint Louis, Missouri 63145
Edward J. Crane, President
(314) 895-6600

OZARK NURSERIES INC.
Post Office Box 557
Tahlequah, Oklahoma 74464
James E. Davis, Chairman and
     President
(918) 456-6134

OZARK PENCIL COMPANY
119 East Commerce Street
Lewisburg, Tennessee 37091

OZARKA WATER COMPANY
630 West Second
Wichita, Kansas 67203

OZARKA WATER COMPANY
(Affiliation of Arrowhead Puritas
     Waters, Inc.)
305 West Nensley Boulevard
Bartlesville, Oklahoma 74003

OZBURN-JANESVILLE
     CORPORATION
133 South Garfield Avenue
Janesville, Wisconsin 53545

OZITE CORPORATION
1755 Butterfield Road
Libertyville, Illinois 60048
Thomas L. Mason, President
(312) 362-8210

OZONE CONFECTIONERS &
     BAKERS SUPPLY COMPANY INC.
55 Bank Street
East Paterson, New Jersey 07407

OZONE SPRING WATERS, INC.
2831 Marais Street
New Orleans, Louisiana 70117
(504) 947-1101

OZONITE (soap)
     See Procter & Gamble Company

Companies and Trade Names

P

P. & A. LAMPS BY INDECOR
(early American lamps, weather instruments, clocks)
See Indecor Inc.

P & C FOOD MARKETS, INC.
(Subsidiary of Pneumo Dynamics Corporation)
Post Office Box 1365
Syracuse, New York 13201
Earl M. Eden, President
(315) 457-9460

P & G (white naphtha soap)
See Procter & Gamble Company

P. & J. PLASTICS, INC.
124 Water Street
Leominster, Massachusetts 01453

P & M BROOM COMPANY
Portales, New Mexico 88130

P & O LINES (North America), INC.
155 Post
San Francisco, California 94108
George M. Turner, President
(415) 397-3700

P. & P. BLUEBERRY PACKING COMPANY
Lunt and Nicholas Streets
Elk Grove Village, Illinois 60007

P & S DESPARD (lighting products)
See Pass & Seymour Inc.

P. & S. LABORATORIES, INC.
Box 61067
436 West Eight Street
Los Angeles, California 90061
(213) 627-1555

P & T LIGHT (whiskey)
See Schenley Industries, Inc.

PAC ENTERPRISES INC.
5045 Torresdale Avenue
Philadelphia, Pennsylvania 19124
(215) 743-7563

PBM (men's apparel)
See Pincus Brothers-Maxwell Inc.

P.G. (cigars)
See Perfecto Garcia & Brothers, Inc.

PGA (golf accessories)
See Victor Golf (Subsidiary of Victor Comptometer Corporation)

P. G. C. (playing cards)
See Stancraft Products

P. G. PROFESSIONAL (golf equipment)
See Professional Golf Company

PH (chemicals for pools)
See Olin Corporation

P.I.E.
See Pacific Intermountain Express Company

P.I.T. FIBERGLASS INC.
1424 East 25th North
Wichita, Kansas 67219
(316) 263-2265

PLA (brush and spray paints)
See Testor Corporation

PLB INTERNATIONAL INC.
17 Newtown Road
Plainview, New York 11803

PM (whiskey)
See National Distillers & Chemical Corporation

P.M.C. CANNING COMPANY, INC.
Box 115
Swedesboro, New Jersey 08085

PMS (amplifiers)
See Pacific Music Supply Company

PPG HIGH FIDELITY (mirrors)
See Pittsburgh Plate Glass Company

PPG INDUSTRIES, INC.
1 Gateway Center
Pittsburgh, Pennsylvania 15222
J.A. Neubauer, President and Chief Operations Officer
(412) 434-3131
See also Barreled Sunlight Paint Company

P.Q. (canned goods)
See Kling Brothers & Fischer Inc.

PRF INDUSTRIES, INC.
See Motor Homes Inc.; Sightseer Corporation; and Travco Corporation

PTL PUBLICATIONS
Box 1277
Tustin, California 92680

PVO INTERNATIONAL, INC.
416 Division Street
Boonton, New Jersey 07005
(201) 334-2900
See also Drew Foods Corporation

PW (bath oils, soap, and powder)
See Pearl-Wick Corporation

Companies and Trade Names

PWI (sports apparel)
See Peter Webber Imports

PA-WRAY PICKLE COMPANY
1403 N.E. Ramsey Street
Minneapolis, Minnesota 55413
(612) 335-8341

PAAS (Easter egg coloring kit)
See Plough, Inc.

PABAFILM (sun-screening agent)
See Owen Laboratories, Inc.

PABCO (linoleum)
See Fibreboard Corporation

PABCO PAINT CORPORATION
1707 64th
Emeryville, California 94608

PABLUM (baby cereal)
See Mead Johnson & Company

PABST BREWING COMPANY
917 West Juneau Avenue
Milwaukee, Wisconsin 53201
James C. Windham, Chairman
(414) 271-0230

PAC-A-MO (men's sportswear)
See Alps Sportswear Manufacturing Company Inc.

PAC ENTERPRISES INC.
5045 Torresdale Avenue
Philadelphia, Pennsylvania 19124
(215) 743-7563

PACCD (canned foods)
See Charles G. Summers, Jr., Inc.

PACE (wood stains)
See International Paint Company Inc.

PACE EDITIONS INC.
115 East 23rd Street
New York, New York 10010
(212) 673-8240

PACE FOODS COMPANY
1414 North San Jacinto
San Antonio, Texas 78207
(512) 735-4241

PACEMAKER (garden tools)
See Hall Industries Inc.

PACEMAKER CORPORATION (boats)
(Subsidiary of Fuqua Industries, Inc.)
Post Office Box 337
River Road, RFD Two
Egg Harbor City,
   New Jersey 08215
John E. Leek, Jr., Chairman of the Board
(609) 965-3000

PACEMAKER CORPORATION
Box 16163
Portland, Oregon 97216

PACEMAKER INNS OF AMERICA INC.
2751 Buford Highway N.E.
Atlanta, Georgia 30324

PACEMAKER JUNIORS INC.
1400 Broadway
New York, New York 10018
(212) 564-0500

PACER (child's vehicle)
See AMF Wheel Goods (Division of AMF Inc.)

PACER (frozen foods)
See Santa Fe-Driscoll Packers Inc.

PACESETTER (garden tools)
See Hall Industries Inc.

PACESETTER INDUSTRIES, INC.
295 Fifth Avenue
New York, New York 10016
Jeffrey E. Britz, Chairman of the Board
(212) 685-6400
See also Lad 'N Dad Slacks, Inc.

PACIFIC (evaporated milk and instant milk powder)
See Fraser Valley Milk Producers Association

PACIFIC (seafood)
See East Point Seafood Company

PACIFIC (tires)
See Uniroyal, Inc.

PACIFIC ARTS MANUFACTURING INC.
Lakeview, Oregon 97630

PACIFIC CLIPPER (canned and frozen foods)
See Agripac, Inc.

PACIFIC COAST BRUSH COMPANY
2030 East Seventh
Los Angeles, California 90021
(213) 489-3390

PACIFIC DEEP (seafood products)
See B & B Fisheries Inc.

PACIFIC ELECTRICORD COMPANY
747 West Redondo Beach Boulevard
Gardena, California 90247
William E. Boyd, Chairman and President
(213) 532-6600

PACIFIC EXECUTIVE GIFTS
1 First Street
Los Altos, California 94022

1046

Companies and Trade Names

PACIFIC FAR EAST LINE, INC.
1 Embarcadero Center
San Francisco, California 94111
John I. Alioto, President
(415) 576-4000

PACIFIC FOOD PRODUCTS
 COMPANY
4200 Airport Way South
Seattle, Washington 98108
(206) 623-8276

PACIFIC FRUIT & PRODUCE
 COMPANY
4103 Second Avenue South
Seattle, Washington 98134
(206) 624-0111

PACIFIC GAME COMPANY
12830 Raymer
North Hollywood, California 91605
J.P. Kayle, President
(213) 875-0535

PACIFIC GAS & ELECTRIC
 COMPANY
77 Beale Street
San Francisco, California 94106
Shermer L. Sibley, Chairman of the
 Board
(415) 781-4211

PACIFIC GOLD (canned foods)
 See California Canners &
  Growers

PACIFIC GUMMED PRODUCTS
 COMPANY
Post Office Box 10578
Portland, Oregon 97210
(503) 223-0310

PACIFIC HARVEST (seafood products)
 See B & B Fisheries Inc.

PACIFIC INTERMOUNTAIN
 EXPRESS COMPANY (P.I.E.)
145th and Clay
Oakland, California 94604
Robert Stier, Chairman of the Board
(415) 452-1616

PACIFIC LUMBER COMPANY
1111 Columbus Avenue
San Francisco, California 94133
Edward M. Carpenter, President
(415) 771-4700

PACIFIC METAL FABRICATORS
3383 Livonia Avenue
Los Angeles, California 90034
(213) 870-5339

PACIFIC MINERAL INDUSTRIES
6000 Sunset Boulevard
Hollywood, California 90028
(213) 464-0255

PACIFIC MUSIC SUPPLY COMPANY
1143 Santee Street
Los Angeles, California 90015
(213) 747-7211

PACIFIC MUTUAL LIFE INSURANCE
 COMPANY
700 Newport Center Drive
Newport Beach, California 92663
Harry G. Bubb, President
(714) 640-3011

PACIFIC NATIONAL BANK OF
 WASHINGTON
1215 Fourth Avenue
Seattle, Washington 98161
John F. Harrigan, Chairman of the
 Board
(206) 292-3111

PACIFIC NORTHWEST BELL
 TELEPHONE COMPANY
821 Second Avenue
Seattle, Washington 98104
Wallace R. Bunn, President
(206) 345-2211

PACIFIC PEARL SEAFOODS, INC.
(Subsidiary of Amfac, Inc.)
1201 Bank of California Building
Seattle, Washington 98164
William Deshler, President
(206) 624-4400

PACIFIC PEARL (seafood)
 See Ivar Wendt

PACIFIC PHARMACEUTICAL
 CORPORATION
21028 West Golden Triangle Road
Sangus, California 91350

PACIFIC POWER & LIGHT
 COMPANY
920 S.W. Sixth Avenue
Portland, Oregon 97204
John Y. Lansing, President
(503) 243-1121

PACIFIC SOAP COMPANY
2532 East 49th Street
Vernon, California 90058
(213) 581-8105

PACIFIC SOUTHWEST AIRLINES
3225 North Harbor Drive
San Diego, California 92101
J. Floyd Andrews, Chairman of
 the Board
(714) 297-4781

PACIFIC STONEWARE INC.
9217 North Peninsular Avenue
Portland, Oregon 97217
(503) 285-2551

PACIFIC TAIWAN ENTERPRISES,
 INC.
3000 El Camino Real
Palo Alto, California 94304

PACIFIC TELEPHONE AND
 TELEGRAPH COMPANY, THE
140 New Montgomery Street
San Francisco, California 94105
Jerome Hull, President
(415) 542-9000
 See also Bell Telephone Company
  of Nevada

PACIFIC TRADING COMPANY,
 INC.
1170 Broadway
New York, New York 10001
(212) 689-8108

Companies and Trade Names

PACIFIC TRAIL SPORTSWEAR
(Division of Apparel, Inc.)
1310 Mercer Street
Seattle, Washington 98109
Larry Mounger, Jr., President
(206) 622-8730

PACIFIC TRAWLER CORPORATION
1945 East Occidental
Santa Ana, California 92705

PACIFIC VEGETABLE OIL
 CORPORATION
Edible Oils Division
130 World Trade Center
San Francisco, California 94111
(415) 362-0990

PACIFIC VITAMIN CORPORATION
12747 Saticoy
North Hollywood, California 91605
Ira Hirsch, Chairman and President
(213) 875-0320

PACIFICO
973 Minna Street
San Francisco, California 94103
(415) 431-1081

PACKAGE PRODUCTS COMPANY,
 INC.
1938 Camden Road
Charlotte, North Carolina 28201

PACKAGING PRODUCTS &
 DESIGN CORPORATION
574 Ferry Street
Newark, New Jersey 07105
Robert B. Winkel, President
(201) 589-5800

PACKAGING SALES
(Division of The Dow Chemical -
 U.S.A.)
The Dow Center
Strosacker Building
Midland, Michigan 48640

PACKARD BELL (televisions,
phonographs)
   See Teledyne Packard Bell

PACKARD ELECTRIC
(Division of General Motors
 Corporation)
Post Office Box 431
Warren, Ohio 44482
B.T. Olson, General Manager
(216) 399-9121

PACKERS CANNING COMPANY
 INC.
Box G
M-40 South
Lawton, Michigan 49065
Ronald O. Packer, President
(616) 624-4681

PACKET LINE (upholstered
furniture)
   See Grand Rapids Leather
     Furniture Company

PACKLANE (latex wall paint)
   See Bondex International

PACON CORPORATION
2525 North Casaloma Drive
Appleton, Wisconsin 54911
Gerard H. Van Hoof, President
(414) 734-9141

PACON MACHINES
 CORPORATION
1285 East Boston Post Road
Mamaroneck, New York 10543
(914) 698-5698

PACOR INDUSTRIES INC.
382 N.E. 191st Street
North Miami Beach, Florida 33162
(305) 652-0808

PACQUIN (hand and skin lotions)
   See Leeming/Pacquin

PACTRA INDUSTRIES, INC.
6725 Sunset Boulevard
Los Angeles, California 90028
A.L. Davenport, Jr., President
(213) 469-7284

PADAWER COMPANY, INC., I.
577 Broadway
New York, New York 10012
(212) 226-1262

PADDINGTON CORPORATION,
 THE
(Subsidiary of Liggett & Myers,
 Inc.)
630 Fifth Avenue
New York, New York 10020
Abraham Rosenberg, President
(212) 541-6610

PADDLE-PADS (eyeglass and
hearing-aid pads)
   See J.I. Morris Company

PADDY (disposable soap pads)
   See Purex Corporation, Ltd.

PADDY (Irish whiskey)
   See Austin, Nichols & Company,
     Inc.

PAECO INC.
500 Market Street
Perth Amboy, New Jersey 08861

PAGE (fence products)
   See ACCO, Page Fence Division

PAGE (napkins, towels, toilet
tissue)
   See Fort Howard Paper Company

PAGE & SHAW (candy)
   See New England Confectionery
     Company

PAGE, ANN
(Division of The Great Atlantic &
 Pacific Tea Company)
500 Ann Page Road
Horseheads, New York 14845

Companies and Trade Names

PAGE BOY COMPANY INC.
2033 Cedar Springs Avenue
Dallas, Texas 75201
(214) 747-3152

PAGE DAIRY COMPANY
Post Office Box 597
Wade and Knapp Streets
Toledo, Ohio 43693
Henry Page, Jr., President and Treasurer
(419) 241-2211

PAGE MILK COMPANY, THE
2200 Sturdevant
Merrill, Wisconsin 54452
Jim C. Page, President
(715) 536-5517

PAGEL'S POPCORN PRODUCTS
Post Office Box 55
Watertown, Wisconsin 53094

PAGER INDUSTRIES INC.
100 Jackson Avenue
Edison, New Jersey 08817

PAGEWRITER PEN COMPANY
30 Lowell Road
Wellesley Hills, Massachusetts 02181

PAGLIACCIO (imported foods)
See Pastene & Company, Inc.

PAGLIERI PARFUMS, INC.
62 Autumnview Road
Williamsville, New York 14221

PAGLO LABORATORIES, INC.
182 Cedar Street
Paterson, New Jersey 07501

PAGODA (canned fish and fruits)
See Roadel Foods Inc.

PAGODA ARTS
51 Aster Drive
New Hyde Park, New York 11040

PAIL-O-CHICKEN
1996 East Street
San Bernardino, California 92405

PAILLARD, INC.
1900 Lower Road
Linden, New Jersey 07036
Ragnar Beyer, President
(201) 381-5600

PAINE COMPANY, THE
501 Westgate Road
Addison, Illinois 60101
C. Dan Polos, Chairman and President
(312) 543-4600

PAINE, WEBBER, JACKSON & CURTIS, INC.
140 Broadway
New York, New York 10005
James W. Davant, Chairman of the Board
(212) 437-2121

PAINT-EZE (paints and paint sundries)
See Pelco Industries Inc.

PAINT MASTER (paints)
See Standard Industrial Products, Inc.

PAINT N KLEEN (paint-remover towelette)
See Brittany House Ltd.

PAINT-O-PLAST (paint)
See Enterprise Paint Manufacturing Company

PAINTMASTER SYSTEMS CORPORATION
121 South Highland Avenue
Pittsburgh, Pennsylvania 15228
(412) 362-4440

PAIR-A-TROOPER (shoes)
See Georgia Boot (Division of United States Industries, Inc.)

PAIR ENTERPRISES INC., RON
24112 Harper Avenue
Saint Clair Shores, Michigan 48080

PAIR-OFFS (jackets and blouses)
See Koret of California, Inc.

PAISANO (wine)
See E. & J. Gallo Winery

PAISLEY FARM
9229 Lake Shore
Mentor, Ohio 44060

PAK-A-ROBE (blankets)
See Faribault Woolen Mill Company

PAK-NIT (knitwear)
See Compax Corporation

PAKI-TEX TRADING CORPORATION
15 Park Row
New York, New York 10038
(212) 233-8020

PAKISTAN INTERNATIONAL AIRLINES CORPORATION
545 Fifth Avenue
New York, New York 10017
M. Rafique Saigol, Manager
(212) 687-7900

PAKLITE (travel accessories)
See Clopay Corporation

PAKS DRUGS, INC.
3435 Bailey Avenue
Buffalo, New York 14215
(716) 835-5532

PAKULA AND COMPANY
218 South Wabash
Chicago, Illinois 60604
Milton Axelrad, President
(312) 939-6460

Companies and Trade Names

PAL (paint)
See National Gypsum Company

PAL (razor blades)
See American Safety Razor Company

PALACE (processed meat products)
See John Morrell & Company

PALACIO DE ORIENTE (canned fish)
See Vicente Puig & Company, Inc.

PALADIN BLACKCHERRY (smoking tobacco)
See American Tobacco Company

PLAZZOLO SON, INC., J.
36 Lakeville Road
New Hyde Park, New York 11040

PALESTINE TRADING COMPANY
115 West 29th Street
New York, New York 10001
(212) 564-0106

PALISANDER (stainless-steel flatware)
See H.E. Lauffer Company, Inc.

PALISSY POTTERY LTD. (earthenware teapots and dinnerware)
See Herbert Van Doorn Company

PALIZZIO HANDBAG INC.
330 Fifth Avenue
New York, New York 10001
(212) 564-5050

PALIZZIO INC.
330 Fifth Avenue
New York, New York 10001
(212) 564-5050

PALL MALL (cigarettes)
See American Tobacco Company

PALM-AIRE (mobile homes)
See Nashua Homes

PALM APIARIES
3247 Marion Street
Fort Myers, Florida 33901

PALM BEACH BEAUTY PRODUCTS COMPANY
2508 Nicollet Avenue South
Minneapolis, Minnesota 55404
Ben B. Kaitz, President
(612) 823-7243

PALM BEACH COMPANY
400 Pike Street
Cincinnati, Ohio 45202
Elmer L. Ward, Jr., President
(513) 241-4260
See also Austin Hill, Ltd.

PALM BROTHERS DECALCOMANIA COMPANY
3736 Regent Avenue
Cincinnati, Ohio 45212
George M. Einsenberg, President
(513) 631-5681

PALMEDICO, INC.
Drawer 3397
Columbia, South Carolina 29203

PALMER CANDY COMPANY
209 Douglas Street
Sioux City, Iowa 51101
Edward C. Palmer, President
(712) 258-5543

PALMER COMPANY, R.M.
77 Second Avenue
West Reading, Pennsylvania 19611
Richard M. Palmer, Chairman and President
(215) 372-8971

PALMER ENTERPRISES, ARNOLD
14 West Mulberry Avenue
Pleasantville, New Jersey 08232

PALMER FIXTURE COMPANY
210 Prairie Avenue
Waukesha, Wisconsin 53186
(414) 542-6608

PALMER JOHNSON INC.
61 Michigan Street
Sturgeon Bay, Wisconsin 54235
(414) 743-4414

PALMER, SOLON
Schooley's Mountain,
New Jersey 07870

PALMER'S SKIN SUCCESS (skin-care products)
See E.T. Browne Drug Company, Inc.

PALMETTO BRUSH & WHISK
(Division of Wooton Fibre Company)
Post Office Box 11
Jacksonville, Florida 32205
(904) 353-0493

PALMETTO GARMENT COMPANY, INC.
Post Office Box 186
Travelers Rest, South Carolina 29690

PALMOLIVE (shaving products, shampoo, soap)
See Colgate-Palmolive Company

PALOMAR (cookware)
See Household Manufacturing Company

PALOMAR (glassware)
See The Lotus Glass Company

PALOMAR (rubber and vinyl floor mats)
See Pretty Products Inc.

PALS (vitamins)
See Clinton (Division of Bristol-Myers Company)

Companies and Trade Names

PALSON MANUFACTURING
  COMPANY
184 Main Street
Worcester, Massachusetts 01608

PALTER DEBS (shoes)
  See Samuels Shoe Company, Inc.

PAM (spray-on pan coating)
  See Boyle-Midway Pam Products
  (Division of American Home
  Products Corporation)

PAMPA (beef products)
  See CAP Sales Corporation

PAMPER (hair products)
  See Gillette Company, Personal
  Care Division

PAMPERIN CIGAR COMPANY
113-115 South Second Street
La Crosse, Wisconsin 54601
(608) 784-3419

PAMPERS (disposable diapers)
  See Procter & Gamble Company

PAN-ALASKA FISHERIES, INC.
Post Office Box 647
Monroe, Washington 98272
Ronald R. Jensen, Chairman &
  President
(206) 743-1176

PAN AMERICAN CIGAR COMPANY
River and First Streets
Hoboken, New Jersey 07030
(201) 792-3838

PAN-AMERICAN LABORATORIES,
  INC.
2347 Fillmore Avenue
New Orleans, Louisiana 70122
(504) 288-0646

PAN AMERICAN SEAFOOD INC.
525 Northern Boulevard
Great Neck, New York 11020

PAN AMERICAN TRADE
  DEVELOPMENT CORPORATION
2 Park Avenue
New York, New York 10016
(212) 481-1800

PAN AMERICAN WORLD AIRWAYS
PanAm Building
New York, New York 10017
William T. Seawell, President
(212) 973-7700
  See also Inter-Continental Hotels

PAN CAKE (makeup)
  See Max Factor & Company

PAN MAGIC (frying-pan coating)
  See AMF Inc.

PAN-O-VISION (electronics)
  See Hoffman Electronics
  Corporation

PAN-PACIFIC FISHERIES
(Division of C.H.B. Foods Inc.)
338 Connery Street
Terminal Island, California 90731
(213) 833-3564

PAN-PACK FOODS
4021 South Sepulveda
Culver City, California 90230

PAN READY (frozen food products)
  See Meal Time Foods, Inc.

PAN REDI (seafood)
  See Trade Winds Company

PAN SHIELD (liquid-silicone pan
coating)
  See Dow Corning Corporation

PAN STIK (makeup)
  See Max Factor & Company

PANASONIC (radios, televisions,
appliances, etc.)
  See Matsushita Electric
  Corporation of America

PANASONIC BUSINESS MACHINES
200 Park Avenue
New York, New York 10017
Akira Harada, President
(212) 973-5700

PANATELA (men's sportswear)
  See Levi Strauss & Company

PANATION TRADE COMPANY
  INC.
160 Fifth Avenue
New York, New York 10010
(212) 691-3344

PANCO LTD.
410 West Coast Highway
Newport Beach, California 92660

PANDA PRINTS, INC.
41 West 25th Street
New York, New York 10010
(212) 741-0772

PANDORA CANNING COMPANY
Sherman Street
Pandora, Ohio 45877
(419) 384-3213

PANDORA PRODUCTIONS INC.
1117 Vicksburg Lane
Wayzata, Minnesota 55391

PANEF MANUFACTURING
  COMPANY INC.
5700 West Douglas Avenue
Milwaukee, Wisconsin 53218
(414) 464-9150

PANEL BRIGHT (panelling and
wood cleaner)
  See Herbert Stanley Company

Companies and Trade Names

PANEL CARE (cleaner/polish for wood paneling)
See Glamour Care Inc.

PANEL GLO (furniture polish)
See Golden Star Polish Manufacturing Company Inc.

PANELGLAS (fiberglas)
See Johns-Manville Fiber Glass, Inc.

PANELGROOVE (building material)
See Masonite Corporation

PANELOC CORPORATION, THE
(Subsidiary of Penn Engineering & Manufacturing Corporation)
Front and Main Streets
Collinsville, Connecticut 06022
(203) 693-8363

PANELTRAC (drapery hardware)
See Kirsch Company

PANFREDI INC.
56 Bowne Avenue
Freehold, New Jersey 07728

PANGBURN COMPANY, INC.
(Subsidiary of Riviana Foods, Inc.)
1900 S.E. Loop 820
Fort Worth, Texas 76101
Frank W. Creager, President
(817) 293-4330

PANIPLUS COMPANY, THE
3406 East 17th Street
Kansas City, Missouri 64127
(816) 483-8600

PANKORA (underwear)
See Chic Lingerie Company, Inc.

PANNETT PRODUCTS, INC.
Box 723
Orleans, Massachusetts 02653

PANNI (potato mix)
See Richter Brothers, Inc.

PANORAMA (shoes)
See International Shoe Company

PANRAY
(Division of Ormont Drug & Chemical Company, Inc.)
520 South Dean Street
Englewood, New Jersey 07631
(201) 567-0820

PANSY ELLEN PRODUCTS INC.
3363 Edward Avenue
Santa Clara, California 95050
(408) 984-3788

PANTALONES (sportswear)
See American Sportsman Manufacturing Company, Inc.

PANTASOTE COMPANY
Post Office Box 1800
Greenwich, Connecticut 06830
Henry W. Wyman, President
(203) 661-0400

PANTATO (food products)
See Douglas Food Corporation

PANTENE COMPANY, THE
(Division of Hoffmann-LaRoche, Inc.)
340 Kingsland Street
Nutley, New Jersey 07110

PANTER COMPANY INC.
12605 Greiner Avenue
Detroit, Michigan 48205
(313) 371-4570

PANTHEON BOOKS
(Division of Random House Inc.)
201 East 50th
New York, New York 10022
(212) 751-2600

PANTHER (lawn and garden supplies)
See Allison-Erwin Company

PANTHER (men's and boys' wear)
See Oxford Industries Inc.

PANTINO (sportswear)
See Maidenform Inc.

PANTRY PRIDE (groceries)
See Robb-Ross Corporation

PANTRY PRIDE SUPERMARKETS
See Food Fair Stores, Inc.

PANTS KING (menswear)
See J. Schoeneman Inc.

PANTSMAKER, INC.
1407 Broadway
New York, New York 10018
Jules Rosen, President
(212) 279-4305

PANTSVILLE PA (sportswear)
See Mister Pants Inc.

PANTYHOSE CORPORATION OF AMERICA
2 Penn Plaza
New York, New York 10001
Nicholas M. Brecher, President
(212) 565-2518

PANZER (lawn and garden tractors)
See Virginia Metalcrafters, Inc.

PAOLI CHAIR COMPANY
Post Office Box 30
Paoli, Indiana 47454
Sherman Heazlitt, President
(812) 723-2791

PAPA's PRIDE (frozen vegetables)
See Crosetti Frozen Foods Inc.

Companies and Trade Names

PAPAYA FOOD PRODUCTS
COMPANY
Post Office Box 74
Redlands, California 92373

PAPCO (seafood)
See Point Adams Packing
Company

PAPEC MACHINE COMPANY
4656 Hamlin Street
Shortsville, New York 14548
(315) 289-3411

PAPEL INTERNATIONAL, PHIL
8623 South Mettler Street
Los Angeles, California 90003
(213) 750-6789

PAPER ART COMPANY, INC.
3500 North Arlington Avenue
Indianapolis, Indiana 46218
William E. Atcheson, President and
Treasurer
(317) 546-1581

PAPER CORPORATION OF
UNITED STATES
488 Madison Avenue
New York, New York 10022
(212) 826-3535

PAPER MANUFACTURES COMPANY
9800 Bustleton Avenue
Philadelphia, Pennsylvania 19115
D.F. O'Neill, President
(215) 673-4500

PAPER MATE COMPANY
(Division of The Gillette Company)
Prudential Tower Building
Boston, Massachusetts 02199
Allan R. Nagle, President
(617) 421-7000

PAPER NOVELTY
MANUFACTURING COMPANY
Post Office Box 1051
166 Henry Street
Stamford, Connecticut 06904
Burt Lee, President
(203) 325-2671

PAPER PRODUCTS
(Division of 3M Company)
3M Center
Saint Paul, Minnesota 55101
(612) 733-1110

PAPER PRODUCTS, INC.
18554 South Susana Road
Compton, California 90221
(213) 774-6250

PAPER SALES CORPORATION
342 Madison Avenue
New York, New York 10017
(212) 661-3770

PAPER SERVICE COMPANY, INC.
Hinsdale, New Hampshire 03451

PAPERCRAFT CORPORATION, THE
Papercraft Park
Pittsburgh, Pennsylvania 15238
Joseph M. Katz, President
(412) 362-8000
See also Lepage's Inc.

PAPERCRAFT INC. (cards, invitations, etc.)
3710 North Richards Street
Milwaukee, Wisconsin 53212

PAPERLYNEN COMPANY, THE
(Subsidiary of White Castle System Inc.)
Post Office Box 1089
Columbus, Ohio 43216

PAPOOSE (portable vacuum cleaners)
See Advance Floor Machine
Company

PAPOOSER (back carriers for infants)
See Century Products Inc.

PAPP COMPANY INC., SIDNEY R.
29 Temple Place
Boston, Massachusetts 02111
(617) 542-4770

PAPPAS & COMPANY, CLEMENT
East Maple Avenue
Cedarville, New Jersey 08311
Dean C. Papas, President and Sales
Manager
(609) 447-3601

PAPYRUS COMPANY
50 Market Street
Kenilworth, New Jersey 07033
(201) 245-1288

PAQUET & COMPANY, INC., M.
17 Battery Place
New York, New York 10004
(212) 269-7281

PAR (foods)
See Clements Foods Company

PAR-FORM ORIGINALS
708 Broadway
New York, New York 10003
Samuel Weisberger, President,
Treasurer and Purchasing Agent
(212) 677-0330

PAR-T-KREME (dehydrated coffee
and whipping cream)
See M & R Food Service
Company

PAR-T-PAK (beverages)
See Royal Crown Cola Company

PAR-T-PAK (frozen shrimp)
See Shell-Tex Fisheries

Companies and Trade Names

PARA INDUSTRIES, INC.
54 Pennsylvania Avenue
Kearny, New Jersey 07032

PARA/METRIC (fishing rods)
See Berkley & Company Inc.

PARA STONE TEX MASONRY
COATING (paint)
See Devoe & Raynolds Company

PARA-TONE, INC.
150 Fencl Lane
Hillside, Illinois 60162
(312) 449-5500

PARA-WELD (epoxy adhesive)
See Parawax Company

PARABOLA (folding tables)
See Cal-Dak Industries Inc.

PARADE (grocery products)
See Red & White International

PARADISE (seafood)
See Shelter Island Oyster
Company Inc.

PARADISE (shoes)
See Brauer Brothers Shoe Company

PARADISE FRUIT COMPANY
1200 West Haines Street
Plant City, Florida 33566
Melvin S. Gordon, President
(813) 752-1155

PARADISO (food products)
See Sun Garden Packing Company

PARADOX (skin-care products)
See DuBarry

PARAEUSAL COMPANY, THE
2420 Glenwood Avenue
Youngstown, Ohio 44511

PARAFLEX (muscle relaxant)
See McNeil Laboratories, Inc.

PARAGON DESIGN INC.
Post Office Box 2188
Waynesboro, Virginia 22980
(703) 942-5116

PARAGON ELECTRIC COMPANY
INC.
See AMF/Paragon Electric
Company Inc.

PARAGON GEARS INC.
20 Cushman Street
Taunton, Massachusetts 02780
Lesie D. Johnson, President and
General Manager
(617) 822-5347

PARAGON NEEDLECRAFT
(Division of National Paragon
Corporation)
385 Fifth Avenue
New York, New York 10016
(212) 683-8000

PARAGON PAINT & VARNISH
CORPORATION
5-49 46th Avenue
Long Island City, New York 11101
George S. Rattner, President
(212) 719-7420

PARAMED INC.
85 Godwin Avenue
Midland Park, New Jersey 07432

PARAMOUNT (cocktail mix)
See United Citrus Products
Corporation

PARAMOUNT (drawing pencils and leads)
See Alvin & Company Inc.

PARAMOUNT (food products)
See Fruitcrest Corporation

PARAMOUNT (frozen seafoods)
See McCallum Sales Ltd.

PARAMOUNT BRUSH COMPANY
2 West Burnside Avenue
Bronx, New York 10453
(212) 584-5800

PARAMOUNT CANDY COMPANY
502 16th Avenue North
Clinton, Iowa 52732

PARAMOUNT CITRUS
ASSOCIATION
11030 Stranwood
San Fernando, California 91341

PARAMOUNT DISTILLERS, INC.
3116 Berea Road
Cleveland, Ohio 44111
R.G. Gottesman, President
(216) 671-6300

PARAMOUNT FOODS, INC.
(Division of Hirsch Brothers &
Company, Inc.)
Picadilly Station
Louisville, Kentucky 41215
Lewis A. Hirsch, President
(502) 969-9363

PARAMOUNT LINE INC., THE
400 Pine Street
Pawtucket, Rhode Island 02863
James Winston, President
(401) 726-0800

PARAMOUNT PHOTO SERVICE,
INC.
72 Honeck
Englewood, New Jersey 07631

PARAMOUNT PICTURES
CORPORATION
(Division of Gulf & Western
Industries, Inc.)
1 Gulf and Western Plaza
New York, New York 10023
Barry Diller, Chairman of the Board
(212) 333-4128

Companies and Trade Names

PARAMOUNT PRODUCE, INC.
97 N.E. Produce Center
Chelsea, Massachusetts 02150

PARAMOUNT RECORDS
(Division of Paramount Pictures, Corporation)
6430 Sunset Boulevard
Hollywood, California 90028
Arnold D. Burk, President
(213) 462-3141

PARAMOUNT WIRE PRODUCTS
1035 Westminster Avenue
Alhambra, California 91803
(213) 570-1601
See also Easy-Way Manufacturing Company

PARAPHERNALIA, INC.
(Subsidiary of Puritan Fashions Corporation)
1250 Broadway
New York, New York 10001
David Strauss, President
(212) 279-5158
See also Young Sportswear, Inc., Diane

PARASEAL (canning wax)
See W. & F. Manufacturing Company, Inc.

PARAWAX COMPANY
1200 Third.
Council Bluffs, Iowa 51501
(712) 328-3028

PARCO COMPOUND (rustproofing process)
See Parker Company

PARDEE COMPANY, THE
261 Madison Avenue
New York, New York 10016
(212) 683-9575

PARENT'S MAGAZINE ENTERPRISES, INC.
52 Vanderbilt Avenue
New York, New York 10017
George J. Hecht, Chairman of the Board
(212) 685-4400

PARFAIT (sauces and condiments)
See H.E. Whitaker Company, Inc.

PARFUM LORLE, INC.
15302 Kercheval Avenue
Grosse Pointe Park, Michigan 48230

PARFUMS BLANCHARD (colognes, perfumes, bath oil, etc.)
See Del Laboratories, Inc.

PARFUMS CORDAY
See Max Factor & Company

PARFUMS DUVELLE, INC.
Box 20125
10825 N.E. Skidmore Street
Portland, Oregon 97220
(503) 254-1442

PARFUMS GIVENCHY INC.
680 Fifth Avenue
New York, New York 10019
(212) 759-0820

PARFUMS HERMES
745 Fifth Avenue
New York, New York 10022
(212) 759-7585

PARFUMS LE GALION, INC.
730 Fifth Avenue
New York, New York 10019
Edward M. Lane, President
(212) 942-2820

PARFUMS ROCHAS, INC.
730 Fifth Avenue
New York, New York 10019
Howard S. Zagor, President
(212) 757-5044

PARFUMS SCHIAPARELLI, INC.
(Division of Del Laboratories)
565 Broad Hollow Road
Farmingdale, New York 11735
Dan Wassong, President
(212) 688-5572

PARFUMS WORTH CORPORATION
5 East 57th Street
New York, New York 10022
(212) 752-4150

PARGO INC.
4300 Raleigh Street
Charlotte, North Carolina 28803
(704) 596-6550

PARIS (sports apparel)
See Gondola Internationale Inc.

PARIS ACCESSORIES FOR MEN
(Division of Kayser-Roth Corporation)
2150 Frontage Road
Des Plaines, Illinois 60018
Walter Stein, President
(312) 296-1111

PARIS-AMERICAN LABORATORIES
1158 Broadway
Seattle, Washington 98122
(206) 323-7503

PARIS BOAT COMPANY
See Roughwater Boats Inc.

PARIS FASHIONS (shoes)
See Brown Group Inc.

PARIS LIGHTING COMPANY, INC.
136 Bowery
New York, New York 10013
(212) 226-7420

PARIS PRESENTS, LTD.
1253 South Michigan Avenue
Chicago, Illinois 60605
(312) 922-6766

Companies and Trade Names

PARISAC (handbags)
See Loriet Fashions Inc.

PARISIAN MAID LINGERIE COMPANY
45 East 30th Street
New York, New York 10016
(212) 679-8236

PARISIAN PRINTS INC.
7 West 30th Street
New York, New York 10001
(212) 524-4200

PARISIEN (cigars)
See Ibis Export Import Company

PARISTYLE FASHIONS ENTERPRISES LTD.
33 East 33rd Street
New York, New York 10016
(212) 683-1760

PARK-ADAMS, INC.
Box 589
Plainfield, New Jersey 07061

PARK & TILFORD DISTILLERS COMPANY
Aladdin, Pennsylvania 15682

PARK AVENUE FOUNDATIONS, INC.
Tyronza, Arkansas 72386

PARK AVENUE IMPORTS
(Division of Joseph E. Seagram & Sons, Inc.)
375 Park Avenue
New York, New York 10022
Eugene Feen, President
(212) 572-7000

PARK AVENUE, INC.
Post Office Box 487
Cordova, Tennessee 38018

PARK, BENZIGER & COMPANY, INC.
674 White Plains Road
Scarsdale, New York 10583
J.B. Benziger, President
(914) 472-3202

PARK CHEMICAL COMPANY
8074 Military
Detroit, Michigan 48204
R.T. Webster, President
(313) 895-7215

PARK CORPORATION, THE
511 Lake Zurich Road
Barrington, Illinois 60010

PARK EDGE FOOD DISTRIBUTORS, INC.
2050 Elmwood Avenue
Buffalo, New York 14207
(716) 874-5380

PARK HALL (canned foods)
See G.L. Webster Company

PARK INC., PHILIP R.
5800 Perkins Road
Oxnard, California 93030
Claud F. Sympson, President
(805) 488-3561

PARK INDUSTRIES, INC.
1200 Park Avenue
Murfreesboro, Tennessee 37130
(615) 896-0600

PARK LANE (whiskey)
See James Barclay & Company, Ltd.

PARK PLASTICS COMPANY
104 East Elizabeth Avenue
Linden, New Jersey 07036
Arthur Lange, President
(201) 486-9300

PARK PLAZA PHARMACEUTICALS, INC.
2200 East 31st Street
Kansas City, Missouri 64109
(816) 921-3000

PARK SHERMAN
(Division of Ketcham & McDougall Inc.)
465 Eagle Rock Avenue
Roseland, New Jersey 07068
(201) 226-6060

PARKAY (margarine)
See Kraft Foods

PARKDALE (processed foods)
See Diamond Fruit Growers, Inc.

PARKE, DAVIS & COMPANY
(Subsidiary of Warner-Lambert Company)
Post Office Box 118
Joseph Campau at the River
Detroit, Michigan 48232
Donald E. O'Neill, President
(313) 567-5300

PARKE, DAVIS & COMPANY
Medical-Surgical Products Division
Post Office Box 368
Greenwood, South Carolina 29646

PARKELP (health foods)
See Philip R. Park, Inc.

PARKER BROTHERS
(Subsidiary of General Mills, Inc.)
190 Bridge Street
Salem, Massachusetts 01970
Edward P. Parker, President
(617) 745-6600

PARKER CANNING COMPANY, W.A.
Box 100
Thaxton, Virginia 24174

Companies and Trade Names

PARKER COMPANY, C.W.
1415 Second Avenue
Des Moines, Iowa 50314
(515) 243-6610

PARKER COMPANY, D.L.
Box 176
Brighton, Michigan 48116

PARKER HERBEX CORPORATION
1 West 37th Street
New York, New York 10018
(212) 244-5975

PARKER HOUSE (coffee)
See White Coffee Corporation

PARKER INDUSTRIES INC.
Box 465
Bohemia, New York 11716
(516) 981-7600

PARKER INDUSTRUES, LEW
Box 7643A
Birmingham, Alabama 35223

PARKER INTERIOR PLANTSCAPE
1325 Terrill Road
Scotch Plains, New Jersey 07076

PARKER LABORATORIES, INC.
103 Elm Street
Newark, New Jersey 07105
(201) 375-2200

PARKER PEN COMPANY, THE
219 East Court Street
Janesville, Wisconsin 53545
George Parker, President
(608) 754-7711

PARKER PRODUCTS INC.
91 Washington Street
Holliston, Massachusetts 01746

PARKER RIVER MARINE INC.
Route One A
Newbury, Massachusetts 01950

PARKER TRADING CORPORATION, THE
25 Victory Boulevard
New York, New York 10004
(212) 425-7606

PARKERHOUSE (margarine)
See Grant Products Ltd.

PARKIN CHEMICAL COMPANY
325 32nd Street
Pittsburgh, Pennsylvania 15201
(412) 566-2150

PARKLAND OF DALLAS, INC.
429 Second Avenue
Dallas, Texas 75226
Robert R. Michlin, President
(214) 823-4163

PARKLANE (latex wall paint)
See Bondex International

PARKMONT PRODUCTS CORPORATION
8000 Cooper Avenue
Building 10
Glendale, New York 11227

PARKS PRODUCTS, INC.
7421 Woodrow Wilson Drive
Hollywood, California 90046
Robert M. Parks, President
(213) 876-5454

PARKS SAUSAGE COMPANY
501 West Hamburg Street
Baltimore, Maryland 21230
Henry G. Parks, Jr., President
(301) 727-2212

PARKSIDE (leather goods)
See Hagerstown Leather Goods Company, Inc.

PARKSMITH
(Division of Universal Marion Corporation)
120 East 23rd Street
New York, New York 10010
(212) 674-7350

PARKVIEW-GEM INC.
6000 Manchester Trafficway Terrace
Kansas City, Missouri 64130
Willard A. Small, President
(816) 363-1800

PARKWAY (automobile accessories)
See Star-Lite Industries

PARKWAY (lawn and garden supplies)
See Midland Cooperatives Inc.

PARKWAY (processed foods)
See Del Mar Food Products Corporation

PARKWAY DISTRIBUTORS, INC.
9 Mear Road
Holbrook, Massachusetts 02343
Leonard Silverman, President
(617) 963-8650

PARKWAY ELECTRONICS
Pierce Hill Road
Vestal, New York 13850

PARKWOOD HOMES, INC.
County Road Eight
Bristol, Indiana 46507
Raymond Bassett, President
(219) 848-4421

PARKWOOD LAMINATES INC.
Box 799
Industrial Park
Lowell, Massachusetts 01851
Frank O'Keefe, Chairman
(617) 459-6161

Companies and Trade Names

PARLAM
(Division of Ormont Drug & Chemical
  Chemical Company, Inc.)
520 South Dean Street
Englewood, New Jersey 07631

PARLIAMENT (cigarettes)
  See Philip Morris, Inc.

PARMA INTERNATIONAL
4651 West 130 Street
Cleveland, Ohio 44135
(216) 252-4414

PARMAN KENDALL CORPORATION
(Subsidiary of Kendall Foods
  Corporation)
Box 458
Goulds, Florida 33170

PARMED PHARMACEUTICALS, INC.
2511 Pine Avenue
Niagara Falls, New York 14301
(716) 284-5666

PARMET COMPANY, INC.,
  JOSEPH
Bridge Street Extension
Catasauqua, Pennsylvania 18032
(215) 264-0533

PARODI CIGAR CORPORATION
1015 North Main Avenue
Scranton, Pennsylvania 18504
Robert J. Keating, President
(717) 344-8566

PARODI CIGAR CORPORATION
H.E. Snyder Division
1015 North Main Avenue
Scranton, Pennsylvania 18504
Robert J. Keating, President
(717) 344-8566

PARR PRODUCTS
825 North Illinois Street
Indianapolis, Indiana 46204
(317) 636-1576

PARRIS MANUFACTURING
  COMPANY
Savannah, Tennessee 38372

PARROTT & COMPANY
215 Market Street
San Francisco, California 94105
J.M. Menzies, President
(415) 495-4900

PARSONS CHEMICAL WORKS
Box 146
Grand Ledge, Michigan 48837

PARSONS' (household products)
  See Armour-Dial, Inc.

PARSONS PAPER
(Division of NVC Company)
84 Sargeant Street
Holyoke, Massachusetts 01040
Edward P. Bagg, III, Division
  Manager
(413) 532-3222

PARTAGLOSS (varnish)
  See McDougall-Butler (Division
    of Bisonite Company, Inc.)

PARTAKE (grocery products)
  See Plee-zing, Inc.

PARTHENON (carpeting)
  See Sequoyah Industries Inc.

PARTI-ADE (food-serving items)
  See Charm House of Gifts

PARTI-BAR (portable bar)
  See Crest Specialty, Inc.

PARTNER (menswear)
  See Barney Sampson Company,
    Ltd.

PARTNER'S CHOICE (whiskey)
  See National Distillers &
    Chemical Company

PARTOUT INTERNATIONAL
  CORPORATION
525 Seventh Avenue
New York, New York 10018
(212) 221-7272

PARTRIDGE (meat products)
  See H.H. Meyer Packing
    Company

PARTY CLUB (snacks and soft
drinks)
  See P & C Food Markets, Inc.

PARTY CURL (home permanent)
  See Procter & Gamble Company

PARTY PACK (glass products)
  See Dominion Glass Company,
    Ltd.

PARTY PACKAGE (stainless cutlery
and serving sets)
  See Lifetime Cutlery Corporation

PARTY-PALETTE (cosmetics)
  See Disc Jockey, Inc.

PARTY PLATTER (warming tray)
  See Kaz Inc.

PARTY PUNCH (wine-base punch
mix)
  See Mogen David Wine
    Corporation

PARTY TIME MANUFACTURING
  COMPANY
421 Parsonage Street
Hughestown, Pennsylvania 18640

PARTY TYME PRODUCTS, INC.
919 Third Avenue
New York, New York 10022
(212) 572-7000

Companies and Trade Names

PARUCA PRODUCTS, INC.
108 Green Street
Brooklyn, New York 11222
(212) 389-0302

PAS (crab meat, frogs' legs, swordfish, halibut)
See Pan American Seafood Inc.

PASADENA RESEARCH LABORATORY
2107 East Villa Street
Pasadena, California 91107
(213) 681-6206

PASCAL COMPANY
2229 N.E. Northrup Way
Bellevue, Washington 98004
(206) 827-4694

PASCHALL LABORATORIES INC.
4116 Rainier Avenue South
Seattle, Washington 98118
(206) 723-7070

PASCO (frozen concentrated juices)
See Lykes Pasco Packing Company

PASCO (imported foods)
See Pastene & Company, Inc.

PASCO MARINE SUPPLY INC.
4425 Fernlee
Royal Oak, Michigan 48073

PASHA (liqueur)
See Park Avenue Imports

PASLODE COMPANY
(Division of Signode Corporation)
8080 McCormick Boulevard
Skokie, Illinois 60076
(312) 583-4500

PASMANTIER COMPANY
224 Fifth Avenue
New York, New York 10001
(212) 679-5454

PASS & SEYMOUR, INC.
50 Boyd Avenue
Syracuse, New York 13209
D.A.A. Ridings, President
(315) 468-6211

PASSPORT (Scotch)
See Calvert Distillers Company

PASTEL LOOK (skin-care products)
See John H. Breck, Inc.

PASTENE & COMPANY INC.
152 Franklin Street
New York, New York 10013
(212) 925-5338

PASTENE WINE & SPIRITS COMPANY INC.
(Subsidiary of Pastene & Company Inc.)
12 First Avenue
Somerville, Massachusetts 02143
(617) 628-5100

PASTORELLI FOOD PRODUCTS INC.
164 North Sangamon
Chicago, Illinois 60607
(312) 666-2041

PASTRY KING (cookies and pastries, flour)
See Acme-Evans Company

PASTURGRO (plant food)
See Swift & Company

PAT & LYN CANDIES
See Standard Specialty Company

PAT FASHIONS INDUSTRIES, INC.
1370 Broadway
New York, New York 10018
Sol Cooper, President
(212) 695-3510

PAT PRINTS INC.
Box 315B
Springfield, Missouri 65801

PAT PRODUCTS
(Division of Ketcham & McDougall Inc.)
465 Eagle Rock Avenue
Roseland, New Jersey 07068

PATAKY, MADAME OLGA
3922 Spruce Street
Philadelphia, Pennsylvania 19104
(215) 386-5985

PATCH (repair material)
See Devcon Corporation

PATCHIT (paints and paint sundries)
See E. Rabinowe & Company

PATCRAFT (carpeting)
See Patcraft Mills Inc.

PATCRAFT MILLS INC.
Post Office Box 1087
Dalton, Georgia 30720
I.V. Chandler, President and Treasurer
(404) 278-2134

PATEK PHILIPPE (watches)
See Henri Stern Watch Agency, Inc.

PATENT CEREALS SALES CORPORATION
Box 571
Danville, Illinois 61832

PATENT NOVELTY COMPANY
Fulton, Illinois 61252

PATENTED PLASTICS INC.
4117 Cloud Avenue
Cleveland, Ohio 44113
(216) 961-6655

Companies and Trade Names

PATENTS DEVELOPMENT QUORUM
9649 Girard Avenue South
Minneapolis, Minnesota 55431
(612) 881-0845

PATERNO IMPORTS, LTD.
2701 South Western Avenue
Chicago, Illinois 60608
Anthony Terlato, President
(312) 247-8000

PATERSON PARCHMENT PAPER
COMPANY
Bristol, Pennsylvania 19007
(215) 945-2200

PATHCOM INC.
24049 South Frampton
Harbor City, California 90710
(213) 325-1290

PATHFINDER (tires)
See Goodyear Tire & Rubber
Company, Inc.

PATHMARK
(Division of Supermarkets General
Corporation)
301 Blair Street
Woodbridge, New Jersey 07095
John O. Whitney, President
(201) 636-2400

PATINO (shoes)
See Don Gustin Shoe Company

PATIO (Mexican foods)
See RJR Foods Inc.

PATIO CHEF (hardwood briquet and
lump charcoal)
See Standard Milling Company

PATON, INC., JOHN
630 Fifth Avenue
New York, New York 10020
(212) 757-6717

PATOU INC., JEAN
(Subsidiary of Borden Inc.)
680 Fifth Avenue
New York, New York 10019
(212) 581-1800

PATRICE UNLTD.
(Division of Cottage Crafts)
Hillside Road
Chester, New Jersey 07930

PATRICIAN (guitars)
See Harmony Company

PATRICIAN FURNITURE COMPANY
1209 Sherman Road
High Point, North Carolina 27260

PATRICIAN HOUSE (perfume,
colognes)
See Tamak Inc.

PATRICIAN PRODUCTS
483 East 99th
Brooklyn, New York 11236
(212) 272-6640

PATRICK CUDAHY, INC.
(Subsidiary of Bluebird Brands, Inc.)
Post Office Box 217
Bernard and Kignan Avenues
Cudahy, Wisconsin 53110
Fred W. Trenkle, President
(414) 744-2000

PATRIOT (mobile homes)
See Marshfield Homes

PATRON TRANSMISSION EXPORT
CORPORATION
129 Grand Street
New York, New York 10013
(212) 226-1144

PATTEN SEED COMPANY
Lakeland, Georgia 31635

PATTERSON (candy products)
See Pet Milk Canada, Ltd.

PATTERSON FROZEN FOODS, INC.
100 West Las Palmas Avenue
Patterson, California 95363
Mario Ielmini, Chairman of the
Board
(209) 892-2611

PATTERSON LABORATORIES, INC.
11930 Pleasant
Detroit, Michigan 48217
(313) 843-4500

PATTERSON PACKING COMPANY
Post Office Box 669
Sanford, North Carolina 27330
O.F. Patterson, Jr., Chairman and
President
(919) 775-5639

PATTERSON SALES COMPANY
Post Office Box 1623
El Paso, Texas 79949

PATTI JEAN (frozen foods)
See Tyson Foods Inc.

PATTI PETITE (dresses)
See Korell Company

PATTON IMPORTS, LTD.
979 Third Avenue
New York, New York 10022
(212) 355-0122

PAUL & COMPANY INC.,
EDWARD P.
525 South Avenue
Plainfield, New Jersey 07060

PAUL & STEIN BROTHERS INC.,
F.H.
5 East 26th Street
New York, New York 10010
(212) 684-6370

PAUL DURAND (saxophones, flutes,
clarinets, picolos)
See Maxwell Meyers Inc.

Companies and Trade Names

PAUL JARMAN (clarinets and other band instruments)
See Southland Musical Merchandise Corporation

PAUL JONES (whiskey)
See Frankfort Distillers Corporation

PAUL-MARSHALL PRODUCTS INC.
1931 Vista Bella Way
Compton, California 90220

PAUL MASSON (wines)
See Browne Vintners Company

PAUL PRODUCTS COMPANY
1204 49th Avenue
Oakland, California 94601

PAUL-REED, INC.
Charlevoix, Michigan 49720

PAUL REUNE (clarinets and flutes)
See Maurice Lipsky Music Company Inc.

PAUL REVERE LIFE INSURANCE COMPANY
18 Chestnut Street
Worcester, Massachusetts 01608
George L. Hogeman, President
(617) 799-4441

PAULA (canned vegetables)
See Girard Inc.

PAULA COMPANY, C.M.
7773 School Road
Cincinnati, Ohio 45242
(513) 791-8105

PAULANN IMPORTS
1174 Industrial Street
Oxnard, California 93030

PAULEN CRYSTAL COMPANY
36-38 White Street
New York, New York 10013
(212) 226-1818

PAULIN PRODUCTS COMPANY
30520 Lakeland Boulevard
Willowick, Ohio 44094
(216) 944-9200

PAULINE GORDON ORIGINALS
See Mardi-Bra Creations Corporation

PAULING'S PHARMACAL COMPANY, INC.
26 Englewood Terrace
Forty Fort, Pennsylvania 18704

PAULMAC PRODUCTS INC.
3111 McFarland Road
Tampa, Florida 33618

PAULUX (glassware, ceramics, wrought-iron and marble chandeliers, lamps, giftware)
See Edward P. Paul & Company Inc.

PAV-LAB, INC.
4701 West 54th Street
Chicago, Illinois 60632
(312) 735-1800

PAVEY ENVELOPE & TAG COMPANY
25 Linden Avenue East
Jersey City, New Jersey 07305
(201) 434-2100

PAVILION (furniture)
See Ficks Reed Company

PAW PAW GRAPE JUICE COMPANY
(Affiliation of Warner Vineyards)
706 South Kalamazoo
Paw Paw, Michigan 49079
See also Michigan Wineries

PAX COMPANY
580 West 13th South
Salt Lake City, Utah 84115
(801) 973-2800

PAX PRODUCTS INC.
100 Water Street
Brooklyn, New York 11201
(212) 875-6301

PAXSON MANUFACTURING COMPANY
State Road above Grant Avenue
Philadelphia, Pennsylvania 19114
(215) 639-0404

PAXTON (cigarettes)
See Philip Morris, Inc.

PAXTON & SONS, INC., F.H.
Box 729
Evanston, Illinois 60204

PAXTON ENTERPRISES
308 Fifth Street
Palacios, Texas 77465

PAY DAY (canned foods)
See Klauber Wangenheim Company

PAY LESS DRUG STORES
8000 Edgewater Drive
Oakland, California 94621
William L. Gherra, Chairman of the Board
(415) 635-9600

PAY LESS DRUG STORES NORTHWEST, INC.
234 N.W. Fifth Avenue
Portland, Oregon 97209
Edward B. Hart, President
(503) 224-8750

PAY LO (canned goods)
See J.G. Pieri Company, Inc.

Companies and Trade Names

PAY'N SAVE CORPORATION
1511 Sixth Avenue
Seattle, Washington 98101
M. Lamont Bean, President
(206) 447-6000

PAYNE COMPANY
(Division of Carrier Corporation)
855 Anaheim-Puente Road
City of Industry, California 91749
William C. Egan, President
(213) 964-1211

PAYNE PUBLISHERS, INC.
2800 Juniper Street
Fairfax, Virginia 22030

PEABODY
802 West Fourth Street
North Manchester, Indiana 46962

PEABODY COAL COMPANY
301 North Memorial Drive
Saint Louis, Missouri 63102
E.R. Phelps, President and Chief Executive Officer
(314) 342-3400

PEACOCK CANNING COMPANY, R.J.
Box Ten
Lubec, Maine 04652

PEACOCK'S (relishes and sauces)
See Howard Food Companies, Inc.

PEANUT CITY (hams)
See Pruden Packing Company

PEANUT SPECIALTY COMPANY
400 West Superior Street
Chicago, Illinois 60610
(312) 787-9893

PEARCE-SIMPSON
(Division of Gladding Corporation)
4701 N.W. 77th Avenue
Miami, Florida 33166
J. Gerald Mayer, President
(305) 592-5550

PEARL (drum/cymbal sets, bongos, congas, castanets, tambourines, accessories, etc.)
See Chicago Musical Instrument Company

PEARL BREWING COMPANY
(Subsidiary of Southdown, Inc.)
312 Pearl Parkway
San Antonio, Texas 78215
E.L. Birdsong, President
(512) 226-0231

PEARL COFFEE & GROCERY COMPANY
675 South High
Akron, Ohio 44311

PEARL DROPS (tooth polish)
See Carter-Wallace, Inc.

PEARL GRANGE FRUIT EXCHANGE
Box 462
Benton Harbor, Michigan 49022

PEARL WASTE MATERIAL COMPANY
62 Greene Street
New York, New York 10012
(212) 431-5959

PEARL-WICK CORPORATION
27-50 First Street
Astoria, New York 11102
Darwin Sussberg, President
(212) 721-3000

PEARL'S QUALITY (canned and frozen foods)
See United Flav-R-Pac Growers, Inc.

PEARS (soap)
See Lever Brothers Company

PEARSON, BEN
(Division of Brunswick Corporation)
Post Office Box 270
Tulsa, Oklahoma 74101
Ralph F. Lafferty, President
(918) 836-5581

PEARSON CANDY COMPANY
(Subsidiary of ITT Continental Baking Company)
2140 West Seventh Street
Saint Paul, Minnesota 55116
James D. Penick, President
(612) 698-0356
See also White Candy Company Inc.

PEARSON CANDY COMPANY
(Division of W.R. Grace & Company)
10101 West Jefferson Boulevard
Culver City, California 90230

PEARSON HANDICRAFTS, HAZEL
4128 Temple City Boulevard
Rosemead, California 91770

PEARSON PRODUCTS
(Division of Schmid Laboratories)
Lackawanna Avenue
West Patterson, New Jersey 07424

PEARSON YACHTS
(Division of Grumman Allied Industries, Inc.)
West Shore Road
Portsmouth, Rhode Island 02871
William H. Shaw, General Manager
(401) 683-1000

PEASE COMPANY
900 Forest Avenue
Hamilton, Ohio 45015
James L. Pease, Jr., President
(513) 867-3333

Companies and Trade Names

PEAU SECHE
(Division of Balm Barr, Inc.)
246 Park Avenue
Bensenville, Illinois 60106

PEAVEY COMPANY
730 Second Avenue, South
Minneapolis, Minnesota 55401
Fredrick H. Corrigan, Chairman of
 the Board
(612) 333-0177

PEAVEY ELECTRONICS
 CORPORATION
611 Tenth Avenue
Meridian, Mississippi 39301
(601) 483-5365

PEAVEY PAPER MILLS, INC.
Warden Avenue East
Ladysmith, Wisconsin 54848
Leland J. Peterson, Chairman and
 President
(715) 532-5541

PEBBLEFORD (whiskey)
 See Schenley Industries, Inc.

PECAN DELUXE CANDY COMPANY
306 West Davis Street
Dallas, Texas 75208
(214) 942-3669

PECAN PRINCE CANDIES, INC.
Highway Number 290
East Waller, Texas 77484

PECHGLO (foundation garments,
lingerie)
 See Vanity Fair Mills, Inc.

PECK & PECK
521 Fifth Avenue
New York, New York 10017
Arnold Cooper, President
(212) 883-6300

PECK & STERBA
(Division of International
 Laboratories, Inc.)
18 Harvard Street
Rochester, New York 14607

PECK INC.
516 Lafayette Road
Saint Paul, Minnesota 55101

PECK, STOW & WILCOX
 COMPANY
(Division of Veeder Industries, Inc.)
217 Center Street
Southington, Connecticut 06489
S.T. Boornazian, President
(203) 628-9621

PECO MANUFACTURING INC.
4707 S.E. 17th Avenue
Portland, Oregon 97202
(503) 233-6401

PECORA CORPORATION
165 Wambold Road
Harleysville, Pennsylvania 19438

PED-I-RUB COMPANY
1700 Exchange
Oklahoma City, Oklahoma 73108

PEDI-BOOTS (shoes and shoe
materials)
 See Bristol Manufacturing
  Corporation

PEDI CANDLES, JUDYTH
200 Atlantic Avenue
Lynbrook, New York 11563

PEDIGREE (sports apparel)
 See Shakespeare Industries

PEDINOL PHARMACAL, INC.
295 Broadway
Bethpage, New York 11714

PEDRICK LABORATORIES
Post Office Box 306
Sand Springs, Oklahoma 74063
(918) 245-1345

PEDRO & SONS INC., CARL
501 North Robert Street
Saint Paul, Minnesota 55101

PEDRO DOMECQ (sherries)
 See Somerset Importers, Ltd.

PEDRO'S (rum)
 See Austin, Nichols & Company,
  Inc.

PEDS PRODUCTS INC.
Post Office Box 5407
3036 Durahart
Riverside, California 92507
(714) 686-3573

PEDWIN (shoes)
 See Brown Group, Inc.

PEE BEE (combs, key chains, key
cases, money clips, luggage tags,
pillboxes, eyeglass holders)
 See Perry Blackburne, Inc.

PEE-GEE (lamps and shades)
 See Philip J. Greenspan Inc.

PEEL & STICK (floor tile)
 See Flintkote Company, Flooring
  Products Division

PEER FOOD PRODUCTS COMPANY
1400 West 46th
Chicago, Illinois 60609
R.C. Buehler, President
(312) 927-1440

PEERLESS (food products)
 See Lodi Canning Company Inc.

Companies and Trade Names

PEERLESS
(Division of Dover Corporation)
Post Office Box 2015
1400 West Ormsby
Louisville, Kentucky 40401
H.L. Ruliffson, President
(502) 636-3711

PEERLESS CHEMICAL COMPANY, INC.
2775 Wilkens Avenue
Baltimore, Maryland 21223
(301) 566-6700

PEERLESS CONFECTION COMPANY
1246-1258 Schubert Avenue
Chicago, Illinois 60614
Robert Picken, Chairman and President
(312) 281-6100

PEERLESS
(Division of American Cement Corporation)
900 Executive Plaza
Detroit, Michigan 48226
(313) 961-6150

PEERLESS-IMPERIAL COMPANY INC.
594 Dean Street
Brooklyn, New York 11238
Walter Kretchmer, President
(212) 622-2606

PEERLESS IMPORTERS, INC.
16 Bridgewater Street
Brooklyn, New York 11222
A. Magliocco, President
(212) 389-7600

PEERLESS PLAYTHINGS COMPANY, INC.
80 Grove Street
Paterson, New Jersey 07503
Irving Hellman, President
(201) 279-4300

PEERLESS SPECIALTY COMPANY
2133 Broadway
Buffalo, New York 14212
(617) 895-1160

PEERLESS STEEL EQUIPMENT COMPANY
Unruh and Hasbrook Avenues
Philadelphia, Pennsylvania 19111
Anton J. Kuhn, Jr., President
(215) 745-0100

PEERLESS TELERAD INC.
37-15 61st Street
Woodside, New York 11377

PEET PACKING COMPANY
6320 State Street
Saginaw, Michigan 48603
Millis L. Peet, President
(517) 845-3021

PEG LEGS (meat products)
See Acme Packing Company

PEG-MAR ASSOCIATES INC.
1 North Orange Avenue
Orlando, Florida 32801

PEISER PRODUCTS COMPANY
1020 Hull Terrace
Evanston, Illinois 60202

PEL-FREEZ RABBIT MEAT, INC.
Rogers, Arkansas 72756

PELAHATCHIE POULTRY COMPANY
Pelahatchie, Mississippi 39145

PELCO INDUSTRIES INC.
Box 11285
Indianapolis, Indiana 46201
(317) 359-0901

PELICAN PRODUCTS COMPANY, INC.
248 McKibbin Street
Brooklyn, New York 11206
(212) 386-1602

PELICAN SALES COMPANY
653 N.E. Northlake Way
Seattle, Washington 98105
(206) 632-9000

PELLFORM (fertilizer)
See Borden, Inc.

PELLGUN (rifles and pistols)
See Crosman Arms Company, Inc.

PELLON CORPORATION
1120 Avenue of the Americans
New York, New York 10036
William M. Klothe, President
(212) 867-9110

PELOUZE SCALE COMPANY
1218 Chicago Avenue
Evanston Illinois 60202
Bob Fisher, President
(312) 328-8330

PEMBERVILLE (food products)
See Hirzel Canning Company

PEMBROOK (whiskey)
See American Distilling Company

PEMBROOKE LINGERIE COMPANY
152 Madison Avenue
New York, New York 10016
(212) 684-7753

PEN ARGYL MILLING COMPANY, INC.
Pen Argyl, Pennsylvania 18072

PEN DEE INC.
3500 Elm Avenue
Portsmouth, Virginia 23704

PEN DOCTOR, THE
128 North Ninth Street
Reading, Pennsylvania 19601

PEN-JEL CORPORATION
2400 Nicholson Avenue
Kansas City, Missouri 64120
(816) 483-1700

PENALJO (women's shoes)
See Hamilton Shoe Company

Companies and Trade Names

PENATEN (baby products)
See Hilary Corporation

PENATHOL LABORATORIES
32370 Shrewsbury
Farmington, Michigan 48024

PENBROOK CONFECTIONS
Emaus and Wood Streets
Middletown, Pennsylvania 17057

PENCO PRODUCTS INC.
(Subsidiary of Alan Wood Steel Company)
Brower Avenue
Oaks, Pennsylvania 19456
Frank J. Spaniel, President
(215) 666-0500

PENDLETON TOOL INDUSTRIES, INC.
(Subsidiary of Ingersoll-Rand Company)
2600 East Nutwood Avenue
Fullerton, California 92631
R.F. Garvey, President
(714) 922-1800

PENDLETON WOOLEN MILLS
218 S.W. Jefferson
Portland, Oregon 97201
C.M. Bishop, Jr., President
(503) 226-4801

PENETRANT (automotive products and accessories)
See Siloo, Inc.

PENETRAY CORPORATION
See North American Philips Lighting Corporation

PENETRO (cough syrup, inhaler, nose drops, etc.)
See Plough Inc.

PENGAD COMPANIES INC.
Box 99
51-55 Oak Street
Bayonne, New Jersey 07002
(201) 436-5625

PENGO CORPORATION
950 Kifer Road
Sunnyvale, California 94086
John G. Benetti, President
(408) 739-8040

PENGUIN BOOKS INC.
72 Fifth Avenue
New York, New York 10011
(212) 924-8801

PENGUIN FROZEN FOODS INC.
540 Frontage Road
Northfield, Illinois 60093

PENGUIN INDUSTRIES, INC.
Post Office Box 97
Parkersburg, Pennsylvania 19365
(215) 384-6000
See also Hoppe, Frank A.

PENHURST PHARMACAL COMPANY
315 East Hunting Park Avenue
Philadelphia, Pennsylvania 19124
(215) 423-2200

PENICK & COMPANY, S.B
1050 Wall Street West
Lyndhurst, New Jersey 07071
J. Verde, President
(201) 935-6600

PENICK & FORD
920 First Street S.W.
Cedar Rapids, Iowa 52404
Paul E. Geiser, President
(319) 398-3700

PENINSULAR LIFE INSURANCE COMPANY
645 Riverside Drive
Jacksonville, Florida 32204
Jack H. Quaritas, President
(904) 358-6000

PENLEY BROTHERS
West Paris, Maine 04289

PENN AMOCO (oils)
See Amoco Oil Company

PENN BEAUTIES (canned foods)
See Avondale Industries, Inc.

PENN CANDY COMPANY
2300 Carpenter Street
Philadelphia, Pennsylvania 19146
(215) 985-9191

PENN CARD & PAPER COMPANY
3436 State Road
Cornwells Heights, Pennsylvania 19020
See also Datacom Supply Company

PENN CENTRAL TRANSPORTATION COMPANY
6 Penn Center Plaza
Philadelphia, Pennsylvania 19104
Jervis Langdon, Jr., President
(215) 594-1000

PENN-CHAMP
Post Office Box 191
Butler, Pennsylvania 16001

PENN CORPORATION
1 Palmer Square
Princeton, New Jersey 08540
Dana A. Hamel, Chairman of the Board
(609) 924-7957

PENN DAIRIES
1801 Hempstead Road
Lancaster, Pennsylvania 17604
J.F. Garber, Jr., President
(717) 394-5601

PENN DALE (groceries)
See Associated Wholesalers, Inc.

Companies and Trade Names

PENN-DALE KNITTING MILLS
148 Madison Avenue
New York, New York 10016
(212) 679-3360

PENN-DIXIE INDUSTRIES INC.
1345 Avenue of the Americas
New York, New York 10019
Jerome Castle, Chairman and
 President
(212) 687-5000

PENN ENGINEERING &
 MANUFACTURING COMPANY
Post Office Box 311
Doylestown, Pennsylvania 18901
K. Arent Swanstrom, Chairman and
 President
(215) 766-8853
 See also Paneloc, Corporation
 The

PENN FISHING TACKLE
 MANUFACTURING COMPANY
3028 West Hunting Park Avenue
Philadelphia, Pennsylvania 19132
(215) 229-9415

PENN FRUIT COMPANY, INC.
Grant and Bluegrass
Philadelphia, Pennsylvania 19115
Rezenol Duryea, President
(215) 673-3500

PENN MAID (food products)
 See Musselman

PENN MANOR (tomato catsup,
tomato puree)
 See Delaware Valley Packing
 Company

PENN MUTUAL LIFE INSURANCE
 COMPANY
Independence Square
Philadelphia, Pennsylvania 19172
Frank F. Tarbox, President
(215) 629-0600

PENN PRODUCTS COMPANY
963 Newark Avenue
Elizabeth, New Jersey 07207

PENN STATE LINE (marking pens,
address books, photo albums,
school supplies, etc.)
 See Majestic Penn State Inc.

PENN STATE MILLS, INC.
361 Gordon Street
Allentown, Pennsylvania 18105
Howard Heiman, President
(215) 434-9456

PENN TRAFFIC COMPANY
319 Washington Street
Johnstown, Pennsylvania 15907
G. Fesler Edwards, President
(814) 536-4411

PENN WAX WORKS, INC.
5200 Unruh Street
Philadelphia, Pennsylvania 19135
James A.G. Beales, President
(215) 332-9400

PENN YAN BOATS, INC.
Waddel Avenue
Penn Yan, New York 14527
Robert B. Stuart, President
(315) 536-4401

PENNACO
(Division of United States Industries
 Inc.)
350 Fifth Avenue
New York, New York 10017
(212) 279-8210

PENNCRAFT (waterproofing paint)
 See J.C. Penney Purchasing
 Corporation

PENNCREST (electrical appliances)
 See J.C. Penney Purchasing
 Corporation

PENNER PROVISION COMPANY
1001 Freyburg Street
Pittsburgh, Pennsylvania 15003
(412) 381-9700

PENNEY COMPANY, INC., J.C.
1301 Avenue of the Americas
New York, New York 10019
Jack B. Jackson, President
(212) 957-4321
 See also Thrift Drug Company

PENNINO MUSIC COMPANY INC.
6421 Industry Way
Westminster, California 92683

PENNMOOR (women's shoes)
 See Midland Shoe Company

PENNSALT CHEMICALS
 CORPORATION
 See Pennwalt Corporation

PENNSBURY POTTERY INC.
Old Tybun Road
Morrisville, Pennsylvania 19067

PENNSY (food products)
 See Conte Inc.

PENNSYLVANIA DUTCH (noodles,
macaroni)
 See Thomas J. Lipton, Inc.

PENNSYLVANIA DUTCH
 COMPANY INC.
Mount Holly Springs,
 Pennsylvania 17065

PENNSYLVANIA DUTCHMAN
(canned foods)
 See Myers Canning Company

PENNSYLVANIA DUTCHMAN
(cigars)
 See G.W. Van Slyke & Horton

1066

Companies and Trade Names

PENNSYLVANIA ELECTRIC
COMPANY
(Subsidiary of General Public
   Utilities Corporation)
1001 Broad Street
Johnstown, Pennsylvania 15907
J.F. Smith, President
(814) 536-6611

PENNSYLVANIA GAS & WATER
COMPANY
30 North Franklin Street
Wilkes-Barre, Pennsylvania 18701
David F. Hansen, President
(717) 824-8711

PENNSYLVANIA GLASS
PRODUCTS COMPANY
434 North Craig Street
Pittsburgh, Pennsylvania 15213
(412) 621-2853

PENNSYLVANIA HOUSE
(Division of General Interiors)
11th Street
Lewisburg, Pennsylvania 17837

PENNSYLVANIA MANUFACTURERS'
ASSOCIATION INSURANCE
COMPANY
Chestnut East Building
Philadelphia, Pennsylvania 19107
F.W. Anton, III, President
(215) 629-5000

PENNSYLVANIA POWER &
LIGHT COMPANY
2 North Ninth Street
Allentown, Pennsylvania 18101
Jack K. Busby, President
(215) 821-5151

PENNSYLVANIA POWER COMPANY
(Subsidiary of Ohio Edison Company)
1 East Washington Street
New Castle, Pennsylvania 16101
Ray E. Semmler, President
(412) 652-5531

PENNSYLVANIA REFINING
COMPANY
Butler, Pennsylvania 16001
John A. Beck, Jr., President
(412) 287-2781

PENNSYLVANIA SCALE COMPANY
21 Graybill Road
Leola, Pennsylvania 17540
A.Y. Johnson, President
(717) 656-2653

PENNTEST PHARMACAL
CORPORATION
Eastern Avenue and Pennex Drive
Verona, Pennsylvania 15147

PENNWALT CORPORATION
Pennwalt Building
3 Parkway
Philadelphia, Pennsylvania 19102
William P. Drake, President
(215) 587-7000
   See also Keystone; Pharmaceu-
      tical; and Pharmacraft

PENNWALT PRESCRIPTION
PRODUCTS
755 Jefferson
Rochester, New York 14623
(716) 271-1000

PENNY CURTIS (baked goods)
   See P & C Food Markets, Inc.

PENNY PENDLETON INC.
10526 Old Olive Street Road
Saint Louis, Missouri 63141
(314) 432-5200

PENNY SAVER (household products)
   See Publix Super Markets, Inc.

PENNY WALKER (sportswear)
   See G., H., & E. Freydberg,
      Inc.

PENNY-WISE (food products)
   See B.F. Trappey's Sons, Inc.

PENNY YOUNG (clothes)
   See Puritan Fashions Corporation

PENNZOIL COMPANY
Pennzoil Place
Houston, Texas 77001
William C. Liedtke, Jr., President
(713) 228-8741

PENOBSCOT SHOE COMPANY
Old Town, Maine 04468
Irving Kagan, President
(207) 827-4431
   See also Old Town Shoe Company
      Company

PENOBSCOT TWO INC.
12700 Reeck
Southgate, Michigan 48195
(313) 287-6600

PENSUPREME (milk and ice cream)
   See Penn Dairies

PENTA PRODUCTS, INC.
425 Second Street
San Francisco, California 94107
(415) 982-2313

PENTAX (photographic equipment)
   See Honeywell Photographic
      Products

PENTEL OF AMERICA LTD.
(Subsidiary of Pentel Company Ltd.)
5422 West Touhy Avenue
Skokie, Illinois 60076

PENTHOUSE (canned foods)
   See Tillie Lewis Foods, Inc.

PENTLAND SALES REPRESENTATIVES
INC.
225 Fifth Avenue, Room 729
New York, New York 10010
(212) 68303625

Companies and Trade Names

PENWICK (whiskey)
See National Distillers & Chemical Corporation

PEOPLE PALS (plastic pools)
See Jetty Products

PEOPLE'S GAS COMPANY
122 South Michigan Avenue
Chicago, Illinois 60603
O.C. Davis, President
(312) 431-4000
See also North Shore Gas Company

PEOPLES DRUG STORES, INC.
6315 Bren Mar Drive
Alexandria, Virginia 22312
S.W. Fantle, Chairman of the Board
(703) 750-6100

PEOPLES LIFE INSURANCE COMPANY
601 New Hampshire Avenue, N.W.
Washington, D.C. 20048
Ernest L. Hogan, President
(202) 337-3000

PEOPLES NATIONAL BANK OF WASHINGTON
1414 Fourth Avenue
Seattle, Washington 98171
Joshu Green, III, President
(206) 344-2300

PEOPLES TRUST OF NEW JERSEY
210 Main Street
Hackensack, New Jersey 07602
Clifford H. Coyman, President
(201) 646-5000

PEORIA PLASTIC COMPANY
9000 North University
Peoria, Illinois 61614
(309) 692-1700

PEP (cereal)
See Kellogg Company

PEP BOYS (MANNY, MOE & JACK)
32nd and Allegheny
Philadelphia, Pennsylvania 19132
Maurice L. Strauss, Chairman of the Board
(215) 229-9000

PEP POTS (peat pots)
See Premier Peat Moss Corporation

PEPE LOPEZ (tequila)
See Brown-Forman Distillers Corporation

PEPE OF MIAMI INC.
738 West 49th Street
Hialeah, Florida 33012

PEPPER MARINE PRODUCTS, PETER
2511 Victoria Avenue
Oxnard, California 93030

PEPPER PRODUCTS INC., PETER
15215 South Broadway
Gardena, California 90248
(213) 770-0517

PEPPERELL (linens)
See West Point Pepperell

PEPPERELL BRAIDING COMPANY, INC.
Post Office Box 67
East Pepperell, Massachusetts 01437
(617) 433-2133

PEPPERIDGE FARM, INC.
(Subsidiary of Campbell Soup Company)
Westport Avenue
Norwalk, Connecticut 06851
R.G. McGovern, President
(203) 847-0456

PEPPERTREE (dresses)
See Oxford Industries, Inc.

PEPPET LABORATORIES
(Division of Hy-Pure, Inc.)
Box 43603
4910 Reading Road
Cincinnati, Ohio 45243
(513) 641-0973

PEPR-OS (snack food)
See General Mills

PEPSI COLA (soft drink)
See PepsiCompany, Inc.

PEPSICOMPANY, INC.
Anderson Hill Road
Purchase, New York 10577
Donald M. Kendall, Chairman of the Board
(914) 253-2000
See also Monsieur Henri Wines Ltd.; and North American Van Lines Inc.

PEPTO-BISMOL (digestive-upset remedy)
See Norwich Pharmacal Company

PEPTONE (food products)
See Wilson & Company, Inc.

PEQUOD (venetian blinds)
See Breneman, Inc.

PEQUOD YACHT CORPORATION
Concord Industrial Park
Concord, New Hampshire 03301

PEQUOT (sheets)
See Springs Mills, Inc.

PER-CLIN ORCHARDS, INC.
Bear Lake, Michigan 49614

PERCO PRODUCTS, INC.
2925 North 77th Avenue
Elmwood Park, Illinois 60635

Companies and Trade Names

PERDUE & ASSOCIATES
2242 Dallas Trade Mart
Dallas, Texas 75207
(214) 748-8651

PERDUE-DEAN INC.
Post Office Box 475
Tavernier, Florida 33070

PEREZ, GREGORY P.
53 Park Place
New York, New York 10007
(212) 233-6860

PERFECT (paints and paint sundries)
See A. Flohr Company Inc.

PERFECT BODY (hair-care products)
See Alberto Culver Company

PERFECT BRASSIERE COMPANY, INC.
180 Madison Avenue
New York, New York 10016
(212) 532-1252

PERFECT HOST (dry cocktail mix)
See Foremost-McKesson

PERFECT NEGLIGEE COMPANY
16 East 34th Street
New York, New York 10016
(212) 686-0818

PERFECT PACKED PRODUCTS COMPANY
6 Xavier Drive
Yonkers, New York 10704

PERFECT PARTS COMPANY, THE
1 North Haven
Baltimore, Maryland 21224
Albert Gross, President
(301) 327-3522

PERFECT PIPE (tobacco)
See John Weisert Tobacco Company

PERFECT PLUS HOSIERY, INC.
5700 McDermott Drive
Berkeley, Illinois 60163
Alex F. Manier, President
(312) 261-1051

PERFECT POWDERS MANUFACTURING COMPANY
140 Talmadge Road
Edison, New Jersey 08817

PERFECT RUBBER SEAT CUSHION COMPANY
6451 Edmund Street
Philadelphia, Pennsylvania 19135
(215) 333-3523

PERFECT SLEEPER (mattress)
See Serta Associates, Inc.

PERFECTFORM CORPORATION
152 Madison Avenue
New York, New York 10016
(212) 684-4450

PERFECTION (baked goods)
See E.F. MacDonald Shopping Bag Food Stores, Inc.

PERFECTION (beer)
See Horlacher Brewing Company

PERFECTION (food products)
See Seneca Foods Corporation

PERFECTION (frozen foods)
See Miss Muffet Foods, Inc.

PERFECTION (macaroni products)
See West Coast Macaroni Manufacturing Company

PERFECTION AMERICAN
(Division of Rexnord Inc.)
Post Office Box 581
Darlington, South Carolina 29532

PERFECTION BISCUIT COMPANY
350 Pearl Street
Fort Wayne, Indiana 46802
H. Leslie Popp, President
(219) 742-8242

PERFECTION MACARONI COMPANY
2704 South Maple Avenue
Fresno, California 93709

PERFECTION PRODUCTS COMPANY
(Division of White Consolidated Industries)
Post Office Box 40
Waynesboro, Georgia 30830
W. Frank Fisher, President
(404) 554-2101

PERFECTO GARCIA & BROTHERS INC.
818 Lake
Evanston, Illinois 60201

PERFORMANCE MARINE
174 Fenna Street
Wollaston, Massachusetts 02170

PERFORMANCE SAILCRAFT CORPORATION
33 Duffy Place
San Rafael, California 94901

PERFORMERS (chairs)
See Douglas Furniture Corporation

PERGANTENE PHARMACAL COMPANY, INC.
1 Lull Street
Worcester, Massachusetts 01602

PERHAM FRUIT CORPORATION
Post Office Box 1314
Yakima, Washington 98901

PERISEAL (paint)
See Luminall Paints, Inc.

Companies and Trade Names

PERK FOODS COMPANY
(Subsidiary of Liggett & Myers, Inc.)
1580 North Northwest Highway
Park Ridge, Illinois 60068
Jack Nester, President
(312) 298-7400

PERKINS ENGINES INC.
24175 Research Drive
Farmington, Michigan 48024
W.D. Winemaster, President
(313) 477-3900

PERKINS MARINE LAMP &
  HARDWARE CORPORATION
16490 N.W. 13th Avenue
Miami, Florida 33164
(305) 621-7525

PERLISH COMPANY, RICHARD
Box 326
Roslyn, New York 11576

PERLITA (seafood)
  See M.S. Cowen Company

PERLITE INSTITUTE, INC.
45 West 45th
New York, New York 10036
(212) 265-2145

PERM-A-TEMP (insulated containers)
  See Thermos (Division of King-
    Seeley Thermos Company)

PERM-COTE (rustproofing compound)
  See Detrex Chemical Industries,
    Inc.

PERMA BROW, INC.
2915 South La Cienega Boulevard
Culver City, California 90230

PERMA-CELL (batteries)
  See General Electric Company,
    Battery Products Section

PERMA-FOAM INC.
605 South 21st Street
Irvington, New Jersey 07111

PERMA-LOC
(Division of Alco)
920 North Wellwood
North Lindenhurst,
  New York 11757

PERMA PRODUCTS COMPANY
816 Mercury
Duncanville, Texas 75110

PERMA-SHARP (knife sharpener)
  See Hacker Instruments Inc.

PERMA-SHARP MANUFACTURING
  CORPORATION
527 West 34th Street
New York, New York 10001
(212) 695-8616

PERMA SHRUB (lawn and garden
supplies)
  See Gordon Industries Inc.

PERMA-STRATE COMPANY, INC.
1255 Lynnfield Road
Memphis, Tennessee 38138
(901) 683-4589

PERMA VENEER (enamels)
  See Standard Industrial Products,
    Inc.

PERMACAST CORPORATION
17825 South Santa Fe Avenue
Compton, California 90221

PERMACEL
(Division of Johnson & Johnson)
United States Highway Number One
New Brunswick, New Jersey 08903
(201) 524-0400

PERMAFLEX PRODUCTS COMPANY
1854 North Front
Philadelphia, Pennsylvania 19122
Wilbur S. Welch, President and
  Treasurer
(215) 739-3243

PERMAGLAS (glass-lined water
heaters and tanks)
  See A.O. Smith Corporation

PERMALIFE GLASS FIBER
(Division of Standard Electric
  Company, Inc.)
3016 Austin Highway
San Antonio, Texas 78218
(512) 655-2210

PERMALUBE (motor oil)
  See Amoco Oil Company

PERMANENT PIGMENTS
(Division of Binney & Smith Inc.)
2700 Highland Avenue
Cincinnati, Ohio 45212
(513) 631-5092

PERMATEX COMPANY INC.
Box 1492
2300 North Florida Mango Road
West Palm Beach, Florida 33401
Constant Benoit, Jr., President
(305) 686-0880

PERMON (vinyl wall covering)
  See Stauffer Chemical Company

PERMUTIT COMPANY
(Division of Sybron Corporation)
East 49 Midland Avenue
Paramus, New Jersey 07653
H.R. Derleth, President and
  General Manager
(201) 262-8900

PERNOD (liqueur)
  See Julius Wile Sons &
    Company, Inc.

1070

Companies and Trade Names

PERPETUAL (carpeting)
See Karastan Rug Mills

PERRIE BORDEAUX (cocktail mixes)
See Peerless Specialty Company

PERRIN, J.B.
(Division of Rohlik, Inc.)
7777 Cortland Avenue
Detroit, Michigan 48204
(313) 933-5367

PERRY BROTHERS, INC.
Post Office Box 28
Lufkin, Texas 75901
W.L. Atwell, President
(713) 634-6686

PERRY CANNING COMPANY
R.F.D. Number Two
Brigham City, Utah 84302
(801) 723-6449

PERRY CANNING COMPANY, H.H.
Montross, Virginia 22520

PERRY CHEMICAL CORPORATION
91-31 Queens Boulevard
Elmhurst, New York 11373

PERRY COMPANY, THE
Post Office Box 6337
Austin, Texas 78702
Edgar Perry, III, Chairman,
   President and Treasurer
(512) 385-0050

PERRY INC., NORMAN
Plymouth, New Hampshire 03264

PERRY LABORATORIES
14713 Gratiot
Detroit, Michigan 48205
(313) 527-9063

PERRY LOU (canned foods)
See Stilwell Foods

PERRY OCEANOGRAPHICS INC.
100 East 17th Street
Riviera Beach, Florida 33404

PERRY'S CANDIES
1020 High Vista Trail West
Webster, New York 14580

PERSON & COVEY, INC.
616 Allen Avenue
Glendale, California 91201

PERSONAL ART COMPANY
45 East 20th Street
New York, New York 10003
(212) 475-8474

PERSONAL CARE
(Division of Gillette Company)
Prudential Tower
Boston, Massachusetts 02199
Marcel C. Durot, President
(312) 467-8000

PERSONAL PRODUCTS COMPANY
(Division of Johnson & Johnson)
Milltown, New Jersey 08850
Jane H. Yates, Vice President
   Consumer Affairs
(201) 524-7744

PERSONALITY (shoes)
See International Shoe Company

PERSONALITY (sunglasses)
See Joy Optical Company

PERSONALIZED CANDLE CORPORATION
Pestalozzi and 13th Streets
Highland, Illinois 62249

PERSONALIZED PAPETERIES
(personalized stationery and informals)
See Royal Imprints Corporation

PERSONNA (razor blades)
See American Safety Razor Company

PERT (toiletries)
See Procter & Gamble Company

PERTS (shoes)
See Musebeck Shoe Company, Inc.

PERTUSSIN (cold remedies)
See Chesebrough-Pond's, Inc.

PERUGINA CHOCOLATE AND CONFECTIONS, INC.
21 Main Street
Little Ferry, New Jersey 07643
John Rovegno, General Manager
(201) 641-3700

PERVO PAINT COMPANY, THE
6624 Stanford Avenue
Los Angeles, California 90001
W.D. Tarlton, President
(213) 758-1147

PESHASTIN FRUIT GROWERS ASSOCIATION
Post Office Box 378
Peshastin, Washington 98847

PESO PLUMA (men's apparel)
See Sagner, Inc.

PEST (bird repellent)
See Animal Repellents, Inc.

PESTER-SCHAEFER OIL COMPANIES
3317 McKinley
Des Moines, Iowa 50321
Jack Pester, Chairman of the Board
(515) 285-9670

PET (electric power tools)
See McGraw-Edison Company,
   Portable Electric Tools
   Division

Companies and Trade Names

PET CHEMICALS, INC.
Box 660, 656
Miami Springs Branch
Miami, Florida 33166
(305) 887-1506

PET, INC.
400 South Fourth Street
Saint Louis, Missouri 63166
Boyd Schenk, President
(314) 621-5400
See also Cyber Corporation; Dentlers; Funsten Nut; Laura Scudder's Snack Foods; Mountain Pass Canning Company; Musselman Fruit Products; Reese Finer Foods, Inc.; Scudder's, Laura; Southland Canning & Packing Company Inc.; Stuckey's, Inc.; and Whitman's Chocolates

PET, INC.
Bakery Operations
1039 Grant Street, S.E.
Atlanta, Georgia 30315
(404) 622-8146

PET, INC.
Dairy Division
2816 Kingsport-Bristol Boulevard
Johnson City, Tennessee 37601
(615) 926-7171

PET, INC.
Funsten Nut Division
400 South Fourth
Saint Louis, Missouri 63166
Boyd F. Schenk, Chairman, President and Chief Executive Officer
(314) 694-2500

PET, INC.
Snack Foods Division
1525 North East
Anaheim, California 92805

PET LABORATORIES
Post Office Box 425
Tustin, California 92680

PETAL (deodorant soap, fabric softener)
See Colgate-Palmolive Company

PETCOR INDUSTRIES INC.
Post Office Box A-369
Muscatine, Iowa 52761

PETER DAWSON (Scotch)
See Julius Wile Sons & Company Inc.

PETER HAND BREWING COMPANY
1000 West North Avenue
Chicago, Illinois 60622
(312) 664-6300

PETER PAN (peanut butter)
See Swift & Company

PETER PAN CANDIES
4400 Jensen
Oakland, California 94601

PETER PAN RECORDS
145 Komorn Street
Newark, New Jersey 07105
Martin Kasin, President
(201) 344-4214

PETER PAN SEAFOODS, INC.
1220 Dexter Horton Building
Seattle, Washington 98104
John P. Bez, President
(206) 624-4344

PETER PAUL, INC.
New Haven Road
Naugatuck, Connecticut 06770
Lloyd W. Elston, President
(203) 729-0221
See also Bachman Chocolate Manufacturing Company; and Johnson

PETER PEPPER MARINE PRODUCTS
2511 Victoria Avenue
Oxnard, California 93030

PETER PEPPER PRODUCTS INC.
15215 South Broadway
Gardena, California 90248
(213) 770-0517

PETER PIPER (groceries)
See Laurans-Standard Grocery Company, Inc.

PETER SCHUYLER (cigars)
See G.W. Van Slyke & Horton

PETER STORM LTD.
Smith Street
Norwalk, Connecticut 06851

PETER STUYVESANT (cigarettes)
See House of Edgeworth

PETERBILT MOTORS COMPANY
(Division of Paccar Inc.)
38801 Cherry Street
Newark, California 94560
Joseph M. Dunn, Division General Manager
(415) 797-3555

PETERBORGH (pianos)
See Manufacturers Centre Holland

PETERBROOK INC.
Candle Mill Village
East Arlington, Vermont 05252

PETERS (ammunition)
See Remington Arms Company, Inc.

PETER'S (chocolate and candy)
See Nestle Company, Inc.

PETERS & SONS, INC., L.D.
1133 Broadway
New York, New York 10010
(212) 255-8580

Companies and Trade Names

PETERS COMPANY, A.K.
230 Park Avenue
New York, New York 10017
(212) 689-0280

PETERSEN LINEN COMPANY
634 South Avenue
Garwood, New Jersey 07027
(212) 244-4165

PETERSEN MANUFACTURING
COMPANY, INC.
DeWitt, Nebraska 68341
Christian Petersen, President
(402) 683-2301

PETERSEN PUBLISHING COMPANY
8490 Sunset Boulevard
Los Angeles, California 90069
F.R. Waingrow, President
(213) 657-5100

PETERSON BABY PRODUCTS
COMPANY
6904 Tunjunga Avenue
North Hollywood, California 91605
Peer Ghent, President
(213) 980-4820

PETERSON COMPANY, JOHN A.
2225 West Commodore Way
Seattle, Washington 98199
(206) 283-9191

PETERSON COMPANY, O.P.
384 Fore Street
Portland, Maine 04111
(207) 772-5334

PETERSON COMPANY, ROBERT H.
2835 Sierra Grande Street
Pasadena, California 91107
(213) 681-9784

PETERSON COMPANY, THE
CHARLES A.
See Peterson Nut Company

PETERSON ELECTRO-MUSICAL
PRODUCTS
11601 South Mayfield Avenue
Worth, Illinois 60482

PETERSON GAMES
1704 Kathleen Avenue
Sacramento, California 95815

PETERSON MANUFACTURING,
A.E.
See Peterson Baby Products
Company

PETERSON NUT COMPANY
917 Carnegie Avenue
Cleveland, Ohio 44115
(216) 861-4353

PETERSON OINTMENT COMPANY
257 Franklin Street
Buffalo, New York 14202
(716) 854-3787

PETERSON SEAFOODS INC.
Box 5470
Charleston, Oregon 97420

PETERSON'S CANDY & ICE
CREAM SHOP
2 Industrial Boulevard
Paoli, Pennsylvania 19301

PETERSONS LTD.
75 Triangle Boulevard
Carlstadt, New Jersey 07072
(201) 939-5400
See also Select Gifts Company
Inc.

PETITES UNLIMITED (dresses)
See Parkland of Dallas, Inc.

PETITJEAN (vegetables)
See A & A Food Products
Corporation

PET'M LABORATORIES
520 Pennsylvania Avenue
Fort Washington, Pennsylvania 19034

PETRI (wines)
See United Vintners Inc.

PETRI CIGAR COMPANY
See Parodi Cigar Corporation

PETRI INTERNATIONAL (USA)
CORPORATION
150 Great Neck Road
Great Neck, New York 11021

PETRINI & COMPANY, INC., D.
281 Franklin
Boston, Massachusetts 02176
(617) 742-2894

PETROCELLI CLOTHES, INC.
28 West 23rd Street
New York, New York 10010
Samuel Silverman, President
(212) 924-7330

PETROF (upright and grand pianos)
See Remeny House of Music Ltd.

PETROLEUM JELLY
See Chesebrough-Ponds, Inc.

PETRUSHKA (Vodka)
See Continental Distilling
Corporation

PETTERS
(Division of Hawker Siddeley Inc.)
7 Delaware Drive
Lake Success, New York 11040

PETTIBONE LABORATORIES
11 East 44th Street
New York, New York 10017
(212) 661-8117

Companies and Trade Names

PETTIT PAINT COMPANY INC.
36 Pine Street
Rockaway, New Jersey 07866
(201) 625-3100

PEUGEOT, INC.
300 Kuller Road
Clifton, New Jersey 07015
Pierre de Montmarin, President
(201) 478-8600

PEUGOT (housewares and electric tools)
See Vanderburgh & Company Inc.

PEXTO (tools)
See Peck, Stow, & Wilcox Company

PEYRIN (sports apparel)
See Gondola Internationale Inc.

PEYTON'S (meat products)
See John Morrell & Company

PEZ-HAAS, INC.
56-16 37th Avenue
Woodside, New York 11377
Curtis J. Allina, Vice President
(212) 476-2700

PFAELZER BROTHERS
(Division of Armour & Company)
4445 West District Boulevard
Chicago, Illinois 60632
Charles Hersheway, Vice President
(312) 927-7100

PFAFF INTERNATIONAL CORPORATION
373 Fifth Avenue
New York, New York 10016
(212) 685-1747

PFALTZ & BAUER INC.
(Subsidiary of Aceto Chemical Company Inc.)
375 Fairfield Avenue
Stamford, Connecticut 06902
Arnold Frankel, President
(203) 357-8700

PFALTZGRAFF COMPANY
140 East Market Street
York, Pennsylvania 17401
(717) 845-5626
See also Buehner-Wanner

PFANSTIEHL LABORATORIES
1219 Glen Rock Avenue
Waukegan, Illinois 60085
(312) 623-0370

PFAUDLER COMPANY, THE
(Division of Sybron Corporation)
West Avenue and Clark Street
Rochester, New York 14603
(716) 235-1000

PFEIFFER (beer)
See Sterling Brewers (Division of G. Heileman Brewing Company, Inc.)

PFEIFFER COMPANY, THE
3965 Laclede Avenue
Saint Louis, Missouri 63108
(314) 371-3000

PFEIFFER'S FOODS, INC.
(Division of International Salt Company)
401 Maryvale Drive
Buffalo, New York 14225
Kascal Peckoff, Vice President
(716) 897-3400
See also Lohmann Foods

PFENING & SNYDER
1075 West Fifth Avenue
Columbus, Ohio 43212
(614) 294-5361

PFIZER, INC.
235 East 42nd Street
New York, New York 10017
Edmund T. Pratt, Jr., Chairman of the Board
(212) 573-2323
See also Coty; Leeming/Pacquin; and Roerig & Company, J.B.

PFLUEGER SPORTING GOODS
Post Office Box 3108
Hallandale, Florida 33009
R.D. Tackett, President
(305) 927-2594

PFRIEMER INC., CHARLES
Centre and Glendale Streets
Easton, Pennsylvania 18042
(215) 258-9221

PHANTOM PRODUCTS, INC.
(electric fishing motors)
See Shakespeare Company

PHANTOMS, INC.
See True Form Foundations, Inc.

PHARM-A-LAB
11751 Levan Road
Livonia, Michigan 48150

PHARMACEUTICAL ASSOCIATES, INC.
Box 8695
Greenville, South Carolina 29604
(803) 277-7282

PHARMACEUTICAL INNOVATIONS, INC.
150 Mount Pleasant Avenue
Newark, New Jersey 07104
(201) 484-7137

PHARMACEUTICS COMPANY
48 West 48th Street
New York, New York 10036
(212) 265-5144

Companies and Trade Names

PHARMACHEM CORPORATION
Broad and Wood Streets
Bethlehem, Pennsylvania 18018
J.L. Kornet, President and Treasurer
(215) 867-4654

PHARMACIA LABORATORIES
800 Centennial Avenue
Piscataway, New Jersey 08854
Donald Cattaneo, President
(201) 469-1222

PHARMACO
(Division of Plough, Inc.)
Kenilworth, New Jersey 07033

PHARMACRAFT
(Division of Pennwalt Corporation)
Post Office Box 1212
Rochester, New York 14603
C.O. Gale, Vice President
(716) 271-1000

PHARMACY GIRL, INC.,
    LABORATORIES
United States Route Seven
Brookfield, Connecticut 06804

PHARMADENT COMPANY, THE
Box 96
Lake Jackson, Texas 77566

PHARMECON, INC.
23550 Haggerty Farmington Hills
Detroit, Michigan 48024
(313) 478-0400

PHARMED, INC.
Riverside Drive
Grundy, Virginia 24614

PHARMEX, INC.
Post Office Box 125
Hollywood, Florida 33022

PHARMICS, INC.
1878 South Redwood Road
Salt Lake City, Utah 84104
(801) 927-4138

PHASE III (soap)
    See Lever Brothers Company

PHELAN-FAUST PAINT
    MANUFACTURING COMPANY
932 Loughborough Avenue
Saint Louis, Missouri 63111
George P. Budke, President
(314) 353-4800

PHELON MAGNAGRIP COMPANY,
    INC.
East Longmeadow,
    Massachusetts 01029

PHELPS & COMPANY, INC., A.E.
410 Waverly Avenue
Brooklyn, New York 11238
(212) 789-0929

PHENIX BOX & LABEL COMPANY
4120 Pennsylvania Street
Kansas City, Missouri 64111
(816) 931-1767

PHIEBIG, INC., ALBERT J.
Box 352
White Plains, New York 10602

PHIFER WIRE PRODUCTS
Post Office Box 1700
2505 Greensboro Avenue
Tuscaloosa, Alabama 35401
Reese Phifer, President
(205) 345-2120

PHIL JACOBS COMPANY, INC.
1331 Oak
Kansas City, Missouri 64106
Phil Jacobs, President
(816) 471-6377

PHIL-MAID INC.
1033 West Van Buren
Chicago, Illinois 60607
(312) 829-2700

PHIL-MAR CORPORATION
1100 East 222nd Street
Cleveland, Ohio 44117
(216) 531-8800

PHIL-O-MATIC COMPANY
Box 832
Springfield, Ohio 45501

PHILADELPHIA (cream cheese)
    See Kraft Foods

PHILADELPHIA (whiskey)
    See Continental Distilling
        Corporation

PHILADELPHIA CANDIES, INC.
1534 East State Street
Sharon, Pennsylvania 16146

PHILADELPHIA CARPET COMPANY
Allegheny Avenue and C
Philadelphia, Pennsylvania 19134
(215) 425-5830

PHILADELPHIA CHEWING GUM
    CORPORATION
Eagle Road
Havertown, Pennsylvania 19083
John H. Daly, Jr., Executive
    Vice President
(215) 449-1700
    See also American Chewing
        Gum Inc.

PHILADELPHIA ELECTRIC COMPANY
2301 Market Street
Philadelphia, Pennsylvania 19101
Robert F. Gilkeson, Chairman of
    the Board
(215) 841-4000

PHILADELPHIA EXTRACT COMPANY
524 West Lindley Avenue
Philadelphia, Pennsylvania 19120
(215) 324-6933

Companies and Trade Names

PHILADELPHIA GEAR
 CORPORATION
King of Prussia, Pennsylvania 19406
Thomas F. Hayes, President
(215) 265-3000

PHILADELPHIA NATIONAL BANK
Broad and Chestnut
Philadelphia, Pennsylvania 19101
G. Morris Dorrance, Chairman of
 the Board
(215) 629-3100

PHILADELPHIA QUARTZ COMPANY
Post Office Box 840
Valley Forge, Pennsylvania 19482
(215) 687-8400

PHILADELPHIA SAVING FUND
 SOCIETY
Coulter and Anderson
Ardmore, Pennsylvania 19003
M. Todd Cooke, President
(215) 629-2000

PHILADELPHIA SEED COMPANY,
 INC.
Post Office Box 230
Chemical and Gravers Road
Plymouth Meeting,
 Pennsylvania 19462
(215) 825-1240

PHILCO-FORD CORPORATION
(Subsidiary of Ford Motor Company)
Union Meeting Road
Blue Bell, Pennsylvania 19422
A.E. Allen, Vice President,
 Consumer Affairs
(215) 646-1900

PHILCRAFT IMPORTS INC.
120 West 28th Street
New York, New York 10001
(212) 686-4490

PHILIP FIBERS & INDUSTRIAL
 CORPORATION, ARTHUR
29 Park Avenue
Manhasset, New York 11030

PHILIP MORRIS, INC.
100 Park Avenue
New York, New York 10017
Ross R. Millhiser, President
(212) 679-1800
 See also American Safety Razor
 Company; and Miller
 Brewing Company

PHILIPPINE PRODUCTS INC.
1609 Broadway
New York, New York 10019

PHILIPS BUSINESS SYSTEMS INC.
(Division of North American
 Philips Corporation)
100 East 42nd Street
New York, New York 10017
(212) 697-3600

PHILIPS COSMETICS, DEBRA
(Division of FlowerModes Ltd.)
20 West 37th Street
New York, New York 10018

PHILIPS ELECTRONIC
INSTRUMENTS
 See North American Philips
 Company Inc.

PHILIPS INDUSTRIES, INC.
4801 Springfield Street
Dayton, Ohio 45401
Robert Levenstein, President
(513) 253-7171

PHILIPS PETROLEUM COMPANY
Philips Building
Bartesville, Oklahoma 74004
W.F. Martin, President
(918) 661-6600
 See also Sealright Company
 Inc.; Seaside Oil Com-
 pany; and Smith Paper
 Company, H.P.

PHILIPS ROXANE LABORATORIES
(Division of Philips Roxane, Inc.)
330 Oak Street
Columbus, Ohio 43215
G.C. Wojta, President
(614) 228-5403
 See also Anchor Laboratories,
 Inc.

PHILLIES (cigars)
 See Bayuk Cigars, Inc.

PHILLIPS (processed food)
 See Hanover Brands Inc.

PHILLIPS & BUTTEROFF
 CORPORATION
813 12th Avenue, North
Nashville, Tennessee 37202
Neal L. Jennings, President
(615) 254-5011

PHILLIPS ART PUBLISHERS INC.
50 Hunt Street
Newton, Massachusetts 02158

PHILLIPS CHEMICAL COMPANY,
CHARLES H.
 See Glenbrook Laboratories

PHILLIPS DRILL COMPANY
Post Office Box 364
Michigan City, Indiana 46360
(219) 874-4217

PHILLIPS FIBERS CORPORATION
(Subsidiary of Phillips Petroleum
 Company)
Box 66
Highway I-85
Greenville, South Carolina 29602
(803) 242-6600

PHILLIPS LABORATORIES, INC.
122 South Gay Street
Knoxville, Tennessee 37902

Companies and Trade Names

PHILLIP'S MILK OF MAGNESIA
(digestive-upset treatment)
See Glenbrook Laboratories

PHILLIPS PETROLEUM COMPANY
Phillips Building
Bartlesville, Oklahoma 74009
C. Douce, President and Chief
   Operations Officer
(918) 661-6600

PHILLIPS PROCESS COMPANY INC.
192 Mill Street
Rochester, New York 14614
(716) 232-1825

PHILLIPS RIBBON & CARBON
   COMPANY
(Division of Labelon Corporation)
10 Chapin Street
Canandaigua, New York 14424

PHILLIPS-VAN HEUSEN
   CORPORATION
1290 Avenue of the Americas
New York, New York 10016
Seymour J. Phillips, Chairman of
   the Board
(212) 541-5200
   See also Joseph & Feiss Com-
       pany; Kennedy's, Inc.;
       Somerset Knitting Mills,
       Inc.; and Windbreaker, Inc.

PHILMAID, INC.
1033 West Van Buren
Chicago, Illinois 60607
(312) 829-2700

PHILMORE MANUFACTURING
   COMPANY
130-01 Jamaica Avenue
Richmond Hill, New York 11418

PHILTEX MANUFACTURING
   COMPANY
First and Ontario
Philadelphia, Pennsylvania 19134
Curt L. Strauss, President
(215) 425-3600

PHINNEY-HALE INC.
Box 5286
Oxnard, California 93030

PHINNEY-WALKER (clocks)
See Semca Corporation

PHOENIX (ale and beer)
See Iroquois Industries, Inc.

PHOENIX (hosiery)
See Kayser-Roth Hosiery
   Company, Inc.

PHOENIX CANDY COMPANY
151-165 35th Street
Brooklyn, New York 11232
Joseph Klein, President
(212) 768-7900

PHOENIX CLOTHES, INC.
(Division of Genesco, Inc.)
Race and Court Streets
Allentown, Pennsylvania 18101
Monte Comer, President
(215) 433-7531

PHOENIX JUICER COMPANY
233 Broadway
New York, New York 10007
(212) 267-2239

PHOENIX MUTUAL LIFE
   INSURANCE COMPANY
1 American Row
Hartford, Connecticut 06115
Robert T. Jackson, President
(203) 278-1212

PHOENIX OIL COMPANY, THE
See Murphy-Phoenix Company,
   The

PHONE-MATE, INC.
335 Maple Avenue
Torrance, California 90503
William Shapren, President
(213) 320-9800

PHONO TRIX (tape recorders)
See Matthew Stuart & Company
   Inc.

PHONOLA (phonograph)
See Telex Corporation, Inc.

PHOTON INC.
355 Middlesex Avenue
Wilmington, Massachusetts 01887
Alfred M. Kerzner, President and
   Chief Executive Officer
(617) 658-9146

PHOTOSUN (glass products)
See Corning Glass Works

PHYSICIANS APPLIANCE
   COMPANY
515 West 75th Street
Kansas City, Missouri 64114
(816) 361-2203

PHYSICIANS FORMULA
   COSMETICS, INC.
4623 San Fernando Road
Glendale, California 91204

PI-LON LABORATORIES, INC.
9016 Van Dyke
Detroit, Michigan 48213
(313) 921-7575

PIAGET (watches)
See North American Watch
   Corporation

PIANOLA (pianos)
See Aeolian Corporation

PIANORGAN (portable electric
organ)
See Unicord Inc.

PIAZZA ELEGANTE (folding and
rigid dining chairs)
See House of Italian Handicrafts,
   Inc.

1077

Companies and Trade Names

PIAZZA ORIGINALS
225 Fifth Avenue
New York, New York 10010
(212) 683-5785

PIC A PAK INC.
1040 Bayview Drive
Fort Lauderdale, Florida 33304

PIC CORPORATION
28 Canfield Street
Orange, New Jersey 07050
See also Jar-it Drill Company;
and Spek-Aid Company

PIC N TIME (food products)
See Watsonville Canning &
Frozen Food Company

PIC-O-MAINE (food products)
See Bessey Foods Corporation

PIC OF THE PACK (food products)
See Williamsburg Canning
Company Inc.

PIC PAC FOOD STORE
4727 Burbank Road
Memphis, Tennessee 38118
(903) 794-0990

PICATO (bass-guitar strings)
See Saint Louis Music Supply
Company Inc.

PICAYUNE (cigarettes)
See Liggett & Myers, Inc.

PICCARD INDUSTRIES INC.,
LUCIEN
180 Madison Avenue
New York, New York 10016
(212) 685-9644

PICCOLINO
(Division of Gino Paoli)
112 West 34th
New York, New York 10001
(212) 868-9420

PICCOLO (men's shirts)
See Gates Shirt Company

PICK-A-DENT CORPORATION
1068 Mission Street
San Francisco, California 94101
(415) 431-1055

PICK HOTELS CORPORATION
532 South Michigan Avenue
Chicago, Illinois 60605
Albert Pick, Jr., Chairman of the
Board
(312) 427-3835

PICK O' THE PATCH (packaged
plants, trees, shrubs, vines)
See Ozark Nurseries Inc.

PICK-UP KAP (campers)
See Winnebago Industries Inc.

PICKANDS, MATHER & COMPANY
See Diamond Shamrock
Corporation

PICKAPEPPA (sauces, vinegars,
chutney)
See J.F. Brady Sales Company

PICKARD INC.
Post Office Box 309
786 Corona Avenue
Antioch, Illinois 60002
Henry A. Pickard, Jr., President
and Treasurer
(312) 395-3800

PICKER INTERNATIONAL
CORPORATION
1275 Mamoroneck Avenue
White Plains, New York 10605

PICKERINGTON CREAMERY, INC.
94 Church Street
Pickerington, Ohio 43147
A. Jerry Good
(614) 837-4311

PICKETT INC.
Box 1515
Santa Barbara, California 93102

PICKWICK (ale)
See Falstaff Brewing Corporation

PICKWICK INTERNATIONAL, INC.
Pickwick Building
135 Crossways Park Drive
Woodbury, New York 11797
Amos Heilicher, President
(516) 364-2900

PICNIC PAX (condiments packed
for picnickers)
See Convenience Products
Corporation

PICO (luggage, travel and desk
accessories)
See Brecher Brothers, Inc.

PICO INTERNATIONAL
CORPORATION
1830 South Hill Street
Los Angeles, California 90015
(213) 749-0203

PICON (aperitif)
See Julius Wile Sons &
Company, Inc.

PICTORIAL PACKAGING
232 South Lake Street
Aurora, Illinois 60507
(312) 897-9165

PICTUREPHONE (visual telephone)
See American Telephone &
Telegraph Company

PICTURESQUE PRODUCTS
1555 Union Center Road
Endicott, New York 13760

PIE KING (baking equipment)
See Barbecue King, Inc.

Companies and Trade Names

PIE MATE (fruit-pie fillings)
See Sun-Rype Products Ltd.

PIEDMONT (cigarettes)
See Liggett & Myers, Inc.

PIEDMONT (grocery items)
See Safeway Stores, Inc.

PIEDMONT (hosiery)
See Rudin & Roth, Inc.

PIEDMONT AVIATION, INC.
Smith-Reynolds Airport
Winston-Salem,
    North Carolina 27102
T.H. Davis, President
(919) 767-5100

PIEDMONT CANDY COMPANY
925 Talbert Boulevard
Lexington, North Carolina 27292

PIEDMONT INDUSTRIES, INC.
1250 Broadway
New York, New York 10001
M.L. Morrow, President
(212) 736-8600

PIEDMONT MOP COMPANY
321 Atando Avenue
Charlotte, North Carolina 28206

PIEDMONT MOULDING COMPANY
Post Office Box 117
Old Atlanta Highway
Conyers, Georgia 30207
(404) 483-7203

PIEDMONT NATURAL GAS
    COMPANY, INC.
4301 Yancey Road
Charlotte, North Carolina 23210
J.D. Pickard, President
(704) 525-5580

PIEL BROTHERS, INC.
(Division of F. & M. Schaefer
    Brewing Company)
Post Office Box 119
Willimansett, Massachusetts 01021
Thomas P. Hawkes, President
(413) 534-7336

PIER 1 IMPORTS, INC.
2520 West Freeway
Fort Worth, Texas 76102
Luther A. Henderson, President
(817) 332-7031

PIERCE & STEVENS CHEMICAL
    CORPORATION
(Subsidiary of Pratt & Lambert
    Company)
710 Ohio Street
Buffalo, New York 14203
Henry E. Jones, President
(716) 856-4910

PIERCE COMPANY, C.S.
278 Montello
Brockton, Massachusetts 02401

PIERCE COMPANY, S.S.
141 Brookline Avenue
Boston, Massachusetts 02167
Robert F. Gammons, President
(617) 536-7600
    See also Kennett Canning
    Company

PIERCE GOVERNOR COMPANY,
    THE
(Division of Avis Industrial
    Corporation)
Post Office Box 2000
Upland, Indiana 46989
(317) 998-2712

PIERCE-PHELPS, INC.
2000 Block North 59th Street
Philadelphia, Pennsylvania 19131
W.G. Pierce, Jr., Chairman of
    the Board
(215) 477-9000

PIERI COMPANY INC., J.G.
601 Bailey Avenue
Buffalo, New York 14206
(716) 825-5000

PIERI DISTRIBUTING COMPANY,
    INC.
1238 North Marshall
El Cajon, California 92020

PIERONI (food products)
See San Giorgio Macaroni Inc.

PIERPONT PRODUCTS COMPANY
156 Lincoln Street
Hingham, Massachusetts 02043

PIERRE (processed foods)
See Ernest Carriere Inc.

PIERRE BALMAIN (men's toiletries)
See Revlon Inc.

PIERRE CARDIN (footwear)
See Kayser-Roth Shoes, Inc.

PIERRE CARDIN (men's shirts)
See Eagle Shirtmakers

PIERRE CARDIN PARFUMS
630 Fifth Avenue
New York, New York 10020
(212) 489-2430

PIERRE CHEVELLE (watches)
See World Wide Watch Company

PIETRUS & SONS COMPANY,
    A.J.
Sleepy Eye, Minnesota 56085

PIGGLY WIGGLY CORPORATION
Post Office Box 149
1010 East Adams
Jacksonville, Florida 32202
W.R. Lovett, Chairman and President
(904) 356-2451

Companies and Trade Names

PIGGLY WIGGLY SOUTHERN, INC.
100 Brinson Road
Vidalia, Georgia 30474
Gerald H. Achenbach, Chairman of the Board
(912) 537-4113

PIGGY BACK (infants' product)
See Strolee of California

PIGGYPAK (juvenile product)
See Himalayan Industries

PIGNOSE INDUSTRIES INC.
8600 Melrose Avenue
Los Angeles, California 90069
(213) 659-1407

PIK-NIK COMPANY
214 Dupont
San Jose, California 95126
(408) 286-2680

PIKE & COMPANY, INC., E.W.
Post Office Box Four
Elizabeth, New Jersey 07207

PIKE & COMPANY, J.J.
R.D. Three
Box 437
Sussex, New Jersey 07461

PIKLE-RITE COMPANY, INC.
Pulaski, Wisconsin 54162

PIKNIK PRODUCTS COMPANY
3806 Day Street
Montgomery, Alabama 36102
(205) 265-1567

PILCHER MANUFACTURING COMPANY, J.V.
715 Gray Street
Louisville, Kentucky 40202

PILE-LIFTER (vacuum cleaner)
See Hild Floor Machine Company

PILGRIM (children's knitwear)
See Shirtees, Inc.

PILGRIM (Rum)
See Fleischmann Distilling Corporation

PILGRIM APPLIANCE COMPANY
Middleboro, Massachusetts 02346

PILGRIM BADGE & LABEL CORPORATION
278 Babcock
Boston, Massachusetts 02215
(617) 782-9300

PILGRIM FARMS, INC.
Post Office Box 440
1430 Western Avenue
Plymouth, Indiana 46563
Charles J. Weidner, President
(219) 936-4061

PILGRIM FOODS INC.
Wilton Road
Greenville, New Hampshire 03048

PILGRIM GLASS CORPORATION, THE
225 Fifth Avenue
New York, New York 10010
(212) 679-5577

PILGRIM PACKING COMPANY
Burnet Avenue and Clark
East Syracuse, New York 13057
Eli Gingold, President
(315) 437-1111

PILGRIM PLASTIC PRODUCTS COMPANY
(Division of Pilgrim Badge & Label Corporation)
278 Babcock Street
Boston, Massachusetts 02215
Herb Segal, President
(617) 782-9300

PILLSBURY COMPANY
608 Second Avenue, South
Minneapolis, Minnesota 55402
James R. Peterson, President
(612) 330-4966
See also Burger King Corporation

PILOT (venetian blinds)
See Breneman, Inc.

PILOT DRUG COMPANY
291 Columbus Avenue
Tuckahoe, New York 10707

PILOT FREIGHT CARRIERS, INC.
North Cherry and Polo
Winston Salem,
    North Carolina 27101
Ruel Yount Sharpe, President
(919) 722-3421

PILOT LIFE INSURANCE COMPANY
Box 20727
Greensboro, North Carolina 27420
L.C. Stephens, Jr., President
(919) 299-4720

PILOT RADIO CORPORATION
(Subsidiary of National Union Electric Corporation)
66 Field Point Road
Greenwich, Connecticut 06830
C. Russell Feldmann, President
(213) 661-1741

PILOT RADIO SALES
(Subsidiary of Mitsubishi International Corporation)
165 West Putnam Avenue
Greenwich, Connecticut 06830

PILSER'S (beer)
See Champale, Inc.

PIN-CURL (home permanent)
See Lander Company, Inc.

PIN-IT (home permanent)
See Procter & Gamble Company

Companies and Trade Names

PINAUD'S (men's and women's toiletries)
See Nestle-LeMur Company

PINCH (Scotch whiskey)
See Renfield Importers, Ltd.

PINCOR (power lawn mower)
See Pioneer Gen-E Motor Corporation

PINCUS BROTHERS, INC.
Independence Mall, East
Philadelphia, Pennsylvania 19106
Irwin Nat Pincus, President
(215) 922-4900

PINE ALL (household products)
See Tumbler Laboratories (Division of Imoco-Gateway Corporation)

PINE BROTHERS (cough drops)
See Life Savers Inc.

PINE CRAFT (furniture)
See Ficks Reed Company

PINE-SOL (household cleaners, etc.)
See American Cyanamid, Household Products Department

PINE STATE KNITWEAR COMPANY
(Subsidiary of Hanes Corporation)
Virginia Street
Mount Airy, North Carolina 27031
Lindsay Holcomb, Sr., Chairman of the Board
(919) 786-6185

PINEHURST (canned foods)
See Bison Canning Company

PINEHURST (carts)
See Molitor, Inc.

PINEHURST LINGERIE
120 East Pritchard Street
Asheboro, North Carolina 27203

PINENOOK (food products)
See R & S Pickle Company Inc.

PINES OF AMERICA INC.
5120 Investment Drive
Fort Wayne, Indiana 46808

PINETREE (produce)
See H.S. Denison & Company

PINEX COMPANY, INC., THE
41 East 57th Street
New York, New York 10022
Alfred Roberts, President
(212) 753-4600

PINK BEAUTY (salmon)
See New England Fish Company

PINK BERRY INDUSTRIES
(Division of Marble King Inc.)
Post Office Box 195
Paden City, West Virginia 26159

PINK CLOUD (laundry products)
See Trager Manufacturing Company, Inc.

PINK COTTAGE CANDIES
Box 438
Mount Dora, Florida 32757

PINK IT (shears and scissors)
See J. Wiss & Sons Company

PINK LADY (paints and paint sundries)
See A. Flohr Company Inc.

PINKERTON TOBACCO COMPANY
3011 Council Street
Toledo, Ohio 43606

PINKERTON'S, INC.
100 Church Street
New York, New York 10007
Edward J. Bednarz, President
(212) 285-4800

PINKHAM MEDICINE COMPANY, LYDIA E.
(Affiliation of Cooper Laboratories Inc.)
Lynn, Massachusetts 01904

PINKNEY PACKAGE COMPANY
Box 2412
Amarillo, Texas 79104

PINNACLE (cigarettes)
See American Brands, Inc.

PINNACLE (food products)
See NCC Food Corporation

PINTO (cigarettes and tobacco)
See Brown & Williamson Tobacco Corporation

PINTO ENTERPRISES INC., FRANK
916 Birmingham Street
Bridgeport, Connecticut 06606
(203) 372-9337

PINTOW INC., DAVID H.
1 Cuttermill Road
Great Neck, New York 11021
(516) 487-3105

PINUS MEDICINE COMPANY
Post Office Box 391
French Lick, Indiana 47432

PIONEER (chain saws)
See Cushman (Division of Outboard Marine Corporation)

PIONEER (cigars)
See M. Marsh & Son

Companies and Trade Names

PIONEER (men's footwear)
See L.B. Evans' Son Company

PIONEER (processed foods)
See Cudahy Company

PIONEER ART GALLERY
See Mockel Gallery, Henry R.

PIONEER CHEESE FACTORY
Renwick, Iowa 50577

PIONEER COMPANY, THE
Qupaw Towers
Ninth and Ferry Streets
Little Rock, Arkansas 72202
John Baumgardner, President
(501) 375-2356

PIONEER FOOD INDUSTRIES, INC.
1000 West Second Street
DeWitt, Arkansas 72042
Finis A. O'Daniel, President
(501) 946-3546

PIONEER GEN-E MOTOR
CORPORATION
5841 West Dickens Avenue
Chicago, Illinois 60639
Robert Graham, President and
Treasurer
(312) 237-4100

PIONEER HI-BRED, INC.
221 North Main
Tipton, Indiana 46072

PIONEER ISLAND CREEK (coal)
See Island Creek Coal Company

PIONEER MANUFACTURING
COMPANY
3053 East 87th Street
Cleveland, Ohio 44104
James H. Schattinger, President,
Treasurer and General Manager
(216) 721-6161

PIONEER NATURAL GAS
COMPANY
Post Office Box 511
Amarillo, Texas 79105
C.I. Wall, Chairman of the Board
(806) 376-4841

PIONEER PIPE COMPANY
65-10 69th Place
Middle Village, New York 11379

PIONEER PRODUCTS COMPANY
28 Gardner Street
Salem, Massachusetts 01970

PIONEER RUBBER COMPANY, THE
(Division of Sherwood Medical
Industries, Inc.)
245 Tiffin Road
Willard, Ohio 44890
(419) 933-2211

PIONEER SAND & GRAVEL
COMPANY
See Lone Star Industries, Inc.,
Northwest Division

PIONEER SOAP COMPANY
470 Carolina Street
San Francisco, California 94107
(415) 861-1188

PIONEER STEEL COMPANY
10608 South Santa Fe Avenue
South Gate, California 90280
(213) 564-3303

PIPE MAJOR (tobacco)
See Brown & Williamson
Tobacco Corporation

PIPER AIRCRAFT CORPORATION
820 East Bald Eagle Street
Lock Haven, Pennsylvania 17745
J.L. Helms, President
(717) 478-6711

PIPER BRACE SALES CORPORATION
811 Wyandotte Street
Kansas City, Missouri 64105
(816) 842-2040
See also Sealtite

PIPER HEIDSIECK (champagne)
See Renfield Importers Ltd.

PIPER HEIDSIECK (tobacco)
See Conwood Corporation

PIPIN HOT (heated serving tray)
See Kenro Corporation

PIPING ROCK (cordials)
See American Distilling
Company, Inc.

PIPING ROCK (men's toiletries)
See Kayser-Roth Hosiery
Company, Inc.

PIQUA ENGINEERING INC.
234 First Street
Piqua, Ohio 45356
(513) 773-2464

PIRANHA BOAT CORPORATION
9970 Banyan Street
Miami, Florida 33157
(305) 233-5554

PIRATE COVE (fruits and vegetables)
See Earl Fruit Company

PIRELLI TIRE CORPORATION
(Subsidiary of Pirelli SPA)
600 Third Avenue
New York, New York 10016
Pierre G. Sierra, President
(212) 490-1300

PISCES (dresses)
See Suzy Perette Dresses, Inc.

Companies and Trade Names

PISGAH PHARMACEUTICALS, INC.
Box 10105
Greenville, South Carolina 29603

PISTACHIO GROWERS
ASSOCIATION
2141 Tuolumne
Fresno, California 93721

PISTOL (processed foods)
See H.P. Cannon & Sons Inc.

PISTOL, INC., A.W.
8-10-12 Drake Avenue
New Rochelle, New York 10805

PIT STOP (auto-care franchise)
See National Auto Wax Systems Inc.

PITCO (frying appliances)
See J.C. Pitman & Sons Inc.

PITLOW COMPANY INC., THE
1045 39th Street
Brooklyn, New York 11219
(212) 871-2080

PITMAN & SONS, INC., J.C.
Post Office Box 501
Bow Junction
Concord, New Hampshire 03302
Lolett Pitman, President
(603) 225-6684

PITMAN-DREITZER
(Division of Lancaster Colony Corporation)
225 Fifth Avenue
New York, New York 10010
(212) 924-7700

PITMAN-MOORE INC.
(Division of Johnson & Johnson)
Bear Tavern Road
Washington Crossing, New Jersey 08560
(609) 737-3700

PITNEY BOWES, INC.
Walnut and Pacific
Stanford, Connecticut 06904
Fred T. Allen, President
(203) 356-5000

PITTSBURGH (paints, brushes)
See PPG Industries

PITTSBURGH BREWING COMPANY
3340 Liberty Avenue
Pittsburgh, Pennsylvania 15201
Louis J. Slais, President
(412) 682-7400

PITTSBURGH CHEMICAL
LABORATORY
Century Building
Pittsburgh, Pennsylvania 15222
(412) 391-0160

PITTSBURGH CORNING
CORPORATION
(Affiliation of PPG Industries)
800 Presque Isle Drive
Pittsburgh, Pennsylvania 15239
R.E. Buckley, Assistant to President
(412) 327-6100

PITTSBURGH NATIONAL BANK
Fifth Avenue at Wood
Pittsburgh, Pennsylvania 15230
Robert C. Milson, President
(412) 355-2000

PITTSBURGH PLATE GLASS
COMPANY
See PPG Industries

PITTSBURGH STAMP COMPANY INC.
817 South Canal Street
Pittsburgh, Pennsylvania 15212
(412) 321-5248

PIXACOL COMPANY
Department DB
Box 38
Avon Lake, Ohio 44012

PIXALL (grooming products)
See Maywood Industries, Inc.

PIXIANA (canned foods)
See Swayzee Packing Company

PIXIE (facial and toilet tissue, diapers, towels)
See Romar Tissue Mills, Inc.

PIXIE (food products)
See Keystone Co-operative Grape Association

PIXIE (juvenile furniture)
See Lullabye Company

PIXIE PAK (food products)
See Flanagan Brothers Inc.

PIZZA FOOD PRODUCTS
CORPORATION, ANTHONY J.
Post Office Box 424
401 East Joe Orr Road
Chicago Heights, Illinois 60411
Anthony J. Pizza, Chairman of the Board
(312) 568-7700

PIZZA HUT, INC.
10225 East Kellogg
Wichita, Kansas 67207
Frank L. Carney, President
(316) 687-4111

PIZZA INN, INC.
2930 Stemmons Freeway
Dallas, Texas 75247
F.J. Spillman, President
(214) 638-7250

PIZZA SPINS (snack foods)
See General Mills, Inc.

PIZZAGETTI N BEEF (spaghetti and beef in pizza sauce)
See American Home Foods

Companies and Trade Names

PLA-FOLD (juvenile furniture)
See All-Luminum Products Inc.

PLA-KRIB (juvenile product)
See Barden & Robeson Corporation

PLACE 'N PRESS (floor tile)
See Armstrong Cork Company

PLACO PRODUCTS COMPANY
Post Office Box 3456
Torrance, California 90510

PLAGWITZ ENTERPRISES
398 Bridlewood Circle
Decatur, Georgia 30030

PLAHELTH ARCH (canvas shoes)
See Uniroyal, Inc., Footwear Division

PLAID (thermos bottles)
See Aladdin Industries, Inc.

PLAID (trading stamps)
See E.F. MacDonald Stamp Company

PLAINWELL CANNING COMPANY
Plainwell, Michigan 49080
Ronald Pell, President, Chief Engineer and Work Manager
(616) 682-6561

PLAISIR (bath oil, dusting powder, perfume, talc, etc.)
See Revlon, Inc.

PLAKIE TOYS INC.
4105 Simon Road
Youngstown, Ohio 44512

PLANO MOLDING COMPANY
113 South Center Avenue
Plano, Illinois 60545
James L. Henning, President and General Manager
(312) 552-3111

PLANT INDUSTRIES, INC.
1235 South State College Boulevard
Anaheim, California 92806
W.R. Tucker, President
(714) 778-3600
See also Sunaid Food Products

PLANT MARVEL LABORATORIES
624 West 119th
Chicago, Illinois 60628
(312) 264-0450

PLANTABBS CORPORATION
Timonium, Maryland 21093
David H. Fulton, Jr., President

PLANTATION (phonograph records)
See Shelby Singleton Corporation

PLANTATION (processed meat products)
See John Morrell & Company

PLANTATION FOODS INC.
Box 887
Waco, Texas 76704

PLANTATION PATTERNS INC.
Post Office Box 31049
Birmingham, Alabama 35222

PLANTERS CLUB (Bourbon)
See Continental Distilling Corporation

PLANTERS PEANUTS
(Division of Standard Brands, Inc.)
Suffolk, Virginia 23434
W.D. Shaw, President
(804) 539-2345

PLAPET TOGS (children's wear)
See Simon & Mogilner Company

PLASBAK (protective sheets, towels, and bibs)
See Graham Manufacturing Company

PLASKOLITE INC.
Box 1497
1770 Joyce Avenue
Columbus, Ohio 43216
Robert I. Yeoman, President
(614) 294-3281

PLASTEX COMPANY
800 North Clark Street
Chicago, Illinois 60610
(312) 787-8358

PLASTI-KOTE COMPANY
(Division of Consolidated Foods Corporation)
1000 Lake Road
Medina, Ohio 44256
(216) 725-4511

PLASTI-LINER COMPANY, INC.
See Brimms Plasti-Liner Company, Inc.

PLASTI MEND (liquid plastic repair and sealer)
See Nip-Co Manufacturing Inc.

PLASTI-MUSIC COMPANY INC.
(Division of C.G. Conn Ltd.)
109 Parker Drive
Evansville, Indiana 47714

PLASTIC BINDING CORPORATION
732 South Sherman
Chicago, Illinois 60605
H. Melnikoff, President
(312) 427-2903

PLASTIC FABRICATORS
127-129 West 24th Street
New York, New York 10011
(212) 924-9124

PLASTIC FABRICATORS INC.
308 Morse Street
Hamden, Connecticut 06517
David A. Beckerman, President
(203) 787-4291

Companies and Trade Names

PLASTIC FINE ARTS OF
   NEW YORK
911 Boulevard East
Weehauken, New Jersey 07087

PLASTIC LACE INC.
65 Walnut
Peabody, Massachusetts 01960

PLASTIC PRODUCTS, INC.
1822 East Franklin
Richmond, Virginia 23223
(804) 644-2355

PLASTIC REEL CORPORATION OF
   AMERICA
640 South Commercial Avenue
Carlstadt, New Jersey 07072
(201) 933-9125

PLASTIC WOOD (filler)
   See Boyle-Midway

PLASTIC WOVEN PRODUCTS INC.
51 Camden Street
Paterson, New Jersey 07503
(201) 742-9282

PLASTICLOTH PRODUCTS INC.
39-08 24th Street
Long Island City, New York 11101

PLASTICOID PRODUCTS INC.
Box 526
Warehouse Point, Connecticut 06088
(203) 623-4471

PLASTICS DEVELOPMENT
   CORPORATION
33091 Calle Perfecto
San Juan Capistrano,
   California 92675

PLASTICS, INC.
Post Office Box 3610
Saint Paul, Minnesota 55165

PLASTICS MANUFACTURING
   COMPANY
2700 South Westmoreland Avenue
Dallas, Texas 75233
(214) 331-5435

PLASTICS RESEARCH & DEVELOP-
   MENT CORPORATION
3601 Jenny Lind Road
Fort Smith, Arkansas 72901
(501) 782-8971

PLASTICS/2000 INC.
12 East Tenth Street
Erie, Pennsylvania 16501
(814) 455-2000

PLASTIMAYD CORPORATION
2204 S.E. Seventh Avenue
Portland, Oregon 97214
(503) 232-5101

PLASTRA TONE (paint)
   See Superior Paint & Varnish
   Corporation

PLASTRON (curtains)
   See Arnel-Plastron

PLASTRON INDUSTRIES
533 Commerce Street
Franklin Lakes, New Jersey 07417
(201) 891-1222

PLATH COMPANY, R.C.
337 N.E. Tenth Street
Portland, Oregon 97232
(503) 232-5509

PLATINE (cologne, dusting powder,
perfume)
   See Dana Perfumes, Inc.

PLATINUM PLUS (razor blades)
   See Gillette Safety Razor
   Company

PLATT LUGGAGE INC.
2301 South Prairie Avenue
Chicago, Illinois 60616
Paul Platt, President and Sales
   Manager
(312) 225-6670

PLATTE VALLEY (vinegar, pickles)
   See Haarman Vinegar & Pickle
   Company

PLATTNER INDUSTRIES INC.
1019 East North Ottawa
North Kansas City, Missouri 64153
(816) 782-4212
   See also Hamilton Skotch

PLAX-N-THINGS
1435 Westwood Hills Road
Saint Louis Park, Minnesota 55426

PLAY-DOH (toy)
   See Kenner Products (Division of
   General Mills Fun Group,
   Inc.)

PLAY-PAL PLASTICS INC.
200 Fifth Avenue
New York, New York 10010
(212) 929-0915

PLAYARD (juvenile furniture)
   See Century Products Inc.

PLAYBOY ENTERPRISES, INC.
919 North Michigan Avenue
Chicago, Illinois 60611
Hugh H. Hefner, President
(312) 751-8000

PLAYCRIB (infants' product)
   See Strolee of California

PLAYDAY (vacuum cleaner)
   See Sunbeam Appliance Company

Companies and Trade Names

PLAYER PIANO COMPANY INC.
620 East Douglas
Wichita, Kansas 67202

PLAYERS CHOICE (combination game set)
See E.S. Lowe Company, Inc.

PLAYGIRL FOUNDATIONS INC.
10 Taylor Street
Freeport, New York 11520

PLAYLAND INDUSTRIES, INC.
112 West 34th Street
New York, New York 10001
Benjamin Levine, President
(212) 564-8540

PLAYMORE (sportswear)
See Warnaco Inc.

PLAYSKOOL, INC.
(Subsidiary of Milton Bradley Company)
4501 West Augusta Boulevard
Chicago, Illinois 60651
James J. Shea, Jr., President
(312) 276-6700

PLAYTEX (rubber gloves, nursers and accessories, tampons, foundation garments)
See International Playtex Corporation

PLAYTIME (canned foods)
See Universal Packers Corporation

PLAYTIMER INDUSTRIES, LTD.
527 West Main Street
Elizabethville, Pennsylvania 17023
Frank F. Idestone, President
(717) 362-8132

PLAZA (groceries, detergents)
See P. D'Aoust, Ltd.

PLAZA (metal arm chairs)
See Lumex Inc.

PLAZA (window shades)
See Breneman, Inc.

PLEASANT THOUGHTS INC.
2100 Section Road
Cincinnati, Ohio 45237
(513) 841-6833

PLEASANT VALLEY WINE COMPANY
Hammondsport, New York 14840
C. Frederic Schroeder, Management Director
(607) 569-2121

PLEAT SEAT (infants' product)
See Gerico Inc.

PLEDGE (furniture polish)
See S.C. Johnson & Son Inc.

PLEETSKIRT (apparel)
See Koret of California, Inc.

PLEETWAY (men's pajamas, loungewear)
See Hansley Industries Inc.

PLESSEY ELECTRONICS CORPORATION
170 Finn Court
Farmingdale, New York 11735

PLESSNER COMPANY, INC., PAUL
Box 7087
Saint Petersburg, Florida 33734

PLEVER INDUSTRIES, INC.
400 Gotham Parkway
Carlstadt, New Jersey 07072
(201) 935-1300

PLEXI-PEG INC.
80-55 250th Street
Bellerose, New York 11426

PLEXIGLAS (plastic sheets, rods, tubes, etc.)
See Rohm & Haas Company

PLEXO PREPARATIONS
220 Eighth Street
Lewistown, Pennsylvania 17044
(717) 248-5834

PLEXTONE CORPORATION OF AMERICA
2141 McCarter Highway
Newark, New Jersey 07104
(201) 484-4443

PLINKIES
588 Lee Street
Glen Ellyn, Illinois 60137

PLIOFLEX (synthetic rubber)
See Goodyear Tire & Rubber Company

PLOGER PACKING COMPANY INC., THE
Box 476
Darien, Georgia 31305

PLOUGH, INC.
(Subsidiary of Schering-Plough, Inc.)
3030 Jackson Avenue
Memphis, Tennessee 38151
R. Lee Jenkins, President
(901) 320-2011
See also Coppertone Corporation; DAP, Inc.; and Pharmaco

PLOW BOY (tobacco)
See Liggett & Myers Inc.

PLOW HORSE (lawn and garden supplies)
See Coast to Coast Stores

PLUESS-STAUFER (NORTH AMERICAN) INC.
1 World Trade Center
New York, New York 10048
(212) 466-0550

Companies and Trade Names

PLUM TREE (import gift shops franchise)
See Aamco Industries Inc.

PLUMB (tools)
See Ames Company

PLUMB, INC., FAYETTE R.
4837 James Street
Philadelphia, Pennsylvania 19137
D. Rumsey Plumb, President
(215) 831-1515

PLUMBER SAVER (drain opener)
See Gillette Company

PLUMITE (drain cleaner)
See Simoniz Company

PLUMROSE, INC.
66 Fadem Road
Springfield, New Jersey 07081

PLUNGE (drain opener)
See Drackett Company

PLURA PLASTICS INC.
27 Newark Way
Maplewood, New Jersey 07040

PLUS (gourmet cookware)
See Gense Import Ltd.

PLUS 5 (varnish)
See Baltimore Copper Paint

PLUS 4 (beverages)
See Monarch-Nugrape Company

PLUS POULTRY, INC.
Post Office Box 430
Siloam Springs, Arkansas 72761

PLUS PRODUCTS
2425 East 38th Street
Los Angeles, California 90058
Gordon MacDonald, President
(213) 582-5144

PLUS WHITE (toothpaste)
See Bishop Industries, Inc.

PLUTO CORPORATION
Post Office Box 391
French Lick, Indiana 47432
(812) 936-9988

PLUTO DOG FURNISHINGS INC.
154-158 Ludlow Street
New York, New York 10002
(212) 475-5503

PLY-FLEX (fishing rods and bow arrows)
See Sportsmen Accessories, Inc.

PLY-GEM INDUSTRIES INC.
182-20 Liberty Avenue
Jamaica, New York 11412
(212) 454-4500

PLYCRAFT CORPORATION
Box 44-S
Walterboro, South Carolina 29488
(803) 538-2277

PLYMOLD (wardrobe trunks)
See Hartmann Luggage Company, Inc.

PLYMOUTH (gin)
See Schenley Industries, Inc.

PLYMOUTH (grocery products)
See Piggly Wiggly Corporation

PLYMOUTH (motor vehicles)
See Chrysler-Plymouth (Division of Chrysler Motors Corporation)

PLYMOUTH (shoes for men)
See Kayser-Roth Shoes, Inc.

PLYMOUTH (tobacco pouches, cigar and cigarette cases)
See Associated Import Corporation

PLYMOUTH CITRUS PRODUCTS COOPERATIVE
Highway 441
Plymouth, Florida 32768
J.R. Graves, Chairman and President
(305) 886-1111

PLYMOUTH CORDAGE
(Division of Columbian Rope Company)
309 West Genesee Street
Auburn, New York 13021

PLYMOUTH GOLF BALL COMPANY
(Subsidiary of Shakespeare Company)
Butler Pike
Plymouth Meeting, Pennsylvania 19462
James G. Hogg, President
(215) 828-7400

PLYMOUTH, INC.
Benigno Boulevard
Bellmawr, New Jersey 08030
(215) 463-7000

PLYMOUTH PINK (liquor)
See Schenley Industries, Inc.

PLYMOUTH ROCK (meat products)
See Ward Foods, Inc.

PLYMOUTH RUBBER COMPANY, INC.
Revere Street
Canton, Massachusetts 02021
Daniel M. Hamilburg, President and Treasurer
(617) 828-0220

Companies and Trade Names

POCASSET PRODUCTS COMPANY
Post Office Box One
Tiverton, Rhode Island 02878

POCKET (stoves)
See Coleman Company, Inc.

POCKET BOOKS, INC.
See Simon and Schuster, Inc., Pocket Books Division

POCKET-MATIC (camera)
See Berkey Keystone (Division of Berkey Photo Inc.)

POCKET PACKET (houseboat)
See Poseidon Corporation

POCKETALK (packet paging system)
See Executone Inc.

POCKMAN
(Division of Chore Time)
Box 1908
Decatur, Alabama 35601

PODAN COMPANY (hardware)
See Baekgaard Ltd.

POE CANDY COMPANY
3600 Leonard Road
Saint Joseph, Missouri 64502

POETRY COLLECTION (cologne, lipstick, toilet soap)
See Yardley of London

POGUE COMPANY, THE H. & S.
(Division of Associated Dry Goods)
Fourth and Race Streets
Cincinnati, Ohio 45202
Edward M. Condon, President
(513) 381-4700

POHLSON GALLERIES INC.
Post Office Box 1627
547 Roosevelt Avenue
Pawtucket, Rhode Island 02863
(401) 722-5086

POINT ADAMS PACKING COMPANY
(Subsidiary of Westgate California Corporation)
Foot of Ford Street
Hammond, Oregon 97121
John Day, President
(503) 861-2226

POINT LAND (canned foods)
See Klauber Wangeheim Company

POINT 'N SHOOT (pocket camera)
See Ponder & Best

POINT OF SALES, INC.
Box 17
Cannon Falls, Minnesota 55009

POINT VIEW (canned foods)
See Furman Canning Company

POIRETTE CORSETS, INC.
115 West 18th Street
New York, New York 10011
Jack E. Robbins, President
(212) 924-3003

POISE (paint)
See The O'Brien Corporation

POLAK'S FRUTAL WORKS, INC.
33 Sprage Avenue
Middletown, New York 10940
(914) 342-1065

POLAMER DRUG COMPANY, INC.
54 Main Street
South River, New Jersey 08882

POLAND (vodka)
See Consolidated Distilled Products Inc.

POLAND SPRING (distilled gin)
See Lawrence & Company, Inc.

POLANER & SON, INC., M.
462 Eagle Rock Avenue
Roseland, New Jersey 07068
Leonard S. Polaner, President
(201) 228-2500

POLAR (frozen vegetables)
See Cedergreen Foods

POLAR BEAR (food products)
See Griffin Grocery Company

POLAR KRAFT MANUFACTURING COMPANY
Drawer 708
Olive Branch, Mississippi 38654
(601) 895-5576

POLAR MANUFACTURING COMPANY
900-908 West Russell Street
Philadelphia, Pennsylvania 19140
(215) 229-7445

POLAR 125 (tires)
See Hercules Tire & Rubber Company

POLAR WARE COMPANY
Lake Shore Road
Sheboygan, Wisconsin 53081
Richard J. Vollrath, President and Treasurer
(414) 458-3561

POLARAD ELECTRONICS CORPORATION
5 Delaware Drive
Lake Success, New York 11040
Robert S. Schlanger, Chairman and President
(516) 328-1100

Companies and Trade Names

POLARIS
(Division of Textron, Inc.)
1225 North County Road 18
Minneapolis, Minnesota 55427
Beverly F. Dolan, President
(612) 546-4252

POLAROID CORPORATION
549 Technology Square
Cambridge, Massachusetts 02139
Edwin H. Land, President
(617) 864-6000

POLE-MASTER (floor-to-ceiling shelving)
See Quaker Industries Inc.

POLE STAR (groceries)
See Compass Foods, Inc.

POLI-GRIP (denture adhesive)
See Block Drug Company, Inc.

POLIDENT (denture cleanser)
See Block Drug Company, Inc.

POLIGNAC (cognac)
See Dennis & Huppert Company

POLISI (bassoons and contrabassoons)
See Ardsley Musical Instrument Corporation

POLKA DOT (milk and ice cream)
See Tom Thumb Food Markets

POLL PARROT (shoes)
See International Shoe Company

POLLACK PRINTING CORPORATION
Pollack Poster Division
877 Main Street
Buffalo, New York 14203
H. William Pollack, President
(716) 884-8204

POLLAK, INC., HENRY
1410 Broadway
New York, New York 10018
Henry Pollak, President and Treasurer
(212) 221-8600

POLLEN CHIA COMMERCE
Box 1468
Santa Monica, California 90406

POLLENEX (health and beauty applicances--vaporizers, steam hair curlers)
See Associated Mills, Inc.

POLLENEX HEALTH APPLIANCE DIVISION
See Associated Mills, Inc.

POLLMAN (bass violins)
See C. Meisel Music Company Inc.

POLLY (food products)
See Taormina Company

POLLY DEBS (women's shoes)
See International Shoe Company

POLLY-FLEX (housewares)
See Republic Molding Corporation

POLLY TRADING CORPORATION
44 Eldridge Street
New York, New York 10002

POLLYANNA (canned foods)
See Silver Creek Preserving Corporation

POLLYANNA PRODUCTS
56 Belmont Street
Carbondale, Pennsylvania 18407

POLO CLUB (dry gin)
See American Distilling Company, Inc.

POLO FOOD PRODUCTS COMPANY
(Division of Allied Mills, Inc.)
601 East Algonquin
Schaumburg, Illinois 60172

POLORIS (dental poultice)
See Block Drug Company, Inc.

POLORON PRODUCTS, INC.
550 Mamaroneck Avenue
Harrison, New York 10528
David Hanania, President
(914) 381-2800

POLSKI-ORZEL (food products)
See Benjamin Lipitz Company

POLSON INTERNATIONAL CORPORATION
290-300 Route Four
East Paterson, New Jersey 07407

POLY-AQUA (epoxy enamel)
See Valspar Corporation

POLY CHOKE COMPANY, INC., THE
Post Office Box 296
Hartford, Connecticut 06101

POLY-GUARD (sheets and pillowcases)
See Unitex Products Inc.

POLY-OLEUM CORPORATION
13531 Greenfield Road
Detroit, Michigan 48227
(313) 838-4280

POLY-OPTICS, INC.
1815 East Carnegie
Santa Ana, California 92705
Richard A. Demmer, President
(714) 546-2250

Companies and Trade Names

POLY SEAL CORPORATION, THE
280 Henderson Street
Jersey City, New Jersey 07302
(201) 432-9562

POLY-TECH
(Division of United States
 Industries, Inc.)
1401 West 94th Street
Minneapolis, Minnesota 554321
(612) 884-7281

POLY-VERSION, INC.
10001 East 54th Street
Tulsa, Oklahoma 74145
(918) 628-0200

POLYCHEM CORPORATION
12 Lyman Street
New Haven, Connecticut 06511

POLYCHEMICAL LABORATORIES
490-498 Hunts Point Avenue
Bronx, New York 10474
(212) 887-0333

POLYCHROME (scissors and shears)
See White Sewing Machine
 Company

POLYCHROME CORPORATION
Paper Products Division
520 Baltimore Avenue
Fernwood, Pennsylvania 19650
(215) 626-4000

POLYCORD (sewing thread)
See Coats & Clark's Sales
 Corporation

POLYDERM (astringent, skin
cleanser, etc.)
See Prince Matchabelli, Inc.

POLYFORM PRODUCTS INC.
9420 West Byron Street
Schiller Park, Illinois 60176

POLYGLAS (tires)
See Goodyear Tire & Rubber

POLYLURE (paint)
See Glidden-Durkee

POLYMED LABORATORIES, INC.
556 West 29th Street
Hialeah, Florida 33012

POLYPLAN CORPORATION
Post Office Box 186
Santa Barbara, California 93103

POLYPOXY (epoxy coating)
See Pettit Paint Company Inc.

POLYTHERM PLASTICS
(Division of Polysar Plastics, Inc.)
1971 Republic Plaza
Middletown, New York 10940
(914) 343-7971

POLYTONE (guitar, bass, cello,
and violin amplifiers and pick-ups)
See Castiglione Accordion &
 Distributing Company

POM POM (cosmetic products)
See Kendall Company

POM POM (enamelware)
See Vefa, Inc.

POM POMS (shoes)
See Foot Flairs Inc.

POMATEX COMPANY, INC.
60 East 42nd Street
New York, New York 10017
(212) 661-3197

POMBAL (wines)
See North America Wines
 Corporation

POMCO (groceries)
See Food International, Inc.

POMEROY'S DEPARTMENT STORES,
 INC.
(Subsidiary of Allied Stores
 Corporation)
Post Office Box 1876
Harrisburg, Pennsylvania 17105
Leon D. Starr, President
(717) 238-1661

POMIDORA (pizza sauce, tomato
puree)
See Delaware Valley Packing
 Company

POMMERELLE (wines)
See American Wine Growers

POMMERY (champagne)
See Somerset Importers, Ltd.

POMONA PRODUCTS COMPANY
(Division of Stokely-Van Camp,
 Inc.)
Post Office Box 57
Griffin, Georgia 30223
Robert L. Rice, President
(404) 228-8456

POMONA TILE MANUFACTURING
 COMPANY
(Division of American Olean
 Company)
216 South Reservoir Street
Pomona, California 91766

POMPANETTE INC.
Box 276
Dania, Florida 33004

POMPANO (wine)
See United Vintners, Inc.

POMPEIA (cologne, perfume, soap)
See Caswell-Massey Company,
 Ltd.

Companies and Trade Names

POMPEIAN, INC.
4201 Pulaski Highway
Baltimore, Maryland 21224
(301) 276-6900

POMPEII (shoes)
See Wolverine World Wide, Inc.

PONCE DE LEON (rum)
See Old Florida Rum Company

POND COMPANY, INC., A.H.
120 East Washington
Syracuse, New York 13202
Robert O. Beadel, President
(315) 472-7741

POND MANUFACTURING COMPANY, THE
80 Bellevue Avenue
Rutland, Vermont 05701

PONDER & BEST, INC.
11201 West Pico Boulevard
Los Angeles, California 90064
John C. Best, Chairman of the Board
(213) 478-1011

PONDERABLES (sports apparel)
See Mighty-Mac

PONDEROSA SYSTEM, INC.
3661 Salem Avenue
Dayton, Ohio 45406
Gerald S. Office, Jr., President
(513) 890-6400

POND'S (makeup, skin-care products, talc, etc.)
See Chesebrough-Pond's, Inc.

PONTIAC MOTORS
(Division of General Motors Corporation)
1 Pontiac Plaza
Pontiac, Michigan 48053
Alex C. Mair, General Manager
(313) 857-5000

PONY (hand tools and furniture)
See O. Ames Company

PONY PET (juvenile product)
See Mapes Industries Inc.

POOL BUTLER BOTTOM VAC (swimming-pool accessory)
See Coastal Chemical Company

POOLE (pianos)
See Aeolian Corporation

POOLE SILVER COMPANY
(Subsidiary of Towle Manufacturing Company)
320 Whittenton Street
Taunton, Massachusetts 02780
Stuart C. Hemingway, Chairman of the Board
(617) 824-7584

POP-R-CORN (snack product)
See General Mills

POP-TARTS (pastry)
See Kellogg Company

POPE PRODUCTS
(Division of Purex Corporation, Ltd.)
212 Gates Road
Little Ferry, New Jersey 07643
Victor Capelouto, Vice President
(201) 641-1710

POPEYE (groceries)
See Stokely-Van Camp, Inc.

POPOV (vodka)
See Heublein Inc.

POPPED-RIGHT, INC.
Box 687
Marion, Ohio 43302
(614) 383-0431

POPPIN' FRESH (food products)
See Pillsbury Company

POPPIN GOOD (popcorn)
See International Multifoods Corporation

POPPY (cookware)
See National Silver Company

POPPY (lawn sprinkler)
See L.R. Nelson Manufacturing Company Inc.

POPPYCOCK (popcorn specialty)
See Ovaltine Food Products

POPPYTRAIL BY METLOX POTTERIES
1200 Morningside Drive
Manhattan Beach, California 90266

POP'S PAL (men's slacks)
See Barrow Manufacturing Company

POPSICLE INDUSTRIES
(Division of Consolidated Foods Corporation)
110 Route Four
Englewood, New Jersey 07631
Edward F. Gaebler, President
(201) 567-8500

POPULAR SERVICES, INC.
128 Dayton Avenue
Passaic, New Jersey 07055
Kenneth Freedman, President
(201) 471-4300

POPYKINS (house slippers)
See Bentley International

PORCE-NAMEL (kitchen furniture)
See Mutschler

PORCELUM (cookware)
See Buehner-Wanner

Companies and Trade Names

PORSCHE (motor vehicles)
See Volkswagen of America, Inc.

PORT-A-BAR (infants' product)
See Port-a-Crib Inc.

PORT-A-BAR (luggage)
See Maximillian Luggage Corporation

PORT-A-CRIB INC.
203 Ramsey Lane
Ballwin, Missouri 63011

PORT-A CRYLIC TABLE (acrylic tables)
See Carrollton Products Company

PORT CLYDE PACKING COMPANY, INC.
Post Office Box E
Hicksville, New York 11802
Irving Zwecker, President
(516) 433-0390
See also Royal River Packing Company; and Stonington Packing Company

PORT HURON PAPER COMPANY
Foot of Washington Avenue
Port Huron, Michigan 48060
Gordon Morseth, President
(313) 982-0191

PORTA-BATH (inflatable portable infant baths)
See Baby Care

PORTA-LITE (battery-operated table lamps)
See Prestigeline

PORTA-PAIR (washer and dryer combination)
See Maytag Company

PORTABILT (kitchens)
See Mutschler

PORTABLE CRIBETTE (infants' product)
See Toidey Company Inc.

PORTABLE ELECTRIC TOOLS
(Division of McGraw-Edison Company)
1200 East State Street
Geneva, Illinois 60134
R.L. Schultz, President
(313) 232-2500

PORTAFRIDGE (portable refrigerator)
See General Thermetics Inc.

PORTAGE (men's shoes)
See Weyenberg Shoe Manufacturing Company

PORTAL (books)
See Warner Press

PORTAL (frozen foods)
See Oxnard Frozen Foods Cooperative

PORTER & COMPANY, R.S.
260 West Broadway
New York, New York 10013
(212) 925-5430

PORTER & DIETSCH, INC.
2453 University Avenue
Saint Paul, Minnesota 55114

PORTER-HAYDEN COMPANY
Post Office Box 476
Edison, New Jersey 08817

PORTER, INC., H.K.
74 Foley Street
Somerville, Massachusetts 02143
Henry K. Porter, President
(617) 776-8200
See also Disston, Inc.; and Thermoid

PORTER'S PRODUCTS
Box 142
Covington, Ohio 45318

PORTFOLIO (soap, shampoo)
See Avon Products, Inc.

PORTLAND FISH COMPANY
301 N.W. Third Avenue
Portland, Oregon 97209
(503) 224-1681

PORTLAND GENERAL ELECTRIC COMPANY
621 S.W. Alder Street
Portland, Oregon 97205
Frank M. Warren, President
(503) 228-7181

PORTLAND PROVISION COMPANY
Columbia and North Burrage
Portland, Oregon 97217
(503) 289-1161

PORTRAIT (cosmetics)
See Yardley of London Inc.

PORTRAIT (home-permanent hair wave)
See Lehn & Fink Products Corporation

PORTRONIC (tools)
See Coleman Systems

POSEIDON CORPORATION
Post Office Box 358
Leeds, Alabama 35094

POSH GIN (liquor)
See Continental Distilling Company

POSLAM (ointment)
See Block Drug Company, Inc.

Companies and Trade Names

POSNER LABORATORIES, INC.
38-19 108th Street
Corona, New York 11368
Karl G. Heinze, President
(212) 478-3200

POST (breakfast foods)
See General Foods Corporation

POST ELECTRIC COMPANY INC.
Post Office Box 335TR
Andover, New Jersey 07821
(201) 786-5350

POST HOUSES RESTAURANTS
See Greyhound Corporation

POST, INC., HERBERT A.
26-30 Borough Place
Woodside New York 11377

POST MARINE COMPANY, INC.
River Road
Mays Landing, New Jersey 08330

POST-O-METER (scales)
See Detecto Scales, Inc.

POST ROAD (carpeting)
See Lees Carpets

POST TIME (men's toiletries)
See Posner Laboratories Inc.

POST TOASTIES (cereal)
See General Foods Corporation

POSTAGE STAMP MACHINE
COMPANY
2008 Utica Avenue
Brooklyn, New York 11234
(212) 241-8500

POSTAL FINANCE COMPANY
814 Pierce
Sioux City, Iowa 51101
D.J. Levitt, Chairman of the Board
(712) 258-0624

POSTALETT (scales)
See Exact Weight Scale Company

POSTAMATIC COMPANY INC.
Post Office Box 279
Lafayette Hill, Pennsylvania 19444
(215) 828-2428

POSTCARD MUSIC
Box 146
Mount Vernon, Kentucky 40456

POSTE (food products)
See Green Bay Food Company

POSTER BROTHERS INC.
(Division of Brown Group Company)
1934 North Washtenaw Avenue
Chicago, Illinois 60647
Harold G. Caro, President
(312) 227-6100

POSTER PRINTS
1899 New Hope Street
Norristown, Pennsylvania 19401

POSTILLION (pipes)
See A. Oppenheimer & Company

POSTING EQUIPMENT
CORPORATION
752 Military Road
Buffalo, New York 14216
(716) 877-1185

POSTLITE (lights)
See Drake Manufacturing
Company

POSTUM (breakfast drink)
See General Foods Corporation

POSTUR-MATIC (metal posture chairs)
See Domore Office Furniture
Inc.

POSTURBILT (furniture)
See Hamilton Manufacturing
Company

POSTURE ARCH POSITIONER
(shoes and shoe materials)
See Bristol Manufacturing
Corporation

POSTURE-RITE (posture chairs)
See Wells Industries

POSTUREPEDIC (mattress)
See Sealy, Inc.

POT BELLY STOVE (lamps)
See Rand Products Company,
Inc.

POT-O-GLOSS (wet-look lip glosses)
See Yardley of London, Inc.

POT POURRI (room spray, sachets, soaps, eau de cologne, scented notes)
See Claire Burke Inc.

POTATO SERVICE INC.
(Subsidiary of American
   Kitchen Foods Inc.)
Box 220
Roslyn Heights, New York 11577

POTLACH (groceries)
See Jacob Hamburger Company,
Inc.

POTLATCH CORPORATION
Post Office Box 3591
1 Maritime Plaza
San Francisco, California 94119
Richard B. Madden, President
(415) 981-5980

Companies and Trade Names

POTLATCH FORESTS, INC.
Consumer Products Division
1290 Avenue of the Americas
New York, New York 10019
See also Northwest Paper Company; and Swanee Paper Company Inc.

POTOCEK ASSOCIATES, M.M.
95 Lockerby Land
Westwood, New Jersey 07675

POTOMAC EDISON COMPANY
(Subsidiary of Allegheny System, Inc.)
Downsville Pike
Hagerstown, Maryland 21740
C.B. Finch, President
(301) 731-3400

POTOMAC ELECTRIC POWER COMPANY
1900 Pennsylvania Avenue N.W.
Washington, D.C. 20068
W. Reid Thompson, President
(202) 872-2000

POTOMAC INSURANCE COMPANY
General Building
414 Walnut Street
Philadelphia, Pennsylvania 19105
Harold Scott Baile, President
(215) 238-5000

POTOSI BREWING COMPANY
Potosi, Wisconsin 53820
(608) 763-2111

POTPOURRI (decorated cookware)
See Gemini International Corporation

POTT (rum)
See James B. Beam Distilling Company

POTTER INSTRUMENT COMPANY, INC.
151 Sunnyside Boulevard
Plainview, New York 11803
J.T. Potter, Chairman
(516) 694-9000

POTTER MANUFACTURING COMPANY
Post Office Drawer 988
Asheboro, North Carolina 27203

POTTERY PLACE
14934 Calvert Street
Van Nuys, California 91401

POTVIN SHOE COMPANY, INC., R.J.
960 Harrison Avenue
Boston, Massachusetts 02118
Arnold Hiatt, President
(617) 440-9300

POULET (French wines)
See Park, Benziger & Company, Inc.

POULTRY PRIDE (frozen chicken products)
See Vineland Processing Company Inc.

POUR & SAVE (frozen foods)
See Patterson Frozen Foods, Inc.

POUR UN HOMME (men's toiletries)
See Caron Corporation

POUST & COMPANY, INC., JACK
745 Fifth Avenue
New York, New York 10022
(212) 752-8580

POWDER-ENE (rug cleaner)
See Van Schroder Manufacturing Company

POWDER HORN (whiskey)
See Heublein Inc.

POWELL (automobile parts)
See International Parts Corporation

POWELL'S INC.
Excelsior Boulevard and Powell Road
Hopkins, Minnesota 55343

POWER-BILT (golf clubs)
See Hillerich & Bradsby Company, Inc.

POWER EXPRESS (tires)
See B.F. Goodrich Company

POWER GEL (tile and grout cleaner)
See Red Devil, Inc.

POWER-HO (garden tractor)
See Bolens (Division of FMC Corporation)

POWER INCORPORATED
12809 Eagle Ridge Drive
Burnsville, Minnesota 55337
(612) 890-1360

POWER PACK (power converter)
See Raritan Engineering Company

POWER PAK (high-intensity lamp)
See Bentley Gifts Inc.

POWER SPRAY (lawn sprinklers)
See H.B. Sherman Manufacturing Company

POWER TOOLS INC.
3771 Sibley Memorial Highway
Saint Paul, Minnesota 55122

Companies and Trade Names

POWER-TRAN OF AMERICA
Box 5534
9320 East South
Houston, Texas 77012
(713) 926-7449

POWERCAR
(Division of Conval Industries Inc.)
See Grand Prix Manufacturing Company

POWERCLEAN (vacuums)
See Dustbane Enterprises, Ltd.

POWERGLIDE (mobile wood shelving)
See Lundia, Myers Industries Inc.

POWERIDE (rechargeable, rideable vehicles)
See Eldon Industries Inc.

POWERITER CUSTOM (portable electric typewriter)
See SCM Corporation

POWERMASTER (hand tools)
See Oxwall Tool Company

POWERMIX (food mixers)
See Westinghouse Electric Corporation

POWERS COMPANY, H.W.
10-24 Medford Street
Boston, Massachusetts 02114
(617) 227-3060

POWERS FIGURE SALON, ELAINE
(Division of Unicare Health Services Inc.)
3201 Orange Grove Avenue
North Highlands, California 95660

POWHATAN (groceries)
See J.W. Wood

POW'R-GRIP (all-purpose adhesive)
See H.B. Fuller Company

POWR-KRAFT (saws)
See Montgomery Ward & Company

POYTHRESS & COMPANY, INC., WILLIAM P.
Box 26946
16 North 22nd Street
Richmond, Virginia 23261
Robert W. Houser, President
(804) 644-8591

PRADO (stainless-steel flatware)
See Cosmos Products

PRAEGER PUBLISHERS
111 Fourth Avenue
New York, New York 10003
David Replogle, President
(212) 255-4100

PRAGER & SUSSBACH COMPANY, INC.
71 West 47th Street
New York, New York 10036
(212) 246-9010

PRAIRIE BELT (canned meats)
See Bryan Brothers Packing Company

PRAIRIE FLOWER (cookware)
See National Silver Company

PRAIRIE VIEW HONEY COMPANY
12303 12th
Detroit, Michigan 48206
(313) 868-6764

PRAISE (deodorant soap)
See Lever Brothers Company

PRAK-T-KAL VAPODYNAMICS CORPORATION
See Purepac Corporation

PRAM INC.
Pram Plaza
Wilmerding, Pennsylvania 15148

PRAM-MOBILE (infants' product)
See Thayer Inc.

PRANG (modeling clay, watercolors, and tempera)
See American Crayon Company

PRANGE COMPANY, H.C.
727 North Eighth Street
Sheboygan, Wisconsin 53081
Henry C. Prange, President
(414) 457-3611

PRATT & AUSTIN COMPANY
642 South Summer Street
Holyoke, Massachusetts 01040
Leonard C. Pratt, President, Treasurer and Advertising Manager
(413) 532-1491

PRATT & LAMBERT, INC.
Box 22
75 Tonawanda Street
Buffalo, New York 14207
Raymond D. Stevens, Jr., President
(716) 873-6000
See also Pierce & Stevens Chemical Corporation

PRAXIS 48 (electric typewriters)
See Olivetti Corporation of America

PRE-FLEX (shoes)
See Mid-States Shoe Company

PRECIOUS BODY (permanent hair-wave products)
See Turner Hall Corporation

PRECIOUS FORM FOUNDATIONS
180 Madison Avenue
New York, New York 10016
(212) 685-0444

Companies and Trade Names

PRECISE IMPORTS CORPORATION
3 Chestnut Street
Suffern, New York 10901

PRECISION PEN COMPANY
7741 Burnet Avenue
Van Nuys, California 91405

PRECISION PRODUCTS INC.
2415 South Grand Avenue
Springfield, Illinois 62708
(217) 528-1311

PRECISION STAPLE CORPORATION
3944 Dearborn Avenue
Sarasota, Florida 33581
(813) 924-3106

PRECISION STEEL EQUIPMENT
 COMPANY
1117 Azusa Canyon Road
West Covina, California 91790

PRECISION TWIST DRILL &
 MACHINE COMPANY
Post Office Box 458
301 Industrial Avenue
Crystal Lake, Illinois 60014
James H. Beck, President and
 Treasurer
(815) 459-2040

PRECISION VALVE CORPORATION
Post Office Box 309
Yonkers, New York 10703
Robert H. Abplanalp, President
(914) 969-6500

PRECO CHEMICAL CORPORATION
55 Skyline Drive
Plainview, New York 11803
(516) 935-9100

PRECO INC.
415 Broadway
Boise, Idaho 83706
(206) 345-9000

PREDICTA (desks)
 See Marble Furniture Company

PREDICTOR (home pregnancy test)
 See Organon Inc.

PREEN (girls' coats)
 See Brand and Puritz

PREFERRED (meat products)
 See Neuhoff Brothers Packers,
  Inc.

PREFERRED (stainless-steel holloware)
 See Latoma, Inc.

PREFERRED FOUNDATIONS INC.
10 Taylor Street
Freeport, New York 11520

PREFERRED PRODUCTS
Box 4153
Normandy Station
Miami Beach, Florida 33141

PREFERRED STOCK (whiskey)
 See Continental Distilling
  Corporation

PREFONTAINES (French wine)
 See Munson Shaw Company

PREGO (bath oil, cologne,
perfume)
 See Rocar

PRELATE (salmon and tuna)
 See Whitney-Fidalgo Seafoods,
  Inc.

PRELL (shampoo)
 See Procter & Gamble Company

PRELUDE (glass products)
 See Viking Glass Company

PREM (canned luncheon meat)
 See Swift & Company

PREMIER (glassware)
 See Libbey (Division of Owens-
  Illinois Inc.)

PREMIER (percussion instruments and
accessories)
 See Selmer (Division of
  Magnavox Company)

PREMIER (portable typewriters)
 See Remington Rand Office
  Machines (Division of Sperry
  Rand Corporation)

PREMIER (sporting goods)
 See American Import Company

PREMIER BAG COMPANY, INC.
Post Office Box 206
700 Pennsylvania Avenue
Lynhurst, New Jersey 07071
Aaron Einhorn, President
(201) 933-2070

PREMIER ELECTRIC COMPANY
1734 Ivanhoe
Cleveland, Ohio 44112
(216) 249-4200

PREMIER INDUSTRIES INC.
Second and Madison Avenue
Covington, Kentucky 41011
(606) 581-1390

PREMIER MALT PRODUCTS, INC.
1137 North Eight Street
Milwaukee, Wisconsin 53201
(414) 271-4272

PREMIER MATERIALS COMPANY
3717 North Halsted Street
Chicago, Illinois 60613
(312) 549-0555

PREMIER PEAT MOSS CORPORATION
25 West 45th Street
New York, New York 10036
Ernst Mayer, President
(212) 757-7606

Companies and Trade Names

PREMIER THREAD COMPANY
345 Thames Street
Bristol, Rhode Island 02809
(401) 253-9000

PREMIERE (glass products)
See Dominion Glass Company, Ltd.

PREMIERE (television)
See Philco-Ford Corporation

PREMIERE
25 Enterprise Avenue
Secaucus, New Jersey 07094

PREMIUM (beer)
See Grain Belt Breweries, Inc.

PREMIUM (meat products)
See Swift & Company

PREMIUM (saltine crackers)
See Nabisco Inc.

PREMIUM PAK (frozen foods)
See Stilwell Foods

PREMO PHARMACEUTICAL LABORATORIES INC.
111 Leuning Street
South Hackensack,
  New Jersey 07606
S. Silverang, President
(201) 343-5800

PREMTEX HOSIERY COMPANY INC.
10 West 33rd Street
New York, New York 10001
(212) 564-0070

PRENTICE CORPORATION
319 New Britain Road
Kensington, Connecticut 06037
Prentice M. Troup, President
(203) 828-4111

PRENTICE-HALL, INC.
Englewood Cliffs,
  New Jersey 07632
Frank J. Dunnigan, President
(201) 592-2000

PREPARATION H (hemorrhoid treatment)
See Whitehall Laboratories

PREPARED FOOD PRODUCTS, INC.
3104 West Main
Whistler, Alamba 36612

PREPO PRODUCTS CORPORATION
225 West Fulton Street
Edgerton, Wisconsin 53534

PRES-TOE-PEN (folding playpens)
See Thayer Inc.

PRESCO FOOD PRODUCTS, INC.
Church Street
Flemington, New Jersey 08822

PRESCOTT COMPANY, J.L.
27 Eighth
Passaic, New Jersey 07055
(201) 777-4200

PRESCRIPTION CONTAINERS, INC.
256 Saint James Place
Brooklyn, New York 11238
(212) 857-8320

PRESCRIPTIONISTS COUNCIL, THE
Box 371
Aurora, Illinois 60507

PRESCUT (glassware)
See Anchor Hocking Corporation

PRESDWOOD
See Masonite Corporation

PRESENTATION SALES CORPORATION
See Kulicke/Contract

PRESERVO (waterproofing materials)
See Astrup Company

PRESIDENT NOVELTY & JEWELRY COMPANY, INC.
104 West 29
New York, New York 10001
(212) 239-1222

PRESIDENTE (brandy)
See Canada Dry Corporation

PRESIDENTIAL (glassware)
See Reha Glass Company

PRESIDENTIAL (tumblers)
See Federal Glass

PRESIDENTIAL HOMES, INC.
Arney's Mount Road
Pemberton, New Jersey 08068
Edward K. Winkler, President
(609) 894-8201

PRESS-TO-TEST (lights)
See Drake Manufacturing Company

PRESSED STEEL TANK COMPANY INC.
(Subsidiary of Norris Industries, Inc.)
Post Office Drawer Ten J
Milwaukee, Wisconsin 53201
J.J. Watson, President
(414) 476-0500

PRESSER COMPANY, C. & L.
49 East 19th Street
New York, New York 10003
(212) 260-6900

PRESSMAN TOY CORPORATION
11 43rd Street
Brooklyn, New York 11232
Edward Pressman, President
(212) 499-6100

Companies and Trade Names

PRESSNER & COMPANY INC., M.
932 Broadway
New York, New York 10010
(212) 254 2484

PRESSURE-FLO (coffee makers)
See Westinghouse Electric Corporation

PRESSURE-MATIC (attachment to form pressure cookers)
See Totila Products Company

PREST 4 LIFE (men's slacks)
See Barrow Manufacturing Company

PREST-O-FLEX (men's shoes)
See Wolverine World Wide, Inc.

PREST-O-MATIC (automatic doors)
See Clark Door Company, Inc.

PREST WHEEL, INC.
(Subsidiary of Griffen Industries, Inc.)
120 Main Street
South Grafton, Massachusetts 01560
Samuel D. Lockshin, President
(617) 839-4466

PRESTIGE (cutlery)
See Lifetime Cutlery Corporation

PRESTIGE (floor wax)
See Du Bois Chemicals (Division of W.R. Grace & Company)

PRESTIGE (rubber and vinyl floor mats)
See Pretty Products Inc.

PRESTIGE FURNITURE CORPORATION
(Subsidiary of Bassett Furniture Industries, Inc.)
Newton, North Carolina 28658
J.E. Bassett, Sr., Chairman of the Board
(704) 464-3354

PRESTIGELINE
(Division of Weiman Company, Inc)
5 Inez Drive
Brentwood, New York 11717
(516) 273-3636
See also Candlelight Enterprises Inc.

PRESTO (electric appliances, personal-care products, vaporizers, portable heaters)
See National Presto Industries, Inc.

PRESTO (fire extinguisher)
See National Dynamics Corporation

PRESTO (rubber cement)
See Columbia Cement Company Inc.

PRESTO (screws, nails, carpet tacks)
See American Tack & Hardware Company Inc.

PRESTO FOODS PRODUCTS, INC.
929 East 14th
Los Angeles, California 90021
Melvin S. Morse, President

PRESTO LOCK COMPANY INC.
100 Outwater Lane
Garfield, New Jersey 07026

PRESTO MIST (atomizers)
See Irving W. Rice & Company, Inc.

PRESTO PRODUCTS, INC.
1843 West Reeve Street
Appleton, Wisconsin 54911
John E. Lynch, President
(414) 739-9471

PRESTO-TEK
(Division of American Gage & Manufacturing Corporation)
551 West Linfoot Street
Wauseon, Ohio 43567
(419) 335-7051

PRESTO-WHIP (instant dessert topping)
See Delsoy Products Corporation

PRESTOLITE COMPANY, THE
(Division of Eltra Corporation)
511 Hamilton Avenue
Toledo, Ohio 43602
D.E. Dobbs, Director of Public Relations
(419) 244-2811

PRESTON CORPORATION, J.A.
71 Fifth Avenue
New York, New York 10003
(212) 255-8484

PRESTON COSMETICS LTD., JO
See Fragranhaus

PRESTON PHARMACEUTICALS, INC.
Dermakon Laboratories Division
568 Pepperidge Tree Lane
Butler, New Jersey 07405

PRESTONE (car-care products)
See Union Carbide Consumer Products Company

PRESTOSEAL MANUFACTURING CORPORATION
37-12 108th Street
Corona, New York 11368

Companies and Trade Names

PRESTYPE INC.
194 Veterans Boulevard
Carlstadt, New Jersey 07072

PRETEXTE (fragrance)
See Lanvin-Charles of The Ritz Inc.

PRETTY (stainless tableware)
See Utica Cutlery Company

PRETTY FACE (cosmetics)
See Chemway Corporation

PRETTY FEET (foot-care product)
See Cooper Laboratories, Inc., Consumer Products Division

PRETTY LIGHT (hair-color preparations and shampoo)
See Alberto-Culver Company

PRETTY NATURALLY
(Division of New York Pencil Company, Inc.)
46-14 Astoria Boulevard
Long Island City, New York 11103
(212) 721-2000

PRETTY PERM (hair permanent)
See Shulton, Inc.

PRETTY PLEASE (foundation garments, lingerie)
See Teenform, Inc.

PRETTY PRODUCTS, INC.
(Subsidiary of Lancaster Colony Corporation)
Cambridge Road
Coshocton, Ohio 43812
J.B. Clift President and General Manager
(614) 622-3522

PREVENT-A-RUN (hosiery wash)
See Fenner Industries, Inc.

PREVUE PRODUCTS, INC.
195 McGregor Street
Manchester, New Hampshire 03102
Zvi R. Cohen, President
(603) 669-2721

PREWAY, INC.
1430 Second Street, North
Wisconsin Rapids, Wisconsin 54494
William Thomas, Jr., President
(715) 423-1100

PRI-PHARMACEUTICALS, INC.
Box 29
Ryder Station
Brooklyn, New York 11234

PRICE & KENSINGTON (English teapots)
See Ebeling & Reuss Company

PRICE & LUCAS COMPANY, INC.
1501 Portland Avenue
Louisville, Kentucky 40203
(502) 585-4036

PRICE CANDY COMPANY
2 West 39th South
Kansas City, Missouri 64111
R.P. Brous, President
(816) 931-4422

PRICE COLD STORAGE & PACKING COMPANY
Box 780
Yakima, Washington 98902

PRICE COMPANY INC., JOHN A.
265 La Salle Avenue
Hasbrouck Heights, New Jersey 07604

PRICE COMPANY, INC., PAUL A.
5 Skillman Street
Roslyn, New York 11576

PRICE IS RIGHT (game)
See Milton Bradley Company

PRICE-MEYERS CORPORATION
1135 Kent Street
Elkhart, Indiana 46514
George E. Price, President
(219) 264-0761

PRICELESS PRODUCTS COMPANY
3115 South Dixie Highway
West Palm Beach, Florida 33405

PRICE'S (cheese)
See Gerber Cheese Company, Inc.

PRICE'S CANDLE COMPANY, LTD.
(English candles and holders)
See Viking-Craft Ltd.

PRIDE (wax)
See S.C. Johnson & Son Inc.

PRIDE COMPANY, INC.
Glen Haven, Wisconsin 53810

PRIDE CREATIONS
Post Office Box D
Carteret, New Jersey 07008

PRIDE 'N JOY (shag-carpet tiles)
See Ozite Corporation

PRIDE OF ARABIA (coffee)
See Loblaw Groceterias Company, Ltd.

PRIDE OF ERIN (Irish whiskey)
See Jules Berman & Associates, Inc.

PRIDE OF EUROPE (hams, luncheon meat)
See Martin Packing Company

PRIDE OF GELDERLAND (canned hams, luncheon meat)
See Meat Trading Company, Inc.

Companies and Trade Names

PRIDE OF HUNGARY (canned foods, groceries)
See Spiceco

PRIDE OF ILLINOIS (canned vegetables)
See Joan of Arc Company

PRIDE OF NELSON (whiskey)
See Schenley Industries, Inc.

PRIDE OF PACIFIC (frozen fruit products)
See Santa Fe-Driscoll Packers, Inc.

PRIDE OF TENNESSEE (whiskey)
See Schenley Industries Inc.

PRIDE OF THE CHESAPEAKE (canned foods)
See J. Langrall & Brother, Inc.

PRIDE OF THE VALLEY (milk, coffee, bread)
See Big Red Markets, Inc.

PRIDE O'MAINE (potato products)
See Taterstate Frozen Foods

PRIDE PAK FOODS, INC.
(Subsidiary of Rogers Brothers Company)
Box 699
Richland, Washington 99352

PRIDE-TRIMBLE CORPORATION
Post Office Box 435
Burbank, California 91503
(213) 843-7171

PRIEBAT COMPANY INC., E.M.
40-28 Murray Street
Flushing, New York 11354

PRILL SILVER COMPANY INC.
836 Broadway
New York, New York 10003
(212) 228-0570

PRIM (women's hosiery)
See Wayne-Gossard Corporation

PRIMA (costume watches)
See Seko Inc.

PRIMA (Italian entrees)
See George A. Hormel & Company

PRIMA DONNA (dresses)
See Donovan-Galvani of Dallas

PRIMATENE (bronchial-asthma remedy)
See Whitehall Laboratories

PRIME (antifreeze)
See Union Carbide Corporation

PRIME (canned dog food)
See General Foods Corporation

PRIME (shaving product)
See Colgate-Palmolive Company

PRIME (steak sauce)
See T. Marzetti Company

PRIME ENVELOPE CORPORATION
272 Sussex Avenue
Newark, New Jersey 07107
(201) 484-5300

PRIME FROZ'N (frozen produce)
See United Foods, Inc.

PRIME MINISTER (cigars)
See Perfecto Garcia & Brothers, Inc.

PRIME QUALITY (seafood)
See Inter-American Foods, Inc.

PRIMECOTE
See Masonite Corporation

PRIMEDICS LABORATORIES
1123 Goodrich Boulevard
Los Angeles, California 90022
(213) 723-2093

PRIMTIF (bath powder, cologne)
See Max Factor & Company

PRIMITIVE ARTISAN INC.
225 Fifth Avenue
New York, New York 10010

PRIMO (beer)
See Joseph Schlitz Brewing Company

PRIMO DEL REY (cigars)
See Moro Cigar Company

PRIMROSE CANDY COMPANY
4111 West Parker Avenue
Chicago, Illinois 60639
(312) 276-9522

PRIMROSE FOUNDATIONS, INC.
See Gluckin & Company, Inc., William

PRIMUS (sports accessories and equipment)
See Ski Country Imports

PRINCE ALBERT (tobacco)
See R.J. Reynolds Tobacco Company

PRINCE BIANCA (men's gift sets)
See Preferred Products

Companies and Trade Names

PRINCE CONSORT (neckwear)
See A. Schreter & Sons
Company, Inc.

PRINCE FREDERIC (men's furnishings)
See Dunleigh Tuxton Corporation

PRINCE GARDNER
(Division of Swank, Inc.)
1234 South Kingshighway Boulevard
Saint Louis, Missouri 63110
William B. MacLeod, President
(314) 535-9500

PRINCE HAMLET (cigars)
See Bayuk Cigars Inc.

PRINCE IGOR (menswear)
See Burma-Bibas Inc.

PRINCE MACARONI
MANUFACTURING COMPANY
Prince Avenue
Lowell, Massachusetts 01853
Joseph P. Pellegrino, President
(617) 457-7674

PRINCE MATCHABELLI
(Division of Chesebrough-Ponds, Inc.)
33 Benedict Place
Greenwich, Connecticut 06830
Edward Sanford, President
(203) 661-2000

PRINCE-MONACO (sunglasses)
See Rayex Corporation

PRINCE-OF-EASE (reclining chair)
See Kittinger Company Inc.

PRINCE RINALDI (men's shirts)
See Gates Shirt Company

PRINCER PHARMACEUTICALS, I.E.
1768 Manor Drive
Irvington, New Jersey 07111

PRINCESS (barware, tableware, silver- and gold-plated accessories)
See West Coast International

PRINCESS (cabinets)
See Akro-Mills Inc.

PRINCESS (hair curler)
See Remington Electric Shaver
(Division of Sperry Rand Corporation)

PRINCESS (high-intensity lamps)
See Tensor Corporation

PRINCESS (lingerie)
See Warnaco, Inc.

PRINCESS CRUISES, INC.
3435 Wilshire Boulevard
Los Angeles, California 90010
Stanley B. McDonald, President
(213) 380-2550

PRINCESS FOUNDATIONS, INC.
451 South Jefferson Street
Orange, New Jersey 07050

PRINCESS HOUSE CLOSET
ACCESSORIES, INC.
(Division of Scovill-Bo-Gene, Inc.)
350 Fifth Avenue
New York, New York 10001
(212) 685-0056

PRINCESS MARCELLA BORGHESE INC.
767 Fifth Avenue
New York, New York 10022
(212) 758-5002

PRINCESS PAT, LTD.
2709 South Wells Street
Chicago, Illinois 60616
(312) 225-2468

PRINCESS PEGGY, INC.
1001 South Adams Street
Peoria, Illinois 61602
R.R. Ruble, President
(309) 673-9167

PRINCESS PLASTIC PRODUCTS INC.
230 Fifth Avenue
New York, New York 10001
(212) 683-8594

PRINCESS RIBBON CORPORATION
601 West 50th Street
New York, New York 10019
(212) 246-5535

PRINCESS TOYS
Post Office Box 311
Boulder, Colorado 80302

PRINCESSE D'ALBERT (bath preparations, eau de toilette, etc.)
See Jean D'Albret

PRINCETON FARMS
(Subsidiary of Princeton Mining Company)
Princeton, Indiana 47670

PRINCETTI (piano accordions)
See Targ & Dinner Inc.

PRINCI VALLI (groceries)
See Kay Bee Food Products, Inc.

PRINCIPLE PLASTICS, INC.
1136 West 135th
Gardena, California 90247
(213) 321-3011

PRINGLE'S (potato chips)
See Procter & Gamble Company

PRINT BAZAAR (women's apparel)
See Country Miss Inc.

Companies and Trade Names

PRINT-O-MATIC COMPANY INC.
724 West Washington Boulevard
Chicago, Illinois 60606
(312) 726-9480

PRINTOGS, LTD.
29-10 Thomson Avenue
Long Island City, New York 11101
Harold Pacht, Chairman of the Board
(212) 392-8855

PRINTZ-BIEDERMAN COMPANY
2230 Superior
Cleveland, Ohio 44114
(216) 241-7600

PRINZ (enamelware)
See Swedish Metalcraft Inc.

PRINZ (motor vehicles)
See Transcontinental Motors, Inc.

PRIOR (beer)
See C. Schmidt & Sons, Inc.

PRIORITY (food products)
See Westgate-California Foods Inc.

PRIPPS (beer)
See North Shore Bottling Company Inc.

PRISCILLA (aluminum cooking utensils)
See Leyse Aluminum Company

PRISCILLA OF BOSTON, INC.
40 Cambridge
Charlestown, Massachusetts 02129
(617) 242-2677

PRISM (stainless steel flatware)
See Georg Jensen Inc.

PRISMATIC (floor tiles)
See GAF Corporation, Floor Products Division

PRISTEEN (feminine hygiene products)
See Warner-Lambert Products

PRITCHARD PHARMACEUTICAL PRODUCTS, INC.
301 Heritage Avenue
Concord, Tennessee 37726

PRITT (glue stick)
See Colgate-Palmolive Company

PRIVATE CELLAR (Bourbon whiskey)
See Hiram Walker, Inc.

PRIVATE STOCK (Bourbon)
See Gooderham & Worts, Ltd.

PRIVATE STOCK (wines and champagnes)
See United Vintners, Inc.

PRIX BLANC (wine)
See Joseph E. Seagram & Sons

PRIX ROUGE (wine)
See Joseph E. Seagram & Sons

PRIZE (produce)
See Central Valley Raisin Company

PRIZE WINNER (electric typewriter)
See Smith-Corona Marchant

PRIZER WARE (procelainized cast-iron cookware)
See Textile Machine Works

PRO (dog and cat foods)
See Pedrick Laboratories

PRO ART PAPER COMPANY INC.
230 Fifth Avenue
New York, New York 10001
(212) 685-9437

PRO BRUSH
(Division of Vistron Corporation)
221 Pine Street
Florence, Massachusetts 01060
(413) 584-1780

PRO GLO (car wax)
See Procter & Gamble Company

PRO GUN 1000 (hair dryer)
See Clairol Inc.

PRO HARDWARE INC.
26 Sixth Street
Stamford, Connecticut 06905

PRO-LINE BOATS INC.
Box 1348
Crystal River, Florida 32629

PRO-MARK CORPORATION
(Subsidiary of Remo Inc.)
10710 Craighead Drive
Houston, Texas 77025
(713) 666-2525

PRO 100 (tennis equipment)
See National Sporting Goods Corporation

PRO-PACE (computers)
See Electronic Associates Inc.

PRO-PAL (baseball set)
See King Athletic Goods Company

PRO-PHARM COMPANY, INC.
121 North Commerce
Russellville, Arkansas 72801

PRO PLUS (golf balls)
See Faultless Rubber Company

PRO-SPORT (athletic products)
See King Athletic Goods Corporation

Companies and Trade Names

PRO STAR (athletic products)
See General Tire & Rubber Company, Athletic Products Division

PRO-TEK-TIV (shoes)
See Curtis-Stephens-Embry Company

PRO-TEM (disposable headrests, table and tray covers, pillowcases, sheets, sleeping bags, towels, wash cloths)
See Kendall Company

PRO 10 (hair-care products)
See Shontex Products Company

PRO-TEN-BEEF (meats)
See Swift & Company

PRO-TEX (closet and travel accessories)
See Clopay Corporation

PROCARE 4 (hair-care products)
See Alberto-Culver Company

PROCEPTION (basal thermometers, ovulation rulers, sperm nutrient)
See Milex Products, Inc.

PROCESSED PLASTIC COMPANY
1001 Aucutt Road
Montgomery, Illinois 60538
(312) 892-7981

PROCINO-ROSSI CORPORATION
46-54 Washington Street
Auburn, New York 13021

PROCOAT (clear-varnish resin)
See Fibre Glass-Evercoat Company Inc.

PROCTOR & GAMBLE COMPANY, THE
301 East Sixth Street
Cincinnati, Ohio 45202
John G. Smale, President
(513) 562-1100
See also Charmin Paper Products Company

PROCTER COMPANY, THE FRED
224 East Eighth Street
Cincinnati, Ohio 45202
(513) 721-1340

PROCTOR-SILEX, INC.
(Subsidiary of SCM Corporation)
700 West Tabor Road
Philadelphia, Pennsylvania 19120
E.P. Larmer, General Manager
(215) 455-8500

PRODUCE UNITRADE INC.
99 Wall Street
New York, New York 10005

PRODUCER SALES CORPORATION
Box 37
Rochester, Washington 98579

PRODUCERS PEANUT COMPANY
Box 250
Suffolk, Virginia 23434
(804) 539-7496

PRODUCERS RICE MILL, INC.
Box 461
Stuttgart, Arkansas 72160

PRODUCT INNOVATIONS, INC.
Post Office Box 94
Forest Park, Illinois 60130

PRODUCT 19 (breakfast cereal)
See Kellogg Company

PRODUCTION (scales)
See Triner Scale & Manufacturing Company

PRODUCTION METALS, INC.
215 14th Street
Jersey City, New Jersey 07302
(201) 656-3220

PRODUCTO MACHINE COMPANY, THE
990 Housatonic
Bridgeport, Connecticut 06606
(203) 367-8675

PRODUCTS INTERNATIONAL COMPANY
220 Fifth Avenue
New York, New York 10001
(212) 683-5250

PRODUCTS OF EXCELLENCE LTD.
483 Park Street
Upper Montclair, New Jersey 07043

PRODUCTS OF THE BEHAVIORAL SCIENCES
1140 Dell Avenue
Campbell, California 95008

PROEN PRODUCTS COMPANY
Ninth and Grayson Streets
Berkeley, California 94710
(415) 848-5504

PROFESSIONAL (inflatable boat)
See Avon Rubber Company Ltd.

PROFESSIONAL AIDS COMPANY
1 North Wacker Drive
Chicago, Illinois 60606
(312) 263-7622

PROFESSIONAL AIDS CORPORATION
535 Port Washington Boulevard
Port Washington, New York 11050

PROFESSIONAL CHEMICAL CORPORATION
11 State Street
Pittsford, New York 14534

1103

Companies and Trade Names

PROFESSIONAL CONVALESCENT
PRODUCTS COMPANY
Ripley, Ohio 45167

PROFESSIONAL GOLF COMPANY
99 Tremont Court
Chattanooga, Tennessee 37405
John M. Tucker, President
(615) 267-5631

PROFESSIONAL PLUS (golf balls)
See Faultless Rubber Company

PROFESSIONAL PRODUCTS
COMPANY
Box 22404
1601 Calhoun
Houston, Texas 77027
(713) 659-3908

PROFESSIONAL TAPE COMPANY,
INC.
144 Tower Drive
Burr Ridge, Illinois 60521
(312) 986-1800

PROFFITT JR., FRANK
Box 67
Todd, North Carolina 28684

PROFILE (bread)
See ITT Continental Baking
Company, Inc.

PROFILE (sports apparel)
See Profile Sports Corporation

PROFILE (toothbrushes)
See Vistron Corporation, Pro
Brush Division

PROFILE SPORTS CORPORATION
1 Profile Plaza
West Lebanon,
New Hampshire 03784
Frederick T. Bedford, III, President
(603) 298-5746

PROFIT LINES, INC.
Box 597
Fair Lawn, New Jersey 07410

PROFIX (women's shoe-heel
protectors)
See International Service
Company

PROFUMO & COMPANY,
INC., L.
350 Broadway
New York, New York 10007
(212) 925-5852

PROGREDO TRADING COMPANY
814 Broadway
New York, New York 10003
(212) 475-8144

PROGRESS FEATHER COMPANY
657 West Lake
Chicago, Illinois 60606
(312) 726-7443

PROGRESS LAWN MOWERS
See Louisville Tin & Stove
Company

PROGRESS PAINT
MANUFACTURING COMPANY
826 West Main Street
Louisville, Kentucky 40202
William Lussky, President
(502) 587-8685

PROGRESSION (oven-to-table ware)
See Noritake Company, Inc.

PROGRESSIVE DISTRIBUTING
Box 211
Pomona, California 91769

PROGRESSIVE DRUGS OF
AMERICA, INC.
6147 Airways Boulevard
Chattanooga, Tennessee 37421

PROGRESSIVE INDUSTRIES, INC.
Box 627
Lake View, Iowa 51450

PROGRESSIVE MEAT PRODUCTS
COMPANY
1009 East Garsfield
Milwaukee, Wisconsin 53212
(414) 562-2080

PROGRESSO FOODS
CORPORATION
100 Cavern Point Road
Jersey City, New Jersey 07305
Nicholas R. Marona, President
(201) 332-8000

PROGRESSUS COMPANY
40 Saint Mary's Place
Freeport, New York 11520

PROJECTS UNLIMITED INC.
3681 Wyse Road
Dayton, Ohio 45414
(513) 890-1918

PROKEM (denture cleanser, mouth-
wash)
See Professional Chemical
Corporation

PROLENS (contact lens wetting
solution)
See Ketchum Laboratories, Inc.

PROLIFE (nail-care product)
See Revlon, Inc.

PROLL PRODUCTS COMPANY
104 Verona Avenue
Newark, New Jersey 07104
(201) 482-1250

PROLONG (floor wax)
See Drackett Company

PROM (home permanent)
See Gillette Company

1104

Companies and Trade Names

PROM-TAC (cold remedy, decongestant, nasal spray)
See Ketchum Laboratories, Inc.

PROMARK
(Division of Wells Lamont Corporation)
332 South Michigan
Chicago, Illinois 60604
(312) 939-5435

PROMENADE (foundation garments, lingerie)
See H.W. Gossard Company

PROMESSE (bath powder, perfume, cologne)
See Max Factor & Company

PROMOTIONAL MERCHANDISING SERVICES, INC.
534 South Glenwood
Glendora, California 91740

PRONTO (cleaner/wax)
See S.C. Johnson & Son, Inc.

PRONTO FILE
(Division of Litton Industries)
640 Whiteford Road
York, Pennsylvania 17405

PRONTO FOOD KITCHENS INC.
Ames, Iowa 50010

PROP-A-ROCK (baby carrier with rocker attachment)
See Infanseat Company

PROP-R-TEMP (air-conditioning units)
See Typhoon Air Conditioning Company

PROPELLAIR (fans for ventilation)
See Robbins & Myers, Inc.

PROPHECY (cologne, dusting powder, sachet, etc.)
See Prince Matchabelli, Inc.

PROPPER (thermometers)
See Ideal Scientific Company, Inc.

PROSLIM (diet mix)
See J.B. Williams Company, Inc.

PROSSER & SON, THOMAS
306 Lydecker Street
Englewood, New Jersey 07631

PROSSER PACKERS, INC.
Prosser, Washington 99350

PROST, INC., ANDRE
Post Office Box 37
Little Neck, New York 11363

PROTAC (nasal spray, troches, etc.)
See Republic Drug Company, Inc.

PROTECT-A-CARE INC.
See PAC Enterprises Inc.

PROTECT-O (baby-care products-diaper pins, fork and spoon, rattles, etc.)
See Reliance Products Corporation

PROTECT-O-COM (intercom system)
See Fasco Industries Inc.

PROTECTA-TOT (juvenile product)
See Hamill Manufacturing Company

PROTECTALL (table pads)
See Bonart Mills Inc.

PROTECTIVE CLOSURES COMPANY, INC.
2150 Elmwood Avenue
Buffalo, New York 14207
Charles Percinal, Jr., President
(716) 876-9855

PROTECTIVE LINING CORPORATION
601 39th Street
Brooklyn, New York 11232
Jerry Dorfman, Chairman, President and Treasurer
(212) 854-3838

PROTECTO (bathroom products, closet deodorizers, moth preventives, vaporizers)
See Klasco Products Company, Inc.

PROTECTOR (intrusion alarm)
See Radatron Corporation

PROTEIN-ETTES (meat substitute)
See Creamette Company

PROTEIN PLUS (cereal)
See General Mills, Inc.

PROTEIN 29 (hairdressing)
See Mennen Company

PROTEIN 21 (hair-care products)
See Mennen Company

PROTEKT YOUR DOOR (door bumpers)
See Unival Corporation

PROTEN (meats)
See Swift & Company

PROTEX (deodorant soap)
See Purex Corporation

1105

Companies and Trade Names

PROTEX WOOD (shingle stain)
See Adelphia Paint & Color Works, Inc.

PROTEXALL CHEMICALS, INC.
Box 424
Port Orange, Florida 32019

PROTO TOOL COMPANY
(Division of Pendleton Tool Industry)
636 32nd Street
Portland, Oregon 97222
B.H. McClain, General Manager
(503) 654-5471

PROUD-FIT (boys' shoes)
See Weinbrenner Shoe Company

PROVEN (tools, housewares and appliances, paints, etc.)
See Pro Hardware, Inc.

PROVENCE (furniture)
See Union National, Inc.

PROVENCE (wines)
See James B. Beam Distilling Company

PROVIDENT LIFE & ACCIDENT INSURANCE COMPANY
Fountain Square
Chattanooga, Tennessee 37402
Henry C. Unruh, Chairman of the Board
(615) 755-1011

PROVIDENT MUTUAL LIFE INSURANCE COMPANY OF PHILADELPHIA
4601 Market Street
Philadelphia, Pennsylvania 19139
Edward L. Stanley, Chairman of the Board
(215) 474-7000

PROVIDENT NATIONAL BANK
Broad and Chestnut
Philadelphia, Pennsylvania 19101
Paul M. Ingersoll, President
(215) 585-5000

PROVINCIAL (glass products)
See Imperial Glass Corporation

PROVINCIAL (melamine products)
See Boonton Molding Company, Inc.

PROWELL ESTATE, T.
18 Pine Street
Steelton, Pennsylvania 17113

PROWL ALARM (security alarms)
See Hall Industries Inc.

PROXIGEL (oral antiseptic)
See Block Drug Company, Inc.

PRUDEN PACKING COMPANY
Post Office Box 1416
Suffolk, Virginia 23434
(804) 539-6261

PRUDEN WOOD PRODUCTS COMPANY
217 Main
Flora, Mississippi 39071

PRUDENCE FOODS INC.
256 Second Avenue
Waltham, Massachusetts 02154

PRUDENTIAL GRACE LINE, INC.
1 New York Plaza
New York, New York 10004
A.T. DeSmedt, President
(212) 623-6000

PRUDENTIAL INSURANCE COMPANY OF AMERICA
Prudential Plaza
Newark, New Jersey 07101
Robert A. Beck, President
(201) 336-1234

PRUDENTIAL PAPER PRODUCTS COMPANY
63-15 Traffic Street
Glendale, New York 11227

PRUF (spray starch)
See Colgate-Palmolive Company

PRUFCOAT (coatings)
See Grow Chemical Coatings Corporation

PRUVO PHARMACAL COMPANY
2018 West Bender Road
Milwaukee, Wisconsin 53209
H. Neal Williams, President
(414) 228-1170

PRYM, INC., WILLIAM
Main Street
Dayville, Connecticut 06241
Thomas J. Mavel, President and Chief Executive Officer
(203) 774-9671

PRYME (hand lotion)
See Jacqueline Cochran, Inc.

PRYOBAR (partition tile)
See United States Gypsum Company

PRYOR MARKING PRODUCTS
21 East Hubbard Street
Chicago, Illinois 60611
(312) 527-2048

PSOREX (antiseborrheic shampoo)
See Jeffrey Martin, Inc.

PUB (glassware)
See Pitman-Dreitzer

PUB (men's toiletries)
See Revlon, Inc.

Companies and Trade Names

PUBLIC SERVICE COMPANY OF COLORADO
550 15th Street
Denver, Colorado 80202
Robert T. Person, President
(303) 571-7511

PUBLIC SERVICE COMPANY OF INDIANA, INC.
1000 East Main Street
Plainfield, Indiana 46168
Hugh A. Barker, President
(317) 839-9611

PUBLIC SERVICE COMPANY OF NEW HAMPSHIRE
1087 Elm Street
Manchester, New Hampshire 03105
William C. Tallman, President
(603) 669-4000

PUBLIC SERVICE COMPANY OF NEW MEXICO
414 Silver Avenue, S.W.
Alburquerque, New Mexico 87103
G.A. Schreiber, President
(505) 842-2700

PUBLIC SERVICE COMPANY OF NORTH CAROLINA
400 Cox Road
Gastonia, North Carolina 28052
B.E. Zeigler, Chairman of the Board
(704) 864-6731

PUBLIC SERVICE COMPANY OF OKLAHOMA
(Subsidiary of Central and South West Corporation)
Post Office Box 201
Tulsa, Oklahoma 74103
R.O. Newman, President
(918) 583-3611

PUBLIC SERVICE ELECTRIC AND GAS COMPANY
80 Park Place
Newark, New Jersey 07101
Robert I. Smith, President
(201) 622-7000

PUBLICKER DISTILLERS PRODUCTS INC.
(Subsidiary of Publicker Industries Inc.)
1429 Walnut
Philadelphia, Pennsylvania 19102
(215) 564-1400

PUBLICKER INDUSTRIES INC.
1429 Walnut
Philadelphia, Pennsylvania 19102
A.E. Lang, President
(215) 564-1400
See also Continental Distilling Corporation

PUBLISHERS CLEARING HOUSE
382 Channel Drive
Port Washington, New York 11050
Anita O. Davis, Director of Consumer Affairs
(516) 883-5432

PUBLISHERS PAPER COMPANY
419 Main Street
Oregon City, Oregon 97045
J.E. Meadows, President
(503) 656-5211

PUBLIX SHIRT CORPORATION
Empire State Building
New York, New York 10016
Sheldon Berdon, President
(212) 695-4700

PUBLIX SUPER MARKETS, INC.
Post Office Box 407
2040 New Tampa Highway
Lakeland, Florida 33802
Charles H. Jenkins, Chairman of the Board
(813) 686-1188

PUCA COMPANY, ANTIMO
413 New York City Terminal Market
Bronx, New York 10474
(212) 887-0332

PUCCI PERFUMES INTERNATIONAL INC., EMILIO
24 East 64th Street
New York, New York 10021
(212) 752-4777

PUDDEX (puddings and cake mixes)
See Enzo Jel Company

PUDDING TREATS (canned pudding)
See General Foods Corporation

PUDDLE PADS (infants' waterproof sheets and pads)
See Plymouth Rubber Company

PUEBLO INTERNATIONAL, INC.
375 Park Avenue
New York, New York 10022
George Toppel, President
(212) 935-1710
See also Hills Supermarkets, Inc.

PUEBLOS (shoes for men)
See Gardiner Shoe Company, Inc.

PUFF N' FLUFF (brushes)
See I. Sekine Company Inc.

PUFFED RICE (cereal)
See Kellogg Company

PUFFED WHEAT (cereal)
See Kellogg Company

PUFFIN (food products)
See General Mills, Inc.

PUFFS (facial tissue)
See Procter & Gamble Company

PUGET SOUND POWER & LIGHT COMPANY
Puget Power Building
Bellevue, Washington 98009
Ralph M. Davis, President
(206) 454-6363

Companies and Trade Names

PUIFORCAT USA LTD.
225 Fifth Avenue
Lower Level
Suite Nine
New York, New York 10010
(212) 683-2541

PUIG & COMPANY, INC., VICENTE
Rosal Lane
Saddlebrook, New Jersey 07662
(212) 993-2246

PULASKI (canned foods)
See Fairfax Food Products

PULASKI (pickles)
See Pikle-Rite Company

PULASKI FURNITURE CORPORATION
Box 1371
Pulaski, Virginia 24301
Colin E. Richardson, Chairman of the Board
(703) 980-7330

PULICI (canned foods)
See Old Ranchers Company

PULL-N-HOIST (electric fence)
See Maes, Inc.

PULL-UMS (juvenile product)
See Marlin Toy Products Inc.

PULLMAN (toiletries)
See Les Parfums de Dana Inc.

PULLMAN COUCH COMPANY
Amory, Mississippi 38821
R. Jackson, President
(601) 256-5641

PULLMAN VACUUM CLEANER CORPORATION
129 Medford Street
Malden, Massachusetts 02148
Jacob Lang, General Manager
(617) 324-7300

PULLUP TABLES COMPANY
8701 Grinnel Avenue
Detroit, Michigan 48213
(313) 571-1770

PULSAR (watches)
See HMW Industries, Inc.

PULVEX (pet products)
See Cooper USA, Inc.

PUMA (sports accessories and equipment)
See Beconta Inc.

PUNCH (cigars)
See F. Palicio & Company, Inc.

PUNCH (detergent)
See Colgate-Palmolive Company

PUNCH N' GRO (flower and vegetable kits)
See Northrup, King & Company

PUN'KIN SEAT (juvenile product)
See Welsh Company

PUP-N-KITTEN (dog and cat food)
See Re-Dan Packing Company

PUP-O (dog food)
See Central Nebraska Packing Company

PUPPET TOES (slipper socks for children)
See Charette Products Corporation

PUPPY CHOW (puppy food)
See Ralston Purina Company

PUPPY LOVE (dog food)
See The Jim Dandy Company

PUPPY PALACE PET SHOPS
See Mars, Inc.

PURASNOW (flour)
See General Mills, Inc.

PURDIE BROTHERS
Dunn, North Carolina 28334

PURDUE FREDERICK COMPANY
99-101 Saw Mill River Road
Yonkers, New York 10701
(914) 968-0100

PURE BEAUTY (makeup)
See Almay Hypo-Allergenic Cosmetics

PURE FOOD COMPANY, INC., THE
Box N
Mamaroneck, New York 10543
Gladys H. Stoll, President
(914) 698-7900

PURE GLUTEN FOOD COMPANY
Post Office Box 24
20 Jerusalem Avenue
Hicksville, New York 11802
(516) 681-2800

PURE GOLD (food products)
See J. Weller Company

PURE MAGIC (makeup)
See Max Factor & Company

PURE MAID (groceries)
See Detroit City Dairy, Inc.

PURE OIL COMPANY, THE
200 East Golf Road
Palatine, Illinois 60067

PURE SILVIKRIN (hair treatment)
See Beecham Products (Division of Beecham, Inc.)

Companies and Trade Names

PURE SUN (fruit juices)
    See Paramount Citrus Association, Inc.

PURELLO (flavoring, extracts)
    See H.W. Wilson Company Ltd.

PURELON LABORATORIES
541 E. Third Street
Mount Vernon, New York 10553

PUREPAC LABORATORIES
    CORPORATION
200 Elmora Avenue
Elizabeth, New Jersey 07207
Adolph D. Storch, President
(201) 527-9100

PUREPAK FOODS INC.
542 LaGuardia Place
New York, New York 10012
(212) 254-7171

PUREX (salt)
    See Morton Salt Company

PUREX CORPORATION, LTD.
5101 Clark Avenue
Lakewood, California 90712
W.R. Tincher, President
(213) 634-3300
    See also Campana Corporation; Grocery Products Group; Pope Products; and Turco Products

PUREX CORPORATION
Grocery Products Group
24600 South Main Street
Carson, California 90744

PUREX LABORATORIES, INC.
West Street
Hanover, New Jersey 07936

PURINA (pet foods)
    See Ralston Purina Company

PURIST (fishing equipment)
    See Shakespeare Sporting Goods

PURITAN (food products)
    See National Preserve Company

PURITAN (glassware)
    See Seneca Glass Company

PURITAN (meat products)
    See Cudahy Company

PURITAN (smoking tobacco)
    See Philip Morris

PURITAN CHEMICAL COMPANY
916 Ashby Street, N.W.
Atlanta, Georgia 30318
William H. Frey, President
(404) 872-0721

PURITAN FASHIONS
    CORPORATION
1400 Broadway
New York, New York 10018
Carl Rosen, President
(212) 695-7900
    See also Paraphernalia, Inc.; and Winston Mills, Inc.

PURITAN MILLS INC.
    See Wellington Puritan Mills, Inc.

PURITAN SPORTSWEAR
    CORPORATION, THE
(Division of Warnaco, Inc.)
Post Office Box 511
813 25th Street
Altoona, Pennsylvania 16603
Lloyd S. Shaper, President
(814) 695-5651

PURITRON (air-purifier range hood)
    See Hamilton Beach Company

PURITY BAKING COMPANY
1007 Bigley Avenue
Charlestown, West Virginia 25302
John D. Smallridge, President
(304) 343-5673

PURITY CHEESE COMPANY
Box 27
Mayville, Wisconsin 53050
(414) 387-4000

PURITY CONFECTIONERY
    COMPANY
15 Flint Avenue
Somerville, Massachusetts 02145
(617) 625-8237

PURITY MILLS
(Division of Stokely-Van Camp, Inc.)
916 Depot Avenue
Dixon, Illinois 61021
L.J. Delehanty, President
(815) 288-3355

PURITY OATS (cereal)
    See General Mills, Inc.

PURITY ORGANICS
30 Mountain Avenue
Monsey, New York 10952

PURITY SUPREME, INC.
312 Boston Road
North Billerica, Massachusetts 01862
Leo Kahn, President
(617) 667-9511

PURNELL'S PRIDE, INC.
Box 1527
301 South Gloster Street
Tupelo, Mississippi 38801
Hugh Purnell, President
(601) 844-3731

PURO COMPANY, INC.
2801-05 Locust
Saint Louis, Missouri 63103
N.E. Wilson, President
(314) 533-1790

Companies and Trade Names

PURO FILTER CORPORATION OF
  AMERICA
21-01 51st Avenue
Long Island City, New York 11101
Richard A. Sloss, President
(212) 729-7900

PUROLATOR, INC.
970 New Brunswick Avenue
Rahway, New Jersey 07065
Paul A. Cameron, President
(201) 388-4000

PURPLE PASSION (soft drink)
  See Canada Dry Corporation

PURR (cat food)
  See Westgate-California Products,
    Inc., Purr Pet Food Division

PURR (fruit)
  See Van Buren County Fruit
    Exchange, Inc.

PURR (hair-care product)
  See Gillette Company, Personal
    Care Division

PURTEX (apparel)
  See Puritan Fashions Corporation

PUSANTEX TRADING
  CORPORATION
15 Park Row
New York, New York 10038
(212) 233-8020

PUSH-BUTTON (locks)
  See Simplex Security Systems

PUSH-BUTTON (spray paint)
  See Marson Corporation

PUSH-BUTTON LILT (home
permanent)
  See Procter & Gamble Company

PUSHOVER (nail enamel)
  See Merle Norman Cosmetics

PUSS 'N BOOTS (cat foods)
  See Quaker Oats Company

PUSSY CAPS (sports apparel)
  See Pussy Caps Company

PUSSY CAPS COMPANY
Box 100
Medina, Washington 98039

PUSSY CAT TOY COMPANY,
  INC.
456 Johnson Avenue
Brooklyn, New York 11237
(212) 497-2414

PUSSYFOOTER (nail enamel)
  See Merle Norman Cosmetics

PUSSYFOOTS (shoes)
  See Penobscot Shoe Company

PUSSYWILLOW (processed foods)
  See Marion Foods Corporation

PUTNAM COUNTY CANNING
  COMPANY
Box 98
Columbus Grove, Ohio 45830

PUTNAM DYES, INC.
301 Oak Street
Quincy, Illinois 62301
T.A. Farley, President
(217) 222-0421

PUTNAM'S SONS, G.P.
200 Madison Avenue
New York, New York 10016
Walter J. Minton, President
(212) 883-5500

PUTT-PUTT GOLF COURSES OF
  AMERICA
Box 5237
Fayetteville, North Carolina 28303

PUZZLE FACTORY (puzzles)
  See Pager Industries Inc.

PY-CO-PAY (toothbrushes, tooth
powder)
  See Block Drug Company, Inc.

PY-O-MY (baking mixes)
  See Gilster-Mary Lee Corporation

PYFERS FOOD CITY
110 East Commercial
Leon, Iowa 50144

PYLON (tapes and tape dispensers)
  See Ben Clements & Sons Inc.

PYR-A-LARM (fire-detection system)
  See Pyrotronics

PYRA-SHELL (plastic fly, bait,
and lure boxes)
  See Shoe Form Company, Inc.

PYRAMID CREATIONS, INC.
2102 Saint Joseph Avenue
Saint Joseph, Missouri 64505

PYRAMID ORCHARDS
5105 West Nob Hill Boulevard
Yakima, Washington 98902

PYRAMID PUBLICATIONS
757 Third Avenue
New York, New York 10022
(212) 754-3100

PYRENE (fire extinguishers)
  See Norris Industries, Fire &
    Safety Equipment Division

Companies and Trade Names

PYREX (glassware)
See Corning Glass Works

PYRO (antifreeze)
See Olin Corporation

PYRO-KURE (flame-resistant vapor barriers)
See St. Regis Paper Company, Laminated & Coated Products Division

PYRO-SANA LABORATORY
3120 South Seventh Street
Saint Louis, Missouri 63118
(314) 773-4251

PYROCERAM (glass products)
See Corning Glass Works

PYROFAX GAS CORPORATION
Post Office Box 2521
921 Main Street
Houston, Texas 77001
J.P. Russell, Executive Vice President
(713) 224-7961

PYROIL COMPANY, INC.
20 Copeland Avenue
La Crosse, Wisconsin 54601
Harold W. McCreight, Preside
See also Warner-Patterson Company

PYROIL-MASTER
(Division of Pyroil Company, Inc.)
445 West Nixon Street
Savage, Minnesota 55478

PYROTECTOR INC.
333 Lincoln Street
Hingham, Massachusetts 02043
(617) 749-3466

PYROTEX CORPORATION
287 Whitney Street
Leominster, Massachusetts 01453
(617) 534-6575

PYROTRONICS
(Subsidiary of Baker Industries)
8 Ridgedale Avenue
Cedar Knolls, New Jersey 07927
(201) 267-1300

PYROZIDE (tooth powder)
See Myers Laboratories, Inc.

Companies and Trade Names

Q

Q.T. (frozen meat products)
See Hi Brand Foods

Q.T. (tanning aids)
See Coppertone Corporation

QT (whiskey)
See Barton Brands, Ltd.

Q-T FOUNDATIONS COMPANY INC.
1 McDermott Place
Bergenfield, New Jersey 07621
Milton Kutzin, President and Treasurer
(201) 384-7000

Q T LAMP (high-intensity lamps)
See Vuette Inc.

Q-TIPS (cotton swabs)
See Chesebrough-Pond's, Inc.

Q-W LABORATORIES
915 West Front Street
Plainfield, New Jersey 07063

QISMET, LTD.
10 East 32nd Street
New York, New York 10016
(212) 679-8060

QUACK-QUACK (children's dinette set)
See Syd Leach Inc.

QUAD-LITE (high-intensity lamps)
See Control Research Inc.

QUADRA-QUE (projector)
See Spindler & Sauppe

QUAFF-AID (hangover treatment)
See Amber Laboratories

QUAKER (rugs)
See Armstrong Cork Company

QUAKER CITY CHOCOLATE & CONFECTIONERY COMPANY, INC.
2901 Grant Avenue
Philadelphia, Pennsylvania 19114
Lester G. Rosskam, Jr., President
(215) 677-6500

QUAKER CITY INDUSTRIES, INC.
301 Mayhill Street
Saddle Brook, New Jersey 07662
Abraham Bosman, President
(201) 438-6600

QUAKER CITY PACKING COMPANY, INC.
104 Union
Allentown, Pennsylvania 18102

QUAKER CITY PHARMACAL COMPANY
129 North Fourth Street
Philadelphia, Pennsylvania 19106
(215) 923-8742

QUAKER HOUSE (rust remover and steam-iron cleaner)
See Jim Bourland Company

QUAKER INDUSTRIES INC.
90 McMillen Road
Antioch, Illinois 60002
Walter W. Block, Jr., President
(312) 395-3300

QUAKER LACE COMPANY
Fourth and Lehigh
Philadelphia, Pennsylvania 19133
Richard N. Bromley, President
(215) 739-1660

QUAKER MAID (food products)
See Great Atlantic & Pacific Tea Company

QUAKER MAID (kitchen appliances)
See Tappan Company

QUAKER OATS COMPANY, THE
Merchandise Mart Plaza
Chicago, Illinois 60654
Robert D. Stuart, Jr., President
(312) 222-7111
See also Fisher-Price Toys; Marx & Company Inc., Louis; and Wolf Brand Products

QUAKER OIL CORPORATION
9060 Latty
Saint Louis, Missouri 63134
(314) 521-3900

QUAKER STATE OIL REFINING CORPORATION
Quaker State Building
Oil City, Pennsylvania 16301
Q.E. Wood, President
(814) 676-1811

QUAL-PAK (fruits and vegetables)
See Hill Brothers, Inc.

QUALICRAFT (shoes)
See Edison Brothers Stores, Inc.

QUALITA (food products)
See Francis C. Stokes Company

QUALITEE (frozen meats)
See Texas Meat Packers

QUALITON
2401 South Main Street
Los Angeles, California 90007
(213) 748-7333

QUALITY (frozen fruit)
See Monroe Frozen Foods Inc. (Subsidiary of Quality Brands Inc.)

Companies and Trade Names

QUALITY (lawn and garden supplies, paints and paint sundries)
See Ace Hardware Corporation

QUALITY (sporting goods, electrical supplies)
See Coast to Coast Stores

QUALITY BAKERS OF AMERICA COOPERATIVE, INC.
1515 Broadway
New York, New York 10036
(212) 790-9200

QUALITY BAKING COMPANY, INC.
50 North Glenwood
Columbus, Ohio 43222

QUALITY BRANDS, INC.
3702 Croton Avenue
Cleveland, Ohio 44115
(216) 361-1120

QUALITY BRONZEWARE INC.
106 Regent Drive
North Kingstown, Rhode Island 02852

QUALITY COSMETICS CORPORATION
316 Dean Street
Brooklyn, New York 11217
(212) 625-1940

QUALITY CRAFTED (luggage)
See Carl Pedro & Sons Inc.

QUALITY INDUSTRIES INC.
5511 Devon Street
Philadelphia, Pennsylvania 19138

QUALITY INNS INTERNATIONAL, INC.
10750 Columbia Pike
Silver Spring, Maryland 20901
Fred E. Ellrod, Jr., President
(301) 593-5600

QUALITY MARINE PRODUCTS INC.
601-607 South Andrews Avenue
Fort Lauderdale, Florida 33301

QUALITY MILLS, INC.
United States 52 South
Mount Airy, North Carolina 27030
John E. Woltz, President
(919) 786-6124

QUALITY PARK PRODUCTS
(Division of Standard Packaging Corporation)
2520 Como Avenue
Saint Paul, Minnesota 55108
(612) 645-0251

QUALITY PRODUCTS MANUFACTURING COMPANY
125 West 157th Street
Gardena, California 90247
(213) 321-3981

QUALITY SHOPPE CANDIES, INC.
Post Office Box 1531
Fort Worth, Texas 76101

QUALITY TOOLS CORPORATION
7750 King Road
Spring Arbor, Michigan 49283
(517) 750-1840

QUALITY WATER INC.
Box 202
Deland, Illinois 61839

QUAM-NICHOLS COMPANY
234 East Marquette Road
Chicago, Illinois 60637
Matt Little, President
(312) 488-5800

QUANTA (calculators)
See Olivetti Corporation of America

QUAPAW CANOE COMPANY
Box 469
600 Newman Road
Miami, Oklahoma 74354
(918) 542-5536

QUARTET MANUFACTURING COMPANY
7131 North Ridgeway Avenue
Lincolnwood, Illinois 60645
(312) 674-1753

QUARTET SALES INC.
236 Fifth Avenue
New York, New York 10001
(212) 686-8911

QUARTZ RADIATION CORPORATION
1275 Bloomfield Avenue
Fairfield, New Jersey 07006
(201) 575-1616

QUASAR CONTEMPORARIES
1750 West Central Road
Mount Prospect, Illinois 60056

QUASAR ELECTRONICS CORPORATION
(Subsidiary of Matsushita Electric Corporation of America)
9401 West Grand Avenue
Franklin Park, Illinois 60131
Robert T. Bloomberg, President

QUE TONIC COMPANY
229 North Euclid Avenue
Princeton, Illinois 61356

QUEEN (hair-care products)
See J. Strickland & Company

QUEEN (household goods)
See Worcester Felt Pad Corporation

QUEEN (rubber products)
See Ace Lite Step Company, Inc.

Companies and Trade Names

QUEEN ANNE (canned vegetables)
See Fox Foods Inc.

QUEEN ANNE (stainless flatware)
See Kirk & Matz Ltd.

QUEEN ANNE CANDY COMPANY
Post Office Box 948
604 Hoffman Street
Hammond, Indiana 46320
E.D. Morando, President
(219) 932-2400

QUEEN BEE (household chemicals)
See Specialty Items Company Inc.

QUEEN CASUALS, INC.
10175 Northeast Avenue
Philadelphia, Pennsylvania 19116
Harvey Saligman, President
(215) 677-3000

QUEEN CHARLOTTE (frozen seafoods)
See McCallum Sales Ltd.

QUEEN CITY BREWING COMPANY
208 Market Street
Cumberland, Maryland 21502
William L. Wilson, President
(301) 722-2882

QUEEN CITY PHARMACAL COMPANY
1040 Marshall Avenue
Cincinnati, Ohio 45225
(513) 541-7731

QUEEN CUTLERY COMPANY
(Subsidiary of Servotronics Inc.)
Box 500
Franklinville, New York 14737
(716) 676-5540

QUEEN FAMILY (vegetables)
See Nash-Finch Company

QUEEN GLASS COMPANY
505 National Highway
La Vale, Maryland 21502
(301) 722-7310

QUEEN HELENE (skin-care products)
See General Therapeutics, Inc.

QUEEN LACE CRYSTAL COMPANY
3 East 27th Street
New York, New York 10016
(212) 686-2780

QUEEN MANUFACTURING COMPANY INC.
4223 West Lake Street
Chicago, Illinois 60624
Donald W. Doherty, President
(312) 638-3600

QUEEN PRODUCTS
(Division of King-Seeley Thermos Company)
505 Front Street
Albert Lea, Minnesota 56007
H. Lee Berghoff, General Manager
(507) 373-3961

QUEEN QUALITY (women's shoes)
See International Shoe Company

QUEENLINER (houseboat)
See Cargile Inc.

QUEEN'S (cosmetics, health and beauty aids)
See J. Strickland & Company

QUEEN'S LACE (toiletries)
See C.P. Baker & Company

QUEEN'S LUSTERWARE LTD.
789 East 91st Street
Brooklyn, New York 11236
(212) 345-2414

QUEENS OF THE SEA
577 14th Street
Oakland, California 94612

QUEENS PRIDE (food products)
See Freezer Queen Foods Inc.

QUEENS ROYAL (canned food products)
See Bright Canning Company Ltd.

QUEENSBORO FARM PRODUCTS, INC.
3513 41st Street
Long Island City, New York 11101
Harvey Y. Miller, President
(212) 786-8900

QUEENSTOWN (canned foods)
See S.E.W. Friel

QUELQUES FLEURS (fragrance)
See Houbigant, Inc.

QUENCH COMPANY, THE
1212 Sixth Avenue
South Seattle, Washington 98134
S.S. Eland, President
(206) 624-4444

QUEST (deodorant)
See Vick Chemical Company

QUEST-SHON MARK BRA COMPANY
89-22 Queens Boulevard
Elmhurst, New York 11373

QUESTOR CORPORATION
1801 Spielbusch Avenue
Toledo, Ohio 43624
Paul Putman, Chairman of the Board
(419) 248-1515
See also Baby Line Company; Infanseat Company; Lullabye Furniture Company; and Spalding

Companies and Trade Names

QUESTOR EDUCATION PRODUCTS COMPANY
1055 Bronx River Avenue
Bronx, New York 10472
(212) 991-9000
See also Tinkertoy

QUESTOR JUVENILE FURNITURE
(Division of Questor Corporation)
95 Chapel
Newton, Massachusetts 02195

QUICK (frozen seafood)
See W.R. Grace & Company

QUICK & EASY (combination opener)
See Vaughan Manufacturing Company

QUICK-BILT (steel shelving)
See Frick-Gallagher Manufacturing Company

QUICK-CLIP (scissors)
See J. Wiss & Sons Company

QUICK CORPORATION OF AMERICA
620 Terminal Way
Costa Mesa, California 92627

QUICK CURLS (curling iron)
See Schick, Inc.

QUICK-CUT (cutlery)
See Scott & Fetzer Company

QUICK FOAM (cleanser)
See Plasti-Kote Company

QUICK MEAL (food products)
See Stokely-Van Camp, Inc.

QUICK MIST (electric hair curlers)
See Sunbeam Appliance Company

QUICK 'N EASY (charcoal and fireplace lighter, spot lifter)
See Penn-Champ

QUICK-N-EASY (frozen meats)
See Ten-Da Brand Frozen Foods, Inc.

QUICK POINT PENCIL COMPANY
1717 Fenpark Drive
Fenton, Missouri 63026

QUICK REFLEXE (fishing rods)
See Gladding Corporation

QUICK-SET, INC.
3650 Woodhead Drive
Northbrook, Illinois 60062
Paul Mooney, President
(312) 498-0700

QUICK-TWIST (brushes)
See Mill-Rose Company, Inc.

QUICK-WAY (insecticides, cleaners, deodorizers, etc.)
See Quick Chemical Corporation

QUICK-X (enamel)
See Steelcote Manufacturing Company

QUICKDRIP (automatic drip-style coffee maker)
See Dart Industries

QUICKEE, INCORPORATED
Front and Bridge
Catasauqua, Pennsylvania 18032
(215) 264-3500

QUICKFOR (serving trays and carts)
See Erik B. Nussbaum

QUICKIE (hair curler)
See Tip Top (Division of Faberge, Inc.)

QUICKSEAL (waterproofing paint)
See Standard Dry Wall Products

QUIET AUTOMATIC BURNER CORPORATION
17 Grove Street
Montclair, New Jersey 07042
J. Gordon Kaveny, President
(201) 744-1500

QUIET FLO (electric fan)
See Gross Mechanical Laboratories Inc.

QUIET-RITER (portable typewriter)
See Sperry Rand Corporation

QUIET WORLD (mild tranquilizer)
See Whitehall Laboratories

QUIGLEY COMPANY, INC.
235 East 42nd Street
New York, New York 10017
(212) 573-3444

QUIK (chocolate bars, morsels, etc.)
See Nestle Company, Inc.

QUIK-BANDS (bandages)
See Rexall Drug Company

QUIK-DRI (carpet)
See Commercial Carpet Corporation

QUIK-HEAT (pool-heating equipment)
See Quiet Automatic Burner Corporation

QUIK-KARD COMPANY INC.
951 Industrial Avenue
Palo Alto, California 94303
(415) 494-6172

QUIK-KUT (shears, trimmers)
See Wallace Manufacturing Corporation

Companies and Trade Names

QUIK 'N SURE (frozen baked goods)
See Buhler Mills, Inc.

QUIKPHONE (phone-answering machine)
See Telefinder Corporation

QUILTED BABY PRODUCTS INC.
177 Main Street
West Orange, New Jersey 07052

QUILTER SOUND COMPANY
1936 Placentia Avenue
Costa Mesa, California 92627

QUIMBY & COMPANY
30 Oakdale Road
Chester, New Jersey 07930
(201) 879-5500

QUINDATA INC.
1011 Route Number 22
Mountainside, New Jersey 07092

QUINLAN PRETZEL COMPANY
Third and Washington
Denver, Pennsylvania 17517
Arthur Nerret, President
(215) 267-7571

QUINN, PAUL D.
21153 Erie Road
Rocky River, Ohio 44116

QUINN POPCORN COMPANY, INC.
Post Office Box 608
Lake View, Iowa 51450

QUINSANA (antiperspirant, foot-care products)
See Mennen Company

QUINTA (wines)
See Heublein, Inc.

QUINTON & SON, INC., GEORGE
Wantagh, New York 11793

QUINTYPE (typewriters)
See Quindata Inc.

QUIP (puddings, shakes, and gelatin)
See Avoset Food Corporation

QUIST (nontarnishable silver-plate items)
See Erik B. Nussbaum

QUIT (thumb-sucking remedy)
See Pharm-A-Lab

QUIX (enamels)
See American Lacquer Solvents Company

QUIX (windshield deicer)
See Household Research Corporation

QUODDY MOCCASINS
(Division of R.G. Barry Corporation)
67 Minot Avenue
Auburn, Maine 04210

QUON-QUON COMPANY
2801 East 12th Street
Los Angeles, California 90023
(213) 264-3400

QUOTA (weight-control product)
See Quaker Oats Company

QURET MANUFACTURING COMPANY
Box 391
Muskegon, Michigan 49443

QWIP (pressurized dairy cream)
See Avoset Food Corporation

Companies and Trade Names

R

R & D/AVANT
Post Office Box C-Seven
New Bedford, Massachusetts 02741

R & G CHEMICAL COMPANY
34 Elm Avenue
Linwood, New Jersey 08221

R & G MARKETS, INC.
523 South 17th
Manhattan, Kansas 66502

R & H (food products)
　　See Richardson & Holland
　　　Corporation

R. & H. GUARANTEE PRODUCTS
　COMPANY
4606-12 West Cermak Road
Cicero, Illinois 60650

R. & K. ORIGINALS
(Division of Jonathan Logan, Inc.)
1400 Broadway
New York, New York 10018
Manny Eagle, President
(212) 736-0900

R & L (fish)
　　See Morse's Foodmarts, Inc.

R. & M. (coin holders, jewelry,
and pillboxes)
　　See Reeve & Mitchell Company,
　　　Inc.

R. & M. LABORATORIES OF
　GEORGIA
Box 44
Avondale Estates, Georgia 30002

R & R (canned food)
　　See William Underwood Company

R. & R. TOY MANUFACTURING
　COMPANY, INC.
Penn Argyl, Pennsylvania 18072

R & S PICKLE COMPANY INC.
154 Terrace Street
Boston, Massachusetts 02120
(617) 445-6300

R & S TOY MANUFACTURING
　COMPANY INC.
344 Maujer Street
Brooklyn, New York 11206
(212) 332-9287

RAI, INC.
37 West 37th Street
New York, New York 10018
Stanley J. Miles, President
(212) 354-6990

R.A.R. (dresses)
　　See Richling, Ades & Richman,
　　　Inc.

RB (boilers, heaters, etc.)
　　See Babcock & Wilcox Company

RBM CONTROLS (electrical
products)
　　See Essex International, Inc.,
　　　Controls Division

RC (soft drinks)
　　See Royal Crown Cola Company

RCA CORPORATION
30 Rockefeller Plaza
New York, New York 10020
Herbert T. Brunn, Vice President,
　Consumer Affairs
(212) 598-5900
　　See also Banquet Foods Corpora-
　　　tion; Cushman & Wakefield,
　　　Inc., Hertz Corporation,
　　　The; National Broadcasting
　　　Company Inc.; and
　　　Random House, Inc.

RCA ELECTRONIC COMPONENTS
(Division of RCA Corporation)
415 South Fifth Street
Harrison, New Jersey 07029

RCA RECORDS
(Division of RCA Corporation)
1133 Avenue of the Americas
New York, New York 10036
Rocco Laginestra, President
(212) 598-5900

RDE IMPORTS
50 Elm Street
Huntington, New York 11743

R.D. FOR MEN
(Division of Bishop Industries)
2345 Vauxhall
Union, New Jersey 07083

R.E.I. (camping equipment)
　　See Recreational Equipment Inc.

RFC (frozen fruit products)
　　See Ranson Fruit Company

R.F.C. (produce)
　　See Regal Fruit Cooperative,
　　　Inc.

RF COMMUNICATIONS
1680 University Avenue
Rochester, New York 14610
Guy W. Neuman, Vice President
　and General Manager
(716) 244-5830

R.F. DEVELOPMENT COMPANY
　LTD.
50 Oldis Street
Rochelle Park, New Jersey 07662

RF STUDIOS (wrought-iron furniture)
　　See Richards Morganthau
　　　Company, Inc.

Companies and Trade Names

R.G. DUN CIGAR CORPORATION
435 North Main
Lima, Ohio 45801

RGM INDUSTRIES INC.
3340 Lillian Boulevard
Titusville, Florida 32780
(305) 269-4720

R.H. COSMETICS CORPORATION
982 East 49th Street
Brooklyn, New York 11203
(212) 856-2222

R-I-D COMPANY, THE
1415 Third Street
Corpus Christi, Texas 78404

RJR ARCHER INC.
220 East Polo Road
Winston-Salem,
    North Carolina 27102
J.H. Corrigan, President
(919) 748-4000

RJR FOODS, INC.
(Subsidiary of R.J. Reynolds
    Industries, Inc.)
401 North Main Street
Winston Salem,
    North Carolina 27106
J. Tylee Wilson, President
(919) 748-4300

RKO GENERAL, INC.
(Subsidiary of General Tire &
    Rubber Company)
1440 Broadway
New York, New York 10018
John B. Poor, Chairman of the
    Board
(212) 764-7000

RKO STANLEY WARNERS
    THEATRES, INC.
1585 Broadway
New York, New York 10036
Matthew Polon, President
(212) 586-8400

R.L. & W. FOODS, INC.
Van Buren, Indiana 46991

R-LINE FOODS, INC.
126 Jefferson Street
Ripon, Wisconsin 54971

RMH INTERNATIONAL, INC.
30 Rockefeller Plaza
New York, New York 10020
(212) 757-5535

RMI (pianos, amplifier/speaker)
    See Allen Organ Company

R.O.W. SALES COMPANY
1365 Academy
Ferndale, Michigan 48220

RP EZ-KLEEN (air filters and air
    conditioners)
    See Research Products
        Corporation

RPM (motor oils and greases)
    See Standard Oil Company of
        California

RPX (hair-care products)
    See Buty Wave Products
        Company

R.S.A. CORPORATION
690 Saw Mill River Road
Ardsley, New York 10502
(914) 693-1818

RSC INDUSTRIES, INC.
Opa Locka Airport
Building 105
Opa Locka, Florida 33054
John Richardson, President
(305) 685-8525
    See also Bergen Wire Rope
        Company

RTC INDUSTRIES, INC.
920 West Cullerton Street
Chicago, Illinois 60608
(312) 243-5300

RV INDUSTRIES INC.
2220 East Carritos
Anaheim, California 92806

R.V.L. (automotive accessories)
    See Norm Weiss Enterprises

RVP (sun-screening agent)
    See Paul B. Elder Company

RW (awnings)
    See Scott & Fetzer Company,
        Carefree Division

R W P (metalware)
    See Wilton-Armetale

RX AMERICAN
Rex-Am Pharmaceuticals Division)
Box 2039
Green Bay, Wisconsin 54306

RA-MATIC (air conditioners)
    See TPI Corporation

RA-PID-GRO (plant food)
    See Ra-Pid-Gro Corporation

RABCO (electric products)
    See Harmon Kardon, Inc.

RABANNE, PACO
9 West 57th
New York, New York 10019
(212) 759-5930

RA-PID-GRO CORPORATION
88 Ossian
Dansville, New York 14437
Mrs. Frances C. Reilly, President
(716) 987-2278

Companies and Trade Names

RABIN-WINTERS
(Division of Brunswig Drug Company)
See BBC Laboratories, Health-Rite Nutritional Products Division

RABINOWE & COMPANY, E.
465 Saw Mill River Road
Yonkers, New York 10701

RACCOON STRAIT YACHT SALES INC.
40 Point San Pedro Road
San Rafael, California 94901

RACE & RACE, INC.
Post Office Box 1400M
Winter Haven, Florida 33880
R.J. Sweitzer, President and Treasurer
(813) 293-4137

RACEMASTER (racing tires)
See M. & H. Tire Company

RACER (cigars)
See Consolidated Cigar Corporation

RACER (sports apparel)
See Skea Ltd.

RACET (dehumidifiers)
See Race & Race Inc.

RACHELLE LABORATORIES, INC.
(Subsidiary of International Rectifier Corporation)
700 Henry Ford Avenue
Long Beach, California 90810
(213) 432-3956

RACINE & COMPANY INC., JULES
85 Executive Boulevard
Elmsford, New York 10573

RACINE GLOVE COMPANY, INC.
Box 368
Rio, Wisconsin 53960
O. Reed Bigelow, President and Purchasing Agent
(414) 992-3131

RACK SERVICE COMPANY, INC.
2601 Newcomb
Monroe, Louisiana 71201

RACK'N FILE (storage file)
See Jayem Sales Corporation

RACO (electrical products)
See All-Steel Equipment Inc.

RACORN (meat products)
See Rath Packing Company

RAD, INC.
375 Park Avenue
New York, New York 10022
(212) 752-0880

RADAR PACKING COMPANY
3675 Air Park
Memphis, Tennessee 38130
(901) 363-3261

RADARANGE (oven products)
See Raytheon Company

RADATRON CORPORATION
2424 Niagara Falls Boulevard
North Tonawanda, New York 14120
John Gambino, President
(716) 731-4171

RADCLIFFE LINGERIE, INC.
136 Madison Avenue
New York, New York 10016
(212) 725-6800

RADI-AIRE (electric fans)
See Reynolds Electric Company

RADIANCE PRODUCTS COMPANY
1839 West Valley
Alhambra, California 91803
(213) 283-5121

RADIANT (glass lighting fixtures)
See Thomas Industries

RADIANT
(Division of Graflex, Inc.)
8220 North Austin Avenue
Morton Grove, Illinois 60053

RADIANT COLOR COATINGS & SPECIALTY PRODUCTS
(Department of Hercules Inc.)
2800 Radiant Avenue
Richmond, California 94804

RADIANT GLO (makeup)
See Apple-Crone Laboratories

RADIANT MANUFACTURING CORPORATION
See Radiant (Division of Graflex, Inc.)

RADIANT PRODUCTS
(Department of The Bouligny Company)
Post Office Box 1059
Monroe, North Carolina 28110

RADIANTFIRES (gas heater)
See General Gas Light Company

RADIATOR LEAK CURE (automotive accessories)
See Kapro Corporation

RADIATOR SPECIALTY COMPANY
1400 West Independence
Charlotte, North Carolina 28208
Isadore D. Blumenthal, President
(704) 377-6555

RADIO CORPORATION OF AMERICA
See RCA Corporation

Companies and Trade Names

RADIO FLYER (children's vehicle)
See Radio Steel & Manufacturing Company

RADIO GARDEN (carts and wheelbarrows)
See Radio Steel & Manufacturing Company

RADIO GIRL (perfume and powder)
See Consolidated Royal Chemical Corporation

RADIO SHACK
(A Tandy Corporation Company)
2617 West Seventh Street
Fort Worth, Texas 76107
Lewis Kornfeld, President
(817) 335-3711

RADIO STEEL & MANUFACTURING COMPANY
6515 West Grand Avenue
Chicago, Illinois 60635
M.A. Pasin, President
(312) 637-7100

RADIO-TYME (men's footwear)
See L.B. Evans' Son Company

RADIOEAR CORPORATION
375 Valley Brook Road
McMurray, Pennsylvania 15317
H.C. Cameron, President
(412) 941-9000

RADO WATCH COMPANY, INC.
(Subsidiary of A. Cohen & Sons Corporation)
27 West 23rd Street
New York, New York 10010
Charles Cohen, President
(212) 675-4400

RAEFORD TURKEY FARMS INC.
Central Avenue
Raeford, North Carolina 28376

RAFAEL MENDEZ (sheet music)
See Koff Music Company

RAFETTO INC., G.B.
87 34th Street
Brooklyn, New York 11232
(212) 499-9000

RAGAN, BRAD, INC.
112 Greenwood Road
Spruce Pine, North Carolina 28777
Bradley E. Ragan, President
(704) 765-9611

RAGAN KNITTING COMPANY
7 Cox Avenue
Thomasville, North Carolina 27360
Amos H. Ragan, Jr., President
(919) 476-7742

RAGGEDY ANDY (disposable diapers)
See Scott Paper Company

RAGGEDY ANDY (musical items)
See Schmid Brothers Inc.

RAGLAND COMPANY, C.B.
600 Thompson Lane
Nashville, Tennessee 37211
James B. Ragland, President
(615) 242-2611

RAGO FOUNDATIONS, INC.
18-15 27th Avenue
Astoria, New York 11102

RAGOZZINO & SON INC., J.
Box 116
Meriden, Connecticut 06450

RAGU PACKING COMPANY
(Division of Chesebrough-Pond's, Inc.)
1680 Lyell Avenue
Rochester, New York 14606
Ralph Cantisano, President
(716) 458-0886

RAHM BROTHERS
Negaunee, Michigan 49866

RAICHLE MOLITOR USA, INC.
200 Saw Mill River Road
Hawthorne, New York 10532

RAID (insecticides)
See S.C. Johnson & Son Inc.

RAIDER (snowmobiles)
See Power Tools Inc.

RAILROAD (pocket watches)
See Ingraham Industries

RAILROAD LINE (underwear and socks)
See William G. Leininger Knitting Company

RAILTON COMPANY, B.A.
111 North Northwest Avenue
Northlake, Illinois 60164
(312) 379-8800

RAIMOND SILVER MANUFACTURING COMPANY, INC.
25 Union Street
Chelsea, Massachusetts 02150

RAIN BARREL (fabric softener)
See S.C. Johnson & Son, Inc.

RAIN-BEAU (fishing gear)
See Brunswick Corporation

RAIN BIRD SPRINKLER MANUFACTURING COMPANY
7045 North Grand Avenue
Glendora, California 91740
Mary E. LaFetra, President
(213) 335-1203

RAIN DROPS (water softener)
See A.E. Staley Manufacturing Company

Companies and Trade Names

RAIN JET CORPORATION
301 South Flower Street
Burbank, California 91503
Gerald W. Frasier, President
(213) 849-2251

RAIN KING (sprinklers)
See Sunbeam Outdoor Company

RAIN-REM (liquid for waterproofing garments)
See Rem Industries, Inc.

RAIN SOFT WATER
CONDITIONING COMPANY
1950 East Estes Avenue
Elk Grove Village, Illinois 60004

RAINBO (bakery products)
See Campbell-Taggert Inc.

RAINBOW (groceries)
See Fleming Foods

RAINBOW (juices and nectars)
See Frozen Fruit Concentrates, Inc.

RAINBOW ART GLASS COMPANY INC., THE
(Division of Viking Glass Company)
1500 Adams Avenue
Huntington, West Virginia 25704

RAINBOW FASHIONS, INC.
1350 Broadway
New York, New York 10018
(212) 925-0761

RAINBOW GRILL (restaurant chain)
See Brody Corporation

RAINBOW IMPORTS, INC.
5-25 48th Avenue
Long Island City, New York 11101
(212) 784-5900

RAINBOW ROCKER (juvenile furniture)
See Gem Manufacturing Corporation

RAINBOW ROOM (restaurant chain)
See Brody Corporation

RAINBOW SPRINGS (seafood)
See Idaho Trout Processors Company

RAINBOW TRADING COMPANY
5-25 48th Avenue
Long Island City, New York 11101
(212) 784-5900

RAINBOW WOOD PRODUCTS, INC.
40-35 21st Street
Long Island City, New York 11101
(212) 392-6888

RAINDRI (water repellent)
See Goorin Brothers Inc.

RAINFAIR, INC.
(Subsidiary of Koracorp Industries, Inc.)
1501 Albert Street
Racine, Wisconsin 53404
John Nikitas, President
(414) 637-1201

RAINGUARD (water repellent)
See National Cleaners Chemical Manufacturing Company

RAINIER BREWING COMPANY
3100 Airport Way, South
Seattle, Washington 98134
E.S. Coombs, Jr., President
(206) 622-2600

RAINSPRAY (underground sprinklers)
See Leisure Group

RAINWAVE (lawn and garden sprinklers, nozzles, and other accessories)
See Melnor Industries

RAINY DAY (windshield wiper blades and refills)
See Anderson Company

RAKE 'N BAG (leaf and grass bagger)
See Hall Industries Inc.

RAKE N SPADE (garden tool)
See Holt-Howard

RALEIGH (cigarettes)
See Brown & Williamson Tobacco Corporation

RALEIGH INDUSTRIES OF AMERICA, INC.
1168 Commonwealth Avenue
Boston, Massachusetts 02134
N.A. Langenfeld, President
(617) 734-0240

RALLO (Marsala wines)
See Munson Shaw Company

RALLY (automobile wax)
See E.I. du Pont de Nemours & Company, Inc.

RALLY (sporting goods)
See Brookfield Sporting Goods Inc.

RALLY
Mirro Marine Division
804 Pecor Street
Oconto, Wisconsin 54153

RALLYE (sports accessories)
See Sport-Obermeyer Ltd.

Companies and Trade Names

RALPH'S FOODS COMPANY
Box 4248
Corpus Christi, Texas 78408

RALS LABORATORIES
480 West Aurora Road
Cleveland, Ohio 44146
(216) 467-1200

RALSTON PURINA COMPANY
835 South Eighth Street
Saint Louis, Missouri 63102
R. Hal Dean, Chairman of the Board
(314) 982-0111
   See also Cardinet Candy Company Inc.; Checkerboard Foods; Foodmaker, Inc.; and Van Camp Sea Food

RAM (hand tools and furniture)
   See O. Ames Company

RAM GOLF CORPORATION
1501 Pratt Boulevard
Elk Grove Village, Illinois 60007
William L. Hansberger, Chairman of the Board
(312) 956-7500

RAM TOOL CORPORATION
2110 West Walnut Street
Chicago, Illinois 60612
John Cutrone, Chairman of the Board
(312) 666-7500

RAMA (lawn and garden supplies)
   See Jaxway Wholesale Supply Company, Inc.

RAMADA INNS, INC.
3838 East Van Buren Street
Phoenix, Arizona 85008
Marion W. Isbell, Chairman of the Board
(602) 275-4000

RAMAR (men's and boys' wear)
   See Oxford Industries, Inc.

RAMIREZ & FERAUD CHILI COMPANY, INC.
130 North Garden
Ventura, California 93001

RAMOS SHRIMP COMPANY
Belt Road
Bayou La Batre, Alabama 36509

RAMP-KING (water skis and accessories)
   See Cut 'N Jump Ski Corporation

RAMPONE (flutes, saxaphones)
   See Gretsch

RAMROD-POLYTRAN, INC.
1010 Doyle
Menlo Park, California 94025

RAMS HEAD (ale)
   See C. Schmidt & Sons, Inc.

RAMSES (contraceptives)
   See Julius Schmid, Inc.

RAMSEY CORPORATION
(Subsidiary of TRW, Inc.)
Post Office Box 513
Saint Louis, Missouri 63166
Charles W. Duffy, President
(314) 227-5371

RAMSON IMPORTS
34 West 33rd
New York, New York 10001
(212) 594-5784

RAMSON TRADING COMPANY, INC.
1185 Broadway
New York, New York 10001
(212) 679-9066

RAMY (ski equipment)
   See Hart Ski Company

RANCH CRAFT (lamps)
   See Dunning Industries Inc.

RANCH HAND (frozen meat)
   See Chip Steak Company

RANCH HOUSE OF AMERICA, INC.
5710 North Federal Highway
Fort Lauderdale, Florida 33308
Nicholas P. Yianilos, President
(305) 946-9100

RANCH OAK (furniture)
   See A. Brandt Company, Inc.

RANCH STYLE (canned foods)
   See Great Western Foods Company

RANCH TABLE (canned and frozen foods)
   See Wilbur-Ellis Company

RANCHERS PACKING CORPORATION
10 Charles Street
Floral Park, New York 11001

RANCHO FRANCISCO (Mexican food products)
   See S & W Fine Foods, Inc.

RAND LTD., JORDAN K.
7625 Hesperia Avenue
Reseda, California 91335

RAND MCNALLY & COMPANY
8255 North Central Park
Skokie, Illinois 60076
Andrew McNally, III, President
(312) 673-9100

RAND PRODUCTS COMPANY INC.
596 Roosevelt Boulevard
Paramus, New Jersey 07652

Companies and Trade Names

RAND RUBBER COMPANY
436 Keap Street
Brooklyn, New York 11211
Leon L. Pine, President and
 Treasurer
(212) 963-2500

RAND SHOES (men's shoes)
 See International Shoe Company

RANDALL
(A Textron Company)
10179 Commerce Park Drive
Cincinnati, Ohio 45246
R. Price, Vice President
(513) 874-8866

RANDALL BEAN
(Division of Randall Chicken
 Products Company
401 South Main Street
Tekonsha, Michigan 49092

RANDALL INSTRUMENTS INC.
1132 Duryea
Irvine, California 92705

RANDALL WINE VINEGAR
 COMPANY, INC.
894 Whittier Street
Bronx, New York 10474
(212) 323-1136

RANDCRAFT (shoes)
 See International Shoe Company

RANDOLPH-RAND CORPORATION
176 Madison Avenue
New York, New York 10016
(212) 685-8080

RANDOLPH-TENNEY INC.
4100 Warren Avenue
Hillside, Illinois 60162

RANDOM HOUSE, INC.
(Subsidiary of RCA Corporation)
201 East 50th Street
New York, New York 10022
Robert L. Bernstein, President
(212) 751-2600
 See also Pantheon Books

RANDOM PRESS
176 East 75th Street
New York, New York 10021
(212) 734-4000

RANDY MANUFACTURING
 COMPANY
32 South Main Street
Randolph, Massachusetts 02368
Saul Komessar, President
(617) 963-7000

RANDY'S (seafood)
 See Brilliant Seafood, Inc.

RANDYS STEAKS INC.
624 East President
Tupelo, Mississippi 38801

RANGAIRE CORPORATION
Post Office Box 177
Cleburne, Texas 76031
J.M. Hill, President
(817) 654-9111
 See also Chambers Corporation

RANGE KLEEN MANUFACTURING
 INC.
Post Office Box 696
Lima, Ohio 45802

RANGE TOP (frozen foods)
 See Pickerington Creamery, Inc.

RANGEMASTER (sporting goods)
 See Bushnell Optical Company

RANGER (steel shelving)
 See Frontier Manufacturing
  Company

RANGER PRODUCTS COMPANY
 (stamp pads, etc.)
Box 828
Red Bank, New Jersey 07701
(201) 747-1060

RANGER PRODUCTS COMPANY,
 INC.
735 Dixwell Avenue
New Haven, Connecticut 06511

RANGER II (outboard motors)
 See Jetco Inc.

RANGER YACHTS
3090 Pullman
Costa Mesa, California 92627
(714) 546-8078

RANGEVENTER (kitchen and
bathroom appliances)
 See The Tappan Company

RANGING, INC.
Post Office Box 9106
Rochester, New York 14625

RANK PRECISION INDUSTRIES
260 North Route 303
West Nyack, New York 10994

RANSBURG INC., HARPER J.
1234 Barth Avenue
Indianapolis, Indiana 46203
Duane H. Williams, President
(317) 634-8712

RANSEE (decanter clocks, shelves)
 See J. Kenneth Zahn

RANSOHOFF'S, INC.
259 Post Street
San Francisco, California 94108
Daniel E. Sachs, President
(415) 392-7500

Companies and Trade Names

RANSON FRUIT COMPANY, INC.
Ranson, West Virginia 25438

RAPCO, INC.
(Subsidiary of Williams
   Manufacturing Company)
500 North Spaulding Avenue
Chicago, Illinois 60624
Yale A. Blanc, President
(312) 826-4444

RAPHAEL (aperitif wine)
   See Julius Wile Sons &
      Company Inc.

RAPHAEL COMPANY INC.,
   EDWIN
Infinity Lane
Holland, Michigan 49423
(616) 396-5246

RAPHAEL OF LONDON, M.
832 Lexington Avenue
New York, New York 10021
(212) 838-0178

RAPID-AMERICAN CORPORATION
711 Fifth Avenue
New York, New York 10022
Meshulam Riklis, President
(212) 752-0100
   See also Cohen & Sons,
      Joseph H.; Cross Country
      Clothes; Leeds Travelwear;
      and McCrory Corporation

RAPID COOL
(Subsidiary of Ardco Inc.)
233 South Berry Street
Brea, California 92621
(714) 529-1731

RAPID-SHAVE (shaving cream)
   See Colgate-Palmolive Company

RAPID-SORTER (cabinets)
   See All Purpose Steel Products
      Company

RAPID TAG & WIRE COMPANY
1116 Ridge Avenue
Pittsburgh, Pennsylvania 15233
(412) 321-3360

RAPIDES LES LACHINE (canned
vegetables)
   See David Lord, Ltd.

RAPTURE (hosiery)
   See William G. Leininger
      Knitting Company

RARE ANTIQUE (straight Bourbon)
   See Four Roses Distillers
      Company

RARITAN ENGINEERING
   COMPANY
1025 North High Street
Millville, New Jersey 08332
(609) 825-4900

RASCAL (motor-scooter minibike)
   See Rupp Industries Inc.

RASCO STORES
(Division of Gamble-Skogmo, Inc.)
2777 North Ontario Street
Burbank, California 91504
H.D. Nelson, President
(213) 843-3773

RASH-BAN (pants for diaper rash)
   See Murray Salk, Inc.

RASHEZE (diaper-rash treatment)
   See Barry-Martin
      Pharmaceuticals, Inc.

RASKAS CANDY COMPANY,
   ANN
Box 603
Englewood, New Jersey 07631

RASMAN PHARMACAL COMPANY
1545 Clinton Place
River Forest, Illinois 60305

RASMUSSEN IMPORT COMPANY
2210 Hennepin Avenue South
Minneapolis, Minnesota 55405
(612) 377-7172

RATCLIFF INDUSTRIES INC.
Box 85
Juneau, Wisconsin 53039

RATELCO INC.
610 Pontius Avenue North
Seattle, Washington 98109
(206) 624-7770

RATH PACKING COMPANY, THE
Elm and Sycamore Streets
Waterloo, Iowa 50703
J.C. Walker, President
(319) 235-8900

RATHCON INC.
2602 Electronic Lane
Dallas, Texas 75220
(214) 350-7721

RATNER CLOTHES FOR MEN
730 13th Street
San Diego, California 92112
Abraham Ratner, Chairman of the
   Board
(714) 234-0111

RATNER, INC., MARC
286 Fifth Avenue
New York, New York 10001
(212) 244-6630

RATSEY & LAPTHORN INC.
East Schofield Street
City Island, New York 10464
Colin E. Ratsey, President and
   Treasurer
(212) 885-1012

RAU FASTENER
(Division of United States
   Industries, Inc.)
99 Sprague
Providence, Rhode Island 02907
(401) 861-7100

Companies and Trade Names

RAUCHER MUSIC COMPANY
5101 Morley Drive
Greendale, Wisconsin 53129

RAUL INTERNATIONAL
 CORPORATION
509 West 56th Street
New York, New York 10019
(212) 247-6520

RAULAND-BORG CORPORATION
3535 West Addison Street
Chicago, Illinois 60618
Harro K. Heinz, President and
 Chief Engineer
(312) 267-1300

RAUSCHENBERGER COMPANY,
 JOHN
193 North Broadway
Milwaukee, Wisconsin 53202
(414) 271-2569

RAVA & SONS, INC., ROSARIO
28 Greene Street
New York, New York 10013
(212) 966-2393

RAVARINO & FRESCHI, INC.
4651 Shaw
Saint Louis, Missouri 63110
A.J. Ravarino, President
(314) 773-2700

RAVE (floor wax)
 See Boyle-Midway

RAVEEN (hair-care products)
 See Supreme Beauty Products
 Company

RAVEN INDUSTRIES INC.
Box 1007
Sioux Falls, South Dakota 57101
David A. Christensen, President
(605) 336-2750
 See also Swing West Ski Wear

RAVENHURST ENTERPRISES
 See Candle Factory, The

RAVENSCROFT, LTD.
(Subsidiary of Anchor Hocking
 Corporation)
Post Office Box 502
Lancaster, Ohio 43130

RAVOX (hearing aids)
 See Zenith Radio Corporation

RAWL ENGINEERING & MANU-
 FACTURING COMPANY INC.
99 Hartford Avenue
Providence, Rhode Island 02909
(401) 861-3480

RAWLINGS SPORTING GOODS
 COMPANY
2300 Delmar Boulevard
Saint Louis, Missouri 63166
Thomas F. O'Brien
(314) 241-2900

RAWLPLUG COMPANY, THE
200 Petersville Road
New Rochelle, New York 10801
Frederic B. Powers, Jr., President
 and Treasurer
(914) 633-6100

RAWSON, INC.
15014 N.E. 90th Street
Redmond, Washington 98052

RAY BAN (sunglasses)
 See Bausch & Lomb Inc.

RAY BROTHERS AND NOBLE
 CANNING COMPANY INC.
Box 314
Hobbs, Indiana 46047

RAY DRUG COMPANY, THE
Box 10285
Oakland, California 94610

RAY GREETING CARD COMPANY,
 DAN
2787 N.W. 34th Street
Miami, Florida 33152
(305) 635-7261

RAY-JET (infrared heaters)
 See Bernardi Brothers, Inc.

RAY-LITE (optical products)
 See Bausch & Lomb Inc.

RAY-NOX (sunburn treatment)
 See Torch Laboratories, Inc.

RAY-O-VAC
(Division of ESB Inc.)
101 East Washington Avenue
Madison, Wisconsin 53703
(608) 252-7400

RAY OIL BURNER COMPANY
1301 San Jose Avenue
San Francisco, California 94112
Russell C. Westover, Jr., President
(415) 333-5800

RAY PACKING COMPANY, L.
Milbridge, Maine 04658

RAY PLASTICS INC.
Mill Circle Road
Winchendon Springs,
 Massachusetts 01477
(617) 297-0088

RAY PROOF CORPORATION
50 Keeler Avenue
Norwalk, Connecticut 06856
(203) 838-4555

RAYBESTOS-MANHATTAN, INC.
100 Oakview Drive
Trumbull, Connecticut 06611
William S. Simpson, President
(203) 371-0101

RAYCO INTERNATIONAL INC.
3200 West Market Street
Akron, Ohio 44313
Gerald Rosenfield, President
(216) 867-5900

Companies and Trade Names

RAYETTE
(Division of Faberge, Inc.)
1345 Avenue of the Americas
New York, New York 10019
(212) 581-3500

RAYEX CORPORATION
133-30 37th Avenue
Flushing, New York 11354
Ray Tunkel, President
(212) 762-5600

RAYGO WAGNER
(Subsidiary of Raygo Inc.)
Post Office Box 20044
4427 N.E. 158 Avenue
Portland, Oregon 97220
Ronald M. Karls, Vice President
   and General Manager
(503) 252-5531

RAYGOLD
(Division of Boise Cascade
   Corporation)
217 East Picadilly Street
Winchester, Virginia 22601
Alvin A. Goldhush, General
   Manager
(703) 667-8611

RAYLINE (auto accessories, etc.)
   See International Manufacturing
   Company

RAYLITE ELECTRIC CORPORATION
305-315 Rider Avenue
Bronx, New York 10451
(212) 292-0400

RAYMODES, INC.
135 Madison Avenue
New York, New York 10016
(212) 683-2300

RAYMOND FOODS, INC.
7540 Croname
Niles, Illinois 60648

RAYMOND HALPERN (lingerie)
   See Movie Star Inc.

RAYMOND PRODUCTS COMPANY
1565 Como Avenue
Saint Paul, Minnesota 55108
(612) 645-0825

RAYMOR, RICHARDS,
   MORGENTHAU COMPANY
734 Grand Avenue
Ridgefield, New Jersey 07657
Everett Winters, President
(212) 689-8184

RAYNOR MANUFACTURING
   COMPANY
Dixon, Illinois 61021
Ray H. Neisewander, President
(815) 288-1431

RAYNOX (cameras)
   See Camera Specialty Company
   Inc.

RAYO CHEMICAL COMPANY
158 State Road East
Westminster, Massachusetts 01473

RAYTHEON COMPANY
141 Spring Street
Lexington, Massachusetts 02173
Thomas L. Phillips, Chairman of
   the Board
(617) 862-6600
   See also Amana Refrigeration,
   Inc.; and Caloric
   Corporation

RAYTHEON MARINE COMPANY
(Subsidiary of Raytheon Company)
676 Island Pond Road
Manchester, New Hampshire 03103

RAZOR-BACK (farm and garden
tools)
   See Union Fork & Hoe Company

RE-DAN PACKING COMPANY,
   INC.
70-10 74th Street
Middle Village, New York 11379
S. Sanders, President
(212) 326-3400

RE-LY-ON METAL PRODUCTS,
INC.
   See Relyon Products Corporation

RE-MAR DRUG COMPANY, INC.
Box 494
Centralia, Illinois 62801

RE-NOVET (disinfectant, air
freshener)
   See Consolidated Chemical Inc.

RE-TAN-ER (leather preservative)
   See Arnold Leather Products
   Company

REA-D-PACK FOODS, INC.
(Subsidiary of Norwich Packing
   Company)
North Norwich, New York 13814

REACO PRODUCTS, INC.
Box 2747
West Durham, North Carolina 27705

READ (canned food)
   See Joan of Arc Company

READ & EMMERICH INC.
110 West 40th Street
New York, New York 10018
(212) 354-0357

READ-FOR-FUN (children's books)
   See Gelles-Widmer Company

READE ORGANIZATION, INC.,
   THE WALTER
Mayfair House
Deal Road
Oakhurst, New Jersey 07755
Sheldon Gunsberg, President
(201) 531-1600

READER'S DIGEST ASSOCIATION,
   INC., THE
Pleasantville, New York 10570
Kent Rhodes, President
(914) 769-7000

Companies and Trade Names

READI-BAKE INC.
190 28th Street S.E.
Grand Rapids, Michigan 49510

READI-SPOTS (bandages)
   See Parke, Davis & Company

READING ANTHRACITE COMPANY
200 Mahantongo
Pottsville, Pennsylvania 17901
John W. Rich, Vice President
(717) 622-5750

READING BREWING COMPANY
Ninth and Laurel Streets
Reading, Pennsylvania 19603
Harry Fischman, President
(215) 374-2231

READING COMPANY
Reading Terminal
Philadelphia, Pennsylvania 19107
C.E. Bertrand, President
(215) 922-6100

READ'S, INC.
2523 Gwynns Falls Parkway
Baltimore, Maryland 21216
Arthur K. Solomon, President
(301) 669-2500

READY DIPS (cheese dips)
   See Kraft Foods

READY-DOUGH (frozen baked goods)
   See Bridgford Foods Corporation

READY REFERENCE PUBLISHING COMPANY
406 West 31st Street
New York, New York 10001
(212) 244-1000

READY RENT-ALL SYSTEMS INC.
100 State Street
Boston, Massachusetts 02109
(617) 227-4650

READY TO EAT (puddings)
   See Sealtest Foods

READY-TO-SERVE (highballs)
   See Lawrence & Company, Inc.

READY-TO-SERVE (puddings)
   See General Mills, Inc.

READY-TO-SPREAD (frostings)
   See General Mills, Inc.

READY TO USE (utensils)
   See Vollrath Company

REAL (hair-care product)
   See Mennen Company

REAL-A-PEEL (housewares)
   See Grayline Housewares

REAL-FORM GIRDLE COMPANY
218 Bedford Avenue
Brooklyn, New York 11211
M. Dorfman, President
(212) 388-6570

REAL FRESH INC.
Box 1551
Visalia, California 93277

REAL FRUIT (canned foods)
   See Wapato Fruit Products, Inc.

REAL FYRE (gas fireplace logs and embers)
   See Robert H. Peterson Company

REAL GOLD (beverage)
   See Coca-Cola Company, Foods Division

REAL JOY (canned foods)
   See J.O. Youngblood Cannery

REAL KILL PRODUCTS
2500 Summit
Kansas City, Missouri 64108
(816) 842-8092

REAL KOSHER SAUSAGE COMPANY, INC.
15 Rivington
New York, New York 10002
(212) 254-5994

REAL MACKENZIE (Scotch)
   See Glenmore Distilleries Company, Inc.

REAL WHIP (frozen nondairy topping)
   See Presto Food Products Inc.

REALEMON FOODS
(Division of Borden, Inc.)
1200 West 37th
Chicago, Illinois 60609
Melvin S. Peters, President
(312) 254-7300

REALEX CORPORATION
2500 Summit Street
Kansas City, Missouri 64108
R. Gordon Martin, President
(816) 842-8092

REALIST, INC.
West 16288 Megal Drive
Menomonee Falls, Wisconsin 53051
Harvey A. Gobis, President
(414) 251-8100
   See also White Instruments, David

REALISTIC (stereo components, etc.)
   See Radio Shack

REALISTIC PRODUCTS COMPANY
1965 South 74th Street
West Allis, Wisconsin 53214

REALITIES (shoes)
   See Oomphies, Inc.

Companies and Trade Names

REALOCK (chain fence)
See C F & I Steel Corporation

REAMES FOODS INC.
8614 Harback
Clive, Iowa 50053

REARDON COMPANY
See Bondex International, Inc.

REARDON LABORATORIES, INC., W.G.
Pleasant View Road
Pleasant Valley, New York 12569
(914) 635-3243

REARDON PRODUCTS
323 North Main Street
Roanoke, Illinois 61561

REASENBERG & SON, A.
385 Clarendon Road
Uniondale, New York 11553

REASOR CORPORATION, THE
500 West Lincoln Street
Charleston, Illinois 61920
William S. Reasor, President
(217) 345-3921

REBCOR
Box 115
Bedford, Texas 76021

REBECCA RUTH CANDY, INC.
Box 64
Frankfort, Kentucky 40601

REBEL (cooked meat products)
See Suzanna's Kitchen Inc.

REBEL (electric guitars)
See Harmony Company

REBEL YELL (Bourbon)
See Somerset Importers, Ltd.

REBER (canned vegetables)
See Aunt Nellie's Foods, Inc.

REBORN PRODUCTS COMPANY
8114 Heacock Lane
Wyncote, Pennsylvania 19095

RECIPE (canned seafoods)
See Peter Pan Seafoods, Inc.

RECLINA-ROCKER (rockers)
See La-Z-Boy Chair Company

RECO INTERNATIONAL CORPORATION
26 South Street
Port Washington, New York 11050

RECO RADI-AIRE (electric fans)
See Reynolds Electric Company

RECOATIT (vinyl coating)
See Marine Development & Research Corporation

RECOBRIGHT (aluminum finish)
See Republic Chemical Company

RECORD BOND (cigars)
See H.L. Neff & Company, Inc.

RECORD CLUB OF AMERICA/ CLUB HEADQUARTERS
York, Pennsylvania 17402
Sigmund Friedman, President
(717) 266-6611

RECORDPLATE COMPANY, INC.
Post Office Box 649
9955 Baldwin Place
El Monte, California 91734
(213) 686-2233

RECOTON CORPORATION
46-23 Crane Street
Long Island City, New York 11101
Herbert H. Borchardt, President
(212) 392-6442

RECREATIONAL ENTERPRISES CORPORATION
3705 S.W. 42nd Place
Gainesville, Florida 32601

RECREATIONAL EQUIPMENT COMPANY
11892 Cardinal Circle
Garden Grove, California 92640

RECREATIONAL EQUIPMENT, INC.
1525 11th Avenue
Seattle, Washington 98122
(206) 323-8333
See also Nord Yachts

RECREATIONAL SERVICES INC.
8111 Gatehouse Road
Falls Church, Virginia 22042

RECREO MANUFACTURING COMPANY, INC.
808 North James Street
Rome, New York 13440

RECRUITS (cigarettes)
See Liggett & Myers Inc.

RECSEI LABORATORIES, THE
633 Tabor Lane
Santa Barbara, California 93103

RECTOR INTERNATIONAL CORPORATION
9 West Prospect
Mount Vernon, New York 10551

RECTORAL COMPANY, THE
313 Crocker Boulevard
Mount Clemens, Michigan 48403

RECTRANS
(Division of White Motor Corporation)
800 Whitney
Brighton, Michigan 48116

Companies and Trade Names

RECYCLE, INC.
3807 Forbes Avenue
Pittsburgh, Pennsylvania 15213
John W. Simpson, Jr., President
(412) 687-1919

RECYCLED DENIMS (caps, halters, bags)
See Variety Wholesale Corporation

RED BALL EXPRESS HOUSEHOLD MOVERS
See American Red Ball Transit Company Inc.

RED BAND (flour)
See General Mills, Inc.

RED BAND (shortening)
See Standard Brands, Inc., Fleischmann Division

RED BARN SYSTEM, INC.
(Subsidiary of Servomation Corporation)
6845 Elm Street
McLean, Virginia 22180
John A. Lee, President
(703) 893-2111

RED BEAUTY (food products)
See Kelley Canning Company Inc.

RED-BIRD (frozen foods)
See Pearl Grange Fruit Exchange Inc.

RED BRAND (fence)
See Keystone Consolidated Industries, Inc.

RED CAP (ale)
See Carling Brewing Company

RED CAP (household products)
See Standard Brush & Broom Company

RED CARPET (fruit)
See Idaho Fruit Sales, Inc.

RED CARPET INNS, INC.
Box 2510
101 Seabreeze Boulevard
Daytona Beach, Florida 32018
Tommy Tucker, Chairman and President
(904) 255-1492

RED CEDAR SHINGLE & HANDSPLIT SHAKE BUREAU
5510 White Building
Seattle, Washington 98101
(206) 623-4881

RED CHEEK, INC.
40 South Buttonwood Street
Fleetwood, Pennsylvania 19522
Daniel D. Unger, President
(215) 944-7661

RED CHIEF (fruit)
See Allstate Apple Exchange, Inc.

RED CHIEF (pet foods)
See Foster Canning Company, Inc.

RED CIRCLE (coffee)
See Great Atlantic & Pacific Tea Company

RED-CLIFF COMPANY
1911 North Clybourn Avenue
Chicago, Illinois 60614
(312) 248-1951

RED COACH GRILLS RESTAURANT
See Howard Johnson Company

RED COMET INC.
2329 West Main
Littleton, Colorado 80120
Max A. Romero, President
(303) 794-1544

RED CROSS (canned foods)
See Furman Canning Company

RED CROSS (evaporated milk)
See Carnation Company

RED CROSS (first-aid needs)
See Johnson & Johnson

RED CROSS (mattresses)
See Southern Cross Industries Inc.

RED CROSS (shoes)
See United States Shoe Corporation

RED CROSS CHEMICAL WORKS, INC.
2338 North Seeley
Chicago, Illinois 60647
(312) 278-6239

RED CROSS MACARONI COMPANY
312 West Grand Avenue
Chicago, Illinois 60610
(312) 644-1061

RED CROSS NURSE (germicide, breath freshener, disinfectant)
See J. Hubbard Company, Inc.

RED DALE (bicycles)
See Chaparral Industries, Inc.

RED DALE COACH COMPANY
15 South Bowen
Longmont, Colorado 80501

RED DEVIL (lighter fluid, flints, charcoal lighters)
See Dome Chemical Corporation

Companies and Trade Names

RED DEVIL, INC.
2400 Vauxhall Road
Union, New Jersey 07083
John L. Lee, Chairman of the Board
(201) 688-6900

RED DIAMOND (tools, hardware, housewares)
See Masback Hardware Company

RED E MADE (prepared food mixes)
See T.A. Faulds Company

RED EAGLE INDUSTRIES, INC.
Post Office Box 616
Amsterdam, New York 12010

RED ENGINE (snack foods)
See McCleary Industries, Inc.

RED FOOT PRODUCTS COMPANY, INC.
20131 Joy Road
Detroit, Michigan 48228
(313) 584-9393

RED FOX (tobacco)
See Conwood Corporation

RED GATE (jams and jellies)
See Lexington Specialty Foods, Inc.

RED GLOW (heat lamp)
See El-Tronics, Inc.

RED GOLD, INC.
Post Office Box 83
Elwood, Indiana 46036

RED GOOSE (shoes)
See International Shoe Company

RED HAWK (farm and garden tools)
See Union Fork & Hoe Company

RED HEAD BRAND CORPORATION
4100 Platinum Way
Dallas, Texas 75237
(214) 330-9134

RED HEART (dog and cat food)
See John Morrell & Company

RED HOOK COLD STORAGE COMPANY
Albany Post Road
Red Hook, New York 12571

RED HOT (hardwood charcoal briquets)
See Standard Milling Company

RED L FOODS CORPORATION
Gloucester, Massachusetts 01930

RED LAMP (high-intensity lamps)
See Roxter Corporation

RED LINE (electric heating pads)
See Northern Electric Company

RED LINE (lubricant)
See Union Oil Company of California

RED-LINE (mattresses and foundations)
See Englander Company, Inc.

RED LINE COMMERCIAL COMPANY INC.
8 Jay
New York, New York 10013
(212) 736-7260

RED LION TABLE COMPANY
Red Lion, Pennsylvania 17356
Edward B. Miller, President
(717) 244-4049

RED LODGE CANNING COMPANY
(Subsidiary of Big Stone Canning Company)
Box 520
Red Lodge, Montana 59068

RED MILL (olives, maraschino cherries, vinegar, prepared mustard)
See Southgate Foods, Inc.

RED MITTEN (canned foods)
See Coloma Cooperative Canning Company

RED MOON (canned foods)
See J. Langrall & Brother, Inc.

RED OWL STORES, INC.
(Subsidiary of Gamble-Skogmo, Inc.)
215 East Excelsior Avenue
Hopkins, Minnesota 55343
Melvin Ross, President
(612) 932-2132

RED PACK (food products)
See California Canners and Growers

RED PAIL (food products)
See Joseph Middleby, Jr., Inc.

RED RAVEN RUBBER COMPANY
237 South Street
Newark, New Jersey 07114
H.K. Dwork, Partner
(201) 621-7676

RED REESE (clocks)
See J. Kenneth Zahn

RED RIBBON (produce)
See Oregon Prune Exchange

RED RIPE (canned foods)
See Tillie Lewis Foods, Inc.

1130

Companies and Trade Names

RED ROBE (canned foods)
See General Grocer Company

RED ROOF INNS INC.
536 South Third Street
Columbus, Ohio 43215
(614) 224-9238

RED ROPE INDUSTRIES
(Division of Sheller-Globe Corporation)
7 Wood Avenue
Bristol, Pennsylvania 19007
Joseph Wexelbaum, President and General Manager
(215) 785-1531
See also Ajax Fibre Envelope Corporation; and Majestic Staple Corporation

RED ROSE (groceries)
See Detroit City Dairy, Inc.

RED ROSE (snuff)
See United States Tobacco Company

RED ROSE (tea)
See Brooke-Bond Foods, Inc.

RED ROSES (cosmetics)
See Yardley of London, Inc.

RED SATIN (whiskey)
See Schenley Industries, Inc.

RED SEA BALSAM COMPANY
12 North Main Street
Fall River, Massachusetts 02720

RED SEAL (canned foods)
See Comly-Flanigan Company

RED SEAL (phonograph records)
See RCA Corporation

RED SEAL POTATO CHIP COMPANY
(Division of T & W Inc.)
Post Office Box 7125
4300 Oneida
Denver, Colorado 80216
Earl S. Wilson, President
(303) 399-2333

RED SHIELD (drills)
See Standard Tool Company

RED SPOT (canned and frozen foods)
See Agripac, Inc.

RED STAR (cake and pie fillings, yeast, baking powder, etc.)
See Universal Foods Corporation

RED STAR (flour)
See General Mills, Inc.

RED STAR COMPANY, THE
Post Office Box 677
Bridgeport, Connecticut 06601
(203) 335-0410

RED STAR EXPRESS LINES OF AUBURN, INC.
24 Wright Avenue
Auburn, New York 13021
John Bisgrove, President
(315) 253-2721

RED STEER (plant food)
See Swift & Company

RED STRIPE (paintbrushes)
See PPG Industries, Inc.

RED SWAN (fruits, vegetables)
See Hilton, Gibson & Miller, Inc.

RED-T-CUT (frozen meats)
See Texas Meat Packers

RED TAG (food products)
See Castle & Cooke Foods

RED TULIP (canned vegetables)
See Spring Garden Wholesale Grocery Company

RED WAVES (seafoods)
See New England Fish Company

RED WHITE AND BLUE (beer)
See Pabst Brewing Company

RED WING (produce)
See Sanger Fruit Growers Association

RED WING COMPANY, INC.
196 Newton Street
Fredonia, New York 14063
Edward C. Steele, President
(716) 672-2114

RED WING SHOE COMPANY, INC.
Red Wing, Minnesota 55066
(612) 388-4791

REDDI-BACON (precooked bacon)
See Hunt-Wesson Foods Inc.

REDDI-MAID (fruit)
See Duffy-Mott Company, Inc.

REDDI-STARCH (spray starch)
See Texize Chemicals Company

REDDI-WIP, INC.
Box 3800
Fullerton, California 92634

REDDY COMPANY INC.
Post Office Box 779
Montpelier, Vermont 05602

Companies and Trade Names

REDEX, INC.
76 North Main Street
Mineral Ridge, Ohio 44440

REDFERN MEATS INC.
(Subsidiary of Redfern Foods Corporation)
1329 Ellsworth Industrial Drive
Atlanta, Georgia 30318
Leon D. Palton, President
(404) 351-0600

REDFOOT PRODUCTS COMPANY, INC.
20131 Joy Road
Detroit, Michigan 48228
J.D. Fundis, President
(313) 584-9797

REDHACKLE (Scotch whiskey)
See Imported Brands, Inc.

REDI-EARTH (garden product)
See W.R. Grace & Company

REDI FOODS
(Division of A. Duda & Sons Inc.)
Box 257
Oviedo, Florida 32765

REDI-LEMON (lemon juice)
See White Rose Tea Inc.

REDI-RECORD PRODUCTS COMPANY INC.
55 Saint Mary's Place
Freeport, New York 11520
Jerome Fleishman, President
(516) 379-2220

REDI-REST COMPANY
Post Office Box 208
Lima, Ohio 45801

REDI-SPUDS OF AMERICA
4959 West 147th Street
Hawthorne, California 90250
Lloyd M. Shapoff, President
(213) 772-5515

REDI-TEA (instant tea)
See Di Giorgio Corporation

REDI-TOASTER
See Knapp-Monarch (Division of The Hoover Company)

REDI-YAM (food products)
See B.F. Trappey's Sons Inc.

REDICEL (food products)
See Redi Foods (Division of A. Duda & Sons Inc.)

REDICUT (frozen foods, meats)
See Colonial Beef Company, Inc.

REDIFORM OFFICE PRODUCTS
(Division of Moore Business Forms, Inc.)
Post Office Box 587
Paramus, New Jersey 07652

REDINGTON & COMPANY INC., J.P.
Post Office Box 954
Scranton, Pennsylvania 18501
(717) 346-7631

REDIQUIK (food products)
See Standard Foods Inc.

REDKEN LABORATORIES, INC.
14721 California Avenue
Van Nuys, California 91401
John E. Meehan, President
(213) 781-4484

REDMAN INDUSTRIES, INC.
2550 Walnut Hill Lane
Dallas, Texas 75229
Lee Posey, President
(214) 350-3761

REDMON SONS & COMPANY, W.C.
Post Office Box Seven
Harrison and Denver
Peru, Indiana 46970
(317) 473-6683

REDPACK (canned tomatoes)
See California Canners & Growers

REDPOINT (cutlery)
See Harvey L. Reid Company, Inc.

REDS TOMALES (Italian foods)
See Lucca Packing Company of California, Inc.

REDWOOD FOOD PACKING COMPANY
Box 630
Redwood City, California 94064

REDWOOD INN (pickles, beans, cherries)
See S & W Fine Foods, Inc.

REDWOOD PRIVACY (fence)
See Colorguard Corporation

REDY MAID (canned foods)
See Venice Maid Company, Inc.

REE-LIEVE PRODUCTS
1355 Millwood Lane
Merrick, New York 11566

REED & BARTON
144 West Britannia Street
Taunton, Massachusetts 02780
Sinclair Weeks, Jr., President
(617) 824-6611

REED & CARNRICK
30 Boright Avenue
Kenilworth, New Jersey 07033
(201) 272-6600

Companies and Trade Names

REED ASSOCIATES INC., ROLAND
Pacific Marina
Alameda, California 94501

REED CANDLE COMPANY
1531 West Poplar
San Antonio, Texas 78285
Peter D. Reed, Chairman
(512) 734-4243

REED CANDY COMPANY
1 Crossroads of Commerce
Rolling Meadows, Illinois 60008
Earl K. Manhold, Jr., President
(312) 259-2600

REED COMPANY, C.A.
(Division of Westvaco Corporation)
99 Chestnut Street
Williamsport, Pennsylvania 17701
M.L. Gleason, Division Manager
(717) 326-9021

REED, INC., PAUL
Charlevoix, Michigan 49720
Paul J.J. Olsen, President
(616) 547-6534

REED INDUSTRIES INC.
340 Blackhawk Park Avenue
Rockford, Illinois 61101
Joseph M. Cvengros, Chairman and President
(815) 968-0451

REED-O-MATIC INC.
2700 East Main Street
Columbus, Ohio 43209
(614) 235-8535

REED STARLINE CARD COMPANY
3331 Sunset Boulevard
Los Angeles, California 90026
(213) 663-3161

REED TOYS, INC.
Union Hill Road
Conshohocken, Pennsylvania 19428

REEDE SEAFOOD COMPANY
98 Cutter Mill Road
Great Neck, New York 11021
(516) 487-9113

REED'S SONS, JACOB
1424 Chestnut
Philadelphia, Pennsylvania 19102
T. Cookenbach, President
(215) 563-5600

REEDSBURG FOODS CORPORATION
Post Office Box 270
Reedsburg, Wisconsin 53959

REEFER-GALLER (insecticide)
See Colgate-Palmolive Company

REELITES (electrical supplies)
See Appleton Electric Company

REENO CHEMICAL CORPORATION
9421 Midland Boulevard
Saint Louis, Missouri 63114
(314) 429-6078

REESE (padlocks)
See Waterbury Lock & Specialty Company

REESE CANDY COMPANY, INC., H.B.
(Subsidiary of Hershey Foods Corporation)
19 East Chocolate Avenue
Hersehy, Pennsylvania 17033
William E. Dearden, President
(717) 534-4200

REESE CHEMICAL COMPANY, THE
10617 Frank Avenue
Cleveland, Ohio 44106
(216) 231-6441

REESE FINER FOODS, INC.
(Division of Pet, Inc.)
Lively Boulevard and Kirk
Elk Grove, Illinois 60007
Morris Kushner, President
(312) 935-3033

REESE PRODUCTS INC.
Box 940
Elkhart, Indiana 46514

REEVE & MITCHELL COMPANY INC.
498 Nepperhan Avenue
Yonkers, New York 10701
(914) 969-1700

REEVE SALES COMPANY
431 Hempstead Avenue
West Hempstead, New York 11552

REEVES-BOWMAN
(Division of Cyclops Corporation)
127 Iron Avenue
Dover, Ohio 44622

REEVES BROTHERS INC.
1271 Avenue of the Americas
New York, New York 10020
J.E. Reeves, Jr., President
(212) 790-8621

REEVES BROTHERS INC.
Consumer Products Division
Box 188
Cornelius, North Carolina 28031

REEVES BROTHERS INC.
Curon Division
1271 Avenue of the Americas
New York, New York 10020
J.E. Reeves, Jr., President
(212) 790-8621

REEVES INTERNATIONAL, INC.
1107 Broadway
New York, New York 10010
(212) 929-5412

Companies and Trade Names

REEVES SOUNDCRAFT
(Division of Reeves Industries Inc.)
15 Great Pasture Road
Danbury, Connecticut 06810

REFLECT-O-SAFETY (automotive accessories)
See Stevens Trading Corporation

REFLECTA (sun-screening makeup)
See Texas Pharmacal Company

RELFECTOR HARDWARE
    CORPORATION
(Division of Spacemaster)
1400 North 25th Avenue
Melrose Park, Illinois 60160
A.R. Umans, President and Treasurer
(312) 345-2500

REFLEXALITE (enamel paint)
See Keystone Paint & Varnish
    Corporation

REFLEXITE (light-reflecting material)
See Luce Corporation

REFRAIN (carpeting)
See Magee Carpet Company

REFRIGIWEAR INC.
71 Inip Drive
Inwood, New York 11696
M. Breakstone, President
(516) 239-7022

REGAL (beer)
See National Brewing Company

REGAL (cocoa)
See C.J. Van Houten & Zoon,
    Inc.

REGAL (food product)
See Zemco Foods Company

REGAL (guitars)
See Harmony Company

REGAL (men's apparel)
See Frank & Meyer Neckwear
    Company

REGAL (paint)
See Benjamin Moore & Company

REGAL (sausage, meats)
See Redfern Meats, Inc.;
    Sausage Division

REGAL (shoes)
See Brown Group Inc.

REGAL ADVERTISING ASSOCIATES
800 Second Avenue
New York, New York 10017
(212) 924-6700

REGAL & WADE MANUFACTURING
    INC.
58-16 57th Road
Maspeth, New York 11378
S. Rael, President
(212) 894-6882

REGAL BAG COMPANY
330 Fifth Avenue
New York, New York 10001
(212) 594-6690

REGAL CHINA CORPORATION
See American Brands, Inc.

REGAL COTE (paints and paint sundries)
See Nelson-Roanoke Corporation

REGAL 8 INNS
Box 1268
Mount Vernon, Illinois 62864

REGAL FIBERGLASS, INC.
3910 N.W. 32nd Avenue
Miami, Florida 33142
(305) 634-6388

REGAL FOODS INC.
4820 Washington Street
Skokie, Illinois 60076

REGAL FRAMES (frames and pictures)
See Intercraft Industries
    Corporation

REGAL FRUIT COOPERATIVE, INC.
Post Office Box 7725
Tonasket, Washington 98855

REGAL GREETINGS
7535 Carolina Lane
Vancouver, Washington 98664

REGAL HARVEST (canned and frozen vegetables)
See Delta Food Processing
    Corporation

REGAL INDUSTRIES INC.
606 Spring Garden
Philadelphia, Pennsylvania 19123
(215) 923-6835

REGAL MANUFACTURING
    COMPANY
3946 West Lawrence Avenue
Chicago, Illinois 60625
(312) 588-4472

REGAL PLASTIC COMPANY
1725 Holmes Street
Kansas City, Missouri 64108
Jerome S. Kivett, President
(816) 421-4020

REGAL SHOE COMPANY
401 South Avenue
Whitman, Massachusetts 02382
J.F. Whitehead, Jr., President
(617) 447-4433

Companies and Trade Names

REGAL SPECIALTY MANUFAC-
TURING COMPANY, THE
241 Wolcott Street
New Haven, Connecticut 06513
Milton Baker, President
(203) 562-5379

REGAL TYPEWRITER COMPANY
INC.
150 New Park Avenue
Hartford, Connecticut 06106

REGAL WARE, INC.
Kewaskum, Wisconsin 53040
James D. Reigle, President
(414) 626-2121

REGALCYCLE (exercise equipment)
See Battle Creek Equipment
Company

REGALE (dog and cat food)
See Quaker City Packing
Company, Inc.

REGAN, EDWARD J.
2531 22nd Avenue
San Francisco, California 94116
(415) 731-0108

REGANSON CARTOON CARDS
5724 East Cambridge
Scottsdale, Arizona 85257

REGARD (wood cleaner and polish)
See S.C. Johnson & Son

REGATTA BOATS
11402 Brookshire Avenue
Downey, California 90241

REGENCY (carpeting)
See Stephen-Leedom Carpet
Company Inc.

REGENCY (cordials)
See Kasser Distillers Products
Corporation

REGENCY (meat)
See Elliott Packing Company

REGENCY (shelves)
See Shelves Unlimited

REGENCY (stack chairs)
See Aladin Plastics Inc.

REGENCY DESIGNERS SHOWCASE
15041 Calvert Street
Van Nuys, California 91409

REGENCY ELECTRONICS, INC.
7707 Records Street
Indianapolis, Indiana 46226
Floyd O. Ritter, President
(317) 547-3581

REGENCY FLOWERS, INC.
34 West 27th Street
New York, New York 10001
(212) 679-8668

REGENCY INTERNATIONAL
BUSINESS CORPORATION
34 West 27th Street
New York, New York 10001
(212) 679-8668

REGENCY THERMOGRAPHERS,
INC.
28 West 23rd
New York, New York 10010
(212) 255-7100

REGENCY THERMOGRAPHERS OF
CALIFORNIA
15041 Calvert Street
Van Nuys, California 91409

REGENCY TRAY SHAPE (TV-table
sets)
See Cal-Dak Industries Inc.

REGENSBURG & SONS, E.
(Division of Bayuk Cigars)
Ninth Street and Columbia Avenue
Philadelphia, Pennsylvania 19122

REGENT (mobile kitchen cabinets)
See Monarch Industries, Inc.

REGENT BABY PRODUCTS
CORPORATION
The Regent Building
43-21 52nd Street
Woodside, New York 11377

REGENT LINE (desks, tables)
See Northwest Metal Products
Company

REGENT MANUFACTURING
CORPORATION
1590 West 34th Place
Hialeah, Florida 33012

REGENT MARINE &
INSTRUMENTATION INC.
1051 Clinton Street
Buffalo, New York 14206
(716) 854-8066

REGENT-SHEFFIELD LTD.
70 Schmitt Boulevard
Farmingdale, New York 11735

REGGIO COMPANY, INC., ABEL
111 West 57th Street
New York, New York 10019
(212) 757-8840

REGGIO COMPANY, STEVE
55 Liberty
New York, New York 10005
(212) 227-4047

REGIME (cosmetics)
See Germaine Monteil
Cosmetiques Corporation

REGINA (Axminster broadlooms)
See American Rug & Carpet
Company Inc.

1135

Companies and Trade Names

REGINA (cookware, gadgets, bakeware)
See G & S Metal Products Company Inc.

REGINA (Italian foods)
See Pastorelli Food Products, Inc.

REGINA (wine and wine vinegars)
See Heublein, Inc.

REGINA CORPORATION, THE
313 Regina Avenue
Rahway, New Jersey 07065
Earl Seitz, President
(201) 381-1000

REGINA GRAPE PRODUCTS COMPANY
Etiwanda, California 91739

REGINA IMPORTS
35 West 31st Street
New York, New York 10001
(212) 564-6787

REGINA PRODUCTS INC.
775 16th Street
Boulder, Colorado 80302

REGISH PRODUCTIONS
16190 Weddel
Taylor, Michigan 48180

REGISTERED FABRICS
475 Fifth Avenue
New York, New York 10017
(212) 684-0728

REGISTRAR (wallets, billfolds)
See Prince Gardner

REGNERY COMPANY, THE HENRY
114 West Illinois Street
Chicago, Illinois 60610
Henry Regenery, Chairman of the Board
(312) 527-3300

REGNIER (cordial)
See Renfield Importers, Ltd.

REGO (electronic equipment)
See Coral, Inc.

REGO SMOKED FISH COMPANY, INC.
69-80 75th
Middle Village, New York 11379

REGOLETTA (concertinas)
See Coast Wholesale Music Company of Los Angeles

REGULA (cameras)
See Burleigh Brooks Optics, Inc.

REHA GLASS COMPANY
4414 Elston Avenue
Chicago, Illinois 60630
(312) 283-7731

REICH, ERICH M.
303 Fifth Avenue
New York, New York 10016
(212) 685-1851

REICH MUSHROOMS INC.
Box 216
Odessa, Missouri 64076

REICHHOLD CHEMICALS, INC.
RCI Building
White Plains, New York 10603
Peter J. Fass, President
(914) 682-5700

REID COMPANY INC., HARVEY L.
150 East 77th
New York, New York 10021
(212) 744-5638

REID MEREDITH, INC.
300 Canal Street
Lawrence, Massachusetts 01840
Samuel L. Highleyman, President
(617) 686-2964

REID-PROVIDENT LABORATORIES INC.
640 Tenth Street N.W.
Atlanta, Georgia 30308
Ferrell S. Ryan, Chairman and Chief Executive Officer
(404) 873-3785

REIDBORD BROTHERS, INC.
5000 Baum Boulevard
Pittsburgh, Pennsylvania 15213
Murray S. Reidbord, President
(412) 687-3000

REIDEMEISTER (wines)
See Jacobi Associates Inc.

REID'S (ice cream)
See Borden Inc.

REILY & COMPANY, WILLIAM B.
Post Office Box 60296
New Orleans, Louisiana 70160
William B. Reily, III, President
(504) 524-6131
See also JFG Coffee Company; and Luzianne Coffee Company

REILY CHEMICAL COMPANY
450 Mandeville
New Orleans, Louisiana 70150
(504) 943-8849

REIMA SET (sports apparel)
See Harju Ski Corporation

REINA CLAIRE
920 43rd Court
Miami Beach, Florida 33140
(305) 538-7254

REINBECK CANNING COMPANY
Reinbeck, Iowa 50669
(319) 345-2132

REINELL INDUSTRIES, INC.
14219 35th Avenue, N.E.
Marysville, Washington 98270
Thomas L. Lynott, President
(206) 659-6226

Companies and Trade Names

REINEMAN COMPANY, FRED M.
36 East 36th Street
New York, New York 10036
(212) 685-9846

REINHOLD (bass violins, violas, violin cellos, and accessories)
See Elger Company

REINHOLD-SILVERSMITHS, D.G.
Millbrook Art Gallery
Mill Hall, Pennsylvania 17751

REINISCH INC., O.
2 Park Avenue
Manhasset, New York 11030

REIS & COMPANY, ROBERT
Empire State Building
New York, New York 10001
Arthur Reis, Jr., President
(212) 695-2500

REISMAN CORPORATION, H.
116 South Second Street
New Hyde Park, New York 11040

REISS WILLIAMS COMPANY
20 Markley Street
Port Reading, New Jersey 07064

REIT-PRICE MANUFACTURING
 COMPANY
522-532 Chestnut Street
Union City, Indiana 47390
(317) 964-5343

REIVERS (cigarettes)
See Brown & Williamson
 Tobacco Corporation

REIZART (crystal)
See Gorham-Reizart

RELAX-A-CURL (hair-care product)
See Ellen Kaye Cosmetics, Inc.

RELAXER (pipes)
See Winton Briar Pipe
 Manufacturing Company

RELAXER (reclining chairs)
See Kroehler Manufacturing
 Company

RELAXON (hassocks)
See Crown Products Company

RELIABLE (meat products)
See Hygrade Food Products
 Corporation

RELIABLE (sports apparel and accessories)
See Halstead Imports Inc.

RELIABLE GLASSWARE & POTTERY
 COMPANY
536 West Erie Street
Chicago, Illinois 60610
(312) 943-2747

RELIABLE KNITTING WORKS
233 East Chicago Street
Milwaukee, Wisconsin 53202
Isabelle Polachek, President
(414) 272-5084

RELIABLE LIFE INSURANCE
 COMPANY
231 West Lockwood Avenue
Webster Groves, Missouri 63119
David D. Chomeau, President
(314) 968-4900

RELIABLE STAMP-O-MATIC
 CORPORATION
4358 South Knox Avenue
Chicago, Illinois 60632
(312) 735-5115

RELIABLE STATIONERS
 MANUFACTURING COMPANY
236 West 26th Street
New York, New York 10001
(212) 255-8550

RELIABLE STORES CORPORATION
3002 Druid Park Drive
Baltimore, Maryland 21215
S. Meyer Barnett, President
(301) 466-8803

RELIABLE TEXTILE COMPANY,
 INC.
1410 Broadway
New York, New York 10018
(212) 563-2374

RELIABLE THREAD COMPANY
602 Broadway
New York, New York 10012
(212) 226-7547

RELIANCE (canned goods)
See National Grocery Company

RELIANCE (coal)
See Peabody Coal Company

RELIANCE (watches)
See Croton Time Corporation

RELIANCE COMPANY, THE
425 Park Avenue South
New York, New York 10016

RELIANCE DENTAL
 MANUFACTURING COMPANY
10316 South Throop Street
Chicago, Illinois 60643

RELIANCE ELECTRIC COMPANY
29325 Chagrin Boulevard
Cleveland, Ohio 44122
B. Charles Ames, President and
 Chief Operations Officer
(216) 266-7000

RELIANCE IMPORTS, INC.
214-18 41st Avenue
Bayside, New York 11361

Companies and Trade Names

RELIANCE INSURANCE COMPANY
4 Penn Center Plaza
Philadelphia, Pennsylvania 19103
A. Addison Roberts, Chairman of the Board
(215) 864-4000

RELIANCE PAPER BOX COMPANY
925 North Third Street
Philadelphia, Pennsylvania 19122
(215) 923-5055

RELIANCE PEN & PENCIL CORPORATION
100 Reliance Avenue
Lewisburg, Tennessee 37091
(615) 359-2586

RELIANCE PRODUCTS CORPORATION
(Subsidiary of Amtel, Inc.)
108 Mason Street
Woonsocket, Rhode Island 02895
Anthony Chrones, President
(401) 769-8230

RELIANCE TRADING CORPORATION OF AMERICA
220 Fifth Avenue
New York, New York 10001
(212) 679-2026

RELOMS (women's apparel)
See Smoler Brothers Inc.

RELSKA (vodka)
See Heublein, Inc.

RELY (tampons)
See Procter & Gamble Company

RELYON PRODUCTS CORPORATION
238 Eagle Street
Brooklyn, New York 11222
(212) 389-6260

REM (cough remedy)
See Block Drug Company, Inc.

REM INDUSTRIES, INC.
7308 Associate Avenue
Cleveland, Ohio 44144
Raymond Connor, President
(216) 281-9520

REMA FOODS, INC.
185 Cross
Fort Lee, New Jersey 07024
(212) 966-3914

REMAR (plastic-furniture cleaners)
See Unicom Products (Division of United Communication Corporation)

REMBRANDT (pipes)
See National Briar Pipe Company, Inc.

REMBRANDT LAMP
4500 West Division Street
Chicago, Illinois 60651
Joseph C. Settimi, President
(312) 278-4500

REMBRANDT SQUARE (shaving products)
See Philips Roxane Laboratories

REMCO INDUSTRIES, INC.
Cape May Street
Harrison, New Jersey 07029
H. Gurbst, President
(201) 484-1700

REMECO MANUFACTURING COMPANY INC.
20 Pine Street
New Rochelle, New York 10801
(914) 632-4665

REMEDIAL (exercise equipment)
See Brown & Bigelow

REMI (ski equipment)
See American Ski Corporation

REMINGTON (chain saws)
See Frost Company

REMINGTON ARMS COMPANY, INC.
(Subsidiary of E.I. DuPont de Nemours & Company)
939 Barnum Avenue
Bridgeport, Connecticut 06602
Philip H. Burdett, President
(203) 333-1112

REMINGTON ELECTRIC SHAVER
(Division of Sperry Rand Corporation)
60 Main Street
Bridgeport, Connecticut 06602
Edward I. Brown, President
(203) 336-2571

REMINGTON RAND OFFICE MACHINES
(Division of Sperry Rand Corporation)
Post Office Box 1000
Blue Bell, Pennsylvania 19422

REMINGTON RAND SYSTEMS
(Division of Sperry Rand Corporation)
Post Office Box 171
Marietta, Ohio 45750

REMIRA (children's clothing)
See William Carter Company

REMOLINO (Mexican foods)
See El Molino Foods Inc.

REMY MARTIN (cognac)
See Renfield Importers, Ltd.

RENA (ski equipment)
See American Ski Corporation

RENAISSANCE (chess sets)
See E.S. Lowe Company, Inc.

RENAISSANCE (desk sets)
See Joshua Meier (Division of W.R. Grace & Company

Companies and Trade Names

RENAISSANCE (dinnerware and glassware)
See Interpace Corporation

RENAISSANCE (leather goods)
See Hugo Bosca Company, Inc.

RENARD (bassoons, oboes, clarinets)
See Fox Products Corporation

RENAULD INTERNATIONAL, LTD.
(Subsidiary of Foster Grant Company, Inc.)
380 River Street
Fitchburg, Massachusetts 01420

RENAULT, INC.
100 Sylvan Avenue
Englewood Cliffs, New Jersey 07632
George Basiliou, General Manager
(201) 461-6000

RENDELL STUDIOS
Ligonier Industrial Park
Ligonier, Indiana 46767

RENE DUMONT (woodwinds)
See Saint Louis Music Supply Company Inc.

RENE DUVAL (brass instruments)
See Buegeleisen & Jacobson Ltd.

RENE, INC.
808 Howell Street
Seattle, Washington 98101

RENE RICHARD (watches)
See Windert Watch Company

RENEE (vegetables, anchovies, sardines)
See A. Sargenti Company Inc.

RENEE CREATIONS INC.
9200 Collins Avenue
Pensauken, New Jersey 08110

RENEE OF HOLLYWOOD
743 Santee Street
Los Angeles, California 90014
Jack Duchowny, President and Treasurer
(213) 627-3761

RENELLI (concertinas)
See Targ & Dinner Inc.

RENETTE FOUNDATIONS CORPORATION
46 West 29th Street
New York, New York 10016
(212) 532-7482

RENFIELD IMPORTERS, LTD.
919 Third Avenue
New York, New York 10022
I.M. Herman, President
(212) 644-2000

RENKEN BOAT MANUFACTURING COMPANY, INC.
808 Folly Road
Charleston, South Carolina 29412

RENNEKER COMPANY INC., H.H.
Post Office Box 9235
San Diego, California 92109
(714) 488-2655

RENNEL COMPANY
Box 151
Northfield, Illinois 60093

RENNER-DAVIS COMPANY
165 Front Street
Chicopee, Massachusetts 01013
Bernard Gold, President and Treasurer
(413) 598-8197

RENNOC CORPORATION
S.E. Boulevard and Sheridan Avenue South
Vineland, New Jersey 08360
(609) 825-7720

RENOIR SLIMWEAR, INC.
See Vassarette

RENOWN FOODS COMPANY
2201 West Highway
McAllen, Texas 78501

RENSIE (clocks)
See Elgin National Industries Inc.

RENSON OF MOUNTAIN VIEW
Mountain View, Arkansas 72560

RENUZIT HOME PRODUCTS COMPANY
3018 Market
Philadelphia, Pennsylvania 19104
(215) 423-2513

RENWAL PRODUCTS COMPANY
(Subsidiary of Learning Aids Group)
1 Newbold Road
Fairless Hills, Pennsylvania 19030
(215) 736-1108
See also Gamescience Corporation

RENZI PLASTIC CORPORATION, A.J.
180 Pond Street
Leominster, Massachusetts 01453
Verginio Renzi, President
(617) 534-8387

REO (lawn mowers)
See Wheel-Horse Products Inc.

REO GLENN (apple products)
See Silveira & O'Connell

REPCO PRODUCTS CORPORATION
7420 State Road
Philadelphia, Pennsylvania 19136
Joseph P. Fanell, Jr., President and Treasurer
(215) 338-1110

Companies and Trade Names

REPEAT-O-TYPE STENCIL MANUFACTURING COMPANY
665 State Highway 23
Wayne, New Jersey 07470
(201) 696-3330

REPEL (heel-resistant floor finish)
See Uncle Sam Chemical Company, Inc.

REPEL (skin-protection creams)
See Divajex

REPLIQUE (bath oil, dusting powder, perfume, talc, etc.)
See Revlon, Inc.

REPLOGLE GLOBES, INC.
1901 North Narragansett Avenue
Chicago, Illinois 60639
William C. Nickels, President
(312) 622-5500

REPRISE (phonograph records)
See Warner Brothers Records, Inc.

REPRODUCTA COMPANY, INC.
11 East 26th Street
New York, New York 10010

REPUBLIC (furnaces, boilers, and switches)
See Autogas Company

REPUBLIC (lawn mower)
See American Lawn Mower Company

REPUBLIC CHEMICAL COMPANY
13068 Saticoy Street
North Hollywood, California 91605

REPUBLIC DRUG COMPANY
175 Great Arrow
Buffalo, New York 14207

REPUBLIC FASTENER PRODUCTS CORPORATION
9-T Commerce Road
Fairfield, New Jersey 07006
(201) 227-1314

REPUBLIC MOLDING CORPORATION
6330 West Touhy Avenue
Chicago, Illinois 60648
Bertram W. Coltman, Jr., President
(312) 647-8977

REPUBLIC NATIONAL BANK OF DALLAS
Pacific, Ervay and Bryant Street
Dallas, Texas 75201
James Keay, Chairman of the Board
(214) 653-5000

REPUBLIC STEEL CORPORATION
Republic Building
Post Office Box 6778
Cleveland, Ohio 44101
W.J. DeLancey, President
(216) 574-7100

REPUBLIC STEEL CORPORATION
Manufacturing Division
Republic Boulevard
Cleveland, Ohio 44101
W.J. DeLancey, President
(216) 574-7100

REQUEST RECORDS INC.
66 Memorial Highway
New Rochelle, New York 10801

RESCUE (soap pads)
See 3M Company

RESEARCH APPLIANCE COMPANY
Pioneer and Hardies Road
Gibsonia, Pennsylvania 15044
(412) 443-5935

RESEARCH ASSOCIATES, INC.
555 East Linden Avenue
Linden, New Jersey 07036
(201) 862-1154

RESEARCH ENTERPRISES INC.
Post Office Box 232
Nutley, New Jersey 07110

RESEARCH GAMES INC.
200 Fifth Avenue
Room 356
New York, New York 10010
(212) 924-7575

RESEARCH INDUSTRIES CORPORATION
Pharmaceuticals Division
1847 West 2300 South
Salt Lake City, Utah 84119
(801) 927-5500

RESEARCH PHARMACAL LABORATORY
1316 Nostrand Avenue
Brooklyn, New York 11226
(212) 856-8962

RESEARCH PRODUCTS COMPANY
Post Office Box 1057
Salina, Kansas 67401

RESEARCH PRODUCTS CORPORATION (filters, humidifiers)
1015 East Washington Avenue
Madison, Wisconsin 53703
J.G. Schutz, Chairman and President
(608) 257-8801

RESEARCH SPECIALTIES COMPANY
Box 1129
Santa Monica, California 90406

RESEARCH SUPPLIES PHARMACEUTICAL CORPORATION
61 Colvin Avenue
Albany, New York 12206

RESERVE (beer)
See Miller Brewing Company

RESERVE SEATING (folding chairs)
See Clarin Corporation

Companies and Trade Names

RESINOL CHEMICAL COMPANY
517 West Lombard Street
Baltimore, Maryland 21201
H. LeRoy Carter, Jr., President
(301) 539-5461

RESISTO (floor wax)
See Uncle Sam Chemical
Company, Inc.

RESISTORUST (paint primer)
See Pettit Paint Company Inc.

RESIWELD (epoxy glue)
See H.B. Fuller Company

RESORT SALES COMPANY
Box 477
Homosassa Springs, Florida 32647

RESPIRATOR (chair cushions)
See Hi-Life Rubber Products Inc.

REST-A-PHONE CORPORATION
Post Office Box 14841
Portland, Oregon 97214
(503) 235-6778

REST-ALL (aluminum chairs)
See Ohio Chair Company

REST EASY (infants' product)
See Earl & Arlington Inc.

RESTAURANT ASSOCIATES
INDUSTRIES, INC.
1540 Broadway
New York, New York 10036
Martin Brody, President
(212) 974-6700

RESTFORM (mattresses)
See Hewitt-Robins

RESTONIC CORPORATION
1010 Jorie Boulevard
Oak Brook, Illinois 60521

RESTOR (hair- and nail-care
products)
See Buty Wave Products
Company

RESTRO (canned peas, corn, and
beans)
See Baker Canning Company

RETAIL CREDIT COMPANY
Post Office Box 4081
1600 Peachtree, N.W.
Atlanta, Georgia 30302
W. Lee Burge, President
(404) 875-8321

RETENTION COMMUNICATIONS
SYSTEM
60 Spruce Street
Paterson, New Jersey 07501
Daniel A. Sherman, President
(201) 742-7200

RETER FRUIT COMPANY
Box 1027
11th and Fir
Medford, Oregon 97501
Raymond R. Reter, President
(503) 772-5256

RETKO PRODUCTS COMPANY
Post Office Box 182
Dover, New Jersey 07801

RETRONOX (antismog device)
See Dana Corporation

REUBEN (meat products)
See Feinberg Distributing
Company, Inc.

REULAND ELECTRIC COMPANY
17969 East Railroad Street
City of Industry, California 91744
(213) 964-6411

REULE, NORMAN L.
Suite 218
Terminal Sales Building
Seattle, Washington 98101
(206) 682-0775

REUTER'S (toiletries)
See Lanman & Kemp-Barclay &
Company, Inc.

REUTHER'S SEA FOOD COMPANY
INC.
Post Office Box 50773
New Orleans, Louisiana 70150
C.G. Reuther, Sr., Chairman &
President
(504) 947-1156

REVAN (woodwinds)
See J.M. Sahlein Music
Company Inc.

REVARK COMPANY INC.
87-27 78th Street
Woodhaven, New York 11421

REVCO DRUG STORES, INC.
1295 Enterprise Parkway
Twinsburg, Ohio 44087
Sidney Dworkin, President
(216) 425-9811

REVCO, INC.
(Subsidiary of Guerdon Industries,
Inc.)
1100 Memorial Drive
West Columbia,
South Carolina 29169
Douglas A. Solley, President
(803) 796-1700

REVCON, INC.
10870 Kalama River Road
Fountain Valley, California 92708
(714) 968-3346

REVEAL (food-roasting wrap)
See Colgate-Palmolive

Companies and Trade Names

REVEL FRAMES INC.
12 West 27th Street
New York, New York 10001
(212) 686-5121

REVELATION (sporting goods)
See Western Auto Supply Company

REVELATION (tobacco)
See Philip Morris, Inc.

REVELATION ART LINEN CORPORATION
38 West 26th Street
New York, New York 10010
Alex Hochstadter, President
(212) 675-8365

REVELATION BRA COMPANY
See Goddess Bra

REVELATIONS (shoes)
See Desco Shoe Corporation

REVELL, INC.
4223 Glencoe Avenue
Venice (Los Angeles), California 90291
Mrs. R. Glaser Lasky, President
(213) 870-7651

REVELLE (band instruments, drum sets, and accessories)
See Pacific Music Supply Company

REVENSCENCE (skin-care product)
See Lanvin-Charles of the Ritz

REVERE (band and orchestral instruments, microphones, music accessories)
See Sorkin Music Company Inc.

REVERE (frozen foods)
See Associated Food Stores, Inc.

REVERE (mobile homes)
See DMH Company

REVERE (rug cushions)
See Allen Industries, Inc.

REVERE (tape recorders)
See 3M Company

REVERE COPPER AND BRASS, INC.
605 Third Avenue
New York, New York 10016
William F. Collins, President
(212) 687-4111

REVERE KNITTING MILLS, INC.
11 Lake Street
Wakefield, Massachusetts 01880
J. Richard Titelman, President
(617) 245-5300

REVERE LANTERN SHOP
Post Office Box 146
New London, Pennsylvania 19360

REVERE SILVER COMPANY
50 Walker Street
New York, New York 10013
(212) 925-8584

REVERE SMOKED FISH COMPANY
222 William
Chelsea, Massachusetts 02150

REVERE SUGAR REFINERY
(Subsidiary of United Brands Company)
333 Medford Street
Charlestown, Massachusetts 02129
Frank A. Monroe, Jr., President
(617) 242-2750

REVERE TENNIS & SPORTS CORPORATION
60 Levning Street
South Hackensack, New Jersey 07606

REVERSE ENGLISH (aftershave lotion, powder, cologne)
See Yardley of London, Inc.

REVILLON, INC.
611 Fifth Avenue
New York, New York 10022
Max Mazerand, Chairman of the Board
(212) 753-4000

REVIV-A-LIFE (oxygen inhalator kit)
See Oxequip Health Industries

REVIVE (suede cleaner)
See Wolverine World Wide, Inc.

REVLON, INC.
767 Fifth Avenue
New York, New York 10022
Michael C. Bergerac, President
(212) 758-5000
See also USV Pharmaceutical Corporation

REVLON-REALISTIC PROFESSIONAL PRODUCTS, INC.
(Subsidiary of Revlon, Inc.)
3274 Beekman Street
Cincinnati, Ohio 45223
(513) 681-8500

REVOLVATOR COMPANY
United States One at 86th Street
North Bergen, New Jersey 07047
Henry S. Germond, III, President
(201) 869-1220

REVOX CORPORATION
155 Michael Drive
Syosset, New York 11791

REWCO (whiskey)
See National Distillers & Chemical Corporation

REX (air purifier)
See Sibert & Company, Inc.

Companies and Trade Names

REX (flour)
　See General Mills, Inc.

REX (meats)
　See Cudahy Company

REX (pet food)
　See Laddie Boy Dog Foods, Inc.

REX (seafood)
　See Norbest, Inc.

REX CHAINBELT, INC.
　See Rexnord, Inc.

REX SALES INC.
1295 Rollins Road
Burlingame, California　94010

REX SHOE COMPANY
1950 Wyoming Avenue
Exeter, Pennsylvania　18643
Jacob Eisenberg, Vice President
(717) 693-3930

REXAIR, INC.
(Subsidiary of LCA Corporation)
1000 Buhl Building
Detroit, Michigan　48226
J.V. Sanders, President
(313) 961-0350

REXALL DRUG COMPANY
(Division of Dart Industries Inc.)
3901 Kingshighway
Saint Louis, Missouri　63115
(314) 383-1234

REXFORD (canned foods)
　See Owensboro Canning
　　Company Inc.

REXFORD PAPER COMPANY
Post Office Box 411
Milwaukee, Wisconsin　53201
(414) 352-1221

REXNORD, INC.
Box 2022
777 East Wisconsin Avenue
Milwaukee, Wisconsin　53202
Robert V. Krihorian, President
(414) 384-3000
　See also Perfection American

REYNOLDS ALUMINUM SUPPLY
　COMPANY
Post Office Box 26885
2015 Staples Mill Road
Richmond, Virginia　23261
(804) 282-2392

REYNOLDS & REYNOLDS
　COMPANY, THE
Dayton, Ohio　45401

REYNOLDS ELECTRIC COMPANY
1800 Madison Street
Maywood, Illinois　60153
Paul H. Rosenberg, Chairman and
　President
(312) 625-2232

REYNOLDS FOODS, INC., R.J.
　See RJR Foods Inc.

REYNOLDS INDUSTRIES, INC.,
　R.J.
401 North Main Street
Winston-Salem,
　North Carolina　27102
William S. Smith, Chairman of
　the Board
(919) 748-4000
　See RJR Foods, Inc.

REYNOLDS METALS COMPANY
6601 West Broad Street
Richmond, Virginia　23230
Richard S. Reynolds, Jr., President
(804) 282-2311
　See also Eskimo Pie Corporation;
　　and Tilo Company, Inc.

REYNOLDS POPCORN COMPANY
Department CB
Osgood, Indiana　47037

REYNOLDS TOBACCO COMPANY,
　R.J.
(Subsidiary of R. J. Reynolds
　Industries, Inc.)
401 North Main Street
Winston-Salem,
　North Carolina　27102
William D. Hobbs, President
(919) 748-4100

REYTON CARDS
114 East Fourth Street
Mount Vernon, New York　10550

REYTRIM MANUFACTURING
　COMPANY
Rayersford, Pennsylvania　19468
Donald O. Bailey, President and
　Treasurer
(215) 948-9500

REZLER & HOWELL COMPANY
2416 Atlantic Avenue
Brooklyn, New York　11233
(212) 345-8889

REZUMAR (canned fish products)
　See Joseph Caragol, Inc.

RHAPSODY (shoes)
　See Brown Group, Inc.

RHEEM MANUFACTURING
　COMPANY
(Subsidiary of City Investing
　Company)
767 Fifth Avenue
New York, New York　10022
W.C. Leone, President
(212) 371-2555

RHEINGOLD (beer)
　See United Beverages Inc.

RHEINGOLD BREWERIES, INC.
36 Forest
Brooklyn, New York　11296
Richard Ahern, President
(212) 386-6600

Companies and Trade Names

RHEINLANDER (beer)
See Rainier Brewing Company

RHINE CASTLE (wine)
See Browne Vintners Company

RHINELANDER (beer)
See Joseph Huber Brewing Company

RHINO HIDE (auto cleaner/polish)
See R.M. Hollingshead Corporation of Canada Ltd.

RHODA LEE, INC.
525 Seventh Avenue
New York, New York 10018
(212) 563-7191

RHODE ISLAND TEXTILE COMPANY
211 Columbus Avenue
Pawtucket, Rhode Island 02861
Glendon M. Elliott, President and Treasurer
(401) 722-3700

RHODES & COMPANY, P.J.
World Trade Center
San Francisco, California 94111
(415) 434-2750

RHODES, INC.
1100 Spring Street
Atlanta, Georgia 30309
Charles D. Collins, Chairman of the Board
(404) 872-7754

RHODES, INC., M.H.
99 Thompson Road
Avon, Connecticut 06001
M.H. Rhodes, Jr., President
(203) 673-3281

RHODES PHARMACAL COMPANY
200 East Ontario Street
Chicago, Illinois 60611
J. Sanford Rose, President
(312) 943-4177

RHODES PIANO
(Division of CBS Musical Instruments)
1300 East Valencia
Fullerton, California 92631

RHODES-SOUTHWEST
(Subsidiary of Amfac, Inc.)
Sears-Rhodes Mall
1801 D. Camelback Road
Phoenix, Arizona 85018

RHUM NEGRITA (rum)
See Carillon Importers, Ltd.

RHUSTICON (poison-ivy and poison-oak treatment)
See American Pharmaceutical Company

RHYTHM MATE (educational musical instruments)
See Elger Company

RHYTHM STEP (ladies' shoes)
See Johnson, Stephens & Shinkle Shoe Company

RIALTO (wines)
See Joeli Wine Distributors, Inc.

RIB STICKERS (dehydrated meals)
See Stow-A-Way Products, Inc.

RIBACK ENTERPRISES INC.
9719 Mason Avenue
Chatsworth, California 91311

RICARD (aperitif)
See Monsieur Henri Wines, Ltd.

RICARDO (corned beef)
See Imperial Commodities Corporation

RICASOLI (Italian wines)
See Browne Vintners Company

RICCADONNA (wines and vermouths)
See James B. Beam Distilling Company

RICCI PARFUMS, NINA
630 Fifth Avenue
New York, New York 10020
(212) 489-2430

RICCIARDI (ice cream)
See Borden Inc.

RICCO (macaroni)
See New Orleans Macaroni Manufacturing Company, Inc.

RICE-A-RONI (rice mixtures)
See Golden Grain Macaroni Company

RICE & COMPANY INC., IRVING W.
11 East 26th
New York, New York 10010
(212) 689-2802

RICE CASTER COMPANY
Post Office Box 675
Defiance, Ohio 43512

RICE CHEX (cereal)
See Ralston Purina Company

RICE COMPANY, A.H.
Pittsfield, Massachusetts 01201
(413) 443-6477

RICE FIT (food product)
See General Foods Corporation

RICE GROWERS ASSOCIATION OF CALIFORNIA
1000 Rice Mill Road
West Sacramento, California 95691

Companies and Trade Names

RICE INC., WILLIAM S.
7-11 Wardwell Street
Adams, New York 13605
(375) 232-4555

RICE KRISPIES (cereal)
See Kellogg Company

RICE MANUFACTURING COMPANY
INC., THE
14941 Oxnard Street
Van Nuys, California 91401

RICE ORIGINALS (food)
See Green Giant Company

RICE TOBACCO COMPANY, S.E.
Box 288
Greenville, Kentucky 42345

RICELAND FOODS, INC.
2020 Park Avenue
Stuttgart, Arkansas 72160
L.C. Carter, Sr., President
(501) 673-6911

RICE'N SPICE (food products)
See Frito-Lay, Inc.

RICH (ice cream)
See Hawthorn Mellody, Inc.

RICH & RARE (Canadian whiskey)
See Gooderham & Worts, Ltd.

RICH CORPORATION, SIDNEY
10-01 44 Road
Long Island City, New York 11101
(212) 784-6268

RICH CREATIONS INC.
73-39 68th Avenue
Middle Village, New York 11379

RICH CROP (canned and frozen foods)
See Utah Packers, Inc.

RICH FLAVORS (food products)
See Santa Clara Packing Company

RICH FOODS INC., LOUIS
Box 288
West Liberty, Iowa 52776

RICH LADDER COMPANY
Post Office Box 120
Carrollton, Kentucky 41008
(502) 732-4211

RICH 'N READY (canned pudding)
See RJR Foods, Inc.

RICH NUT (canned foods)
See Western Food Products Company

RICH PRODUCTS CORPORATION
1149 Niagara
Buffalo, New York 14213
Robert E. Rich, President
(716) 883-3211
See also Coffee Rich, Inc.

RICHARD, ANDRE
(Division of Ar. Winarick Inc.)
158 Linwood Plaza
Fort Lee, New Jersey 07024

RICHARD FOODS CORPORATION
4520 West James Place
Melrose Park, Illinois 60160
(312) 345-2335
See also Fearn Soya Foods

RICHARD HUDNUT
(Subsidiary of Warner-Lambert Company)
201 Tabor Road
Morris Plains, New Jersey 07950
Stuart K. Hensley, President
(201) 285-0234

RICHARD INC., PAUL
Post Office Box 5407
3036 Durahart
Riverside, California 92507
(714) 686-3573

RICHARD INDUSTRIES, INC.
5140 N.E. 12th
Fort Lauderdale, Florida 33308

RICHARD QUILES (classic guitars)
See Hough & Kohler Ltd.

RICHARD'S (wines)
See Canandaigua Industries Company, Inc.

RICHARDS, INC., CARYL
See Faberge, Inc.

RICHARDS KNITTING MILLS, JONATHAN
719 Walnut
Boulder, Colorado 80302

RICHARDS LTD., ARTHUR
29 West 56th Street
New York, New York 10019
(212) 247-2300

RICHARDS MORGENTHAU COMPANY
See Raymor/Richards Morgenthau Company

RICHARDS PAPER COMPANY, S.P.
1130 Bankhead Avenue N.W.
Atlanta, Georgia 30318
(404) 875-4571

RICHARDS PHARMACEUTICAL COMPANY
Box 1129
Santa Monica, California 90406

Companies and Trade Names

RICHARDS ROSEN ASSOCIATES, INC.
29 East 21st Street
New York, New York 10010
(212) 777-3017

RICHARDSON & HOLLAND CORPORATION
1001 John Street
Seattle, Washington 98109
Eugene R. Holland, Chairman and President
(206) 623-7740

RICHARDSON & ROBBINS (canned chicken products)
See William Underwood Company

RICHARDSON COMPANY, THE
2400 East Devon Avenue
Des Plaines, Illinois 60018
(312) 297-3570
See also Kelite Chemical Corporation

RICHARDSON COMPANY THOMAS D.
(Division of Beatrice Foods, Inc.)
Atlantic and I
Philadelphia, Pennsylvania 19134
W.J. Powers, President
(215) 426-9200

RICHARDSON CONTROLS CORPORATION
410 Tidewater Drive
Warwick, Rhode Island 02889

RICHARDSON CORPORATION
1069 Lyell Avenue
Rochester, New York 14606
William N. Thompson, President
(716) 254-8822

RICHARDSON HOMES CORPORATION
Post Office Box 1048
2421 South Nappanee
Elkhart, Indiana 46514
Stanley F. Stitgen, President
(219) 523-1030

RICHARDSON-MERRELL, INC.
122 East 42nd Street
New York, New York 10017
H. Robert Marschalk, President
(212) 769-2222

RICHBRAU (beer)
See Queen City Brewing

RICHCO (paints and paint sundries)
See Norman & Sons Inc.

RICHELAIT (powdered milk for infants)
See Goodwin Drug Company, Inc.

RICHELIEU (groceries)
See Consolidated Foods Corporation

RICHFORD SPECIALTIES INC.
2521 Long Beach Road
Oceanside, New York 11572

RICHLEIGH (carpeting)
See Bigelow-Sanford Inc.

RICHLING, ADES & RICHMAN, INC.
520 Eighth
New York, New York 10018
(212) 695-4390

RICHLUBE (motor oil)
See Atlantic Richfield Company

RICHLYN LABORATORIES
3725 Castor Avenue
Philadelphia, Pennsylvania 19124
(215) 289-2220

RICHMAID (dairy products)
See Albany Public Markets, Inc.

RICHMAN BROTHERS
(Subsidiary of F.W. Woolworth Company)
1600 East 55th
Cleveland, Ohio 44103
Donald J. Gestenberger, President
(216) 431-0200

RICHMAR PRODUCTS, INC.
Box 9608
21360 Center Ridge
Cleveland, Ohio 44140
(216) 331-3326

RICHMARK (hosiery)
See McCubbin Hosiery, Inc.

RICHMOND (milk)
See Dolly Madison Industries, Inc.

RICHMOND CANDY COMPANY
(Subsidiary of La Salle Candy Company)
3311 West Montrose Avenue
Chicago, Illinois 60618
(312) 267-2980

RICHMOND PRESSED METAL WORKS INC.
506-12 Maury Street
Richmond, Virginia 23224
(804) 233-8371

RICHMOND RING COMPANY
Richmond Road
Souderton, Pennsylvania 18964
(215) 855-2609

RICHMOND SCHOOL FURNITURE COMPANY
705 East 18th Street
Muncie, Indiana 47302
(316) 288-6624

RICHMONT (hand tools)
See Dresser Industries SK Tools Hand Tool Division

Companies and Trade Names

RICH'S, INC.
45 Broad, S.W.
Atlanta, Georgia 30303
Harold Brockey, Chairman of the
 Board
(404) 522-4636
    See also Richway, Inc.

RICHTER BROTHERS, INC.
355 Michele Place
Carlstadt, New Jersey 07072
Kurt G. Richter, President
(201) 935-6850

RICHTER LTD., CLARE
680 Fifth Avenue
New York, New York 10019
(212) 355-4600

RICHVALE (fruit)
    See Wapato Fruit Products, Inc.

RICHWAY, INC.
(Subsidiary of Rich's, Inc.)
Post Office Box 50359
Atlanta, Georgia 30302
John Weitnauer, President
(404) 525-5961

RICHWOOD (wood shelves)
    See Kenmore Industries

RICKBORN INDUSTRIES INC.
175 Route Nine
Bayville, New Jersey 08721

RICKEL, INC.
4800 Main Street
Kansas City, Missouri 64112
E.J. Rickel, Chairman and President
(816) 561-5912

RICKERT INC., BEN
100 Asia Place
Carlstadt, New Jersey 07072

RICKIE TICKIE INC.
704 Silver Spur Road
Rolling Hills, California 90274

RICKMAN (motorcycles)
    See Birmingham Small Arms
     Company, Inc.

RICK'S (flavoring extracts)
    See C & D Flavor Company

RICKSHA BOY (canned fish,
vegetables, and fruits)
    See Roadel Foods, Inc.

RICO CORPORATION
Post Office Box 3266
Victory Center Station
North Hollywood, California 91609
(213) 767-7030

RICOH (photographic equipment)
    See Braun North America

RICOH TIME CORPORATION
2000 North Mills Street
Orlando, Florida 32803
Cliff M. Fried, President
(305) 843-7400

RICORY (instant coffee)
    See Nestle Company, Inc.

RICOSALI (Italian wine)
    See Browne Vintners Company

RID-JID (casual furniture)
    See General Housewares
     Corporation, Leisure
     Furniture Group

RID-O-LITER (automotive
accessories)
    See A.G. Busch & Company
     Inc.

RID-X (cesspool and septic-tank
cleaner)
    See D-Con Company, Inc.

RIDDELL, INC.
1151 West Roscoe Street
Chicago, Illinois 60657
E.L. Morgan, President
(312) 929-4200

RIDDLE LABORATORIES
(Division of King Pharmaceutical
 Company, Inc.)
26 North 77th Street
Birmingham, Alabama 35206

RIDER (infants' product)
    See Strolee of California

RIDGE HOMES
(Division of Evans Products
 Company, Inc.)
Conshohocken, Pennsylvania 19428
Hillard Madway, President
(215) 825-4000

RIDGE TOOL COMPANY, THE
(Subsidiary of Emerson Electric
 Company)
400 Clark Street
Elyria, Ohio 44035
C.L. Mikovitch, President
(216) 323-5581
    See also Supreme Products
     Corporation

RIDGEMONT COMPANY, THE
Route Six
Brewster, New York 10509

RIDGEWAY (furniture)
    See Gravely Furniture Company,
     Inc.

RIDGEWOOD (whiskey)
    See Hiram Walker, Inc.

RIDGEWOOD FINE CHINA
COMPANY
1110 Chestnut Street
Burbank, California 91502

RIDGID (tools)
    See Ridge Tool Company

Companies and Trade Names

RIDGWAYS (tea)
See General Foods Corporation

RIDIN HI (auto seat)
See Toidey Company

RIDINGER ASSOCIATES
20700 Dearborn Street
Chatsworth, California 91311

RIDZ (dog repellent)
See Boyle-Midway

RIEBANDT VANE STEERING
Box 2153
Department YBG
Idyllwild, California 92349

RIEBER (sports accessories and equipment)
See Haugen Nordic Products

RIECK'S (ice cream)
See National Dairy Products Corporation

RIEGEL PRODUCTS CORPORATION
Frenchtown
Milford, New Jersey 08848
John E. Griffith, President
(201) 995-2411

RIEGEL TEXTILE CORPORATION
1457 Cleveland Street
Greenville, South Carolina 29606
R.E. Coleman, Chairman
(803) 242-6050

RIEGEL TEXTILE CORPORATION
Consumer Products Division
Post Office Box 6807
Greenville, South Carolina 29606
(803) 242-6050

RIEGEL TEXTILE CORPORATION
Convenience Products Division
Post Office Box 929
Aiken, South Carolina 29801

RIEKE CORPORATION
500 West Seventh Street
Auburn, Indiana 46706
M.E. Rieke, President
(219) 925-3700

RIEKER INSTRUMENT COMPANY
Box 52
Holgar Industrial Park
Sycamore and Mill Streets
Clifton Heights, Pennsylvania 19018
(215) 622-4545

RIEKES-CRISA CORPORATION
1818 Leavenworth
Omaha, Nebraska 68102
Max Riekes, President
(402) 341-9848

RIES BIOLOGICALS
3190-J Airport Loop Drive
Costa Mesa, California 92626
(213) 625-7321

RIES BOTTLING WORKS, JACOB
112 West Third Avenue
Shakopee, Minnesota 55379

RIES-HAMLY, INC.
29360 Grandview
Mount Clemens, Michigan 48043

RIESCO MANUFACTURING & IMPORT COMPANY
158 West Hubbard Street
Chicago, Illinois 60610
(312) 467-6565

RIFKIN & SONS, WILLIAM
143 Madison Avenue
New York, New York 10016
(212) 679-3590

RIGGIN & ROBBINS, INC.
Foot of Ogden Avenue
Port Norris, New Jersey 08349

RIGGS NATIONAL BANK OF WASHINGTON, D.C.
1503 Pennsylvania Avenue, N.W.
Washington, D.C. 20005
John M. Christie, Chairman of the Board
(202) 624-2000
See also Central Charge Service, Inc.

RIGHT-AWAY FOODS CORPORATION
Box 184
Edinburg, Texas 78539
(512) 383-3877

RIGHT CHOICE (food products)
See Glen-Webb & Company

RIGHT DRESS (garden products)
See MacAndrews & Forbes Company

RIGHT GUARD (deodorant)
See Gillette Toiletries Company

RIGHT ON (aftershave, cologne, shave lather)
See Posner Laboratories, Inc.

RIGHT TIME (soups)
See General Foods Corporation

RIGHTO (canned foods)
See Reinbeck Canning Company

RIGID-BAK-R-FOAM (insulated aluminum siding)
See Alsco Anaconda Inc.

RIGID FORM INC.
121 South Kallock
Richmond, Kansas 66080

RIGIDENT (denture cleanser, retainer)
See Wickman Pharmaceutical Company, Inc.

Companies and Trade Names

RIGIDIZED METALS CORPORATION
658 Ohio Street
Buffalo, New York 14203
Richard S. Smith, Jr., President
(716) 856-9060

RIGO CHEMICAL COMPANY
Post Office Box 1188
638 Benton Avenue
Nashville, Tennessee 37202
Robert Hughes, General Manager
(615) 297-3591

RIGOLETTO (cigars)
See M & N Cigar Manufacturers Inc.

RIKER LABORATORIES
(Subsidiary of 3M Company)
19901 Nordhoff Street
Northbridge, California 91325
Charles R. Adams, Vice President and General Manager
(213) 341-1300

RIL-SWEET (saccharin)
See Plough Inc.

RILEY-BEAIRD INC.
Box 1115
601 Benton Kelly Street
Shreveport, Louisiana 71102
William E. Adams, President and General Manager
(318) 868-4441

RILEY CANDY COMPANY, INC.
1412 West Third Avenue
Spokane, Washington 99204

RIMMEL, INC.
566 Grand Avenue
Englewood, New Jersey 07631

RINALDI (shoes)
See Schwartz & Benjamin, Inc.

RINALDO ROSSI (breadstick-making) equipment)
See Lehara Corporation

RINEX (shoes)
See Uniroyal, Inc.

RING AROUND PRODUCTS, INC.
Post Office Box 589
Montgomery, Alabama 36101
Edward V. Welch, President
(205) 365-5971

RING CANDY COMPANY
115 South Frederick Street
Baltimore, Maryland 21202

RING DING (cake products)
See Drake Bakeries

RINGER (men's knit sportshirts)
See Stedman Manufacturing Company

RINGERS DUTCHOCS, INC.
See Dutchocs International, Inc.

RINGLING BROTHERS-BARNUM & BAILEY COMBINED SHOWS, INC.
1015 18th Street, N.W.
Washington, D.C. 20036
Irvin Feld, President
(202) 833-2700

RINGSBY TRUCK LINES, INC.
3201 Ringsby Court
Denver, Colorado 80216
Hugh Shurtleff, President
(303) 222-5761

RINN & CLOOS (cigars)
See Gesty Trading and Manufacturing Corporation

RINSA RAMA (hair-care product)
See The Fleetwood Company

RINSE AWAY (dandruff treatments)
See Alberto-Culver Company

RINSE 'N VAC (rug and carpet cleaners)
See Liggett & Myers Inc., Earl Grissmer Company, Inc. Division

RINSO (detergent)
See Lever Brothers Company

RIO DEL MAR FOOD, INC.
160 Sansome
San Francisco, California 94104
(415) 421-6902

RIO D'ORO (food products)
See Tropicana Products Inc.

RIO-FRIO (seafoods)
See San Antonio Foreign Trading Company, Inc.

RIO GLEN (fruit)
See Silveira & O'Connell

RIO JR (accordions)
See Excelsior Accordions, Inc.

RIONDO (rums)
See Renfield Importers, Ltd.

RIP TIDE (frozen seafood)
See Bayou Foods

RIPA (bicycle products)
See Joseph Caragol, Inc.

RIPCORD (window shades)
See Breneman, Inc.

RIPE-N-GROW SUNLITE (planter and gro-lux tube)
See Hall Industries Inc.

Companies and Trade Names

RIPLEY & GOWEN COMPANY, INC.
67 Mechanic Street
Attleboro, Massachusetts 02703
Emilio G. Gautieri, Jr., President
(617) 222-0060

RIPLEY COMPANY, INC.
1 Factory
Middletown, Connecticut 06457
Frank A. Rudolph, Chairman and President
(203) 346-6677

RIPOLIN (paint)
See Glidden-Durkee (Division of SCM Corporation)

RIPON FOODS, INC.
Oshkosh Street
Ripon, Wisconsin 54971
John E. Bumby, President
(414) 748-3151

RIPON INDUSTRIES, INC.
(Subsidiary of Medalist Industries)
Waupun, Wisconsin 53963
W.R. Murphy, President
(414) 324-5566

RIPPLE (sauces for ice cream)
See Balch Flavor Company, Inc.

RIPPLE (wine)
See E. & J. Gallo Winery

RIPPON CANDY COMPANY, D.J.
1229 Harding Avenue
Hershey, Pennsylvania 17033

RISDON MANUFACTURING COMPANY
Risdon Street
Naugatuck, Connecticut 06770
Christopher H. Buckley, Chairman and President
(203) 729-8231

RISE (shaving lather)
See Carter-Wallace, Inc.

RISHEL FURNITURE COMPANY J.K.
1201 West Third Street
Williamsport, Pennsylvania 17701
Richard E. Mellish, President
(717) 326-4178

RISQUE (shoes)
See Brown Group, Inc.

RISTMASTER (watchbands)
See Kestenman Brothers Manufacturing Company

RITCHIE & SONS INC., E.S.
Oak Street
Pembroke, Massachusetts 02359
(617) 826-5131

RITCHIE COMPANY INC., B.C.
15 Exchange Place
Jersey City, New Jersey 07302
(212) 344-2323

RITCHIE GROCER COMPANY
Post Office Box 100
319 South Washington Street
El Dorado, Arkansas 71730
John S. Benson, President
(501) 863-8191

RITE (hand tools)
See Seco Tool Company, Ltd.

RITE (liquid wax)
See W.R. Grace Company

RITE-A-WAY INDUSTRIES INC.
See Interstate Inns

RITE AID CORPORATION
Trindle and Railroad
Shiremanstown, Pennsylvania 17091
Alex Grass, Chairman of the Board
(717) 761-2633

RITE AUTOTONICS CORPORATION
3485 South La Cienega Boulevard
Los Angeles, California 90016
Edward Schwartz, President
(213) 836-7900

RITE-HITE (posture chairs and stools)
See Dependable Manufacturing Company

RITE-LINE CORPORATION
172 Rollins Avenue
Rockville, Maryland 20852
(301) 881-3000

RITE-MADE PAPER CONVERTERS
1501 West 29th
Kansas City, Missouri 64108
(816) 753-7870

RITE-OFF CORPORATION
40 Cain Drive
Plainview, New York 11803

RITE-SPOT (cabinets and files)
See Gordon L. Hall Company

RITE STYLE (handbags)
See Olla Industries

RITEPOINT
9400 Watson Road
Crestwood, Missouri 63126
(314) 842-1000

RITESTARTS (shoes)
See Dr. Posner Shoe Company Inc.

RITEWAY (heaters and furnaces)
See Virginia Metalcrafters, Inc.

RITON COMPANY, A.
512 Third Avenue
New York, New York 10016
(212) 532-4857

Companies and Trade Names

RITORNELLE, INC.
520 Fifth Avenue
New York, New York 10036
(212) 682-5844

RITTENBAUM INC., MAX
Post Office Box 43526
600 Wharton Circle S.W.
Atlanta, Georgia 30336
(404) 691-7133

RITTENHOUSE (whiskey)
See Continental Distilling Corporation

RITTENHOUSE PAPER COMPANY
2600 North Clybourn Avenue
Chicago, Illinois 60614
(312) 935-5550

RITTER & RITTER IMPORTERS INC.
5 East 33rd Street
New York, New York 10016
(212) 751-5920

RITTER COMPANY, P.J.
(Division of Curtice-Burns, Inc.)
Quality Lane
Bridgeton, New Jersey 08302
Alfred H. Funke, Jr., President
(609) 451-6500

RITTER, HEIDE E.
8300 South 20th Street
Oak Creek, Wisconsin 53154

RITTS COMPANY, HERBERT
2221 South Sepulveda
Los Angeles, California 90064
Herbert Ritts, Chairman and President
(213) 272-3226

RITZ (crackers)
See Nabisco, Inc.

RITZ (rotisserie)
See Son-Chief Electrics Inc.

RITZENTHALER COMPANY, JOHN
40 Portland Road
West Conshohocken, Pennsylvania 19428
(215) 825-9321

RIVAL MANUFACTURING COMPANY
36th and Bennington
Kansas City, Missouri 64129
I. H. Miller, President
(816) 861-1000

RIVAL PET FOODS
(Division of Associated Products, Inc.)
7830 West 71st Street
Bridgeview, Illinois 60455
Harry L. Gadau, President
(312) 594-6600

RIVCO (uniforms)
See Riverside Manufacturing Company

RIVER (rice)
See Riviana Foods, Inc.

RIVER FOODS INC.
Box 448
La Crosse, Wisconsin 54601

RIVER GARDEN (canned fruits)
See Plainwell Canning Company

RIVER VALLEY (frozen foods)
See Allied-Langield Company, Inc.

RIVERS & GILMAN MOULDED PRODUCTS
Box 206
Hampden, Massachusetts 04444
(207) 862-3600

RIVERSIDE (frozen turkeys)
See Ralston-Purina Company

RIVERSIDE CHEMICAL COMPANY
(Division of Cook Industries, Inc.)
855 Ridge Lake Boulevard
Memphis, Tennessee 38117
Douglas Kelly, Jr., President
(901) 767-8810

RIVERSIDE MANUFACTURING COMPANY
Post Office Box 460
Moultrie, Georgia 31768
William C. Vereen, Jr., President
(912) 985-5210

RIVERSIDE PAPER CORPORATION
800 South Lawe Street
Appleton, Wisconsin 54911
R.J. Turek, President
(414) 733-6651

RIVETO MANUFACTURING COMPANY
59 River Street
Orange, Massachusetts 01364
(617) 544-2551
See also Stencil Company

RIVIANA FOODS, INC.
2777 Allen Parkway
Houston, Texas 77019
William H. Lane, President
(713) 529-3251
See also Hebrew National Kosher Foods, Inc.; Hill's; and Pangburn Company Inc.

RIVIERA (food products)
See Lucca Packing Company of California Inc.

RIVIERA (furniture)
See Finkel Outdoor Products Inc.

RIVIERA CRUISER
(Division of LML Engineering & Manufacturing Corporation)
607-617 South Chauncey Street
Columbia City, Indiana 46725

Companies and Trade Names

RIVIERA FOODS
360 Harbor Way
South San Francisco,
   California 94080
(415) 761-3533

RIVIERA MANUFACTURING
2819 West 28th Street
Grand Rapids, Michigan 49509

RIVIERA WIGS INC.
2530 El Camino Real
Mountain View, California 94040

RIVNUT (tools)
   See B.F. Goodrich Company

RIVOLI CORSET COMPANY, INC.
   See Vanity Corset Company

RIXIE PAPER PRODUCTS, INC.
Post Office Box 155
Stowe, Pennsylvania 19464

RIXON ELEKTRONICS, INC.
(Subsidiary of Sangamo Electric
   Company)
2120 Industrial Parkway
Silver Spring, Maryland 20904
Maurice W. Horrell, President
(301) 622-2121

RIZ (dry lubricant)
   See Shaler Company

RO-MAY (canned foods)
   See Elsa Canning Company

RO-PAUL DRUG CORPORATION
185-12 Hillside Avenue
Jamaica, New York 11432
(212) 526-1121

RO-TEL (canned foods)
   See Elsa Canning Company

RO-TRIM (exercise equipment)
   See Battle Creek Equipment
      Company

ROAD AMERICA (automotive
accessories)
   See Wells Manufacturing
      Corporation

ROAD BOSS (trucks)
   See White Motor Corporation

ROAD KING (tires)
   See Dayton Tire & Rubber
      Company

ROAD MASTER (tires)
   See Cooper Tire and Rubber
      Company

ROAD RANGER (recreational
vehicles)
   See Kit Manufacturing Company

ROAD-RUNNER (automotive parts)
   See Goerlich's

ROAD RUNNER (bicycle)
   See Iverson Cycle Corporation

ROADEL FOODS, INC.
Hunts Point
Food Distribution Center
New York, New York 10474
(212) 378-1000

ROADGRIPPER (rubber products)
   See Carlisle Corporation

ROADLINER (travel trailer)
   See Redman Industries, Inc.

ROADMARK (tires)
   See Kelly Springfield Tire
      Company

ROADMASTER (bicycles)
   See AMF, Inc.

ROADSIDE FARMS (food products)
   See Theresa Friedman & Sons
      Inc.

ROAMER (power vacuum)
   See Advance Floor Machine
      Company

ROAMER-MEDANA WATCH
CORPORATION
   See Medana Watch Corporation

ROANOKE APPLE PRODUCTS
COMPANY
314-A South Jefferson
Roanoke, Virginia 24011
(703) 344-3711

ROANOKE MILLS, INC.
505 Sixth Street, S.W.
Roanoke, Virginia 24007
William T. King, President
(703) 389-9311

ROARING SPRING BLANK BOOK
COMPANY
740 Spang Street
Roaring Spring, Pennsylvania 16673
Robert R. Hoover, President
(814) 224-2111

ROAST'N BOAST (sauce mix and
roasting bag)
   See General Foods

ROB BOY COMPANY, INC.
34 West 33rd Street
New York, New York 10021
Allen L. Boorstein, President
(212) 947-8100

ROBB ROSS CORPORATION
301 Wall
Sioux City, Iowa 51102

Companies and Trade Names

ROBBIE BURNS (Scotch whiskey)
See Carillon Importers, Ltd.

ROBBIE RIVERS (dresses and sportswear)
See Bobbie Brooks, Inc.

ROBBINS & COMPANY INC., D.
127 West 17th Street
New York, New York 10011
(212) 929-9124

ROBBINS & MYERS, INC.
1345 Lagonda Avenue
Springfield, Ohio 45501
Fred G. Wall, President
(513) 323-6461
See also Hunter Fan & Ventilating Company

ROBBINS ENTERPRISES
160 Fifth Avenue
New York, New York 10010
(212) 929-2101

ROBBINS INDUSTRIES
507 Washington Street
Lynn, Massachusetts 01903

ROBBY LEN
(Division of Genesco, Inc.)
New Haven, Connecticut 06510
Louis Brumberger, President
(203) 777-5531

ROBE D'UN SOIR (dusting powder, eau de toilette, hair spray, etc.)
See Carven Parfums

ROBERK
(Division of Parker-Hannifin Corporation)
88 Long Hill Cross Road
Shelton, Connecticut 06484

ROBERT (oboes and English horns)
See Dorn & Kirschner Band Instrument Company

ROBERT BRUCE, INC.
(Division of Consolidated Foods, Inc.)
C and Westmoreland Streets
Philadelphia, Pennsylvania 19134
Ronald Stevens, President
(215) 426-0300

ROBERT BURNS (cigars)
See General Cigar Company

ROBERT DANIELS & COMPANY
3 Caesar Place
Moonachie, New Jersey 07074

ROBERT DENNEY (men's toiletries)
See Frances Denney

ROBERT MANUFACTURING COMPANY
1001 East 23rd Street
Hialeah, Florida 33013

ROBERT PETERS (dresses)
See Ginsburg & Abelson, Inc.

ROBERT SCHAFER (menswear)
See Burma-Bibas Inc.

ROBERTET, INC., P.
37 West 65th Street
New York, New York 10023
(212) 873-6400

ROBERTS
(Division of Gabriel Industries Inc.)
1 Maxson Drive
Old Forge, Pennsylvania 18518

ROBERTS & GRANCELLI INC.
West Kerley Corners Road
Tivoli, New York 12583

ROBERTS & PORTER INC.
4140 West Victoria Avenue
Chicago, Illinois 60646
Keith D. Nickoley, President
(312) 588-3700

ROBERTS & ROBERTS
1275 Rollins Road
Burlingame, California 94010

ROBERTS BROTHERS INC.
Box 877
Winter Haven, Florida 33880

ROBERTS COLONIAL HOUSE INC.
570 West 167th Street
South Holland, Illinois 60473
(312) 331-6233

ROBERTS COLOR PRODUCTIONS, MIKE
2023 Eighth Street
Berkeley, California 94710

ROBERTS CONSOLIDATED INDUSTRIES, INC.
(Subsidiary of Champion International)
600 North Baldwin Park Boulevard
City of Industry, California 91749
(213) 338-7311

ROBERTS, CUSHMAN & COMPANY
129 West 22nd Street
New York, New York 10011
(212) 242-5170

ROBERTS FARMS, BYRON T.
Evesboro Road and Route 73
Marlton, New Jersey 08059

ROBERTS FIG COMPANY
Post Office Box 216
Pinedale, California 93650
Donald Roberts, President
(209) 439-3145

ROBERTS, INC., STANLEY
230 Fifth Avenue
New York, New York 10036
(212) 889-4250

Companies and Trade Names

ROBERTS NUMBERING MACHINE
(Division of Heller Roberts
   Instruments Corporation)
700 Jamaica Avenue
Brooklyn, New York 11208
(212) 647-4600

ROBERTS RUBBER COMPANY,
   WELDON
(Subsidiary of A.W. Faber-Castell
   Pencil Company)
351 Sixth Avenue
Newark, New Jersey 07107
(201) 482-7812

ROBERTS, SANFORD & TAYLOR
   COMPANY
Box 818
Sherman, Texas 75090

ROBERTSHAW CONTROL COMPANY
1701 Byrd Avenue
Richmond, Virginia 23230
Ralph S. Thomas, President
(804) 282-9561
   See also Lux Time

ROBERTSON (airplanes)
   See Curtiss-Wright Corporation

ROBERTSON (port wine)
   See Julius Wile Sons &
      Company, Inc.

ROBERTSON COMPANY, H.H.
2 Gateway Center
Pittsburgh, Pennsylvania 15222
Douglas A. Jones, President and
   Chief Executive Officer
(412) 281-3200

ROBERTSON FACTORIES, INC.
33 Chandler Avenue
Taunton, Massachusetts 02780
C. Stuart Robertson, President
(617) 824-4061

ROBERTSON PAPER BOX
   COMPANY, INC.
Montville, Connecticut 06353
Ralph A. Powers, Jr., President
   and Chief Operations Officer
(203) 848-9231

ROBERTSON PHOTO MECHANIX
   INC.
(Subsidiary of Log Etronics, Inc.)
250 Wille Road
Des Plaines, Illinois 60018
Meade Kendrick, General Manager
(312) 827-7711

ROBERTSON, SHEARER B.
Appomattox, Virginia 24522

ROBERTSON STEEL & IRON
   COMPANY, THE
700 Kent Road
Batavia, Ohio 45103
(513) 732-2000

ROBERTSON'S (preserves)
   See Heublein, Inc.

ROBERTSON'S YELLOW LABEL
(Scotch whiskey)
   See Kobrand Corporation

ROBESON CUTLERY COMPANY,
   INC.
(Division of Van Dyck International
   Corporation)
Buffalo Road
Castille, New York 14427
A.J. Zupert, General Manager
(716) 493-2502

ROBETOWN ROBES, INC.
1350 Broadway
New York, New York 10018
(212) 431-5825

ROBIN FOOTWEAR CORPORATION
208 North Division Street
Mount Union, Pennsylvania 17066
Charles Femia, President
(814) 542-2545

ROBIN GREETINGS
1269 Rand Road
Des Plaines, Illinois 60016

ROBIN HARDWARE CORPORATION
35-03 31st Street
Long Island City, New York 11106
(212) 721-8994

ROBIN HOOD (ale and beer)
   See August Wagner Breweries
      Inc.

ROBIN HOOD (bicycles)
   See Raleigh Industries of
      America, Inc.

ROBIN HOOD (flour, mixes)
   See International Multifoods

ROBIN HOOD (shoes)
   See Brown Group, Inc.

ROBINETTE (shoes)
   See Brown Group, Inc.

ROBINS COMPANY, INC., A.H.
1407 Cummings Drive
Richmond, Virginia 23220
W.L. Zimmer, III, President
(804) 257-2000
   See also Caran Corporation;
      Chap Stick Company;
      Miller-Morton Company;
      Vio Bin Corporation; and
      Whittier Laboratories, Inc.

ROBINS INDUSTRIES
   CORPORATION
15-58 127th Street
College Point, New York 11356

ROBINSON & COMPANY INC.,
   GEORGE A.
Brightford Road
East Rochester, New York 14445
(716) 586-5432

Companies and Trade Names

ROBINSON CANNING COMPANY, INC.
Post Office Box 4248
New Orleans, Louisiana 70118
H.R. Robinson, President
(504) 341-4246

ROBINSON, COMPANY, J.W.
(Division of Associated Dry Goods Corporation)
7th and Grand
Los Angeles, California 90017
James Slayden, President
(213) 628-0333

ROCHAS (perfumes)
See Parfums Rochas, Inc.

ROBINSON COMPANY, M.W.
Laurel Brook Road
Rockfall, Connecticut 06481

ROBINSON CONSUMER PRODUCTS
Post Office Box 893
Meriden, Connecticut 06450

ROBINSON LABORATORY, INC.
355 Brannan Street
San Francisco, California 94107
Michael J. Cousins, Jr., President
(415) 982-8438

ROBINSON-LLOYDS, LTD.
100 Fairchild Avenue
Plainview, New York 11803

ROBINSON-RANSBOTTOM POTTERY COMPANY, THE
Roseville, Ohio 43777
J.A. Ransbottom, President
(614) 697-7355

ROBINSON REMINDERS
171 Elm Street
Westfield, Massachusetts 01085
John W. Robinson, Chairman, President and Treasurer
(413) 562-9993

ROBINSON SPONGE COMPANY, INC.
2769 West 15th Street
Brooklyn, New York 11224
Alvin Kaplan, President
(212) 996-7505

ROBITUSSIN (cough remedies)
See A.H. Robins Company, Inc.

ROBLEE (shoes)
See Brown Group, Inc.

ROBO JR. (knife sharpener)
See Alden Speare's Sons Company

ROBO TROL (outboard motors)
See Minn-Kota Manufacturing Company

ROBOT (photo equipment)
See Karl Heitz, Inc.

ROBOTGUARD (alarm systems)
See Telecommunications Corporation of America

ROBY & COMPANY INC., JOHN W.
10020 14th Avenue S.W.
Seattle, Washington 98146
(206) 767-3420

ROCHE COMPANY, INC., PAUL C.
11 Park Place
New York, New York 10007
(212) 227-8288

ROCHE LABORATORIES
(Division of Hoffmann-La Roche)
Roche Park
Nuttley, New Jersey 07110

ROCHE-THOMAS COMPANY
27196 East Tenth Street
Highland, California 92346

ROCHELLE FURNITURE MANUFACTURING COMPANY
Rochelle, Illinois 61068
(815) 562-6516

ROCHESTER GAS AND ELECTRIC CORPORATION
89 East Avenue
Rochester, New York 14649
Francis E. Drake, Jr., Chairman of the Board
(716) 546-2700

ROCHESTER GERMICIDE COMPANY
333 Hollenbeck Street
Rochester, New York 14621
Herbert J. Chamberlain, President
(716) 266-2250

ROCHESTER PAPER
(Division of King-Seeley Thermos Company)
Mill Street
Rochester, Michigan 48063
H.R. O'Donnell, President
(313) 651-8121

ROCHESTER PRODUCTS
(Division of General Motors Corporation)
Post Office Box 1790
1000 Lexington Avenue
Rochester, New York 14603
John R. Wilson, Jr., General Manager
(716) 254-5050

ROCHESTER TELEPHONE CORPORATION
100 Midtown Plaza
Rochester, New York 14646
George S. Beinetti, Chairman of the Board
(716) 325-9851

ROCHESTER WIRE-O BINDING COMPANY
171 York Street
Rochester, New York 14611
(716) 235-2343

Companies and Trade Names

ROCK (wines)
See Schenley Industries, Inc.

ROCK-A-CHAIR (furniture)
See Master Woodcraft Inc.

ROCK-A-TOT (infant chairs)
See Comfy-Babe

ROCK-KNIT (men's coats)
See Goodstein Brothers & Company, Inc.

ROCK OF AGES CORPORATION
(Subsidiary of Nortek, Inc.)
Barre, Vermont 05641
R.S. Gillette, President
(802) 476-3115

ROCK RIVER MANUFACTURING CORPORATION
120 North Franklin Street
Janesville, Wisconsin 53545
(608) 754-6956

ROCK SPRING (beverages)
See Jacob Ries Bottling Works, Inc.

ROCKBRIDGE (carpeting)
See Lees Carpets

ROCKCOTE (paints)
See Valspar Corporation

ROCKET (guitars)
See Harmony Company

ROCKET (wine)
See Schenley Industries, Inc.

ROCKET RESEARCH CORPORATION
York Center
11441 Willows Road
Redmond, Washington 98052
B.F. Beckleman, President
(206) 885-5000

ROCKET WAVE (hair-care products)
See Faberge, Inc.

ROCKFORD (tomato products)
See Sharp Canning, Inc.

ROCKFORD TEXTILE MILLS, INC.
McMinnville, Tennessee 37110

ROCKING HORSE (phonograph records)
See Ambassador Record Corporation

ROCKING K FOODS, INC.
9420 Sorenson
Santa Fe Springs, California 90670

ROCKINGHAM (meat products)
See Shen-Valley Meat Packers Inc.

ROCKINGHAM POULTRY MARKETING COOPERATIVE
Broadway, Virginia 22815
Dave Van Meter, President
(703) 896-7001

ROCKLAND LEATHER GOODS CORPORATION
10 West 33rd Street
New York, New York 10001
(212) 279-5537

ROCKMONT ENVELOPE COMPANY
(Division of Pak Well Corporation)
3500 Rockmont Drive
Denver, Colorado 80217
(303) 433-7331

ROCKVILLE INTERNATIONAL
225 Fifth Avenue
New York, New York 10010
(212) 725-4845

ROCKWARE, INC.
See Kirsch Company

ROCKWELL-BARNES COMPANY
2101 Greenleaf Avenue
Elk Grove Village, Illinois 60007
Gordon J. Juttner, President
(312) 437-1600

ROCKWELL INTERNATIONAL CORPORATION
Power Tool Division
600 Grant Street
Pittsburgh, Pennsylvania 15219
Robert Anderson, President and Chief Executive Officer
(412) 565-2000
See also Whit-Craft Houseboat

ROCKWELL PHARMACAL COMPANY
33 Virginia Avenue
West Nyack, New York 10994

ROCKY MOUNTAIN MUSIC DISTRIBUTORS
955 Decatur
Denver, Colorado 80204
(303) 825-4321

ROCKY MOUNTAIN PHARMACAL COMPANY
Box 7373
Phoenix, Arizona 85011

ROD RIGGER INC.
Box 836
Eau Gallie, Florida 32935

RODA MANUFACTURING COMPANY
38 Livonia Avenue
Brooklyn, New York 11212
(212) 345-2000

RODALE MANUFACTURING COMPANY INC.
Sixth and Minor Streets
Emmaus, Pennsylvania 18049
Robert L. Horstman, President
(215) 965-9071

RODDA CANDY COMPANY
1300 Stefko Boulevard
Bethlehem, Pennsylvania 18017

Companies and Trade Names

RODDENBERY COMPANY, INC., W.B.
Post Office Box 60
Cairo, Georgia 31728
J.B. Roddenbery, Sr., President
(912) 377-2102

RODDICK TOOL COMPANY INC.
1023 North Pauline Street
Anaheim, California 92801
(714) 772-1801

RODE (sports accessories)
See Eiger Mountain Sports

RODELLE LABORATORIES, INC.
2700 Arapahoe Street
Denver, Colorado 80205
(303) 534-5844

RODENBECK MARINE MANUFACTURING
5410 Brighton Drive
Fort Wayne, Indiana 46825

RODENSTOCK (optical products, photographic lenses)
See King Photo Corporation

RODEO (meat products)
See John Morrell & Company

RODERICH PAESOLD (string and fretted musical instruments)
See York Musical Instrument Company, Inc.

RODEWAY INNS OF AMERICA
Post Office Box 34736
Dallas, Texas 75234
C. Huston Bell, President
(214) 243-1021

RODIN INDUSTRIES INC.
820 South Washington Avenue
Scranton, Pennsylvania 18501
Sidney H. Rodin, President
(717) 346-7045

RODISCO (lighting fixtures)
See Heifetz Company, Inc.

RODMAN-TRANSEUROPA INC.
80 South Early Street
Alexandria, Virginia 22304

RODNEY ELEVATOR COMPANY
Fort Morgan, Colorado 80701

RODNEY KENT (giftware and housewares)
See Krischer Metal Products Company, Inc.

RODRIGUEZ & COMPANY INC., J.M.
225 South Marginal Road
Fort Lee, New Jersey 07024
(212) 344-3114

RODS FOOD PRODUCTS, INC.
2443 East 27th
Los Angeles, California 90058
Waldon Calamia, President
(213) 583-4223

ROE (shoes)
See Cannon Shoe Company

ROE & SONS INC., JUSTUS
217 River Avenue
Patchogue, New York 11772

ROEGELEIN PROVISION COMPANY
1700 South Brazos
San Antonio, Texas 78206
William Roegelein, Jr., President
(512) 225-2631

ROERIG & COMPANY, J.B.
(Division of Pfizer, Inc.)
235 East 42nd Street
New York, New York 10017
(212) 573-2323

ROESBERY PRODUCTS, LTD.
413 West Idaho Street
Boise, Idaho 83702

ROFFE-RENE INC.
808 Howell Street
Seattle, Washington 98101
(206) 622-0456

ROGER & GALLET
12 Potter Avenue
New Rochelle, New York 10801

ROGER REPRESENTATIVES
5 Robins Nest Lane
Larchmont, New York 10538

ROGERS (electronic products)
See North American Philips Company

ROGERS (paint products)
See Sherwin-Williams Company

ROGERS (silverware)
See Oneida Ltd. Silversmiths

ROGERS BROTHERS COMPANY, INC.
3100 Rollendet
Idaho Falls, Idaho 83401
R.B. MacLean, President
(208) 522-0110
See also Pride Pak Foods, Inc.

ROGERS CANDY COMPANY
315 West Mercer Street
Seattle, Washington 98119
(206) 284-7676

ROGERS COMPANY, W.T.
Post Office Box 4327
Madison, Wisconsin 53711

ROGERS' DRUG COMPANY
122-20 Merrick Road
New York, New York 10023
(212) 528-1000

Companies and Trade Names

ROGERS DRUMS
(Division of CBS Musical Instruments)
1300 East Valencia
Fullerton, California 92631

ROGERS FAMILY RESTAURANTS INC., ROY
(Subsidiary of Marriott Corporation)
5161 River Road
Washington, D.C. 20016
(202) 986-5364

ROGERS, LUNT & BOWLEN COMPANY
Federal and Norwood
Greenfield, Massachusetts 01301
Denham C. Lunt, Jr., President
(413) 774-2774

ROGERS PARK LABORATORY
3623 Seven Mile Lane
Baltimore, Maryland 21208

ROGERS PEET COMPANY
479 Fifth Avenue
New York, New York 10017
Paul H. Wright, President
(212) 682-8170

ROGERS SILVER COMPANY, INC., F.B.
(Subsidiary of National Silver Industries, Inc.)
414 West Water Street
Taunton, Massachusetts 02780
Bernard Bernstein, President
(617) 824-6981

ROGERS STERLING (silverware)
See Insilco Corporation

ROGERS VINEGAR COMPANY
Box 218
Rogers, Arkansas 72756

ROGERS WALLA WALLA, INC.
Box 998
Seventh and Rose
Walla Walla, Washington 99362
B.L. Davis, President
(509) 525-8390

ROGUE RIVER ORCHARDS OREGON, LTD.
1311 North Central Avenue
Medford, Oregon 97501

ROGUE RIVER PACKING CORPORATION
Box 456
Medford, Oregon 97501

ROHM AND HAAS COMPANY
Independence Mall, West
Philadelphia, Pennsylvania 19105
Vincent L. Gregory, President
(215) 592-3000
See also Warren-Teed Pharmaceuticals, Inc.; and Whitmoyer Laboratories, Inc.

ROHNER (sports apparel)
See Max Hurni Importer Inc.

ROI-TAN (cigars)
See American Cigar

ROISMAN, MAX
1308 West 130th Street
Gardena, California 90247

ROK MAN TRADING COMPANY, INC.
1225 Broadway
New York, New York 10001
(212) 686-8588

ROKA (salad dressing)
See Kraft Foods

ROKA INTERNATIONAL CORPORATION
437 West 16th Street
New York, New York 10011
(212) 989-0130

ROKEACH & SONS, INC., I.
551 Grand Street
New York, New York 10002
Monroe Nash, President
(212) 677-4480

ROKON, INC.
160 Emerald Street
Keene, New Hampshire 03431
Edward R. Hampson, President
(603) 352-7341

ROL-A-PAK (aluminum foil)
See Kaiser Aluminum & Chemical Corporation

ROL-EZE (knife sharpeners)
See Alden Speare's Sons Company

ROL GLO (paints)
See Mary Carter Industries Inc.

ROL-RULER COMPANY
1217 Durham Road
Riegelsville, Pennsylvania 18077

ROL-TOP (overhead doors)
See Kinnear Corporation

ROLA CHAIR (high chairs)
See Peterson Baby Products

ROLAMECH INC.
3713 North 75th Street
Scottsdale, Arizona 85251

ROLAND (cocktail specialties, canned fruits, vegetables, fish, and meats)
See American Roland Food Corporation

ROLAND (rhythm instruments, electronic pianos, synthesizers, and effects pedals)
See Sorkin Music Company Inc.

ROLAND INDUSTRIES, INC.
2280 Chaffee Drive
Saint Louis, Missouri 63141
(314) 567-3800

Companies and Trade Names

ROLAND MARINE, INC.
50 Broadway
New York, New York 10004
(212) 269-1075

ROLANE (hosiery)
   See Kayser-Roth Hosiery
   Company, Inc.

ROLATAPE CORPORATION
4221 Redwood Avenue
Los Angeles, California 90066
(213) 822-2057

ROLEX (watches)
   See American Rolex Watch
   Corporation

ROLF'S (leather goods)
   See Amity Leather Products
   Company

ROLIT (knife sharpener)
   See Housewares American
   Corporation

ROLITE (recreational equipment)
   See Larson Industries, Inc.

ROLL-A-BELT (seat belts)
   See Borg-Warner Corporation

ROLL DIPPERS COMPANY
207 Conant Street
Maumee, Ohio 43537
(419) 893-6212

ROLL FOLD (chairs)
   See J.P. Redington & Company

ROLL KING (golf carts)
   See A.J. Industries Inc.

ROLL RITE (tobacco and cigarette papers)
   See House of Edgeworth

ROLLA-HEAD (custom venetian blinds)
   See Eastern Products Corporation

ROLLABOUT (infants' product)
   See Thayer Inc.

ROLLAWAY (luggage)
   See United States Luggage
   Corporation

ROLLEI OF AMERICA INC.
100 Lehigh Drive
Fairfield, New Jersey 07006
(201) 227-6425

ROLLER DERBY SKATE CORPORATION
311 West Edwards Street
Litchfield, Illinois 62056
(217) 324-3961

ROLLER PERM (home permanent)
   See Gillette Company

ROLLERSISER (exercise and reducing equipment)
   See Matador Industries, Inc.

ROLLFAST (bicycles and roller skates)
   See D.P. Harris Hardware &
   Manufacturing Company

ROLLING ROCK (beer)
   See Latrobe Brewing Company

ROLLING WEST (canned foods)
   See Western Farmers Association

ROLLINS, INC.
2170 Piedmont Road, N.E.
Atlanta, Georgia 30324
O. Wayne Rollins, Chairman of
   the Board
(404) 873-2355

ROLLOHOME CORPORATION
1515 North Central Avenue
Marshfield, Wisconsin 54449
John Bertschie, President
(715) 384-2161

ROLLOP (cameras and lenses)
   See Geiss-America

ROLLS-ROYCE, INC.
75 West Century Road
Paramus, New Jersey 07652
George W. Lewis, President
(201) 265-8300

ROLNCO
5600 Lincoln Drive
Edina, Minnesota 55436

ROLOFF MANUFACTURING CORPORATION
Box 271
400 Gertrude Street
Kaukauna, Wisconsin 54130
Harold W. Roloff, President and
   Treasurer
(414) 766-3501

ROMA (mandolins, lutes)
   See Eastern Music Company

ROMA (pasta products)
   See Skinner Macaroni Company

ROMA (wine)
   See Schenley Industries, Inc.

ROMALON (hose)
   See Virginia Maid Hosiery
   Mills Inc.

ROMAN BRIO (men's toiletries)
   See Leeming/Pacquin

ROMAN CLEANSER COMPANY
2700 East McNichols Road
Detroit, Michigan 48212
(313) 891-0700

Companies and Trade Names

ROMAN MEAL COMPANY
2101 South Tacoma Way
Tacoma, Washington 98411
Charles W.H. Matthaci, President
(206) 475-0964

ROMAN PRODUCTS CORPORATION
330 Phillips Avenue
South Hackensack,
   New Jersey 07606
Joseph H. Hoyt, President
(201) 499-1700

ROMANELLI IMPORTS
59 West 56th Street
New York, New York 10019
(212) 265-8518

ROMANO & SCHREIBER
   CORPORATION
54 West 37th Street
New York, New York 10018
(212) 279-1382

ROMANOFF (caviar)
   See Riviana Foods, Inc.

ROMANOFF (vodka)
   See Fleischmann Distilling
   Corporation

ROMANTICA BY VICTOR COSTA
(dresses)
   See Suzy Perette Dresses, Inc.

ROMAR INTERNATIONAL
   CORPORATION
350 Fifth Avenue
New York, New York 10018
(212) 564-1260

ROMEO (fruit products)
   See Frigid Food Products, Inc.

ROMEO SALTA (frozen Italian food)
   See Pet, Inc.

ROMP AND REST (baby bouncers)
   See Comfort Lines Inc.

ROMP-O-MANUFACTURING
   COMPANY
560 Eldorado Drive
Macon, Georgia 31204

ROMULUS (sports apparel)
   See Max Hurni Importer Inc.

RON BIENEN (handbags)
   See Bienen-Davis Inc.

RON-SON MUSHROOM PRODUCTS
Ellis Street and Deptford Road
Glassboro, New Jersey 08028

RON-VIK, INC.
800 Colorado Avenue South
Minneapolis, Minnesota 55416
(612) 545-0276

RONAY INC.
1 East 33rd Street
New York, New York 10016
(212) 679-4740

RONCO FOODS
800 South Barksdale
Memphis, Tennessee 38114
(901) 272-1705

RONCO TELEPRODUCTS, INC.
919 North Michigan Avenue
Chicago, Illinois 60611
Ronald M. Popeil, Chairman of
   the Board
(312) 645-0111

RONDELLI (accordions)
   See Massimino Music Studio

RONLEY INDUSTRIES INC., C.
532 Cherry Lane
Floral Park, New York 11001

RONNIE PACKAGING COMPANY
4301 New Brunswick Avenue
South Plainfield,
   New Jersey 07080

RONRICO (Puerto Rican rum)
   See General Wine & Spirits
   Company

RONSEN PIANO HAMMER
   COMPANY INC.
Post Office Box 188
Boiceville, New York 12412

RONSON CORPORATION
1 Ronson Road
Woodbridge, New Jersey 07095
Louis V. Aronson, II, President
(201) 634-5000

RONZONI FOODS, INC.
50 Ludy Street
Hicksville, New York 11801

RONZONI MACARONI COMPANY,
   INC.
50-02 Northern Boulevard
Long Island City, New York 11101
Emanuele Ronzoni, Jr., President
(212) 278-3500

ROOF FIX (protective coatings)
   See Monsey Products Company

ROOF WHITE (paints and paint
sundries)
   See Gable-Tite Products
   Company Inc.

ROOS/ATKINS, INC.
(Division of Genesco, Inc.)
799 Market Street
San Francisco, California 94103
George Karatsis, President
(415) 397-4000

ROOSTER (groceries)
   See Pasquale Brothers Ltd.

ROOSTER (snuff)
   See United States Tobacco
   Company

Companies and Trade Names

ROOSTER, INC.
714 Market Street
Philadelphia, Pennsylvania 19106
Jerome B. Myers, President
(215) 925-9933

ROOT CANDLE COMPANY, THE
537 South Flores Street
San Antonio, Texas 78204
(512) 223-2948

ROOTES MOTORS, INC.
See Chrysler Motors Corporation

ROOTO CORPORATION, THE
33094 West Eight Mile Road
Farmington, Michigan 48024
J.S. Moon, President
(313) 476-6111

ROPAT-CASLON, INC.
12616 Chadron Avenue
Hawthorne, California 90025
(213) 973-7104

ROPER CORPORATION
1905 West Court Street
Kankakee, Illinois 60901
Charles M. Hoover, President
(815) 939-3641
See also Sardis Luggage Company

ROPER PECAN COMPANY
Post Office Box 150
Hickman, Kentucky 42050

ROQUEFORT ASSOCIATION
41 East 42nd Street
New York, New York 10017
(212) 687-2064

ROR CHEMICAL COMPANY
338 East 16th
New York, New York 10003
(212) 534-2998

RORER-AMCHEM, INC.
See Amchem Products, Inc.

RORER, INC., WILLIAM H.
500 Virginia Drive
Fort Washington,
 Pennsylvania 19034
J.W. Eckman, President and
 Chief Executive Officer
(215) 628-6800

ROSA FOOD PRODUCTS
 COMPANY
1312 Federal
Philadelphia, Pennsylvania 19147
(215) 467-2214

ROSA JANE (syrup, coffee, tea,
margarine)
See Cole Brothers Company

ROSA PEN COMPANY
155 Park Avenue
Lyndhurst, New Jersey 07071
(201) 939-1112

ROSAL LABORATORIES
7408 West Chester Pike
Upper Darby, Pennsylvania 19082
(215) 528-6436

ROSALINDA INC.
260 West 39th Street
New York, New York 10018
(212) 563-6111

ROSANNA KNITTED SPORTSWEAR,
 INC.
(Subsidiary of Warnaco, Inc.)
1410 Broadway
New York, New York 10018
William J. O'Brien, President
(212) 947-8876

ROSARITA MEXICAN FOODS
 COMPANY
(Division of Beatrice Foods
 Company)
Post Office Box 1427
310 South Extension Road
Mesa, Arizona 85201
Clevel Langston, General Manager
(602) 964-8751

ROSCO (pet foods)
See Lewis Food Company

ROSCO TOOLS INC.
100 Landing Avenue
Smithtown, New York 11787
(516) 265-2200

ROSCREA PARTS CORPORATION
1249 Washington Boulevard
Seventh Floor
Detroit, Michigan 48226

ROSE (canned meats, chili)
See Foell Packing Company

ROSE (fruits)
See Sanger Fruit Growers
 Association

ROSE & COMPANY, INC.,
 DOUGLAS
4620 Ten Avenue
Temple, Pennsylvania 19560

ROSE & COMPANY INC., J.
23-49 Borden Avenue
Long Island City, New York 11101
(212) 392-1077

ROSE & CROWN (tobacco)
See S.S. Pierce Company

ROSE CONFECTIONS
1415 Fifth Street South
Hopkins, Minnesota 55343

ROSE CROIX (canned vegetables
and fruits)
See Michigan Fruit Canners,
 Inc.

ROSE-DERRY COMPANY
95 Chapel
Newton, Massachusetts 02195

Companies and Trade Names

ROSE FRUIT (canned foods)
See Lyons Canning Company Inc.

ROSE HARDWARE INC., L.
219 Snediker Avenue
Brooklyn, New York 11207
(212) 342-0162

ROSE LAIRD (skin- and hair-care products, makeup)
See R.H. Laird Manufacturing Company Inc.

ROSE-LEE INC.
5 East Fourth Street
Wilmington, Delaware 19801

ROSE MARIE REID (swimsuits)
See Jonathan Logan

ROSE PACKING COMPANY, INC.
4900 South Major Avenue
Chicago, Illinois 60638
(312) 458-9300

ROSE PRODUCTS COMPANY
2500 Valley Road
Reno, Nevada 89502

ROSE ROYAL (frozen dessert)
See Ward Foods, Inc.

ROSE-X (household cleaners, polishes)
See J.L. Prescott Company

ROSELINE (wines)
See Julius Wile Sons & Company, Inc.

ROSELLE STUDIOS INC.
300 West Central Avenue
Roselle, Illinois 60172

ROSEMAN COMPANY, JACK
307 Fifth Avenue
New York, New York 10016
(212) 684-0237

ROSEMAN MOWER CORPORATION
2300 Chestnut Avenue
Glenview, Illinois 60025
James E. Hoffman, President
(312) 729-2300

ROSEMARY CANDY COMPANY
352 Niagara Street
Buffalo, New York 14201
(716) 853-5563

ROSEMARY UNDERWEAR MANUFACTURING COMPANY
657 Broadway
New York, New York 10012
(212) 254-0877

ROSEMONT (fruit)
See H.F. Byrd, Inc.

ROSEMONT (shoes)
See G.H. Bass & Company

ROSEN COMPANY, E.
1005 Main Street
Pawtucket, Rhode Island 02860
(401) 726-4500

ROSEN MANUFACTURING COMPANY, S.
616 Plant Street
Utica, New York 13504

ROSENAU BROTHERS, INC.
Fox and Roberts Avenue
Philadelphia, Pennsylvania 19129
Louis V. Ajmo, President
(215) 223-6500

ROSENBERG BROTHERS, INC.
102 Landing Avenue
Smithtown, New York 11787

ROSENBERG COMPANY, MORRIS
644 East Ninth Street
Los Angeles, California 90015
(213) 627-8855

ROSENBERG PREMIUMS, MYER
221 North LaSalle Street
Chicago, Illinois 60601
(312) 263-5589

ROSENBLATT, INC., D.B.
912 Currie Avenue
Minneapolis, Minnesota 55403
Justin L. Rosenblatt, Sr., Chairman and President
(612) 336-2601

ROSENBLOOM & COMPANY INC., MORRIS
228 South Avenue
Rochester, New York 14604
(716) 232-2660

ROSENFELD INC., HARRY
1 East 33rd Street
New York, New York 10016
(212) 683-3332

ROSENHIRSCH COMPANY INC., H.
51 Bank
Stamford, Connecticut 06901
(203) 359-1034

ROSENOW PAPER COMPANY INC.
1 Mill Street
Menasha, Wisconsin 54952

ROSENSTEIN, INC., NETTIE
400 Madison Avenue
New York, New York 10017
Tedd Thomas, President
(212) 371-6300

ROSENTHAL
(Division of A.W. Faber-Castell Pencil Company, Inc.)
Post Office Box 7099
41 Dickerson Street
Newark, New Jersey 07107
(201) 484-4141

ROSENTHAL U.S.A. LTD.
411 East 76th Street
New York, New York 10021
(212) 249-1400

Companies and Trade Names

ROSENVINGE (sports apparel)
See Imports International Inc.

ROSE'S (tonic water, bitter lemon, lime juice, etc.)
See Schwepps (USA), Ltd.

ROSES & MYRRH, INC.
51 Weaver Street
Greenwich, Connecticut 06830

ROSE'S STORES, INC.
218-220 Garnett Street
Henderson, North Carolina 27536
Lucius H. Harvin, President
(919) 438-6161

ROSETTE DOLL COMPANY
217 Jackson Street
Lawrence, Massachusetts 01841

ROSKO & ROSKO (canned foods)
See Old Ranchers Company

ROSLER (upright and grand pianos)
See Remeny House of Music Ltd.

ROSMAR MANUFACTURING COMPANY
1826 South Washtenaw
Chicago, Illinois 60608
(312) 762-4411

ROSOFF (food products)
See R & S Pickle Company Inc.

ROSS (bicycle)
See Chain Bike Corporation

ROSS (snowplows, etc.)
See The Burch Corporation

ROSS & COMPANY, MARK
3131 19th Street
San Francisco, California 94103
(415) 285-5500

ROSS APOLLO (bicycle)
See Chain Bike Corporation

ROSS ASSOCIATES, INC., ABBE
241 Normandy Road
Massapequa, New York 11590

ROSS BAKERIES, INC., BETSY
1325 Bluefield Avenue
Bluefield, West Virginia 24701

ROSS CHEMICAL & MANUFACTURING COMPANY
8459 Melville
Detroit, Michigan 48217
(313) 842-8200

ROSS COMPANY, FRANK B.
6-10 Ash Street
Jersey City, New Jersey 07304
Dorothy A. Siebert, President
(201) 433-4512

ROSS COMPANY SYDNEY
(Division of Sterling Drug, Inc.)
90 Park Avenue
New York, New York 10016
T.P. Serpa, President
(212) 972-4141

ROSS CORPORATION, ROBB
301 Wall
Sioux City, Iowa 51102

ROSS ENGINEERING MACHINERY
(Division of Midland-Ross Corporation)
Post Office Box 751
New Brunswick, New Jersey 08903
E.J. Kurie, Manager
(201) 356-6000

ROSS INDUSTRIES, INC.
Post Office Box 2152
Wichita, Kansas 67201
G.M. Ross, President
(316) 267-6281

ROSS LABORATORIES
(Division of Abbott Laboratories)
(Pharmaceuticals)
625 Cleveland
Columbus, Ohio 43216
(614) 228-5281

ROSS LABORATORIES, INC.
(Underwater electronic equipment)
3138 Fairview Avenue East
Seattle, Washington 98102
(206) 324-3950

ROSS-MATTHAI CORPORATION
2235 Sisson
Baltimore, Maryland 21211

ROSS PACKING COMPANY
Box 128
Selah, Washington 98942
K.E. Steinhilb, President
(509) 697-7233

ROSSELLA (fruits, tomato paste)
See Louis Metafora Company, Inc.

ROSSETT MANUFACTURING CORPORATION
740 Broadway
New York, New York 10003
(212) 777-2067

ROSSI (vermouth and wines)
See Renfield Importers, Ltd.

ROSSI QUALITY FOOD PRODUCTS, INC.
1775 Rohlwing Road
Rolling Meadows, Illinois 60008
Donald Rossi, President
(312) 956-8220

ROSSIGNOL SKI COMPANY
Industrial Road
Williston, Vermont 05495
Jean Pierre Rosso, President
(802) 863-2511

Companies and Trade Names

ROSSINI (coffee mugs, hibachis, salad bowls, ashtrays, dishes, etc.)
See Ross Products

ROSSKOPF (skis)
See Sport-Obermeyer Ltd. U.S.A.

ROSSLI (tobacco and cigars)
See Gesty Trading & Manufacturing Corporation

ROSZELL'S (dairy products)
See National Dairy Products Corporation

ROTAFLEX (lighting fixtures)
See The Heifetz Company Inc.

ROTARY BUSINESS FORMS INC.
590 Lane Avenue
Memphis, Tennessee 38102
(901) 523-0058

ROTARY PRINTING COMPANY
1950 Earle Street
Norwalk, Ohio 44857
(419) 668-4821

ROTH AMERICAN, INC.
200 Fifth Avenue
New York, New York 10010
(212) 741-2010

ROTH & LIEBMANN, INC.
401 Broadway
New York, New York 10013
(212) 925-2020

ROTH CLOTHES, LOUIS
1140 South Flower
Los Angeles, California 90015
H. Roth, President
(213) 749-6081

ROTH GREETING CARDS
7900 Deering Avenue
Canoga Park, California 91304

ROTH JOHNSON DRUG COMPANY
143 North Water Street
Decatur, Illinois 62523

ROTH LEATHER GOODS CORPORATION, MAX
583 Broadway
New York, New York 10012
(212) 431-6717

ROTHMANS (cigarettes)
See House of Edgeworth

ROTHSCHILD (Scotch and brandy)
See Paramount Distillers, Inc.

ROTHSCHILD BROTHERS INC.
1307 Washington
Saint Louis, Missouri 63103
(314) 231-8508

ROTHSCHILD CHATEAU (wines)
See Munson Shaw Company

ROTHSCHILD'S MEDICAL & SURGICAL SUPPLIES
805 East Genesee Street
Syracuse, New York 13210
(315) 475-5181

ROTHWELL-GATRELL FRUIT COMPANY
Charles Town Road
Martinsburg, West Virginia 25401

ROTO-BROIL CORPORATION OF AMERICA
29 Riverside Avenue
Newark, New Jersey 07104
Albert Klinghoffer, President
(201) 485-0300

ROTO-HOE & SPRAYER COMPANY
100 Auburn Road
Newbury, Ohio 44065
(216) 564-2294

ROTO-PHOTO COMPANY
2835 North Western Avenue
Chicago, Illinois 60618
(312) 235-7766

ROTO-ROOTER CORPORATION
300 Ashworth Road
West Des Moines, Iowa 50265
Henry G. Peterson, President
(515) 277-6251

ROTOR TOOL
(Division of Cooper Industries, Inc.)
26300 Lakeland Boulevard
Cleveland, Ohio 44132
F.X. Linsenmeyer, President
(216) 731-8888

ROUGH RIDER, INC.
2321 Oak Street
Napa, California 94558
Morton Rothman, President
(707) 224-7961

ROUGHWATER BOATS INC.
13442 Bali Way
Marina Del Rey, California 90291

ROUND THE CLOCK (fruit drinks)
See Hanover Brands, Inc.

ROUND-THE-CLOCK HOSIERY
(Pennaco - Division of United States Industries, Inc.)
350 Fifth Avenue
New York, New York 10001
Tom Good, President
(212) 279-8210

ROUNDUP (processed foods)
See Cudahy Company

ROUNDUP COMPANY
(Subsidiary of Fred Meyer, Inc.)
1212 Front Avenue
Spokane, Washington 99202
Virgil Campbell, President
(509) 534-0451

Companies and Trade Names

ROUNDY'S, INC.
11300 West Burleigh
Wauwatosa, Wisconsin 53201
Vincent R. Little, President
(414) 453-8200

ROUSANA COMPANY, INC., THE
195 Allwood Road
Clifton, New Jersey 07012

ROUSE PORCELAIN COMPANY
300 Third Street
Trenton, New Jersey 08611

ROUSSEL CORPORATION
155 East 44th Street
New York, New York 10017
(212) 697-5820

ROUX LABORATORIES, INC.
3733 University Avenue
Jacksonville, Florida 32207
Norman Kagan, President
(904) 731-3050

ROWE-DE ARMOND INC.
1702 Airport Highway
Toledo, Ohio 43609

ROWE FURNITURE CORPORATION
239 Rowan Street
Salem, Virginia 24153
D.E. Rowe, Jr., Chairman of the Board
(703) 389-8671

ROWE INTERNATIONAL, INC.
(Subsidiary of Triangle Industries, Inc.)
75 Troy Hills Road
Whippany, New Jersey 07981
D.J. Barton, President
(201) 887-0400

ROWE 'L-EZY (lawn edger/trimmer)
See Proen Products Company

ROWE MANUFACTURING COMPANY
614 West Third Street
Galesburg, Illinois 61401
(309) 342-4171

ROWE RIDE (mower and tiller)
See Jari Corporation

ROWELL LABORATORIES, INC.
Baudette, Minnesota 56623
Theodore H. Rowell, Jr., President and Treasurer
(218) 634-1866

ROWEN, INC.
1261 Fifth Avenue
New York, New York 10029
(212) 889-0441

ROWEX (exercise equipment)
See Battle Creek Equipment Company

ROWOCO INC.
111 Calvert Street
Harrison, New York 10528

ROWSE INC.
Wilton Road
Greenville, New Hampshire 03048
Paul E. Weamer, President
(603) 878-2100

ROXANNE SWIM SUITS COMPANY, INC.
(Division of Milady Brassiere & Corset Company, Inc.)
1411 Broadway
New York, New York 10018
Hyman Bernstein, President
(212) 679-8060

ROXBURY CARPET COMPANY
4900 Hooker Road
Chattanooga, Tennessee 37407

ROXEY (pet foods)
See Shurfine-Central Corporation

ROXHALL TIME CORPORATION
43 West 24th Street
New York, New York 10010
(212) 929-7103

ROXTER CORPORATION
10-11 40th Avenue
Long Island City, New York 11101
(212) 392-5060

ROY (appliances)
See White Consolidated Industries, Inc.

ROY J. MAIER (reed instruments)
See Rico Corporation

ROY LOGAN (shoes)
See Cannon Shoe Company

ROY ROGERS FAMILY RESTAURANTS INC.
(Subsidiary of Marriott Corporation)
5161 River Road
Washington, D.C. 20016
(202) 986-5364

ROYAL (baby carriages)
See Supreme Enterprises Ltd.

ROYAL (canned fish)
See Reede Seafood Company

ROYAL (canned fruits and vegetables)
See Oceana Canning Company

ROYAL (cigars)
See Consolidated Cigar Corporation

ROYAL (clarinets, drum sets)
See Empire Music Company Inc.

ROYAL (cookware)
See Hagemeyer Industries Inc.

Companies and Trade Names

ROYAL (cosmetics)
See Consolidated Royal Chemical Corporation

ROYAL (food products)
See Standard Brands, Inc.

ROYAL (golf balls)
See Uniroyal Inc.

ROYAL (lawn equipment)
See King O'Lawn Inc.

ROYAL (optical products)
See Royal Optical

ROYAL (soups)
See Royal Caterers

ROYAL (watches)
See Endura Time Corporation

ROYAL AGES (Scotch whiskey)
See Paddington Corporation

ROYAL ALASKAN (seafood)
See Pan-Alaska Fisheries, Inc.

ROYAL AMBER (beer)
See George Wiedermann Brewing Company, Inc.

ROYAL AMERICAN (whiskey)
See American Distilling Company Inc.

ROYAL AMERICAN CORPORATION
Box 543
Racine, Wisconsin 53401

ROYAL AMERICAN FOODS
See Hollister Canning Company

ROYAL APPLIANCE MANUFACTURING COMPANY
650 Alpha Drive
Highland Heights, Ohio 44143
(216) 449-6150

ROYAL ASCOT (gin)
See Old Boone Distillery Company

ROYAL AUTOLINE (hand tools and screwdrivers)
See Royal Merchandise Company

ROYAL BANQUET (Scotch whiskey)
See Gooderham & Worts, Ltd.

ROYAL BRAND (cutlery)
See National Silver Company

ROYAL BRASS CORPORATION
429 12th Street
Brooklyn, New York 11215
(212) 768-1500

ROYAL BUSINESS FORMS INC.
Simon Street
Nashua, New Hampshire 03060
W.W. Zechel, President, Chief Executive Officer and Treasurer
(603) 889-2192

ROYAL CASTLE SYSTEM, INC.
3800 62nd Street, N.W.
Miami, Florida 33147
C. Roberts Whitney, Chairman of the Board
(305) 887-8121

ROYAL CATERERS
2027 Sherman Street
Hollywood, Florida 33020

ROYAL CATHAY TRADING COMPANY
1301-1325 Folsom Street
San Francisco, California 94103
(415) 863-1466

ROYAL CHEF (cookware)
See Enterprise Aluminum Company

ROYAL CHEF (frozen foods)
See Stilwell Foods

ROYAL CHEF (seafood)
See Guilford Packing Company Inc.

ROYAL CHINA, INC.
(Subsidiary of Jeanette Corporation)
60 South 15th Street
Sebring, Ohio 44672
M. Silverburg, President
(216) 938-2155

ROYAL CHROME (housewares)
See V.C.A. Corporation, Federal Housewares Division

ROYAL CIRCLE (cigars)
See A.J. Golden Inc.

ROYAL CLUB (liquor)
See Schenley Industries, Inc.

ROYAL COPENHAGEN (men's toiletries)
See Swank Inc.

ROYAL COPENHAGEN PROCELAIN CORPORATION
8 Westchester Plaza
Elmsford, New York 10523

ROYAL CORD (tires)
See Uniroyal Inc.

ROYAL COURT (seafood)
See K & C Food Sales

ROYAL CROSS (food products)
See A. Giurlani & Brother

Companies and Trade Names

ROYAL CROWN (men's toiletries)
　See J. Strickland & Company

ROYAL CROWN COLA COMPANY
41 Perimeter Center East, N.E.
Atlanta, Georgia 30346
Donald A. MacMahon, President
(404) 394-6120

ROYAL CRYSTAL
47-02 Metropolitan Avenue
Maspeth
New York, New York 10001
(212) 366-9485

ROYAL CUP INC.
2401 North First Avenue
Birmingham, Alabama 35203

ROYAL CUSHION COMPANY INC.
71 Field Street
Brockton, Massachusetts 02401
(617) 586-2099

ROYAL-DELTA (cookware)
　See Hagemeyer Industries Inc.

ROYAL DOULTON TABLEWARES, LTD.
　See Doulton and Company, Inc.

ROYAL DRU (enamel and iron cookware)
　See The Pfaltzgraff Company

ROYAL DUTCH (pewter)
　See Blue Delft Company, Inc.

ROYAL DUTCH (pipes)
　See Riesco Manufacturing & Import Company

ROYAL FAMILY (linens)
　See Cannon Mills Company

ROYAL FARMS (canned foods)
　See Tabor City Foods, Inc.

ROYAL FASHION (curtains and bedspreads)
　See Robertson Factories, Inc.

ROYAL FOUNDATIONS, INC.
　See Wear Rite Brassiere Company

ROYAL GARNET (frozen foods)
　See United Flav-R-Pac Growers, Inc.

ROYAL GATE (vodka)
　See Haas Brothers

ROYAL GEM (food products)
　See Morgan Packing Company Inc.

ROYAL-GLOBE INSURANCE COMPANIES
150 William Street
New York, New York 10038
J. Roy Nicholas, President
(212) 732-8400

ROYAL GREENLAND (seafood)
　See Danland Seafood Corporation

ROYAL GUARD (men's socks)
　See Silver Knit Industries, Inc.

ROYAL GUEST (groceries)
　See Independent Grocers Alliance of America

ROYAL HAEGER LAMP COMPANY
(Division of The Haeger Potteries Inc.)
7 Maiden Lane
Dundee, Illinois 60118
Joseph F. Estes, President
(312) 926-3441

ROYAL HARVEST (canned and frozen vegetables)
　See Delta Food Processing Corporation

ROYAL HAWAIIAN MACADAMIA NUT COMPANY
(Division of Castle & Cooke, Inc.)
Box 2990
Honolulu, Hawaii 96813
William M. Hale, President
(808) 548-6611

ROYAL HOUSE FOOD PRODUCTS COMPANY
386 West Broadway
New York, New York 10012
(212) 966-2722

ROYAL IMPORTS, INC.
(Subsidiary of Jeannette Corporation)
41 Madison Avenue
New York, New York 10010
(212) 532-9181

ROYAL IMPRINTS CORPORATION
Ligonier Industrial Park
Ligonier, Indiana 46767

ROYAL INDEX TAB COMPANY
10 West Third Street
New York, New York 10012
(212) 254-7983

ROYAL INDUSTRIES
Tetrafluor Division
980 South Arroyo Parkway
Pasadena, California 91109
J.R. Johnson, President
(213) 681-1176
　See also Hinson; and Interstate

ROYAL INNS OF AMERICA, INC.
4855 North Harbor Drive
San Diego, California 92106
Harry Henke, III, President
(714) 224-8201

ROYAL INTERNATIONAL VITAMINS
(Division of Royal Vita-Ceuticals, Inc.)
45 Lispenard Street
New York, New York 10013
(212) 226-5817

Companies and Trade Names

ROYAL JAMAICA (cigars)
See Pan American Cigar Company

ROYAL JEFF (menswear)
See Lord Jeff Knitting Company Inc.

ROYAL LASSIE MILLS, LTD.
105-29 63rd Drive
Flushing, New York 11375

ROYAL LIGHTING (fixtures)
See DeSoto, Inc., Home Accessories Division

ROYAL LONDON LTD.
225 Fifth Avenue
New York, New York 10010
(212) 683-7323

ROYAL MAID, INC.
Post Office Drawer 30
Hazlehurst, Mississippi 39083
(601) 894-1771

ROYAL MANOR (canned goods)
See Loblaw Inc.

ROYAL MERCHANDISE COMPANY
(Division of Royal United Corporation)
13-15 131st Street
College Point, New York 11356

ROYAL NORSEMAN
1024 Commonwealth Avenue
Bristol, Virginia 24201

ROYAL OAK (wall-mount shelving systems)
See Kirsch Company

ROYAL OAKS (mobile home)
See Kit Manufacturing Company

ROYAL OPTICAL COMPANY INC.
748 Coleman Avenue
San Jose, California 95110
(408) 297-5616

ROYAL PAPER CORPORATION
210-216 11th Avenue
New York, New York 10001
Morton H. Baron, President and Treasurer
(212) 924-3400

ROYAL PAPER PRODUCTS INC.
Caln Road
Coatesville, Pennsylvania 19320
(215) 384-3400

ROYAL PASTEL MINK (furs)
See Emba Mink Breeders Association

ROYAL PERCUSSION (musical percussion instruments)
See Magnamusic-Baton Inc.

ROYAL PORT (wines)
See Barnes Wines, Ltd.

ROYAL PRIDE (apple products)
See Hallberg Canning Corporation

ROYAL PRINCE (bicycles)
See AMF, Inc.

ROYAL PRODUCTS
1516 Lake Street
Minneapolis, Minnesota 55408
(612) 724-7447

ROYAL PURPLE (canned and frozen foods)
See United Flav-R-Pac Growers, Inc.

ROYAL PURPLE (perfume, dusting powder, cologne)
See Herb Farm Shop, Ltd.

ROYAL RACER (sleds)
See Garton Company

ROYAL RED (seafood)
See North Pacific Processors Inc.

ROYAL REGIMENT (men's toiletries)
See Max Factor & Company

ROYAL RIVER PACKING COMPANY
(Division of Port Clyde Packing Company Inc.)
Box 237
Yarmouth, Maine 04096

ROYAL RIVIERA (pears)
See Harry and David, Inc.

ROYAL ROBES, INC.
16 East 34th Street
New York, New York 10016
Harry H. Greenberg, President
(212) 689-5410

ROYAL ROSE (canned vegetables)
See David Lord, Ltd.

ROYAL ROSE (gas ranges)
See J. Rose & Company Inc.

ROYAL RUBY (domestic glassware)
See Anchor Hocking Corporation

ROYAL SABLE LINE (carving and steak sets)
See W.R. Case & Sons Cutlery Company

ROYAL SAILBOATS COMPANY
4252 Oriole Lane
Daytona Beach, Florida 32019

ROYAL SCOT (bicycles)
See Stuyvesant Bicycle Company

ROYAL SCOT (tobacco)
See G.A. Georgopulo & Company

Companies and Trade Names

ROYAL SCOTT (motor oils)
See MacMillan Ring-Free Oil Company

ROYAL SCOTT (whiskey)
See Foriegn Vintages, Inc.

ROYAL SEAL (hand tools)
See Royal Merchandise Company

ROYAL SHERRY (wines)
See Barnes Wines, Ltd.

ROYAL SHIELD (hair-care products)
See J. Strickland & Company

ROYAL SILVER (men's toiletries)
See Cosmetco

ROYAL SILVER MANUFACTURING COMPANY INC.
3300 Chesapeake Boulevard
Norfolk, Virginia 23513
(804) 855-6004

ROYAL SNACK (food products)
See Vita Food Products Inc.

ROYAL-SOUDERS, INC.
520 Lonoke
Dayton, Ohio 45401
(513) 253-7461

ROYAL STAR (drums and accessories)
See Elger Company

ROYAL STATIONERY COMPANY
13010 County Road Six
Minneapolis, Minnesota 55441
Paul J. Sundberg, Jr., President
(612) 544-3671

ROYAL SUNDRIES CORPORATION
344 Broadway
New York, New York 10013
(212) 227-3352

ROYAL SUPREME (scissors and shears)
See National Silver Company

ROYAL SWEDISH (stainless flatware and holloware)
See Gense Import, Ltd.

ROYAL TELMAST (TV antennas)
See Lance Industries

ROYAL TIVOLI (tobacco)
See House of Edgeworth

ROYAL TYPEWRITER COMPANY
(Division of Litton Industries)
150 New Park Avenue
Hartford, Connecticut 06106
Ronald L. White, President
(203) 233-2621

ROYAL VALLEY (food products)
See Avon Foods Ltd.

ROYAL VIKING (lager beer)
See G. Heileman Brewing Company

ROYAL VODKA (liquor)
See Fleischmann Distilling Corporation

ROYAL WOOLYN (cold-water soap)
See Andrew Jergens Company

ROYAL WORCESTER PORCELAIN COMPANY, INC.
11 East 26th Street
New York, New York 10010
Raymond Zrike, President
(212) 683-7130

ROYALCHROME (metal furniture)
See Royalmetal Corporation

ROYALCOTE
See Masonite Corporation

ROYALE (cleaner wax)
See Morton-Norwich Products, Inc.

ROYALE (folding doors)
See American Accordion-Fold Doors, Inc.

ROYALE CREST (men's toiletries)
See Bourjois, Inc.

ROYALFLEX (rubber hose)
See Uniroyal Inc.

ROYALIST (cigars)
See Bayuk Cigars, Inc.

ROYALIST (infants' product)
See Strolee of California

ROYALITE (plastic products)
See Uniroyal, Inc.

ROYALMETAL CORPORATION
1 Park Avenue
New York, New York 10016
(212) 686-3500

ROYALSHIRE (luggage and portable bars)
See Ever Wear Inc.

ROYALTY HOUSE (foods)
See Robb-Ross Corporation

ROYALTY INDUSTRIES
601 West 27th Street
Hialeah, Florida 33010

ROYALWEVE (carpets)
See Mand Carpet Mills

Companies and Trade Names

ROYCE CHEMICAL COMPANY
17 Carlton Avenue
East Rutherford, New Jersey 07073
A.J. Royce, President
(201) 438-5200

ROYCE COMPANY
14603 Dorchester Avenue
Dolton, Illinois 60419

ROYDEN PRODUCTS
51 Seneca Street
Weedsport, New York 13166

ROYDON WEAR, INC.
(Subsidiary of Coordinated Apparel)
1409 East Oak Street
McRae, Georgia 31055
R.T. Lewis, President
(912) 868-6444

ROYFAX
(Division of Litton Industries Inc.)
150 New Park Avenue
Hartford, Connecticut 06106
(203) 523-0726

ROYKEN (sports accessories and equipment)
See Janoy Inc.

ROYLCRAFT (shelf paper, place mats, doilies)
See Standard Packaging Corporation

ROYLON, INC.
225 Fifth Avenue
New York, New York 10010
(212) 683-7323

ROYMAC (melamine products)
See Brookpark-Royalon, Inc.

ROYOX (household cleaner)
See Royce Chemical Company

ROYSON SHAVINOL, INC.
456 West Frontage Road
Northfield, Illinois 60093

ROYSTER COMPANY
Post Office Drawer 1940
Norfolk, Virginia 23510
Charles F. Burroughs, Jr., President
(804) 622-4783

ROYTEX, INC.
390 Fifth Avenue
New York, New York 10018
Milton Fried, President
(212) 695-3830

ROYTYPE
(Division of Litton Business Systems Inc.)
1031 New Britain Avenue
West Hartford, Connecticut 06110
E.W. Ferris, President
(203) 523-4881

RU-EX INC.
2453 University Avenue
Saint Paul, Minnesota 55114
(612) 646-1848

RU-LA SALES INC.
Box Five
Winston-Salem,
   North Carolina 27102

RUB-R-CLAD (masonry paint)
See Adelphi Paint & Color Works, Inc.

RUBBER FABRICATORS, INC.
(Subsidiary of B.F. Goodrich Company)
Commercial Avenue
Richwood, West Virginia 26261
Robert L. Schnurr, President
(304) 846-0231

RUBBER FABRICS COMPANY
270 Park Avenue South
New York, New York 10010
(212) 477-6610

RUBBER QUEEN (rubber housewares)
See Pretty Products, Inc.

RUBBER TOP (rug cushions)
See Allen Industries, Inc.

RUBBERMAID, INC.
1147 Akron Road
Wooster, Ohio 44691
Donald Noble, Chairman of the Board
(216) 264-6464

RUBBERSET COMPANY
(Division of The Sherwin-Williams Company)
Post Office Box 231
Crisfield, Maryland 21817
George Heidt, Jr., Vice President
(301) 968-1050

RUBEL & COMPANY
208 Fifth Avenue
New York, New York 10010
(212) 683-4400

RUBENS (brushes)
See M. Grumbacher, Inc.

RUBENS ORIGINALS
726 Santa Fe Avenue
Los Angeles, California 90021
(213) 627-9388

RUBENSTEIN FOODS, INC.
1111 Hall Street
Dallas, Texas 75204
M.D. Rubenstein, President
(214) 824-6261

RUBIN & SONS, J.M.
180 Madison Avenue
New York, New York 10016
(212) 683-3789

RUBIN GRAIS AND SONS, INC.
200 North Artesian Avenue
Chicago, Illinois 60612
Edward Grais, President
(312) 738-0606

Companies and Trade Names

RUBIN SONS, INC., J.
Box 188
Chicopee, Massachusetts 01014

RUBINOFF & COMPANY, H.
See Baker Brands

RUBINSTEIN, INC., HELENA
300 Park Avenue
New York, New York 10022
(212) 751-9100

RUBY (canned foods)
See A.L. Stewart & Sons

RUBY (erasers and indelible pencils)
See Eberhard Faber

RUBY BEE (preserves, jams, etc.)
See Beatrice Foods

RUBY KIST (canned foods)
See Clement Pappas & Company

RUCKER PHARMACAL COMPANY, INC.
Box 6200
6540 Line Avenue
Shreveport, Louisiana 71106
Johnny B. Rucker, Chairman and President
(318) 868-6562

RUDD MANUFACTURING COMPANY
3929 Cleveland Avenue
Saint Louis, Missouri 63110
Eugene Rudd, President
(314) 865-2339

RUDD-MELIKIAN, INC.
Warminster, Pennsylvania 18974

RUDDER (seafood)
See Blue Channel Corporation

RUDIN & ROTH, INC.
45 West 34th Street
New York, New York 10001
Sid Brodkin, President
(212) 695-5950

RUDIN NEEDLECRAFT, LTD.
45 West 34th Street
New York, New York 10001
(212) 947-8316

RUDSON-WOOD INC.
1133 Broadway
New York, New York 10010
(212) 675-1117

RUFFINO (Chianti wine)
See Schieffelin & Company

RUG CLEAN (aerosol rug cleaner)
See W.J. Hagerty & Sons, Ltd., Inc.

RUG CRAFTERS
3895 South Main
Santa Ana, California 92707

RUG GARD (rug shampoo)
See Flagship Products, Inc.

RUG HUGGER (canister vacuum cleaner)
See Regina Company

RUGBEE (cleaning agent)
See S.C. Johnson & Son

RUGER (pistols and revolvers)
See Sturm, Ruger & Company, Inc.

RUGG MANUFACTURING COMPANY
105 Newton Street
Greenfield, Massachusetts 01301
Allen D. Rugg, President
(413) 773-5471

RUGG, RUGG & JACKEL MUSIC COMPANY
Post Office Box 389
Felton, California 95018

RUGGED TOOLS (tools, lawn and garden supplies, etc.)
See S & R International Inc.

RUGGEDWEAR (floor resurfacer and patch)
See Flexrock Company

RUINART (champagne)
See Schieffelin & Company

RULE INDUSTRIES INC.
Cape Ann Industrial Park
Gloucester, Massachusetts 01930
(617) 281-0440

RULE PRODUCTS
175 Grist Mill Lane
Great Neck, New York 11023

RULO LEATHER ART COMPANY
(Division of Alpha Handbag Corporation)
615 West 131st Street
New York, New York 10027
(212) 286-6700

RULON (hosiery)
See Rudin & Roth, Inc.

RUM & MAPLE TOBACCO CORPORATION
See House of Edgeworth

RUM CARIOCA (rum)
See Schenley Industries, Inc.

RUM RIVER (cigars)
See House of Windsor

RUMBLE SEAT (stroller seats)
See Peterson Baby Products

Companies and Trade Names

RUMBO (cigarettes)
See G.A. Georgopulo & Company, Inc.

RUMEUR (fragrance)
See Lanvin-Charles of the Ritz, Inc.

RUMFORD (high-intensity lamp)
See Tensor Corporation

RUMFORD COMPANY, THE
900 Wabash Avenue
Terre Haute, Indiana 47801

RUNABOUT (portable televisions)
See Philco-Ford Corporation

RUNIN'S EMPIRE FOOD DISTRIBUTORS INC.
101 East Third
Mount Vernon, New York 10550

RUNNING GREETING CARD STUDIO
1020 Park Street
Paso Robles, California 93446

RUPP INDUSTRIES, INC.
1776 Airport Road
Mansfield, Ohio 44903
Edmund L. Fachtman, Jr., President
(419) 522-5732

RUSCO INDUSTRIES, INC.
Post Office Box 202
Northvale, New Jersey 07647
Jack Catain, Jr., President
(201) 767-8880

RUSCOE COMPANY, W.J.
483 Kenmore Boulevard
Akron, Ohio 44301
(216) 253-8148

RUSH INC., GRACE A.
3715 Madison Road
Cincinnati, Ohio 45209
(513) 871-4477

RUSHTON (canoe)
See Old Town Canoe Company

RUSHTON COMPANY, THE
1275 Ellsworth Industrial Drive
Atlanta, Georgia 30325
(404) 355-9220

RUSKETS (food product)
See Loma Linda Foods

RUSKIN (china pattern)
See Cumbow China Decorating Company

RUSKIN (cigars)
See Bayuk Cigars, Inc.

RUSS TOGS, INC.
1411 Broadway
New York, New York 10018
Louis E. Rousso, Chairman of the Board
(212) 695-2155
See also Kaufmann, R. & M.; and Youthcraft/Charmfit

RUSSELL, BURDSALL & WARD BOLT AND NUT COMPANY
Midland Avenue
Port Chester, New York 10573

RUSSELL CAPO INC., BILL
2130 Ferger Avenue
Fresno, California 93704

RUSSELL CORPORATION
Alexander City, Alabama 35010
Eugene C. Gwaltney, President
(205) 234-4251

RUSSELL CORPORATION, F.L.
Sterling Road
Mount Marion, New York 12456
(914) 246-4921

RUSSELL FISHERIES, INC.
6 Eastman Place
Melrose, Massachusetts 02176

RUSSELL HARRINGTON CUTLERY COMPANY
(Subsidiary of Hyde Manufacturing Company)
44 River
Southbridge, Massachusetts 01550
(617) 764-4371

RUSSELL HOSIERY MILLS, INC.
Russell Drive
Star, North Carolina 27356
Charles J. Russell, President
(919) 428-2131

RUSSELL MOCCASIN COMPANY, W.C.
285 S.W. Franklin
Berlin, Wisconsin 54923

RUSSELL-NEWMAN MANUFACTURING COMPANY, INC.
Post Office Box 2306
Denton, Texas 76201
Frank M. Martino, President
(817) 382-2531

RUSSELL STOVER CANDIES
1004 Baltimore Avenue
Kansas City, Missouri 64105
Louis L. Ward, President
(816) 842-9240

RUSSET FARMS (potato products)
See American Potato Company

RUSSKAYA (vodka)
See National Distillers & Chemical Corporation

RUSSKIT (scale-model racing cars)
See American Russkit Company

RUSSO BROTHERS UNDERWEAR COMPANY
580 Broadway
New York, New York 10012
(212) 226-5190

Companies and Trade Names

RUSSWOOD, INC.
4600 West Washington Boulevard
Los Angeles, California 90016
(213) 937-6134

RUST COMPANY, INC., FRANK
207 East Woodward Road
Englishtown, New Jersey 07726

RUST CRAFT GREETING CARDS, INC.
Rust Craft Park
Dedham, Massachusetts 02026
Marshall L. Berkman, President
(617) 325-9600
See also Greetings Inc.; Muench-Kreuzer Candle Company; and National Artcrafts Inc.

RUST CURE (automotive accessories)
See Kapro Corporation

RUST-ERASER (cleaner for rusted metals)
See Coricone Corporation

RUST JELLY (antirust product)
See Devcon Corporation

RUST MASTER SALES CORPORATION
Post Office Box 1269
Worcester, Massachusetts 01601
John F. Hampshire, President
(617) 753-4768

RUST-OLEUM CORPORATION
2301 Oakton Street
Evanston, Illinois 60204
Donald W. Fergusson, President
(312) 869-1100

RUST PATROL (rust remover)
See Dow Corning Corporation

RUST SALES COMPANY
East 61 Avenue and Franklin Street
Denver, Colorado 80210
Maurice A. Rust, President
(303) 287-3203

RUSTAIN PRODUCTS INC.
745 Midland Avenue
Fairlawn, New Jersey 07410

RUSTAKE (chain-link fencing with wood slats)
See Cyclone Fence Sales

RUSTIC (canned fruits and vegetables)
See Michigan Fruit Canners, Inc. Inc.

RUSTICANA (pipes)
See Winston Briar Pipe Manufacturing Company

RUSTY (canned pet foods)
See Hi-Vi Dog Food Company

RUTGERS UNIVERSITY PRESS
New Brunswick, New Jersey 08903

RUTH (cast-aluminum mailboxes)
See Gordon Associates Inc.

RUTH ANNE (hosiery)
See Kayser-Roth Hosiery Company, Inc.

RUTHERFORD FOOD CORPORATION
200 Grand
Kansas City, Missouri 64106
Bernice Rutherford Hanback, President and Treasurer
(816) 221-8433

RUTLAND FIRE CLAY COMPANY
Curtis Avenue
Rutland, Vermont 05701
Donald A. Perkins, President and Treasurer
(802) 775-5519

RUTLEDGE (stainless-steel flatware)
See Cosmos Products

RUXTON (playing cards)
See Arrco Playing Card Company

RUZA CREATIONS (leather goods)
See Elegant Leather Goods Inc.

RYDER SYSTEM, INC.
3600 N.W. 82nd Avenue
Miami, Florida 33166
Leslie O. Barnes, President
(305) 593-3726

RYEBROOK (whiskey)
See Heublein Inc.

RYKOFF & COMPANY, S.E.
761 Terminal Street
Los Angeles, California 90021
Roger W. Coleman, President
(213) 622-4131

RYKRISP (crackers)
See Ralston-Purina Company

RYSSIN COMPANY, J.W.
1489 Folsom Street
San Francisco, California 94103
(415) 626-0810

RYSTAN COMPANY, INC.
470 Mamaroneck Avenue
White Plains, New York 10605

RYTEX COMPANY, THE
432 North Capitol Avenue
Indianapolis, Indiana 46206
(317) 634-5588

Companies and Trade Names

S

S & A (insurance)
See State Mutual Life Assurance Company of America

S & B UNDERGARMENT COMPANY
513 Broadway Avenue
New York, New York 10012
(212) 966-3590

S & E CHEMICAL COMPANY
1847 West Carroll Avenue
Chicago, Illinois 60612
(312) 666-7171

S & F TOOL COMPANY
Box 1546
Costa Mesa, California 92626

S. & G. (silver plate)
See Kirk & Matz, Ltd.

S & H (trading stamps)
See Sperry & Hutchinson Company

S & M (tobacco)
See Liggett & Myers Inc.

S. & M. LABORATORIES CORPORATION
1025 Randolph
Oak Park, Illinois 60302

S & R INTERNATIONAL INC.
Box 1638
1501 Hertel Avenue
Buffalo, New York 14216
(716) 835-3016

S & R PUBLICATIONS
2430 20th Street N.W.
Washington, D.C. 20009

S. & S. BRUSH MANUFACTURING COMPANY
915 Broadway
New York, New York 10010
(212) 260-5959

S & S DRUG COMPANY
20-12 Seagirt Boulevard
Far Rockaway, New York 11691

S & S MANUFACTURING COMPANY INC.
Box 114
Elkhart, Indiana 46514

S. & S. PRODUCTS, INC.
West Grand Avenue
Lima, Ohio 45801
Robert I. Brown, President
(419) 225-5040

S & W FINE FOODS, INC.
1730 South El Camino Real
San Mateo, California 94402
Ian W. Murray, President
(415) 574-4200

S & W MOP COMPANY
East Railroad
Grantville, Georgia 30220

SAC CORPORATION
Post Office Box 916-T
2530 Morgan
Parsons, Kansas 67357
(316) 421-3100

S-B MANUFACTURING COMPANY, LTD.
11320 Watertown Plank Road
Milwaukee, Wisconsin 53226
Donald A. Schultz, Manager Partner
(414) 771-3500

SCM CORPORATION
299 Park Avenue
New York, New York 10017
Paul H. Elicker, President
(212) 752-2700
See also Allied Paper Inc.; Baltimore Copper Paint; Durkee Famous Foods; Gates Office Papers; Glidden-Durkee; Proctor-Silex, Inc.; and Shetland-Lewyt

SCOA INDUSTRIES, INC.
35 North Fourth Street
Columbus, Ohio 43215
Herbert H. Schiff, President
(614) 221-5421

S E R (groceries)
See S.E. Rykoff & Company

S-G (locks and security devices)
See Sargent & Greenleaf Inc.

SGA SCIENTIFIC INC.
735 Broad Street
Bloomfield, New Jersey 07003
William O. Geyer, President and Manager
(201) 748-6600

SI BRAND (insulating tape)
See Superior Insulating Tape Company

S.I.D. SCANDINAVIAN INTERIOR DESIGN, INC.
Box 643
Racine, Wisconsin 53401

SJC DESIGN
1816 Kansas Avenue
McKeesport, Pennsylvania 15131

S-K FORMS COMPANY
919 Walnut Street
Philadelphia, Pennsylvania 19107
(215) 627-0235

SK SUREKILL (insecticide)
See Mutual Products Company

S. K. TEAKWOOD (home and table accessories)
See The Holdings Inc.

Companies and Trade Names

S-K TOOLS
(Division of Dresser Industries, Inc.)
5725 N.E. River Road
Chicago, Illinois 60031
R.I. Allen, President
(312) 693-4320

SL SPRAY BOMBS (paints and paint sundries)
See State-Leed Distributors

S.L.C. CORPORATION
1711 Anaheim
Costa Mesa, California 92627

SLS (baby powder)
See St. Lawrence Starch Company, Ltd.

S.M.D. (weight-control preparations)
See Fleetwood Company

S.M.S. INDUSTRIES, INC.
Box 755
Highlands, Texas 77562

S.M.S. SALES COMPANY INC.
350 Fifth Avenue
New York, New York 10016
(212) 695-6188

S.O. ETTES (soap pads)
See Miles Laboratories Inc., Household Products Division

S.O.S. (first-aid spray)
See Columbia Medical Company

S.O.S. (scouring pads)
See Miles Laboratories, Inc., Household Products Division

SS (telephone intercoms)
See Fanon Electronics

S.S.A. ENTERPRISES
7304 East Adams
Paramount, California 90723

S S ARTIST MATERIALS, INC.
712 North State Street
Chicago, Illinois 60610
(312) 787-2005

S S C & B, INC.
1 Dag Hammerskjold Plaza
New York, New York 10017
Alfred J. Seaman, President
(212) 644-5000

SSI (trays and containers)
See Schaefer System International, Inc.

SSM CORPORATION
5050 Poplar Avenue
Memphis, Tennessee 38157
(901) 767-1131

S.S.P. EPICURE (pipes)
See S.S. Pierce Company

S. S. PIERCE COMPANY
141 Brookline Avenue
Boston, Massachusetts 02215
Robert F. Gammons, President
(617) 536-7600

S.S.S. COMPANY
71 University Avenue, S.W.
Atlanta, Georgia 30302
Lamar Swift, President
(404) 521-0857

SSS INTERNATIONAL (phonograph records)
See Shelby Singleton Corporation

STP CORPORATION
1400 West Commercial Boulevard
Fort Lauderdale, Florida 33310
Craig A. Nalen, President
(305) 771-1010

S/V TOOL COMPANY INC.
206 West Sixth
Newton, Kansas 67114

S-W (heating and cooling units)
See Typhoon Air Conditioning Company

SW INDUSTRIES, INC.
Rhode Island Hospital Trust Building
Providence, Rhode Island 02903
Thomas M. Leonard
(401) 272-7000

SWB COMPANY, INC.
28 Cedar Street
Canton, Massachusetts 02021

S.W.T. (sleeping aid)
See Ray Drug Company

SAAB-SCANIA OF AMERICA, INC.
Saab Drive
Orange, Connecticut 06477
Jonas C. Kjellberg, President
(203) 795-5671

SAAD, ISAAC
22 West 48th Street
New York, New York 10036
(212) 575-8975

SAALFIELD PUBLISHING COMPANY
Saalfield Square
Akron, Ohio 44301
Henry R. Saalfield, President
(216) 434-3451

SAARINOX (stainless cookware)
See King Housewares Inc.

SABA PHARMACAL PRODUCTS
Box 4273
Santa Barbara, California 93103

SABATIER (knives)
See Rowoco Inc.

Companies and Trade Names

SABENA BELGIAN WORLD
  AIRLINES
125 Community Drive
Great Neck, New York 11021
Pierre Dils, Vice President
(516) 466-6100

SABER (motors)
  See The Louis Allis Company

SABLE SERIES (desks and modular groups)
  See Anderson Desk Manufacturing Company

SABRA (women's shoes)
  See Simora Shoe Company Inc.

SABRE (portable typewriters)
  See Royal Typewriter Company

SABRE SAW CHAIN INC.
Box 272
La Salle Station
Niagara Falls, New York 14304

SABROSO COMPANY
Box 129
Medford, Oregon 97501

SAC CORPORATION
2530 Morgan
Parsons, Kansas 67357

SACCONI (musical-instrument rosin, peg compound, shoulder pads, tailpiece adjusters)
  See R.W. Service & Supplies Inc.

SACHS LABORATORIES, DR.
(Division of Garon Inc.)
2232 South Pulaski Road
Chicago, Illinois 60623
(312) 521-2232

SACHS NEW YORK, INC.
330 Bruckner Boulevard
Bronx, New York 10454
Richard C. Sachs, President
(212) 635-5300

SACONY (sportswear, foundations for women)
  See S. Augstein & Company

SACRAMENTO FOODS
(Division of Borden, Inc.)
Post Office Box 2470
North Seventh and Richards Boulevard)
Sacramento, California 95811
Thomas H. Richards, Jr., President
(916) 441-1241

SACRAMENTO PHARMACAL
  COMPANY
Box 4548
South Lake Tahoe, California 95705

SACRO-EASE (seat pad)
  See McCarty's Sacro-Ease

SADDLE BACKS (slacks for men and boys)
  See Chadbourn, Inc.

SADDLE CLUB (men's furnishings)
  See Knothe Brothers Company Inc.

SADDLE SEAT (infants' product)
  See Westland Plastics Inc.

SADEK IMPORT COMPANY, CHARLES
225 Fifth Avenue
New York, New York 10010
(212) 679-8121

SAENGER COMPANY INC., MARCEL
113-14 72nd Road
Forest Hills, New York 11375
(212) 263-4474

SAF-AIRE (heaters)
  See South Wind (Division of Stewart-Warner Corporation)

SAF-T-CUSHION (rubber floor mats)
  See Flexi-Mat Corporation

SAF-T-CUT (abrasive products)
  See Bay State Abrasives

SAF-T-GUARD (entrance mats)
  See National Floor Products Company

SAF-T-NEE (boys' clothing)
  See Hortex Inc.

SAF-T-NOB (infant safety device)
  See Reed Industries Inc.

SAF-T-SAW (saws)
  See Spartan Saw Works Inc.

SAF-TE (paint remover)
  See Wilson-Imperial Company

SAFA (sports apparel)
  See A & T Ski Company

SAFARI (all-terrain vehicle)
  See Air-Lec Industries

SAFARI (first-aid kits)
  See Acme Cotton Products Company, Inc.

SAFARI (portable typewriter)
  See Royal Typewriter Company

SAFCO (automotive accessories)
  See A.G. Busch & Company Inc.

SAFCO (fruits)
  See Interamerican Fruit & Produce Corporation

1176

Companies and Trade Names

SAFCO PRODUCTS COMPANY
7425 Laurel Avenue South
Golden Valley, Minnesota 55426

SAFE (drain cleaner)
　See Circle Research Laboratories

SAFE FLIGHT INSTRUMENT
　CORPORATION
Box 550
White Plains, New York 10602
Leonard M. Greene, President
(914) 946-9500

SAFE-MADE (wood folding
furniture and porch gates, etc.)
　See C.J. Johnson Company

SAFE TM (oven cleaner)
　See Circle Research Laboratories,
　　Inc.

SAFE-T-PLAY (safety sports
equipment)
　See Cosom (Division of ITT
　　Thermotech)

SAFE-T-SEAT (car seats)
　See Peterson Baby Products
　　Company

SAFECO INSURANCE COMPANY
　OF AMERICA
Safeco Plaza
Seattle, Washington 98185
Gordon H. Sweany, President
(206) 545-5000

SAFEDGE (glassware)
　See Owens-Illinois Inc.

SAFEGARD CORPORATION, THE
315 East 15th Street
Covington, Kentucky 41011
(606) 431-7650

SAFEGUARD (soap)
　See Procter & Gamble Company

SAFEGUARD (wet mop)
　See Bouras Mop Manufacturing
　　Company

SAFELOCK (juvenile product)
　See Mapes Industries Inc.

SAFELON CORPORATION
167 Sawmill River Road
Yonkers, New York 10701
Ernest Eckstein, Chairman and
　President
(914) 423-4000

SAFETECH (saws)
　See Stanadyne/Capewell

SAFETY BRAKER (automotive safety
device)
　See Sem Products Inc.

SAFETY ENVELOPE
　MANUFACTURING COMPANY
709 West Juneau Avenue
Milwaukee, Wisconsin 53201
(414) 276-3663

SAFETY FIRST SHOES INC.
Ninth and Greenleaf
Allentown, Pennsylvania 18105

SAFETY-FLARE (automotive
accessories)
　See A.G. Busch & Company
　　Inc.

SAFETY LABORATORIES, INC.
220 N.E. 68th Street
Miami, Florida 33138
(305) 758-2571

SAFETY PACKAGING
　CORPORATION
66 DeForest Avenue
Hanover, New Jersey 07936

SAFETY-PEN (infants' product)
　See Stacy Manufacturing
　　Company Inc.

SAFETY ROLL (can opener)
　See Vaughan Manufacturing
　　Company

SAFETY-SEALED (home and wall
heaters)
　See South Wind (Division of
　　Stewart-Warner Corporation)

SAFETY SHELL (juvenile product)
　See Peterson Baby Products

SAFETY TENDER (chairs)
　See Wear-Ever Baby Carriage
　　Company, Inc.

SAFEWAY STORES, INC.
Fourth and Jackson Streets
Oakland, California 94604
W.S. Mitchell, President
(415) 444-4711

SAFF-O-LIFE (safflower oil)
　See General Mills, Inc.

SAFFOLA (margarine, mayonnaise,
salad and cooking oil)
　See Pacific Vegetable Oil
　　Corporation, Edible Oils
　　Division

SAFIE BROTHERS PICKLE COMPANY
52365 North Gratiot
New Baltimore, Michigan 48047

SAFRAN & GLUCKSMAN INC.
8 West 30th Street
New York, New York 10001
Benjamin P. Safran, President and
　Treasurer
(212) 684-6434

SAFTIPREME (tires)
　See Hercules Tire & Rubber
　　Company

SAGA (watches)
　See The United States Time
　　Corporation

Companies and Trade Names

SAGA INC.
Post Office Box 4267
Albuquerque, New Mexico 87106

SAGA-MOC (men's footwear)
See L.B. Evans' Son Company

SAGE-ALLEN & COMPANY, INC.
900 Main Street
Hartford, Connecticut 06103
Lafayette Keeney, President
(203) 278-2570

SAGE COMPANY, EDWIN R.
60 Church
Cambridge, Massachusetts 02138

SAGE LABORATORIES, INC.
3 Huron Drive
Natick, Massachusetts 01760
Theodore Saad, Chairman and
 President
(617) 653-0844

SAGEBRUSH (carpeting)
See Magee Carpet Company

SAGER BROTHERS
133 West 24th Street
New York, New York 10011
(212) 243-2464

SAGINAW FURNITURE SHOPS,
 INC.
7300 Lehigh Avenue
Chicago, Illinois 60648
V. Gagliano, General Manager
(312) 775-0747

SAGNER, INC.
Sagner Avenue
Frederick, Maryland 21701
Arnold Sagner, President
(301) 662-1000

SAHADI & COMPANY, INC., A.
200 Carol Place
Moonachie, New Jersey 07074

SAHARA (men's footwear)
See L.B. Evans' Son Company

SAHARA (portable typewriter)
See Royal Typewriter Company

SAHARA-NEVADA CORPORATION
Post Office Box 14066
2535 Las Vegas Boulevard South
Las Vegas, Nevada 89114
(702) 735-2111

SAHLEIN MUSIC COMPANY,
 J.M.
1174 Howard Street
San Francisco, California 94103
(415) 621-0626

SAIL-FAST INC.
337 Water Street
Warren, Rhode Island 02885

SAIL LOFT, THE
302 1/2 Seminole Street
Clearwater, Florida 33515

SAIL MANUFACTURING
(Division of MFG Boat Company)
55 Fourth Avenue
Union City, Pennsylvania 16438

SAIL 'N SKI (boating jackets,
water-ski belts)
See Texas Water Crafters

SAIL RESEARCH ASSOCIATES
26410 Birchfield Avenue
Palos Verdes Peninsula,
 California 90274

SAILBOATS & FITTINGS INC.
Box 6595
Richmond, Virginia 23230
(804) 321-6106

SAILING TECHNOLOGY
 COMPANY
Box 20352
San Diego, California 92120

SAILMASTER (outboard motors)
See Intermarine Agency

SAILRITE KITS
2010 Lincoln Boulevard
Venice, California 90291

SAINBERG & COMPANY INC.
18 West 18th Street
New York, New York 10011
(212) 924-4310

ST. BRUNO (tobacco)
See American Tobacco Company

ST. CHARLES (brandy)
See James B. Beam Distilling
 Company

ST. CHARLES (cigars)
See Garcia y Vega, Inc.
 (Division of Bayuk Cigars
 Inc.)

ST. CHARLES (coffee)
See American Coffee Company,
 Inc.

ST. CHARLES (food products)
See Hi-Country Processors

ST. CHARLES MANUFACTURING
 COMPANY
1611 East Main Street
Saint Charles, Illinois 60174
R.A. MacNeille, President
(312) 584-3800

ST. CLAIR MANUFACTURING
 CORPORATION
120 25th Avenue
Bellwood, Illinois 60104
E.C. Friesendorf, Chairman and
 President
(312) 547-7500

ST. CROIX (food products)
See Friday Canning Corporation

Companies and Trade Names

ST. CROIX CORPORATION
9909 South Shore Drive
Minneapolis, Minnesota 55441
(612) 544-9161

ST. ETIENNE (sports apparel)
See Gondola Internationale, Inc.

ST. IVES (men's clothes)
See Phoenix Clothes, Inc.

ST. JAMES (pipes)
See Comoy's of London

ST. JAMES (scotch whiskey)
See Buckingham Corporation

ST. JAMES RHUM (rum)
See Dreyfus, Ashby & Company

ST. JOE VALLEY (food products)
See Ralph Sechler & Son Inc.

ST. JOHNS (men's toiletries)
See DuBarry

ST. JOSEPH (aspirin, epsom salt, nose drops, vitamins, etc.)
See Plough Inc.

ST. JOHNSBURY TRUCKING COMPANY
38 Main Street
Saint Johnsbury, Vermont 05819
Martin N. Zabarsky, President
(802) 748-8131

ST. LAURENT (Canadian whiskey)
See Old Boone Distillery Company

ST. LAURENT BROTHERS, INC.
1101 North Water Street
Bay City, Michigan 48706

ST. LOUIS CRAYON & HANDLE COMPANY
9420 Watson Industrial Park
Saint Louis, Missouri 63126
(314) 962-7273

ST. LOUIS HARDWARE MANUFACTURING COMPANY
10230 Page Industrial Boulevard
Saint Louis, Missouri 63132
(314) 427-7922

ST. LOUIS MUSIC SUPPLY COMPANY
1400 Ferguson Avenue
Saint Louis, Missouri 63133
(314) 727-4512

ST. LOUIS PENCIL COMPANY
1881 South Hanley Road
Saint Louis, Missouri 63144
(314) 645-7444

ST. LOUIS-SAN FRANCISCO RAILWAY
906 Olive Street
Saint Louis, Missouri 63101
R.C. Grayson, President
(314) 241-7800

ST. MARTINS (preserves)
See International Marketing Services, Inc.

ST. MARYS (woolens, blankets)
See Fieldcrest Mills, Inc.

ST. MORITZ (binoculars)
See Manhattan Novelty Corporation

ST. MORITZ (ski equipment)
See Anderson & Thompson Ski Company

ST. MORITZ (cigarettes)
See House of Edgeworth

ST. PAUL COMPANIES
385 Washington Street
Saint Paul, Minnesota 55102
C.B. Drake, Jr., President
(612) 221-7911

ST. PIERRE & PATTERSON MANUFACTURING COMPANY
234 Victoria Street
Costa Mesa, California 92627

ST. RAPHAEL (aperitif wine)
See Renfield Importers Ltd.

ST. REGIS PAPER COMPANY
150 East 42nd Street
New York, New York 10017
William R. Haselton, President
(212) 697-4400

ST. REGIS PAPER COMPANY
Consumer Products Division
Box 1107
Marion, Indiana 46952

ST. REGIS PAPER COMPANY
Laminated & Coated Products Division
Attleboro, Massachusetts 02703

ST. REGIS PAPER COMPANY
Wire Tie Division
2910 East 75th Street
Cleveland, Ohio 44104
(216) 271-4700

ST. REMY (brandy)
See Renfield Importers, Ltd.

ST. THOMAS, INC.
Saint Thomas Place
Gloversville, New York 12078
James W. St. Thomas, President
(518) 454-3115

STE. MICHELLE (wines)
See American Wine Growers

Companies and Trade Names

SAKAI TRADING NEW YORK INC.
417 Fifth Avenue
New York, New York 10016
(212) 683-1840

SAKRETE, INC.
Post Office Box 17087
Saint Bernard Station
Cincinnati, Ohio 45217
Arthur C. Avril, President
(513) 242-3644

SAKS FIFTH AVENUE
(Division of Gimbel Brothers, Inc.)
611 Fifth Avenue
New York, New York 10022
Allan R. Johnson, Chairman of the
  Board
(212) 421-2000

SAKURA (guitars)
  See Midwest Musical Instrument
  Company

SAL-COH PRODUCTS COMPANY
Box 6706
Clearlake Highlands,
  California 95422

SAL HEPATICA (laxative)
  See Bristol-Myers Company

SALAD BOWL (salad dressing)
  See Kraft Foods

SALAD-MAID (food cutter)
  See Foodco Appliance
  Corporation

SALAD QUEEN (food products)
  See Piknik Products Company

SALAD-WARE (bowls, forks, and
spoons)
  See Gitsware Corporation

SALADA FOODS, INC.
(Subsidiary of Kellogg Company)
10 New England Executive Park
Burlington, Massachusetts 01801
W.M. Wilbur, President
(617) 273-2180

SALADMASTER CORPORATION
131 Howell
Dallas, Texas 75207
Gilbert Flocker, President
(214) 747-4238

SALAMANCA HERB SALVE
545 Center Street
Salamanca, New York 14779

SALAMANDER (shoes)
  See Anre Inc.

SALANT CORPORATION
330 Fifth Avenue
New York, New York 10001
Joseph Lipshie, Chairman of the
  Board
(212) 594-9700

SALASNEK FISHERIES, INC.
2140 Wilkins Street
Detroit, Michigan 48207
(313) 961-6066

SALEM (cigarettes)
  See R.J. Reynolds Tobacco
  Company

SALEM CARPET MILLS, INC.
I-40 at Linville Road
Winston-Salem,
  North Carolina 27101
W. Douglas Foster, President
(919) 784-9280

SALEM CASUALS (handbags)
  See Dorle Handbags

SALEM CHINA COMPANY, THE
Box 110
Salem, Ohio 44460
J. Harrison Keller, President
(216) 332-4655

SALEM CLOCK COMPANY, INC.
12 Jefferson Avenue
West Hartford, Connecticut 06110
(203) 523-1921

SALEM COMPANY
1539 Waughtown Street
Winston-Salem,
  North Carolina 27107
Richard Steele, President
(919) 788-4901

SALEM FRUIT GROWERS
  COOPERATIVE ASSOCIATION
Box Three
Greenford, Ohio 44422

SALEM, INC., K.T.
325 West Bowery
Akron, Ohio 44307

SALEM LABS, INC.
215 Avery Avenue
Morganton, North Carolina 28655

SALEM PHARMACAL
Box 125
Naugatuck, Connecticut 06770

SALEM TOOL COMPANY, THE
767 South Elsworth Avenue
Salem, Ohio 44460
James H. Wilson, Jr., Treasurer
(216) 337-3416

SALEM'S OLD FASHIONED
  CANDIES, INC.
93 Canal Street
Salem, Massachusetts 01970

Companies and Trade Names

SALERNO-MEGOWEN BISCUIT COMPANY
7777 North Caldwell Avenue
Chicago, Illinois 60648
Charles L. Sullivan, President
(312) 967-6200

SALES AND DEVELOPMENT CORPORATION
105 Marigold Street
Rocky Mount, North Carolina 27801

SALES PRODUCERS ASSOCIATES
603 South Front Street
Memphis, Tennessee 38102
(903) 526-1409

SALICE (sports accessories)
See Vener Associates Inc.

SALIENT FLAVORING CORPORATION
48-25 Metropolitan Avenue
Brooklyn, New York 11237
(212) 386-0302

SALIGNAC (cognac)
See Park, Benziger & Company, Inc.

SALINA COFFEE HOUSE INC.
113 North Seventh Street
Salina, Kansas 67401

SALINAS VALLEY WAX PAPER COMPANY
Box 68
1111 Abbott Street
Salinas, California 93901
(408) 424-2747

SALING MANUFACTURING COMPANY
440 Framington Avenue
Unionville, Connecticut 06085
(203) 673-5752

SALINITRO LABORATORIES
58 East Gate
Manhasset, New York 11030

SALISBURY & COMPANY, W.H.
7520 North Long Avenue
Skokie, Illinois 60076
William H. Salisbury, President
(312) 679-6700

SALISBURY ARTISANS, INC.
Box 424
Salisbury, Connecticut 06068

SALK, INC., MURRAY
119 Braintree
Boston, Massachusetts 02134
(617) 782-4030

SALLMANN (sports apparel)
See Max Hurni Importer Inc.

SALLY HANSEN (cuticle remover, lip gloss, etc.)
See Del Laboratories

SALLY STITCH (dress form)
See Harrison-Hoge Industries Inc.

SALLY'S (groceries)
See Lewis Grocer Company

SALM-HARLEY CORPORATION
1169 Eagan Industrial Road
Saint Paul, Minnesota 55121
(612) 454-6900

SALMANSON COMPANY
215 Lexington Avenue
New York, New York 10016
(212) 689-3030

SALMON DERBY (seafoods)
See New England Fish Company

SALOMON (ski equipment)
See Anderson & Thompson Ski Company

SALOMON & BROTHER, INC., L.A.
14 Vandeventer Avenue
Port Washington, New York 11050
(516) 883-6100

SALOMON & SON, INC., M.W.
1140 Saint Charles Avenue
New Orleans, Louisiana 70130
(504) 525-6154

SALOMON/NORTH AMERICA INC.
7 Dearborn Road
Peabody, Massachusetts 01960

SALON FINISH (hair-care products)
See John H. Breck, Inc.

SALON FORMULA (wig-care products)
See House of Style

SALSBURY LABORATORIES
500 Gilbert Street
Charles City, Iowa 50616
(515) 257-2422

SALTERINI-GALLO
2605 East Kilgore Road
Kalamazoo, Michigan 49003
Howard W. Kosier, President
(616) 349-1521

SALTON, INC.
1260 Zerega Avenue
Bronx, New York 10462
Lewis L. Salton, President
(212) 931-3900

SALTY BAY (frozen seafood)
See Old Salt Seafoods, Inc.

SALUTE (soft drink)
See Dr. Pepper Company

Companies and Trade Names

SALUTI INTERNATIONAL LTD.
119 West 40th Street
New York, New York 10018
(212) 354-1300

SALVAJOR COMPANY, THE
4530 East 75th Terrace
Kansas City, Missouri 64132
(816) 363-1030

SALVATORE'S (food products)
See Silver State Foods Inc.

SALVATORI
(Division of Genesco)
440 Englewood Avenue S.W.
Atlanta, Georgia 30315
(404) 622-9331

SALVO (detergents)
See Procter & Gamble Company

SAM CLAY (whiskey)
See J.T.S. Brown Distillers Company

SAM THOMPSON (whiskey)
See Schenley Industries, Inc.

SAMBO'S RESTAURANTS, INC.
3760 State Street
Santa Barbara, California 93105
Wayne G. Kees, President
(805) 687-6777

SAMCO SPORTSWEAR INC.
211 East Fourth Street
Saint Paul, Minnesota 55101
(612) 226-2775

SAMET & WELLS INC.
1725 West Farms Road
Bronx, New York 10460
(212) 329-7160

SAMMANN COMPANY, INC.
704 West Ninth Street
Michigan City, Indiana 46360

SAMOA (outdoor light)
See Swivelier Company, Inc.

SAMOCA (cameras)
See Scopus (Division of Beskey Photo)

SAMOVAR (Vodka)
See Boaka Kompaniya

SAMPCO INC.
221 North LaSalle Street
Chicago, Illinois 60601
(312) 346-1506

SAMPSON COMPANY, LTD., BARNEY
40 West 57th Street
New York, New York 10019
(212) 541-5420

SAM'S (dressings and seasonings)
See Werner Food Specialties

SAMS & COMPANY, HOWARD W.
(Subsidiary of International Telephone & Telegraph Corporation)
4300 West 62nd Street
Indianapolis, Indiana 46268
Stanley S. Sills, President
(317) 291-3100
See also Bobbs-Merrill Company

SAMSILL BROTHERS PLASTIC CORPORATION
Post Office Box 15066
Glencrest Station
Fort Worth, Texas 76119
(817) 536-1906

SAMSON (paint)
See Luminall Paints, Inc.

SAMSON (planters)
See Reliable Glassware & Pottery Company, Inc.

SAMSON CORDAGE WORKS
470 Atlantic Avenue
Boston, Massachusetts 02210
Jerry J. Jones, President
(617) 426-6550

SAMSONITE CORPORATION
(Division of Beatrice Foods)
11200 East 45th Avenue
Denver, Colorado 80217
Richard W. Hanselman, President
(303) 344-2000

SAMUELS DISTILLERY, T.W.
Deatsville, Kentucky 40016
S.L. Westerman, President
(502) 348-3951

SAMUELS PRODUCTS INC.
3929 Virginia Avenue
Cincinnati, Ohio 45227
(513) 271-4545

SAMUELS SHOE COMPANY
(Division of Brown Group)
4940 Northrup Avenue
Saint Louis, Missouri 63110
Edward R. Samuels, President
(314) 865-1966

SAMURAI (cutlery)
See Albert Kessler & Company

SAMURI (seafoods)
See Arista Industries Inc.

SAN ANTONIO FOREIGN TRADING COMPANY
84 NE Loop 410
San Antonio, Texas 78216
(512) 349-2453

SAN BENITO (food products)
See Hollister Canning Company

Companies and Trade Names

SAN DIEGO GAS & ELECTRIC
   COMPANY
101 Ash Street
San Diego, California   92112
Walter A. Zitlau, President
(714) 232-4252

SAN DIEGO TRUST & SAVINGS
   BANK
(Subsidiary of San Diego Financial
   Corporation)
540 Broadway
San Diego, California   92101
Thomas W. Sefton, President
(714) 235-5151

SAN FELIPE (wines)
   See Excelsior Wine & Spirits
   Corporation

SAN GABRIEL (wines, brandies,
etc.)
   See Cucamonga Vineyard
   Company

SAN GIORGIO (rainwear for men)
   See Bill & Caldwell, Inc.

SAN GIORGIO (sports accessories
and equipment)
   See Cortina Ski Company Inc.

SAN GIORGIO MACARONI, INC.
(Subsidiary of Hershey Foods
   Corporation)
Eighth and Water Streets
Lebanon, Pennsylvania   17042
Joseph P. Viviano, President
(717) 273-7641
   See also Giovanni Foods

SAN HYGENE FURNITURE
   MANUFACTURING COMPANY
   See Schubert Industries, Inc.

SAN JUAN (frozen and canned
seafoods)
   See New England Fish Company

SAN JUAN ISLANDS CANNERY
Box 459
La Conner, Washington   98257

SAN JUAN PACKERS, INC.
Box 487
Bellingham, Washington   98225
   See also Everson Canning
   Company

SAN LAU (cushions and pillows)
   See George Koch Sons, Inc.

SAN-MAN (sleeping aid)
   See Plough, Inc.

SAN MARCO (ski boots)
   See Sport-Obermeyer Ltd., USA

SAN MARTIN VINEYARDS
   CORPORATION
Post Office Box 53
San Martin, California   95046
Fred A. Lico, President
(408) 683-2672

SAN MATIAS (Tequila)
   See Clan Importers, Inc.

SAN NICOLA (food products)
   See Stanislaus Food Products
   Company

SAN PAOLO (chianti wine)
   See Park, Benziger & Company,
   Inc.

SAN PEDRO LABORATORIES
110 North Medina
San Antonio, Texas   78207
(512) 226-6051

SAN SOUCI (cigars)
   See Perfecto Garcia & Brothers,
   Inc.

SAN TELMO CIGAR COMPANY
(Division of B & M Tobacco
   Company)
723 South Madison Avenue
Bay City, Michigan   48706

SANABALM COMPANY
4923 North Darrah Street
Philadelphia, Pennsylvania   19124
(215) 744-2742

SANALAC (instant nonfat dry milk)
   See Sanna, Inc.

SANCHEZ (guitars)
   See Buegeleisen & Jacobson Ltd.

SANDALSTONE COMPANY, THE
Box 703
Wheaton, Illinois   60187

SANDCASTLE SWIMWEAR
(Division of Kayser-Roth Corporation)
110 East Ninth Street
Los Angeles, California   90015
James B. Garkie, President
(213) 623-6219

SANDELL COMPANY, THE
Post Office Box 1887
Wilmington, Delaware   19899

SANDEMAN (port and sherry wines)
   See W.A. Taylor & Company

SANDERS MANUFACTURING
   COMPANY
Sanders Block
Nashville, Tennessee   37201
(615) 254-6611

SANDERSON FARMS, INC.
208 Beacon Street
Laurel, Mississippi   39440
D.R. Sanderson, Sr., President
(601) 649-4030

Companies and Trade Names

SANDEY COMPANY
496 Teaneck Road
Ridgefield Park, New Jersey 07660

SANDIA PHARMACEUTICALS INC.
2329 Wisconsin Avenue N.E.
Suite K
Albuquerque, New Mexico 87110

SANDLER COMPANY, A.
New England Industrial Center
Needham Heights,
 Massachusetts 02194
Joseph Bloom, President
(617) 444-5500

SANDMAN MOTELS, INC.
2082 Business Center Drive
Irvine, California 92664

SANDOZ INC.
59 State Highway Ten
East Hanover, New Jersey 07936
Dr. A. Frey, President
(201) 386-1000
 See also Delmark Company;
  and Dorsey Laboratories

SANDOZ PHARMACEUTICALS
(Division of Sandoz Inc.)
59 State Highway Ten
East Hanover, New Jersey 07936
(201) 386-1000

SANDRITE (paintbrushes)
 See American Brush Company,
  Inc.

SANDS, TAYLOR & WOOD
 COMPANY
130 Fawcett
Cambridge, Massachusetts 02138
Frank E. Sands, II, President and
 Treasurer
(617) 876-8422

SANDSTONE CREATIONS INC.
Post Office Box 4103
Mesa, Arizona 85201

SANDUNES (men's footwear)
 See Kayser-Roth Shoes Inc.

SANDVIK STEEL INC.
1702 Nevins Road
Fair Lawn, New Jersey 07410
Peter Wickmertz, President and
 Treasurer
(201) 797-6200

SANDWICH-MASTER (fast-food
franchise)
 See Stand 'n Snack of America
  Inc.

SANDWOOD (kitchen and hostess
accessories)
 See National Silver Company

SANDY MAC DONALD (Scotch)
 See American Distilling
  Company, Inc.

SANDY MCGEE (men's and boys'
shoes)
 See Genesco Inc.

SANDY MCGLEEM (paint)
 See Baltimore Paint and
  Chemical Corporation

SANDY SCOT (Scotch)
 See Federal Distillers, Inc.

SANDY SUE (fruit)
 See Idaho Fruit Sales Inc.

SANEK (barber and beauty products)
 See Kimberly-Clark Corporation

SANFLIPPO & SON, JOHN B.
300 East Touhy
Des Plaines, Illinois 60018
(312) 298-1510

SANFORD CORPORATION
2740 Washington Boulevard
Bellwood, Illinois 60104
Charles W. Lofgren, President
(312) 378-4814

SANGAMON COMPANY
Rural Route Four
Taylorville, Illinois 62568
(217) 824-2261

SANGER CITRUS ASSOCIATION
L and Tenth
Sanger, California 93657

SANGER FRUIT GROWERS
 ASSOCIATION
1028 Academy
Sanger, California 93657

SANGER-HARRIS STORES
(Division of Federated Department
 Stores, Inc.)
Pacific and Akard
Dallas, Texas 75222
Alan Gilman, Chairman of the
 Board
(214) 651-2345

SANGO CHINA COMPANY
212 Fifth Avenue
New York, New York 10010
(212) 532-2840

SANGRAY CORPORATION
Post Office Box 2388
Pueblo, Colorado 81004

SANGRIA ROSE (wine)
 See Joseph E. Seagram & Sons

SANI-COLORS (shoe polish)
 See Hollywood Shoe Polish
  Company, Inc.

SANI-FLUSH (cleanser)
 See Boyle-Midway, Inc.

1184

Companies and Trade Names

SANI-MIST INC.
3018 Market Street
Philadelphia, Pennsylvania 19104
(215) 387-2210

SANI-TOP (bowls and food servers)
　See Thermalene 73

SANI-WAX COMPANY
1500 Plantation Drive
Dallas, Texas 75235
Wayland Boles, President
(214) 637-0450

SANI-WHITE (shoe polish)
　See Hollywood Shoe Polish, Inc.

SANITAIR (pipes)
　See Winston Briar Pipe
　　　Manufacturing Company

SANITAIRE (insect repellent)
　See Campbell Chemicals, Inc.

SANITARY COMPANY, INC.
　See Sanitary Soap Company, Inc.

SANITARY SOAP COMPANY, INC.
104 Railroad Avenue
Paterson, New Jersey 07501

SANITATION EQUIPMENT INC.
615 South Fourth Street
Elkhart, Indiana 46514

SANITEK PRODUCTS, INC.
3959 Goodwin Avenue
Los Angeles, California 90039
(213) 245-6781

SANITOR MANUFACTURING
　COMPANY
1221 West Centre Avenue
Kalamazoo, Michigan 49002
(616) 327-3001

SANITOY INC.
150 Roosevelt Place
Palisades Park, New Jersey 07650
(201) 947-8005

SANITUBE COMPANY, THE
Radio Circle
Mount Kisco, New York 10549

SANIWAX PAPER COMPANY
436 North Park Street
Kalamazoo, Michigan 49006
James A. Hummel, President
(616) 342-0221

SANKA (decaffeinated coffee)
　See General Foods Corporation

SANKYO SEIKI (AMERICA) INC.
149 Fifth Avenue
New York, New York 10010
(212) 260-0200

SANNA, INC.
(Division of Beatrice Foods Company)
Post Office Box 1587
910 Wingra Drive
Madison, Wisconsin 53701
F.L. Sanna, President
(608) 257-0281

SANO (cigarettes, tobacco)
　See United States Tobacco
　　　Company

SANRAL PRODUCTS COMPANY
Box 1113
Tryon, North Carolina 28782

SANS EGAL (groceries)
　See Institutional Mart

SANS SOUCI LINGERIE
　See American Manufacturing
　　　Corporation, Inc.

SANSABELT (men's slacks)
　See Jaymar-Ruby, Inc.

SANSONE FOOD PRODUCTS
　COMPANY, INC.
149 Hull Street
Brooklyn, New York 11233
(212) 455-0126

SANSUI ELECTRONICS
　CORPORATION
32-17 61st Street
Woodside, New York 11377

SANTA (spray paint, spray snow, etc.)
　See Chase Products Company

SANTA ANA (food products)
　See Hollister Canning Company

SANTA CLARA PACKING
　COMPANY
Box 1149
625 North Ninth Street
San Jose, California 95108
W. Harlow Waggoner, President
(408) 295-2570

SANTA FE (cigars)
　See Universal Cigar Corporation

SANTA FE (wines)
　See United Vintners, Inc.

SANTA FE-DRISCOLL PACKERS
　INC.
9454 Wilshire Boulevard
Beverly Hills, California 90212

SANTA FE TRAIL TRANSPORTATION
　COMPANY
433 East Waterman Street
Wichita, Kansas 67201
Charles J. Nassimbene, President
(316) 264-3306

SANTA MARIA CHILI INC.
700 West Orange
Santa Maria, California 93454

Companies and Trade Names

SANTA PAULA (processed foods)
See Case-Swayne Company Inc.

SANTA ROSA (canned foods)
See Mission-Harlingen Canning Company, Inc.

SANTA ROSA SHOE COMPANY
3033 Coffey Lane
Santa Rosa, California 95402
Ernest J. Freeman, President
(707) 544-8000

SANTA SOFIA (Italian wines)
See Frederick Wildman & Sons, Ltd.

SANTIAM (food products)
See Stayton Canning Company, Co-operative

SANTIBA (beverage mixers)
See Coca-Cola Company

SANTINI BROTHERS, INC.
1405 Jerome Avenue
Bronx, New York 10452
Godfrey F. Santini, President
(212) 293-7000

SANTONE INDUSTRIES, INC.
Post Office Box 21380
San Antonio, Texas 78221
Harold M. Scherr, President
(512) 924-4821

SANYO ELECTRIC INC.
1200 West Walnut Street
Compton, California 90220

SANZENO (wines)
See Winegate Imports Inc.

SAPARITO (canned foods)
See Stanislaus Food Products Company

SAPO ELIXIR CHEMICAL COMPANY
9870 Big Bend Boulevard
Kirkwood, Missouri 63122
(314) 965-1171

SAPOLIN PAINTS, INC.
201 East 42nd Street
New York, New York 10017
E. Albert Eckart, Jr., President
(212) 867-1300

SAPORO (sports accessories and equipment)
See Eiger Mountain Sports

SAPORTA TRADING AGENCY CORPORATION
1457 Broadway
New York, New York 10036
(212) 947-4771

SAPPHIRE (hosiery)
See Kayser-Roth Company, Inc.

SARA INDUSTRIES
146 North Prince Street
Lancaster, Pennsylvania 17603

SARA LEE (frozen products)
See Kitchens of Sara Lee, Inc.

SARABHAI AGENCIES
30 Rockefeller Plaza
New York, New York 10020
(212) 757-8450

SARAH COVENTRY, INC.
(Subsidiary of C.H. Stuart & Company)
Sarah Coventry Parkway
Newark, New Jersey 14513
Rex W. Wood, President
(315) 331-1580

SARAH JANE (dry food mixes)
See April Corporation

SARAMAE LINGERIE, INC.
503 Broadway
New York, New York 10012
(212) 966-0020

SARAN WRAP (plastic wrap)
See Dow Chemical Company

SARANAC GLOVE COMPANY
1263 Main Street
Green Bay, Wisconsin 54305

SARANDOS DEODORANTS COMPANY, INC.
8209 Dunlap
Houston, Texas 77036
(713) 772-1073

SARATOGA (beans)
See Standard Brands, Inc.

SARATOGA (food products)
See Tulkoff's Horseradish Products Company

SARATOGA (meat products)
See John Morrell & Company

SARATOGA (pipes)
See Whitehall Products, Inc.

SARATOGA (tires)
See Duddy Tire Company

SARATOGA VICHY SPRING COMPANY
Box 565
Rural Delivery 4
Geyser Road
Saratoga Springs, New York 12866
(518) 584-6363

SARCO COMPANY, INC.
(Division of White Consolidated Industries, Inc.)
1951 26th Street S.W.
Allentown, Pennsylvania 18105
Albert Burnett, President
(215) 797-5830

Companies and Trade Names

SARD (binoculars)
See Kollsman Instrument Corporation

SARDE (basketware, woodenware, rugs, and tapestries)
See Holladay International

SARDEAU, INC.
Galloping Hill Road
Kenilworth, New Jersey 07033

SARDINETTE (seafood)
See Norbest Inc.

SARDIS LUGGAGE COMPANY
(Division of Roper Company)
17 West Hightower Street
Sardis, Mississippi 38666
Joe M. Scott, President
(601) 487-1211

SARDO TEXTILE CORPORATION
113 West 30th Street
New York, New York 10001
(212) 695-4680

SARGEANT ACNOID PHARMACEUTICAL COMPANY
Highland Mills, New York 10930

SARGENT & COMPANY
(Subsidiary of Walter Kidde & Company)
100 Sargent Drive
New Haven, Connecticut 06509
Stanley R. Cullen, President
(203) 562-2151

SARGENT & COMPANY
Hand Tool Division
100 Sargent Drive
New Haven, Connecticut 06509
Leonard T. Riccardo, President
(203) 562-2151

SARGENT & GREENLEAF, INC.
24 Seneca Avenue
Rochester, New York 14621
Henry C. Miller, President
(716) 467-3200

SARGENT ART
(Division of The Mead Corporation)
100 East Diamond Avenue
Hazleton, Pennsylvania 18201
(717) 454-3596

SARGENT INDUSTRIES
Stillman Seal Division
1901 Building
Century City, California 90067
Dan Burns, President
(213) 277-9111

SARGENT PAINT, INC.
323 West 15th Street
Indianapolis, Indiana 46206
(317) 635-7501

SARGENT-SOWELL INC.
1185 108th Street
Grand Prairie, Texas 75050
(214) 647-1525

SARGENTI COMPANY INC., A.
453 West 17th Street
New York, New York 10011
(212) 989-5555

SARGENTO CHEESE COMPANY, INC.
320 Pine Street
Elkhart, Wisconsin 53020

SARGENT'S DRUG STORE
23 North Wabash Avenue
Chicago, Illinois 60602
(312) 726-4770

SARKES TARZIAN, INC.
East Hillside Drive
Bloomington, Indiana 47403
Sarkes Tarzian, President
(812) 332-7251

SARNA INC., S.S.
225 Fifth Avenue
New York, New York 10010
(212) 924-3703

SARNE HANDBAG COMPANY INC.
20 West 33rd Street
New York, New York 10001
(212) 594-4130

SARNS MACHINE
Southwest Harbor, Maine 04679

SARON PHARMACAL CORPORATION
1640 Central South
Saint Petersburg, Florida 33712

SARRIA (wines)
See Robinson-Lloyds, Ltd.

SARTEL (copper and steel cookware)
See King Housewares, Inc.

SASIENI OF LONDON, INC.
33 Union Square West
New York, New York 10003
(212) 242-0258

SASKA SPORTS INDUSTRIES
185 Valley Drive
Brisbane, California 94005
David T. O'Neal, Jr., President
(415) 467-9286

SASSMANN (harpsichords, clavichords)
See Gregoire Harpsichord Shop

SASSONE WHOLESALE GROCERIES COMPANY INC.
1706 Bronxdale Avenue
Bronx, New York 10462
(212) 792-2828

SASTRI (sports apparel)
See Halstead Imports Inc.

Companies and Trade Names

SATEJEAU (wines)
See Dreyfus, Ashby & Company

SATELLITE (clocks)
See The Cincinnati Time Recorder Company

SATELLITE SOAP COMPANY
17826 East Warren Avenue
Detroit, Michigan 48224
(313) 882-2244

SATELLITE SYSTEMS INC.
3710 Washington Boulevard
Indianapolis, Indiana 46205
(317) 638-7551

SATELLITE-2001 (portable electric typewriters)
See Adler Business Machines Inc.

SATICOY FOODS CORPORATION
Box 4547
Saticoy, California 93003

SATIN FINISH (varnish)
See Pettit Paint Company Inc.

SATIN GLOSS (floor wax)
See Uncle Sam Chemical Company, Inc.

SATIN SHEATH (body and hand cream)
See Carter-Wallace, Inc.

SATIN SOFT COSMETICS
2170 Piedmont Road N.E.
Atlanta, Georgia 30324
(404) 875-3511

SATINA (laundry finish)
See Miles Laboratories Inc.

SATINSHEEN (men's furnishings)
See Knothe Brothers Company, Inc.

SATINTONE (latex paints)
See Conchemco, Inc.

SATISFACTION (food products)
See Mount Royal Industries

SATTLER'S INC.
998 Broadway
Buffalo, New York 14212
Ralph H. Wilcove, President
(716) 894-2345

SATTONA (varnish)
See McDougall-Butler (Division of Bisonite Company, Inc.)

SATURA (bath oil, cleansing lotion, skin freshener, etc.)
See Dorothy Gray, Ltd.

SATURN (chairs)
See Fixtures Manufacturing Corporation

SATURN AIRWAYS, INC.
International Airport
Post Office Box 2426
Oakland, California 94614
Howard K. Howard, President
(415) 635-4200

SATURN II (luggage)
See Samsonite Corporation

SATURNA (folding and mobile tables)
See Mitchell Manufacturing Company

SAU-SEA FOODS, INC.
1000 Saw Mill River Road
Yonkers, New York 10710
Ernest J. Schoenbrun, President
(914) 969-5922

SAUCE FROSTED (frozen vegetables)
See Green Giant Company

SAUCE-QUIK (instant white sauce)
See Ac'cent International

SAUCY BERRY (canned fruits)
See Shenandoah Apple Co-Operative, Inc.

SAUCY SUSAN PRODUCTS, INC.
104 Woodside Avenue
Briarcliff Manor, New York 10510
Emanuel L. Adelman, President
(914) 762-1300

SAUDER MANUFACTURING CORPORATION
600 Middle Street
Archbold, Ohio 43502
(419) 445-7670

SAUER COMPANY, THE C.F.
2000 West Broad Street
Richmond, Virginia 23220
(703) 350-5786

SAUER'S (spices, condiments)
See C.F. Sauer Company

SAUK CITY CANNING COMPANY
401 J.Q. Adams Street
Sauk City, Wisconsin 53580
(608) 643-6442

SAUL BROTHERS & COMPANY, INC.
820 Spring Street, N.W.
Atlanta, Georgia 30308
David Saul, President
(404) 881-1833

SAUNA (beer)
See Bosch Brewing Company

SAUNAGLASS (portable steam-vapor bath)
See Cromar Company

SAUNDER'S (rabbit repellent, snake-bite kit)
See Lotshaw Company

Companies and Trade Names

SAUNDERS (Scotch whiskey)
    See Intercontinental Wines & Spirits, Ltd.

SAUNDERS COMPANY, W.B.
West Washington Square
Philadelphia, Pennsylvania 19106
(215) 574-4700

SAUNDERS DISTRIBUTORS, INC.
28-32 North Main
Minot, North Dakota 58701

SAUPIQUET (canned vegetables and fish)
    See O.K. Simson Company

SAUS-OS (snack food)
    See General Mills, Inc.

SAUTER LABORATORIES
(Division of Hoffman-La Roche Inc.)
340 Kingsland Road
Nutley, New Jersey 07110

SAUZA (Tequila)
    See Munson Shaw Company

SAV-A-BRUSH (paintbrush restorer)
    See Red Devil Inc.

SAV-A-STOP, INC.
2050 Art Museum Drive
Jacksonville, Florida 32207
B.E. Griffin, Chairman
(904) 768-3411
    See also Top Dollar Store, Inc.

SAV-COTE CHEMICAL LABORATORIES, INC
Box 770
Lakewood, New Jersey 08701

SAV-LIN (napkins, place mats, tray covers, bath mats)
    See Freeman Paper Company

SAV-ON-DRUGS, INC.
4818 Lincoln Boulevard
Marina Del Rey, California 90291
Ira D. Brown, President
(213) 823-5454

SAVE-WAVE (swim caps)
    See Kleinert's, Inc.

SAVABLAZE (nonflammable paint remover)
    See The Savogran Company

SAVADA BROTHERS, INC.
34 West 33rd Street
New York, New York 10001
Morton J. Savada, President
(212) 594-9330

SAVAGE (men's toiletries)
    See Panco Ltd.

SAVAGE ARMS
(Division of Emhart Corporation)
Westfield, Massachusetts 01085
H.R. Clark, President
(413) 562-2361

SAVAGE COMPANY
1814 Burr Parkway
Dodge City, Kansas 67801

SAVAGE INC., FRANK L.
17 East 37th Street
New York, New York 10016
(212) 679-1860

SAVAGE LABORATORIES INC.
Box 700
Bellaire, Texas 77401

SAVANNAH FOODS & INDUSTRIES, INC.
Post Office Box 339
Savannah Bank Building
Savannah, Georgia 31402
W.W. Sprague, Jr., President
(912) 234-1261
    See also Jim Dandy Company

SAVANNAH SUGAR REFINERY
(Division of Savannah Food & Industries, Inc.)
Post Office Box 339
Savannah, Georgia 31402
(912) 234-1261

SAVARESE (relishes and sauces)
    See Howard Food Companies, Inc.

SAVARIN (coffee)
    See S.A. Schonbrunn & Company Inc.

SAVARIN COFFEES AND TEAS
    See S.A. Schonbrunn & Company, Inc.

SAVE THE BABY (baby products)
    See William W. Lee & Company, Inc.

SAVILLE ORGAN CORPORATION
2901 Shermer Road
Northbrook, Illinois 60062
James A. Brandt, President
(312) 272-7070

SAVILLE ROW (carpeting)
    See Magee Carpet Company

SAVIN BUSINESS MACHINES CORPORATION
Columbus Avenue
Valhalla, New York 10595
Robert K. Low, President
(914) 769-9550

SAVOGRAN COMPANY, THE
Box 130
259 Lenox Street
Norwood, Massachusetts 06062
Carl O. Olson, President
(617) 762-5400

SAVOIA (food products)
    See Gattuso Corporation Ltd.

Companies and Trade Names

SAVOL DRUG COMPANY
128 East 45th Street
Brooklyn, New York 11203
(212) 493-0509

SAVON FOOD COMPANY
3651 NW 51st Street
North Miami Beach, Florida 33142
(305) 634-2449

SAVONA (pipes)
See Comoy's of London

SAVORY (food products)
See Wilson & Company Inc.

SAVORY EQUIPMENT COMPANY
Post Office Box 610
349 Essex Road
Neptune, New Jersey 07753
(201) 922-0044

SAVOY (men's dress shirts)
See Merrill-Sharpe Ltd.

SAWACO (sports apparel)
See Halstead Imports Inc.

SAWGRASS (produce)
See S.M. Jones Farms, Inc.

SAWHILL TUBULAR
(Division of Cyclops Corporation)
Post Office Box 11
Sharon, Pennsylvania 16146
(412) 347-7771

SAWSMITH (radial-arm saw)
See Magna American Corporation

SAWYER (slide projectors)
See Sawyer (Division of GAF Corporation)

SAWYER CANOE COMPANY
234 State Street
Oscoda, Michigan 48750

SAWYER FRUIT & VEGETABLE & COLD STORAGE
Box 268
Bear Lake, Michigan 49614

SAWYER-TOWER PRODUCTS INC.
76 Stanley Avenue
Watertown, Massachusetts 02172
Robert P. Fanning, General Manager
(617) 926-1200

SAWZALL (power saws)
See Milwaukee Electric Tool Corporation

SAXET (canned goods)
See Allen Canning Company

SAXON ADHESIVE PRODUCTS, INC.
880 Garfield Avenue
Jersey City, New Jersey 07305
(201) 451-1979

SAXON BUSINESS PRODUCTS INC.
Red Road at N.W. 139th Street
Miami Lakes, Florida 33014

SAXON DISTRIBUTORS & CANDY KITCHENS
Box 54
Wellington, Alabama 36279

SAXON INDUSTRIES, INC.
450 Seventh Avenue
New York, New York 10001
Myron P. Berman, President
(212) 736-3663

SAXON PAPER NEW YORK
(Division of Saxon Industries, Inc.)
30-10 Starr Avenue
Long Island City, New York 11101
(212) 937-6100

SAXONETTE (men's furnishings)
See Knothe Brothers Company Inc.

SAXONWARE (oven-to-table ware)
See Glanson Company

SAXONY (groceries)
See Institutional Wholesalers, Inc.

SAXONY PRODUCTS INC.
2301 East 55th Street
Los Angeles, California 90058
(213) 588-6111

SAXTON (fruit)
See Idaho Fruit Sales Inc.

SAXTON INC.
11727 Mississippi Avenue
Los Angeles, California 90025
(213) 272-1484

SAY-LU, INC.
149 Madison Avenue
New York, New York 10016
(212) 686-5217

SAYKLLY'S CANDIES
1815 Third Avenue North
Escanaba, Michigan 49829

SAYLOR'S CHOCOLATES, INC., MISS
1001 81st Avenue
Oakland, California 94621

SAYOUR COMPANY, ELIAS
31 East 31st Street
New York, New York 10016
(212) 686-7560

SAZERAC COMPANY, INC.
Post Office Box 52821
328 North Cortez Street
New Orleans, Louisiana 70150
Stephen Goldring, President
(504) 486-6228
See also Dennis & Huppert Company

Companies and Trade Names

SCABBARD (men's wallets)
See Charles Doppelt & Company Inc.

SCACCIANOCE & COMPANY
1165 Burnett Place
New York, New York 10059
(212) 991-4462

SCALAMANDRE SILKS, INC.
37-24 24th Street
Long Island City, New York 11101
Franco Scalamandre, President
(212) 361-8500

SCALP HIGENE DRUG COMPANY
281 North Grant Avenue
Columbus, Ohio 43215
(614) 221-0636

SCALPMASTER (hairbrushes)
See B & S Industries Inc.

SCAN (sports accessories and equipment)
See Trak Inc.

SCAN AM IMPORT INC.
1306 First Street South
Great Falls, Montana 59405

SCAN, INC.
13850 Saticoy Street
Van Nuys, California 91402

SCAN-PLAST INDUSTRIES INC.
54 East 54th Street
New York, New York 10022
(212) 755-0422

SCANDAL (fragrance)
See Lanvin-Charles of the Ritz Inc.

SCANDECOR INC.
1105 Industrial Highway
Southampton, Pennsylvania 18966

SCANDIA (cookware)
See West Bend Company

SCANDIA (tobacco)
See Lane Limited

SCANDIA FONDUE (melamine plates and platters)
See Kenro Corporation

SCANDIA GLASS WORKS
Box 302
Kenova, West Virginia 25530

SCANDIA HOUSE ENTERPRISES, INC.
Post Office Box 1711
Hialeah, Florida 33010

SCANDIA SPECIALTIES INC.
Southwest Cutoff
Auburn, Massachusetts 01501

SCANDIA TRADING COMPANY INC.
15 Lowell Avenue
Winchester, Massachusetts 01890

SCANDIA TRAY SHAPE (TV-table sets)
See Cal-Dak Industries, Inc.

SCANDIC (cheese)
See A.V. Olsson Trading Company, Inc.

SCANDICRAFTS INC.
4550 Calle Alto
Camarillo, California 93010

SCANDINAVIAN AIRLINES
138-02 Queens Boulevard
Jamaica, New York 11435
B. John Heistein, General Manager
(212) 657-8000

SCANLI COMPANY, THE
137 Green Wood Avenue
Bethel, Connecticut 06801

SCANNON, LTD.
666 Fifth Avenue
New York, New York 10019
Bent Rasmussen, President
(212) 246-3070

SCARLET KING (canned fruits and vegetables)
See Sales Producers Associates, Inc.

SCARNE GAMES INC., JOHN
4319 Meadowview Avenue
North Bergen, New Jersey 07047

SCARVES BY VERA, INC.
417 Fifth Avenue
New York, New York 10016
Vera Neumann, President
(212) 532-8000

SCATS (footwear)
See SCOA Industries, Inc.

SCENE-O-RAMA (wallpaper)
See Wall Trends, International

SCENT-SATION INC.
22 West 32nd Street
New York, New York 10001
(212) 244-4125

SCERBO & SONS INC., FRANK
140 Plymouth Street
Brooklyn, New York 11201
Albert Scerbo, President
(212) 852-5959

SCHAAFF (bicycles)
See Beacon Cycle & Supply Company

Companies and Trade Names

SCHACHT RUBBER
  MANUFACTURING COMPANY
238 Polk Street
Huntington, Indiana 46750
William F. Schacht, II, President
(219) 356-4900

SCHAEFER BREWING COMPANY,
  F. & M.
430 Kent Avenue
Brooklyn, New York 11211
William J. Schoen, President
(212) 387-7000

SCHAEFER SYSTEM
  INTERNATIONAL, INC.
311 East Park Street
Moonachie, New Jersey 07074

SCHAEFFER ASSOCIATES, INC.
411 Fifth Avenue
New York, New York 10016
(212) 683-7426

SCHAERF COMPANY, HENRY C.
2 Prince
Brooklyn, New York 11201
(212) 925-7564

SCHAFFER GROCERY
  CORPORATION, S.
27 Weymen Avenue
New Rochelle, New York 10805
Samuel Schaffer, President
(914) 235-7000

SCHAIBLE'S BAKERY INC.
2400 Northhampton Street
Easton, Pennsylvania 18042
John F. Schaible, President and
  General Manager
(215) 258-7131

SCHALK CHEMICALS, INC.
2400 Vauxhall Road
Union, New Jersey 07083
Harry Kyger, Jr., President
(201) 688-6900

SCHALL & COMPANY
200 Fifth Avenue
New York, New York 10010
(212) 989-4477

SCHAPER MANUFACTURING
  COMPANY
(Division of Kusan, Inc.)
9909 South Shore Drive
Minneapolis, Minnesota 55441
W.L. Garrity, President
(612) 544-9161

SCHATZ (clocks)
  See Coehler-Coptex Company

SCHATZ MANUFACTURING
  COMPANY, THE
Fairview Avenue
Poughkeepsie, New York 12601
James E. Neighbors, Jr., President
  and Treasurer
(914) 452-6000

SCHAUMBURGER, INC., CHARLES
145 Coolidge
Englewood, New Jersey 07631

SCHEEL, INC., WILLIAM H.
38 Franklin Street
Brooklyn, New York 11222
(212) 389-3480

SCHEEL YACHTS INC.
1 South Main Street
Rockland, Maine 04841

SCHEIB AUTO PAINT SHOPS,
  EARL
8737 Wilshire Boulevard
Beverly Hills, California 90211
Earl Scheib, President
(213) 652-4880

SCHEIBE COMPANY, R.R.
Post Office Box Seven
Brockton, Massachusetts 02403

SCHEITLER (sports apparel)
  See Max Humi Importer, Inc.

SCHELL, INC.
242 West McMicken Avenue
Cincinnati, Ohio 45214
(513) 621-0188

SCHELLING HARDWARE COMPANY
  INC.
734 Willow Avenue
Hoboken, New Jersey 07030

SCHENKELAARS (trumpets,
cornets, trombones)
  See St. Louis Music Supply
    Company, Inc.

SCHENLEY INDUSTRIES, INC.
(Subsidiary of Glen Alden
  Corporation)
888 Seventh Avenue
New York, New York 10019
Howard S. Feldman, President
(212) 957-2200

SCHERPS GROCER SUPPLY INC.
1135 South Lamar Street
Dallas, Texas 75215
(214) 742-1311

SCHERING CORPORATION
(Subsidiary of Schering-Plough
  Corporation)
Galloping Hill Road
Kenilworth, New Jersey 07033
Francis J. Gleason, President
(201) 931-2000
  See also American Scientific
    Laboratories

SCHERING DIAGNOSTICS
(Division of Schering Corporation)
40 Markley Street
Port Reading, New Jersey 07064

SCHERK FRENCH COSMETIC, INC.
3605 Kingsbridge Avenue
Bronx, New York 10463
(212) 546-2606

Companies and Trade Names

SCHERL & ROTH INC.
(Division of C.G. Conn, Ltd.)
1729 Superior Avenue
Cleveland, Ohio 44114
(216) 861-7640

SCHERMACK PRODUCTS
CORPORATION
228 Chandler Pontiac
Detroit, Michigan 48202
(313) 333-7147

SCHERMERHORN'S (tobacco)
See Faber, Coe & Gregg, Inc.

SCHIAPARELLI (cologne, dusting powder, perfume)
See Parfums Schiaparelli, Inc.

SCHIAPARELLI (hosiery)
See Kayser-Roth Hosiery Company, Inc.

SCHIAPARELLI (men's shirts)
See Eagle Shirtmakers

SCHIAPARELLI (watches)
See World Wide Watch Company, Inc.

SCHIAVONE-BONOMO
CORPORATION
Fort of Jersey Avenue
Jersey City, New Jersey 07302
Alfred T. Sforza, President
(201) 333-4300

SCHICK, INC.
1901 Avenue of the Stars
Los Angeles, California 90067
Frank H. Seyer, President
(213) 553-3366

SCHICK SAFETY RAZOR COMPANY
(Division of Warner-Lambert Company)
10 Webster Road
Milford, Connecticut 06460
E.L. Whitney, President
(203) 878-9351

SCHICKHAUS (meats)
See Swift & Company

SCHIEFFELIN & COMPANY
30 Cooper Square
New York, New York 10003
William J. Schieffelin, III, President
(212) 777-3311
See also Almay, Inc.

SCHIFF (shoes)
See SCOA Industries, Inc.

SCHIFF BIO-FOOD PRODUCTS
Moonachie Avenue
Moonachie, New Jersey 07074

SCHIFF, LUDWIG L.
93 Patton Boulevard
New Hyde Park, New York 11040

SCHIFF, WALTER M.
134 Haven Avenue
New York, New York 10032
(212) 923-7631

SCHIFFMANN COMPANY, R.
1734 North Main Street
Los Angeles, California 90031
(213) 221-4167

SCHIFTAN INC., ALFRED
460 Park Avenue South
New York, New York 10016
(212) 532-1984

SCHILDKRAUT-MILLER INC.
35 West 35th Street
New York, New York 10001
(212) 594-9606

SCHILKE MUSIC PRODUCTS INC.
529 South Wabash Avenue
Chicago, Illinois 60605
(312) 922-0230

SCHILLER & ASMUS INC.
1525 Merchandise Mart
Chicago, Illinois 60654
(312) 644-7747

SCHILLING (spices)
See McCormick & Company, Inc.

SCHIMMEL (food products)
See Red Wing Company, Inc.

SCHINDLER'S PEANUT PRODUCTS, INC.
4500 College Avenue
College Park, Maryland 20740
(301) 864-5005

SCHIPPERS (tobacco)
See Faber, Coe & Gregg, Inc.

SCHIRMER, INC., G.
(Subsidiary of Macmillan, Inc.)
866 Third Avenue
New York, New York 10022
Rudolph E. Schirmer, Chairman of the Board
(212) 935-5100

SCHLAGE LOCK COMPANY
Post Office Box 3324
2201 Bayshore Boulevard
San Francisco, California 94119
Marron Kendrick, President
(415) 467-1100

SCHLEGEL CORPORATION
1555 Jefferson Road
Rochester, New York 14601
Richard L. Turner, Chairman, President and Chief Executive Officer
(716) 244-1000

SCHLENZIG COMPANY, E.
801 East Tenth Avenue
Denver, Colorado 80218

SCHLICK, INC.
See Scrip, Inc.

1193

Companies and Trade Names

SCHLORER'S INC., MRS.
Scotts Lane
Philadelphia, Pennsylvania 19129
(215) 848-2505

SCHLOTTERBECK & FOSS
COMPANY
117 Preble
Portland, Maine 04101
(207) 772-4660

SCHLUDERBERG-KURDLE
COMPANY
See Esskay Quality Meat
Company

SCHLITZ BREWING COMPANY,
JOSEPH
235 West Galena Street
Milwaukee, Wisconsin 53212
Robert A. Uihlein, Jr., President
(414) 224-5000

SCHLUETER MANUFACTURING
COMPANY
4700 Goodfellow Boulevard
Saint Louis, Missouri 63120
Walter J. Schlueter, President
(314) 385-3800

SCHLUMBERGER, LTD.
277 Park Avenue
New York, New York 10017
Jean Riboud, Chairman of the Board
(212) 350-9400
See also Weston Instruments,
Inc.

SCHMID BROTHERS, INC.
55 Pacella Park Drive
Randolph, Massachusetts 02368
Paul A. Schmid, Chairman and
President
(617) 961-3000

SCHMID LABORATORIES
Lackawanna Avenue
West Paterson, New Jersey 07424
See also Pearson Products

SCHMID-SCHLENKER (clocks)
See Coehler-Coptex Company

SCHMIDT (beer)
See G. Heileman Brewing
Company, Inc.

SCHMIDT & SONS, INC., C.
127 Edward Street
Philadelphia, Pennsylvania 19123
Carl E. von Czoernig, President
(215) 627-5800

SCHMIDT COMPANY, A.O.
2100 Bryant Street
San Francisco, California 94110
(415) 824-7466

SCHMIDT DISPLAY
MANUFACTURING COMPANY
2516 Superior Avenue
Sheboygan, Wisconsin 53081

SCHMIDTMAN COMPANY
Post Office Box 157
702 Jay Street
Manitowoc, Wisconsin 54220
(414) 682-0146

SCHMITT COMPANY, INC.,
PETER J.
Post Office Box Two
2775 Broadway
Buffalo, New York 14240
Robert S. Abels, President
(716) 897-2121

SCHMUGLES (juvenile furniture)
See Mobi Corporation

SCHNADIG CORPORATION
4820 West Belmont Avenue
Chicago, Illinois 60641
Lawrence K. Schnadig, President
(312) 545-2300

SCHNAPP ENTERPRISES
70 Franklin Avenue
Brooklyn, New York 11205
(212) 625-0114

SCHNEIBLE COMPANY
Post Office Box 100
712 Thomas Street
Holly, Michigan 48442
(313) 634-8211

SCHNEIDER MANUFACTURING
COMPANY, C.J.
1622 Roosevelt
Toledo, Ohio 43607
(419) 536-0006

SCHNEIDER METAL
MANUFACTURING COMPANY
1805 South 55th Avenue
Chicago, Illinois 60650
(312) 242-2980

SCHNEIERSON & SON, A.J.
389 Fifth Avenue
New York, New York 10016
(212) 686-4330

SCHNELL & COMPANY, INC., H.
238 New York City Terminal
Market
Hunts Point, New York 10474

SCHNITZELBANK (German beer
steins)
See American Bravo Company

SCHNUCK MARKETS, INC.
12921 Enterprise Way
Bridgeton, Missouri 63044
Donald O. Schnuck, President
(314) 291-5400

SCHNUR & COHAN, INC.
112 Madison Avenue
New York, New York 10016
(212) 684-4187

SCHOBER ORGAN CORPORATION,
THE
43 West 61st Street
New York, New York 10023
Richard H. Dorf, President
(212) 586-7552

Companies and Trade Names

SCHOCK CORPORATION, W.D.
3502 South Greenville Street
Santa Ana, California 92704

SCHOELLKOPF COMPANY, THE
806 Jackson
Dallas, Texas 75202
George H. Norsworthy, President
(214) 747-0611

SCHOEN & SONS INC.,
 ISAAC A.
249 West 29th Street
New York, New York 10001
(212) 564-0122

SCHOENEMAN, INC., J.
9818 Reisterstown Road
Owings Mills, Maryland 21117
(301) 363-0100

SCHOENFELD (tea)
 See Pfeiffer Company

SCHOLL (German wines)
 See International Vintage Wines

SCHOLL, INC.
213 West Schiller Street
Chicago, Illinois 60610
William H. Scholl, President
(312) 642-7200
 See also Arno Adhesive Tapes,
 Inc.

SCHOLZ HOMES, INC.
(Subsidiary of Inland Steel Company)
2001 North Westwood
Toledo, Ohio 43607
Julius J. Cohen, President
(419) 531-1601

SCHONBRUNN & COMPANY,
 INC., S.A.
(Subsidiary of American-Maize
 Products Company)
Grand and Ruby Avenues
Palisades Park, New Jersey 07650
William Ziegler, III, Chairman of
 the Board
(201) 943-0600

SCHONEBERGER & SONS
3422 West Lake
Chicago, Illinois 60624
(312) 533-2733

SCHONFELD COMPANY, INC., S.
401 Hackensack Avenue
Hackensack, New Jersey 07601
(212) 966-2933

SCHOOL BELL (alarm clocks)
 See Ingraham Industries

SCHOOL BOY (food products)
 See Pacific Food Products
 Company

SCHOOL DAYS (food products)
 See Stokely-Van Camp Inc.

SCHOOL PICTURES, INC.
Post Office Box 570
Jackson, Mississippi 39205
Robert M. Hearin, President
(601) 984-2081

SCHOOL STATIONERS
 CORPORATION
Neenah, Wisconsin 54956

SCHOOLTIME (composition books,
loose-leaf fillers, notebooks,
tablets, ruled papers)
 See Roaring Spring Blank Book
 Company

SCHOR PARCRAFT INC.
122 Eighth Street
Passaic, New Jersey 07055
A. Weinstein, President
(201) 773-0840

SCHOTT (ale)
 See Iroquois Industries, Inc.

SCHOTT-ZWIESEL GLASS INC.
11 East 26th Street
New York, New York 10010
(212) 689-5560

SCHOTTENSTEIN STORES
 CORPORATION
(Subsidiary of E.L. Schottenstein &
 Sons, Inc.)
3251 Westerville Road
Columbus, Ohio 43207
Alvin E. Schottenstein, President
(614) 471-4711

SCHOWANEK BEADS LTD.
280 Madison Avenue
New York, New York 10016
(212) 689-2499

SCHRADE (cutlery)
 See Imperial Knife Associated
 Companies Inc.

SCHRADER CORPORATION, ABE
530 Seventh Avenue
New York, New York 10018
Abe Schrader, Chairman of the
 Board
(212) 564-9194

SCHRAFFT CANDY COMPANY
(Subsidiary of Gulf & Western
 Industries)
529 Main Street
Charlestown, Massachusetts 02129
J. Jaffe, President
(617) 242-2700

SCHRAMM, INC.
901 East Virginia
West Chester, Pennsylvania 19380
Leslie B. Schramm, President
(215) 696-2500

SCHRATZ PRODUCTS, INC.
253 East Milwaukee
Detroit, Michigan 48202
(313) 873-6770

SCHREIBER COMPANY, A.H.
10 West 33rd Street
New York, New York 10001
(212) 564-2700

Companies and Trade Names

SCHREIBER MILLS, INC.
802 Mitchell Avenue
Saint Joseph, Missouri 64503
(816) 279-1631

SCHRETER & SONS COMPANY, INC., A.
16 South Eutaw Street
Baltimore, Maryland 21201
Sidney H. Schreter, President
(301) 685-3400

SCHRODER & SCHYLER (wines)
See Dreyfus, Ashby & Company

SCHROEDER & TREMAYNE, INC.
1711 Delmar Boulevard
Saint Louis, Missouri 63103
(314) 421-4460

SCHUBERT INDUSTRIES, INC.
680 Miami Street
Akron, Ohio 44311
J.R. Schubert, President
(216) 434-6621

SCHUCO TOY COMPANY, INC.
1107 Broadway
New York, New York 10010
(212) 243-0803

SCHUEMANN LABORATORIES
480 West Aurora Road
Cleveland, Ohio 44146
(216) 467-1200

SCHULER CHOCOLATES, INC.
1000 West Fifth Street
Winona, Minnesota 55987
William C. Schuler, President and General Manager
(507) 454-3433

SCHULMERICH CARILLONS, INC.
Carillon Hill
Sellersville, Pennsylvania 18960
Kenneth G. McGrath, Chairman, President and Treasurer
(215) 257-2771

SCHULT MOBILE HOME CORPORATION
(Subsidiary of Inland Steel Company)
1800 South Main Street
Elkhart, Indiana 46514
Walter E. Wells, President
(219) 825-5881

SCHULTZ BROTHERS COMPANY
800 North Church Street
Lake Zurich, Illinois 60047
C.H. Schultz, President
(312) 438-3900

SCHULTZ COMPANY
11730 Northline
Saint Louis, Missouri 63043
(314) 567-4545

SCHULTZ HONEY FARMS
Ripon, Wisconsin 54971

SCHULTZ SAV-O STORES, INC.
2215 Union Avenue
Shaboygan, Wisconsin 53081
Howard C. Dickelman, President
(414) 457-4433

SCHULZE & BURCH BISCUIT COMPANY
1133 West 35th
Chicago, Illinois 60609
P.J. Boyle, President
(312) 927-6622

SCHUMACHER & COMPANY, F.
919 Third Avenue
New York, New York 10022
C. Richard Brose, President
(212) 371-4500
See also Waverly Fabrics

SCHUSTER, REED
6041 Harrison Avenue
Cincinnati, Ohio 45211
(513) 574-6161

SCHUURING AND LANG ASSOCIATES
15-112 Merchandise Mart
Chicago, Illinois 60654
(312) 642-6950

SCHUYLER (food products)
See H.C. Hemingway & Company Inc.

SCHWAAB STAMP & SEAL COMPANY
11415 West Burleigh Street
Milwaukee, Wisconsin 53210
(414) 771-4150

SCHWAB AND COMPANY, DAVID E.
417 Fifth Avenue
New York, New York 10016
(212) 679-2828

SCHWAB COMPANY, A.H.
1831 Avenue H
Saint Louis, Missouri 63129
(314) 544-1100

SCHWARTZ & BENJAMIN, INC.
200 Locust Street
Lynn, Massachusetts 01902
Arthur R. Schwartz, President and Treasurer
(617) 595-5600

SCHWARTZ & SONS VICTORIAN CANDY COMPANY, J.
2042-50 North Tenth Street
Philadelphia, Pennsylvania 19122
(215) 765-8657

SCHWARTZ EXPORT IMPORT LTD., GENE
252-24 Northern Boulevard
Little Neck, New York 11362

SCHWARTZ, INC., S. BERNARD
140 Cedar Street
New York, New York 10006
(212) 267-5419

Companies and Trade Names

SCHWARTZ MANUFACTURING
COMPANY
1000 School Street
Two Rivers, Wisconsin 54241
Harlan A. Schwartz, President
(414) 793-1375

SCHWARTZ SHOWELL
CORPORATION
470 South Front
Columbus, Ohio 43215
(614) 221-3301

SCHWARZ, F.A.O.
(Division of W.R. Grace Company)
745 Fifth Avenue
New York, New York 10022
Raymond S. Reed, President
(212) 688-2200

SCHWED COMPANY INC.,
CHARLES B.
509 Fifth Avenue
New York, New York 10017
(212) 687-0890

SCHWEIGER INDUSTRIES, INC.
116 West Washington Street
Jefferson, Wisconsin 53549
J.R. Schweiger, President
(414) 674-2440

SCHWEITZER & COMPANY,
NATHAN
824 Washington
New York, New York 10011
(212) 243-3900

SCHWEPPES U.S.A., LTD.
(Subsidiary of Schweppes, Ltd.)
1200 High Ridge Road
Stamford, Connecticut 06905
Robert E. Ix, President
(203) 329-0911
   See also Cadbury Corporation

SCHWINN BICYCLE COMPANY
1856 North Kostner Avenue
Chicago, Illinois 60639
Frank V. Schwinn, President
(312) 227-3000

SCHWOB MANUFACTURING
COMPANY
945 Broadway
Columbus, Georgia 31901
Mrs. Simon Schwob, President
(404) 323-9521

SCIABICA & SONS, NICK
Camellia Way
Modesto, California 95351

SCIENCE PRODUCTS COMPANY,
INC.
5801 North Tripp Avenue
Chicago, Illinois 60646
(312) 583-3171

SCIENTIFIC INDUSTRIES INC.
70 Orville Drive
Bohemia, New York 11716
Lowell A. Kleiman, President
(516) 567-4700

SCIENTIFIC INSTRUMENTS, INC.
632 South F Street
Lake Worth, Florida 33460
(305) 585-9451

SCIENTIFIC SILVER SERVICE
CORPORATION
35-30 61st Street
Woodside, New York 11377

SCIENTIFIC TOYS INC.
17 Scott Street
Utica, New York 13501

SCIO POTTERY COMPANY
Post Office Box 565
Scio, Ohio 43988
Gertrude P. Reese, President
(614) 945-3111

SCOA INDUSTRIES, INC.
35 North Fourth
Columbus, Ohio 43215
Herbert H. Schiff, President
(614) 221-5421

SCOLDING LOCKS CORPORATION
Box 858
1520 West Rogers Avenue
Appleton, Wisconsin 54911
P.F. Skaer, President
(414) 733-5561

SCONZA CANDY COMPANY
919 81st Avenue
Oakland, California 94621

SCOOPER DOOPER
7820 Airport Highway
Pennsauken, New Jersey 08109

SCOOPSTER (housewares)
   See Bloomfield Industries, Inc.

SCOOTER JET (infants' product)
   See Kewaunee Equipment
   Company

SCOPE (mouthwash)
   See Procter & Gamble Company

SCOPUS
(Division of Berkey Photo)
25-20 Brooklyn-Queens Expressway
West
Woodside, New York 11377

SCORE (hairdressing, hair spray)
   See Clinton (Division of Bristol-
   Myers Products)

SCORPION, INC.
(Subsidiary of Fuqua Industries, Inc.)
Box 300
Crosby, Minnesota 56441
Harvey Paulson, President
(218) 546-5125

SCOT LAD FOODS, INC.
1 Scot Lad Lane
Lansing, Michigan 60438
Walter R. Schaub, President
(312) 895-2300
   See also Chilton Canning
   Company

1197

Companies and Trade Names

SCOT TIES, LTD.
14 East 38th Street
New York, New York 10016
M. Blum, President
(212) 243-8660

SCOT-TUSSIN PHARMACAL COMPANY
50 Clemence Street
Cranston, Rhode Island 02920
Salvatore G. Scotti, President and Treasurer
(401) 942-8555

SCOTCH (tapes, dispensers, sewing notions, etc.)
See 3M Company

SCOTCH-BRITE (pot scourers)
See 3M Company

SCOTCH CRAFT (sports apparel)
See United Knitwear Company Inc.

SCOTCH GAME CALL COMPANY, INC.
60 Main
Oakfield, New York 14125
(716) 948-3241

SCOTCH-IRISH (tobacco)
See John Weisert Tobacco Company

SCOTCH KING (snuff)
See United States Tobacco Company

SCOTCH MIXTURE (tobacco)
See Faber, Coe & Gregg, Inc.

SCOTCH-TRED (floor covering)
See 3M Company

SCOTCH TUMBLER (menswear)
See Jantzen Inc.

SCOTCHGARD (fabric protector)
See 3M Company

SCOTKINS (paper napkins)
See Scott Paper Company

SCOTS (footwear)
See SCOA Industries, Inc.

SCOT'S GOLD (gin)
See Schenley Industries, Inc.

SCOTSMAN (folding chairs)
See Bela Seating Company Inc.

SCOTSMAN (ice machines, drink dispensers)
See Queen Products (Division of King-Seeley Thermos Company)

SCOTT & FETZER COMPANY, THE
14600 Detroit Avenue
Lakewood, Ohio 44107
Ralph Schey, President
(216) 228-6200
See also American Lincoln; Campbell Hansfeld Company; and Kirby Company

SCOTT & FETZER COMPANY, THE
Douglas Division
141 Railroad Street
Bronson, Michigan 49028

SCOTT & SONS COMPANY, O.M.
(Subsidiary of ITT Corporation)
333 North Maple Street
Marysville, Ohio 43040
F. Leon Herron, Jr., Chairman of the Board
(513) 642-6015

SCOTT-ALISON PHARMACEUTICAL
581 Sagamore
Teaneck, New Jersey 07666

SCOTT AVIATION
225 Erie Street
Lancaster, New York 14086
Edward J. Fierle, President
(716) 683-5100

SCOTT BOAT COMPANY, INC.
Box 68
Thawville, Illinois 60968

SCOTT COMPANY INC., ROBERT T.
20436 N.E. 15th Court
North Miami Beach, Florida 33162
(305) 651-0114

SCOTT-CORD LABORATORIES INC.
23 Englewood Avenue
Englewood, New Jersey 07631

SCOTT COUNTY (food products)
See Morgan Packing Company Inc.

SCOTT, FORESMAN & COMPANY
1900 East Lake Avenue
Glenview, Illinois 60025
Darrel E. Peterson, Chairman of the Board
(312) 729-3000

SCOTT GLASS COMPANY
Post Office Box 152
Fort Smith, Arkansas 72901
(918) 436-2421

SCOTT GRAPHICS INC.
(Subsidiary of Scott Paper Company)
Holyoke, Massachusetts 01040
W.S. Wesson, President
(413) 536-7800

SCOTT, INC., H.H.
111 Powder Mill Road
Maynard, Massachusetts 01754
Solomon Boucai, President
(617) 897-8801

Companies and Trade Names

SCOTT MANUFACTURING
    COMPANY
Box 61
Amarillo, Texas   79105

SCOTT MOLDING COMPANY
Box 2958
Sarasota, Florida   33578

SCOTT NATIONAL (food products)
    See Burns Foods, Ltd.

SCOTT PAPER COMPANY
Scott Plaza
Philadelphia, Pennsylvania   19113
Charles D. Dickey, Jr., Chairman
(215) 521-5000
    See also Warren Company, S.D.

SCOTT PETERSEN (meat products)
    See John Morrell & Company

SCOTT SCIENTIFIC INC.
Post Office Box 2121
Fort Collins, Colorado   80521

SCOTT SPECIALTIES, INC.
1810 L Street
Belleville, Kansas   66935

SCOTT TOBACCO COMPANY,
    INC.
Box 658
Bowling Green, Kentucky   42101
Henry H. Baird, President
(502) 842-5727

SCOTT U.S.A. INC.
(Subsidiary of Clorox Company)
Box 187
Sun Valley, Idaho   83353
James E. Tobin, President
(208) 726-4541

SCOTTIE (pet foods)
    See Old Mother Hubbard Dog
        Food Company, Inc.

SCOTTISH & NEWCASTLE
    IMPORTERS COMPANY
640 West Colorado Boulevard
Glendale, California   91204
Michael Dixon, President
(213) 245-0381

SCOTTISH CRAFTS AND
    INDUSTRIES, INC.
Box 803
Montauk, New York   11954

SCOTTISH INNS OF AMERICA,
    INC.
104 Bridgewater Road
Knoxville, Tennessee   37919
William J. Dooner, President
(615) 693-6611

SCOTTISSUE (bathroom tissue)
    See Scott Paper Company

SCOTT'S (dressings and seasonings)
    See Werner Food Specialties

SCOTTS (outboard motors)
    See McCulloch Corporation

SCOTT'S LIQUID GOLD, INC.
4880 Havana Street
Denver, Colorado   80239
Jerome Goldstein, President
(303) 373-4860

SCOTTY (motorized children's
vehicles)
    See Grand Prix Manufacturing
        Company, Inc.

SCOTTY (space savers)
    See Sanjo Utility Manufacturing
        Company Inc.

SCOTTY PEN COMPANY
78 First Street
San Francisco, California   94105
(415) 982-1172

SCOTTY'S INC.
Post Office Box 939
Winter Haven, Florida   33880
James W. Sweet, Chairman of the
    Board
(813) 299-1111

SCOUT (electric outboard motor)
    See Evinrude Motors

SCOUT (twin-floating head razor)
    See North American Philips
        Corporation

SCOUT CABIN (groceries)
    See E. Bierhaus & Sons

SCOVILL MANUFACTURING
    COMPANY
Scovill Square
99 Mill Street
Waterbury, Connecticut   06720
Malcolm Baldrige, Chairman of
    the Board
(203) 757-6061
    See also Ajax Hardware Corpora-
        tion; Coradco Window &
        Door; Dominion Electric
        Corporation; Hamilton-
        Beach; Lightcraft of
        California, Inc.; and
        Nutone

SCOVILL MANUFACTURING
    COMPANY
Sewing Notions Group
Buckingham
Waterbury, Connecticut   06710
(203) 757-6061

SCOVILL MANUFACTURING
    COMPANY
Dritz, John & Sons Division
350 Fifth Avenue
New York, New York   10001
(212) 947-3100

SCRABBLE (crossword game)
    See Selchow & Righter Company

Companies and Trade Names

SCRAM (moth preventives, deodorants)
See Frank J. Curran-Esquire Chemical Company

SCRANTON ALUMINUM MANUFACTURING COMPANY
1011-1015 Capouse Avenue
Scranton, Pennsylvania 18509
(717) 347-6080

SCRANTON BAKER SUPPLY COMPANY
Rocky Glen Road
Moosic, Pennsylvania 18501

SCRAP MASTER (food waste disposer)
See Salvajor Company

SCREAMING YELLOW ZONKERS (popcorn specialty)
See Ovaltine Food Products

SCREEN-A-SHOW (cassette projector)
See Kenner Products

SCREEN GEMS
(Division of Columbia Pictures Industries, Inc.)
711 Fifth Avenue
New York, New York 10022
John H. Mitchell, President
(212) 751-4432

SCREEN-KING (general hardware)
See Allied Hardware Services Inc.

SCRIBNER'S SONS, CHARLES
597 Fifth Avenue
New York, New York 10017
Charles Scribner, Jr., President
(212) 486-2700

SCRIP, INC.
101 South Street
Peoria, Illinois 61602

SCRIPTO, INC.
Box 4847
423 Houston Street, N.E.
Atlanta, Georgia 30302
Herbert W. Sams, Chairman
(404) 523-8511

SCRIPTOMATIC INC.
2030 Upland Way
Philadelphia, Pennsylvania 19131
(215) 878-9600

SCRIVNER-BOOGAART, INC.
Post Office Box 26146
1101 S.E. 59th Street
Oklahoma City, Oklahoma 73126
J.V. Smith, President

SCROLL (aluminum furniture)
See Keller-Scroll Inc.

SCROLLCRAFT INC.
480 East Water Street
Urbana, Ohio 43078

SCROPPO COMPANY, GIUSEPPE
19 Rector Street
Staten Island, New York 10310
(212) 248-4500

SCRU-DRILL (combined electric drill and screwdriver)
See Black & Decker Manufacturing Company

SCRUGGS PHARMACAL COMPANY, INC.
611 Moore Street
Marion, Alabama 36756

SCUDDER'S, LAURA
(Division of Pet, Inc.)
1525 North Raymond Avenue
Anaheim, California 92803

SCUF PRUF (heel protectors)
See Eastern Seaboard Plastics, Inc.

SCUFFABLES (slippers)
See R.G. Barry Corporation

SCUFFY (pet-store franchise)
See American Pet Company

SCULPTRA WAX (paints and paint sundries, toys, hobbies, etc.)
See Fitzgerald Enterprises, Inc.

SCULPTURA (chrome serving ware)
See Kromex

SCULPTURA (plastic chairs)
See Clarin Corporation

SCULPTURED (aluminum chairs)
See Emeco Industries Inc.

SCUPPERNONG (wine)
See Canandaigua Industries Company, Inc.

SCUTL (lawn-care products)
See O.M. Scott & Sons Company

SCUTTLEBUTT (girls' sportswear)
See L. Wohl & Company

SEA & AIR PRODUCTS INC.
Box 821
South Norwalk, Connecticut 06856

SEA & SHORE (synthetic-turf carpet)
See Ozite Corporation

SEA & SKI CORPORATION
(Subsidiary of Smith Kline & French Laboratories)
1500 Spring Garden Street
Philadelphia, Pennsylvania 19101
Peter Godfrey, Chairman of the Board
(215) 854-4000

Companies and Trade Names

SEA BEACH (seafoods)
See Biloxi Canning & Packing Company, Inc.

SEA BEE (canned seafood products)
See Universal Packers Corporation

SEA BRAND (frozen seafood)
See National Sea Products (United States) Corporation

SEA BREEZE (frozen foods)
See Alberti Foods, Inc.

SEA BREEZE LABORATORIES, INC.
Post Office Box 15598
Pittsburgh, Pennsylvania 15244
John H. Weisbrod, President
(412) 923-2626

SEA-CAL (septic-tank and cesspool cleaner)
See Activated Chemicals & Products Company

SEA CLEAR (all-purpose cleaner)
See Newport Supply Company

SEA COAST (canned and frozen foods)
See Coast Counties Canning Company

SEA COAST COMPANY, INC.
Box 502
315 Seal Avenue
Biloxi, Mississippi 39533
(601) 436-3344

SEA COVE (seafood)
See Wally Sea Products Corporation

SEA-CREST (houseboat)
See Aluminum Cruisers Inc.

SEA CREST (mobile home)
See Kit Manufacturing Company

SEA FASHIONS (women's beachwear)
See Marlyle Swimwear Corporation

SEA GEM (frozen seafood)
See Coldwater Seafood Corporation

SEA GULL (seafoods)
See Webeco Foods, Inc.

SEA HARVEST PACKING COMPANY
Box 818
Brunswick, Georgia 31520
Charles Wesley Wells, General Manager
(912) 264-3212

SEA HAUL (canned fish)
See K.J. Preiswerck Ltd.

SEA HAVEN (seafood)
See Washington Crab Producers Inc.

SEA-HORSE (outboard motors)
See Johnson Motors

SEA HORSE CORRAL
Box 1477
Coral Gables, Florida 33134

SEA ISLAND (salad dressing)
See Kraftco Corporation

SEA ISLAND THREAD CORPORATION
476 Broadway
New York, New York 10013
(212) 226-7037

SEA ISLE PRODUCTS, INC.
995 N.W. 72nd Street
Miami, Florida 33150
(305) 836-1010

SEA JACKET (paints)
See Gloucester Paints, Inc.

SEA KING (canned foods)
See Marion Foods Corporation

SEA KING (men's toiletries)
See Old 97 Company

SEA KING (shoes)
See Bristol Manufacturing Corporation

SEA-LAND SERVICE, INC.
(Subsidiary of McLean Industries Inc.)
Post Office Box 900
Edison, New Jersey 08817
Paul F. Richardson, President
(201) 494-2500

SEA-LECT (seafood)
See Revere Smoked Fish Company

SEA LIGHTFUL (seafood)
See Rubenstein Foods Inc.

SEA LINE (marine products)
See West Products

SEA LORD (seafood)
See Westfair Foods Ltd.

SEA-LUX (repair and maintenance material for boats)
See Woolsey Marine Industries

SEA MAID (seafoods)
See Sau-Sea Foods, Inc.

Companies and Trade Names

SEA MARK (men's swimwear)
See Hansley Industries Inc.

SEA MATE PRODUCTS COMPANY
Box Three
West Pittston, Pennsylvania 18643

SEA MIST (lemonade and lemon products)
See Ventura Coastal Corporation

SEA 'N' AIR BUSINESS CASE MANUFACTURERS
106 East Tenth Street
Saint Paul, Minnesota 55101
(612) 224-5381

SEA NYMPH BOATS
Box 298
Syracuse, Indiana 46567
(219) 457-3131

SEA PAK CORPORATION
Box 667
Saint Simons Island, Georgia 31522
H.J. Cofer, Jr., President and Chief Executive Officer
(912) 639-8691

SEA PAL DISTRIBUTING COMPANY
17023 Hawthorne Boulevard
Lawndale, California 90260

SEA-PREME (seafood)
See Allied Institutional Distributors

SEA RAY BOATS
925 North Lapeer Road
Oxford, Michigan 48051

SEA ROCK (seafood)
See Washington Crab Producers Inc.

SEA ROVER MARINE
1301 Bay Street S.E.
Saint Petersburg, Florida 33701

SEA SCAMP (small boats, rowboats, dinghies, etc.)
See Aero-Nautical, Inc.

SEA SCAPE (life preservers)
See Gentex Corporation

SEA SENSORS INC.
422 East Warren Lane
Inglewood, California 90302

SEA SHELL INDUSTRIES INC.
701 N.W. 12th Street
Miami, Florida 33125
(305) 324-1567

SEA SIREN (rubber swim caps)
See Pretty Products Inc.

SEA SNACK COMPANY
1400 North American
Philadelphia, Pennsylvania 19122
(215) 769-6800

SEA SPIKE ANCHORS INC.
994 Fulton Street
Farmingdale, New York 11735
(516) 249-2241

SEA SPORT (safety vests)
See Gentex Corporation

SEA SPRITE BOAT COMPANY, INC.
Box 160
Crescent City, Illinois 60928

SEA STAR (frozen seafood)
See Coldwater Seafood Corporation

SEA STAR (swimwear)
See Leading Lady Foundations, Inc.

SEA-SWING (stove)
See Bremer Manufacturing Company Inc.

SEA TASTY (seafood)
See Gorton, Slade & Company, Inc.

SEA-TEC RESEARCH INC.
4154 Santa Monica Boulevard
Los Angeles, California 90029
(213) 661-2138

SEA-TEMP INSTRUMENT COMPANY
19250 East Colima Road
La Puente, California 91748

SEA TIES
Box 186
Westport, Connecticut 06880

SEA TREASURE (seafood)
See Inter-American Foods Inc.

SEABARTS
Box One
Willoughby, Ohio 44094

SEABIRD (seafood)
See Point Adams Packing Company

SEABIRD INDUSTRIES
1775 West Okeechobee Road
Hialeah, Florida 33010
W.C. Runnstrom, President
(305) 885-1555

SEABOARD ALLIED MILLING CORPORATION
200 Boylston Street
Newton, Massachusetts 02167
H.H. Bresky, President and Chief Executive Officer
(617) 332-8492

SEABOARD COAST LINE RAILROAD COMPANY
3600 West Broad Street
Richmond, Virginia 23230
W. Thomas Rice, Chairman
(804) 359-6911

Companies and Trade Names

SEABOARD MARINE
212 Montauk Highway
Islip, New York 11751

SEABOARD PACKING COMPANY
(Subsidiary of Stinson Canning Company)
Prospect Harbor, Maine 04669

SEABOARD SEED COMPANY
Post Office Box 106
1 Quality Lane
Bristol, Illinois 60512
G.H. Valentine, Jr., President
(312) 553-5801

SEABOARD WORLD AIRLINES
John Kennedy International Airport
Jamaica, New York 11430
Richard M. Jackson, President
(212) 995-8900

SEABORNE SYSTEMS INC.
100 Merrick Road
Rockville Center, New York 11570

SEABREEZE (gin and tonic)
See Seagram Distillers Corporation

SEABREEZE (seafood)
See Guilford Packing Company Inc.

SEABREEZE MARINE CORPORATION, INC.
See Lyn-Craft Boat Company

SEABRIGHT (marine equipment)
See Newport Supply Company

SEABROOK FARMS COMPANY
(Subsidiary of Seabrook Foods, Inc.)
Seabrook, New Jersey 08302
James M. Seabrook, President
(609) 455-1000

SEABROOK FOODS, INC.
(Subsidiary of Springs Mills, Inc.)
321 Plant Street
Montezuma, Georgia 31063
Murry P. Berger, President
(912) 472-8101
See also Carnation Seafoods; and Southern Frozen Foods, Inc.

SEACO (outboard motors)
See Eska Company

SEACRAFT INC.
24400 S.W. 137th Avenue
Princeton, Florida 33030

SEAFARER (fishing and sailing vests)
See Gentex Corporation

SEAFARER (flotation jackets)
See Canor Plarex, Inc.

SEAFARER FIBERGLASS YACHTS, INC.
760 Park Avenue
Huntington, New York 11743
Brian B. Acworth, President
(516) 427-6670

SEAFORTH CORPORATION
(Division of Nestle-LeMur Company)
529 Fifth Avenue
New York, New York 10036
(212) 867-8900

SEAFRESH (seafood)
See National Sea Products (United States) Corporation

SEAFROST (frozen seafood)
See McCallum-Legaz Fish Company Inc.

SEAGER'S (gin)
See Dreyfus, Ashby & Company

SEAGRAM & SONS, INC., JOSEPH E.
(Subsidiary of Centenary Distillers, Inc.)
375 Park Avenue
New York, New York 10022
Jack Yogman, President
(212) 572-7000
See also Browne Vintners Company; Calvert Distillers Company; Four Roses Distillers Company; General Wine & Spirits Company; Park Avenue Imports; and Summit Marketing Company

SEAGRAM DISTILLERS COMPANY
(Division of Joseph E. Seagram & Sons, Inc.)
375 Park Avenue
New York, New York 10022
(212) 572-7000

SEAGREN PRODUCTS, INC.
3623 Fort Hamilton Parkway
Brooklyn, New York 11218
(212) 853-3300

SEAGULL MARINE SALES
1851 McGaw Avenue
Irvine, California 92705

SEAKANDEE (fish and seafoods)
See Trans-Oceanic Distributing Corporation

SEAL (life jackets)
See Gentex Corporation

SEAL-ALL (adhesive, glue, cement)
See Allen Products Corporation

SEAL-COTE (corrosion-control agent)
See CRC Chemicals

Companies and Trade Names

SEAL, INC.
251 Roosevelt Drive
Derby, Connecticut 06418
Donald D. Hundt, President and
 Chief Executive Officer
(203) 735-8741

SEAL 'N CURE (automotive
accessories)
 See Kapro Corporation

SEAL-O-MATIC (steel cookware)
 See Regal Ware, Inc.

SEAL-O-MATIC/FLASH COMPANY
272 Sussex Avenue
Newark, New Jersey 07107
(201) 481-6500

SEAL OF PURITY (food color,
extracts, and glucose)
 See William H. Siegmann
  Company

SEAL TEK INC.
3000 West 16th Avenue
Hialeah, Florida 33012

SEALAIR (aluminum windows)
 See Kawneer Company

SEALD-SWEET GROWERS, INC.
Post Office Box 2349
Tampa, Florida 33601
D. Victor Knight, President
(813) 223-7411

SEALED POWER CORPORATION
2001 Sanford
Muskegon, Michigan 49444
Edward I. Schalon, President
(616) 726-3261

SEALINE (paints)
 See Pettit Paint Company, Inc.

SEALMASTER (tank balls)
 See Radiator Specialty Company

SEALRIGHT COMPANY, INC.
(Subsidiary of Phillips Petroleum
 Company)
605 West 47th Street
Kansas City, Missouri 64112
A.M. Hull, President
(816) 531-6666

SEALSWEET (fruit juices)
 See Golden Gem Growers Inc.

SEALTEST FOODS
(Division of Kraftco Corporation)
Woodland Avenue and 43rd Street
Philadelphia, Pennsylvania 19104
John M. Steiner, President
(215) 243-2000

SEALTITE
(Division of Piper Brace Sales
 Corporation)
811 Wyandotte
Kansas City, Missouri 64105
(816) 842-2040

SEALY, INC.
Merchandise Mart
Chicago, Illinois 60654
Howard G. Haas, President
(312) 944-1915

SEAMAN FISHERIES, INC.
Powell Avenue
Bayou La Batre, Alabama 36509

SEAMASTER (liferaft)
 See Datrex Inc.

SEAMATE CORPORATION
2601 East Oakland Park Boulevard
Fort Lauderdale, Florida 33306

SEAMLESS HOSPITAL PRODUCTS
 COMPANY
(Division of Dart Industries)
253 Hallock Avenue
New Haven, Connecticut 06503
V.F. Mendillo, President
(203) 787-2211

SEAMLOC LOMA-LOOM CARPET
 COMPANY
165 West Putman Avenue
Greenwich, Connecticut 06830
(212) 683-6321

SEAMPRUFE (lingerie)
 See Charles Komar & Sons, Inc.

SEAPACK
(Division of W.R. Grace &
 Company)
Box 667
Saint Simons Island, Georgia 31522
H.J. Cofer, Jr., President
(912) 638-8691

SEARCH (spray antiseptic)
 See Bristol-Myers Company

SEARCHLIGHT (processed seafood)
 See New England Fish Company

SEARER RUBBER COMPANY
125 North Union Street
Akron, Ohio 44304
(216) 253-9492

SEARLE & COMPANY, G.D.
Searle Parkway
Skokie, Illinois 60076
William G. Analyan, President
(312) 982-7000

SEARS, ROEBUCK AND COMPANY
Sears Tower
Chicago, Illinois 60684
Arthur M. Wood, Chairman of the
 Board
(312) 875-2500
 See also Allstate Insurance
  Company

SEASIA
422 South Main
Seattle, Washington 98104

Companies and Trade Names

SEASIDE OIL COMPANY
(Subsidiary of Phillips Petroleum
  Company)
Post Office Drawer S
Santa Barbara, California 93102

SEASON (canned and packaged
foods)
  See I. Epstein & Sons, Inc.

SEASON-ALL (spices and seasonings)
  See McCormick & Company, Inc.

SEASON-ALL INDUSTRIES, INC.
Route 119 South
Indiana, Pennsylvania 15701
Frank Gorell, President
(412) 349-4600

SEASONS FAVORITE (fruit products)
  See California Farm Products

SEASTAR, INC.
91 North Franklin Street
Hempstead, New York 11550

SEASWEET CRABMEAT COMPANY
Crystal River, Florida 32629

SEATON INDUSTRIES INC.
996 Mackinaw Highway
Pellston, Michigan 49769

SEATRACE COMPANY, THE
Box 363
Gadsden, Alabama 35902

SEATRON INC.
Box 13102
Fort Lauderdale, Florida 33316
(305) 522-8556

SEATTLE BOX COMPANY
401 Spokane
Seattle, Washington 98134
(206) 623-0362

SEATTLE FIRST NATIONAL BANK
Post Office Box 3586
1001 Fourth
Seattle, Washington 98124
William M. Jenkins, Chairman of
  the Board
(206) 583-3131

SEATTLE TENT & FABRIC
  PRODUCTS COMPANY
900 North 137th Street
Seattle, Washington 98133
Roger W. Jones, President
(206) 364-8900

SEAVIEW (food products)
  See Ralston Purina Company

SEAWARD COMMERCE COMPANY
19 West 44th Street
New York, New York 10036
(212) 986-1636

SEAWAY (groceries)
  See Great Scot, Inc.

SEAWAY FOOD TOWN, INC.
1020 Ford Street
Maumee, Ohio 53537
(419) 893-9401

SEAWAY SUPPLY COMPANY
4201 Redwood Avenue
Los Angeles, California 90066
(213) 821-8071

SEAZUN (kelp products)
  See Ocean Labs, Inc.

SEBACLEAN COMPANY, THE
528 Monroe Avenue
Glencoe, Illinois 60022

SEBAGO, INC.
Mechanic Street
Westbrook, Maine 04092
Daniel J. Wellehan, President and
  Treasurer
(207) 854-8474

SEBASTIAN STUDIO INC.
13 Bassett Street
Marblehead, Massachusetts 01945

SEBASTIAN'S INTERNATIONAL,
  INC.
312 Bank of Washington Building
Spokane, Washington 99201

SEBASTOPOL COOPERATIVE
  CANNERY
Box 241
Sebastopol, California 95472

SEBRING (pocket watches)
  See Ingraham Industries

SEBRING INDUSTRIAL
  CORPORATION
Post Office Box 467
Sebring, Florida 33870
(813) 385-8441

SECHLER & SON INC., RALPH
RFD Number One
Saint Joe, Indiana 46785

SECOND CHEF INC.
2715 Brooklyn Avenue
Fort Wayne, Indiana 46804

SECRET (deodorant)
  See Procter & Gamble Company

SECRET CHANGE (face cream,
hair-care product)
  See Andrew Jergens Company

SECRET CHARM BRA INC.
180 Madison Avenue
New York, New York 10016
(212) 684-2232

SECRET OF VENUS (bath powder,
perfume, etc.)
  See Parfums Weil Paris, Inc.

Companies and Trade Names

SECRETER (ear receiver)
See Maico Hearing Instruments

SECURITY (juvenile product)
See Mapes Industries Inc.

SECURITY (timers)
See Jules Racine & Company, Inc.

SECURITY BLANKET COMPANY
18320 Clifftop Way
Malibu, California 90265

SECURITY ENGINEERING
15 Buford Road
Peabody, Massachusetts 01960

SECURITY MILLS INC.
(Division of Conagra Inc.)
Post Office Box 671
Knoxville, Tennessee 37901
(615) 524-3061

SECURITY PACIFIC NATIONAL BANK
(Subsidiary of Pacific Security Corporation)
333 South Hope Street
Los Angeles, California 90071
Frederick G. Larkin, Jr., Chairman of the Board
(213) 613-6211

SEDCO INDUSTRIES INC.
1352 South Borchard Avenue
Santa Ana, California 92705

SEDCO-SPORT EDUCATIONAL DEVICES COMPANY
See Sports Educational Devices Company

SEDGEFIELD (men's and boys' sportswear)
See Blue Bell, Inc.

SEDGWICK MACHINE WORKS, INC.
Foot of Prospect Street
Poughkeepsie, New York 12602
(914) 454-5400

SEE-A-SHOW (viewer)
See Kenner Products

SEE-LINE COMPANY
Post Office Box 2765
Amarillo, Texas 79105

SEE SAFE (plastic products)
See Phillips Films Company, Inc.

SEE-THRU (clear, heat-resistant ovenware)
See Jeannette Glass Company

SEEBURG CORPORATION, THE
1500 North Dayton Street
Chicago, Illinois 60622
(312) 642-0800
See also King Musical Instruments

SEEBURG INDUSTRIES, INC.
767 Fifth Avenue
New York, New York 10022
Louis J. Nicastro, Chairman of the Board
(212) 751-5300

SEED-TAPE (seeds)
See Ferry-Morse Seed Company

SEEDBURO EQUIPMENT COMPANY
1022 West Jackson Boulevard
Chicago, Illinois 60607
(312) 738-3700

SEEDMAN COMPANY INC.
104-01 Foster Avenue
Brooklyn, New York 11236
(212) 272-3270

SEELBACH COMPANY, INC., K.C.
Post Office Box 15
Rhinebeck, New York 12572

SEEMAN BROTHERS, INC.
Seabrook, New Jersey 08302

SEE'S CANDY SHOPS, INC.
3423 LaCinego Boulevard
Los Angeles, California 90016
Charles N. Huggins, President
(213) 870-3761

SEGGERMAN SLOCUM INC.
15 James Street
New Haven, Connecticut 30112
H. Turner Slocum, President and Treasurer
(203) 777-3461

SEGGIO (stack and gang chairs)
See Hank Loewenstein Inc.

SEGO (reducing aid)
See Pet, Inc.

SEIBERLING LATEX PRODUCTS
4500 S.E. 59th Street
Oklahoma City, Oklahoma 73135
Robert Greenberg, President
(405) 672-2301

SEIBERLING TIRE & RUBBER COMPANY, THE
(Subsidiary of Firestone Tire & Rubber Company)
Barberton, Ohio 44203
J.L. Cumming, President
(216) 745-1111

SEIDEN BRASS & GIFTWARE
225 Fifth Avenue
New York, New York 10010
(212) 522-4497

SEIDENBERG (cigars)
See S. Frieder & Sons Company

Companies and Trade Names

SEIDLITZ (paint)
See Conchemco, Inc.

SEIDNER'S MAYONNAISE
26 Friendship
Westerly, Rhode Island 02891
(401) 596-7721

SEIFERT'S INC.
109 West Washington Street
Washington, Iowa 52353
William J. Seifert, Chairman of the Board
(319) 653-5448

SEIKI CORPORATION
18-39 42nd Street
Astoria, New York 11105

SEIKO BUSINESS MACHINE
(Division of C. Itoh & Company, Inc.)
270 Park Avenue
New York, New York 10017
(212) 953-5455

SEIKO TIME CORPORATION
640 Fifth Avenue
New York, New York 10019
Masahiro Sekimoto, Vice President
(212) 977-2800

SEILER CORPORATION, THE
153 Second Avenue
Waltham, Massachusetts 02154
(617) 890-6200

SEILER'S OF NEW ENGLAND
153 Second Avenue
Waltham, Massachusetts 02154
James R. Cochrane, President
(617) 890-6200

SEILON (plastics)
See Seiberling Tire & Rubber Company

SEINSHEIMER COMPANY, H.A.
400 Pike Street
Cincinnati, Ohio 45202
James P. Ahern, President
(513) 241-6100

SEKAI MANUFACTURING COMPANY INC.
350 Fifth Avenue
New York, New York 10001
(212) 695-0200

SEKINE COMPANY, INC., I.
200 Park Avenue South
New York, New York 10003
Leon A. Feder, Chairman and President
(212) 674-6333

SEKISUI PRODUCTS INC.
1800 West Blancke Street
Linden, New Jersey 07036

SEKO INC.
282 West 24th Street
Hialeah, Florida 33010

SEL-MOR GARMENT COMPANY, INC.
1717 Olive Street
Saint Louis, Missouri 63103
Marc A. Seldin, President
(314) 421-3312

SEL-TOX (insecticides, pesticides)
See Nott Manufacturing Company, Inc.

SELANDIA (stainless steel and pewter)
See Walter Fleisher Company, Inc.

SELBY (shoes)
See United States Shoe Corporation

SELBY FURNITURE HARDWARE COMPANY
15-21 East 22nd Street
New York, New York 10010
(212) 673-4097

SELCHOW & RIGHTER COMPANY
2215 Union Boulevard
Bayshore, New York 11706
C. Ellsworth Tobias, President
(516) 666-7390

SELECT (timers and chronographs)
See Jules Racine & Company, Inc.

SELECT-A-SCENT (scented paints)
See Foy-Johnston Inc.

SELECT-A-SPEDE (motors)
See The Louis Allis Company

SELECT EDITIONS (men's suits, sportscoats)
See Martil Clothing Company

SELECT GIFTS COMPANY, INC.
(Division of Peterson's Ltd.)
75 Triangle Boulevard
Carlstadt, New Jersey 07073

SELECT WARES INC.
325 East 58th Street
New York, New York 10022
(212) 688-5404

SELECTA (ham and pork products)
See Jaka Ham Company, Inc.

SELECTAVISION MAGTAPE
(video recorder/player)
See RCA Corporation

SELECTIVE LEATHER NOVELTIES COMPANY INC.
50 West 29th Street
New York, New York 10001

Companies and Trade Names

SELECTRA INC.
28 West 005 Industrial Avenue
Barrington, Illinois 60010

SELECTRIC (electric typewriter)
   See International Business
      Machines Corporation

SELECTRON (paints)
   See PPG Industries, Inc.

SELECTRON (photo-slide changers)
   See Bell & Howell Company

SELECTROSLIDE (projector)
   See Spindler & Sauppe

SELF-SERVER SALES, INC.
213 Admiral Street
Providence, Rhode Island 02908

SELFIX INC.
311 West Superior Street
Chicago, Illinois 60610
(312) 337-7190
   See also Maggie Magnetic

SELICK INC., C.H.
17 Edgewood Road
Red Bank, New Jersey 07701

SELIG MANUFACTURING
   COMPANY, INC.
(Subsidiary of Simmons Company)
52 Green Street
Leonminster, Massachusetts 01453
Robert H. Wexler, President
(617) 537-9111

SELL-O MANUFACTURING INC.
1505 South Ninth
Sheboygan, Wisconsin 53081

SELLECK WATERCYCLE
   CORPORATION
Post Office Box 366
Boca Raton, Florida 33432
(305) 395-3303

SELLRIGHT GIFTWARES
   CORPORATION
225 Fifth Avenue
New York, New York 10010
(212) 685-5451

SELL'S (liver pate)
   See William Underwood
      Company

SELLWELL (canned meats)
   See Loyal Packing Company

SELMER
(Division of Magnavox Company)
Box 310
1119 North Main Street
Elkhart, Indiana 46518
H. William Petersen, President
(219) 264-4141

SELSI COMPANY INC.
40 Veterans Boulevard
Carlstadt, New Jersey 07072

SEM PRODUCTS INC.
Sem Lane and Shoreway Road
Belmont, California 94002

SEMCA CORPORATION
Hamilton Clock Division
Box Eight
East Petersburg, Pennsylvania 17520

SEMINOLE PAPER & PRINTING
   COMPANY
60 N.W. Third Street
Miami, Florida 33101
(305) 379-8481

SEMINOLES (moccasins, slippers)
   See Hiawatha Shoe Company

SEMMERLING MANUFACTURING
   CORPORATION
700 North Wolf Road
Wheeling, Illinois 60090

SEMPCO INC.
201 North Eighth Street
West Branch, Michigan 48661

SEMPER PAPER COMPANY
40-14 24th Street
Long Island City, New York 11101
(212) 383-2826

SEMPLE COMPANY
1000 South Broad
Philadelphia, Pennsylvania 19146
(215) 735-4334

SEN-DURE PRODUCTS INC.
25 Moffitt Boulevard
Bay Shore, New York 11706

SENATE CLUB (cigars)
   See Parodi Cigar Corporation

SENATOR (calculating machine)
   See General Trading Company
      Inc.

SENATOR (cigars)
   See Gesty Trading &
      Manufacturing Corporation

SENATOR (fishing reels)
   See Penn Fishing Tackle
      Manufacturing Company

SENATOR CORBY (blended whiskey)
   See James Barclay & Company,
      Ltd.

SENATORS CLUB (whiskey, gin,
and vodka)
   See Laird & Company

SENECA FOODS CORPORATION
74 Seneca Street
Dundee, New York 14837
Arthur Wolcott, President
(607) 243-7171
   See also Marion Foods
      Corporation

Companies and Trade Names

SENECA GLASS COMPANY
Post Office Box 855
709 Beechurst Avenue
Morgantown, West Virginia 26505
John W. Weimer, President,
 Treasurer and General Manager
(304) 292-7121

SENECA KNITTING MILLS
 COMPANY, INC.
Seneca Falls, New York 13148
F.J. Souhan, President
(315) 568-9441

SENECA KRAUT & PICKLING
 COMPANY INC.
Box 97
Phelps, New York 14532
(315) 548-8311

SENECA TEXTILE
(Division of United Merchants &
 Manufacturers Inc.)
200 Madison Avenue
New York, New York 10016
(212) 686-6200

SENG COMPANY, THE
 See Hoover-Seng Company

SENGBUSCH COMPANY
2222 West Clybourn
Milwaukee, Wisconsin 53233
Frederick G. Sengbusch, President
 and Treasurer
(414) 933-7650

SENIOR EXECUTIVE (motor homes)
 See Executive Industries Inc.

SENNETT CANDY COMPANY
Box 2481
Memphis, Tennessee 38102

SENNHEISER ELECTRONIC
 CORPORATION
10 West 37th
New York, New York 10018
(212) 239-0190

SENOKOT (laxative)
 See Purdue Frederick Company

SENORET CHEMICAL COMPANY
631 Leffingwell Avenue
Saint Louis, Missouri 63122
(314) 966-2394

SENSATION CORPORATION, THE
7577 Burlington
Ralston, Nebraska 68127

SENSATIONAL (pipes)
 See Winston Briar Pipe
  Manufacturing Company

SENSI-DRY (clothes dryer)
 See Hotpoint

SENSODYNE (toothpaste for
sensitive gums)
 See Block Drug Company Inc.

SENSORMATIC ELECTRONICS
 CORPORATION
2040 Sherman Street
Hollywood, Florida 33020
David R. Humble, Vice President
(305) 920-6030

SENTINEL (first-aid products)
 See Forest City Products Inc.

SENTINEL (hardware and
housewares)
 See Puretec Inc.

SENTRY (safes)
 See John D. Brush Company
  Inc.

SENTRY CHEMICAL COMPANY
3645 Oakcliff Road
Doraville, Georgia 30340

SENTRY FENCES
(Division of Texas Steel & Wire
 Corporation)
2002 Brittmoore
Houston, Texas 77043
(713) 462-2638

SENTRY HARDWARE CORPORATION
33 Public Square Building
Cleveland, Ohio 44113
(216) 621-2045

SENTRY INSURANCE & MUTUAL
 COMPANY
1421 Strongs Avenue
Stevens Point, Wisconsin 54481
John W. Joanis, Chairman of the
 Board
(715) 344-2345

SENTRY 24-HOUR TIMER
 See General Electric Company

SENTRYBOX (fire-resistant chest
and safe)
 See John D. Brush Company Inc.

SEPP IMPORT AGENCIES, JOHN E.
381 Park Avenue South
New York, New York 10010
(212) 683-2840

SEQUOYAH INDUSTRIES INC.
4545 North Lincoln Boulevard
Oklahoma City, Oklahoma 73105
James L. Fesperman, President
(405) 528-7821

SER-VAC (insulated serving ware)
 See West Bend Thermo-Serv, Inc.

SERAC (sports apparel and
accessories)
 See Super-Visor Corporation

SERANO (food products)
 See B.F. Trappey's Sons Inc.

Companies and Trade Names

SERBIN FASHIONS, INC.
3480 N.W. 41st Street
Miami, Florida 33142
Lewis I. Serbin, Chairman of the Board
(305) 635-0607

SERCO (groceries)
See S.E. Rykoff & Company

SERENE HIGHNESS (pillows and mattress pads)
See Celanese Corporation

SGT. PEPPER SALES
2800 East Miraloma Avenue
Anaheim, California 92806

SERGEANTS (pet-care products)
See Miller-Morton Company

SERMA COMPANY
7517 20th Avenue
Brooklyn, New York 11214
(212) 232-0101

SERMAN & COMPANY, INC., M.
1411 Broadway
New York, New York 10018
Michael Serman, President
(212) 244-0125

SERNAU INC., PAUL E.
236 Fifth Avenue
New York, New York 10001
(212) 686-8911

SERO OF NEW HAVEN
1290 Avenue of the Americas
New York, New York 10019
Seymour Shapiro, President
(212) 246-4209

SERON MANUFACTURING COMPANY
254 Republic Avenue
Joliet, Illinois 60435
(815) 725-1502

SERRA SHARP (dressmakers' shears)
See Marks Specialties Inc.

SERRANO (men's toiletries)
See Swank Inc.

SERTA INC.
666 Lake Shore Drive
Chicago, Illinois 60611
Alan H. Goff, President
(312) 787-6000

SERUMS & VACCINES OF AMERICA
(Division of Murai Laboratories, Inc.)
301 Almeria Avenue
Coral Gables, Florida 33134

SERUTAN (laxative)
See J.B. Williams Company Inc.

SERV-AGEN CORPORATION
1101 Frankford Avenue
Philadelphia, Pennsylvania 19125
(215) 739-2500

SERV-IT (aluminum platter)
See West Bend Aluminum Company

SERV-U-RITE (canned foods)
See Krier Preserving Company

SERVAIDES (paper towels, place mats, table covers)
See Erving Paper Mills

SERVBEST FOODS INC.
1256 Old Skokie Road
Highland Park, Illinois 60035

SERVEL (air conditioners)
See Arkla Industries, Inc.

SERVE'N STYLE (folding carts)
See General Housewares Corporation Leisure Furniture Group

SERVESS (paints and paint sundries)
See Cotter & Company

SERVESSWARE (kitchenware)
See Ace Manufacturing Company, Inc.

SERVETTES (folding tray tables)
See Quaker Industries Inc.

SERVI-CARS (motor vehicles)
See Harley-Davidson Motor Company

SERVICE AUTOMATICS, INC.
95 Grant Avenue
Copiague, New York 11726

SERVICE MERCHANDISE COMPANY, INC.
2968 Foster Creighton Drive
Nashville, Tennessee 37204
Raymond Zimmerman, President
(615) 259-4214

SERVICE PRODUCTS, INC.
5900 West 51st Street
Chicago, Illinois 60638
(312) 767-2360

SERVICE RECORDER COMPANY, THE
(Division of Sycon Corporation)
959 Cheney Avenue
Marion, Ohio 43302
(614) 382-5771

SERVICEMASTER INDUSTRIES INC.
2300 Warrenville Road
Downers Grove, Illinois 60515
(312) 964-1300

Companies and Trade Names

SERVIS PAPER
(Division of Calibrated Charts
   Corporation)
56 Harvester Avenue
Batavia, New York 14020

SERVISCO
470 Mundet Place
Hillside, New Jersey 07205
Nathaniel Cohen, President
(201) 964-7500

SERVIT FOODS CORPORATION
100-05 92nd Avenue
Richmond Hill, New York 11418

SERVO CORPORATION OF
   AMERICA
111 New South Road
Hicksville, New York 11802
Henry Blackstone, Chairman,
   President and Treasurer
(516) 938-9700

SERVOMATION CORPORATION
777 Third Avenue
New York, New York 10017
Allan P. Lucht, President
(212) 751-2650
   See also Red Barn System, Inc.

SERVUS RUBBER COMPANY, THE
1136 Second Street
Rock Island, Illinois 61201
Richard L. Schulz, President
(309) 786-7741

SESAMEE (box and luggage locks,
padlocks)
   See Corbin Cabinet Lock

SESSIONS
(Division of United Metal Goods
   Manufacturing Company)
379 DeKalb Avenue
Brooklyn, New York 11205
(212) 789-6200

SESSIONS CLOCK COMPANY
58 East Main Street
Forestville, Connecticut 06010

SESSIONS COMPANY, INC.
Post Office Box 1336
108 West College Avenue
Enterprise, Alabama 36330
(205) 347-9551

SET-N-GO (tile)
   See Sikes Corporation, Florida
   Tile Division

SETH THOMAS
(Division of General Time
   Corporation)
135 South Main Street
Thomaston, Connecticut 06787
Ron E. Weaver, General Manager
(203) 283-5881

SETHNESS PRODUCTS COMPANY
444 North Lake Shore Drive
Chicago, Illinois 60611
Charles H. Sethness, Jr., Chairman,
   and President
(312) 527-4755

SETON NAME PLATE
   CORPORATION
592 Boulevard
New Haven, Connecticut 06505
Fenmore R. Seton, President
(203) 772-2520

SETON PHARMACEUTICAL
   COMPANY
2697 Merrick Road
Bellmore, New York 11710

SETTLER (meat products)
   See Omaha Steaks International

SETWELL COMPANY, THE
Woodmere Avenue
Traverse City, Michigan 49684

SEVEN CHIMES (whiskey)
   See M.S. Walker, Inc.

7 CROWN (whiskey)
   See Seagram-Distillers Company

7-ELEVEN (food-store franchise)
   See Southland Corporation

7-FARMS (groceries)
   See S.M. Flickinger Company

SEVEN-ITE (protective auto
coating)
   See E.I. du Pont de Nemours &
   Company Inc.

SEVEN-MINUTE (dinners)
   See Thomas J. Lipton Inc.

707 COMPANY, THE
1530 Stillwell Avenue
Bronx, New York 10461
(212) 823-8300

SEVEN SEAS (men's slacks)
   See Anthony Gesture

SEVEN SEAS (men's toiletries)
   See Faberge, Inc.

SEVEN SEAS (salad dressings)
   See Anderson Clayton Foods

SEVEN SEAS (tobacco)
   See John Weisert Tobacco
   Company

SEVEN SEAS ARTS
1254 East Miner Road
Mayfield Heights, Ohio 44124

SEVEN SEAS INDUSTRIES
Post Office Box 616
Westport, Connecticut 06880

SEVEN STAR (whiskey)
   See Gooderham & Worts, Ltd.

7 STEERS RESTAURANTS
691 Peachtree Street N.E.
Atlanta, Georgia 30308
(404) 874-7777

Companies and Trade Names

SEVEN-UP COMPANY, THE
121 South Meramee Avenue
Saint Louis, Missouri 63105
Ben H. Wells, Chairman of the Board
(314) 863-7777

SEVENSTRAND TACKLE MANUFACTURING COMPANY
14799 Chestnut
Westminster, California 92683

SEVENTEEN INC.
33 Virginia Avenue
West Nyack, New York 10994

76 (gasoline)
See Union Oil Company of California

SEVERA'S (cough remedy, soap, first-aid ointment)
See Myers Laboratories, Inc.

SEVERIN (trumpets, cornets, trombones, French horns, saxophones, etc.)
See Peate Musical Supplies Ltd.

SEVIGNY'S CANDY, INC.
West Hanover, Massachusetts 02339

SEVILLE OLIVE COMPANY
633 South Anderson
Los Angeles, California 90023
(213) 261-2218

SEW MAGIC (children's sewing machine)
See Mattel, Inc.

SEWARD FISHERIES
(Affiliation of Petersburg Fisheries Inc.)
4215 21st Avenue West
Seattle, Washington 98119
(206) 282-0988

SEWARD LUGGAGE MANUFACTURING COMPANY
(Subsidiary of Dayco Corporation)
434 High Street
Petersburg, Virginia 23803
G.F. Liebscher, President
(703) 733-5111

SEWHANDY (miniature sewing machine)
See Singer Company

SEXAUER MANUFACTURING COMPANY, J.A.
10 Hamilton Avenue
White Plains, New York 10601
(914) 948-0224

SEXTON & COMPANY, JOHN
(Division of Beatrice Foods Company)
222 South Riverside Plaza
Chicago, Illinois 60606
M. Sexton, President
(312) 648-1100

SEYMOUR (scissors and shears)
See American Cutlery & Hardware Company Inc.

SEYMOUR CANNING COMPANY
Box Five
Seymour, Wisconsin 54165

SEYMOUR FOODS INC.
Box 1220
First and Kansas
Topeka, Kansas 66601
M.J. Chamberlain, President
(913) 233-4181

SEYMOUR MANUFACTURING COMPANY
Fifth and Broadway
Seymour, Indiana 47274
Willis S. Hobson, President
(812) 522-2900

SEYMOUR OF SYCAMORE INC.
917 Crosby Avenue
Sycamore, Illinois 60178
Edward H. Seymour, President
(815) 895-9101

SEYMOUR PRODUCTS CORPORATION
109 River Street
Seymour, Connecticut 06483

SGT.
See Sergeant

SHA-LEM, INC.
1229 South 12th Street
Virginia, Minnesota 55792

SHACHIHATA INC. USA
6731 Variel Avenue
Canoga Park, California 91303

SHACKMAN & COMPANY, B.
85 Fifth Avenue
New York, New York 10003
(212) 989-5162

SHACO PRODUCTS, INC.
125 Rivington Street
New York, New York 10002
(212) 475-7200

SHADIGREEN (lawn seed)
See Associated Producers Inc.

SHADOTONE (paints)
See Cook Paint & Varnish Company

SHADOWLINE, INC.
Lenoir Road
Morganton, North Carolina 28655
Sherrod Salsbury, President
(704) 437-3821

SHADY BROOK (canned foods)
See Carlton Clifton & Sons

Companies and Trade Names

SHADY LANE (dresses)
See Bleeker Street Apparel Corporation

SHAER SHOE CORPORATION
Canal and Dow
Manchester, New Hampshire 03101
David L. Shaer, President
(603) 625-8566

SHAFFER, CLARKE & COMPANY
424 Madison Avenue
New York, New York 10017
(212) 688-0795

SHAFFORD COMPANY, THE
225 Fifth Avenue
New York, New York 10010
(212) 685-7966

SHAG-A-MO (men's sportswear)
See Alps Sportswear Manufacturing Company Inc.

SHAGMASTER (floor-care products)
See Premier Electric Company

SHAHAF PRESS INC.
10 Canal Street
Bristol, Pennsylvania 19007

SHAI (bath powder, perfume, toilet water, etc.)
See Rosal Laboratories, Ltd.

SHAINBERG COMPANY, SAM
(Subsidiary of Interco, Inc.)
1325 Warford Street
Memphis, Tennessee 38112
Herbert Shainberg, Chairman of the Board
(901) 458-1121

SHAKE-A-PUDD'N (pudding mix)
See Standard Brands Inc.

SHAKE 'N BAKE (seasoned coating mixes)
See General Foods Corporation

SHAKER LABORATORIES
(Division of Sherwood Laboratories)
1601 East 361st Street
Willoughby, Ohio 44094

SHAKERTOWN CORPORATION
Winlock, Washington 98596

SHAKESPEARE (cigars)
See General Cigar Company

SHAKESPEARE COMPANY
Box 246
1801 Main Street
Columbia, South Carolina 29201
Stephen W. Trewhella, President
(803) 779-5800
See also Columbia Products Company; and Plymouth Golf Ball Company

SHAKESPEARE INDUSTRIES
100 Dorset Street
Burlington, Vermont 05401

SHAKEY'S, INC.
(Subsidiary of Great Western United Corporation)
333 West Hampden Avenue
Englewood, Colorado 80110
Michael Bosell, Chairman of the Board
(303) 761-3431

SHAKLEE PRODUCTS
1900 Powell Street
Emeryville, California 94608
J. Gary Shansby, President
(415) 428-8000

SHALAM IMPORTS INC.
29 West 30th Street
New York, New York 10001
(212) 695-1315

SHALEEN (hosiery)
See Chadbourn Inc.

SHALER COMPANY, THE
(Subsidiary of National Rivet & Manufacturing Company)
Waupun, Wisconsin 53963
John A. Zeratsky, President
(414) 324-5511

SHALIMAR (perfumes)
See Guerlain Inc.

SHALOM (pipes)
See Mastercraft Pipes, Inc.

SHALOM (wine)
See Old Monastery Wine Company Inc.

SHALOM BROTHERS ORIENTAL RUG COMPANY
245 Fifth Avenue
New York, New York 10016
(212) 686-0026

SHAMOKIN DRESS COMPANY
1012 North Shamokin Street
Shamokin, Pennsylvania 17872
Lawton W. Shroyer, President
(717) 648-4617

SHAMPOOETTE (shampoo recliner for children)
See Roseal Company

SHAMPOOZER (rug and upholstery shampoo)
See Carbona Products Company

SHAMROCK (waffles, pies, potato products, condiments)
See Morrison & McCluan

SHANAN COMPANY INC., STEPHEN
Post Office Box 461
Bellaire, Texas 77401

SHANBARGER, CHARLES C.
Box 142
Stewartstown, Pennsylvania 17363

Companies and Trade Names

SHANE UNIFORM COMPANY, INC.
Post Office Box 6106
2015 West Maryland Street
Evansville, Indiana 47712
Sidney A. Shane, President
(812) 423-1133

SHANNON MANUFACTURING COMPANY
Box 736
5510 Cleon Avenue
North Hollywood, California 91603
(213) 877-7166

SHAPELY (men's shirts)
See Mack Shirt Corporation

SHAPELY BEAUTIES (pillows)
See Pop-Arts, Inc.

SHARELLE (perfumes and colognes)
See House of Hampton Perfumes

SHARK BRAND (cutlery)
See Bahco Tools, Inc.

SHARKTOOTH (fishing gear)
See Sportsmen's Industries, Inc.

SHARON LABS, INC.
703 Welch Road
Palo Alto, California 94304

SHARON STEEL CORPORATION
Post Office Box 291
Sharon, Ohio 16146
Victor Posner, Chairman, President and Chief Executive Officer
(216) 448-4011

SHARP CANNING INC.
150 Hickory
Rockford, Ohio 45882

SHARP COMPANY, STANLEY
1261 Broadway
New York, New York 10001
(212) 683-6120

SHARP ELECTRONICS CORPORATION
10 Keystone Place
Paramus, New Jersey 07652
K. Saitoh, President
(201) 265-5600

SHARPE AUDIO
(Division of Scintex Inc.)
John Glen TR
Amherst Industrial Park
Buffalo, New York 14150
(716) 691-6910

SHARPSHOOTER (sporting firearms)
See The High Standard Manufacturing Corporation

SHASHI IMPORTS
215 West 98th Street
New York, New York 10025

SHASTA BEVERAGES
(Division of Consolidated Foods Corporation)
26901 Industrial Boulevard
Hayward, California 94545
William Meyers, President
(415) 783-3200

SHATTERPROOF GLASS CORPORATION
4815 Cabot Avenue
Detroit, Michigan 48210
Arthur M. Acker, President
(313) 582-6200

SHAVE BOMB (shaving products)
See American Safety Razor Company

SHAVEMASTER (electric shaver)
See Sunbeam Appliance Company

SHAVER JET (shaver for use in autos)
See Parks Products, Inc.

SHAVER MANUFACTURING COMPANY
Graettinger, Iowa 51342
(712) 859-3536

SHAVETTE (leg-shaving product)
See Julie Marie, Inc.

SHAVEX (shavers)
See Electro Engineering Products Company, Inc.

SHAW (furniture)
See General Interiors Corporation

SHAW COMPANY, MUNSON
(Division of National Distillers & Chemical Corporation)
99 Park Avenue
New York, New York 10016
(212) 949-5000

SHAW CRAFT
Stokes Road
Rural Delivery 3
Indian Mills, New Jersey 08088

SHAW CREATIONS INC.
6 West 32nd Street
New York, New York 10001
Morris Shaw, President
(212) 695-3092

SHAW, INC., M.T.
Coldwater, Michigan 49036
M.T. Shaw, Jr., President
(517) 278-2361

SHAW LABORATORIES
Box 3311
Youngstown, Ohio 44512

SHAW-WALKER COMPANY, THE
Muskegon, Michigan 49443
Shaw Walker, President
(616) 722-7211
See also Master-Craft Corporation

Companies and Trade Names

SHAWMUT BANK OF BOSTON
40 Water
Boston, Massachusetts 02106
D. Thomas Trigg, President
(617) 742-4900

SHAWNEE CANNING COMPANY
Cross Junction, Virginia 22625

SHAWNEE MILLING COMPANY
401 South Broadway
Shawnee, Oklahoma 74801
Leslie A. Ford, President
(405) 273-7000

SHE BRA BRASSIERE COMPANY
1178 Broadway
New York, New York 10001
(212) 683-8460

SHEAFFER PEN COMPANY, W.A.
(Division of Textron, Inc.)
301 Avenue H
Fort Madison, Iowa 52627
Louis S. Bishop, President
(319) 372-3300

SHEBOYGAN PAPER BOX
COMPANY
716 Clara Avenue
Sheboygan, Wisconsin 53081
Robert H. Liebl, Chairman,
President and Sales Manager
(414) 458-8373

SHEDD-BARTUSH FOODS, INC.
(Division of Beatrice Foods,
Company)
14401 Dexter Boulevard
Detroit, Michigan 48238
Adam J. Schubel, President
(313) 868-5810

SHEER ENERGY (hosiery)
See Hanes Hosiery, Inc.

SHEER MAGIC (makeup)
See Campana Corporation

SHEER PUFFERY (cosmetics)
See Coty

SHEFFIELD (cigarettes)
See United States Tobacco
Company

SHEFFIELD (motor vehicles)
See Colt Industries Inc.

SHEFFIELD (razor blades)
See Perma-Sharp Manufacturing
Corporation

SHEFFIELD BRONZE PAINT
CORPORATION
17814 Waterloo Road
Cleveland, Ohio 44119
Sanford Gross, President
(216) 481-8330

SHEFFIELD CHEMICAL
(Operation of Kraftco Corporation)
2400 Morris Avenue
Union, New Jersey 07083

SHEFFIELD TUBE CORPORATION,
THE
170 Broad Street
New London, Connecticut 06320
Peter Kyle Sheffield, President
(203) 442-4451

SHEFFIELD WATCH CORPORATION
330 West 34th Street
New York, New York 10001
Marvin Richter, Vice President
(212) 695-5300

SHEFFLER MERCHANDISE
COMPANY
999 Central Avenue
Woodmere, New York 11598

SHELBURNE INDUSTRIES, INC.
Box 158
Shelburne, Vermont 05482
Richard A. Snelling, President
(802) 985-3321
See also Barrecrafters Inc.

SHELBY (bicycles)
See AMF, Inc.

SHELBY (food products)
See Oceana Canning Company

SHELBY METAL PRODUCTS
COMPANY
110 Broadway
Shelby, Ohio 44875
W.H. Kinnaird, President
(419) 342-6526

SHELBY SINGLETON
CORPORATION, THE
3106 Belmont Boulevard
Nashville, Tennessee 37212

SHELBY WILLIAMS INDUSTRIES,
INC.
325 North Wells Street
Chicago, Illinois 60610
Herbert L. Roth, President
(312) 527-3500

SHELDON AND COMPANY INC.,
H.D.
104 Fifth Avenue
New York, New York 10011
(212) 924-6920

SHELDONS', INC.
Post Office Box 508
Antigo, Wisconsin 54409
A.L. Sheldon, President
(715) 623-2382

SHELF-N-EDGE (shelving)
See The Ullman Company, Inc.

SHELF-O-LITE (shelf lights)
See Hobby Hill Inc.

SHELFLEX (modular shelving)
See RTC Industries Inc.

Companies and Trade Names

SHELL CHEMICAL COMPANY
(Division of Shell Oil Company)
Post Office Box 2463
1 Schell Plaza
Houston, Texas 77001
(713) 220-6161

SHELL FIXTURES (lighting fixtures)
See Decorative Imports

SHELL OIL COMPANY
Post Office Box 2463
1 Shell Plaza
Houston, Texas 77001
John F. Bookout, President
(713) 220-6161

SHELL-TEX FISHERIES
(Subsidiary of Grand Caillou
Packing Company Inc.)
Box 1672
Brownsville, Texas 78520

SHELLER-GLOBE CORPORATION
1505 Jefferson Avenue
Toledo, Ohio 43697
Chester Devenow, President
(419) 255-8840
See also Globe-Weis System
Company; and Red Rope
Industries

SHELLY (meat products)
See A. Szelogowski & Son, Inc.

SHELLY BROTHERS, INC.
116 Courtland Street
Lansdale, Pennsylvania 19466

SHELTER COVE (canned seafood)
See The Tom Lazio Fish
Company Inc.

SHELTER ISLAND OYSTER
COMPANY INC.
Sterling Avenue
Greensport, New York 11944
John L. Plock, Jr., President
(516) 477-1170

SHELTER RESOURCES
CORPORATION
See Lancer Mobile Homes, Inc.;
and Winston Industries, Inc.

SHELTERDOVE, LYDIA
Post Office Box 13268
Oakland, California 94611

SHELTON-WARE INC.
133 West 20th Street
New York, New York 10011
(212) 924-5290

SHELTORS (men's coats)
See Uniroyal, Inc.

SHELV-IT-ALL (steel shelving)
See S.A. Hirsh Manufacturing
Company

SHELVES UNLIMITED
See Gale's/Shelves Unlimited

SHEN-VALLEY MEAT PACKERS
INC.
Timberville, Virginia 22853

SHENANDOAH (whiskey)
See National Distillers &
Chemical Corporation

SHENANDOAH APPLE
CO-OPERATIVE, INC.
Post Office Box 435
Fairmont Avenue
Winchester, Virginia 22601
H. Delmer Robinson, Jr., President
(703) 662-0331

SHENANDOAH CANDIES
5422 North Miami Avenue
Miami, Florida 33127
(305) 751-0803

SHENANDOAH CANDY
COMPANY, INC.
1425 Amherst
Winchester, Virginia 22601

SHENANDOAH VALLEY POULTRY
COMPANY, INC.
560 Northern Boulevard
Great Neck, New York 11021
Charles T. Ferrara, President
(516) 829-9000

SHENANGO CHINA
(Division of Interpace Corporation)
New Castle, Pennsylvania 16103

SHENANIGANS (shoes)
See Desco Shoe Corporation

SHEPARD LABORATORIES
500 Virginia Drive
Fort Washington, Pennsylvania 19034

SHEPARD-NILES CRANE AND
HOIST CORPORATION
(Subsidiary of Vulcan, Inc.)
250 North Genessee Street
Montour Falls, New York 14865
Lynn Carter, President
(607) 568-3921

SHEPHERD, LTD., IMOGENE
9011 Grand
River Grove, Illinois 60171
(312) 456-1400

SHEPHERD PRODUCTS U.S. INC.
203 Kerth Street
Saint Joseph, Michigan 49085

SHEPHERD TOBACCO COMPANY
Ridgeville Corners, Ohio 43555

SHEPPARD & MYERS, INC.
(Subsidiary of The Hanover Shoe,
Inc.)
118 Carlisle Street
Hanover, Pennsylvania 17331
A.C. Blunt, III, President
(717) 637-6631

SHEPPARD'S MILL
Greensboro, Florida 32330

Companies and Trade Names

SHER-MART-CANDLE
MANUFACTURING COMPANY
404-410 Stokes Avenue
Trenton, New Jersey 08638

SHERATON (groceries)
See Leon Supply Company

SHERATON CORPORATION
470 Atlantic Avenue
Boston, Massachusetts 02210
Howard P. James, President
(617) 482-1250

SHERATON HOTELS & MOTOR
INNS
See ITT Sheraton Corporation of
America

SHERATON LABORATORIES INC.
374 Reed
Santa Clara, California 95050
(408) 249-6285

SHERATON MANOR (mobile homes)
See Redman Industries, Inc.

SHERBROOK MARYLAND (straight
rye whiskey)
See Gooderham & Worts, Ltd.

SHERBROOKE (shoes)
See Brown Group, Inc.

SHERIDAN (beer and stout)
See Walter Brewing Company

SHERIDAN FLOURING MILLS
Sheridan, Wyoming 82801

SHERIDAN SILVER COMPANY,
INC.
90 Ingell Street
Taunton, Massachusetts 02780
Harold Wolfson, President
(617) 824-6906

SHERMAN BROTHERS CANNING
COMPANY
East Jordan, Michigan 49727

SHERMAN COMPANY, NAT
1400 Broadway
New York, New York 10018
(212) 391-8000

SHERMAN MANUFACTURING
COMPANY, H.B.
(Division of Wolverine Industries
Inc.)
207 West Michigan Avenue
Battle Creek, Michigan 49014
Frank Steketee, Vice President and
General Manager
(616) 964-7012

SHERMAN UNDERWEAR MILLS
152 Madison Avenue
New York, New York 10016
(212) 684-7090

SHERMAN, WHITE & COMPANY,
INC.
205 Murray Street
Fort Wayne, Indiana 46801

SHERMANS BRITCHES INC.
(menswear)
See Arthur Richards Ltd.

SHERRILL CORPORATION, THE
River Avenue
Mexico, Indiana 46958
(317) 872-4121

SHERRY INC., LOUIS
18 West Putnam Avenue
Greenwich, Connecticut 06830

SHERU BEAD CURTAIN &
JEWELRY DESIGNERS
49 West 38th Street
New York, New York 10018
(212) 730-0766

SHERWIN CANDY COMPANY
14657 Lull Street
Van Nuys, California 91405

SHERWIN WILLIAMS COMPANY,
THE
101 Prospect Avenue, N.W.
Cleveland, Ohio 44115
W.O. Spencer, Chairman of the
Board
(216) 566-2000
See also Acme Quality Paints
Inc.; Lucas & Company,
John; Martin-Senour
Company; and Sprayon
Products, Inc.

SHERWOOD (camping trailers)
See A-T-O, Inc.

SHERWOOD (processed foods)
See Arkell Foods Ltd.

SHERWOOD ELECTRONIC
LABORATORIES
4300 North California Avenue
Chicago, Illinois 60618
John A. Snow, President
(312) 478-7300

SHERWOOD INDUSTRIES, INC.
110 Lyman Street
Holyoke, Massachusetts 01040

SHERWOOD LABORATORIES, INC.
1601 East 361st Street
Willoughby, Ohio 44094
See also Borotar Chemical
Company; and Shaker
Laboratories

SHERWOOD MEDICAL INDUSTRIES
1831 Olive
Saint Louis, Missouri 63103
H.E. Wickstra, President
(314) 621-7788
See also Pioneer Rubber Company

Companies and Trade Names

SHERWOOD OVERSEAS
　CORPORATION
Box 793
Manhasset, New York 11030

SHERYL PHARMACEUTICALS, INC.
2303 Schuetz Road
Saint Louis, Missouri 63141
(314) 567-1544

SHETLAINE (men's sportswear)
　See Alps Sportswear Manufacturing Company Inc.

SHETLAND (floor-care products)
　See Premier Electric Company

SHETLAND-LEWYT
(Division of SCM Corporation)
2000 Walnut
Philadelphia, Pennsylvania 19103
(215) 564-2704

SHIELD (food products)
　See B.F. Trappey's Sons, Inc.

SHIELD BRAND (tools)
　See Standard Tool Company

SHIELD INDUSTRIES, R.W.
9461 Jefferson Boulevard
Culver City, California 90230

SHIGOTO INDUSTRIES LTD.
350 Fifth Avenue
New York, New York 10001
(212) 695-0200

SHILLCRAFT (rug outfits)
　See A. & H. Shillman Company, Inc.

SHILLITO COMPANY, JOHN
(Division of Federated Department Stores, Inc.)
Seventh and Race Streets
Cincinnati, Ohio 45202
Edward H. Selonick, President
(513) 381-7000

SHILLMAN COMPANY, INC.,
　A. & H.
500 North Calvert Street
Baltimore, Maryland 21202
(301) 539-0430

SHIM (skin- and hair-care products)
　See W.L. Vomack Inc.

SHIMMERICK (cosmetics)
　See Yardley of London, Inc.

SHIMMERSTICKS (lipsticks)
　See Cosmair, Inc.

SHIMMY SHINS (depilatory, shaving cream)
　See Alberto-Culver Company

SHIN SHAMS (pantyhose)
　See Burlington Industries, Inc.

SHINDANA TOYS
(Division of Operation Bootstrap Inc.)
6107 South Central Avenue
Los Angeles, California 90001
(213) 231-9387

SHINING ARMOR (enamel)
　See Illinois Bronze Powder & Paint Company

SHINTOA INTERNATIONAL, INC.
277 Park Avenue
New York, New York 10017
(212) 826-2180

SHIOCTON KRAUT COMPANY
(Subsidiary of Bush Brothers & Company)
Shiocton, Wisconsin 54170
(414) 986-3816

SHIP AHOY (frozen seafood)
　See New England Fish Company

SHIP "N" SHORE, INC.
Aston, Pennsylvania 19014
Richard L. Freundlich, President
(215) 494-2000

SHIPASHORE INC.
1313 East Jefferson Boulevard
Mishawaka, Indiana 46544

SHIPENDEC (marine enamels)
　See Pettit Paint Company Inc.

SHIPMATE (boat trailers)
　See Simek Manufacturing Inc.

SHIPMATE (heating equipment, stoves, etc.)
　See Richmond Ring Company

SHIPYARD CRAFTS
Box 171
San Lorenzo, California 94580

SHIR-BACK (curtains and drapes)
　See Cameo Curtains, Inc.

SHIRE-TEX (slacks)
　See Davenshire, Inc.

SHIREY COMPANY
1917 Stanford
Greenville, Texas 75401
David Shirey, President
(214) 455-5235

SHIRI (bath oil, cologne, perfume, etc.)
　See Sabrina Fragrances, Ltd.

SHIRLEE MANUFACTURING
　COMPANY
Broad and Willow
Terre Hill, Pennsylvania 17581

Companies and Trade Names

SHIRLEY OF ATLANTA, INC.
4200 Shirley Drive, S.W.
Atlanta, Georgia 30336
Sylvan A. Makeover, Chairman of
  the Board
(404) 691-6400

SHIRTCRAFT (clothing)
  See Oxford Industries, Inc.

SHIRTEES, INC.
350 Fifth Avenue
New York, New York 10001
(212) 564-8420

SHIRTREE (sportswear)
  See Mister Pants, Inc.

SHISEIDO COSMETICS (AMERICA) LTD.
540 Madison Avenue
New York, New York 10022
(212) 752-2644

SHIVA (artists' colors)
  See Morilla Company

SHLANSKY & COMPANY, INC., LOUIS
500 Seventh Avenue
New York, New York 10018
Milton Shlansky, President
(212) 564-6425

SHO-BUD (drums, guitars, and amplifiers)
  See Gretsch

SHO-WALL (movable room dividers)
  See Brewster Corporation

SHOCKING (women's toiletries)
  See Parfums Schiaparelli, Inc.

SHOE CORPORATION OF AMERICA
  See SCOA Industries, Inc.

SHOE FORM COMPANY
26-30 Aurelius Avenue
Auburn, New York 13021
Frank P. De Witt, President
(315) 253-6285

SHOE OF GUARANTEED COMFORT (shoes)
  See Allen-Edmonds Shoe Corporation

SHOE SAVER (shoe covers)
  See Dow Corning Corporation

SHOECRAFT, INC.
603 Fifth Avenue
New York, New York 10017
Andrew H. Rosenthal, President
(212) 755-5871

SHOETOWN (shoes)
  See The Felsway Corporation

SHOLOM GREETING COMPANY INC.
26 South Sixth Avenue
Mount Vernon, New York 10550

SHONEY'S BIG BOY ENTERPRISES, INC.
1727 Elm Hill Pike
Nashville, Tennessee 37210
Raymond Danner, President
(615) 254-5201

SHONTEX PRODUCTS COMPANY
2915 South La Cienega Boulevard
Culver City, California 90230
Howard Soloman, President
(213) 870-5725

SHOP-KING (hand and power tools)
  See Allied Hardware Services Inc.

SHOP RITE FOODS, INC.
2401 West Marshall Drive
Grand Prairie, Texas 75050
E.W. Keeling, President
(214) 263-3311

SHOP-VAC CORPORATION
(Division of Craftool, Inc.)
2323 Reach Road
Williamsport, Pennsylvania 17701
(717) 326-0503

SHOPCRAFT (tools)
  See McGraw-Edison Company, Portable Electric Tools Division

SHOPMATE (tools)
  See McGraw-Edison Company, Portable Electric Tools Division

SHOPMOR (groceries)
  See Daitch Crystal Dairies, Inc.

SHOPPER (infants' product)
  See Peterson Baby Products

SHOPPING BAG (soap products, mayonnaise, corned beef)
  See E.F. MacDonald Shopping Bag Food Stores Inc.

SHOPSMITH (power tools)
  See Magna American Corporation

SHOPWELL, INC.
400 Walnut Avenue
Bronx, New York 10454
Martin Rosengarten, President
(212) 665-6200

SHORE ACRES (food products)
  See North East Packing Corporation

Companies and Trade Names

SHORE CHEMICAL COMPANY, INC.
Boston Post Road
Madison, Connecticut 06443

SHORE INDUSTRIES, INC.
See Superior Sleeprite

SHORELINE SEAFOODS, LTD.
Hookers Point
Tampa, Florida 33605

SHORELL INC., IRMA
509 Madison Avenue
New York, New York 10022
(212) 759-5236

SHORT MILLING COMPANY, J.R.
233 South Wacker Drive
Chicago, Illinois 60606
Jeffrey R. Short, Jr., President
(312) 876-7070

SHORT SNORTER (beer)
See Horlacher Brewing Company

SHORT STOP CONVENIENCE MARTS INC.
5310 Cleveland Avenue
Columbus, Ohio 43229
(614) 882-8500

SHORTRIP (luggage, travel and desk accessories)
See Brecher Brothers, Inc.

SHOSHA CARDS
141 East 88th Street
New York, New York 10028
(212) 879-4940

SHOT OF STEAM (steam irons)
See Sunbeam Appliance Company

SHOW & TELL PRODUCTS
17657 Ridge Creek
Cleveland, Ohio 44136
(216) 238-5511

SHOW BOAT (canned foods)
See Bush Brothers & Company

SHOWCARD MACHINE COMPANY
320 West Ohio Street
Chicago, Illinois 60610
(312) 944-3829

SHOWCASE (luggage)
See Eastern Case Company, Inc.

SHOWCASE (multiple long-play records)
See Pickwick International Inc.

SHOWER FRESH LTD.
100 Tokeneke Road
Darien, Connecticut 06820

SHOWER TO SHOWER (body powder)
See Johnson & Johnson

SHOWERFOLD (tub and shower enclosures)
See Kinkead Industries, Inc.

SHOWERITE (tub and shower enclosures)
See Theodore Efon Manufacturing Company

SHOWOFF (rainwear)
See Trident Sales Company

SHOX STOK CORPORATION
Spencerville, Indiana 46788

SHRAGER & SONS, LOUIS
2314 North American Street
Philadelphia, Pennsylvania 19133

SHRED ALL (food-waste disposer)
See Whirl-A-Way Company

SHRED-O-MAT (salad maker)
See Rival Manufacturing Company

SHRIMP-BAKE (prepared frozen seafood)
See Eat-All Frozen Food Company, Inc.

SHRIMP BOATS
Lanier Plaza
Macon, Georgia 31202

SHRIMP-MEX (seafood)
See M.S. Cowen Company

SHRUBSOLE CORPORATION, S.J.
104 East 57th Street
New York, New York 10022
(212) 753-8920

SHU-MAK-UP
(Division of Advance Color Corporation)
800 South Vail Avenue
Los Angeles, California 90054
(213) 723-5233

SHUFORD MILLS, INC.
Post Office Box 2228
Hickory, North Carolina 28601
Harley F. Shuford, Sr., President
(704) 328-2131

SHUGLOVS (women's rubber footwear)
See B.F. Goodrich Company, Footwear & Flooring Division

SHUKSAN FROZEN FOODS INC.
204 First Street
Lynden, Washington 98264

SHULER INTERNATIONAL INC.
5241 Greenhurst Extension
Cleveland, Ohio 44137
(216) 587-6626

SHULSINGER BROTHERS, INC.
21 East Fourth Street
New York, New York 10012
(212) 475-3637

Companies and Trade Names

SHULTON, INC.
(Subsidiary of American Cyanamid Company)
687 Route 46
Clifton, New Jersey 07013
A.L. Munsell, President
(201) 546-7000
See also Nitine Inc.

SHUMAN PLASTIC INTERNATIONAL
35 Neoga
Depew, New York 14043

SHUN (repellent for dogs and cats)
See William Cooper & Nephews, Inc.

SHUN (tobacco deterrent)
See Sacramento Pharmacal Company

SHUPTRINE COMPANY
Post Office Box 5126
Savannah, Georgia 31403
(912) 232-8303

SHUR EDGE (cutlery)
See Robeson Cutlery Company, Inc.

SHUR-LOK CORPORATION
1300 East Normandy Place
Santa Ana, California 92705
F.W. Rohe, President
(714) 547-8891

SHUR-SAVE (health and beauty aids)
See Hereth Food Mart, Inc.

SHUR-TRED (antiskid product)
See Permaflex Products

SHUR UP (men's socks)
See Kayser-Roth Hosiery Company, Inc.

SHUR WOOD (wood products)
See Robeson Cutlery Company, Inc.

SHURE BROTHERS, INC.
222 Hartrey Avenue
Evanston, Illinois 60204
S.N. Shure, President
(312) 328-9000

SHUREGOOD (fruit)
See Washington Fruit & Produce Company

SHURFINE-CENTRAL CORPORATION
2100 North Mannheim Road
Northlake, Illinois 60164
R.G. Avischious, President
(312) 681-2000

SHURLOCK (shingles)
See Flintkote Company

SHUTTLE (skin-care products)
See Unique Products Company

SI BON (bath oil, cologne, soap, etc.)
See Monico, Inc.

SIAM SILVER (rings, bracelets, pendants)
See Quality Bronzeware Inc.

SIAMESE IMPORTS COMPANY
71 Plandome Road
Manhasset, New York 11030

SIBER HEGNER & COMPANY, INC.
1250 Broadway
New York, New York 10001
(212) 563-5213

SIBERIAN SALMON EGG COMPANY
4660 East Marginal Way South
Seattle, Washington 98134
(206) 762-2620

SIBERT & COMPANY, INC.
8 Livingston Street
Newark, New Jersey 07103
(201) 242-3230

SIBLEY, LINDSAY & CURR COMPANY
(Division of Associated Dry Goods Corporation)
228 Main Street, East
Rochester, New York 14604
William E. Lee, President
(716) 232-7700

SIBONEY (cigars)
See Perfecto Garcia & Brothers, Inc.

SIBONEY (rum)
See Schenley Industries, Inc.

SIBS ASSOCIATES INC.
35 Haddon Avenue
Shrewsbury, New Jersey 07701

SICALY (freeze-dried foods)
See I.G. Koryn, Inc.

SICHEL (French wines)
See Schieffelin & Company

SICILLIAN GOLD (wine)
See Paterno Imports Ltd.

SICO INC.
Post Office Box 1169
7525 Cahill Road
Minneapolis, Minnesota 55435
Kermit H. Wilson, President and Treasurer
(612) 941-1700

SID JEROME (women's dresses)
See Smoler Brothers, Inc.

SIDE-BY-SIDE (outboard motors)
See Jetco Inc.

Companies and Trade Names

SIDLEY COMPANY
88 First Street
San Francisco, California 94105
(415) 421-3188

SIDNEY SAILBOATS
4057 Lincoln Boulevard
Venice, California 90291

SIEGEL COMPANY, INC.,
HENRY I.
16 East 34th Street
New York, New York 10016
Jesse Siegel, President
(212) 685-8700

SIEGEL COMPANY, INC., JACOB
642 North Broad
Philadelphia, Pennsylvania 19130
(215) 763-4000

SIEGEL, FRANK C.
475 Fifth Avenue
New York, New York 10017
(212) 685-1470

SIEGWERK (cookware)
See Hagemeyer Industries Inc.

SIELING URN & BAG COMPANY
927 West Huron
Chicago, Illinois 60622
(312) 421-1024

SIEMENS CORPORATION
186 Wood Avenue, South
Iselin, New Jersey 08830
Otto J. Dax, President
(201) 494-1000

SIERRA (cigarettes)
See Brown & Williamson Tobacco Corporation

SIERRA (lawn and garden supplies)
See Hall Distributing Company

SIERRA (saws)
See G.W. Griffin Company

SIERRA CHEMICAL COMPANY
Box 275
Newark, California 94560

SIERRA FIRE EQUIPMENT
COMPANY
3804 South Broadway Place
Los Angeles, California 90037
(213) 232-3131

SIERRA PACIFIC INDUSTRIES
1990 North California Boulevard
Walnut Creek, California 94596
A.A. Emmerson, President
(415) 933-6440

SIERRA PACIFIC POWER COMPANY
100 East Moana Lane
Reno, Nevada 89510
Neil W. Plath, Chairman of the Board
(702) 789-4011

SIESTA (decaffeinated instant coffee)
See Standard Brands Inc.

SIFERS CHEMICALS INC.
112 West Jackson
Iola, Kansas 66749

SIFERS VALOMILK CONFECTION
COMPANY
See Hoffman Candy Company

SIG MANUFACTURING INC.
Route One
Box One
Montezuma, Iowa 50171
(515) 623-5154

SIGARETTO (cigars)
See Petri Cigar Company

SIGHT GUARD (lamps)
See Electrix, Inc.

SIGHT LIGHT (lamps)
See M.G. Wheeler Company Inc.

SIGHT-SAVER (desk lamps)
See Laurel Lamp Manufacturing Company Inc.

SIGHT SAVERS (eyeglass cleaners, nose and temple pads)
See Dow Corning Corporation

SIGHTMASTER (desk light)
See Art Specialty Company Inc.

SIGHTSEER CORPORATION
(Subsidiary of PRF Industries, Inc.)
Mid-Ohio Industrial Park
Newark, Ohio 43055
Peter R. Fink, President
(614) 928-6215

SIGMA (acoustic and electric guitars)
See C.F. Martin Organization

SIGMA ENGINEERING COMPANY
11320 Burbank Boulevard
North Hollywood, California 91601
(213) 877-0187

SIGMA LEATHER INC.
99 Madison Avenue
New York, New York 10016
(212) 679-8000

SIGMA MARKETING SYSTEMS INC.
225 Fifth Avenue
New York, New York 10010
(212) 725-4844

SIGMA PHARMACEUTICAL
CORPORATION
Box 977
342 Madison Avenue
New York, New York 10017
(212) 986-0245

SIGMAN MEAT COMPANY, INC.
6000 West 54th Avenue
Arvada, Colorado 80217

Companies and Trade Names

SIGNA CORPORATION
Box 501
Decatur, Indiana 46733

SIGNA-CRAFT
(Division of Crownmark Corporation)
166 Valley Street
Providence, Rhode Island 02909

SIGNAL (smoked hams)
See Heath Meat Company, Inc.

SIGNAL COMPANIES, INC., THE
9665 Wilshire Boulevard
Beverly Hills, California 90212
William E. Walkup, Chairman of the Board
(213) 278-7400
See also Mack Trucks, Inc.

SIGNAL OFFICE PRODUCTS COMPANY
66 Erna Avenue
Milford, Connecticut 06460

SIGNAL OIL & GAS COMPANY
2800 North Loop, West
Houston, Texas 77018
W.H. Thompson, Jr., President
(713) 686-9261

SIGNAL-U MANUFACTURING COMPANY
(Division of Cooper Industries Inc.)
250 Railroad Street
Canfield, Ohio 44406
(216) 533-5535

SIGNALTONE CORPORATION
34039 Schoolcraft Road
Livonia, Michigan 48150
(313) 425-3120

SIGNATURE (aftershave, cologne)
See Max Factor & Company

SIGNATURE (band instruments)
See DEG Music Products Inc.

SIGNATURE (canned foods)
See Hickmott Canning Company

SIGNATURE (electric guitars)
See Micro-Frets Corporation

SIGNATURE (major appliances)
See Montgomery Ward & Company

SIGNATURE GREETINGS
457 Kramer Road
Dayton, Ohio 45419

SIGNATURE QUALITY (meats)
See Roegelein Provision Company

SIGNATURES (shoes)
See Brockton Footwear, Inc.

SIGNET (band instruments and accessories)
See Selmer (Division of Magnavox Company)

SIGNET (food products)
See NCC Food Corporation

SIGNET (mirrors)
See Carolina Mirror Corporation

SIGNET (portable typewriters)
See Royal Typewriter Company

SIGNET MARINE KITS ASSOCIATES
Box 91
Wilton, Connecticut 06897

SIGNET SCIENTIFIC COMPANY
Box 6489
Burbank, California 91505

SIGNORICCI (men's toiletries)
See Nina Ricci

SIKA CHEMICAL CORPORATION
875 Valley Brook Avenue
Lyndhurst, New Jersey 07071
Paul Meeske, President
(201) 933-8800

SIKES CORPORATION
Post Office Box 447
608 Prospect Street
Lakeland, Florida 33802
James W. Sikes, President
(813) 683-5431

SIL-O-ETTE (beds)
See Burton-Dixie Corporation

SIL-O-ETTE SALES CORPORATION
200 Madison Avenue
New York, New York 10016
Lawrence P. O'Reilly, President
(212) 685-5050

SILA-LUX (enamels)
See International Paint Company Inc.

SILASTIC (silicone rubber products)
See Dow Corning Corporation

SILBO STEEL CORPORATION
10 Columbus Circle
New York, New York 10019
(212) 265-0022

SILENCE IS GOLDEN (cough remedies)
See Hillside (Division of Bristol-Myers Products)

SILENT BREEZE (ventilating fans)
See Holcomb & Hoke Manufacturing Company, Inc.

SILENT NIGHT (body powder, deodorant, etc.)
See Countess Maritza Cosmetic Company

Companies and Trade Names

SILENT SIOUX CORPORATION
208 Eighth S.W.
Orange City, Iowa 51041

SILENT 67 (air-conditioning furnace)
　See Fraser & Johnston Company

SILENT WATCHMAN CORPORATION
4861 McGraw
Columbus, Ohio 43207
(614) 491-5200

SILER CITY MILLS, INC.
Post Office Box 249
118 West Second Street
Siler City, North Carolina 27344
Dannis Sawyer, President and
　General Manager
(919) 742-2166

SILEX (coffee-making equipment)
　See Bloomfield Industries Inc.

SILF SKIN GIRDLES
14 Pelham Parkway
Pelham, New York 10803

SILHOUETTE (housewares and appliances)
　See Gamble-Skogmo Inc.

SILHOUETTE (luggage)
　See Samsonite Corporation

SILHOUETTE (reducing aid)
　See Thompson Medical Company, Inc.

SILHOUETTES
2020 East Seventh Street
Los Angeles, California 90021
(213) 627-0021

SILICARE (medicated hand cream)
　See Revlon, Inc.

SILICONE SEAL (adhesives)
　See General Electric Company, Silicone Products

SILICONIX INC.
2201 Laurelwood Road
Santa Clara, California 95054
Richard E. Lee, President and
　Treasurer
(408) 246-8000

SILITE, INC.
2600 North Pulaski Road
Chicago, Illinois 60639
(312) 489-2600

SILITEX (paints)
　See Upson Company

SILK 'N HOLD (hair-care product)
　See John H. Breck Inc.

SILK 'N SATIN (bath products)
　See Leeming/Pacquin

SILK SHEEN (hair conditioners)
　See Helena Rubinstein, Inc.

SILKEN LEGS (aerosol shave cream for women)
　See Colgate-Palmolive Company

SILKO NEW IMPROVED PRODUCTS COMPANY
2121 Ninth Avenue South
Birmingham, Alabama 35205

SILKY-SOFT (fabric softener and liquid detergent)
　See Mayflower Super Foods

SILL FARMS MARKET
Route One
Lawrence, Michigan 49064

SILLCOCKS-MILLER COMPANY
41 West Parker Avenue
Maplewood, New Jersey 07040

SILLS PRODUCTS COMPANY, INC.
Box 807
Woodward, Oklahoma 73801

SILLY PUTTY MARKETING
Box 741
187 Union Avenue
New Haven, Connecticut 06503
(203) 562-4115

SILOO INC.
393 Seventh Avenue
New York, New York 10001
(212) 695-3190

SILTEX (men's furnishings)
　See Knothe Brothers Company Inc.

SILTON BROTHERS, INC.
3535 South Broadway
Los Angeles, California 90007
Fred Silton, President
(213) 233-7151

SILVA-CHROME (trays and serving pieces)
　See Forman Family Inc.

SILVA COMPANY
(Division of Johnson Diversified Inc.)
2466 North State Road 39
La Porte, Indiana 46350

SILVA INC.
Highway 39 North
La Porte, Indiana 46350

SILVA THINS (cigarettes)
　See American Tobacco Company

SILVAGNI (concertinas)
　See J.M. Sahlein Music Company Inc.

SILVALITE (religious pendants)
　See Panation Trade Company, Inc.

1224

Companies and Trade Names

SILVATRIM CORPORATION OF
AMERICA
Box 396
South Plainfield, New Jersey 07080

SILVECO PRODUCTS, INC.
2502-14 Milwaukee Avenue
Chicago, Illinois 60647
(312) 489-0130

SILVEIRA & O'CONNELL
Post Office Box 320
Sebastopol, California 95472

SILVER & COMPANY, FRED
145 Sussex Avenue
Newark, New Jersey 07103
(201) 621-8848

SILVER BEAM (lantern)
See Dorco Manufacturing Inc.

SILVER-BRITES (aluminum paint)
See Sherwin Williams Company

SILVER CENTURY (outboard motors)
See Intra Corporation

SILVER CITY GLASS COMPANY
INC., THE
122 Charles Street
Meriden, Connecticut 06450
William D. Schultz, President,
Treasurer and Sales Advertising
Manager
(203) 235-7911

SILVER CREEK ORCHARDS
Tyro, Virginia 22976

SILVER CREEK PRESERVING
CORPORATION
Box 64
Howard Street
Silver Creek, New York 14136
W.W. Wilson, President
(716) 934-2687

SILVER CROWN (fruit products)
See Landsman Packing Company
Inc.

SILVER CUP (groceries)
See Central Grocers
Co-Operative Inc.

SILVER CUP (tobacco)
See Whitehall Products Inc.

SILVER CURL (home permanent)
See Gillette Company

SILVER DEW (gin)
See Old Boone Distillery
Company

SILVER DIP (tarnish remover)
See Vigilant Products Company,
Inc.

SILVER DUST (detergent)
See Lever Brothers Company

SILVER FLEECE INC.
Box B
Port Clinton, Ohio 43452

SILVER FLOSS FOODS
Eagle Street
Phelps, New York 14532
Eugene W. Hermenet, President
(315) 548-9461

SILVER FOX (phonograph records)
See Shelby Singleton Corporation

SILVER GATE (canned foods)
See Klauber Wangenheim
Company

SILVER GRILLE (processed foods)
See Diamond Fruit Growers,
Inc.

SILVER/GULFSTREAM INC.
(Division of Hart, Schaffner &
Marx)
5000 South Ohio Street
Michigan City, Indiana 46360

SILVER GULL (gasoline)
See Seaside Oil Company

SILVER HILL PRODUCTS
310 Northern Boulevard
Great Neck, New York 11021

SILVER KING (tractors)
See Fate-Root-Heath Company

SILVER KNIT HOSIERY MILLS INC.
High Point, North Carolina 27260
Robert Silver, President
(919) 883-1491

SILVER LABEL (Bourbon)
See Glenmore Distilleries
Company, Inc.

SILVER LAKE COMPANY
99 High
Boston, Massachusetts 02210
(617) 426-6332

SILVER LINE (tools, paints, paint
sundries, etc.)
See Essex Machine Sales
Company Inc.

SILVER MEDAL (food products)
See McCormick & Company Inc.

SILVER METAL PRODUCTS INC.
1868 National Avenue
Hayward, California 94545

SILVER MILL FROZEN FOODS,
INC.
Box 155
Eau Claire, Michigan 49111

Companies and Trade Names

SILVER NIP (citrus products)
See Ben Hill Griffin Inc.

SILVER PINE LABORATORIES
319 North Main
Spring Valley, New York 10977

SILVER PLATE 'N POLISH (replating product for silver plate)
See Vigilant Products Company, Inc.

SILVER QUEEN INC.
2419 Felts Avenue
Nashville, Tennessee 37211
(615) 256-2380

SILVER-REY (groceries)
See S.E. Rykoff & Company

SILVER RIBBON (food products)
See Baxter Canning Company Ltd.

SILVER RUN (canned foods)
See J. Langrall & Brother, Inc.

SILVER SAVER (canned foods)
See Western Food Products Company

SILVER SEAL PHARMACAL INC.
5792 S.W. Eighth Street
Miami, Florida 33144
(305) 266-1616

SILVER SERVICE (meat, provisions)
See Red Owl Stores, Inc.

SILVER SHEEN (hosiery)
See Lynchburg Hosiery Mills, Inc.

SILVER SHIELD (groceries)
See W.H. Bintz Company

SILVER SKILLET FOOD PRODUCTS COMPANY
Post Office Box 168
7450 North Saint Louis Avenue
Skokie, Illinois 60076
David R. Lansky, President
(312) 675-8440

SILVER SPRINGS CITRUS COOPERATIVE
Box 1046
Winter Garden, Florida 32787

SILVER SPRUCE (canned foods)
See Fort Lupton Canning Company

SILVER STATE FOODS INC.
3725 Jason
Denver, Colorado 80211
(303) 433-0210

SILVER STREAK (sleds)
See Garton Company

SILVER STREAK TRAILER COMPANY
2319 North Chico Avenue
El Monte, California 91733
Kenneth E. Neptune, President
(213) 444-2646

SILVER TOP (beer)
See C. Schmidt & Sons, Inc.

SILVER TOUCH (hair-care products)
See Helena Rubinstein, Inc.

SILVER WEDDING (gin)
See Schenley Industries, Inc.

SILVER WHITE (groceries)
See P. Fahey Inc.

SILVERAMA (silver-plate trays, bowls, sugar-and-creamers)
See Philcraft Imports

SILVERBRITE (silver polish)
See Boyle-Midway

SILVERBROOK FOODS INC.
Box 2855
Wilmington, Delaware 09805

SILVERCRAFT COMPANY INC.
680 Dudley
Boston, Massachusetts 02210
(617) 282-3200

SILVERDUST (detergents)
See Lever Brothers Company

SILVERFLEX (insulation)
See Suflex Corporation

SILVERLEAF (lard)
See Swift & Company

SILVERLINE, INC.
2300 12th Street South
Moorhead, Minnesota 56560

SILVERSEAL (paints and paint sundries)
See E. Rabinowe & Company

SILVERTON MARINE CORPORATION
120 Kettle Creek Road
Toms River, New Jersey 08753

SILVERTONE (televisions)
See Sears Roebuck and Company

SILVERTOP (Scotch)
See Brown-Forman Distillers Corporation

SILVERTOWN (tires and tubes)
See B.F. Goodrich Company

SILVERTROL (outboard motors)
See G. & R. Industries Inc.

Companies and Trade Names

SILVETTA (guitars, recorders)
See FG Enterprises

SILZLE COMPANY INC., E.A.
Box 711
Anaheim, California 92805

SIMCA (motor vehicles)
See Chrysler Motors Corporation

SIMCO COMPANY, INC., THE
920 Walnut Street
Lansdale, Pennsylvania 19446
Dolph Simons, Chairman, President and Advertising Manager
(215) 368-2220

SIMCO-MOSS (cutlery)
See S.I. Moss Company, Inc.

SIMEK MANUFACTURING INC.
Townsend Avenue
Johnstown, New York 12095

SIMER PUMP COMPANY
5960 Main Street N.E.
Minneapolis, Minnesota 55432
(612) 566-5666

SIMERL, R.A.
Instrument Division
238 West Street
Annapolis, Maryland 21401
(301) 849-8667

SIMI WINERY INC.
Healdsburg, California 95448

SIMM-R-MATIC (electric frying pan)
See Westinghouse Electric Corporation

SIMMER SERVER (electric trays)
See Cornwall Corporation

SIMMON OMEGA
25-20 Brooklyn-Queens Expressway, West
Woodside, New York 11377
Fred Simmon, President
(212) 932-4040

SIMMONS COMPANY
Post Office Box 49000
Atlanta, Georgia 30340
Robert P. Tyler, Jr., President
(404) 449-5000
See also Bloomcraft

SIMMONS COMPANY
Contract Division
1870 Merchandise Mart
Chicago, Illinois 60654
(312) 644-1540

SIMMONS COMPANY
Hausted Division
Post Office Box 190
Medina, Ohio 44256
(216) 723-3271

SIMMONS COMPANY
Juvenile Products Division
New London, Wisconsin 54961

SIMMONS INC., DOROTHY
200 Varick Street
New York, New York 10014
(212) 924-3300

SIMMONS MACHINE TOOL CORPORATION
1700 North Broadway
Albany, New York 12201
Charles A. Simmons, III, President and Secretary
(518) 462-5431

SIMON & MOGILNER COMPANY
1420 14th, S.W.
Birmingham, Alabama 35211
David Betten, President
(205) 781-3661

SIMON & SCHUSTER, INC.
630 Fifth Avenue
New York, New York 10020
Richard E. Snyder, President
(212) 245-6400
See also Trident Press

SIMON CANDY COMPANY
31 North Spruce Street
Elizabethtown, Pennsylvania 17022

SIMON COMPANY, A. & R.
23 West 73rd Street
New York, New York 10023
(212) 874-4084

SIMON COMPANY, M. & D.
(Division of Bobbie Brooks, Inc.)
3830 Kelley Avenue
Cleveland, Ohio 44114
(216) 391-6969

SIMON, GEORGE
507 Fifth Avenue
New York, New York 10017
(212) 682-3872

SIMON HANDBAGS INC.
40 East 32nd Street
New York, New York 10016
(212) 679-4150

SIMON IMPORTS INC.
175 Eighth Avenue
New York, New York 10011
(212) 989-4929

SIMON PRODUCTS COMPANY
3003 Hirsch Avenue
Melrose Park, Illinois 60160
(312) 681-8980

SIMON SAYS (phonograph records)
See Westminster Recording Company, Inc.

SIMON SIMPLE ORIGINALS INC.
430 Tompkins Street
Orange, New Jersey 07050

Companies and Trade Names

SIMONDS BOATS
Box 671
Southbridge, Massachusetts 01550

SIMONE COMPANY INC., THE
See Leading Lady Foundations

SIMONETTA (cosmetics)
See Chesebrough-Pond's, Inc.

SIMONIN'S SONS, INC., C.F.
Belgrade and Tioga Streets
Philadelphia, Pennsylvania 19134
McNair Evans, President
(215) 426-2300

SIMONIZ COMPANY
See Texize Chemicals, Inc.

SIMONSON COMPANY, WILMOT H.
10 Henshaw
Woburn, Massachusetts 01801

SIMPLE SIMON (frozen dessert)
See Ward Foods, Inc.

SIMPLEX
(Division of Lava-Simplex Internationale Inc.)
1735 North Ashland
Chicago, Illinois 60622
(312) 384-2600

SIMPLEX SECURITY SYSTEMS
10 Front Street
Collinsville, Connecticut 06022
David Creedon, President
(203) 693-8391

SIMPLICITY MANUFACTURING COMPANY, INC.
(Subsidiary of Allis-Chalmers Corporation)
500 North Spring Street
Port Washington, Wisconsin 53074
A.F. Hurley, President
(414) 282-5535

SIMPLICITY PATTERN COMPANY, INC.
200 Madison Avenue
New York, New York 10016
Harold Cooper, President
(212) 481-3737

SIMPLOT COMPANY, J.R.
Post Office Box 2777
Boise, Idaho 83701
John M. Dahl, President
(208) 336-2110

SIMPSON-BOSWORTH COMPANY
2531-39 North Ashland Avenue
Chicago, Illinois 60614
(312) 528-8787

SIMPSON COMPANY
1470 Doolittle Drive
San Leandro, California 94577
(415) 562-7775

SIMPSON ELECTRONICS, INC.
2295 N.W. 14th Street
Miami, Florida 33125
William S. Simpson, President
(305) 633-3261

SIMPSON-LAWRENCE (anchors)
See Seagull Marine

SIMPSON TABLET COMPANY
Post Office Box 1008
Everett, Washington 98201

SIMPSON TIMBER COMPANY
900 Fourth Avenue
Seattle, Washington 98164
Gilbert L. Oswald, President
(206) 292-5000

SIMPSON'S
950 Clement Street
San Francisco, California 94118

SIMRAD INC.
Labriola Court
Armonk, New York 10504

SIMS (cigarettes)
See Nat Sherman Company

SIMS (sports accessories and equipment)
See Janoy Inc.

SIMSON COMPANY, O.K.
84 Daisy Farm Drive
New Rochelle, New York 10804

SINAREST (sinus medication)
See Pharmacraft

SINCERELY YOURS (foundation garments, lingerie)
See Glamorise Foundations, Inc.

SINCLAIR & VALENTINE COMPANY
(Division of Martin Marietta Corporation)
120 Charlotte Place
Englewood Cliffs, New Jersey 07632

SINCLAIR GLASS
520 North Michigan
Chicago, Illinois 60611
(312) 644-9133

SINCLAIR INDUSTRIES INC.
1317 Kentucky Avenue
Saint Louis, Missouri 63110
(314) 535-6335

SINCLAIR MANUFACTURING COMPANY
6120 Detroit Avenue
Toledo, Ohio 43612
James Brown, President
(419) 478-4131

SINCLAIR PHARMACAL COMPANY
Drawer D
Fishers Island, New York 06390

SINE-AID (sinus-headache tablets)
See Johnson & Johnson

Companies and Trade Names

SINE-OFF (sinus medication)
　See Menley & James Laboratories

SINEX (nasal spray)
　See Vick Chemical Company

SING (deodorant soap)
　See Purex Corporation, Ltd.

SINGER BUSINESS MACHINES
15287 Hesperian Boulevard
San Leandro, California 94578
(415) 483-6480

SINGER COMPANY, INC., S.J.
1133 Broadway
New York, New York 10010
(212) 243-7792

SINGER COMPANY, INC., THE
30 Rockefeller Plaza
New York, New York 10020
Joseph B. Flavin, President
(212) 581-4800
　See also Controls Company of
　America; and Society for
　Visual Education, Inc.

SINGER ORIGINALS INC., ARLENE
102 Shoreview Drive
Yonkers, New York 10710

SINGER, WILLIAM H.
Post Office Box 95
Cheltenham, Pennsylvania 19012

SINGING NEEDLES, INC.
(Subsidiary of the William Carter
　Company)
40 Glen Brook Road
Leola, Pennsylvania 17540

SINGLE FORGE (sporting goods)
　See York Cutlery Company Inc.

SINGLE SERV (groceries)
　See W.T. Lynch Foods, Ltd.

SINGLES BY GERBER (single-
serving food product for adults)
　See Gerber Products Company

SINGLETON PACKING
CORPORATION
Post Office Box 2819
Tampa, Florida 33601
Edward C. Cutcheon, President
(813) 247-1171

SINKMASTER (food-waste disposer)
　See Whirl-A-Way Company

SIOUX HONEY ASSOCIATION
509 Plymouth Street
Sioux City, Iowa 51102
Harry Rodenberg, President
(712) 258-0638

SIOUX TOOLS, INC.
2801-2999 Floyd Boulevard
Sioux City, Iowa 51102
Frank O. Albertson, President
(712) 252-0525

SIPPIT CUPS INC.
Post Office Box 2065
Hollywood, Florida 33022

SIPSTER (whiskey)
　See Glenmore Distilleries
　Company

SIR BRUCE (men's hose)
　See Iselin Jefferson-Woodside

SIR JAC (apparel)
　See Stahl-Urban Company

SIR MALCOLM (Scotch whiskies)
　See Sazerac Company, Inc.

SIR PERIOR (menswear)
　See Haspel Brothers Inc.

SIR SPEEDY INC.
Post Office Box 1790
892 West 16th Street
Newport Beach, California 92663
James Merriam, Chairman and
　President
(714) 642-9470

SIR STEAK (restaurant franchise)
　See Goody's Food Systems

SIR WALTER (shoes)
　See Craddock-Terry Shoe
　Corporation

SIR WALTER RALEIGH (tobacco and
accessories)
　See Brown & Williamson
　Tobacco Corporation

SIR WINSTON (pipes)
　See Winston Briar Pipe
　Manufacturing Company

SIRCO INTERNATIONAL
CORPORATION
700 South Fulton Avenue
Mount Vernon, New York 10550
(914) 664-4400

SIRIS PRODUCTS CORPORATION,
A.J.
780 East 134th Street
Bronx, New York 10454
Ted Scheiber, President
(212) 292-2500

SIROCCO (cologne, perfume)
　See Lucien Lelong

SIROIL LABORATORIES
(Division of The Denver Chemical
　Manufacturing Company)
35 Commerce Road
Stamford, Connecticut 06904

SISKA PRODUCTS
194 Oak Ridge Drive
Oak Harbor, Ohio 43449

Companies and Trade Names

SISSY (trunks)
   See Seward Luggage (Division of Dayco Corporation)

SIT-A-PON (juvenile seats)
   See Kantwet Company

SIT EASY (chairs)
   See Waco Products Inc.

SITASONS INTERNATIONAL INC.
284 Fifth Avenue
New York, New York 10001
(212) 594-5177

SITKA (seafood)
   See Pelican Sales Company

SITMAR CRUISES
3303 Wilshire Boulevard
Los Angeles, California 90010
John P. Bland, President
(213) 381-5941

SITTIN SOX (socks)
   See Hanover Glove Company

SITTING PRETTY (disposable diapers)
   See United States Industries, Inc.

SITTLER'S CANDIES INC., MRS.
5130 West 26th Street
Cicero, Illinois 60650

6 BELLS (seafood)
   See The Gorton Corporation

SIX SIXTY SIX CORPORATION
Post Office Box 251
Clawson, Michigan 48017

1600 LINE (metal desks, tables)
   See General Fireproofing Company

SIXTEEN LABORATORIES, INC.
Valleybrook Road
Chester Heights, Pennsylvania 19017

1670 (Scotch whiskey)
   See Hudson's Bay Company, Wine & Spirit Division

"61" (paints, varnishes, enamels, and lacquers)
   See Pratt & Lambert, Inc.

66 RESERVE (whiskey)
   See J.T.S. Brown Distillers Company

SIZZLE MAID (broiler/server)
   See Forman Family, Inc.

SIZZLER FAMILY STEAK HOUSES
12731 West Jefferson Boulevard
Los Angeles, California 90066
(213) 390-6241

SKAGG'S COMPANIES, INC.
212 West 13th Street
Salt Lake City, Utah 84110
L.S. Skaggs, President
(801) 487-4751

SKALNY BASKET COMPANY INC., L.
655 Pullman Avenue
Rochester, New York 14615
(716) 254-7907

SKAMPER (recreational vehicles)
   See AMF Inc.

SKAMPER (small boats--rowboats, dinghies, etc.)
   See Aero-Nautical Inc.

SKAN LABORATORIES
767 West Woodburn Drive
Los Angeles, California 90049
(213) 681-6749

SKANDIA FOODS, INC.
4507 North Ravenswood Avenue
Chicago, Illinois 60640
(312) 561-6853

SKANE KNIT INC.
120 South Main Street
Uxbridge, Massachusetts 01569

SKASOL CORPORATION
112 Glencoe
Webster Groves, Missouri 63119
(314) 961-7100

SKAT-KITTY (motor scooter)
   See Projects Unlimited, Inc.

SKATE MOBILE (roller skates)
   See Samsonite Corporation

SKEA LTD.
55 Stag Lane
Greenwich, Connecticut 06830

SKELETON (outdoor fireplace units and accessories)
   See Hancock Iron Works

SKELLY OIL COMPANY
(Subsidiary of Getty Oil Company)
Oil Center Building
1437 South Boulder
Tulsa, Oklahoma 74102
James E. Hara, President
(918) 584-2311

SKI (canned and frozen seafood)
   See Olfisco, Inc.

SKI BOGGAN (water-sports equipment)
   See Formex Corporation

SKI COUNTRY IMPORTS
2370 West Main Street
Littleton, Colorado 80120

Companies and Trade Names

SKI-DADDLER (snowmobiles)
  See AMF Inc.

SKI-DOO (snowmobiles and accessories)
  See Bombardier Ltd.

SKI ENTERPRISES LTD.
100 Front Street
Keeseville, New York 12944

SKI HUT
1615 University Avenue
Berkeley, California 94703

SKI IMPORTS (sports apparel, accessories, and equipment)
  See Herbert G. Schwarz Ski Imports

SKI-KART (boat trailers)
  See Lenox (Division of Hoover Ball & Bearing Company

SKI-MASTER (water skis and accessories)
  See Texas Recreation Corporation

SKI SKINS (sports apparel)
  See Allen-A Company

SKI USA (sports apparel, accessories, and equipment)
  See Imports International Inc.

SKI-WHIZ (snowmobiles)
  See Massey-Ferguson Inc.

SKIDELSKY & COMPANY, INC., S.S.
685 Grand Avenue
Ridgefield, New Jersey 07657

SKIDLESS COMPOUND (skid-proof finish)
  See Pettit Paint Company Inc.

SKIDPROOF (floor wax)
  See Consolidated Chemical Inc.

SKIFF (first-aid kits)
  See Acme Cotton Products Company, Inc.

SKIL CORPORATION
5033 Elston Avenue
Chicago, Illinois 60630
John W. Sullivan, President
(312) 286-2000

SKIL-CRAFT CORPORATION
325 West Huron Street
Chicago, Illinois 60610
Martin Kramer, President
(312) 642-6661

SKILCRAFT (brooms, mops, markers, iron-board covers, etc.)
  See Industries of the Blind Inc.

SKILLET DINNERS (prepared food mixes)
  See Hunt-Wesson Foods, Inc.

SKILLET MAGIC (packaged dinners)
  See McCormick & Company, Inc.

SKIMER (sports apparel)
  See Skea Ltd.

SKIN BRACER (men's toiletries)
  See Mennen Company

SKIN CLINIC (medicated toiletries)
  See Noxell Corporation

SKIN CULTURE COMPANY
130 West 42nd Street
New York, New York 10036
(212) 730-0660

SKIN DEW (toiletries)
  See Helena Rubinstein, Inc.

SKINNER & KENNEDY COMPANY
9451 Natural Bridge
Saint Louis, Missouri 63134
J. Howard Pecker, President
(314) 426-2800

SKINNER COMPANY, INC., S.P.
225 Fifth Avenue
New York, New York 10010
(212) 741-8100

SKINNER MACARONI COMPANY
6848 F Street
Omaha, Nebraska 68117
William A. Henry, President
(402) 331-7000

SKINNY DIP (cologne, bath oil, bubble bath, etc.)
  See Leeming/Pacquin

SKINNY-MINI (laundry center)
  See Frigidaire (Division of General Motors Corporation)

SKINNY-MINNY (food products)
  See Sunaid Food Products

SKINTEX (bandages, cotton, tape, methiolate)
  See The Scholl Manufacturing Company, Inc.

SKIP (floor cleaner and wax)
  See Chemex Industries, Inc.

SKIPPER (seafood)
  See Wally Sea Products Corporation

SKIPPY (peanut products)
  See Best Foods

SKIPS (smoking substitute in lozenge form)
  See Chex Company

Companies and Trade Names

SKIROULE (snowmobiles)
See Coleman Company Inc.

SKIROW BROTHERS
932 West Dakin Street
Chicago, Illinois 60613
(312) 935-1711

SKITTLE-POOL (game)
See Aurora Products Corporation

SKIVVIES (underwear)
See Norwich Mills

SKLENARIK MUSICAL STRING COMPANY
Box 90
South Norwalk, Connecticut 06856

SKOKIE SAW & TOOL COMPANY
10415 United Parkway
Schiller Park, Illinois 60176

SKOL (tanning aids)
See J.B. Williams Company, Inc.

SKOL (vodka)
See J.A. Dougherty's Sons Inc., Distillers

SKOLNIK, ARTHUR
160 Fifth Avenue
New York, New York 10010
(212) 929-1969

SKOOKUM PACKERS ASSOCIATION, INC.
Post Office Box 487
Wenatchee, Washington 98801

SKOOT COMPANY
681 South Washington Boulevard
Hamilton, Ohio 45013

SKOR-MOR CORPORATION
6390 Cindy Lane
Carpinteria, California 93013

SKOTCH GRILL (outdoor grills)
See Hamilton-Skotch Corporation

SKRAM (insect repellent)
See Conwood Corporation

SKRATCH STIKS (polish)
See GC Electronics Company

SKRIP (pens, ink)
See W.A. Sheaffer Pen Company

SKRUZIT (screwdrivers)
See W.E. Bassett Company

SKUTTLE MANUFACTURING COMPANY
150 West Summit
Milford, Michigan 48042
David B. Powers, President and Treasurer
(313) 684-1415

SKY (menthol cigarettes)
See Philip Morris Inc.

SKY CAP (luggage)
See Platt Luggage Inc.

SKY CHIEF (gasoline)
See Texaco, Inc.

SKY HOST (hotels)
See International Airport Hotel System Inc.

SKY LARK (kite)
See Airplane Kite Company

SKY LARK (light whiskey)
See Fleischmann Distilling Corporation

SKY-PAK (attache cases)
See The Lifton Manufacturing Corporation

SKY-SKOOTER (playground equipment)
See Gym Dandy Inc.

SKY-WAY COMMUNICATIONS
10833 East Jefferson
Detroit, Michigan 48214
(313) 823-0711

SKY-WAY PRODUCTS
739 East New York Avenue
Brooklyn, New York 11203
(212) 772-0442

SKYCRAFT (boat trailers)
See Long Manufacturing N.C. Inc.

SKYLAND FOOD CORPORATION
Box 250
Delta, Colorado 81416

SKYLAND INTERNATIONAL CORPORATION
2001 Wheeler Avenue
Chattanooga, Tennessee 37406
Colon W. York, President
(615) 629-2531

SKYLARK (bread)
See Safeway Stores, Inc.

SKYLARK (portable typewriter)
See Royal Typewriter Company

SKYLINE CORPORATION
2520 By-Pass Road
Elkhart, Indiana 46514
A.J. Decio, Chairman of the Board
(219) 294-6521

SKYMATE (luggage)
See Hartmann Luggage Company, Inc.

SKYRIDER (men's and boys' shoes)
See Genesco, Inc.

Companies and Trade Names

SKYSCRAPER (ladies' shoes)
    See A.C. Shoes & Accessories, Inc.

SKYWAY (clothing)
    See Manhattan Shirt Company

SKYWAY (food products)
    See Bama Food Products

SKYWAY LUGGAGE COMPANY
Skyway Center
Seattle, Washington 98121
Henry Kotkins, President
(206) 623-5300

SLADE COMPANY, D. & L.
(Division of Brady Enterprises Inc.)
Box 99
East Weymouth, Massachusetts 02189
(617) 337-5000

SLADE COMPANY, INC., CHARLES F.
160 Van Rensselaer Street
Buffalo, New York 14210
(716) 852-8156

SLAKNIT (men's trousers)
    See Hansley Industries Inc.

SLALOM SKIWEAR, INC.
4 Eastern Avenue
Newport, Vermont 05855
Stephen W. Crisafulli, President
(802) 334-7958

SLANT/FIN CORPORATION
100 Forest Drive
Greenvale, New York 11548
Melvin Dubin, President
(516) 484-2600

SLATER ELECTRIC, INC.
45 Sea Cliff Avenue
Glen Cove, New York 11542
Herbert A. Slater, President
(516) 671-7000

SLATER, N.G.
220 West 19th Street
New York, New York 10011

SLAUGHTER COMPANY, T.C.
Reedville, Virginia 22539
    See also Huff & Puff Pet Foods Inc.

SLAX (apparel)
    See B.V.D. Company Inc.

SLAX LEISURE (footwear)
    See Kayser-Roth Shoes, Inc.

SLAYMAKER LOCK COMPANY, THE
115 South West End Avenue
Lancaster, Pennsylvania 17603
Samuel C. Slaymaker, Chairman of the Board
(717) 394-7141

SLEATER COMPANY INC., JOHN C.
310 Fifth Avenue
New York, New York 10001
Robert T. Le Brecht, President
(212) 563-1320

SLEEP-EZE (sleeping aid)
    See Whitehall Laboratories

SLEEP-HAVEN (mattresses)
    See Logan Company

SLEEP EYE SHADE COMPANY
828 Mission Street
San Francisco, California 94103
(415) 362-8185

SLEEP-TITE (sleepwear)
    See Colonial Textile Manufacturing Corporation

SLEEPY EYE (frozen poultry and eggs)
    See A.J. Pietrus & Sons Company

SLEEPY RIDER (car-seat recliners for infants)
    See Bunny Bear Inc.

SLEEX (men's slacks)
    See Esquire Sportswear Manufacturing Corporation

SLEIGH BELL (snowsuits)
    See LoBel Company

SLENCIL COMPANY
(Division of Riveto Manufacturing Company)
36 South Main Street
Orange, Massachusetts 01364

SLENDER (beverage)
    See Virginia Dare Extract Company, Inc.

SLENDER (reducing aid)
    See Carnation Company

SLENDER-X (reducing aids)
    See Progressive Drugs of America, Inc.

SLENDERELLA (diet foods)
    See Louis Sherry, Inc.

SLENDERELLA (hosiery)
    See Munsingwear, Inc.

SLESINGER, INC., CHARLES
609 Fifth Avenue
New York, New York 10017
(212) 758-0130

SLICKCRAFT BOAT COMPANY
(Division of AMF, Inc.)
500 East 32nd Street
Holland, Michigan 49423
Leon R. Slikkers, President
(616) 384-4634

SLIDE-A-FOLD (sliding doors)
    See Homeshield Industries, Inc.

Companies and Trade Names

SLIDE-A-WAY SHELVES (shelves for cabinets, doors, etc.)
See Dennis Mitchell Industries

SLIDE-LOK (infant safety devices)
See Reed Industries Inc.

SLIDE 'N SPLASH (plastic pool)
See Coleco Industries, Inc.

SLIDE-RIDE (plaything)
See Gym-Dandy Inc.

SLIM JIM (frozen food)
See North Pacific Canners & Packers, Inc.

SLIM JIM, INC.
(Subsidiary of General Mills, Inc.)
1 Bala Avenue
Bala Cynwyd, Pennsylvania 19004

SLIM MASTER (exercise equipment)
See Central Quality Industries, Inc.

SLIM-MINT (reducing aids)
See Thompson Medical Company, Inc.

SLIM-O-MATIC (weight and sauna belts)
See Home Equipment Manufacturing Company

SLIMFOLD (stepstools)
See Comfort Lines Inc.

SLIMMETRY, INC.
16 Main Street
Newark, New Jersey 07105

SLIMU (men's posture garments)
See Munsingwear Inc.

SLINGSHOT BASEBALL COMPANY
Box 366
Godfrey, Illinois 62035

SLINKY (plaything)
See James Industries Inc.

SLIP GARD (slip-proofing liquid for bath tub)
See Reily Chemical Company

SLIP SEAL COMPANY, THE
1325 Redondo Avenue
Long Beach, California 90804
(213) 597-8431

SLIPICONE (silicone lubricant)
See Dow Corning Corporation

SLIPMATES (slip and blouse combination)
See Blue Swan-Milsan Industries

SLIPREE (dry lubricant)
See Unival Corporation

SLITS (apparel)
See A-1 Kotzin Company

SLOAN GLASS INC.
Box 182
Culloden, West Virginia 25510
Charles T. Sloan, Chairman and President
(304) 743-9101

SLOAN VALVE COMPANY
10500 Seymour Avenue
Franklin Park, Illinois 60131
Charles C. Allen, President and Chief Executive Officer
(312) 671-4300

SLOANE, INC., W. & J.
414 Fifth Avenue
New York, New York 10018
Leonard J. Novogrod, President
(212) 695-3800

SLOCUM COMPANY, T.A.
Boston Post Road
Madison, Connecticut 06443

SLOMONS LABORATORIES INC.
32-45 Hunters Point Avenue
Long Island City, New York 11101
(212) 784-0205

SLOPPY JOE (Mexican foods)
See Gebhardt Mexican Foods Company

SLUMBER KING (mattresses)
See Simmons Company

SLUMBER PRODUCTS CORPORATION
1429 Riverside Street
Memphis, Tennessee 38109
Ronald C. Haas, President
(901) 948-4471

SLUMBER/SOFA (convertible furniture)
See Victor Stanley Inc.

SLUMBER SOX (sleeping and lounging socks)
See Reliable Knitting Works

SLUMBER SWING (infants' product)
See Century Products Inc.

SLUMBERFLEX (mattresses)
See Burton-Dixie Corporation

SLUMBERTOGS, INC.
135 Madison Avenue
New York, New York 10016
(212) 686-0560

SMALL BOAT SHOP
Box 808
Sandy Hook, Connecticut 06482

Companies and Trade Names

SMALL COMPANY, P.A. & S.
1100 North Sherman Street
York, Pennsylvania 17405
L. Doyle Ankrum, President and
  Chief Operation Officer
(717) 755-1976

SMALL WONDER (baby products)
  See Shaklee Products

SMALLEY & WILLIAM, INC.
806 Lexington Avenue
New York, New York 10021
(212) 838-2502

SMART & FINAL IRIS COMPANY
(Division of Thriftimart, Inc.)
4700 South Boyle Avenue
Vernon, California 90058
Lewis O. Mullin, General Manager
(213) 737-8452

SMART SET (closet accessories)
  See Ashland Products Company,
    Inc.

SMART SET (foam dishes, plates, bowls, trays)
  See Polytherm Plastics (Division of Polysar Plastics, Inc.)

SMART SET GLOVES LTD.
45 West 38th Street
New York, New York 10018
(212) 868-7640

SMART TIME (loungewear)
  See Eastern Isles, Inc.

SMARTAIR (sportswear)
  See Rainfair, Inc.

SMARTONE (paint)
  See Luminall Paints, Inc.

SMART'S (food products)
  See Canvin Products Ltd.

SMARTY PANTS (shorts, halters, sweaters, t-shirts)
  See Koret of California, Inc.

SMASHER (aluminum tennis racket)
  See Spalding

SMEAD MANUFACTURING COMPANY
600 East Tenth
Hastings, Minnesota 55033
E.C. Hoffman, President and
  Treasurer
(612) 437-4111

SMELTZER ORCHARD COMPANY
Frankfort, Michigan 49635
James H. Brian, President and
  Sales Manager
(616) 882-4421

SMETHPORT SPECIALTY COMPANY
1 Magnetic Avenue
Smethport, Pennsylvania 16749

SMILE COMPANY
5624 West Raymond Street
Indianapolis, Indiana 46241
(317) 243-3521

SMILER COMPANY, ED
1407 Broadway
New York, New York 10018
(212) 244-1165

SMILEY HATS INC.
423 Overmeyer Road
Sparks, Nevada 89431

SMILING SCOT
1266 Goodale Boulevard
Columbus, Ohio 43212
(614) 486-9657

SMIRNOFF BEVERAGE & IMPORT COMPANY
  See Heublein, Inc.

SMITH & BIRD
1 World Trade Center
New York, New York 10048
(212) 432-0107

SMITH & NICHOLS, INC.
620 Central Avenue
Carlstadt, New Jersey 07072
(201) 438-3194

SMITH & PETERS
Eighth and Somerset
Philadelphia, Pennsylvania 19133
(215) 225-1035

SMITH & SON INC., SEYMOUR
1940 Justin Street
Oakville, Connecticut 06779
(203) 274-2558

SMITH & WATSON INC.
305 East 63rd Street
New York, New York 10021
(212) 355-5615

SMITH & WESSON
(Division of Bangor Punta
  Operations, Inc.)
2100 Roosevelt Avenue
Springfield, Massachusetts 01101
James L. Oberg, President
(413) 736-0323

SMITH-ALSOP PAINT & VARNISH COMPANY
630 North Third Street
Terre Haute, Indiana 47808
Lee A. Roads, President
(812) 234-2680

SMITH, BARNEY & COMPANY, INC.
1345 Avenue of the Americas
New York, New York 10019
Robert A. Powers, Chairman of the
  Board
(212) 333-7200

SMITH BROTHERS (cough drops)
  See American Chicle Company

Companies and Trade Names

SMITH BROTHERS
100 North Franklin
Port Washington, Wisconsin 53074

SMITH BROTHERS
MANUFACTURING COMPANY
526 Howard Street
Carthage, Missouri 64836
Clayton E. Smith, President
(417) 358-5955

SMITH CABINET
MANUFACTURING COMPANY
East Market Street
Salem, Indiana 47167
Chester M. Smith, President
(812) 883-3111

SMITH CAPE COD PRODUCTS
Route 28
West Dennis, Massachusetts 02670

SMITH CARPETS, ALEXANDER
919 Third Avenue
New York, New York 10022
(212) 486-9480

SMITH CHEMICAL COLOR
COMPANY
104-20 Dunkirk
Jamaica, New York 11412
(212) 454-9400

SMITH COMPANY, CLAYTON E.
See Goldsmith Company

SMITH COMPANY, H.E.
139 South 15th Street
Newark, New Jersey 07107
(201) 484-0900

SMITH COMPANY INC., THE H.B.
57 Main
Westfield, Massachusetts 01085
Edwin E. Smith, Chairman and
  President
(413) 562-9631

SMITH COMPANY, J.
  HUNGERFORD
(Subsidiary of United Brands
  Company)
Prudential Center
Boston, Massachusetts 02199
Robert H. Maclachlan, President
(617) 262-3000

SMITH COMPANY, JOHN A.
Box 86
Oconomowoc, Wisconsin 53066

SMITH COMPANY, THE S.K.
2857 North Western Avenue
Chicago, Illinois 60618
L. Richard Smith, President and
  Treasurer
(312) 276-3790

SMITH-CORONA MARCHANT
(Division of SCM Corporation)
299 Park Avenue
New York, New York 10017
(212) 752-2700

SMITH CORPORATION, A.O.
3533 North 27th
Milwaukee, Wisconsin 53201
J.R. Parker, President
(414) 447-4000

SMITH-DOUGLASS (Division of
Borden Chemical Company)
  See Borden, Inc.

SMITH ENTERPRISES, INC.
Industrial Park
Box 188
Rock Hill, South Carolina 29730

SMITH-GATES CORPORATION
New Britain Avenue
Farmington, Connecticut 06032
Richard J. Gates, President
(203) 677-2657

SMITH GLASS COMPANY, L.E.
1900 Liberty Street
Mount Pleasant, Pennsylvania 15666
(412) 547-3544

SMITH GOGGLE COMPANY
Box 74
Sun Valley, Idaho 83353

SMITH HOUSE
(Division of Universal Enterprises)
1000 Atando Avenue
Charlotte, North Carolina 28206

SMITH INC., DAVID H.
Bubier Street
Lynn, Massachusetts 01901

SMITH INC., E. ERRETT
58-51 Maspeth Avenue
Maspeth, New York 11378

SMITH INC., JAY
292 State Street East
Westport, Connecticut 06880

SMITH JUNIOR (food products)
  See H.A. Johnson Company

SMITH, KLINE & FRENCH
  LABORATORIES
1500 Spring Garden Street
Philadelphia, Pennsylvania 19101
D. VanRoden, President
(215) 564-2400

  See also Avoset Food Corpora-
    tion; Mehley & James
    Laboratories; Norden
    Laboratories Inc.; and Sea
    & Ski Corporation

SMITH LABORATORY, B.W.
Box 1408
Hattiesburg, Mississippi 39401

SMITH LABORATORY, INC., THE
811 Wyandotte
Kansas City, Missouri 64105
(816) 842-1711

SMITH-LEE COMPANY, INC.
537 Fitch Street
Oneida, New York 13421
Leslie B. Arnold, President
(315) 363-2500

Companies and Trade Names

SMITH, LYNN
9H1 Atlanta Merchandise Mart
Atlanta, Georgia 30303
(404) 688-7139

SMITH MANUFACTURING
  COMPANY, INC., ROBERT
6507 Salt Lake Avenue
Bell, California 90201
(213) 585-8679

SMITH, MILLER & PATCH, INC.
(Division of Cooper Laboratories
  Inc.)
401 Joyce Kilmer Avenue
New Brunswick, New Jersey 08902

SMITH PAPER COMPANY, H.P.
(Subsidiary of Phillips Petroleum
  Company)
5001 West 66th
Chicago, Illinois 60638
(312) 767-8000

SMITH PRODUCE COMPANY
Route 250 South
Fairmont, West Virginia 26554

SMITH PRODUCTS COMPANY,
  C.G.
Box 1016
Blytheville, Arkansas 72315

SMITH TRUSS COMPANY INC.,
  THE
1119-23 West Tenth Street
Topeka, Kansas 66604
(913) 354-8548

SMITH-VALSPAR (marine paints)
  See Valspar Corporation

SMITH WHOLESALE DRUG
  COMPANY
Box 1779
Spartanburg, South Carolina 29301

SMITHERS (food products)
  See Milani Foods Inc.

SMITHERS COMPANY, THE
Marvin Avenue
Kent, Ohio 44240

SMITHFIELD HAM & PRODUCTS
  COMPANY, INC., THE
Smithfield, Virginia 23430
J.C. Sprigg, Jr., President
(804) 357-2121

SMITHKLINE CORPORATION
1500 Spring Garden Street
Philadelphia, Pennsylvania 19101
R.F. Dee, President and Chief
  Executive Officer
(215) 854-4000

SMITHS' (clocks, watches, timers
and time-keeping devices, barometer movements, and barometer
fitups)
  See C. Brook Flowers

SMITH'S PIE COMPANY, MRS.
Charlotte and South Streets
Pottstown, Pennsylvania 19464

SMITH'S TRANSFER CORPORATION
Post Office Box 1000
Staunton, Virginia 24401
R.R. Smith, Chairman of the Board
(703) 886-6231

SMITHSONIAN PUZZLE SERIES
  See Selchow & Righter Company

SMO-KING PRODUCTS INC.
111 Pioneer Street
Brooklyn, New York 11231
(212) 624-2676

SMOKADOR PRODUCTS COMPANY
(Division of Baylis Industries Inc.)
470 West First Avenue
Roselle, New Jersey 07203
(201) 241-5300

SMOKE CRAFT, INC.
Post Office Box 36
850 West 30th Street
Albany, Oregon 97321
William L. Milckelson, Chairman
  and President
(503) 926-8831

SMOKED ALASKAN SEAFOODS
Box 13
Clam Gulch, Arkansas 99568

SMOKED FOOD PRODUCTS
  COMPANY, INC.
2100 North Mill Street at Duncan
  Avenue
Jackson, Mississippi 39202

SMOKEMASTER PIPES
(Subsidiary of United States
  Tobacco Company)
Box 21244
Greensboro, North Carolina 27420

SMOKE LUMBER COMPANY
Post Office Box 65
Sixth and Clunette
New Paris, Indiana 46553
(219) 831-2103

SMOKER PRODUCTS INC.
2724 Southwell
Dallas, Texas 75209
(214) 243-1001

SMOKY CANYON MEAT
  PRODUCTS COMPANY
2120 Holland-Sylvania Road
Toledo, Ohio 43615

SMOKY MOUNTAIN (food products)
  See M. Light & Son

SMOLER & SONS, BORIS
3021 North Pulaski
Chicago, Illinois 60624
Hy Smoler, President
(312) 283-8000

Companies and Trade Names

SMOLER BROTHERS, INC.
2300 Wabansia Avenue
Chicago, Illinois 60647
Jerry Smoler, President
(312) 384-1200

SMOOTH AMERICAN (gin)
See Schenley Industries, Inc.

SMOOTH EEZ (tights for women, swimsuits)
See Sondra Manufacturing Company, Inc.

SMOOTHIE (neckwear)
See A. Schreter & Sons Company, Inc.

SMOOTHIE (produce)
See Pacific Fruit & Produce Company

SMOOTHY (paints)
See Leonard Company

SMUCKER COMPANY, J.M.
Post Office Box 280
Strawberry Lane
Orrville, Ohio 44667
Paul H. Smucker, Chairman of the Board
(216) 682-0015
See also California Farm Products; and Madison Company, The H.W.

SNACK JARS (fruits and puddings)
See Duffy-Mott Company

SNACK LOAF (bakery goods)
See Kitchens of Sara Lee

SNACK MATE (cheese spreads)
See Nabisco, Inc.

SNACK-N-SNOOZE (infants' product)
See Castle Industries Inc.

SNACK PAK (canned puddings and fruits)
See Hunt-Wesson Foods Inc.

SNACKIN' CAKES (cake mixes)
See General Mills, Inc.

SNAG-PROOF (waterproof and canvas rubber-soled footwear)
See Servus Rubber Company

SNAP-CUT (lawn tools)
See Seymour Smith & Son Inc.

SNAP-E-TOM (tomato cocktail)
See Heublein, Inc.

SNAP ON (pipe insulation)
See Gustin Bacon (Division of Certain-Teed Products Corporation)

SNAP-ON (solid-vinyl siding)
See Mastic Corporation

SNAP-ON TOOLS CORPORATION
2801 80th Street
Kenosha, Wisconsin 53140
Robert L. Grover, Chairman of the Board
(414) 654-8681

SNAPIT (electrical supplies)
See Cable Electric Products Inc.

SNAPOUT FORMS COMPANY
357 Washington Street
Chardon, Ohio 44024
W.L. Carson, President
(216) 285-3123

SNAPPER (men's ties)
See Beau Brummell Ties

SNAPPER (mower)
See McDonough Power Equipment, Inc.

SNARK PRODUCTS, INC.
1580 Lemoine Avenue
Fort Lee, New Jersey 07024
A. Roth, President
(201) 869-5000

SNELLING & SNELLING INC.
2 Industrial Boulevard
Paoli, Pennsylvania 19301
Robert O. Snelling, Chairman, President and Chief Executive Officer
(215) 644-8100

SNELLINGS & MINOR
319 William Street
Fredericksburg, Virginia 22401

SNELLIT (fishing tackle)
See Gem Enterprises

SNICKERS (candy)
See Mars, Inc.

SNIDER'S (condiments)
See Hunt-Wesson Foods, Inc.

SNIP'N STICK (carpets)
See Ozite Corporation

SNIPPY (electric scissors)
See Ungar (Division of Eldon Industries, Inc.)

SNO-BALL (flavoring syrup)
See Cajun Chef Products

SNO BALLS (snack cakes)
See ITT Continental Baking Company Inc.

SNO BALLS (sports accessories)
See Jack Martin Company

SNO-BAN (ice- and snow-melting compound)
See Todd Chemical Company, Inc.

1238

Companies and Trade Names

SNO BOL (bathroom-bowl cleaner)
See A.E. Staley Manufacturing Company

SNO BOY (juice)
See Di Giorgio Corporation

SNO-BRITE (rice products)
See Blue Ribbon Rice Mills, Inc.

SNO-CO BERRY PAK
1301 Fourth Street
Marysville, Washington 98270

SNO-FLOK (flocking kit for trees, wreaths, etc.)
See General Mills Inc.

SNO JET
(Division of Conroy of Canada, Inc.)
Box 594
Burlington, Vermont 05401
(802) 878-5301

SNO-KAP (canned and frozen foods)
See Mushroom Co-operative Canning Company

SNO-PAK INC.
Post Office Box 510
Barberton, Ohio 44203

SNO-SPUN (vegetables)
See Rogers Brothers Company

SNO-THRO (snowmobiles)
See Ariens Company

SNO-TOG (sports apparel)
See Free Trade Center Inc.

SNOBOY (fruit)
See Pacific Fruit & Produce Company

SNOCRAFT
(Division of Garland Manufacturing Company)
46 Water Street
Saco, Maine 04072
Harry P. Garland, II, President
(207) 283-3693

SNOKIST GROWERS, INC.
Post Office Box 1587
18 West Meade Avenue
Yakima, Wisconsin 98901
Roy Salverda, President
(509) 453-5631

SNOOPY (dog foods)
See Interstate Bakeries Corporation

SNOOPY POWER TOOTHBRUSH
See Kenner Products

SNOOTIE (sun-screening agent)
See Sea & Ski Corporation

SNOOZ-ALARM (alarm clock)
See General Electric Company

SNOOZER (infants' product)
See Swyngomatic Industries

SNOOZER (men's furnishings)
See Knothe Brothers Company Inc.

SNOW-BIRD (snow blowers, lawn mowers)
See Frost Company

SNOW-BLO (bicycle power package, churns and mowers, etc.)
See Sensation Corporation

SNOW CHAMP (snow blowers)
See Sunbeam Outdoor Company

SNOW CHEF (frozen foods)
See Trappe Frozen Foods Corporation

SNOW CORPORATION
4350 McKinley Court
Omaha, Nebraska 68112
Adrian L. Fasse, President
(402) 453-2200

SNOW CROP (frozen juices)
See Coca-Cola Company

SNOW FOOD PRODUCTS
(Division of Borden, Inc.)
Post Office Box F
Old Orchard Beach, Maine 04064
Richard R. Brown, President
(207) 883-4321

SNOW-GIRL (frozen vegetables)
See John Inglis Frozen Foods Company

SNOW MACHINE INTERNATIONAL LTD.
Route 17
Tuxedo, New York 10987

SNOW MIST (seafood)
See New England Fish Company

SNOW OWL (fruit)
See Perham Fruit Corporation

SNOW PROOF (water repellent)
See Ski Country Imports

SNOW PUP (snow thrower)
See The Toro Company

SNOW STAR (ice cream)
See Safeway Stores Inc.

SNOW WHITE (cosmetics)
See Chap Stick Company

Companies and Trade Names

SNOWBIRD (seafood)
See Acadia Fisheries Inc.

SNOWCHEF (frozen foods)
See Cliffdale Corporation

SNOWCO (boat trailers)
See The Snow Company

SNOWCREST (food products)
See Burns Foods Ltd.

SNOWDON, INC.
South Main Street
Osceola, Iowa 50213

SNOWDRIFT (vegetable shortening)
See Hunt-Wesson Foods, Inc.

SNOWFLAKE (discloths, kitchen towels)
See Opelika Manufacturing Corporation

SNOWFLAKE (fruit)
See Columbia River Orchards Company

SNOWITE (automotive accessories)
See Go-Jo Industries Inc.

SNOWVALE (food products)
See Burns Foods Ltd.

SNOWY (bleach)
See Gold Seal Company

SNUG HARBOR BOAT WORKS
10121 Snug Harbor Road
Saint Petersburg, Florida 33702

SNUG-L-REST (infants' bedding)
See Family Tree Inc.

SNUG 'N DRY (infant sheets and pads)
See Plymouth Rubber Company Inc.

SNUG-TREDS (slippers)
See R.G. Barry Corporation

SNUGGIE (sports robe)
See Kemp Manufacturing Company

SNUGGLE-BUG (baby carriages and seats)
See Welsh Company

SNUGLI COTTAGE INDUSTRIES INC.
Box 685
Evergreen, Colorado 80439

SNYDER, M.L.
(Division of Boss Manufacturing Company)
221 West First
Kewanee, Illinois 61443
(309) 852-2131

SNYDER MANUFACTURING COMPANY
22 and Ontario
Philadelphia, Pennsylvania 19140
(215) 228-3000

SNYDER MANUFACTURING COMPANY, INC., H.P.
203 West Main Street
Little Falls, New York 13365
Harry W. Snyder, Chairman of the Board
(315) 823-3300

SNYDER PACKING COMPANY
Rural Delivery 2
Delta, Pennsylvania 17314
(717) 456-5024

SNYDER TRAILER COMPANY
100 Elm Street
Butler, Ohio 44822

SNYDER WOODCRAFT COMPANY
128 South Monroe Street
Blissfield, Michigan 49228

SNYDERS (health and beauty aids)
See Red Owl Stores, Inc.

SNYDERS POTATO CHIPS
(Division of Curtice-Burns Inc.)
Box 85
Berlin, Pennsylvania 15530

SO BIGS (protein food for toddlers)
See Gerber Products Company

SO GOOD INCORPORATED
8550 West Bryn Mawr
Chicago, Illinois 60631
(312) 693-7175

SO GOOD POTATO CHIP COMPANY
4190 Hoffmeister
Saint Louis, Missouri 63125
A. Elmer Leeker, Jr., President
(314) 631-2020

SO HELP ME HANNAH LABORATORIES
2574 El Camino Real North
Salinas, California 93901

SO-LITE (oil paint)
See Warren Paint and Color Company

SO MAID (household products)
See Standard Brush & Broom Company

SO-RITE MANUFACTURING & SUPPLY COMPANY INC.
Post Office Box 6097
Raleigh, North Carolina 27608

SO SOOTHING (first-aid spray)
See Chase Products Company

Companies and Trade Names

SO-TEN (meat tenderizer)
See J. Strickland & Company

SOAK N RINSE (soaps)
See Carolina Soap & Candle Makers

SOBAX (electronic calculators)
See Sony Corporation of America, Business Products Division

SOBEL SUPPLY INC.
10 West 47th Street
New York, New York 10036
(212) 246-5820

SOBIESKI (food products)
See Pikle-Rite Company Inc.

SOBRANIE BLACK RUSSIAN (cigarettes)
See G.A. Georgopulo & Company, Inc.

SOCCER ASSOCIATES
Post Office Box 634
New Rochelle, New York 10802

SOCCER SPORT SUPPLY COMPANY INC.
1745 First Avenue
New York, New York 10028
(212) 427-6050

SOCIABLES (crackers)
See Nabisco Inc.

SOCIAL SUPPER INC.
Main Street
Dresden, Ohio 43821
See also Stylecraft Products

SOCIALITE (luggage)
See United States Luggage Corporation

SOCIALITES (shoes)
See United States Shoe Corporation

SOCIETE CANDY COMPANY
800 Western Avenue
Seattle, Washington 98104
Charles H. Brown, President
(206) 623-0160

SOCIETY BRAND LTD. (menswear)
See Hart Schaffner & Marx

SOCIETY FOR VISUAL EDUCATION, INC.
(Subsidiary of The Singer Company, Inc.)
1345 West Diversey Parkway
Chicago, Illinois 60614
Walter Johnson, President
(312) 525-1500

SOCIETY HILL (groceries)
See Supreme Food Distributors

SOCIETY LINGERIE COMPANY
Springland and Roeske Avenues
Michigan City, Indiana 46360
Irving J. Levin, President and Treasurer
(219) 872-7206

SOCIETY NATIONAL BANK OF CLEVELAND
127 Public Square
Cleveland, Ohio 44114
J. Maurice Struchen, Chairman of the Board
(216) 861-4000

SOCK-EEZ (foot socks)
See Sondra Manufacturing Company, Inc.

SOCKING (hosiery)
See Rudin & Roth, Inc.

SOCONY (gasoline)
See Mobil Oil Corporation

SODAR (crabgrass eradicator)
See Nott Manufacturing Company, Inc.

SODERBERG MANUFACTURING COMPANY INC.
20821 Currier Road
Walnut, California 91789
(714) 595-1291

SODICO INC.
Post Office Box 666
Greer, South Carolina 29651

SODOMA FARMS
213 Gordon Road
Brockport, New York 14420

SODUS FRUIT FARM INC.
(Subsidiary of Sodus Packing Corporation)
Box 160
Sodus, New York 14551
James K. Albright, President
(315) 483-6903

SOF-GLO (light dimmers)
See Home Equipment Manufacturing Company

SOF-SPREAD (margarine)
See Lever Brothers Company

SOF' STROKE (shaving product)
See Mennen Company

SOF-TRED (rubber matting)
See Superior Rubber Manufacturing (Division of Superior Rubber Supply Corporation)

SOFAIR (skin-care product)
See Chap Stick Company

SOFETTE (lounger)
See La-Z-Boy Chair Company

Companies and Trade Names

SOFFER, Y.E.
67-08 Austin
Forest Hills, New York 11375
(212) 896-0762

SOFFITS (panels)
See Upson Company

SOFLENS (contact lens)
See Bausch & Lomb Inc.

SOFRITO (food product)
See William Underwood Company

SOFSEAT (stool cushions)
See Perfect Rubber Seat Cushion Company

SOFSKIN, INC.
595 Madison Avenue
New York, New York 10022
Alfred Roberts, President
(212) 753-4600

SOFSPRA (car wash)
See ALD, Inc.

SOFT & DRI (antiperspirant)
See Gillette Toiletries Company

SOFT MAGIC (pantyhose)
See Fruit of the Loom, Inc.

SOFT WALKS (shoes for men)
See Gardiner Shoe Company, Inc.

SOFT-WEVE (toilet tissue)
See Scott Paper Company

SOFTASILK (flour)
See General Mills, Inc.

SOFTEX (baby pants)
See Kleinert's Inc.

SOFTIQUE (bath products)
See Clinton (Division of Bristol-Myers Company)

SOFTONE TUFIDE (luggage)
See Stebco Products Corporation

SOFTRED (floor covering)
See GAF Corporation

SOFTSKIN TOYS INC.
1907 Park Avenue
New York, New York 10035
(212) 534-7074

SOHARI (women's shoes)
See Johansen Brothers Shoe Company, Inc.

SOHIO (petroleum products)
See Standard Oil Company (Ohio)

SOHMER AND COMPANY, INC.
31 West 57th Street
New York, New York 10019
Harry J. Sohmer, Jr., President
(212) 753-9235

SOHO (phonograph records)
See Dagonet Records

SOHO GALLERY (note papers)
See Charles Zahn-Import Merchant

SOIL-OFF (cleaner)
See Economics Laboratory, Inc.

SOILAX (washing and cleaning compounds)
See Economics Laboratory Inc.

SOILEAU (canned foods)
See Bruce Foods Corporation

SOILTEST INC.
(Subsidiary of Cenco Inc.)
2205 Lee Street
Evanston, Illinois 60202
Theodore W. Van Zelst, President
(312) 869-5500

SOKOL (food products)
See Mount Rose Canning Company Inc.

SOKOL (sports accessories and equipment)
See Eiger Mountain Sports

SOKOL & COMPANY
5315 Dansher Road
La Grange, Illinois 60525
(312) 482-8250

SOL (food products)
See Belle-Sommers

SOL CATAMARANS INC.
1932 East Pomona Street
Santa Ana, California 92705

SOL DE MALLORCA (Spanish wines)
See Munson Shaw Company

SOLA BASIC INDUSTRIES INC.
Post Office Box 753
Milwaukee, Wisconsin 53201
Frank M. Roby, Chairman and President
(414) 276-1480
See also Guth Lighting

SOLANO (menswear)
See Haspel Brothers Inc.

SOLAR (canned foods)
See Fruit Belt Canning Company Inc.

Companies and Trade Names

SOLAR FOOD PRODUCTS
COMPANY, INC.
51-02 23rd Street
Long Island City, New York 11101
(212) 729-2382

SOLAR LABORATORIES, INC.
Dayton, Virginia 22821

SOLAR-MATIC (sunglasses)
  See Bachmann Brothers, Inc.

SOLAR OINTMENT COMPANY
36 West Broad Street
Hazleton, Pennsylvania 18201

SOLAR SALT COMPANY
270 Crossroad Square
Salt Lake City, Utah 84115
(801) 484-5273

SOLAR SET (furniture)
  See Fixture Manufacturing
  Corporation

SOLAR SUNTAN PRODUCTS
CORPORATION
5300 N.W. 167th Street
Miami Beach, Florida 33138
(305) 757-6549

SOLARAMA (shatterproof sunglasses)
  See Bachmann Brothers, Inc.

SOLARAY RIVIERA (electric
blankets)
  See George W. Endress
  Company Ltd.

SOLARBONNE
Box 274
Gilbertsville, New York 13776

SOLAREX (sunglasses)
  See Bachmann Brothers

SOLARI AMERICA INC.
45 West 45th Street
New York, New York 10036
(212) 581-4480

SOLARI MANUFACTURING, INC.
1670 Cordova
Los Angeles, California 90007
(213) 731-6313

SOLARINE COMPANY, THE
(Subsidiary of Divex Inc.)
4201 Pulaski Highway
Baltimore, Maryland 21224
Robert S. Ginsburg, President
(301) 327-5010

SOLARIS (credenzas, desks, tables)
  See Chromcraft Corporation

SOLARITE (paint and art colors)
  See Bondex International

SOLARIUM (rugs)
  See Armstrong Cork Company

SOLART (framed original oil
paintings)
  See S.P. Solomons Decorative
  Art Company

SOLARTOGS (clothes)
  See Princess Peggy, Inc.

SOLDER SEAL (automotive radiator
repair product)
  See Radiator Specialty Company

SOLE SECRET (hosiery)
  See Virginia Maid Hosiery
  Mills, Inc.

SOLETTE (medicated makeup)
  See Kay Preparations Company,
  Inc.

SOLID JET SPRAY (rinse aid for
diswashers)
  See Economics Laboratory, Inc.

SOLID KUMFORT CORPORATION
Post Office Box 1228
Fort Wayne, Indiana 46801

SOLIGOR (photographic lenses and
accessories)
  See Allied Impex Corporation

SOLINA (electronic organs)
  See Manufacturers Centre Holland

SOLITAIRE (canned foods)
  See Great Western Foods
  Company

SOLO (margarine)
  See Monarch Fine Foods
  Company, Ltd.

SOLO CUP COMPANY, THE
1505 East Main Street
Urbana, Illinois 61801
L.J. Hulseman, President
(217) 384-1800

SOLOMONS DECORATIVE ART
  COMPANY, S.P.
1180 Broadway Avenue
New York, New York 10001
(212) 684-0290

SOLV-O (soap, oils, and
disinfectants)
  See Masury-Columbia Company

SOLVENE (adhesive-tape remover)
  See Day-Baldwin

SOLVENTOL (household wall and
paint cleaner)
  See Rooto Corporation

Companies and Trade Names

SOLVENTOL CHEMICAL PRODUCTS, INC.
13177 Huron River Drive
Romulus, Michigan 48174
R.W. Huffman, President
(313) 941-3800

SOLVIT CHEMICAL COMPANY, INC.
7001 Raywood Road
Madison, Michigan 53713
(608) 222-8624

SOLVO-RUST (rust penetrant)
See Permatex Company Inc.

SOMA (analgesic/muscle relaxant)
See Wallace Pharmaceuticals

SOMERDALE (food products)
See Seabrook Farms Company

SOMERSET IMPORTERS, LTD.
(Subsidiary of Norton Simon, Inc.)
100 Park Avenue
New York, New York 10017
John E. Heilmann, President
(212) 679-0900

SOMERSET KNITTING MILLS, INC.
(Subsidiary of Phillips-Van Heusen Corporation)
700 Spring Garden Street
Philadelphia, Pennsylvania 19123
Donald E. Cutler, President
(215) 922-7700

SOMETHING ELSE (home permanent)
See Dorothy Gray, Ltd.

SOMETIME (sofa)
See Jamison Bedding, Inc.

SOMINEX (sleeping aid)
See J.B. Williams Company, Inc.

SOMMER MAID CREAMERY, INC.
Doylestown, Pennsylvania 18901

SON-CHIEF ELECTRICS, INC.
41 Meadow Street
Winsted, Connecticut 06098
Donal F. Fitzgerald, President
(203) 379-2741

SON-NEL INC.
1990 Embarcadero
Oakland, California 94604

SONA FOOD PRODUCTS COMPANY, INC.
3712 Cerritos
Los Alamitos, California 90720
Nat Ross, President
(213) 431-1379

SONAR RADIO CORPORATION
73 Wortman Avenue
Brooklyn, New York 11207
Jack Babkes, President
(212) 649-8000

SONATA (music lamp)
See Cannon Products Inc.

SONATA (perfume, toilet water, etc.)
See Countess Maritza Cosmetic Company, Inc.

SONDRA MANUFACTURING COMPANY, INC.
350 Fifth Avenue
New York, New York 10001
(212) 947-6850

SONEETA (hair-care products)
See Thomas Holmes Corporation

SONESTA INTERNATIONAL HOTELS CORPORATION
390 Commonwealth Avenue
Boston, Massachusetts 02215
Roger P. Sonnabend, Chairman of the Board
(617) 536-2700

SONGO SHOE MANUFACTURING CORPORATION
34 Diamond Street
Portland, Maine 04101
Abe W. Berkowitz, President
(207) 773-1741

SONNENSCHEIN HOP COMPANY, J.
15 East 40th Street
New York, New York 10016
(212) 689-8790

SONNY BOY (groceries)
See McClintoch Trunkey Company

SONOR (percussion instruments and accessories)
See M. Hohner Inc.

SONORAMIC (magnetic tape, cassettes, cartridges)
See Robins Industries Corporation

SONOTEER (speaker system)
See Koss Corporation

SONOTONE CORPORATION
Elmsford, New York 10523
Marilyn E. Costello, Vice President
(914) 592-9600

SONY CORPORATION OF AMERICA
9 West 57th Street
New York, New York 10019
Harvey L. Schein, President
(212) 571-5800

SONY CORPORATION OF AMERICA
Business Products Division
47-47 Van Dam Street
Long Island, New York 11101
(212) 361-8600

Companies and Trade Names

SOO LINE RAILROAD COMPANY
Soo Line Building
Minneapolis, Minnesota 55440
Leonard H. Murray, President
(612) 332-1261

SOOTH 'N HEAL (medicated cream)
See Foods Plus, Inc.

SOOTHE (eye decongestant)
See Burton, Parsons & Company, Inc.

SOPHIE MAE CANDY
(Division of Fine Products Company Inc.)
317 North Avenue N.E.
Atlanta, Georgia 30308
(404) 874-0868

SOPHISTICRAT (footwear)
See Frank Brothers-Fenn Feinstein

SOPHISTO CAT (pet supplies)
See Lowes, Inc.

SOPIC EXPORT & COMMISSION CORPORATION
70 West 40th
New York, New York 10018
(212) 947-8718

SOPTRA FABRICS CORPORATION
70 West 40th Street
New York, New York 10018
(212) 947-8718

SORBOL COMPANY
39 South Main Street
Mechanicsburg, Ohio 43044

SORENSIN INC., ARNOLD
401 Hackensack Avenue
Hackensack, New Jersey 07601

SORG PAPER COMPANY
901 Manchester Avenue
Middletown, Ohio 45042
D.M. Yost, Chairman and President
(513) 422-3661

SORG PRODUCTS COMPANY INC.
(Affiliation of Sorg Paper Company)
Bridge and Gerber Streets
Ligonier, Indiana 46767
(219) 894-4131

SORIANO LTD.
Post Office Box 95
High Point, North Carolina 27261

SORKIN ENTERPRISES
11 Broadway
New York, New York 10004
(212) 797-1206

SORKIN MUSIC COMPANY INC.
370 Motor Parkway
Hauppauge, New York 11787

SORMANI, INC.
Post Office Box 403
Greenwich, Connecticut 06830

SORRENTO (carpeting)
See Stephen-Leedom Carpet Company Inc.

SORRENTO (dairy products)
See Frigo Cheese Corporation

SORTILEGE (perfume, toilet water)
See Parfums Le Galion, Inc.

SOSS MANUFACTURING COMPANY
21777 Hoover Road
Warren, Michigan 48089
(313) 536-8220

SOTTILE MANUFACTURING COMPANY
Beech Avenue
Patton, Pennsylvania 16668

SOUND BUSINESS FORMS
1930 Patterson
Bronx, New York 10473
(212) 893-4800

SOUND CITY/KELSEY (sound equipment, musical instruments, amplifiers, etc.)
See Dallas Music Industries USA Ltd.

SOUND-O-GRAM (phonograph)
See Brownie Manufacturing Company

SOUND PACKING COMPANY
Rural Free Delivery 1
Merritt, North Carolina 28556

SOUND POST INC., THE
1239 Chicago Avenue
Evanston, Illinois 60202

SOUNDER (organ)
See Hammond Organ Company

SOUNDESIGN CORPORATION
34 Exchange Place
Jersey City, New Jersey 07302
Ely E. Askenazi, President
(201) 434-1050

SOUNDSCRIBER CORPORATION, THE
Simm Lane
Newton, Connecticut 06470
Stephen J. Ziff, President
(203) 426-2585

SOUP IN A POUCH (frozen soup)
See Kold Kist, Inc.

SOUP-MEIN (soup)
See Golden Grain Macaroni Company

SOUR PUSS (cocktail mixes)
See Dell Products Corporation

Companies and Trade Names

SOUSSA (cigarettes)
See G.A. Georgopulo & Company, Inc.

SOUTH ATLANTIC DISTRIBUTORS COMPANY
1225 Broadway
New York, New York 10001
(212) 889-6744

SOUTH BEND TACKLE COMPANY, INC.
See Gladding Corporation

SOUTH BEND TOY MANUFACTURING COMPANY
(Subsidiary of Milton Bradley Company)
3300 West Sample Street
South Bend, Indiana 46627
Louis R. Chreist, Jr., President
(219) 289-9275

SOUTH CAMDEN IRON WORKS
1029 Van Hook Street
Camden, New Jersey 08104

SOUTH CAROLINA ELECTRIC & GAS COMPANY
328 Main Street
Columbia, South Carolina 29218
Arthur M. Williams, President
(803) 779-1234

SOUTH CAROLINA NATIONAL BANK
Post Office Box 168
Columbia, South Carolina 29202
John H. Lumpkin, Chairman of the Board
(803) 765-3000

SOUTH CENTRAL BELL TELEPHONE COMPANY
(Subsidiary of American Telephone & Telegraph Company)
Post Office Box 771
Birmingham, Alabama 35201
W. Cecil Bauer, President
(205) 328-2311

SOUTH COAST CORPORATION
1420 Carondelet Building
New Orleans, Louisiana 70130
J.L. Dickson, President
(504) 525-5171

SOUTH COAST RICE MILLING COMPANY
Box 771
Crowley, Louisiana 70526

SOUTH COAST SEACRAFT
Box 1674
Shreveport, Louisiana 71165

SOUTH EASTERN CORDAGE COMPANY
Post Office Box 234-T
Cleveland, Tennessee 37311
(615) 476-4544

SOUTH GEORGIA PECAN COMPANY
Box 609
Valdosta, Georgia 31601
(912) 244-1321

SOUTH JERSEY GAS COMPANY
1 South Jersey Plaza
Folsom, New Jersey 08037
William A. Gemmel, President
(609) 561-9000

SOUTH SHORE FOOD INC.
National Boulevard at West Pine
Long Beach, California 11561

SOUTH SHORE PACKING CORPORATION, THE
Box Three
5117 South Street
Vermilion, Ohio 44089
Stratton L. Appleman, President
(216) 967-3141

SOUTH WIND
(Division of Stewart-Warner Corporation)
1514 Drover Street
Indianapolis, Indiana 46222
(317) 632-8411

SOUTHALL'S FOOD PRODUCTS
Cranberry Highway
Route Six A
East Sandwich, Massachusetts 02537

SOUTHAMPTON (clocks)
See Franklin Instrument Company

SOUTHAMPTON MARINE CORPORATION
Route 73 and Lafayette
Berlin, New Jersey 08009

SOUTHCOM INTERNATIONAL INC.
2210 Meyers Avenue
Escondido, California 92025
(714) 746-1141

SOUTHDOWN, INC.
950 Tenneco Building
Houston, Texas 77002
W.S. Chadwick, President
(713) 228-8921
See also Judson Candies, Inc.; and Pearl Brewing Company

SOUTHEASTERN FABRICATORS INC.
4525 East Tenth Lane
Hialeah, Florida 33013

SOUTHEASTERN LABORATORIES
4005 Post Street
Jacksonville, Florida 32205

SOUTHEASTERN MILLS INC.
Box 908
Rome, Georgia 30161
(404) 232-6528

SOUTHEASTERN TELEPHONE COMPANY
(Subsidiary of Central Telephone Company)
1201 N Street
Lincoln, Nebraska 68501
Clarence H. Ross, President
(402) 475-5941

Companies and Trade Names

SOUTHEASTERN TRAILWAYS, INC.
1820 West 16th Street
Indianapolis, Indiana 46202
Ben D. Kramer, President
(317) 635-8671

SOUTHERLAND (menswear)
See J. Schoeneman Inc.

SOUTHERN (canned foods)
See Columbus Foods Inc.

SOUTHERN AIRWAYS, INC.
Atlanta Airport
Atlanta, Georgia 30320
Frank W. Hulse, Chairman of the Board
(404) 766-5321

SOUTHERN BAKERIES COMPANY
See Southern Daisy Industries Inc.

SOUTHERN BELL TELEPHONE & TELEGRAPH COMPANY
67 Edgewood Avenue, S.E.
Atlanta, Georgia 30303
L. Edmund Rast, President
(404) 529-8611

SOUTHERN BELLE (canned meats)
See Mid South Packers Inc.

SOUTHERN BELLE (citrus products)
See H.P. Hood & Sons, Florida Citrus Division

SOUTHERN BELLE (salad dressings, sandwich spreads)
See J.H. Filbert Inc.

SOUTHERN BELLE FROZEN FOODS INC.
Box 3823
Jacksonville, Florida 32206

SOUTHERN BISCUIT COMPANY
Box 27487
900 Terminal Drive
Richmond, Virginia 23261
David O. Clark, President
(804) 355-7801

SOUTHERN BRANDS INC.
Box 151
Saint Martinsville, Louisiana 70582

SOUTHERN CALIFORNIA EDISON COMPANY
2244 Walnut Grove Avenue
Rosemead, California 91770
Jack K. Horton, Chairman of the Board
(213) 572-1212

SOUTHERN CALIFORNIA FIRST NATIONAL BANK
Post Office Box 1311
San Diego, California 92112
Richard T. Silverman, President
(714) 294-4647

SOUTHERN CALIFORNIA GAS COMPANY
810 South Flower Street
Los Angeles, California 90017
H.P. Letton, Jr., President
(213) 689-2345

SOUTHERN CALIFORNIA WOOD PRODUCTS INC.
3989 Centinela Avenue
Los Angeles, California 90066
(213) 870-6934

SOUTHERN CENTRAL COMPANY
736 South Dudley Street
Memphis, Tennessee 38102
(901) 774-3873

SOUTHERN CHAMPION TRAY COMPANY
Box 4066
Compress Street
Chattanooga, Tennessee 37405
(615) 267-2179

SOUTHERN CHOICE (food products)
See Brundidge Foods Inc.

SOUTHERN COFFEE & RESTAURANT SUPPLY COMPANY
704 North Hudson
Oklahoma City, Oklahoma 73102
(405) 232-7584

SOUTHERN COMFORT CORPORATION
1220 North Price Road
Saint Louis, Missouri 63132
F.E. Fowler, III, President
(314) 993-6606

SOUTHERN CONFECTIONERS, INC.
Brookhaven Boulevard
Columbus, Georgia 31906

SOUTHERN CONNECTICUT GAS COMPANY
880 Broad Street
Bridgeport, Connecticut 06609
John R. Hungerford, President
(203) 368-6781

SOUTHERN CROSS INDUSTRIES, INC.
Post Office Box 1597
290 Hunter, S.E.
Atlanta, Georgia 30301
William M. Caldwell, Chairman of the Board
(404) 688-2154

SOUTHERN CROSS MARKETING
Box 66
Corona del Mar, California 92625

SOUTHERN DAISY INDUSTRIES, INC.
Post Office Box 2206
1259 Greene Street
Augusta, Georgia 30903
R.E. Brown, Chairman of the Board
(404) 722-2238

SOUTHERN DESK COMPANY
Hickory, North Carolina 28601

Companies and Trade Names

SOUTHERN DRUG & MANU-
FACTURING COMPANY
Box 2506
Knoxville, Tennessee 37901

SOUTHERN FABRICATORS
CORPORATION
Post Office Box 7321
Shreveport, Louisiana 71107

SOUTHERN FLAVORING COMPANY
Bedford, Virginia 24523

SOUTHERN FLAVORS (flavoring extracts)
See C & D Flavor Company

SOUTHERN FOLDER & INDEX
COMPANY
Post Office Drawer 1232
El Dorado, Arkansas 71730
(501) 863-5184

SOUTHERN FROZEN FOODS, INC.
(Division of Seabrook Foods, Inc.)
Plant Street
Montezuma, Georgia 31063
Preston C. Williams, Jr., President
(912) 472-8101

SOUTHERN FRUIT DISTRIBUTORS, INC.
Post Office Box 8367
1 West Pine Loch Avenue
Orlando, Florida 32806
Austin A. Caruso, President
(305) 859-3550

SOUTHERN GEM (food products)
See Bush Brothers & Company

SOUTHERN GOLD (margarine)
See Shedd-Bartush Foods, Inc.

SOUTHERN GOLD CITRUS
PRODUCTS, INC.
Box 7538
Orlando, Florida 32804

SOUTHERN HIGHLAND
DULCIMERS COMPANY
1010 South 14th Street
Slaton, Texas 79364

SOUTHERN INDIANA GAS &
ELECTRIC COMPANY
20-24 N.W. Fourth Street
Evansville, Indiana 47741
Dorris W. Vaughn, President
(812) 424-6411

SOUTHERN INDUSTRIES
CORPORATION
Post Office Box 1685
Mobile, Alabama 36601
D.E. Dawson, Jr., President
(205) 438-3531

SOUTHERN IOWA MANUFAC-
TURING COMPANY
Post Office Box 448
103 Furnas Drive
Osceola, Iowa 50213
(515) 342-2166
See also Kaper Krafts

SOUTHERN MANOR (food products)
See Lexington Specialty Foods Inc.

SOUTHERN MILLS INC.
585 Wells Street S.W.
Atlanta, Georgia 30312
(404) 524-1991

SOUTHERN NATURAL GAS
COMPANY
Post Office Box 2563
Birmingham, Alabama 35203
John S. Shaw, Jr., President
(205) 325-7410

SOUTHERN NEW ENGLAND
TELEPHONE
227 Church
New Haven, Connecticut 06506
Alfred W. Van Sinderen, President
(203) 771-5200

SOUTHERN PACIFIC COMPANY
1 Market Company
San Francisco, California 94105
B.F. Biaggini, President
(415) 362-1212

SOUTHERN PACKING COMPANY
INC.
909 South Carey Street
Baltimore, Maryland 21223
William E. Lamble, President and Treasurer
(301) 752-0020

SOUTHERN PHARMACAL
COMPANY, INC.
8901 Lawn Avenue
Brentwood, Missouri 63144

SOUTHERN PRECISION
INSTRUMENT COMPANY
3419 East Commerce Street
San Antonio, Texas 78219
(512) 224-5801

SOUTHERN PRIDE (flavored Bourbon)
See American Distilling Company, Inc.

SOUTHERN PRIDE (frozen meat products)
See Hi Brand Foods

SOUTHERN QUEEN (shortening)
See Anderson Clayton Foods

SOUTHERN RAILWAY COMPANY
920 15th Street, N.W.
Washington, D.C. 20005
W. Graham Claytor, Jr., President
(202) 628-4460

Companies and Trade Names

SOUTHERN ROLL (margarine)
See Shedd-Bartush Foods Inc.

SOUTHERN SEAS (tuna)
See Wilbur-Ellis Company

SOUTHERN SHELL FISH COMPANY
(Subsidiary of Norton Simon Inc.)
Harvey, Louisiana 70058
(504) 341-5631

SOUTHERN STAR (meats)
See Klarer of Kentucky, Inc.

SOUTHERN STATES COOPERATIVE, INC.
Seventh and Main Streets
Richmond, Virginia 23213
James L. Campbell, President
(804) 782-1000

SOUTHERN STATES PHARMACEUTICAL COMPANY
Box 606
Highlands, North Carolina 28741

SOUTHERN STRAW MANUFACTURING COMPANY
4415 Wendell Drive N.W.
Atlanta, Georgia 30336

SOUTHERN STYLE (food products)
See Garcia Canning Company

SOUTHERN STYLE FOODS, INC.
2905 Armory Drive
Nashville, Tennessee 37204

SOUTHERN UNION GAS COMPANY
Fidelity Union Tower
Dallas, Texas 75201
N.P. Chestnut, President
(214) 748-8511

SOUTHGATE FOODS, INC.
2842 Cromwell Road
Norfolk, Virginia 23513
(804) 853-4321

SOUTHLAND CANNING & PACKING COMPANY, INC.
(Subsidiary of Pet Inc.)
800 Edwards Avenue
New Orleans, Louisiana 70123
(504) 733-6991
See also Orleans Seafood Company

SOUTHLAND COFFEE COMPANY, INC.
1 Washington Avenue, S.W.
Atlanta, Georgia 30303
J.D. Anderson, President
(404) 688-1870

SOUTHLAND CORPORATION, THE
2828 North Haskell Avenue
Dallas, Texas 75204
Jere W. Thompson, President
(214) 828-7011
See also Barricini, Inc.

SOUTHLAND FROZEN FOODS, INC.
1 Linden Place
Great Neck, New York 11021
D. Herman Kennedy, Chairman of the Board
(516) 466-3200

SOUTHLAND MOWER COMPANY, INC.
Old Montgomery Highway
Selma, Alabama 36701
B.L. Peak, President
(205) 874-7406

SOUTHLAND MUSICAL MERCHANDISE CORPORATION
Post Office Box 6125
Greensboro, North Carolina 27405

SOUTHLAND OIL COMPANY
Savannah State Docks
Savannah, Georgia 31408
Norman A. McGee, President
(912) 964-1811

SOUTHLAND STATES (battery)
See General Battery Corporation

SOUTHLAND SUPREME (lawn and garden supplies, sporting goods)
See Gooch-Edenton Hardware Inc.

SOUTHMOST (frozen produce)
See United Foods, Inc.

SOUTHWEST AIRLINES
3300 Love Field Drive
Dallas, Texas 75235
M. Lamar Muse, President
(214) 630-5511

SOUTHWEST FOREST INDUSTRIES
Packaging Division
2939 Vail Avenue
Los Angeles, California 90040
(213) 724-2711

SOUTHWEST GAS CORPORATION
Post Office Box 1450
Las Vegas, Nevada 89101
W.M. Laub, President
(702) 876-7011

SOUTHWEST PECAN COMPANY
Box 1116
Bristow, Oklahoma 74010

SOUTHWEST PHARMACEUTICALS
8516 South 18th
Fort Smith, Arkansas 72901

SOUTHWEST TABLET MANUFACTURING COMPANY
2110 Corinth Street
Dallas, Texas 75215
Bernard W. Mathiew, General Manager
(214) 421-7681

SOUTHWESTERN BELL TELEPHONE COMPANY
1010 Pine
Saint Louis, Missouri 63101
Zane E. Barnes, President
(314) 247-9800

Companies and Trade Names

SOUTHWESTERN CANDY
  COMPANY, INC., THE
Post Office Box 877
Jackson, Tennessee 38301

SOUTHWESTERN DRUG
  CORPORATION
8000 John W. Carpenter Freeway
Dallas, Texas 75222
C.C. Hopper, President
(214) 631-2440

SOUTHWESTERN ELECTRIC POWER
  COMPANY
428 Travis Street
Shreveport, Louisiana 71156
James L. Stall, President
(318) 222-2141

SOUTHWESTERN LIFE INSURANCE
  COMPANY
Post Office Box 2699
Dallas, Texas 75221
William H. Seay, President
(214) 742-9101

SOUTHWESTERN PUBLIC SERVICE
  COMPANY
Sixth and Tyler Street
Amarillo, Texas 79170
Roy Tolk, President
(806) 378-2121

SOUTHWICK (men's clothes)
  See Grieco Brothers, Inc.

SOUTHWORTH COMPANY
Front Street
West Springfield,
  Massachusetts 01089
John H. Southworth, President and
  Treasurer
(413) 732-5141

SOVEREIGN (banjos, guitars,
mandolins, ukuleles)
  See Harmony Company

SOVEREIGN (outboard motors)
  See Outboard Marine Corporation

SOVEREIGN (plastic cutlery)
  See Maryland Plastics, Inc.

SOVEREIGN (trumpets, trombones,
etc.)
  See Boosey & Hawkes Ltd.

SOVEREIGN METAL
  CORPORATION
10 East 40th Street
New York, New York 10016
(212) 532-8280

SOVEREIGN PAPER
  CORPORATION
Post Office Box 398
Suffern, New York 10901

SOVEREIGN PLAYING CARD &
  NOVELTY CORPORATION
10-05 35th Avenue
Long Island City, New York 11106
(212) 545-2659

SOYALAC (infant formula)
  See Loma Linda Food Company

SPA (bath products)
  See Products of Excellence Ltd.

SPACE COMMAND 100 (remote-
control portable color TV)
  See Zenith Radio Corporation

SPACE MAKER (radio intercom)
  See Westinghouse Electric
    Corporation

SPACE MATE (air conditioners)
  See Philco-Ford Corporation

SPACE-MATE (luggage)
  See Atlantic Products
    Corporation

SPACE SAVER (desk lamps)
  See Cannon Products Inc.

SPACE SAVER (housewares)
  See Grayline Housewares

SPACE SAVER
(Division of Clarin Corporation)
2650 North Greenfield Avenue
North Chicago, Illinois 60064
(312) 689-0575

SPACE TONE (electric guitars)
  See Micro-Frets Corporation

SPACEFOOD (dehydrated meat,
vegetables, fruit, etc.)
  See Epicure Foods, Inc.

SPACEHOPPERS (children's boots
and rubbers)
  See Torch Rubber Company

SPACEMASTER (folding doors)
  See Modernfold Industries, Inc.

SPACKLIT (paints and paint
sundries)
  See E. Rabinowe & Company

SPADA DISTRIBUTING COMPANY
1137 S.E. Union Avenue
Portland, Oregon 97214
(503) 234-9215

SPADEMAN RELEASE SYSTEM
21 Karen Road
Belmont, California 94002

SPAETH DISPLAYS, INC.
423 West 55th Street
New York, New York 10019
(212) 489-0770

SPALDING (shoes)
  See B.A. Corbin & Son
    Company

Companies and Trade Names

SPALDING
(Division of Questor Corporation)
Meadow Street
Chicopee, Massachusetts 01014
Paul F. Collins, President
(413) 536-1200

SPAM (meat product)
See George A. Hormel & Company

SPANADA (wine)
See E. & J. Gallo Winery

SPANDEX
Elm Square
Andover, Massachusetts 01810

SPANGLER CANDY COMPANY
400 North Portland Street
Bryan, Ohio 43506
Harlan G. Spangler, President
(419) 636-4221

SPANGLER COMPANY, E.J.
1237 North Howard
Philadelphia, Pennsylvania 19101
Bruce S. Parkinson, President
(215) 634-8820

SPANISH GERANIUM (fragrance)
See Lanvin-Charles of the Ritz Inc.

SPANISH GUITAR (men's cologne and aftershave lotion)
See Textron, Inc.

SPANISH LADY (canned Spanish foods)
See Candle-Light Foods Inc.

SPANISH MANUFACTURERS ASSOCIATION OF THE US INC.
666 North Lake Shore Drive
Space 314
Chicago, Illinois 60611

SPANISH STONE (inlaid vinyl flooring)
See Congoleum-Nairn Inc.

SPANNAR INC.
Grandy, Minnesota 55029

SPANNER INC., G.O.
20 Church Street
Montclair, New Jersey 07042

SPAR-KOOL (frozen foods)
See Newton Foods Inc.

SPARCLIN (enamel)
See Hooker Paint Manufacturing Company

SPARCRAFT INC.
770 West 17th Street
Costa Mesa, California 92627

SPARKLE (automotive products)
See The Ward Products Corporation

SPARKLE 'N GLOW (shampoo)
See Helene Curtis Industries, Inc.

SPARKLENE (brushes, brooms, mops)
See H. Hertzberg & Son Inc.

SPARKLER (carpeting)
See Magee Carpet Company

SPARKLET DEVICES, INC.
(Division of The Hoover Company)
3402 Morganford Road
Saint Louis, Missouri 63116
(314) 773-0400

SPARKLETS (food products)
See Kelley, Fanquhar & Company

SPARKLETTS DRINKING WATER CORPORATION
(Subsidiary of Foremost-McKesson Inc.)
4500 York Boulevard
Los Angeles, California 90041
Burton N. Arnds, Jr., President
(213) 258-2747

SPARKLIN (enamel)
See Hooker Paint Manufacturing Company

SPARKLING (tea)
See Piggly Wiggly Corporation

SPARKLING SPRING MINERAL WATER COMPANY
1629 Park Avenue West
Highland Park, Illinois 60035

SPARKLING WAVE (seafood)
See Union Fish Company

SPARKS (whiskey)
See Heublein Inc.

SPARKS GAME & TOY COMPANY INC.
Post Office Box 2361
Pikeville, Kentucky 41501

SPARKY OF CHICAGO
1006 South Michigan Avenue
Chicago, Illinois 60605
(312) 341-1920

SPARTA BRUSH COMPANY, INC.
402 South Black River Street
Sparta, Wisconsin 54656
(608) 269-2151

SPARTAN (boat trailers)
See C & F Machine Works Inc.

SPARTAN (pipes)
See Yello-Bole Pipes, Inc.

Companies and Trade Names

SPARTAN (TV's and radios)
See Magnavox Corporation

SPARTAN FOOD SYSTEMS, INC.
Interstate 85
Frontage Road
Spartanburg, South Carolina 29302
Jerome Johnson Richardson, President
(803) 579-1220

SPARTAN PLASTICS INC.
Post Office Box 67-T
1845 South Cedar Street
Holt, Michigan 48842
(517) 694-3911

SPARTAN SAW WORKS INC.
152 Fisk Avenue
Springfield, Massachusetts 01107
(413) 733-2127

SPARTAN STORES INC.
Produce Division
1111 44th Street S.E.
Grand Rapids, Michigan 49508
Glen Catt, President
(616) 538-6550

SPARTANS INDUSTRIES, INC.
350 Fifth Avenue
New York, New York 10016
Marshall Rose, President
(212) 997-8800

SPARTUS (kitchen tools)
See Regent-Sheffield Ltd.

SPARTUS CORPORATION
(Subsidiary of Walter Kidde & Company, Inc.)
730 West Lake Street
Chicago, Illinois 60606
(312) 263-0235

SPARVAR (aerosol paint and coatings)
See Krylon (Department of Borden Inc.)

SPASAVER (stainless-steel shelving)
See Eastern Steel Rack Company

SPATIAL LIGHT (aluminum lamp shades and louvers)
See Lustro Metal Inc.

SPATINI COMPANY
47th and Brown
Philadelphia, Pennsylvania 19139
(215) 222-3055

SPATOLA-THOMPSON, INC.
Delaware Avenue and Miffin
Philadelphia, Pennsylvania 19148
(215) 389-8600

SPATZ BINDING COMPANY
See Star Binding & Trimming Corporation

SPAULDING & FROST COMPANY INC.
108 Main Street
Fremont, New Hampshire 03044
(603) 895-3372

SPAULDING FIBRE COMPANY, INC.
310 Wheeler
Tonawanda, New York 14152

SPAULDING'S INC.
Box 10009
Saint Petersburg, Florida 33733

SPE-DE-WAY PRODUCTS COMPANY INC.
8000 N.E. 14th Place
Portland, Oregon 97217
(503) 285-8371

SPEAK EASY (breath freshener)
See American Safety Razor Company

SPEAKER CORPORATION, J.W.
3059 North Weil
Milwaukee, Wisconsin 53212
John A. Speaker, President
(414) 264-0500

SPEAKMAN COMPANY
301 East 30th Street
Wilmington, Delaware 19899
Willard A. Speakman, III, President
(302) 764-7100

SPEAR ENGINEERING COMPANY
3107 Stone Avenue
Colorado Springs, Colorado 80907
(303) 634-2801

SPEAR PRODUCTS COMPANY
(Division of Jerome Electric Corporation)
391 Lakeside Avenue
Orange, New Jersey 07050

SPEARE'S SONS COMPANY, THE ALDEN
24 Webster Avenue
Somerville, Massachusetts 02143

SPEARS (arts, crafts, and games)
See Lesney Products Corporation

SPEAS COMPANY
2400 Nicholson Avenue
Kansas City, Missouri 64120
(816) 483-1700

SPEC-T (cough suppressant, decongestant, etc.)
See Squibb Products Company

SPECIAL (compact manual typewriters)
See Adler Business Machines Inc.

SPECIAL CHEMICALS
(Division of Winthrop Laboratories)
90 Park Avenue
New York, New York 10016
(212) 972-4141

Companies and Trade Names

SPECIAL FOODS INC.
426 West Avenue
Red Wing, Minnesota 55066

SPECIAL K (cereal)
See Kellogg Company

SPECIAL MORNING (breakfast drink)
See Carnation Company

SPECIAL SECTIONS, INC.
2266 Tillotson Avenue
Bronx, New York 10469
(212) 325-6666

SPECIAL SENATOR (fishing reels)
See Penn Fishing Tackle Manufacturing Company

SPECIAL-T (processed fruits)
See Bakers' Specialties Ltd.

SPECIAL "T" HOSIERY COMPANY
2 Penn Plaza
New York, New York 10001
Nicholas M. Brecher, President
(212) 565-4844

SPECIALIZED COATINGS, INC.
62 Broadway
Passaic, New Jersey 07056

SPECIALTY BRANDS, INC.
850 Montgomery Street
San Francisco, California 94133
Toby Schreiber, President
(415) 397-7550

SPECIALTY CANDY COMPANY, INC.
429 South Caton Avenue
Baltimore, Maryland 21229

SPECIALTY FOOD DISTRIBUTORS
250 Carol Place
Moonachie, New Jersey 07074

SPECIIALTY FOODS CORPORATION
Post Office Box 71
Johnson City, New York 13790
(607) 729-3593

SPECIALTY FRANCHISES, INC.
57-01 32 Avenue
Woodside, New York 11377

SPECIALTY INK COMPANY, INC.
20 Dunton Avenue
Deer Park, New York 11729
(516) 586-3666

SPECIALTY ITEMS COMPANY INC.
1075 Curtis Street
Menlo Park, California 94025

SPECIALTY PRINTING COMPANY
8556 West Nine Mile Road
Oak Park, Michigan 48237

SPECIALTY PRODUCTS COMPANY
433 Bourbon Street
New Orleans, Louisiana 70130
(504) 523-7326

SPECIALTY SEWN PRODUCTS INC.
240 Old Country Road
Hicksville, New York 11801

SPECO, INC.
3946 Willow Road
Schiller Park, Illinois 60176
Charles W. Hess, President and General Manager
(312) 678-4240

SPECTACULAR PRODUCTS
1101 North Fourth Street
Cannon Falls, Minnesota 55009

SPECTOR FREIGHT SYSTEM, INC.
205 West Wacker Drive
Chicago, Illinois 60606
K.J. Younger, President
(312) 236-7220

SPECTOR, INC., WILLIAM & SIDNEY
580 Eighth Avenue
New York, New York 10018
(212) 947-0540

SPECTOR WOOL STOCK CORPORATION
225 Lafayette
New York, New York 10012
(212) 226-3477

SPECTRA-STRIP CORPORATION
7100 Lampson Avenue
Garden Grove, California 92642
(714) 892-3361

SPECTRACIDE (plant-care product)
See Ciba-Geigy Corporation

SPECTRUM (brushes)
See Avalon Industries Inc.

SPECTRUM IMPORTS, INC.
2121 Broadway
New York, New York 10023
(212) 362-8000

SPEED (cement)
See Louisville Cement Company

SPEED COAT (coating for fiberglass boat bottoms)
See Sailing Technology Company

SPEED DEMON (paint applicators, caulking compound, etc.)
See Red Devil Inc.

SPEED GRAPHIC (cameras)
See Graflex, Inc.

SPEED KING (skates)
See Hustler Corporation

SPEED O PRINT (photocopier)
See Speed O Print Business Machines Corporation

Companies and Trade Names

SPEED-O-PRINT BUSINESS
  MACHINES CORPORATION
1801 West Larchmont Avenue
Chicago, Illinois 60613
Abe Samuels, President
(312) 477-2000

SPEED QUEEN
(Division of McGraw-Edison
  Company)
Shepard Street
Ripon, Wisconsin 54971
Glenn S. Olinger, President
(414) 748-3121

SPEED QUEEN (washers and dryers)
  See Speed Queen

SPEED-REX (enamels)
  See Celanese Corporation

SPEED-SPRED (fertilizer distributor)
  See Calhoun Manufacturing
  Company, Inc.

SPEED SWEEP (brushes and brooms)
  See Milwaukee Dustless Brush
  Company

SPEED-TONE (paints)
  See Consolidated Paint &
  Varnish Corporation

SPEEDI-DRI
(Department of Engelhard Minerals &
  Chemicals Corporation)
Menlo Park
Edison, New Jersey 08817
(201) 321-5000

SPEEDI-HEAT (stainless-steel-clad
cookware)
  See Everedy Company, Inc.

SPEEDIMPEX U.S.A. INC.
23-16 40th Street
Long Island City, New York 11104
(212) 786-4706

SPEEDLINER COMPANY
7633 South Western Avenue
Chicago, Illinois 60620
(312) 737-2446

SPEEDLINER MARINE COMPANY
Sixth and Oak Streets
Saint Joseph, Missouri 64503

SPEEDRACK INC.
5300 Simpson
Skokie, Illinois 60076
(312) 966-5100

SPEEDSHAVER (electric shaver)
  See North American Phillips
  Company

SPEEDY (lawn mower)
  See American Lawn Mower
  Company

SPEEDY-CLEAN (chrome cookware)
  See Everedy Company, Inc.

SPEEDY SPRAYER (paint sprayer)
  See W.R. Brown Corporation

SPEEDY-SPREAD (fertilizer spreader)
  See General Metals, Inc.

SPEER, INC.
Post Office Box 896
1023 Snake River Avenue
Lewiston, Idaho 83501
Raymond G. Speer, President
(208) 743-8574

SPEERT INC.
35 West 35th Street
New York, New York 10001
(212) 947-7758

SPEIDEL CORPORATION
(Division of Textron Company)
70 Ship Street
Providence, Rhode Island 02902
Robert S. Kennedy, President
(401) 421-8600

SPEK-AID COMPANY
(Division of Pic Corporation)
30 Canfield Street
Orange, New Jersey 07050

SPENCER CALIFORNIA
Box 470
Tehachapi, California 93561

SPENCER COMPANY, INC.
450 Summer Street
Boston, Massachusetts 02210
C. Charles Marran, President
(617) 542-8120

SPENCER FOODS, INC.
225 West 21st Street
Spencer, Iowa 51301
G.L. Pearson, Chairman of the
  Board
(712) 262-4250

SPENCER GIFTS, INC.
1601 Albany Avenue
Atlantic City, New Jersey 08401
J. Eugene Brog, President
(609) 345-5934

SPENCER, INC., R.L.
719 South Los Angeles
Los Angeles, California 90014
(213) 627-5201

SPENCER INDUSTRIES, INC.
135 West 50th Street
New York, New York 10020
G.W. Spencer, President
(212) 582-0220
  See also Casual Sportswear
  Company Inc.

SPENCER-MURRAY CORPORATION
Box 48
Swarthmore, Pennsylvania 19081

SPENCER, WILLIAM
Creek Road
Rancocas Woods, New Jersey 08060
(609) 235-1830

Companies and Trade Names

SPERRY (flour)
See General Mills, Inc.

SPERRY & HUTCHINSON
COMPANY, THE
330 Madison Avenue
New York, New York 10017
Joanna C. Maitland, Director,
Consumer Affairs
(212) 983-5531
See also American/Drew Furniture Companies; Bigelow-Sanford, Inc.; Daystrom Furniture, Inc.; Gunlocke, Company, Inc.; Lea Industries, Inc.; and State National Bank of Connecticut

SPERRY COMPANY INC., JOHN H.
115 Sandwich Street
Plymouth, Massachusetts 02360

SPERRY COMPANY, J.
7 West Second Street
Kingsley, Iowa 51028

SPERRY RAND CORPORATION
The Sperry Rand Building
1290 Avenue of the Americas
New York, New York 10019
J.P. Lyet, Chairman of the Board
(212) 956-2121
See also Remington Electric Shaver; Remington Rand Office Machines; Remington Rand System

SPERRY RAND CORPORATION
New Holland Division
New Holland, Pennsylvania 17557
Kenneth F. Thompson, President
(717) 354-1121

SPERRY REMINGTON
(Division of Sperry Rand Corporation)
60 Main Street
Bridgeport, Connecticut 06602
F.M. Pistilli, President
(203) 336-3571

SPERRY TOP SIDER
(Division of Uniroyal Inc.)
Box 338
Naugatuck, Connecticut 06770
(203) 729-6333

SPERRY VICKERS
Box 302
Troy, Michigan 48084
John T. Burns, President
(313) 576-3000

SPERRY'S (meat products)
See Swift & Company

SPERTI DRUG PRODUCTS, INC.
(Division of Cooper Hewitt Electric Company)
7 Sperti Drive
Fort Mitchell, Kentucky 41017
Robert Montgomery, President
(606) 331-0800
See also Stanley Drug Products, Inc.

SPIBRO (seafood)
See Rego Smoked Fish Company, Inc.

SPIC AND SPAN (household cleaner)
See Procter & Gamble Company

SPICE (venetian blinds)
See Breneman, Inc.

SPICE CRAB (apples, pears, etc.)
See Michigan Fruit Canners, Inc.

SPICE GARDEN (aluminum canister sets)
See Kromex

SPICE ISLANDS
850 Montgomery
San Francisco, California 94133
(415) 397-7550

SPICE KING CORPORATION
6009 Washington Boulevard
Culver City, California 90203

SPICE OF LIFE (spices)
See Hygrade Food Products Corporation

SPICE O'LIFE (cooking and serving ware)
See Corning Glass Works

SPICE SERVICE INC.
170 Stewart Avenue
Brooklyn, New York 11237
(212) 456-7096

SPICE TREE (spice grinders)
See Dudley Kebow Inc.

SPICECO
900 Passaic Avenue
East Newark, New Jersey 07029

SPIEGEL BROTHERS COMPANY
313 Sixth Avenue
McKeesport, Pennsylvania 15132

SPIEGEL, INC.
(Subsidiary of Beneficial Corporation)
2511 West 23rd Street
Chicago, Illinois 60608
Harry A. Johnson, Chairman of the Board
(312) 927-5600

SPIEGL FOODS, INC.
Post Office Box 1491
1219 Abbott
Salinas, California 93901
James L. Rankin, President
(408) 422-4751

SPIEWAK & SONS, INC., I.
2 Penn Plaza
New York, New York 10001
Gerald Spiewak, President
(212) 695-1620

Companies and Trade Names

SPIFFY (picnic jugs)
See Hamilton-Skotch Corporation

SPIL-GARD (ice trays)
See Inland Manufacturing (Division of General Motors Corporation)

SPILL-STOP MANUFACTURING COMPANY
1509 West LeMoyne Street
Melrose Park, Illinois 60160
(312) 345-2200

SPIN-A-TEST COMPANY
Post Office Box 823
Pleasanton, California 94566

SPIN BLEND (salad dressing)
See CPC International Inc.

SPIN CURLERS (hair permanent)
See Gillette Company, Personal Care Division

SPIN-IN (fishing equipment)
See Tradewinds, Inc.

SPINDLER & SAUPPE
13034 Saticoy
North Hollywood, California 91605
(213) 764-1800

SPINDLER & SONS INC., AUGUST
7 Commerce Drive
Cranford, New Jersey 07016

SPINDRIFT
(Division of N.I.C.)
Post Office Box 7078
Fort Lauderdale, Florida 33304

SPINFISHER (fishing reels)
See Penn Fishing Tackle Manufacturing Company

SPINNAKER (tobacco)
See Theodorus Niemeyer, Inc.

SPINNERIN SPORTS BY GUSTI
Box 134
Burlington, Wisconsin 53105

SPINNERIN YARN COMPANY, INC.
30 Wesley Street
South Hackensack, New Jersey 07606
Herman Ruegger, President
(201) 343-5900

SPIRAL BINDING COMPANY INC.
10 Columbus Circle
New York, New York 10019
George E. Roth, President
(212) 397-1630

SPIRAL KILLER (archery equipment)
See Miller Ski Company

SPIRATONE INC.
135-06 Northern Boulevard
Flushing, New York 11354
(212) 886-2000

SPIRE OF CALIFORNIA (men's sport shirts)
See Grunwald-Marx, Inc.

SPIRIT OF NORWAY (canned fish)
See Norbest Inc.

SPIRITE INDUSTRIES
150 South Dean Street
Englewood, New Jersey 07631
Harvey Bernstein, President
(201) 871-4910

SPIRITUAL SKY SCENTED PRODUCT PRODUCTS
3959 Landmark Street
Culver City, California 90230

SPIRT & COMPANY
(Division of Nutrion Corporation)
Box 1496
Reading, Pennsylvania 19603

SPITZ COMPANY, INC., THE PAUL
461 Timpson Place
Bronx, New York 10455
(212) 665-6800

SPIVEY BROTHERS SAUCE COMPANY, INC.
1324 Louisiana Avenue
Shreveport, Louisiana 71101
(318) 222-1588

SPLASH REFRESHER (bath lotion, deodorant, and aftershave lotion)
See Yardley of London, Inc.)

SPLENDOR FORM BRASSIERE, INC.
632 Broadway
New York, New York 10012
Joseph Delman, President
(212) 777-7262

SPLINTER PICKLE COMPANY, INC.
4001 West Loomis Road
Milwaukee, Wisconsin 53221
(414) 282-9300

SPLITKEIN (sports accessories and equipment)
See Sportco Inc.

SPO-CHAM (wet mops, dust clothes)
See Zelinkoff Company

SPOACRAFT
(Division of Bischoff Chemical Corporation)
220 Miller Road
Hicksville, New York 11801

SPOAN (shaving cream and deodorant soap)
See Bristol-Myers

SPODE, INC.
26 Kennedy Boulevard
East Brunswick, New Jersey 08816
George Barker, President
(201) 846-1227

Companies and Trade Names

SPOHN MEDICAL COMPANY
202 North Main Street
Goshen, Indiana 46526
(219) 533-4670

SPOILER YACHTS INC.
Box 2289
Costa Mesa, California 92626

SPOKANE DRY GOODS COMPANY
(Subsidiary of Marshall Field &
  Company)
West 710 Riverside Avenue
Spokane, Washington 99201
H.W. Bacon, General Manager
(509) 747-3311

SPOKANE PORTLAND & SEATTLE
  RAILWAY
(Subsidiary of Burlington Northern,
  Inc.)
1101 N.W. Hoyt Street
Portland, Oregon 97209
Louis W. Menk, President
(503) 221-1300

SPOLA FIBRES INTERNATIONAL
729 Madison Street
Hoboken, New Jersey 07030

SPONHOLZ KUNO
350 West 55th Street
New York, New York 10019
(212) 265-3777

SPOONIK (combination spoon/fork/
knife)
    See Kirk International

SPORODYNE COMPANY
304 Vermont Avenue
Dayton, Ohio 45404

SPORT-CRAFT INC.
Box 351
Perry, Florida 32347

SPORT KING (binoculars)
    See Swift Instruments Inc.

SPORT KING (sporting firearms)
    See High Standard Manufacturing
      Corporation

SPORT-KING (sporting goods)
    See Allied Hardware Services
      Inc.

SPORT LIFE (shoes)
    See Herbst Shoe Manufacturing
      Company

SPORT-OBERMEYER, LTD, USA
Box 130
Aspen, Colorado 81611
Klaus F. Obermeyer, President
(303) 925-3037

SPORT SHELF
Post Office Box 634
New Rochelle, New York 10802

SPORTADE (energy drink)
    See Becton, Dickinson &
      Company

SPORTCASTER COMPANY INC.
Pioneer Square Station
Box 4000
Seattle, Washington 98104
(206) 624-2214

SPORTCO INC.
Depot Street
Wilton, Maine 04294

SPORTJAMA (men's pajamas)
    See Varsity Pajamas

SPORTLEIGH-HALL (coats)
    See Country Miss Inc.

SPORTOCASINS (shoes)
    See G.H. Bass & Company

SPORTOWELS INC.
901 North 27th Street
Milwaukee, Wisconsin 53208
(414) 342-6675

SPORTS (shoes)
    See Bristol Manufacturing
      Corporation

SPORTS EDUCATIONAL DEVICES
  COMPANY
Box 386
Corona del Mar, California 92625
(714) 673-5711

SPORTS ILLUSTRATED
92 Tokeneke Road
Darien, Connecticut 06820

SPORTS MARINE COMPANY
122 Broad Boulevard
Cuyahoga Falls, Ohio 44221

SPORTSCASTERS (shoes)
    See Old Town Shoe Company

SPORTSCOACH CORPORATION
9134 Independence
Chatsworth, California 91311

SPORTSCRAFT LEATHER (handbags)
    See Fancy Industries Inc.

SPORTSET (sportswear)
    See Puritan Fashions Corporation

SPORTSMAN (automotive bicycle
carriers)
    See Mijon Company Inc.

SPORTSMAN (flashlights)
    See Ray-O-Vac (Division of
      ESB Inc.)

SPORTSMAN (freezers)
    See Frigibar Industries Inc.

1257

Companies and Trade Names

SPORTSMAN (rear-engine rider/mower)
See Toro Company

SPORTSMAN (sporting goods)
See Philip S. Olt Company

SPORTSMAN (walkie-talkies)
See RCA Corporation

SPORTSMAN (whiskey)
See Schenley Industries, Inc.

SPORTSMAN ATHLETIC TRUSS
Box 355
Noblesville, Indiana 46060

SPORTSMAN'S WORKSHOP
834 Gillespie Avenue
Sarasota, Florida 33578

SPORTSMASTER (toys, hobbies, sporting goods, etc.)
See Liberty Distributors Group

SPORTSMASTER RV (recreational vehicle)
See Kit Manufacturing Company

SPORTSMEN ACCESSORIES, INC.
434 Grand Street
Bridgeport, Connecticut 06604
(203) 579-0686

SPORTSMEN'S CANNERY
Box 11
Winchester Bay, Oregon 97467

SPORTSMEN'S INDUSTRIES INC.
7878 N.W. 103rd Street
Hialeah Gardens, Florida 33016

SPORTSMEN'S SEAFOODS
(Subsidiary of Union Fish Company)
1617 Quivira Road
San Diego, California 92108
(714) 224-3551

SPORTSTER (lanterns)
See Garrity Industries, Inc., Dynatron Division

SPORTSTER (outboard motors)
See Evinrude Motors

SPORTSVIEW (binoculars)
See Bushnell Optical Company

SPOT (dog food)
See J.M. Schneider Ltd.

SPOT (dry cleaner)
See Red Devil Inc.

SPOT AWAY (foam rug cleaner)
See Bissell Inc.

SPOTLESS TOWN (paints and paint sundries)
See Belknap Inc.

SPOTNAILS, INC.
1100 Hicks Road
Rolling Meadows, Illinois 60008
G. Villwoch, Executive Vice President
(312) 259-1620

SPRAINT (aerosol paints and sundries)
See Kerr Chemicals, Inc.

SPRATT WOODWIND SHOP, JACK
199 Sound Beach Avenue
Old Greenwich, Connecticut 06870

SPRATT'S (dog and cat foods)
See General Mills, Inc.

SPRAY-DAY-LITE (paint)
See Glidden-Durkee (Division of SCM Corporation)

SPRAY 'N VAC (foam rug cleaner)
See Glamorene Products Corporation

SPRAY 'N WASH (laundry prespotter)
See Texize Chemicals, Inc.

SPRAY NET (hair spray)
See Helene Curtis Industries Inc.

SPRAY-O-NAMEL (aerosol spray paint)
See Illinois Bronze Powder & Paint Company

SPRAY-PLA (brush and spray paints)
See Testor Corporation

SPRAY-VAR (varnish)
See Blair Art Products

SPRAYBOND (paints and paint sundries)
See E. Rabinowe & Company

SPRAYING SYSTEMS COMPANY
North Avenue at Schmale Road
Wheaton, Illinois 60187
Fred W. Wahlin, President
(312) 665-5000

SPRAYON PRODUCTS, INC.
(Subsidiary of The Sherwin Williams Company)
26300 Fargo Avenue
Bedford Heights, Ohio 44146
W.C. Fine, President
(216) 292-7400

SPRAYWAY, INC.
484 Vista
Addison, Illinois 60101
(312) 261-5553

SPRAZ COMPANY
Box 775
Enquirer Building
Cincinnati, Ohio 45201
(513) 381-3939

Companies and Trade Names

SPRAZIT (fire extinguishers)
See Plasti-Kote Company

SPREAD-AWAY (spreaders)
See Kelly Ryan Equipment-Blair Manufacturing Company

SPREAD-EAGLE FARM FOODS
Klingerstown, Pennsylvania 17941

SPREADABLES (meat-salad sandwich spread)
See Carnation Company

SPRECKELS SUGAR
(Division of Amstar Corporation)
50 California Street
San Francisco, California 94111
(415) 362-5600

SPRED SATIN (paint)
See Glidden-Durkee (Division of SCM Corporation)

SPREE (deodorant soap, laundry detergent)
See Colgate-Palmolive Company

SPRING (cigarettes)
See Lorillard Corporation

SPRING (food products)
See Southland Frozen Foods

SPRING AIR COMPANY, THE
666 North Lakeshore Drive
Chicago, Illinois 60611
Arlen Tennyson, President
(312) 944-4390

SPRING BROTHERS COMPANY, INC.
218 Little Falls Road
Cedar Grove, New Jersey 07009

SPRING CENTER (canned foods)
See Albro Packing Company

SPRING CITY KNITTING COMPANY
(Division of Cluett, Peabody & Company)
475 North Lewis Road
Royersford, Pennsylvania 19468
A.Y. Noojin, Jr., President
(215) 948-9400

SPRING GARDEN (food products)
See Southern Packing Company Inc.

SPRING GARDEN (whiskey)
See National Distillers & Chemical Corporation

SPRING GARDEN WHOLESALE GROCERY COMPANY
61 Greylock Avenue
Belleville, New Jersey 07109

SPRING GLORY (shampoo, soap, etc.)
See Caswell-Massey Company, Ltd.

SPRING HILL (whiskey)
See National Distillers & Chemical Corporation

SPRING LEDGE FARMS
Rural Delivery 3
Dundee, New York 14837

SPRING RIVER (dairy products)
See Carthage Creamery

SPRINGBOK EDITIONS
(Division of Hallmark Cards Inc.)
Post Office Box 1556
Kansas City, Missouri 64141
(816) 274-5111

SPRINGDALE FOOD COMPANY
Box 279
Sayre, Oklahoma 73662

SPRINGER-PENGUIN INC.
11 Brookdale Place
Mount Vernon, New York 10550
(914) 699-3200

SPRINGER PUBLISHING COMPANY
200 Park Avenue South
New York, New York 10003
(212) 475-2494

SPRINGFIELD (canned and frozen foods)
See Certified Grocers of California

SPRINGFIELD (sporting firearms)
See Savage Arms (Division of Emhart Corporation)

SPRINGFIELD LEATHER PRODUCTS COMPANY
230 North Fountain Avenue
Springfield, Ohio 45504
Robert N. Lupfer, President
(513) 325-1519

SPRINGFIELD SUGAR AND PRODUCTS COMPANY
1120 Harvey Lane
Suffield, Connecticut 06078
See also New England Grocer Supply Company

SPRINGFIELD TABLET MANUFACTURING COMPANY
Box 1425
Springfield, Missouri 65805
K.G. Wells, President
(816) 862-6638

SPRINGFLOWERS (dusting powder, foam bath, and talc)
See Yardley of London

SPRINGHOUSE FARMS (frozen vegetables)
See John Inglis Frozen Foods Company

Companies and Trade Names

SPRINGS MILLS, INC.
Fort Mill, South Carolina 29715
H. William Close, Chairman of the Board
(803) 547-2901
See also Seabrook Foods, Inc.

SPRINGTIME (canned foods)
See Barbey Packing Company

SPRINGTIME (frozen vegetables)
See Patterson Frozen Foods, Inc.

SPRINGTIME (pantyware)
See Woodpecker Products

SPRINGWATER (canned foods)
See North Pacific Canners & Packers, Inc.

SPRINGWOUND (alarm clocks)
See Robertshaw Controls Company

SPRITE (folding kayak)
See Amerimex Corporation

SPRITE (lawn mowers)
See The S.P. Lummus Supply Company

SPRITE (motor vehicles)
See J.S. Inskip, Inc.

SPRITE (portable typewriters)
See Royal Typewriter Company

SPRITE (soft drink)
See Coca Cola USA

SPRITZER (faucet spray)
See The Faucet-Queens Inc.

SPRUANCE COMPANY, THE GILBERT
Tioga and Richmond
Philadelphia, Pennsylvania 19134
Robert M. Cox, President
(215) 739-6172

SPRUCE SPRAY (paint)
See Seymour of Sycamore

SPRUCE UP (household brushes)
See Wright-Bernet Inc.

SPRY (shortening)
See Lever Brothers Company

SPUD (cigarettes)
See Philip Morris, Inc.

SPUD QUEEN (potato products)
See J.R. Simplot Company

SPUDNUT, INC.
450 West 17th Street
Salt Lake City, Utah 84115
Duane R. Wold, President
(801) 487-4176

SPUNTEX (hosiery)
See Dart Industries

SPUR (cigarettes)
See Liggett & Meyers Inc.

SPUR (gasoline)
See Murphy Oil Corporation

SQUARE DEAL (fertilizer)
See Borden, Inc.

SQUARE-PEN (infants' product)
See Stacy Manufacturing Company Inc.

SQUARE SHOOTER (cameras)
See Polaroid Corporation

SQUEEGEE-VACS (floor machine)
See The Cello Chemical Company

SQUEEZ-A-SNACK (cheeses)
See Kraftco Corporation

SQUEEZ-KLIP (fasteners, tools, cutters, kits)
See Republic Fastener Products Corporation

SQUEEZE (soft drink)
See National Fruit Flavor Company

SQUEEZE-MEEZ (puddings)
See Hunt-Wesson Foods, Inc.

SQUIBB CORPORATION
40 West 57th Street
New York, New York 10019
D. Barry Davis, President
(212) 489-2000
See also Dobbs Houses, Inc.; Lanvin-Charles of the Ritz, Inc.; and Life Savers Inc.

SQUIBB, E.R.
Post Office Box 4000
Lawrenceville-Princeton Road
Princeton, New Jersey 08540
C.A. Faden, President
(609) 921-4000

SQUIBB-TAYLOR INC.
10807 Harry Hines Boulevard
Dallas, Texas 75220
(214) 357-4591

SQUIER COMPANY, V.C.
(Division of CBS Musical Instruments)
35 South Edison Street
Battle Creek, Michigan 49015
(616) 968-8191

SQUIRE (mobile homes)
See Marshfield Homes

1260

Companies and Trade Names

SQUIRES (cigars)
　　See House of Windsor, Inc.

SQUIRES INKWELL COMPANY
Grand and East Railroad
Verona, Pennsylvania 15147

SQUIRREL BRAND COMPANY
17 Boardman Street
Cambridge, Massachusetts 02139
Hollis G. Gerrish, President, Sales
　　Manager and Purchasing Agent
(617) 547-1481

SQUIRT COMPANY, THE
4610 Van Nuys Boulevard
Sherman Oaks, California 91403
Herbert B. Bishop, President
(213) 789-8121

SSS-T! (steam-iron cleaner, rust remover, metal cleaner, room deodorizer, etc.)
　　See Fast Chemical Products
　　　Corporation

ST.
　　See Saint

STA-BRITE (tarnish preventive)
　　See Rudd Manufacturing Company

STA-BRITE, INC.
Box 544
Lucedale, Mississippi 39452

STA-CLOSE (safety lock)
　　See Toidey Company, Inc.

STA-DRI (waterproofing paint)
　　See American Sta-Dri Company

STA-DRI PRODUCTS
147-47 Sixth Avenue
Whitestone, New York 11357

STA-FLO (starch)
　　See A.E. Staley Manufacturing
　　　Company

STA-HOT (food warmers)
　　See Cory Corporation

STA-LUBE INC.
3039 Ana Street
Compton, California 90221
William J. Stabler, President
(213) 537-5650

STA-PREST (jeans and jackets)
　　See Levi Strauss & Company

STA-PUF (fabric softener)
　　See A.E. Staley Manufacturing
　　　Company

STA-PUT (nonskid spray for rugs)
　　See Cling-Surface Company

STA-RITE GINNIE LOU, INC.
South Fifth and Charles Street
Shelbyville, Illinois 62565
G. Noel Bolinger, President
(217) 774-3921

STA-RITE INDUSTRIES, INC.
234 South Eighth Street
Delavan, Wisconsin 53115
Henry S. Lauterbach, President
(414) 728-5551
　　See also Webster Electric
　　　Company, Inc.

STA-SAF (juvenile products)
　　See Waukegan Baby Seat
　　　Company Inc.

STA-SHARP (scissors and shears)
　　See Acme United Corporation

STA-SLIM (food product)
　　See Dean Foods Company

STA-TITE (paints and paint sundries)
　　See Gable-Tite Products
　　　Company Inc.

STA-WITE, INC.
4054 Mystic Valley Parkway
Medford, Massachusetts 02155

STAC-A-DRAWER (small-parts cabinets)
　　See Akro-Mills Inc.

STACK N ADD (sectional-shelving room dividers)
　　See Quaker Industries Inc.

STACK-SHELF (storage cabinets)
　　See Dolin Metal Products Inc.

STACKDOOR (folding doors)
　　See American Accordion-Fold
　　　Doors, Inc.

STACKMASTER (small-parts cabinets)
　　See Union Steel Chest
　　　Corporation

STACO (desk pad, desk blotter, letter opener, memo pad, work organizer)
　　See Robinson Reminders-Staco

STACOAT (paint)
　　See Luminall Paints, Inc.

STACOR CORPORATION
285 Emmet Street
Newark, New Jersey 07114
Nigel Harlen, President
(201) 242-6600

STACY-ADAMS (men's shoes)
　　See Weyenberg Shoe
　　　Manufacturing Company

Companies and Trade Names

STACY FABRICS CORPORATION
469 Seventh Avenue
New York, New York 10018
(212) 239-3300

STACY MANUFACTURING
COMPANY INC.
82 Willis Avenue
Bronx, New York 10454
(212) 292-8553

STADELMAN FRUIT COMPANY
Post Office Box 1313
Yakima, Washington 98901

STADIUM (brass instruments and guitars)
See Maurice Lipsky Music Company Inc.

STAEDTLER, INC., J.S.
Post Office Box 68
Montville, New Jersey 07045
(201) 335-1800

STAFF SALES INC.
103 Dutchess Turnpike
Poughkeepsie, New York 12403

STAFF SUPERMARKET ASSOCIATES
333 Jericho Turnpike
Jericho, New York 11753

STAFFORD-REEVES, INC.
626 Greenwich
New York, New York 10014
Leon Juster, President
(212) 924-2600

STAG (beer)
See Carling Brewing Company

STAG (cigars)
See P. Lorillard Company

STAGE DELICATESSEN
850 Seventh Avenue
New York, New York 10019
(212) 246-7164

STAGG (meat products)
See Rocking K Foods Inc.

STAHL INC., PHILIP
10 First Street
Pelham, New York 10803

STAHL SOAP CORPORATION
17 Forrest
Brooklyn, New York 11206
(212) 585-3050

STAHL-URBAN COMPANY
Brookhaven, Mississippi 39601
N.E. Wilson, Jr., President
(601) 833-5561

STAINED GLASS COLOR-ART INC.
Post Office Box 80
Delafield, Wisconsin 53018

STAINLESS METAL PRODUCTS
COMPANY INC.
1000 Cromwell Road
Chattanooga, Tennessee 37411
(615) 892-3720

STAINLESS METALS, INC.
19-42 42nd
Long Island City, New York 11705
Martin H. Sommer, President and Treasurer
(212) 728-7555

STAIR (elevator)
See Sedgwick Machine Works

STAK-UP (small-parts cabinets)
See Jayem Sales Corporation

STAKEES (meat)
See Heath Meat Company, Inc.

STAKMORE, INC.
200 Lexington Avenue
New York, New York 10016
Milton Schankman, President
(212) 683-7544

STAL-LAVAL INC.
400 Executive Boulevard
Elmsford, New York 10523
(914) 592-4710

STALEY, MANUFACTURING
COMPANY, A.E.
2200 East Eldorado Street
Decatur, Illinois 62521
Donald E. Nordlund, President
(217) 423-4411

STALKER-NAFEY CORPORATION
3590 Oceanside Road
Oceanside, New York 11572

STALWART (shaving cream)
See Procter & Gamble Company

STAMAS BOATS INC.
300 Pampas Avenue
Tarpon Springs, Florida 33589

STAMBOVSKY CHEMICALS
517 Arnold Avenue
Point Pleasant, New Jersey 08742

STAMFORD (canned food products)
See Bright Canning Company Ltd.

STAMM BOAT COMPANY
1746 Milwaukee Avenue
Delafield, Wisconsin 53108

STAMPEDE (men's toiletries)
See Sears, Roebuck & Company

STAMPING LEAF (paints)
See Kurz-Hastings, Inc.

STAN-GARD (chain-link fences)
See Robertson Steel & Iron Company

STAN SMITH (sportswear)
See Duofold Inc.

Companies and Trade Names

STANADYNE/CAPEWELL
60 Governor Street
Hartford, Connecticut 06102

STANBACK COMPANY, LTD.
1500 South Main Street
Salisbury, North Carolina 28144
T.M. Stanback, Partner
(704) 633-9231

STANBEL INC.
100 Tapley Street
Springfield, Massachusetts 01104

STANCE (slacks)
See H.R. Kaminsky & Sons Inc.

STANCE INDUSTRIES INC.
1425 37th Street
Brooklyn, New York 11218
(212) 853-2700

STANCO
Post Office Box 233
West Simsbury, Connecticut 06092

STANCOR (electrical products)
See Essex International Inc.,
Controls Division

STANCRAFT PRODUCTS
1621 East Hennepin
Minneapolis, Minnesota 55414

STAND 'N SNACK OF AMERICA INC.
1851 Executive Center Drive
Jacksonville, Florida 32207

STANDARD (hardware)
See Shelby Metal Products
Company

STANDARD (premium beer)
See F. & M. Schaefer Brewing
Company

STANDARD (snuff)
See United States Tobacco
Company

STANDARD (telescopes, binoculars, etc.)
See 3M Company

STANDARD & POOR'S CORPORATION
(Subsidiary of McGraw-Hill, Inc.)
345 Hudson Street
New York, New York 10014
Brenton W. Harries, President
(212) 924-6400

STANDARD ANTISEPTICS CORPORATION
Box 528
West Hempstead, New York 11552

STANDARD BRANDS, INC.
625 Madison Avenue
New York, New York 10022
Henry Weigl, Chairman of the Board
(212) 759-4400
See also Planters Peanuts; and
Wile Sons & Company,
Inc., Julius

STANDARD BRANDS PAINT COMPANY
4300 West 190th Street
Torrance, California 90509
John De Gregory, President
(213) 772-2371

STANDARD BRIEF CASE COMPANY INC.
28 West 25th Street
New York, New York 10010
(212) 255-6370

STANDARD BRUSH & BROOM COMPANY
Portland, Indiana 47371
(317) 726-8128

STANDARD CANDY COMPANY
443 Second Avenue North
Nashville, Tennessee 37201
Jimmy Miller, President
(615) 256-3186

STANDARD CELLULOSE &
NOVELTY COMPANY, INC.
90-02 Atlantic Avenue
Ozone Park, New York 11416

STANDARD CHEMICAL
MANUFACTURING COMPANY
Post Office Box 3844
701 South 42nd
Omaha, Nebraska 68103
James M. Paxson, President
(402) 558-4606

STANDARD COATED PRODUCTS
(Department of American Cyanamid
Company)
120 East Fourth Street
Cincinnati, Ohio 45202
Fred G. Ledlow, President
(513) 721-1000

STANDARD DAIRY PRODUCTS OF
WILSON JONES
(Division of Swingline, Inc.)
1000 South Elmora Avenue
Elizabeth, New Jersey 07207
(201) 353-8900

STANDARD DISTILLERS PRODUCTS, INC.
310 East Lombard
Baltimore, Maryland 21202
Andrew W. Merle, Jr., President
and Treasurer
(301) 752-0123

STANDARD DOLL COMPANY
23-83 31 Street
Long Island City, New York 11105
(212) 721-7787

STANDARD DRUG PRODUCTS INC.
Box 124
Zionsville, Indiana 46077

Companies and Trade Names

STANDARD DRY WALL PRODUCTS
7800 N.W. 38th Street
Miami, Florida 33166
(305) 592-2081

STANDARD DUPLICATING
 MACHINE CORPORATION
1935 Revere Beach Parkway
Everett, Massachusetts 02149
L. Guy Reny, President and
 Treasurer
(617) 387-5070

STANDARD ELECTRIC MANUFAC-
 TURING CORPORATION
135 Haddon Avenue
West Berlin, New Jersey 08091
(609) 767-0220

STANDARD FOODS INC.
1101 East Washington Street
Louisville, Kentucky 40206
(502) 587-8877

STANDARD FRUIT & STEAMSHIP
COMPANY
 See Castle & Cooke Foods

STANDARD FURNITURE
 MANUFACTURING COMPANY
Highway 31 South
Bay Minnette, Alabama 36507
William M. Hodgson, Jr., President
(205) 937-6741
 See also Emeco

STANDARD GLASS MANUFAC-
 TURING COMPANY, THE
West Fifth and Pierce Avenues
Lancaster, Ohio 43130

STANDARD-GREY TEXTILE
 TRADING CORPORATION
15 Park Row
New York, New York 10038
(212) 233-8020

STANDARD HOMEOPATHIC
COMPANY
204 West 131st Street
Los Angeles, California 90061
(213) 321-4884

STANDARD HOUSEHOLD
PRODUCTS CORPORATION
 See Spandex

STANDARD INDUSTRIAL
 PRODUCTS, INC.
(Subsidiary of George Koch Sons,
 Inc.)
Post Office Box 325
1500 Park Street
Evansville, Indiana 47704
Roderic M. Koch, President
(812) 423-3127

STANDARD INTERNATIONAL
CORPORATION
 See Standex International
 Corporation

STANDARD-KEIL HARDWARE
 MANUFACTURING COMPANY
Box 169
Route 34 at Garden State Parkway
Allenwood, New Jersey 08720
Alfred Klein, President
(201) 449-3700

STANDARD KNITTING MILLS,
 INC.
(Division of Chadbourn, Inc.)
Washington and Mitchell
Knoxville, Tennessee 37901
James E. Gettys, President
(615) 546-3211

STANDARD KOLLSMAN
INDUSTRIES, INC.
 See Kollsman Instrument
 Corporation

STANDARD LABORATORIES
(Division of Warner-Lambert
 Pharmaceutical Company)
201 Tabor Road
Mount Plains, New Jersey 07950

STANDARD MANIFOLD COMPANY
333 West Lake Street
Chicago, Illinois 60606
Howard J. MacKenzie, President
(312) 263-2075

STANDARD MATTRESS COMPANY,
THE
801 Windsor Street
Hartford, Connecticut 06101
N. Aaron Naboicheck, President
(203) 549-2000

STANDARD MEDICAL COMPANY
101 West Abbott Street
Lansford, Pennsylvania 18232

STANDARD MILLING COMPANY
1009 Central
Kansas City, Missouri 64105
R. Hugh Uhlmann, President
(816) 221-8200

STANDARD MOTOR PRODUCTS,
 INC.
37-18 Northern Boulevard
Long Island City, New York 11101
Bernard Fife, President
(212) 392-0200

STANDARD NOVELTY WORKS
722 Market Street
Duncannon, Pennsylvania 17020
(717) 834-3031

STANDARD OIL COMPANY OF
 CALIFORNIA
225 Bush Street
San Francisco, California 94104
H.J. Haynes, Chairman of the
 Board
(415) 894-7700
 See also Chevron Chemical
 Company; and Chevron
 Oil Company

Companies and Trade Names

STANDARD OIL COMPANY OF
INDIANA
200 East Randolph Drive
Chicago, Illinois 60601
John E. Swearingen, Chairman of
the Board
(312) 856-6111
See also American Oil Company;
and Amoco Oil Company

STANDARD OIL COMPANY OF
KENTUCKY
(Subsidiary of Standard Oil Company
of California)
Starks Building
Louisville, Kentucky 40202
W.J. Price, President
(502) 587-7531

STANDARD OIL COMPANY OF
NEW JERSEY
See Exxon Corporation

STANDARD OIL COMPANY OF
OHIO
Midland Building
Cleveland, Ohio 44115
Charles E. Spahr, Chairman of the
Board
(216) 575-4141
See also Vistron Corporation

STANDARD PACKAGING
CORPORATION
(Subsidiary of Saxon Industries, Inc.)
450 Seventh Avenue
New York, New York 10001
Mryon P. Berman, President
(212) 736-3663

STANDARD PAPER
MANUFACTURING COMPANY
Post Office Box 1554
First and Hull Street
Richmond, Virginia 23212
Horace B. Faber, Jr., President
(804) 232-1273

STANDARD PRESSED STEEL
COMPANY
Jenkintown, Pennsylvania 19046
John R. Selby, Sr., President
(215) 884-7300
See also Hallowell

STANDARD PRODUCTS COMPANY,
THE
2130 West 110th Street
Cleveland, Ohio 44102
James S. Reid, Jr., President
(216) 281-8300

STANDARD PRODUCTS
CORPORATION
856 Main Street
New Rochelle, New York 10801
William H. Weber, President
(914) 235-7200

STANDARD PYROXOLOID
CORPORATION
Willow Street
Fitchboro, Massachusetts 01420
(617) 345-7705

STANDARD REGISTER COMPANY
626 Albany Street
Dayton, Ohio 45401
D.F. Whitehead, President
(513) 223-6181

STANDARD SEWING EQUIPMENT
CORPORATION
(Subsidiary of White Consolidated
Industries)
203 Broadway Avenue
New York, New York 10007
(212) 673-2669

STANDARD SPECIALTY COMPANY
1028 44th Avenue
Oakland, California 94601
(415) 532-3096

STANDARD STAMPING COMPANY,
INC.
146 West 29th Street
New York, New York 10001
(212) 947-8666

STANDARD TANK & SEAT
COMPANY
308-20 North Front
Camden, New Jersey 08102
(609) 963-0270

STANDARD TERRY MILLS INC.
110 East Broad Street
Souderton, Pennsylvania 18964
(215) 723-8121

STANDARD WINE & LIQUOR INC.
2615 Brooklyn-Queens Expressway
Woodside, New York 11377

STANDBY (canned foods)
See Pacific Fruit & Produce
Company

STANDEE SEATS (nursery chairs)
See Questor Juvenile Furniture
(Division of Questor
Corporation)

STANDEX INTERNATIONAL
CORPORATION
615 South Columbus Avenue
Mount Vernon, New York 10550

STANDEX LABORATORIES
585 West Second Avenue
Columbus, Ohio 43215
(614) 294-4443

STANDEY ARTS (lamps)
See J.B. Hirsch Company, Inc.

STANDISH (men's shoes)
See George E. Keith Company

STANDWOOD CORPORATION
2417 North Davidson Street
Charlotte, North Carolina 28205
Thomas Roboz, President
(704) 372-5320

Companies and Trade Names

STANFORD PROFESSIONAL
   PRODUCTS CORPORATION
Post Office Box 456
Norristown, Pennsylvania 19404

STANFORD SALES INC.
240 South 16th Street
Sebring, Ohio 44672

STANGE COMPANY
342 North Western Avenue
Chicago, Illinois 60612
T.R. Miles, President
(312) 733-6945

STANGL POTTERY COMPANY
Post Office Box 2080
Trenton, New Jersey 08607
Frank H. Wheaton, Jr., President
(609) 695-8538

STANISLAUS FOOD PRODUCTS
   COMPANY
12th and D
Modesto, California 95352
Edna B. Piciullo, Chairman and
   President
(209) 522-7201
   See also Suzy-Bel Canning
   Company Inc.

STANISLAUS IMPORTS INC.
75 Arkansas Street
San Francisco, California 94107
(415) 431-7122

STANLABS, INC.
Post Office Box 3108
232 S.E. Oak Street
Portland, Oregon 97208
(503) 234-0432

STANLEY (steel thermos bottles)
   See Aladdin Industries

STANLEY BLACKER INC.
19th and Allegheny Avenue
Philadelphia, Pennsylvania 19132
(212) 247-1133

STANLEY DRUG PRODUCTS, INC.
(Division of Sperti Drug Products)
232 S.E. Oak Street
Portland, Oregon 97208
Leigh M. Standish, President
(503) 234-0432

STANLEY FURNITURE COMPANY,
   INC.
Stanleytown, Virginia 24168
James Van Vleck, President
(703) 629-7561

STANLEY HOME PRODUCTS, INC.
333 Western Avenue
Westfield, Massachusetts 01085
Homer G. Perkins, President
(413) 562-3631
   See also Frederick-Willys

STANLEY, INC., OSCAR M.
60 East 42nd Street
New York, New York 10017
(212) 697-0383

STANLEY KNIGHT CORPORATION
1600 East Birchwood Avenue
Des Plaines, Illinois 60018
R.A. Schneider, President and
   Treasurer
(312) 296-5586

STANLEY ORCHARDS, INC.
Modena, New York 12548

STANLEY ROBERTS INC.
230 Fifth Avenue
New York, New York 10001

STANLEY TOOLS
(Division of The Stanley Works)
600 Myrtle Street
New Britain, Connecticut 06050
Richard C. Hastings, Jr., President
   and General Manager
(203) 225-5111

STANLEY WORKS, THE
195 Lake Street
New Britain, Connecticut 06050
D.W. Davis, President
(203) 225-5111

STANLEY KNITTING MILLS, INC.
Post Office Drawer 479
Main Street Extension
Oakboro, North Carolina 28129
John P. Rogers, President
(704) 485-3311

STANSBURY CHEMICAL COMPANY
1929 Aurora Avenue North
Seattle, Washington 98109
(206) 283-5450

STANTON MAGNETICS INC.
Terminal Drive
Plainview, New York 11803

STANTON PHARMACAL COMPANY
127 South Fifth Street
Steubenville, Ohio 43952

STANWELL CAVENDISH (tobacco)
   See Peterson's Ltd.

STANWELL TRADING COMPANY,
   INC.
212 Fifth Avenue
New York, New York 10010
(212) 683-8140

STANZEL COMPANY, VICTOR
Box 28
Schulenberg, Texas 78956

STAPLE SALES, INC.
46-09 11th Street
Long Island City, New York 11101
(212) 392-2231

STAPLE SPECIALISTS INC.
124 West Lincoln Avenue
Mount Vernon, New York 10550

Companies and Trade Names

STAPLETON COMPANY, J.H.
217 North Broadway
Milwaukee, Wisconsin 53202
(414) 276-1031

STAPLETON-SPENCE PACKING
  COMPANY
1810 South Seventh
San Jose, California 95112
(408) 297-8815

STAPLEX COMPANY, THE
777 Fifth Avenue
Brooklyn, New York 11232
(212) 768-2335

STAR (drums and accessories)
  See Elger Company

STAR (fruit)
  See John A. Nicodemus Estate

STAR (kosher wine)
  See Fredonia Products Company, Inc.

STAR (liquor)
  See Schenley Industries Inc.

STAR (meat products, lard, peanut oil, salad oil)
  See Armour and Company

STAR (roses)
  See Conard-Pyle Company

STAR BAND COMPANY
Broad and Commerce Streets
Portsmouth, Virginia 23707
Leon Cardon, President
(804) 393-6061
  See also Wilmsen Inc.

STAR BINDING & TRIMMING
  CORPORATION
935 Broadway
New York, New York 10010
(212) 254-4425

STAR BRAND (produce)
  See Stanley Orchards, Inc.

STAR BRAND (shoes)
  See International Shoe Company

STAR-BRITE FURNITURE
  CORPORATION
69 Jefferson Street
Stanford, Connecticut 06902
(203) 327-1800

STAR-BRITE STUDIOS INC.
501 Columbus Avenue
Building 113
South Base Industrial Park
Norman, Oklahoma 73069

STAR BRONZE COMPANY
Post Office Box 568
Alliance, Ohio 44601
(216) 823-1550

STAR CASE COMPANY
225 Fifth Avenue
New York, New York 10010
(212) 686-3400

STAR CHEF (frozen foods)
  See Oxford Corporation

STAR CHEMICAL COMPANY, INC.
360 Shore Drive
Hinsdale, Illinois 60521
(312) 654-8650

STAR CHOCOLATE & NOVELTIES
(Division of Chocolate and Candy Industries)
19 Columbia Street
Hudson, New York 12534

STAR CLIPPER (houseboat)
  See Jack Powles International Marine Ltd.

STAR CROSS (food products)
  See Hirzel Canning Company

STAR DESK PAD COMPANY INC.
367 Southern Boulevard
Bronx, New York 10454
(212) 635-9100

STAR FILTER COMPANY
30669 West Eight Mile Road
Livonia, Michigan 48152

STAR FOUNDATIONS, INC.
  See Q-T Foundations

STAR HILL DISTILLING COMPANY
Star Hill Farm
Loretto, Kentucky 40037
T. William Samuels, President
(502) 865-2881

STAR INDUSTRIES INC.
17155 Van Wagoner Road
Spring Lake, Michigan 49456
Robert A. Fuller, Chairman,
  President and Work Manager
(616) 842-2600

STAR-KIST FOODS, INC.
(Subsidiary of H.J. Heinz Company)
582 Tuna Street
Terminal Island, California 90731
Joseph J. Bogdanovich, President
(213) 548-4411

STAR-LITE (dried fruits)
  See Central California Raisin Packing Company, Inc.

STAR LITE (freeze-dried foods)
  See Armour & Company

STAR-LITE (illuminated makeup mirror)
  See Monaco Optical Rayex Corporation

STAR LITE INDUSTRIES
915 South Mateo Street
Los Angeles, California 90021
Morton Steinberg, President
(213) 627-1321

Companies and Trade Names

STAR MANUFACTURING
   COMPANY
100 Water Street
Leominster, Massachusetts 01453
Robert Padovano, President and
   Sales Manager
(617) 537-2437

STAR MARKET COMPANY
(Division of Jewel Companies, Inc.)
625 Mount Auburn Street
Cambridge, Massachusetts 02138
John M. Mugar, Chairman of the
   Board
(617) 491-3000

STAR MERCHANDISE COMPANY
   INC.
11130-36 Chandler Boulevard
North Hollywood, California 91601
(213) 877-4778

STAR OF THE WEST MILLING
   COMPANY
231 Hubinger
Frankenmuth, Michigan 48734
Edward Weis, President
(517) 652-9971

STAR PHARMACEUTICALS INC.
206 Chanin Building
16499 N.E. 19th Avenue
North Miami Beach, Florida 33162
(305) 949-1612

STAR PHARMACEUTICALS, INC.
Box 4161
506 Nandina Lane
Atlanta, Georgia 30338
(404) 394-1709

STAR PIN COMPANY
273 Canal Street
Shelton, Connecticut 06484
Harold H. Porter
(203) 734-2521
   See also De Long Products

STAR PLASTICS INC.
826-828 Broadway
New York, New York 10003
(212) 674-5910

STAR SUPERMARKETS, INC.
175 Humboldt Street
Rochester, New York 14610
W.E. Fearnley, Chairman of the
   Board
(716) 288-5050

STAR TEXTILE AND RESEARCH
   INC.
Nonwoven Division
47 Fuller Road
Albany, New York 12203
(518) 459-1080

STAR ZEPHYR (windmills)
   See Flint & Walling, Inc.

STARCRAFT COMPANY
(Division of Bangor Punta
   Operations, Inc.)
2703 College Avenue
Goshen, Indiana 46526
William G. Christmas, President
(219) 533-0481

STARCROSS, INC.
Box 647
128 Cumberland Avenue
Easley, South Carolina 29640
Roy C. McCall, Jr., President
   and Treasurer
(803) 859-6345

STARDUST INC.
145 Madison Avenue
New York, New York 10016
Joel Seiff, President
(212) 686-1919
   See also Helen of Troy Inc.

STARFIRE (pipes)
   See Dr. Grabow Pre-Smoked
      Pipes, Inc.

STARFIRE IMPERIAL (tires)
   See Cooper Tire and Rubber
      Company

STARFIRE INDUSTRIES
619 South 600 West
Salt Lake City, Utah 84101
(801) 355-2949

STARFLITE (molded luggage)
   See Sardis Luggage Company

STARFLITE (outboard motors)
   See Evinrude Motors

STARFLYTE (home tools)
   See McGraw-Edison Company,
      Portable Electric Tools
      Division

STARK CALENDARS INC.
100 Bissel Street
Joliet, Illinois 60434
(815) 723-0654

STARK CARPET CORPORATION
979 Third Avenue
New York, New York 10022
(212) 752-9000

STARK COMPANY, HOWARD B.
Candy Lane and Hickory Street
Pewaukee, Wisconsin 53072
William Stark, President
(414) 691-0600

STARK'S COMPANY, INC.
Midway, Kentucky 40347

STARLET (batons and twirling
accessories)
   See Star Line Baton Company
      Inc.

STARLET (campers)
   See S & S Manufacturing
      Company Inc.

STARLIGHT (electric heating pads)
   See Northern Electric Company

1268

Companies and Trade Names

STARLIGHT (glass lighting fixtures)
See Thomas Industries

STARLIGHT (seafood)
See New England Fish Company

STARLINE
(Subsidiary of Chromalloy American)
300 West Front
Harvard, Illinois 60033
Stephen G. Burritt, President
(815) 943-4441

STARLITE (toy typewriters)
See Western Stamping Corporation

STARMARINE
1931 Embarcadero
Oakland, California 94606
Bruce A. Wilson, President
(415) 841-4493

STARR SPRINGS (canned foods)
See Stilwell Foods

STARRETT COMPANY, THE L.S.
1-165 Crescent Street
Athol, Massachusetts 01331
Douglas R. Starrett, President
(617) 249-3551

STARRETT CORPORATION
4522 West Ohio Avenue
Tampa, Florida 33614
(817) 877-5321

STARS 'N STRIPES (thermos bottles, lunch kits)
See Aladdin Industries, Inc.

STARTREK INC.
711 South University Avenue
Provo, Utah 84601

STASCO (toilet seats, etc.)
See Standard Tank & Seat Company

STATE FAIR (bakery products)
See Zinsmaster Baking Company

STATE FAIR (canned foods)
See Sacramento Foods

STATE FAIR (cookware)
See Ekco Housewares Company

STATE FAIR (preserves, peanut butter, syrup)
See Home Brands, Inc.

STATE FARM MUTUAL AUTOMOBILE INSURANCE COMPANY
1 State Farm Plaza
Bloomington, Illinois 61701
Edward B. Rust, President
(309) 662-2311

STATE LABS INC.
215 Park Avenue South
New York, New York 10003
(212) 677-8400

STATE-LEED DISTRIBUTORS
1014 Meriden Road
Waterbury, Connecticut 06710

STATE MUTUAL LIFE ASSURANCE COMPANY OF AMERICA
440 Lincoln Street
Worcester, Massachusetts 01605
W. Douglas Bell, President
(617) 852-1000

STATE NATIONAL BANK OF CONNECTICUT
(Subsidiary of Sperry & Hutchinson Company)
State National Tower
Bridgeport, Connecticut 06605
Benjamin Blackford, Chairman
(203) 333-1131

STATE STREET BANK & TRUST COMPANY
225 Franklin Street
Boston, Massachusetts 02101
William S. Edgerly, President
(617) 786-3000

STATESMAN (billfolds, purses)
See Buxton Inc.

STATESMAN (high-intensity lamps)
See Roxter Corporation

STATESMAN (tobacco)
See Comoy's of London

STATESMAN SERIES (wood desks)
See Jasper Table Company Inc.

STATI-CHEK (carpeting)
See Bigelow-Sanford Inc.

STATIONERS' GUILD OF AMERICA
255 Kings Highway
Haddonfield, New Jersey 08033

STATIONERS LOOSE LEAF COMPANY
246 East Chicago Street
Milwaukee, Wisconsin 53201
John G.H. Lotter, President and Treasurer
(414) 276-4747

STATIONERS MANUFACTURING COMPANY
420 South Ballinger Street
Fort Worth, Texas 76101
L.H. McDaniel, Jr., President
(817) 332-8311

STATIONWAGON (apparel)
See Princess Peggy, Inc.

STATLER (shoes)
See Genesco, Inc.

Companies and Trade Names

STATTON FURNITURE MANUFACTURING COMPANY
East First Street
Hagerstown, Maryland 21740
Philip B. Statton, President
(301) 739-0360

STAUFFER CHEMICAL COMPANY
Westport, Connecticut 06880
H.B. Morley, President
(203) 226-1511

STAUFFER CHEMICAL COMPANY
Plastics Division
Newburgh, New York 12550

STAVER WESTPORT INC.
123 Pleasant Street
Westport, New York 12993

STAY CHEMICAL COMPANY
4385 Davison Road
Flint, Michigan 48506

STAY FRESH (spray starch)
See Penn-Champ

STAY LONG (hair spray, lipstick)
See Helena Rubinstein, Inc.

STAY NATURAL (permanent hair color)
See Realistic Company

STAY OPEN (insulated baby carpet)
See Fashioncraft-Excello

STAY-TITE PRODUCTS COMPANY, INC.
14703 Industrial Avenue
Cleveland, Ohio 44137
(216) 663-4350

STAYFREE (sanitary napkins)
See Personal Products Corporation

STAYNER CORPORATION
2391 West Winton
Hayward, California 94545
Ramon Buchling, Chairman and President
(415) 785-4000

STAYSHARP (electric shaver)
See Schick Inc.

STAYTON CANNING COMPANY, CO-OPERATIVE
Box 458
930 West Washington Street
Stayton, Oregon 97383
Harvey A. Kendell, Chairman and President
(503) 769-2101

STE.
See Sainte

STEADIFEED (baby bottles, nipples, etc.)
See Searer Rubber Company

STEAK & ALE RESTAURANTS OF AMERICA, INC.
Post Office Box 22102
Dallas, Texas 75222
Lou Neeb, Vice President, Operations
(214) 661-0312

STEAK & BREW, INC.
(Subsidiary of Longchamps, Inc.)
230 Park Avenue
New York, New York 10017
Lawrence Ellman, President
(212) 490-7000

STEAK N SHAKE, INC.
1 Indiana Square
Indianapolis, Indiana 46204
Robert P. Cronin, President
(309) 636-4401

STEAK PRYME (seasonsings and food additives)
See Jacob Associates, Inc.

STEAK SUPREME (steak sauce)
See Heublein, Inc.

STEAM-N-SPRAY (travel iron)
See Knapp-Monarch (Division of The Hoover Company)

STEAM-O-MATIC (irons, etc.)
See Rival Manufacturing Company

STEAM-R-DRY (iron)
See Knapp-Monarch (Division of The Hoover Company)

STEAM ROLLERS (hair curlers)
See Remington Electric Shaver (Division of Sperry Rand Corporation)

STEAM TABLE (food products)
See Bush Brothers & Company

STEAMARVEL (cookware)
See Aero Industrial Company Inc.

STEAMATIC INC.
1601 109th Street
Grand Prairie, Texas 75050

STEAMETTE (fabric dewrinkler)
See Associated Mills

STEAMEZE (vaporizing inhalant)
See Sacramento Pharmacal Company

STEARN CREATIONS, INC.
1 West 64th Street
New York, New York 10023
(212) 873-2693

Companies and Trade Names

STEARNS & FOSTER COMPANY, THE
Wyoming and William
Cincinnati, Ohio 45215
R.G. Brierley, President
(513) 821-0700
See also Franklin Furniture Company, The

STEARNS ELECTRIC PASTE COMPANY
220 South State Street
Chicago, Illinois 60604
(312) 939-2115

STEARNS MANUFACTURING COMPANY
(Division of Versa Technologies)
30th at Division
Saint Cloud, Minnesota 56301

STEBCO PRODUCTS CORPORATION
3950 South Morgan Street
Chicago, Illinois 60609
Edward B. Stein, President
(312) 254-3800

STECKER CHEMICALS INC.
500 Barnett Place
Ho-Ho-Kus, New Jersey 07423
Herbert C. Stecker, President, Treasurer and Manager Director
(201) 445-0433

STEDE INC.
Box 28
Northfield, Illinois 60093

STEDI-EYE (telescope)
See Fraser-Volpe Corporation

STEDMAN MANUFACTURING COMPANY
Asheboro, North Carolina 27203
W.D. Stedman, President
(919) 625-2141

STEDMAN WHOLESALE DISTRIBUTORS INC.
6600 Oakcrest Drive
Beaumont, Texas 77708

STEEL CERAMIC (enamel cookware)
See Herman Dodge & Son

STEEL CITY CORPORATION, THE
190-200 North Meridian Road
Youngstown, Ohio 44501

STEEL CRAFT TOOLS
(Division of Daido Corporation)
875 Centennial Avenue
Piscataway, New Jersey 08854

STEEL GRIP SAFETY APPAREL COMPANY INC.
700 Garfield
Danville, Illinois 61832
Tom McGuirk, President
(217) 442-6240

STEELCASE, INC.
1120 36th Street, S.E.
Grand Rapids, Michigan 49508
Robert C. Pew, President
(616) 247-2710

STEELCOTE MANUFACTURING COMPANY
3418 Gratiot
Saint Louis, Missouri 63103
(314) 771-8053

STEELCRAFT MANUFACTURING COMPANY
(Subsidiary of American Standard Inc.)
9017 Blue Ash Road
Cincinnati, Ohio 45242
Robert E. Levinson, President
(513) 791-8800

STEELE CANNING COMPANY INC.
Box S
Springdale, Arkansas 72764
(501) 756-6111

STEELGARD (steel-belted radial tires)
See Goodyear Tire & Rubber Company

STEELWOOD (modular furniture)
See Robert John Company

STEERHEAD (cutlery)
See Goodell Company

STEFFEN & COMPANY, INC., M.
7667 West 95th Street
Hickory Hills, Illinois 60457
(312) 598-8131

STEFFEN DAIRY FOODS COMPANY
700 East Central Street
Wichita, Kansas 67201
Owen C. McEwen, President
(316) 267-4221

STEGMAIER BREWING COMPANY
152 East Market
Wilkes-Barre, Pennsylvania 18701
(717) 822-8171

STEGNER FOOD PRODUCTS COMPANY
5 Chile Hill Drive
Cincinnati, Ohio 45238
(513) 922-1125

STEGOR (stainless flatware)
See Gorham

STEGS PRODUCTS, INC.
12500 South Inglewood Avenue
Hawthorn, California 90250

STEIGER, INC., ALBERT
1477 Main Street
Springfield, Massachusetts 01102
Albert E. Steiger, President
(413) 781-4211

STEIN & DAY, INC.
7 East 48th Street
New York, New York 10017
Sol Stein, President
(212) 753-7285

STEIN BLOCH (men's suits)
See Fashion Park, Inc.

Companies and Trade Names

STEIN FISH COMPANY
115 East Fourth
Pueblo, Colorado 81002

STEIN, HALL & COMPANY, INC.
(Subsidiary of Celanese Corporation
 of America)
12-10 Jackson Avenue
Long Island City, New York 11101
(212) 784-6164

STEIN TOBLER EMBROIDERY
 COMPANY
403 35th Street
Union City, New Jersey 07087

STEINBOCK (cheese)
 See Merchants Trading Company,
  Inc.

STEINER, INC., S.S.
655 Madison Avenue
New York, New York 10021
S. Stinor Gimbel, President
(212) 838-8900

STEINFELD'S PRODUCTS COMPANY
10001 North Polk Avenue
Portland, Oregon 97203
(503) 286-5811

STEINFELDT-THOMPSON
 COMPANY INC.
Box 98
Dania, Florida 33004
(305) 922-3187

STEINGENBERGER (German wines)
 See Munson Shaw Company

STEINHARDT & BROTHER INC., A.
716 Madison
New York, New York 10021
(212) 838-7000

STEINWAY & SONS
(Division of CBS Musical
 Instruments)
Steinway Place
Long Island City, New York 11105
(212) 721-2600

STELAZINE (tranquilizer)
 See Smith, Kline & French
  Company

STELBER INDUSTRIES, INC.
33 West Hawthorne Avenue
Valley Stream, New York 11580
Philip Steller, Chairman of the
 Board
(516) 561-0050

STELLA (guitars)
 See The Harmony Company

STELLA D'ORO BISQUIT
 COMPANY, INC.
184 West 237th Street
Bronx, New York 10463
Felice Zambetti, President
(212) 549-3700

STELLA FAGIN CORPORATION
31 East 31st Street
New York, New York 10016
(212) 686-0372

STELLAMCOR
331 Madison Avenue
New York, New York 10017
(212) 687-8160

STELLAR INDUSTRIES, INC.
610 Newport Center Drive
Newport Beach, California 92660
A.A. Gale, Jr., President
(714) 640-0100

STELLAROPTICS (fiber-optic lamps)
 See Dixson Inc., Creative
  Decor Group

STELLO PRODUCTS INC.
78 East Market Street
Spencer, Indiana 47460
(812) 829-2246

STEMLEY CANNING COMPANY
North Star-Fort Laramie Road
New Weston, Ohio 45348

STEMPEL MANUFACTURING
 COMPANY
2830 Roberta Street
Dallas, Texas 75203
(214) 942-8413

STEN-O-MATE PRODUCTS INC.
(Division of Modern Ribbon &
 Carbon Company)
128-30 North Tenth Street
Philadelphia, Pennsylvania 19107
(215) 922-1545

STENDIG, INC.
510 East 62nd Street
New York, New York 10021
(212) 838-6050

STENNO RIBBON & CARBON
 MANUFACTURING COMPANY
6600 North Saint Louis Avenue
Portland, Oregon 97203
(503) 286-8313

STEP-LITE (hosiery)
 See Virginia Maid Hosiery
  Mills Inc.

STEP 'N FETCH (booster/step stools)
 See Century Products Inc.

STEP N GO (dresses)
 See Huntington Industries, Inc.

STEP-ON (waste receptacles)
 See The F.H. Lawson Company

STEP SAVER (clean-and-shine floor
product)
 See S.C. Johnson & Son, Inc.

Companies and Trade Names

STEPHAN COMPANY, THE
1850 West McNab Road
Fort Lauderdale, Florida 33309
Richard W. Stephan, President
(305) 971-0600

STEPHANIE IMPORTS INC.
1140 Broadway
New York, New York 10001
(212) 679-4820

STEPHANO BROTHERS
Post Office Box 308
Spring House, Pennsylvania 19477
Stephen C.S. Stephano, President
(215) 643-5105

STEPHAN'S CANDY COMPANY
82 Wentworth Street
Charleston, South Carolina 29401

STEPHEN-LEEDOM CARPET
    COMPANY, INC.
919 Third Avenue
New York, New York 10022
Arthur A. Nestler, President
(212) 758-6000

STEPHENS MANUFACTURING
    COMPANY, W.E.
400 First Avenue South
Nashville, Tennessee 37201

STEPHENS MARINE, INC.
345 North Yosemite Street
Stockton, California 95201
Theodore Stephens, President
(209) 466-8691

STEPPETTES (shoes)
    See Musebeck Shoe Company,
        Inc.

STERA-KLEEN (denture cleaner)
    See Block Drug Company, Inc.

STERE-O-CRAFT (tape recordings)
    See Scopus (Division of Berkey
        Photo)

STEREO REALIST (photo equipment)
    See Realist, Inc.

STEREODEON (stereo/hi-fi unit)
    See Guild Radio & Television
        Corporation

STERI-PAD (gauze pads)
    See Johnson & Johnson

STERIMED BRAND
(Division of Ketchum Laboratories)
26 Edison Street
Amityville, New York 11701

STER'L DRI CORPORATION, THE
10 Central Street
Saxonville, Massachusetts 01701

STERLING (baseballs and softballs)
    See Tober Baseball
        Manufacturing Company Inc.

STERLING (guitars, accordions,
banjos, drums)
    See Atlas Accordions, Inc.

STERLING (lawn and garden
supplies)
    See Fones Brothers Hardware
        Company

STERLING (portable typewriters)
    See Smith-Corona Marchant

STERLING (salt)
    See International Salt Company

STERLING & HUNT (menswear)
    See Hart Schaffner & Marx

STERLING BLEND (tobacco)
    See Liggett & Myers Inc.

STERLING BREWERS
(Division of G. Heileman Brewing
    Company)
1301 Pennsylvania Avenue
Evansville, Indiana 47708

STERLING CARBON & RIBBON
    COMPANY
99 Hudson Street
New York, New York 10013
(212) 226-6491

STERLING CHINA COMPANY
12th Street
Wellsville, Ohio 43968
William T. Pomeroy, President
(216) 532-1544

STERLING COMPANY, THE
2801 Locust Street
Saint Louis, Missouri 63103
(314) 533-1790

STERLING COOPERATIVE, INC.
Sterling Co-Op Road
Sterling, New York 13156

STERLING DRUG, INC.
90 Park Avenue
New York, New York 10016
W. Clark Wescoe, Chairman of the
    Board
(212) 972-4141
    See also Breon Laboratories,
        Inc.; Cook-Waite Labora-
        tories, Inc.; d-Con Com-
        pany, Inc.; Dorothy Gray-
        Tussy, Ltd.; Glenbrook
        Laboratories; Gray Tussy
        Ltd., Dorothy; Hallemite,
        Lehn & Fink Industrial
        Products; Lehn & Fink
        Products Company; Ross
        Company, Sydney; and
        Winthrop Laboratories

STERLING ELECTRONICS
    CORPORATION
4201 S.W. Freeway
Houston, Texas 77027
R. Larry Snider, President
(713) 623-6600

Companies and Trade Names

STERLING HUNT COMPANY
Box 157
South Dartmouth,
  Massachusetts 02748

STERLING MANUFACTURING
Post Office Box 410
Mansfield, Massachusetts 02048
(617) 339-8033

STERLING PACKING
  CORPORATION
131 Railroad
Garden City Park, New York 11040

STERLING PLASTICS COMPANY
(Division of Borden Chemical
  Company)
253 Sheffield Street
Mountainside, New Jersey 07092
Charles A. Metzen, General
  Manager
(201) 233-7600

STERLING PRECISION
  CORPORATION
319 Clematis Street
West Palm Beach, Florida 33401
Matthew E. Carroll, President
(305) 655-9700

STERLING PRODUCTS COMPANY
  INC.
1689 Oakdale Avenue
West Saint Paul, Minnesota 55118
(612) 455-6691

STERLING PRODUCTS
  INTERNATIONAL INC.
(Subsidiary of Sterling Drug Inc.)
90 Park Avenue
New York, New York 10016
(212) 972-4141

STERLING PUBLISHING COMPANY
419 Park Avenue South
New York, New York 10016
(212) 532-7160

STERLING PULP & PAPER
  COMPANY
Dells Dam
1200 Forest Street
Eau Claire, Wisconsin 54701
Walter Gold, President
(715) 834-3461

STERLING STORES COMPANY,
  INC.
Post Office Box 2301
6500 Forbing Road
Little Rock, Arkansas 72203
Dave Grundfest, Sr., President
(501) 565-4661

STERLING'S DELUXE (coffee, tea)
  See M. & S. Gordon Company,
    Inc.

STERN & STERN, INC.
71 Fifth Avenue
New York, New York 10003
(212) 741-0550

STERN & STERN TEXTILES INC.
1359 Broadway
New York, New York 10018
E.M. Stern, Jr., President
(212) 947-6244

STERN BROTHERS
(Affiliation of Allied Stores, Inc.)
Bergen Mall
Paramus, New Jersey 07652
Lawrence J. Stern, President
(201) 845-5500

STERN HATS & SPORTSWEAR
  CORPORATION
38 Irving Street
Framingham, Massachusetts 01701

STERN, INC., LUCIEN L.
220 Fifth Avenue
New York, New York 10001
(212) 679-5323

STERN INC., WALTER
Box 571
65-T Manorhaven Boulevard
Port Washington, New York 11050
(516) 883-8743

STERN-MAID NITEWEAR, INC.
135 Madison Avenue
New York, New York 10016
(212) 686-5480

STERN PARFUMS INC., MILTON
40 West 57th Street
New York, New York 10019
(212) 765-2060

STERN WATCH AGENCY, INC.,
  THE HENRI
10 Rockefeller Plaza
New York, New York 10020
Werner Sonn, President
(212) 581-0870

STERNCO INDUSTRIES INC.
722 Cross
Harrison, New Jersey 07029

STERNER COMPANY, CURT L.
124-17 Metropolitan Avenue
Kew Gardens, New York 11415

STERNIMPEX, INC.
43-17 216th Street
Bayside, New York 11361

STERNO INC.
(Division of Colgate-Palmolive
  Company)
300 Park Avenue
New York, New York 10022
(212) 751-1200

STERN'S NURSERIES, INC.
404 William
Geneva, New York 14456

Companies and Trade Names

STERWIN CHEMICALS, INC.
90 Park Avenue
New York, New York 10016
(212) 972-4141

STETSON CORPORATION
Stetson Park
Lincoln, Illinois 62656

STETSON HAT COMPANY, INC.
Whitaker and Leonard Road
Saint Joseph, Missouri 64502
Gary Rosenthal, President
(816) 233-8031

STEUBEN (glass products)
See Corning Glass Works

STEUBENVILLE POTTERY COMPANY, THE
Post Office Box 110
Canonsburg, Pennsylvania 15317

STEURY CORPORATION
310 Steury Avenue
Goshen, Indiana 46526
(219) 533-8671

STEVEN FOUNDATIONS, INC., J.
882 Third Avenue
Brooklyn, New York 11232
(212) 888-9606

STEVEN INC., DAVID G.
37 West 47th Street
New York, New York 10036
(212) 246-1311

STEVEN MANUFACTURING COMPANY
East Fourth Street
Hermann, Missouri 65041
(314) 486-5494

STEVENS (firearms)
See Savage Arms (Division of Emhart Corporation)

STEVENS & COMPANY, INC., J.P.
1185 Avenue of the Americas
New York, New York 10036
Whitney Stevens, President
(212) 575-2000
    See also United Elastic Company

STEVENS & THOMPSON PAPER COMPANY
Middle Falls
Greenwich, New York 12834
R.B. Stevens, President
(518) 692-2211

STEVENS CANNING COMPANY
2757 West 6000 South
Roy, Utah 84067
Angus Stevens, President
(801) 825-6765

STEVENS COMPANY, R.B. & C.G.
Jonesport, Maine 04649

STEVENS HOSIERY
1185 Avenue of the Americas
New York, New York 10036
(212) 575-3400

STEVENS INDUSTRIES, INC.
Dawson, Georgia 31742
Matthew E. Williams, President
(912) 995-2111

STEVENS JOY OF CALIFORNIA
407 East Pico Boulevard
Los Angeles, California 90015
Benjamin Stevens, President
(213) 747-7223

STEVENS, PERFUMER, WILLIAM
10202 Douglas Avenue
Des Moines, Iowa 50322
(515) 276-7366

STEVENS TRADING CORPORATION
206 West First Street
Mount Vernon, New York 10550

STEVENSON INDUSTRIES
400 Lawndale Drive S.W.
Winston-Salem, North Carolina 27104

STEWART (drums and accessories)
See Buegeleisen & Jacobson Ltd.

STEWART (food products)
See Piknik Products Company

STEWART & COMPANY
(Division of Associated Dry Goods Corporation)
Howard and Lexington
Baltimore, Maryland 21201
Norbert R. Christel, President
(301) 727-6060

STEWART & COMPANY INC., R.A.
85 White Street
New York, New York 10013
(212) 962-6060

STEWART & SONS, A.L.
Cherryfield, Maine 04622
(207) 546-2616

STEWART & STEVENSON SERVICES INC.
Box 1637
4516 Harrisburg Boulevard
Houston, Texas 77011
C. Jim Stewart, President
(713) 923-2161

STEWART CANDY COMPANY
330 Albany Avenue
Waycross, Georgia 31501
(912) 283-1970

STEWART COMPANY, W.W.
400-410 West Second
Sedalia, Missouri 65301
R.J. Lindstrom, President
(816) 827-0352

Companies and Trade Names

STEWART-MACDONALD MANUFACTURING INC.
Box 900
Athens, Ohio 45701

STEWART-SIMMONS, INC.
Box 459
Mason City, Iowa 50401

STEWART SWIMWEAR, ELISABETH
7533 South Garfield
Bell Gardens, California 90201

STEWART-WARNER CORPORATION
1826-52 Diversey Parkway
Chicago, Illinois 60614
Bennett Archambault, President
(312) 883-6000
See also Bassick; South Wind; and Thor Power Tool Company

STEWART-WARNER CORPORATION
Heating and Air Conditioning Division
320 North Patterson Street
Lebanon, Indiana 46052
(317) 482-5500

STEWART'S DRIVE-INS
1420 Crestmont Avenue
Camden, New Jersey 08103

STEWARTS PRIVATE BLEND FOODS
4110 Wrightwood Avenue
Chicago, Illinois 60639
Donald R. Stewart, President
(312) 489-2500

STICHT COMPANY, INC., HERMAN H.
27 Park Place
New York, New York 10007
(212) 732-8163

STICK NO MOR (window and drawer lubricant)
See Boyle-Midway

STIEFEL LABORATORIES, INC.
Oak Hill, New York 12460
Werner K. Stiefel, President
(518) 239-6901

STIEFF COMPANY, THE
800 Wyman Park Drive
Baltimore, Maryland 21211
Rodney G. Stieff, President
(301) 338-1200

STIEVATERS'
750 Battery Street
San Francisco, California 94111

STIFFEL COMPANY, THE
(Division of Beatrice Foods)
700 North Kingsberry
Chicago, Illinois 60610
Fred Phillips, President

STIL-TOPS (sports apparel)
See Scandia Trading Company Inc.

STILES, INC., R.L.
66 Montvale Avenue
Stoneham, Massachusetts 02180

STILLBROOK (whiskey)
See American Distilling Company, Inc.

STILLCO LABORATORIES
Post Office Box 991
Sarasota, Florida 33578

STILLICIOUS (food products)
See National Flavors, Inc.

STILLMAN COMPANY, INC., THE
323 East Galena Boulevard
Aurora, Illinois 60505

STILWELL FOODS
Box 432
Stilwell, Oklahoma 74960

STIM-U-DENTS, INC.
14035 Woodrow Wilson Avenue
Detroit, Michigan 48238
(313) 869-2390

STIM-U-PLANT, INC.
2077 Parkwood Avenue
Columbus, Ohio 43219
(614) 267-1296

STIMSON LUMBER COMPANY
See Forest Fiber Products Company

STIMSONITE AUTOMOTIVE PRODUCTS
(Division of Amerace Corporation)
Ace Road
Butler, New Jersey 07405

STINSON CANNING COMPANY
Prospect Harbor, Maine 04669
Charles B. Stinson, President
(207) 963-5565
See also Seaboard Packing Company

STIR-N-SERV (packaged dinner)
See Golden Grain Macaroni Company

STIRLING-EVEREST CORPORATION
1212 Dielman Industrial Court
Saint Louis, Missouri 63132
(314) 994-9262

STITZEL-WELLER DISTILLERY COMPANY
See Somerset Importers Ltd.

STIX, BAER & FULLER
(Division of Associated Dry Goods Corporation)
603 Washington Avenue
Saint Louis, Missouri 63101
J.A. Baer, II, Chairman of the Board
(314) 231-6500

Companies and Trade Names

STO-BINS (small-parts bins)
See Sempco Inc.

STOCK (sweet and dry vermouth, brandy, cordials, etc.)
See Distillerie Stock U.S.A. Ltd.

STOCK LABELS
126 John Street
South Amboy, New Jersey 08879

STOCK MODEL PARTS
(Division of Designatronics Inc.)
54 South Denton Avenue
New Hyde Park, New York 11040
(516) 328-0200

STOCKINETTE (hosiery)
See Burlington Industries Inc.

STOCKTON (food products)
See Tillie Lewis Foods Inc.

STOKELY-VAN CAMP, INC.
941 North Meridan Street
Indianapolis, Indiana 46206
Alfred J. Stokely, President
(317) 631-2551
See also Capital City Products Company; Kuner-Empson Company; Pomona Products Company; and Purity Mills

STOKES ASSOCIATES, E.D.
1213 East 33rd Street
Cleveland, Ohio 44114
(216) 687-0768

STOKES CANNING COMPANY
378 Osage
Denver, Colorado 80223
(303) 623-5331

STOKES COMPANY, FRANCIS C.
Box 278
Vincentown, New Jersey 08088

STOLL CANDY COMPANY
1854 Russell Boulevard
Saint Louis, Missouri 63104
(314) 772-0952

STONE & COMPANY, LTD., H.
321 Millburn
Millburn, New Jersey 07041
Harvey Stone, President
(201) 379-7535

STONE AGE (children's vehicles)
See AMF Inc.

STONE, BOB
Miami Merchandise Mart
Miami, Florida 33126
(305) 261-3221

STONE ENTERPRISES, GILBERT
4305 Beverly Glen Boulevard
Sherman Oaks, California 91403

STONE HAVEN (mobile home)
See Kit Manufacturing Company

STONE HOUSE INC.
800 Park Avenue
Keene, New Hampshire 03431

STONE HOUSE OF MAX SCHUSTER, INC.
1212 Avenue of the Americas
New York, New York 10036
(212) 582-3880

STONE INDUSTRIAL
(Subsidiary of J.L. Clark Manufacturing Company)
51st Avenue and Cree Lane
College Park, Maryland 20740
James B. Platt, Jr., President
(301) 474-3100

STONE MANUFACTURING COMPANY
Post Office Box 3725
Park Place
Greenville, South Carolina 29608
Eugene E. Stone, III, President
(803) 242-6300

STONE MINERAL & PALLET CORPORATION
Post Office Box Nine
Northport, New York 11768

STONECUTTER MILLS CORPORATION
Sprindale, North Carolina 28160
Adin H. Rucker, President
(704) 631-2341

STONEDEN IMPORTS, LTD.
1133 Broadway
New York, New York 10010
(212) 929-5290

STONER'S INK & CHEMICAL COMPANY
Box 127
Quarryville, Pennsylvania 17566
(717) 786-7355

STONEWARE DESIGNS WEST
3056 Bandini Boulevard
Los Angeles, California 90023
(213) 263-9053

STONEWARE ORIGINALS (dinnerware, casseroles, cookie jars)
See Pacific Stoneware Inc.

STONEY CREEK (canned foods)
See Niagara Food Products Ltd.

STONEY HILL (pickle products, fruit juices, mixes)
See Grantham Foods, Ltd.

STONHARD COMPANY
Park Avenue
Maple Shade, New Jersey 08052

Companies and Trade Names

STONINGTON PACKING
COMPANY
(Division of Port Clyde Packing
Company Inc.)
Stonington, Maine 04681
Irving Zwecker, President, Sales
and Advertising Manager
(207) 367-2331

STOP & SAVE TRADING STAMP
CORPORATION
(Subsidiary of Grand Union
Company)
125 Phillips Avenue
South Hackensack,
New Jersey 07606

STOP & SHOP COMPANIES, INC.,
THE
393 D Street
Boston, Massachusetts 02210
Sidney R. Rabb, Chairman of the
Board
(617) 463-7000

STOP-IT (paints)
See Tamms Industries Company

STOP LEAK (protective coating)
See Monsey Products Company

STOP-SHOCK (antistatic rug spray)
See Carbona Products Company

STOP-STEP (ladders)
See Cramer Industries Inc.

STOP-ZIT (thumb-sucking deterrent)
See Purepac Corporation

STOPLITE (window shades)
See Breneman, Inc.

STOR A PACK (food products)
See Bernard Food Industries Inc.

STOR-MOR (trash compactor)
See Amana Refrigeration Inc.

STOR-RITE METAL PRODUCTS
865 West North Avenue
Chicago, Illinois 60622
(312) 642-5678

STORCASE (bookcases)
See Borroughs (Division of Lear
Siegler Inc.)

STORCH CORPORATION, BEN
5-22 Lyncrest Avenue
Fair Lawn, New Jersey 07410

STORE KRAFT MANUFACTURING
COMPANY, THE
Box 807
Beatrice, Nebraska 68310

STORER BROADCASTING
COMPANY
1177 Kane Concourse
Miami Beach, Florida 33154
Peter Storer, President
(305) 866-0211

STORM KING FRUIT GROWERS
SALES CORPORATION
Milton, New York 12547

STORM LTD., PETER
Smith Street
Norwalk, Connecticut 06851

STORMOGRAPH (barometers)
See Taylor Instrument/Sybron
Corporation

STORMS COMPANY, H.M.
561 Grand Avenue
Brooklyn, New York 11238
(212) 622-0460

STORY & CLARK PIANO
COMPANY
7373 North Cicero Avenue
Lincolnwood, Illinois 60646
(312) 675-2000

STORYBOOK (shoes for children)
See Genesco, Inc.

STORZ BREWING COMPANY
See Grain Belt Breweries, Inc.

STOTTER INC., H.J.
246 Fifth Avenue
New York, New York 10001
(212) 689-9800

STOUDT'S DRUGS
154 North Ninth Street
Reading, Pennsylvania 19601

STOUFFER FOODS
(Division of The Stouffer
Corporation)
5750 Harper Road
Cleveland, Ohio 44139
(216) 248-0700

STOUFFER RESTAURANT & INN
(Division of Stouffer Corporation)
1375 Euclid Avenue
Cleveland, Ohio 44115
Thomas G. Stauffer, President
(216) 861-3450

STOVE TOP (stuffing mix)
See General Foods Corporation,
Jell-O Division

STOVER CANDIES INC., RUSSELL
1004 Baltimore
Kansas City, Missouri 64105
(816) 842-9240

STOVER LABORATORIES
2080 Mountain Boulevard
Oakland, California 94611

STOW-A-WAY PRODUCTS
103 Ripley Road
Cohasset, Massachusetts 02025

Companies and Trade Names

STOW-DAVIS FURNITURE
  COMPANY
25 Summer Avenue, N.W.
Grand Rapids, Michigan 49504
Allen I. Hunting, President
(616) 456-9681

STOWARE INC.
Box 207
Stowe, Vermont 05672

STOWAWAY (infants' product)
  See Strolee of California

STOWAWAYS (cookware)
  See Dart Industries Inc.

STOWAY (folding table-and-stool
unit)
  See Midwest Folding Products

STOWBOAT
665 South 31st Street
Richmond, California 94804

STOY INC.
279 East 44th Street
Penthouse East
New York, New York 10017
(212) 986-4994

STRACHMAN ASSOCIATES INC.
520 Eighth Avenue
New York, New York 10018
(212) 695-5688

STRADIVARI (cologne, dusting
powder, etc.)
  See Prince Matchabelli, Inc.

STRADIVARIUS (concertinas and
accordions)
  See Brown Distributing Company

STRADOLIN (guitars, basses,
mandolins, banjos)
  See Sorkin Music Company Inc.

STRAIGHT ARROW (produce)
  See Stadelman Fruit Company

STRAIGHT ARROW PUBLISHERS
  INC.
625 Third Street
San Francisco, California 94107
(415) 362-4730

STRAITS PHARMACAL COMPANY
Elm Street
Cheboygan, Michigan 49721

STRAND (garage doors)
  See Marmon Group, Inc.

STRAND BAKING COMPANY
212 East Main
Marshalltown, Iowa 50158

STRASER CANDY COMPANY
1442 Blake Street
Denver, Colorado 80202

STRASSBURGER COMPANY,
  WALTER
180 Madison Avenue
New York, New York 10016
(212) 683-1020

STRATFORD (cigarettes)
  See United States Tobacco
    Company

STRATFORD-COOKSON COMPANY
2000 Sullivan Road
College Park, Georgia 30337
C. Allen Wagner, Jr., Chairman,
  President and Treasurer
(404) 768-0184

STRATFORD FARMS (preserves,
jellies, prune juice)
  See Theresa Friedman & Sons

STRATHMORE PAPER COMPANY
(Division of Hammermill Paper
  Company)
Front Street
West Springfield,
  Massachusetts 01089
John G. Gallup, President
(413) 568-9111

STRATO-VARIOUS PRODUCTS INC.
9041 Hensley
Sterling Heights, Michigan 48078

STRATOJAC (jackets)
  See Winer Manufacturing
    Company, Inc.

STRATOLOUNGER (chair)
  See Stratford Company

STRATTON AIR ENGINEERING
  SQUADRON KITES
12821 Martha Ann Drive
Los Alamitos, California 90720

STRATTON & TERSTEGGE
  COMPANY, INC.
Main and 16th Streets
Louisville, Kentucky 40201
J.L. Meagher, President
(502) 584-5311

STRATTON OF LONDON INC.
9 East 37th Street
New York, New York 10016
(212) 532-1416

STRATTON TRADING
  CORPORATION
261 Stratton Road
New Rochelle, New York 10804

STRAUB & COMPANY, INC.,
  PAUL A.
Quinnipiac Street
Wallingford, Connecticut 06492

Companies and Trade Names

STRAUB & COMPANY, W.F.
5520 North Northwest Highway
Chicago, Illinois 60630
John W. Straub, President
(312) 763-5520

STRAUBEL PAPER COMPANY
615 University
Green Bay, Wisconsin 54305
Louis A. Straubel, President
(414) 432-4851

STRAUS-ARTYS CORPORATION
45 North Station Plaza
Great Neck, New York 11022

STRAUS COMPANY, THE HENRY
9345 Princeton Glendale Road
Cincinnati, Ohio 45206
(513) 874-5200

STRAUS MITTELDORFER INC.
41 Madison Avenue
New York, New York 10010
(212) 565-5207

STRAUSS & COMPANY, F.J.
3900 Westside Avenue
North Bergen, New Jersey 07047
(212) 675-8757

STRAUSS & COMPANY, LEVI
98 Battery Street
San Francisco, California 94106
Peter E. Haas, President
(415) 391-6200

STRAUSS COMPANY INC., D.
29 West 36th Street
New York, New York 10018
(212) 868-0100

STRAUSS, ERNST
217 East Eighth Street
Los Angeles, California 90014
Paul Scott, President
(213) 623-8112

STRAUSS STORES CORPORATION
5306 Grand Avenue
Maspeth, New York 11378
L.S. Strauss, President
(212) 386-5000

STRAWBRIDGE & CLOTHIER
Eighth and Market Streets
Philadelphia, Pennsylvania 19105
Randall E. Copeland, President
(215) 922-7100

STRAYER COIN BAG COMPANY INC.
1024 Fifth Avenue
New Brighton, Pennsylvania 15066
(412) 846-2600

STRAYLINE PRODUCTS COMPANY
Box 4124
336 Putnam Avenue
Hamden, Connecticut 06514
(203) 562-6866

STREAMLINE BEAUTY (mattress)
See White Cross Sleep Products

STREAMLINE BUTTON, INC.
234 West 39th
New York, New York 10018
(212) 947-7484

STREAMLINER (portable typewriters)
See Remington Rand Office Machines (Division of Sperry Rand Corporation)

STREATER STORE FIXTURES, INC.
(Division of Litton Industries)
26 North Fifth Street
Minneapolis, Minnesota 55403
(612) 335-8961

STREET KING (skates)
See Roller Derby Skate Corporation

STREETT & COMPANY, INC., J.D.
144 Weldon Parkway
Maryland Heights, Missouri 63043
Newell A. Baker, Chairman and President
(314) 432-6600

STRETCH (latex paints)
See Tamms Industries Inc.

STRETCH & SEW INC.
Post Office Box 185
Eugene, Oregon 97401
Ann Person, President
(503) 686-9961

STRETCH LEVI'S (jeans)
See Levi Strauss & Company

STRETCH 'N FIT (pantyhose)
See Stevens Hosiery

STRETCH 'N SEAL (food wrapping)
See Colgate-Palmolive Company

STRETCHINI, INC.
(Division of Bobbie Brooks, Inc.)
112 West 34th Street
New York, New York 10001
Irving Hochberg, President
(212) 868-0550

STREVE (belts and watchbands)
See Buxton Inc.

STREVELL-PATERSON COMPANY
Box 1048
1401 South Seventh West
Salt Lake City, Utah 84110
V.J. Kuhre, President
(801) 486-6961

STRI-DEX (acne treatment)
See Lehn & Fink Consumer Products

Companies and Trade Names

STRIBBONS LTD.
99 Powrhse Road
Roslyn Heights, New York 11577
(212) 895-5560

STRICK OF HOLLYWOOD
806 South Robertson Boulevard
Los Angeles, California 90035
(213) 655-9650

STRICKLAND & COMPANY, J.
Post Office Box 2841
1400 Ragan
Memphis, Tennessee 38102
Mildred B. Long, President
(901) 942-1575

STRICKLANDS GIFTS
Logan Square Shopping Center
Norristown, Pennsylvania 19401

STRICKLER BROTHERS
580 Fifth Avenue
New York, New York 10036
(212) 246-7595

STRICKMEISTER (sports apparel)
See Max Humi Importer Inc.

STRIDE (food products)
See Southland Frozen Foods

STRIDE RITE CORPORATION
960 Harrison Avenue
Boston, Massachusetts 02118
Arnold S. Hiatt, President
(617) 440-9300
See also Weber Shoe Company

STRINGFELLOW SUPPLY COMPANY
1015 South Main Street
Gainesville, Florida 32601

STRIP-LAY (self-adhesive vinyl tiles)
See Joseph Katz Floor
Coverings Company, Inc.

STRIP PAK (paint remover)
See Savogran Company

STRIP-SEAL (weather stripping)
See Tremco Manufacturing
Company

STRIPP (floor-wax stripper)
See Advance Chemical Company, Inc.

STROBE NOVELTY
2136A Mott Avenue
Far Rockaway, New York 11691

STROEHMANN BROTHERS
COMPANY
1685 Four Mile Drive
Williamsport, Pennsylvania 17701
Harold J. Stroehmann, Jr.,
President
(717) 326-3311

STROH BREWERY COMPANY, THE
909 East Elizabeth Street
Detroit, Michigan 48201
Peter W. Stroh, President
(313) 961-5840

STROHEIM & ROMANN
10 West 20th Street
New York, New York 10011
(212) 691-0700

STROHMEYER & ARPE COMPANY
1 World Trade Center
Suite 4967
New York, New York 10048
D. H. Fraser, President
(212) 432-6150

STROLEE OF CALIFORNIA, INC.
19067 South Reyes Avenue
Compton, California 90221
Paul C. Smith, President
(213) 537-5801

STROMBECK MANUFACTURING
COMPANY
51st Street and Fourth Avenue
Moline, Illinois 61265
Frederick K. Strombeck, President
(309) 764-7475

STROMBECKER CORPORATION
600 North Pulaski Road
Chicago, Illinois 60624
Myron B. Shure, President
(312) 638-1000
See also Tootsietoy

STROMBERG-CARLSON
CORPORATION
(Subsidiary of General Dynamics
Corporation)
Box 987
100 Carlson Road
Rochester, New York 14603
Leonard A. Muller, President and
Chief Operations Officer
(716) 482-2200

STROMBERG PRODUCTS
(Division of Mite Corporation)
446 Blake Street
New Haven, Connecticut 06515
(203) 387-2572

STROMEYER COMPANY, J.
See Strohmeyer & Arpe Company

STRONG & LONG (nail hardener
and conditioner)
See Helena Rubinstein, Inc.

STRONG, CARLISLE & HAMMOND
(Division of White Consolidated
Industries)
11760 Berea Road
Cleveland, Ohio 44111
(216) 252-4000

STRONG COBB ARNER OF
CALIFORNIA INC.
7200 Vineland Avenue
Sun Valley, California 91352

STRONGBARN (roofing and siding)
See Granite City Steel Company

STRONGHEART PRODUCTS
(Division of Doric Corporation)
Post Office Box 2009
Kansas City, Kansas 66110
(913) 621-4909

Companies and Trade Names

STRONGIN & SONS
1101 West Armitage Avenue
Chicago, Illinois 60614
(312) 929-4700

STRONGLAS (insulated containers)
See Thermos (Division of King-Seeley Thermos Company)

STROUSE COMPANY, THE ADLER
78 Olive
New Haven, Connecticut 06507
Stephen D. Wayne, President
(203) 777-3484

STROUT PLASTICS INC.
9611 James Avenue South
Minneapolis, Minnesota 55431
(612) 881-8673

STRUBEL DRUGS
4517 18th Avenue
Kenosha, Wisconsin 53140

STRUCTO
(Division of King-Seely Thermos Company)
Route 75
Freeport, Illinois 61032
F.W. Voss, President
(815) 232-2111

STRUCTO-THE EARTL COMPANY
See Ertl Company, The

STRUCTURAL DEVELOPMENT CORPORATION
See Artini Arts Inc.

STRUCTURAL INDUSTRIES
96 New South Road
Hicksville, New York 11590

STRUM & DRUM INC.
177 Hintz Road
Wheeling, Illinois 60090

STRUTHERS-DUNN INC.
Lambs Road
Pitman, New Jersey 08071
J.L. Pfeffer, President
(609) 589-7500

STRYER, NORBERT
104-20 Queens Boulevard
Forest Hills, New York 11375
(212) 896-4718

STRYGLER & COMPANY INC., H.S.
595 Madison Avenue
New York, New York 10022
(212) 758-4100

STRYPE, INC., FRED C.
60 Glen Avenue
Glen Rock, New Jersey 07452
(212) 349-0463

STRYPEEZE (paint and varnish remover)
See The Savogran Company

STUART (groceries)
See South Shore Foods Inc.

STUART & COMPANY, INC., C.H.
165 East Union Street
Newark, New York 14513
See also Sarah Coventry, Inc.

STUART HALL COMPANY, INC.
2121 Central Street
Kansas City, Missouri 64108
Charles G. Hanson, President
(816) 221-8480
See also Whiting Stationery Company

STUART, INC.
500 Robert Street
Saint Paul, Minnesota 55101

STUART McGUIRE COMPANY, INC.
115 Brand Road
Salem, Virginia 24153
Cabell Brand, President
(703) 389-8121

STUART NYE SILVER SHOP
Post Office Box 9068
Asheville, North Carolina 28805

STUART PHARMACEUTICALS
(Division of ICI America Inc.)
3411 Silverside Road
Wilmington, Delaware 19810
(302) 575-3000

STUART'S (laxative, ointment, suppositories, etc.)
See Consolidated Royal Chemical Corporation

STUCKEY'S, INC.
(Division of Pet, Inc.)
Post Office Box 370
Eastman, Georgia 31023
Williamson S. Stuckey, President
(912) 374-4381

STUD (smoking tobacco)
See R.J. Reynolds Tobacco Company

STUDIO 45 (portable typewriters)
See Olivetti Corporation of America

STUDIO 49 (musical instruments)
See Magnamusic-Baton Inc.

STUDIO GIRL (cosmetics)
See Helene Curtis Industries, Inc.

STUDIO ONE
1899 New Hope Street
Norristown, Pennsylvania 19401

Companies and Trade Names

STUDIO TWELVE
150 Baker Street
Costa Mesa, California 92626

STUDY-CRAFT
Tusson Research Center
Route 1-683
Belle Chasse, Louisiana 70037

STUFFED SHELLS (frozen meat- or cheese-filled pasta)
See Stouffer Foods

STUFFED SHIRT-STUFFED JEANS
1407 Broadway
New York, New York 10018

STUR-DEE (work clothes)
See Stahl-Urban Company

STURDEE (porch gates, clothes dryers)
See Mapes Industries Inc.

STURDY DOG FOOD COMPANY, INC.
116 East Alameda
Burbank, California 91502

STURGES MANUFACTURING COMPANY
Sunset and Railraod Avenue
Utica, New York 13502
Edwin T. Weiss, President and Treasurer
(315) 732-6159

STURGIS COMPANY
(Subsidiary of General Fireproofing Company)
Box 100
Sturgis, Michigan 49091

STURM & SCHEINBERG, INC.
(Affiliation of DeLuxe Girdlecraft Company, Inc.)
45 West 25th
New York, New York 10010
(212) 929-4565

STURM-RUGER & COMPANY, INC.
Lacey Place
Southport, Connecticut 06490
William B. Ruger, President
(203) 259-7843

STURTEVANT COMPANY, THE F.C.
227 Shunpike Road
Cromwell, Connecticut 06416

STUYVESANT BICYCLE COMPANY
10 East 13th
New York, New York 10003
(212) 254-5200

STYL-O-VIN (wallpaper)
See Wall Trends, International

STYLAIRE (folding tables and chairs, serving carts, etc.)
See Hamilton Cosco, Inc.

STYLE (hair-care products)
See The House of Style

STYLE (paints and paint sundries)
See Van Camp Hardware & Iron Company Inc.

STYLE CHIEF (work clothes)
See Chadbourn, Inc.

STYLE-CRAFTERS INC.
See Gladding Style-Crafters Inc.

STYLE EYES OF CALIFORNIS
855 Hinckley Road
Burlingame, California 94010

STYLE KING (clocks)
See Cuckoo Clock Manufacturing Company

STYLE LINE (toothbrushes)
See Lever Brothers Company

STYLE LITE (lamps)
See Brite Lite Lamps Corporation

STYLE UNDIES INC.
See Dale Inc., Jennifer

STYLECRAFT OF BALTIMORE
(Division of L. Gordon & Son Inc.)
1800 Johnson Street
Baltimore, Maryland 21230
(301) 539-4547

STYLECRAFT PRODUCTS
(Division of Social Supper, Inc.)
Main Street
Dresden, Ohio 43821

STYLECRAFT STUDIOS INC.
622 1/2 Main Street
Coshocton, Ohio 43812

STYLEGIRL, INC.
683 Broadway
New York, New York 10012
(212) 254-8080

STYLEPRIDE (shoes)
See Edison Brothers Stores, Inc.

STYLER (hair appliance)
See Master Appliance Corporation

STYLERITE (buttons, sequins, beads, appliques)
See Lidz Brothers Inc.

STYLEWRITER (dip-pen writing sets, ribbons, and carbons)
See Carter's Ink Company

STYLEX INC.
620 Cooper Street
Delanco, New Jersey 08075
(609) 461-5600

Companies and Trade Names

STYLINE (tray table sets, wastebaskets, etc.)
See Quaker Industries Inc.

STYLUME (furniture)
See Scott Paper Company

STYSON, INC.
543 West 23rd Street
New York, New York 10011
(212) 242-3210

STYX (cosmetics)
See Coty

SUAVE (hair-care products)
See Helene Curtis Industries, Inc.

SUAVE SHOE CORPORATION
14100 60th Avenue, N.W.
Miami Lakes, Florida 33014
David Egozi, Chairman
(305) 822-7880

SUB-OX-INE CHEMICAL COMPANY
20-12 Seagirt Boulevard
Far Rockaway, New York 11691

SUB-ZERO (pocket adding machine)
See Alexander-Addimax

SUB-ZERO FREEZER COMPANY INC.
Post Office Box 4130
4717 Hammersley Road
Madison, Wisconsin 53711
Lawrence C. Bakke, President
(608) 271-2233

SUBARU OF AMERICA, INC.
7040 Central Highway
Pennsauken, New Jersey 08109
Harvey H. Lamm, President
(609) 665-3344

SUBITO (dairy products)
See Frigo Cheese Corporation

SUBLIME (AM/FM stereos, cassette tape recorders, police worldwide multiband radios, car stereo-tape players, men's and women's umbrellas)
See Ramson Trading Company, Inc.

SUBLIME (food products)
See Tillie Lewis Foods Inc.

SUBMARINE RESEARCH LABS INC.
(Division of North American)
11 Porter Cove Road
Hingham, Massachusetts 02043
(617) 749-0900

SUBMARINER (binoculars)
See American Foreign Industries

SUBOX COATINGS
(Division of BWC Corporation)
Broad and 14th Street
Carlstadt, New Jersey 07072
(201) 438-0600

SUBTRACT (balanced food for weight control)
See General Mills

SUBURBAN MANUFACTURING COMPANY
Post Office Box 399
Dayton, Tennessee 37321
A.R. Spreen, President
(615) 775-2131

SUBURBAN PROPANE GAS CORPORATION
State Highway 10
Whippany, New Jersey 07981
Mark Anton, Chairman of the Board
(201) 887-5300

SUBURBAN TRUST COMPANY
6495 New Hampshire Avenue
Hyattsville, Maryland 20783
Joseph Richards, Jr., Chairman of the Board
(301) 270-5000

SUBURBANITE (tires)
See Goodyear Tire & Rubber Company

SUBURBIA (menswear)
See Haspel Brothers Inc.

SUBWAY PRODUCTIONS INC.
12 Irving Street
Framingham, Massachusetts 01701

SUCARYL (reducing aids)
See Abbott Laboratories, Consumer Products Division

SUCCESS (floor wax)
See Lever Brothers Company

SUCCESS (foreign-language cards)
See Gibson Greeting Cards Inc.

SUCCESS (lawn mower)
See American Lawn Mower Company

SUCCESS GREETING CARD COMPANY, INC.
882 Third Avenue
Brooklyn, New York 11232
(212) 499-7532

SUCHARD CHOCOLATE, INC.
Box 111
Villa Park, Illinois 60181

SUCREST CORPORATION
120 Wall Street
New York, New York 10005
Robert M. Rapaport, President
(212) 344-4920
See also Colonial Molasses Company of Louisiana Inc.

SUCRETS (cough and cold remedies)
See Calgon Consumer Products Company, Inc.

SUDBURY LABORATORY
Box 2886
572 Dutton Road
Sudbury, Massachusetts 01776
Frank D. Walker, President and Treasurer
(617) 443-8844

Companies and Trade Names

SUDDEN ACTION (breath freshener)
See Whitehall Laboratories

SUE BRETT INC.
1400 Broadway
New York, New York 10018
(212) 391-4800

SUE CORY
See Helene Curtis Industries, Inc.

SUEDE SAVER
See Dow Corning Corporation

SUFFOLK (pipes)
See Whitehall Products, Inc.

SUFFRAGE (hair conditioners, hair spray)
See Cosmair, Inc.

SUFLEX CORPORATION
57th Street and Broadway
Woodside, New York 11377

SUFRIN INC., I. AND M.
2500 Jane Street
Pittsburgh, Pennsylvania 15203
(412) 481-7000

SUGAR CREEK (dairy foods)
See Breakstone Sugar Creek Foods

SUGAR-LO COMPANY
2001 Bacharach Boulevard
Atlantic City, New Jersey 08401

SUGAR 'N SPICE (stretch knitwear)
See A.H. Schreiber Company, Inc.

SUGAR PRODUCTS COMPANY
2322 East 37th
Los Angeles, California 90058
(213) 588-1221

SUGAR ROSE CANNING COMPANY
Box 2129
Tampa, Florida 33601

SUGARBUSH FARM
Pastures Road
Woodstock, Vermont 05091

SUGARDALE FOODS, INC.
1600 Harmont Avenue, N.E.
Canton, Ohio 44705
David J. Lanvin, President
(216) 455-5253

SUGARLESS CANDY CORPORATION OF AMERICA
3537 West North
Chicago, Illinois 60647
(312) 227-7676

SUGIMOTO PEARL COMPANY, INC., S.
16 East 52nd Street
New York, New York 10022
(212) 759-4845

SUIVANTE (suits and costumes)
See Ernst Strauss

SULFODENE (foot soap)
See Combe Chemical, Inc.

SULKA & COMPANY, A.
405 Park Avenue
New York, New York 10022
John T. McCaffrey, President
(212) 758-3030

SULLIVAN MANUFACTURING & SALES CORPORATION
Box 666
5031 Paxton Street
Hammond, Indiana 46325
(219) 931-9060

SULPHO-NAPHTHOL COMPANY, THE
(Subsidiary of Samuel Cabot, Inc.)
1 Union Street
Boston, Massachusetts 02108
Samuel Cabot, President
(617) 723-7740

SULRAY PRODUCTS
(Division of Thomas Holmes Corporation)
Benson East
Jenkintown, Pennsylvania 19046

SULTANA (grocery products)
See Ann Page (Division of The Great Atlantic & Pacific Tea Company)

SUMITOMO SHOJI AMERICA, INC.
345 Park Avenue
New York, New York 10022
(212) 935-7000

SUMMER GARDEN (canned vegetables)
See Draper Foods Inc.

SUMMER MAGIC (women's toiletries)
See Old 97 Company

SUMMER SHEER (pantyhose)
See Hanes Hosiery Sales Inc.

SUMMERAIRE (portable space heaters)
See Clayton Manufacturing Company

SUMMERS & REID, INC.
United States Highway 50 West
Brownstown, Indiana 47220
(812) 358-3000

SUMMERS JR., INC., CHARLES G.
50 High Street
New Freedom, Pennsylvania 17349
Thomas S. Summers, President
(717) 235-3821

1285

Companies and Trade Names

SUMMERS LABORATORIES, INC.
Morris Road and Wissahickon Creek
Fort Washington, Pennsylvania 19034
(215) 646-1477

SUMMERTIME (tobacco)
See Liggett & Myers Inc.

SUMMIT (table wine)
See Geyser Peak Winery

SUMMIT IMPORT CORPORATION
491 Greenwich
New York, New York 10013
(212) 226-1662

SUMMIT MARKETING COMPANY
(Division of Joseph E. Seagram & Sons, Inc.)
375 Park Avenue
New York, New York 10022
Seymour Feit, President
(212) 572-7962

SUMMIT ORGANIZATION, INC.
385 Fifth Avenue
New York, New York 10016
Robert Solof, President
(212) 532-8160

SUMMIT SILVER, INC.
(Subsidiary of W.M.F. of America Inc.)
236 Fifth Avenue
New York, New York 10001
(212) 889-1525

SUMMY-BIRCHARD COMPANY
1834 Ridge Avenue
Evanston, Illinois 60204

SUMNER COMPANY, W.S.
5936 Pillsbury Avenue South
Minneapolis, Minnesota 55419
(612) 861-1854

SUN & FUN
Route One
North Attleboro,
   Massachusetts 02760

SUN BATH (tanning aid)
See Revlon, Inc.

SUN BELL (canned foods)
See C. Itoh & Company

SUN BLEST (grocery products)
See Stokely-Van Camp of Canada, Ltd.

SUN BRAND (curry powder, chutnies, mango slices, poppadums)
See Edward Benneche, Inc.

SUN CHEMICAL CORPORATION
200 Park Avenue
New York, New York 10017
Norman E. Alexander, Chairman of the Board
(212) 986-5500
   See also Artistic Manufacturing Company

SUN CHEMICAL CORPORATION
Chemicals Group
222 South Marginal Road
Fort Lee, New Jersey 07024

SUN CHEMICAL CORPORATION
Dyna-Foam Division
Ellenville, New York 12428

SUN CLOTHES, INC.
26th and Reed
Philadelphia, Pennsylvania 19146
Thomas Levin, President
(215) 336-5400

SUN COAST CANNING COMPANY
Post Office Box 818
Fort Meade, Florida 33841

SUN COUNTRY (air freshener)
See S.C. Johnson & Son Inc.

SUN-E-BOY BRANDS, INC.
120 New Hyde Park Road
Franklin Square, New York 11010

SUN ELECTRIC CORPORATION
6323 North Avondale Avenue
Chicago, Illinois 60631
Russell R. Malik, President
(312) 631-6000

SUN FLO (skin-care products)
See Emilio Pucci Perfumes

SUN FROST (insulated cups and tumblers)
See Federal Tool & Plastic

SUN GARDEN PACKING COMPANY
Box 6180
1582 South First Street
San Jose, California 95150
(408) 297-1185

SUN-GLO (floor finish and wax)
See Twi-Lag Chemical Company

SUN GLO CORPORATION
See Lamplight Products, Inc.

SUN-GRAZE (canned meats)
See International Food Products Company

SUN HARBOR INDUSTRIES
Purr Pet Food Division
1995 Bay Front
San Diego, California 92112

SUN JOY (frozen foods)
See Frank S. Oliver & Son

SUN KING (carpets)
See Lees Carpets

SUN-LITE ELECTRO COMPANY
Box 188
Perrine, Florida 33157

SUN LUCK (groceries)
See Seasia

1286

Companies and Trade Names

SUN-MAID RAISIN GROWERS OF CALIFORNIA
13525 South Bethel Avenue
Kingsburg, California 93631
R.F. Light, President
(209) 897-5861

SUN OIL COMPANY
240 Radnor-Chester Road
Saint Davids, Pennsylvania 19087
H. Robert Sharbaugh, President
(215) 985-1600

SUN POWER (batteries)
See Battery Systems, Inc.

SUN PRODUCTS CORPORATION
(Subsidiary of Talley Industries, Inc.)
366 Fairview Avenue
Barberton, Ohio 44203
Richey Smith, President
(216) 753-2231

SUN RAY HAIR PREPARATION COMPANY
15-03 209th Street
Bayside, New York 11360

SUN-RAY INDUSTRIES
8136 Liberty Road
Baltimore, Maryland 21207
(301) 944-7085

SUN RED (food products)
See Naas Foods Inc.

SUN RIPE (jams, jellies, etc.)
See Lexington Specialty Foods, Inc.

SUN-RISE CLOCKS
(Division of Nelson McCoy Pottery Company)
Roseville, Ohio 43777

SUN RISE INC.
Marshall, Minnesota 56258

SUN SENSOR (goggles and glasses)
See Jack Martin Company

SUN SET (portable TV)
See Sony Corporation of America

SUN SIP (citrus products)
See Ben Hill Griffin Inc.

SUN VALLEY MELMAC (melamine dinnerware)
See Stetson Corporation

SUNAID FOOD PRODUCTS
(Subsidiary of Plant Industries Inc.)
3615 N.W. 60th Street
Miami, Florida 33142
(305) 635-1381

SUNAIR ELECTRONICS INC.
3101 S.W. Third Avenue
Fort Lauderdale, Florida 33315
Evertt A. Cooper, President
(305) 525-1501

SUNBEAM (automobiles)
See Chrysler-Plymouth (Division of Chrysler Corporation)

SUNBEAM (bakery products)
See Waldensian Bakeries, Inc.

SUNBEAM (bread products)
See Schaible's Sunbeam Bakery

SUNBEAM (motorcycles and bicycles)
See BSA, Inc.

SUNBEAM (paintbrushes)
See Ideal Brushes Inc.

SUNBEAM APPLIANCE COMPANY
(Division of Sunbeam Corporation)
2001 South York Road
Oak Brook, Illinois 60521
S.M. Bohmbach, President
(312) 654-1900

SUNBEAM CORPORATION
5400 West Roosevelt Road
Chicago, Illinois 60650
Robert P. Gwinn, Chairman of the Board
(312) 854-3500
See also Hanson Scale Company; Hurst Performances, Inc.; Northern Electric Company; and Oster Corporation

SUNBEAM OUTDOOR COMPANY
(Division of Sunbeam Corporation)
2001 South York Road
Oak Brook, Illinois 60521
Austin Cunningham, President
(312) 654-1900

SUNBELL CORPORATION
Post Office Box 7447
1503 Central Avenue
Albuquerque, New Mexico 87104
(505) 243-5636

SUNBIRD INDUSTRIES INC.
5368 Sterling Center Drive
Westlake Village, California 94015

SUNCHASER MARINE
23635 South Dixie Highway
Princeton, Florida 33030

SUNCOAST STUDIOS
909 N.E. Third Avenue
Fort Lauderdale, Florida 33304

SUNCRAFT (wood fences, furniture, and supplies)
See Habitant Fence

SUNDAE SNACK (food products)
See Eat-All Frozen Food Company

SUNDIAL (infants' product)
See Questor Juvenile Products Ltd.

SUNDIAL (no-wax floors)
See Armstrong Cork Company

1287

Companies and Trade Names

SUNDIAL (shoes)
See International Shoe Company

SUNDOWN (venetian blinds)
See Breneman Inc.

SUNDOWNERS (slippers)
See R.G. Barry Corporation

SUNDQUIST FRUIT COLD STORAGE
302 North First Avenue
Yakima, Washington 98902
Ralph Sundquist, President
(509) 457-8164

SUNFISH (one-design or class sailboat)
See AMF Alcort

SUNFLECTORS (sun reflector)
See Tropical Tan Products Company

SUNFLOWER (wine)
See Huntington & Rice Inc.

SUNFROST (insulated thermal products)
See Federal Tool & Plastic

SUNGLOW (margarine)
See Sunnyland Refining Company

SUNKIN & SON, INC., S.
46-50 West 29th
New York, New York 10001
(212) 686-5880

SUNKIST GROWERS, INC.
Post Office Box 7888
Van Nuys, California 91409
Roy Utke, President
(213) 986-4800
See also Lemon Products

SUNLAND MARKETING, INC.
3000 Sand Hill Road
Menlo Park, California 94025
Frank R. Light, President
(415) 854-2322

SUNLIGHT (butter, eggs, etc.)
See Cudahy Company

SUNLINE (umbrellas and furniture)
See Finkel Outdoor Products Inc.

SUNLITE PRODUCTS COMPANY INC.
Box 418
Belleview, Florida 32620
James G. Kirkland, President
(904) 245-2571

SUNN MUSICAL EQUIPMENT COMPANY
(Subsidiary of Hartzel Corporation)
Amburn Industrial Park
Tualatin, Oregon 97062

SUNNIDAY (vacuum cleaner)
See Sunbeam Appliance Company

SUNNY (dairy products)
See Carthage Creamery Company

SUNNY (groceries)
See B.A. Railton Company

SUNNY BANK (margarine)
See Safeway Stores, Inc.

SUNNY BROOK (whiskey)
See National Distillers & Chemical Corporation

SUNNY DAY (flour, baking mixes, coffee, tea, spices, detergents)
See Community Cash Stores

SUNNY DAY (maps)
See Wellington Puritan Mills Inc.

SUNNY DOODLES (cake products)
See Drake Bakeries

SUNNY FARM (processed foods)
See Ernest Carriere Inc.

SUNNY HILL (straight Kentucky Bourbon)
See Waterfill & Frazier Distillery Company

SUNNY JIM (food products)
See Pacific Food Products Company

SUNNY LEA (canned foods)
See Vineland Canning Company, Ltd.

SUNNY MORN (coffee)
See Independent Grocers Alliance of America

SUNNY SQUARE (groceries)
See P & C Food Markets, Inc.

SUNNYBROOK (insecticides, etc.)
See SSM Corporation

SUNNYDALE (margarine)
See Shedd-Bartush Foods, Inc.

SUNNYDALE FARMS, INC.
400 Stanley Avenue
Brooklyn, New York 11207
Stanley Eisenberg, President
(212) 257-1100

SUNNYFIELD (food products)
See Great Atlantic & Pacific Tea Company

Companies and Trade Names

SUNNYLAND FOODS
Post Office Box 1138
Thomasville, Georgia 31792
L.B. Harvard, President
(912) 226-1611

SUNNYLAND JUICE CORPORATION
(Division of Di Giorgio Corporation)
605 East Commercial
Anaheim, California 92801

SUNNYLAND REFINING COMPANY
3330 Tenth Avenue North
Birmingham, Alabama 35234

SUNNYVIEW FARMS (food products)
See Dickinson Company

SUNOCO (petroleum products)
See Sun Oil Company

SUNPROOF (paint)
See PPG Industries, Inc.

SUNRAY STOVE COMPANY
435 Park Avenue
Delaware, Ohio 43015
Robert M. Leach, II, President and
  Chief Executive Officer
(614) 363-1381

SUNRISE (pipes)
See Comoy's of London

SUNRISE FOOD PRODUCTS INC.
2330 Utah Avenue
El Segundo, California 90245
Henry E. Goldich, President
(213) 772-6117

SUNRISE HOME JUICES, INC.
10-40 Beach 22nd
Far Rockaway, New York 11691

SUNRISE MARKETING
  CORPORATION
Post Office Box 24041
Fort Lauderdale, Florida 33307

SUNRISE PRODUCTS INC.
Box 1659
Fort Pierce, Florida 33450

SUNROC CORPORATION
Glen Riddle, Pennsylvania 19037
Orville C. Morrison, President
(215) 459-1100

SUNSET (books)
See Lane Magazine & Book
  Company

SUNSET (canned foods)
See Bessey Foods Corporation

SUNSET (cordials and wines)
See Consolidated Distilled
  Products, Inc.

SENSET GIFT HOUSEWARES INC.
35 Elliott Street
Athens, Ohio 45701

SUNSET GOLD (grocery products)
See Piggly Wiggly Corporation

SUNSET HILLS PHARMACY
7007 Three Chopt Road
Richmond, Virginia 23226
(804) 288-4893

SUNSET HOUSE
(Subsidiary of Broadway-Hale
Stores)
12800 Culver Boulevard
Los Angeles, California 90066
Roy Hedberg, President
(213) 823-6333

SUNSHADE CORPORATION
Box 2127
Sunnyvale, California 94087

SUNSHEEN (paints)
See Standard Industrial Products,
  Inc.

SUNSHINE (cooked meat products)
See Suzanna's Kitchen Inc.

SUNSHINE (juices and drinks)
See Dell Products Corporation

SUNSHINE (phonograph records)
See Ambassador Record
  Corporation

SUNSHINE ART STUDIOS INC.
45 Warwick Street
Springfield, Massachusetts 01101

SUNSHINE BISCUITS, INC.
(Subsidiary of American Brands Inc.)
245 Park Avenue
New York, New York 10017
Edward J. Jennings, Jr., President
(212) 557-7000
  See also Bell Brand Foods, Inc.

SUNSHINE FARMS (butter, eggs,
poultry)
  See Sherman, White & Company,
    Inc.

SUNSHINE SALES
106 Sauls Street
Lake City, South Carolina 29560

SUNSHINE STATE (frozen fruit
juice)
  See Winter Garden Citrus
    Products Co-operative

SUNSHINE STATE COSMETICS,
  INC.
Box 10184
Orlando, Florida 32809

SUNSHINE UNLIMITED
Post Office Box 4759
Panorama City, California 91412

SUNSWEET (canned foods)
See Duffy-Mott Company

Companies and Trade Names

SUNSWEET GROWERS, INC.
1050 South Diamond Street
Stockton, California 95201
A.L. Buffington, President
(209) 465-0201

SUNTONE (wrought-iron furniture)
See George Koch Sons

SUNWARM INC.
Post Office Box 3808
Kingsport, Tennessee 37662
(615) 247-9176

SUNWAY (canned foods)
See Charles C. Shanbarger

SUNWEAVE (window shades)
See Hough Manufacturing
Corporation

SUPER BALL (toy)
See Wham-O Manufacturing
Company

SUPER CEDAR (closet lining)
See George C. Brown &
Company

SUPER-CHEF (bakeware)
See Wear-Ever Aluminum Inc.

SUPER CHIEF (tires)
See Mohawk Rubber Company

SUPER COOLANT (antifreeze)
See Dow Chemical Company

SUPER-CREME (pudding and filling)
See Griffin & Company, Inc.

SUPER CUTTER (lawn and garden supplies)
See Coast to Coast Stores

SUPER D DRUGS
1887 Latham Street
Memphis, Tennessee 38106
Peter Formanek, President
(901) 775-2300

SUPER DUPER (grocery and dairy products)
See S.M. Flickinger Company Inc.

SUPER EBONETTES (household gloves)
See Pioneer Rubber Company

SUPER EDGE (kitchen cutlery)
See Utica Cutlery Company

SUPER 8 (coffee)
See Hafner Coffee Company

SUPER 8 MOTELS INC.
Post Office Box 1456
Aberdeen, South Dakota 57401

SUPER-FOAM (rug cushions)
See Allen Industries, Inc.

SUPER FOOD SERVICES INC.
3185 Elbee Road
Dayton, Ohio 45439
C. Elwood Shaffer, President
(513) 294-1731

SUPER-FORM BRASSIERE, INC.
451 South Jefferson Street
Orange, New Jersey 07050

SUPER GLAZE RESIN SPRAY (paints and paint sundries)
See Zim's Inc.

SUPER-GLO (spray furniture wax)
See Penn-Champ

SUPER GLOSFAST (interior and exterior enamel)
See Textron, Inc.

SUPER GROOM (hair-care products)
See M & W Manufacturing
Company

SUPER HARD SHELL (automobile waxes)
See Turtle Wax Inc.

SUPER-HOLD (denture adhesive)
See Harry J. Bosworth Company

SUPER KEM-TONE (paints)
See Sherwin-Williams Company

SUPER KEY-TEX (paints)
See Keystone Bronze Paint
Corporation

SUPER KLEEN FLOOR (floor polish)
See S.C. Johnson & Son Inc.

SUPER KROME (aluminum paint)
See Sheffield Bronze Paint
Corporation

SUPER LUSTA (housewares and appliances, etc.)
See Essex Machine Sales
Company Inc.

SUPER M (menthol cigarettes)
See American Tobacco Company

SUPER MARKET (food products)
See Stayton Canning Company,
Co-operative

SUPER MAX (hair dryer)
See Gillette Company, Personal
Care Division

SUPER MOIST (cosmetics)
See Germaine Monteil
Cosmetiques Corporation

SUPER MOTRAC (tires)
See Mohawk Rubber Company

Companies and Trade Names

SUPER NO-NOX (gasoline)
See Gulf Oil Corporation

SUPER PLY (paints)
See Glidden-Durkee (Division of SCM Corporation)

SUPER POT (slow cooker)
See Oster Corporation

SUPER POWER II (air conditioners)
See Philco-Ford Corporation

SUPER SAHARA (waterproofing paints)
See United States Paint, Lacquer & Chemical Company

SUPER SATIN PLUS (paint)
See Columbia Paint Company

SUPER SAVE (bakery goods, coffee, ginger ale)
See Gordons Super Markets, Ltd.

SUPER SAVER (processed foods)
See Acme Markets Inc.

SUPER SCOOPERS (snack products)
See Snack Products Inc.

SUPER-SENSITIVE MUSICAL STRING COMPANY
R.R. Two
Sarasota, Florida 33577

SUPER SHAVER (pencil sharpener)
See Sterling Plastics Company

SUPER SHEEN (cosmetics)
See Germaine Monteil Cosmetiques Corporation

SUPER SHEER (makeup)
See Noxell Corporation

SUPER SILICONE (spray lubricant)
See Unival Corporation

SUPER SOFT (buoyant cushions, water-ski belts)
See Texas Water Crafters

SUPER STAR PRODUCTS
16209 Mack Avenue
Detroit, Michigan 48224
(313) 881-9380

SUPER STARFIRE (tires)
See Cooper Tire and Rubber Company

SUPER STRAP (watchbands)
See Brite Industries Inc.

SUPER SUDS (soap powder)
See Colgate-Palmolive Company

SUPER SWEEP (carpet sweepers)
See Bissell Inc.

SUPER-TEX (paints)
See Vita-Var Company

SUPER TIRE ENGINEERING COMPANY
7255 Crescent Boulevard
Camden, New Jersey 08101

SUPER VALU STORES, INC.
101 Jefferson Avenue, South
Hopkins, Minnesota 55343
Jack J. Crocker, President
(612) 935-8844

SUPERB (shoes and shoe materials)
See Bristol Manufacturing Corporation

SUPERBA (Italian foods)
See Lucca Packing Company of California, Inc.

SUPERBA CRAVATS, INC.
216 Andrews Street
Rochester, New York 14604
Allan S. Lerner, President
(716) 325-5440

SUPERBA MILLS
Hancock Street and Montgomery Avenue
Philadelphia, Pennsylvania 19122
(215) 739-1668

SUPERBLOW HAIR CARE CENTER (hair-care appliance)
See General Electric Company

SUPERBOWL PET FOODS, INC.
57-18 48th Street
Maspeth, New York 11378

SUPERCALE (sheets, pillowcases, etc.)
See Wamsutta Mills

SUPERCAMBO (cameras)
See Burleigh Brooks Optics Inc.

SUPEREX ELECTRONICS CORPORATION
151 Ludlow Street
Yonkers, New York 10705
Daniel Shulman, President
(914) 965-6906

SUPERFINE (canned foods)
See Charles G. Summers Jr., Inc.

SUPERFINE (shortening)
See Drew Foods Corporation

SUPERFINE (sugar)
See Godchaux-Henderson Sugar Company, Inc.

SUPERGANIC NATURAL PRODUCTS
200 Elmora
Elizabeth, New Jersey 07207

Companies and Trade Names

SUPERGLOW (cosmetics)
See Germaine Monteil
 Cosmetiques Corporation

SUPERGRIP (bobby pins, hairpins, hair-waving devices)
See Gaylord Products, Inc.

SUPERIDE (shock absorbers)
See General Motors Corporation

SUPERIOR (canned foods)
See Avondale Industries, Inc.

SUPERIOR (groceries, meats)
See Gainers, Ltd.

SUPERIOR (tools, lawn and garden supplies, paints and paint sundries)
See Ace Hardware Corporation

SUPERIOR ALUMINUM PRODUCTS INC.
Box 445
Russia, Ohio 45363

SUPERIOR BEDDING COMPANY
2525 Medford
Los Angeles, California 90033
Victor Erenberg, Chairman of the Board
(213) 225-5651

SUPERIOR CHEMICAL INTERNATIONAL, INC.
18063 James Couzens
Detroit, Michigan 48235

SUPERIOR ELECTRIC COMPANY INC.
383 Middle Street
Bristol, Connecticut 06010
William P. Carpenter, President
(203) 582-9561

SUPERIOR ELECTRIC PRODUCTS CORPORATION
Nash Road
Cape Girardeau, Missouri 63701
James A. Bauerle, President
(314) 335-6647

SUPERIOR FABRICATORS INC.
314 West Superior Street
Chicago, Illinois 60610
(312) 642-5610

SUPERIOR FIREPLACE COMPANY
Post Office Box 2066
4325 Artesia Avenue
Fullerton, California 92633
Courtney Moe, President
(714) 521-7302

SUPERIOR FOODS, INC.
9001 Chancellor Row
Dallas, Texas 75247
Durward H. Meenach, President
(214) 631-7970

SUPERIOR FRUIT & CONFECTIONS
240 Center
Staten Island, New York 10306
(212) 987-1000

SUPERIOR HONEY COMPANY
10920 Garfield Avenue
South Gate, California 90280

SUPERIOR INDUSTRIES INTERNATIONAL INC.
14721 Keswick Street
Van Nuys, California 91405
Louis L. Borick, Chairman and President
(213) 781-4973

SUPERIOR INSULATING TAPE COMPANY
1975 Walton Road
Saint Louis, Missouri 63114
(314) 426-3800

SUPERIOR LINGERIE COMPANY
105 Madison Avenue
New York, New York 10016
Oscar Cohen, Chairman of the Board
(212) 685-7900

SUPERIOR MARKING EQUIPMENT COMPANY
1800 West Larchmont Avenue
Chicago, Illinois 60613
(312) 935-6025

SUPERIOR MATCH COMPANY
7530 South Greenwood Avenue
Chicago, Illinois 60619
Merrill L. Nash, President and Chief Executive Officer
(312) 723-2800

SUPERIOR MATERIALS, INC.
111 Broadway
New York, New York 10006
(212) 233-8944

SUPERIOR METAL INDUSTRIES
509 Front Avenue
Saint Paul, Minnesota 55117

SUPERIOR MOTELS INC.
Post Office Drawer S
Hollywood, Florida 33022

SUPERIOR MOTOR HOMES
1200 East Kibby
Lima, Ohio 45802

SUPERIOR NUT COMPANY, INC.
119 Pearl Street
Boston, Massachusetts 02110

SUPERIOR NUTRITIONAL COMPANY
2530 Polk Street
Union, New Jersey 07083

Companies and Trade Names

SUPERIOR PAINT & VARNISH
CORPORATION
200 East Market
Scranton, Pennsylvania 18509
(717) 343-4340

SUPERIOR PET PRODUCTS, INC.
321 Summer Street
Boston, Massachusetts 02210
Richard J. Phelps, President and
 Treasurer
(617) 482-3900

SUPERIOR PETTICOAT COMPANY
5727 Hudson Boulevard
North Bergen, New Jersey 07047

SUPERIOR PLASTICS INC.
1660 Old Deerfield Road
Highland Park, Illinois 60035
Richard S. Bezark, President
(312) 831-5200

SUPERIOR PRODUCTS COMPANY
 See Globe-Superior Inc. (Division of American Biltrite
 Rubber Company, Inc.)

SUPERIOR RUBBER
 MANUFACTURING
(Division of Superior Rubber Supply
 Corporation)
501 West 82nd Street
Chicago, Illinois 60620
(312) 488-4040

SUPERIOR SLEEPRITE
(Division of Shore Industries, Inc.)
759 South Washtenaw Avenue
Chicago, Illinois 60612
Harry M. Shore, President
(312) 632-4545

SUPERIOR TABBIES INC.
1719 South Elmhurst Road
Elk Grove Village, Illinois 60007

SUPERIOR TAPE CORPORATION
22 Romanelli Avenue
South Hackensack,
 New Jersey 07606
(201) 489-2011

SUPERIOR TEA & COFFEE
 COMPANY
2278 North Elston Avenue
Chicago, Illinois 60614
Earl Cohn, Chairman of the Board
(312) 489-1000

SUPERIOR TOY & MANUFAC-
 TURING COMPANY
1447 West Montrose Avenue
Chicago, Illinois 60613
(312) 929-1300

SUPERLECTRIC (electric heaters)
 See Superior Electric Products
 Corporation

SUPERLUX, LTD.
79 Madison Avenue
New York, New York 10016
(212) 889-3740

SUPERMARINE PRODUCTS
 COMPANY
1 Johnson Drive
Department BG
Raritan, New Jersey 08869
(201) 526-0255

SUPERMKT (frozen foods)
 See United Flav-R-Pac Growers,
 Inc.

SUPERMARKETS GENERAL
 CORPORATION
301 Blair Road
Woodbridge, New Jersey 07095
Milton Perlmutter, President
(201) 636-2400

SUPERMATIC (sporting firearms)
 See The High Standard
 Manufacturing Corporation

SUPERMIX (paints and paint
sundries)
 See Our Own Hardware Company

SUPERPOSED (shotguns)
 See Browning

SUPERSCOPE, INC.
8150 Vineland Avenue
Sun Valley, California 91352
Joseph S. Tushinsky, President
(213) 767-9750

SUPERSPORT (binoculars)
 See Watrous & Company, Inc.

SUPERSTAR 100 (automatic organs)
 See Zachary Musical Instruments

SUPERSWEET (feeds)
 See International Multifoods
 Corporation

SUPERTRED (cleaning compounds,
waxes, etc.)
 See S.C. Johnson & Company

SUPERTURF (lawn seed)
 See Mock Seed Company

SUPERVISORS, INC.
125-10 Queens Boulevard
Kew Gardens, New York 11415

SUPERWINCH INC.
Connecticut Route 52
Putnam, Connecticut 06260
(203) 928-7787

SUPP-HOSE (support hosiery)
 See Kayser-Roth Hosiery
 Company, Inc.

SUPPER TIME (frozen prepared foods)
 See Southland Frozen Foods,
 Inc.

Companies and Trade Names

SUPPLE'S SONS, J.
Bayou Gould, Louisiana 70716
Edward T. Supple, President

SUPPLEX
(Division of Amerace Esna
Corporation)
8929 Columbus Pike
Washington, Ohio 43085
(419) 562-0601

SUPPOSITORIA LABORATORIES
135 Florida Street
Farmingdale, New York 11736

SUPR-LITE (stepladders)
See Watling Ladder Company

SUPRANEIGE (sports apparel)
See Alpine Crafts Company Inc.

SUPREME (air conditioners)
See Westinghouse Electric
Corporation

SUPREME (drums, amplifiers, PA
systems, and microphones)
See Peate Musical Supplies Ltd.

SUPREME (fruit drinks)
See Tropicana Products, Inc.

SUPREME (hand and power tools)
See Famport Hardware Company

SUPREME (hosiery)
See Virginia Maid Hosiery Mills

SUPREME (wine)
See House of Old Molineaux,
Inc.

SUPREME BEAUTY PRODUCTS
COMPANY
820 South Michigan
Chicago, Illinois 60605
(312) 664-9255

SUPREME CUTLERY
(Division of Sigma Marketing
Systems)
225 Fifth Avenue
New York, New York 10010
(212) 725-4844

SUPREME ENTERPRISES LTD.
(Division of Min-Dee Distributors
Inc.)
Post Office Box 130
Syosset, New York 11791

SUPREME EQUIPMENT &
SYSTEMS CORPORATION
170 53rd Street
Brooklyn, New York 11232
Philip Frederick, Chairman and
President
(212) 492-7777

SUPREME FOOD DISTRIBUTORS
331-337 Fitzwater
Philadelphia, Pennsylvania 19147
(215) 925-1965

SUPREME FOODS COMPANY, INC.
34 Morelia Avenue
Knoxville, Tennessee 37917
(615) 524-2533

SUPREME MILLS SALES COMPANY
INC.
2927 Lomita Boulevard
Torrance, California 90509

SUPREME PHARMACEUTICAL
COMPANY
354 Mercer
Jersey City, New Jersey 07302

SUPREME PRODUCTS
CORPORATION
(Subsidiary of The Ridge Tool
Company)
2222 South Calumet Avenue
Chicago, Illinois 60616
R.L. San Soucie, Chairman of the
Board
(312) 326-2000

SUPREME STEEL EQUIPMENT
CORPORATION
See Supreme Equipment &
Systems Corporation

SUPREME WEAR COMPANY
683 Broadway
New York, New York 10012
(212) 254-8080

SURACE, PAUL
16 Court
Brooklyn, New York 11241
(212) 875-3745

SURCO PRODUCTS, INC.
1040 East 33rd Street
Hialeah, Florida 33013
Bob Surloff, President
(305) 691-5971

SURE CORRAL (fence products)
See Fi-Shock Inc.

SURE-FLEX (rubber products)
See Carlisle Corporation

SURE-JELL (powdered fruit pectin)
See General Foods Corporation

SURE-START (automotive product)
See Pyroil-Master (Division of
Pyroil Company, Inc.)

SURE TOUCH (razor blade)
See Gillette Company

SURETY RUBBER COMPANY, THE
North High
Carrollton, Ohio 44615
J.L. Hall, President and Secretary
(216) 627-2166

SUREX (deodorant bar soap)
See Purex Corporation, Ltd.

Companies and Trade Names

SURF (cold-water detergent)
See Lever Brothers Company

SURF PRIDE (frozen seafood)
See Old Salt Seafoods Inc.

SURF SIDE (gin, vodka, and rum)
See Old Florida Rum Company

SURFA-SELE (protective coating)
See Rust-Oleum Corporation

SURFGLAS INC.
1009 South Hathaway Street
Santa Ana, California 92705

SURFSET INC.
35 Haddon Avenue
Shrewbury, New Jersey 07701

SURGITUBE PRODUCTS
CORPORATION
83 North Summit Street
Tenafly, New Jersey 07670

SURPRISE/CORDE
200 Madison Avenue
New York, New York 10016
(212) 532-0810

SURREY ORIGINALS
108-22 Queens Boulevard
Forest Hills, New York 11375
(212) 897-5864

SURVEYOR (electronic calculator)
See Monroe, The Calculator Company

SURVEYOR (motor homes)
See Futura Industries Inc.

SURVIVAL SYSTEMS INC.
Box 273
Ontario, California 91761

SUSAN KAY CANDIES
MANUFACTURING COMPANY
517-19 33rd
Parkersburg, West Virginia 26101

SUSAN OF CALIFORNIA, INC.
2020 East Seventh Street
Los Angeles, California 90021
(213) 627-0021

SUSAN SMITH (golf equipment)
See Professional Golf Company

SUSAN TYLER (handbags)
See Kadin Brothers Inc.

SUSANA (groceries)
See Sassone Wholesale Groceries Company, Inc.

SUSIE-Q RESTAURANTS, INC.
770 South Adams
Birmingham, Michigan 48011

SUSIS (tripods)
See AIC Photo Inc.

SUSQUEHANNA GLASS COMPANY
731 Avenue H
Columbia, Pennsylvania 17512
Edward J. Rowen, Jr., President
(717) 684-2155

SUSSE CHALET (hotel/motel chain)
See Chalet Susse International Inc.

SUSSEX (canned foods)
See H.P. Cannon & Sons Inc.

SUSSEX-MAID (frozen foods)
See Vita-Frost Foods Inc.

SUTER'S SALES COMPANY
Post Office Box 327
Sycamore, Illinois 60178

SUTLIFF & CASE COMPANY, INC.
Box 838
Peoria, Illinois 61601

SUTLIFF TOBACCO COMPANY
(Division of Consolidated Cigar Corporation)
600 Perdue Avenue
Richmond, Virginia 23224
(804) 233-7668

SUTPHEN INC., DUNCAN
Box 83
Old Lyme, Connecticut 06731

STEPHEN MARINE CORPORATION
Edison Road
Lake Hopatcong, New Jersey 07849

SUTTER COMPANY INC.,
PETER M.
Box 927
Sausalito, California 94965

SUTTON & SONS INC., I.S.
200 Fifth Avenue
New York, New York 10010
(212) 563-2258

SUTTON COMPANY
7310 Bay Parkway
Brooklyn, New York 11204
(218) 236-6567

SUTTON MANUFACTURING
CORPORATION
112 West Wilson Avenue
Norfolk, Virginia 23510
(703) 622-6313

SUTTON MANUFACTURING INC.
109 Sylvania Place
South Plainfield, New Jersey 07080

SUTTON POINT (carpeting)
See Stephen-Leedom Carpet Company Inc.

Companies and Trade Names

SUTTONS BAY (fruit products)
  See Frigid Food Products, Inc.

SUVA GROUP (rattan and wicker)
  See Decorative Imports

SUVEREN (sports accessories and equipment)
  See Silva Company

SUWANEE (food trays)
  See Southern Champion Tray Company

SUWANEE (seafood)
  See New England Fish Company

SUWANNEE DRUG COMPANY
128 Central Avenue
Newberry, Florida 32669

SUZAN (food products)
  See Clements Foods Company

SUZANNA'S KITCHEN INC.
4300 Pleasantdale Road
Doraville, Georgia 30340

SUZETTE (food products)
  See Old Fashioned Kitchen Inc.

SUZUKI MOTOR CORPORATION
    UNITED STATES
13767 Freeway Drive
Santa Fe Springs, California 90670

SUZY-BEL CANNING COMPANY, INC.
(Subsidiary of Stanislaus Food Products)
South Delsea Drive
Port Elizabeth, New Jersey 08348

SUZY STAR
135 Madison Avenue
New York, New York 10016
(212) 686-5480

SVEDEN HOUSE INTERNATIONAL INC.
89 Providence Highway
Westwood, Massachusetts 02090

SVEND JENSEN OF DENMARK, INC.
1010 Boston Post Road
Rye, New York 10580

SWAGGER (men's trousers)
  See Irving Greenberg

SWAIN'S (barbecue sauce, dressings)
  See Smoked Food Products Company, Inc.

SWAN (alcohol, first-aid items, espom salts, peroxide)
  See Cumberland Manufacturing Company

SWAN (liquid detergent)
  See Lever Brothers Company

SWAN ISLAND (seafood)
  See Noon Hour Food Products, Inc.

SWAN PENCIL COMPANY INC.
221 Park Avenue South
New York, New York 10003
(212) 254-7950

SWAN PRODUCTS COMPANY INC.
1107 Broadway
New York, New York 10010
(212) 741-9400

SWAN RUBBER
(Division of Amerace Esna Corporation)
Post Office Box 509
8929 Columbus Pike
Washington, Ohio 43085
C.A. Rivasi, President
(614) 548-6511

SWANEE PAPER COMPANY, INC.
(Subsidiary of Potlatch Forests, Inc.)
1290 Avenue of the Americas
New York, New York 10019
Edmund Pearlman, President
(212) 581-2000

SWANK (food products)
  See Knapp-Sherrill Company

SWANK, INC.
6 Hazel Street
Attleboro, Massachusetts 02703
Marshall Tulin, President
(617) 222-3400
  See also Prince Gardner

SWANS DOWN (cake flour and cake mix)
  See General Foods Corporation

SWAN'S LABORATORIES
Box 418
Andrews, North Carolina 28901

SWANSON (prepared foods)
  See Campbell Soup Company

SWAYZEE PACKING COMPANY
Sayzee, Indiana 46986
(317) 922-7996

SWEATERVILLE U.S.A. (women's sweaters)
  See Old Colony Knitting Mills, Inc.

SWEDA INTERNATIONAL
(Division of Litton Industries)
34 Maple Avenue
Pine Brook, New Jersey 07058
J.P. Francini, President
(201) 575-8100

SWEDEN FREEZER
    MANUFACTURING COMPANY
3401 17th Avenue West
Seattle, Washington 98119
Harvey S. Swenson, President
(206) 283-9200

Companies and Trade Names

SWEDISH CRUCIBLE STEEL COMPANY, Plastic Division
See Olsonite Corporation

SWEDISH FOOD PRODUCTS
652 West Randolph
Chicago, Illinois 60606
(312) 728-1177

SWEDISH METALCRAFT INC.
204 Leonia Avenue
Bogota, New Jersey 07603

SWEDISH PLASTIC RUGS (carpeting)
See Scandia Specialties Inc.

SWEDISH SHAMPOO LABORATORIES
14 East 38th Street
New York, New York 10016
(212) 685-7026

SWEDISH TANNING SECRET (tanning aids)
See Leeming/Pacquin

SWEEN CHEMICAL CORPORATION
2854 115 Lane N.W.
Coon Rapids, Minnesota 55433

SWEENEY MANUFACTURER, INC., W.R.
340 South Broadway
Salisbury, Missouri 65281
(816) 388-6417

SWEENEY SEED COMPANY
Mount Pleasant, Michigan 48858

SWEEP MASTER (lightweight electric vacuum)
See Bissell Inc.

SWEEP STAKES (jams, jellies, condiments, etc.)
See C.H.B. Foods Inc.

SWEET BRIER (fruits and vegetables)
See Midland Grocery Company

SWEET CANDY COMPANY
Post Office Box 2008
224 South First West
Salt Lake City, Utah 84104
(801) 363-6701

SWEET CHICK (frozen poultry)
See Mar-Jac, Inc.

SWEET LIFE (food products)
See Springfield Sugar and Products Company

SWEET MISS (tomatoes and juices)
See Dextra Corporation

SWEET-N-FRESH (processed foods)
See Case-Swayne Company Inc.

SWEET 'N LOW (beverage)
See Monarch-Nugrape Company

SWEET 'N LOW (sugar substitute)
See Cumberland Packing Company

SWEET SLUMBER (bedding)
See Jamison Bedding, Inc.

SWEET SUE KITCHENS INC.
Post Office Box 974
Athens, Alabama 35611

SWEET SUSAN (jams, jellies, condiments, etc.)
See C.H.B. Foods Inc.

SWEET TIP TOP (tobacco)
See Liggett & Myers Inc.

SWEET TREAT (liquor)
See Schenley Industries, Inc.

SWEET-X (drain cleaner)
See Rooto Corporation

SWEETHEART (bread)
See Interstate Brands Corporation

SWEETHEART (fabric softener, liquid detergent, soap, bleach)
See Purex Corporation, Ltd.

SWEETHEART (facial sauna)
See Pollenex Health Appliance (Division of Associated Mills, Inc.)

SWEETHEART CUP
(Division of Maryland Cup Corporation)
10100 Reisterstown Road
Owings Mills, Maryland 21117
(301) 363-1111

SWEETHEART PLASTICS
(Division of Maryland Cup Corporation)
1 Burlington Avenue
Wilmington, Massachusetts 01887
Samuel Shapiro, President
(617) 658-9100

SWEETNIN (food products)
See Tillie Lewis Foods Inc.

SWEETSTEPS (shoes)
See Edison Brothers Stores, Inc.

SWEL (frosting mix)
See RJR Foods, Inc.

SWEPCO TUBE CORPORATION
1 Clifton Boulevard
Clifton, New Jersey 07011
Paul A. Tobelmann, President
(201) 778-3000

SWERDLOFF & COMPANY
43 Homer
Mattapan, Massachusetts 02126

SWERL (detergent)
See Colgate-Palmolive Company

SWIBO (cutlery)
See International Edge Tool Company

Companies and Trade Names

SWIFT & COMPANY
115 West Jackson Boulevard
Chicago, Illinois 60604
Charles C. Olcott, President
(312) 431-2000
  See also Derby Foods, Inc.;
  Treasure Cave; and Vickers
  Petroleum Corporation

SWIFT & SONS, INC., M.
50 Love Lane
Hartford, Connecticut 06101
(203) 522-1181

SWIFT EDIBLE OIL COMPANY
(Division of Swift & Company)
115 West Jackson Boulevard
Chicago, Illinois 60604
(312) 431-2000

SWIFT INDUSTRIES, INC.
241 Curry Follow Road
Pittsburgh, Pennsylvania 15236
Ira H. Gordon, President
(412) 892-0700

SWIFT INSTRUMENTS, INC.
952 Dorchester Avenue
Boston, Massachusetts 02125
Humphrey H. Swift, President
(617) 436-2960

SWIFTEE (paint rollers and trays)
  See Colonial Brush Manufacturing
  Company Inc.

SWIFT'NING (shortening)
  See Swift & Company

SWIFTWATER (food products)
  See Bumble Bee Seafoods

SWIM N' STRUT JUNIORS
(swimwear)
  See Peter Pan Swimwear &
  Sportswear

SWIM-PACK (children's swim vests)
  See Martin Marine Company

SWIMOBILE (water-sports equipment)
  See Chris-Craft Marine
  Accessories

SWIMQUIP, INC.
(Subsidiary of Weil-McLain
  Company)
3301 Gilman Road
El Monte, California 91732
D.F. Benson, General Manager
(213) 443-4211

SWIMRITE, INC.
15330 Oxnard Street
Van Nuys, California 91408
James H. Edmiston, President
(213) 782-7772

SWINDLE & SONS COMPANY,
  D.W.
Post Office Box 8021
201 R. Hart Lane
Nashville, Tennessee 37207
(615) 228-3471

SWING-A-WAY
  MANUFACTURING COMPANY
4100 Beck Street
Saint Louis, Missouri 63116
I.L. Rhodes, Chairman of the Board
(314) 773-1487

SWING INC., D. THOMPSON
Price, Maryland 21656
(301) 556-6633

SWING-'N-PEN (infants' product)
  See Stacy Manufacturing
  Company Inc.

SWING-N-SET (plaything)
  See Gym-Dandy Inc.

SWING N TWIST (exercise and
reducing equipment)
  See Matador Industries Inc.

SWING-TIMER (clocks)
  See Howard Miller Clock
  Company

SWING-UP STEP COMPANY
Box 5345
Beaumont, Texas 77702

SWING WEST SKI WEAR
(Division of Raven Industries Inc.)
Box 1007
Sioux Falls, South Dakota 57105

SWINGER (diaper hampers)
  See Century Products Inc.

SWINGER (pantyhose, tights, socks)
  See Landenberger Associated
  Mills

SWINGER (recreational vehicles)
  See Monitor Coach Company

SWINGLINE, INC.
(Subsidiary of American Brands,
  Inc.)
32-00 Skillman Avenue
Long Island City, New York 11101
John H. Behr, President
(212) 361-8555
  See also Ace Fastener Company;
  Marson Corporation; and
  Wilson Jones Company

SWINGMASTER (juvenile product)
  See Jenkintown Metal Products
  Inc.

SWINGSTER (jackets)
  See Nat Nast Inc.

SWINGSTER (phonographs)
  See Kerner Products

SWIRL INC.
1411 Broadway
New York, New York 10018
(212) 564-8890
  See also Models Coat Inc.

SWISH (detergents, cleaners, etc.)
  See Curley Company, Inc.

Companies and Trade Names

SWISHER & SON, INC., JNO. H.
Post Office Box 2230
Jacksonville, Florida 32203
(904) 353-4311

SWISS AMERICAN TRADING
COMPANY
351 Greenwich Street
New York, New York 10003
(212) 431-6599

SWISS CHALET FOOD PRODUCTS
(Division of Consolidated American
Industries, Inc.)
Post Office Box 800
Wichita, Kansas 67201
George Ablah, Chairman of the
Board
(316) 267-3201

SWISS COLONY, THE
1112 Seventh Avenue
Monroe, Wisconsin 53566
Kurt Schwager, Vice President
(608) 328-8400

SWISS HARMONY INC.
847 West Jackson Street
Chicago, Illinois 60607
(312) 666-3311

SWISS KNIGHT (cheese)
See Gerber Cheese Company,
Inc.

SWISS MISS (desserts)
See Pet, Inc.

SWISS MISS (instant cocoa mix)
See Sanna, Inc.

SWISS PINE IMPORTING
COMPANY INC.
3545 Webster
Bronx, New York 10467
(212) 798-3400

SWISS TREAT (groceries)
See W.T. Lynch Foods Ltd.

SWISSAIR
608 Fifth Avenue
New York, New York 10020
Claude Christie, General Manager
(212) 995-3800

SWISSART CANDY COMPANY
218 29th Street
Brooklyn, New York 11232
(212) 868-4971

SWISSCO (music boxes and
novelties)
See Elpa Marketing Industries
Inc.

SWISSMART INC.
444 Madison Avenue
New York, New York 10022
(212) 751-3768

SWISSTEX COMPANY
220 61st Street
West New York, New Jersey 07093

SWITZER CANDY COMPANY
(Division of Beatrice Foods
Company)
621 North First
Saint Louis, Missouri 63102
B. Robert Kill, President
(314) 421-3474

SWITZER-CRAFT, INC.
7109 Pinegree Road
Crystal Lake, Illinois 60014
Russell M. Switzer, Chairman of
the Board
(815) 459-2460

SWIV-L-TILT (television)
See Zenith Radio Corporation

SWIVELIER COMPANY INC.
33 Route 304
Nanuet, New York 10954
Nathan R. Schwartz, President
(914) 623-3471

SWIVELTIES (accent and spot
lighting fixtures)
See Fostoria-Fannon Inc.

SWIVLER (athletic shoes)
See Wolverine World Wide Inc.

SWIZZELS, INC.
803 Clinton Street
Hoboken, New Jersey 07030

SWYNGOMATIC INDUSTRIES
Main Street
Elverson, Pennsylvania 19520

SYBIL MILLS, INC.
611 Rose Street
Williamsport, Pennsylvania 17701

SYBRON CORPORATION
1100 Midtown Tower
Rochester, New York 14604
William G. von Berg, President
(716) 546-4040
See also Taylor Instrument; and
Thermolyne Corporation

SYCAMORE MOBILE HOMES INC.
Box 496
Goshen, Indiana 46526

SYCOR, INC.
100 Phoenix Drive
Ann Arbor, Michigan 48104
Samuel N. Irwin, Chairman and
President
(313) 971-0900

SYDNEY DESIGNS (loungewear)
See Ed Smiler Company

SYLER, INC.
Dickman (Box B)
Plymouth, Indiana 46563

SYLRAY UNDERWEAR COMPANY
Independence Street
Orwigsburg, Pennsylvania 17961
(717) 366-0537

Companies and Trade Names

SYLVAN CHEMICAL CORPORATION
Post Office Box 998-A
616 Palisade Avenue
Englewood Cliffs, New Jersey 07632
(201) 567-8900

SYLVANIA ELECTRIC PRODUCTS, INC.
See GTE Sylvania

SYLVANIA SHOE MANUFACTURING CORPORATION
350 South Street
McSherrystown, Pennsylvania 17344
Irving Pearlstein, President
(717) 637-3874

SYMBRA*ETTE, INC.
23 Janis Way
Scotts Valley, California 95066

SYMCO (food products)
See Flanagan Brothers Inc.

SYMMONS INDUSTRIES INC.
31 Brooks Drive
Braintree, Massachusetts 02184
Paul C. Symmons, President and Treasurer
(617) 848-2250

SYMONS FROZEN FOODS INC.
Box 577
Centralia, Washington 98531

SYMONS SAILING INC.
255 South Ketcham Avenue
Amityville, New York 11701

SYMPATICO (men's cologne and aftershave lotion)
See Textron, Inc.

SYMPHONIA (accordions)
See J.M. Greene Music Company Ltd.

SYMPHONY (music lamps)
See Cannon Products Inc.

SYMPHONY CLASSICS (women's apparel)
See Bobbie Brooks, Inc.

SYN-CORDION MUSICAL INSTRUMENT CORPORATION
32-73 Steinway Street
Long Island City, New York 11103
(212) 278-7422

SYNCOM (hi-fi and stereo equipment)
See Bose Corporation

SYNEK STUDIO
99 Spring Street
New York, New York 10012
(212) 226-4215

SYNERGISTICS RESEARCH CORPORATION
650 Avenue of Americas
New York, New York 10019
(212) 989-9707

SYNESTRUCTICS INC.
9559 Irondale Avenue
Chatsworth, California 91311

SYNITE (synthetic enamels)
See Mobil Chemical Company

SYNKOLOID COMPANY, THE
Post Office Box 60937
2945 Maria
Los Angeles, California 90060
(213) 636-1211

SYNTEX LABORATORIES, INC.
Stanford Industrial Park
Palo Alto, California 94304
Richard Rogers, President
(415) 855-5844
See also Borden Pharmaceutical Products

SYRACUSE CHINA CORPORATION
2900 Court Street
Syracuse, New York 13201
Robert J. Theis, Chairman, President and Chief Executive Officer
(315) 455-5671

SYRACUSE ORNAMENTAL COMPANY, INC.
See Syroco

SYRO STEEL COMPANY
1170 North State Street
Girard, Ohio 44420
(216) 545-4373

SYROCO
(Division of Dart Industries, Inc.)
State Fair Boulevard
Syracuse, New York 13201
Adolph Sebell, President
(315) 635-9911

SYSTEMATIC LEARNING CORPORATION
52 Hook Road
Bayonne, New Jersey 07002

SYSTEMS MANUFACTURING CORPORATION
13 Broad Street
Binghamton, New York 13904

SZELAGOWSKI & SON, INC., A.
755 Baily Avenue
Buffalo, New York 14240
Walter L. Hegeman, President
(716) 825-7000

Companies and Trade Names

T

T & G (produce)
  See Warren Wagner, Inc.

T & R MACHINE COMPANY, INC.
Box 17691
Orlando, Florida 32810

TBI PRODUCTS INC.
36 Cutler Street
Stonington, Connecticut 06378

T-BALL JOTTER (ball-point pen)
  See Parker Pen Company

TCA (thermometers)
  See Thermometer Corporation of America

T.C.B. (toiletries)
  See Alberto-Culver Company

T.C. GREEN LTD. (English ovenproof cookware)
  See Herbert Van Doorn Company

TCO INDUSTRIES, INC.
315 Continental Avenue
Dallas, Texas 75207
M.E. Moore, President
(214) 748-4411

TC-65 SERIES (folding table and chair combination)
  See Sico Inc.

TC-28 (T-shirts)
  See Munsingwear, Inc.

T-CRAFT BOAT COMPANY, INC.
Box 1206
Titusville, Florida 32780

T.E.S.T. INC.
19428 Londelius Street
Northridge, California 91324

TFF (frozen foods)
  See Trappe Frozen Foods Corporation

T-FAL (cookware)
  See Mouli Manufacturing Corporation

TFI COMPANIES, INC.
  See Tastee Freez International Inc.

T-4-L (foot powder, medicated soap, etc.)
  See Sorbol Company

T G & Y STORES COMPANY
3815 North Santa Fe
Oklahoma City, Oklahoma 73125
Raymond A. Young, Chairman of the Board
(405) 528-3141
  See also Gosselin Stores Company, Inc.

T.I.M.E.-DC, INC.
(Subsidiary of National City Lines, Inc.)
Post Office Box 2550
Lubbock, Texas 79408
Rex R. Davis, President
(806) 747-3131

TM (steel shelving systems)
  See Airway Products Corporation

TMA COMPANY
1020 Noel Avenue
Wheeling, Illinois 60090
Daniel J. Domin, President
(312) 537-5700

TM-3 (paint remover)
  See Dartworth Inc.

T.N. DICKINSON COMPANY, THE
36 West Point Road
East Hampton, Connecticut 06424

TNT FOOD PRODUCTS, INC.
Post Office Box 98
Lawrence, Kansas 66044

T.P. ENTERPRISES
1313 Chalet Avenue
Anaheim, California 92802

TPI CORPORATION
Box T,
Carroll Reese Station
Johnson City, Tennessee 37601
(615) 929-3151
  See also Electri-Heat

T-ROUSERS (men's clothing)
  See Oxford Industries, Inc.

TRW, INC.
23555 Euclid Avenue
Cleveland, Ohio 44117
R.F. Mettler, President
(216) 383-2121
  See also Marlin-Rockwell; and Ramsey Corporation

TTS (water skis and accessories)
  See Western Wood Manufacturing Company

T.T.T. (hair- and scalp-care products)
  See Tin-Tone Cosmetic Company

TV (groceries)
  See Fleming Foods

TV CONVERTA SEAT (juvenile furniture)
  See Gay Products Inc.

TV MANUFACTURERS OF AMERICA
1020 Noel Avenue
Wheeling, Illinois 60090

Companies and Trade Names

TVP (textured vegetable protein)
See Archer Daniels Midland Company

TVR CARS OF AMERICA, LTD.
572 Merrick Road
Lynbrook, New York 11563

TV-TIME FOODS, INC.
6570 North Sheridan Road
Chicago, Illinois 60626
John Bishop, President
(312) 743-8600

T.W.A.
See Trans World Airlines, Inc.

TA-KO-MA (canned foods)
See Green Bay Canning Corporation

TAAKA (vodka)
See Sazerac Company, Inc.

TAB (soft drink)
See Coca Cola USA

TAB PRODUCTS COMPANY
2690 Hanover Street
Palo Alto, California 94304
Harry W. Le Claire, President
(415) 493-5790

TABAC BLOND (eau de cologne, eau de toilette, extract)
See Caron Corporation

TABAGO (aftershave)
See Shulton Inc.

TABASCO (hot sauce)
See McIlhenry Company

TABBY (cat food)
See Lipton Pet Foods, Inc.

TABLE CHEF (portable food warmer)
See Ronson Corporation

TABLE-ETTE (chess table)
See Pacific Game Company

TABLE HI (infant seat)
See Toidey Company, Inc.

TABLE KING (frozen and canned foods)
See Super Food Services, Inc.

TABLE MATES (infants' product)
See Stacy Manufacturing Company Inc.

TABLE PRIDE (food products)
See San Juan Packers Inc.

TABLE QUEEN (frozen foods)
See Albany Frosted Foods, Inc.

TABLE READY (meats)
See Swift & Company

TABLE ROCK (produce)
See Associated Fruit Company

TABLE ROCK LABORATORIES, INC.
Box 1968
Greenville, South Carolina 29602

TABLE TALK PIE (food product)
See Beech-Nut, Inc.

TABLE TESTED (frozen foods)
See Frozen Foods (Division of Stokely-Van Camp Inc.)

TABLE TOGS
Post Office Box 10527
2523 Farrington
Dallas, Texas 75207
(214) 630-4481

TABLE TOPS (frozen foods)
See Northwest Cold Pack Company

TABLEMATE (nondairy creamer)
See Carnation Company

TABLEWARE INC.
Belmont Drive
Somerset, New Jersey 08873

TABLOTHERM (heated serving tray)
See Gemini International Corporation

TABOR CITY FOODS INC.
Tabor City, North Carolina 28463

TABU (bath oil, cologne, hair spray, perfume, etc.)
See Dana Perfumes, Inc.

TACA INTERNATIONAL AIRLINES, S.A.
New Orleans International Airport
Kenner, Louisiana 70062
Claude E. Taylor, Vice President
(504) 729-4551

TACKLE (acne treatment)
See Colgate-Palmolive Company

TACKMASTER (leather conditioner and cleaner)
See Dairy Association Company, Inc.

TACKS (outdoor footwear)
See G.H. Bass & Company

TACO BELL
2424 Moreton Street
Torrance, California 90505
Robert L. McKay, President
(213) 534-1211

Companies and Trade Names

TACONIS (pipe tobacco)
See Brown & Williamson
Tobacco Corporation

TADS (slacks)
See H.R. Kaminsky & Sons Inc.

TAD'S ENTERPRISES, INC.
119 West 42nd Street
New York, New York 10036
Don Townsend, President
(212) 524-4840

TAFFALURE (shower curtains)
See Kleinert's Inc.

TAFT BROADCASTING COMPANY
1906 Highland
Cincinnati, Ohio 45219
Charles S. Mechem, Jr., Chairman
of the Board
(513) 721-1414

TAGUS (copperware)
See Inline Products Inc.

TAHITI BOATS INC.
2 Robert Lennox Drive
Northport, New York 11768

TAHITIAN LIME (men's toiletries)
See Alberto-Culver Company

TAHITIAN TREAT (beverage)
See Canada Dry Corporation

TAIL-R-CUT (seafood)
See Frionor Kitchens Inc.

TAIL WAGGER (dog food)
See Allied Mills, Inc.

TAILOR-D CLOTHING, INC.
2901 Court A
Tacoma, Washington 98401
M. John Slikas, President
(206) 272-4184

TAILOR INC., JUNE
Box 125
Hartland, Wisconsin 53029

TAITTINGER (champagnes)
See Kobrand Corporation

TAJ IMPORTING COMPANY
1355 Market Street
San Francisco, California 94103
(415) 863-8058

TAJ MAHAL
(Division of Supercraft India)
14-21 150th Street
Whitestone, New York 11357

TAK-A-TASTE (canned fruit)
See J.R. May Company

TAKASAGO USA, INC.
41-12 38th Street
Long Island City, New York 11101
(212) 937-7730

TAKASHIMAYA, INC.
509 Fifth Avenue
New York, New York 10017
Tetsutaro Iida, President
(212) 682-1900

TAKE 'N TAPE (cassette player/
recorder)
See Matsushita Electronic
Corporation of America

TAL (bath oil, cologne, perfume)
See Sabrina Fragrances, Ltd.

TALBOT KNITTING MILLS
Sixth and Hiester
Reading, Pennsylvania 19603
Edward Coopersmith, President
(215) 929-4761

TALISMAN YACHTS
170 West Providencia Avenue
Burbank, California 91503

TALK-A-PHONE COMPANY
5013 North Kedzie Avenue
Chicago, Illinois 60625
A. Liberman, President
(312) 539-1100

TALK O' TEXAS BRANDS INC.
435 South Oakes
San Angelo, Texas 76901

TALKING DEVICES COMPANY
406 South Boulder
Tulsa, Oklahoma 74103
(918) 587-4641

TALLEY INDUSTRIES, INC.
3500 North Greenfield Road
Mesa, Arizona 85201
Frank G. Talley, President
(602) 969-7411
See also Eska Company; and
Sun Products Corporation

TALLFELLOW (menswear)
See Lord Jeff Knitting Company
Inc.

TALL'N SLIM (cigars)
See United States Tobacco
Company

TALLOCH (Scotch whiskey)
See Van Munching & Company,
Inc.

TALMADGE FARMS
Lovejoy, Georgia 30250

TALMAN YACHT COMPANY
521 Water Street
Warren, Rhode Island 02885

TALON
(Division of Textron, Inc.)
626 Arch Street
Meadville, Pennsylvania 16335
E.L. Caldwell, Jr., President
(814) 337-1281

Companies and Trade Names

TALON ADHESIVES
160 Passaic Avenue
Kearny, New Jersey 07032
(201) 998-7511

TALSOL CORPORATION
4677 Dewitt Drive
Cincinnati, Ohio 45218
(503) 874-5151

TALWIN (analgesic)
See Winthrop Laboratories

TAM O'SHANTER (tobacco)
See G.A. Georgopulo & Company

TAMA (guitars and drums)
See Elger Company

TAMAK INC.
3328 S.E. Hawthorne Boulevard
Portland, Oregon 97214

TAME (hair-care products)
See Gillette Company

TAMI, INC.
(Subsidiary of Athlone Industries, Inc.)
100 California Street
San Francisco, California 94111
Richard B. Simkalo, President
(415) 956-3330

TAMIAMI TRAIL TOURS, INC.
445 East Tenth Avenue
Hialeah, Florida 33011
R.A. Foster, President
(305) 885-2781

TAMICO FOODS, INC.
4502 West Osborne
Tampa, Florida 33614

TAMMS INDUSTRIES
1222 Ardmore Avenue
Itasca, Illinois 60143
James A. Marko, President
(312) 773-2350

TAMMY LOUNGEWEAR LTD.
31 East 31st Street
New York, New York 10016
(212) 686-3900

TAMPA BAY (food products)
See Treasure Isle Inc.

TAMPA CUBS (cigars)
See Parodi Cigar Corporation

TAMPA ELECTRIC COMPANY
Post Office Box 111
Tampa, Florida 33601
Hugh L. Culbreath, President
(813) 876-4111

TAMPA NUGGETT (cigars)
See Havatampa Cigar Corporation

TAMPAX, INC.
5 Dakota Drive
Lake Success, New York 11040
Thomas F. Casey, Chairman of the Board
(516) 437-8800

TANAC (cold-sore treatment)
See Commerce Drug Company, Inc.

TANATEX CHEMICAL COMPANY
(Division of Sybron Corporation)
Page and Schuyler Avenues
Lyndhurst, New Jersey 07071

TANDBERG OF AMERICA, INC.
8 Third Avenue
Pelham, New York 10803
Kjell S. Hoel, President
(914) 273-9150

TANDLER TEXTILE CORPORATION
104 West 40th Street
New York, New York 10018
(212) 730-1212

TANDY CORPORATION
2727 West Seventh Street
Fort Worth, Texas 76107
John A. Wilson, President
(817) 335-2551
See also Merribee Company; and Tex Tan Walhausen Company

TANFASTIC (tanning aids)
See Sea & Ski Corporation

TANG (breakfast drink)
See General Foods Corporation

TANG BINDER CORPORATION
1001 Roosevelt Avenue
Carteret, New Jersey 07008

TANGEE (women's toiletries)
See Luft-Tangee, Inc.

TANGER CREIGHTON, INC.
350 Fifth Avenue
New York, New York 10001
S.K. Tanger, President
(212) 695-9250

TANGERINE (melamine products)
See Boonton Molding Company, Inc.

TANGLEFOOT COMPANY, THE
314 Straight Avenue S.W.
Grand Rapids, Michigan 49504
(616) 459-4130

TANGO (shoes)
See Brauer Brothers Shoe Company

TANNEL (knit dresses)
See Ginsburg & Abelson, Inc.

Companies and Trade Names

TANNEN FOOD COMPANY, INC.
Albany Post Road
Hyde Park, New York 12538

TANNER OF NORTH CAROLINA
Rutherfordton, North Carolina 28139
James T. Tanner, President
(704) 287-4206

TANNER PECAN COMPANY,
  INC., B.C.
Box 7188
Mobile, Alabama 36607

TANNHAUSER COMPANY,
  ERWIN B.
1776 Broadway
New York, New York 10019
(212) 582-5465

TANNING RESEARCH
832 Halekanwila Street
Honolulu, Hawaii 96814
(808) 524-0510

TANNISHA GREETING CARDS
91-35 193rd Street
Hollis, New York 11423

TANNOY (AMERICA) LIMITED
1756 Ocean Avenue
Bohemia, New York 11716

TANO, INC.
21 East 33rd Street
New York, New York 10016
(212) 684-2896

TANTALINE (company)
  See Willoform Manufacturing
    Company Inc.

TANYA HAWAII CORPORATION
345 Park Avenue
Suite 1639
New York, New York 10022
(212) 644-2100

TANYANA OF CALIFORNIA
1242 North Clybourn Avenue
Burbank, California 91505

TAORMINA COMPANY
225 South 13th
Donna, Texas 78537
(512) 464-3328

TAP-ICER
(Division of Waldon Inc.)
5 Lafayette Avenue
Summit, New Jersey 07901

TAP 'N SET (alarm clocks)
  See General Electric Company

TAPADERA MOTOR INNS
Raley Building
Pendleton, Oregon 97801

TAPE DISPENSER PRODUCTS
Seymour Avenue and Hawkins Street
Derby, Connecticut 06418

TAPE, INC.
Box 1069
Green Bay, Wisconsin 54305
(414) 499-0601

TAPE INDEXES INC.
Evergreen, Colorado 80439

TAPE TAB (disposable diapers)
  See Kendall Company, Consumer
    Division

TAPER-FLITE (water skis and
accessories)
  See Nash Manufacturing, Inc.

TAPPAN COMPANY, THE
Tappan Park
Mansfield, Ohio 44901
W. Richard Tappan, President
(419) 529-6744
  See also Whirl-A-Way Company

TAPPE BROTHERS
4883 East Harvey Avenue
Fresno, California 93727

TAR-GON (tooth whitener)
  See Commerce Drug Company,
    Inc.

TAR RESIDUALS INTERNATIONAL,
  INC.
122 East 42nd Street
New York, New York 10017
(212) 867-0116

TARA (food products)
  See Talmadge Farms

TARANTELLE (bath oil, cologne,
perfume, etc.)
  See Miahati, Inc.

TAREYTON (cigarettes)
  See American Tobacco Company

TARG & DINNER INC.
4100 West 40th Street
Chicago, Illinois 60632
(312) 254-8424

TARGET (hardware, housewares,
paints, etc.)
  See Dash Sales Corporation

TARGET (tobacco)
  See Brown & Williamson
    Tobacco Corporation

TARGET SPORTSWEAR, INC.
(Division of Target Menswear, Inc.)
1290 Avenue of the Americas
New York, New York 10019
Jesse Bayer, President
(212) 541-6800

TARGETWARE (housewares)
  See Borden Chemical Company

Companies and Trade Names

TARMAC PRODUCTS, INC.
38 West 32nd Street
New York, New York 10001
(212) 695-3439

TARNI-SHIELD (tarnish preventive and cleaner)
See 3M Company

TARRSON COMPANY
2762 North Claybourn Avenue
Chicago, Illinois 60614
Philip I. Rosenberg, President
(312) 348-6906

TART & CREAMY (food products)
See Bama Food Products

TARTAN (groceries)
See Alfred Lowry & Brother

TARTAN (tanning aids)
See McKesson & Robbins Drug Company

TARTAN MARINE COMPANY
320 River Street
Grand River, Ohio 44045
(216) 357-5592

TASCO (housewares)
See The Turner & Seymour Manufacturing Company

TASCO SALES INC.
1075 N.W. 71st Street
Miami, Florida 33138
(305) 836-3551

TASIBEL (sisal boucle carpeting)
See Continental Importing Company

TASK-MASTER (lighting fixtures)
See Benjamin (Division of Thomas Industries Inc.)

TASSAWAY, INC.
Post Office Box N
155 South Robertson Boulevard
Beverly Hills, California 90213
Richard Griebel, President
(213) 391-5503

TAST-T (sausage, bologna, and frankfurters)
See Glazier Packing Company

TASTE AMERICA RECIPES (frozen vegetables)
See Green Giant Company

TASTE O'SEA (fish)
See O'Donnell-Usen Fisheries Corporation

TASTE SEALED (food products)
See NCC Food Corporation

TASTE-TELLS (food products)
See P. Herold & Sons

TASTE X (food product)
See Standard Brands, Inc.

TASTEE FREEZ INTERNATIONAL, INC.
(Subsidiary of TFI Companies, Inc.)
1515 Mount Prospect Road
Des Plaines, Illinois 60018
George N. Mitros, President
(312) 694-3900

TASTEFUL (canned foods)
See National Fruit Canning Company

TASTEMAKER MILLS
1185 Avenue of the Americas
New York, New York 10036
(212) 575-3464

TASTEMARK (dairy products and ice cream)
See Foremost Foods Company

TASTERS CHOICE (freeze-dried coffee)
See Nestle Company, Inc.

TASTI DIET (canned foods)
See Tillie Lewis Foods, Inc.

TASTI-FRESH (groceries)
See Independent Wholesale Grocers

TASTI-PAC (food products)
See Bush Brothers & Company

TASTY BAKING COMPANY
2801 Hunting Park Avenue
Philadelphia, Pennsylvania 19129
Paul R. Kaiser, Chairman of the Board
(215) 228-4200

TASTY BLEND (frozen food)
See Jacob Associates, Inc.

TASTY BURGERS (dog food)
See Strongheart Products

TASTY FOODS, INC.
Post Office Box 5546
Denver, Colorado 80217

TASTY PAK (food products)
See Friday Canning Corporation

TASTY POPS (dairy and poultry products)
See Wilson & Company, Inc.

TASTY RICH (food products)
See Food Specialties Inc.

TASTY TOPPINGS, INC.
Post Office Box 728
Columbus, Nebraska 68601

TASTY TREAT (fruit)
See George F. Joseph

Companies and Trade Names

TASTYSNACK, INC.
222 West Main Street
Windsor Park, Pennsylvania 17366
(717) 244-3750

TAT ENGINEERING CORPORATION
744 Washington Avenue
West Haven, Connecticut 06516

TATA INCORPORATED
425 Park Avenue
New York, New York 10022
(212) 751-5620

TATCHER, ERNEST
79 N.W. 92nd Street
Miami, Florida 33147
(305) 751-1390

TATE & LYLE (syrups)
See Perry H. Chipurnoi

TATE PRODUCT DEVELOPMENT
 COMPANY, RAYMOND F.
21423 Pacific Coast Highway
Malibu, California 90265

TATER BAKER (electric baker)
See Everedy Company

TATER BOY (food products)
See Rogers Walla Walla Inc.

TATERSTATE FROZEN FOODS
(Division of Agway Inc.)
Box 218
Wade Road
Washburn, Maine 04786
William H. Prigmore, President
(207) 455-3741

TATO-MIX (food products)
See Douglas Food Corporation

TATRA SHEEP CHEESE COMPANY
15 Harrison Street
New York, New York 10013
(212) 925-7583

TAUNTON-VALE (kitchen accessories)
See Schiller & Asmus Inc.

TAURUS (acrylic floor finish)
See Fuld-Stalfort, Inc.

TAUSCHER & SEITZ (women's dresses)
See James A. Trodden Associates, Inc.

TAVA (liqueur)
See Smirnoff Beverage & Import Company

TAVENER RUTLEDGE (fruit drops)
See The Paul Spitz Company, Inc.

TAVERN (cigars)
See Jacobs Cigar Company

TAWN LTD.
(Division of Foremost-McKesson)
Box 448
Bridgeport, Connecticut 06602
(203) 334-9809

TAX MAN INC.
639 Massachusetts Avenue
Cambridge, Massachusetts 02139

TAX OFFICES OF AMERICA
Box 4098
Waterbury, Connecticut 06714

TAYCO PRODUCTS (ice buckets, bar sets, wine racks)
See George E. Taylor Company, Inc.

TAYLOR (tools, lawn and garden supplies)
See Dealer Supply Company Inc.

TAYLOR & COMPANY, C.S.
Davenport, Florida 33837

TAYLOR & COMPANY, W.A.
(Subsidiary of Hiram Walker, Inc.)
825 South Bayshore Drive
Miami, Florida 33131
Edward Roth, President
(305) 577-5300

TAYLOR & GASKIN INC.
Marine Products Division
6440 Mack Avenue
Detroit, Michigan 48207
(313) 925-9550

TAYLOR & NG
480 Ninth Street
San Francisco, California 94103
(415) 864-3660

TAYLOR & SLEDD, INC.
7420 Ranco Road
Richmond, Virginia 23228
(804) 262-8614

TAYLOR BEDDING
 MANUFACTURING COMPANY
401-419 West Second Street
Taylor, Texas 76574
L.D. Hammack, President
(512) 352-6311

TAYLOR BROTHERS INC.
308 East First
Winston-Salem,
 North Carolina 27101
(919) 722-8171

TAYLOR CHAIN COMPANY,
 INC., S.G.
Box 1009
Hammond, Indiana 46325
(219) 932-2220

TAYLOR CHAIR COMPANY
75 Taylor Street
Bedford, Ohio 44146
J.T. Meals, President
(216) 232-0700

Companies and Trade Names

TAYLOR COMPANY, FRANK F.
Post Office Box 636
Old Leestown Road
Frankfort, Kentucky 40601
Frankie Taylor, President
(502) 223-2311

TAYLOR COMPANY, INC.,
 GEORGE E.
225 Fifth Avenue
New York, New York 10010
(212) 685-2870

TAYLOR COMPANY, INC.,
 NELSON A.
West Ninth Avenue
Gloversville, New York 12078
Willard H. Taylor, President
(518) 725-0681

TAYLOR CORPORATION, E.E.
Freeport, Maine 04032

TAYLOR ENTERPRISE
20442 Kenworth
Huntington Beach, California 92646

TAYLOR-EVANS SEED COMPANY
(Subsidiary of Diamond Shamrock
 Corporation)
Box 480
505 South 87th Avenue
Tulia, Texas 79088
L.J. Dye, President
(806) 995-4111

TAYLOR IMPORTING COMPANY
 See Taylor Linen Company Inc.

TAYLOR INC., LOU
330 Fifth Avenue
New York, New York 10001
(212) 868-7767

TAYLOR INSTRUMENT
(Division of Sybron Corporation)
Arden, North Carolina 28704
Leo M. Storey, Jr., President
(704) 684-8111

TAYLOR LOCK COMPANY
2034 West Lippincott
Philadelphia, Pennsylvania 19132
Jerome Schwartz, President
(215) 223-7766

TAYLOR LTD., EDWARD
(Division of Glenwood Laboratories)
83 North Summit Street
Tenafly, New Jersey 07670

TAYLOR MACHINE WORKS
Highway 15 North
Louisville, Mississippi 39339
William A. Taylor, Jr., President
(601) 773-3421

TAYLOR MAID (fruit)
 See Fruit Growers Service
  Company

TAYLOR OF LONDON (pomanders
and toiletries)
 See Schmid Brothers Inc.

TAYLOR PACKING COMPANY,
 INC., JOHN W.
Hallwood, Virginia 23359
B.M. Bull, President
(804) 824-3431

TAYLOR RENTAL CORPORATION
570 Cottage Street
Springfield, Massachusetts 01104
Jay D. Chapin, President
(413) 781-7730

TAYLOR, SMITH & TAYLOR
 COMPANY, THE
Box 1028
East Liverpool, Ohio 43920

TAYLOR TOT
Post Office Box 636
Frankfort, Kentucky 40601

TAYLOR WINE COMPANY, INC.
County Route 88
Hammondsport, New York 14840
George A. Lawrence, Chairman
 of the Board
(607) 569-2111

TAYLORED CALIFORNIA
2528 East 37th Street
Los Angeles, California 90011
(213) 589-9161

TAYSTEE (bread)
 See American Bakeries Company

TAYSTEE (macaroni products)
 See United States Macaroni
  Manufacturing Company, Inc.

TE TREE (foot cream, ointment, oil)
 See Metabolic Products
  Corporation

TEA & TOAST (cup, saucer, and
plate stand)
 See Endicott-Seymour of Ann
  Arbor

TEA ASSOCIATION OF THE U.S.A.
 INC.
230 Park Avenue
New York, New York 10017
(212) 725-1934

TEA FOR TWO (tea)
 See Royal House Food Products
  Company

TEA HOUSE (tea)
 See McCormick & Company,
  Inc., Schilling Division

TEA KETTLE (freeze-dried foods)
 See Oregon Freeze Dry Foods
  Inc.

Companies and Trade Names

TEAC CORPORATION OF AMERICA
7733 Telegraph Road
Montebello, California 90640
George DeRado, President
(213) 726-0303

TEACHERS (Scotch whiskey)
See Schieffelin & Company

TEACHERS INSURANCE & ANNUITY
ASSOCIATION OF AMERICA
(TIAA)
730 Third Avenue
New York, New York 10017
Thomas C. Edwards, President
(212) 490-9000

TEACHERS PROTECTIVE MUTUAL
LIFE INSURANCE COMPANY
116-118 North Prince
Lancaster, Pennsylvania 17603

TEACHING CONCEPTS INC.
230 Park Avenue
New York, New York 10017
(212) 757-8030

TEAKETTLE (AM transistor radio)
See Guild Radio & Television
Corporation

TEAKITE (lamp bases)
See Angelo Brothers Company

TEAKOE (tea makers)
See Ekco Home Products Company

TEAM CENTRAL INC.
720 29th Avenue S.E.
Minneapolis, Minnesota 55414
(612) 331-8511

TEAM-MATE (clocks)
See Westclox

TEATIME PRODUCTS COMPANY,
THE
3845 North Ravenswood
Chicago, Illinois 60613
(312) 472-7860

TECH (beer)
See Pittsburgh Brewing Company

TECH/NAUTIC CORPORATION
700 Parsippany Road
Parsippany, New Jersey 07054
(201) 386-1444

TECHMATIC (razors)
See Gillette Safety Razor
Company

TECHNICAL HOME STUDY
SCHOOLS
1500 Cardinal Drive
Little Falls, New Jersey 07424
George Duryea, General Manager
(201) 256-4512

TECHNICAL PAPER CORPORATION
729 Boylston Street
Boston, Massachusetts 02116
(617) 266-6070

TECHNICAL PRODUCTS COMPANY
1532 Locust Street
Walnut Creek, California 94596

TECHNICAL TAPE CORPORATION
1 Le Fevre Lane
New Rochelle, New York 10801
Gerald Sauler, President and Chief
Executive Officer
(914) 235-1000
See also Tuck Industries Inc.

TECHNICOLOR INC.
6311 Romaine Street
Hollywood, California 90038
William McKenna, Chairman and
President
(213) 462-6111

TECHNIDYNE INC.
2578 First Street
Livermore, California 94550

TECHNILUBE
Post Office Box 453
Napa, California 94558

TECHNIQUES IN WOOD INC.
8-10 Cairn Street
Rochester, New York 14611
(716) 328-3800

TECHNITE (saws)
See Stanadyne/Capewell

TECHNO TRUCK MANUFACTURING
COMPANY
20850 Saint Clair Avenue
Cleveland, Ohio 44117
(216) 692-3110

TECHNOS (watches)
See Holzer Watch Company Inc.

TECHNYGRAPH COMPANY
36 Skokie Highway
Highland Park, Illinois 60035

TECHSOY (soy products)
See Dirigo Corporation

TECLA COMPANY, INC.
11374 Schaefer Highway
Detroit, Michigan 48227
(313) 834-8083

TECNAR (binoculars and telescopes)
See Swift Instruments Inc.

TECNICA (footwear)
See Vener Associates Inc.

TECNIQUE (hair-care products)
See Shulton, Inc.

TECNUS (footwear)
See Vener Associates Inc.

TECUMSEH PRODUCTS COMPANY
Ottawa and Patterson Streets
Tecumseh, Michigan 49286
W.E. Macbeth, President
(313) 423-8411

Companies and Trade Names

TEDDY (tobacco)
See Gesty Trading and Manufacturing Corporation

TEDDY-TOT (auto seats for babies)
See International Manufacturing Company

TEDRUTH PLASTICS CORPORATION
Box 607
Tedruth Plaza
Farmingdale, New Jersey 07727
(201) 681-7777

TED'S (root bear)
See Monarch-Nugrape Company

TEE-PAK, INC.
2 North Riverside Plaza
Chicago, Illinois 60606
L.E. Russell, President
(312) 782-2020

TEE PEE OLIVES INC.
60 East 42nd Street
New York, New York 10016
(212) 986-8816

TEEM (beverage)
See Pepsi-Cola Company

TEEN (handbags)
See Mighty Midget Leather Goods

TEEN QUEEN (groceries)
See Creasey Company of Kentucky

TEEN SET (misses' coats)
See New York Girl Coat Company, Inc.

TEEN TYPE (shoes)
See Dr. Posner Shoe Company, Inc.

TEENA PAIGE FASHIONS, INC.
1375 Broadway
New York, New York 10018
Morris T. Golder, President
(212) 695-8085

TEENCHARM, INC.
40 Triangle Boulevard
Carlstadt, New Jersey 07072
(201) 933-8400

TEENFORM, INC.
40 Triangle Boulevard
Carlstadt, New Jersey 07072
Morton Sloate, President
(201) 933-8400

TEENIE WEENIE (canned vegetables)
See Oconomowoc Canning Company

TEEPEE HEET (sports heaters)
See Silent Sioux Corporation

TEGRIN (medicated skin cream, shampoo, and soap)
See B.C. Remedy Company

TEICH & COMPANY INC., CURT
1733 West Irving Park Road
Chicago, Illinois 60613
Norman Goldman, Executive Vice President and Secretary
(312) 281-0606

TEJAS MANUFACTURING & SUPPLY INC.
5025 College Street
Beaumont, Texas 77707

TEKMAR CORPORATION
1346 Washington Boulevard
Stamford, Connecticut 06902

TEKTRONIX, INC.
Tektronix Industrial Park
Beaverton, Oregon 97005
Earl Wantland, President
(503) 644-0161

TEL-A-CORDER (telephone-answering device)
See Electronic Concepts Laboratories Inc.

TELANSWERPHONE (telephone-answering service)
See Lin Broadcasting Corporation

TELATTACK (electric protection service)
See American District Telegraph Company

TELAUTOGRAPH CORPORATION
8700 Bellanca Avenue
Los Angeles, California 90045
Bernard Briskin, President and Treasurer
(213) 641-3690

TELCOR INSTRUMENTS, INC.
17785 Sky Park Circle
Irvine, California 92664
(714) 549-3397

TELE-CONTROL (telephone device for turning on or off appliances)
See Electronic Concepts Laboratories Inc.

TELE-TONE COMPANY INC.
444 South Ninth Avenue
Mount Vernon, New York 10550

TELECOM (intercom system)
See Webster Electric Company Inc.

TELECTRO SYSTEMS CORPORATION
96-18 43rd Avenue
Corona, New York 11368
Harry Sussman, President and Sales Manager
(212) 651-8900

Companies and Trade Names

TELECTRON INC.
(Subsidiary of Paklo Companies)
Broward County Airport
Fort Lauderdale, Florida 33310
L.L. Colasurdo, President
(305) 525-6711

TELEDYNE AERO-CAL
(Subsidiary of Teledyne Inc.)
528 East Mission Road
San Marcos, California 92069
(714) 744-1131

TELEDYNE AQUA TEC
1730 East Prospect Street
Fort Collins, Colorado 80521
A.E. Rouse, President
(303) 484-1352

TELEDYNE BIG BEAM
(Subsidiary of Teledyne Inc.)
290 East Prairie Street
Crystal Lake, Illinois 60014
C.J. Ortmeyer, Vice President
(815) 459-6100

TELEDYNE, INC.
1901 Avenue of the Stars
Los Angeles, California 90067
Henry E. Singleton, Chairman of the Board
(213) 277-3311
See also Acoustic Research, Inc.; and Argonaut Insurance Company

TELEDYNE-OSTER
(Subsidiary of Teledyne Inc.)
1340 East 289th Street
Wickliffe, Ohio 44092
(216) 943-3500

TELEDYNE PACKARD BELL
12333 West Olympic Boulevard
Los Angeles, California 90064
R.L. Kiernan, President
(213) 272-6141

TELEDYNE PINES
(Subsidiary of Teledyne Inc.)
601 West New York Street
Aurora, Illinois 60506
A.K. Stewart, President
(312) 896-7701

TELEDYNE POST
(Subsidiary of Teledyne Inc.)
700 N.W. Highway
Des Plaines, Illinois 60016
Joseph D'Annunzio, President
(312) 299-1111

TELEDYNE SPRAGUE ENGINEERING
(Subsidiary of Teledyne Inc.)
19300 South Vermont Avenue
Gardena, California 90248
(213) 327-1610

TELEDYNE WISCONSIN MOTOR
1910 South 53rd Street
Milwaukee, Wisconsin 53246
A.A. Erlinger, President
(414) 384-5800

TELEFINDER CORPORATION
822B Challenge Drive
Concord, California 94520

TELEFLEX INC.
Church Road
North Wales, Pennsylvania 19454
L.K. Black, President and Chief Executive Officer
(215) 699-4861

TELEMARK (ski equipment)
See A & T Ski Company

TELEMATIC (intercom phone system)
See Dictograph Products Inc.

TELEPRO INDUSTRIES INC.
3 Olney Avenue
Cherry Hill, New Jersey 08034

TELESCOPE FOLDING FURNITURE COMPANY, INC., THE
Church Street
Granville, New York 12832
Henry J.W. Vanderminden, III, President
(518) 642-1100

TELESCOPEX (photographic equipment)
See Acme Lite Manufacturing Company

TELETALK (intercom systems)
See Webster Electric Company Inc.

TELETHERM (electric protection service)
See American District Telegraph Company

TELETIME (liquid-crystal watches)
See Gruen Watch Company

TELETONE COMPANY, INC.
444 South Ninth Avenue
Mount Vernon, New York 10550
I. Rothman, President
(914) 699-2100

TELETYPE CORPORATION
(Subsidiary of Western Electric Company)
5555 Touchy Avenue
Skokie, Illinois 60076
Floyd C. Boswell, President
(312) 982-2000

TELEX CORPORATION
41st and Sheridan
Tulsa, Oklahoma 74101
Roger M. Wheeler, Chairman of the Board
(918) 627-2333

TELEX COMMUNICATIONS
(Division of The Telex Corporation)
9600 Aldrich Avenue South
Minneapolis, Minnesota 55420
(612) 884-4051

Companies and Trade Names

TELFA (sterile pads)
See Kendall Company

TELKEE INC.
Route Number 452
Glen Riddle, Pennsylvania 19037

TELL CHOCOLATE NOVELTIES
CORPORATION
3052-78 West 21st
Brooklyn, New York 11224
(212) 266-4651

TELL CITY CHAIR COMPANY
Tell City, Indiana 47586
(812) 547-3491

TEM TASTY (seafood)
See Gorton, Slade & Company, Inc.

TEMCO, INC.
4101 Charlotte Avenue
Nashville, Tennessee 37202
M.A. Rice, President
(615) 297-7551

TEMDE (household-lighting equipment)
See Koch & Lowy Inc.

TEMO CANDY COMPANY, C.L.
495 West Exchange Street
Akron, Ohio 44302

TEMP-MAT (insulation)
See Pittsburgh Corning Corporation

TEMP-MATE (thermometers)
See Sapphire Products Inc.

TEMPCO QUILTERS
414 First Avenue South
Seattle, Washington 98104
(206) 623-4194

TEMPERGLAS (glass containers)
See Brockway Glass Company

TEMPEST (radios, tape recorders, phonographs, high-intensity lamps, dry batteries)
See Azad International Inc.

TEMPLATE (modular desks and credenzas)
See Lehigh-Leopold Furniture Company

TEMPLE CORPORATION
7905 Calumet Avenue
Munster, Indiana 46321

TEMPLE-STUART COMPANY
Holman Street
Baldwinville, Massachusetts 01436
Benjamin F. Stuart, President
(617) 939-5342

TEMPLETON, KENLY & COMPANY
16th and Gardner Road
Broadview, Illinois 60153
R.A. Ward, Chairman, President and Treasurer
(312) 865-1500

TEMPLINE (thermometers)
See Republic Drug Company, Inc.

TEMPMASTER (air conditioners)
See Otasco

TEMPO (beer)
See G. Heileman Brewing Company, Inc.

TEMPO (books)
See Grosset & Dunlap Inc.

TEMPO (cigarettes)
See R.J. Reynolds Tobacco Company

TEMPO (speakers)
See Oxford Speaker Company

TEMPO (sports accessories and equipment)
See Silva Company

TEMPO (TV-table sets)
See Cal-Dak Industries, Inc.

TEMPO (trumpets, saxophones, clarinets, etc.)
See King Musical Instruments

TEMPO CHEMICAL COMPANY
47-02 Fifth Street
Long Island City, New York 11101
(212) 784-3374

TEMPO LINGERIE
136 Madison Avenue
New York, New York 10016
(212) 725-6800

TEMPO OF CALIFORNIA (men's sportswear)
See American Sportsman Manufacturing Company

TEMPO PRODUCTS COMPANY
6200 Cochran Road
Cleveland, Ohio 44139
(216) 248-1450

TEMPO/VOGUE (housewares)
See Kromex

TEMPOS (insulated containers)
See Thermos (Division of King-Seeley Thermos Company)

TEMPOS (shoes for women)
See Brown Group, Inc.

TEMPTOR (food products)
See Big Stone Canning Company

Companies and Trade Names

TEMT (food product)
  See Dubuque Packing Company

TEN-DA BRAND FROZEN FOODS, INC.
Birney Avenue
Route 11
Moosic, Pennsylvania 18507
Harry Kanoff, Chairman and President
(717) 457-6742

TEN DAY BEAUTY SET (shampoo and conditioning cream)
  See Tintair, Inc.

TEN FORTY (portable typewriters)
  See Remington Rand Office Machines (Division of Sperry Rand Corporation)

TEN HIGH (whiskey)
  See Hiram Walker, Inc.

TEN-O-SIX (facial cleanser, shampoo)
  See Bonne Bell, Inc.

TEN TWENTY (tobacco)
  See Lane Limited

TENCO (coffee)
  See Coca-Cola Company

TEND-R-AGED (meat tenderizer)
  See Meat Seasonings, Inc.

TENDER (inflatable boat)
  See Hispania Motors Inc.

TENDER COOK (seasonings, sauces, extracts)
  See Burgie Foods Company

TENDER FACE (liquid preshave)
  See J.B. Williams Company Inc.

TENDER-GUARDIAN (infants' product)
  See Stacy Manufacturing Company Inc.

TENDER KARE (juvenile products)
  See Pines of America Inc.

TENDER LEAF (tea)
  See Standard Brands

TENDER LOVING CARE (fabric softener)
  See Colgate-Palmolive Company

TENDER TIDE (food products)
  See Mark 7 Seafood & Industries

TENDER TOUCH (skin-care products)
  See Helene Curtis Industries, Inc.

TENDER VITTLES (cat products)
  See Ralston Purina Company

TENDERAGE (food products)
  See Big Stone Canning Company

TENDERPAK (food products)
  See King Pharr Canning Operations Inc.

TENDERSWEET (canned vegetables)
  See Schepps Grocer Supply, Inc.

TEND'R MILD (food products)
  See Rath Packing Company

TENDRA (meat tenderizer)
  See Marx Pure Foods Inc.

TENEX COMPANY
125 Third Avenue S.E.
Cedar Rapids, Iowa 52401

TENNA-GROUN (lighting arrestor)
  See Layton Industries

TENNA MANUFACTURING COMPANY, THE
19201 Cranwood Parkway
Cleveland, Ohio 44128
Harvey Ludwig, Chairman of the Board
(216) 475-1400

TENNA-ROTOR (antenna rotator)
  See Alliance Manufacturing Company Inc.

TENNANT SONS & COMPANY OF NEW YORK, C.
100 Park Avenue
New York, New York 10017
Sidney E. Sweet, President
(212) 679-1300

TENNECO, INC.
Tenneco Building
Post Office Box 2511
Houston, Texas 77001
Bruce B. Conway, Director of Consumer Affairs and Community Relations
(713) 229-4211
  See also Case Company, J.I.; and Davis Manufacturing, Inc.

TENNECO CHEMICALS, INC.
(Division of Tenneco, Inc.)
Park 80 Plaza West
Saddle Brook, New Jersey 07662
R.H. Marks, President
(201) 646-3800

TENNESSEE (food products)
  See Winter Garden Inc.

TENNESSEE DULCIMER WORKS
(Division of Tut Taylor Music Inc.)
500 Arlington Avenue
Nashville, Tennessee 37210

TENNESSEE FARM (meat products)
  See Neuhoff Brothers Packers, Inc.

Companies and Trade Names

TENNESSEE INDUSTRIES
201 Jackson State Bank Building
Jackson, Tennessee 38301

TENNESSEE MAT COMPANY
1400 Third Avenue South
Nashville, Tennessee 37210
(615) 254-8381

TENNESSEE PHARMACEUTICAL
  COMPANY
Box 16396
1231 Raines Road East
Memphis, Tennessee 38116
(901) 379-0302

TENNESSEE TISSUE MILLS
507 Mapleleaf Drive
Metro Industrial Park
Nashville, Tennessee 37210
(615) 889-6794

TENNESSEE WALKER (whiskey)
  See Schenley Industries Inc.

TENNSCO CORPORATION
Post Office Box 606
Dickson, Tennessee 37055
(615) 446-8035

TENNYSON (cigarettes)
  See American Brands, Inc.

TENNYSON (cigars)
  See G.W. Van Slyke & Horton

TENSION ENVELOPE
  CORPORATION
19th and Campbell Streets
Kansas City, Missouri 64108
E. Bertram Berkley, President
(816) 471-3800

TENSON (sports apparel)
  See Vener Associates Inc.

TENSOR CORPORATION
333 Stanley Avenue
Brooklyn, New York 11207
Jay Monroe, President
(212) 649-2000

TEPROMARK INTERNATIONAL INC.
206 Mosher Avenue
Woodmere, New York 11598
(516) 569-4533

TER MAR INC.
Box 998
Lehigh Acres, Florida 33936

TERADO CORPORATION
1068 Raymond Avenue
Saint Paul, Minnesota 55108
(612) 646-2868

TERESA (food products)
  See NCC Food Corporation

TERI (paper towels)
  See Kimberly-Clark Corporation

TERMINAL SALES CORPORATION
12871 Eaton Avenue
Detroit, Michigan 48227
(313) 491-0606

TERMINAL TRANSPORT COMPANY
248 Chester Avenue, S.E.
Atlanta, Georgia 30316
John F. Spickerman, President
(404) 524-5831

TERMINEX INTERNATIONAL, INC.
(Affiliation of Cook Industries, Inc.)
2185 Democrat Road
Memphis, Tennessee 38118
Henry M. Tobey, President
(901) 396-8600

TERRA-LITE (soil conditioner)
  See W.R. Grace & Company,
    Construction Products
    Division

TERRA MAJOR (ovenware, serving
ware)
  See Peter Breck Corporation

TERRA NEW (polishes, waxes)
  See S.C. Johnson & Son

TERRA SANCTA GUILD
Post Office Box 1776
Broomall, Pennsylvania 19008

TERRA-TWILL (men's coats)
  See Isaac Cohen & Son
    Clothes Company Inc.

TERRA-VERDE (lawn and garden
supplies)
  See Arett Sales Corporation

TERRACE CERAMICS INC.
Post Office Box 2068
Zanesville, Ohio 43701

TERRAMAR INDUSTRIES LTD.
Box 114
Pelham, New York 10803

TERRATRAC (tractors)
  See J.I. Case Company

TERREPLANE MOUNTAIN
  COMPANY, THE
Box Six
Longbranch, Washington 98351

TERRIER (towels)
  See Sardo Textile Corporation

TERRY PRODUCTS, INC.
(Subsidiary of Forest Laboratories,
  Inc.)
963 Newark Avenue
Elizabeth, New Jersey 07208

Companies and Trade Names

TESSER DISPOSABLE PRODUCTS
COMPANY
307 East 44th Street
New York, New York 10017
(212) 687-2066

TESSINA (cameras)
See Karl Heitz, Inc.

TEST CORPORATION
Post Office Box Five
Dania, Florida 33004
Robert Graf, President
(305) 920-7800

TEST LABORATORIES, INC.
7121 Canby Avenue
Reseda, California 91336

TESTED PAPERS OF AMERICA
230 North Michigan Avenue
Chicago, Illinois 60601
(312) 726-1163

TESTED PRODUCTS COMPANY
3901 North Kingshighway Boulevard
Saint Louis, Missouri 63115
(314) 383-1234

TESTOR CORPORATION, THE
620 Buckbee
Rockford, Illinois 61101
Charles D. Miller, President
(815) 962-6654

TESTRITE INSTRUMENT COMPANY,
INC
135 Monroe Street
Newark, New Jersey 07105
(201) 589-6767

TETERS FLORAL PRODUCTS
COMPANY
1425 South Lillian Avenue
Bolivar, Missouri 65613
H. Tiffin Teters, President
(417) 326-7654

TETLEY (tea)
See Beech-Nut, Inc.

TETROID COMPANY, INC.
1 Utica Street
Hamilton, New York 13346

TEWELES SEED COMPANY
1600 Oregon Street
Muscatine, Iowa 52761
Robert L. Teweles, President
(319) 263-0142

TEX (beer)
See Jackson Brewing Company

TEX-KNIT (ironing-board covers)
See Textile Mills Company

TEX 'N' JEANS (boys' apparel)
See Mann Manufacturing
Company

TEX TAN WELHAUSEN COMPANY
(Division of Tandy Corporation)
Post Office Box 431
Yoakum, Texas 77995
Carson R. Thompson, President
(512) 293-2311

TEXACO, INC.
135 East 42nd Street
New York, New York 10017
John K. McKinley, President
(212) 953-6000

TEXACORT (scalp-care product)
See Texas Pharmacal Company

TEXAN (flashlights, lanterns, etc.)
See Fulton Manufacturing
Company

TEXAS & PACIFIC RAILWAY
(Subsidiary of Missouri Pacific
Railroad Company)
210 North 13th Street
Saint Louis, Missouri 63103
John H. Lloyd, President
(314) 622-0123

TEXAS BOOT COMPANY
(Division of United States Shoe
Corporation)
Lebanon, Tennessee 37087
Harry Vise, Chairman of the Board
(615) 444-5440

TEXAS CHILI COMPANY
3313 North Jones
Fort Worth, Texas 76106
(817) 626-0983

TEXAS CITRUS EXCHANGE
Box 480
Edinburg, Texas 78539

TEXAS COFFEE COMPANY
3300 Point Arthur Road
Beaumont, Texas 77705
(713) 835-3434

TEXAS COMMERCE BANK
712 Main Street
Houston, Texas 77001
John T. Cater, President
(713) 236-4865

TEXAS ELECTRIC SERVICE
COMPANY
Seventh and Lamar Streets
Fort Worth, Texas 76102
W.G. Marquardt, President
(817) 336-9411

TEXAS FARM PRODUCTS COMPANY
915 South Fredonia
Nacogdoches, Texas 75961
Joe Wright, President
(713) 564-3711

TEXAS FEATHERS INC.
Post Office Box 1118
Brownwood Industrial Park
Brownwood, Texas 76801
William C. Carpenter, President
(915) 646-1504

TEXAS GOLD (citrus products)
See Bordo Products Company

Companies and Trade Names

TEXAS INTERNATIONAL AIRLINES, INC.
8451 Lockheed Street
Houston, Texas 77017
Francisco A. Lorenzo, President
(713) 644-3471

TEXAS MAGIC (food products)
See Knapp-Sherrill Company

TEXAS PETE (food products)
See T.W. Garner Food Company

TEXAS PHARMACAL COMPANY
(Subsidiary of Werner-Lambert Company)
Box 1659
307 East Josephine Street
San Antonio, Texas 78206
Ward S. Hagan, President
(512) 223-3281

TEXAS POWER & LIGHT COMPANY
Fidelity Union Life Building
Post Office Box 6331
Dallas, Texas 75222
J.F. Skelton, President
(214) 748-5411

TEXAS RECREATION CORPORATION
Box 539
Wichita Falls, Texas 76307

TEXAS-TENNESSEE INDUSTRIES INC.
See Igloo Corporation

TEXASWARE
See Plastics Manufacturing Company

TEXFAB TRADING CORPORATION
15 Park Row
New York, New York 10038
(212) 233-8020

TEXIZE CHEMICALS COMPANY
(Division of Morton-Norwich Products, Inc.)
Post Office Box 368
Greenville, South Carolina 29602
Jack F. Mayer, President
(803) 277-4021

TEXJOY (coffee)
See Texas Coffee Company

TEXOLITE (wall paint)
See United States Gypsum Company

TEXOMA (lawn and garden supplies, sporting goods)
See Roberts Sanford & Taylor Company

TEX'S ROLL-O'-DOUGH (novelty)
See Grove Tex Industries

TEXSTAR PLASTICS
Post Office Box 1530
Grand Prairie, Texas 75051
E.I. Jones, President
(214) 263-4111

TEXSUN (soft drink)
See Royal Crown Cola Company

TEXSUN CORPORATION
(Subsidiary of Royal Crown Cola Company)
522 South Texas Boulevard
Weslaco, Texas 78596
Howard Lombard, President
(512) 968-2141

TEXTILE IMPORT CORPORATION
135 West 50th Street
New York, New York 10020
(212) 581-2840

TEXTILE MACHINE WORKS
Foundry Division
Box 1382
Reading, Pennsylvania 19603

TEXTILE MILLS COMPANY
1066 Clinton Avenue
Irvington, New Jersey 07111
Herb Glatt, President
(201) 399-1500

TEXTOE (hosiery, pantyhose)
See Premtex Hosiery Company Inc.

TEXTOL COMPANY INC.
753 North Britain Road
Irving, Texas 75060

TEXTONE (plastic paint)
See United States Gypsum Company

TEXTROL (protein additive for baked goods)
See Central Soya

TEXTRON, INC.
40 Westminster Street
Providence, Rhode Island 02903
G. William Miller, Chairman of the Board
(401) 421-2800
See also Alvin Company; Bostitch; Eaton Paper Company; Gorham Company; Gorham-Reizart; Homelite Company; Maico Hearing Instruments; Polaris; Sheaffer Pen Company, W.A.; Speidel Corporation; and Talon

TEXTURED YARN COMPANY INC.
Post Office Box 376
Route One
Kennet Square, Pennsylvania 19348
Ira Schwartz, President
(215) 444-5400

THACHER MARINE INC.
Box 340
Lisle, Illinois 60532

Companies and Trade Names

THAI IMPORTS
Post Office Box 35
Essex, Massachusetts 01929

THALHIMER BROTHERS, INC.
615 East Broad Street
Richmond, Virginia 22319
William B. Thalhimer, Jr.,
   Chairman of the Board
(703) 643-4211

THALLMATES (shoes)
   See Desco Shoe Corporation

THAMES PECAN COMPANY, H.M.
Box 2206
Mobile, Alabama 36601

THANK YOU (canned fruits and vegetables)
   See Michigan Fruit Canners, Inc.

THANX LABORATORIES, INC.
Bradford, Pennsylvania 16701

THARAUD & SON, JUSTIN
Post Office Box 190
Maplewood, New Jersey 07040

THAT DESIGNING WOMAN (boutique specialties and costume jewelry)
   See Frieda Gratzon

THAT DOUBLE SEAT PANTY (panties)
   See Isaacson-Carrico Manufacturing Company

THAT MAN (men's toiletries)
   See Revlon, Inc.

THATCHER GLASS
   MANUFACTURING COMPANY
(Division of Dart Industries Inc.)
2 Corporate Park Drive
White Plains, New York 10604
(914) 694-5900

THAT'S MY COLOR (hair coloring)
   See Shulton, Inc.

THAWZ (windshield deicer)
   See Household Research Corporation

THAYER COMPANY, HENRY
61 Moulton Street
Cambridge, Massachusetts 02138
(617) 876-3313

THAYER, INC.
205 School Street
Gardner, Massachusetts 01440
Catherine Theis, President
(617) 632-2780

THAYER, INC. (drug products)
   See Mitchum-Thayer, Inc.

THAYER SCALE
(Division of Cutler-Hammer, Inc.)
Thayer Park
Pembroke, Massachusetts 02359
Frank S. Hyer, President
(617) 826-2371

THELMA LU'S INC.
5823 Lomas Boulevard N.E.
Albuquerque, New Mexico 87110

THEOBALD INDUSTRIES
Foot of Sanford Avenue
Kearny, New Jersey 07032
Harry Theobald, President
(201) 991-6500

THEONEX (tree-would dressing, gardening books)
   See Hydroponic Chemical Company

THER-A-PEDIC ASSOCIATES INC.
225 North Avenue
Garwood, New Jersey 07027

THERA-BLEM (acne treatment)
   See Noxell Corporation

THERA-MEDIC INC.
168 Rose Drive
Birmingham, Alabama 35215

THERA-PLAST COMPANY, INC.
132 Nassau
New York, New York 10038
(212) 233-6036

THERADYNE CORPORATION
Post Office Box 458
Jordan, Minnesota 55352
Richard D. Moroney, President
(612) 266-4263

THERLAND DRUG COMPANY
20 Farmington Avenue
Hartford, Connecticut 06105

THERMA-WARE (tumblers, cups, mugs, steins)
   See Giftsware Corporation

THERMABOOT (shoes and shoe materials)
   See Bristol Manufacturing Corporation

THERMADOR
(Division of Norris Industries)
5119 South District Boulevard
Los Angeles, California 90040
A.S. Fernandez, President
(213) 588-6131

THERMAFLO (heated blanket)
   See Fieldcrest Mills, Inc.

THERMAKOOL (insulated tumblers)
   See Kraftware Corporation

THERMALENE PRODUCTS INC.
Post Office Box 709
Deland, Florida 32720
(904) 734-6075

Companies and Trade Names

THERMASOL, LTD.
101 Park Avenue
New York, New York 10011
Murray Altman, President
(212) 684-7766

THERMI-WEAR (insulated tumblers and cups)
  See J.P. Gits Moulding Company

THERMO-CHEM CORPORATION
Post Office Box 15457
8141 East 44th Street
Tulsa, Oklahoma 74115
(918) 836-8841

THERMO CHINA (food warmers)
  See Cornwall Corporation

THERMO ELECTRON ENGINE CORPORATION
711 East 15 Mile Road
Sterling Heights, Michigan 48077
(313) 264-1200

THERMO-FAX (office machines)
  See 3M Company

THERMO-JAC (sportswear)
  See Grove Company

THERMO-JAR (insulated container)
  See Aladdin Industries Inc.

THERMO KING CORPORATION
314 West 90th Street
Minneapolis, Minnesota 55420
J.C. Sheehan, President
(612) 887-2300

THERMO-SERV COMPANY
(Division of West Bend)
2939 Sixth Avenue North
Anoka, Minnesota 55303
(612) 421-2224

THERMO TRAY (electric food warmers)
  See Cornwall Corporation

THERMOCAP (electric heating cap)
  See Kaz, Inc.

THERMOFILTER (pipes)
  See Whitehall Products, Inc.

THERMOGAS, INC.
(Subsidiary of Mapco, Inc.)
4509 East 14th
Des Moines, Iowa 50333
M. Maher, Vice President
(515) 265-3431

THERMOID
(Division of H.K. Porter Company, Inc.)
Porter Building
Pittsburgh, Pennsylvania 15219
R.W. Davison, General Manager
(412) 391-1800

THERMOLIER (unit heaters)
  See ITT Grinnell Corporation

THERMOLITE (lamps)
  See Emeralite (Division of NL Corporation)

THERMOLYNE CORPORATION
(Subsidiary of Sybron Corporation)
2555 Kerper Boulevard
Dubuque, Iowa 52001
B.S. Payne, Jr., President
(319) 556-2241

THERMOMETER CORPORATION OF AMERICA
(Division of A-T-O, Inc.)
567 East Pleasant Street
Springfield, Ohio 45505
J.B. Twiggs, President
(513) 325-0456

THERMOPANE (insulating glass)
  See Libbey-Owens-Ford Company

THERMOPHORE (exercise equipment)
  See Battle Creek Equipment Company

THERMOS
(Division of King-Seeley Thermos Company)
Thermos Avenue
Norwich, Connecticut 06360
(203) 887-1671

THERMOSEAL GLASS CORPORATION
400 Water Street
Gloucester City, New Jersey 08030
(609) 456-3109

THERMOTAINER (roll and food warmer)
  See McGraw Edison Company

THERMOTAPE (heater)
  See Smith-Gates Corporation

THERMOWAVE (hair-setting lotion)
  See Clairol, Inc.

THERMWELL PRODUCTS COMPANY, INC.
150 East Seventh Street
Paterson, New Jersey 07524
David B. Gerstein, President
(201) 271-5000

THETFORD CORPORATION
2300 Washtenaw
Ann Arbor, Michigan 48106
Ronald J. Sargent, Co-Chairman and President
(313) 769-6000

THEURGENE CHEMICAL COMPANY
11325 Olson Highway
Minneapolis, Minnesota 55427

THEXTON MANUFACTURING COMPANY
7019 Oxford Street
Minneapolis, Minnesota 55426
(612) 920-1650

THIBAUD (oboes)
  See DEG Music Products Inc.

Companies and Trade Names

THIBAULT MILLING COMPANY
Tenth and Fairpoint
Little Rock, Arkansas 72202
(501) 372-7232

THIBOUVILLE (clairnets)
  See Ardsley Musical Instruments
      Corporation

THICK & FROSTY (milk shake)
  See General Foods

THICK & THIRSTY (paper towels)
  See Kimberly-Clark Corporation

THEMANN BROTHERS, INC.
500 York Street
Cincinnati, Ohio 45214
(503) 241-6124

THIES PACKING COMPANY, INC.
Post Office Box 49
South Main Street
Great Bend, Kansas 67530
J.M. Thies, President
(316) 792-1311

THINGS FROM RED MOUNTAIN
Red Mountain Road Seven
Arlington, Vermont 05250

THINKING PIANIST-ORGANIST
(musical instruction method)
  See Raucher Music Company

THINLINE (watchbands)
  See Speidel

THINZ (diet food)
  See Alva/Amco Pharmacal
      Companies, Inc.

THIOKOL CORPORATION
Post Office Box 27
Bristol, Pennsylvania 19007
(215) 946-9150

THIRD EYE
210 East 36th Street
New York, New York 10016
(212) 532-1768

THIRST AID (food products)
  See Joseph Middleby, Jr., Inc.

THIRSTEE SMASH (fruit drinks)
  See Borden, Inc., Dairy &
      Services Division

38 (varnish)
  See Pratt & Lambert, Inc.

THISTLE (Scotch)
  See Monsieur Henri Wines, Ltd.

THOFRA
Post Office Box 308
Sausalito, California 94965

THOM MCAN (shoes)
  See Melville Shoe Corporation

THOMAS' (baked goods)
  See Thomas Frozen Foods

THOMAS & COMPANY INC.,
  P.L.
393 Seventh Avenue
New York, New York 10001
(212) 947-7475

THOMAS & HOWARD COMPANY
1942 Laurel Street
Columbia, South Carolina 29202
T. Howard Timberlake, President
(803) 788-5520

THOMAS & SONS INC., WILLIAM
Slocum Avenue
Ridgefield, New Jersey 07657
  See also Avant Products

THOMAS & THOMPSON COMPANY
101 East Baltimore Street
Baltimore, Maryland 21202
(301) 727-2960

THOMAS A. EDISON (major
appliances)
  See McGraw-Edison Company

THOMAS COFFEE COMPANY
525 East Hillcrest Road
York, Pennsylvania 17403

THOMAS COMPANY, THE
485 Smith Street
Farmingdale, New York 11735
(516) 293-8600

THOMAS HOLMES CORPORATION
Suite B-Six
Benson East
Jenkintown, Pennsylvania 19046
  See also Sulray Products

THOMAS INDUSTRIES, INC.
207 East Broadway
Louisville, Kentucky 40202
T.R. Fuller, President
(502) 582-3771
  See also Benjamin Electric
      Manufacturing Company

THOMAS ORGAN COMPANY
(Division of Warwick Electronics,
Inc.)
7310 North Lehigh Avenue
Chicago, Illinois 60648
Thomas Archer, General Manager
(312) 647-0770

THOMAS PAPER COMPANY INC.,
  P.L.
393 Seventh Avenue
New York, New York 10001
(212) 947-7475

THOMAS SANITARY PRODUCTS
  COMPANY
35 South College
Akron, Ohio 44308

Companies and Trade Names

THOMAS, SETH
(Division of General Time
  Corporation)
135 South Main
Thomaston, Connecticut 06787

THOMAS STUART (menswear)
  See J. Schoeneman Inc.

THOMAS TEXTILE, INC.
112 West 34th Street
New York, New York 10001
Thomas J. Swartz, President
(212) 947-7591

THOMAS U.S.A. LTD.
411 East 76th Street
New York, New York 10021
(212) 249-1400

THOMAS WEBB (lead crystal)
  See Crown Lynn Ceramics (USA)
    Ltd.

THOMASTON MILLS
Thomaston, Georgia 30286
William H. Hightower, Jr.,
  Chairman of the Board
(404) 647-7131

THOMASVILLE FURNITURE
  INDUSTRIES, INC.
(Subsidiary of Armstrong Cork
  Company)
Thomasville, North Carolina 27360
Tom A. Finch, President
(919) 475-1361

THOMPSON (mirrors)
  See Paul D. Quinn

THOMPSON (sprinklers)
  See Leisure Group

THOMPSON (whiskey)
  See Schenley Industries, Inc.

THOMPSON BOAT COMPANY
Highway 41
Peshtigo, Wisconsin 54157
Saul Padek, President
(715) 582-4515

THOMPSON CANDY COMPANY,
  THE
80 South Vine Street
Meriden, Connecticut 06450
Knowlton H. White, President
(203) 235-2541

THOMPSON COMPANY,
  GEORGE S.
366 Coral Circle
El Segundo, California 90245

THOMPSON COMPANY, THE
  HENRY G.
277 Chapel
New Haven, Connecticut 06505
Walter L. Wise, Jr., President
(203) 772-0770

THOMPSON COMPANY, INC.,
  E.A.
1333 Gough Street
San Francisco, California 94109
Edward A. Thompson, President
(415) 346-8610

THOMPSON COMPANY, J.
  WALTER
420 Lexington Avenue
New York, New York 10017
Don Johnston, President
(212) 686-7000

THOMPSON COMPANY, JOHN R.
(Subsidiary of Green Giant
  Company)
29 West Randolph Street
Chicago, Illinois 60601
J.R. Sebastian, President
(312) 298-8500

THOMPSON COMPANY,
  WILLIAM T.
23529 South Figueroa Street
Wilmington, California 90745
William T. Thompson, President
(213) 830-5550

THOMPSON DESIGNS INC.
445 Factory Road
Addison, Illinois 60101

THOMPSON FARMS COMPANY
1440 West 47th Street
Chicago, Illinois 60609
John E. Thompson, Chairman and
  President
(312) 927-6020

THOMPSON-HAYWARD CHEMICAL
  COMPANY
(Subsidiary of North American
  Philips Company)
5200 Speaker Road
Kansas City, Kansas 66106
P.L. Lonnecker, President
(913) 321-3131

THOMPSON, INC., M.R.
767 Fifth Avenue
New York, New York 10022
(212) 752-5700

THOMPSON INDUSTRIES
  COMPANY
2501 East Magnolia
Phoenix, Arizona 85034
(602) 275-4711

THOMPSON INTERNATIONAL,
  INC.
200 East Thomas Road
Phoenix, Arizona 85012
(602) 264-6231

THOMPSON MEDICAL COMPANY,
  INC.
919 Third Avenue
New York, New York 10022
Moses Ratowsky, President
(212) 688-4420

Companies and Trade Names

THOMPSON PACKAGING
NOVELTIES INC.
(Division of James Thompson
Company)
1133 Avenue of the Americas
New York, New York 10036
(212) 757-4120

THOMPSON'S (malted milk)
See Borden, Inc.

THOMPSON'S (prepared food mix)
See Hushpuppy Corporation of
America, Inc.

THOMPSON'S (waterproofing and
sealing compound)
See E.A. Thompson Company
Inc.

THOMSON COMPANY
1290 Avenue of the Americas
New York, New York 10019
J. Gordon Buss, Chairman of the
Board
(212) 581-7590

THOMSON INDUSTRIES, INC.
1029 Plandome Road
Manhasset, New York 11030
John B. Thomson, President
(516) 883-8000

THOR (batteries)
See General Battery Corporation

THOR POWER TOOL COMPANY
(Subsidiary of Stewart Warner
Corporation)
175 North State Street
Aurora, Illinois 60505
Bennett Archambault, President
(312) 898-8000

THORCO (mirrors)
See Richards Morganthou
Company, Inc.

THORENS (record changers, music
works, etc.)
See Elpa Marketing Industries

THORN (pipes)
See Yello-Bole Pipes, Inc.

THORN CANDY
MANUFACTURING COMPANY
413 Fillmore Street
Amarillo, Texas 79101

THORNE'S (Scotch)
See Hiram Walker, Inc.

THORNTON MINOR OINTMENT
COMPANY
Box 498
Excelsior Springs, Missouri 64024

THORO-FED (pet foods)
See Kal Kan Foods Inc.

THORO PRODUCTS COMPANY
6611 West 58th Place
Arvada, Colorado 80002

THORO SYSTEM (protective
coatings)
See Standard Dry Wall Products,
Inc.

THOROBRED COMPANY, INC.,
THE
Waynesville, Ohio 45068

THOROFARE MARKETS, INC.
Post Office Box 120
Youngstown, Ohio 44501
T.L. Harshbarger, President
(216) 792-9051

THOROFOM (carpet and upholstery
shampoo)
See J.W. Gibson Company Inc.

THOROGOOD (work shoes)
See Weinbrenner Shoe Company

THOROSEAL (waterproofing paint)
See Standard Dry Wall Products

THOROUGHBRED REMEDY
CORPORATION
251 Hempstead Turnpike
Elmont, New York 11003

THORPE INC., DOROTHY C.
7990 San Fernando Road
Sun Valley, California 91352
(213) 875-1151

THORPE INDUSTRIES INC.
1137 Route 22
Mountainside, New Jersey 07092

THORSON SOAP LAKE PRODUCTS
COMPANY
Soap Lake, Washington 98851

THOUGHT FACTORY
Post Office Box 5515
Sherman Oaks, California 91413

THRALL-MATES (shoes)
See Desco Shoe Corporation

THREADS, INC.
Bessemer City Road
Gastonia, North Carolina 28054
Dan Maddox, President
(704) 867-7271

3 BEARS (wine)
See Southland Wine Company

THREE BEES (honey and honey
spread)
See Sioux Honey Association

THREE B's LTD., THE
Post Office Box One
Great Falls, Virginia 22066

3-C (canned foods)
See Clement Pappas & Company

Companies and Trade Names

THREE CAPTAINS (cutlery)
See P.R. Myers & Company

THREE CASTLES (tobacco)
See American Tobacco Company

3-D WEST
Box 692
Payette, Idaho 83661

THREE DAGGER (Jamaica rum)
See Schieffelin & Company

THREE DIAMOND (food and fish products)
See Mitsubishi International Corporation

THREE FEATHERS (whiskey and gin)
See Schenley Industries Inc.

THREE FISH BRAND (seafood)
See Mutual Fish Company Inc.

3-IN-ONE OIL (household oil, motor oil, lubricant)
See Boyle-Midway

THREE LITTLE KITTENS (cat food)
See Lipton Pet Foods, Inc.

3M COMPANY
3M Center
Saint Paul, Minnesota 55101
F.M. Metcalfe, Vice President, Consumer Affairs
(612) 733-1670
See also Broemmel Pharmaceuticals, Riker Laboratories Inc; Commercial Tape & Gift Wrap; and Paper Products

THREE MOUNTAINEERS, INC.
40 Simpson Street
Asheville, North Carolina 28803
Hugh C. Brown, Jr., Chairman of the Board
(704) 253-9851

THREE NEW YORKERS (closet and boudoir accessories)
See Invento Products Corporation

3P INDUSTRIES, INC.
Post Office Box 242
Oakland, New Jersey 07436

THREE SISTERS (canned foods)
See D. Thompson Swing, Inc.

THREE STAR (cognac)
See Belgrave, Ltd.

THREE STAR (food products)
See NCC Food Corporation

THREE STAR (seafood)
See Norwegian Fish Importers, Inc.

THREE UNDER (shirts, sweaters)
See Jantzen Inc.

THRIF-T-PAK (vegetables)
See Patterson Frozen Foods Inc.

THRIFT DRUG COMPANY
(Division of J.C. Penney Company, Inc.)
615 Alpha Drive
Pittsburgh, Pennsylvania 15238
Louis L. Avner, President
(412) 781-5373

THRIFT VALUE (lawn and garden tools)
See Douglas Products

THRIFTEE (adhesives, paints, polishes, masking and electric tapes, etc.)
See Copper Chemicals Company

THRIFTEE (mops)
See W.E. Kautenberg Company

THRIFTCHECK SERVICE COMPANY
(Division of Diebold Inc.)
700 Dowd Avenue
Elizabeth, New Jersey 07201

THRIFTIMART, INC.
1837 South Vermont
Los Angeles, California 90006
Robert E. Laverty, Chairman of the Board
(213) 732-6271

THRIFTMONEY (pantyhose)
See Kayser-Roth Hosiery Company Inc.

THRIFTY (hardware, sporting goods, electrical supplies)
See Coast to Coast Stores

THRIFTY DRUG STORES, INC.
5051 Rodeo Road
Los Angeles, California 90016
L.H. Straus, President
(213) 293-5111

THRIFTY RENT-A-CAR SYSTEM
2400 North Sheridan Road
Tulsa, Oklahoma 74115

THRILL (liquid detergent)
See Procter & Gamble Company

THRIVO COMPANY, INC.
919 North Front
Philadelphia, Pennsylvania 19123
(215) 925-4356

THRU-STYLE (vinyl asbestos tile)
See Congoleum-Nairn, Inc.

THRU-WALL (air conditioners)
See Sunwarm Inc.

THUMBELINA (frozen shrimp)
See Ward Foods, Inc.

Companies and Trade Names

THUNDERBIRD (men's coats)
See Goodstein Brothers & Company, Inc.

THUNDERBIRD JR. (motor vehicles)
See Grand Prix Manufacturing Company, Inc.

THUNDERBIRD PRODUCTS CORPORATION
Post Office Box 501
Decatur, Indiana 46733
(219) 724-9111

THUNDERWEAR (underwear and sportswear)
See Duofold Inc.

THURMAN'S INC.
3916 Crooked Run Road
North Versailles, Pennsylvania 15137
Frank W. Creager, President
(412) 664-4128

THURON INDUSTRIES
(Subsidiary of Zoecon Inc.)
12200 Denton Drive
Dallas, Texas 75234
(214) 247-7141

THURSTON MOTOR LINES, INC.
601 Johnston Road
Charlotte, North Carolina 28201
Doc J. Thurston, Jr., President
(704) 334-2813

THYMO BORINE LABORATORY
3100 West Villard Avenue
Milwaukee, Wisconsin 53209
(414) 462-6710

THYMOLAC COMPANY
32 Skillen Street
Buffalo, New York 14207
(716) 876-8218

THYSSEN STEEL/NEW YORK
1114 Avenue of the Americas
New York, New York 10036
(212) 764-0500

TI-DEE (mops, applicators, buckets, brooms)
See Emsco-Erie

TIA MARIA (coffee liqueur)
See W.A. Taylor & Company

TIA MARIA (food products)
See Hickmott Canning Company

TIARA (gold or platinum flatware)
See The Lotus Glass Company

TIARA (portable televisions)
See Philco-Ford Corporation

TIARA (tables)
See Gordon's, Inc.

TIBER PRESS
40 East 12th Street
New York, New York 10003
(212) 777-8383

TICHENOR ANTISEPTIC COMPANY, DR. G.H.
Box 53374
1700 Baronne Street
New Orleans, Louisiana 70113
(504) 523-7377

TICHNOR BROTHERS, INC.
1249 Boylston Street
Boston, Massachusetts 02215
Robert M. Tichnor, President and General Manager
(617) 226-7010

TICKYTRON (cameras)
See Camera Specialty Company Inc.

TID-BIT (meat snacks)
See Fairmont Foods Company

TID-BIT PRODUCTS COMPANY
17212 Miles Avenue
Cleveland, Ohio 44128
(216) 751-0777

TIDBITS (women's shoes)
See Midland Shoe Company

TIDDY'S (Canadian liqueur)
See Twenty One Brands, Inc.

TIDE (detergent)
See Procter & Gamble Company

TIDE CRAFT INC.
Box 796
Minden, Louisiana 71055

TIDE RIDE BOARDING RAMPS
2340 West Eighth Lane
Hialeah, Florida 33010

TIDEWATCH YACHTS INC.
98 Preston Terrace
Marshfield, Massachusetts 02050

TIDEWATER BOATS INC.
Box 1571
Annapolis, Maryland 21404

TIDY HOUSE PRODUCTS
See Church & Dwight Company, Inc.

TIE BREAKER (tennis rackets)
See Rawlings Sporting Goods Company

TIE-IT-ON (produce)
See F.H. Cubberly Fruit Company

TIE-TIE PRODUCTS
See CPS Industries Inc.

Companies and Trade Names

TIEDEMANNS (tobacco)
See Overseas Commodex Corporation

TIERNEY SPECIALTIES
1021 El Camino Avenue
Stockton, California 95207

TIERRA (furniture)
See Consolidated Furniture Industries

TIFFANY (chairs)
See Dennix Products Company

TIFFANY & COMPANY
Fifth Avenue and 57th Street
New York, New York 10022
Henry B. Platt, President
(212) 755-8000

TIFFANY APPAREL, INC.
152 Madison Avenue
New York, New York 10016
(212) 683-1820

TIFFIN GLASS COMPANY, INC.
(Subsidiary of Interpace Corporation)
Fourth Avenue and Vine Street
Tiffin, Ohio 44883

TIFFINY UNIFORMS
7144 Furnace Branch Road
Glen Burnie, Maryland 21061
(301) 761-5775

TIGER (batteries)
See Hamway Import Company

TIGER (cheese)
See Atalanta Trading Corporation

TIGER (thumbtacks, paper fasteners, staples, and parcel handles)
See Noesting Pin Ticket Company Inc.

TIGER BRAND (ale and porter)
See C. Schmidt & Sons, Inc.

TIGER BRITCHES (men's slacks)
See Barrow Manufacturing Company

TIGER COMPANY INC., F.S.
325 West Jackson Boulevard
Chicago, Illinois 60606
(312) 263-3521

TIGER HEAD (ale)
See C. Schmidt & Sons, Inc.

TIGER PAW (tires)
See Uniroyal, Inc.

TIGER ROSE (wine)
See Kasser Distillers Products Corporation

TIGER TAMER (furniture)
See Burris Industries, Inc.

TIJUANA SMALLS (cigars)
See General Cigar Company

TILE-GLO (tile cleaner)
See Hadco Corporation

TILE-TEX (tile and flooring products)
See The Flintkote Company

TILLAMOOK COUNTY CREAMERY ASSOCIATION
Post Office Box 313
Tillamook, Oregon 97141
Roy Dunn, President
(503) 842-4481

TILLER MASTER
Box 1901
Newport Beach, California 92663

TILLERS (garden tractors)
See MTD Products Inc.

TILLEY LADDERS COMPANY INC., JOHN S.
100 Second Street
Watervliet, New York 12189
Lewis S. Howland, President
(518) 273-0030

TILLIE LEWIS FOODS, INC.
(Subsidiary of Ogden Corporation)
Fresno and Charter Way
Stockton, California 95201
Arthur H. Heiser, President
(209) 946-4011

TILLOTSON-PEARSON INC.
Post Office Box 60
Route 136
Warren, Rhode Island 02885
E.A. Person, President
(401) 245-1200

TILLY TAILS (seafood)
See East Coast Fisheries Inc.

TILO (tile cleaner)
See Pactra Industries, Inc.

TILO COMPANY, INC.
(Subsidiary of Reynolds Metals Company)
347 Longbrook Avenue
Stratford, Connecticut 06497
Emmet B. Thompson, President
(203) 375-3331

TILT-A-BABE (infants' product)
See International Manufacturing Company

TILT ALARM (security alarm)
See Hall Industries Inc.

TILTON & COOK COMPANY
38 Spruce Street
Leominster, Massachusetts 04153
George H. Cook, Jr., President
(617) 534-8389

Companies and Trade Names

TIMARK
801 South Elmhurst Avenue
Mount Prospect, Illinois 60056

TIMBER ENGINEERING COMPANY
5530 Wisconsin Avenue
Washington, D.C. 20015
Ralph H. Glass, President
(202) 654-8288

TIMBERLAND PRODUCTS
COMPANY, INC.
11801 Industrial Area Drive
Jacksonville, Florida 32218

TIMBERLANE MANUFACTURING
COMPANY
2571 Timber Lane
Dayton, Ohio 45414

TIMBERLINE (cologne and aftershave)
See Mem Company

TIMBERLINE (sportswear for men)
See Brill Brothers, Inc.

TIMBERLINE ARTISTS PUBLISHING
INC.
2130 South Platte River Drive
Denver, Colorado 80223

TIME & TIDE INC.
Box 127
Boca Raton, Florida 33432

TIME-AID (timer with buzzer)
See Paragon Electric Company,
Inc.

TIME-ALL (appliance timer)
See International Register
Company

TIME CAPSULE (solid-state liquid-
crystal digital watch)
See Elgin Watch Company Inc.

TIME, INC.
Time and Life Building
New York, New York 10020
James R. Shepley, President
(212) 586-1212

TIME MACHINE (home hair dryer)
See Schick, Inc.

TIME SAVER (ammonia, vinegar,
sauces)
See Erbrich Products, Inc.

TIME SAVER (mops)
See W.E. Kautenberg Company

TIME SAVER FOOD STORES, INC.
5243 Canal Boulevard
New Orleans, Louisiana 70124
(504) 486-7221

TIME SAVER TOOL CORPORATION
7006 Indianapolis Boulevard
Hammond, Indiana 46323

TIME SAVING PRODUCTS (tools,
lubricants)
Post Office Box 218-A
Villanova, Pennsylvania 19085
(215) 527-4320

TIME-SAVING PRODUCTS
(Division of Com-Pak Chemical
Corporation)
223 South Holmes Street
Shakopee, Minnesota 55379

TIME TESTED (paints)
See Glidden-Durkee (Division
of SCM Corporation)

TIMELY (food products)
See NCC Food Corporation

TIMELY TOYS, INC.
61 Greenpoint Avenue
Brooklyn, New York 11222
Stanley B. Zimmerman, President
(212) 383-4444

TIMES MIRROR COMPANY, THE
Times Mirror Square
Los Angeles, California 90053
Robert Erburn, President
(213) 625-2345
See also Abrams, Inc., Harry
N.; New American
Library, Inc.; and
Newsday, Inc.

TIMESAVER (suits)
See Koret of California, Inc.

TIMEX (watchbands)
See Harline, Inc.

TIMEX CORPORATION
Waterbury, Connecticut 06720
Martin Siem, President
(203) 758-1911

TIMKEN COMPANY, THE
1835 Dueber Avenue, S.W.
Canton, Ohio 44706
H.E. Markley, President
(216) 453-4511

TIMPTE INDUSTRIES, INC.
5990 North Washington Street
Denver, Colorado 80216
Thomas W. Gamel, President
(303) 893-3366

TIN-TONE COSMETIC COMPANY
Box 152
Rural Free Delivery 4
Saugerties, New York 12477

TINA MARINA (dresses)
See Puritan Fashions Corporation

TINDER BOX INTERNATIONAL INC.
1723 Cloverfield Boulevard
Santa Monica, California 90404

TING (acne treatment)
See Pharmacraft

Companies and Trade Names

TINGLEY RUBBER CORPORATION
200 South Avenue
South Plainfield, New Jersey 07080

TINKERBELL (children's toiletry sets)
   See Tom Fields Ltd.

TINKERTOY
(Division of Questor Education
   Products Company)
1055 Bronx River Avenue
Bronx, New York 10472
(212) 991-9000

TINTAIR, INC.
430 Myrtle Avenue
Bridgeport, Connecticut 06604
(203) 368-2538

TINTEX (fabric dye)
   See Knomark, Inc.

TINTILLATE (hair-care products)
   See Helena Rubinstein, Inc.

TINY-LITE (flashlights)
   See Brownie Manufacturing
      Company

TINY TIM (pipes)
   See Buescher's Cob Pipes

TINY TOT (exercisers, bottle bibs, swings, etc. for infants)
   See Village Manufacturing
      Corporation

TINYLITE (lights)
   See Drake Manufacturing
      Company

TIO PEPE (sherry)
   See Austin, Nichols & Company,
      Inc.

TIONA (cigars)
   See S. Frieder & Sons Company

TIP (cigars)
   See Lorillard (Division of Loew's
      Theatres Inc.)

TIP-A-DENT (tooth-care product)
   See Pick-A-Dent Corporation

TIP-O-MINT (cigars)
   See General Cigar Company,
      Inc.

TIP TONI (hair permanent)
   See Gillette Company, Personal
      Care Division

TIP TOP (bakery products)
   See Ward Foods, Inc.

TIP TOP (citrus beverage)
   See Doric Foods Corporation

TIP TOP (fruits, vegetables)
   See Seneca Foods Corporation

TIP TOP (juicer)
   See Rival Manufacturing Company

TIP-TOP (seafood)
   See F.J. O'Hara & Sons Inc.

TIP TOP
(Division of Faberge, Inc.)
16th and Cuming Street
Omaha, Nebraska 68102
(402) 348-9150

TIP TOP CANNING COMPANY
Box 106
Tipp City, Ohio 45371
(513) 667-3713

TIPARILLO (cigars)
   See General Cigar Company

TIPO (wine)
   See United Vintners Inc.

TIPPA (portable typewriters)
   See Adler Business Machines
      Inc.

TIPPERMINT (cigars)
   See General Cigar Company,
      Inc.

TIPPY'S TACO HOUSE INC.
2853 West Illinois
Dallas, Texas 75233
(214) 331-4406

TIPSCO COMPANY INC.
99 Tracy Place
Hewlett, New York 11557

TIPSTER (cigars)
   See Bayuk Cigars, Inc.

TIPTON (cigars)
   See American Cigar

TIQUE/TONE (paint)
   See Bruning Paint Company,
      Inc.

TISKET-TASKET (toiletries)
   See Avon Products, Inc.

TISSOT WATCH COMPANY
(Division of Omega Watches)
301 East 57th Street
New York, New York 10022
Robert E. Morris, President
(212) 753-5100

TITAN (battery)
   See General Battery Corporation

TITAN (folding chairs)
   See Hampden Specialty Products
      Corporation

TITAN (ironstone)
   See Lipper International Inc.

Companies and Trade Names

TITAN (money safes)
See Gary Safe Company

TITAN (portable electric heater)
See Rival Manufacturing Company

TITAN (tools, lawn and garden supplies, electrical supplies)
See Budrow & Company

TITAN EDGE (hand and power tools)
See Budrow & Company

TITAN PLASTICS CORPORATION
129 Hudson Avenue
New York, New York 10013
(212) 966-4330

TITCHE-GOETTINGER
(Subsidiary of Allied Stores)
Main, Elm and Saint Paul
Dallas, Texas 75201
Harvey Sanford, President
(214) 748-4811

TITEFLEX
(Division of Atlas Corporation)
603 Hendee Street
Springfield, Massachusetts 01109
Robert O. Cooling, President
(413) 739-5631

TITELITE (lights)
See Drake Manufacturing Company

TITLEIST (golf balls)
See Acushnet Sales Company

TOAST-R-CAKE (toaster cakes)
See Thomas Frozen Foods

TOASTEES (toaster cakes)
See Howard Johnson Grocery Products

TOAST'EM (frozen pastries)
See General Foods Corporation

TOASTETTES POP-UPS (fruit-flavored toaster products)
See Nabisco, Inc.

TOASTMASTER (electrical appliances)
See McGraw-Edison Company

TOASTWICHES (frozen food)
See General Mills, Inc.

TOBACCO CANDY (sugarless candy with a tobacco flavor for former smokers)
See Sugarless Candy Corporation of America

TOBER BASEBALL MANUFACTURING COMPANY INC.
Box 210
Rockville, Connecticut 06066

TOBER-SAIFER SHOE MANU-FACTURING COMPANY, INC.
1520 Washington Avenue
Saint Louis, Missouri 63103
Harold E. Tober, President
(314) 421-2030

TOBI INC. (contemporary home furnishings)
See Trans-Ocean-Bridge, Inc.

TOBIAS (trousers and tops)
See A-1 Kotzin Company

TOBIN PACKING COMPANY, INC.
900 Maple Street
Rochester, New York 14611
John Watson, President
(716) 436-4600

TOBLER (chocolates and hard candy)
See Chocolat Tobler American Corporation

TOBY THE TIGER (toy chests)
See Safco Products Company

TODAY (cigarettes)
See Brown & Williamson Tobacco Corporation

TODAY (irons)
See Sunbeam Corporation

TODAYS (canned foods)
See Del Monte Corporation

TODAYS CHOICE (potato chips, flour, and mayonnaise)
See Associated Grocers of Alabama, Inc.

TODD (tools)
See M.W. Robinson Company

TODD CHEMICAL COMPANY, INC.
9 Chelsea Place
Great Neck, New York 11022

TODD COMPANY, A.M.
Box 711
Kalamazoo, Michigan 49005
(616) 343-2603

TODD COMPANY, INC., E.M.
Hermitage Road and Lehigh
Richmond, Virginia 23220
(703) 359-5051

TODD ENTERPRISES INC.
530 Wellington Avenue
Cranston, Rhode Island 02910
(401) 467-2750

TODD SHIPYARDS CORPORATION
1 State Street Plaza
New York, New York 10004
(212) 344-6900

TODDLERS EDUCATION INC.
240 West 40th Street
New York, New York 10018

Companies and Trade Names

TODDLETIME (baby clothes)
See J.C. Penney Company

TODDY (cold-water coffee maker)
See Tracy Dawson & Associates

TODRIN, MOSES
259 West 30th Street
New York, New York 10001
(212) 244-6225

TOE-FLEX (foot remedies)
See Scholl, Inc.

TOGIAK FISHERIES INC.
2366 Eastlake Avenue East
Seattle, Washington 98102
(206) 329-5910

TOIDEY COMPANY INC., THE
4320 Ardmore Avenue
Fort Wayne, Indiana 46804

TOILETRIES
(Division of the J.B. Williams
 Company Inc.)
767 Fifth Avenue
New York, New York 10022
(212) 752-5700

TOILETTE (toilet trainers and seats)
See Century Products Inc.

TOKAY (tea)
See New Orleans Import
 Company, Ltd.

TOKAY (tobacco)
See A. Oppenheimer & Company

TOKELAND (seafood)
See Nelson Crab, Inc.

TOKO (skis and wax)
See Medalist Sports International

TOLEDO EDISON COMPANY
300 Madison Avenue
Toledo, Ohio 43652
John P. Williamson, President
(419) 259-5000

TOLEDO METAL FURNITURE
 COMPANY
1100 Hastings Street
Toledo, Ohio 43607
R.E. Surface, President
(419) 536-4651

TOLIBIA CHEESE, INC.
45 East Scott Street
Fond du Lac, Wisconsin 54935
(414) 921-3500

TOLL ROAD (restaurant franchise)
See Marriott Corporation

TOLLYCRAFT CORPORATION
2200 Clinton Avenue
Kelso, Washington 98626
Robert M. Tollefson, Chairman of
 the Board
(206) 383-5160

TOLONA PIZZA PRODUCTS
 CORPORATION
2501-13 West Armitage Avenue
Chicago, Illinois 60647
Francis Ponticelli, President
(312) 489-5050

TOM BURNS (whiskey)
See Barton Brands, Ltd.

TOM CAT MEN'S TOILETRIES
22 East 17th Street
New York, New York 10003
(212) 242-4443
See also Emboy Company

TOM MOORE (cigars)
See Bayuk Cigars, Inc.

TOM MOORE (whiskey)
See Barton Brands, Ltd.

TOM SAWYER (boys' wear)
See Elder Manufacturing Company

TOM SAWYER (children's toys)
See Avalon Industries, Inc.

TOM SAWYER MOTOR INNS
3142 Third Avenue North
Saint Petersburg, Florida 33713

TOM SCAT (cat deterrent)
See Pierpont Products Company

TOM SWIFT (shoes)
See Herbst Shoe Manufacturing
 Company

TOM THUMB (canned foods)
See Draper Canning Company

TOM THUMB (canned foods)
See Tony Downs Foods Company

TOM THUMB FOOD MARKETS
6700 Penn Avenue South
Richfield, Minnesota 55423

TOM THUMB STORES, INC.
(Subsidiary of Cullum Companies,
 Inc.)
14303 Inwood Road
Dallas, Texas 75240
Jack W. Evans, President
(214) 351-3751

TOM TOM (fruits)
See United Marketing Exchange

TOM-TOM LABORATORIES
413 Sharp
Glenwood, Iowa 51534

TOMA (chocolates)
See Mason Candy Company

TOMAHAWK (ale)
See Iroquois Industries, Inc.

Companies and Trade Names

TOMATO MAGIC (canned foods)
  See Stanislaus Food Products Company

TOMCO INC.
Post Office Box 308L
Racine, Wisconsin 53401
V.T. Thomas, General Manager
(414) 639-2233

TOMELLEM COMPANY
Lock Box 45
Calico Rock, Arkansas 72519

TOMIC GOLF & SKI MANUFACTURING INC.
23102 Mariposa Avenue
Torrance, California 90502

TOMLINSON OF HIGH POINT, INC.
305 West High Avenue
High Point, North Carolina 27260
William A. Tomlinson, President
(919) 885-2121

TOMMEE TIPPEE (infant accessories)
  See Westland Plastics, Inc.

TOMMIES (pajamas)
  See Chadbourn Inc.

TOMMY TRAVELER (luggage, travel and desk accessories)
  See Brecher Brothers, Inc.

TOMMY TUCKER (groceries)
  See Thomas & Howard Company

TOMMY TUCKER INC.
Post Office Box 28
Tarzana, California 91356

TOMMY'S SPANISH FOODS, INC.
2030 East Walnut
Fullteron, California 92631

TOMORROW (cigarettes)
  See Brown & Williamson Tobacco Corporation

TOMOS (outboard motors)
  See Recreational Equipment Company

TOMPKINS LABEL SERVICE
3207 Frankford Avenue
Philadelphia, Pennsylvania 19134
(215) 739-4509

TOM'S FOODS, LTD.
(Subsidiary of General Mills, Inc.)
Eighth Street and Tenth Avenue
Columbus, Georgia 31901
J.W. Feighner, President
(404) 323-2721

TON-HI (produce)
  See Regal Fruit Cooperative Inc.

TON-TEX CORPORATION
247 Pearl Street N.W.
Grand Rapids, Michigan 49502
William H. Beaman, Jr., President and Treasurer
(616) 456-1737

TONE (guitar-string lubricant, guitar polish and cleaner, lacquer polish/protector, mouthpiece cleaner, etc.)
  See Chem-Pak Inc.

TONE (toilet soap)
  See Armour & Company

TONEKA (corn remover, cough syrup, soap, etc.)
  See Cel-Ton-Sa Medicine Company

TONELLI (accordions and accessories)
  See Empire Music Company Inc.

TONETIC (paint and varnish)
  See Pratt & Lambert, Inc.

TONETTE (home permanent)
  See The Gillette Company

TONETTE (musical training instruments)
  See Chicago Musical Instrument Company

TONI (hair-care products)
  See Gillette Company, Personal Care Division

TONI TODD (dresses)
  See R. & M. Kaufmann

TONKA CORPORATION
10505 Wayzata Boulevard
Minneapolis, Minnesota 55343
Dale R. Olseth, President
(612) 544-9171
  See also Vogue Dolls, Inc.

TONKA TOYS
(Division of Tonka Corporation)
5300 Shoreline Boulevard
Mound, Minnesota 55364
(612) 472-8000

TONKIN (sports accessories and equipment)
  See Vener Associates Inc.

TONY KENT (boys' wear)
  See Santone Industries, Inc.

TOOLKRAFT CORPORATION
Plainfield Street
Chicopee, Massachusetts 01013
Joseph Deliso, President
(413) 737-3591

TOOLMASTER (pocket tool kit)
  See Bayes Manufacturing Company, Inc.

1329

Companies and Trade Names

TOOTAL (men's hosiery)
See Bill & Caldwell, Inc.

TOOTSIE ROLL INDUSTRIES, INC.
7401 South Cicero Avenue
Chicago, Illinois 60629
Melvin Gordon, President
(312) 581-6100

TOOTSIETOY
(Division of Strombecker Corporation)
600 North Pulaski
Chicago, Illinois 60624
(312) 638-1000

TOP-ALL (frozen foods)
See Pearl Grange Fruit
Exchange Inc.

TOP BRASS (hair-care products and deodorant)
See Revlon, Inc.

TOP CHOICE (dog food)
See General Foods Corporation

TOP DOG (meats)
See Sigman Meat Company, Inc.

TOP DOLLAR STORE, INC.
(Subsidiary of Sav-a-Stop, Inc.)
Jasper, Alabama 35501
J.G. Mitnick, President
(205) 384-5526

TOP FLAVOR (food products)
See National Preserve Company

TOP FLIGHT INDUSTRIES, INC.
6831 South Bell
Chicago, Illinois 60636
(312) 737-0370

TOP FLIGHT STAINLESS (cutlery)
See Burrell Cutlery Company, Inc.

TOP-FLITE (stainless-steel tableware)
See Stanley Roberts Company

TOP FLITE MODELS, INC.
2635 South Wabash Avenue
Chicago, Illinois 60616
M. Schlesinger, President
(312) 842-3381

TOP FROST (shrimp, turkeys, chicken dinners)
See Topco Associates Inc.

TOP-HAT (air freshener, knife sharpener, refrigerator deodorants, etc.)
See Earle Harmon Products Inc.

TOP JOB (household cleaner)
See Procter & Gamble Company

TOP MARK (frozen produce)
See United Foods, Inc.

TOP MILLS INC.
112 West 34th Street
New York, New York 10001
(212) 564-4762

TOP MOST (coffee, canned foods)
See General Grocer Company

TOP NOTCH (rubber footwear)
See Uniroyal, Inc.

TOP-O-MART CLOTHES COMPANY
217 Peach Street
Vineland, New Jersey 08360
Mrs. Josephine Barse, President
(609) 692-7920

TOP PRO (tennis equipment)
See National Sporting Goods Corporation

TOP QUALITY (groceries)
See Kothe, Wells & Bauer Company, Inc.

TOP SECRET (hair-color restorer)
See Albin of California Inc.

TOP SECRET (wallets)
See Craftsman Billfolds

TOP VALUE ENTERPRISES, INC.
3085 Woodman Drive
Dayton, Ohio 45420
William P. Rynyan, President
(513) 298-0333

TOPANGA SUN PRODUCTS
Post Office Box 124
Topanga, California 90290

TOPAZ HOSIERY MILLS INC.
350 Fifth Avenue
New York, New York 10001
(212) 695-0525

TOPAZE (cookware)
See Wheaton-Durand, Inc.

TOPCO ASSOCIATED INC.
7711 Gross Point
Skokie, Illinois 60076
Robert D. Fenn, President and General Manager
(312) 676-3030

TOPCON (cameras)
See Paillard Inc.

TOPEKA (mowers)
See American Hoist & Derrick Company

TOPICALS (shoes)
See Edison Brothers Stores, Inc.

TOPIT COMPANY
365 Broadway
Hillsdale, New Jersey 07642

Companies and Trade Names

TOPLESS (lipstick)
See Coty

TOPLINER (infants' product)
See Strolee of California

TOPMOST (food products)
See General Grocer Company

TOPP COLA COMPANY
Crestmont and Haddon Avenues
Camden, New Jersey 08103

TOPP ELECTRONICS, INC.
4201 N.W. 77th Avenue
Miami, Florida 33166
Louis Topp, Chairman of the Board
(305) 887-6201

TOPPER (automotive vinyl-top refinish)
See Sem Products Inc.

TOPPER (men's ties)
See Beau Brummel Ties

TOPPER (ski equipment)
See Turski Corporation

TOPPER CORPORATION
107 Trumbull Street
Elizabeth, New Jersey 07206
Henry D. Clarke, Jr., President
(201) 351-4400

TOPPING TIME (food products)
See Eat-All Frozen Food Company

TOPPS CHEWING GUM, INC.
254 36th Street
Brooklyn, New York 11232
Joel J. Shorin, President
(212) 768-8900

TOPPS PRODUCTS CORPORATION
(Division of Cole National Corporation)
930 Newark Avenue
Jersey City, New Jersey 07306

TOPRITER DIVISION INC.
175 Pearl Street
Brooklyn, New York 11201
(212) 858-6204

TOPS (shoes)
See Bristol Manufacturing Corporation

TOPS FOR TOTS (infants' product)
See Thayer Inc.

TOPS MANUFACTURING COMPANY INC.
1 Park Lane
Mount Vernon, New York 10552

TOPSAIL (men's sportswear)
See Alps Sportswear Manufacturing Company Inc.

TOPSALL (canned foods)
See Hungerford Packing Company, Inc.

TOPSPOT TOY COMPANY INC.
200 Fifth Avenue
New York, New York 10010
(212) 989-0050

TOPSY'S INTERNATIONAL, INC.
215 East 18th Street
Kansas City, Missouri 64108
James T. House, President
(816) 221-2511

TOPWAVE (seafood products)
See Pan-Pacific Fisheries

TOR INTERNATIONAL INC.
393 North Corona Street
Denver, Colorado 80218

TORCH LABORATORIES INC.
542 Industrial Park Drive
Yeadon, Pennsylvania 19050

TORI INTERNATIONAL ENTERPRISES INC.
764 Industrial Way
San Carlos, California 94070

TORIC (tools, electrical supplies)
See Bass & Sons Inc.

TORIGIAN LABORATORIES
218-20 98th Avenue
Queens Village, New York 11429

TORINO (Italian foods)
See J. Ossola Company

TORINO (men's shoes)
See Arthur M. Leopold Inc.

TORINO (pipes)
See Comoy's of London

TORK TIME CONTROLS INC.
1 Grove Street
Mount Vernon, New York 10551

TORO BRAVO (wines)
See Wine Merchants Ltd.

TORO COMPANY, THE
8111 Lyndale Avenue South
Bloomington, Minnesota 55420
David T. McLaughlin, President
(612) 888-8801

TORONADO (water skis and accessories)
See Medalist Water Sports

TOROWARE (cooking utensils)
See Leyse Aluminum Company

1331

Companies and Trade Names

TORQUE MANUFACTURING
COMPANY
712 North 34th Street
Seattle, Washington 98103
(206) 632-5700

TORRE PRODUCTS COMPANY,
INC.
479 Washington
New York, New York 10013
(212) 925-8989

TORRES (wines)
　See Charles Morgensten &
　Company

TORRINGTON COMPANY
59 Field Street
Torrington, Connecticut 06790
R.G. O'Connell, President
(203) 482-9511

TORSCH CANNING COMPANY
Milford, Delaware 19963
(302) 422-8075

TORSION BALANCE COMPANY
125 Ellsworth Street
Clifton, New Jersey 07012
C.S. Wesley, President
(201) 473-6900

TORTOLANI CRISLU
141 Nevada
El Segundo, California 90245
(213) 332-3444

TORTUE (body and bath cosmetics)
　See Polly Bergen Company

TOSCANELLI (cigars)
　See Petri Cigar Company

TOSCANY IMPORTS LTD.
245 Fifth Avenue
New York, New York 10016
Harold Pothtar, President
(212) 683-9576

TOSHIBA AMERICA, INC.
280 Park Avenue
New York, New York 10017
Yoshihiro Nagatake, President
(212) 557-0200

TOSHOKU AMERICA INC.
551 Fifth Avenue
New York, New York 10017
(212) 661-5400

TOSSE & COMPANY, INC., E.
Box 150
Englewood, New Jersey 07631

TOSS'EMS (disposable bottles)
　See Evenflo Products

TOT-L-JUMPER (juvenile product)
　See Kewaunee Equipment
　Company

TOT-ROCKER (juvenile furniture)
　See Century Products Inc.

TOT SEAT (juvenile product)
　See Toidey Company Inc.

TOT WALKER (walker for infants)
　See Dennis Mitchell Industries

TOTAL (cereal)
　See General Mills, Inc.

TOTAL-CARE MACHINE WORKS
INC.
330 Tompkins Avenue
Staten Island, New York 10304
(212) 442-2176

TOTAL LEONARD, INC.
East Superior Street
Alma, Michigan 48801
Phillipe Dunoyer, President
(517) 463-1161

TOTELINE (serving trays)
　See Rockwell International
　Toteline Products

TOTEM BAGS (plastic bags)
　See Gulf Oil Corporation

TOTEM POLE (seafoods)
　See Ivar Wendt Inc.

TOTEM SEA FOODS COMPANY
Tenakee Springs, Arkansas 99841

TOTES, INC.
East Kemper Road
Loveland, Ohio 45140
Bradford E. Phillips, President
(513) 683-6000

TOTINO'S FINER FOODS
7350 Commerce Lane
Fridley, Minnesota 55432
Rod Miley, President
(612) 571-7350

TOTIZO, INC.
360 North Bedford Drive
Beverly Hills, California 90210

TOTLINER (juvenile product)
　See Hedstrom Company

TOTS COMPANY
99 Tracy Place
Hewlett, New York 11557

TOTSY MANUFACTURING
COMPANY INC.
Biegelow Street
Holyoke, Massachusetts 01040
(413) 536-0510

TOUCH-A-MATIC (lamps)
　See Eagle Electric Manufacturing
　Company Inc.

TOUCH & GLOW (makeup)
　See Revlon, Inc.

1332

Companies and Trade Names

TOUCH & SEW (sewing machines)
See Singer Company

TOUCH DOWN (pens)
See W.A. Sheaffer Pen Company

TOUCH-N-COOK (electric range)
See Frigidaire (Division of General Motors Corporation)

TOUCH OF SWEDEN (body lotion)
See Dow Chemical Company

TOUCH-TRONIC (electric toothbrush)
See Teledyne Aqua Tec

TOUCHE (touch-operated lamp)
See Hall-Barkan Opticon

TOUCH'N TONE (colored aluminum paint)
See Master Bronze Powder Company, Inc.

TOUCH'N'TOAST (toaster)
See Sunbeam Appliance Company

TOUR-A-BED (travel cribs)
See Questor Juvenile Furniture (Division of Questor Corporation)

TOURAINE PAINTS, INC.
1760 Revere Beach Parkway
Everett, Massachusetts 02149
John S. Anderson, President
(617) 387-4690

TOURNAMENT (marine products-- boats accessories, fishing gear, etc.)
See August Spindler & Sons Inc.

TOURNAMENT (tennis equipment)
See National Sporting Goods Corporation

TOURNEAU, INC.
500 Madison Avenue
New York, New York 10022
Saul Sadow, President
(212) 758-3265

TOURNEUR CUSTOM COSMETICS
542 LaGuardia Place
New York, New York 10012
(212) 254-8440

TOURNUS (copperware)
See Schiller & Asmus Inc.

TOUROBE (luggage)
See Hartmann Luggage Company, Inc.

TOVARISCH (liquors)
See American Distilling Company, Inc.

TOWER (typewriter)
See Sears Roebuck & Company

TOWER CANDY COMPANY
1388 West 70th Street
Cleveland, Ohio 44102
(216) 651-4468

TOWER INDUSTRIES, INC.
10643 South Norwalk Boulevard
Santa Fe Springs, California 90670
James Stull, President
(213) 944-9911

TOWLE MANUFACTURING COMPANY
260 Merrimac Street
Newburyport, Massachusetts 01959
E.W. Mulligan, President
(617) 462-7111
See also Ellis-Barker Silver Company; and Poole Silver Company

TOWLSAVER, INC.
2639 South Garfield Avenue
Los Angeles, California 90040
(213) 728-7317

TOWMOTOR CORPORATION
(Subsidiary of Caterpillar Tractor Company)
7111 Tyler Boulevard
Mentor, Ohio 44060
George Wellner, President
(216) 255-5611

TOWN (toiletries for men)
See McKesson & Robbins Drug Company

TOWN & COUNTRY (dinnerware)
See Stangl Pottery Company

TOWN & COUNTRY (men's coats)
See Goodstein Brothers & Company, Inc.

TOWN & COUNTRY (men's sportswear)
See Gordon & Ferguson Company

TOWN & COUNTRY (pipes)
See Bradberry Briar Pipe Corporation

TOWN & COUNTRY (snow tires)
See Firestone Tire & Rubber Company

TOWN & COUNTRY LINEN CORPORATION
295 Fifth Avenue
New York, New York 10001
(212) 889-7911

TOWN & COUNTRY SHOES, INC.
7745 Carondelet
Clayton, Missouri 63105
John D. Lipscomb, President
(314) 862-1500

TOWN & COUNTRY MOBILE HOMES, INC.
First Wichita National Bank Building
Wichita Falls, Texas 76307
Barry Donnell, President
(817) 723-5523

Companies and Trade Names

TOWN & TERRACE (decorated kitchenware)
See Vollrath Company

TOWN-AIRE (carpet tiles)
See Ozite Corporation

TOWN CLUB (whiskey)
See American Distilling Company, Inc.

TOWN CRIER (AM/FM radio, lamps)
See Guild Radio & Television Corporation

TOWN CRIER (dairy products)
See Churny Company, Inc.

TOWN FOOD COMPANY
Beverly Hills, California 90212

TOWN HALL (coffee, tea)
See Community Cash Stores

TOWN HALL (pipes)
See Comoy's of London

TOWN HOUSE (cookware)
See West Bend Company

TOWN HOUSE (crackers)
See Keebler Company

TOWN MANOR (mobile homes)
See Marshfield Homes

TOWN 'N' TERRACE (carpeting)
See Ozite Corporation

TOWN SQUARE (frozen cakes and pies)
See Hawthorn Mellody, Inc.

TOWN SQUARE (women's shoes)
See Midland Shoe Company

TOWN TAVERN (liquor)
See National Distillers & Chemical Corporation

TOWNE CLUB BEVERAGE CORPORATION
2101 East 12 Mile Road
Warren, Michigan 48092

TOWNE, PAULSEN & COMPANY, INC.
140 East Duarte Road
Monrovia, California 91016
James R. Mallen, President
(213) 359-9331
See also American Laboratories

TOWNECRAFT, INC.
23 Omaha Street
Dumont, New Jersey 07628
E.H. Barbaris, President
(201) 385-7400

TOWNSEND ENGINEERING COMPANY
Box 1433
2425 Hubbell Street
Des Moines, Iowa 50317
(515) 265-8181

TOWNSEND MANUFACTURING COMPANY, H.P.
Post Office Box 10319
Brook Street
West Hartford, Connecticut 06110
Robert P. Nichols, President and Treasurer
(203) 233-2611

TOWT-LOW (campers)
See Ratcliff Industries Inc.

TOY TINKERS
(Division of A.G. Spaulding & Brothers Inc.)
807 Greenwood Street
Evanston, Illinois 60201

TOYO (perfumes and colognes)
See House of Hampton Perfumes

TOYOMENKA, INC.
361 County Avenue
Secaucus, New Jersey 07094
(212) 564-1090

TOYOSHIMA & COMPANY INC.
303 Fifth Avenue
New York, New York 10016
(212) 685-3227

TOYOTA (guitars)
See Rocky Mountain Music Distributors

TOYOTA MOTOR SALES, U.S.A., INC.
Post Office Box 2991
2055 West 190th Street
Torrance, California 90509
I. Kodaira, President
(213) 532-5010

TOYS "R" US
See Interstate Stores, Inc.

TRAC II (razor)
See Gillette Company

TRACIES COMPANY, THE
102 Cabot Street
Holyoke, Massachusetts 01040
Robert R. Ehrlich, President and Treasurer
(413) 533-7141

TRACK KING (shoes)
See Bristol Manufacturing Corporation

TRACKSTER (all-terrain vehicle)
See Cushman, OMC-Lincoln

TRACTOR CHAIR LTD.
Post Office Box 402
Soquel, California 95073

TRACY-LUCKEY COMPANY, INC.
102 Hicks
Harlem, Georgia 30814

Companies and Trade Names

TRACY PHARMACAL COMPANY
1600 Fernpark
Saint Louis, Missouri 63141
(314) 343-8200

TRADE WINDS (frozen seafoods)
See Sea Pack Corporation

TRADE WINDS (tobacco)
See Amar Blends Company

TRADE WINDS COMPANY
1211 Depot Street
Manawa, Wisconsin 54949
Philip M. Meldahl, President and General Manager
(414) 596-2505

TRADER VIC'S FOOD PRODUCTS, INC.
1545 Park Avenue
Emeryville, California 94608
V. J. Bergeron, III, President
(415) 658-9722

TRADERS PROTEIN
(Division of Traders Oil Mill Company)
Box 1837
3501 South Jennings
Fort Worth, Texas 76101
(817) 923-4641

TRADERS SERVICE CORPORATION
1 World Trade Center
New York, New York 10048
(212) 432-1590

TRADESCOPE (radios)
See Trade Unlimited, Inc.

TRADEWAYS INC.
5226 Fairlawn Avenue
Baltimore, Maryland 21215
(301) 664-7000

TRADEWIND (houseboat)
See Boatel Company Inc.

TRADEWIND INDUSTRIES, INC.
Highway 54 West
Liberal, Kansas 67901

TRADEWINDS (repair and maintenance material for boats)
See Woolsey Marine Industries

TRADEWINDS, INC.
Box 1191
Tacoma, Washington 98401

TRADITION (cigars)
See Bayuk Cigars, Inc.

TRAGACANTH IMPORTING CORPORATION
141 East 44th Street
New York, New York 10017
(212) 697-3216

TRAGER MANUFACTURING COMPANY INC.
1200 Wheeler Avenue
Scranton, Pennsylvania 18510
(717) 346-7351

TRAIL-BREAKER (motorcycle)
See Rokon Inc.

TRAIL OR FLOAT CORPORATION
6438 Bonner Drive
Vancouver, Washington 98665

TRAILBLAZER (juvenile product)
See Moulded Products Inc.

TRAILBLAZER
(Division of Wick Building Systems, Inc.)
211 South Central Avenue
Marshfield, Wisconsin 54449
John F. Wick, President
(715) 387-3471

TRAILBLAZER CAMPING
Post Office Box 5110
Taylorsville Road
Statesville, North Carolina 28677
John Clerici, President
(704) 872-3601

TRAILHOPPER (minibike)
See United States Suzuki Motor Corporation

TRAILORSHIPS (highway trailers)
See Sea-Land Service, Inc.

TRAILWISE (camping equipment)
See Ski Hut

TRAINE (rifles)
See Parris Manufacturing Company

TRAK INC.
3250 Riverside Drive
Columbus, Ohio 43221

TRAK INC. (sports equipment)
Shawsheen Village Station
Andover, Massachusetts 01810

TRAMPEZE (shoes)
See Penobscot Shoe Company

TRAMPS
See Brown & Williamson Tobacco Corporation

TRANE COMPANY, THE
3600 Pammel Creek Road
La Crosse, Wisconsin 54601
Thomas Hancock, Chairman of the Board
(608) 782-8000

TRANE COMPANY, THE
Transport Division
Box 989
2740 Gunter Park Drive
Montgomery, Alabama 36109
(205) 279-8680

Companies and Trade Names

TRANQUIL AID (tranquilizer tablets)
See Thompson Medical Company, Inc.

TRANS CARIBBEAN AIRWAYS
See American Airlines, Inc.

TRANS INTERNATIONAL AIRLINES
(Subsidiary of Transamerica Corporation)
Oakland International Airport
Oakland, California 94614
Henry P. Huff, President
(415) 577-6000

TRANS/MATCH INC.
Post Office Box 370
2 Third Street
Kenner, Louisiana 70062
(504) 721-9356

TRANS-OCEAN-BRIDGE, INC.
1608 Washington Plaza
Reston, Virginia 22070

TRANS-OCEANIC SALES COMPANY
6 Harrison Street
New York, New York 10013
(212) 925-5737

TRANS WORLD AIRLINES, INC.
605 Third Avenue
New York, New York 10016
Charles C. Tillinghast, Jr., Chairman of the Board
(212) 557-3000
See also Canteen Corporation; and Hilton International Company

TRANS-WORLD SERVICE INC.
106 South Chestnut Street
Derry, Pennsylvania 15627

TRANSAIRCO, INC.
3200 West Market Street
Akron, Ohio 44313
Andre J. Andreoli, President
(216) 867-5023

TRANSAMERICA CORPORATION
600 Montgomery Street
San Francisco, California 94111
John R. Beckett, President
(415) 983-4000
See also Lyon Moving & Storage Company; Occidental Life Insurance Company of California; Trans International Airlines; United Artists Corporation; and United Artists Records, Inc.

TRANSAMERICA INSURANCE COMPANY
1150 South Olive Street
Los Angeles, California 90015
Edwin Seaman, President
(213) 749-3051

TRANSATLANTIC ANIMAL BY-PRODUCTS CORPORATION
38 Edgemere
Pelham Manor, New York 10803
(212) 994-7308

TRANSCIENCE CORPORATION
200 Fifth Avenue
New York, New York 10010
(212) 989-3772

TRANSCO PLASTICS CORPORATION
26100 Richmond Road
Cleveland, Ohio 44146
Herbert V. Sharlitt, President and Sales Manager
(216) 292-4700

TRANSCON LINES
101 Continental Avenue
El Segundo, California 90245
Lee R. Sollenbarger, President
(213) 640-1800

TRANSICORDER (cameras)
See Camera Specialty Company Inc.

TRANSILWRAP COMPANY
2615 North Paulina Street
Chicago, Illinois 60614
(312) 528-8000

TRANSIT TRADING CORPORATION
196 West Broadway
New York, New York 10005
(212) 925-1020

TRANSITEXIM, INC.
487 Broadway
New York, New York 10013
(212) 226-3680

TRANSOCEAN IMPORTING
2290 Panorama Drive
Salt Lake City, Utah 84117

TRANSOGRAM COMPANY, INC.
200 Fifth Avenue
New York, New York 10010
Joseph Bruna, President
(212) 675-1500

TRANSPAC SERVICES-GOPLACO, INC.
17 Simonson Place
Farmingdale, New York 11735

TRANSPORT OF NEW JERSEY
180 Boyden Avenue
Maplewood, New Jersey 07040
John J. Guihooley, Chairman of the Board
(201) 622-7000

TRANSPOS-A-CHORD
5334 Woodman Avenue
Van Nuys, California 91401

TRANSWORLD TRADING COMPANY
565 Fifth Avenue
New York, New York 10017
(212) 697-8770

Companies and Trade Names

TRANTER MANUFACTURING INC.
105 Fort Pitt Boulevard
Pittsburgh, Pennsylvania 15222
W. Parke Tranter, President and Treasurer
(412) 261-0600

TRANZFORM, INC.
1312 Hudson Street
Hoboken, New Jersey 07030

TRAP-HANDIS (marching bongos, suspended cymbals, marching timbali, etc.)
See Drumland/Ralph Kester Inc.

TRAPPE OF ASPEN
(Division of Woodstream Corporation)
Box 327
Front and Locust Streets
Lititz, Pennsylvania 17543
(717) 626-2125

TRAPPEY'S SONS, INC., B.F.
Post Office Box 400
Trappey Building
New Iberia, Louisiana 70560
William J. Trappey, President
(318) 369-6311

TRAPPIST CANDIES
Saint Benedict's Monastery
Snowmass, Colorado 81654

TRAPPIST PRESERVES
Saint Joseph's Abbey
Spencer, Massachusetts 01562

TRASH MASHER (waste compacter)
See Whirlpool Corporation

TRASHMASHER (trash-can carrier)
See J.G. Wilson Corporation

TRATTORIA DI ROMA (food products)
See NCC Food Corporation

TRAUB COMPANY
1934 McGraw Avenue
Detroit, Michigan 48208
E.A. Duncan, President
(313) 896-0789

TRAUM, INC., DAVID
85 Tenth Avenue
New York, New York 10011
J.B. Caron, President
(212) 255-7600

TRAV (soap powder)
See Canaan Products, Inc.

TRAV-L-BAR (portable bar)
See Ever-Wear Inc.

TRAV-L-CRIB (infants' product)
See Kantwet Company

TRAV-L-EEZ (juvenile product)
See Kewaunee Equipment Company

TRAVACO LABORATORIES INC.
345 Eastern Avenue
Chelsea, Massachusetts 02150
(617) 884-7740

TRAVCO CORPORATION
(Subsidiary of PRF Industries, Inc.)
6894 Maple Valley Road
Brown City, Michigan 48416
Peter R. Fink, President
(313) 346-2725

TRAVEL AIRE (portable air coolers)
See International Metal Products

TRAVEL DROWSE (clock)
See General Time Corporation, Westclox Division

TRAVEL MATES (travel accessories)
See Treasure Masters Corporation

TRAVEL MATES INC.
574 Fifth Avenue
New York, New York 10036
(212) 221-6565

TRAVEL MODES (packaged dresses)
See Flower Modes Ltd.

TRAVEL-TIER (auto-top carriers)
See The Martin Company

TRAVEL TYKE (baby carriages and seats)
See Welsh Company

TRAVELAIRE (briefcases, luggage)
See Friedberg-Grunauer Company Inc.

TRAVELALL (vehicle)
See International Harvester Company

TRAVELER (campers)
See Delta Industries Inc.

TRAVELERS CORPORATION
1 Tower Square
Hartford, Connecticut 06115
Morrison S. Beach, President
(203) 277-0111

TRAVELERS EXPRESS COMPANY, INC.
(Subsidiary of The Greyhound Corporation)
15 South Fifth Street
Minneapolis, Minnesota 55402
Arthur S. Moore, President
(612) 332-7481

TRAVELER'S MANUFACTURING & SALES COMPANY
22 Liberty Street
Quincy, Massachusetts 02169

TRAVELER'S TRUNKS (men's and ladies' swimwear)
See Inn Supplier Corporation

Companies and Trade Names

TRAVELIER INDUSTRIES INC.
Box 9036
Station A
Greenville, South Carolina 29604

TRAVELODGE INTERNATIONAL, INC.
250 Travelodge Drive
El Cajon, California 92090
Roger L. Manfred, President
(714) 442-0311

TRAVELPAD (heating pad)
See Kaz Inc.

TRAVERS TOOL COMPANY
25-26 50th Street
Long Island City, New York 11101
(212) 932-9400

TRAVERSE CITY CANNING COMPANY
Box 427
3710 Cass Road
Traverse City, Michigan 49684
(616) 946-4860

TRAVIS MILLS CORPORATION
1071 Sixth Avenue
New York, New York 10018
(212) 564-1940

TRAV'L-TRAIL (trailer-lighting connector kits)
See Belden Corporation, Consumer Products Division

TRAVLIN'COOLER (portable beverage refrigerator)
See Glacierware, Inc.

TRAVOY CORPORATION
540 South San Jacinto
San Jacinto, California 92383

TRAW COMPANY
2015 Anthony Avenue
Bronx, New York 10457
(212) 583-5840

TREAD STRAIGHT (shoes)
See Brown Group, Inc.

TREADEASY (shoes)
See P.W. Minor & Son, Inc.

TREADWAY COMPANIES, INC.
140 Market Street
Paterson, New Jersey 07505
Daniel Parke Lieblich, President
(201) 881-7900

TREASURE (books)
See Grosset & Dunlap, Inc.

TREASURE CAVE
(Division of Swift & Company)
Box 247
Faribault, Minnesota 55021

TREASURE CHEST (frozen foods)
See King Shrimp Company, Inc.

TREASURE CHEST (insulated chests)
See Victor Systems

TREASURE CRAFT
2320 North Alameda Street
Compton, California 90222

TREASURE GREETINGS INC.
See Artistic Card Publishing Corporation

TREASURE HUNT (pipes)
See Buescher's Cob Pipes

TREASURE ISLE, INC.
Route 574 and Gallagher Road
Dover, Florida
Marshall E. Levinson, President
(813) 752-1141

TREASURE MASTERS CORPORATION
1 Treasure Lane
Derry, New Hampshire 03038

TREASURE PAK (citrus fruits)
See Hunt Brothers Cooperative, Inc.

TREASURE VALLEY (foods)
See Di Giorgio Corporation

TREASURE OF THE UNIVERSE
230 Fifth Avenue
New York, New York 10001
(212) 583-5328

TREASURGARD (personal safes)
See Herring-Hall-Marvin Safe Company

TREASURY (health and beauty products)
See Thrift Drug Company

TREAT COMPANY, INC.
1 Meadow
Brooklyn, New York 11206
(212) 497-5190

TRED-LITE (footwear)
See Cambridge Rubber Company

TREE TOP, INC.
Post Office Box 248
Selah, Washington 98942
R.E. Ward, President
(509) 697-7251

TREEKOTE (tree-wound dressing, pruning and grafting compounds)
See Walter E. Clark & Son

TREESWEET PRODUCTS COMPANY
1044 East Fourth Street
Santa Ana, California 92702
R.E. Graves, President
(714) 542-1173

TREET (canned meat)
See Armour and Company

Companies and Trade Names

TREET (razor blades)
　See American Safety Razor
　　Company

TREITEL & COMPANY, INC., N.
244 West 30th Street
New York, New York 10001
(212) 736-6138

TREJAN (scrubber/vacuum)
　See Dustbane Enterprises, Ltd.

TRELOCK (padlocks and chain locks)
　See Hamilton Import Corporation

TREMCO INC.
10701 Shaker Boulevard
Cleveland, Ohio 44104
Leigh Carter, President and Chief
　Executive Officer
(216) 229-3000

TREND (bookshelf/room divider)
　See Hirsh Company

TREND (cigars)
　See Stephano Brothers

TREND (detergent)
　See Purex Corporation, Ltd.

TREND INDUSTRIES
11337 West Melrose Street
Franklin Park, Illinois 60131
(312) 455-4350

TREND MILLS
(Division of Champion International
　Inc.)
Redmond Road
Rome, Georgia 30161

TRENDAR (menstrual-discomfort
remedy)
　See Whitehall Laboratories

TRENDSETTER (menswear)
　See J. Schoeneman Inc.

TRENDSETTER FOOTWEAR
CORPORATION
　See Wolverine World Wide, Inc.

TRENKLE COMPANY, INC., H.
1225 Central
Dubuque, Iowa 52001
(319) 582-3629

TRENT (floor coverings)
　See American Biltrite Rubber
　　Company

TRENT PHARMACEUTICALS, INC.
8 Westchester Plaza
Elmsford, New York 10523

TREVARNO
(Division of Hexcel Corporation)
11711 Dublin Boulevard
Dublin, California 94566
(415) 828-4200

TREVILLE, INC.
360 Allwood Road
Clifton, New Jersey 07012

TREWAX COMPANY
5631 Mesmer Avenue
Culver City, California 90230
Jason A. Reitzin, President
(213) 390-3591

TREXLER PARK (groceries)
　See Lehigh Wholesale Grocery
　　Company

TREXWARE (plastic products)
　See Centrex Corporation

TRI-CAL LABORATORIES
20-12 Seagirt Boulevard
Far Rockaway, New York 11691

TRI-CHAIR (infants' product)
　See Thayer Inc.

TRI-G COMPANY
1731 Washington Boulevard
Venice, California 90291

TRI-LIGHT (draperies)
　See Plastic Products, Inc.

TRI-LITE (high-intensity lamp)
　See Eagle Electric Manufacturing
　　Company, Inc.

TRI-OUR (produce, canned foods)
　See Snokist Growers

TRI-SONIC INC.
4025 Marina Drive
Fort Worth, Texas 76135
(817) 237-7101

TRI-STATE MILLING COMPANY
426 Omaha Street
Rapid City, South Dakota 57701
(605) 342-6172

TRI-STATE MOTOR TRANSIT
COMPANY
East Seventh Road
Joplin, Missouri 64801
George F. Boyd, Sr., President
(417) 624-3131

TRI-STATE PHARMACEUTICAL
COMPANY
Box 3177
Springfield, Missouri 65804

TRI-TAPER (luggage)
　See American Luggage Works,
　　Inc.

TRI-VALLEY GROWERS
100 California
San Francisco, California 94106
(415) 445-1600

TRI-WAY PUBLICATIONS
Post Office Box 10516
Tampa, Florida 33609

Companies and Trade Names

TRIACTIN (antacid)
See Norwich Pharmacal Company

TRIANGLE (shoes)
See International Shoe Company

TRIANGLE CORPORATION
Cameron Road
Orangeburg, South Carolina 29115
H. Arthur Bellows, Jr., President
(803) 534-7010
See also Utica Tool Company Inc.

TRIANGLE INDUSTRIES
1919 Vineburn Avenue
Los Angeles, California 90032
(213) 233-1201
See also Rowe International Inc.

TRIANGLE MANUFACTURING COMPANY
519 West Pratt Street
Baltimore, Maryland 21201
George Fisher, President
(301) 539-7159

TRIANGLE PACIFIC CORPORATION
9 Park Place
Great Neck, New York 11021
Morton Howard, President
(516) 482-2600

TRIANGLE PACKAGE MACHINERY COMPANY
6655 West Diversey
Chicago, Illinois 60635
(312) 889-0200

TRIANGLE PUBLICATIONS, INC.
250 King of Prussia Road
Radnor, Pennsylvania 19088
W.H. Annenberg, President
(215) 688-7400

TRIANGLE RUBBER COMPANY INC.
Post Office Box 532
Goshen, Indiana 46526
(219) 533-3118

TRIANGLE SHOE COMPANY
Post Office Box 1391
Kingston, Pennsylvania 18704
Aaron Weiss, President
(717) 288-4545

TRIANGLE UNDERWEAR CORPORATION
149 Madison Avenue
New York, New York 10016
(212) 725-2585

TRIANON (enameled cookware)
See King Housewares Inc.

TRIBORO QUILT MANUFACTURING CORPORATION
451 Broadway
New York, New York 10013
(212) 966-2662

TRIBUNE (carpeting)
See Lees Carpets

TRIBUNO WINES, INC.
(Subsidiary of Coca-Cola Bottling Company of New York)
100 Hancock Street
Lodi, New Jersey 07644
John L. Tribuno, President
(201) 777-5110

TRICASCO LABORATORIES
Route Two
Winamac, Indiana 46996

TRICO-LON (men's underwear, pajamas, and robes)
See Munsingwear Inc.

TRICO MANUFACTURING CORPORATION
2948 North Fifth
Milwaukee, Wisconsin 53212
D.R. Jung, President
(414) 264-3410

TRICO PRODUCTS CORPORATION
817 Washington Street
Buffalo, New York 14203
R.J. Oshei, President
(716) 852-5700

TRICOLATOR MANUFACTURING COMPANY
Bellmore, New York 11710
Leo B. Rudin, President
(516) 221-5300

TRID-N-TRU TOYS INC.
1135 East Truslow Avenue
Fullerton, California 92631

TRIDENT (cigarettes)
See Brown & Williamson Tobacco Corporation

TRIDENT (sugarless gum and mints)
See American Chicle Company

TRIDENT PRESS
(Division of Simon & Schuster, Inc.)
630 Fifth Avenue
New York, New York 10020
Herbert M. Alexander, President
(212) 245-6400

TRIED & TRUE (hair coloring)
See Max Factor & Company

TRIFARI KRUSSMAN & FISHEL, INC.
16 East 40th Street
New York, New York 10016
Louis F. Krussman, President
(212) 679-0220

TRIGO (rum)
See Park, Benziger & Company, Inc.

TRIKCOMBO (jackets and blouses)
See Koret of California, Inc.

TRIKSHORT (women's wear)
See Koret of California, Inc.

Companies and Trade Names

TRILLIUM LINGERIE
135 Madison Avenue
New York, New York 10016
(212) 585-7382

TRIM (beer)
See The Genesee Brewing Company, Inc.

TRIM-ALL (reducing aid)
See Pacific Pharmaceutical Corporation

TRIM-FIT (men's slacks)
See Gale Sobel Company, Inc.

TRIM TEEN (dresses)
See L. Gidding & Company, Inc.

TRIMAC SALES INC.
Box Three
Danvers, Massachusetts 01923

TRIMAL LABORATORIES
7029 Willoughby Avenue
Hollywood, California 90038
(213) 874-8885

TRIMARAN DESIGN CENTER
4230 Glencoe Avenue
Marina del Rey, California 90291

TRIMARC CORPORATION
4415 West Harriston Street
High Point Office Plaza
Hillside, Illinois 60162

TRIMBLE PRODUCTS INC.
Yodkin Road
Southern Pines,
    North Carolina 28387

TRIMCYCLE (exercise equipment)
See Battle Creek Equipment Company

TRIMFIT, INC.
10450 Drummond Road
Philadelphia, Pennsylvania 19154
Arnold Kramer, Sr., Chairman of the Board
(215) 632-3000

TRIMFOOT COMPANY
(Subsidiary of Endicott Johnson Corporation)
Trimfoot Terrace
Farmington, Missouri 63640
Donald M. Epstein, President
(314) 756-4504

TRIMLINE (shears and scissors)
See J. Wiss & Sons Company

TRIMLITE INSTAMATIC (pocket cameras)
See Eastman Kodak Company

TRIMOUNT CLOTHING COMPANY
18 Station Street
Boston, Massachusetts 02120
Pat Picariello, President
(617) 427-3610

TRIMTEX
(Division of William E. Wright Company)
402 Park Avenue
Williamsport, Pennsylvania 17701
(717) 326-9135

TRINA, INC.
Ace Street
Fall River, Massachusetts 02722
Clara Rose, President
(617) 678-7601

TRINDL PRODUCTS INC.
1807-11 South Clark
Chicago, Illinois 60616
Edward R. Johnson, President
(312) 842-7716

TRINER CORPORATION, JOSEPH
4053 West Taylor
Chicago, Illinois 60624
(312) 638-2006

TRINER SCALE & MANUFACTURING COMPANY
2714 West 21st Street
Chicago, Illinois 60608
Theodore T. Jansey, President
(312) 376-9100

TRINIDAD BEAN & ELEVATOR COMPANY
2401 East Second Avenue
Denver, Colorado 80206
Wayne L. Van Vlett, President
(303) 399-6986

TRINOVID (binoculars)
See E. Leitz Inc.

TRIO (prepared foods - potatoes, gravy)
See Carnation Company

TRIO CHEMICAL WORKS INC.
341-47 Scholes Street
Brooklyn, New York 11206
(212) 497-3595

TRIO MANUFACTURING COMPANY
101 South Union Street
Griggsville, Illinois 62340
(217) 833-2393

TRIO SPORTING GOODS MANUFACTURING COMPANY
1621-29 West Carroll Avenue
Chicago, Illinois 60612
(312) 243-6655

TRION, INC.
Post Office Box 760
McNeill Road
Sanford, North Carolina 27330
Edgar W. Meyers, President
(919) 775-2201

TRIOS (shoes)
See International Shoe Company

Companies and Trade Names

TRIPAK (luggage)
See Schell Inc.

TRIPLE-A (paint rollers)
See Bestt Rollr Inc.

TRIPLE-A (paints, varnishes, enamels, lacquers)
See Quigley Company, Inc.

TRIPLE A (whiskey)
See Schenley Distillers Company

TRIPLE AAA ROOT BEER COMPANY
Box 1027
Oklahoma City, Oklahoma 73101
(405) 236-1616

TRIPLE A SPECIALTY COMPANY
5750 West 51st Street
Chicago, Illinois 60638
Eugene B. Raymond, President
(312) 458-7200

TRIPLE ACTION (cough and cold remedies)
See Jay Drug Company

TRIPLE-C (canvas footwear)
See Converse Rubber Company

TRIPLE CHECK (household needs)
See Worcester Felt Pad Corporation

TRIPLE COLA (beverages)
See Frank's Beverages

TRIPLE-CUSHION (mattresses)
See Slumber Products Corporation

TRIPLE PLAY PAL (combination folding table and carrying bag)
See Re-Ly-On Metal Products Inc.

TRIPLE SEAL (weather stripping)
See The WeatherProof Company

TRIPLE T ENTERPRISES INC.
10335 Ironwood Road
Palm Beach Gardens, Florida 33403

TRIPLE TESTED (binoculars)
See Bushnell Optical Company

TRIPLE XXX CORPORATION
109 Eighth Street
Orange, Texas 77630

TRIPLETOE (hosiery)
See Bullock Hosiery Company, Inc.

TRIPLETT CORPORATION
286 Harmon Road
Bluffton, Ohio 45817
William R. Triplett, President and Chief Executive Officer
(419) 358-5015

TRIPOD (collapsible dryer)
See Artmoore Company, Inc.

TRIPOLEY KING (game)
See Cadaco Inc.

TRIPPE MANUFACTURING COMPANY
133 North Jefferson
Chicago, Illinois 60606
(312) 346-3040

TRIPPER INDUSTRIES INC.
1533 Monrovia Avenue
Newport Beach, California 92660

TRIPURE SPRING WATER COMPANY
3355 N.W. 73rd Street
Miami, Florida 33147
(305) 691-8680

TRISCUIT (crackers)
See Nabisco, Inc.

TRISSI INC.
1411 Broadway
New York, New York 10018
(212) 354-2000

TRITLE LABORATORIES
(Division of Blistex, Inc.)
700 Enterprise Drive
Oak Brook, Illinois 60521

TRITON (gas, oil)
See Union Oil Company of California

TRITON (photographic equipment)
See Scopus (Division of Berkey Photo)

TRITON MARK I (binoculars)
See Swift Instruments Inc.

TRITON WATER SYSTEMS INC.
1761 Kaiser Avenue
Irvine, California 92664
(714) 556-0330

TRITT, INC., OLGA
424 Park Avenue
New York, New York 10022
Harold P. Davidson, President
(212) 755-8379

TRIUM INC.
11000 West Colfax
Denver, Colorado 80215

TRIUMPH (automobiles)
See British Leyland Motors, Inc.

TRIUMPH (beer)
See Grain Belt Breweries, Inc.

TRIUMPH (bicycles)
See Raleigh Industries of America, Inc.

Companies and Trade Names

TRIUMPH (motorcycles)
See Birmingham Small Arms Company

TRIUMPH HOSIERY MILLS INC.
1114 Avenue of the Americas
New York, New York 10036
(212) 869-9800

TRIUMPH INTERNATIONAL, INC.
330 Fifth Avenue
New York, New York 10001
(212) 239-1380

TRIUMPH MOTORCYCLES
Post Office Box 275
Duarte, California 91010
Dr. Felix Kalinski, President
(213) 359-3221

TRIX (cereal)
See General Mills, Inc.

TROEMNER, INC., HENRY
6825 Greenway Avenue
Philadelphia, Pennsylvania 19142
(215) 724-0800

TROGDON FURNITURE COMPANY
Post Office Box 727
Toccoa, Georgia 30577
George C. Trogdon, President
(404) 886-9403

TROJAN LUGGAGE COMPANY
2070 Channel Avenue
Memphis, Tennessee 38113
Leo Brody, President
(901) 948-6725

TROJAN, YACHTS
(Division of Whittaker Corporation)
Box 1571
Lancaster, Pennsylvania 17604
James R. McQueen, Jr., President
(717) 397-2471

TROKELL'S (pharmaceuticals)
See Humphreys Pharmacal, Inc.

TROL (men's toiletries)
See Knomark, Inc.

TROLLING PAL (fishing gear)
See Dewitt Plastics

TROMBOLITE (lighting fixture)
See ITT Lighting Fixture
(Division of ITT Corporation)

TROMMERS WHITE LABEL (beer)
See Piel Brothers

TRONA (fumigant)
See Kerr-McGee Corporation

TROOST (tobacco)
See Faber, Coe & Gregg, Inc.

TROPHY (sporting firearms)
See High Standard Manufacturing Corporation

TROPHY (thermometers)
See Ideal Scientific Company, Inc.

TROPI-KAI (low-calorie fruit drink)
See Castle & Cook Foods

TROPI-TEX (men's suits)
See House of Worsted-Tex

TROPIC-AIRE (electric heaters)
See Bersted Manufacturing
(Division of McGraw Edison Company)

TROPIC-FAIR COMPANY
(Affiliation of the Gorton Corporation)
7501 N.W. 25th Avenue
Miami, Florida 33147

TROPIC FRESH (food products)
See Parman Kendall Corporation

TROPIC GARDEN (food products)
See Knapp-Sherrill Company

TROPIC ROYAL (woven rattan furniture)
See Otto Gerdau Company

TROPIC SURF (soft drink)
See Pepsi-Cola Company

TROPIC TREND (canned and frozen foods)
See Citrus World, Inc.

TROPIC-WAVE (hair appliance)
See Master Appliance Corporation

TROPICAL PAINT COMPANY
1246 West 70th Street
Cleveland, Ohio 44102
(216) 651-5900

TROPICAL SEA (South Sea merchandise)
See Benson's Import Corporation

TROPICAL SOAP COMPANY
Box 31673
11422 Harry Hines
Dallas, Texas 75231
(214) 243-1991

TROPICAL TAN PRODUCTS COMPANY
15 Milburn
Hicksville, New York 11801

TROPICANA IMPORTS
313 Depot Street
Youngwood, Pennsylvania 15697

TROPICANA POOLS, INC.
3600 East Colonial Avenue
Orlando, Florida 32803
Terrance McLaughlin, President
(305) 841-2881

Companies and Trade Names

TROPICANA PRODUCTS, INC.
Post Office Box 338
Bradenton, Florida 33505
Anthony T. Rossi, President
(813) 747-4461

TROPIGAS INTERNATIONAL
CORPORATION
2151 Le Jeune Road
Coral Gables, Florida 33134
R.W. Stewart, President
(305) 445-1421

TROPITONE FURNITURE COMPANY
Commerce Boulevard
North Highway 301
Bert Baker, Sr., President
(813) 355-2715

TROPIX TOGS, INC.
333 N.W. 22nd Lane
Miami, Florida 33127
Sam Kantor, President
(305) 573-8316

TROT-A-LONG (juvenile product)
See Kewaunee Equipment Company

TROTTER (shoes)
See Old Town Shoe Company

TROUBADOR PRESS
385 Fremont
San Francisco, California 94105
(415) 397-3717

TROUBLE (aftershave, cologne)
See Mennen Company

TROUGH-VEYOR (food-waste disposer)
See Salvajor Company

TROUSERS BY BARRY
40 West 55th Street
New York, New York 10019
(212) 247-4055

TROUT COMPANY, FREDERICK
Interstate 85, Exit 276
Greenville, South Carolina 29607

TROY CHEMICAL COMPANY, INC., THE
Corral Park
Mount Kisco, New York 10549

TROY INDUSTRIES, INC.
1735 Cortland Court
Addison, Illinois 60101
(312) 495-0960

TROY MILLS INC.
Jaffrey Road
Troy, New Hampshire 03465
F. Fuller Ripley, President
(603) 242-7711

TROY SUNSHADE COMPANY, THE
(Division of Hobart Manufacturing Company)
612 Grant Street
Troy, Ohio 45373
Eugene Shook, Manager
(513) 335-0065

TROY-VET
(Division of Trojan Laboratories, Inc.)
Box 675
Norwalk, California 90650

TRU-ADE COMPANY, THE
488 Madison Avenue
New York, New York 10022
Lee C. Ward, Jr., President
(212) 832-7205

TRU BALANCE CORSETS, INC.
136 Madison Avenue
New York, New York 10016
(212) 689-3153

TRU-BLU COOPERATIVE ASSOCIATION
New Lisbon, New Jersey 08064

TRU-FIT (gloves)
See Heyman Corporation

TRU-FLAVOR (canned foods)
See Swayzee Packing Company

TRU-GLO (liquid makeup)
See House of Westmore Inc.

TRU GOLD (groceries)
See Scrivner-Boogaart, Inc.

TRU HEALTH
10 Taylor Street
Freeport, New York 11520

TRU-NOTE (food products)
See NCC Food Corporation

TRU-PAK PRODUCTS COMPANY, INC.
317 Maple Street
Rutherfordton, North Carolina 28139

TRU POINT PRODUCTS, INC.
140 Baker Street
Coloma, Michigan 49038
(616) 468-4611

TRU-RITE INC.
43 Hall Street
Brooklyn, New York 11205
(212) 858-7040

TRU-SPOT (flashlights)
See Ekco Products Inc.

TRU-STITCH FOOTWEAR
(Division of Wolverine World Wide, Inc.)
123 Catherine Street
Malone, New York 12953
Benjamin B. Bregman, President
(518) 483-3800

TRU-TEMP (thermometers)
See Thermometer Corporation of America

Companies and Trade Names

TRU-TEST (tools, hardware, housewares, sporting goods, etc.)
See Cotter & Company

TRU-TEX CANDY COMPANY
1511 Manor Road
Austin, Texas 78722

TRU-VUE (mirrors)
See Metaltex Inc.

TRU-VUE (photographic viewer)
See Consumer Photo (Division of GAF Corporation)

TRU-WHITE (decorative light bulbs)
See Duro-Lite Lamps, Inc.

TRUBYTE (artificial teeth)
See Dentsply International, Inc.

TRUC INTERNATIONAL INC.
Woodstock Hill, Connecticut 06218

TRUCCO, INC., A.J.
343-344 NYC Terminal Market
Bronx, New York 10474
(212) 887-3060

TRUCKER (ski equipment)
See Super-Visor Corporation

TRUDY TOYS COMPANY INC.
35 Lois Street
Norwalk, Connecticut 06856

TRUE (cigarettes)
See Lorillard Corporation

TRUE FORM FOUNDATION COMPANY, INC.
Quarry and Hamilton Streets
Darby, Pennsylvania 19023
Herbert Barg, President
(215) 532-2157

TRUE SONIC (hearing aid)
See Dahlberg Electronics Inc.

TRUE TEMPER CORPORATION
(Subsidiary of Allegheny Ludlum Industries, Inc.)
1623 Euclid Avenue
Cleveland, Ohio 44115
Herbert C. Graves, President
(216) 696-3366

TRUE TONE (housewares and appliances)
See Western Auto Supply Company

TRUECRAFT TOOL
(Division of Daido Corporation)
875 Centennial Avenue
Piscataway, New Jersey 08854
(201) 885-1850

TRUEFLIGHT MANUFACTURING COMPANY INC.
Manitowish Waters, Wisconsin 54545
(715) 543-8451

TRUESDELL COMPANY, THE P.S.
1015 Marion Road
Columbus, Ohio 43207
(614) 443-4608

TRUETONE (televisions)
See Western Auto Supply Company

TRUETT LABORATORIES
(Division of Southwestern Drug Corporation)
13450 Harry Hines Boulevard
Dallas, Texas 75234
(214) 247-9631

TRUFLEX (tablecloths, shower curtains)
See Plasticloth Products Inc.

TRUGLO (liquid makeup)
See House of Westmore, Inc.

TRULON (curtains)
See Beacon Looms, Inc.

TRULY FINE (groceries)
See Safeway Stores

TRUMAC LABORATORIES, INC.
Box 3752
Oak Park, Michigan 48237

TRUMP (bridge sets, card tables, chairs)
See Ernest Products Corporation

TRUMP (hand garden tools)
See Woodstream Corporation

TRUMP PLASTICS INC.
712 Melvin Avenue
Cuyahoga Falls, Ohio 44221

TRUSSELL MANUFACTURING COMPANY INC.
190 Cottage Street
Poughkeepsie, New York 12602
Donald F. Marsh Brooklyn, President
(914) 454-6200

TRUST COMPANY OF GEORGIA
1 Park Place
Atlanta, Georgia 30303
A.H. Sterne, President
(404) 588-7711

TRUSTWORTHY (tools, hardware, building materials, paints, etc.)
See Liberty Distributors Group

TRUSTY (dog food)
See SMS Industries Inc.

TRUXTON, INC., C.O.
1458-60 Haddon Avenue
Camden, New Jersey 08103

Companies and Trade Names

TRUZZOLINO'S FOOD PRODUCTS
COMPANY
Box 3416
Butte, Montana 59701

TRYET-NC (driveway cleaner)
See Edco Chemicals Company

TRYLON PRODUCTS CORPORATION
2750 North Wolcott Avenue
Chicago, Illinois 60614
(312) 248-5614

TRYLON UNDERWEAR COMPANY
600 Broadway
New York, New York 10012
Sidney Schnapp, President
(212) 226-7820

TRYSIL (sports accessories and
equipment)
See Eiger Mountain Sports

TUB-'N-TABLE (infants' product)
See Stacy Manufacturing
Company Inc.

TUBBS CORDAGE COMPANY
Box 709
Orange, California 92666

TUBBY (bath seats for children)
See Century Products Inc.

TUBE ROSE (sweet Scotch snuff)
See Brown & Williamson
Tobacco Corporation

TUBED PRODUCTS, INC.
186 Pleasant Street
Easthampton, Massachusetts 01027
William H. Auerswald, President
(413) 527-1250

TUBORG (beer)
See Carling Brewing Company
(Massachusetts)

TUBULAR SPECIALTIES, INC.
654 Madison Avenue
New York, New York 10021
(212) 421-0818

TUCK INDUSTRIES INC.
(Division of Technical Tape
Company)
1 Le Fevre Lane
New Rochelle, New York 10801
Gerald Sauler, President and Chief
Executive Officer
(914) 235-1000

TUCKER DUCK & RUBBER
COMPANY
Kelley Highway and North 27th
Street
Fort Smith, Arkansas 72901
W.L. Carter, President, Treasurer
and General Manager
(501) 782-8662

TUCKER FREIGHT LINES, INC.
1415 South Olive Street
South Bend, Indiana 46619
Samuel Raitzin, Chairman of the
Board
(219) 288-4441

TUCKER GARMENTS INC.
34 Front Street
Indian Orchard,
   Massachusetts 01051

TUCKER INC., TOMMY
Post Office Box 28
Tarzana, California 91356

TUCKER TIES INC.
385 Fifth Avenue
New York, New York 10016
(212) 686-6070

TUCKO SALES COMPANY
114 North Tennessee
McKinney, Texas 75069

TUCSON GAS & ELECTRIC
COMPANY
220 West Sixth Street
Tucson, Arizona 85701
J. Luther Davis, President
(602) 622-6661

TUDOR ARMS (cigars)
See S. Frieder & Sons Company

TUDOR GAMES, INC.
176 Johnson
Brooklyn, New York 11201
Norman A. Sas, President
(212) 624-0910

TUEROS (cigars)
See Consolidated Cigar
Corporation

TUF BOY (lawn and garden
supplies, housewares and appliances)
See L.J. Kingsley Company

TUF-FLEX (saws)
See Millers Falls Company

TUF-N-TUDY (mats and matting)
See Crown Industries

TUF WHITE (cookware)
See West Bend Company

TUFF INDUSTRIES INC.
11455 Warnen Road
Hazelwood, Missouri 63043

TUFF-KOTE DINOL INC.
13650 East Ten Mile Road
Warren, Michigan 48089
(313) 776-5000

TUFF-LITE CORPORATION
216 Tingley Lane
Edison, New Jersey 08817
(201) 757-9500

Companies and Trade Names

TUFF-TEX (tile)
　See Flintkote Company, Flooring Products

TUFF-TRED (rubber products)
　See Oliver Tire & Rubber Company

TUFFIES (trash-can liners)
　See Poly-Tech (Division of United States Industries, Inc.)

TUFFLEX (cushions and protective padding)
　See Conwed Corporation

TUFFY (heavy-duty vacuum cleaner)
　See Sunbeam Appliance Company

TUFFY (scouring pads)
　See Miles Laboratories Inc.

TUFIDE (luggage)
　See Stebco Products Corporation

TUFT-WELD (juvenile product)
　See Little Tyke Products Company

TUFTWOVEN WEEK (rugs)
　See Mohasco Industries Inc.

TUGON CHEMICAL CORPORATION
Box 31
Cross River, New York 10518

TULANE (sportswear)
　See J.H. Bonck Company, Inc.

TULIO (guitars)
　See Manhattan Novelty Corporation

TULIP (paper cups and dispensers)
　See Lily-Tulip

TULIP (produce)
　See Perham Fruit Corporation

TULIP (room dividers and decorative panels)
　See Forms, Inc.

TULLAMORE DEW (Irish whiskey)
　See Heublein Inc.

TULSA PIZZA COMPANY
912 West Admiral
Tulsa, Oklahoma 74127

TULSHED (tools, general hardware)
　See Hardware Distributors Inc.

TUMBLER LABORATORIES
(Division of Imoco-Gateway Corporation)
Plum and West Streets
Baltimore, Maryland 21230
(301) 752-6245

TUMBLETWIST (rugs)
　See Wunda Weve Carpet Company

TUMS (antacid)
　See Lewis-Howe Company

TUMWATER (produce)
　See Cashmere Fruit Exchange

TUNA BONUS (soy-protein extender)
　See A.E. Staley Manufacturing Company

TUNGSEAL (varnish)
　See McCloskey Varnish Company

TUNIS COMPANY INC., BEN
Nursery Lane
Rye, New York 10580

TUPPERWARE HOME PARTIES
(Division of Dart Industries, Inc.)
Box 2353
Orlando, Florida 32802
Joe Hara, President
(305) 847-3111

TURBO (insulation materials)
　See Brand-Rex Company

TURBO MARINE PRODUCTS
Box 622
Salina, Kansas 67401

TURBO-OVEN (kitchen appliance)
　See S.W. Farber

TURBO-WAVE (hair appliance)
　See Master Appliance Corporation

TURCO PRODUCTS
(Division of Purex Corporation Ltd.)
24600 South Main Street
Wilmington, California 90744
Walter Applewhite, Vice President
(213) 775-2111

TURF-KING (lawn and garden supplies)
　See Allied Hardware Services Inc.

TURF LABORATORIES
Box 425
Tustin, California 92680

TURNAMATIC (high chairs)
　See Bunny Bear Inc.

TURNBULL CONE MACHINE COMPANY
1404 Carter
Chattanooga, Tennessee 37401

Companies and Trade Names

TURNER & SEYMOUR MANU-
  FACTURING COMPANY, THE
100 Lawton Street
Torrington, Connecticut 06790
Allen M. Sperry, Chairman and
  President
(203) 489-9214

TURNER COMPANY
(Division of Olin Company)
821 Park Avenue
Sycamore, Illinois 60178
R.C. Mehken, General Manager
(815) 895-4545

TURNER HALL CORPORATION
175 Great Neck Road
Great Neck, New York 11021
Melvin Finkelstein, President
(516) 466-6310
  See also Admiracion

TURNER MANUFACTURING
  COMPANY
2309 South Keeler Avenue
Chicago, Illinois 60623
(312) 277-8800

TURSKI CORPORATION
8 Henshaw Street
Woburn, Massachusetts 01801

TURTLE CREEK ARTIFICIAL
  FLOWERS
647 Axminster-Watson Industrial
  Park
Saint Louis, Missouri 63126
(314) 343-5262

TURTLE WAX, INC.
5655 West 73rd Street
Chicago, Illinois 60638
Carl F. Schmid, President
(312) 284-8300

TUSCO MUSHROOM PRODUCTS
  INC.
Route One
Beach City, Ohio 44608

TUSSY COSMETICS
680 Fifth Avenue
New York, New York 10019
(212) 247-4100

TUTTLE LAW PRINT INC.
7 Court Square
Rutland, Vermont 05701

TUTTLE SILVERSMITHS
340 Quinnipiac Street
Wallingford, Connecticut 06492
(203) 269-4401

TUTTLE'S ELIXIR COMPANY
Radio Circle
Mount Kisco, New York 10549

TUVACHE PERFUMES INC.
40 West 57th Street
New York, New York 10019
(212) 582-5805

TUXEDO (tobacco)
  See American Tobacco Company

TVARSCKI (gins)
  See American Distilling
    Company, Inc.

TWEED (bath oil, cologne,
perfume, etc.)
  See Yardley of London, Inc.

TWEED (smoking tobacco)
  See United States Tobacco
    Company

TWEEN'S TEENS (shoes)
  See Viner Brothers, Inc.

TWEET (instant orange breakfast
drink)
  See Sanna, Inc. (Division of
    Beatrice Foods Company)

TWELVE SIGNS INC.
3369 South Robertson Boulevard
Los Angeles, California 90034
(213) 553-8000

TWENTIETH CENTURY-FOX FILM
  CORPORATION
10201 West Pico Boulevard
Los Angeles, California 90035
Dennis Stanfill, President
(213) 277-2211

TWENTIETH CENTURY
  MANUFACTURING COMPANY
9231 Penn Avenue South
Minneapolis, Minnesota 55431
(612) 884-3211

TWENTIETH CENTURY VARIETIES
  INC.
511 East 164th Street
Bronx, New York 10456
(212) 585-3208

20TH CENTURY WEAR, INC.
149 Madison Avenue
New York, New York 10016
(212) 684-4822

20 BELOW (freezer wrap)
  See H.P. Smith Paper Company

20 CARATS (bath oil, cologne,
dusting powder, etc.)
  See Dana Perfumes, Inc.

20-GRAND (ale)
  See Sterling Brewers (Division of
    G. Heileman Brewing
    Company, Inc.)

20 MULE TEAM (borax)
  See United States Borax &
    Chemical Corporation

Companies and Trade Names

TWENTY-ONE BRANDS, INC.
(Subsidiary of Foremost-McKesson, Inc.)
75 Rockefeller Plaza
New York, New York 10019
C.R. Margolis, President
(212) 582-5500
See also Brooks Distilling Company, Ezra

TWENTY-ONES (fashion shoes for women)
See Genesco, Inc.

TWI-LAG CHEMICAL COMPANY
76 Grand Avenue
Brooklyn, New York 11205
(212) 638-5860

TWIGGY (soaps, shampoo, lipstick, nail polish)
See Yardley of London, Inc.

TWILL COMPANY, INC., THE
2207 Bonnie Drive
Stevensville, Michigan 49127

TWILL-O-WEVE (menswear)
See J. Schoeneman Inc.

TWIN BB (food products)
See Springdale Food Company

TWIN CITY SHELLAC COMPANY
338 Flushing Avenue
Brooklyn, New York 11205
(212) 855-0505

TWIN COUNTY GROCERS, INC.
145 Talmadge Road
Edison, New Jersey 08817
Leroy Davidson, President
(201) 287-4600

TWIN FAIR, INC.
1 Twin Fair Corporate Center
Buffalo, New York 14240
Harold A. Egan, Jr., President
(716) 683-0770

TWIN HARBORS (seafood)
See Ivar Wendt Inc.

TWIN-LITE (rechargeable flashlights)
See Garrity Industries, Inc., Dynatron Division

TWIN-O-MATIC (waffle baker)
See Manning-Bowman (Division of McGraw-Edison Company)

TWIN PINE CARD COMPANY
Box 2053
313 Throckmorton
Fort Worth, Texas 76102
(817) 335-2945

TWIN SEAL (whiskey)
See Hiran Walker Incorporated

TWIN TREES GARDENS
Route 44
Salisbury, Connecticut 06068

TWINKIES (snack cakes)
See ITT Continental Baking Company Inc.

TWINKLE (copper cleaner and silver cream)
See Drackett Company

TWINKLE SEAT (infants' product)
See The Toidey Company Inc.

TWINKLE TOES (shoes, rubber footwear, slippers)
See Lida Trading Corporation

TWINKLE UNDERGARMENT CORPORATION
600 Broadway
New York, New York 10012
(212) 925-1850

TWINSON COMPANY
433 LaPrenda Road
Los Altos, California 94022

TWISSORS (tweezers with scissor handles)
See Kurlash Company, Inc.

TWITCHELL COMPANY, S.
Crestmont and Haddon Avenue
Camden, New Jersey 08103
Paul J. Samuelenas, President
(609) 966-3075

TWO CUP (coffee)
See Loblaw Groceterias Company, Ltd.

TWO GUYS (department stores)
See Vornado, Inc.

TWO OCEANS (prepared frozen seafood)
See Eat-All Frozen Food Company, Inc.

TWO-TIMER (men's watch)
See Zodiac Watch Company

TWO-TIMER (twenty-hour timing device)
See Vocaline Company of America Inc.

2-TON (adhesive)
See Devcon Corporation

221B BAKER STREET (tobacco)
See Fireside Tobacco Corporation

TWOROGER, INC., JOHN
249 West 34th Street
New York, New York 10001
(212) 563-7796

TWO'S COMPANY INC.
33 Bertel Avenue
Mount Vernon, New York 10550

TWYTEX (fabrics)
See John Heathcoat & Company, Inc.

Companies and Trade Names

TY-D-BOL (automatic toilet-bowl cleaner)
See Knomark, Inc.

TY-DATA INC.
109 Northeastern Boulevard
Nashua, New Hampshire 03060
William F. Brine, Jr., President and Treasurer
(603) 889-1155

TYCO (baking mixes, canned foods, spices, cleaning needs)
See Tyler & Simpson Company

TYCO INDUSTRIES, INC.
(Division of Consolidated Foods Corporation)
Woodbury Heights, New Jersey 08097
Richard E. Grey, President
(609) 845-4600

TYCOON (molded attaché cases)
See Leather Specialty Company

TYDEE (folding nursery chairs equipped with disposable bags)
See Tesser Disposable Products Company

TYKIE TOY, INC.
Post Office Box 38
Conley, Georgia 30027

TYLER & SIMPSON COMPANY
2020 Industrial Boulevard
Norman, Oklahoma 73069

TYLER FARMS (food products)
See Athens Canning Company

TYLER REFRIGERATION
(Division of Clark Equipment Company)
1329 Lake Street
Niles, Michigan 49120

TYLERCRAFT INC.
1439 Montauk Highway
Oakdale, New York 11769

TYMETER (clocks)
See Pennwood Numechron Company-Tymeter Electronics

TYNAMITE (flashlights)
See Baudinet International Corporation

TYNDALE, INC.
(Subsidiary of Hamilton Cosco, Inc.)
311 Bruckner Boulevard
New York, New York 10454
Robert Fox, President
(212) 292-0680

TYPE-OUT CORPORATION
43 East 59th Street
New York, New York 10022
(212) 758-2080

TYPHOO (tea)
See A & A Food Products Corporation

TYPHOON (lighters)
See Ronson Corporation

TYPHOON AIR CONDITIONING
(Division of Hupp, Inc.)
1135 Ivanhoe Road
Cleveland, Ohio 44110
H.D. Weller, President
(216) 851-6200

TYREE, CHEMIST, INC., J.S.
120 Westhampton Avenue
Washington, D.C. 20027
(202) 336-5700

TYROL USA
100 Front Street
Keeseville, New York 12944

TYROLEANS (shoes)
See G.H. Bass & Company

TYROLIA (wine)
See E. & J. Gallo Winery

TYSON FOODS, INC.
Post Office Box E
2210 West Oaklawn Drive
Springdale, Arkansas 72764
Don Tyson, President
(501) 756-4000

TYSON-WHITE LABORATORIES
613 Merritt Street
Nashville, Tennessee 37203
(615) 242-0528

Companies and Trade Names

U

UDGA, INC.
2453 University Avenue
Saint Paul, Minnesota 55114
(612) 646-1848

U-DRIVE-IT (toy dashboard)
See Schaper Manufacturing Company Inc.

U-FILE-M BINDER MANUFACTURING COMPANY INC.
Post Office Box 206
Lafayette, New York 13084

U-FRY-EM (seafood)
See Frionor Kitchens Inc.

U.G.L. (aluminum-roof paint)
See United Gilsonite Laboratories

U-HAUL RENTAL SYSTEM
Post Office Box 21502
Phoenix, Arizona 85036
Paul J. Kelley, Public Relations Manager
(602) 263-6011

UHU PRODUCTS CORPORATION
105 East 29th Street
New York, New York 10016
(212) 689-9133

UM (automotive accessories)
See Ultramotive Corporation

UMC INDUSTRIES, INC.
72 Wall Street
New York, New York 10005
H. Ridgely Bullock, President
(212) 344-8050

UNCO
Box 129
Mamaroneck, New York 10543

U.P.C. (canned seafood products)
See Universal Packers Corporation

UPD (computer)
See Data Technology Inc.

U.P.S. (scales)
See Pelouze Scale Company

U.S.
See United States

U-SELECT-IT, INC.
Box 1395
Des Moines, Iowa 50305
(515) 277-5397

USM CORPORATION
140 Federal Street
Boston, Massachusetts 02107
William S. Brewster, Chairman of the Board
(617) 542-9100

USV PHARMACEUTICAL CORPORATION
(Subsidiary of Revlon, Inc.)
1 Scarsdale Road
Tuckahoe, New York 10707
J.H. Williford, Chairman of the Board
(914) 779-6300

UTA FRENCH AIRLINES
9841 Airport Boulevard 1000
Los Angeles, California 90045
Jean Marie Sauvage, General Representative, North America
(213) 649-1810

U-TRI DISTRIBUTORS
2501 West Redondo Beach
Gardena, California 90249
(213) 321-5241

U/V (fire-detection system)
See McGraw-Edison Company

U-VEE (aerial)
See Ward Products Corporation

U. W. PRODUCTS COMPANY
Box 5693
Nashville, Tennessee 37208

UARCO INC.
West County Line Road
Barrington, Illinois 60010
Gregson L. Barker, President
(312) 381-7000

UCAGCO (dinnerware)
See United China & Glass Company

UEBE CANNING COMPANY
Rural Free Delivery 5
Harrison, Arkansas 72601

UGENE (processed fruits and vegetables)
See Agripac, Inc.

UHE COMPANY, INC., GEORGE
76 Ninth Avenue
New York, New York 10011
(212) 929-0870

UKULELE (food products)
See Castle & Cooke Foods

ULI (sports apparel)
See Peter Webber Imports

ULLMAN COMPANY, INC., THE
319 McKibbin Street
Brooklyn, New York 11206
Martin C. Poppe, President
(212) 497-3700

ULMANN COMPANY, BERNHARD
(Division of Indian Head, Inc.)
30-20 Thomson Avenue
Long Island City, New York 11101
Sidney G. Wasch, President
(212) 786-2500

Companies and Trade Names

ULMER INC., CHARLES
175 City Island Avenue
City Island, New York 10464
(212) 885-1700

ULMER PHARMACAL COMPANY, THE
1400 Harmon Place
Minneapolis, Minnesota 55403
(612) 332-7745

ULRICH (wines)
    See Jacobi Associates Inc.

ULSA COMPANY
365 Lisbon Street
Lewiston, Maine 04240

ULSTER (knives)
    See Imperial Knife Associated Companies, Inc.

ULSTER WEAVING COMPANY LTD., THE
118 Madison Avenue
New York, New York 10016
(212) 684-5534

ULTIMA (gourmet foods)
    See Invento Products Corporation

ULTIMA (stainless-steel products)
    See Gense Import Ltd.

ULTIMA II (cosmetics, skin-care products, aromatics, etc.)
    See Revlon Inc.

ULTIMATE (coolers)
    See Island Equipment Corporation

ULTIMILER (tires)
    See Mohawk Rubber Company

ULTISSIMA (brushes, brooms, mops, dusters, etc.)
    See Craftsman Brush Company Inc.

ULTRA (shampoo, sun-screening agent)
    See Caswell-Massey Company, Ltd.

ULTRA BANN 5000 (deodorant)
    See Bristol-Myers Company

ULTRA BRITE (toothpaste)
    See Colgate-Palmolive Company

ULTRA CUSTOM PAK, INC.
614 West 51st Street
New York, New York 10019
(212) 582-5088

ULTRA DELUXE (whiskey)
    See Schenley Industries, Inc.

ULTRA-FEMININE (hormone-cream products)
    See Helena Rubinstein, Inc.

ULTRA/50 (polyester carpet)
    See Trend Mills

ULTRA-MATIC (suitcase and garment bag)
    See Lark Luggage Corporation

ULTRA POWER (batteries)
    See Wonder Corporation of America

ULTRA RICH (shampoo, conditioner)
    See Cosmair, Inc.

ULTRA SHEEN (hair-care products)
    See Johnson Products Company, Inc.

ULTRA TRADE
Box 4125
Fremont, California 94538

ULTRA VELLUX (blankets)
    See L. L. Bean Inc.

ULTRA-VIOLET PRODUCTS
5114 Walnut Grove
San Gabriel, California 91776
Paul B. Warren, President
(213) 285-3123

ULTRA WAVE (hair-care products)
    See Johnson Products Company, Inc.

ULTRALITE (glass-fiber insulation)
    See Gustin-Bacon (Division of Certain-teed Products Corporation)

ULTRALUCENT (makeup)
    See Max Factor and Company

ULTRAMOTIVE CORPORATION
Box 291
Bethel, Vermont 05032

ULTRATONE (bongos, congas, castanets, cymbals, triangles, tambourines, etc.)
    See Chicago Musical Instrument Company

ULTRONIC (portable electric typewriter)
    See Royal Typewriter Company

UMATILLA CIRTUS GROWERS ASSOCIATION
Post Office Box J
Umatilla, Florida 32784

UMBROLLER (foldable baby strollers)
    See Cross River Products Inc.

UN-POLLUTER (no-phosphate detergent)
    See Gold Seal Company

Companies and Trade Names

UNAGUSTA CORPORATION
(Subsidiary of Welbilt Corporation)
Welch Road
Waynesville, North Carolina 28786
Herbert J. Broner, President
(704) 456-3581

UNCAS MANUFACTURING
  COMPANY
623 Atwells Avenue
Providence, Rhode Island 02901
Stanley Sorrentino, President
(401) 421-0680

UNCLE BEN'S FOODS
(Division of Mars, Inc.)
Box 1752
Houston, Texas 77001
J.J. Coady, President
(713) 497-1970

UNCLE JACK'S (preserves, peanut butter, syrup)
  See Home Brands Inc.

UNCLE JIM'S (sauces)
  See Prepared Food Products, Inc.

UNCLE MILTON INDUSTRIES INC.
10459 West Jefferson Boulevard
Culver City, California 90230
(213) 870-9334

UNCLE SAM (refuse cans)
  See Reeves-Bowman Division (Cyclops Corporation)

UNCLE SAM BREAKFAST FOOD
  COMPANY
4201 North 28th Avenue
Omaha, Nebraska 68111
John M. McGowan, President
(402) 451-4567

UNCLE SAM CHEMICAL COMPANY
  INC.
575-577 West 131st Street
New York, New York 10027
Herman Schwartz, Chairman and
  President
(212) 286-2510

UNCLE STEVE'S (processed foods)
  See Food Products, Inc.

UNCLE WILLIE (cigars)
  See T. E. Brooks & Company

UNCO
Box 129
Mamaroneck, New York 10543

UNDERSEA WINDOW-FLOAT
(water-sports equipment)
  See Chris-Craft Marine Accessories

UNDERWOOD (typewriters, etc.)
  See Olivetti Corporation of America

UNDERWOOD COMPANY,
  WILLIAM
1 Red Devil Lane
Watertown, Massachusetts 02172
Alice Liddell, Director, Consumer Affairs
(617) 926-1350

UNDERWOOD GLASS COMPANY
6120 Jefferson Highway
New Orleans, Louisiana 70123
(504) 733-6755

UNEEDA BISCUIT (crackers)
  See Nabisco Inc.

UNEEDA DOLL COMPANY, INC.
200 Fifth Avenue
New York, New York 10001
Sam Sklarsky, President
(212) 675-3313

UNGAR
(Division of Eldon Industries, Inc.)
233 East Manville Street
Compton, California 90220
William L. Nehrez, President and
  General Manager
(213) 774-5950

UNGER & ASSOCIATES, HENRY
1206 South Maple Avenue
Los Angeles, California 90015
(213) 744-1711

UNGER & COMPANY, INC.,
  WILLIAM
230 Fifth Avenue
New York, New York 10001
(212) 532-0689

UNGUENTINE (burn remedies, first-aid preparations, hemorrhoid treatments)
  See Norwich Pharmacal Company

UNI-CARD (Division of Chase Manhattan Bank, N.A.)
  See Bankamericard

UNI-FLEX (adjustable lamps)
  See O.C. White Company

UNI/FLEX (first-aid equipment)
  See Medical Supply Company

UNI-LUX (lamps)
  See Luxo Lamp Corporation

UNI/MAG (barometers)
  See Taylor Instrument Companies

UNI-PAK (glass products)
  See Owens-Illinois

UNI-SEAL (frames)
  See Vance Industries, Inc.

UNI-SERV CORPORATION
  See Bankamericard

UNI-VISION (photo albums)
  See C.R. Gibson Company

Companies and Trade Names

UNIBRAZE CORPORATION
7502 West State Route 41
Covington, Ohio 45318
William G. Tanner, President
(513) 473-2006

UNIBRAZE INTERNATIONAL INC.
(Subsidiary of Unibraze Corporation)
60 South Avenue
Fanwood, New Jersey 07023

UNICA (seafood)
See Peter Pan Seafoods Inc.

UNICAN CORPORATION
915 Hartford Pike
Shrewsbury, Massachusetts 01546
Joseph C. O'Donnell, President and Treasurer
(617) 844-4581

UNICAP (vitamins)
See Upjohn Company

UNICARE HEALTH SERVICE INC.
See Elaine Powers Figure Salon

UNICO (freezers)
See Universal Cooperatives Inc.

UNICOM (intercom system)
See Dictograph Products Inc.

UNICOM PRODUCTS
(Division of United Communication Corporation)
3362 Long Beach Road
Oceanside, New York 11572

UNICOM SYSTEMS INC.
10670 North Tantau
Cupertino, California 95014

UNICORD, INC.
(Subsidiary of Gulf & Western Industries, Inc.)
75 Frost
Westbury, New York 11590
Sidney Hack, President
(516) 333-9100

UNICUBE CORPORATION
(Subsidiary of Gordon Tube Products Company, Inc.)
1290 Oak Point Avenue
Bronx, New York 10474
(212) 378-2400

UNIFIBRES, INC.
14 East 60th Street
New York, New York 10022
(212) 838-4740

UNIFLEX (steel shelving)
See Bernard Franklin Company Inc.

UNIFLEX INC.
474 Grand Boulevard
Westbury, New York 11590
Herbert Barry, President
(516) 997-7300

UNIFLITE, INC.
Ninth and Harris
Bellingham, Washington 98225
John L. Thomas, President
(202) 676-6200

UNIFLO (motor oil)
See Exxon Company

UNIFLOW MANUFACTURING COMPANY
1525 East Lake Road
Erie, Pennsylvania 16512
Thomas L. Kuebler, Chairman and President
(814) 453-6761

UNIFORM (shoes)
See Penobscot Shoe Company

UNIFORMAT (fiberglass)
See Ferro Corporation

UNIFRAME (portable tables)
See Peabody Seating Company Inc.

UNIJAX INC.
Envelope Division
Gulf Life Tower
Jacksonville, Florida 32207
Walter L. Moore, President and Chief Executive Officer
(904) 398-3181

UNIMED, INC.
Route 202 South
Morristown, New Jersey 07960

UNIMETRICS INC.
1534 Old Country Road
Plainview, New York 11803

UNION (seafood)
See Deep Sea Shrimp Importing Company, Inc.

UNION (stereo consoles)
See JVC America, Inc.

UNION BANK
445 South Figueroa Street
Los Angeles, California 90017
Harry J. Volk, Chairman of the Board
(213) 687-6877

UNION CAMP CORPORATION
1600 Valley Road
Wayne, New Jersey 07470
Samuel M. Kinney, Jr., President
(201) 628-9000

UNION CARBIDE CORPORATION
(Consumer Products)
New York, New York 10017
William S. Sneath, Jr., President
(212) 551-2345

1354

Companies and Trade Names

UNION CENTRAL LIFE
INSURANCE COMPANY
Mill and Waycross
Cincinnati, Ohio 45240
John A. Lloyd, Chairman of the
Board
(513) 825-1880

UNION CHEMICAL COMPANY
INC.
Union, Maine 04862

UNION
(Division of Miles Laboratories)
900 19th Street
Granite City, Illinois 62040
(618) 451-7730

UNION ELECTRIC COMPANY
1 Memorial Drive
Saint Louis, Missouri 63166
Charles J. Dougherty, President
(314) 621-3222

UNION ENVELOPE COMPANY
Post Office Box 27007
Richmond, Virginia 23261
Ralph Nesbit, President
(703) 358-5555

UNION FISH COMPANY
100 Bush
San Francisco, California 94104
(415) 392-6313
　　See also Sportsmen's Seafoods

UNION FORK & HOE COMPANY,
THE
500 Dublin Avenue
Columbus, Ohio 43215
Edward Durell, Chairman of the
Board
(614) 228-1791

UNION HALL (whiskey)
　　See Kasser Distillers Products
　　　　Corporation

UNION JACK CUT PLUG (tobacco)
　　See House of Edgeworth

UNION LEADER (tobacco)
　　See Lorillard (Division of
　　　　Loew's Theatres)

UNION MANUFACTURING
COMPANY
110 West 11th Street
Los Angeles, California 90015
Albert P. Harris, President
(213) 749-5066

UNION MUTUAL LIFE
INSURANCE COMPANY
2211 Congress Street
Portland, Maine 04112
Colin C. Hampton, President
(207) 775-4411

UNION NATIONAL BANK OF
PITTSBURGH
Fourth at Wood
Pittsburgh, Pennsylvania 15222
Richard D. Edwards, President
(412) 644-8111

UNION-NATIONAL, INC.
226 Crescent
Jamestown, New York 14701
Alldor M. Nord, President
(716) 487-1165

UNION NOVELTY COMPANY,
INC.
149 Fifth Avenue
New York, New York 10010
Frank P. Jager, President and
Secretary
(212) 673-2121

UNION OIL COMPANY OF
CALIFORNIA
461 Boylston
Los Angeles, California 90017
Fred L. Hartley, President
(213) 486-7600

UNION PACIFIC RAILROAD
345 Park Avenue
New York, New York 10022
Frank E. Barnett, Chairman of the
Board
(212) 593-1700

UNION PEN & PENCIL COMPANY
175 Clearbrook Road
Elmsford, New York 10523
Morton Tenny, General Manager
(914) 592-2000

UNION PIN COMPANY
170 Lake Street
Winsted, Connecticut 06098
(203) 379-3397

UNION PLANTERS NATIONAL
BANK
67 Madison Avenue
Memphis, Tennessee 38147
Richard A. Trippeer, Jr.,
President
(901) 523-6000

UNION RUBBER AND ASBESTOS
COMPANY
Post Office Box 1040
Allen and Donohue Streets
Trenton, New Jersey 08606
(609) 396-9328

UNION 76
(Division of Union Oil Company
of California)
200 East Golf Road
Palatine, Illinois 60067
W.S. McConnor, President
(312) 529-7676

UNION STEEL CHEST CORPORATION
LeRoy, New York 14482

UNION TRUST COMPANY
Church and Elm
New Haven, Connecticut 06502
Thomas F. Richardson, President
(203) 497-4500

UNION TRUST COMPANY OF
MARYLAND
Baltimore and Saint Paul
Baltimore, Maryland 21203
William H. Cowie, Jr., President
(301) 332-5416

Companies and Trade Names

UNION UNDERWEAR COMPANY
(Subsidiary of Northwest Industries, Inc.)
6300 Sears Tower
Chicago, Illinois 60602
John B. Holland, Chairman of the Board
(212) 581-9700

UNION WADDING COMPANY
125 Goff Avenue
Pawtucket, Rhode Island 02862
Kenneth W. Washburn, President
(401) 725-3500

UNIPAS INC.
1303 Jefferson Boulevard
Warwick, Rhode Island 02886
(401) 739-6660

UNIPOLE (adjustable slotted pole)
See Howard Accessories Inc.

UNIPOXY (epoxy adhesive)
See Kristal Kraft Inc.

UNIQUE (floor wax)
See Simoniz Company

UNIQUE (ice cracker)
See Tap-Icer (Division of Waldon Inc.)

UNIQUE FURNITURE MAKERS, INC.
1665 Stadium Drive
Winston-Salem, North Carolina 27107
John S. Creech, President
(919) 784-7140

UNIQUE INDUSTRIES
4061 N.E. Fifth Terrace
Fort Lauderdale, Florida 33308

UNIQUE PURE FOODS CORPORATION
160 Passaic Avenue
Kearny, New Jersey 07032

UNIQUE THINGS INC.
Box 381
Sudbury, Massachusetts 01776

UNIROYAL
Chemical Division
Elm Street
Naugatuck, Connecticut 06770

UNIROYAL
407 North Main Street
Mishawaka, Indiana 46544
(219) 255-2181

UNIROYAL
Footwear Division
58 Maple
Naugatuck, Connecticut 06770
(203) 729-0261

UNIROYAL, INC.
1230 Avenue of the Americas
New York, New York 10020
David Beretta, Chairman of the Board
(212) 489-4000
See also Heller, Inc., William; Latex Fiber Industries, Inc.; Masland Duraleather Company; Mishawaka Rubber Company, Inc.; and Sperry Top Sider

UNISHOPS, INC.
21 Caven Point Avenue
Jersey City, New Jersey 07305
Herbert I. Wexler, President
(201) 433-0100

UNISORB (disposable diapers, underpads, tissues)
See Parke, David & Company, Medical-Surgical Products Division

UNISORB (dusting powder)
See Dermik Laboratories, Inc.

UNISTRAND (fiberglass)
See Ferro Corporation

UNISTRUT CORPORATION
4118 South Wayne
Wayne, Michigan 48184
Rhett W. Butler, President
(313) 721-4040

UNIT PORTIONS, INC.
176 Cherry Valley Road
West Hampstead, New York 11552

UNIT WALL (aluminum curtain-wall systems)
See Kawneer Company

UNITAS (food products)
See Elias Pando S.A. de C.V.

UNITED AIR LINES (UAL)
Box 66100
Chicago, Illinois 60666
Richard J. Ferris, President
(312) 952-4000
See also Western International Hotels

UNITED ART COMPANY, INC.
28 Randolph Street
Boston, Massachusetts 02118
(617) 426-1350

UNITED ARTISTS CORPORATION
(Subsidiary of Transamerica Corporation)
729 Seventh Avenue
New York, New York 10019
Eric R. Pleskow, President
(212) 575-3000

UNITED ARTISTS RECORDS, INC.
(Subsidiary of Transamerica Corporation)
6920 Sunset Boulevard
Los Angeles, California 90028
Michael Stuart, President
(213) 461-9141

UNITED ARTISTS THEATRE CIRCUIT, INC.
1700 Broadway
New York, New York 10019
Robert A. Naify, President
(212) 765-2800

Companies and Trade Names

UNITED BALTIC CORPORATION
17 Battery Place
New York, New York 10004
(212) 269-8337

UNITED BANK OF DENVER
1740 Broadway
Denver, Colorado 80217
John D. Hershner, President
(303) 861-8811

UNITED BASKET COMPANY INC.
1064 DeKalb Avenue
Brooklyn, New York 11221
(212) 455-2800

UNITED BEAN COMPANY
Box 185
Eaton, Indiana 47388

UNITED BENEFIT LIFE INSURANCE
  COMPANY
Dodge at 33rd
Omaha, Nebraska 68131
Conrad S. Young, President
(402) 342-7600

UNITED BEVERAGES INC.
41 East 42nd Street
New York, New York 10017
Richard I. Ahern, President and
  Chief Executive Officer
(212) 687-0790

UNITED BRANDS COMPANY
200 Park Avenue
New York, New York 10017
Wallace Booth, President
(212) 490-8630
    See also A&W International
    Inc.; Chiquita Brands,
    Inc.; Hungerford Smith
    Company, J.; Morrell &
    Company, John; and Revere
    Sugar Refinery

UNITED BRANDS INC.
1212 East Maple Road
Troy, Michigan 48084

UNITED BUYING SERVICE
(consumer buying)
    See Rollins, Inc.

UNITED CABINET CORPORATION
14th and Aristokraft Streets
Jasper, Indiana 47546

UNITED CALIFORNIA BANK
(Affiliate of Western Bancorporation)
707 Wilshire Boulevard
Los Angeles, California 90017
Joseph J. Pinola, President
(213) 624-0111

UNITED CANNING CORPORATION
212 State Line Road
East Palestine, Ohio 44413

UNITED CARD COMPANY
1101 North Carnegie
Rolling Meadows, Illinois 60008
(312) 259-6000

UNITED-CARR INC.
(Division of TRW Inc.)
31 Ames Street
Cambridge, Massachusetts 02142
(617) 547-4900

UNITED CHINA & GLASS
  COMPANY
Post Office Box 51510
4500 Tchoupitoulas Street
New Orleans, Louisiana 70150
(504) 891-5881
    See also Orleans Silver Company

UNITED CITRUS PRODUCTS
  CORPORATION
951 Providence Highway
Norwood, Massachusetts 02062

UNITED COATINGS
3050 North Rockwell
Chicago, Illinois 60618
(312) 583-3700

UNITED COMB & NOVELTY
  COMPANY
161 Sixth Street
Leominister, Massachusetts 01453
(617) 537-2096

UNITED CRAFTS OF CALIFORNIA
800 Fish Canyon Road
Duarte, California 91010

UNITED CRAFTSMEN, INC.
1400 State Avenue
Cincinnati, Ohio 45214
(513) 471-0111

UNITED CUTLERY & HARDWARE
  PRODUCTS COMPANY
108 East 16th Street
New York, New York 10003
(212) 473-7745

UNITED ELASTIC COMPANY
(Division of J.P. Stevens &
  Company)
1185 Avenue of the Americas
New York, New York 10036
(212) 575-2000

UNITED FARM BUREAU MUTUAL
  INSURANCE COMPANY
130 East Washington Street
Indianapolis, Indiana 46204
George Doup, President
(317) 263-7200

UNITED FLAV-R-PAC GROWERS
  INC.
    See Stayton Canning Company,
    Co-op

UNITED FOODS, INC.
5050 Poplar Avenue
Memphis, Tennessee 38117
(901) 683-3502
    See also Dulany Foods Inc.;
    Inglis Frozen Foods Company,
    John; and Winter Garden
    Freezer Company

Companies and Trade Names

UNITED FRUIT COMPANY
(Division of United Brands Company)
Prudential Center
800 Boyston Street
Boston, Massachusetts 02199
Eli M. Black, President
(617) 262-3000

UNITED FRUIT GROWERS ASSOCIATION
Palisade, Colorado 81526

UNITED FUR BROKERS
258 West 29th Street
New York, New York 10001
(212) 244-8667

UNITED GAS, INC.
1200 Milam Street
Houston, Texas 77002
Jackson C. Hinds, President
(713) 228-5111

UNITED GILSONITE LABORATORIES
Jefferson Avenue and New York
Scranton, Pennsylvania 18501
(717) 344-1202

UNITED GROCERS COMPANY
1630 Cody Street
Brooklyn, New York 11227
(212) 821-9220

UNITED ILLUMATING COMPANY, THE
80 Temple Street
New Haven, Connecticut 06506
John D. Fassett, President
(203) 777-7981

UNITED INDUSTRIES INC.
Post Office Box 231
Southington, Connecticut 06489

UNITED INDUSTRIES OF COLORADO INC.
3512 North Tejon
Colorado Springs, Colorado 80907

UNITED INNS, INC.
2300 Clark Tower
Memphis, Tennessee 38137
William C. Cockroft, Chairman
(901) 767-2880

UNITED KNITWEAR COMPANY, INC.
1384 Broadway
New York, New York 10018
(212) 354-2920

UNITED MARKETING EXCHANGE
Box 118
Delta, Colorado 81416

UNITED MASK & NOVELTY COMPANY
70-02 70th Avenue
Glendale, New York 11227
(212) 821-1816

UNITED METAL RECEPTACLE CORPORATION
14th and Laurel Streets
Pottsville, Pennsylvania 17901
(717) 622-7715

UNITED METALGOODS MANUFACTURING COMPANY
379 De Kalb Avenue
Brooklyn, New York 11205
Harold Levy, President
(212) 789-6200

UNITED MINERAL & CHEMICAL CORPORATION
129 Hudson
New York, New York 10013
Alexander Lipetz, President
(212) 966-4330

UNITED NATURAL GAS COMPANY
308 Seneca Street
Oil City, Pennsylvania 16301
John A. Comet, President
(814) 644-1251

UNITED PACIFIC INSURANCE COMPANY
728 Saint Helens Avenue
Tacoma, Washington 98401
John J. Savage, President
(206) 383-1481

UNITED PARCEL SERVICE OF NEW YORK
643 West 43rd Street
New York, New York 10036
James McLauglin, President
(212) 695-7500

UNITED PHARMACAL CORPORATION
103 River Street
Cambridge, Massachusetts 02139

UNITED PHARMACEUTICALS, INC.
1064 44th Avenue
Oakland, California 94601

UNITED PIECE DYE WORKS, THE
Post Office Box 279
Cranbury, New Jersey 08512
Harry M. Wellott Jr., President and Chief Executive Officer
(609) 448-8440

UNITED PLASTIC PRODUCTS COMPANY
Route 130
Florence, New Jersey 08518

UNITED PLASTICS INC.
Post Office Box 567
Paxton, Illinois 60957

UNITED RECORDING ELECTRONICS INDUSTRIES
11922 Valerio Street
North Hollywood, California 91605
(213) 764-1500

UNITED RICE MILLING PRODUCTS COMPANY INC.
1667 Tchoupitoulas Street
New Orleans, Louisiana 70150
(504) 525-5146

Companies and Trade Names

UNITED SALES COMPANY
Post Office Box 636
Reading, Pennsylvania 19603

UNITED SALT CORPORATION
2000 West Loop South
Houston, Texas 77027
James H. Tichenor, President
(713) 626-5400

UNITED STAPLE COMPANY INC.
5-15 48th Avenue
Long Island City, New York 11101
(212) 786-0478

U.S. (tires, rubber footwear, etc.)
See Uniroyal, Inc.

UNITED STATES BEDDING
COMPANY, THE
Wabash and Vandalia Streets
Saint Paul, Minnesota 55104
Edward L. Bronstein, Sr., Chairman
(612) 646-7221
See also Englander Company, Inc.

UNITED STATES BORAX &
CHEMICAL CORPORATION
3075 Wilshire Boulevard
Los Angeles, California 90010
Steffne Miller, Consumer Affairs
Coordinator
(213) 381-5311

U.S. CASTER CORPORATION
9999 West 75th Street
Overland Park, Kansas 66204
(913) 631-4900

UNITED STATES CERAMIC TILE
COMPANY
1375 Raff Road, S.W.
Canton, Ohio 44710
John Haggarty, President
(216) 477-8511

U.S. CHEWING GUM
MANUFACTURING COMPANY
730 45th Avenue
Oakland, California 94601
(415) 261-8323

U.S. CLUB (whiskey)
See National Distillers &
Chemical Corporation

U.S. CRAYON COMPANY
226 West Ontario Street
Chicago, Illinois 60610
(312) 787-6855

U.S. ENTERPRISES CORPORATION
832 Sansome
San Francisco, California 94111
(415) 986-2026

UNITED STATES ENVELOPE
COMPANY
(Subsidiary of Westvaco
Corporation)
Post Office Box 3300
Memorial Industrial Park
Springfield, Massachusetts 01101
Hans P. Stillbolt, President
(413) 736-7211

U.S. ENVELOPE COMPANY
Paper Cup Division
68 Prescott Street
Worcester, Massachusetts 01605

U.S. ETHICALS, INC.
37-02 48th Avenue
Long Island City, New York 11101
(212) 786-8606

U.S. EXPANSION BOLT
COMPANY
500 State Street
York, Pennsylvania 17405
(717) 843-0875

U.S. FIBER GLASS CORPORATION
4016 Crystal Lake Road
McHenry, Illinois 60050

U.S. FIDELITY & GUARANTEE
COMPANY
100 Light Street
Baltimore, Maryland 21202
Williford Gragg, President
(301) 547-3300

U.S. FIRE INSURANCE COMPANY
OF NEW YORK
110 William Street
New York, New York 10038
B.P. Russell, Chairman of the
Board
(212) 233-1100

U.S. GAMES SYSTEMS INC.
468 Park Avenue South
New York, New York 10016
(212) 685-4300

U.S. GELATINE COMPANY
Palmer Street
Gowanda, New York 14070
(716) 532-3344

UNITED STATES GYPSUM
COMPANY
101 South Wacker Drive
Chicago, Illinois 60606
Edward W. Duffy, President
(312) 321-4000
See also Kinkead Industries,
Inc.; and Warren Paint
& Color

U.S. HOME CORPORATION
1 Countryside Office Park
Clearwater, Florida 33515
Ben F. Harrison, President
(813) 736-7111

U.S. INDUSTRIAL CHEMICALS
COMPANY
(Division of National Distillers &
Chemical Corporation)
99 Park Avenue
New York, New York 10016
Clifford E. Oman, Vice President
and General Manager
(212) 697-0700

Companies and Trade Names

U.S. INDUSTRIAL PRODUCTS
 CORPORATION
96-12 43rd Avenue
Corona, New York 11368
(212) 335-3300

U.S. INDUSTRIES, INC.
250 Park Avenue
New York, New York 10017
I. John Billera, Chairman
(212) 697-4141
  See also Cardinal Cottons
   Corporation; Delwood
   Furniture Company; Georgia
   Boot; Gloray Knitting Mills,
   Inc.; Health Industries,
   Inc.; Import Associates;
   Oomphies Inc.; Pennaco;
   Poly-Tech; Rau Fastener;
   Round-the-Clock Hosiery;
   and Western Mobile Homes,
   Inc.

U.S. LACE PAPER WORKS, INC.
417 Union Avenue
Brooklyn, New York 11211
(212) 387-3003

U.S. LINE COMPANY
22 Main Street
Westfield, Massachusetts 01085
(413) 562-3629

UNITED STATES LINES, INC.
1 Broadway
New York, New York 10004
B.N. Ames, Chairman of the Board
(212) 344-5800

UNITED STATES LUGGAGE
 CORPORATION
951 Broadway
Fall River, Massachusetts 02724
Sydney S. Feinberg, Chairman of
 the Board
(617) 675-7883

U.S. MACARONI MANUFACTURING
 COMPANY
East 601 Pacific Avenue
Spokane, Washington 99202
(509) 747-2085

U.S. MARINE COATINGS INC.
Box 5425
Sarasota, Florida 33529

U.S. METALITE CORPORATION
405 Farabee Drive
Lafayette, Indiana 47902
(317) 447-6874

U.S. NATIONAL BANK OF
 OREGON
321 S.W. Sixth Avenue
Portland, Oregon 97204
Robert E. Mitchell, President
(503) 225-6111

UNITED STATES NATIONAL BANK
 OF SAN DIEGO
190 Broadway
San Diego, California 92112
James F. Mulvaney, President
(714) 234-4311

UNITED STATES NAVIGATION
 INC.
17 Battery Place
New York, New York 10004
Edward Oelsner, Jr., President
(212) 269-6000

UNITED STATES ORIENT
 AGENCIES INC.
110 West 40th Street
New York, New York 10018
(212) 563-5876

UNITED STATES PACKAGING
 CORPORATION
506 Clay
LaPorte, Indiana 46350

U.S. PAINT, LACQUER &
 CHEMICAL COMPANY
(Subsidiary of Grow Chemicals
 Corporation)
2101 Singleton Street
Saint Louis, Missouri 63103
J.M. Dilschneider, President and
 Treasurer
(314) 621-0525

U.S. PENCIL & STATIONERY
 COMPANY
(Division of Cadence Industries
 Corporation)
21 Henderson Drive
West Caldwell, New Jersey 07006
(201) 227-5100

UNITED STATES PHARMACAL
 COMPANY
(Division of Garden Pharmaceuticals
 Inc.)
2647 Grand Avenue
Bellmore, New York 11710

U.S. PIONEER ELECTRONICS
 CORPORATION
178 Commerce Street
Carlstadt, New Jersey 07072

U.S. PIPE & FOUNDRY COMPANY
(Subsidiary of Jim Walter
 Corporation)
3300 First Avenue North
Birmingham, Alabama 35202
W.L. Turner, President
(205) 254-7000

UNITED STATES PLAYING CARD
 COMPANY, THE
(Subsidiary of Diamond International
 Corporation)
Park and Beech Streets
Cincinnati, Ohio 45212
(513) 731-0220

U.S. PLYWOOD
(Division of Champion International
 Corporation)
777 Third Avenue
New York, New York 10017
John A. Ball, President
(212) 935-3500

UNITED STATES PRODUCTS INC.
1105 Front Street N.E.
Salem, Oregon 97308

UNITED STATES PUMICE COMPANY
2890 Empire Boulevard
Burbank, California 91504
(213) 834-8553

Companies and Trade Names

U.S. RUBBER RECLAIMING
COMPANY, INC.
Post Office Box 54
Vicksburg, Mississippi 39180
Benjamin R. Wendrow, President
(601) 636-5457

U.S. SCHOOL OF MUSIC, INC.
See Macmillan, Inc.

U.S. SHOE CORPORATION
1658 Herald Avenue
Cincinnati, Ohio 45207
Philip G. Barach, President
(513) 841-4111
See also Cincinnati Shoe Company; Freeman Shoe Company; Freeman-Toor Corporation; Marx & Newman Company, Inc.; Texas Boot Company; and Vaisey-Bristol Shoe Company, Inc.

U.S. SLICING MACHINE
COMPANY, INC.
1 Berkel Drive
La Porte, Indiana 46350
P.F.A. Wulff, President
(219) 362-3165

UNITED STATES STEEL
CORPORATION
600 Grant Street
Pittsburgh, Pennsylvania 15230
Edgar Speer, Chairman of the Board
(412) 433-1121

U.S. SUZUKI MOTOR
CORPORATION
13767 Freeway Drive
Santa Fe Springs, California 90670
K. Iizuka, Vice President
(213) 921-4461

UNITED STATES TELEPHONE
COMPANY
444 Park Avenue South
New York, New York 10016
(212) 889-4885

U.S. TOBACCO COMPANY
100 West Putnam Avenue
Greenwich, Connecticut 06830
Louis A. Bantle, President
(203) 661-1100
See also Cadillac Pet Foods, Inc.; Circus Foods; Grabow Pre-Smoked Pipes Inc.; House of Windsor, Inc.; Lummis & Company; and Smokemaster Pipes

U.S. TRUST COMPANY OF NEW YORK
45 Wall Street
New York, New York 10005
Charles W. Buek, President
(212) 425-4500

U.S. YACHT PAINT COMPANY
Box 96
Roseland, New Jersey 07068

UNITED STATIONERS SUPPLY
COMPANY
1900 South DesPlaines Avenue
Forest Park, Illinois 60130

UNITED STELLAR INDUSTRIES
131 Sunnyside Boulevard
Plainview, New York 11803

UNITED TECHNICAL INSTITUTE
See Career Academy, Inc.

UNITED TELEPHONE COMPANY
OF FLORIDA
1520 Lee Street
Fort Myers, Florida 33902
E.P. Kittinger, President
(813) 334-1311

UNITED TELEPHONE COMPANY
OF MISSOURI
2330 Johnson Drive
Shawnee Mission, Kansas 66205
C.D. Ehinger, President
(913) 236-9900

UNITED TELEPHONE COMPANY
OF OHIO
665 Lexington Avenue
Mansfield, Ohio 44907
R.H. Snedaker, Jr., President
(419) 755-8011

UNITED TELEPHONE COMPANY
OF PENNSYLVANIA
1170 Harrisburg Pike
Carlisle, Pennsylvania 17013
Lawrence G. Wigbels, President
(717) 243-6312

UNITED THREAD MILLS
CORPORATION
146 Greene Street
New York, New York 10012
(212) 966-4440

UNITED TRACTOR COMPANY
Post Office Box 358
116 North 15th Street
Chesterton, Indiana 46304
(219) 926-1186

UNITED TRADE REPRESENTATIVES,
INC.
1775 Broadway
New York, New York 10019
(212) 489-8970

UNITED ULTRAMARiNE &
CHEMICAL COMPANY
2 Terminal Road
New Brunswick, New Jersey 08902

UNITED VAN LINES, INC.
Betty Malone Relocation Center
1 United Drive
Fenton, Missouri 63026
Carol A. Sellew, Manager, Marketing Communications
(314) 326-3100
(800) 325-3870

Companies and Trade Names

UNITED VINTNERS, INC.
(Subsidiary of Heublein, Inc.)
601 Fourth Street
San Francisco, California 94107
Donna L. Sheppard, Consumer
  Relations Coordinator
(415) 421-3213
  See also International Vintage
  Wines; and Morgo Wine
  Company

UNITED VIRGINIA BANK
Ninth and Main
Richmond, Virginia 23219
Joseph A. Jennings, Chairman
  of the Board
(804) 771-5000

UNITEK CORPORATION
2724 South Peck Road
Monrovia, California 91016

UNITEX PRODUCTS INC.
(Subsidiary of Angelica Corporation)
Fourth and Seminole Streets
Lester, Pennsylvania 19113
Cal Batchelor, Vice President
(215) 521-3300

UNITHERM (unit heaters)
  See Clarage Fan Company

UNITOG COMPANY
1004 Baltimore Avenue
Kansas City, Missouri 64105
Dutton Brookfield, President
(816) 474-7000

UNITREE CORPORATION
812 Borden Road
Cheektowaga, New York 14225

UNITY BUYING SERVICE COMPANY
810 South Broadway
Hicksville, New York 11802
Albert Friedman, President
(516) 433-9100

UNIVAL CORPORATION
157 Summerfield Street
Scarsdale, New York 10583
Jerome Berk President
(914) 725-0200

UNIVAR CORPORATION
1600 Norton Building
Seattle, Washington 98104
James H. Wiborg, President
(206) 447-5911

UNIVERSAL (car radios and
stereos)
  See Matsushita Electric
  Corporation of America

UNIVERSAL (electrical appliances)
  See General Electric
  Company

UNIVERSAL (enamel cookware)
  See Atlas Originals

UNIVERSAL (freezers)
  See Universal Cooperatives
  Inc.

UNIVERSAL (sewing machines)
  See Standard Sewing
  Equipment Corporation

UNIVERSAL CIGAR CORPORATION
660 Madison Avenue
New York, New York 10021
Edward Gropper, Chairman and
  President
(212) 753-5700

UNIVERSAL COOPERATIVES, INC.
111 Glamorgan Street
Alliance, Ohio 44601
Glenn Franklin, President
(216) 821-5770

UNIVERSAL DRUG PRODUCTS
568 Broad Avenue
Ridgefield, New Jersey 07657

UNIVERSAL EDUCATION & VISUAL
  ARTS
(Division of Universal City Studios,
  Inc.)
100 Manetto Hill Road
Plainview, New York 11803
(516) 433-2656

UNIVERSAL FIELD EQUIPMENT
  COMPANY INC.
Mira Loma Space Center,
  Building 811A
Mira Loma, California 91752

UNIVERSAL FILING SYSTEMS,
  INC.
(Division of Visible Computer
  Supply Corporation)
9865 Derby Lane
Westchester, Illinois 60153

UNIVERSAL FOODS CORPORATION
433 East Michigan Street
Milwaukee, Wisconsin 53201
Robert T. Foote, Chairman of the
  Board
(414) 271-6755

UNIVERSAL FOUNDATIONS, INC.
  See Glucken & Company,
  Inc., William

UNIVERSAL FOUNTAIN BRUSH
  COMPANY
Post Office Box 295
Saint Petersburg, Florida 33731
(813) 894-3027

UNIVERSAL FOUNTAIN PEN &
  PENCIL COMPANY
694 Metropolitan Avenue
Brooklyn, New York 11211
(212) 384-1317

UNIVERSAL GENEVE (watches)
  See Holzer Watch Company Inc.

UNIVERSAL IMPORTERS INC.
70 Orchard Drive
North Salt Lake, Utah 84054
(801) 363-2653

Companies and Trade Names

UNIVERSAL IMPORTS COMPANY
Industrial Cold Storage Building
American and Berk Streets
Philadelphia, Pennsylvania 19122
(215) 427-1717

UNIVERSAL MERCHANDISE
 CORPORATION
321 West 13th Street
New York, New York 10014
(212) 675-1390

UNIVERSAL MILKING MACHINE
 MANUFACTURING
(Division of Universal Cooperatives,
 Inc.)
408 First Avenue S.W.
Albert Lea, Minnesota 56007
(507) 373-3922

UNIVERSAL MODEL PRODUCTS
 COMPANY INC.
3919 M Street
Philadelphia, Pennsylvania 19124
(215) 537-9994
 See also Gem Models

UNIVERSAL MOTORS
(Division of Medalist Industries)
1552 Harrison Street
Oshkosh, Wisconsin 54901
Norman J. Fischer, President
(414) 231-4100

UNIVERSAL OIL PRODUCTS
 COMPANY
10 UOP Plaza
Des Plaines, Illinois 60016
(312) 391-2000

UNIVERSAL PACKERS
 CORPORATION
804 East Third
Oxnard, California 93030

UNIVERSAL PAPER GOODS
 COMPANY
7171 Telegraph Road
Los Angeles, California 90040
(213) 685-6220

UNIVERSAL PICTURES
445 Park Avenue
New York, New York 10022
Henry H. Marten, President
(212) 759-7500

UNIVERSAL PRODUCING
 COMPANY
Fairfield, Iowa 52556
R.R. Stewart, Jr., President
(515) 472-5161

UNIVERSAL PROMOTIONS, INC.
407 South Dearborn
Chicago, Illinois 60605
(312) 427-4814

UNIVERSAL RESILITE
43 Polk Avenue
Hempstead, New York 11550

UNIVERSAL-RUNDLE
 CORPORATION
Box 960
New Castle, Pennsylvania 16103
J.W. Sant, President
(412) 658-6631

UNIVERSAL SECURITY
 INSTRUMENTS INC.
2829 Potee Street
Baltimore, Maryland 21225
Michael Kovens, President
(301) 355-9000

UNIVERSAL STATUARY
 CORPORATION
850 North Ogden Avenue
Chicago, Illinois 60622
L. Lucchesi, President
(312) 666-1155

UNIVERSAL SURGICAL
400 N.E. 191st Street
Miami, Florida 33162
(305) 652-0810

UNIVERSAL-390 (standard
 typewriters)
 See Adler Business Machines
  Inc.

UNIVERSAL TIME
437 North Fifth Street
Springfield, Illinois 62702

UNIVERSAL TRACTOR-EQUIPMENT
 CORPORATION
Box 5489
928 North Meadow Street
Richmond, Virginia 23220
(804) 353-7806

UNIVERSAL WATER SYSTEMS,
 INC.
(Subsidiary of The Coca-Cola
 Company)
1425 Hawthorne Lane
West Chicago, Illinois 60185
W.E. Bergmann, President
(312) 231-7170

UNIVERSE (tables)
 See Reflector Hardware
  Corporation-Spacemaster

UNIVERSE FOODS COMPANY
161 Park Avenue
Paterson, New Jersey 07509

UNIVERSITY (canned foods)
 See Eisner Food Stores

UNIVERSITY CLUB (malt liquor)
 See Miller Brewing Company

UNIVERSITY COMPUTING
 COMPANY
(Subsidiary of Wyly Corporation)
7200 Stemmons Parkway
Dallas, Texas 75247
Donald Thomson, President and
 Chief Executive Officer
(214) 637-5010

UNIVERSITY DRUG COMPANY
 INC.
609 North Grand Boulevard
Saint Louis, Missouri 63103
(314) 533-5941

Companies and Trade Names

UNIVERSITY GUILD (men's double knit clothing)
See Louis Goldsmith Inc.

UNIVEX LOOSELEAF CORPORATION
2200 East Empire Avenue
Benton Harbor, Michigan 49022

UNIVIS, INC.
(Subsidiary of Itek Corporation)
3301 S.W. Ninth Avenue
Fort Lauderdale, Florida 33315

UNIVOR MANUFACTURING CORPORATION, THE
101-23 44th Avenue
Corona, New York 11368

UNIWELD PRODUCTS INC.
2850 Ravenswood Road
Fort Lauderdale, Florida 33312
(305) 583-6743

UNLIMITED BEAUTY, INC.
State Road
Route 6
North Dartmouth, Massachusetts 02747

UNLIMITED IMPORTS INC.
472 Third Avenue
San Diego, California 92101

UNMASK LTD.
2915 South LaCienega Boulevard
Culver City, California 90230

UPJOHN COMPANY, THE
7000 Portage Road
Kalamazoo, Michigan 49001
William Hubbard, President
(616) 382-4000
See also Asgrow Mandeville Company; and Asgrow Seed Company

UPLAND INDUSTRIES INC.
115 Sixth Street
Upland, Pennsylvania 19015
John Kuc, President and Sales Manager
(215) 874-4261

UPLAND LEMON GROWERS ASSOCIATION
392 East A Street
Upland, California 91786
C. Harper Brubaker, President
(714) 985-7265

UPPER DECK (canned foods)
See Fall River Canning Company

UPPER TEN (soft drink)
See Royal Crown Cola Company

UPSHER-SMITH LABORATORIES
529 South Seventh Street
Minneapolis, Minnesota 55415
(612) 332-0467

UPSON COMPANY, THE
Upson Point
Lockport, New York 14094
James J. Upson, President
(716) 434-8881

UPSON TOOLS INC.
Post Office Box 4750-T
99 Ling Road
Rochester, New York 14612
(716) 663-5373

UPTIGHT (toiletries)
See Clairol, Inc.

UPTOWNER INNS INC.
1415 Fourth Avenue
Huntington, West Virginia 25701

URBANA MILLS COMPANY
Box 312
716 Miami Street
Urbana, Ohio 43078
Donald H. Schultz, President and Treasurer
(513) 653-5211

URBANI, PAUL A.
130 Graf Avenue
Trenton, New Jersey 08638

URIS BUILDING CORPORATION
850 Third Avenue
New York, New York 10022
Andrew J. Frankel, President
(212) 688-8200

UROLLIT (men's hats)
See Bailey Hat Company

URSIN SEAFOODS INC.
Box 492
Kodiak, Arkansas 99615

USALITE (flashlights, batteries, etc.)
See Bright Star Industries

USAPHARM CORPORATION
520 South Dean Street
Englewood, New Jersey 07631

USEN PRODUCTS COMPANY
See Lipton Pet Foods, Inc.

USHLER'S GREEN STRIPE (Scotch whiskey)
See Brown-Forman Distillers Corporation

USYLIN CORPORATION
578 Chestnut Street
Lynn, Massachusetts 01904

Companies and Trade Names

UTAH-IDAHO SUGAR COMPANY
Beneficial Life Building
Salt Lake City, Utah 84110
Rowland M. Cannon, President
(801) 328-9031

UTAH PACKERS, INC.
2404 Washington Boulevard
Ogden, Utah 84401

UTAH POWER & LIGHT COMPANY
1407 West North Temple
Salt Lake City, Utah 84116
Edward M. Naughton, Chairman
   of the Board
(801) 350-3535

UTAH'S FAVORITE (canned tomato
products)
   See Woods Cross Canning
        Company

UTE (seafood)
   See Stein Fish Company

UTE LINER INC.
145 West 4500 South
Murray, Utah 84107
(801) 262-4611

UTEXIQUAL
(Division of Executive Designs,
   Inc.)
Box 59 B
Mount Laurel Road
Morrestown, New Jersey 08057
(609) 235-0220

UTICA (sheets and pillowcases)
   See J.P. Stevens & Company,

UTICA CLUB (beer)
   See West End Brewing
        Company

UTICA CUTLERY COMPANY
820 Noyes Street
Utica, New York 13502
A. Edward Allen, Jr., President
(315) 733-4663

UTICA-DUXBAK CORPORATION
815 Noyes
Utica, New York 13502
Gilbert H. Jones, President
(315) 797-0050

UTICA MUTUAL INSURANCE
COMPANY
Utica, New York 13503
Victor T. Ehre, President
(315) 735-3321

UTICA TOOL COMPANY, THE
(Subsidiary of Triangle Corporation)
Cameron Road
Orangeburg, South Carolina 29115
R. William Metzger, President
(803) 534-7010

UTILITIES ENGINEERING
INSTITUTE
   See Macmillan, Inc.

UTILITY CHEMICAL COMPANY
Sixth and Waite Streets
Paterson, New Jersey 07524
Bernard H. Lehner, President
(201) 274-2800

UTILITY COMPANY, INC.
10 West 33rd
New York, New York 10001
(212) 279-1775

UTILITY METAL PRODUCTS
COMPANY INC.
117 Elliot Street
Beverly, Massachusetts 01915
(617) 922-0581

UTILIVAR (paint)
   See McDougall-Butler
        (Division of Bisonite
        Company, Inc.)

UTINSLOW MANUFACTURING
(Division of Watsco Inc.)
1800 West Fourth
Hialeah, Florida 33010

UTOPIA COACH INC.
Post Office Box 1282
Elkhart, Indiana 46514
(219) 522-7705

UTZ POTATO CHIP COMPANY
   INC.
Hanover, Pennsylvania 17331

Companies and Trade Names

V

V.B. LABORATORIES
269 Monticello Avenue
Jersey City, New Jersey 07306

V.C.A. CORPORATION
Federal Housewares Division
3600 West Pratt Avenue
Chicago, Illinois 60645
(312) 267-3060
See also Federal Tool & Plastic

VDO INSTRUMENTS
116 Victor Avenue
Detroit, Michigan 48203
(313) 883-2676

V-8 (cocktail vegetable juice)
See Campbell Soup Company

V.F. CORPORATION
1047 North Park Road
Wyomissing
Reading, Pennsylvania 19610
Manford O. Lee, Chairman of the Board
(215) 378-1151
See also Berkshire International Corporation; Kay Windsor, Inc.; Lee Company, Inc., H.D.; and Vanity Fair Mills, Inc.

V-4 EMBOSSED (window shades)
See Breneman, Inc.

VIP (fluorescent lamps)
See Lightolier Inc.

V.I.P. (foundation garments, lingerie)
See Olga Company

VIP (frozen foods)
See Fadler Company

V.I.P. (tobacco)
See House of Edgeworth

V.I.P. IMPORTS, LTD.
320 Fifth Avenue, Room 1004
New York, New York 10001
(212) 563-0715

V.I.P. INDUSTRIES INC.
1543 14th Street
Santa Monica, California 90404
(213) 871-0828

VLN CORPORATION
1374 East 51st Street
Cleveland, Ohio 44103
David H. Cogan, President
(216) 744-7646

V-M CORPORATION
305 Territorial Road
Benton Harbor, Michigan 49002
Victor A. Miller, President
(616) 925-8841

VMR (meat extender)
See Nabisco Inc.

V-O (whiskey)
See Seagram Distillers Company

VO 5 (hair-care products)
See Alberto Culver Company

VRC VITAMIN RESEARCH CORPORATION
See Vitamin Research Corporation

VSA VISUAL SALES AIDS
34-21 56th Street
Woodside, New York 11377
(212) 478-0400

V.S.C. (canned fruits and vegetables)
See Vancouver Supply Company, Ltd.

VWR UNITED CORPORATION
See Univar Corporation

VAC-U-RIG (power tools)
See Milwaukee Electric Tool Corporation

VACATION (campers)
See Delta Industries Inc.

VACATIONER (luggage)
See Seward Luggage

VACHERON & CONSTANTIN (watches and scientific instruments)
See Longines-Wittnauer Watch Company, Inc.

VACHON (preserves, pie filling, mustard, etc)
See Diamond Products Ltd.

VACMASTER (vacuum cleaners)
See Bigelow-Sanford, Inc.

VACOL (storm windows, screens, etc.)
See V.E. Anderson Manufacturing Company, Inc.

VACU-BLAST CORPORATION
Post Office Box 885
Belmont, California 94002
(415) 592-2121

VACU-DRY COMPANY
5801 Christie Street
Emeryville, California 94608
Kenneth P. Gill, President
(415) 654-0116

VACUETTE (vacuum cleaner)
See Scott & Fetzer Company

VACULATOR (coffee makers)
See Hill-Shaw Company

Companies and Trade Names

VACUUM CLEANER CORPORATION
OF AMERICA
  See Cordomatic

VAGABOND MOTOR HOTELS
  INC.
1810 State Street
San Diego, California 92101
I. Ronald Horowitz, President and
  Vice Chairman
(714) 232-6274

VAHLSING, INC.
Route 130
Robbinsville, New Jersey 08691
F.H. Vahlsing, Jr., Chairman and
  President
(609) 586-7000

VAIR-E-BEST CANDIES
16057 Hamilton
Detroit, Michigan 48203

VAISEY-BRISTOL SHOE COMPANY,
  INC.
(Division of United States Shoe
  Corporation)
Monett, Missouri 65708
Norton Saidleman, President
(417) 235-3122

VAL (paints and paint sundries)
  See E. Rabinowe & Company

VAL-A-PAK (luggage)
  See Atlantic Products
    Corporation

VAL DEZ (guitars)
  See Buegeleisen & Jacobson Ltd.

VAL D'OR (dinnerware pattern)
  See Ebeling & Reuss Company

VAL MODE LINGERIE, INC.
102 Madison Avenue
New York, New York 10016
Melvin Morris, President
(212) 684-4270

VAL-TEST DISTRIBUTORS INC.
Riverside Plaza Building
400 West Madison Street
Chicago, Illinois 60606
(312) 372-2250

VALAGRAPH COMPANY
6905 East Oslo Circle
Buena Park, California 90622

VALAMONT (canned foods)
  See National Fruit Canning
    Company

VALCO COMPANY
1311-15 Ann Avenue
Saint Louis, Missouri 63104
(314) 776-2660

VALCRAFT, INC.
Box 166
Morgantown, West Virginia 26505

VALDON (frozen foods)
  See Red Owl Stores, Inc.

VALDOSTA DRUG COMPANY
Box 1287
Valdosta, Georgia 31601

VALE (apples and pears)
  See Butler Trading Company,
    Inc.

VALE CHEMICAL COMPANY, INC.;
  THE
1201 Liberty Street
Allentown, Pennsylvania 18102
(215) 433-7579

VALENCIA (food products)
  See Lindsay International

VALENSI, LANGE, INC.;
  RANDOLPH E.
422 Taconic Road
Greenwich, Connecticut 06830

VALENTI, GARY
55-72 61st Street
Maspeth, New York 11378

VALENTINE (furniture)
  See Kroehler Manufacturing
    Company

VALENTINE (paints, varnishes,
enamels)
  See Valspar Corporation

VALENTINE & STRAUSS INC.
  See Valentine Sales Inc.

VALENTINE COMPANY
Post Office Box 7360
3414 West Leigh
Richmond, Virginia 23221
(804) 358-4012

VALENTINE SALES INC.
111 West 40th Street
New York, New York 10018
(212) 354-5455

VALENTINE-SEAVER (furniture)
  See Kroehler Manufacturing
    Company

VALENTINES (women's shoes)
  See Genesco, Inc.

VALET (razor blades)
  See Gillette Safety Razor
    Company

VALET (tie racks)
  See Crest Specialty

VALET PAC (grooming kit)
  See H.C. Cook Company

VALETONE (dry-cleaning franchise)
  See One Hour Valetone of
    America Inc.

Companies and Trade Names

VALHAR CHEMICAL CORPORATION
277 Greenwich Avenue
Greenwich, Connecticut 06830

VALIANT (cigarettes)
See Brown & Williamson Tobacco Corporation

VALIANT (cookware)
See Wear-Ever Aluminum Inc.

VALIANT (men's leather wear)
See Salvatori

VALID PROCESS COMPANY
459 West 15th Street
New York, New York 10011
(212) 675-5216

VALIENT (health and beauty aids)
See Hinky Dinky Stores

VALLE FRERES (wines)
See International Vintage Wines

VALLE VERDE (milk products)
See Maple Island Inc.

VALLE'S STEAK HOUSES
660 Forest Avenue
Portland, Maine 04103
Donald Valle, Chairman of the Board
(207) 775-6571

VALLEY (food products)
See Arnold Pickle & Olive Company

VALLEY (shoes)
See Johansen Brothers Shoe Company, Inc.

VALLEY DISTRIBUTING COMPANY
2540 North 29th Avenue
Phoenix, Arizona 85009
Jacob E. Heneger, President
(602) 269-1451

VALLEY EVAPORATING COMPANY
Box 16
Yakima, Washington 98901
(509) 453-7169

VALLEY FAIR CORPORATION
260 Bergen Turnpike
Little Ferry, New Jersey 07643
Philip Ganguzza, President
(201) 488-4000

VALLEY FARMS (frozen foods)
See McCain Foods, Ltd.

VALLEY FIG GROWERS
2028 South Third Street
Fresno, California 93702
William H. Corbett, President
(209) 237-3893

VALLEY FORGE (beer)
See C. Schmidt & Sons, Inc.

VALLEY FORGE FLAG COMPANY
1 Rockefeller Plaza
New York, New York 10020
Abraham Liberman, Chairman and President
(212) 586-1776

VALLEY FORGE PRODUCTS
150 Roger Avenue
Inwood, New York 11696
(516) 239-1900

VALLEY GEM (food products)
See Bush Brothers & Company

VALLEY-HI (frozen foods)
See Northwest Cold Pack Company

VALLEY HONEY ASSOCIATION
Box 1241
Stockton, California 95201

VALLEY LABORATORIES
Box 116
Spring Valley, New York 10977

VALLEY LAKE FARMS (meat products)
See Frigid Freeze Foods, Inc.

VALLEY NATIONAL BANK OF ARIZONA
141 North Central Avenue
Phoenix, Arizona 85004
G.F. Bradley, President
(602) 261-2900

VALLEY PACKERS INC.
Box 97
Puyallup, Washington 98371

VALLEY PAPER COMPANY
Holyoke, Massachusetts 01040

VALLEY VIEW ORCHARDS
Peckville Road
Shelburne, Massachusetts 01370

VALLEYCREST (carpeting)
See Bigelow-Sanford Inc.

VALMOR PRODUCTS COMPANY, THE
2411 South Prairie Avenue
Chicago, Illinois 60616
(312) 225-7215

VALSPAR CORPORATION, THE
1101 South Third Street
Minneapolis, Minnesota 55415
C.A. Wurtele, Chairman of the Board
(612) 332-7371

VALU-LINE (beefsteaks)
See L.B. Darling & Company, Inc.

VALU-PLUS (air fresheners, deodorant, hair spray, oven cleaner, etc.)
See Chase Products Company

Companies and Trade Names

VALUAIRE (heating equipment)
See Auer Register Company

VALUE (rubber products)
See Rand Rubber Company

VALULINE (kitchen thermometers)
See Taylor Instrument Companies (Consumer Products Division)

VALVOLINE OIL COMPANY
(Division of Ashland Oil, Inc.)
Post Office Box 391
Ashland, Kentucky 41101
John F. Boehm, President
(606) 329-3333

VAM (hairdressing)
See Colgate-Palmolive Company

VAN BAALEN PACIFIC CORPORATION
393 Fifth Avenue
New York, New York 10016
George Cooper, President
(212) 684-0672

VAN BENNETT FOOD INC.
415 Gregg Avenue
Reading, Pennsylvania 19062

VAN BOURGONDIEN & SONS, K.
Box A
Babylon, New York 11702

VAN BRITE (wax and dry-cleaning soap)
See Adco, Inc.

VAN BRODE MILLING COMPANY, INC.
20 Cameron Street
Clinton, Massachusetts 01510
W.H. Crowley, President
(617) 365-4541

VAN BUREN COUNTY FRUIT EXCHANGE
Box 116
Hartford, Michigan 49057

VAN CAMP HARDWARE & IRON COMPANY INC.
Box 1094
5201 West 86th Street
Indianapolis, Indiana 46206
(317) 291-8090

VAN CAMP SEA FOOD
(Division of Ralston Purina Company)
835 South Eighth Street
Checkerboard Square
Saint Louis, Missouri 63102
Richard Atchison, Vice President
(314) 982-3648

VAN CAMP'S (canned foods)
See Stokely-Van Camp Inc.

VAN CLEFF STUDIOS INC.
580 Riverside Avenue
Westport, Connecticut 06880

VAN COMPANY-QUALITY CARD COMPANY
Post Office Box 141
Huntingdon Valley, Pennsylvania 19006

VAN DAM
(Division of Miner Industries Inc.)
200 Fifth Avenue
New York, New York 10010
Thomas Van Dam, General Division and Sales Manager
(212) 691-9400

VAN DE KAMP (bread)
See General Host Corporation

VAN DINE & COMPANY, PETER D.
Post Office Box 8
Annapolis, Maryland 21404
(301) 867-0575

VAN DOORN COMPANY, THE HERBERT
1355 Market Street
San Francisco, California 94103
(415) 861-5139

VAN DORN (electric tools)
See Black & Decker Manufacturing Company

VAN DOW-FENTON, INC.
225 Fifth Avenue
New York, New York 10010
(212) 683-2782

VAN DUTCH PRODUCTS CORPORATION
2417 Third Avenue
Bronx, New York 10451
E.J. Lowry, President and Treasurer
(212) 292-0300

VAN DYCK (cigars)
See General Cigar Company

VAN DYKE (pencils, erasers, leads)
See Eberhard Faber

VAN GELDER-FANTO CORPORATION
420 Lexington Avenue
New York, New York 10017
(212) 490-3950

VAN HEES ORCHARDS
Post Falls, Idaho 83854

VAN HEUSEN (men's apparel)
See Phillips Van Heusen Corporation

VAN HEUSEN/WINDBREAKER (men's outerwear)
See Windbreaker Inc.

1369

Companies and Trade Names

VAN HOLTEN & SON, INC.
J.G.
Post Office Box 66
703 West Madison Street
Waterloo, Wisconsin 53594
E. Jerry Van Holten, President
(414) 478-2144

VAN HOUTEN (candy)
See Peter Paul, Inc.

VAN HOUTEN & ZOON, C.J.
105 Hudson Street
New York, New York 10013
Harry G. Grover, Jr., President
(212) 924-7101

VAN LUIT & COMPANY, ALBERT
4000 Chevy Chase Drive
Los Angeles, California 90039
(213) 245-5106

VAN MELLE, INC.
Post Office Box 401
South Sudbury, Massachusetts 01776

VAN MERRITT COMPANY
2415-49 West 21st
Chicago, Illinois 60608
(312) 847-7000

VAN MUNCHING & COMPANY, INC.
51 West 51st Street
New York, New York 10019
L. van Munching, President
(212) 265-2685

VAN NOSTRAND REINHOLD COMPANY
(Division of Litton Educational Publishing, Inc.)
450 West 33rd Street
New York, New York 10001
Robert E. Ewing, President
(212) 594-8660

VAN PELS INC., MAX
10 Columbus Circle
New York, New York 10019
(212) 586-6020

VAN RAALTE COMPANY, INC.
(Subsidiary of Cluett Peabody & Company)
417 Fifth Avenue
New York, New York 10016
John J. McCarthy, President
(212) 689-4200

VAN ROOY COFFEE COMPANY
2900 Detroit Avenue
Cleveland, Ohio 44113
(216) 771-1220

VAN SAN CORPORATION
1180 Centre Drive
City of Industry, California 91748
(714) 595-7487

VAN SLYKE & HORTON, G.W.
Drawer 111
Red Lion, Pennsylvania 17356

VAN VALKENBURG COMPANY, L.D.
Post Office Box 190
Holyoke, Massachusetts 01040
(413) 536-7400

VAN WYCK PRODUCTS COMPANY, INC.
120 South Euclid Street
Pasadena, California 91101
(213) 681-4823

VANCE INDUSTRIES, INC.
7401 West Wilson Avenue
Chicago, Illinois 60656
Wayne E. Toussaint, Chairman and President
(312) 867-8161

VANCO (tools, lawn and garden supplies, electrical supplies)
See Van Camp Hardware & Iron Company Inc.

VANCO COMPANY
925 Lake Avenue
Gothenburg, Nebraska 69138

VANDA (cosmetics and toiletries)
See Dart Industries

VANDALIA (health and beauty aids)
See Red Owl Stores, Inc.

VANDERBILT PRODUCTS INC.
585 Dean Street
Brooklyn, New York 11238
(212) 622-2700

VANDERBURGH & COMPANY INC.
11 Broadway
New York, New York 10004
(212) 422-1226

VANDERFLIT (wine)
See Renfield Importers, Ltd.

VANDERHORST CANNERY
430 West South Street
Saint Marys, Ohio 45885
Thomas A. Vanderhorst, President
(419) 394-5236

VANDERLAAN TILE COMPANY, INC.
103 Park Avenue
New York, New York 10017
(212) 532-0362

VANEE FOODS
5418 McDermott Drive
Berkeley, Illinois 60163

VANGUARD (cigarettes)
See Brown & Williamson Tobacco Corporation

VANGUARD (men's slippers)
See L.B. Evans' Son Company

VANGUARD (shoes)
See Melville Shoe Corporation

VANGUARD (sports accessories)
See Alpine Crafts Company Inc.

Companies and Trade Names

VANGUARD (thermos bottles, lunch kits)
See Aladdin Industries, Inc.

VANGUARD BUSINESS FURNITURE INC.
(Division of Vanguard Diversified Inc.)
10 Java Street
Brooklyn, New York 11222
(212) 383-2500

VANGUARD INC.
1251 East Wisconsin Avenue
Pewaukee, Wisconsin 53072
(414) 691-3320

VANGUARD INSURANCE COMPANY
2727 Turtle Creek Boulevard
Dallas, Texas 75219
John F. Knight, President
(214) 528-0301

VANGUARD LABORATORIES
(Division of Midway Medical Company)
415 Samson Street
Glasgow, Kentucky 42141

VANGUARD PRESS, INC., THE
424 Madison Avenue
New York, New York 10017
Evelyn Shrifte, President
(212) 753-3906

VANGUARD RECORDING SOCIETY, INC.
71 West 23rd Street
New York, New York 10010
Seymour Solomon, President
(212) 255-7732

VANGUARD SHOE STORES
See Melville Shoe Corporation

VANGUARD STUDIOS INC.
20746 Dearborn Street
Chatsworth, California 91311
Stuart C. Burr, President and Chief Executive Officer
(213) 341-4115

VANIA SPORTSWEAR (handmade Greek robes, caftans, blouses)
See Art Originals Ltd.

VANISH (toilet-bowl cleaner)
See Drackett Company

VANITY CORSET COMPANY, INC.
1115 Broadway
New York, New York 10010
(212) 924-8550

VANITY FAIR (cigarettes)
See Stephano Brothers

VANITY FAIR (luggage)
See Hartmann Luggage Company, Inc.

VANITY FAIR (mattresses)
See Burton-Dixie Corporation

VANITY FAIR INDUSTRIES INC.
170 Michael Drive
Syosset, New York 11791

VANITY FAIR MILLS, INC.
(Subsidiary of VF Corporation)
1047 North Park Road
Wyomissing, Pennsylvania 19610
M.O. Lee, Chairman of the Board
(215) 376-7201

VANITY FAIR PAPER SALES CORPORATION
(Subsidiary of Groveton Papers Company)
Groveton, New Hampshire 03582
C.C. Wemyss, President
(603) 636-1154

VANKNIT (shirts)
See Phillips-Van Heusen Corporation

VANLAARHOVEN ASSOCIATES
7318 Melrose
Buena Park, California 90620

VANLEIGH FURNITURE SHOWROOMS, INC.
4900 Hampden Lane
Bethesda, Maryland 20014
A.I. Van Wye, President
(301) 657-3900

VANMAR PAPER & ENVELOPE COMPANY INC.
50 Maple Street
Norwood, New Jersey 07648

VANN ENTERPRISES INC.
Post Office Box 267
Woodstock, New York 12498

VANO (fabric finish, liquid and spray starch)
See Purex Corporation, Ltd.

VANTAGE (cigarettes)
See R.J. Reynolds Tobacco Company

VANTAGE (clocks and watches)
See Hamilton Watch Company

VANTAGE (handbags)
See Boonton Handbag Company Inc.

VANTAGE HOUSE, INC.
See Bristol-Myers Company

VANTAGE PRESS, INC.
516 West 34th Street
New York, New York 10001
Arthur Kleinwald, President
(212) 736-1767

Companies and Trade Names

VANTAGE PRODUCTS INC.
1017 Valencia Street
San Francisco, California 94110
(415) 826-4545

VAP-O-CLEAN (vaporizer-cleanser tablets)
See DeVilbiss Company

VAPEX (paint and varnish)
See Pratt & Lambert, Inc.

VAPINEZE RESEARCH LABORATORIES
1026 North Fairfax
Hollywood, California 90046
(213) 654-3476

VAPON, INC.
23 Fairfield Place
West Caldwell, New Jersey 07006

VAPOR BRITE (oven cleaner)
See Copper-Brite, Inc.

VAPOR CORPORATION
6420 West Howard Street
Chicago, Illinois 60648
(312) 631-9200

VAPOR MASTER (vaporizers and other electrical appliances)
See Hankscraft Company

VAPORETTE CHEMICAL CORPORATION
12200 Denton Drive
Dallas, Texas 75234
(214) 243-2321

VAPORUB
See Vick Chemical Company

VARAFLAME (lighters)
See Ronson Corporation

VARGAS (diamonds)
See Harry Winston, Inc.

VARI-COLOR DUPLICATOR COMPANY
435 South Lincoln, Department B
Shawnee, Oklahoma 74801
(405) 273-5410

VARI-LINE INDUSTRIES INC.
Post Office Box 609
Tenafly, New Jersey 07670

VARIAN ASSOCIATES
611 Hansen Way
Palo Alto, California 94303
Norman F. Parker, President and Chief Executive Officer
(415) 493-4000

VARIG AIRLINES
485 Lexington Avenue
New York, New York 10017
J. L. Yanow, Sales Manager
(212) 883-6161

VARIGRAPH INC.
Box 690
Madison, Wisconsin 53701
(608) 256-4816

VARITYPER
(Division of Addressograph Multigraph Corporation)
11 Mount Pleasant Avenue
East Hanover, New Jersey 07936
H.N. Norris, General Manager
(201) 887-8000

VARMAC MANUFACTURING COMPANY INC.
4201 Redwood Avenue
Los Angeles, California 90066
George A. Hine, President
(213) 821-8071

VARMOR (paint and varnish)
See Pratt & Lambert, Inc.

VARON HANDBAGS LTD.
15 East 32nd Street
New York, New York 10016
(212) 532-4117

VARSITY PAJAMAS
(Division of Knothe Brothers Company Inc.)
24 West 40th Street
New York, New York 10018
(212) 391-0550

VARSITY TOWN (men's clothes)
See H.A. Seinsheimer Company

VARTA (batteries)
See Hemispheres Industries Inc.

VASA (ski equipment)
See Fullplast Ski America

VASELINE (petroleum jelly, hair-care products, gauze, etc.)
See Chesebrough-Pond's, Inc.

VASSAR CORPORATION, THE
585 Gerard Avenue
Bronx, New York 10451

VASSARETTE
(Division of Munsingwear, Inc.)
718 Glenwood Avenue
Minneapolis, Minnesota 55405
A. Byron Reed, President
(612) 374-4220

VAT GOLD (whiskey)
See National Distillers & Chemical Corporation

VAT 69 (Scotch whiskey)
See Munson Shaw Company

VAUBAN (vegetables)
See Louis Ender Inc.

VAUGHAN & BUSHNELL MANUFACTURING COMPANY
11414 Maple Avenue
Hebron, Illinois 60034
Howard A. Vaughan, Jr., President
(815) 648-2446

Companies and Trade Names

VAUGHAN-BASSETT FURNITURE
    COMPANY
(Division of Elkin Furniture
    Company)
Galax, Virginia 24333
Carlisle W. Higgins, Jr., President
(703) 236-6161

VAUGHAN MANUFACTURING
    COMPANY
900 North Kilpatrick Avenue
Chicago, Illinois 60651
Ralph Robinson, President
(312) 261-8200

VAUGHAN'S SEED COMPANY
5300 Katrine Avenue
Downers Grove, Illinois 60515
Gager T. Vaughan, President
(312) 969-6300

VAUGHN CARDS OF CALIFORNIA
6001 Canyonside Road
La Crescenta, California 91014

VAVALON U.S. SPICE, INC.
Molasses Hill Road
Lebanon, New Jersey 08833

VAX (vacuum flasks and picnic
sets)
    See Glanson Company

VAZOHIST (cough and cold
remedies)
    See Lamb & Berlin Inc.

VE-VE INC.
14047 Azurite Street
Anoka, Minnesota 55303

VEC/TRAK RESEARCH &
    DEVELOPMENT CORPORATION
186 East Main Street
Elmsford, New York 10523

VECERE & COMPANY, ROBERT A.
900 South Clinton Avenue
Trenton, New Jersey 08611

VECTA CONTRACT COMPANY
740 West Mockingbird Lane
Dallas, Texas 75247
(214) 631-2880

VECTA GROUP INC.
2605 East Kilgore Road
Kalamazoo, Michigan 49003
(616) 349-1521

VECTOR (slide rules)
    See Keuffel & Esser Company

VEDRA (moisturizing cream, hand
and body lotion)
    See Madison Laboratories

VEEDER INDUSTRIES, INC.
799 Main Street
Hartford, Connecticut 06102
Andrew J. Rebmann, President
(203) 278-5960
    See also Peck, Stow &
    Wilcox Company

VEEKEN PHARMACEUTICAL
    PRODUCTS
(Division of Veeken Laboratories,
    Inc.)
116-23 Jamaica Avenue
Richmond Hill, New York 11418

VEERMAN INTERNATIONAL
    COMPANY
950 Third Avenue
New York, New York 10022
(212) 644-1350

VEFA, INC.
    See Caspari

VEG-ALL (canned foods)
    See Larsen Company

VEGA (banjos and accessories)
    See C.F. Martin Organisation

VEGA DEL REY (cigars)
    See G.W. Van Slyke & Horton

VEGA INDUSTRIES, INC.
East Brighton Avenue
Syracuse, New York 13205
Robert W. Cranshaw, President
(315) 478-5701

VEGA TRADING COMPANY,
    INC.
54 West 24th Street
New York, New York 10010
(212) 741-8850

VEGEMATO (vegetable juice)
    See RJR Foods, Inc.

VEGEMITE (food product)
    See Kraftco Corporation

VEGIE (produce)
    See Pacific Fruit & Produce
    Company

VEGIOLA (food products)
    See Pastorelli Food Products
    Inc.

VEL (soap)
    See Colgate-Palmolive Company

VEL-O-MATIC (automatic-dishwasher
product)
    See Colgate Palmolive Company

VELASQUES (cigars)
    See G.A. Georgopulo &
    Company, Inc.

VELCRO CORPORATION
(Subsidiary of American Velcro, Inc.)
681 Fifth Avenue
New York, New York 10022
(212) 751-2144

Companies and Trade Names

VELDENT COMPANY, THE
Box 966
Menlo Park, California 94025

VELLEMAN CORPORATION
2 Pennsylvania Place
New York, New York 10001
(212) 868-7215

VELLO PRODUCTS
Lyndonville, Vermont 05851

VELLUX (blanket)
See West Point Pepperell

VELON (plastic products)
See Firestone Plastics Company

VELOUR (interior paints)
See Celanese Corporation

VELSCO INC.
180 Berry Street
Brooklyn, New York 11211
(212) 782-7959

VELSICOL CHEMICAL
CORPORATION
(Subsidiary of Northwest Industries, Inc.)
341 East Ohio Street
Chicago, Illinois 60611
Robert M. Morris, Chairman and President
(312) 467-5700

VELVA FLOCK (paints and paint sundries)
See Industriline Company

VELVATEX (rubber mats and runners)
See National Floor Products Company

VELVEETA (cheese)
See Kraft Foods

VELVET (men's shoes)
See International Shoe Company

VELVET (pens and pencils)
See Venus Esterbrook Corporation

VELVET (tobacco)
See Liggett & Myers Inc.

VELVET CLOUD (tobacco)
See Amar Blends Company

VELVET-O'DONNELL
CORPORATION
30111 Schoolcraft
Livonia, Michigan 48150
Thomas Klein, President and Secretary
(313) 937-0600

VELVET PHARMACAL COMPANY
OF MALVERNE
Box 22
Malverne, New York 11565

VELVET STEP (women's shoes)
See International Shoe Company

VEN KING (porcelain oven-to-table ware)
See Europa Commerce Inc.

VEND MASTER (microwave ovens)
See Litton Industries (Atherton Division)

VENDO COMPANY, THE
7400 East 12th Street
Kansas City, Missouri 64126
Walter C. Gummere, Chairman, President and Chief Executive Officer
(816) 483-7400

VENDOME EXCLUSIVES INC.
55 Webster Avenue
New Rochelle, New York 10801

VENDRAMINI (sports accessories and equipment)
See M.R.D. and Associates Inc.

VENER ASSOCIATES INC.
98 Westport Avenue
Norwalk, Connecticut 06851

VENETIANAIRE CORPORATION
OF AMERICA
490 Nepperhan
Yonkers, New York 10701

VENICE IMPORTING COMPANY
66 North Sixth Street
Brooklyn, New York 11211
(212) 388-8420

VENICE INDUSTRIES, INC.
1407 Broadway
New York, New York 10018
Al Paris, Chairman of the Board
(212) 563-7950

VENICE MAID COMPANY
North Mill Road
Vineland, New Jersey 08360
Lawrence Pepper, President
(609) 691-2100

VENIDA PRODUCTS CORPORATION
120 East 16th Street
New York, New York 10003
(212) 477-8190

VENINI LTD.
169 East 61st Street
New York, New York 10021
(212) 355-0680

VENTRE PACKING COMPANY, INC.
373 Spencer
Syracuse, New York 13204

Companies and Trade Names

VENTURA (cigarettes)
See Brown & Williamson Tobacco Corporation

VENTURA COASTAL CORPORATION
Box 69
Ventura, California 93001

VENTURA DISTRIBUTORS
Post Office Box 283
Bayside, New York 11361

VENTURA FARMS (frozen vegetables)
See Oxnard Frozen Foods Corporation

VENTURA TRAVELWARE, INC.
32-33 47th Avenue
Long Island City, New York 11101
Walter Bialo, President
(212) 392-6200

VENTURE (camping trailers)
See Starcraft Company

VENTURE (hairdressing)
See Beecham Products Inc.

VENTURE (portable televisions)
See Philco-Ford Corporation

VENTURE PRODUCTS, INC.
Box 20
Mansfield, Massachusetts 02048

VENTURI, INC.
1610 Rollins Road
Burlingame, California 94010

VENUS (groceries)
See Lone Star Institutional Grocers

VENUS (venetian blinds)
See Breneman, Inc.

VENUS CORPORATION
147 South Franklin Avenue
Valley Stream, New York 11582

VENUS ESTERBROOK CORPORATION
730 Fifth Avenue
New York, New York 10019
(212) 265-0370

VENUS INDUSTRIES, INC.
2200 West Lawrence Avenue
Chicago, Illinois 60625
Louis Roston, President
(312) 728-9200

VENUS LAMP (adjustable arm lamps)
See Vantage Products Inc.

VENUTI (piano accordions)
See Sorkin Music Company Inc.

VER-NAL CANNING COMPANY
1044 West Mendocino Avenue
Stockton, California 95204

VER SLUIS CELERY COMPANY, LEWIS W.
445 Drexel
Kalamazoo, Michigan 49007

VERA (clothing)
See Manhattan Shirt Company

VERA (scarves and blouses)
See Scarves by Vera, Inc.

VERA-SHARP (cheese)
See Borden Foods

VERANA (liqueur)
See Schieffelin & Company

VERBENA (fruits and vegetables)
See Earl Fruit Company

VERBRIDGE & SON INC., J.H.
Williamson, New York 14589

VERD-A-RAY (insect-repellent lamps)
See Lear Siegler, Inc.

VERDE SHOE CORPORATION
See Wolverine World Wide, Inc.

VERDURA (paint and varnish)
See Pratt & Lambert, Inc.

VERFRANCE, INC.
1133 Broadway
New York, New York 10010
(212) 929-0809

VERGEZ (Bordeaux wines)
See Dreyfus, Ashby & Company

VERGO (wart remover)
See Daywell Laboratories Corporation

VERI-BEST (food products)
See Gordon Pickle Company

VERI-SHARP (kitchen cutlery)
See Imperial Knife Associated Companies, Inc.

VERIBEST (canned meats)
See Armour & Company

VERICHROME (film)
See Eastman Kodak Company

VERITY SOUTHALL
6041 Variel Avenue
Woodland Hills, California 91364

VERMILLION INC.
1207 South Scenic Avenue
Springfield, Missouri 65802

Companies and Trade Names

VERMONT EVAPORATOR
COMPANY
Box 650
Ogdensburg, New York 13669

VERMONT FARMS (griddle-cake mix, maple spread, candy)
See American Maple Products Corporation

VERMONT MAID (syrups)
See RJR Foods Inc.

VERMONT MAPLE ORCHARDS, INC.
Burlington, Vermont 05401

VERMONT MARBLE COMPANY
61 Main Street
Proctor, Vermont 05765
F. Ray Keyser Jr., President
(802) 459-3311

VERMONT ORIGINALS
East Hardwick, Vermont 05836

VERMONT PLASTICS INC.
Post Office Box 572
35 Blanchard Court
Montpelier, Vermont 05602
(802) 223-5012

VERMONT-WARE
Hinesburg, Vermont 05461

VERMOUTH INDUSTRIES OF
AMERICA, INC.
See Tribuno Wines, Inc.

VERNAT (vermouth and aperitif)
See Somerset Importers, Ltd.

VERNAY PRODUCTS INC.
Yellow Springs, Ohio 45387

VERNCO CORPORATION
1804 22nd Street
Columbus, Indiana 47201
(812) 372-9901

VERNEDALE (peanut butter, juices, mayonnaise)
See Harris-Teeter Super Markets

VERNELL'S FINE CANDIES
(Division of Golden Grain Macaroni Company)
1825 Westlake Avenue North
Seattle, Washington 98109
(206) 283-8200

VERNON COMPANY, S.E. & M.
(Division of Mead Corporation)
801 Newark Avenue
Elizabeth, New Jersey 07208

VERNON LABORATORIES, INC.
508 Franklin Avenue
Mount Vernon, New York 10551
(914) 699-3131

VERNONWARE
(Division of Metlox Potteries)
1200 Morningside Drive
Manhattan Beach, California 90266

VERNORS, INC.
4501 Woodward Avenue
Detroit, Michigan 48201
Leonard Heilman, President
(313) 684-3020

VERONA (dresses and suits)
See Puritan Fashions Corporation

VERONA (piano accordions)
See Sorkin Music Company Inc.

VERONEX (perlite plant propagator, vermiculite, volcanic sand)
See Hydroponic Chemical Company, Inc.

VERPLEX COMPANY, THE
(Subsidiary of U.S. Industries, Inc.)
Kane Street
Scranton, Pennsylvania 18505
R.H. Benedict, President
(717) 961-5331

VERRAZZANO (Italian wines)
See Dreyfus, Ashby & Company

VERSA BOX
(Division of Toccoa Metal Products Company)
Box 610
Toccoa, Georgia 30577

VERSA TABLE (folding table)
See Re-Ly-On Metal Products Inc.

VERSANATRONIC (ranges)
See General Electric Company

VERSITOP (tables)
See D & M Products Company

VERTIFLOW (heaters)
See Young Radiator Company

VERTIGRAPHIX (photographic equipment)
See Visual Graphics Corporation

VERVE (phonograph records)
See Metro-Goldwyn-Mayer, Inc.

VERY IMPORTANT PRODUCTS
INC.
3901 Westerly Place, Suite 101
Newport Beach, California 92660

VERY SPORT (footwear)
See Otto Gmeiner

VERYFINE (fruit)
See New England Apple Products Company

Companies and Trade Names

VESELY COMPANY
2101 North Lapeer Road
Lapeer, Michigan 48446
Eugene L. Vesely, Chairman of
   the Board
(313) 664-9961

VESPRE (feminine-hygiene
deodorant)
   See Personal Products
      Corporation

VESTA CORSET COMPANY
25 South Street
McGraw, New York 13101

VESTA GLASS COMPANY
Post Office Box 1426
Corning, New York 14830

VESTAL LABORATORIES
(Division of Chemed Corporation)
4963 Manchester Avenue
Saint Louis, Missouri 63100
F.J. Pollinow, Jr., President
(314) 535-1810

VESUVIO (accordions)
   See Atlas Accordions Inc.

VETERAN (tobacco)
   See American Tobacco
      Company

VETERAN TOOL AND SUPPLY
   COMPANY
3A Howard Street
New York, New York 10013
(212) 925-0940

VETERANO (brandy)
   See Munson Shaw Company

VETERINARY
(Division of Cutter Laboratories)
Box 998
Shawnee Mission, Kansas 66201

VETO (deodorant)
   See Colgate-Palmolive Company

VETS (dog and cat food)
   See Perk Foods Company

VEUVE CLIQUOT (champagne)
   See Joseph Garneau Company

VEXILAR INC.
9345 Penn Avenue South
Minneapolis, Minnesota 55431
(612) 884-5291

VI-JON LABORATORIES INC.
6300 Etzel Avenue
Saint Louis, Missouri 63133
(314) 721-2990

VIBELLI (men's footwear)
   See Baker-Benjes Inc.

VIBRA MAT (vibrator)
   See Denticator Company

VIBRA TOUCH (massager)
   See Master Appliance
      Corporation

VIBRANT (skin-care products)
   See Aditi, Inc.

VIBRATECHNIQUES CORPORATION
101 Park Avenue
New York, New York 10017
(212) 679-7459

VIBRATOR REED COMPANY INC.
(Division of Musical Instrument
   Corporation of America)
Hanover, Pennsylvania 17331

VIBRO-TOOL (tools)
   See Burgess Vibrocrafters, Inc.

VIBROSAGE (electric vibrator)
   See Beauty Appliance
      Corporation

VICEROY (cigarettes)
   See Brown & Williamson
      Tobacco Corporation

VICHY (beverages)
   See Saratoga Vichy Spring
      Company

VICHY CELESTINS (health waters)
   See Health Waters, Inc.

VICK CHEMICAL COMPANY
10 Westport Road
Wilton, Connecticut 06897
(203) 762-2222

VICKERS PETROLEUM CORPORATION
(Subsidiary of Swift & Company)
Post Office Box 2240
Wichita, Kansas 67202
R.D. Phillips, President
(316) 267-0311

VICKY VAUGHN (junior dresses)
   See R. & M. Kaufmann

VICO (ceramic tile, marble
products, and slate)
   See Amsterdam Corporation

VICON FARM MACHINERY INC.
5898 Poplar Hall Drive
Norfolk, Virginia 23502

VICOR (floor tile)
   See Flintkote Company
      (Flooring Products)

VICTAULIC COMPANY OF
   AMERICA
3100 Hamilton
South Plainfield, New Jersey 07080
Joseph E. St. Clair, President
   and Treasurer
(201) 752-0600

Companies and Trade Names

VICTOR (seafood)
See Mavar Shrimp & Oyster Company, Ltd.

VICTOR (sporting firearms)
See High Standard Manufacturing Corporation

VICTOR BROTHERS INC.
Usonia Road
Pleasantville, New York 10570
(914) 769-0630

VICTOR COMPTOMETER CORPORATION
3900 North Rockwell Street
Chicago, Illinois 60618
Albert C. Buehler, Jr., President
(312) 539-8200
See also Bear Archery; Daisy Heddon; Ertl Company; and Heddon's Sons, James

VICTOR EQUIPMENT COMPANY
(Subsidiary of Pacific Lumber Company)
44 Montgomery Street
San Francisco, California 94104
Turner G. Brashear, President
(415) 421-3000

VICTOR GOLF
(Subsidiary of Victor Comptometer Corporation)
8350 North Lehigh Avenue
Morton Grove, Illinois 60053
J.T. Butz, President
(312) 966-6300

VICTOR KRAUT INC.
Box 15
Marietta, New York 13110

VICTOR SAW WORKS INC.
(Subsidiary of Clemson Brothers Inc.)
22 Cottage Street
Middletown, New York 10940
William A. Schrade, President
(914) 343-4177

VICTOR STANLEY INC.
Post Office Box 93
Dunkirk, Maryland 20754
Stanley Skalka, Chairman, President and Treasurer
(301) 855-8300

VICTOR SYSTEMS
(Division of Remington Rand Office Systems)
4300 Janitrol Road
Columbus, Ohio 43228

VICTORI & COMPANY, INC.; JOSEPH
644 Greenwich Street
New York, New York 10014
(212) 691-1080

VICTORIA (sherry)
See Twenty One Brands, Inc.

VICTORIA CROSS (shoes)
See Tober-Saifer Shoe Manufacturing Company, Inc.

VICTORIA DISTRIBUTORS
Post Office Box 753
Lancaster, Pennsylvania 17604

VICTORIA PACKING CORPORATION
433 East 100th
Brooklyn, New York 11236
Joseph Aquilina, Chairman and President
(212) 649-1635

VICTORIA SHAW (dresses and suits)
See Puritan Fashions Corporation

VICTORIA STATION, INC.
150 Chestnut Street
San Francisco, California 94111
Richard J. Bradley, President
(415) 981-8649

VICTORIA SUSAN CONFECTIONS (candy)
See Herman Goelitz Company

VICTORIA VOGUE, INC.
8000 Cooper Avenue
Glendale, New York 11227

VICTORIA WICKERWARE
2255 Computer Avenue
Willow Grove, Pennsylvania 19090

VICTORIAN CANDY COMPANY
2042-50 North Tenth Street
Philadelphia, Pennsylvania 19122
(215) 765-2507

VICTORIAN KEEPSAKES
Box 202
Green Creek, New Jersey 08219

VICTORIAVILLE (hockey sticks)
See Kendall Company

VICTORIOUS-FEIKA INC.
Post Office Box 78
Charlottesville, Virginia 22902

VICTORIUS INC. (wall accessories)
See Virginia Metalcrafters Inc.

VICTORS (cough drops)
See Vick Chemical Company

VICTORY (food products)
See Musselman

VICTORY ARTWARES COMPANY
1170 Broadway
New York, New York 10001
(212) 686-2244

VICTORY BRAND (dog and cat food)
See Calo Pet Foods

Companies and Trade Names

VICTORY CHEMICAL COMPANY
728-30 North Second Street
Philadelphia, Pennsylvania 19123
(215) 627-4676

VICTORY FRUIT PRODUCTS
COMPANY
4433 West Grenshaw Street
Chicago, Illinois 60624
(312) 826-0410

VICTORY MARKETS, INC.
54 East Main Street
Norwich, New York 13815
Charles A. Smith, Jr., President
(607) 335-4711

VICTORY MERCHANDISE
COMPANY, INC.
220 Fifth Avenue
New York, New York 10001
(212) 686-1376

VICTORY OPTICAL MANUFAC-
TURING COMPANY
Mulberry Place
Newark, New Jersey 07105
Anthony J. Bartolotta, President
(201) 643-7844

VICTROLA (phonographs,
phonograph records)
See Radio Corporation of
America RCA

VIDENT (denture cleaner)
See Vick Chemical Company

VIDEOCLOCK (household timers)
See General Electric Company

VIE-DEL COMPANY
Box 2896
Fresno, California 93745

VIENNA BEAUTY PRODUCTS
COMPANY
347 Leo Street
Dayton, Ohio 45404

VIENNA MODERN (stainless-steel flatware)
See W.M.F. of America Inc.

VIENNA SAUSAGE MANUFAC-
TURING COMPANY
2501 North Damen
Chicago, Illinois 60647
William Ladany, President
(312) 278-7800

VIERK WATER COMPANY
18145 Lorence Avenue
Lansing, Illinois 60438

VIETTI FOODS COMPANY, INC.
636 Southgate Street
Nashville, Tennessee 37204
(615) 244-7864

VIEW-MASTER (photographic viewer)
See GAF Corporation
(Consumer Photo Division)

VIEWLEX, INC.
810 Seventh Avenue
New York, New York 10019
Andrew Galef, President
(212) 541-6980

VIGILANT PRODUCTS COMPANY, INC.
855 Bloomfield Avenue
Glen Ridge, New Jersey 07028
(201) 748-3530

VIGO (dog and cat foods)
See Pedrick Laboratories

VIGOR COMPANY
(Division of B. Jadow & Sons Inc.)
53 West 23rd Street
New York, New York 10010
(212) 741-9500

VIGORO (fertilizer)
See Swift & Company

VIGORTONE PRODUCTS
COMPANY
(Division of Beatrice Foods, Company)
931 Blairs Ferry Road, N.E.
Cedar Rapids, Iowa 52406
Arthur D. Swarzentruber, President
(319) 393-3310

VIKING (seafood)
See Lyon Food Products, Inc.

VIKING (seafoods and breads)
See Swedish Food Products

VIKING (thermal blankets)
See Sibs Associates Inc.

VIKING BOAT COMPANY
(Subsidiary of Coachmen Industries, Inc.)
Coachmen Drive
Middlebury, Indiana 46540
Thomas H. Corson, President
(219) 825-5854

VIKING CARPETS, INC.
10 West 33rd Street
New York, New York 10001
Wolfe R. Nichols, President
(212) 564-7600

VIKING FOODS INC.
600 Columbia Road
Dorchester, Massachusetts 02125

VIKING GLASS COMPANY
Post Office Box 29
New Martinsville, West Virginia 26155
Eugene Miller, President and Treasurer
(304) 455-2900
See also Rainbow Art Glass Company

VIKING IMPORT HOUSE INC.
412 S.E. Sixth Street
Fort Lauderdale, Florida 33301

Companies and Trade Names

VIKING IMPORTRADE, INC.
225 Fifth Avenue
New York, New York 10010
(212) 679-5577

VIKING INSTRUMENTS INC.
See Moeller Instruments Company

VIKING MANUFACTURING COMPANY, INC.
68-70 Middlesex Avenue
Natick, Massachusetts 01760

VIKING OAK (furniture)
See American Furniture Company (Indiana)

VIKING PRESS, INC., THE
625 Madison Avenue
New York, New York 10022
Thomas H. Guinzburg, President
(212) 755-4330

VIKO (cooking utensils)
See Mirro Aluminum Company

VIKO FURNITURE CORPORATION
Eldred, Pennsylvania 16731
Robert S. Warner, President

VIKOA, INC.
See Coral, Inc.

VILDMARK (sports apparel)
See Janoy Inc.

VILETTAS ARTS & SOUVENIRS
592 N.E. Chestnut Street
Roseburg, Oregon 97470

VILLAGE BATH PRODUCTS
See Minnetonka Laboratories Inc.

VILLAGE BLACKSMITH
(Division of McGraw-Edison Company)
1200 East State Street
Geneva, Illinois 60134
(312) 232-2500

VILLAGE CHEF (cookware)
See West Bend Company

VILLAGE INN PANCAKE HOUSE INC.
400 West 48th Avenue
Denver, Colorado 80216
(303) 892-5858

VILLAGE KITCHEN FOODS, INC.
2827 Nagle
Dallas, Texas 75206
(214) 357-5747

VILLAGE MANUFACTURING CORPORATION
443 Saint John Street
Pleasanton, California 94566
(415) 846-2330

VILLAGE PARK (lawn and garden supplies)
See American Hardware Supply Company

VILLAGE SQUIRE (groceries)
See Fayette County Grocers Association, Inc.

VILLAGE SQUIRE (men's sportswear)
See M. & D. Simon Company

VILLAGE SUPER MARKETS, INC.
733 Mountain Avenue
Springfield, New Jersey 07081
Nicholas Sumas, President
(201) 467-2200

VILLAGER FOODS, INC.
Industrial Parkway
Jackson, Minnesota 56143

VILLAGER INDUSTRIES INC.
(Subsidiary of Jonathan Logan Inc.)
1411 Broadway
New York, New York 10018
(212) 594-3250

VILLAWARE (plastic housewares)
See Federal Tool & Plastic

VILLAZON COMPANY
3104 North Armenia
Tampa, Florida 33607
Frank Llaneza, President
(813) 879-2291

VILLENCY INC., MAURICE
250 South Service Road
Roslyn Heights, New York 11577

VILLOM (ski equipment)
See A & T Ski Company

VILTER MANUFACTURING CORPORATION
2217 South First Street
Milwaukee, Wisconsin 53207
Albert A. Silverman, Chairman, President and Chief Executive Officer
(414) 744-0111

VIM (air purifiers)
See Master Appliance Corporation

VIM (detergent)
See Lever Brothers Company

VIM (produce)
See Warren Wagner Inc.

VIM (scissors and shears)
See J. Wiss & Sons Company

VIMCO MANUFACTURING COMPANY INC.
Vermont Street
Holland, New York 14080
(716) 537-2216

Companies and Trade Names

VIMY (processed foods)
See Ernest Carriere Inc.

VIN-L-KOTE (paints and paint sundries)
See Gable-Tite Products Company Inc.

VINCENT BACH (brass and band instruments and accessories)
See H. & A. Selmer Ltd.

VINCENT BAR-NONE COMPANY, INC.
2661 Walnut
Denver, Colorado 80205
(303) 534-3251

VINCENT GIFT BOX COMPANY
Box 294
Westwood, Massachusetts 02090

VINCENTI & COMPANY, D.
Box 188
Kennett Square, Pennsylvania 19348

VINCENZO (Italian-type vegetables, cheeses, sausage, soups)
See Pieri Distributing Company, Inc.

VINCOR (tile)
See Flintkote Company (Building Materials Division)

VINDALE CORPORATION
4999 Northcutt Place
Dayton, Ohio 45414
Paul Riedel, President
(513) 833-2151

VINE KIST (food products)
See J. Weller Company

VINE RIPE (tomato products)
See Fettig Canning Corporation

VINEFRESH (cranberry products)
See Indian Trail Cranberry Company

VINELAND LABORATORIES, INC.
2285 East Landis Avenue
Vineland, New Jersey 08360
(609) 691-2411

VINELAND PROCESSING COMPANY INC.
Evelyn and Gershall Avenues
Norma, New Jersey 08347

VINER BROTHERS, INC.
304 Hancock Street
Bangor, Maine 04401
John J. Coleman, President
(207) 945-9423

VINEWOOD (rattan furniture)
See Hurricane International

VINEYARD YACHTS INC.
Box 149
Vineyard Haven, Massachusetts 02568

VINING BROOM COMPANY, INC.
2530 Columbus Avenue
Springfield, Ohio 45501
(513) 324-5596

VINO-FINO (wines)
See California Wine Association

VINO ROYAL (wines)
See United Vinters, Inc.

VINTAGE (books)
See Random House Inc.

VINTAGE ENTERPRISES, INC.
3825 Northeast Expressway
Atlanta, Georgia 30340
Thomas S. Cheek, President
(404) 458-3144

VINTAGE FOODS INC.
Box 5
Bailey, Michigan 49303

VINTERO SALES CORPORATION
80 Wall Street
New York, New York 10005
(212) 422-2583

VINTEX TEXTURE (paints)
See Bondex International, Inc.

VINTNER (table and dessert wines)
See Michigan Wineries Inc.

VINTNERS PRIDE (fruit products)
See Ermey Vineyards Inc.

VINYA (wines)
See Heublein, Inc.

VINYL PLASTICS, INC.
3123 South Ninth Street
Sheboygan, Wisconsin 53081
Robert E. Kohler, President
(414) 458-4664

VINYLGLAS (insulation)
See Suflex Corporation

VINYLMAID (plastic-coated housewares)
See Artistic Wire Products Company, Inc.

VIOBIN CORPORATION
(Subsidiary of A.H. Robins Company)
226 West Livingston
Monticello, Illinois 61856
Ezra Levin, President
(217) 762-2561

VIOLA (cameras)
See Camera Specialty Company Inc.

VIOLET (produce)
See Perham Fruit Corporation

Companies and Trade Names

VIOLET PACKING COMPANY
123 Railroad Avenue
Williamstown, New Jersey 08094

VIQUET CREME-OIL LTD.
6224 Broadway
Chicago, Illinois 60626
(312) 465-8030

VIRCO MANUFACTURING
CORPORATION
15134 South Vermont Avenue
Los Angeles, California 90044
Donald C. Heyl, President
(213) 532-3570

VIRGINIA (pork products)
See Genoa Packing Company

VIRGINIA BEST (groceries)
See Norfolk Packing Company, Inc.

VIRGINIA CHEMICALS, INC.
3340 West Norfolk Road
Portsmouth, Virginia 23703
Harry W. Buchanan, Chairman and President
(804) 484-5000

VIRGINIA CRAFTS, INC.
Keysville, Virginia 23947
Robert Hertford, President
(804) 736-8405

VIRGINIA DARE (wine)
See Canandaigua Industries Company, Inc.

VIRGINIA DARE EXTRACT
COMPANY, INC.
882 Third Avenue
Brooklyn, New York 11232
Howard Smith, President
(212) 788-1766

VIRGINIA ELECTRIC & POWER
COMPANY
7th East Franklin Street
Richmond, Virginia 23261
T. Justin Moore, Jr., President
(804) 771-3225

VIRGINIA FOODS, INC.
Bluefield, Virginia 24605

VIRGINIA GLASS PRODUCTS
CORPORATION
Box 5431
Martinsville, Virginia
William C. Beeler, President
(703) 956-3131

VIRGINIA HALL, INC.
4331 PioNono Avenue
Macon, Georgia 31206

VIRGINIA LEE (processed foods)
See Acme Markets Inc.

VIRGINIA MAID HOSIERY MILLS, INC.
28 Jefferson Avenue, South
Pulaski, Virginia 24301
Raymond R. Rice, President
(703) 980-6220

VIRGINIA METAL PRODUCTS
(Division of Gray Manufacturing Company)
51 Patrick
Orange, Virginia 22960
(703) 672-2800

VIRGINIA METALCRAFTERS, INC.
1010 East Main Street
Waynesboro, Virginia 22980
Willard A. Foster, President
(703) 942-8205

VIRGINIA NATIONAL BANK
1 Commercial Place
Norfolk, Virginia 23510
C.A. Cutchins, III, President
(804) 441-4000

VIRGINIA OAK TANNERY SALES
CORPORATION
419 Park Avenue South
New York, New York 10016
Stephan J. Blaut, President
(212) 686-2821

VIRGINIA PEANUT COMPANY, THE
515 West Lombard Street
Baltimore, Maryland 21201
(301) 727-2777

VIRGINIA REEL (meat products)
See Cudahy Company

VIRGINIA SEAFOODS INC.
Irvington, Virginia 22480

VIRGINIA SLIMS (cigarettes)
See Philip Morris, Inc.

VIRGINIA SYRUP & PRODUCTS
Box 385
Salem, Virginia 24153

VIRGINIA TELEPHONE &
TELEGRAPH COMPANY
12 N Street
Lincoln, Nebraska 68501
Clarence H. Ross, President
(402) 475-5921

VIRGINIA TROUT COMPANY, INC.
Monterey, Virginia 24465

VIRGINIANS (cigars)
See M. Marsh & Son

VIRKOTYPE CORPORATION
111 Rock Avenue
Plainfield, New Jersey 07063
(201) 756-7170

Companies and Trade Names

VIRTAL PHARMACEUTICAL
   COMPANY
Box 2929
Brightwood Road
New Haven, Connecticut 06515
(203) 387-0064

VIRTUE OF CALIFORNIA
19801 South Santa Fe
Compton, California 90221
George B. Maitland, President
(213) 774-2775

VISA-DOME (thermometers)
   See Thermometer Corporation
        of America

VISCOL COMPANY, THE
2200 South Central Expressway
Dallas, Texas 75215
(214) 421-4137

VISCOUNT (billfolds)
   See Enger-Kress Company

VISCOUNT (electronics products)
   See Consolidated Merchandising
        Company

VISCOUNT (home/portable organs)
   See J.M. Greene Music
        Company Ltd.

VISCUSI WHOLESALE GROCERS
819 Kings Road
Schenectady, New York 12303

VISIBLE FILE
(Division of Red-Rope Industries Inc.)
Wood Avenue
Bristol, Pennsylvania 19007

VISINE (eyedrops)
   See Leeming/Pacquin

VISION HOSIERY MILLS
Belmont, North Carolina 28012
Walter Lineberger, President
(704) 825-5383

VISION-WRAP INDUSTRIES, INC.
250 South Hicks Road
Palatine, Illinois 60067
(312) 359-5000

VISIRECORD SYSTEMS
(Division of Barry Wright
   Corporation)
54 Railroad Avenue
Copiague, New York 11726

VISITATION HOME MADE CANDIES
2300 Springhill Avenue
Mobile, Alabama 36607

VISON COSMETIQUES
   LABORATORY
Post Office Box 348
Littleton, New Hampshire 03561

VISTA (auto wash, wax)
   See Texize Chemicals Company

VISTA (bicycles)
   See National Independent
        Distributors Associates Inc.

VISTA D' TAMPA (cigars)
   See General Cigar Company

VISTA INSURANCE COMPANY
   See Ford Motor Credit
        Company

VISTA LABORATORIES INC.
3243 Espanola Drive
Sarasota, Florida 33580

VISTA VINYL (fatigue mats)
   See Harte & Company, Inc.

VISTASCOPE (cameras)
   See J.L. Galef & Son, Inc.

VISTRON CORPORATION
(Subsidiary of Standard Oil
   Company, Ohio)
350 Midland Building
Cleveland, Ohio 44115
D. G. Stevens, President
(216) 575-4141
   See also Pro Brush

VISU-FLEX COMPANY
1641 West Collins Avenue
Orange, California 92667
(714) 633-2142

VISUAL ART INDUSTRIES, INC.
Wayne & Windrim Avenues
Philadelphia, Pennsylvania 19144
(215) 329-3980
   See also Weber Company, F.

VISUAL CREATIONS
25 Hamilton Drive
Novato, California 94797

VISUAL DESIGN MANUFACTURING
   COMPANY INC.
6335 Skyline Drive
Houston, Texas 77027
(714) 783-7100

VISUAL DYNAMICS INC.
Brightwaters, New York 11718

VISUAL GRAPHICS CORPORATION
5701 Northwest 94th Avenue
Tamarac, Florida 33313
Miltorn J. Zorn, Chairman,
   President and Chief Executive
   Officer
(305) 722-3000

VISUAL PANOGRAPHICS
Post Office Box 5640
Arlington, Texas 76011

VITA (fruit products)
   See National Papaya Company

Companies and Trade Names

VITA-BARK INC.
(Subsidiary of Di Giorgio
    Corporation)
1880 South River Road
West Sacramento, California 95691

VITA ELIXIR COMPANY, INC.
Box 9026
Atlanta, Georgia 30314
(404) 523-5974

VITA FILTERS (cigarettes)
    See Brown & Williamson
        Tobacco Corporation

VITA FOOD PRODUCTS, INC.
(Subsidiary of Brown & Williamson
    Tobacco Corporation)
Hunts Point District Center
Bronx, New York 10474
E.F. Lewis, President
(212) 378-1000

VITA-FROST FOODS, INC.
1135 North Plymouth
Allentown, Pennsylvania 18103

VITA INTERNATIONAL, LTD.
55 West 42nd Street
New York, New York 10036
(212) 564-5386

VITA PAKT-CITRUS PRODUCTS
    COMPANY
Box 309
707 North Barranca
Covina, California 91723
(213) 686-1260

VITA-SAVER (cookware)
    See Aero Industrial Company
        Inc.

VITA SUN (food products)
    See Hawaiian Sun Products Inc.

VITA-TONE (hearing aids)
    See Univis Company

VITA-VAR COMPANY
Post Office Box 494
New Brunswick, New Jersey 08903

VITA YUMS (candy vitamin)
    See Jeffrey Martin, Inc.

VITABATH
(Division of Beecham, Inc.)
65 Industrial, South
Clifton, New Jersey 07012
W. Petley, President
(201) 778-9000

VITAGLIANO & COMPANY,
    ANTONIO
1118 Kossuth Avenue
Utica, New York 13501

VITALES ITALIAN FOODS INC.
2814 North Rice Street
Saint Paul, Minnesota 55113
(612) 484-7206

VITALINOX, INC.
94 Garth Road
Scarsdale, New York 10583

VITALIS (men's hair-grooming
products)
    See Bristol-Myers Company

VITALITY (citrus products)
    See Lykes Pasco Packing
        Company

VITALITY (shoes)
    See International Shoe Company

VITAMIN FOOD COMPANY, INC.
187 Sylvan Avenue
Newark, New Jersey 07104
(201) 484-8434

VITAMIN RESEARCH CORPORATION
2026 South Fourth Street
Philadelphia, Pennsylvania 19148
(215) 462-4526

VITAMINS BY SPIRT, INC.
39 Prospect Street
Waterbury, Connecticut 06702

VITAMIX PHARMACEUTICALS INC.
    See Cooper Laboratories

VITAPOINTE (hair-care product)
    See Clairol, Inc.

VITARINE COMPANY INC., THE
227-15 North Conduit
Springfield Gardens, New York 11413

VITO-GRAPHIC (maps and globes)
    See Weber Costello

VITONEX (cut-flower preserver)
    See Hydroponic Chemical
        Company, Inc.

VITOS PRODUCTS
17808 Tourny Road
Los Gatos, California 95030

VITRALITE (enamel)
    See Pratt & Lambert, Inc.

VITRO DYNAMICS INC.
114 Beach Street
Rockaway, New Jersey 07866
(201) 625-1707

VIVA (paper napkins, towels)
    See Scott Paper Company

VIVA (photo albums)
    See Joshua Meier (Division of
        W.R. Grace & Company)

VIVA AMERICANA (shoes)
    See U.S. Shoe Corporation

Companies and Trade Names

VIVARA (dusting powder, eau de cologne, perfume, etc.)
See Emilio Pucci Perfumes, International, Inc.

VIVARIN (stimulant tablets)
See J.B. Williams Company

VIVE LE BAIN (bath products)
See Shulton, Inc.

VIVI (cosmetics)
See Nu-Masca Cosmetics

VIVIANE WOODARD CORPORATION
(Subsidiary of General Foods Corporation)
14621 Titus Avenue
Panorama City, California 91412
Loren Smith, President
213) 782-3310

VIVITAR (photographic equipment)
See Ponder & Best

VLASIC FOODS, INC.
33200 West 14 Mile Road
West Bloomfield, Michigan 48033
Russell H. Post, President
(313) 851-9400

VO-TOYS, INC.
321 Rider Avenue
Bronx, New York 10451
Arthur A. Hirschberg, President
(212) 665-1313

VOCALINE COMPANY OF AMERICA INC.
Old Saybrook, Connecticut 06475

VODKOFF (vodka)
See American Distilling Company, Inc.

VOGARELL PRODUCTS
1212 West Washington Boulevard
Los Angeles, California 90007
(213) 748-6287

VOGART CRAFTS CORPORATION
230 Fifth Avenue
New York, New York 10001
Eli J. Siegal, President
(212) 481-9020

VOGEL-PETERSON COMPANY
Post Office Box 90
Route 83 and Madison Street
Elmhurst, Illinois 60126
(312) 279-7123

VOGEL SALES CORPORATION
920 Connecticut Avenue
Bridgeport, Connecticut 06601
(203) 368-4646

VOGEL SONS, S.
191 Park Avenue
East Hartford, Connecticut 06108

VOGELZANG BROTHERS
879 Central Avenue
Holland, Michigan 49423

VOGT MANUFACTURING CORPORATION
100 Fernwood Avenue
Rochester, New York 14621
(716) 381-7070

VOGUE (chrome servingware)
See Kromex

VOGUE (cigarettes)
See Stephano Brothers

VOGUE (curtains and draperies)
See Robertson Factories, Inc.

VOGUE (groceries)
See S. Vogel Sons

VOGUE (sports apparel)
See M.R.D. Associates Inc.

VOGUE BASKET COMPANY
709 Dartmouth Street
South Dartmouth, Massachusetts 02748

VOGUE COSMETIC PRODUCTS
Post Office Box 215
682 West 17th Street
Costa Mesa, California 92627
Howard P. Gray, President
(714) 548-8747

VOGUE DOLLS, INC.
(Subsidiary of Tonka Corporation)
37 Washington Street
Melrose, Massachusetts 02176
Edwin W. Nelson, Jr., President
(617) 662-6300

VOGUE-LITES (portable lamps)
See Swivelier Company Inc.

VOGUE PATTERN SERVICE
161 Sixth Avenue
New York, New York 10013
(212) 620-2596

VOGUE RATTAN MANUFACTURING COMPANY, INC.
(Division of General Housewares Corporation)
Fairman Road
Lexington, Kentucky 40505
Roger A. Denne, General Manager
(606) 255-3346

VOGUE SHOE, INC.
3660 South Hill Street
Los Angeles, California 90007
Seymour C. Fabrick, President
(213) 232-8191

VOGUE WATCH STRAP CREATIONS
94 Spring Street
New York, New York 10012
(212) 962-3762

Companies and Trade Names

VOHANN OF CALIFORNIA INC.
Box 2066
Capistrano Beach, California 92624

VOICE OF MUSIC (musical instruments)
See V-M Corporation

VOISIN CANNING COMPANY INC., THE
Box 450
Houma, Louisiana 70360

VOIT (sports equipment)
See AMF Voit Inc.

VOL-ADE INC.
4226 Shangri-La Drive
Knoxville, Tennessee 37914

VOLA (sports accessories)
See Alpine Crafts Company Inc.

VOLAND CORPORATION
27 Centre Avenue
New Rochelle, New York 10801

VOLARE (cosmetics)
See Upjohn Company

VOLKART BROTHERS, INC.
90 Crossways Park West
Woodbury, New York 11797

VOLKSWAGEN OF AMERICA, INC.
818 Sylvan Avenue
Englewood Cliffs, New Jersey 07632
J. Stuart Perkins, President
(212) 736-5510

VOLLMER & SONS INC.
N.E. of Bozeman
Bozeman, Montana 59715

VOLLRATH COMPANY, THE
1236 North 18th Street
Sheboygan, Wisconsin 53081
(414) 457-4851

VOLUME SHOE CORPORATION
3515 East Sixth Street
Topeka, Kansas 66607
Louis Pozez, President
(913) 233-5171

VOLUNTEER (groceries)
See Robert Orr & Company

VOLVO, INC.
Volvo Drive
Rockleigh, New Jersey 07647
Bjorn Ahlstrom, President
(201) 768-7300

VOLVO WESTERN DISTRIBUTING, INC.
1955 West 190th Street
Torrance, California 90509
Robert J. Sinclair, President
(213) 770-1550

VOMACK, INC., W.L.
19 Hoover Street
Inwood, New York 11696
(516) 371-2600

VON DAMM INC., F.H.
900 Grand Street
Brooklyn, New York 11211
(212) 782-2722

VON EICKEN'S THREE STAR (tobacco)
See G.A. Georgopulo & Company

VON RUDEN MANUFACTURING COMPANY
(Subsidiary of W.S.I.)
Post Office Box 507-T
2100 Park Drive
Owatonna, Minnesota 55060
(507) 451-9736

VON SCHRADER COMPANY
1600 Junction Avenue
Racine, Wisconsin 53403
Francis von Schrader, President
(414) 634-1956

VON'S GROCERY COMPANY
10150 Lower Azusa Road
El Monte, California 91731
Charles T. Von der Ahe, Chairman of the Board
(213) 579-1400

VOORHIS-TIEBOUT COMPANY
Barry Town Road
Red Hook, New York 12571
(914) 758-2441

VORNADO, INC.
174 Passaic Street
Garfield, New Jersey 07026
Solomon Rogoff, President
(201) 773-4000
See also Meyenberg Milk Products Company

VOROS, PHILIP & PHYLLIS
1007 North New Hampshire
Los Angeles, California 90029
(213) 661-3625

VORTA SYSTEMS INC.
Box 613
Round Lake, Illinois 60073

VOSE (pianos)
See Aeolian Corporation

VOSPER INC.
500 Barnett Place
Ho-Ho-Kus, New Jersey 07423

VOSS (washing machines)
See Midwest International Inc.

VOSTRA (ski equipment)
See Miller Ski Company

VOTE (toothpaste)
See Bristol-Myers Products
Hillside Division

VUARNET (sports accessories)
See Herbert G. Schwarz Ski
Imports

VUDOR (shades)
See Breneman, Inc.

VUE INC.
485 West First Avenue
Roselle, New Jersey 07203

VUETTE INC.
Vuette Building
46 Railroad Avenue
Glen Head, New York 11545

VULCAN (lawn mowers)
See Southland Mower Company

VULCAN BINDER & COVER
(Division of Ebsco Industries, Inc.)
Post Office Box 29
Vincent, Alabama 35178
(205) 672-2241

VULCAN CORPORATION
6 East Fourth Street
Cincinnati, Ohio 45202
J. Howard Frazer, President
(513) 621-2850

VULCAN SAFETY RAZOR
CORPORATION
238 Burnett Avenue
Maplewood, New Jersey 07040

VULCAN-VOLNER MANUFAC-
TURING CORPORATION
924 McDonald Avenue
Brooklyn, New York 11218
(212) 854-1978

Companies and Trade Names

W

W. & F. MANUFACTURING COMPANY, INC.
251 Seneca Street
Buffalo, New York 14204
Robert E. Grahner, President
(716) 856-3600

W & H MANUFACTURERS
Post Office Box 255
Industrial Site
Nebraska City, Nebraska 68410
(402) 873-5207

WD-40 COMPANY
1061 Cudahy Place
San Diego, California 92110
John S. Barry, Chairman, President and Treasurer
(714) 275-1400

W.F. (stainless flatware and holloware)
See Walter Fleisher Company, Inc.

W.F.R. RIBBON CORPORATION
115 West 18th Street
New York, New York 10011
(212) 924-4675

WGA (coffee)
See Washington Grocers Association Inc.

WIX CORPORATION
Post Office Box 1967
Gastonia, North Carolina 28052
Leon G. Alexander, President
(704) 864-6711

W-K IMPORTS INC.
Post Office Box 280
Dover, Pennsylvania 17315

WMF OF AMERICA, INC.
236 Fifth Avenue
New York, New York 10001
Otto Spiekermann, President
(212) 684-5696
See also Fraser's; and Summit Silver, Inc.

W. M. I. CORPORATION
3725 West Lunt Avenue
Lincolnwood, Illinois 60645

WSO MIRACLE FORMULA (moisture- and rust-inhibitor)
See Watsco Inc.

W-10 (canned vegetables)
See Lombardi Food Company

WW GRINDER CORPORATION
2955 North Market Street
Wichita, Kansas 67219
F.J. Mankoff, President
(316) 838-4229

WABA COMPANY
Post Office Box 1907
Beverly Hills, California 90213
(213) 273-0319

WACHOVIA BANK & TRUST COMPANY, NORTH AMERICA
Third and Main Streets
Winston-Salem, North Carolina 27101
John G. Medlin, Jr., President
(919) 748-5000

WACHTEL MUSIC PRODUCTS
1766 Halleck Place
Columbus, Ohio 43209

WACO PRODUCTS INC.
450 North Leavitt Street
Chicago, Illinois 60612
(312) 829-6565

WACOM CORPORATION
1271 Avenue of the Americas
New York, New York 10020
(212) 581-9150

WACONIA SORGHUM COMPANY
Post Office Box 1227
Cedar Rapids, Iowa 52406
(319) 366-6236

WADDELL COMPANY, INC., THE
Box 18
South Washington Street
Greenfield, Ohio 45123
Dean T. Waddell, President
(513) 981-3642

WADE PHARMACAL COMPANY
2115 59th Street
Saint Louis, Missouri 63110

WADERS, RALPH
24-30 41st Street
Astoria, New York 11103

WADHAMS & COMPANY
S.E. Milwaukee Expressway at Pheasant Court
Portland, Oregon 97222
(503) 654-9551

WAECO (canned foods)
See Wapato Fruit Products Inc.

WAFFLE HOUSE INC.
2133 La Vista Executive Park
Tucker, Georgia 30084
Joe W. Rogers, Jr., President
(404) 934-1800

WAGGONER CANDY COMPANY
308 Trinity Lane
Nashville, Tennessee 37207

WAGNER (cast-iron cookware)
See General Housewares Corporation Cookware Group

Companies and Trade Names

WAGNER (fruit drinks)
See A. E. Staley Manufacturing Company

WAGNER & SONS, JOHN
Ivyland, Pennsylvania 18974

WAGNER AWNING & MANUFACTURING COMPANY, THE
2658 Scranton Road
Cleveland, Ohio 44113
J. H. Jordan, President and Treasurer
(216) 861-5400

WAGNER COMPANY, INC., E.L.
554 Post Road
Darien, Connecticut 06821
E.P. Wagner, President
(203) 655-2531

WAGNER ELECTRIC CORPORATION
(Subsidiary of Studebaker Corporation)
100 Misty Lane
Parsippany, New Jersey 07054
Richard W. Vieser, President
(201) 386-9300

WAGNER INC., WARREN
1100 North Avenue A
Crystal City, Texas 78839

WAGNER MANUFACTURING COMPANY, E.R.
4611 North 32nd Street
Milwaukee, Wisconsin 53209
Robert S. Wagner, President
(414) 871-5080

WAGNER PRODUCTS
(Division of E.R. Wagner Manufacturing Company)
331 Riverview Drive
Hustisford, Wisconsin 53034
(414) 349-3271

WAGON TRAIL (food products)
See Holsum Foods

WAGON TRAIN (canned foods)
See Tony Downs Foods Company

WAHBA COMPANY, CHARLES J.
56 West 45th Street
New York, New York 10036
(212) 661-0330

WAHL CLIPPER CORPORATION
2902 North Locust Street
Sterling, Illinois 61081
W.P. Wahl, President
(815) 625-6525

WAIT-CAHILL COMPANY
704-32 North Monroe Street
Decatur, Illinois 62522

WAITING MOTHER (maternity bras, panties, and girdles)
See Leading Lady Foundations, Inc.

WAKE-UP (aftershave lotion and cologne
See Nestle-LeMur Company

WAKE-UP (skin-care products)
See Helena Rubinstein, Inc.

WAKE UP 'N LIVE (body rub)
See Bristol-Myers Company

WAKEFERN FOOD CORPORATION
600 York Street
Elizabeth, New Jersey 07207
Sylvia Nadel, Manager, Consumer Affairs and Communications
(201) 527-3300

WAKEFIELD (smoking tobacco)
See Philip Morris Inc.

WAKEFIELD BEARING CORPORATION
29 Foundry
Wakefield, Massachusetts 01880
Nathaniel D. Clapp, President and Manager
(617) 245-1828

WAKEFIELD ENGINEERING INC.
Audubon Road
Wakefield, Massachusetts 01880
Thomas D. Coe, President and Treasurer
(617) 245-5900

WAKEFIELD SEAFOODS, INC.
4215 21st Street West
Seattle, Washington 98119
(206) 284-5257

WAL-JAN SURGICAL PRODUCTS, INC.
395 Atlantic Avenue
East Rockaway, New York 11518

WAL-MART STORES, INC.
702 S.W. Eighth Street
Bentonville, Arkansas 72712
Sam M. Walton, Chairman of the Board
(501) 273-7741

WAL-RICH CORPORATION
35-12 Skillman Avenue
Long Island City, New York 11101
(212) 784-8024

WALBEAD INC.
38 West 37th Street
New York, New York 10018
S. Wallach, President
(212) 564-7070

WALBORG CORPORATION
149 Madison Avenue
New York, New York 10016
(212) 689-4222

WALBRO CORPORATION
6242 Garfield Avenue
Cass City, Michigan 48726
W.E. Walpole, President
(517) 872-2131
See also Dupree Products

WALBUCK CRAYON COMPANY
Andover, Massachusetts 01810
(617) 475-0032

1389

Companies and Trade Names

WALCO-LINK CORPORATION
Routes 3 and 46
Clifton, New Jersey 07013
(201) 471-1070
See also Link Company, O.E.

WALDBAUM COMPANY, MILTON G.
Wakefield, Nebraska 68784

WALDBURGER (sports apparel)
See Free Trade Center

WALDECH (beer)
See Theodore Hamm Company

WALDEN FARMS INC.
1209 West Saint George Avenue
Linden, New Jersey 07036

WALDENSIAN BAKERIES, INC.
Box 220
Valdes, North Carolina 28690
John P. Rostan, Jr., President and General Manager
(704) 874-2136

WALDES KOHINOOR, INC.
47-16 Austel Place
Long Island City, New York 11101
George Waldes, President
(212) 392-3100

WALDMAN, INC., TIBOR J.
35 Park Avenue
New York, New York 10016
(212) 683-0773

WALDORFS (cigars)
See Perfecto Garcia & Brothers, Inc.

WALDRON LTD., FRED L.
550 North Nimitz Highway
Honolulu, Hawaii 96817
(808) 538-6984

WALES (antacid, mouthwash, toothache remedy, etc.)
See Winsale Drug Company

WALES (leather goods)
See Columbia Walescraft Ltd.

WALES FLANNEL (men's furnishings)
See Knothe Brothers Company Inc.

WALGREEN COMPANY
200 Wilmot Road
Deerfield, Illinois 60015
C.R. Walgreen, III, President
(312) 948-5000

WALK-EZE (foot-care products)
See Sacramento Pharmacal Company

WALK-OVER (shoes)
See George E. Keith Company

WALKA BOUNCER (baby bouncer)
See Thayer Inc.

WALKER & ASSOCIATES, INC., MARVIN L.
347 Madison Avenue
New York, New York 10017
(212) 686-0480

WALKER & COMPANY, INC., J.H.
22 West First Street
Mount Vernon, New York 10550

WALKER & SON, W.H.
Clintondale, New York 12512

WALKER & ZANGER, INC.
179 Summerfield Street
Scarsdale, New York 10583

WALKER BUTTER & EGG COMPANY
20 Harrison Street
New York, New York 10013
(212) 966-5424

WALKER COMPANY, B.B.
Post Office Box Drawer 1167
Asheboro, North Carolina 27203
Marshall R. Williams, President
(919) 629-1411

WALKER COMPANY, FRANK, R.
5030 North Harlem Avenue
Chicago, Illinois 60656
(312) 867-7070

WALKER COMPANY, THE
East Main Street
Middleboro, Massachusetts 02346

WALKER CORPORATION & COMPANY INC.
Easthampton Place and North Collingwood Avenue
Syracuse, New York 13201
(315) 463-4511

WALKER FOODS INC.
237 North Mission Road
Los Angeles, California 90033

WALKER-GORDON LABORATORY COMPANY
Princeton Road
Plainsboro, New Jersey 08536
Henry W. Jeffers III, President
(609) 799-1234

WALKER, INC., M.S.
35 Wareham Street
Boston, Massachusetts 02118
Leo Allen, President
(617) 423-6300

WALKER-JUMPER (stroller)
See Peterson Baby Products Company

Companies and Trade Names

WALKER MANUFACTURING
& SALES CORPORATION
1711-1717 Penn
Saint Joseph, Missouri 64507

WALKER MANUFACTURING
COMPANY
(A Tenneco Company)
1201 Michigan Boulevard
Racine, Wisconsin 53402
T.G. Cook, President
(414) 632-8871

WALKER MANUFACTURING
COMPANY, THE MADAME
C.J.
617 Indiana Avenue
Indianapolis, Indiana 46202
(317) 631-7143

WALKER PHARMACAL COMPANY
4200 Laclede Avenue
Saint Louis, Missouri 63108
(314) 533-9600

WALKER-SCOTT CORPORATION
Fifth Avenue at Broadway
San Diego, California 92101
Barry P. Knudson, President
(714) 233-8282

WALKER STORES, W.E.
Post Office Box 9407
Jackson, Mississippi 39206
William E. Walker, Chairman of
 the Board
(601) 956-5330

WALKING SPRINKLER (lawn
sprinkler)
   See National Manufacturing
    Company (Nebraska)

WALL-LENK MANUFACTURING
COMPANY
Post Office Box 3349, Department
 A-19
Greenville Highway
Kinston, North Carolina 28501
E.G. Oppenheimer, President
(919) 527-4186

WALL-LITES (lighted pictures)
   See Hobby Hill Inc.

WALL MANUFACTURING
COMPANY
Kinston, North Carolina 28501

WALL-O-VIN (wall coverings)
   See Columbus Coated Fabrics
    Company

WALL-ROGALSKY MILLING
COMPANY
416 North Main Street
McPherson, Kansas 67460
John B. Wall, President and
 Chief Executive Officer
(316) 241-2410

WALL ROPE WORKS
Broad Street and Railroad Avenue
Beverly, New Jersey 08010
(609) 877-1800

WALL-STREETER SHOE COMPANY
26 Union Street
North Adams, Massachusetts 01247
Robert E. Wall, President
(413) 663-3751

WALL-TEX (fabric wall covering)
   See Columbus Coated Fabrics
    Company

WALL-TO-WALL (rug shampooer and
shampoo)
   See Bissell Inc.

WALL TRENDS, INC.
17 Mileed Way
Avenel, New Jersey 07001
Michel Marq, President
(201) 382-8600

WALLA WALLA (food products)
   See Rogers Walla Walla Inc.

WALLA WALLA GRAIN GROWERS
Post Office Box 310
George and Jefferson
Walla Walla, Washington 99362
Martin Buchanan, President
(509) 525-6510

WALLACE, DAVIS COMPANY
1070 Sherman Avenue
Hamden, Connecticut 06514
(203) 248-6375

WALLACE FOODS INC.
2855 Whipple Avenue N.W.
Canton, Ohio 44708

WALLACE MANUFACTURING
CORPORATION
21 Manning Road
Thompsonville, Connecticut 06082
Edward M. Wallace, President
 and Treasurer
(203) 745-1634

WALLACE-MURRAY
CORPORATION
299 Park Avenue
New York, New York 10017
Charles V. Myers, President
(212) 758-4000
   See also Heller Tool

WALLACE PENCIL COMPANY
2001 South Hanley Road
Saint Louis, Missouri 63144
(314) 644-5010

WALLACE PHARMACEUTICALS
(Division of Carter-Wallace, Inc.)
Half Acre Road
Cranbury, New Jersey 08512

WALLACE SILVERSMITHS
(Division of Hamilton Watch
 Company)
340 Quinnipiac Street
Wallingford, Connecticut 06492
Robert F. Wilson, President
(203) 269-4401

1391

Companies and Trade Names

WALLACH INC., ROLF
Sherman, Connecticut 06784

WALLAU, INC., ALEX LEE
Harbor View Avenue
Stamford, Connecticut 06902

WALLDECOR
41 Madison Avenue
New York, New York 10010
(212) 686-3990

WALLERSTEIN COMPANY
(Division of Baxter Laboratories Inc.)
6301 Lincoln Avenue
Morton Grove, Illinois 60053
Claude J. Grunewald, President
(312) 965-4700

WALLERSTEIN TEXTILES, INC.
419 Park Avenue
New York, New York 10016
(212) 683-8355

WALLEY CLEGG COMPANY
(Subsidiary of Heublein, Inc.)
1420 McPherson
Oxford, Alabama 36201
Dewey E. Walley, President
(205) 831-4381

WALLHIDE (paint)
See PPG Industries, Inc.

WALLINGFORD ORCHARDS, B.H.
Box 200
Auburn, Maine 04210

WALLIS COMPANY, MARVIN G.
5014 Mendell Street
Fairfax, Virginia 22030
(703) 273-0813

WALLKYD (wall enamel)
See Reichhold Chemicals, Inc.

WALLSTREETER (luggage)
See Baltimore Luggage Company

WALLY FRANK LTD.
344 Madison Avenue
New York, New York 10017
(212) 349-3366

WALLY SEA PRODUCTS CORPORATION
400 C Street
Boston, Massachusetts 02110
(617) 357-5010

WALNUT ACRES INC.
Penns Creek, Pennsylvania 17862

WALNUT BLEND (tobacco)
See John Middleton Inc.

WALNUT GROVE PRODUCTS
(Division of W.R. Grace & Company)
Second and Linn
Atlantic, Iowa 50022
W. Rodgers, General Manager
(712) 243-1030

WALNUT HILL (food products)
See Fry Foods Inc.

WALNUT HILL (slacks)
See Petrocelli Clothes Inc.

WALPAT COMPANY
Box 34
Westboro, Massachusetts 01581

WALSH COMPANY, INC., THE JOHN D.
66 Glen Avenue
Glen Rock, New Jersey 07452
(201) 444-3133

WALSH-JAMAICA
89-74 165th Street
Jamaica, New York 11432
(212) 523-3219

WALSTROM PRODUCTS
105 Bay Street
Harbor Springs, Michigan 49740

WALT DISNEY PRODUCTIONS, INC.
500 South Buena Vista Street
Burbank, California 91503
Donn B. Tatum, Chairman of the Board
(213) 849-3411

WALT WHITMAN (fruits, vegetables, jellies, etc.)
See Camden Grocers Exchange

WALTER, BEN
450 Seventh Avenue
New York, New York 10001

WALTER BREWING COMPANY, THE
Hickory and Lacrosse
Post Office Box 236
Pueblo, Colorado 81001
Edmund B. Koller, President
(303) 544-6354

WALTER CARPET MILLS
(Division of Ludlow Corporation)
14641 East Con Julian Road
Industry, California 91749
Stephen Walter, President
(213) 968-1464

WALTER CORPORATION, JIM
See Briggs; Celotex Corporation; Luminous Ceilings, Inc.; and Miami Carey

WALTER MACHINE COMPANY, THE
84 Cambridge Avenue
Jersey City, New Jersey 07307
(201) 656-5654

WALTER-MORTON (men's clothes)
See Hickey-Freeman Company, Inc.

1392

Companies and Trade Names

WALTER MOTOR TRUCK
COMPANY
School Road
Voorhesville, New York   12186
(518) 765-2321

WALTER'S FOOD DISTRIBUTORS,
INC.
2175 South 162nd Street
New Berlin
Milwaukee, Wisconsin   53151
(414) 782-3150

WALTERS INC., BEN
4600 East 11th Avenue
Hialeah, Florida   33013
(305) 681-6618

WALTHAM CHEMICAL COMPANY
817 Moody
Waltham, Massachusetts   02154
R.L. Keenan, President and
    Treasurer
(617) 893-1810

WALTHAM WATCH COMPANY
400 South Jefferson Street
Chicago, Illinois   60606
Sid M. Phillips, Vice President
(312) 454-0010

WALTON LABORATORIES
(Division of Melnor Industries)
1 Carol Place
Moonachie, New Jersey   07074
Eugene C. Okin, President
(201) 641-5700

WALTON MARCH
Box 340
1620 Old Deerfield Road
Highland Park, Illinois   60035
Jeffrey L. Fried, President
(312) 831-2200

WAMPOLE LABORATORIES
(Division of Denver Chemical
    Manufacturing Company)
35 Commerce Road
Stamford, Connecticut   06904

WAMPUM (corn chips, etc).
    See Pet Inc. Snack Foods
        Division

WAMSUTTA MILLS
(Division of M. Lowenstein & Sons)
111 West 40th Street
New York, New York   10018
William M. Fine, President
(212) 560-5000

WANAMAKER, JOHN
13th and Market Streets
Philadelphia, Pennsylvania   19101
Robert D. Harrison, President
(215) 422-2000

WAND ART (comb/brush sets and
mirrors)
    See R. Dakin & Company)

WANG LABORATORIES, INC.
836 North Street
Tewksbury, Massachusetts   01876
An Wang, President
(617) 851-4111

WANTZ CONSUMER PRODUCTS
(Division of Illinois Water
    Treatment Company)
840 Cedar Street
Rockford, Illinois   61105

WAPACO (cherry and apple
products)
    See Wayne Packing Company,
        Inc.

WAPATO FRUIT PRODUCTS, INC.
Post Office Box 127
Wapato, Washington   98951

WAPLES-PLATTER COMPANY
Post Office Box 1350
Fort Worth, Texas   76118
James D. Sweeney, President
(817) 284-9321
    See also Great Western Foods
        Company

WARA INTERCONTINENTAL
COMPANY
20101 West Eight Mile Road
Detroit, Michigan   48219
(313) 535-9110

WARD (men's hats)
    See Bill & Caldwell, Inc.

WARD & SON, E. WALDO
Box 266
273 East Highland
Sierra Madre, California   91024
(213) 355-1218

WARD CANDY COMPANY
(Subsidiary of Ward Foods Inc.)
2 Penn Plaza
New York, New York   10001
(212) 594-5400

WARD CHOCOLATE COMPANY
Margaret and James Streets
Philadelphia, Pennsylvania   19137
Bernhard S. Blumenthal, Chairman
(215) 535-7766

WARD FOODS, INC.
1000 Skokie Boulevard
Wilmette, Illinois   60091
William Howlett, President
(312) 256-5600
    See also Johnston Company,
        Inc., Robert A.; and
        Ward Candy Company

WARD HILL (shoes)
    See Gardiner Shoe Company,
        Inc.

WARD INC., JOHN J.
23-08 Jackson Avenue
Long Island City, New York   11101
(212) 784-7332

WARD-JOHNSTON, INC.
(Subsidiary of Ward Foods, Inc.)
2 Penn Plaza
New York, New York   10001
Alvin L. Erlich, President
(212) 564-1010

Companies and Trade Names

WARD LA FRANCE INTERNATIONAL INC.
Grand Central Avenue and 11th Street
Elmira Heights, New York 14902
Everett E. Baldwin, President
(607) 733-5631

WARD MANUFACTURING INC., SAMUEL
29 Melcher Street
Boston, Massachusetts 02210
(617) 426-6720

WARD PRODUCTS CORPORATION, THE
Edson Street
Amsterdam, New York 12010
(518) 842-7220

WARD SCHOOL BUS MANUFACTURING, INC.
Conway, Arkansas 72032
Charles D. Ward, President
(501) 327-7761

WARD TERRY & COMPANY
70 Rio Grande Boulevard
Denver, Colorado 80201
Donald J. Thurman, President
(303) 266-3181

WARDS COMPANY, INC.
2040 Thalbro Street
Richmond, Virginia 23230
Alan Wurtzel, President
(804) 257-4292

WARD'S COVE PACKING COMPANY, INC.
88 Hamlin
Seattle, Washington 98102
A.W. Brindle, President
(206) 323-3200

WARING PRODUCTS
(Division of Dynamics Corporation of America)
New Hartford, Connecticut 06057
Milton Stohl, President
(203) 379-0731

WARMEL, INC.
56 East 11th Street
New York, New York 10003
(212) 533-1177

WARMETTE (electric food-warming trays)
   See Jasco Products Inc.

WARN INDUSTRIES
19450 68th Avenue South
Kent, Washington 98031
T.L. Warn, President
(206) 854-5350

WARNACO, INC.
350 Lafayette Street
Bridgeport, Connecticut 06602
Linwood E. Melton, President
(203) 333-1151
   See also Cresco Manufacturing Company; Hathaway Company, C.F.; Puritan Sportswear Corporation; Rosanna Knitted Sportswear Inc.; and White Stag Manufacturing Company

WARNE & COMPANY, INC., FREDERICK
101 Fifth Avenue
New York, New York 10003
(212) 675-1151

WARNER & SWASEY COMPANY, THE
11000 Cedar Avenue
Cleveland, Ohio 44106
Joseph T. Bailey, President
(216) 368-5000

WARNER BROTHERS, INC.
(Subsidiary of Warner Communications, Inc.)
4000 Warner Boulevard
Burbank, California 91505
Frank Wells, President
(213) 843-6000

WARNER BROTHERS RECORDS, INC.
3701 Warner Boulevard
Burbank, California 91505
Joe Smith, President
(213) 843-8688

WARNER-CHILCOTT LABORATORIES
   See Warner-Lambert Company

WARNER COMMUNICATIONS, INC.
10 Rockefeller Plaza
New York, New York 10020
Steven J. Ross, President
(212) 484-8000
   See also Atlantic Recording Corporation

WARNER DRUG COMPANY
2713 Franklin Road
Nashville, Tennessee 37204

WARNER GEAR
(Division of Borg-Warner Corporation)
1106 East Seymour Street
Muncie, Indiana 47302
Richard T. Brown, President and General Manager
(317) 284-8411

WARNER-JENKINSON COMPANY
2526 Baldwin Street
Saint Louis, Missouri 63106
(314) 531-1500

WARNER-LAMBERT COMPANY
201 Tabor Road
Morris Plains, New Jersey 07950
Ward S. Hagan, President
(201) 540-2000
   See also American Chicle Company; American Optical Corporation; Parke, Davis & Company; Richard Hudnut; Schick Safety Razor Company; and Texas Pharmacal Company

Companies and Trade Names

WARNER MANUFACTURING
COMPANY
13435 Industrial Park Boulevard
Minneapolis, Minnesota 55441
F.P. Warner, President
(612) 559-4740

WARNER-PATTERSON COMPANY
(Subsidiary of Pyroil Company)
Box 1438
LaCrosse, Wisconsin 54601

WARNER PRESS
Post Office Box 2499
1200 East Fifth Street
Anderson, Indiana 46011
Donald A. Noffsinger, President
 and Publisher
(317) 644-7221

WARNER'S
(Division of Warnaco Group)
325 Lafayette Street
Bridgeport, Connecticut 06602
Philip J. Lamoureux, President
(203) 333-1151

WARP BROTHERS
(Division of Flex-O-Glass, Inc.)
1100 North Cicero
Chicago, Illinois 60651
Delbert Christensen, President
(312) 261-5200

WARREN CHEMICAL PRODUCTS
 COMPANY
2671 Youngstown Road
Warren, Ohio 44484

WARREN COMPANY, S.D.
(Division of Scott Paper Company)
225 Franklin Street
Boston, Massachusetts 02101
Charles W. Schmidt, President
(617) 423-7300

WARREN CORPORATION, THE
519 Rudder
Saint Louis, Missouri 63144
(314) 343-8300

WARREN DADO TOOL COMPANY
 INC.
29811 Eight Mile
Livonia, Michigan 48152

WARREN INDUSTRIES INC.
120 South Rancho Avenue
San Bernardino, California 92410

WARREN PAINT & COLOR
(Division of U.S. Gypsum
 Company)
700 Wedgewood Avenue
Nashville, Tennessee 37202
(615) 295-6655

WARREN PAPER PRODUCTS
 COMPANY
3200 South Street
Lafayette, Indiana 47905
Warren N. Eggleston, President
 and Treasurer
(317) 447-2151

WARREN PETROLEUM
 CORPORATION
(Subsidiary of Gulf Oil Corporation)
1350 South Boulder
Tulsa, Oklahoma 74102
John T. McDonnell, President
(918) 584-7121

WARREN-SHERER
(Division of Kysor Industrial
 Corporation)
Post Office Box 1436
905 Memorial Drive S.E.
Atlanta, Georgia 30301
(404) 688-1601

WARREN-TEED PHARMACEUTICALS,
 INC.
(Subsidiary of Rohm & Haas
 Company)
1 Gibralter Place
Horsham, Pennsylvania 19044
W.P. Ambrogi, President
(215) 674-9800

WARRIOR (mobile homes)
 See Nashua Homes

WARRIOR (tools, paints, and
paint sundries)
 See Moore-Handley Inc.

WARRIOR FIBERGLASS PRODUCTS
 INC.
Box 29
Fayette, Alabama 3555

WARRIOR SURGICAL SUPPLY
(Subsidiary of S.H. Camp
 Company)
Warrior, Alabama 35180

WARSAW CUT GLASS COMPANY
Post Office Box 293
Warsaw, Indiana 46580
(219) 267-6581

WARSHAW MANUFACTURING
 COMPANY INC.
4000 First Avenue
Brooklyn, New York 11232
Norman London, Chairman and
 President
(212) 965-6200

WARWICK (cutlery)
 See Regent-Sheffield Ltd.

WARWICK CLUB GINGER ALE
 COMPANY, INC.
108 Pond Street
West Warwick, Rhode Island 02893

WARWICK ELECTRONICS, INC.
(Subsidiary of Whirlpool Corporation)
7300 North Lehigh Avenue
Chicago, Illinois 60648
Robert F. Gunts, President
(312) 774-6400
 See also Thomas Organ
  Company

WASA RY-KING, INC.
1200 High Ridge Road
Stamford, Connecticut 06905

Companies and Trade Names

WASATCH CHEMICAL
(Division of Entrada Industries Inc.)
1979 South Seventh West
Salt Lake City, Utah 84106
(801) 972-8800

WASH & CARE (skin medication)
See Glenbrook Laboratories

WASHBURN (guitars, banjos)
See Boosey & Hawkes Ltd.

WASHBURN CANDY CORPORATION, F.B.
137 Perkins Avenue
Brockton, Massachusetts 02402

WASHINGTON ALUMINUM COMPANY, INC.
(Subsidiary of Easco Corporation)
Knecht Avenue and P.R.R.
Baltimore, Maryland 21229
D. Mc Phee, President
(301) 242-1000

WASHINGTON CHOCOLATE COMPANY
1064 Fourth Avenue South
Seattle, Washington 98134
(206) 622-1760

WASHINGTON COMPANY, THE
2055 North Main Street
Washington, Pennsylvania 15301

WASHINGTON CRAB PRODUCERS INC.
109 Dock Street
Westport, Washington 98505

WASHINGTON ETHICAL SOCIETY
7750 16th Street N.W.
Washington, D.C. 20012
(202) 882-6650

WASHINGTON FISH & OYSTER COMPANY, INC.
Pier 54
Seattle, Washington 98104
(206) 624-6888

WASHINGTON FORGE INC.
28 Harrison Avenue
Englishtown, New Jersey 07726
(201) 446-7777

WASHINGTON FRUIT & PRODUCE COMPANY
Post Office Box 1588
Yakima, Washington 98901

WASHINGTON FRUIT GROWERS, INC.
529 South Wenatchee Avenue
Wenatchee, Washington 98801

WASHINGTON GAS & LIGHT COMPANY
1100 H Street, N.W.
Washington, D.C. 20080
Paul E. Reichardt, President
(202) 750-4440

WASHINGTON GROCERS ASSOCIATION INC.
Box 396
Meadow Lands, Pennsylvania 15347

WASHINGTON GROUP, INC.
Post Office Box 1015
3068 Trenwest Drive
Winston-Salem, North Carolina 27103
Smith Bagley, President
(919) 765-9540

WASHINGTON KNITTING MILLS
152 Madison Avenue
New York, New York 10016
(212) 679-4544

WASHINGTON MANUFACTURING COMPANY
218-228 Second Avenue, North
Nashville, Tennessee 37203
T.W. Comer, President
(615) 244-0600

WASHINGTON MILLS
Post Office Box 1015
Winston-Salem, North Carolina 27102

WASHINGTON NATIONAL INSURANCE COMPANY
1630 Chicago Avenue
Evanston, Illinois 60201
E.E. Cragg, President
(312) 866-7900

WASHINGTON NATURAL GAS COMPANY
815 Mercer Street
Seattle, Washington 98111
James A. Thorpe, President
(206) 672-6767

WASHINGTON POST COMPANY
1150 15th Street N.W.
Washington, D.C. 20071
Katharine Graham, Chairman of the Board
(202) 223-6000

WASHINGTON PRODUCTS CORPORATION
201 Eastview Drive
Cleveland, Ohio 49141
(216) 398-9620

WASHINGTON RHUBARB GROWERS ASSOCIATION
Box 537
Sumner, Washington 98390

WASHINGTON STATE FRUIT COMMISSION
Box 2696
Yakima, Washington 98902

WASHINGTON WATER POWER COMPANY
East 1411 Mission Avenue
Spokane, Washington 99202
Wendell J. Satre, President
(509) 489-0500

WASKITOLI REEL COMPANY
1800 Tribune Tower
Oakland, California 94612

WASSELL ORGANIZATION, INC.
See Visirecord Systems

Companies and Trade Names

WASTE KING
(Division of Norris Industries, Inc.)
3300 East 50th
Los Angeles, California 90058
(213) 583-6161

WATCHEMOKET OPTICAL
    COMPANY
232 West Exchange
Providence, Rhode Island 02903
George Dickson, President
(401) 421-1314

WATCO (tools, hardware,
sporting goods)
    See Watkins Cottrell Company

WATCO-DENNIS CORPORATION
Michigan Avenue and 22nd Street
Santa Monica, California 90404
(213) 870-4781

WATER DEVIL (water skis and
accessories)
    See Wellington Puritan Mills
         Inc.

WATER KING (water conditioner)
    See Sta-Rite Industries, Inc.
         Water Treatment Division

WATER MAID (rice)
    See Riviana Foods Inc.

WATER MASTER COMPANY
13 South Third
New Brunswick, New Jersey 08904
Marvin Cheiten, Partner
(201) 247-1900

WATER PIK (oral-hygiene appliance)
    See Teledyne Aqua Tec

WATER REFINING COMPANY,
    INC.
500 North Verity Parkway
Middletown, Ohio 45042
Ronald D. Baker, Chairman of the
    Board
(513) 423-9421

WATER SOLUBLE PRODUCTS
7321 North Ridgeway Avenue
Skokie, Illinois 60076

WATERBURY (watches)
    See United States Time
         Corporation

WATERBURY LOCK & SPECIALTY
    COMPANY
205 Broad Street
Milford, Connecticut 06460
John E. Peterson, Jr., Chairman
    of the Board
(203) 874-1666

WATERFILL & FRAZIER (whiskey)
    See Double Springs Distillers
         Inc.

WATERFOG (nozzles and sprinkler
systems)
    See E.W. Bliss (A Gulf &
         Western Company)

WATERFORD COOKWARE (enamelled
cast iron)
    See IDG International
         Designers Group Inc.

WATERFORD GLASS INC.
225 Fifth Avenue
New York, New York 10010
(212) 686-4450

WATERMAN-BIC PEN
CORPORATION
    See Bic Pen Corporation

WATERMAN FRUIT PRODUCTS
    COMPANY, INC.
35 North Road
Ontario Center, New York 14520
(315) 524-2211

WATERS CONLEY COMPANY,
INC.
    See Telex Corporation, Inc.,
         The

WATERS MANUFACTURING INC.
533 Boston Post Road
Wayland, Massachusetts 01778
Robert A. Waters, President
(617) 358-2777

WATERSPAR (paint)
    See PPG Industries, Inc.

WATHENA (food products)
    See Clements Foods Company

WATJEN INC., LOUIS
60 East 42nd Street
New York, New York 10017
(212) 697-6485

WATKINS COTTRELL COMPANY
109-125 South 14th Street
Richmond, Virginia 23219
Edwin Raleigh Courtney, Chairman
    and President
(804) 678-6536

WATKINS PRODUCTS, INC.
150 Liberty Street
Winona, Minnesota 55987
David F. King, President
(612) 507-8150

WATKINS SALT COMPANY, INC.
518 East Fourth Street
Post Office Box 150
Watkins Glen, New York 14891
Franklin R. Hinman, President
(315) 535-2713

WATLING LADDER COMPANY
111 South Meramec Avenue
Saint Louis, Missouri 63105
(314) 727-4426

WATNEY (beer)
    See Original Beer Importing
         and Distributing Company,
         Inc.

Companies and Trade Names

WATROUS & COMPANY, INC.
110 East 23rd Street
New York, New York 10010
(212) 473-7789

WATSCO INC.
1800 West Fourth Avenue
Hialeah, Florida 33010
Albert H. Nahmad, Chairman and
  President
(305) 885-1911

WATSON (home elevators)
  See Crane Carrier Corporation

WATSON COMPANY, T.E.
Box 3829
Sarasota, Florida 33578

WATSON MANUFACTURING
  COMPANY
335 Harrison Street
Jamestown, New York 14701
John H. O'Brien, President and
  Chief Executive Officer
(716) 484-0171

WATSON PRODUCTS COMPANY
2917 Oak Brook Hills
Oak Brook, Illinois 60521

WATSONVILLE CANNING &
  FROZEN FOOD COMPANY
Box 990
Watsonville, California 95076

WATSONVILLE EXCHANGE, INC.
Watsonville, California 95076

WATT FABRICS, INC., ADAM
1412 Broadway
New York, New York 10018
(212) 221-1046

WATT POTTERY COMPANY, THE
101-115 China Street
Crooksville, Ohio 43731

WATT-SAVER (light bulb)
  See Duro-Test Corporation

WAUKEGAN BABY SEAT
  COMPANY INC.
1125-27 Washington Street
Waukegan, Illinois 60085

WAUKESHA MOTOR COMPANY
West Saint Paul Avenue
Waukesha, Wisconsin 53186
R.A. D'Amour, President
(414) 547-3311

WAUSAU HOMES, INC.
901 North Cherry
Wausau, Wisconsin 54401
Earl Schuette, President
(715) 675-2311

WAUSAU PAPER MILLS COMPANY
Brokaw, Wisconsin 54417
William V. Arvold, President
(715) 675-3361

WAVE KING (seafood)
  See Hallmark Fisheries

WAVE MASTER (lawn and garden
  sprinklers, nozzles, and other
  accessories)
  See Melnor Industries

WAVERLY (rugs)
  See Mohasco Industries, Inc.

WAVERLY FABRICS
(Division of F. Schumacher &
  Company)
58 West 40th
New York, New York 10018
(212) 644-5900

WAVERLY INDUSTRIES INC.
428 Miller Avenue
Brooklyn, New York 11207

WAVERLY MINERAL PRODUCTS
  COMPANY
(Division of Johnson-March
  Corporation)
3018 Market
Philadelphia, Pennsylvania 19104
(215) 387-2210

WAVERLEY MIXTURE (tobacco)
  See American Tobacco Company

WAVERLY PRODUCTS (ashtrays,
  banks, wastebaskets)
  See Consolidated Molded
    Products Corporation

WAVERLY WAFERS (crackers)
  See Nabisco Inc.

WAWONA FROZEN FOODS INC.
3789 East Alluvial
Clovis, California 93612

WAX-O-MATIC (floor waxer)
  See Master Manufacturing
    Company

WAXOFF (wax remover)
  See Red Devil Inc.

WAXTEX (waxed paper and bags)
  See American Can Company
    Consumer Products

WAY-RITE (scales)
  See Hanson Scale Company

WAYNE CANDIES INC.
(Division of W.R. Grace &
  Company)
1501 East Berry Street
Fort Wayne, Indiana 46803
Peter Mildred, Vice President
(219) 742-1211

Companies and Trade Names

WAYNE GOSSARD CORPORATION
North 22nd Street
Humboldt, Tennessee 38343
Robert B. Colbert, Jr., President
(901) 784-3211
See also Archer Mills, Inc.;
Gossard Company, H.W.;
Heritage Sportswear; and
May Hosiery Mills

WAYNE NAUTICAL HANDCRAFTS
21 Cypress Drive
Swansea, Massachusetts 02777

WAYNE PACKING COMPANY, INC.
Box 128
Sodus, New York 14551

WAYNE POULTRY COMPANY
110 North Wacker Drive
Chicago, Illinois 60606
(312) 346-5060

WAYSIDE INDUSTRIES
55 Howland Street
Marlborough, Massachusetts 01752

WEAR BEST (leather goods)
See Leather Specialty Company

WEAR DATED (mark for guaranteed apparel)
See Monsanto Company

WEAR-EVER ALUMINUM, INC.
(Subsidiary of Aluminum Company of America)
1089 Eastern Avenue
Chillicothe, Ohio 45601
J.S. Hamilton, President
(614) 775-9100

WEAR-EVER BABY CARRIAGE COMPANY, INC.
1250 Atlantic Avenue
Brooklyn, New York 11216
(212) 778-8400

WEAR MASTER (paint)
See Standard Industrial Products, Inc.

WEAR-RITE BRASSIERE COMPANY
See Bi-Flex International

WEAREVER (writing instruments)
See David Kahn, Inc.

WEARRA (men's footwear)
See Baker-Benjes Inc.

WEARWELL (door mats)
See Tennessee Mat Company

WEATHA-COTE (men's apparel)
See Maurice Holman Inc.

WEATHER BIRD (shoes)
See International Shoe Company

WEATHER CHEK (protective coating)
See Monsey Products Company

WEATHER-COTE (weatherproofing compound)
See Goodyear Tire & Rubber Company

WEATHER MASTER (tires)
See Cooper Tire and Rubber Company

WEATHER MASTER (waterproofing materials)
See Astrup Company

WEATHER-MATES (weather instruments)
See Westclox (Division of General Time)

WEATHER-TWIN (air conditioners)
See Embassy Industries Inc.

WEATHER WATCHERS (thermometer-barometer)
See Kraftware Corporation

WEATHER WAX (car cleaner)
See S.C. Johnson & Son, Inc.

WEATHERBY, INC.
2781 Firestone Boulevard
South Gate, California 90280
Roy E. Weatherby, President
(213) 569-7186

WEATHERLY COMPANY, W.H.
225 North Water Street
Elizabeth City, North Carolina 27909

WEATHERMASTER (outdoor finishes)
See Standard Industrial Products Inc.

WEATHERTRON (heat pump system)
See General Electric Company Air Conditioning Division

WEAVER & SON, W.J.
Circleville, Ohio 43113

WEAVER INC., VICTOR F.
403 South Custer Avenue
New Holland, Pennsylvania 17557
Victor F. Weaver, President
(717) 354-4211

WEAVER POTATO CHIP COMPANY
1600 Center Park Road
Lincoln, Nebraska 68512

WEAVEWOOD INC.
7520 Wayzata Boulevard
Minneapolis, Minnesota 55426
(612) 544-3136

WEBAIR (air conditioner)
See Walter Kidde & Company

Companies and Trade Names

WEBBER IMPORTS, PETER
Box 309
Farmington, Maine 04938

WEBB'S CITY, INC.
128 Ninth Street, South
Saint Petersburg, Florida 33705
Fred B. Scott, President
(813) 894-7151

WEBCO (art materials)
See Weber Costello

WEBCOR ELECTRONICS
1815 Troy Street
New Albany, Indiana 47150

WEBECO FOODS, INC.
6966 N.W. 36th Avenue
Miami, Florida 33147
(305) 691-6515

WEBER (beer)
See G. Heileman Brewing Company, Inc.

WEBER (food products)
See Stevens Canning Company

WEBER (pianos)
See Aeolian Corporation

WEBER & COMPANY, INC., A.C.
216 North Canal
Chicago, Illinois 60606
A.C. Weber, President
(312) 346-0414

WEBER BRIARS, INC.
140 Cator Avenue
Jersey City, New Jersey 07305
(201) 433-5300

WEBER COMPANY, F.
(Division of Visual Arts Industries Inc.)
Wayne & Windrim Avenues
Philadelphia, Pennsylvania 19144
(215) 329-3980

WEBER COSTELLO
1900 North Narragansett Avenue
Chicago, Illinois 60639
J.C. Sinderal, President
(312) 889-2300

WEBER FOOD PRODUCTS COMPANY
6710 East Florence Avenue
Bell Gardens, California 90202

WEBER MANUFACTORY, JON
4140 Pearl Road
Cleveland, Ohio 44109
(216) 351-6971

WEBER MARKING SYSTEMS INC.
711 West Algonquin Road
Arlington Heights, Illinois 60005
Joseph A. Weber, Jr., President
(312) 439-8500

WEBER PLASTICS INC.
1039 Ellis
Stevens Point, Wisconsin 54481
(715) 344-9080

WEBER, RAYMOND W.
2724 Mahoning Avenue
Youngstown, Ohio 44509

WEBER SHOE COMPANY
(Division of Stride-Rite Corporation)
Tipton, Missouri 65081
Arnold Hiatt, President
(314) 433-5511

WEBER TACKLE COMPANY
1039 Ellis Street
Stevens Point, Wisconsin 54481
Earl Parkman, President
(715) 344-9080

WEBER'S (bread)
See Interstate Brands Corporation

WEBLON INC.
4 Westchester Plaza
Elmsford, New York 10523
(914) 592-4244

WEBSTER (cigars)
See Bayuk Cigars, Inc.

WEBSTER (slacks)
See Spencer Industries, Inc.

WEBSTER ADVERTISING PRODUCTS
5515 Fairlane Drive
Cincinnati, Ohio 45227
(513) 272-0110

WEBSTER & WILCOX (silver)
See Insilco Corporation

WEBSTER CLOTHES, INC.
1800 Woodlawn Drive
Baltimore, Maryland 21207
Samuel Feldman, President
(301) 944-8811

WEBSTER COMPANY, G.L.
(Subsidiary of Kane-Miller Corporation)
Cheriton, Virginia 23316
Stanley Reehling, President
(804) 331-2200

WEBSTER COMPANY, H.K.
32 West
Lawrence, Massachusetts 01841
Dean K. Webster, President
(617) 686-4131

WEBSTER COMPANY INC., THE
262 Broadway
North Attleboro, Massachusetts 02761

WEBSTER COMPANY, WILLIAM A.
Box 18358
Memphis, Tennessee 38118

Companies and Trade Names

WEBSTER DRUG PRODUCTS, INC.
139 Webster Avenue
Providence, Rhode Island 02909

WEBSTER ELECTRIC COMPANY, INC.
(Subsidiary of Sta-Rite Industries, Inc.)
1900 Clark
Racine, Wisconsin 53403
J.C. McAlvay, President
(414) 633-3511

WEBSTER SEED & SUPPLY, INC.
Post Office Box 86
Marienthal, Kansas 67863

WECO TRADING COMPANY
40-35 Ithaca Street
Elmhurst, New York 11373

WED-LOK (diamond rings)
See Granat Brothers

WEDAC (rust remover)
See West Chemical Products, Inc.

WEDDING PLANNER COMPANY
Post Office Box 371
Monrovia, California 91016

WEDDING VEIL (German wine)
See Austin, Nichols & Company, Inc.

WEDEMEYER INC., HENRY
41 Madison Avenue
New York, New York 10010
(212) 686-3790

WEDGE-A-GATE (juvenile product)
See Port-a-Crib Inc.

WEDGEWOOD POOLS
See Ideal Recreational Products

WEDGIE (aluminum ware)
See Flambeau Products Corporation

WEDGWOOD & SONS, INC. JOSIAH
(Subsidiary of Wedgwood, Ltd.)
555 Madison Avenue
New York, New York 10022
Raymond Smyth, President
(212) 755-3950

WEE BURN (Scotch)
See Austin, Nichols, & Company, Inc.

WEE CARE (juvenile car seats)
See Strolee of California

WEE WALKER (infants' shoes)
See Trimfoot Company

WEE WINKIES (children's clocks)
See Westclox (Division of General Time)

WEED-B-GONE (agricultural and garden chemicals)
See Chevron Chemical Company

WEE JUNS (shoes)
See G.H. Bass & Company

WEEKS & LEO COMPANY, INC.
4000 N.W. 100th Street
Des Moines, Iowa 50322
(512) 276-1586

WEEMS & PLATH INC.
48 Maryland Avenue
Annapolis, Maryland 21401
(301) 263-6700

WEEN (thumb-sucking deterrent)
See Manhattan Drug Company, Inc.

WEERES INDUSTRIES INC.
Box 98
Saint Cloud, Minnesota 56301

WEGMAN COMPANY, S.J.
35 Wilbur Street
Lynbrook, New York 11563

WEIBEL CHAMPAGNE VINEYARDS
Post Office Box 3095
Fremont, California 94538
Fred E. Weibel, President
(415) 656-2340

WEIGHT WATCHERS INTERNATIONAL, INC.
800 Community Drive
Manhasset, New York 11050
Albert Lippert, President
(516) 627-9200

WEIL & DURRSE INC.
200 Madison Avenue
New York, New York 10016
(212) 679-0035

WEIL & SCHOENFELD FABRICS INC.
See Reliable Textile Company Inc.

WEIL BROTHERS
82 Wall Street
New York, New York 10005
(212) 269-2551

WEIL CERAMICS & GLASS, INC.
225 Fifth Avenue
New York, New York 10010
(212) 532-5685

WEIL, INC., CLIFF
Erie Road
Mechanicsville, Virginia 23111
Henry Gunst, Sr., President
(804) 746-1321

Companies and Trade Names

WEIL-MCLAIN COMPANY, INC.
10400 North Central Expressway
Box 31349
Dallas, Texas 75231
Guy M. Foote, President
(214) 369-1777
    See also Swimquip, Inc.

WEILER CORPORATION, MORRIS W.
10 West 47th Street
New York, New York 10036
(212) 757-2410

WEIMAN COMPANY, THE
4801 West Paterson Avenue
Chicago, Illinois 60646
Richard D. Goddard, President
(312) 286-1121
    See also Prestigeline

WEINBERG IMPORT COMPANY, H.
126-08 Jamaica Avenue
Richmond Hill, New York 11418

WEINBRENNER SHOE COMPANY
(Division of Bata Shoe Company, Inc.)
Polk Street
Merrill, Wisconsin 54452
James V. Greenlee, President
(715) 536-5521

WEINGARTEN, INC., J.
600 Lockwood Street
Houston, Texas 77001
Bernard Weingarten, President
(713) 928-5551

WEINSTEIN COMPANY, A.J.
100 Rosslyn Road
Carnegie, Pennsylvania 15106
Fred D. Weinstein, President
(412) 923-1166

WEIR (heating and air-conditioning equipment)
    See Meyer Furnace Company

WEISERT TOBACCO COMPANY, JOHN
1120 South Sixth Street
Saint Louis, Missouri 63104
(314) 421-1197

WEISFIELD'S INC.
800 South Michigan Street
Seattle, Washington 98108
Leslie D. Rosenberg, President
(206) 767-5090

WEISS (sports apparel)
    See Beconta Inc.

WEISS & SONS, INC., MAX
45 Cedar Street
Stamford, Connecticut 06904

WEISS AND BIHELLER MERCHANDISE CORPORATION
40 West 20th Street
New York, New York 10011
(212) 929-7453

WEISSMAN COMPANY INC., BETH
260 Smith Street
Farmingdale, New York 11735

WEISSMILLER MANUFACTURING COMPANY
38 Furnace Road
Wernersville, Pennsylvania 19565

WEKSLER INSTRUMENTS CORPORATION
80 Mill Road
Freeport, New York 11520
Alvin Marks, President
(516) 623-0100

WELBILT CORPORATION
57-18 Flushing Avenue
Maspeth, New York 11378
Henry Hirsch, Chairman of the Board
(212) 386-4300
    See also Unagusta Corporation

WELCH (electric clocks)
    See Sessions Clock Company

WELCH COMPANY, JAMES O.
810 Main Street
Cambridge, Massachusetts 02139

WELCH FOODS, INC.
Westfield, New York 14787
R. Craig Campbell, President
(716) 326-3131

WELCH'S (candy)
    See Nabisco, Inc.

WELCOME WORLD CREATIONS
(Division of Kalman Development Corporation)
510 Thrush Drive
Dresher, Pennsylvania 19025

WELDIT CORPORATION
44 West 18th
New York, New York 10011
(212) 989-0800

WELDON (tobacco)
    See S.S. Pierce Company

WELDON FARM PRODUCTS INC.
880 Third Avenue
New York, New York 10022
(212) 751-6055

WELDON ROBERTS RUBBER COMPANY
(Subsidiary of A.W. Faber-Castell Pencil Company)
351 Sixth Avenue
Newark, New Jersey 07107
(201) 482-7812

WELDON, WILLIAMS & LICK
711 North A Street
Fort Smith, Arkansas 72901
S.W. Jackson, President
(501) 783-4114

Companies and Trade Names

WELDONA, INC.
1 Newark Street
Hoboken, New Jersey 07030

WELDWOOD (glue, partitions)
See Champion International
Corporation

WELL MADE (food products)
See Silver Foods Inc.

WELL MADE MANUFACTURING
COMPANY
Sixth and East Streets
Easton, Pennsylvania 18042

WELL OF YOUTH (skin-care
products)
See Apple-Crone Laboratories

WELLA CORPORATION, THE
524 Grand Avenue
Englewood, New Jersey 07631
Eugen Megerle, President
(201) 569-1020

WELLCO ENTERPRISES, INC.
Post Office Box 188
Waynesville, North Carolina 28786
Rolf Kaufman, President
(704) 456-3545

WELLCOME BRAND
See Burroughs-Welcome

WELLCRAFT MARINE CORPORATION
8151 Bradenton Road
Sarasota, Florida 33580

WELLER (tools)
See Cooper Group Weller
Division

WELLER COMPANY, THE J.
Box 30
Oak Harbor, Ohio 43449
(419) 898-2551

WELLINGTON (beers and stout)
See Walter Brewing Company

WELLINGTON (pipes)
See William Demuth &
Company

WELLINGTON BOATS INC.
7591 Wilson Boulevard
Jacksonville, Florida 32210

WELLINGTON IMPORTERS LTD.
340 Kennedy Drive
Hauppauge, New York 11787

WELLINGTON PRODUCTS
Box 1141
Baltimore, Maryland 21203

WELLINGTON PURITAN MILLS
INC.
Post Office Box 521
Madison, Georgia 30650
(404) 342-1916

WELLINGTON SYNTHETIC FIBRES
INC.
Plastic Woven Products Division
33-49 Whelan Road
East Rutheford, New Jersey 07073
Richard C. Wellington, President
(201) 742-9282

WELLONS CANDY COMPANY,
INC.
(Division of Flora Mir Candy
Corporation)
Post Office Box 677
Dunn, North Carolina 28334

WELLS & SON, W.S.
Box 512
Wilton, Maine 04294

WELLS FARGO BANK
464 California Street
San Francisco, California 94120
Richard P. Cooley, President
(415) 396-0123

WELLS-GARDNER ELECTRONICS
CORPORATION
2701 North Kildare Avenue
Chicago, Illinois 60639
Grant Gardner, President
(312) 252-8220

WELLS INDUSTRIES
Post Office Box 230
Michigan City, Indiana 46360

WELLS MANUFACTURING
CORPORATION
2-26 South Brooke Street
Fond du Lac, Wisconsin 54935
R.L. Ridley, President
(414) 922-5900

WELLS YACHTS INC.
Foot of Commercial Street
Marblehead, Massachusetts 01945

WELLWORTH PICKLE COMPANY
74-86 Florida Avenue
Paterson, New Jersey 07503

WELS INDUSTRIES INC.
160 East 56th Street
New York, New York 10022
(212) 758-2611

WELSH COMPANY
1535 South Eighth
Saint Louis, Missouri 63104
Albert D. Welsh, Jr., President
(314) 231-8822

WELT/SAFE-LOCK INC.
2400 West Eighth Lane
Hialeah, Florida 33010
(305) 885-6401

WELTER, INC., HENRY C.
1412 Broadway
New York, New York 10018
(212) 695-3091

Companies and Trade Names

WELTY COMPANY
2700 West 50th Street
Chicago, Illinois 60632
(312) 778-4000

WELTY PEN & REPAIR COMPANY
302 South Second Street
Champaign, Illinois 61820

WEMBLEY INDUSTRIES, INC.
966 South White Street
New Orleans, Louisiana 70125
Sidney Pulitzer, President
(504) 822-3700

WEN PRODUCTS INC.
5812 Northwest Highway
Chicago, Illinois 60631
(312) 763-6060

WENATCHEE-BEEBE ORCHARD COMPANY
Post Office Box 878
Chelan, Washington 98816

WENCHOW IMPORTING COMPANY
439 Third Avenue
New York, New York 10016
(212) 689-8667

WENCZEL TILE COMPANY
Klagg Avenue
Trenton, New Jersey 08618
Chester L. Wenczel, President
(609) 599-4503

WENDELL BROOKS CHOCOLATES (candy)
See Standard Chocolates, Inc.

WENDT-BRISTOL COMPANY
1159 Dublin Road
Columbus, Ohio 43212
(614) 486-9411

WENTE BROTHERS
5565 Tesla Road
Livermore, California 94550
Karl L. Wente, President
(415) 447-3603

WENTWORTH (fine china)
See Metasco, Inc.

WENTWORTH (lighting fixtures)
See Hallmark Accessories, Inc.

WENZEL COMPANY, THE
1280 Research Boulevard
Saint Louis, Missouri 63132
William Wenzel, President
(314) 993-4000

WERCO (tambourines)
See White Eagle Rawhide Manufacturing Company

WERNER COMPANY, INC., R.D.
Post Office Box 580
77 Osgood Road
Greenville, Pennsylvania 16125
L.L. Werner, President
(412) 588-8600

WERNER CONTINENTAL, INC.
2500 West County Road, "C"
Roseville, Minnesota 55113
John N. Hall, President
(612) 633-0220

WERNER ENTERPRISES COMPANY
3214 Taylor Street N.E.
Minneapolis, Minnesota 55418

WERNER LABORATORIES, INC.
1112 57th Street
Kenosha, Wisconsin 53140

WERNER PRODUCTS INC.
11420 Parkside Road
Chardon, Ohio 44024

WERNET'S (denture adhesive, plate brush)
See Block Drug Company, Inc.

WERNICK COMPANY, MARVIN
960 South Los Angeles Street
Los Angeles, California 90013
(213) 623-5437

WERTHON, INC., K.H.
161 William Street
New York, New York 10038
(212) 267-1775

WESBRO (shoes)
See International Shoe Company

WESCO (paints)
See National Gypsum Company

WESCO ELECTRICAL COMPANY INC.
(Division of Atlee Corporation)
27 Olive
Greenfield, Massachusetts 01301

WESCO INDUSTRIES INC.
121 Carver Avenue
Westwood, New Jersey 07675

WESCOSA INC.
186 South Dillon Avenue
Campbell, California 95008

WESLEY-JESSEN
37 South Wabash Avenue
Chicago, Illinois 60603
(312) 346-2000

WESLEY PHARMACAL COMPANY, INC., THE
4831-33 Rising Sun Avenue
Philadelphia, Pennsylvania 19120
(215) 324-6566

WESSANEN INC.
715 Park Avenue
East Orange, New Jersey 07017

Companies and Trade Names

WESSEL (hardware)
See Shelburne Industries, Inc.

WESSEL, DUVAL & COMPANY, INC.
1 World Trade Center
New York, New York 10048
Bernard T. Keogh, President and Treasurer
(212) 432-1940

WESSON (cooking oil, salad dressings, etc)
See Hunt-Wesson Foods Inc.

WEST & COMPANY OF LOUISIANA, INC.
Post Office Drawer G
Minden, Louisiana 71055
C.O. West, President
(318) 377-1975

WEST AGRO-CHEMICAL, INC.
(Subsidiary of West Chemical Products, Inc.)
4216 West Street
Long Island City, New York 11101
Thomas Z. Van Raalte, President
(212) 784-2424

WEST BAY (canned foods)
See Traverse City Canning Company

WEST BAY BOAT YARD INC.
Box 2379
Burlington, North Carolina 27215

WEST BEND COMPANY
(Subsidiary of Dart Industries, Inc.)
400 Washington Street
West Bend, Wisconsin 53095
J.J. Keenan, President
(414) 334-2311
See also Coppercraft Guild; and Thermo-Serv Company

WEST BEND EQUIPMENT CORPORATION
Post Office Box 497
West Bend, Wisconsin 53095
Richard A. Klumb, President
(414) 334-5561

WEST BEND THERMO-SERV INC.
2939 Sixth Avenue North
Anoka, Minnesota 55303

WEST BEST (canned foods)
See Commission Company, Inc.

WEST CHEMICAL PRODUCTS, INC.
42-16 West Street
Long Island City, New York 11101
M. Peter Schweitzer, President
(212) 784-2424

WEST COAST CHAIN MANUFACTURING COMPANY
2242 East Foothill Boulevard
Pasadena, California 91107
(213) 681-6358

WEST COAST GROWERS & PACKERS, INC.
1445 Nebraska Avenue
Selma, California 93662
D.R. Hoak, Jr., President
(209) 896-2140

WEST COAST INTERNATIONAL
161 West 33rd Street
Los Angeles, California 90007
(213) 747-7916

WEST CREST (fruit products)
See Diamond Fruit Growers Inc.

WEST-CUT (cutlery)
See Western Cutlery Company

WEST END BREWING COMPANY
811 Edward Street
Utica, New York 13503
Walter J. Matt, President
(315) 732-3181

WEST FARMS (food products)
See Kelley, Farquhar & Company

WEST FOODS, INC.
Box 428
Soquel, California 95073

WEST INDIES PRIDE (seafood)
See Gulfstream Packing Company, Inc.

WEST KNITTING CORPORATION
514 North Washington Street
Wadesboro, North Carolina 28170
Fulton A. Huntley, President
(704) 694-4131

WEST MILL CLOTHES, INC.
45 West 18th Street
New York, New York 10011
Harvey Weinstein, President
(212) 255-6640

WEST PENN POWER COMPANY
800 Cabin Hill Drive
Greensburg, Pennsylvania 15601
C.B. Finch, President
(412) 837-3000

WEST POINT (carpeting)
See Stephen-Leedom Carpet Company Inc.

WEST POINT PEPPERELL
Post Office Box 71
West Tenth Street
West Point, Georgia 31833
Joseph L. Lanier, Jr., President
(205) 756-7111

Companies and Trade Names

WEST POINT PEPPERELL
Lantuck Nonwoven Fabrics Department
1221 Avenue of the Americas
New York, New York 10020
(212) 354-9150

WEST POINT PEPPERELL CARPET & RUG
(Division of West Point Pepperell)
120 East Morris Street
Dalton, Georgia 30720
William J. Dixon, President
(404) 278-1100

WEST PRODUCTS COMPANY
161 Prescott Street
East Boston, Massachusetts 02128
Frederick W. Bowers, President and Treasurer
(617) 569-5100

WEST VIRGINIA GLASS SPECIALTY COMPANY, INC.
Drawer 510
Weston, West Virginia 26452
John Pertz, President
(304) 269-2842

WEST VIRGINIA PULP AND PAPER COMPANY
See Westvaco Corporation

WEST VIRGINIA WIRE PRODUCTS INC.
106 Oak Street
Saint Albans, West Virginia 25177

WEST-WARD PHARMACEUTICALS INC.
745 Eagle Avenue
Bronx, New York 10456
George S. Greene, President
(212) 585-7777

WESTALL-RICHARDSON (cutlery)
See Regent-Sheffield Ltd.

WESTBERG MANUFACTURING COMPANY
3402 Western Way
Sonoma, California 95476
V. Luther Westberg, President
(707) 938-4723

WESTBROOK (guitars, mandolins)
See J.M. Sahlein Music Company Inc.

WESTBRYTE (floor wax)
See West Chemical Products

WESTBURY FASHIONS
1400 Broadway
New York, New York 10018
Hy Rabin, Chairman of the Board
(212) 564-0500
See also Hoot Owl Junior Petite Dresses

WESTCHESTER (chickens, meats, soups)
See Pure Food Company, Inc.

WESTCHESTER (mobile homes)
See Conchemco Inc. Homes Group

WESTCHESTER VETERINARY PRODUCTS
(Division of Combe Chemical Company, Inc.)
180 Mamaroneck Avenue
White Plains, New York 10601

WESTCLOX
(Division of General Time Corporation)
LaSalle, Illinois 61301
R.B. Hally, General Manager
(815) 224-5000

WESTCO (can openers)
See Turner & Seymour Manufacturing Company

WESTCO PRODUCTS
1654 Long Beach Avenue
Los Angeles, California 90021
(213) 748-5415

WESTCOTT NUT PRODUCTS
93-97 Coit Street
Irvington, New Jersey 07111

WESTERFIELD LABORATORIES
3941 Brotherton Road
Cincinnati, Ohio 45209
(513) 271-8260

WESTERGAARD & COMPANY, INC., B.
357-363 36th Street
Brooklyn, New York 11232
(212) 388-3870

WESTERLY MARINE CONSTRUCTION, LTD.
c/o Andrew Gemeny & Son
5809 Annapolis Road
Hyattsville, Maryland 20784
(301) 779-6190

WESTERN (beer)
See Cold Spring Brewing Company

WESTERN AIR LINES, INC.
6060 Avion Drive
Los Angeles, California 90009
Fred Benninger, Chairman of the Board
(213) 646-2345

WESTERN ARMS (shotguns)
See Ithaca Gun Company, Inc.

WESTERN AUTO SUPPLY COMPANY
(Subsidiary of Beneficial Corporation)
2107 Grand Avenue
Kansas City, Missouri 64108
L.A. Fults, President
(816) 421-5382

Companies and Trade Names

WESTERN BED PRODUCTS
544 Casanova Street
Bronx, New York 10474
(212) 329-7418

WESTERN BOAT BUILDING
 CORPORATION
2556 East 11th Street
Tacoma, Washington 98421

WESTERN CANNING COMPANY
Box 387
Second and Grant Streets
(303) 384-4441

WESTERN CARBON PAPER
 MANUFACTURING COMPANY
3700 Whittier Boulevard
Los Angeles, California 90023
(213) 262-5111

WESTERN CASUALTY & SURETY
 COMPANY
14 East First Street
Fort Scott, Kansas 66701
Thomas M. Mayhew, President
(316) 223-1100

WESTERN CEREAL COMPANY
Billings, Montant 59101

WESTERN CHAIN COMPANY
1807 West Belmont Avenue
Chicago, Illinois 60657
(312) 472-2212

WESTERN COIL & ELECTRICAL
 COMPANY
Hobby-Time Division
215 State Street
Racine, Wisconsin 53403
(414) 632-4741

WESTERN CUTLERY COMPANY
Box 391
Boulder Industrial Park
Boulder, Colorado 80301
Harvey N. Platts, President
(303) 442-4023

WESTERN DRESSING INC.
Box 920
Oak Park, Illinois 60303

WESTERN ELECTRIC (hearing aids)
 See Graybar Electric Company,
  Inc.

WESTERN ELECTRIC COMPANY,
 INC.
(Subsidiary of American Telephone
 and Telegraph Company)
195 Broadway
New York, New York 10007
Donald E. Procknow, President
(212) 571-2345
 See also Teletype Corporation

WESTERN FARMERS ASSOCIATION
201 Elliott Avenue West
Seattle, Washington 98119
(206) 284-8500

WESTERN FILAMENT INC.
4680 San Fernando Road
Glendale, California 91204
(213) 247-5880

WESTERN FLYER (toys, hobbies,
etc.)
 See Western Auto Supply
  Company

WESTERN FOOD PRODUCTS
 COMPANY
Box 1524
Hutchinson, Kansas 67501
(316) 665-5541

WESTERN GLOBE PRODUCTS, INC.
8985 Venice Boulevard
Los Angeles, California 90034
Robert William, President
(213) 870-6923

WESTERN GOLD (canned foods)
 See Great Western Foods
  Company

WESTERN GOLD & PLATINUM
(Subsidiary of W.B. Driver Company)
525 Harbor Boulevard
Belmont, California 94002
Peter W. Smith, President
(415) 592-9440

WESTERN INTERNATIONAL HOTELS
(Subsidiary of United Airlines)
Olympic Hotel
Seattle, Washington 98111
Harry Mullikin, President
(206) 447-5000

WESTERN IRRIGATION &
 MANUFACTURING INC.
3558 Highway 99 North
Eugene, Oregon 97402

WESTERN KING (barbecues,
braziers, and accessories)
 See Big Boy Manufacturing
  Company, Inc.

WESTERN LOOSE LEAF
 COMPANY
150 Industrial Way
Brisbane, California 94005
(415) 468-4550

WESTERN MANUFACTURING
 COMPANY
1266 South Orchard Road,
 Department O-72
Aurora, Illinois 60506
Paul H. Adair, President
(312) 897-8458

WESTERN MASSACHUSETTS
 ELECTRIC COMPANY
174 Brush Hill Avenue
West Springfield, Massachusetts
 01089
Lelan F. Sillin, Jr., President
(413) 785-5871

Companies and Trade Names

WESTERN MOBILE HOMES, INC.
(Subsidiary of U.S. Industries, Inc.)
1185 Oak Street
Lakewood, Colorado 80215
G. McGough, President
(303) 238-8191

WESTERN MOTELS INC.
See Best Western Motels

WESTERN MUSIC SPECIALTY
COMPANY
Box 1389
Grand Junction, Colorado 81501

WESTERN NATIONAL PRODUCTS
869 West 15th
Newport Beach, California 92660

WESTERN NATURAL GROWERS
INC.
Box 209
Ulysses, Kansas 67880

WESTERN PACIFIC RAILROAD
526 Mission Street
San Francisco, California 94105
Alfred E. Perlman, Chairman
(415) 982-2100

WESTERN PANCAKE HOUSE
4080 South High Street
Columbus, Ohio 43207
(614) 491-2974

WESTERN PAPER GOODS
COMPANY
4890 Spring Grove Avenue
Cincinnati, Ohio 45232
George A. Biehle, President
(513) 542-4700

WESTERN PHARMACAL COMPANY
1537 South Main
Salt Lake City, Utah 84115
(801) 466-4621

WESTERN PLAYING CARD
COMPANY
1220 Mound Avenue
Racine, Wisconsin 53404

WESTERN PRECIPITATION
(Division of Joy Manufacturing
Company)
4565 Colorado Boulevard
Los Angeles, California 90039
William G. Henke, Vice
President and General Manager
(213) 240-2300

WESTERN PRODUCTS INC.
Post Office Box 745
Orange, Connecticut 06477

WESTERN PROVISION MARKETS
21 West 21st Street
Erie, Pennsylvania 16502

WESTERN PUBLISHING COMPANY,
INC.
1220 Mound Avenue
Racine, Wisconsin 53404
G.J. Slade, President
(414) 633-2431

WESTERN QUARRY TILE COMPANY
2428 Dallas Street
Los Angeles, California 90031
(213) 222-2641

WESTERN RESEARCH
LABORATORIES
301 South Cherokee
Denver, Colorado 80223
(303) 733-7207

WESTERN RODEO (jeans)
See Hicks-Ponder Company

WESTERN SCHOOL EQUIPMENT
COMPANY
510 East Airline Way
Gardena, California 90247
(213) 770-0730

WESTERN STAMPING
CORPORATION
2218 Enterprise Avenue
Jackson, Michigan 49203
L.N. Masters, President and
Chief Executive Officer
(517) 787-9800

WESTERN STAR MILL COMPANY
316 North Santa Fe
Salina, Kansas 67401
(913) 825-1541

WESTERN STATES BANKCARD
ASSOCIATION
100 Northpoint
San Francisco, California 94133
Hal W. Sconyers, President
(415) 391-1430

WESTERN STATES ENVELOPE
COMPANY
Post Office Box 2048
Milwaukee, Wisconsin 53201
George F. Moss, President
(414) 781-5540

WESTERN STONEWARE
521 West Sixth Avenue
Monmouth, Illinois 61462
(309) 734-2161

WESTERN SUPPLY COMPANY
Box 237
West Covina, California 91790

WESTERN TRADITION
Box 1500
Boulder, Colorado 80302

WESTERN UNION INTERNATIONAL
26 Broadway
New York, New York 10004
Edward A. Gallagher, President
(212) 363-6400

Companies and Trade Names

WESTERN UNION TELEGRAPH COMPANY, THE
1 Lake Street
Upper Saddle River, New Jersey 07458
Mary Gardiner Jones, Vice President, Consumer Affairs
(201) 825-1100

WESTERN VALLEY (groceries)
See Associated Grocers

WESTERN WOOD MANUFACTURING COMPANY
6077 S.W. Lakeview Boulevard
Lake Oswego, Oregon 97034
(503) 639-7644

WESTFIELD MAID (food products)
See Seneca Foods Corporation

WESTGATE-CALIFORNIA FOODS INC.
See Sun Harbor Industries

WESTHEIMER COMPANY INC., SOL
24 East 18th Street
New York, New York 10003
(212) 947-9568

WESTINGHOUSE BROADCASTING COMPANY, INC.
(Subsidiary of Westinghouse Electric Corporation)
90 Park Avenue
New York, New York 10016
D.H. McGannon, President
(212) 983-6500

WESTINGHOUSE CREDIT CORPORATION
(Subsidiary of Westinghouse Electric Corporation)
3 Gateway Center
Pittsburgh, Pennsylvania 15222
M.K. Evans, President
(412) 255-4100

WESTINGHOUSE ELECTRIC CORPORATION
Westinghouse Building
Gateway Center
Pittsburgh, Pennsylvania 15222
Charles E. Hammond, President, Consumer Products
(412) 255-3800
See also Econo-Car International, Inc.; and Longines-Wittnauer Watch Company, Inc.

WESTINGHOUSE LAMP
(Division of Westinghouse Electric Corporation)
Westinghouse Plaza
Bloomfield, New Jersey 07003

WESTLAND-PHYSICS
Post Office Box 25088
Portland, Oregon 97225

WESTLAND PLASTICS, INC.
800 North Mitchell Road
Newbury Park, California 91320

WESTLEY INDUSTRIES
(Division of Norandex, Inc.)
5300 Harvard Avenue
Cleveland, Ohio 44105
(216) 641-5490

WESTMARK (cookware and appliances)
See West Bend Company

WESTMARK (cutlery)
See Western Cutlery Company

WESTMINSTER (flutes)
See Pennino Music Company Inc.

WESTMINSTER CORPORATION
790 East Baltimore Boulevard
Westminster, Maryland 21157
Alvin London, President
(301) 848-5600

WESTMINSTER INDUSTRIES INC.
220 Fifth Avenue
New York, New York 10010
(212) 683-6035

WESTMINSTER RECORDING COMPANY, INC.
(Subsidiary of ABC Records)
1330 Avenue of the Americas
New York, New York 10019
J. Lasken, President
(212) 581-7777

WESTMINSTER SPORTS
32-21 Downing Street
Flushing, New York 11354
(212) 762-8300

WESTMORE (cosmetics)
See House of Westmore, Inc.

WESTMORELAND GLASS COMPANY
Grapeville, Pennsylvania 15634
(412) 523-5481

WESTMORLAND (sterling)
See Wear-Ever Aluminum, Inc.

WESTON COMPANY, BYRON
Dalton, Massachusetts 01226
(413) 684-1234

WESTON INSTRUMENTS, INC.
(Subsidiary of Schlumberger, Ltd.)
614 Frelinghuysen Avenue
Newark, New Jersey 07114
Howard J. Warnken, President
(201) 243-4700

WESTON LABORATORIES, INC.
Box 218
Ottawa, Illinois 61350

WESTON'S (Scotch whiskey)
See National Distillers & Chemical Corporation

Companies and Trade Names

WESTOURS, INC.
100 West Harrison
Seattle, Washington 98101
H.J. Musiel, President
(206) 623-1683

WESTPAC (frozen foods)
See United Flav-R-Pac Growers, Inc.

WESTPHAL (toiletries)
See Essex Chemical Corporation Consumer Products Division

WESTPHAL IMPORT CORPORATION, G.A.
34 West 27th Street
New York, New York 10001
(212) 684-2630

WESTPHALIA (enamel cookware)
See Herman Dodge & Son

WESTPOINT (toys, hobbies, sporting goods, etc)
See Cotter & Company

WESTPORT PRIDE (seafood)
See North Pacific Processors Inc.

WESTRAVEN TILE COMPANY
45 Gunther Avenue
Yonkers, New York 10704

WESTRIP (paint remover)
See West Chemical Products

WESTSAIL CORPORATION
1626 Placentia Avenue
Costa Mesa, California 92627

WESTVACO CORPORATION
299 Park Avenue
New York, New York 10017
David L. Luke, III, President
(212) 688-5000
See also Reed Company, C.A.; and United States Envelope Company

WESTVACO CORPORATION
C.A. Reed Division
Williamsport, Pennsylvania 17701

WESTWAY PETITE JRS (dresses)
See Lorch Westway Corporation

WESTWOOD (wood-grained plastic serving and insulated ware)
See Thermo-Serv Company

WESTWOOD, INC.
Mill Street
Southbridge, Massachusetts 01550
Louis C. Broughton, President
(617) 764-3252

WESTWOOD INDUSTRIES INC.
177 Genessee Avenue
Paterson, New Jersey 07503
(201) 271-4700

WESTWOOD PHARMACEUTICALS INC.
468 Dewitt Street
Buffalo, New York 14213
Frank R. Nero, Jr., President
(716) 882-8484

WET ONES (moist towelettes)
See Lehn & Fink Consumer Products

WET PAINT (high-gloss enamel)
See Illinois Bronze Powder & Paint Company

WET-PROOF (infants' product)
See Barden & Robeson Corporation

WETTERAU FOODS INC.
8400 Pershall Road
Hazelwood, Missouri 63043

WEXFORD (glassware)
See Anchor Hocking Corporation

WEXFORD HALL (men's belts)
See Buxton Inc.

WEXLER & COMPANY, DAVID
823 South Wabash Avenue
Chicago, Illinois 60605
(312) 427-0560

WEYENBERG SHOE MANUFACTURING COMPANY
234 East Reservoir Avenue
Milwaukee, Wisconsin 53201
Robert Feitler, President
(414) 374-8900
See also Nunn-Bush Shoe Company

WEYERHAEUSER COMPANY
2525 South 336th Street
Federal Way, Washington 98002
Norton Clapp, Chairman of the Board
(206) 924-2345

WEYMAN'S (tobacco)
See American Tobacco Company

WEYMOUTH LABORATORIES
972 Commercial Street
East Weymouth, Massachusetts 02189

WFF'N PROOF LEARNING GAMES ASSOCIATES
1490 US South Boulevard
Ann Arbor, Michigan 48104

WHALEY PECAN COMPANY
Box 332
Troy, Alabama 36081

WHAM-O MANUFACTURING COMPANY
835 East El Monte Street
San Gabriel, California 91778
Richard P. Knerr, Vice President
(213) 287-9681

Companies and Trade Names

WHANTON CLOCKS (decorator clocks)
See J. Kenneth Zahn

WHARTON LABORATORIES, INC.
(Division of U.S. Ethicals, Inc.)
37-02 48th Avenue
Long Island City, New York 11101
(212) 786-8606

WHEARY LINE (luggage)
See Hartmann Luggage Company, Inc.

WHEAT PRODUCTS COMPANY
4201 North Nevada Avenue
Colorado Springs, Colorado 80907

WHEATENA (hot wheat cereal)
See Standard Milling Company

WHEATIES (cereal)
See General Mills, Inc.

WHEATLEY (frozen foods)
See Omstead Foods Ltd.

WHEATON INDUSTRIES
Wheaton Avenue
Millville, New Jersey 08332
Frank H. Wheaton, Jr., President
(609) 825-1400

WHEATON PRODUCTS
1501 North Tenth Street
Millville, New Jersey 08332

WHEATON VAN LINES, INC.
Post Office Box 55191
2525 East 56th
Indianapolis, Indiana 46025
E.S. Wheaton, Chairman of the Board
(317) 255-3131

WHEEL CAMPER CORPORATION
580 West Burr Oak Street
Centerville, Michigan 49032
Ora E. Miller, President
(616) 467-9025

WHEEL-HORSE PRODUCTS, INC.
515 West Ireland Road
South Bend, Indiana 46614
Cecil Pond, Chairman of the Board
(219) 291-3112

WHEEL-LOK (trailer accessory)
See Campbell Chain Company

WHEELDEX INC.
1000 North Division Street
Peekskill, New York 10566

WHEELEES INC.
931 Liberty Street
Jacksonville, Florida 32206

WHEELER COMPANY, INC., M.G.
10 Lexington Avenue
Greenwich, Connecticut 06830
(203) 869-5404

WHEELING CORRUGATING COMPANY
(Division of Wheeling-Pittsburgh Steel Corporation)
1134 Market Street
Wheeling, West Virginia 26003
(304) 234-0000

WHEELOCK SIGNALS, INC.
273 Branchport Avenue
Long Branch, New Jersey 07740
Thomas H. Shriver, President
(201) 222-6880

WHIFF 'N POUFF (colognes, perfumes, hair tonics, etc.)
See Hattie Carnegie Perfumes

WHIFF 'N RUB (men's cosmetics)
See Viviane Woodard Corporation

WHINK PRODUCTS COMPANY
Post Office Box 230
Eldora, Iowa 50627
(515) 858-3456

WHIP (organ)
See Whippany Melosonic Corporation

WHIP N CHILL (pudding mixes)
See General Foods Corporation

WHIPPANY MELO-SONIC CORPORATION
(Subsidiary of Aerosystems Technology Corporation)
1275 Bloomfield Avenue
Fairfield, New Jersey 07006
(201) 575-0141

WHIPPLE COMPANY, THE
Natick, Massachusetts 01760
(617) 653-2660

WHIRL-A-WAY COMPANY
(Division of Tappan Company)
Post Office Box 4146
4240 East La Palma
Anaheim, California 92803
B.F. Blough, General Manager
(714) 524-7770

WHIRLPOOL CORPORATION
Lake Shore and Monte Road
Benton Harbor, Michigan 49022
John Platts, President
(616) 926-5000
See also Appliance Buyers Credit Corporation; Heil-Quaker Corporation; and Warwick Electronics, Inc.

WHIRLWIND (floor-care products)
See Premier Electric Company

WHIRLWIND (hand-held hair dryer)
See Schick, Inc.

WHIRLWIND (juvenile product)
See Gym Dandy Inc.

WHIRLWIND (ovens)
See Universal Oil Products Company

Companies and Trade Names

WHIRLWIND (rotary mowers)
See Toro Company

WHISK-AWAY (brooms, mops, brushes)
See Zephyr Manufacturing Company

WHISK AWAY (rust remover)
See W.W. Stewart Company

WHISPER CLEAN (dishwashers)
See Hotpoint

WHISPER DRIVE (blender)
See Ronson Corporation

WHISTLE (household cleaner)
See Bristol-Myers Company

WHISTLE SEAT (juvenile furniture)
See Group 7 Inc.

WHISTLES (snack food)
See General Mills, Inc.

WHIT-CRAFT HOUSEBOAT
(Division of North American Rockwell)
24 Laird Street
Winona, Minnesota 55987

WHIT SALES COMPANY
102 South Colony Road
Newport News, Virginia 23602

WHITAKER COMPANY INC., H.E.
1841 North 19th Street
Philadelphia, Pennsylvania 19121
(215) 769-6767

WHITAKER, W. THEODORE
1218 Lenox Road
Jenkintown, Pennsylvania 19046
(215) 884-3362

WHITBREAD (ale)
See Bedford Importers Ltd.

WHITE (gas heaters)
See Bradford-White Corporation

WHITE & BAGLEY COMPANY, THE
Post Office Box 706
150 Worcester Center Boulevard
Worcester, Massachusetts 01608
Herbert P. Bagley II, President
(617) 791-3201

WHITE & COMPANY, INC., L.N.
225 West 34th Street
New York, New York 10001
(212) 239-7474

WHITE & GOLD (cigars)
See A.J. Golden Inc.

WHITE & WYCKOFF (stationery)
See Westab

WHITE ASH (cigars)
See Parodi Cigar Corporation

WHITE BALLOON (whiskey)
See James B. Beam Distilling Company

WHITE CANDY COMPANY INC.
(Subsidiary of Pearson Candy Company, Minnesota)
1396 San Mateo Avenue South
San Francisco, California 94080
(415) 871-8094

WHITE CANDY COMPANY, INC.
BOB
208 East Olin Street
Madison, Wisconsin 53713

WHITE CAP
(Division of Continental Can Company, Inc.)
1819 North Major Avenue
Chicago, Illinois 60639
(312) 637-2000

WHITE CARD CORPORATION
76 Atherton Street
Boston, Massachusetts 02130
(617) 522-6500

WHITE CASTLE SYSTEM, INC.
Post Office Box 1498
555 West Goodale
Columbus, Ohio 43216
Edger W. Ingram, Jr., President
(614) 228-5781
See also Paperlynen Company

WHITE CLOUD (bathroom tissue)
See Procter & Gamble Company

WHITE CLOVER DAIRY COMPANY
Route 3
Kaukauna, Wisconsin 54130
Earl A. Gilling, President and Treasurer
(414) 766-3517

WHITE COFFEE CORPORATION
11-50 44th Road
Long Island City, New York 11101
(212) 361-1600

WHITE COMPANY, O.C.
15-21 Hermon Street
Worcester, Massachusetts 01608
R.L. May, President
(617) 755-8621

WHITE CONSOLIDATED INDUSTRIES, INC.
11770 Berea Road
Cleveland, Ohio 44111
Edward S. Reddig, Chairman of the Board
(216) 252-3700
See also Gibson Appliance Corporation; Hupp, Inc.; Kelvinator Appliance Company; Perfection Products Company; and Saraco Company, Inc.

Companies and Trade Names

WHITE CORPORATION, I.J.
210 Sherwood Avenue
Farmingdale, New York 11735
(516) 293-2211

WHITE CROSS (bandages, gauze, tapes, etc.)
See American White Cross Laboratories

WHITE CROSS (insurance plan)
See Bankers Life & Casualty

WHITE CROSS SLEEP PRODUCTS
N.E. Corner H and Lycoming
Philadelphia, Pennsylvania 19124
(215) 289-5556

WHITE EAGLE RAWHIDE
    MANUFACTURING COMPANY
2340 West Nelson Street
Chicago, Illinois 60618
(312) 327-6795

WHITE FARM EQUIPMENT
    COMPANY
(Subsidiary of White Motor Corporation)
2625 Butterfield Road
Oak Brook, Illinois 60521
R.E. Kidder, President
(312) 887-0110

WHITE FASHIONS INC., MORRIS
362 Fifth Avenue
New York, New York 10001
(212) 564-1900

WHITE FLASH (gasoline)
See Atlantic Richfield Company

WHITE FOODS, INC., MARTHA
110 21st Avenue, South
Nashville, Tennessee 37203
Cohen T. Williams, Chairman of the Board
(615) 327-4961

WHITE FREIGHTLINER
(Division of White Motor Corporation)
5400 North Basin Avenue
Portland, Oregon 97217
(503) 285-0536

WHITE FURNITURE COMPANY
Mebane, North Carolina 27302
Stephen A. White, President
(919) 563-1217

WHITE GREASE (lubricants, paints)
See Plasti-Kote Company

WHITE HART (rum)
See Julius Wile Sons & Company, Inc.

WHITE HEATHER (Scotch)
See Clan Importers, Inc.

WHITE HEN PANTRY
666 Industrial Drive
Elmhurst, Illinois 60126

WHITE HOUSE (apple products)
See National Fruit Product Company Inc.

WHITE INSTRUMENTS, DAVID
(Division of Realist Inc.)
N 93, West 16288 Megal Drive
Menomonee Falls, Wisconsin 53051

WHITE KING, INC.
(Subsidiary of Los Angeles Soap Company)
617 East First
Los Angeles, California 90054
DeWitt A. Barton, President
(213) 627-5011

WHITE KNIGHT (seafood)
See Caleb Haley & Company, Inc.

WHITE LABORATORIES, INC.
Kenilworth, New Jersey 07033

WHITE LACE (bath oil, perfume, etc.)
See De Heriot, Inc.

WHITE LILY (flour, mixes)
See Great Western Sugar Company

WHITE MAGIC (laundry products)
See Safeway Stores, Inc.

WHITE METAL ROLLING &
    STAMPING CORPORATION
84 Moultrie Street
Brooklyn, New York 11222
H. Lamberg, President
(212) 389-4134

WHITE MINK (toiletries)
See Dart Industries

WHITE MIST (body powder, toilet water, perfume, etc.)
See Countess Maritza Cosmetic Company, Inc.

WHITE MOTOR CORPORATION
100 Erieview Plaza
Cleveland, Ohio 44114
S.E. Knudsen, President
(216) 523-5800
See also Euclid, Inc.

WHITE MOUNTAIN (storage and wardrobe cabinets)
See Maine Manufacturing Company

WHITE ORCHID (cigars)
See A.J. Golden Inc.

WHITE OWL (cigars)
See General Cigar Company

Companies and Trade Names

WHITE PHLOX (perfume, dusting powder, cologne)
See Herb Farm Shop Ltd.

WHITE RABBIT DYE COMPANY
4800 North Broadway
Saint Louis, Missouri 63147
(314) 231-1035

WHITE RAIN (hair spray, shampoo)
See Gillette Company

WHITE ROCK CORPORATION
215 Van Dyke Street
Brooklyn, New York 11231
Alfred Y. Morgan, President
(212) 625-0300

WHITE ROSE (canned foods)
See Di Giorgio Corporation

WHITE ROSE (cosmetics, beauty aids)
See J. Strickland & Company

WHITE ROSE TEA, INC.
1501 Park Avenue
Linden, New Jersey 07036

WHITE SANDS (bath oil, dusting powder, perfume, etc.)
See Ritornelle, Inc.

WHITE SATIN (sugar)
See Amalgamated Sugar Company

WHITE SEAL (seafood)
See Union Fish Company

WHITE SEAL (whiskey)
See Calvert Distillers Company

WHITE SEWING MACHINE COMPANY
11750 Berea Road
Cleveland, Ohio 44111
R.E. Lavery, President
(216) 252-3300

WHITE SHOULDERS (perfume)
See Evyan Perfumes, Inc.

WHITE STAG (camping equipment)
See Hirsch Weis Canvas Products Company

WHITE STAG (pipes)
See Bradberry Briar Pipe Corporation

WHITE STAG MANUFACTURING COMPANY
(Division of Warnaco, Inc.)
5100 S.E. Harney Drive
Portland, Oregon 97206
John Detjens, President
(503) 777-1711
See also Hirsch-Weis Canvas Products Company

WHITE STAR CONCENTRATES COMPANY
223 S.E. Third Avenue
Portland, Oregon 97214
(503) 233-4678

WHITE-STOKES COMPANY
3615 Jasper Place
Chicago, Illinois 60609
(312) 523-7540

WHITE STORES, INC.
Knoxville, Tennessee 37917

WHITE STORES INC.
39-10 Call Field Road
Wichita Falls, Texas 76308

WHITE SWAN UNIFORMS, INC.
21 Saint Casimir Avenue
Yonkers, New York 10701
Robert L. Cooper, President
(914) 965-3190

WHITE TIP (cigars)
See Jacobs Cigar Company

WHITE TRUCKS
(Division of White Motor Corporation)
842 East 79th
Cleveland, Ohio 44101
(216) 621-7284

WHITE WOLF (vodka)
See Clan Importers Inc.

WHITEFIELD'S (ointment)
See Barry-Martin Pharmaceuticals, Inc.

WHITEHALL (drums, flutes, xylophones, percussion accessories, etc.)
See David Wexler & Company

WHITEHALL INC.
350 Hudson Street
New York, New York 10014
(212) 924-3131

WHITEHALL INDUSTRIES INC.
Whitehall Building
East Rockaway, New York 11518
William H. Benson, President and Treasurer
(516) 593-5700

WHITEHALL LABORATORIES
(Division of American Home Products Corporation)
685 Third Avenue
New York, New York 10017
George De Mott, General Manager
(212) 986-1000

WHITEHALL METAL STUDIOS INC.
8786 Water Street
Montague, Michigan 49437
(616) 893-5205

WHITEHALL PRODUCTS, INC.
(Subsidiary of Bloch Brothers Tobacco Company)
4000 Water Street
Wheeling, West Virginia 26003
(304) 232-4000

Companies and Trade Names

WHITEHALLS (shoes for men)
See Kayser-Roth Shoes, Inc.

WHITEHOUSE MANUFACTURING
COMPANY
(Division of Opelika Manufacturing
Corporation)
361 West Chestnut
Chicago, Illinois 60610
Donald P. Cohen, President
(312) 664-8300

WHITEHOUSE PRODUCTS, INC.
360 Furman
Brooklyn, New York 11201
William L. Lawson, Jr., President
(212) 625-3570

WHITE'S ELECTRONICS
1011 Pleasant Valley Road
Sweet Home, Oregon 97386
Kenneth G. White, Sr., President
(503) 367-2138

WHITESTONE PRODUCTS
(Division of IPCO Hospital Supply
Corporation)
40 Turner Place
Piscataway, New Jersey 08854
(201) 752-2700
See also Osti Products Company Inc.

WHITFIELD PICKLE COMPANY
See Alaga Whitfield Foods Inc.

WHITING
(Division of Milton Bradley Company)
443 Shaker Road
East Longmeadow, Massachusetts
01028
(413) 525-6411

WHITING & DAVIS COMPANY
23 West Bacon Street
Plainville, Massachusetts 02762
Peter P. Aransky, President
(619) 699-4411

WHITING MILK COMPANY
570 Rutherford Avenue
Charlestown, Massachusetts 02129
Harold W. Masteller, President
(617) 242-2860

WHITING-PLOVER PAPER
COMPANY
Stevens Point, Wisconsin 54481
(715) 344-3100

WHITING STATIONERY COMPANY
(Division of Stuart Hall Company
Inc.)
2121 Central
Kansas City, Missouri 64108
(816) 221-8480

WHITLEY POPCORN COMPANY
24 Princeton Road
Trenton, Missouri 64683
(816) 359-2238

WHITLOCK PROCESS COMPANY,
C.G.
2520 South Grant East
Springfield, Illinois 62703

WHITMAN GENERAL
CORPORATION
39 Main Street
Terryville, Connecticut 06786
(203) 583-1847

WHITMAN'S CHOCOLATES
(Division of Pet, Inc.)
Post Office Box 688
9701 Roosevelt Boulevard
Philadelphia, Pennsylvania 19105
James W. Nixon, President
(215) 464-6000

WHITMIRE RESEARCH
LABORATORIES, INC.
3568 Tree Court Industrial
Boulevard
Saint Louis, Missouri 63122
H.E. Whitmire, President
(314) 225-5371

WHITMOYER LABORATORIES, INC.
(Subsidiary of Rohm & Haas
Company)
19 North Railroad Street
Myerstown, Pennsylvania 17067
William P. Ambrogi, President
(717) 866-2151

WHITNEY (watches)
See Alpha Watch Company

WHITNEY BLAKE COMPANY
1565 Dixwell Avenue
New Haven, Connecticut 06514
(203) 288-8281

WHITNEY BROTHERS COMPANY
6 Water Street
Marlborough, New Hampshire 03455
Griffin M. Stabler, President
(603) 876-3331

WHITNEY-FIDALGO SEAFOODS,
INC.
2360 West Commodore Way
Seattle, Washington 98199
Sam Rubinstein, President
(206) 285-0300

WHITNEY NAMEPLATE COMPANY
524 Main Street
West Springfield, Massachusetts
01105
(413) 733-2009

WHITNEY'S CANNERY &
DISTRIBUTING COMPANY
6955 S.W. Garden Home Road
Portland, Oregon 97223
(503) 244-1117

WHITSON (food products)
See Kimbell Foods Inc.

WHITTAKER, CLARK & DANIELS,
INC.
1000 Coolidge Street, South
Plainfield, New Jersey 07080
Clarence V. Driscoll, President
(201) 561-6100

Companies and Trade Names

WHITTAKER CORPORATION
10880 Wilshire Boulevard
Los Angeles, California 90024
Joseph F. Alibrandi, President
(213) 475-9411
See also Bertram Yacht
Corporation; Columbia
Yacht; Crown Aluminum
Industries Corporation;
Kettenburg Marine, Inc.;
and Trojan Yachts

WHITTAKER LABORATORIES, INC.
Box 551
Peekskill, New York 10566

WHITTEMORE POLISH COMPANY
125 North Water Street
Milwaukee, Wisconsin 53208
(414) 276-6190

WHITTEN COMPANY, INC., J.O.
134 Cross Street
Winchester, Massachusetts 01890
William I. Garfinkle, President
(617) 729-4200

WHITTIER LABORATORIES, INC.
(Subsidiary of A.H. Robins
  Company, Inc.)
69 Rawls Road
Des Plaines, Illinois 60018
(312) 299-2206

WHIZ MANUFACTURING COMPANY
141 Hinsdale Street
Brooklyn, New York 11207
(212) 342-4100

WHIZ ON (housewares, paints,
paint sundries, etc.)
See A. Flohr Company Inc.

WHIZZ-ZZ (housewares and
appliances)
See Carr Products Company
Inc.

WHOLE-SUM PRODUCTS
COMPANY
223 Arch Street
Philadelphia, Pennsylvania 19106
(215) 627-3747

WHOPPER (food products)
See Rogers Walla Walla Inc.

WHORTON PHARMACAL
COMPANY, INC.
4202 Gary Avenue
Fairfield, Alabama 35064

WHYTE & MACKAY (Scotch
whiskey)
See Dennis & Huppert Company

WIATT COMPANY INC.,
NORMAN
3221 South Hill Street
Los Angeles, California 90017
Harold Sonners, President
(213) 748-6303

WIC SALES
Post Office Box 172
Yonkers, New York 10702

WICHITA FLOUR MILLS
COMPANY, THE
701 East 17th
Wichita, Kansas 67214
(316) 267-7311

WICK BUILDING SYSTEM
See Marshfield Homes; and
Trailblazer

WICK DRY (sports apparel)
See Dorfman-Pacific
Company Inc.

WICK-O-LITE (decorative lamps)
See North American Electric
Lamp Company

WICKER (cologne, perfume, soap,
etc)
See Prince Matchabelli, Inc.

WICKER (spices, etc.)
See Frank Foods Company

WICKES CORPORATION
110 West A Street
San Diego, California 92101
E.L. McNeely, President
(714) 238-0304
See also Monitor Coach
Company; and Woodard
Sons, Inc., Lee L.

WICKES CORPORATION
Yorktowne Division
Post Office Box 231
Red Lion, Pennsylvania 17356

WICKES HOMES
(Division of Wickes Corporation)
401 West Street
Argos, Indiana 46501
E.L. McNeely, President
(219) 892-5171

WICKFIELD (homes)
See Marshfield Homes

WICKFORD SHIPYARD
125 Steamboat Avenue
North Kingstown, Rhode Island 02852

WICKMAN CORPORATION, THE
10325 Capital Avenue
Oak Park, Michigan 48237
(313) 548-3822

WICKMAN PHARMACEUTICAL
COMPANY, INC.
302 East Stevens Avenue
Santa Anna, California 92707
(714) 556-8834

1416

Companies and Trade Names

WIDDER & COMPANY, J.
110 Fifth Avenue
New York, New York 10011
(212) 243-2500

WIDDER CORPORATION
1 Depot Plaza South
Mamaroneck, New York 10543
(914) 698-3770

WIDE AWAKE SHIRT COMPANY
2047 Kutztown Road
Reading, Pennsylvania 19603
(215) 921-0651

WIDE 'N WONDERFUL (watch-bands)
See Vogue Watch Strap Creations, Inc.

WIDE ONE (rug shampooer and floor polisher)
See SCM Corporation

WIDE SPAN (shelving)
See Penco Products Inc.

WIDMAYER & JUNGLING INC.
116 36th Street
Union City, New Jersey 07087
(201) 864-8457

WIDMER'S WINE CELLARS, INC.
Naples, New York 14512
Ernest I. Reveal, Chairman of the Board
(315) 574-6311

WIEBOLDT STORES, INC.
1 North State
Chicago, Illinois 60602
Arthur K. Muenze, President
(312) 782-1500

WIEDEMANN BREWING COMPANY, INC., THE GEORGE
(Division of G. Heileman Brewing Company)
601 Columbia Street
Newport, Kentucky 41071
G.T. Schurter, General Manager
(606) 261-3710

WIEGAND, EDWIN L.
(Division of Emerson Electric Company)
7500 Thomas
Pittsburgh, Pennsylvania 15208
William H. Davis, President and Chief Executive Officer
(412) 242-6400

WIEGARDT BROTHERS
Ocean Park, Washington 98640
(206) 665-4151

WIEMER'S INC.
541 Fairfield Avenue
Bridgeport, Connecticut 06604
(203) 368-3634

WIEN CONSOLIDATED AIRLINE, INC.
International Airport
Anchorage, Arkansas 99502
Sigurd Wien, Chairman of the Board
(907) 279-8657

WIENER CORPORATION
5725 Powell Street
Harahan, Louisiana 70183
N. Sidney Wiener, President
(504) 733-7055

WIENER LACES INC.
295 Fifth Avenue
New York, New York 10016
Lester J. Wiener, President
(212) 684-5870

WIFFLE BALL INC., THE
275 Bridgeport Avenue
Shelton, Connecticut 06484
(203) 735-4643

WIGHT'S SHERBROOK (rye and bourbon whiskey)
See Goodeham & Worts, Ltd.

WIGWAM (drugstore chain)
See Pay Less Drug Stores

WIGWAM MILLS, INC.
3402 Crocker Avenue
Sheboygan, Wisconsin 53081
R.E. Chesebro, Jr., President
(414) 457-5551

WIKLER (shoes for children)
See Brown Group, Inc.

WIL-DEX (tools)
See XLO Tool & Abrasive Products

WILAMET (canned foods)
See Agripac, Inc.

WILARDY ORIGINALS INC.
117 36th Street
Union City, New Jersey 07087

WILBERT PRODUCTS COMPANY, INC.
805-15 East 139th Street
Bronx, New York 10454
William A. Dalan, President
(212) 635-0500

WILBUR CHOCOLATE COMPANY
48 North Broad Street
Lititz, Pennsylvania 17543
J.A. Buzzard, President
(717) 626-2154

WILBUR COON (women's shoes)
See P.W. Minor & Son, Inc.

WILBUR-ELLIS COMPANY
320 California
San Francisco, California 94104
Carter P. Thacher, President
(415) 421-1775

1417

Companies and Trade Names

WILCOX-CRITTENDEN
699 Middle Street
Middletown, Connecticut 06457
(203) 632-2600

WILCOX MARINE PRODUCTS INC.
948 N.W. 44th Street
Fort Lauderdale, Florida 33309

WILCOX-MITCHELL ENTERPRISES
710 Sanson Street
Philadelphia, Pennsylvania 19106
(215) 925-3932

WILCOXSON REMEDY COMPANY
640 South Tanglewood
Springfield, Ohio 45504

WILD CAT TWIST (tobacco)
See American Tobacco Company

WILD CHERRY (tobacco)
See Lane Ltd.

WILD IRISH ROSE (wine)
See Canandaigua Industries Company, Inc.

WILD MOSS (men's toiletries)
See Mennen Company

WILD SURF (men's toiletries)
See Sea & Ski Corporation

WILD TURKEY (whiskey)
See Austin Nichols & Company, Inc.

WILDERNESS CARDS
2963 Linden
Berkeley, California 94705

WILDLIFE INTERNATIONALE INC.
10900 Deerfield Road
Cincinnati, Ohio 45242
(513) 891-5600

WILDMAN & SONS, LTD., FREDERICK
21 East 69th Street
New York, New York 10021
Frederick S. Wildman, Chairman
(212) 288-8000

WILDROOT (hairdressing)
See Colgate-Palmolive Company

WILE & COMPANY, M.
(Subsidiary of Hart Schaffner & Marx)
77 Goodell
Buffalo, New York 14203
(716) 852-8280
See also Johnny Carson Apparel, Inc.

WILE SONS & COMPANY, INC. JULIUS
(Subsidiary of Standard Brands, Inc.)
320 Park Avenue
New York, New York 10022
Neil L. Bianchini, President
(212) 752-4800

WILEY & SONS, INC., JOHN
605 Third Avenue
New York, New York 10016
W. Bradford Wiley, Chairman of the Board
(212) 867-9800

WILEY PRODUCTS, INC.
7925 North Kolmar
Skokie, Illinois 60076

WILGOR MILLS
Fifth & Williams Street
Bethlehem, Pennsylvania 18015

WILHOLD GLUES, INC.
8707 Miller Grove Drive
Santa Fe Springs, California 90670
C. Willcox Comegys, Sr., President
(213) 692-0911

WILKE, A.
1804 Decatur Street
Brooklyn, New York 11227
(212) 821-4449

WILKES (food products)
See Sunlite Products Company Inc.

WILKES (hosiery)
See Hanes Hosiery Sales, Inc.

WILKE'S (tobacco)
See A. Oppenheimer & Company, Inc.

WILKINS & SONS (preserves)
See Shaffer, Clarke & Company

WILKINS COFFEE COMPANY
3131 Pennsy Drive
Landover, Maryland 20785
Paul R. Benner, President
(301) 322-3000

WILKINS COMPANY, INC., THE
214-220 Groton Avenue
Cortland, New York 13045
Ralph R. Wilkins, President
(607) 756-7548

WILKINS-ROGERS, INC.
27 Frederick Road
Ellicott City, Maryland 21043
S.H. Rogers Jr., President
(202) 621-1144

WILKINSON (pipes)
See Bradberry Briar Pipe Corporation

Companies and Trade Names

WILKINSON PUBLISHING
COMPANY LTD.
35-25 35th Street
Long Island City, New York 11101
(212) 937-3800

WILKINSON SWORD, INC.
1121 Bristol Road
Mountainside, New Jersey 07092

WILL & BAUMER CANDLE
COMPANY INC.
Post Office Box 711
Syracuse, New York 13201
(315) 451-1000

WILL-BURT COMPANY, THE
Orrville, Ohio 44667
W.B. Baer, President
(216) 682-7015

WILL-O-WISP (menswear)
See J. Schoeneman Inc.

WILLAMETTE VALLEY
MANUFACTURING COMPANY
1475 Maxwell Road
Eugene, Oregon 97402

WILLARD (automotive batteries)
See ESB Inc.

WILLARD BOAT WORKS
1300 Logan Avenue
Costa Mesa, California 92626

WILLARD-FAIRCHILD CORPORATION
530 Seventh Avenue
New York, New York 10018

WILLARD'S CHOCOLATES LTD.
122 Arsenal Street
Watertown, Massachusetts 02172

WILLCOX & COMPANY, R.E.B.
88 Pine Street
New York, New York 10005
(212) 425-2100

WILLEN DRUG COMPANY
18 North High Street
Baltimore, Maryland 21202
(301) 752-1865

WILLET STAINED GLASS
STUDIOS
10 East Moreland Avenue
Philadelphia, Pennsylvania 19118
E. Crosby Willet, President
(215) 247-5721

WILLEY'S CARBIDE TOOL
COMPANY
See XLO Tool & Abrasive
Products

WM. ALLEN (cigars)
See Pan American Cigar
Company

WILLIAM BYRD (groceries)
See Snellings & Minor

WM. KNABE (pianos)
See Aeolian Corporation

WM. LEWIS & SON (violins, violas,
cellos, etc.)
See Chicago Musical
Instrument Company

WM. PENN (cigars)
See General Cigar Company,
Inc.

WILLIAM PENN (whiskey)
See Gooderham & Worts, Ltd.

WM. ROGERS & SON (silver-plate
products)
See Insilco Corporation

WILLIAM TELL (food products)
See Columbia Products Inc.
(Washington)

WILLIAMHOUSE-REGENCY, INC.
28 West 23rd Street
New York, New York 10010
Martin R. Lewis, President
(212) 691-2000

WILLIAMHOUSE SALES COMPANY
1710 Flushing Avenue
Brooklyn, New York 11237
(212) 366-7100

WILLIAMS (foot-care products)
See Majestic Drug Company

WILLIAMS & COMPANY, INC.,
DWIGHT S.
40 East 34th Street
New York, New York 10016
Robert D. Williams, President
(212) 683-9037

WILLIAMS & HUMBERT (sherries)
See Julius Wile Sons &
Company, Inc.

WILLIAMS BROTHERS PICKLE
COMPANY
16150 Brookpark Road
Cleveland, Ohio 44135
(216) 267-2666

WILLIAMS, BROWN & EARLE INC.
906 Chestnut Street
Philadelphia, Pennsylvania 19107
(215) 923-1800

WILLIAM'S CANDY COMPANY
18 Main Street
Somerville, Massachusetts 02145

WILLIAMS CHEMICAL COMPANY
2018 West Bender Road
Milwaukee, Wisconsin 53209
(414) 374-2130

Companies and Trade Names

WILLIAMS COMPANIES, THE
National Bank of Tulsa Building
Tulsa, Oklahoma 74103
John H. Williams, Chairman of
the Board
(918) 583-1711

WILLIAMS COMPANY, THE
Post Office Box 309
251 West High
London, Ohio 43140
(614) 852-1511

WILLIAMS COMPANY, INC., J.B.
(Subsidiary of Nabisco, Inc.)
767 Fifth Avenue
New York, New York 10022
M.B. Rosenhaus, Chairman of
the Board
(212) 752-5700

WILLIAMS CRAFT INC.
Box 1288
Arlington, Texas 76010

WILLIAMS FOOD PRODUCTS, INC.
119 Railroad Avenue
Olean, New York 14760

WILLIAMS FOODS, INC.
1900 West 47th Place
Kansas City, Missouri 64055
Conrad Hock, Jr., President
(816) 531-4811

WILLIAMS FURNACE COMPANY
14960 Firestone Bouelvard
La Mirada, California 90638
L.P. MacHarg, Chairman of the
Board
(714) 521-6500

WILLIAMS FURNITURE
CORPORATION
Fulton Street
Sumter, South Carolina 29150
(803) 775-7311

WILLIAMS GUN SIGHT
COMPANY
Davison, Michigan 48243
Dick Williams, Chairman of the
Board
(313) 653-2131

WILLIAMS, ICHABOD T.
200 East 66th Street
New York, New York 10021
(212) 452-4896

WILLIAMS LABORATORY
Box 101
Oradell, New Jersey 07649

WILLIAMS MANUFACTURING
COMPANY, THE
Gallia & Campbell
Portsmouth, Ohio 45662
John D. Monroe, President
(614) 353-5111
See also Rapco, Inc.

WILLIAMS OFFICE FURNITURE
COMPANY
47 West 34th Street
New York, New York 10001
(212) 695-6766

WILLIAMS PECAN PRODUCTS
COMPANY
2875 19th
Gulfport, Mississippi 39501

WILLIAMSBURG (paint)
See Martin-Senour Company

WILLIAMSBURG REPRODUCTIONS
(brass and iron accessories)
See Virginia Metalcrafters Inc.

WILLIAMSBURG RESTORATION INC.
Williamsburg, Virginia 23185

WILLIAMSON & COMPANY, D.D.
Box 6001
Louisville, Kentucky 40206

WILLIAMSON COMPANY, THE
3500 Madison Road
Cincinnati, Ohio 45209
W.D. Wilder, President
(513) 731-1343

WILLIAMSON CANDY COMPANY
4701 West Armitage Avenue
Chicago, Illinois 60639
(312) 227-4000

WILLIAMSON-DICKIE
MANUFACTURING COMPANY
509 West Vickery Boulevard
Fort Worth, Texas 76104
J. Don Williamson, President
(817) 336-7201

WILLIAMSON INC., GARFIELD
1072 West Side Avenue
Jersey City, New Jersey 07306

WILLIAMSON JUICE CORPORATION
337 Railroad Avenue
Williamson, New York 14589

WILLIAMSPORT MILK PRODUCTS
COMPANY
216 Market
South Williamsport, Pennsylvania
17707

WILLM (Alsatian wines)
See Julius Wile Sons &
Company, Inc.

WILLOBROOK (seafood)
See Young's Market Company

WILLOFORM MANUFACTURING
COMPANY
6 East 32nd Street
New York, New York 10016
Jack Stern, President
(212) 689-0618

Companies and Trade Names

WILLOUGHBY-PEERLESS CAMERA
    STORES
110 West 32nd Street
New York, New York 10001
Erich Hirschfield, President
(212) 564-1600

WILLOW ASSOCIATES
c/o William R. Bannon
18 Stewart Road
Needham, Massachusetts 02192

WILLOW SPRINGS (whiskey)
    See J.T.S. Brown Distillers
        Company

WILLOW WARE (cookware and
ceramics)
    See Holt-Howard

WILLPOWER (smoking deterrent)
    See Carter-Wallace, Inc.

WILLS COMPANY, THE
301 Fourth Avenue S.E.
Waseca, Minnesota 56093

WILL'S, INC.
Box 1336
Bismarck, North Dakota 58501

WILLSON (tubas, baritone horns,
fluegelhorns)
    See DEG Music Products Inc.

WILLSON, INC., R.B.
250 Park Avenue
New York, New York 10017
F. H. Mattutat, President and
    Treasurer
(212) 986-6977

WILLSON PRODUCTS
Post Office Box 622
Reading, Pennsylvania 19603
(215) 376-6161

WILLWOOD (chocolates)
    See Adolph Goldmark & Sons
        Corporation

WILMINGTON TRUST COMPANY
Tenth and Market Streets
Wilmington, Delaware 19801
William W. Geddes, President
(302) 655-4011

WILMOD COMPANY INC.
200 West 57th Street
New York, New York 10019
(212) 586-6450

WILMOT MILLS
105 Madison Avenue
New York, New York 10016
(212) 532-6100

WILMSEN INC.
(Division of Star Band Company
    Inc.)
800 Broad Street
Portsmouth, Virginia 23707

WILSCO (shortening)
    See Wilson & Company, Inc.

WILSEY FOODS, INC.
633 South Mission Road
Los Angeles, California 90023
Robert Morgan, President
(213) 264-2160

WILSHIRE (light fixtures)
    See Newell Companies Inc.

WILSON (juvenile product)
    See Carriage Craft Company

WILSON (whiskey)
    See Four Roses Distillers
        Company

WILSON & COMPANY, INC.
(Subsidiary of LTV Corporation)
4545 North Lincoln Boulevard
Oklahoma City, Oklahoma 73105
Kenneth J. Griggy, President
(405) 525-4743
    See also New England
        Provision Company Inc.

WILSON & COMPANY, INC.,
    THOMAS
261 Madison Avenue
New York, New York 10016
Robert R. Giebel, President
(212) 986-9000

WILSON & SONS INC., R.R.
1329 Youngstown Road S.E.
Warren, Ohio 44484

WILSON & WOLFER, INC.
14833 East Jefferson Street
Detroit, Michigan 48125
(313) 822-5474

WILSON CANDY COMPANY
408 Harrison Avenue
Jeannette, Pennsylvania 15644

WILSON CHEMICAL COMPANY,
    A.L.
1050 Harrison Avenue
Kearny, New Jersey 07032
(201) 997-3300

WILSON, COMPANY, INC., THE
    H.W.
950 University Avenue
Bronx, New York 10452
Leo M. Weins, President and
    Treasurer
(212) 588-8400

WILSON CORPORATION, H.
555 West Taft Drive
South Holland, Illinois 60473

Companies and Trade Names

WILSON CORPORATION, THE
J.G.
Post Office Box 599
Norfolk, Virginia 23501
D.E. Clark, President
(703) 545-7341

WILSON EXPORT & IMPORT
CORPORATION
17 Battery Place
New York, New York 10004
(212) 269-3570

WILSON FISHERIES, B.H.
Battery Street
Eastport, Maine 04631
(207) 853-2828

WILSON FREIGHT COMPANY
3636 Follett Avenue
Cincinnati, Ohio 54223
David M. Gantz, President
(513) 681-5600

WILSON GARMENT
MANUFACTURING COMPANY,
INC.
337 South Franklin
Chicago, Illinois 60606
Harold Rosenberg, President
(312) 427-1568

WILSON-IMPERIAL COMPANY
115 Chestnut Street
Newark, New Jersey 07105
James Molloy, President
(201) 589-6050

WILSON JONES COMPANY
(Division of Swingline)
6150 Touhy Avenue
Chicago, Illinois 60648
John P. Clark, President and Chief
Executive Officer
(312) 774-7700
See also Cooke & Cobb
Products

WILSON LABORATORIES
2660 Bond Street
Park Forest South, Illinois 60466

WILSON LAUREL FARMS, INC.
(Subsidiary of Wilson & Company,
Inc.)
4545 North Lincoln Boulevard
Oklahoma City, Oklahoma 73105
Francis J. Zurek, President
(405) 521-9611

WILSON MANUFACTURING
CORPORATION
Packer Street
Sunbury, Pennsylvania 17801

WILSON MILK COMPANY
(Division of Diehl, Inc.)
2174 Seymour Avenue
Cincinnati, Ohio 46219
(513) 731-4438

WILSON NURSERIES INC., C.E.
Post Office Box 400
Jacksonville, Texas 75766

WILSON PRODUCTS COMPANY
1811 West 1700 South
Salt Lake City, Utah 84104
(801) 972-5633

WILSON PRODUCTS COMPANY,
INC., THE
Tyrone, Pennsylvania 16686

WILSON ROLLIN COMPANY, THE
Box 7433
North Station
Memphis, Tennessee 38107
(901) 525-2628

WILSON-SINCLAIR COMPANY
Gelatin Division
Plummer Street and Wentworth
Avenue
Calumet City, Illinois 60409

WILSON SPECIALTIES COMPANY
INC.
90 Ingell Street
Taunton, Massachusetts 02780

WILSON SPORTING GOODS
COMPANY
2233 West Street
River Grove, Illinois 60171
Thomas P. Mullaney, President
(312) 456-6100

WILTON (carpets)
See Magee Carpet Company

WILTON ARMETALE
18th and Franklin Streets
Columbia, Pennsylvania 17512

WILTON CORPORATION
Packaging Division
2400 East Devon Avenue
Des Plaines, Illinois 60018
Alex J. Vogl, Chairman and
President
(312) 827-7700

WILTON ENTERPRISES INC.
833 West 115th Street
Chicago, Illinois 60643
Norman Wilton, President
(312) 785-1144

WIMPFHEIMER & SON, INC., M.
250 West 57th Street
New York, New York 10019
(212) 586-7506

WIN-ALL (canned foods)
See Wapato Fruit Products, Inc.

WIN-SET (hair-care products)
See Winslow Manufacturing
(Division of Watsco Inc.)

WIN YOU (foods)
See Clements Foods Company

WINARICK, INC., A.R.
225 Park Avenue, South
New York, New York 10003
Jules Winarick, President
(212) 673-5552
See also Luft-Tangee, Inc.;
and Richard, Andre

Companies and Trade Names

WINCHESTER (cigars)
  See R.J. Reynolds Industries Inc.

WINCHESTER (roller skates, firearms, ammunition)
  See Olin Corporation

WINCHESTER-AUBURN MILLS
Rainbow Products Division
200 Merrimac
Woburn, Massachusetts 01801
(617) 935-4110

WINCO AFFILIATES, INC.
316 Dean Street
Brooklyn, New York 11217
(212) 625-1940

WIND & WEATHER (bath oil)
  See Lehn & Fink Products Company

WIND CORPORATION
1111 Post Road
Riverside, Connecticut 06878

WIND DRIFT (toiletries for men)
  See Mem Company, Inc.

WIND SONG (bath oil, cologne, etc.)
  See Prince Matchabelli, Inc.

WINDBREAKER, INC.
(Division of Phillips-Van Heusen Corporation)
1290 Avenue of the Americas
New York, New York 10019
Daniel Keisman, President
(212) 541-5200

WINDERS & GEIST, INC.
Box 83088
Lincoln, Nebraska 68501
(402) 477-3133

WINDERT WATCH COMPANY
448 South Hill Street
Los Angeles, California 90013
(213) 626-7688

WINDEX (cleaner)
  See Drackett Company

WINDJAMMER (men's sportswear)
  See Alps Sportswear Manufacturing Company Inc.

WINDLITE (lighter)
  See Ronson Corporation

WINDMILL (linoleum and vinyl floor coverings)
  See Joseph Katz Floor Coverings Company, Inc.

WINDMILLS (swimwear)
  See A.H. Schreiber Company, Inc.

WINDOR SECURITY MANUFACTURING INC.
1695 Boone Avenue
Bronx, New York 10460
(212) 328-3700

WINDOW CLEEN (cleaner)
  See Standard Industrial Products, Inc.

WINDOW ZIPPER (product for opening stuck windows)
  See Red Devil Inc.

WINDRIFT (toiletries)
  See Mem Company, Inc.

WINDSOR (cigars)
  See G.W. Van Slyke & Horton

WINDSOR (pipes)
  See Sasieni of London, Inc.

WINDSOR (plastic wall tile)
  See Miraplas Tile Company

WINDSOR (whiskey)
  See National Distillers & Chemical Corporation

WINDSOR BROOM COMPANY
218 Pine Street
Hamburg, Pennsylvania 19526
(215) 562-3030

WINDSOR CARD COMPANY
223 West Erie Street
Chicago, Illinois 60610
(312) 642-6244

WINDSOR WAX COMPANY, INC.
611 Newark
Hoboken, New Jersey 07030
(201) 659-1700

WINE & SCHULZ INC.
903 Samuel Street
Louisville, Kentucky 40204

WINE ANTIQUES INC.
667 Madison Avenue
New York, New York 10021
(212) 759-5685

WINE MERCHANTS LTD.
4560 Buckley Road
Syracuse, New York 13212
(315) 652-8681

WINEGARD COMPANY
3000 Kirkwood Street
Burlington, Iowa 52601
John Winegard, President
(319) 753-0121

WINEGATE IMPORTS INC.
19-40 Flushing Avenue
Ridgewood, New York 11237

WINEMASTERS (wine)
  See Guild Wine Company

Companies and Trade Names

WINER MANUFACTURING
COMPANY, INC.
4433 Calumet Avenue
Hammond, Indiana 46327
Louis Winer, President
(219) 932-1751

WING (archery equipment)
See AMF, Inc.

WINGFOOT (lawn mowers)
See American Lawn Mower
Company

WINGS (cigarettes)
See Brown & Williamson
Tobacco Corporation

WINIG SLIPPER CORPORATION
Gloversville, New York 12078
Norbert Winig, President
(518) 725-0665

WINK (soft drink)
See Canada Dry Corporation

WINK-AWAKE (alarm clock)
See Sunbeam Appliance
Company

WINK, JR'S
112 Madison Avenue
New York, New York 10016
(212) 683-7940

WINK-N-WAKE (infants' product)
See Kantwet Company

WINKELMAN STORES, INC.
25 Parsons Street
Detroit, Michigan 48201
Stanley J. Winkelman, President
(313) 833-6900

WINKELS (pantyhose)
See Charles H. Bacon Company,
Inc.

WINKIE (juvenile product)
See Welsh Company

WINKING CHEF (frozen foods)
See Texas Meat Packers

WINKY'S DRIVE-IN RESTAURANTS
See Jiffy Foods Corporation

WINMOR LABORATORIES, INC.
Box 236
Bohemia, New York 11716

WINN-DIXIE GREENVILLE, INC.
(Subsidiary of Winn-Dixie Stores,
Inc.)
2819 Wade Hampton Boulevard
Greenville, South Carolina 29602
G.H. Derisco, President
(803) 244-2310

WINN-DIXIE LOUISIANA, INC.
(Subsidiary of Winn-Dixie Stores,
Inc.)
600 Edwards Avenue
New Orleans, Louisiana 70123
Tine W. Davis, President
(504) 733-6720

WINN-DIXIE STORES, INC.
5050 Edgewood Court
Jacksonville, Florida 32203
Bert L. Thomas, President
(904) 783-1800
See also Astor Products, Inc.

WINNEBAGO INDUSTRIES, INC.
Consumer Information Department
1909 East Cornell
Peoria, Illinois 61614
John V. Hanson, President
(515) 582-3535

WINNECONNE CORPORATION
Reeseville, Wisconsin 53579

WINNER CORPORATION
Box 667
First and Pickert Streets
Dickson, Tennessee 37055
Charles E. Bradley, President
(615) 446-3781

WINN'S STORES, INC.
1235 Gembler Road
San Antonio, Texas 78219
Lynn H. Spears, President
(512) 333-4224

WINONA KNITTING MILLS, INC.
Winona, Minnesota 55987
Leslie R. Woodworth, President
(507) 454-4381

WINPOWER MANUFACTURING
COMPANY
1207 First Avenue East
Newton, Iowa 50208
(515) 792-1301

WINROSS COMPANY, INC.
Box 422
65 Atlantic Avenue
Rochester, New York 14607
(716) 244-9233

WINS FAVOR (food products)
See Burnette Farms Packing
Company

WINSALE DRUG COMPANY
214 Taaffe Place
Brooklyn, New York 11205
(212) 622-1875

WINSLOW (shaving cream and
vitamins)
See Household Research
Corporation

WINSLOW COMPANY, THE
Post Office Box 578B
Osprey, Florida 33559

Companies and Trade Names

WINSTON (cigarettes)
See R.J. Reynolds Tobacco Company

WINSTON (wine)
See Fredonia Products Company Inc.

WINSTON BRIAR PIPE MANUFACTURING COMPANY
116 North Eighth
Lindenhurst, New York 11757

WINSTON, INC., HARRY
718 Fifth Avenue
New York, New York 10019
(212) 245-2000

WINSTON INDUSTRIES, INC.
(Subsidiary of Shelter Resources Company)
Box 347
Double Springs, Alabama 35553
Robert Richards, President
(205) 489-5056

WINSTON MILLS, INC.
(Subsidiary of Puritan Fashions Corporation)
1372 Broadway
New York, New York 10018
Irving Nelson, President
(212) 594-1100

WINSTON PHARMACAL CORPORATION
64 East Sanford Boulevard
Mount Vernon, New York 10550

WINSTON PHARMACEUTICALS, INC.
4706 Kirk Road
Winston-Salem, North Carolina 27103

WINT-O-GREEN (flavor of Life Savers candy)
See Beech-Nut, Inc.

WINTA (frozen vegetables)
See Cascade Foods, Inc.

WINTER (pianos)
See Aeolian Corporation

WINTER EMERGENCY & TOOL KIT (roadside emergency unit)
See Dynamic Classics Ltd.

WINTER GARDEN CITRUS PRODUCTS CO-OP
Winter Garden, Florida 32787

WINTER GARDEN FREEZER COMPANY
(Subsidiary of United Foods, Inc.)
Post Office Box 119
Dawson Avenue
Bells, Tennessee 38006
James I. Tankersley, President
(901) 663-2341

WINTER HILL (juices, cider, vinegar)
See Rowse, Inc.

WINTER, INC., JACK
8100 North Teutonia Avenue
Milwaukee, Wisconsin 53209
Jack A. Winter, President
(414) 354-4100
See also Dorothy Dean

WINTER PATROL (tires)
See UniRoyal Tire Company

WINTER VALLEY (frozen produce)
See United Foods, Inc.

WINTER WONDER (sunglasses)
See Del Laboratories Inc.

WINTERBOURNE & COMPANY, S.
38 Richmond Terrace
Staten Island, New York 10301
(212) 447-5116

WINTERCLEAT (tires)
See General Tire & Rubber Company

WINTERMARK (tires)
See Kelly Springfield Tire Company

WINTERMINT (tobacco)
See Conwood Corporation

WINTHROP-ATKINS COMPANY, INC.
35 East Main Street
Middleboro, Massachusetts 02346
Donald K. Atkins, President and Treasurer
(617) 947-4600

WINTHROP-HANNAN (shoes)
See International Shoe Company

WINTHROP LABORATORIES
(Division of Sterling Drug, Inc.)
90 Park Avenue
New York, New York 10016
John P. Pfeiffer, President
(212) 972-4141
See also Special Chemicals

WINTON COMPANY, INC., RALPH
20 North High Street
Baltimore, Maryland 21202
(301) 752-1865

WIP (sports accessories and equipment)
See Vener Associates Inc.

WIRE-O CORPORATION
205 Cottage Street
Poughkeepsie, New York 12601
A.F. Brook, President
(914) 454-8200

WIRE ROPE CORPORATION OF AMERICA INC.
See Leschen Wire Rope Company

Companies and Trade Names

WIRE SALES COMPANY
4630 West 54th Street
Chicago, Illinois 60632
L.S. Baness, President, Chief
  Executive Officer and Treasurer
(312) 767-2500

WIREMOLD COMPANY, THE
Woodlawn Street
West Hartford, Connecticut 06110
John D. Murphy, President
(203) 233-6251

WIRTH COMPANY, INC.
2000 National Avenue
Hayward, California 94545

WISCO (automobile accessories)
  See ESB Inc.

**WISCONSIN ALUMINUM
    FOUNDRY COMPANY, INC.**
838 South 16th Street
Manitowoc, Wisconsin 54220
Bernard Schwartz, President
(414) 682-8286

WISCONSIN CLUB (beer)
  See Jos. Huber Brewing
       Company

**WISCONSIN DISTRIBUTING
    COMPANY OF NEENAH, INC.**
1000 Lyndale Avenue
Neenah, Wisconsin 54956

**WISCONSIN ELECTRIC POWER
    COMPANY**
231 West Michigan Street
Milwaukee, Wisconsin 53201
Charles S. McNeer, President
(414) 273-1234

WISCONSIN FOODS, INC.
128 Kentucky Street
Sturgeon, Wisconsin 54235

WISCONSIN GAS COMPANY
(Subsidiary of American Natural
Gas Company)
626 East Wisconsin Avenue
Milwaukee, Wisconsin 53201
Robert M. Hoffer, President
(414) 276-6720

**WISCONSIN PHARMACAL
    COMPANY**
2535 South 170th Street
New Berlin, Wisconsin 53151
(414) 786-2370

**WISCONSIN POWER & LIGHT
    COMPANY**
222 West Washington Avenue
Madison, Wisconsin 53703
James R. Underkofler, President
(608) 252-3311

**WISCONSIN PUBLIC SERVICE
    CORPORATION**
700 North Adams Street
Green Bay, Wisconsin 54305
P.D. Ziemer, President
(414) 432-3311

WISCONSIN SHOE COMPANY
1039 South Second
Milwaukee, Wisconsin 53204
D.L. Reeder, Jr., President
(414) 672-1670

**WISCONSIN STATE CANNERS
    COMPANY**
Pickett, Wisconsin 54964
(414) 589-2262

**WISCONSIN TELEPHONE
    COMPANY**
(Affiliate of Bell Telephone System)
722 North Broadway
Milwaukee, Wisconsin 53202
Gustave H. Moede, Jr., President
(414) 456-3000

WISCONSIN TISSUE MILLS INC.
Post Office Box 489
Menasha, Wisconsin 54952
James E. Asmuth, President
(414) 725-7031

WISE FOODS
(Division of Borden, Inc.)
228 Rasely Street
Berwick, Pennsylvania 18603
C.L. Daley, President
(717) 752-4561

**WISE-UP COMPANY OF
    AMERICA**
Post Office Box 162
11 Nunly Court
Staten Island, New York 10304
(212) 447-8829

WISER'S (Canadian whiskey)
  See Corby Distilleries Ltd.

**WISE'S HOMEOPATHIC
    PHARMACY**
4200 Laclede
Saint Louis, Missouri 63108
(314) 533-9600

WISH-BONE (salad dressings)
  See Thomas J. Lipton, Inc.

WISHBONE (fast-food franchise)
  See Munford Inc.

WISK (heavy-duty liquid blue
detergent)
  See Lever Brothers Company

WISLA (canned foods)
  See Albro Packing Company

WISP (nylon stockings)
  See Van Raalte Company, Inc.

WISS & SONS COMPANY, J.
400 West Market Street
Newark, New Jersey 07107
Paul G. Richards, President
(201) 622-4670

WISTEL (polyester knitted dresses)
  See Saporta Trading Agency
       Corporation

1426

Companies and Trade Names

WISTERIA HOSIERY MILLS
310 South Main Street
Saluda, South Carolina 29138

WISTONE (deeptone table covers, napkins, place mats, coasters)
See Wisconsin Tissue Mills, Inc.

WITCO CHEMICAL CORPORATION
277 Park Avenue
New York, New York 10017
William Wishnick, Chairman of the Board
(212) 644-6300

WITE-OUT PRODUCTS INC.
10114 Bacon Drive
Beltsville, Maryland 20705
(301) 937-5353

WITHERBY (tools)
See John H. Graham & Company, Inc.

WITT COMPANY, THE
4454 Steel Place
Cincinnati, Ohio 45209
Stuart J. Swensson, Jr., President
(513) 871-5700

WITT MANUFACTURING COMPANY
Box 7646
Springwells Station
Detroit, Michigan 48209
(313) 841-5080

WITTE HARDWARE COMPANY
704 North Second Avenue
Saint Louis, Missouri 63102
(314) 241-1038

WITTER & COMPANY, INC., DEAN
45 Montgomery
San Francisco, California 94106
William M. Witter, Chairman of the Board
(415) 392-7200

WITTICH'S
211 East Main Street, Department CB
Circleville, Ohio 43113

WITTNAUER (watches and cameras)
See Longines-Wittnauer Watch Company, Inc.

WITTUR & COMPANY, H.
1024-1026 Emerson Street
Evanston, Illinois 60204

WIZARD (charcoal lighter, deodorizers)
See Boyle-Midway

WIZARD (foot-care product)
See Trimfoot Company

WIZARD (paint, power tools, appliances, etc.)
See Western Auto Supply Company

WIZARD (vacuum cleaners)
See Western Auto Supply Company

WOC-O-MOCS (shoes)
See G.H. Bass & Company

WODKA WYBOROWA (Polish vodka)
See Schieffelin & Company

WOEBER MUSTARD MANUFACTURING COMPANY
561 East Madison Avenue
Springfield, Ohio 45503

WOELFFEL COMPANY INC., RICHARD
10120 Imperial Avenue
Cupertino, California 95014

WOHL & COMPANY L.
(Division of Kate Greenaway Industries, Inc.)
1333 Broadway
New York, New York 10018
(212) 947-4320

WOHL SHOE COMPANY
(Division of Brown Group, Inc.)
8350 Maryland Avenue
Clayton, Missouri 63105
Ben Peck, President
(314) 863-9000

WOLCO (canned foods)
See Woldert Canning Company

WOLDERT CANNING COMPANY
818 West Erwin Street
Tyler, Texas 75701
(214) 592-6571

WOLF BRAND PRODUCTS
(Subsidiary of Quaker Oats Company)
Box 617
Corsicana, Texas 75110
Herbert H. Johnson, President
(214) 874-5601

WOLF BROTHERS CIGARS
(Division of House of Windsor)
Windsor, Pennsylvania 17366

WOLF, INC., HOWARD B.
3809 Parry Avenue
Dallas, Texas 75226
Howard B. Wolf, President
(214) 823-9941

WOLF LTD., LEE
1422 Washington Street
Manitowoc, Wisconsin 54220

WOLF MANUFACTURING COMPANY
6101 West Washington Boulevard
Culver City, California 90230

Companies and Trade Names

WOLFF PRODUCTS COMPANY
1150 Broadway
New York, New York 10001
(212) 686-4590

WOLF'S HEAD OIL REFINING
COMPANY
(Division of Pennzoil United)
Wolf's Head Building
Oil City, Pennsylvania 16301
Glenn E. Scott, President
(814) 645-1231

WOLFSET & COMPANY, INC.,
I.B.
137 Fifth Avenue
New York, New York 10010
(212) 477-1539

WOLIN COMPANY, THE
486 Derby Avenue
West Haven, Connecticut 06516

WOLLENBERGER MANUFACTURING
& DISTRIBUTING CORPORATION
91 The Promenade
Glen Head, New York 11545

WOLLENSAK (photographic equipment, tape recorders, etc.)
See 3M Company

WOLLMODE (sports apparel)
See Max Hurni Importer Inc.

WOLSEY COMPANY
15110 East Nelson Street
City of Industry, California 91744
(213) 336-4575

WOLTRA COMPANY, INC., THE
150 West 22nd Street
New York, New York 10011
(212) 675-4199

WOLTZ (cosmetics)
See R.H. Cosmetics Corporation

WOLVERINE CAMPER COMPANY
801 East Cedar Avenue
Gladwin, Michigan 48624

WOLVERINE HOUSEHOLD
PRODUCTS INC.
818 Front Avenue N.W.
Grand Rapids, Michigan 49504

WOLVERINE KNITTING MILLS
120 North Jackson Street
Bay City, Michigan 48706
Henry E. Schwartz, President
(517) 893-6541

WOLVERINE TOY
Booneville, Arkansas 72927
James L. Lehren, President
(501) 675-2000

WOLVERINE WORLD WIDE, INC.
9341 Cortland Drive, N.E.
Rockford, Michigan 49351
Thomas D. Gleason, President
(616) 866-1561
See also Tru-Stitch Footwear

WOMANS FRIEND (washers and dryers)
See Centrex Corporation

WOMETCO ENTERPRISES, INC.
316 North Miami Avenue
Miami, Florida 33128
Mitchel Wolfson, President
(303) 374-6262

WONDER (bread, snack foods)
See ITT Continental Baking
Company

WONDER (paint remover)
See Wilson-Imperial Company

WONDER BOOKS INC.
51 Madison Avenue
New York, New York 10010
(212) 689-9200

WONDER CORPORATION OF
AMERICA
1082 Post Road
Darien, Connecticut 06820

WONDER-FOIL (foil for home freezer)
See Anaconda Aluminum
Company

WONDER LAC (lacquers)
See E.I. du Pont de Nemours
& Company, Inc.

WONDER MAID, INC.
(Division of Mutual Garment
Company)
1724 Locust
Saint Louis, Missouri 63103
H.B. Wittcoff, President
(314) 231-8530

WONDER-1-COAT (exterior house paints)
See Celanese Corporation

WONDER ORANGE COMPANY
5626 West Raymond Street
Indianapolis, Indiana 46241
(317) 243-3521

WONDER PRODUCTS COMPANY
Collierville, Tennessee 38017
Donald E. Toussaint, President
(901) 853-2242

WONDER WARE (steel cookware)
See Regal Ware, Inc.

WONDER WHEEL (exerciser)
See General Home Products

WONDER WRAP (food wrap)
See Scott Paper Company

WONDERALLS
600 First Avenue, North
Minneapolis, Minnesota 55403
G.J. Rosenberg, President
(612) 339-7141

Companies and Trade Names

WONDERFUL DREAM SALVE CORPORATION
Box 223
Croswell, Michigan 48422
  See also Kondon Manufacturing Company

WONDERFUL WORLD (carpets)
  See Lees Carpets

WONDERODS (fishing equipment)
  See Shakespeare Sporting Goods

WONDURA PRODUCTS INC.
109 Avenue L
Newark, New Jersey 07105
(201) 589-2260

WONG'S (frozen Chinese foods)
  See RJR Foods, Inc.

WOOD & COMPANY, VAN
1555 West Embassy Street
Anaheim, California 92802

WOOD & SELICK COCONUT COMPANY
162 East 64th Street
New York, New York 10021
(212) 688-3600

WOOD & SONS (dinnerware)
  See Herman C. Kupper Inc.

WOOD COMPANY, C.G.
438 Church Street
Girard, Pennsylvania 16417
(814) 774-4204

WOOD DESIGN, INC.
Beechwood Avenue
French Lick, Indiana 47546

WOOD GALLERIE (floor lamps)
  See Rand Products Company, Inc.

WOOD, INC., J.R.
(Subsidiary of Lenox, Inc.)
216 East 45th Street
New York, New York 10017
F.L. Campbell, President
(212) 687-2420

WOOD, J.W.
Lynchburg, Virginia 24504

WOOD MANUFACTURING COMPANY, A.R.
Post Office Box 218
Luverne, Minnesota 56156
(507) 283-4411

WOOD MET (wood and metal floor lamps)
  See Georgian Lighting Studios Inc.

WOOD-MOSAIC PRODUCTS
(Division of Olinkraft Inc.)
Post Office Box 21159
5000 Crittenden Drive
Louisville, Kentucky 40221
David B. Hilley, Vice President and General Manager
(502) 363-3531

WOOD PRODUCTS COMPANY
2640 East Del Amo Boulevard
Compton, California 90021
(213) 636-0691

WOOD-REGAN INSTRUMENT COMPANY INC.
Nutley, New Jersey 07110
(201) 667-2460

WOOD STEEL COMPANY, ALAN
Conshohocken, Pennsylvania 19428

WOODALL INDUSTRIES, INC.
(Subsidiary of Libby-Owens-Ford Company)
7565 East McNichols Road
Detroit, Michigan 48234
Wesley R. Johnson, President
(313) 365-9000

WOODARD CORPORATION, VIVIANE
(Subsidiary of General Foods Corporation)
14621 Titus Avenue
Panorama City, California 91412
(213) 782-3310

WOODARD SONS, INC., LEE L.
(Subsidiary of Wickes Corporation)
317 Elm Street
Owosso, Michigan 48867
John H. Hekman, President
(517) 723-7881

WOODBINE (cigarettes)
  See G.A. Georgopulo & Company, Inc.

WOODBURY (men's and women's toiletries)
  See Andrew Jergens Company

WOODBURY INDUSTRIES CORPORATION
87 Engineers Drive
Hicksville, New York 11801

WOODBURY PEWTERERS
Route 6
Woodbury, Connecticut 06798

WOODCO CORPORATION
Paterson Plank Road and 34th
North Bergen, New Jersey 07047
(201) 863-1200

WOODCRAFT EQUIPMENT COMPANY
Box 110
1450 West Lexington Street
Independence, Missouri 64051
Kenneth B. Smith, Jr., President and Treasurer
(816) 252-9612

WOODCRAFTER (furniture polish)
  See Colgate-Palmolive Company

1429

Companies and Trade Names

WOODCROFTERY SHOPS INC.
School Boulevard 2
Wayland, New York 14572
W.T. Morris, President
(716) 728-5121

WOODFLEX (folding doors)
See American-Accordion-Fold Doors Inc.

WOODGARD (paints and paint sundries)
See Merchants & Manufacturers Supply Inc.

WOODHEAD COMPANY, DANIEL
3411 Woodland Drive
Northbrook, Illinois 60062
Robert S. LaMantia, President and Chief Executive Officer
(312) 272-7990

WOODHILL CHEMICAL SALES COMPANY
18731 Cranwood Parkway
Cleveland, Ohio 44128
Victor Gelb, President
(216) 475-3600

WOODHUE (men's and women's toiletries)
See Faberge, Inc.

WOODLAND STUDIOS INC.
Route 5
Perryville, Missouri 63775

WOODLAWN (steak-knife and carving sets)
See Carvel Hall

WOODMAN (horseradish, beet relish, seafood cocktail)
See Grant Products, Ltd.

WOODS BROTHERS COFFEE COMPANY, INC.
Post Office Box 181
Blue Ridge Park for Industry
3404 Aerial Way Drive
Roanoke, Virginia 24002
Robert W. Woods, Sr., President
(703) 342-3425

WOODS CROSS CANNING COMPANY
Box J
Clearfield, Utah 84015
(801) 825-0621

WOODSTREAM CORPORATION
69 North Locust Street
Lititz, Pennsylvania 17543
Chester M. Woolworth, Chairman of the Board
(717) 626-2125
See also Trappe of Aspen

WOODWARD & LOTHROP
10th, 11th, F and G, N.W.
Washington, D.C. 20013
Edwin K. Hoffman, President
(202) 347-5300

WOODWARD, INC., PATTY
860 South Los Angeles Street
Los Angeles, California 90014
J.E. McCloskey, President
(213) 620-9640

WOODWAY TOY COMPANY INC.
Post Office Box 757
Friendswood, Texas 77546

WOOLAMA (menswear)
See Lord Jeff Knitting Company Inc.

WOOLCO DEPARTMENT STORES
See F.W. Woolworth Company

WOOLITE (cold-water wash)
See Boyle-Midway

WOOLMASTER (cold-water wash)
See Reen'O Chemical Corporation

WOOLNO, INC.
(Division of Gund Manufacturing Company)
200 Fifth Avenue
New York, New York 10010
Jack Swedlin, Chairman of the Board
(212) 675-7750

WOOLRICH WOOLEN MILLS
Woolrich, Pennsylvania 17779
Roswell Brayton, President
(717) 769-6464

WOOLSEY MARINE INDUSTRIES INC.
100 Saw Mill Road
Danbury, Connecticut 06810
Herbert W. Evans, Jr., President
(203) 792-6300

WOOLWORTH COMPANY, F.W.
Woolworth Building
233 Broadway
New York, New York 10007
Edward F. Gibbons, President
(212) 227-1000
See also Anderson-Little Company Inc.; Kinney Shoe Corporation; and Richman Brothers

WOOSTER BRUSH COMPANY, THE
604 Madison Avenue
Wooster, Ohio 44691
(216) 264-4440

WORCESTER (lawn mowers)
See Savage Arms (Division of Emhart Corporation)

WORCESTER (pewter, crystal, and silver)
See Royal Worcester Porcelain Company

Companies and Trade Names

WORCESTER BAKING COMPANY
43 Mason
Worcester, Massachusetts 01610

WORCESTER FELT PAD
CORPORATION
11 Brackett Court
Worcester, Massachusetts 01604
(617) 752-1981

WORCESTER PRESSED STEEL
COMPANY
100 Barber Avenue
Worcester, Massachusetts 01606
Benjamin M. Pacek, President
and Director
(617) 853-6000

WORD INC.
4800 West Waco Drive
Waco, Texas 76703

WORD POPCORN COMPANY,
INC.
212 Peachtree
Scottsboro, Alabama 35768

WORKSHOP CARDS
Box 526
Concord, New Hampshire 03301

WORLD AIRWAYS, INC.
Oakland International Airport
Oakland, California 94614
Edward J. Daly, Chairman of the
Board
(415) 577-2000

WORLD ART COMPANY
823 N.E. Second Avenue
Fort Lauderdale, Florida 33304

WORLD BESTOS COMPANY
(Division of Firestone Tire &
Rubber Company)
1112 South 25th Street
New Castle, Indiana 47362
(317) 529-4790

WORLD BOOK ENCYCLOPEDIA
See Field Enterprises
Educational Corporation

WORLD CANDIES INC.
185 30th Street
Brooklyn, New York 11232
(212) 768-8100

WORLD CARPETS, INC.
401 South Green Street
Dalton, Georgia 30720
S. Shaheen, President
(404) 278-8000

WORLD DRYER CORPORATION
5700 McDermott
Berkely, Illinois 60163
(312) 449-6950

WORLD FOODS (gourmet foods)
See Holly World Foods, Inc.

WORLD OF COLOR (spray paint)
See Ideal Brushes Inc.

WORLD TOY HOUSE
(Division of Telmont Corporation)
408 Saint Peter
Saint Paul, Minnesota 55102
Warren Gochenour, President
(612) 227-7701

WORLD VISION (illuminated globes)
See Replogle Globes

WORLD WIDE (earplugs, household
gloves, ice bags, pacifiers, etc.)
See Danor Industries, Inc.

WORLD WIDE (frozen foods)
See Frozen Foods (Division
of Stokely-Van Camp Inc.)

WORLD WIDE EQUIPMENT
CORPORATION
3612 West Lincoln Highway
Olympia Fields, Illinois 60461

WORLD WIDE MANUFACTURING
INC.
8817 S.W. 131st Street
Miami, Florida 33144
(305) 235-5585

WORLD'S FAIR (towels, clothespins,
rolling pins, utility tongs)
See Forster Manufacturing
Company Inc.

WORLD'S FINEST CHOCOLATE,
INC.
(Division of Cook Chocolate
Company)
2521 West 48th Street
Chicago, Illinois 60632
Edmond Opler, President
(312) 847-4600

WORLDWIDE COMPUTER SERVICES
INC.
22 Purchase Street
Rye, New York 10580

WORSTED-TEX (men's suits)
See House of Worsted-Tex

WORTH (furniture)
See Gravely Furniture
Company, Inc.

WORTH BAT COMPANY
(Division of Lannom Manufacturing
Company Inc.)
Tullahoma, Tennessee 37388

WORTH COMPANY, THE
Post Office Box 88
Stevens Point, Wisconsin 54481
Robert Worth, President
(715) 344-6081

WORTH CROWING ABOUT (candy)
See Goelitz Confectionary
Company

Companies and Trade Names

WORTH ENTERPRISES, HELEN
106 East 31st Street
New York, New York 10016
(212) 532-2185

WORTH PARFUMS CORPORATION
5 East 57th Street
New York, New York 10022
Jerome A. Landsman, President
(212) 752-4150

WORTHINGTON (boat accessories)
See Spindrift

WORTHINGTON (food products)
See Worthington Foods, Inc.

WORTHINGTON FOODS, INC.
(Division of Miles Laboratories, Inc.)
900 Proprietors Road
Worthington, Ohio 43085
James L. Hagle, President
(614) 885-9511

WORTHMORE (aluminum cooking utensils)
See Mirro Aluminum Company

WORTZ COMPANY
201 South Fifth Street
Fort Smith, Arkansas 72901
Victor L. Cary, President
(501) 785-2831

WOS-WIT (groceries)
See Kresge Farm Food Packers

WOW (luggage)
See Hartmann Luggage Company, Inc.

WRANGLER (albums, books, and desk accessories)
See Strathmore Sales Inc.

WRANGLER (sportswear)
See Blue Bell, Inc.

WRAP-N-HOLD (heating pads)
See Westinghouse Electric Corporation

WRAP-ON COMPANY
341 West Superior
Chicago, Illinois 60610
(312) 822-0450

WRAP-RITE (aluminum foil)
See Wax-Rite Products Company

WRAP-TURES GIFT WRAP INC.
Post Office Box 9151
Panorama Branch
Penfield, New York 14526

WRAPAROUND (heating pads)
See Kaz Inc.

WRAPP CLEAT INC.
Clark Street
Old Saybrook, Connecticut 06475

WRAY (Jamaican rum)
See Schieffelin & Company

WREN (alarm clock by Springwound)
See Robertshaw Controls Company

WREN PHARMACEUTICALS, INC.
Box 8203
Greenville, South Carolina 29604

WRENS GROCERY COMPANY
Wrens, Georgia 30833

WRETCHED MESS NEWS INC., THE
1950 Mountain Boulevard
Oakland, California 94611

WRIEDT INC.
13900 South Norwalk Boulevard
Norwalk, California 90650

WRIGHT (gas heaters)
See International Metal Products

WRIGHT (gasoline-powered blade and chain saws)
See Thomas Industries, Inc.

WRIGHT (menswear and boys' wear)
See Oxford Industries, Inc.

WRIGHT & COMPANY, INC. E.T.
379 Liberty Street
Rockland, Massachusetts 02370
James P. Giblin, President
(617) 878-0420

WRIGHT & COMPANY, J.A.
68 Dunbar Street
Keene, New Hampshire 03431
(603) 352-2625

WRIGHT & MCGILL COMPANY
4245 East 46th Avenue
Denver, Colorado 80216
Mrs. M.F. McGill, President
(303) 321-1481

WRIGHT-BERNET INC.
1524 Bender Avenue
Hamilton, Ohio 45011
Robert G. Bernet, President
(513) 867-8008

WRIGHT COMPANY, INC., THE E.H.
2900 Oak Street
Kansas City, Missouri 64108
James R. Reynolds, Jr., President
(413) 436-7732

WRIGHT COMPANY, WILLIAM E.
South Street
West Warren, Massachusetts 01092
George M. Stevens, President and Chief Executive Officer
(413) 436-7732
See also Trimtex

1432

Companies and Trade Names

WRIGHT SALES COMPANY, J.C.
5933 Sixth Avenue South
Seattle, Washington 98108
(206) 763-1220

WRIGHTCO CORPORATION
2730 N.W. First Avenue
Boca Raton, Florida 33432

WRIGHT'S (shampoo, soap)
   See Caswell-Massey Company, Ltd.

WRIGHTWAY MANUFACTURING COMPANY
371 East 116th Street
Chicago, Illinois 60628
(312) 468-4700

WRIGLEY, JR., COMPANY, WILLIAM
410 North Michigan Avenue
Chicago, Illinois 60611
William Wrigley, President
(312) 644-2121
   See also Amurd Products Company

WRIGLEY PHARMACEUTICAL COMPANY
123 Fifth Avenue
New York, New York 10003
(212) 674-1433

WRINKLES-AWAY (hand steamers)
   See West Bend Company

WRISLEY COMPANY, ALLEN B.
129 Medford
Malden, Massachusetts 02148

WRITE BROTHERS (ball-point pens and pencils)
   See Paper-Mate Company

WRITE INC.
420 Lexington Avenue
New York, New York 10017
William D. Glover, President and Treasurer
(212) 532-6171

WRITE LITE (flashlight and pen combination)
   See Brownie Manufacturing Company

WUNDA WEVE CARPET COMPANY
(Division of Dan River, Inc.)
2200 Poinsett Highway
Greenville, South Carolina 29602
R.C. Crawford, President
(803) 877-2021

WUNDAGLIDE (ironing-board covers)
   See Starcross Inc.

WUNDER (ski equipment)
   See Herbert G. Schwarz Ski Imports

WUNDERBRAU (beer)
   See Erie Brewing Company

WUNDERHOSE (pantyhose)
   See Olga Company

WUNDERLE, INC., PH.
Eighth and Somerset Streets
Philadelphia, Pennsylvania 19133
J. Mackie Wunderle, President and Treasurer
(215) 225-1035

WUNDERLICH-DIEZ CORPORATION
State Highway 17
Hasbrouck Heights, New Jersey 07604

WUNDERWEAR MILLS, INC.
385 Gerard Avenue
Bronx, New York 10451

WURLITZER COMPANY, THE
105 West Adams Street
Chicago, Illinois 60603
W.N. Herleman, President
(312) 263-3373

WURZBURGER HOFBRAU (Bavarian beer)
   See Original Beer Importing Distributing Company, Inc.

WYANDOTTE (cleaner and polish)
   See BASF Wyandotte Corporation

WYANDOTTE TABLET COMPANY
1100 West Third Avenue
Columbus, Ohio 43212
(614) 291-7693

WYE CHEMICALS INC.
1185 Bristol Road
Warminster, Pennsylvania 18974

WYETH LABORATORIES
(Subsidiary of American Home Products Corporation)
Box 8299
Philadelphia, Pennsylvania 19101
Charles J. Kern, President
(215) 688-4400

WYLDE FLOUR COMPANY, INC., SAM
1526 Utah Avenue
Seattle, Washington 98134
(206) 624-6363

WYLER FOODS
(Division of Borden Foods)
2301 Shermer Road
Northbrook, Illinois 60062
W. Stephen Dee, President
(312) 498-6200

WYLER WATCH CORPORATION
315 Park Avenue, South
New York, New York 10010
Victor A. Wyler, President
(212) 777-5002

WYMAN & SON, JASPER
Millbridge, Maine 04658
(207) 546-2311

WYNN OIL COMPANY
2600 East Nutwood Avenue
Azusa, California 91702
Wesley E. Bellwood, President
(714) 992-2000

WYNTON BRASSIERE COMPANY
227 58th Street
Brooklyn, New York 11220
(212) 439-5083

WYNWOOD SAN (soap, cologne, and aftershave)
   See Gentlemen's Choice

WYOMISSING CORPORATION
Seventh and Reading Streets
Reading, Pennsylvania 19602
Lawrence P. Kelley, President
(215) 376-2891
   See also Narrow Fabric Company

WYTHEVILLE PACKING COMPANY, INC.
Cassell Road
Wytheville, Virginia 24382

Companies and Trade Names

X

X-ACTA (pocket adding machine)
See Alvin & Company Inc.

X-ACTO INC.
48-41 Van Dam Street
Long Island City, New York 11101
(212) 392-3333

X-CEL (lawn and garden supplies)
See Spaulding's Inc.

X-DRIN (appetite depressant)
See Pharmex, Inc.

XL (processed foods)
See Ernest Carriere Inc.

X-L (tools, housewares, paints, sporting goods, etc.)
See Witte Hardware Company

XL (whiskey)
See Schenley Industries, Inc.

XLO TOOL & ABRASIVE PRODUCTS
Post Office Box 274A
Detroit, Michigan 48232
J.W. Groomes, Vice President
(313) 867-3600

X LABORATORIES INC.
1801 Estes Avenue
Elk Grove Village, Illinois 60007
(312) 439-4410

X NINETY (siding)
See Masonite Corporation

X-PANDO CORPORATION
43-15 36th Street
Long Island City, New York 11101
(212) 784-7180

X-PEL PRODUCTS COMPANY
516 Lafayette Building
South Bend, Indiana 46601

X-PLORER (flashlights)
See Fulton Manufacturing Company

X-POTENTIAL ENTERPRISES
17819 Joshua Circle
Fountain Valley, California 92708

X700 IMPAKTA MAGICUBE (cameras and photo accessories)
See Imperial Camera Corporation

X-WAX
(Division of Micro-Therapeutics Inc.)
330 West 58th Street
New York, New York 10019
(212) 582-6833

XXX (frozen foods)
See Fred's Frozen Foods, Inc.

XANADU (bath oil, cologne, hand and body lotion, etc)
See Faberge, Inc.

XANTECH CORPORATION
13038 Saticoy Street
North Hollywood, California 91605
(213) 983-0811

XCELITE INC.
Bank Street
Orchard Park, New York 14127

XEROX CORPORATION
Stamford, Connecticut 06904
C. Peter McColough, Chairman of the Board
(203) 329-8711
See also Ginn & Company

XPLORER MOTOR HOME
(Division of Frank Industries Inc.)
3950 Burnsline Road
Brown City, Michigan 48416

XTERMINATOR PRODUCTS CORPORATION
171 Monticello
Jersey City, New Jersey 07304

XTTRIUM LABORATORIES, INC.
415 West Pershing Road
Chicago, Illinois 60609
(312) 268-5800

Y

Y & S CANDIES, INC.
45 Cardinal Drive
Westfield, New Jersey 07091
C.A. Smylie, President
(201) 654-4100

Y K K ZIPPER (USA) INC.
1251 Valley Brook Avenue
Lyndhurst, New Jersey 07071
(201) 935-4200

YMM (men's slacks)
See Jaymar-Ruby, Inc.

YACHT AIR (cooling and heating units)
See Richard Industries Inc.

YACHT CLUB (groceries)
See Consolidated Foods Corporation

YACHT CONSTRUCTORS INC.
7030 N.E. 42nd Avenue
Portland, Oregon 97218
(503) 287-5794

YACHTCRAFT
(Division of Islander Yachts Inc.)
777 West 17th Street
Costa Mesa, California 92627

YACOBELLIS, CHARLES
45 Sutton Place South
New York, New York 10022
(212) 753-9321

YAGER DRUG COMPANY
430 West Mulberry Street
Baltimore, Maryland 21201
(301) 685-8542

YAKA (cigarettes)
See G.A. Georgopulo & Company, Inc.

YAKETYS (shoes)
See Midwest Footwear, Inc.

YAKIMA FRUIT & COLD STORAGE COMPANY
Post Office Box 91
Yakima, Washington 98901

YAKIMA VALLEY GRAPE PRODUCERS
Box 520
Grandview, Washington 98930

YALE (locks)
See Eaton Corporation

YALE (tires and batteries)
See Union Oil Company of California

YALE ENGINEERING COMPANY
12405 Woodruff Avenue
Downey, California 90241
Edward Di Loreto, Chairman and President
(213) 923-7262

YALE EXPRESS SYSTEM, INC.
215 County Avenue
Secaucus, New Jersey 07094
James F. Crosby, President

YAMAHA INTERNATIONAL CORPORATION
6600 Orangethorpe Avenue
Buena Park, California 90620
Hiroshi Kawashima, President
(714) 522-9011

YAMAKI (classical and steel-string guitars)
See Castiglione Accordion & Distributing Company

YANIGANS (women's shoes)
See International Shoe Company

YANKEE (food products)
See Wayside Industries

YANKEE ARTISTS INC.
47 Main Street
Keene, New Hampshire 03431

YANKEE CUTTER (lawn and garden supplies)
See Frost Company

YANKEE INC.
320 Main Street
Dublin, New Hampshire 03444

YANKEE MARINE PRODUCTS INC.
63 North Cherry Street
Wallingford, Connecticut 06492

YANKEE METAL PRODUCTS CORPORATION
25 Grand Street
Norwalk, Connecticut 06851
Milton Putterman, President
(203) 847-5841

YANKEE MOTOR COMPANY
2910 Campbell Avenue
Schenectady, New York 12301
John A. Taylor, President
(518) 372-4726

YANKEE YACHTS INC.
2724 South Grand
Santa Ana, California 92705

YAO SHIH-CHIN CORPORATION
342 Madison Avenue
New York, New York 10017
(212) 697-5336

YAPRE CRAVATS INC.-HERBERT BERGHEIM
99 Madison Avenue
New York, New York 10016
(212) 684-5588

Companies and Trade Names

YAR-CRAFT INC.
1213 20th Avenue
Menominee, Michigan 49858

YARD BOSS (lawn mower)
   See White Motor Corporation

YARD GUARD (insecticide)
   See S.C. Johnson & Son, Inc.

YARD-MAN
1410 West Granson Street
Jackson, Michigan 49202

YARD MASTER (garden products)
   See S.C. Johnson & Son, Inc.

YARDLEY ASSOCIATES INC.
122 York Road
Jenkintown, Pennsylvania 19046

YARDLEY OF LONDON, INC.
700 Union Boulevard
Totowa, New Jersey 07511
William D. Hunt, President
(201) 256-3100

YARD'N GARDEN (tools)
   See Union Fork & Hoe Company

YARDNEY ELECTRIC CORPORATION
82 Mechanic Street
Pawcatuck, Connecticut 02891
Americo W. Petrocelli, President
   and Chief Executive Officer
(203) 599-1100
   See also Hol-Gar Manufacturing
   Corporation

YASHICA, INC.
50-17 Queens Boulevard
Woodside, New York 11377
Kenji Sakuma, President
(212) 446-5566

YASUTOMO & COMPANY
24 California Street
San Francisco, California 94111
(415) 981-4326

YATES BLODGETT
Penn Yan, New York 14527

YAVNER BROTHERS COMPANY, INC.
211 West 24th Street
Norfolk, Virginia 23517

YAZOO MANUFACTURING COMPANY INC.
Post Office Box 4207
3607 Livingston Road
Jackson, Mississippi 39216
(601) 366-6421

YE OLDE STYLE (groceries)
   See W.T. Lynch Foods Ltd.

YE OLDE TAVERN CHEESE COMPANY, INC.
3949 West Lake
Chicago, Illinois 60624
Dennis J. Burke, President
(312) 533-8170

YE OLDE VIRGINIA (tobacco)
   See Peterson's Ltd.

YE OLE VIRGINNY (meat products)
   See Joel E. Harrell, Inc.

YEAGER SPECIALTY COMPANY
Post Office Box 250
Blountsville, Alabama 35031

YEAR ROUNDER (handbags)
   See Henry-Richards Company Inc.

YEAR'S WEAR (work clothes)
   See W.E. Stephens Manufacturing Company

YEAST PRODUCTS, INC.
455 Fifth Avenue
Paterson, New Jersey 07514

YEE HOP & COMPANY, LTD., C.Q.
125 King
Honolulu, Hawaii 96817
(808) 538-6951

YELLOW BOW (food products)
   See Sun Garden Packing Company

YELLOW DRAGON (ski equipment)
   See Jacobs Corporation

YELLOW-FLASH (electric lanterns)
   See Justrite Manufacturing Company

YELLOW FREIGHT SYSTEM, INC.
10990 Roe Avenue
Shawnee Mission, Kansas 66207
Donald L. McMorris, President
(913) 383-3000

YELLOW ROSE (cigars by Villiger A.G.)
   See Gesty Trading & Manufacturing Corporation

YELLOW ROSE (grocery products)
   See Dixieland Food Stores, Inc.

YELLOWSTONE (whiskey)
   See Glenmore Distilleries Company, Inc.

YERG INC.
85 Washington Avenue
Belleville, New Jersey 07109
(201) 459-4041

YEUELL INC., E.V.
2 Adele Road
Woburn, Massachusetts 01801
(617) 933-2984

YEUNG COMPANY, SAM
1 World Trade Center
New York, New York 10048
(212) 432-9335

Companies and Trade Names

YIELD HOUSE
(Division of Standard International Corporation)
Route 16 and 302
North Conway, New Hampshire 03860
M. Joseph Dunn, President
(603) 356-5507

YOAKUM PACKING COMPANY, LTD.
Yoakum, Texas 77995

YODELERS
(Division of Somersworth Manufacturing Company)
Somersworth, New Hampshire 03878

YODER COMPANY
5500 Walworth Avenue
Cleveland, Ohio 44102
Douglas O. Yoder, President
(216) 631-0520

YONKERS LABORATORIES
923 Old Nepperhan Avenue
Yonkers, New York 10703

YOO HOO CHOCOLATE BEVERAGE CORPORATION
600 Commercial Avenue
Carlstadt, New Jersey 07072
Max A. Geller, President
(201) 933-0070

YORK (cigarettes)
See Lorillard

YORK
(Division of Borg-Warner Corporation)
South Richland Avenue
York, Pennsylvania 17405
J.W. Kennedy, President
(717) 846-7890

YORK ARCHERY
1450 West Lexington
Independence, Missouri 64051
K.B. Smith, President
(816) 252-9612

YORK COMPANY INC., OTTO H.
42 Intervale Road
Parsippany, New Jersey 07054
(201) 263-2200

YORK COMPANY, L.T.
440 East Helm Street
Brookfield, Missouri 64628
R. Stanley Ladley, President
(816) 258-2291

YORK CONE COMPANY
615 South Pine Street
York, Pennsylvania 17403
(717) 845-2619

YORK COUNTY (food products)
See W.E. Bittinger Company Inc.

YORK CUTLERY COMPANY INC.
286-288 West Market
York, Pennsylvania 17401

YORK DRUG COMPANY, INC.
21 North Congress Street
York, South Carolina 29745

YORK GRAPHIC ARTS INC.
216 Ridge Road
Villa Park, Illinois 60181

YORK IMPERIAL (cigars)
See G.W. Van Slyke & Horton

YORK MUSICAL INSTRUMENT COMPANY INC.
(Subsidiary of Tolchin Instruments Inc.)
55 Marcus Drive
Melville, New York 11746

YORK STREET FLAX SPINNING COMPANY
21 West 38th Street
New York, New York 10018
(212) 221-6440

YORK TEEN (misses' coats and suits)
See New York Girl Coat Company, Inc.

YORKAIRE (air conditioners)
See Borg-Warner Corporation York Division

YORKANA CIGAR COMPANY
131-35 North Penn Street
York, Pennsylvania 17404

YORKRAFT, INC.
550 South Pine
York, Pennsylvania 17403

YORKTOWN (shoes)
See Gardiner Shoe Company Inc.

YORKTOWNE
(Division of Wickes Corporation)
Post Office Box 231
Red Lion, Pennsylvania 17356
Leigh Bench, President
(717) 244-4011

YORKVILLE (tea, coffee, spices)
See Universal Coffee Corporation

YORKVILLE, INC.
Ciro Road
North Branford, Connecticut 06471
(203) 488-2558

YORKVILLE INDUSTRIES
55 Motor Avenue
Farmingdale, New York 11735

YOSELOFF, PUBLISHER, THOMAS
(Division of A.S. Barnes & Company Inc.)
Cranbury, New Jersey 08512

YOST CANDY COMPANY, THE
Dalton, Ohio 44618

Companies and Trade Names

YOUNG & COMPANY, F.E.
8057 Stony Island Avenue
Chicago, Illinois 60617
(312) 221-7188

YOUNG & RUBICAM, INC.
285 Madison Avenue
New York, New York 10017
Edward N. Nay, President
(212) 953-2000

YOUNG-IN-BUILD (men's double knit clothing)
See Louis Goldsmith Inc.

YOUNG, INC., HENRY M.
1182 Broadway
New York, New York 10001
(212) 532-5650

YOUNG, INC., W.F.
111 Lyman Street
Springfield, Massachusetts 01103
Sally Fenelon Young, President
(413) 737-0201

YOUNG LIFE (shoes)
See Tober-Saifer Shoe Manufacturing Company, Inc.

YOUNG LOOK (cosmetics)
See Lehn & Fink Products Company

YOUNG LOOK, INC.
See Renee of Hollywood

YOUNG MISS MORTON, INC.
14 East 32nd Street
New York, New York 10016
(212) 686-3257

YOUNG 'N FREE (bubble bath, cologne, hand and body lotion, etc.)
See Youth Care, Inc.

YOUNG NATURALS (dresses and suits)
See Puritan Fashions Corporation

YOUNG PEOPLE'S RECORDS
See Greystone Corporation

YOUNG RADIATOR COMPANY
2825 Four Mile Road
Racine, Wisconsin 53404
Fred M. Young, President and General Manager
(414) 639-1010

YOUNG SPORTSWEAR, INC., DIANE
(Subsidiary of Paraphernalia, Inc.)
525 Seventh Avenue
New York, New York 10018
David B. Strauss, Jr., President
(212) 563-7979

YOUNG TIMERS, INC.
520 Eighth Avenue
New York, New York 10018
Ralph Kurtz, President
(212) 244-4514

YOUNG VIEWPOINT (women's dresses)
See Ginsburg & Abelson, Inc.

YOUNG YEARS MANUFACTURING COMPANY INC.
Post Office Box 747
Brookline, Massachusetts 02147

YOUNGBLOOD CANNERY, J.O.
Box 31
Burton, South Carolina 29902

YOUNGDALE (juvenile shoes)
See International Shoe Company

YOUNGER MANUFACTURING COMPANY
3788 South Broadway Place
Los Angeles, California 90007
(213) 232-2345

YOUNGER THAN SPRINGTIME (skin-care products)
See Aquamint Laboratories

YOUNGFELLOW (cigars)
See R.G. Dun Cigar Corporation

YOUNGS DRUG PRODUCTS CORPORATION
865 Centennial Avenue
Piscataway, New Jersey 08854
John C. MacFarlane, President
(201) 885-5777

YOUNGS MANUFACTURING COMPANY
Line Lexington, Pennsylvania 18932

YOUNG'S MARKET COMPANY
500 South Central
Los Angeles, California 90013
(213) 629-5571

YOUNGSTOWN KITCHENS
(Division of Mullins Manufacturing Corporation)
South Ellsworth Avenue
Salem, Ohio 44460
Robert Brisell, President
(216) 337-8771

YOUNGSTOWN SHEET AND TUBE COMPANY
(Subsidiary of Lykes-Youngstown Corporation)
Post Office Box 900
7655 Market Street
Youngstown, Ohio 44501
Frank A. Nemec, Chairman, President and Chief Executive Officer
(216) 758-6411

Companies and Trade Names

YOUNKER BROTHERS, INC.
Seventh and Walnut Streets
Des Moines, Iowa 50309
Morey Sostrin, Chairman
(515) 244-1112

YOUR EXCELLENCY (men's toiletries)
See Evyan Perfumes, Inc.

YOUR VERY OWN (wedding invitations, personalized paper products)
See E. Errett Smith Inc.

YOU'RE THE FIRE (fragrance)
See Yardley of London

YOUTH CARE, INC.
107 Trusbull Street
Elizabeth, New Jersey 07206

YOUTH-DEW (bath oil, cologne, perfume, etc).
See Estee Lauder, Inc.

YOUTH 25 (cosmetics)
See Irma Shorell, Inc.

YOUTHCRAFT/CHARMFIT
(Division of Russ Togs, Inc.)
90 Park Avenue
New York, New York 10016
Lionel N. Bloomfield, President
(212) 768-0125

YOUTHCRAFT COATS & SUITS, INC.
801 Broadway
Kansas City, Missouri 64105
Leon Karosen, President
(816) 221-9300

YOUTHFORM COMPANY
257 Trinity Avenue S.W.
Atlanta, Georgia 30303
(404) 681-1252

YOUTHMORE ORIGINAL (coats)
See Wilson Garment Manufacturing Company, Inc.

YOUTHQUAKE (dresses)
See Puritan Fashions Corporation

YUBA INDUSTRIES, INC.
277 Park Avenue
New York, New York 10017
Ezra J. Denerstein, President
(212) 922-4660

YUBAN (coffee)
See General Foods Corporation

YULETIDE ENTERPRISES INC.
108 New South Road
Hicksville, New York 11802
Perry Feuer, President
(212) 895-0150

YULETIDE KREATIONS INC.
1107 Broadway
New York, New York 10010
(212) 686-3349

YVES SAINT LAURENT (toiletries)
See Lanvin-Charles of the Ritz, Inc.

1440

Companies and Trade Names

Z

Z.B.T. (baby-care products)
   See Glenbrook Laboratories

ZABALA (shotguns)
   See J.L. Galef & Son, Inc.

ZACHARY MUSICAL
   INSTRUMENTS
5 Eastmans Road
Parsippany, New Jersey 07054

ZACK (cigarettes)
   See Lorillard

ZAGREB (imported foods)
   See Baltic Trading Company

ZAHN-IMPORT MERCHANT,
   CHARLES
Box 149
Milford, New Hampshire 03055

ZAHN, J. KENNETH
225 Fifth Avenue
New York, New York 10010
(212) 684-6472

ZAIMA INTERNATIONAL
949 Broadway
New York, New York 10010
(212) 777-8370

ZALE CORPORATION
3000 Diamond Park Drive
Dallas, Texas 75247
Donald Zale, President
(214) 634-4011
   See also Butler's Shoe
      Corporation; Levine Department Store; and
      Maling Brothers Inc.

ZALOOM & COMPANY, INC.,
   JOSEPH A.
(Subsidiary of Biddle Purchasing
Company)
8 Jay Street
New York, New York 10013
(212) 431-6700

ZAMPA, INC.
410 Ocean Avenue
Lynbrook, New York 11563

ZANESVILLE STONEWARE
   COMPANY
309 Pershing Road
Zanesville, Ohio 43701
Milman H. Linn, Jr., President,
   Secretary and Treasurer
(614) 452-7441

ZAP (insect electrocutors)
   See Gardner Manufacturing
      Company

ZAPATO FOODS INC.
730 Hennepin Avenue
Minneapolis, Minnesota 55403
Marno McDermott, President
(612) 239-0471

ZARLENE IMPORTS
516 Fifth Avenue
New York, New York 10036
(212) 221-5872

ZAUSNER FOODS CORPORATION
Post Office Box 1146
1190 U.S. Highway 22
Mountainside, New Jersey 07092
Sol Zausner, President and
   Treasurer
(201) 233-1211

ZAYRE CORPORATION
Framingham, Massachusetts 01701
Stanley H. Feldberg, President
(617) 630-5000

ZAX CORPORATION
10 Otterson Street
Nashua, New Hampshire 03060
(603) 889-4126

ZEBCO/CONSUMER
(Division of Brunswick Corporation)
Post Office Box 270
Tulsa, Oklahoma 74101
Ralph F. Lafferty, President
(918) 836-5581

ZEBRA (water skis and accessories)
   See Gladding Corporation

ZECOL, INC.
3270 South Third
Milwaukee, Wisconsin 53207
(414) 483-6400

ZECRON INTERNATIONAL
350 Fifth Avenue
New York, New York 10001
(212) 736-4300

ZEE BEST (food products)
   See Zemco Foods Company,
      Inc.

ZEFF (hairdressing, shampoo,
soaps)
   See Chesebrough-Pond's, Inc.

ZEGA (watches)
   See Seko Inc.

ZEGERS, INC.
16727 Chicago Avenue
Lansing, Illinois 60438
(312) 474-7700

ZEHNER PACKING COMPANY
South West Street
Bellevue, Ohio 44811
Robert C. Zehner, President
   and Treasurer
(419) 483-6790

ZEIGLER CONTROLS INC.
17810 South Western Avenue
Gardena, California 90248
(213) 324-2932

Companies and Trade Names

ZEISS, INC., CARL
444 Fifth Avenue
New York, New York 10018
Siegfried Kessler, President
(212) 736-6070

ZELAN (water repellents)
See E.I. du Pont de Nemours
& Company, Inc.

ZELINKOFF COMPANY
300 West Murdock Avenue
Wichita, Kansas 67203
Milton A. Zelinkoff, Owner and
Chief Executive Officer
(316) 264-7378

ZELITE CORPORATION
342 Madison Avenue
New York, New York 10017
(212) 986-0245

ZELL-AIRE CORPORATION
(Subsidiary of Zellers Laboratories)
Reading, Pennsylvania 19603
E.G. Zellers, President
(215) 372-9579

ZELL COMPANY
327 Main
Norwalk, Connecticut 06852
(203) 847-3818

ZELLER CORPORATION
Post Office Box 278
1307 Baltimore Road
Defiance, Ohio 43512
Robert C. Zeller, Jr., President
(419) 784-2244

ZELLERBACH PAPER COMPANY
55 Hawthorne Street
San Francisco, California 94105
(415) 761-1212

ZEMCO FOODS COMPANY, INC.
(Division of H. Zemsky & Sons)
665 Perry Street
Buffalo, New York 14210
(716) 826-6400

ZEMMER COMPANY, INC., THE
231 Hulton Road
Oakmont, Pennsylvania 15139
(412) 828-5240
See also Moore Kirk
Laboratories Inc.

ZEMO (soap, ointment)
See Plough Inc.

ZENITH (meat products)
See Elliott Packing Company

ZENITH-GODLEY COMPANY, INC.
176 Duane
New York, New York 10013
(212) 925-3600

ZENITH IGNITION
Box 22
Seneca Falls, New York 13148

ZENITH LABORATORIES, INC.
140 LeGrand Avenue
Northvale, New Jersey 07647
Benjamin Wiener, Chairman,
President and Chief Executive
Officer
(201) 767-1700

ZENITH MOVADO TIME
CORPORATION
610 Fifth Avenue
New York, New York 10020
Nathan Jurist, President
(212) 247-0111

ZENITH RADIO CORPORATION
1900 North Austin Avenue
Chicago, Illinois 60639
Nathan W. Aram, Vice President,
Consumer Affairs
(312) 745-2000

ZEP MANUFACTURING
CORPORATION
3008 Olympic Industrial Boulevard
Atlanta, Georgia 30080
H. Maziar, President
(404) 352-1680

ZEPHYR (electric shaver)
See Manning, Bowman (Division
of McGraw-Edison Company)

ZEPHYR (zippers)
See Talon, Inc.

ZEPHYR-FLYTE (rubber products)
See Carlisle Corporation

ZEPHYR MANUFACTURING
COMPANY
400-410 West Second Street
Sedalia, Missouri 65301
Robert J. Lindstrom, President
(816) 827-0352

ZEPHYR PRODUCTS INC.
Narrows Road
Wareham, Massachusetts 02571

ZEREGA'S SONS, INC., A.
Fair Lawn, New Jersey 07410

ZEREX (antifreeze)
See E.I. du Pont de Nemours
& Company, Inc.

ZERO (food products)
See Sunaid Food Products

ZERO (sports apparel, accessories,
and equipment)
See Hanover Glove Company

ZERO KING (family sportswear)
See B.W. Harris Manufacturing
Company

ZERO KIST (frozen vegetables and
potatoes)
See Prosser Packers, Inc.

ZERO MANUFACTURING COMPANY
811 Duncan Avenue
Washington, Missouri 63090
(314) 239-6721

Companies and Trade Names

ZERO-MAX
Division of Zero-Max Industries)
2845 Harriet Avenue South
Minneapolis, Minnesota 55408
(612) 827-6261

ZERO PAK (food products)
See C.M. McLean Ltd.

ZERONE (antifreeze)
See E.I. du Pont de Nemours & Company, Inc.

ZEST (soap)
See Procter & Gamble Company

ZESTEE (food products)
See Jewett & Sherman Company

ZETA (tires)
See Uniroyal Inc.

ZHIVAGO (vodka)
See Fleischmann Distilling Corporation

ZIABICKI IMPORT COMPANY
Post Office Box 994
Racine, Wisconsin 53405

ZICKOS CORPORATION
11844 West 85th Street
Lenexa, Kansas 66214

ZIDREP LABORATORIES
Box 137
257 Franklin Street
Buffalo, New York 14212
(716) 853-2255

ZIEBART AUTO TRUCK
RUSTPROOFING
Post Office Box 1248
Warren, Michigan 48090

ZIEGLER COMPANY, GEORGE
408 West Florida Street
Milwaukee, Wisconsin 53204
(414) 276-2490

ZIEGLER PHARMACAL CORPORATION
484 Delaware Avenue
Buffalo, New York 14202
(716) 884-3309

ZIFF-DAVIS PUBLISHING COMPANY
1 Park Avenue
New York, New York 10016
William Ziff, Chairman of the Board
(212) 679-7200

ZILDJIAN COMPANY, AVEDIS
Post Office Box 198
Accord, Massachusetts 02018

ZIMBER METALS CORPORATION
633 Third Avenue
New York, New York 10017
(212) 687-1460

ZIMMER HOMES CORPORATION
777 S.W. 12th Avenue
Pompano Beach, Florida 33060
Paul H. Zimmer, President
(305) 943-7600

ZIM'S INC.
240 East Second South
Salt Lake City, Utah 84107
(801) 359-5821

ZINSMASTER BAKING COMPANY
2900 Park
Minneapolis, Minnesota 55407
Aaron J. Peterson, President
(612) 823-6244

ZINSSER & COMPANY, INC., WILLIAM
31 Belmont Drive
Somerset, New Jersey 08873
Gardner R. Cunningham, President and Treasurer
(201) 469-8100

ZION FOODS CORPORATION
478-484 Austin Place
Bronx, New York 10455
Edwin Anderson, President
(212) 292-5500

ZION'S CO-OPERATIVE MERCANTILE INSTITUTION
2200 South 900 West Street
Salt Lake City, Utah 84137
Oakley S. Evans, President
(801) 321-6179

ZIP (ball-point pens, erasers)
See Venus Esterbrook Corporation

ZIP (camera)
See Polaroid Corporation

ZIP-A-BABE (baby harness with zippers)
See Life Manufacturing Company Inc.

ZIP QUICK CRISPS (ready-to bake fruit desserts)
See Michigan Fruit Canners, Inc.

ZIP-STRIP (paint and varnish remover)
See Star Bronze Company

ZIPLOC (storage bags)
See Dow Chemical Company

ZIPLON (zippers)
See Y K K Zipper (USA) Inc.

Companies and Trade Names

ZIPOUT INC.
3115 Auburn Street
Rockford, Illinois 61103

ZIPPER (boots and shoes)
See B.F. Goodrich Company

ZIPPO MANUFACTURING
COMPANY
36 Barbour Street
Bradford, Pennsylvania 16701
George G. Blaisdell, President
(814) 362-4541

ZIRIN LABORATORIES
INTERNATIONAL
199 West 24th Street
Hialeah, Florida 33010

ZITA CREATIONS (handbags)
See Excellent Bag Corporation

ZITNER COMPANY, S.
3140 North 17th Street
Philadelphia, Pennsylvania 19132
(215) 229-4990

ZIZANIE (men's toiletries)
See Kayser-Roth Hosiery
Company Inc.

ZOBRIST COMPANY, INC., J.C.
Box 1128
Charleston, West Virginia 25324

ZODIAC (ball-point pens)
See Paper-Mate Company

ZODIAC (cologne, aftershave)
See Beauty Basics, Inc.

ZODIAC OF NORTH AMERICA
INC.
11 Lee Street
Annapolis, Maryland 21401

ZODIAC WATCH COMPANY
(Division of Edward Trauner, Inc.)
7 Westchester Plaza
Elmsford, New York 10523
Richard Trauner, President
(914) 592-9000

ZOELLER COMPANY
3280 Old Millers Lane
Louisville, Kentucky 40216
(502) 772-2584

ZOES MANUFACTURING
COMPANY, INC., C.A.
168 North Sangamon Stree
Chicago, Illinois 60607
(312) 666-4018

ZOLKIND & SONS, INC.
1623 Utica Avenue
Brooklyn, New York 11234
(212) 388-3602

ZONOLITE (insulation)
See W.R. Grace & Company
Construction Products
Division

ZOOM PLUS (hair detangler and styler/dryer)
See General Electric Company

ZOOM III Z (rechargeable flashlights)
See Garrity Industries, Inc.
Dynatron Division

ZOOMATIC (cameras)
See Bell & Howell Company

ZOTOS INTERNATIONAL, INC.
100 Tokeneke Road
Darien, Connecticut 06820
Ralph L. Evans, Jr., President
(203) 655-8911

ZOTOX (poison-ivy and poison-oak treatment)
See Commerce Drug Company, Inc.

ZUBACK'S BOAT WORKS
Highway 35
Morgan, New Jersey 08879

ZUCCA (canned foods)
See Ronzoni Foods, Inc.

ZUCKER CORPORATION, CHARLES
31 Mercer Street
New York, New York 10013
(212) 226-6133

ZULEGER (bassoons)
See DEG Music Products Inc.

ZUM ZUM
1540 Broadway
New York, New York 10036
(212) 974-6712

ZUNDAPP (motorcycles)
See McCormack International
Motors, Inc.

ZURD (pesticides)
See Murd Company

ZURICH INSURANCE COMPANY
11 West Jackson Boulevard
Chicago, Illinois 60604
Neville Pilling, Chairman of the
Board
(312) 922-3124

ZURN INDUSTRIES, INC.
2214 West Eighth Street
Erie, Pennsylvania 16512
Frank W. Zurn, Chairman of the
Board
(814) 455-0921

ZWICKER KNITTING MILLS
410-418 North Richmond Street
Appleton, Wisconsin 54911
Lloyd Paul, Chairman of the Board
(414) 739-3691

ZWIESEL DISTRIBUTORS, INC.
 See Schott-Zwiesel Glass, Inc.

ZYLINDER (stainless-steel flatware)
 See W-K Imports Inc.

ZYNOLYTE PRODUCTS COMPANY
15700 South Avalon Boulevard
Compton, California 90224
Leo Diamond, President
(213) 321-6964

SECTION V

SELECTED BIBLIOGRAPHY

The bibliography is divided into five parts according to the form of the material: Directories, Bibliographies, Abstracts and Indexes; Books and Pamphlets; Periodicals and Newsletters; Continuing Publications Series; and Audiovisual Materials. Within each part, arrangement is alphabetical by title. Entries for publications include wherever feasible, the full title; date; edition; author, editor, or compiler; publisher's or distributor's name and address; number of pages; and brief description of content. For audiovisual materials (primarily films and filmstrips), the entry usually includes the title, type of material, color or black and white, sound, duration, sponsor or producer, and name and address of the distributor, as well as a brief annotation of content.

The bibliography includes materials published in English in the United States since 1960, and audiovisual materials released within the last ten years. Although some of the publications were intended for use in a limited geographical area, they serve as illustrations of their type and so may be of interest to individuals in other parts of the country as well.

Directories, Bibliographies, Abstracts and Indexes

THE ANGRY BUYER'S COMPLAINT DIRECTORY. 1974. By Jack White, Gary Yanker, and Harry Steinberg. Peter H. Wyden, Incorporated, 750 Third Avenue, New York, New York 10017. 294 p.

The first section consists of a guide giving pointers on complaining and marshalling help in dealing with consumer disputes. The second section is a directory of national organizations, state, regional, and local groups handling consumer problems.

BIBLIOGRAPHY: CORPORATE RESPONSIBILITY FOR SOCIAL PROBLEMS. 1973-. Annual. Bank of America, 555 California Building, San Francisco, California 94104.

An annotated bibliography of materials concerned with corporate responses to current social problems. Includes books, articles, reports, speeches, and other pertinent material. The subject arrangement is by topics such as: Community Relations and Urban Affairs, Employment, Energy, Pollution, and Recycling.

BIBLIOGRAPHY OF RESEARCH ON CONSUMER AND HOMEMAKING EDUCATION. 1970. By Anna M. Gorman and Joel H. Magisos. Bibliography series number 6. Center for Vocational and Technical Education, Ohio State University, 1900 Kenny Road, Columbus, Ohio 43210. 71 p.

Presents bibliographic information, prices, and availability of research publications produced from 1966 to 1970. Entries are arranged under the following topics: Consumer Education; Disadvantaged; Evaluation; Homemaking Education; Research Methodology; Teacher Education; Vocational Educational Programs; and Wage Earning Home Economics.

BUYER'S GUIDE TO ENVIRONMENTAL MEDIA; A Directory of Books, Magazines, Films, and Information Sources. 1973. Environment Information Center, Incorporated, 124 East 39th Street, New York, New York 10016. 64 p.

Categories of materials listed include air pollution, contamination, energy, environmental education, food and drugs, land use, noise pollution, oceans, renewable resources, solid waste, water pollution, and wildlife. Bibliographic citations are given for books published during 1969 to 1973, and for periodicals and films that were currently available.

CALL FOR ACTION; A Survival Kit for New Yorkers. 1975. Revised and updated. By Muriel Sohmer, Myrel Winston, and Sue Lifton. Quadrangle/The New York Times Book Company, 10 East 53rd Street, New York, New York 10022. 402 p.

A directory of government, commercial, volunteer, charitable, and religious organizations which can be helpful to people with problems or special interests, primarily in the New York metropolitan area. Arranged under such topics as: Addiction, Aged, Business Advice, Children/Youth, Consumer, Discrimination, Education, Health, Housing, Licenses/Records/Permits, Recreation, Transportation, and Welfare/Social Services.

CAPITAL CONTACTS IN CONSUMERISM. 1976. Edited by Diane Zapanta. Fraser/Ruder & Finn, 1701 K Street, N.W., Washington, D.C. 20006. 233 p.

A directory to important consumer contacts in the executive and legislative branches of federal and state governments, consumer organizations, corporations, associations, and the consumer press. Lists programs, services, names, addresses, and phone numbers of consumer affairs people. Also includes a ten-page bibliography.

COMPLAINT DIRECTORY FOR CONSUMERS, 1977. Everybody's Money, CUNA, Incorporated, Box 431B, Madison, Wisconsin 53701. 55 p.

Gives addresses of federal, state, and local government agencies, senators and representatives, radio and television broadcasters, food producers, product manufacturers, and other places to address complaints or request information.

CONSERVATION DIRECTORY, 1976; A List of Organizations, Agencies, and Officials Concerned with Natural Resource Use and Management. 1976. 21st edition. By Gloria H. Decker. National Wildlife Federation, 1412 16th Street, N.W., Washington, D.C. 20036. 235 p.

Gives addresses, telephone numbers, officials, publications, and activities of organizations dealing with the environment. Arranged under the headings: U.S. Federal Departments, Offices and Agencies; International, National, Interstate Organizations and Commissions; State, Territorial Agencies and Citizen's Groups; Canadian Federal Government Agencies;

Directories, Bibliographies, Abstracts and Indexes

Canadian National Citizen's Groups; Canadian Provincial Government Departments and Citizens Groups. Also includes a listing of colleges and universities offering major programs in the environmental sciences, a directory of fish and game commissioners and directors in the United States and Canada, and bibliographic material.

CONSUMER ACTION'S AUTO INSURANCE GUIDE. 1976. San Francisco Consumer Action, 26 Seventh Street, San Francisco, California 94103.

A survey of 14 insurance companies in California reveals the spread in cost of auto insurance premiums and various types of coverage offered. A comprehensive shopper's guide to auto insurance in California.

CONSUMER BIBLIOGRAPHY. 1976. By Susan Samuel. Office of Fair Trading, Chancery House, Chancery Lane, London, England. 43 p.

A selective listing of materials on consumer credit, advertising, consumer education, consumerism, and marketing. Arrangement is by subject, subdivided by type of material. Materials covered include bibliographies, directories, abstracting and indexing tools, journals, statistics, books, and articles published in Great Britain, Canada, and the United States mostly since 1970.

CONSUMER BIBLIOGRAPHY. 1976. By the Montgomery County Office of Consumer Affairs, 24 Maryland Avenue, Rockville, Maryland 20850. 37 p.

Lists books available at the various branches of the Montgomery County Public Library. Arranged by subjects, including advertising, automobiles, aviation safety, credit, drugs, food, health, housing, insurance, money management, and protective regulations.

CONSUMER COMPLAINT ACTION GUIDE. 1973. 2nd edition. By the Complaint Committee of the Virginia Citizens Consumer Council, Incorporated, Post Office Box 3103, Alexandria, Virginia 22302. 89 p.

Provides guidelines on how to write a letter of complaint and where to send it. Offers suggestions on avoiding difficulties and resolving consumer dissatisfaction with advertising, airlines, appliances, automobiles, cleaning, credit, department stores, door-to-door sales, furniture, housing, insurance, mail orders, repairs, toys, utilities, and many other topics. Lists names and addresses of local, state, and national organizations that aid consumers in resolving complaints.

CON$UMER COMPLAINT GUIDE, 1977. c1976. By Joseph Rosenbloom. Macmillan Information, 866 Third Avenue, New York, New York 10022. 497 p.

Part I, The Consumer in the Marketplace, offers advice to follow before making purchases. Part II, How and to Whom to Complain, explains how to go about complaining and enlisting help from many different types of organizations. Part III, Who's Who in the Marketplace, lists names, addresses, phone numbers, and officials of companies and brand names of their products.

CONSUMER EDUCATION BIBLIOGRAPHY. 1971. By the U.S. Office of Consumer Affairs and the New York Public Library. Superintendent of Documents, U.S. Government Printing Office, Washington, D.C. 20402. 192 p.

An annotated list of over 4,000 books, pamphlets, periodical articles, audiovisual aids, and teachers' materials relating to consumer interests. They are arranged under such topics as consumer protection, consumer and the environment, money management, consumer goods and services, consumer education. Teaching materials in English and Spanish are included. Contains sections on government and private consumer organizations, trade and business associations, and land grant universities.

CONSUMER EDUCATION CATALOG. 1976. Social Studies School Service, 10,000 Culver Boulevard, Culver City, California 90230.

A comprehensive bibliography of various types of teaching materials for use in consumer education. Includes paperback books and other publications, filmstrips, multimedia kits, and other audiovisual materials.

CONSUMER GUIDE: 1974 BEST BUYS & DISCOUNT PRICES. 1974. Publications International, Limited,

Directories, Bibliographies, Abstracts and Indexes

3323 West Main Street, Skokie, Illinois 60076. 386 p.

Describes best buys in automobiles and a variety of major and minor applicances. Tabulates comparative retail prices, discount prices, and dealer costs. Gives recommended makes and models in each product category.

CONSUMER INFORMATION; An Index of Selected Federal Publications of Consumer Interest. Quarterly. Compiled by the U.S. General Service Administration's Consumer Product Information Center. Public Documents Distribution Center, Pueblo, Colorado 81009.

Each quarterly edition of the Consumer Information Index lists approximately 200 federal publications selected for particular interest to consumers. Most of the publications tell how to buy, use, and care for consumer products, such as appliances, automobiles, clothing. Others discuss such subjects as child care, health and safety, home maintenance, nutrition, and consumer and environmental protection. About 75 per cent of the publications are free or cost no more than $.50. Formerly called Consumer Product Information.

CONSUMER PROTECTION DIRECTORY; A Comprehensive Guide to Consumer Protection Organizations in the United States and Canada. 1975. 2nd edition. Edited by Sally R. Osberg and Thaddeus C. Trzyna. Marquis Academic Media, 200 East Ohio Street, Chicago, Illinois 60611. 466 p.

Provides information on government and private organizations concerned with consumer protection in the United States and Canada. The first part is a "User's Guide" arranged by subject topics. Other sections deal with United States federal and state government organizations, national private organizations, Canadian, international, and major foreign organizations. A second edition, along with Environmental Protection Directory, of the one-volume Directory of Consumer Protection and Environmental Agencies published in 1973.

CONSUMER PROTECTION GUIDE, 1977. c1976. By Joseph Rosenbloom. Macmillan Information, 866 Third Avenue, New York, New York 10022. 398 p.

A directory dealing with 55 different types of services, including accountants, architects, automobile repairs, banks, health insurance, dentists, doctors, employment agencies, funeral services, hospitals, hotels, household moving, insurance, lawyers, nursing, public utilities, real estate, schools, investments, appliance repairs, travel, and transportation. Information on each topic usually includes a brief overview of the type of service, education and other qualifications required for practice, complaint procedures, and directories of state licensing boards and professional associations. Other information on criteria for selecting a service, fees, specialties, contracts, and federal laws is presented, also.

A CONSUMER'S DICTIONARY OF COSMETIC INGREDIENTS. 1976. New revised and expanded edition. By Ruth Winter. Crown Publishers, Incorporated, 419 Park Avenue South, New York, New York 10016. 256 p.

Describes the chemical properties of ingredients of deodorants, shaving creams, lipsticks, skin creams, and other popular cosmetic products. Warns against harmful additives.

CONSUMERS DIRECTORY, 1973-1974. 3rd edition. The International Organization of Consumers Unions, 9 Emmastraat, The Hague, Netherlands. 160 p.

An international directory of consumer organizations arranged by country. For each organization the address, date founded, aims, main activities, publications, membership, finances, and principal officers are listed. A section on consumer periodicals published in various countries is included.

A CONSUMER'S DIRECTORY OF PRINCE GEORGE'S COUNTY DOCTORS. 1974. By Public Citizen, Incorporated, and the Health Research Group, 1346 Connecticut Avenue, N.W., Washington, D.C. 20036. 116 p.

Presents information on doctors' fees, education, accessibility, details of practice and tests administered, medication and immunization procedures. The cooperating doctors are grouped by geographic area within the county and listed under the type of practice, such as dermatology, general practice, internal medicine. For each area a list is given of non-responding and uncooperative doctors.

CONSUMER'S GUIDE TO QUEENS DOCTORS. 1976.

Directories, Bibliographies, Abstracts and Indexes

Edited by Nancy Kramer. New York Public Interest Research Group, College Union 307, Queen's College, Flushing, New York 11367.

Lists the office hours, billing practices, hospital affiliations, and other information for more than 300 general practitioners and general internists practicing in Queens County, New York. Based on a telephone survey of doctors who cooperated with the project. Includes information about house calls.

CONSUMERS INDEX TO PRODUCT EVALUATIONS AND INFORMATION SOURCES. Quarterly. Pierian Press, Post Office Box 1808, Ann Arbor, Michigan 48106.

Provides access to evaluations and informational articles about consumer products in periodicals. Pamphlets, books, and other sources of information are also indexed. Citations are arranged under such topics as: aircraft, appliances, automobiles, bicycles, boats, cameras, campers, carpets, clothing, food, insurance, motorcycles, paints, television sets, toys, travel information, and similar subjects. Annual cumulative indexes are available.

CONSUMERS UNION NEWS DIGEST. Semimonthly. By Consumers Union of United States, Incorporated. Consumers Union News Digest, Orangeburg, New York 10962.

Surveys the current literature, providing digests of articles from about 150 publications regularly scanned. Each issue contains about 50 digests. Presented in newsletter format.

DEVELOPING A RESOURCE CENTER IN CONSUMER EDUCATION: An Annotated Bibliography. 1971. Compiled by Thomas Garman, Floyd L. Crank, and Julienne V. Cochran. Northern Illinois University, Business Education Department, De Kalb, Illinois 60115.

Contains more than 1,300 entries for audiovisual materials, arranged under 18 subject categories. Also lists names and addresses of about 100 consumer organizations offering free or inexpensive materials and source of financing for each organization.

DIRECTORY OF FEDERAL, STATE, COUNTY, AND CITY GOVERNMENT CONSUMER OFFICES. 1976.

4th edition. By the U.S. Department of Health, Education, and Welfare's Office of Consumer Affairs. Superintendent of Documents, U.S. Government Printing Office, Washington, D.C. 20402. 32 p.

Lists consumer offices and consumer divisions within government organizations with addresses, telephone numbers, names and titles of people to contact. The offices and divisions were specifically established to handle consumer complaints, supply information, enforce consumer laws, conduct consumer educational programs, and represent consumer interests in other ways.

DIRECTORY OF GOVERNMENT AGENCIES SAFEGUARDING CONSUMER AND ENVIRONMENT. 1975. 6th edition. Serina Press, 70 Kennedy Street, Alexandria, Virginia 22305. 135 p.

Lists federal and state regulatory agencies under headings such as: air pollution, automobile safety, consumer product safety, consumer protection, environmental protection, food and drugs, food service, insurance, land sales and real estate, meat and poultry surveillance, movement of household effects, noise abatement, oil spills and hazardous substances, pesticides, radiation, waste management, water pollution, weights and measures. Names, addresses, and phone numbers are given for regulatory offices and people to contact.

DIRECTORY OF VOLUNTARY CONSUMER ORGANIZATIONS; A Selected Listing of Nongovernmental Organizations at the Local, State, and National Level. 1976. By the U.S. Department of Health, Education, and Welfare's Office of Consumer Affairs, State and Local Programs Division, Washington, D.C. 20201. 41 p.

Lists nonprofit organizations formed for consumer advocacy or protection and also organizations dedicated to serving the needs of special population groups, such as socio-economic, elderly, ethnic, women, etc.

EATER'S DIGEST; The Consumer's Factbook of Food Additives. 1972. By Michael F. Jacobson. Doubleday & Company, Incorporated, 501 Franklin Avenue, Garden City, New York 11530. 260 p.

Discusses why food additives are used, how they are tested, and what effects they have on consumers. A close-up look at food additives gives detailed

Directories, Bibliographies, Abstracts and Indexes

information on about 100 different additives. A close-up look at foods tells about ingredients and their proportions in a large variety of foods.

THE ENERGY INDEX. 1973-. Annual. Environment Information Center, Incorporated, 124 East 39th Street, New York, New York 10016.

Catalogs key information on critical energy issues: resources, conversion technology, consumption, and environmental impact. Indexes more than 2,000 abstracts by subject and author. Documents can be retrieved in hard copy or microfiche cards. Includes a list of energy books and films available, texts of energy laws, a list of energy-related patents, and texts of official policy statements.

ENERGY INFORMATION ABSTRACTS. 1976-. Bimonthly. Environment Information Center, Incorporated, 124 East 39th Street, New York, New York 10016.

Contains abstracts arranged under about 20 topics including: economics, policy and planning, research and development, resources and reserves, petroleum and natural gas resources, coal resources, unconventional resources, solar energy, fuel processing, fuel transport and storage, electric power generation, electric power storage and transmission, nuclear resources and power, thermonuclear power, consumption and conservation, industrial consumption, transportation consumption, residential consumption and environmental impact. The abstracting service covers about 1,000 periodicals in the energy field, as well as reports, conference proceedings, government documents, and new books. Indexed by subject, SIC code, source, and author.

ENVIRONMENT ABSTRACTS. 1970-. Monthly. Editors: James G. Kollegger and Alain R. Carr. Environment Information Center, Incorporated, 124 East 39th Street, New York, New York 10016.

Deals with ecological and pollution problems in about 20 categories of interest. Coverage includes approximately 3,500 international journals, government documents, conference papers, technical and research reports, books, and films. Provides multiple-entry subject, industry, and author indexes. Cited documents can be retrieved in hard copy or microfiche cards. Formerly called Environment Information Access.

ENVIRONMENT, U.S.A.; A Guide to Agencies, People, and Resources. 1974. Compiled and edited by the Onyx Group, Incorporated. R. R. Bowker Company, 1180 Avenue of the Americas, New York, New York 10036. 451 p.

Contains chapters on government and private environmental organizations, consultants, environmental officers of U.S. corporations, labor unions and the environment, environmental employment, education programs, libraries, fund-raising, law, conferences and meetings, films, newspapers, radio, and television. Includes a bibliography and a glossary.

ENVIRONMENTAL PROTECTION DIRECTORY. 1975. 2nd edition. Edited by Thaddeus C. Trzyna. Marquis Academic Media, 200 East Ohio Street, Chicago, Illinois 60611. 526 p.

Presents information about federal and state agencies and private organizations engaged in environmental protection activities. Contains a User's Guide arranged by subject topics. Also includes sections on Canadian, international, and major foreign organizations. A second edition, along with Consumer Protection Directory, of the one-volume Directory of Consumer Protection and Environmental Agencies published in 1973.

ENVIRONMENTAL QUALITY ABSTRACTS. 1975-. Quarterly. Editor: Christine Maddox. Data Courier, Incorporated, 620 South Fifth Street, Louisville, Kentucky 40202.

Includes abstracts from about 200 periodicals published in English primarily in the United States. The abstracts are arranged under the topics: public policy, population and health, conservation and endangered species, resources and recycling, and energy resources. Also includes a digest of current news on environmental quality, a book review section, and environmental updates for each main subject section.

ENVIRONMENTAL VALUES, 1860-1972; A Guide to Information Sources. 1976. By Loren C. Owings. Man and the Environment Information Guide Series, volume 4. Gale Research Company, Book Tower, Detroit, Michigan 48226. 324 p.

An annotated bibliography of material about American attitudes concerning nature and the human environment. Some of the topics covered are: Man and Nature in

Directories, Bibliographies, Abstracts and Indexes

America, Conservation and the Idea of Wilderness, Conservation and the Preservation of Natural Beauty, Conservation and the Ecological Ethic, Camping and Outdoor Life.

GUIDE TO FEDERAL CONSUMER SERVICES. 1976. By the U.S. Department of Health, Education, and Welfare's Office of Consumer Affairs. Superintendent of Documents, U.S. Government Printing Office, Washington, D.C. 20402. 39 p.

Describes the consumer services of federal agencies and departments. Provides information on component organizations, purposes, principal laws administered, functions for consumers, how they are performed, and how to obtain service.

A GUIDE TO SOURCES OF CONSUMER INFORMATION. 1973. By Sarah M. Thomas and Bernadine Weddington. Information Resources Press, 2100 M Street, N.W., Washington, D.C. 20037. 177 p.

Part I, Published Information, includes books, directories, bibliographies, documents, indexes, and periodicals published in the United States since 1960. Part II, Organizations, contains descriptions of federal, state, and local government organizations, and national associations and companies concerned with consumer interests. The entries include information about publications and audiovisual materials.

INFORMATION FOR EVERYDAY SURVIVAL; What You Need and Where to Find It. 1976. Compiled by Priscilla Gotsick, Sharon Moore, Susan Cotner, and Joan Flanery. American Library Association, 50 East Huron Street, Chicago, Illinois 60611. 403 p.

An annotated listing of materials that contain information helpful in solving everyday problems. Books, pamphlets, films, filmstrips, tapes, games, and records are listed alphabetically by title in thirteen major categories: aging, children, community, education, family, free time, health, home, jobs, law and government, money management, self and others, and transportation. Each major category is divided into subcategories. The table of contents and index provide access to subject areas covered.

MAIL ORDER USA; A Consumer's Guide to over 1,500 Top Mail Order Catalogs in the United States and Canada. 2nd edition. By Dorothy O'Callaghan. Mail Order USA, Post Office Box 19083, Washington, D.C. 20036.

Contains names, addresses, and specialties of business firms publishing catalogs which are available at little or no cost. Arranged by categories such as housewares, gifts, sporting goods, clothes, hardware, needlecrafts, garden supplies, toys, and hobbies.

THE MERCHANT AND THE POOR: A SELECTED BIBLIOGRAPHY. 1970. Compiled by Marian O. Boner. Exchange Bibliography #129. Council of Planning Librarians, Post Office Box 229, Monticello, Illinois 61856. 5 p.

A bibliography on consumer problems of the poor, including entries on consumer credit, finance, legal protection, education, and related topics. Arranged by main entry. Gives bibliographic data.

NATIONAL MAIL ORDER CATALOG DIRECTORY. 1976. C & M Enterprises, Post Office Box 24, Staten Island, New York 10304.

Gives names, addresses, and specialties of business firms that do business by mail and publish comprehensive catalogs. The entries are arranged by topics such as housewares, sporting goods, gifts, clothes, hardware, toys and hobbies, garden supplies, stereo equipment, health foods, government surplus, and other categories.

PEOPLE'S YELLOW PAGES. 1976. Vocations for Social Change, 353 Broadway, Cambridge, Massachusetts 02139.

An annotated directory to business concerns that care about customer satisfaction. Most of the enterprises listed tend to be cooperatives or collectives or nonprofit groups. Arranged by categories, including sections on jobs, health, landlords. Covers the New England area; similar directories are being prepared in other areas.

PEOPLE'S YELLOW PAGES OF AMERICA. 1974. By Scott R. French. Richard Heller & Son, Incorporated, 90 Daisy Farms Drive, New Rochelle, New York 10804. 256 p.

Directories, Bibliographies, Abstracts and Indexes

A directory of "non-rip-off, people-oriented groups, services, and facilities throughout the United States." Arranged by topics such as bikes, clinics, communes, co-ops, electronics, energy, health, housing, legal, peace, prisoners, switchboards, volunteers, wilderness, women, youth. Includes many small, recently established organizations. Emphasis is on groups interested in helping people and performing honest service.

POLLUTION ABSTRACTS. 1970-. 6 times a year. Pollution Abstracts, Incorporated, 620 South Fifth Street, Louisville, Kentucky 40202.

Presents abstracts of articles, reports, proceedings, and books on environmental topics, such as air and water pollution, solid wastes, noise pollution, pesticides, radiation, and general environmental quality. Each issue contains subject and author indexes. Annual cumulative indexes are also available. Photocopies of most of the material abstracted can be obtained.

REFERENCE GUIDE FOR CONSUMERS. 1975. By Nina David. R. R. Bowker Company, 1180 Avenue of the Americas, New York, New York 10036. 327 p.

Part I consists of an annotated bibliography of multimedia materials arranged by subject areas. Part II describes government and private organizations active in the consumer field in the United States and Canada. Part III lists consumer columns in newspapers in the United States and Canada.

A RESOURCE DIRECTORY OF SELECTED CONSUMER EDUCATION MATERIALS FOR GRADES K-8. 1976. State Board of Education, Program Planning & Development Section, 100 North First Street, Springfield, Illinois 62777. 39 p.

An annotated bibliography listing books, periodicals, resource guides, films, filmstrips, multimedia kits and other materials for consumer education.

S.O.S. - SAVE ON SHOPPING! Shopper Recommended Good Buys for '75. 1975. By Iris Ellis, Post Office Box 96, Dearborn, Michigan 48121. 200 p.

A directory of factory outlet and sample stores in the United States and Canada arranged by state and city. Lists names, addresses, telephone numbers, the types of products on sale, discounts offered, times of special sales, and type of payment accepted.

SELECTED AND ANNOTATED BIBLIOGRAPHY OF REFERENCE MATERIAL IN CONSUMER CREDIT. 1972. National Consumer Finance Association, 1000 16th Street, N.W., Washington, D.C. 20036.

Lists textbooks, monographs, study guides; published and unpublished articles, addresses, and papers; pamphlets and booklets; audiovisual materials; and proceedings of state and national consumer credit conferences.

SELECTED GUIDE TO MAKE-IT, FIX-IT, DO-IT-YOURSELF BOOKS. 1973. Edited by Susan Nueckel. Fleet Press Corporation, 156 Fifth Avenue, New York, New York 10010. 213 p.

An annotated bibliography for people interested in using and enjoying skills and techniques usually reserved for professional workers. Arranged by field of interest, such as archaeology, dieting, childbirth.

SELECTED U.S. GOVERNMENT PUBLICATIONS. Monthly. Superintendent of Documents, U.S. Government Printing Office, Washington, D.C. 20402.

Presents annotated lists of new publications for sale by the U.S. Government Printing Office. Each issue contains sections featuring such topics as food, health, environment, energy, education, recreation, transportation, taxes, and employment.

SOURCE CATALOG: COMMUNICATIONS. 1971. By Source, Incorporated. Swallow Press, Incorporated, 1139 South Wabash Avenue, Chicago, Illinois 60605. 118 p.

Shares information about groups, projects, books, and films applicable to the movement to liberate America and return its control to the people. The catalog is designed to encourage the building of creative working relationships among people through intensified communication. Describes projects and resources in the areas of mass media, art, music, theater, film, television, radio, periodicals, printing-publishing, language, libraries, and community communications.

Directories, Bibliographies, Abstracts and Indexes

SOURCE CATALOG: COMMUNITIES/HOUSING. 1972. By Source, Incorporated. Swallow Press, Incorporated, 1139 South Wabash Avenue, Chicago, Illinois 60605. 255 p.

Assists people in locating resource tools - organizations, strategies, books, and films - that will enable them to improve their housing and communities. Contains sections on organizing for basic tenant rights, legal aid, public housing, open housing, elderly and handicapped, temporary housing, rural and urban housing.

TRADE NAMES DICTIONARY. 1976. Edited by Ellen T. Crowley. 2 volumes. Gale Research Company, Book Tower, Detroit, Michigan 48226.

A guide to trade names, brand names, product names, coined names, model names, and design names, with addresses of their manufacturers, importers, marketers, or distributors. Covers: apparel, appliances, automobiles, beverages, candy, cosmetics, decorative accessories, drugs, fabrics, food, furniture, games, glass products, hardware, jewelry, paper products, pet supplies, tobacco products, toys, and other consumer-oriented items. Trade names and company names are interfiled in one alphabetical arrangement.

WASHINGTON INFORMATION DIRECTORY. 1977-78. Edited by Robert E. Healy. Congressional Quarterly, Incorporated, 1414 22nd Street, N.W., Washington, D.C. 20037.

Presents sources of information in 16 subject areas, including health and consumer affairs; employment and labor; energy; housing and urban affairs; individual assistance programs; law and justice; natural resources, environment and agriculture. Key government agencies, personnel, and congressional committees are given for each major topic. Additional government and private organizations and committees are arranged by subtopics. At the end of each major section a bibliography contains references to books, periodicals, and other pertinent material arranged by title. New editions have been produced annually.

THE WHOLE WASHINGTON HANDBOOK; Where to Go and What to Know in the Metropolitan Area. 1975. By Marion Ein and Alice Shabecoff. Robert B. Luce, Incorporated, 2000 N Street, N.W., Suite 103, Washington, D.C. 20036. 350 p.

A comprehensive index to services, agencies, programs, and activities available in the Washington, D.C., area. Arranged under 20 subject topics including adoption, children, community, consumer, education, the elderly, employment, environment, the handicapped, legal, licenses, municipal services, recreation, taxes, transportation. Each entry gives the name, address, and phone number and describes the services offered by the organization.

Books and Pamphlets

AIR TRAVEL BARGAINS; How to Get the Lowest Fares on All Airlines World Wide & U.S.A. 1975. 10th edition. By Jim Woodman. Air Travel Bargains Worldwide Guidebook, Post Office Box 897, Coconut Grove, Miami, Florida 33133.

Gives details about special bargain fares offered by various airlines. Explains the advantages of traveling at off-seasons, with stopovers, on charter flights, on special category fares, and on bargain air tours all over the world. New features are fly-drive bargains and air-sea bargains.

ALL ABOUT AUCTIONS. 1975. By L. G. Hewitt. Chilton Book Company, 201 King of Prussia Road, Radnor, Pennsylvania 19089.

Discusses the purposes, organization, procedures, and advantages of auctions. Tells about the sources and quality of merchandise offered, the functions of auctioneers, useful bidding techniques, and how to avoid common mistakes when bidding at an auction.

AMERICA THE BEAUTIFUL; A Modern Guide to Sex, Security, and the Soft Buck. 1968. Edited by Joel Lieber. David White, Incorporated, 60 East 55th Street, New York, New York 10022. 207 p.

A book about money and sex, American-style, and outrageous but successful selling practices. Tells how the merchants of sex and security prey on our fears and anxieties, sexual frustrations, and naiveté to exploit gullible buyers from the cradle to the grave.

THE AMERICAN CONSUMER; Issues and Decisions. 1973. By Herbert M. Jelley and Robert O. Herrmann. Gregg Division of McGraw-Hill Book Company, 1221 Avenue of the Americas, New York, New York 10020. 502 p.

A consumer education text designed to help the student recognize his needs, gather pertinent data, and make intelligent decisions. Emphasizes controversial consumer issues and problems involved in choosing products and services - from furniture and vacation trips to cars and life insurance.

THE AMERICAN FOOD SCANDAL; Why You Can't Eat Well on What You Earn. 1974. By William Robbins. William Morrow & Company, Incorporated, 105 Madison Avenue, New York 10016. 280 p.

Explains how giant corporations and conglomerates have gained a stranglehold on food growing, processing, and selling. Shows why consumers must pay super prices in the supermarket for foods lacking in taste and variety. Reveals the health hazards in eating American processed foods, the high cost of political payoffs and government grain deals, and the effects of politics on food inspection and inflation.

AN ANALYSIS OF EMPLOYMENT AGENCY PRACTICES IN MONTGOMERY AND PRINCE GEORGE'S COUNTIES, MARYLAND; A MaryPIRG Report. 1974. By John Vitarello. Maryland Public Interest Research Group, Room 0137, Armory, University of Maryland, College Park, Maryland 20742. 39 p.

Uncovers unethical and illegal activities of many employment agencies. Explores four different problem areas: sex discrimination, bait and switch advertising, handling of fee contracts, and agency fees. Includes MaryPIRG's findings, recommendations for action, and advice to consumers for each problem area.

ANSWERS TO YOUR EVERYDAY MONEY QUESTIONS. 1968. By Lorraine L. Blair. Henry Regnery Company, 180 North Michigan Avenue, Chicago, Illinois 60601. 200 p.

Offers specific advice on saving, investing, house purchasing, bargain hunting, using credit, buying a car, taxes, and even on becoming a millionaire. Stresses learning to use money in the most effective way to achieve personal goals.

AUTO REPAIR FRAUDS; How to Prevent Your Car from Driving You to the Poorhouse. 1976. By Monty Norris. Arco Publishing Company, Incorporated, 219 Park Avenue, South, New York, New York 10003. 187 p.

Tells how to avoid auto repair gyp artists and also how to take care of your car for best service and fewer repairs. Includes addresses of organizations to write to for help in the United States and Canada.

THE BARGAIN HUCKSTERS. 1962. By Ralph Lee Smith. Thomas Y. Crowell Company, 666 Fifth

Books and Pamphlets

Avenue, New York, New York 10019. 236 p.

Exposes the schemes and tricks of hucksters offering false bargains and misleading advertising. Discusses "bait and switch" tactics, fictitiously high "list prices", deceptive telephone and door-to-door sales. Describes the snares and traps laid by unscrupulous car dealers, home improvement schemers, and funeral directors. Warns consumers about mail order frauds, phony charities, and misleading advertising.

BE A SMART SHOPPER. 1974. By Kathlyn Gay. Julian Messner, 1 West 39th Street, New York, New York 10018. 64 p.

A book for juveniles explaining choices for consumers, various types of purchases, reasons for buying, "ballyhoo" advertising, how to find the best buy, and protections for consumers. Attractive format and illustrations. Ends with eight steps for action to become a responsible consumer.

THE BEST. 1974. By Peter Passell and Leonard Ross. Farrar, Straus and Giroux, Incorporated, 19 Union Square West, New York, New York 10003. 169 p.

A compendium of advice about the best products, places, services, sayings, and various other oddities. Short entries, rather whimsical, are arranged more or less alphabetically. Includes cameras, peanut butter, bicycles, champagne, vacation spots and restaurants, diets, museums, and a myriad of other topics.

BETTER TIMES. 1975. Edited by Frances Cerra. Doubleday & Company, Incorporated, 501 Franklin Avenue, Garden City, New York, New York 11530. 319 p.

Explores possibilities and solutions for dealing with consumer problems of the seventies. Includes articles on food, clothing, shelter, energy, credit, health, jobs, government aid, legal advice, and travel suggestions. Contains charts, diagrams, tables, special tips, and other aids for consumers.

THE BILLION $ SWINDLE, FRAUDS AGAINST THE ELDERLY. 1969. By Amram Ducovny. Fleet Press, 156 Fifth Avenue, New York, New York 10010. 252 p.

Reviews problems uncovered by Senate investigations. Points out areas where fraud has been practiced against the elderly.

THE BOOM IN GOING BUST. 1968. By George Sullivan. Macmillan Company, 866 Third Avenue, New York, New York 10022. 215 p.

Defines bankruptcy and explains the various types. Examines the typical bankrupt and analyzes the reasons why be became one. Surveys the problems of credit, collection, and debt. Describes the advantages and disadvantages of bankruptcy and how to file a petition. Explains the pitfalls, the fees, the legal, financial, and social ramifications of being declared a bankrupt.

BREAK THE BANKS: A SHOPPER'S GUIDE TO BANKING SERVICES. 1973. San Francisco Consumer Action, 312 Sutter Street, San Francisco, California 94108. 63 p.

Contains much valuable information on banking services provided in California. Helps people in other areas to shop wisely for bank services.

BRIDE'S: BUYERS' GUIDE FOR YOUNG HOMEMAKERS. 1972. Consumer Guide, Skokie, Illinois. Distributed by Doubleday & Company, Incorporated, 501 Franklin Avenue, Garden City, New York 11530. 97 p.

Contains brief chapters on food preparation appliances, clocks, cookware and kitchen utensils, home care appliances, money management, supermarket shopping, dinnerware, furniture, silverware, etc. Describes and rates various brands of household products.

BUSINESS AND CONSUMER EDUCATION CASE STUDIES. 1976. Phi Chapter, Delta Pi Epsilon, 254 Peik Hall, University of Minnesota, Minneapolis, Minnesota 55455. 30 p.

Consumer case studies illustrate situations that students experienced in the fields of credit, money management, banking and finance, rights and responsibilities, insurance, and related topics. The first 23 of the 58 case studies are concerned with the business environment, business enterprise, and labor relations.

Books and Pamphlets

BUSINESS AND THE CONSUMER; The Creative Interface. 1971. By Peter Weaver, Miles W. Kirkpatrick, and H. Bruce Palmer. Volume 4 of the American University Lectures in Business-Government Relations. School of Business Administration, American University, Washington, D.C. 20016. 57 p.

A group of lectures focusing on the problems, needs, and evolving trends of consumerism. The first lecture deals with the consumerism complex of businessmen, bureaucrats, and buyers. The second discusses the Federal Trade Commission as an adversary on behalf of consumers. The third lecture suggests "progressive enterprise" as an alternative way of dealing with modern consumerism.

BUY IT RIGHT; A Shoppers Guide to Home Furnishings. 3rd edition. 1974. By Jan Brown. Career Institute, Consumer Services Division, 555 East Lange Street, Mundelein, Illinois 60060. 172 p.

Offers tips on buying furniture, including bedding, carpeting, draperies, lighting, and other home furnishings. Gives advice on decorating and furniture maintenance. Contains guides to plastics, fibers, and fabrics, and checklists for shopping.

BUY IT RIGHT! An Introduction to Consumerism. 1974. By Jean Ende and Clifford J. Earl. E. P. Dutton & Company, 201 Park Avenue South, New York, New York 10003. 207 p.

Tells what to watch for in buying food, cars (new and used), clothing, furniture, a house, repairs, insurance, and credit. Gives advice about budgets and what to do if cheated.

BUY NOW, PAY LATER. 1961. By Hillel Black. William Morrow & Company, Incorporated, 105 Madison Avenue, New York, New York 10016. 240 p.

Reports on consumer credit practices. Reveals intricacies and various devices used to conceal from the consumer what he is required to pay. Investigates the meaning of debt living and how it affects individual lives.

BUYER BEWARE! 1965. By Fred Trump. Abingdon Press, 201 Eighth Avenue South, Nashville, Tennessee 37203. 207 p.

Exposes deceptive advertising and selling practices. Presents reliable information on hundreds of schemes designed to defraud consumers. Tells how they operate, how to avoid being victimized, and what to do if you are.

BUYER BEWARE! A Report on Product Safety and the Cost of Credit in the Retail Industry. 1973. Council on Economic Priorities, 84 Fifth Avenue, New York, New York 10011.

Reveals that many unsafe products are still on the market, such as children's sleepwear not labelled flame-retardant, power tools without double insulation, unsafe lawnmowers, mattresses not labelled flame-retardant, and hazardous toys. Discloses wide variations in methods of computing finance credit charges in different states and companies. Reports on incomplete, confusing information on credit agreements.

BUYING LOTS FROM DEVELOPERS. 1974. By the U.S. Department of Housing and Urban Development. Superintendent of Documents, U.S. Government Printing Office, Washington, D.C. 20402. 32 p.

Cautions prospective buyers to know their rights, know the developer, find out facts about the lot, and be aware of nine dishonest sales practices. Explains the Interstate Land Sales Act of 1968 and tells how to complain if cheated in a transaction covered by the Act.

CAN YOU BE SURE OF YOUR EXPERTS? A Complete Manual on How to Choose and Use Doctors, Lawyers, Brokers - and All the Other Experts in Your Life. 1969. By Roger A. Golde. Macmillan Company, Collier-Macmillan Canada Limited, 1125b Leslie Street, Don Mills, Ontario, Canada. 243 p.

Tells how to get good advice from experts - doctors, lawyers, accountants, investment brokers, teachers, or architects. Each chapter ends with a summary of points to consider in selecting and evaluating a type of professional for expertise.

Books and Pamphlets

CAPTAINS OF CONSCIOUSNESS; Advertising and the Social Roots of the Consumer Culture. 1976. By Stuart Ewen. McGraw-Hill Book Company, Incorporated, 1221 Avenue of the Americas, New York, New York 10020.

Explores the development of mass consumption and modern advertising in the early twentieth century. Explains the use of advertising by capitalists as a mechanism to control social values and manipulate the daily lives of consumers.

CASH AND CREDIT. 1974. By Moses Campbell, Jr. Vantage Press, 516 West 34th Street, New York, New York 10001. 55 p.

Examines many facets of the credit system and explains why cash payments result in large savings. Contains chapters on money lenders, collection agencies, credit cards, bankruptcy, buying a home, mortgage foreclosure, truth in lending, and the philosophy of profit.

CAVEAT EMPTOR! An Introductory Analysis of Consumer Problems. 1975. By Roger M. Swagler. D.C. Heath and Company, 125 Spring Street, Lexington, Massachusetts 02173. 269 p.

Explains consumer problems created by affluence and a large, complex marketplace. Discusses consumer economics, fraud, psychic enjoyment in consumption, evaluating choices, future developments, the need for information, advertising, consumer organization, government protection, the plight of low-income consumers, and the need for a "buyer beware" attitude. Includes study questions, suggested projects, and bibliographies at the end of each chapter.

THE CHALLENGE OF CONSUMERISM; A Symposium. 1971. The Conference Board, Incorporated, 845 Third Avenue, New York, New York 10022. 90 p.

A collection of reports presented at a marketing conference. Deals with business and government responsibilities to consumers, rising consumer expectations, advertising myths, consumer activism, responsible promotion policies, improving consumer products and services, educating and protecting the consumer.

CHAMPAGNE LIVING ON A BEER BUDGET; How to Buy the Best for Less. 1968. By Mike and Marilyn Ferguson. G.P. Putnam's Sons, 200 Madison Avenue, New York, New York 10016. 271 p.

Gives tricks of the trade in living well on a modest income. Tells about shopping for true bargains, such as off-season items.

THE CHEMICAL ADDITIVES IN BOOZE. 1972. By Michael Jacobson and Joel Anderson. Center for Science in the Public Interest, 1757 S Street, Northwest, Washington, D.C. 20036. 38 p.

Advocates government action on labeling regulations and on eliminating harmful substances from alcoholic beverages. Discusses the use of cobalt salts in beer production leading to fatalities in 1966, and a preservative in some wines that generates a cancer-causing agent called urethan. Questions the regular use in liquor of coloring and flavoring agents like glycyrrhizin, whose physiological effects have not been adequately tested.

THE CHEMICAL FEAST; Nader Task Force Report on the Food and Drug Administration. 1970. Edited by James S. Turner. Grossman Publishers, 625 Madison Avenue New York, New York 10022. 273 p.

Decries the lack of control over careless use of pesticides and other chemicals which pollute the environment.

CITIZEN NADER. 1972. By Charles McCarry. Saturday Review Press, 201 Park Avenue, South, New York, New York 10003. 335 p.

Traces Nader's progress from the publication of <u>Unsafe at any Speed</u> through the enactment of various reform measures in the fields of safety, health, pollution control, and government responsiveness to consumer interests. Details his work with Congressional committees, the pressure tactics he has used, his extensive speaking engagements, and Nader's Raiders.

THE CLAIMS GAME. 1969. By Vladimir P. Chernik. Sherbourne Press, Incorporated, Award Books, 235 East 45th Street, New York, New York 10017. 208 p.

Gives information on secrets of settling, winning, and collecting insurance claims on your own.

A COMMONSENSE GUIDE TO DOCTORS, HOSPITALS AND MEDICAL CARE. 1964. By R. H. Blum. Macmillan Publishing Company, 866 Third Avenue, New York, New York 10022. 333 p.

A practical handbook for consumers seeking information on medical care. Provides advice on how to select and use a doctor, how to change doctors or arrange a consultation, how to choose a hospital, and how to make a choice between medical insurance plans.

Books and Pamphlets

THE COMPLETE FOOD HANDBOOK. 1976. By Rodger P. Doyle and James L. Redding. Grove Press, 196 West Houston Street, New York, New York 10014. 318 p.

A buying guide and reference tool presenting important information on how to avoid health hazards and economic pitfalls in shopping for food products.

THE CONSUMER. 1970. Compiled by Gerald Leinwand. Pocket Books Division of Simon & Schuster, Incorporated, 630 Fifth Avenue, New York, New York 10020. 190 p.

Points out the difficulties the consumer faces in making wise choices. Explains the problems of grade labeling and comparison shopping. Part One presents an overview; Part Two includes selected readings on consumer problems.

THE CONSUMER ADVOCATE VERSUS THE CONSUMER. 1972. By Ralph K. Winter, Jr. American Enterprise Institute for Public Policy Research, 1150 17th Street, Northwest, Washington, D.C. 20036. 16 p.

Discusses the ideology of consumerism and the cure offered by the consumer advocate. Questions the soundness of the ideology of consumerism. Argues that the cure of consumer advocacy - a consumer protection agency - is worse than the disease.

THE CONSUMER AND CORPORATE ACCOUNTABILITY. 1973. Edited by Ralph Nader. Harcourt, Brace, Jovanovich, Incorporated, 757 Third Avenue, New York, New York 10017. 375 p.

Presents articles documenting the costs in diminished health, safety, and consumer income caused by unscrupulous business practices. Includes chapters on: Corporate Disregard for Life; Truth versus Profits in Advertising; Consumer Waste and Frustration; Compulsory Consumption; The Regulatory-Industrial Complex; Protection of the Poor; Dissent from Within; The New Accountability: An Agenda for Action.

THE CONSUMER AND HIS DOLLARS. 1975. 3rd revised edition. By David Schoenfeld and Arthur A. Natella. Oceana Publications, Incorporated, 75 Main Street, Dobbs Ferry, New York 10522.

A high school and college textbook designed to develop an awareness of the importance of making wise consumer decisions. Alerts the reader to watch for pitfalls and to consider carefully the choices available to him.

CONSUMER BEWARE! Your Food and What's Been Done to It. 1971. By Beatrice Trum Hunter. Simon & Schuster, 630 Fifth Avenue, New York, New York 10020. 442 p.

Explains adverse effects of food processing and production methods. Emphasizes the importance of good, wholesome food for good health. Suggests ways to counteract the present trend toward unhealthful foods.

THE CONSUMER BOOK OF HINTS & TIPS. 1977. By Richard Trubo. Jonathan David Publishers, Incorporated, 68-22 Eliot Avenue, Middle Village, New York 11379.

CONSUMER BUYING FOR BETTER LIVING. 1961. By Cleo Fitzsimmons. John Wiley & Sons, Incorporated, 605 Third Avenue, New York, New York 10016. 546 p.

Deals with basic problems in purchasing goods. Aids consumers in understanding the market and their position in it. Offers advice on buying food, housing, clothing, and equipment, as well as health, transportation, recreation, and insurance services.

CONSUMER CHOICE: The Economics of Personal Living. 1977. By Andrew J. Allentuck and Gordon E. Bivens. Harcourt, Brace, Jovanovich, Incorporated, 757 Third Avenue, New York, New York 10017. 525 p.

Discusses consumer choices in the fields of credit, insurance, investments, food, shelter, clothing. Also deals with careers, taxes, estate planning, checking accounts, nutrition, transportation, corporations and social responsibility, values and life styles.

CONSUMER CHOICE IN THE AMERICAN ECONOMY. 1967. By Carolyn Shaw Bell. Random House,

Books and Pamphlets

Incorporated, 201 East 50th Street, New York, New York 10022. 429 p.

Discusses how the "scarce means" of consumer purchasing power is apportioned among the many alternatives of spending and saving. Chapter 9 deals with consumer information, credit, protection, and warranties.

THE CONSUMER COMPLAINT DIRECTORY. 1973. By Jack White, Gary Yanker, and Robert Greenfield. Peter H. Wyden, Incorporated, Publisher. Distributed by David McKay Company, Incorporated, 750 Third Avenue, New York, New York 10017.

Three Columbia University lawyers show how to cut red tape and get results when consumers face problems such as a late Social Security check, crooked television repairman, or phone that doesn't work. Tells how to use the many new weapons available to consumers.

CONSUMER CREDIT REFORM. 1970. Edited by Clark C. Havighurst. Library of Law & Contempotary Problems. Oceana Publications, Incorporated, 75 Main Street, Dobbs Ferry, New York 10522. 160 p.

Presents papers from a symposium held at Duke University. Traces the remarkable growth in consumer credit from 1954 to 1968. Includes discussions on consumer credit in the affluent society, legislative control of consumer credit transactions, revolving credit and credit cards, and the new federal attack on the loan shark problem.

CONSUMER ECONOMIC PROBLEMS. 1977. 9th edition. By Roman F. Warmke and Eugene D. Wyllie. South-Western Publishing Company, 5101 Madison Road, Cincinnati, Ohio 45227.

A college textbook relating personal economic decision-making to the total economy. Includes sections on: Money Management, The Consumer and the Market, Protection through Insurance, and Problems of Obtaining a Home.

CONSUMER ECONOMICS. 1974. By James F. Niss. Prentice-Hall, Incorporated, Englewood Cliffs, New Jersey 07632. 193 p.

Discusses consumer economics in relation to daily decision-making processes. Contains chapters on: budgeting, techniques of choice making, buying goods and services, consumer credit, economics of housing, income distribution, occupations and occupational choice, insurance and investments, and case studies in family financial planning.

CONSUMER FINANCE. 1977. By Louis J. DeSalvo. John Wiley & Sons, Incorporated, 605 Third Avenue, New York, New York 10016. 350 p.

Deals with consumer management, consumer spending, and consumer planning. In addition to these three major sections, appendices contain addresses of government and nongovernment consumer organizations.

CONSUMER FINANCE: A CASE HISTORY IN AMERICAN BUSINESS. 1970. By Irving S. Michelman. Augustus M. Kelley Publishers, 305 Allwood Road, Clifton, New Jersey 07012. 336 p.

Reviews the social and economic forces and ideas involved in the growth of consumer credit in the twentieth century. Gives a history of abusive practices and attempts to regulate financial dealings to protect consumers. Gives an account of the consumer finance industry and the installment way of life.

CONSUMER GUIDE TO PRODUCT INFORMATION. 1977. Edited by Bess Myerson. Bristol-Myers Company, 345 Park Avenue, New York, New York 10022. 122 p.

Describes types of products available and their safe and proper use. Major topics covered are: non-prescription drugs, nutritional products, household products, personal care products, and personal care appliances. For each type of product "important safeguards" are enumerated. Also includes short sections on prescription drugs, aerosols, writing an effective complaint letter, and a listing of Bristol-Myers consumer products.

CONSUMER GUIDE TO USED AND SURPLUS HOME APPLIANCES AND FURNISHINGS. 1973. By Patricia Wilson. Houghton Mifflin Company, 2 Park Street, Boston, Massachusetts 02107. 182 p.

Offers many useful tips on the availability of used

Books and Pamphlets

and surplus household goods, what to look for in specific items such as sewing machines and vacuum cleaners, and types of guarantees available. A handy guide for budget-conscious shoppers.

CONSUMER HEALTH: PRODUCTS AND SERVICES. 1976. By Jessie Helen Haag. Lea & Febiger, 600 South Washington Square, Philadelphia, Pennsylvania 19106. 268 p.

Provides information to enable the consumer to make wise decisions concerning purchases of health products and services. Part I, Consumer Beware! warns about quackery, food faddism, cults and fallacies, questionable health care, and health advertising. Part II, Wise Consumer, discusses health insurance, prescription and over-the-counter drugs, consumer protection agencies, physicians, dentists, nurses, and hospitals.

THE CONSUMER IN AMERICAN SOCIETY: ADDITIONAL DIMENSIONS. 1974. 5th edition. Compiled by Jack L. Taylor, Jr. and Arch W. Troelstrup. McGraw-Hill Book Company, Incorporated, 1221 Avenue of the Americas, New York, New York 10020. 451 p.

Part 1 contains articles on the modern consumer in our society, decision-making, advertising, and money management. Part 2 discusses budgeting, consumer credit, buying food, clothing, housing, automobiles, health care, insurance, savings and investments, and taxes. Part 3 includes informative articles on consumer protection and the international consumer movement.

CONSUMER INFORMATION HANDBOOK: EUROPE AND NORTH AMERICA. 1974. By Hans B. Thorelli and Sarah V. Thorelli. Praeger Special Studies in International Economics and Development. Praeger Publishers, 111 Fourth Avenue, New York, New York 10003. 525 p.

A study of independent consumer information programs carried on by private and public organizations in the North Atlantic community of nations. Part I covers Prototype Consumer Information Programs; Part II contains Surveys of Countries; Part III discusses International Organizations. Gives details of the history, structure, programs, finances, publications, and activities of the consumer organizations. Published in cooperation with Consumer Research Institute.

CONSUMER INFORMATION SYSTEMS & CONSUMER POLICY. 1977. By Hans B. Thorelli and Sarah V. Thorelli. Ballinger Publishing Company, 17 Dunster Street, Harvard Square, Cambridge, Massachusetts 02138.

An in-depth analysis of the experiences, problems, and prospects of independent consumer information programs. Focuses on clusters of subject matter rather than on organizations and countries.

CONSUMER PROBLEMS AND MARKETING PATTERNS IN LOW-INCOME NEIGHBORHOODS: AN EXPLORATORY STUDY. 1969. By Robert J. Holloway and Richard N. Cardozo. Graduate School of Business Administration, University of Minnesota, Minneapolis, Minnesota 55455. 62 p.

A study of the problems of poor people and their buying habits as consumers. Concentrates on marketing problems in low-income neighborhoods in Minneapolis and Saint Paul. Examines the problems of retailers and the adequacy of their efforts to serve low-income neighborhoods. Offers conclusions and recommendations for solving problems of low-income groups and the retailers who sell to them.

CONSUMER PROTECTION; A Symposium. 1972. Da Capo Press, Incorporated, 227 West 17th Street, New York, New York 10011. 137 p.

Presents symposium papers on provisions of the proposed Uniform Consumer Credit Code (U3C); enforceability of the U3C; limiting the use of negotiable notes and waiver-of-defense clauses in consumer sales; consumer protection under the Uniform Commercial Code; and increasing low-income consumer buying and borrowing power by cooperative action.

CONSUMER PROTECTION IN THE STATES. 1970. By the Council of State Governments, Iron Works Pike, Lexington, Kentucky 40505. 39 p.

Discusses consumer problems related to the marketing system, health and safety, deceptive and fraudulent selling, and credit abuses. Contains sections titled: What Are the Consumers' Problems?; How Should the Consumer be Protected?; and What the States are Doing.

Books and Pamphlets

CONSUMER PROTECTION LABS. 1975. By Melvin Berger. John Day Company, Incorporated, 257 Park Avenue South, New York, New York 10010.

A study of the methods used by scientists in various government, industry, and nonprofit private laboratories for the purpose of consumer protection. Describes scientists at work inspecting, testing, analyzing, and researching the properties and effects of foods, drugs, and other products used by consumers.

CONSUMER PROTECTION: REPORTING SERVICE. 1973. By Donald P. Rothschild and David W. Carroll. W. H. Anderson Publishing Company, 646 Main Street, Cincinnati, Ohio 45201. Looseleaf.

A reporting service produces supplements every six months to update the looseleaf binder material. Part One deals with law techniques for consumer protection at the federal, state, local, and private levels. Part Two covers federal government administration of consumer protection statutes. Part Three discusses state protection of the consumer. Part Four deals with local consumer protection. And Part Five outlines consumer protection activities by private institutions.

CONSUMER SKILLS. 1977. By Irene Oppenheim. Bennett Publishing Company, 102 Charles Street, Boston, Massachusetts 02114.

THE CONSUMER SURVIVAL BOOK; How to Fight Inflation. 1976. By Marvin L. Bittinger. Barron's Educational Services, Incorporated, 113 Crossways Park Drive, Woodbury, New York 11797. 216 p.

Contains many useful tips on how to save money on food, clothing, housing and home maintenance, automobiles, taxes, legal aid, and similar topics.

CONSUMER SURVIVAL KIT. 1975. Adapted by John Dorfman from the television series by the Maryland Center for Public Broadcasting. Praeger Publishers, 111 Fourth Avenue, New York, New York 10003.

A guide to values in the marketplace: what to look for and what to avoid in food, clothing, housing, transportation, and other goods and services.

CONSUMER SWINDLERS AND HOW TO AVOID THEM. 1970. By John L. Springer. Henry Regnery Company, 180 North Michigan Avenue, Chicago, Illinois 60610. 246 p.

Catalogues the major kinds of deception practiced upon American consumers. Describes the swindlers and their methods and tells how to detect fraudulent activities by repairmen, home improvement contractors, investment companies, real estate firms, medical quacks, and credit organizations. Discusses mail and phone swindles, "bargain sales", and pitfalls to avoid in signing contracts.

CONSUMERISM: A NEW AND GROWING FORCE IN THE MARKETPLACE. 1970. 3rd edition. By Burson-Marsteller Public Relations, 1776 K Street, Northwest, Washington, D.C. 20006. 52 p.

Discusses activities of consumer forces and their organizations. Summarizes consumer legislation in the sixties and proposed consumer laws. Suggests constructive attitudes businessmen should adopt and steps they can take in their own self-interest and in the broader public interest. Tabulates reference data on consumer protection laws in effect and under consideration, personalities in the consumer movement, government agencies with consumer-related responsibilities, consumer product testing organizations, and data concerning private consumer organizations.

CONSUMERISM; A New Force in Society. 1976. Edited by Mary Gardiner Jones and David M. Gardner. Lexington Books, D.C. Heath & Company, 125 Spring Street, Lexington, Massachusetts 02173. 201 p.

Based on a conference on consumer forces, the book contains 18 papers presented together with summaries of discussions following each presentation.

CONSUMERISM: SEARCH FOR THE CONSUMER INTEREST. 1971. Edited by David A. Aaker and George S. Day. The Free Press, 866 Third Avenue, New York, New York 10022. 442 p.

A collection of articles discussing key issues of consumerism. Part One views the scope of the problem from several perspectives. Part Two considers the availability and quality of prepurchase information. Part Three deals with aspects of the purchase transaction, such as prices and credit terms. Part Four covers post-purchase performance. Part Five discusses discrimination against disadvantaged consumers.

CONSUMERISM: THE ETERNAL TRIANGLE; Business, Government, and Consumers. 1973. Edited by Barbara B. Murray. Goodyear Publishing Company, Incorporated, Pacific Palisades, California 90272. 469 p.

A selection of articles on consumerism, government regulations, credit, packaging, marketing, advertising, warranties, and consumer practices of the poor. The reprinted articles emphasize social, economic, and marketing aspects of consumerism as related to government legislation.

CONSUMERISM; Viewpoints from Business, Government, and the Public Interest. 1972. Edited by Ralph M. Gaedeke and Warren W. Etcheson. Canfield Press, 850 Montgomery Street, San Francisco, California 94133. 401 p.

Part One traces antecedents of the new consumer movement and discusses major policy questions. Part Two reviews backgrounds and issues of the consumer movement in the United States. Part Three examines the positions of advocates of increased government involvement in consumer protection. Part Four deals with responses of business to demands for more consumer protection and prospects for detente through self-regulation.

CONSUMERS ALL: The Yearbook of Agriculture. 1965. By the U.S. Department of Agriculture. Superintendent of Documents, U.S. Government Printing Office, Washington, D.C. 20402. 496 p.

Provides many useful facts and advice about housing, furniture and equipment, finances, yards and gardens, clothing, food, recreation, and safety.

CONSUMERS ALMANAC & CALENDAR. 1977. Compiled by the National Consumers League, 1028 Connecticut Avenue, Northwest, Suite 522, Washington, D.C. 20036. 120 p.

A center calendar section lists important dates and accomplishments in the consumer movement. Flanking sections give brief summaries of past efforts and present needs for correcting abuses in the food industry, chemical additives, cosmetics, drugs, regulatory agencies, advertising, automobiles, health, energy, frauds, small claims court, and related topics.

A CONSUMER'S ARSENAL. 1976. By John Dorfman. Praeger Publishers, Incorporated, 111 Fourth Avenue, New York, New York 10003. 270 p.

The first part of this manual on consumerism gives recommended tactics for making written or telephoned complaints. The second part describes the functions of consumer agencies in each state and lists their addresses. The last section provides an encyclopedic arrangement of 50 common consumer problems and advice on how to solve them. The problems concern such topics as advertising, buying clubs, encyclopedias, and vocational schools.

CONSUMER'S BUYING GUIDE; How to Get Your Money's Worth. 1973. By the Association of Better Business Bureaus. Benjamin Company, Incorporated, 485 Madison Avenue, New York, New York 10022. 205 p.

A guide to spending money more wisely by shopping for real value, spotting faulty merchandise, understanding contracts and basic facts about borrowing and financing. Explains the public information program conducted by Better Business Bureaus.

THE CONSUMER'S CATALOG OF ECONOMY & ECOLOGY. 1974. By Jeanne Bendick and Robert Bendick. McGraw-Hill Book Company, Incorporated, 1221 Avenue of the Americas, New York, New York 10020. 160 p.

Discusses consumer skills that help people become good bargainers and make the best choices. Gives detailed information on food, household goods, outdoor gear, clothes, tools, and repair jobs.

CONSUMERS DENTAL BIBLE - Tooth or Consequences. 1974. 3rd edition revised. By Jack L. Anderson and others. Project P, Incorporated, 448 Edgewood Court, Neenah, Wisconsin 54956. 176 p.

Offers advice on selecting a dentist, avoiding false teeth, controlling dental fear, reducing dental bills, preventing dental disease, and good nutrition. Discusses tooth structure and the reasons behind recommended practices. Includes a glossary of dental terms. Written by a group of dentists, physicians, and psychologists.

Books and Pamphlets

A CONSUMER'S GUIDE TO BANKRUPTCY. 1975. By Herbert S. Denenberg. Pilot Books, 347 Fifth Avenue, New York, New York 10016. 24 p.

A concise and informative booklet explaining the advantages, disadvantages, procedures, and costs of going bankrupt.

THE CONSUMER'S GUIDE TO BANKS. 1975. By Gordon L. Weil. Stein and Day Publishers, 7 East 48th Street, New York, New York 10017.

Reviews various practices, services, and special gimmicks of American banks. Discusses differences in charges for services rendered and advises shopping around for the best value. Tells how banking customers can protect their interests and use beneficial approaches in dealing with banks.

THE CONSUMER'S GUIDE TO BETTER BUYING. 1972. Revised edition. By Sidney Margolius. Pocket Books, Incorporated, Simon & Schuster, Incorporated, 630 Fifth Avenue, New York, New York 10020. 436 p.

Offers tips on how to buy almost anything. Also gives suggestions for proper maintenance of products. Tells how to find the best values in manufactured goods, food, insurance, and numerous other products and services.

CONSUMER'S GUIDE TO FIGHTING BACK. 1976. By Morris J. Bloomstein. Dodd, Mead, and Company, 79 Madison Avenue, New York, New York 10016. 296 p.

Discusses many different types of consumer problems. Tells how to prevent problems with purchases and services and how to go about retaliating against rip-offs. Includes sample complaint letters for various types of grievances.

THE CONSUMER'S GUIDE TO INSURANCE BUYING. 1970. By Vladimir P. Chernik. Sherbourne Press, 1640 South La Cienega Boulevard, Los Angeles, California 90035. 288 p.

A guide for selecting a suitable insurance plan. Describes each type of insurance, the pros and cons involved, and which represents the best choice.

CONSUMERS' GUIDE TO PRESCRIPTION PRICES. 1973. By William Gulick. Consumer Age Press, Post Office Box 279, Syracuse, New York 13214. 300 p.

A useful handbook to help make the buyer of prescription drugs more knowledgeable. Tells how to read a prescription, how to estimate the price, and who makes the product. Does not include the generic names of brand name drugs.

CONSUMER'S GUIDE TO PRODUCT SAFETY. 1971. Edited by Ronald Bruce. Award Books, 235 East 45th Street, New York, New York 10017. 252 p.

An edited reprint of the Final Report of the National Commission on Product Safety published in June, 1970. Reports on the hearings, investigations, and studies of hazards inherent in various types of consumer products. Presents a careful analysis of how standards are set by government, industry, and independent groups. Discusses federal, state, and local laws and regulations and offers recommendations for improvement.

THE CONSUMER'S HANDBOOK. 1974. Revised and updated. Edited by Paul Fargis. Hawthorn Books, Incorporated, 260 Madison Avenue, New York, New York 10016. 244 p.

Provides basic information on various aspects of homemaking and household management and shows how the consumer can use this information to save time and money. The major sections cover: finances, houses, furnishings, food, clothing, equipment, and outdoor purchases, such as patios and landscaping.

THE CONSUMER'S HANDBOOK; 100 Ways to Get More Value for your Dollars. 1971. By the Staff of the National Observer. Dow Jones Books, Post Office Box 300, Princeton, New Jersey 08540. 205 p.

Contains material compiled from The National Observer from 1969 to 1971 to aid the discriminating shopper. Presents suggestions and guidelines for shopping wisely in seven subject areas: automotive, education, health and safety, food and household, investments, recreation and hobbies, and miscellaneous. Also offers tips on maintenance and repair and proper use for better and more economical service.

Books and Pamphlets

CONSUMERS IN TROUBLE; A Study of Debtors in Default. 1974. By David Caplovitz. Free Press, Division of Macmillan Publishing Company, 866 Third Avenue, New York, New York 10022. 352 p.

Presents a victim's view of the consumer credit system. Tells why debtors default on their obligations and what happens to them after they default. Describes abusive collection practices and credit laws that favor creditors.

THE CONSUMERS UNION REPORT ON LIFE INSURANCE: A Guide to Planning and Buying the Protection You Need. 1973. Revised 1972 edition. By the Editors of Consumer Reports. Grossman Publishers, 625 Madison Avenue, New York, New York 10022. 135 p.

A thorough investigation of the life insurance business, various types of policies, and the purposes for which they are intended. Provides a guide to determine how much life insurance a person should have. Contains charts and tables comparing particular companies and the types of coverage offered. An appendix provides a worksheet for determining the reader's resources and estimating his future needs.

THE CONSUMER'S WORLD: Buying, Money Management, and Issues. 1974. By E. Thomas Garman and Sidney W. Eckert. McGraw-Hill Book Company, Incorporated, 1221 Avenue of the Americas, New York, New York 10020. 451 p.

Examines basic consumer problems, effective consumer buying practices, and future planning through savings, investments, life insurance, and understanding taxes. Deals with many different types of goods and services and explores the best ways of utilizing them.

THE CONSUMING PUBLIC. 1968. Edited by Grant S. McClellan. H.W. Wilson Company, 950 University Avenue, Bronx, New York 10452. 219 p.

A collection of articles grouped into five sections: The Citizen as Consumer; The Role of Government as Protector; Business and Consumer Protection; Consumer Concerns; and The Consumer Interest Movement. Each section contains an editor's introduction discussing aspects of consumerism.

THE COST OF DYING; And What You Can Do about It. 1974. By Raymond Paavo Arvio. Harper & Row Publishers, Incorporated, 10 East 53rd Street, New York, New York 10022. 159 p.

Offers encouragement, guidance, and practical advice about the formation and operation of nonprofit memorial societies and cooperative funeral homes as alternatives to exploitation by the funeral industry. Advocates advance planning and low-cost funerals through member-owned and controlled organizations.

COUNSEL FOR THE DECEIVED; Case Studies in Consumer Fraud. 1972. By Philip G. Schrag. Pantheon Books, Random House, Incorporated, 201 East 50th Street, New York, New York 10022. 200 p.

Documents in six case histories the schemes of the "commercial underworld". Exposes consumer frauds and the inability of the legal system to secure justice through timely response. Describes mail order abuses, door-to-door sales of shoddy merchandise, and other rackets.

THE CREDIT JUNGLE. 1971. By Al Griffin. Henry Regnery Company, 180 North Michigan Avenue, Chicago, Illinois 60601. 230 p.

Decries the abuses of consumer credit. Points out the real costs of using short-term, relatively high-interest personal credit. Discusses credit cards, revolving charge accounts, automotive financing and other installment plans, juvenile credit, credit land sales, credit bureaus, and collectors.

THE DARK SIDE OF THE MARKETPLACE; The Plight of the American Consumer. 1968. By Warren Grant Magnuson and Jean Carper. Prentice-Hall, Incorporated, Route 9W, Englewood Cliffs, New Jersey 07632. 240 p.

Part One covers topics concerned with the consumer's economic welfare, while Part Two discusses the protection of his health and safety. Presents examples illustrating problems encountered by consumers.

THE DAY THE PIGS REFUSED TO BE DRIVEN TO MARKET; Advertising and the Consumer Revolution. 1974. By Robin Wight. Random House, Incorporated, 201 East 50th Street, New York, New York 10022. 230 p.

Books and Pamphlets

Describes an international revolt of consumers against being pushovers, or gullible pigs driven to market. Tells how and where the consumer revolution grew, the ideologies contributing to its growth, activities in many countries, and how the movement can be expected to spread.

THE DISADVANTAGED CONSUMER. 1975. By Alan R. Andreasen. Free Press, 866 Third Avenue, New York, New York 10022. 366 p.

Part I discusses the disadvantaged consumer, particularly poor and black people. Part II deals with characteristics and problems of the disadvantaged marketplace. Part III covers price discrimination in the inner city and exploitation of the disadvantaged. Part IV offers possible solutions to problems of the disadvantaged consumer.

THE DOLLAR SQUEEZE AND HOW TO BEAT IT. 1970. By George Sullivan. Macmillan Company, 866 Third Avenue, New York, New York 10022. 213 p.

Offers advice on planning your spending, borrowing and investing, adding a second income, handling debts - even the right way to go bankrupt. The chapter on "Buymanship" provides many helpful hints on shopping for food, clothing, furniture, and houses.

DOLLARS AND SENSE; The Teen-Age Consumer's Guide. 1975. By Elizabeth McGough. William Morrow and Company, Incorporated, 105 Madison Avenue, New York, New York 10016. 160 p.

Offers guidance for teen-agers on how to handle money, find a job, understand pitfalls in advertising, spot health and cosmetic frauds, and shop wisely for clothing, food, cars, and other major purchases. Explains how to save and borrow, points out legal rights, and tells how to complain effectively.

$$$ AND SENSE; Your Complete Guide to Wise Buying. 1965. By Ella Gale. Fleet Publishing Corporation, 156 Fifth Avenue, New York, New York 10010. 283 p.

Shows in detail how to save money on food, clothing, furniture, linens, houses, and household equipment. Contains practical tips on how to spot the good buy or the poor value. Explains how to figure true interest rates and how to shop around for the best credit.

EARTH FOODS. 1972. By Lee Fryer and Dick Simmons. Follett Publishing Company, 1010 West Washington Boulevard, Chicago, Illinois 60607. 180 p.

Presents a plea for safe, nutritious foods grown by ecologically sound farm technology. Tells how to put natural nutrition back into foods and how to guard against harmful chemicals. Includes recipes designed to give good nutrition. Explains how to obtain good, nutritional foods at the lowest possible cost.

EAT YOUR HEART OUT: Food Profiteering in America. 1974. By Jim Hightower. Crown Publishers, Incorporated, 419 Park Avenue South, New York, New York 10016. 294 p.

Advocates a return to family farms, independent processors, mom and pop stores, family restaurants, farmers' markets, good taste, high nutritive value, and fair food prices. Documents the many devices used by giant corporations to dish out new food products at high cost and low value to consumers.

EATING RIGHT FOR LESS; Consumers Union's Practical Guide to Food and Nutrition for Older People. 1975. By the editors of Consumer Reports. Consumers Union, Orangeburg, New York 10962. 80 p.

Explains how an older person can eat well on a little more than $10 per week. Contradicts some common advice for food shoppers, and explodes some myths about nutrition and health.

ECONOMICS FOR CONSUMERS. 1977. 7th edition. By Leland J. Gordon and Stewart M. Lee. D. Van Nostrand Company, 450 West 33rd Street, New York, New York 10001. 701 p.

Explores the consumer's role in the economy, consumer behavior, the marketing and pricing process, personal finance, and buymanship. Emphasizes patterns influencing consumer behavior. Includes chapters on state and federal government organizations active in the consumer field. A college textbook, with a teacher's manual available.

Books and Pamphlets

ENOUGH! The Revolt of the American Consumer. 1972. By Doris Faber. Farrar, Straus and Giroux, 19 Union Square West, New York, New York 10003. 184 p.

Gives anecdotes and descriptions of many aspects of the consumer movement and the people who fought against shoddy and unsafe food and products, air pollution, untested drugs, and deceptive practices. Discusses protective agencies and a new awareness among private citizens of the need to safeguard the public interest.

ESCAPE FROM THE MONEY TRAP. 1973. By Henry B. Clark. Judson Press, Valley Forge, Pennsylvania 19481. 124 p.

Shows how to reappraise values and find deeper fulfillment by avoiding the race for material possessions and a more affluent way of life. Points out how we can use our economic resources in a Christian way.

EXPERT CONSUMER: A COMPLETE HANDBOOK. 1977. By Eisenberger. Prentice-Hall, Incorporated, Englewood Cliffs, New Jersey 07632.

FACTS ABOUT MERCHANDISE. 1967. 2nd edition. By William Boyd Logan and Helen M. Moon. Prentice-Hall, Incorporated, Route 9W, Englewood Cliffs, New Jersey 07632. 372 p.

Provides information about retail products such as fabrics, leather products, plastics, wearing apparel, home furnishings, toys, and foods. Includes dictionary and bibliography sections, a teacher's manual, and film lists.

THE FAMILY AS CONSUMERS. 1965. By Irene Oppenheim. Macmillan Company, 866 Third Avenue, New York, New York 10022. 318 p.

A college textbook dealing with consumer economics and family finance. Presents comprehensive information on problems involved in family spending and consumption.

THE FAMILY GUIDE TO BETTER FOOD AND BETTER HEALTH. 1971. By Ronald M. Deutsch. Meredith Corporation, 716 Locust Street, Des Moines, Iowa 50336. 277 p.

Discusses the effects of food on health - on bodily growth, function, and survival. Aids in choosing food wisely for better health.

THE FAMILY GUIDE TO SUCCESSFUL MOVING. 1968. By Carl Warmington. Association Press, 291 Broadway, New York, New York 10007. 95 p.

Answers practical and important questions on ways to cut moving costs, what to sell or leave behind, loss and damage insurance, choosing a mover, systematic packing, local and long distance moving. Provides helpful advice on locating housing and settling into a new community. Includes several checklists of items to remember.

THE FIGURE FINAGLERS. 1974. By Robert S. Reichard. McGraw-Hill Book Company, Incorporated, 1221 Avenue of the Americas, New York, New York 10020. 274 p.

Educates the consumer in constructive use of statistics to separate fact from fiction and useful figures from misleading ones. Attempts to classify and analyze the many ways an unsuspecting user of statistics can be duped. Discusses credit and advertising distortions, prices, cost of living, and related topics.

A FINANCIAL GUIDE FOR THE SELF-EMPLOYED. 1972. By John Ellis. Henry Regnery Company, 180 North Michigan Avenue, Chicago, Illinois 60601. 228 p.

Discusses such subjects as taxes, insurance, and retirement plans. Offers helpful advice on handling paperwork, collecting overdue bills, and similar topics. Includes a bibliography with brief annotations of books and pamphlets.

FINANCIAL SELF-DEFENSE. 1969. By John L. Springer. McGraw-Hill Book Company, Incorporated, 1221 Avenue of the Americas, New York, New York 10020. 201 p.

A guide to basic problems of personal finance. Discusses taxes, credit insurance, frauds and rackets, inflation, and investments.

Books and Pamphlets

FOOD AND THE CONSUMER. 1973. By Amihud Kramer. AVI Publishing Company, Incorporated, Post Office Box 831, Westport, Connecticut 06880. 256 p.

Explains the nature of available food supplies, methods of preparation, packaging, and marketing, and their value in satisfying nutritional and aesthetic requirements. Discusses safety and health hazards of foods, their convenience, possibilities of recycling, and foods of the future. Also discusses nutrition and the general nutritional status of the American population. Includes a chapter on techniques followed by the food industry and the government in protecting the consumer against misbranding and adulteration of packaged foods.

FOOD BUYING; Marketing Information for Consumers. 1962. By Carlton E. Wright. Macmillan Company, 866 Third Avenue, New York, New York 10022. 410 p.

Presents food and marketing information to aid in enlightened decision-making in feeding a family or buying food for an institution. Gives details on what a consumer should consider in shopping for food; comparison of various brands, labels, and grades; seasonal factors in food price and supply; and cost per food serving.

FOOD COLORS. 1972. By Michael F. Jacobson. Center for Science in the Public Interest, 1757 S Street, Northwest, Washington, D.C. 20036. 25 p.

Reports on the use of chemicals derived from coal tar dyes as coloring agents in food. Points out the dangers to consumers and the deceptions involved in food color additives. Includes tabulated data on food colors other than coal tar dyes. The report is based on a section of the author's book, Eater's Digest: The Consumer's Factbook on Food Additives.

THE FOOD CO-OP HANDBOOK; How to Bypass Supermarkets to Control the Quality and Price of Your Food. 1975. The Co-op Handbook Collective. Houghton Mifflin, 2 Park Street, Boston, Massachusetts 02107. 382 p.

FOOD CO-OPS; An Alternative to Shopping in Supermarkets. 1976. By William Ronco. Beacon Press, 25 Beacon Street, Boston, Massachusetts 02108. 188 p.

Urges consumers to form neighborhood cooperative food stores or food distribution centers in order to free members from the economic tyranny and inferior foods of the supermarket system. Describes various food co-ops and their methods of operation.

FOOD CO-OPS FOR SMALL GROUPS. 1975. By Tony Vellela. Workman Publishing Company, Incorporated, 231 East 51st Street, New York, New York 10022. 173 p.

FOR THE PEOPLE; A Consumer Action Handbook. 1977. By Joanne Anderson. Addison-Wesley, Reading, Massachusetts 01867. 352 p.

Describes more than 15 consumer action projects from Ralph Nader's associates that can be carried out in any local community. Provides step-by-step guidelines and practical information for launching successful campaigns on such projects as finding and eliminating energy waste, lowering utility bills, improving nursing home conditions, and comparing grocery prices. The introduction was written by Ralph Nader.

FORMING CONSUMER ORGANIZATIONS. 1972. By the U.S. Office of Consumer Affairs. Superintendent of Documents, U.S. Government Printing Office, Washington, D.C. 20402. 32 p.

A booklet of instructions for forming voluntary groups to work on consumer problems in local communities. The three parts tell how to form an organization, how to operate an organization, and how to get it going with suggested programs and projects.

FRAUDS, SWINDLES, AND RACKETS; A Red Alert for Today's Consumers. 1971. By Robert S. Rosefsky. Follett Publishing Company, 1010 West Washington Boulevard, Chicago, Illinois 60607. 338 p.

Examines enterprises involving outright fraud; obtaining money under false pretenses. The six parts deal with mail order and "get-rich-quick" schemes; home improvement rackets; land swindles; easy credit; assorted sneaky schemes and swindles; and "who's doing what to whom, and for whom?" Explains various recurring patterns and characteristics that are Snake Oil Sam's tricks of the trade.

GETTING THE MOST FOR YOUR MONEY; How to Beat the High Cost of Living. 1970. By Anthony Scaduto. David McKay Company, Incorporated, 750 Third Avenue, New York, New York 10017. 241 p.

Aids the shopper to soften the impact of rising prices by getting the most for his dollar. Offers advice on shopping for food, clothing, cars, household equipment, vacations, educations, legal and health services. Cautions against marketplace rackets, credit gouges, crooked advertising, mail frauds, dishonest salesmen and repairmen.

GETTING YOUR SHARE. 1977. Edited by Consumers Guide Editors. Simon & Schuster, Incorporated, 630 Fifth Avenue, New York, New York 10020.

THE GHETTO MARKETPLACE. 1969. Edited by Frederick D. Sturdivant. Free Press, 866 Third Avenue, New York, New York 10022. 316 p.

A collection of articles and other materials dealing with problems confronting the urban poor on the economic front. Tells about injustices and difficulties encountered in the purchase of goods.

GOING BROKE AND HOW TO AVOID IT. 1972. By Leonard M. Groupe. Thomas Y. Crowell Company, 666 Fifth Avenue, New York, New York 10019. 213 p.

Advises "the affluent poor" on credit traps, how to get a better deal, how to handle bill collectors, how to avoid being cheated, where to get financial and legal help, when not to declare bankruptcy, and how to figure a budget that works.

THE GREAT AMERICAN FOOD HOAX. 1971. By Sidney Margolius. Walker & Company, 720 Fifth Avenue, New York, New York 10019. 216 p.

Discusses the rising cost of food and the lack of value received. Points out that the nutrition level is declining as food costs go up. Gives tips on thrifty shopping for nutritional foods and how to avoid impulse shopping, rip-offs, and "empty" calories.

GUIDE FOR THE RESPONSIBLE CONSUMER. 1972. American Association of University Women, 2401 Virginia Avenue, Northwest, Washington, D.C. 20037. 12 p.

Presents brief but inclusive articles on common frauds and deceptive practices, protective measures available to the public, legislation designed for consumer protection, where to turn for redress of grievances, reconciling consumption with ecological concerns, and also a consumer's code of ethics.

GUIDE TO CONSUMER SERVICES; Consumers Union's Advice on Selected Financial and Professional Services. 1977. By the Editors of Consumer Reports. Consumers Union of the United States, Incorporated, 256 Washington Street, Mount Vernon, New York 10550. 372 p.

A compendium of recent revised and updated Consumer Reports on how to obtain good service when shopping for credit, auto repairs, dentists, doctors, other health services, title insurance for a house, an apartment, and many other professional and financial services.

GUIDE TO PERSONAL FINANCE; A Lifetime Program of Money Management. 1975. 2nd edition. By Richard J. Stillman. Prentice-Hall, Incorporated, 9W, Englewood Cliffs, New Jersey 07632. 493 p.

HANDBOOK FOR THE HOME - 1973 YEARBOOK OF AGRICULTURE. 1973. By the U.S. Department of Agriculture. Superintendent of Documents, U.S. Government Printing Office, Washington, D.C. 20402. 388 p.

Contains general and specific information on housing, home furnishings, family problems, and community affairs. Presents hundreds of "how-to" tips on spending money wisely.

HANDBOOK OF SYSTEM AND PRODUCT SAFETY. 1972. By Willie Hammer. Prentice-Hall, Route 9W, Englewood Cliffs, New Jersey 07632. 351 p.

Books and Pamphlets

Gives methods of analysis, preparation, and solutions for insuring the safety of systems and products <u>before</u> the user is exposed to them. Techniques developed for the aeronautics and astronautics industries are applied to industrial, motor vehicle, railroad, mine, and nuclear safety. The principal technique presented is the use of blocked figures listing outstanding principles, tasks, examples, and guidelines to follow. The text supplements the figures by giving practical examples of successes or failures when safety considerations were followed or neglected.

HANDLING YOUR MONEY. 1970. By Anthony Scaduto. David McKay Company, Incorporated, 750 Third Avenue, New York, New York 10017. 236 p.

Presents advice on wise use of money in obtaining housing, shopping for credit, consolidating loans, paying taxes, and making investments.

HEALTH: A CONSUMER'S DILEMMA. 1970. By Robert E. Kime. Wadsworth Publishing Company, Incorporated, 10 Davis Drive, Belmont, California 94002. 68 p.

Explores health products advertising, quackery, health insurance, choosing and using medical services. Serves as a guide in making wise decisions about health.

HEALTH FOODS: FACTS AND FAKES. 1973. By Sidney Margolius. Walker Publishing Company, 720 Fifth Avenue, New York, New York 10019. 293 p.

Offers much useful information enabling the reader to save on his food bill without sacrificing good nutrition. Includes valuable appendices, references, and a glossary of nutrition and health food firms.

THE HEALTH HUCKSTERS. 1960. By Ralph Lee Smith. Thomas Y. Crowell Company, 666 Fifth Avenue, New York, New York 10019. 248 p.

Reveals how false and misleading advertising persuades the American public to spend tremendous sums on food, drugs, and cosmetics that have no real benefit. Tells about hucksters in vitamins and minerals, dentifrices and cold cures, arthritis remedies, cosmetics, cigarette filters, and food fads.

HEALTH, QUACKERY & THE CONSUMER. 1976. By Warren E. Schaller and Charles R. Carroll. W.B. Saunders Company, West Washington Square, Philadelphia, Pennsylvania 19105. 426 p.

Examines the health care delivery system in the United States, economic costs, prevention of health problems, and utilization of health services. Also discusses quackery - questionable health practices, practitioners, and products - and protection against various types of quackery. A third area focuses on possibilities for improving the health care delivery system and fostering consumer health education. Each chapter ends with discussion questions and activities and a list of references.

THE HEALTH ROBBERS. 1976. Edited by Stephen Barrett, M.D., and Gilda Knight. George F. Stickley Company, 210 West Washington Square, Philadelphia, Pennsylvania 19106. 350 p.

Attacks medical quackery, health fads and frauds, dangerous gadgets, self-serving lobbies, and other problems confronting consumers. Cautions them to protect their money and their health. Each of the 24 chapters is written by an expert in a specialized field.

HELP: The <u>Useful Almanac</u>. 1976-77. Edited by Arthur E. Rowse. Consumer News, Incorporated, 813 National Press Building, Washington, D.C. 20045. 410 p.

Opens with chapters on how to get help on consumer problems from nongovernment and government organizations. Presents much useful information in categories such as appliances, clothing, furnishings, housing, transportation and travel, death and burial, banking and borrowing, insurance and pensions, charities, taxes, food, health care, hazardous products, utilities, automobiles, and communications. Offers help in solving daily problems, compares products and performance records, explains how to apply for Social Security, Medicare, Medicaid, and food stamps.

THE HIDDEN ASSASSINS. 1966. By Booth Mooney. Follett Publishing Company, 1010 West Washington Boulevard, Chicago, Illinois 60607. 230 p.

Deals with food additives, food quackery, and similar food problems. Discusses what can be done to correct the problems involved.

Books and Pamphlets

HIT & RUN; The Rise - and Fall? - of Ralph Nader. 1975. By Ralph de Toledano. Arlington House, Incorporated, 81 Centre Avenue, New Rochelle, New York 10801. 160 p.

A critique of Ralph Nader's activities, publications, fundraising and expenditures, press relations, war on the automobile, reports, congressional studies, environmental crusade, legislative contributions, and other aspects of his "consumerism". Describes Nader as a manipulative "powerist" who has done more harm than good.

HOME BUYER'S GUIDE. 1970. By Jack Wren. Barnes and Noble, Harper and Row Publishers, 10 East 53rd Street, New York, New York 10022. 259 p.

Teaches how to select, finance, and sell a home. Financial checklists for buyers and sellers are included in appendices. Also contains glossaries on building construction and legal terms.

HOT WAR ON THE CONSUMER. 1969. Edited by David Sanford. Pitman Publishing Corporation, 6 East 43rd Street, New York, New York 10017. 280 p.

A collection of articles by Ralph Nader and others taken from The New Republic. Explores the ways in which the consumer is buffeted about. Contains sections on food and drugs, big business malpractices, safety, and insurance.

HOUSEHOLD DECISION-MAKING. 1961. Edited by Nelson N. Foote. Consumer Behavior, Volume IV. New York University Press, Washington Square, New York, New York 10003. 349 p.

Papers presented at a conference cover household decision-making regarding changes in family composition, saving and borrowing, allocation and spending, buying and choice of brands, husband-wife roles and careers, and related topics concerned with consumer behavior. Participants in the conference were primarily consumption economists and family sociologists.

HOW TO AVOID A REAL ESTATE AGENT. 1969. By Ruth Mayer and Lucille Bowman. William Morrow & Company, Incorporated, 105 Madison Avenue, New York, New York 10016. 110 p.

Offers a step-by-step explanation of the details involved in buying or selling a house without a real estate agent. Describes how to arrive at a realistic price, where and when to advertise, and what information to have available for prospective buyers. Tells how to go about cleaning the house and grounds and preparing them for inspection.

HOW TO BEAT INFLATION BY USING IT. 1970. By Donald I. Rogers. Arlington House, Incorporated, 81 Centre Avenue, New Rochelle, New York 10801. 211 p.

Offers down-to-earth advice on methods of combatting inflation through wise investments, sensible buying habits, resistance to conspicuous consumption, practical purchases of clothing, furniture, housing, cars, and food.

HOW TO BUY A USED CAR. 1967. By Charles R. Jackson. Chilton Book Company, 201 King of Prussia Road, Radnor, Pennsylvania 19089. 90 p.

Offers guidance from an old "pro" to help amateur buyers deal with professional sellers of used cars. Tells the tricks of the trade, what to look into and under, and how to buy the used car that is right for you safely and economically. Discusses advertising and dealers, used car condition and guarantees, negotiating and buying, trade in's, and used care financing.

HOW TO BUY A USED CAR. 1975. By Donald MacDonald. Berkley Publishing Corporation, 200 Madison Avenue, New York, New York 10016. 188 p.

Presents basic facts and valuable advice about used-car buying. Includes information concerning engines and transmissions, best buys, depreciation, reconditioning, dealers, private party sales, try outs, needed repairs, accessories, financing and insurance, warranties, and recreational vehicles.

HOW TO BUY AT AUCTION. 1972. By Michael De Forrest. Simon & Schuster, 630 Fifth Avenue, New York, New York 10020. 224 p.

Covers every phase of auction sales, including what

can be bought, how to find a good auction, how to act at an auction. Gives many pointers on factors involved in making successful bids and what to avoid in buying at auctions in order to achieve maximum fun and profit.

HOW TO BUY FURNITURE. 1972. By Donna Difloe. P.F. Collier, Incorporated, 866 Third Avenue, New York, New York 10022. 143 p.

Presents information on the purposes intended for various types of furniture, materials used, and methods of construction. Discusses requirements for living room, bedroom, and other furniture. Contains chapters on furniture displays, how to examine furniture, and how to deal with salespeople, interior decorators, and deliverymen. Also considers budgets and the purchase of used furniture.

HOW TO BUY MAJOR APPLIANCES. 1973. By Charles Klamkin. Henry Regnery Company, 180 North Michigan Avenue, Chicago, Illinois 60601. 186 p.

Guides the consumer through the pitfalls of appliance shopping and explains how to choose best values in each appliance category. Contains chapters on how to purchase a refrigerator, freezer, washer, dryer, dishwasher, stove, television set, stereo system, compact appliance, garbage disposal, air conditioner and dehumidifier. Recommends specific makes and models for each type of appliance.

HOW TO GET A DOLLAR'S VALUE FOR A DOLLAR SPENT. 1964. By Arthur Milton. Citadel Press, 120 Enterprise Avenue, Secaucus, New Jersey 07094. 190 p.

Discusses installment buying, loans, mortages, food and home purchases, stocks and bonds, insurance, pensions, and related topics. Tells how to get more "living value" from your present income.

HOW TO GET MORE FOR YOUR MONEY IN RUNNING YOUR HOME. 1968. By Merle E. Dowd. Parker Publishing Company, Incorporated, West Nyack, New York 10994. 263 p.

Helps the home dweller achieve maximum cost effectiveness through controlling expenses for heating and cooling, water and lights, insurance, home equipment, furnishings, interior decorating, landscaping, and maintenance. Tells how to prevent losses by being prepared for emergencies, how to shop for a home, remodel economically, and get more for your home when you sell it.

HOW TO GET $100,000 WORTH OF SERVICES FREE, EACH YEAR, FROM THE U.S. GOVERNMENT. 1975. By E. Joseph Cossman. Frederick Fell Publishers, Incorporated, 386 Park Avenue South, New York, New York 10016.

Explains how to take advantage of the many services offered by the federal government to businesses, organizations, and individuals. Includes mailing addresses of government agencies and a bibliography.

HOW TO GET OUT OF DEBT AND STAY OUT OF DEBT. 1971. By Merle E. Dowd. Henry Regnery Company, 180 North Michigan Avenue, Chicago, Illinois 60601. 280 p.

Shows how to gain control of the family finances by determining the extent of the debt problem, getting rid of debts, finding outside help, avoiding crooked agencies, and devising a plan for getting the most out of the resources available.

HOW TO GET 20 TO 90% OFF ON EVERYTHING YOU BUY. 1966. By Jean and Cle Kinney. Parker Publishing Company, Incorporated, West Nyack, New York 10994. 255 p.

Offers realistic advice on how to face up to economic limitations and become a better purchasing agent for yourself and your family. The four parts of the book are titled: Beefing Up Your Cash on Hand; Specific Ways to Save on Almost Anything; How to Cut Back Expenses in Ten Vital Areas; and Let the Joneses Keep Up with You.

HOW TO INVEST IN BEAUTIFUL THINGS WITHOUT BEING A MILLIONAIRE; How the Clever Consumer Can Outthink the Tastemakers. 1971. By Elaine Cannel. David McKay Company, Incorporated, 750 Third Avenue, New York, New York 10017. 244 p.

Explains what to look for and what to avoid in buying and selling jewelry, silver, furniture, antiques, art objects, fabrics, lamps, appliances, china and glassware. Discusses selection, appraisals, insurance, resale value, supply and demand, labels and hallmarks of things of beauty.

HOW TO LIVE BETTER ON LESS; A Guide for Waste Watchers. 1974. By Barbara Jurgensen. Augsburg Publishing House, 426 South Fifth Street, Minneapolis, Minnesota 55415.

HOW TO LIVE CHEAP BUT GOOD. 1971. By Martin Poriss. American Heritage Press, 330 West 42nd Street, New York, New York 10036. 319 p.

A guide to good value at low cost in housing, moving, furniture, food, home repairs, utilities, health care, clothing, and other purchases. Gives many practical pointers as well as special checklists on hiring movers, furniture repair, pressuring a landlord to make repairs, food storage, and other topics.

HOW TO LIVE ON NOTHING. 1961. By Joan Ranson Shortney. Doubleday & Company, Incorporated, 501 Franklin Avenue, Garden City, New York 11530. 456 p.

Tells how to eat, dress, furnish your home, find shelter, do repair work, save heat, make gifts, vacation on pennies, and live on practically nothing. Includes chapters on staying healthy, making the most of social benefits, and how to make something out of nothing by using throwaways.

HOW TO MANAGE YOUR MONEY. 1964. By Edward T. Imparato and Charles L. Hyde. A. S. Barnes and Company, Incorporated, Post Office Box 421, Cranbury, New Jersey 08512. 301 p.

Plots a journey toward financial success by controlling one's standard of living, using a budget, checking accounts, life insurance, real estate, stocks and bonds, and an over-all financial plan. Explains how to live within one's means and how to increase those means by careful budgeting, sound investments, and practical savings.

HOW TO PAY LOTS LESS FOR LIFE INSURANCE... AND BE COVERED FOR AS MUCH AND AS LONG AS YOU WANT. 1971. By Max Fogiel. Research & Education Association, 342 Madison Avenue, New York, New York 10017. 208 p.

A brief, practical guide to various types of life insurance written by an insurance consultant agent.

HOW TO REDUCE YOUR MEDICAL BILLS. 1970. By Ruth Winter. Crown Publishers, Incorporated, 419 Park Avenue South, New York, New York 10016. 248 p.

Presents some proven solutions to use in dealing with the problems of medical costs and proposes other solutions. Includes at the end of each chapter an annotated list of suggestions on how to obtain effective health care. Also includes a list of health-related organizations, statistical tables on medical personnel, information on physician-assistant training programs, and names and addresses of community health centers.

HOW TO SAVE MONEY WHEN YOU BUY AND DRIVE YOUR CAR. 1967. By Merle E. Dowd. Parker Publishing Company, Incorporated, West Nyack, New York 10994. 227 p.

Part One tells how to cut costs when buying a new or used car. Part Two explains ways to save on car operating expenses, such as gasoline, oil, tires, batteries, insurance, repairs and maintenance. Includes many money-saving and dollar-stretching tips to control the costs of buying and maintaining a car.

HOW TO SET UP A HEALTH SERVICES INFORMATION CENTER. 1976. National Consumers League, 1028 Connecticut Avenue, Northwest, Suite 522, Washington, D.C. 20036. 24 p.

Gives step-by-step procedures for setting up a center for collecting and disseminating information about a community's health facilities. Using nursing homes as one example, the manual tells how to gather government inspection records, develop digests from them, make appendices of pertinent government regulations, sample records, and a bibliography. Offers advice on running the center with volunteer staffing.

HOW TO SHAKE THE MONEY TREE. 1966. By Robert Metz. G. P. Putnam's Sons, 200 Madison Avenue, New York, New York 10016. 277 p.

Books and Pamphlets

Discusses high and low interest rates and offers rules to guide the borrower seeking low-cost loans. Explains criteria used by bankers and other lenders. Comments on lending practices in the 50 states and pitfalls for borrowers in the various jurisdictions. Evaluates credit unions, finance companies, and bankers as lenders.

HOW TO START YOUR OWN FOOD CO-OP (With a Little Help from Your Friends). 1974. By Gloria Stern. Walker and Company, 750 Fifth Avenue, New York, New York 10019. 214 p.

Explains the advantages of cooperative buying, various types of cooperative clubs and stores, how to start a co-op, and how to go about buying foods for a co-op. Includes sections giving names and locations of cooperatives and of wholesale food suppliers.

HOW YOU CAN BEAT INFLATION. 1970. By David L. Markstein. McGraw-Hill Book Company, Incorporated, 1221 Avenue of the Americas, New York, New York 10020. 226 p.

Presents advice on stretching dollars to counteract their shrinking value caused by inflation. Gives detailed information to consider in choosing food, shelter, services, and investments.

IF IT DOESN'T WORK, READ THE INSTRUCTIONS. 1970. By Charles Klamkin. Stein & Day Publishers, 7 East 48th Street, New York, New York 10017. 191 p.

Attempts to help the consumer become a more sophisticated, less gullible buyer in the purchase of major appliances. Discusses various manufacturers and good and bad points concerning their products.

IN OUR TIME. 1968. By Paul H. Douglas. Harcourt, Brace & World, Incorporated, 757 Third Avenue, New York, New York 10017. 228 p.

Deals with various economic matters affecting consumers, such as injustices in the tax structure, exploitation of natural resources, expenses and ethical problems of politicians, and credit practices that confuse consumers. The last four chapters present an in-depth study of the problems of poverty. The book is based on a series of lectures by the late Senator from Illinois.

IN THE BANK...OR UP THE CHIMNEY. 1976. By the U.S. Department of Housing and Urban Development. U.S. Government Printing Office, Washington, D.C. 20402. 69 p.

Discusses many different ways of insulating your home and explains how to determine quickly what improvements your individual house does or does not need. Gives directions on how the homeowner can insulate windows, doors, attic, walls, floors, crawl spaces, and basement and provides simple diagrams to aid in doing the work. Also shows how to estimate insulation costs and resulting savings for each region and major metropolitan area in the United States.

IN THE MARKETPLACE; Consumerism in America. 1972. Edited by the Editors of Ramparts Magazine. Canfield Press, 850 Montgomery Street, San Francisco, California 94133. 245 p.

A collection of articles exploring the seamy side of the American economic system. Part I describes increasingly lethal, shoddy products and shyster deals. Part II discusses services and regulation, including transportation and medical services. Part III deals with advertising media, promotion, and exploitation.

THE INFORMATION SEEKERS; An International Study of Consumer Information and Advertising Image. 1975. By Hans B. Thorelli, Helmut H. Becker, and Jack Engledow. Ballinger Publishing Company, 17 Dunster Street, Harvard Square, Cambridge, Massachusetts 02138. 373 p.

Presents the results of a large-scale field survey of subscribers to testing journals as well as general consumers in Germany and the United States. Compares consumer attitudes to independent information programs, such as product testing, quality marks, and labeling, and to advertising.

THE INNOCENT CONSUMER VS. THE EXPLOITERS. 1967. By Sidney Margolius. Trident Press, 630 Fifth Avenue, New York, New York 10020. 240 p.

Discusses the pitfalls that await ignorant consumers and how to avoid exploitation stemming from shady credit practices, stifling of competition, false advertising, deceptive packaging, lack of quality grading, and other ills.

Books and Pamphlets

THE INTELLIGENT BUYER AND THE TELLTALE SELLER. 1968. By Dexter Masters. Alfred A. Knopf, Incorporated, 201 East 50th Street, New York, New York 10022. 246 p.

Traces the history of traders and advertising. Gives insights on the base nature and irresponsibility of modern commercial pressures, their origins, development, and probable future. Written by a former director of Consumers Union and editor of Consumer Reports, the book illuminates the nature of selling and sellers, advertising and advertisers.

THE INTELLIGENT CONSUMER. 1973. By Christopher and Bonnie Weathersbee. E. P. Dutton & Company, 201 Park Avenue South, New York, New York 10003. 366 p.

A down-to-earth guide for consumers who strive to obtain true value for money spent and at the same time conserve natural resources. Contains numerous suggestions on a wide variety of products.

THE INTELLIGENT CONSUMER; How Not to Be a "Connedsumer". 1975. By Gershon Wheeler. Reston Publishing Company, Post Office Box 547, Reston, Virginia 22090. 176 p.

Gives pointers for intelligent handling of life insurance, savings and checking accounts, charge accounts, automobile purchase and repair, appliances, housing, estates, record keeping, and similar matters. Tells how to avoid fraud and theft and how to find good value.

THE INVESTIGATION OF RALPH NADER; General Motors vs. One Determined Man. 1972. By Thomas Whiteside. Arbor House Publishing Company, Incorporated, 757 Third Avenue, New York, New York 10017. 255 p.

A detailed account of the surveillance of Ralph Nader by agents of General Motors after Nader's campaign for safe automobiles exposed negligence by the company. Includes testimony given at a special hearing of a Senate subcommittee, the settlement made by General Motors, and many ramifications of the investigation.

KNOW YOUR MERCHANDISE. 1975. 4th edition. By Isabel Barnum Wingate and others. McGraw-Hill Book Company, Incorporated, 1221 Avenue of the Americas, New York, New York 10020.

A textbook for classes in consumer buying and business retailing. Discusses merchandise information obtained from labels, advertisements, and other sources. Contains two parts: Part I, Textiles; and Part II, Non-Textiles. Presents many details about the attributes and manufacture of products.

LAW AND THE CONSUMER. 1969. By Robert Berger and Joseph Teplin. Justice in Urban America Series. Houghton Mifflin Company, 2 Park Street, Boston, Massachusetts 02107. 101 p.

Discusses contracts, credit, advertising, bargains and various ways of buying goods and services. Explains basic principles of consumer law and how consumers can help themselves. Includes discussion and review questions and ideas for study projects.

LAWSUITS WITHOUT LAWYERS. 1973. Allegheny County Bureau of Consumer Affairs, Jones Law Building, Pittsburgh, Pennsylvania 15219. 49 p.

Assists the average consumer in bringing a small claims action in Allegheny County without the use of a lawyer. Much of the information is applicable elsewhere as well.

LEGAL PROTECTION FOR THE CONSUMER. 1973. 2nd edition of volume previously written by Paul Crown. By Stanley Morganstern. Legal Almanac Series, No. 52. Oceana Publications, Incorporated, 75 Main Street, Dobbs Ferry, New York 10522. 128 p.

Covers state and federal legislation concerned with consumer protection. Discusses the intelligent purchase of goods, appliances, and services. Tells how to deal with work-at-home gyps, unordered merchandise, door-to-door salespeople, francises, and guarantees, and how to be an alert consumer in general.

LET THE SELLER BEWARE. 1969. By James Bishop, Jr. and Henry W. Hubbard. The National Press, Incorporated, 128 C Street, Northeast, Washington, D.C. 20002. 195 p.

Discusses efforts to identify and correct injustices in the American marketplace. Points out present problems of danger, deception, and doubt encountered by consumers.

LIVING ON LESS AND LIKING IT MORE. 1976. By Maxine Hancock. Moody Press, 820 North LaSalle Street, Chicago, Illinois 60610. 158 p.

Tells how to cut costs. Gives down-to-earth advice on how to live well on a reduced budget and find satisfaction in modest living.

MAIL FRAUD LAWS PROTECTING: CONSUMERS, INVESTORS, BUSINESSMEN, PATIENTS, STUDENTS. 1973. By the U.S. Postal Service. Superintendent of Documents, U.S. Government Printing Office, Washington, D.C. 20402. 28 p.

Presents information about various types of mail frauds such as chain-referral schemes, fake contests, home

Books and Pamphlets

improvement fraud, debt consolidation, auto insurance fraud, retirement homes, missing heir schemes, charity rackets, and unordered merchandise. Also discusses shady business franchises, vending machines, distributorships, work-at-home schemes, phony business directories, fake newspapers, advance fees, medical frauds, and fraudulent correspondence schools. The last section gives brief descriptions of fraud areas in which postal inspectors conduct investigations.

MAKE THE MOST OF YOUR INCOME. 1961. By John L. Springer. Prentice-Hall, Incorporated, Route 9W, Englewood Cliffs, New Jersey 07632. 214 p.

Shows how to get better satisfaction for your money by making a spending plan, buying and using credit wisely, investing savings, obtaining protection through insurance, and preparing in advance for retirement. Offers inside business tips from financial experts.

MAKING IT; The Encyclopedia of How to Do It for Less. 1975. By Arnold and Connie Krochmal. Drake Publishers, Incorporated, 381 Park Avenue South, New York, New York 10016.

Gives advice about ways of saving money on food, clothes, furniture, housing, appliances, vacations, leisure activities, medical care, finances, and other topics of interest to consumers.

MAN AND FOOD. 1970. By Magnus Pyke. McGraw-Hill Book Company, Incorporated, 1221 Avenue of the Americas, New York, New York 10020. 256 p.

A study of nutrition and food technology in relation to human wellbeing. Consists of 3 parts: Part 1, Commodities selected as food; Part 2, Developments in the understanding of nutrition; and Part 3, Food technology, present and future.

MANAGE YOUR MONEY AND LIVE BETTER; Get the Most from Your Dwindling Dollars. 1971. By David L. Markstein. McGraw-Hill Book Company, Incorporated, 1221 Avenue of the Americas, New York, New York 10020. 252 p.

Explains how to take stock of assets available and stretch dollars by careful planning, tax savings, and elimination or reduction of many types of expenditures. One chapter gives a detailed tour of "How the Smart Shopper Shops." Others offer checklists of money saving do's and don't's to use when considering appliances, automobiles, housing, health, education, and investments.

THE MEDICAL MESSIAHS. 1967. By James Harvey Young. Princeton University Press, Box 231, Princeton, New Jersey 08540. 460 p.

Presents a comprehensive treatment of the concurrent growth of modern medical science and pseudo-medical nonsense in twentieth century America. Discusses trends in quackery along with the broad practice of self-medication.

THE MEDICINE SHOW; Consumers Union's Practical Guide to Some Everyday Health Problems and Health Products. 1974. Revised edition. By the Editors of Consumer Reports. Consumers Union of the United States, Incorporated, 256 Washington Street, Mount Vernon, New York 10550. 384 p.

Discusses a wide variety of health problems, possible causes, good, bad, and indifferent products used to treat them. Gives advice on buying prescription drugs, stocking a medicine cabinet, choosing a doctor and a hospital, and other useful medical topics.

MOTORCYCLES: A Buyer's and Rider's Guide. 1974. Revised edition. By Al Griffin. Henry Regnery Company, 180 North Michigan Avenue, Chicago, Illinois 60601.

Presents a brief history of motorcycling, an appraisal of gangs and associations, information about accessories, a close look at relevant legislation, and a discussion of the economics of motorcycle riding, including insurance coverage. Describes and rates various makes and models of motorcycles. Appendices list state laws, local clubs, outlawed gangs, speed records, piston displacement equivalents, motorcycle periodicals, and names and addresses of motorcycle distributors.

MOBILE HOMES; The Low-Cost Housing Hoax. 1975. By the Center for Auto Safety. Grossman Publishers, 625 Madison Avenue, New York, New York 10022. 220 p.

Provides information on how the mobile home industry operates. Exposes abuses such as high costs and low quality, excessive financing charges, freedom-restricting

Books and Pamphlets

regulations in mobile home parks, and high risk of personal injury or death from winds and fire. Concludes with an outline for corrective action by consumers, industry, and government.

THE MONOPOLY MAKERS; Ralph Nader's Study Group Report on Regulation and Competition. 1973. Edited by Mark J. Green. Grossman Publishers, 625 Madison Avenue, New York, New York 10022. 400 p.

Gives a detailed account of how the United States Government has participated in the formation and protection of monopolies. Nine contributors analyze the techniques used and the abuse of authority by regulatory agencies and sometimes the legislative branch of the federal government. Shows how free enterprise, competition, and open markets have been stifled by self-serving interests in communications, transportation, public utilities, the maritime industry, pharmaceuticals, energy fuels, and foreign trade.

MOVING: A Commonsense Guide to Relocating Your Family. 1970. By Edith Ruina. Funk & Wagnalls Publishing Company, Incorporated, 666 Fifth Avenue, New York, New York 10019.

Presents information on how to go about selling a home, packing possessions, scheduling a move, and making legal and financial arrangements. Also gives advice about relocating in a new area and adjusting to the new environment.

MOVING AHEAD WITH GROUP ACTION; The Buying Club. 1966. Cooperative League of the U.S.A., 59 East Van Buren Street, Chicago, Illinois 60605. 61 p.

Explains how to organize and operate a buying club in order to save money by buying at wholesale prices. Gives simple, complete, step-by-step instructions for forming a cooperative.

MUSINGS ON MONEY; How to Make Dollars Out of Sen$e. 1976. By Eliot Janeway. David McKay Company, 750 Third Avenue, New York, New York 10017. 118 p.

Contains 35 short chapters on such topics as earning, borrowing, lending, saving, spending, investing, and giving away money.

NEW CONSUMERISM: SELECTED READINGS. 1973. Edited by William T. Kelley. Grid, Incorporated, 4666 Indianola Avenue, Columbus, Ohio 43214. 578 p.

Contains selected readings on the history of the consumer movement, the position of the consumer in the marketplace, malefactors in industry, the impact of consumerism on industry, reactions of industry, new departures in consumer protection, how business is abused by consumers, new social responsibilities of business, and consumerism in 1990.

THE NEW HANDBOOK OF PRESCRIPTION DRUGS: Official Names, Prices, and Sources for Patient and Doctor. 1975. Revised edition. By Richard Burack, M.D. Ballantine Books, Incorporated, 201 East 50th Street, New York, New York 10022.

Discusses in an introduction issues of importance in prescribing and using medication, such as the advisability of using reliable single-entity drugs available by official (or generic) name at relatively little cost. Lists about 60 basic drugs which are used in treating 90 per cent or more of the patients examined by doctors. An extensive Prescription Drug List gives fuller information about the basic generic drugs as well as numerous brand name drugs and their effectiveness. The last section gives widely varying prices of different manufacturers.

NUTRITION SCORECARD: Your Guide to Better Eating. 1974. By Michael F. Jacobson and Wendy Wilson. Center for Science in the Public Interest, 1757 S Street, Northwest, Washington, D.C. 20009. 102 p.

Discusses nutrients in food, companies that make and advertise foods, and rating of nutritional values by use of food scorecards. Gives nutritional scores for various types of foods, including soups, vegetables, grain foods, protein foods, fresh fruits, beverages, snacks, dairy products, breakfast foods, and desserts. A condensed version of the book is available as a booklet, Food Scorecard.

OPEN REALITY; The Way Out of Mimicking Happiness. 1974. By Richard Altschuler and Nicholas Regush. G. P. Putnam's Sons, 200 Madison Avenue, New York, New York 10016. 224 p.

Describes how the corporate consumer system and mass

Books and Pamphlets

media have imposed a conception of reality on us and defined the "good life." They have been very successful in making us believe that happiness can be achieved only by buying new products and services. Tells how corporations have pervaded every aspect of our lives, such as sex, marriage, leisure, religion, and politics, to convince us that happiness is a consumable commodity. Shows ways to stop mimicking happiness and create new life possibilities based on personal needs and personal ideas of happiness.

ORGANIZING FOR HEALTH CARE: A Tool for Change. 1974. By the Source Collective. Source Catalog Series, No. 3. Beacon Press, Incorporated, 25 Beacon Street, Boston, Massachusetts 02108.

PAYING THROUGH THE EAR; A Report on Hearing Health Care Problems. 1973. By Public Citizen's Retired Professional Action Group, 2000 P Street, Northwest, Washington, D.C. 20036.

Reports on inadequate services, products, and information in the hearing aid industry. Also accuses the industry of recommending aids to people who do not need them and falsely exaggerating the benefits of their devices.

PERSONAL ECONOMICS. 1977. By Fred F. Bartok and Edward B. Lee, Jr. Holbrook Press, 470 Atlantic Avenue, Boston, Massachusetts 02210. 436 p.

Offers advice concerning budgeting, purchasing clothing, appliances and furniture, entertainment, leisure, cars, housing, credit, insurance, investments, taxes, keeping records, retirement and estate planning.

PERSONAL FINANCE AND CONSUMER ECONOMICS. 1976. By R. Robert Rosenberg and R. V. Naples. McGraw-Hill Book Company, Incorporated, 1221 Avenue of the Americas, New York, New York 10020. 199 p.

Deals with such topics as budgeting, buying, saving, insuring, investing, making out income tax and Social Security forms. Includes approximately 500 solutions to problems concerned with these topics. Part of the Schaum's Outline Series.

PERSONAL MONEY MANAGEMENT. 1977. Second edition. By Thomas E. Bailard, David L. Biehl, and Ronald W. Kaiser. Science Research Associates, Incorporated, 1540 Page Mill Road, Palo Alto, California 94304. 621 p.

Covers such topics as budgeting, insurance, income taxes, credit, housing, investments, and retirement planning. For use as a college textbook.

THE PLOT TO MAKE YOU BUY. 1968. By John Fisher. McGraw-Hill Book Company, Incorporated, 1221 Avenue of the Americas, New York, New York 10020. 209 p.

Discusses the effects of marketing practices and the deliberate plots to persuade consumers to buy products, such as programs of planned obsolescence. Appeals for controls on the tremendous power and enormous amounts of money available to organized marketing interests.

THE POLITICS OF CONSUMER PROTECTION. 1971. By Mark V. Nadel. Bobbs-Merrill Company, Incorporated, Subsidiary of Howard W. Sams & Company, 4 West 58th Street, New York, New York 10019. 257 p.

Provides a brief history of consumer protection policy, a critical analysis of the role of federal agencies and Congress in consumer protection, and a study of consumer advocates and the press in bringing about consumer protection measures.

THE POOR PAY MORE; Consumer Practices of Low-Income Families. 1967. By David Caplovitz. The Free Press, 866 Third Avenue, New York, New York 10022. 225 p.

A report of the Bureau of Applied Social Research, Columbia University, on the buying patterns of poor people. Exposes unfair selling practices and other problems confronting the poor.

PRETENDERS TO THE THRONE. 1976. By Lucy Black Creighton. D. C. Heath & Company, Lexington Book Division, 125 Spring Street, Lexington, Massachusetts 02173. 142 p.

Bolsters the statement that "the consumer movement has accomplished very little" with a historical study,

Books and Pamphlets

an economic analysis, a critique of Ralph Nader, and an analysis of consumer education and consumer advocacy. Includes bibliographical references.

PRODUCT PERFORMANCE AND SERVICING; An Examination of Consumer Problems and Business Responses. 1973. By the National Business Council for Consumer Affairs, U.S. Department of Commerce, Washington, D.C. 20230. 46 p.

Reports on the reasons for consumer dissatisfaction with the performance and servicing of selected consumer durable products. Includes recommendations for specific activities by manufacturers before, during, and after sale of their products.

PRODUCT QUALITY, PERFORMANCE, AND COST. 1972. By the National Academy of Engineering, 2101 Constitution Avenue, Northwest, Washington, D.C. 20418. 154 p.

Reports on a symposium and workshops dealing with such topics as consumer needs; product performance; consumer preferences; product quality; information exchange between user, manufacturer, and regulatory agencies; government performance as developer, manufacturer, and customer; the function of governments in the consumer product area.

PRODUCT SAFETY IN HOUSEHOLD GOODS. 1968. Edited by F. Reed Dickerson. Bobbs-Merrill Company, Incorporated, Subsidiary of Howard W. Sams & Company, 4 West 58th Street, New York, New York 10019. 190 p.

A report of the Seminar in Legislation at Indiana University School of Law. Discusses consumer protection, product hazards, improving product safety, and compensating the injured consumer.

PROTECTING CONSUMER INTERESTS; Private Initiative and Public Response. 1976. Edited by Robert N. Katz. Ballinger Publishing Company, 17 Dunster Street, Harvard Square, Cambridge, Massachusetts 02138. 300 p.

An edited version of papers presented at a three-day symposium on who speaks for the consumer and when and where they will be heard. The 17 topics by 19 contributors deal with standards, self-regulation, the press, redress of grievances, legal services, insurance regulatory agencies, public policy, and related issues.

PROTECTING YOUR HOUSING INVESTMENT. 1973. By the U.S. Department of Housing and Urban Development. Consumer Information, Pueblo, Colorado 81009.

Describes how household utility systems work, what to do in case of emergencies, the structure of a house, and how to check for wear and tear. Distinguishes between jobs that should be tackled as routine maintenance and repairs that require the services of a professional. Discusses special problems such as pest control, the effects of moisture, and shrinkage and expansion.

PROUDLY WE HAIL; Profiles of Public Citizens in Action. 1975. By Kenneth Lasson. Grossman Publishers, 625 Madison Avenue, New York, New York 10022. 244 p.

The first section details the efforts of public citizens and public servants acting alone to expose and correct abuses by private companies and government organizations. The second section describes attempts to bring about reforms by people acting together in groups, as professionals, in government, and in business and labor.

PSYCHOLOGY AND CONSUMER AFFAIRS. 1977. By Milton L. Blum. Harper & Row Publishers, Incorporated, 10 East 53rd Street, New York, New York 10022. 328 p.

Explains psychological aspects of buyer-seller-maker transactions in order to improve the consumer's understanding. Interprets consumer psychology and shows how consumers are generally at a disadvantage in dealing with sellers and manufacturers.

A PUBLIC CITIZEN'S ACTION MANUAL. 1973. By Donald K. Ross. Grossman Publishers, 625 Madison Avenue, New York, New York 10022.

Emphasizes large issues of public interest such as taxes, health care, and civil rights. Gives detailed instructions on how to evaluate a small claims court, how to deal with a bait-and-switch merchant, how to fight racial and sex discrimination, and similar problems. Includes sample letters to be sent to government officials and businesses to complain or to get action.

Books and Pamphlets

THE RADICAL CONSUMER'S HANDBOOK. 1972. By Goody L. Solomon. Ballantine Books, Incorporated, 201 East 50th Street, New York, New York 10022. 174 p.

A guide explaining consumers' rights in the marketplace. Stresses the importance of understanding these rights and the protective laws and regulations designed to aid consumers. Lists trade associations which cooperate with the U.S. Office of Consumer Affairs in resolving complaints. Also lists city, county, state, and federal agencies, explaining their work in handling consumer problems. Tells how to write letters of complaint and where to send them.

RATING THE DIETS. 1973. By Theodore Berland. Consumer Guide, Skokie, Illinois 60076. 386 p.

A comprehensive study of all sorts of diet plans. Rates more than three dozen diet programs for safety and effectiveness. Discusses the roles of diet pills, diet doctors, and diet organizations. Gives a clear explanation of the scientific basis of dieting for an understanding of the essential differences among low carbohydrate, high protein, and high fat diets. Tells not only what to eat to lose weight, but why. Contains sample diets and calorie charts.

THE REGULATED CONSUMER. 1971. By Mary Bennett Peterson. Nash Publishing, 9255 Sunset Boulevard, Los Angeles, California 90069. 271 p.

Focuses on the question of whether regulation is a boon or bane to the consumer. Examines the roles of federal regulatory agencies: the Food and Drug Administration, Federal Trade Commission, National Labor Relations Board, Interstate Commerce Commission, Civil Aeronautics Board, and Federal Communications Commission. Points out that government intervention in the name of helping the consumer generally hurts the consumer.

SAFETY IN THE MARKETPLACE; A Program for the Improvement of Consumer Product Safety. 1973. By the Sub-Council on Producr Safety of the National Business Council for Consumer Affairs. Superintendent of Documents, U.S. Government Printing Office, Washington, D.C. 20402. 82 p.

A report containing analyses, conclusions, and recommendations on ways of improving product safety. Discusses manufacturing activities and product safety, product safety standards, retail and service activities related to product safety, and public safety awareness programs. Also includes information about product testing laboratories, trade associations, government and other organizations and their contributions to improved product safety.

SAVE YOUR HEALTH AND YOUR MONEY: A Doctor's Answers to Today's High Health Costs. 1971. By Patrick J. Doyle. Acropolis Books, Limited, Colortone Building, 2400 17th Street, Northwest, Washington, D.C. 20009. 240 p.

Presents information on how to evaluate and select physicians, dentists, hospitals, and health insurance policies. Tells how to keep drug costs down. Explains where and how to obtain free medical information and services.

THE SCREWING OF THE AVERAGE MAN. 1974. By David Hapgood. Doubleday & Company, 501 Franklin Avenue, Garden City, New York 11530. 323 p.

Describes an endless series of swindles the average man encounters in the fields of banking, the stock market, insurance, law, health, automobiles and accessories, pensions, nursing homes, government monopolies, subsidies, and taxes. Tells how the rich and powerful rig the system to benefit themselves at the expense of the average man.

ENE WITH DOLLARS. 1967. By Charles Neal. Doubleday & Company, Incorporated, 501 Franklin Avenue, Garden City, New York 11530. 393 p.

Counsels the consumer on how to solve financial problems before they start. Consists of four parts: Part I, Managing your income, or the ins and outs of money; Part II, Managing your spending, or where the money goes; Part III, Managing your debts, or the art of using credit; and Part IV, Managing your assets, or how to build security.

THE SERVICE SOCIETY AND THE CONSUMER VANGUARD. 1974. By Alan Gartner and Frank Riessman. Harper & Row Publishers, Incorporated, 10 East 53rd Street, New York, New York 10022. 266 p.

Analyzes major economic changes in our society,

Books and Pamphlets

movements, and ideas. Examines the emergence of a new service phase following the agricultural and industrial phases of economic development. Emphasizes the role of the consumer as producer and user of education, health, safety, welfare, and personal services.

SHOPPER'S GUIDE. 1974 Yearbook of Agriculture. By the U.S. Department of Agriculture. Superintendent of Documents, U.S. Government Printing Office, Washington, D.C. 20402. 358 p.

Presents guidelines for making shopping decisions. Tells how to compare brands and products available to make the right selections for the shopper's needs. Six sections deal with food, home improvements, household appliances, gardening, recreation, and services such as moving, repairs, and credit.

A SHOPPER'S GUIDE TO LAWYERS. 1973. By Herbert S. Denenberg. Insurance Department, Harrisburg, Pennsylvania, or Consumer Insurance, Department KF, 813 National Press Building, Washington, D.C. 20004.

Explains what to look for and to look out for when choosing and dealing with lawyers. Gives practical tips on how to cross examine a lawyer before selecting one, how to establish a reasonable fee, and ways of communicating with a lawyer and maintaining a good relationship. One of a series of guides to various kinds of services.

THE SHOPPER'S GUIDEBOOK TO LIFE INSURANCE, HEALTH INSURANCE, AUTO INSURANCE, HOMEOWNER'S INSURANCE, DOCTORS, DENTISTS, LAWYERS, PENSIONS, ETC. 1974. By Herbert S. Denenberg. Consumer News, Incorporated, 813 National Press Building, Washington, D.C. 20004. 156 p.

Chapters on various types of insurance discuss types of coverage for automobiles, snowmobiles, homes, mobile homes, life insurance, and health insurance. Additional chapters give consumer advice concerning surgery, hospital rights, dentistry, lawyers, pensions, and nuclear power. A compilation of useful information contained in over 20 Shopper's Guides originally published since 1971 by the Pennsylvania Insurance Department to enlighten and protect the public by providing important facts and advice.

SMART SHOPPER'S GUIDE. 1965. By Aileen Snoddy. Arco Publishing Company, Incorporated, 219 Park Avenue South, New York, New York 10003. 143 p.

A buyer's guide designed to aid in choosing major purchases. Presents specific facts on design, performance, and engineering for use in comparing items considered for purchase. Also includes important questions that should be asked before buying.

SO YOU WANT TO BUY A HOUSE. 1970. By Al Griffin. Henry Regnery Company, 180 North Michigan Avenue, Chicago, Illinois 60601. 244 p.

Discusses points to consider in purchasing a house: cost, size, construction, age, neighborhood, schools, taxes, community facilities, floor plan, financing, and real estate services. Gives numerous helpful details to aid in making a wise housing investment.

SO YOU WANT TO BUY A MOBILE HOME. 1970. By Al Griffin. Henry Regnery Company, 180 North Michigan Avenue, Chicago, Illinois 60601. 182 p.

Presents information on design, construction, dealers, financing, and sites for locating mobile homes. Includes a list of mobile home manufacturers and the types of units built by each manufacturer.

SOCIAL ISSUES OF MARKETING IN THE AMERICAN ECONOMY. 1971. By Y. Hugh Furuhashi and E. Jerome McCarthy. Grid, Incorporated, 4143 North High Street, Columbus, Ohio 43214. 119 p.

Presents many different points of view and shifting notions about the consumer's place in our market-directed economy. Discusses freedom of choice, product quality and safety, guarantees and warranties, deceptive advertising, price discrimination, and the meeting of consumer demands.

SOWING THE WIND; A Report from Ralph Nader's Center for Study of Responsive Law on Food Safety and the Chemical Harvest. 1972. By Harrison Wellford. Grossman Publishers, 625 Madison Avenue, New York, New York 10022. 384 p.

Reports on the application of chemical technology to agriculture and its implications for food safety. Criticizes the role of the Department of Agriculture, its

Books and Pamphlets

domination by agribusiness and other entrenched interests, its secrecy, and its lack of concern for the consumer's interest in wholesome meat, the meat inspector's interest in enforcing the meat laws, and the chicken farmer's interest in escaping the status of corporate peonage. Publicizes the failure to protect the public interest in preventing long-term hazards to human and environmental health from agricultural chemicals and federal pesticide campaigns.

THE SPENDERS. 1960. By Steuart Henderson Britt. McGraw-Hill Book Company, Incorporated, 1221 Avenue of the Americas, New York, New York 10020. 293 p.

Tells about how products are marketed and advertised to influence consumers. Discusses consumer motives, choices, actions and reactions.

STRATEGY FOR PERSONAL FINANCE. 1977. By Larry R. Lang and Thomas H. Gillespie. McGraw-Hill Book Company, Incorporated, 1221 Avenue of the Americas, New York, New York 10020. 608 p.

Five major sections deal with financial planning, keeping records, and choosing a career; developing resources and managing money; consumer purchases of automobiles, housing, and other major items; insurance; and an extensive section on investments.

SUPER THREATS; How to Sound like a Lawyer & Get Your Rights on Your Own. 1977. By John N. Striker and Andrew O. Shapiro. Rawson Associates Publishers, Incorporated. Distributed by Atheneum Publishers, 122 East 42nd Street, New York, New York 10017.

SUPERMARKET COUNTER POWER. 1973. By Adeline Garner Shell. Warner Paperback Library, Warner Press, 75 Rockefeller Plaza, New York, New York 10019. 209 p.

Discusses points to consider in wise food shopping. Covers many subjects, such as junk foods, coupons and specials to avoid, over-advertising, and the inadvisability of carrying too rigid a shopping list.

THE SUPERMARKET HANDBOOK: ACCESS TO WHOLE FOODS. 1973. By Nikki and David Goldbeck. Harper & Row Publishers, Incorporated, 10 East 53rd Street, New York, New York 10022. 430 p.

A basic guide on how to select, evaluate, and prepare supermarket products to get maximum nutrition, purity, economy, and variety. Bridges the gap between "health foods" and super-processed foods, showing how to use standard supermarket fare to best advantage.

THE SUPERMARKET TRAP; The Consumer and the Food Industry. 1970. By Jennifer Cross. Indiana University Press, 10th and Morton Streets, Bloomington, Indiana 47401. 258 p.

Analyzes the packaging and advertising techniques of the food industry. Explains how supermarkets are laid out to stimulate additional buying; the special promotions used; and the various persuasions based on the shopper's habits, needs, and desires.

SUPERSHOPPER; A Guide to Spending and Saving. 1971. By David and Marymae Klein. Praeger Publishers, Incorporated, 111 Fourth Avenue, New York, New York 10003. 175 p.

Aids in developing skillful and sophisticated shoppers. Teaches how to get good value for money spent, and how to acquire sales resistance toward unwanted items. Main topics covered are: Getting Your Money, Saving Your Money, Spending Your Money, and Getting the Most for Your Money.

SYLVIA PORTER'S MONEY BOOK; How to Earn It, Spend It, Save It, Invest It, Borrow It - and Use It to Better Your Life. 1975. By Sylvia Porter. Doubleday & Company, Incorporated, 501 Franklin Avenue, Garden City, New York 11530. 1105 p.

Gives detailed advice on a great many aspects of consumer economics. Part I, Everyday Matters, covers food, shelter, clothing, transportation, health, vacations, etc. Part II, Milestones, deals with marriage, children, divorce, wills, and funerals. Part III, Managing Your Money, discusses investments. Part IV, Your Rights and How to Get Them, advises consumers on their rights and where to get help when needed.

TAKE CARE OF YOURSELF; A Consumer's Guide

Books and Pamphlets

to Medical Care. 1976. By Donald M. Vickery and James F. Fries. Addison-Wesley Publishing Company, Incorporated, Jacob Way, Reading, Massachusetts 01867. 288 p.

A medical guide providing quick instructions for such ailments as hoarseness, cuts, nose bleeds, poisoning, burns, etc. Uses 68 flow charts with yes or no questions and appropriate procedures to follow, including whether to see a doctor or try home treatment first.

THE THUMB ON THE SCALE; Or the Supermarket Shell Game. 1967. By A. Q. Mowbray. J. B. Lippincott Company, East Washington Square, Philadelphia, Pennsylvania 19105. 178 p.

Exposes supermarket packaging abuses, misleading advertising, and manipulation of the public for profit. Discusses various deceptive practices and government attempts to regulate packaging, labeling, product safety and effectiveness, deceptive advertising, and other matters of concern to the supermarket shopper.

200,000,000 GUINEA PIGS; New Dangers in Everyday Foods, Drugs, and Cosmetics. 1972. By John G. Fuller. G. P. Putnam's Sons, 200 Madison Avenue, New York, New York 10016. 320 p.

Warns consumers how they are being treated as guinea pigs "to be caged, tagged, fed, and drugged for the sake of exploitative profit." Points out dangers from food additives, harmful or ineffective drugs, poisonous, unsanitary, and unsafe products. Decries the indifference of industrial leaders who put profits ahead of consumer health and welfare.

THE USED CAR GAME: A Sociology of the Bargain. 1973. By Joy Browne. Lexington Books, D.C. Heath and Company, 125 Spring Street, Lexington, Massachusetts 02173. 184 p.

A study of used car salesmen and the way they bargain with customers on a used car lot. Shows the sociological and psychological factors that influence the participants as they bargain and interact with each other.

THE VULNERABLE AMERICANS. 1966. By Curt Gentry. Doubleday & Company, Incorporated, 501 Franklin Avenue, Garden City, New York 11530. 333 p.

Exposes a whole spectrum of swindles from false advertising through various con tricks, bait and switch sales, shoddy door-to-door sales, mail fraud, inflated credit interest, land fraud, and medical quackery. Tells about a variety of thieving tricks against companies and individuals. A final chapter explains how to avoid being taken by outright fraud and deceptive practices and discusses government measures to protect consumers.

THE WASTE MAKERS. 1960. By Vance Packard. David McKay Company, Incorporated, 750 Third Avenue, New York, New York 10017. 340 p.

Reveals how productivity is being maintained by strategies such as "planned obsolescence" and "product death". Explains who the waste makers are, how they operate, and their impact on dwindling natural resources, on America's survival as an honest supplier in the export market, and on the consumer's pocketbook, system of values, and whole way of life.

WEIGHTS AND MEASURES AND THE CONSUMER; Third National Survey of State Weights and Measures Legislation, Administration, and Enforcement (1969). 1970. By Leland J. Gordon. Consumers Union of United States, 256 Washington Street, Mount Vernon, New York 10550. 252 p.

Evaluates existing state laws and enforcement powers. Discusses administration of measurement laws, what consumers need to know about weights and measures, and what consumers can do to receive fair treatment.

WHAT TO DO WITH YOUR BAD CAR: An Action Manual for Lemon Owners. 1971. By Ralph Nader, Lowell Dodge, and Ralf Hotchkiss. Grossman Publishers, 625 Madison Avenue, New York, New York 10022. 175 p.

Tells how to reduce your chances of buying a defective car. Points out types of things to consider before making the purchase. Explains various courses of action to take if you do buy a "lemon".

WHAT WE EAT TODAY; The Food Manipulators vs. the People. 1972. By Michael and Sheilagh

Books and Pamphlets

Crawford. Stein and Day Publishers, 7 East 48th Street, New York, New York 10017. 192 p.

Reveals how the manipulation and processing of food can be biologically harmful and cause gradual damage to the brain. Discusses chronic diseases related to diet in technically advanced and other societies. Compares animal and human nutrition in various parts of the world, the development of deficiencies, and the results of poor nutrition.

WHAT YOU SHOULD KNOW BEFORE YOU BUY A CAR. 1968. By Anthony Till. Sherbourne Press, Incorporated, 1640 South La Cienega Boulevard, Los Angeles, California 90035. 235 p.

Section I, the New Car, explains how to choose a new car and new car dealer, avoid misleading advertisements and unethical practices, and obtain reasonable financing. Section II, The Used Car, discusses used car dealers, where used cars come from, book value, advertising, financing, and guarantees.

WHAT YOU SHOULD KNOW BEFORE YOU HAVE YOUR CAR REPAIRED. 1970. By Anthony Till. Sherbourne Press, 1640 South La Cienega Boulevard, Los Angeles, California 90035. 166 p.

Explains how to go about protecting oneself from bad practices in the automobile repair business. Includes a Flat-Rate Book that lists prices for major and minor repair jobs.

WHISTLE BLOWING; The Report of the Conference on Professional Responsibility. 1972. Edited by Ralph Nader, Peter J. Petkas, and Kate Blackwell. Grossman Publishers, 625 Madison Avenue, New York, New York 10022. 302 p.

Presents the results of a conference that brought together leading exponents of "whistle blowing". A person who "blows the whistle" exposes the organization he serves if it is involved in corrupt, illegal, fraudulent, or harmful activity. Section I contains four keynote speeches by Ralph Nader and others. Section II describes actions taken by various whistle blowers in the fields of harmful radiation, automobile safety, food additives, unsafe drugs, and defense abuses. Section III discusses "Prescriptions for Change", and Section IV presents "Strategies for Whistle Blowers".

WHO PUT THE CON IN CONSUMER? 1972. By David Sanford. Liveright Publishing Corporation, 386 Park Avenue South, New York, New York 10016. 166 p.

Points out that increases in profit margins by companies shortchange the consumer in food quality and quantity, and the high cost of television sets, drugs, housing, repair work, and service in general. The last chapter, "Fighting Back", advises the consumer on methods of redressing grievances.

THE WHOLE TRUTH ABOUT ECONOMY DRIVING. 1976. By Doug Roe. H. P. Books, Post Office Box 5367, Tucson, Arizona 85703.

Tells how to run a car economically, keep it in good shape; and what to do in emergencies. Contains chapters on pumping your own gas, avoiding rip-offs, buying and selling cars. Contains many photos, charts, and tips on car repair and maintenance.

WISE HOME BUYING. 1975. By the U.S. Department of Housing and Urban Development. Consumer Information, Pueblo, Colorado 81009. 36 p.

Gives pointers on shopping for a house, inspecting your selection, financing and purchasing, and keeping the property in good condition. Includes a glossary and addresses of field offices of HUD.

YOU AND YOUR MONEY. 1977. Revised edition. By Dorothy Y. Goble. Steck-Vaughn Company, 807 Brazos, Post Office Box 2028, Austin, Texas 78768. 58 p.

Presents practical information and advice concerning money management and good habits in consumer buying.

YOU ARE A CONSUMER - OF CLOTHING. 1967. By Pauline Bertie Gillette Garrett and Edward J. Metzer. Ginn and Company, 191 Spring Street, Lexington, Massachusetts 02173. 177 p.

A textbook on the consumer's role in purchasing clothing. Tells how to get his money's worth, where to buy, and where to get help when something goes wrong.

YOUR HOME FURNISHINGS DOLLAR. 1973. Money Management Institute, Household Finance Corporation, Prudential Plaza, Chicago, Illinois 60601. 40 p.

Contains many useful tips on how to buy furniture. Includes questions to ask on those slippery warranties.

Periodicals and Newsletters

THE ACTION FACTION. 1977-. Monthly. Editors: Sherry Lindquist and Gary Rosenberg. Paul H. Douglas Consumer Research Center, Incorporated, 1012 14th Street, N.W., Washington, D.C. 20005. Free to consumer groups.

Discusses topics of current interest to consumers, such as the Agency for Consumer Protection legislation, the Senate Nutrition Committee Report, "lifeline" utility rates, and government decisions affecting consumers. Also covers state and local news concerning consumer groups, ideas for activities, and fundraising suggestions. A new publication supported by a grant from the U.S. Department of Health, Education, and Welfare's Office of Consumer Education.

THE ADVOCATE. Bimonthly. Editor: Samuel J. Parker, Jr. Metropolitan Washington Planning and Housing Association, 1225 K Street, N.W., Washington, D.C. 20005. $10 per year includes membership dues.

A newsletter analyzing government action in the housing field, local planning and housing issues, equal housing opportunities, neighborhood preservation, and District of Columbia housing policies. Points out special needs of the poor and programs that assist or detract from meeting those needs.

AIR AND WATER NEWS. 1957-. Weekly. Editor: Steven Ross. McGraw-Hill Book Company, Incorporated, 1221 Avenue of the Americas, New York, New York 10020. $145 per year.

Reports on pollution of air, water, and land. Presents brief articles on such topics as solid waste, land use, recycling, and noise control, as well as environmental pollution of water and air.

AIR POLLUTION NOTES. 1970-. Bimonthly. Editor: Franklin B. Flower. Rutgers University, College of Agriculture and Environmental Science, New Brunswick, New Jersey 08903. Free.

AIR QUALITY CONTROL DIGEST. 1969-. 10 times per year. Editor: Dr. Arthur D. Even. Wayne State University, Scientific and Technical Information Center, Detroit, Michigan 48202. $45 per year.

AMERICAN COUNCIL ON CONSUMER INTERESTS NEWSLETTER. 9 times a year. Editor: Stewart M. Lee. American Council on Consumer Interests, 162 Stanley Hall, University of Missouri, Columbia, Missouri 65201. $6 per year.

Presents brief news items on Council business, activities of other consumer organizations, federal and state consumer action, and items of general interest in the consumer field. Includes an annotated listing of journal articles, books, pamphlets, films and filmstrips, and other consumer resource materials.

BUYER'S GUIDE ANNUAL; Consumer Discount Price Guide. Annual. Arco Publishing Company, Incorporated, 219 Park Avenue South, New York, New York 10003. $1.75 per year.

Gives information about many different kinds of consumer products. Offers advice to prospective buyers and lists discount prices.

CENTER FOR SCIENCE IN THE PUBLIC INTEREST NEWSLETTER. Quarterly. Center for Science in the Public Interest, 1757 S Street, N.W., Washington, D.C. 20009. $5 per year.

Reports on public interest projects such as the annual Food Day, petitions to regulatory agencies, analyses of energy consumption, and nuclear hazards. Includes news items about consumer action for public health, and information about reports available from CSPI and other publications.

CHANGING TIMES. Monthly. Editor: Sidney Sulkin. Kiplinger Washington Editors, Incorporated, 1729 H Street, N.W., Washington, D.C. 20006. $9 per year.

"The Kiplinger Service for Families," Changing Times carries short articles of practical interest in the fields of money management, housing, food, science, medicine, safety, children, religion, and the arts, in addition to articles on taxes, insurance, advertising, real estate, investments, interest rates, and product evaluations. Includes special features such as Your Questions Answered, Things to Write For, and News behind the Ads.

CONSERVATION FOUNDATION LETTER. Monthly. Editor: Rice Odell. The Conservation Foundation,

Periodicals and Newsletters

1717 Massachusetts Avenue, N.W., Washington, D.C. 20036. $10 per year.

A newsletter reporting on environmental issues. Each monthly report is devoted to a special topic, such as energy problems, land use legislation, budgeting of environmental programs, food supply problems, waste disposal, resource depletion, air, water, and noise pollution.

THE CONSERVATIONIST. Bimonthly. Editor: John J. DuPont. New York State Department of Environmental Conservation, 50 Wolf Road, Albany, New York 12233. $3.50 per year.

Contains articles of interest to hikers, hunters, fishermen, and others interested in enjoying and protecting the outdoors. The supplement, Environmental Quality News, and other features discuss air and water pollution, recycling, smokeless combustion, fire protection, solid waste disposal, land use legislation, and similar topics.

THE CONSUMER - AT THE BOTTOM OF THE TOTEM POLE. 1976. 4th quarter issue of the magazine Viewpoint. Industrial Union Department, AFL-CIO, 815 16th Street, N.W., Washington, D.C. 20006. 32 p. $.50.

Seven articles cover such topics as pocketbook protection, gaining a voice in the marketplace, food stamps, credit protection laws, food policy, consumer representation in government, and ways to be heard. This entire issue of Viewpoint is devoted to consumer topics.

CONSUMER ALERT. 1971-. Monthly. By the U.S. Federal Trade Commission. Superintendent of Documents, U.S. Government Printing Office, Washington, D.C. 20402. Free.

A newsletter put out for consumer protection. Reports on FTC hearings concerning labeling practices, pricing regulations, fair practices in installment sales and credit disclosure, misleading advertising, and similar topics.

Consumer Bulletin
    Name changed to CONSUMERS' RESEARCH MAGAZINE

CONSUMER CLOSE-UPS. 9 times a year. Cornell University, College of Human Ecology, Department of Consumer Economics & Public Policy, Ithaca, New York 14853.

CONSUMER EDUCATION FORUM. 3 times a year. Editor: Herbert M. Jelley. American Council on Consumer Interests, 162 Stanley Hall, University of Missouri, Columbia, Missouri 65201. Free with $10 membership fee.

Contains brief articles by educators on teaching methods used for consumer education. Describes field trips, conferences, and creating teaching materials. Presents new approaches to the study of personal finance, meal planning, product purchases, pollution problems, truth-in-lending, and similar topics.

CONSUMER FEDERATION OF AMERICA NEWS. Monthly. Editor: Kathleen Sheekey. Consumer Federation of America, 1012 14th Street, N.W., Washington, D.C. 20005. $20 per year.

Focuses on national bills in Congress, news about regulatory agencies, CFA activities, and news concerning state and local consumer organizations.

CONSUMER NEWS. Semimonthly. Managing Editor: Marion Ciaccio. By the U.S. Department of Health, Education and Welfare's Office of Consumer Affairs. Superintendent of Documents, U.S. Government Printing Office, Washington, D.C. 20402. $4 per year.

Covers activities of all regulatory agencies and federal consumer legislation. Reports on such topics as the proposed Consumer Protection Agency, unfair sales practices, air and water pollution, airline ticket regulations, product safety, labeling and packaging. Discusses new federal regulations and lists new publications. A supplement, Consumer Register, summarizes major consumer proposals before federal agencies, including deadlines for comments.

CON$UMER NEW$WEEKLY. Weekly. Editor: Arthur E. Rowse. By Consumer News, Incorporated, 813 National Press Building, Washington, D.C. 20045. $15 per year.

Features "news you can use from the Nation's Capital".

Periodicals and Newsletters

A newsletter giving current information on U.S. government committee meetings, agency actions, speeches, status of legislation, and administrative decisions. Includes helpful advice, safety information, news concerning developments in the fields of energy, recall of products, auto insurance, medicine, misleading advertising, food contamination, and other areas of consumer interest. Formerly called U.S. Consumer.

CONSUMER PROTECTION NEWS. 1970-. Monthly. Editor: Cornelia Olive. North Carolina Office of the Attorney General, Box 629, Raleigh, North Carolina 27602.

CONSUMER PROTECTION NEWSLETTER. 1973-. Quarterly. Editor: Mareatha Counts. Attorney General, Dexter Horton Building, Seattle, Washington 98104.

CONSUMER REPORTS. Monthly. By Consumers Union of United States, Incorporated, 256 Washington Street, Mount Vernon, New York 10550. $11 per year.

Provides advice for purchasers and ratings of specific models produced by different manufacturers. Compares cars, appliances, bicycles, foods, household goods, luggage, services such as life insurance, and many other items of importance to consumers. Includes a cumulative index. The December issue is the Buying Guide Issue, which rates products as Acceptable or Not Acceptable and describes their advantages and disadvantages.

CONSUMER TIPS. Quarterly. Purchase Power, Incorporated, 303 West 42nd Street, New York, New York 10036.

CONSUMER TRENDS. 1963-. Semimonthly. Editor: James A. Ambrose. Consumer Trends, Incorporated, 375 Jackson Avenue, Saint Louis, Missouri 63130. $25 per year.

Presents news articles, comments, and predictions concerning consumer credit and financial matters. Reports on legal and legislative affairs in the field of consumer finance.

CONSUMER VIEWS. Monthly. Citibank, 399 Park Avenue, New York, New York 10022. Free.

A newsletter offering advice about the management of personal and family finances. Each issue covers a special topic concerned with consumer products or services, such as car maintenance and repair, family expenditures, insurance, retirement plans, and similar subjects.

CONSUMERS DIGEST. Bimonthly. Editor: Arthur Darack. Consumers Digest, Incorporated, 6316 North Lincoln Avenue, Chicago, Illinois 60659. $7 per year.

Presents a compilation of reports on purchasing various products and services, including houses, cars, insurance, etc. Includes shopping tips and discount prices on products, as well as business and job opportunities. Reports news about new products, financial news, and consumer news briefs. Two Price Buying Directories each year list discount prices of products and names of dealers offering the discounts.

CONSUMERS' RESEARCH MAGAZINE. Monthly. Technical Director and Editor: F.J. Schlink. By Consumers' Research, Incorporated, Washington, New Jersey 07882. $9 per year.

Articles compare types of products and brands put out by various manufacturers in order to help the consumer make a wise choice in purchasing such items as carpets, hair sprays, stereo systems, irons, cameras, stereo sets, toasters, automobiles, etc. Specific information is given for various models and brands tested by the Consumers' Research organization and rated A. Recommended, B. Intermediate, or C. Not recommended. Ratings of products are featured in the October Handbook of Buying Issue. Formerly called Consumer Bulletin.

CONSUMERS VOICE. 1966-. Monthly. Editor: Max Weiner. Consumers Education and Protective Association International, Incorporated, 6048 Ogontz Avenue, Philadelphia, Pennsylvania 19141.

CURRENT CONSUMER; The Continuing Guide to Consumer Education. 1976-. 9 times a year. Curriculum Innovations, Incorporated, 501 Lake Forest Avenue, Highwood, Illinois 60040. $3.25 per year.

Periodicals and Newsletters

A consumer magazine for junior and senior high school students. Covers a variety of topics concerned with products and services, health care, taxes, credit, copyrights, and suggestions for saving money. Includes a question-and-answer section.

ENVIRONMENT. 10 times a year. Editors: Julian McCaull, Sheldon Novick, and Kevin P. Shea. Scientists' Institute for Public Information, 560 Trinity Avenue, Saint Louis, Missouri 63130. $12.75 per year.

Carries articles on energy policies, land use, food manipulation, pollution, nuclear risks, water control, pesticides, hazardous materials, and similar topics concerning the environment.

ENVIRONMENT ACTION BULLETIN. Biweekly. Editor: Jerome Goldstein. Rodale Press, Incorporated, 33 East Minor Street, Emmaus, Pennsylvania 18049. $12 per year.

Reports on government policies concerning the environment, activities of cooperatives, air and water pollution, nuclear radiation dangers, alternative energy sources, current environmental legislation, and other topics related to environment action.

ENVIRONMENT AND BEHAVIOR. Quarterly. Editor: Gary H. Winkel. Sage Publications, Incorporated, 275 South Beverly Hills Drive, Beverly Hills, California 90212. $15 per year.

Covers topics related to conservation of the environment, such as air pollution, litter control, forest management, recycling waste material, and water pollution. Also publishes articles on reactions of people to their environment, emphasizing the value of open space and unspoiled wilderness.

ENVIRONMENT REPORT. 1970-. Semimonthly. Publisher: A. Kranish. Trends Publishing, Incorporated, 330 National Press Building, Washington, D.C. 20004. $60 per year.

Covers national and international news and developments concerning ecology, environment, and pollution control with emphasis on national policy, research, and development.

ENVIRONMENT REPORTER. 1970-. Weekly. Managing Editor: Morris A. Ward. Bureau of National Affairs, Incorporated, 1231 25th Street, N.W., Washington, D.C. 20037. $485 per year.

Reports on federal and state legislation, programs, regulations, and court decisions concerning water and air pollution control, solid wastes, water supply, agricultural, mineral, and marine resources. The Current Development section comes out weekly; reference supplements are issued as required.

ENVIRONMENTAL ACTION. 1970-. Biweekly. Editors: Deborah Baldwin and Don Cullimore. Environmental Action, Incorporated, 1346 Connecticut Avenue, N.W., Suite 731, Washington, D.C. 20036. $15 per year ($10 to students and senior citizens).

Surveys environmental issues, problems, and solutions. Carries articles on such topics as energy conservation, solid waste disposal, prevention of pollution, preservation of coastlines, nuclear power plants, the transportation of hazardous substances, the electric utility industry and "acid rain," automotive emissions, and product safety. Regular features include Eco Notes, Government-Environment, Business Briefs, and a book review.

ENVIRONMENTAL AFFAIRS. 1971-. Quarterly. Editor-in-Chief: Mary Lee Warren. Environmental Affairs, Incorporated, of Boston College Law School, 885 Centre Street, Newton Centre, Massachusetts 02159. $20 per year.

Presents scholarly discussions on such topics as: the economics of recycling, estimating emission control costs, limiting the demand for energy, the pesticides controversy, thermal discharge and radioactive waste from nuclear power plants, preserving rural land and public beaches, and various aspects of water pollution.

ENVIRONMENTAL QUALITY MAGAZINE. 1970-. Quarterly. Publisher: Ira Ritter. Environmental Awareness Associates, Incorporated, 6464 Canoga Avenue, Woodland Hills, California 91364. $10 per year.

Concerned with environmental and ecological problems such as natural resources, industrial wastes, federal and state government legislation, consumer protection, urban problems, endangered species, activities of regulatory agencies, and related topics.

Periodicals and Newsletters

ENVIRONMENTAL SCIENCE & TECHNOLOGY. Monthly. Editor: Russell F. Christman. American Chemical Society, Editorial and Subscription Service Department, 1155 16th Street, N.W., Washington, D.C. 20036. $15 per year to nonmembers, $10 per year to members.

Covers current topics of interest concerning conservation and cleanup of the environment. Recycling, air and water pollution, oil spill technology, industrial pollution reduction, sewage treatment, energy supplies, noise pollution, and similar subjects are discussed in scientific and technical articles.

EVERYBODY'S MONEY; The Credit Union Magazine for Consumers. Quarterly. Credit Union National Association, Incorporated, Post Office Box 431, Madison, Wisconsin 53594. $1.25 per year.

Features brief, illustrated articles on such topics as pollution control, travel tips, mobile homes, food, clothing, truth-in-lending, cosmetics, insurance, banking services, and other items of consumer interest.

FAMILY HEALTH. Monthly. Editor: Dalma Heyn. Family Communications, Incorporated, 149 Fifth Avenue, New York, New York 10010. $6.95 per year.

Contains popular, illustrated articles on various health and nutrition topics, such as arthritis, yogurt, exercise, birth control, depression, diets, asthma, cancer, meat substitutes, care of eyes and teeth. Includes many question and answer features. Incorporates Today's Health Magazine, following a merger in April, 1976.

FAMILY SAFETY. Quarterly. Editor: Robert Meyer. National Safety Council, 444 North Michigan Avenue, Chicago, Illinois 60611. $2.50 per year.

Presents articles on such topics as child poisoning, ladder sense, getting lost, poisonous plants, safe driving, explosive vapors, injuries from falls, fires, and other family safety hazards. Illustrates examples of injury-producing situations.

FDA CONSUMER. 10 times a year. By the U.S. Department of Health, Education, and Welfare's Food and Drug Administration. Consumer Information, Pueblo, Colorado 81009. $8.55 per year.

Informs consumers about the safety and usefulness of a large variety of foods and additives, medicines, cosmetics, medical devices, and electronic products. Tells about the latest scientific and regulatory developments. Previously known as FDA Papers. A subject index is available covering the issues from 1967 through 1975.

FOOD CHEMICAL NEWS. Weekly. Editor: Louis Rothschild, Jr. Food Chemical News, Incorporated, 420 Colorado Building, 1341 G Street, N.W., Washington, D.C. 20005. $250 per year.

Reports news of food additives, pesticides, color additives, veterinary drugs, and other food chemicals. Covers the activities and rulings of federal government agencies concerned with the regulation of food products: the Food and Drug Administration, Department of Agriculture, Environmental Protection Agency, Federal Trade Commission, and also Congressional action.

FRONTLINE. Bimonthly. Editor: Arlene Alligood. Common Cause, 2030 M Street, N.W., Washington, D.C. 20036. $15 per year membership fee.

Monitors legislation concerning consumers, reporting on voting records and other information about Congressmen, activities of lobbyists, legislative status of Common Cause issues, results of surveys, and other news about federal and state government. Alerts members to take action, especially on federal legislation, and gives an update on Common Cause activities.

IN COMMON. Quarterly. Editor: Georgianna Rathbun. Common Cause, 2030 M Street, N.W., Washington, D.C. 20036. $15 per year membership fee.

Reports from Washington on Common Cause involvement in national issues. Covers legislation, Congressional committee activities, judicial matters, accountability of executive departments and regulatory agencies, activities of lobbyists, and similar topics.

JOINT ACTION IN COMMUNITY SERVICE VOLUNTEER. 5 times a year. Editor: Ted Orme. Joint Action in Community Service, Incorporated, 500

Periodicals and Newsletters

Madison National Bank Building, 1730 M Street, N.W., Washington, D.C. 20036. Free.

Reports news concerning Job Corps training and placement programs for disadvantaged youths. Contains news about the JACS organization and activities of the volunteers. Carries brief articles on such topics as the U.S. Employment Service, proposed legislation to provide income tax deductions for volunteer workers, financial and consumer advice for Job Corpsmen, advice on solving housing problems, and similar subjects.

THE JOURNAL OF CONSUMER AFFAIRS. Semi-annual. Editor: Joseph N. Uhl. American Council on Consumer Interests, 238 Stanley Hall, University of Missouri, Columbia, Missouri 65201. $6 per year.

Features articles by professional economists and educators on such topics as personal and family finance, warranties, deceptive practices, consumer education, consumer product safety standards, product quality and prices, food shopping, real estate transactions. Includes abstracts and listings of new books.

JOURNAL OF ENVIRONMENTAL QUALITY. 1972-. Quarterly. Editor: J.D. Menzies, 677 South Segoe Road, Madison, Wisconsin 53711. $10 per year.

JOURNAL OF HOME ECONOMICS. 5 times a year. Editor: Honor Fairman. American Home Economics Association, 2010 Massachusetts Avenue, N.W., Washington, D.C. 20036. $13 per year.

Carries articles on food, clothing, housing, family relations, roles of women, energy use, child abuse, and other subjects of interest to the consumer, as well as home economics teaching methods and housework projects.

JOURNAL OF PRODUCTS LIABILITY. 1976-. Quarterly. Editors-in-Chief: Verne L. Roberts and Joseph W. Cotchett. Pergamon Press, Incorporated, Maxwell House, Fairview Park, Elmsford, New York 10523. $50 per year.

Publishes papers concerned with product safety and liability, including legal and technical aspects, engineering, medicine, aviation, clothing, automobiles, and a wide assortment of consumer goods. Covers prosecution and defense of products liability actions, analyses of accident causation, product failures, appropriate designs to minimize failure or encourage safety of products.

KONSUM. Quarterly. Editor: Art Danforth. The Cooperative League of the USA, 1828 L Street, N.W., Suite 1100, Washington, D.C. 20036. Free to leadership of consumer co-ops affiliated with the Cooperative League of the USA.

Presents news items, publications, and ideas of interest to leaders of cooperatives. Discusses briefly such topics as buying clubs, state and federal government actions affecting consumers, cost of living, consumer information programs, credit unions, etc. Disseminates information about activities of cooperatives in this country and abroad.

LEGISLATIVE LOOKOUT. 5 times a year. Editor: Ellen Griffee. American Association of University Women, 2401 Virginia Avenue, N.W., Washington, D.C. 20037. $2.50 per year.

A newsletter reporting on government programs and legislation concerning such topics as the Equal Rights for Women amendment, environmental issues, health matters, pregnancy benefits for working women, energy conservation, and other national issues. Concerned with elimination of all forms of discrimination and the status of legislation affecting women.

LIFE & HEALTH. Monthly. Editor: Don Hawley. Review and Herald Publishing Association, 6856 Eastern Avenue, N.W., Washington, D.C. 20012. $8 per year.

Publishes illustrated, popular articles on health, nutrition, and child care topics such as digestion and elimination of food, exercise, smoking, traffic fatalities, vitamins, causes of disease, diets, baby care, heart attacks, eyesight, and a variety of diseases and ailments.

MODERN MATURITY. Bimonthly. American Association of Retired Persons, 215 Long Beach Boulevard, Long Beach, California 90801. $3 per year includes association membership.

Carries articles on drug prices, eye care, annuities,

Periodicals and Newsletters

ways to save estate taxes, and other topics of special interest to older persons. Also presents many hobby ideas, such as courtwatching, gardening, reading sea stories, preparing picnics, and nature photography. Consumer tips, brief news items, and puzzles are regular features.

MONEYSWORTH. Fortnightly. Editor: Junius Ellis. Publisher: Ralph Ginzburg. Moneysworth, 251 West 57th Street, New York, New York 10019. $10 per year.

Short articles describe new consumer products and services. Offers tips on how to save money, and counsels consumers on management of personal finances. Prints articles on such topics as gas mileage of cars, air travel bargains, medical and dental developments, employment, insurance, education, energy, appliances, cost of living, investments and savings, how to sue without a lawyer, and various product evaluations.

NATIONAL CONSUMERS LEAGUE BULLETIN. Bimonthly. Editor: April Moore. National Consumers League, 1028 Connecticut Avenue, N.W., Suite 522, Washington, D.C. 20036. $15 per year membership fee.

Presents consumer news concerning food, advertising and labeling, health, energy, insurance, finances, legislation, pension reform, action by regulatory agencies, and activities of local and national consumer activists.

NOT MAN APART. Biweekly. Editor: Tom Turner. Friends of the Earth, 529 Commercial Street, San Francisco, California 94111. $10 per year.

A newsletter reporting on environmental affairs, such as energy conservation, noise pollution, waste management, nuclear power plants, preserving coastlines, pesticides, water and air pollution control, strip mining, and similar topics. Regular features include Congress In-Action, Canadian Environmental Notes, Reviews, and Letters.

NUTRITION ACTION. 1974-. Monthly. Editor: Gina Moreland. Center for Science in the Public Interest, 1757 S Street, N.W., Washington, D.C. 20009. $10 per year.

Reports on new developments and advances in the field of nutrition. Exposes corporation food products and activities that are detrimental to good health. Also covers nutrition action taken by trade organizations and by government agencies.

NUTRITION TODAY. Bimonthly. Editor and publisher: Cortez F. Enloe, Jr., M.D. Nutrition Today, Incorporated, Post Office Box 465, Annapolis, Maryland 21404. $12.50 per year.

A publication and "principal benefit" of the Nutrition Today Society. Discusses various issues in the field of nutrition, such as the role of dietary fiber, food additives, infant feeding practices, medicine and nutrition, and the uses of vitamin C in preventing colds, cancer, and other conditions. Includes book reviews and news about people, places, and things in the nutrition world.

OCCUPATIONAL OUTLOOK QUARTERLY. Quarterly. Editor: Melvin C. Fountain. U.S. Department of Labor, Bureau of Labor Statistics, Occupational Outlook Service, Washington, D.C. 20212. $4 per year.

Contains articles on career preparation, job search, job safety, various types of jobs, and careers in many different fields. Presents overviews of special jobs for special needs, jobs with service programs, jobs with agencies, and similar topics.

PEOPLE & ENERGY. 1975-. Monthly. Center for Science in the Public Interest, 1757 S Street, N.W., Washington, D.C. 20009. $10 per year.

Presents news, resource information, and analyses of key developments in the energy field. Reports on national and local energy policies, and citizen action undertaken to help solve the nation's energy problems. Provides feature articles and news items on such issues as reforming utility rates, development of solar and wind energy, nuclear power proliferation, energy conservation, environmental protection, social impacts, and how to get involved.

THE PUBLIC INTEREST. Quarterly. Editors: Irving Kristol and Nathan Glazer. Publisher: Warren Demian Manshel. National Affairs, Incorporated, 10 East 53rd Street, New York, New York 10022. $9.50 per year.

Periodicals and Newsletters

Articles by educators and others discuss such topics as government regulation, education, corporate management, urban problems, medical care, health insurance, the court system, national economic planning, housing, transportation, firearms regulation, crime and punishment, ethnic progress, and other areas of public interest.

RETIREMENT LIVING. Monthly. Editor-in-Chief: Roy Hemming. Retirement Living Publishing Company, Incorporated, Whitney Communications Corporation Magazine Division, 150 East 58th Street, New York, New York 10022. $7.95 per year.

Carries popular articles of interest to retired persons on topics such as housing, health, finances, home repairs, hobbies, nutrition, travel, recreation, adult education, insurance, shopping, taxes, government policies and programs. Special departments include questions and answers about retiring, the law, money, investments, health, taxes, and consumer concerns.

THE SIGHT-SAVING REVIEW. Quarterly. Editor-in-Chief: Joseph J. Kerstein. National Society for the Prevention of Blindness, Incorporated, 79 Madison Avenue, New York, New York 10016. $10 per year.

Presents articles that aid in preventing blindness by pointing out various potential hazards, such as toys that can blind children. Tells about programs for screening and treatment of glaucoma, cataracts, and other eye ailments. Also discusses proper use of contact lenses, microscopes, studies on causes of blindness, noncompliance with medical advice, corneal transplantation, retinal detachment, occupational safety, night blindness, and related topics.

Today's Health
    Name changed to FAMILY HEALTH

U.S. Consumer
    Name changed to CON$UMER NEW$WEEKLY

U.S. Food and Drug Administration Consumer
    See FDA CONSUMER

U.S. JOURNAL OF DRUG AND ALCOHOL DEPENDENCE. 1977-. Monthly. Co-Editors: Gary Seidler and Milan Korcok. U.S. Journal of Drug and Alcohol Dependence, 7541 Biscayne Boulevard, Miami, Florida 33138. $20 per year ($12 per year for students).

Covers a wide range of issues in the areas of alcohol and other drug misuse. Reports on public and private measures for detecting drug use and ways of combatting dependence on drugs and rehabilitating addicts.

VOICE FOR CHILDREN. 10 times a year. Editor: Henry Blue. Day Care & Child Development Council of America, Publications Department, 622 14th Street, N.W., Washington, D.C. 20005. $12 per year.

Prints articles on all phases of child care programs by public and voluntary agencies. Discusses their establishment and operation, current legislation, activities, problems encountered, and publications of interest in upgrading standards.

WASHINGTON CONSUMERS' CHECKBOOK. 1976-. Quarterly. President: Robert M. Krughoff. Washington Center for the Study of Services, 1910 K Street, N.W., Suite 303, Washington, D.C. 20006. $14 per year.

Counsels consumers in the Washington area about high quality, reasonably priced services. Each issue is devoted to a topic such as health services, auto services, money services, home maintenance, child care, television and hi-fi repairs, bargain stores, kennels, employment agencies, household movers, and other types of services. A nonprofit magazine free of advertising and outside influences. Supported by funds from Consumers Union and the U.S. Office of Consumer Affairs.

WOMEN'S EQUITY ACTION LEAGUE WASHINGTON REPORT. Bimonthly. Editor: Leslie Gladstone. Women's Equity Action League, National Capital Chapter, 733 15th Street, N.W., Suite 200, Washington, D.C. 20006. $10 per year.

A newsletter with brief articles about recent Congressional action on topics of interest to women, such as abortion legislation, pensions, minimum wage proposals, sex bias, equal opportunity, health care, pregnancy benefits, etc. Contains a tabulated section on Status of Legislation Affecting Women. Available also as a supplement to Women Today.

Continuing Publication Series

AGRICULTURE INFORMATION BULLETINS. By the U.S. Department of Agriculture. Superintendent of Documents, U.S. Government Printing Office, Washington, D.C. 20402.

Inexpensive or free booklets and pamphlets on home and garden, hobbies, foods, fabrics, and materials from agricultural research. Single copies are free. Titles include: Insects and Diseases of Vegetables in the Home Garden; How to Control Wind Erosion; Your Water Supply and Forests; Fats in Food and Diet; Cooking for Small Groups; Consumer Products by Design; Building Hobby Greenhouses; Windbreaks for Conservation; Selecting and Raising Rabbits; Horsemanship and Horse Care; Soils and Septic Tanks; and others.

AGRICULTURE YEARBOOKS. By the U.S. Department of Agriculture. Superintendent of Documents, U.S. Government Printing Office, Washington, D.C. 20402.

Each yearbook covers a topic of general interest to the public and contains many short articles on subjects such as varied uses of plants, improvement of environment and housing, benefits of agricultural research, protection for consumers, etc. Prices average about $3.50. Titles include: Handbook for the Home; Shoppers' Guide; Consumers All; That We May Eat; The Face of Rural America; Landscape for Living; A Good Life for More People; Science for Better Living; Protecting Our Food; A Place to Live; and others.

CONSUMER AID SERIES. By the U.S. Department of Transportation's National Highway Traffic Safety Administration. Superintendent of Documents, U.S. Government Printing Office, Washington, D.C. 20402.

Compiled each year from data furnished by vehicle manufacturers. Published for use with the agency's Consumer Information Series. Titles include: Brakes, A Comparison of Braking Performance for Passenger Cars; Tires, A Comparison of Tire Reserve Load for Passenger Cars; Acceleration and Passing Ability.

CONSUMER BULLETINS. By the U.S. Federal Trade Commission, Distribution and Duplication Branch, Sixth Street & Pennsylvania Avenue, N.W., Washington, D.C. 20580.

Booklets present information on consumer rights and warnings about unfair business practices. Single copies are free. Titles include: Unordered Merchandise; Mail Order Insurance; Risks in Raising Chinchillas; Freezer Meat Bargains; The Fair Credit Reporting Act; Look for That Label; and others.

CONSUMER GUIDES. Edited by Consumer Guide Magazine Editors. New American Library, 1301 Avenue of the Americas, New York, New York 10019.

A series of paperbound books giving information about consumer products and advice to prospective purchasers about best values. The guides discuss advantages and disadvantages of various types of products and rate them for purchase, giving reasons for the recommendations. Average price of the paperbacks is about $2. Titles include: 1977 Consumer Buying Guide; 1977 Cars; Complete Buying Guide to Ski Equipment; Complete Buying Guide to Stereo & Tape Recorders; Complete Guide to Used Cars; Complete Guide to Golf Equipment; Food - the Brand Name Game; How It Works & How to Fix It; Photographic Equipment; Sewing Machine & Fabric Buying; Complete Guide to Tennis Equipment; and others.

CONSUMER INFORMATION SERIES. By the Council of Better Business Bureaus, Incorporated, 1150 17th Street, N.W., Washington, D.C. 20036.

Free booklets provide tips on the selection and use of many types of products and services, as well as warnings against various schemes used to defraud consumers. Some of the booklets are published jointly with the Electronic Industries Association. Titles include: Consumer Tips on Electronic Calculators; Tips on Refunds and Exchanges; Tips on Buying a Used Car; Tips on Car Repair; Tips on Tires; Tips on Television Sets; Tips on Buying a Mobile Home; Facts on Computer Careers; Tips on Work-at-Home Schemes; Tips on Home Improvements; Tips on Drycleaning; and others.

CONSUMER INFORMATION SERIES. By the U.S. Department of Transportation's National Highway Traffic Safety Administration. Superintendent of Documents, U.S. Government Printing Office, Washington, D.C. 20402.

Compiled each year from data furnished by vehicle manufacturers, the series presents Performance Data for New Passenger Cars and Motorcycles. Intended

Continuing Publication Series

for use with the related Consumer Aid Series.

CONSUMER INFORMATION SERIES. By the U.S. General Services Administration. Consumer Information, Public Documents Distribution Center, Pueblo, Colorado 81009.

Inexpensive booklets designed to share federal government information about consumer products with consumers in order to aid them in making better selections and use of various types of products. Titles include: Everyday Hand Tools; Pots and Pans; Car Care and Service; Portable Dehumidifiers; Household Cleaners; Power Hand Tools; and others.

CONSUMER MEMOS. By the U.S. Food and Drug Administration, HFG-20, 5600 Fishers Lane, Rockville, Maryland 20852.

A series of free publications supplying current and useful information about food, drugs, additives, and cosmetics. Titles include: Facts about Food Poisoning; Nitrates and Nitrites; Safety of Cooking Utensils; Some Questions and Answers about Canned Foods; Caffeine; Aspirin; Self-Medication; Quackery; Laetrile; Hexachlorophene; Food Colors (Color Additives); Cosmetics; Facts about "Tanning" Products; Antibiotics and the Foods You Eat; Available Consumer Memos; Brochures Available from FDA; and others.

CONSUMER SURVIVAL KITS. By Consumer Survival Kit television program, Box 1975, Owings Mills, Maryland 21117. $1 per kit.

Each kit contains a synopsis of information presented on the television program as well as reprints of articles, pamphlets, and topical material relating to the program's subject. The subjects covered in the program series include: small claims courts, home security systems, taxes, investment frauds, advertising, prescription drugs, insurance, auto repair, employment, nursing homes, new cars, education costs, tenants' rights, and other consumer topics. The three-year series contains 78 booklets, and free publication lists are available for 1975, 1976, and 1977.

CONSUMER TIPS. By the Montgomery County Office of Consumer Affairs, 24 Maryland Avenue, Rockville, Maryland 20850.

A series of free printed cards with do's and dont's for consumers. Titles include: Appliance Service; It's Your Move; Door-to-Door Sales; Getting the Best Prescription Drug Buy; Your New Home or Condominium; Health Clubs; Home Improvement Work; Buying a Car; Toys and Toy Safety; Basement Waterproofing; Auto Repair Checklist; and others.

ECO-TIPS. By Concern, Incorporated, 2233 Wisconsin Avenue, N.W., Washington, D.C. 20007.

Brief inexpensive leaflets present concise information on what individual consumers can do to preserve the environment and protect themselves from various forms of pollution. Titles include: Toxic Substances; Ozone: The Earth's Protective Shield; Energy Alternatives; Land Use; Automobile Pollution; Solid Waste; Drinking Water Alert; Energy Conservation; Food * Chemicals * Health; and others.

EDUCATIONAL PAMPHLETS. By Case Western Reserve University, Bureau of Business Research. Disbributed by the Money Management Institute, Household Finance Corporation, Prudential Plaza, Chicago, Illinois 60601.

Booklets written by specialists in various fields of consumer interest, published by the Bureau of Business Research, and available at low cost through the Money Management Institute. Titles include: Consumer Credit Facts for You; Small Loan Laws of the United States; and others.

EVALUATIVE STUDIES. American Enterprise Institute for Public Policy Research, 1150 17th Street, N.W., Washington, D.C. 20036.

Pamphlets by various scholars and specialists present in-depth studies of government programs and major national and international problems. Average price is about $3. Titles include: Regulation of Advertising by the FTC; The Occupational Safety and Health Act: Its Goals and Achievement; Redistribution and the Welfare System; Regulation of Auto Safety; Regulation and Drug Development; Food Stamps and Nutrition; Public Employment Programs; Veterans Administration Hospitals; Public Housing; Recovery from Natural Disasters; Urban Renewal; America's Housing Problem; and others.

Continuing Publication Series

FACT BOOKLETS. By Better Business Bureau, Educational Division, 1150 17th Street, N.W., Washington, D.C. 20036.

Low-cost booklets on business, merchandise, and financial subjects published to aid consumers with everyday money management problems and their business relationships. Titles include: Facts about Health Insurance; Facts You Should Know about Borrowing; and others.

FACT SHEETS. By the U.S. Consumer Product Safety Commission, Washington, D.C. 20207.

Leaflets describing characteristics, dangers, and misuse of hazardous products of various kinds. Single copies are available free of charge from the Commission. Titles include: Toys; Bicycles; Oven Cleaners; Vinyl Chloride; Cribs; High Chairs; Baby Walkers; Electrical Products; Fireworks; Flammable Fabrics; Flammable Liquids; Furnaces; Smoke Detectors; Pressure Cookers; Mobile Homes; Swimming Pools; Snowmobiles; and others.

FARMERS BULLETINS. By the U.S. Department of Agriculture. Superintendent of Documents, U.S. Government Printing Office, Washington, D.C. 20402.

Inexpensive booklets cover topics of interest to farmers working on a small or large scale. Titles include: Home Heating Systems, Fuels, Controls; Beef Cattle Breeds; Growing Raspberries; Growing Blackberries; Roofing Farm Buildings; Part-Time Farming; Raising Guinea Fowl; Catfish Farming; How to Control a Gully; Controlling Tomato Diseases; Strawberry Varieties in the United States; Building a Pond; Raising Geese; and others.

FDA CONSUMER MEMOS. By the U.S. Department of Health, Education, and Welfare's Food and Drug Administration, HFG-20, 5600 Fishers Lane, Rockville, Maryland 20852.

Each memo presents current and useful information on a topic concerned with foods, drugs, cosmetics, or related subjects. A publication list is available, the leaflets are free, and titles include: Facts about Food Poisoning; Nitrates and Nitrites; Food Standards; Safety of Cooking Utensils; Aspirin; Caffeine; Self-Medication; Cosmetics; Facts about "Tanning" Products; and others.

FDA CONSUMER REPRINTS. By the U.S. Department of Health, Education, and Welfare's Food and Drug Administration, Office of Public Affairs, 5600 Fishers Lane, Rockville, Maryland 20852.

A series of articles reprinted from FDA Consumer. Single copies are free. Each reprint deals with a topic concerned with the safety and usefulness of foods and additives, medicines, cosmetics, medical devices, and electronic products. Discusses current scientific and regulatory developments. Titles include: Making Food Labels More Informative; Plentiful Protein from the Sea; The Cyclamate Story; and others.

FDA PUBLIC SURVEYS. By the U.S. Department Health, Education, and Welfare's Food and Drug Administration. National Technical Information Service, 5285 Port Royal Road, Springfield, Virginia 22151.

Reports of survey results concerned with safety, regulation, and information about foods, drugs, and cosmetics. Prices vary. Titles include: Food and Nutrition Knowledge and Beliefs; A Study of Health Practices and Opinions; Consumer Perception of Safety of Foods, Drugs, and Cosmetics; and others.

FTC BUYER'S GUIDES. By the U.S. Federal Trade Commission, Distribution and Duplication Branch, Sixth Street & Pennsylvania Avenue, N.W., Washington, D.C. 20580.

Free leaflets offer advice on pitfalls that await consumers and how to avoid fraud of various types. Titles include: Care Labels; Sold Out Supermarket Specials; Don't Be Gypped; Protection for the Elderly; Freezer Meat Bargains; Look for That Label; Unordered Merchandise; Franchise Business Risks; and others.

GUIDES TO GETTING THINGS DONE IN THE VISUAL ENVIRONMENT. By the Center for the Visual Environment, 1795 Massachusetts Avenue, N.W., Washington, D.C. 20036.

Each booklet contains basic information to be used by citizens and organizations to protect their neighborhoods from visual pollution and to restore and enhance the visual elements of their environment. Prices average about $1.50. Titles include: A Guide to Neighborhood Ecology; A Guide to More Green;

Continuing Publication Series

Legal Tools and the Visual Environment; Signs and Billboards; Designs for Good Neighborhoods; Funds for Neighborhood Conservation; Benefits of Recycling Buildings; and others.

HEALTH INFORMATION SERIES. By the U.S. Department of Health, Education, and Welfare's Public Health Service. Superintendent of Documents, U.S. Government Printing Office, Washington, D.C. 20402.

Small, inexpensive booklets on various diseases and health problems. Titles include: Hearing Loss; Cataract & Glaucoma; Headache; Epilepsy; Pyorrhea and Other Gum Diseases; Dizziness; and others.

HEW CONSUMER INFORMATION SERIES. By the U.S. Department of Health, Education, and Welfare. Superintendent of Documents, U.S. Government Printing Office, Washington, D.C. 20402.

The series deals with the selection and use of products and services relating to health, safety, and education. The booklets represent the cooperative efforts of experts in government, business, professional, and consumer groups. The first booklet in the series, Tooth Care, is illustrated and written in a clear, easy-to-read style suitable for adults and children.

HOME AND GARDEN BULLETINS. By the U.S. Department of Agriculture. Superintendent of Documents, U.S. Government Printing Office, Washington, D.C. 20402.

A series of inexpensive leaflets providing practical information for homemakers and gardeners. Titles include: Keeping Food Safe to Eat; Better Lawns; Nutritive Value of Foods; Beekeeping for Beginners; Food and Your Weight; Renovate an Old House?; Family Fare; Drainage around Your Home; Home Canning of Fruits and Vegetables; Home Freezing of Fruits and Vegetables; Mulches for Your Garden; Soaps and Detergents for Home Laundering; Selecting and Growing Shade Trees; Growing Vegetables; A Guide to Budgeting for the Retired Couple; Removing Stains from Fabrics; and others.

ILLUSTRATED PAMPHLET SERIES. By the U.S. Consumer Product Safety Commission, Washington, D.C. 20207.

A free series of publications describing hazards associated with the use of various consumer products. Titles include: Crib Safety; Locked-Up Poisons; Celebrate--But Safely; The Swing That Swung Back; Childhood Poisonings; For Kids' Sake...Think Toy Safety; Safe Use of Electrical Toys; and others.

LEAFLETS SERIES. By the U.S. Department of Agriculture. Superintendent of Documents, U.S. Government Printing Office, Washington, D.C. 20402.

Inexpensive leaflets containing practical hints for small farmers and homemakers. Titles include: Food for Fitness; What to Do When Your Home Freezer Stops; Silverfish and Firebrats; Blight of Pears, Apples, and Quinces; The House Fly; Trout Farming; Raising a Few Cattle for Beef; Keeping a Cow; Growing Black Walnuts for Home Use; Muskmelons for the Garden; and others.

MIND YOUR MONEY. By the Money Management Institute of Household Finance Corporation, Prudential Plaza, Chicago, Illinois 60601.

A series of inexpensive leaflets on management of family income, planning expenditures to the best advantage, and how to buy wisely. Titles include: When You Shop; When You Use Credit; and others.

MODEL OF CONSUMER ACTION SERIES. By the National Consumers League, 1028 Connecticut Avenue, N.W., Suite 522, Washington, D.C. 20036.

Low-cost pamphlets outline objectives and procedures for various types of consumer action. The basic Model of Consumer Action can be used to deal with any consumer issue. Other titles are: Health Services; and Food Marketing System.

MONEY MANAGEMENT SERIES. Edited by the Money Management Institute of Household Finance Corporation, Prudential Plaza, Chicago, Illinois 60601.

Inexpensive booklets offer advice on how to stretch

Continuing Publication Series

dollars in order to get the best values for your money. Titles include: Your Home Furnishings Dollar; Your Recreation Dollar; Your Food Dollar; Your Clothing Dollar; Your Budget; Your Equipment Dollar; Your Shelter Dollar; Children's Spending; Your Automobile Dollar; and others.

NBS CONSUMER INFORMATION SERIES. By the U.S. Department of Commerce's National Bureau of Standards. Superintendent of Documents, U.S. Government Printing Office, Washington, D.C. 20402.

Illustrated, inexpensive pamphlets provide information to aid in choosing and using consumer products to the best advantage. Presents results of practical value from NBS research on measurement and standards. Titles include: Tires, Their Selection and Care; Making the Most of Your Energy Dollars; What about Metric?; Smoke Detectors; Facts about Hearing and Hearing Aids; Adhesives for Daily Use; and others.

PROGRAM AIDS. By the U.S. Department of Agriculture. Superintendent of Documents, U.S. Government Printing Office, Washington, D.C. 20402.

Inexpensive leaflets and pamphlets offer practical suggestions on a variety of household and other subjects. Titles include: Safe Use of Pesticides; Color It Green with Trees; Backpacking in the National Forests; Farm Operating Loans; Farm Ownership Loans; Home Improvement and Repair Loans; Invite Birds to Your Home; People, Cities, and Trees; Buying a New Sewing Machine; Cooking for Two; Simple Home Repairs...Inside; Food and Nutrition; and others.

PUBLIC ADVISORY SERIES. By the U.S. Interstate Commerce Commission. Superintendent of Documents, U.S. Government Printing Office, Washington, D.C. 20402.

A series of leaflets issued to inform the householder of his rights and the mover's obligations in transporting household goods. Titles include: Householder's Guide to Accurate Weights; Arranging Transportation for Small Shipments; People on the Move; Lost or Damaged Household Goods; and others.

PUBLIC AFFAIRS PAMPHLETS. By the Public Affairs Committee, 381 Park Avenue South, New York, New York 10016.

An inexpensive series of pamphlets, by Sidney Margolius and other authors, covering social and economic problems, child development and family relations, mental and physical health, and intergroup relations. Titles include: Buyer, Be Wary!; Your Child and Money; How to Finance Your Home; A Guide to Consumer Credit; How to Get Good Medical Care; Consumer's Guide to Health Insurance; The Responsible Consumer; Health Foods: Facts and Fakes; Housing: A Nationwide Crisis; Population and the American Future; The Challenge of Inflation and Recession; Making Products Safer; and others.

SERIES FOR ECONOMIC EDUCATION. By the Federal Reserve Bank of Philadelphia, Public Information Department, Philadelphia, Pennsylvania 19101.

Free booklets on various aspects of the economic system provide understandable explanations of complex issues for average citizens. Titles include: The Price System; The Mystery of Economic Growth; Automation; The New Poverty; The National Debt; Inflation and/or Unemployment; Truth in Lending; The Growth of Government; Economic Man vs. Social Man; and others.

TECHNICAL FACT SHEETS. By the U.S. Consumer Product Safety Commission, Washington, D.C. 20207.

Free leaflets provide information about potential hazards concerned with the use of various kinds of consumer products. Titles include: Fluorocarbons; Aluminum Wiring; Bicycle Regulations; and others.

U.S. Federal Trade Commission Buyer's Guides
See FTC BUYER'S GUIDES

U.S. Food and Drug Administration Consumer Memos
See FDA CONSUMER MEMOS

U.S. Health, Education, and Welfare Consumer Information Series
See HEW CONSUMER INFORMATION SERIES

U.S. National Bureau of Standards Consumer Information Series
See NBS CONSUMER INFORMATION SERIES

WE WANT YOU TO KNOW ABOUT... By the U.S. Food and Drug Administration, HFG-20, 5600 Fishers Lane, Rockville, Maryland 20852.

A series of free brochures providing advice to consumers on food and drug problems. Titles include: Nutrition Labels on Food; Foodborne Illness; Cooking Utensils; Medicines without Prescriptions; Prescription Drugs; Labels on Medicines; Adverse Reactions to Medicines; and others.

Audiovisual Materials

ADVERTISING AND THE CONSUMER. 1973. 35mm filmstrip. 86 frames. Color. With phonodisc, 18 minutes. Jacoby/Storm Productions. Released by Current Affairs Films, 24 Danbury Road, Wilton, Connecticut 06897.

Explains how advertising gives useful information but also plays upon desires and fears in influencing the consumer. Tells of the expressed need for more regulation by the advertiser himself, government, or private agencies to counteract deceptive practices. Produced in cooperation with the Council of Better Business Bureaus. Part of the series Buyer beWise.

ADVERTISING AND YOU. 1974. 35mm filmstrip. 96 frames. Color. With phonodisc, 13 minutes. Centron Corporation. Released by Centron Educational Films, 1621 West Ninth Street, Lawrence, Kansas 66044.

Shows the consumer how to avoid false advertising pitches and how to evaluate advertising messages. Part of the series Consumer Education for the Elementary Grades.

THE ALL-AMERICAN CONSUMER. 1972. 35mm filmstrip. 63 frames. Color. With phonodisc, 12 minutes. Doubleday Multimedia, 1371 Reynolds Avenue, Santa Ana, California 92705.

Follows a product from its development by a manufacturer to its introduction in the marketplace. Highlights the positive and negative values of advertising, and the ways in which consumers can protect themselves when buying advertised products. Part of the Consumer Education Series.

AMERICA FOR SALE. 1973. 16mm film. Black and white. Sound. 27 minutes. NET Division, Educational Broadcasting Corporation. Released by Indiana University Audio-Visual Center, Bloomington, Indiana 47401.

Explores the practices of unscrupulous real estate salesmen and land developers as duped buyers recount the tactics used to make them buy worthless land. Warns potential buyers to look at the land they plan to buy and to hire lawyers to read contracts before a sale.

THE ANATOMY OF A SALE. 1972. 35mm filmstrip. 100 frames. Color. With phonodisc, 17 minutes. Consumer Information Services, Sears, Roebuck and Company. Released by Association-Sterling Films, 866 Third Avenue, New York, New York 10022.

Examines the structure of the buying-selling situation and the underlying and interacting factors between consumers and retailers. Shows how the buyer and the seller operate, how they relate, how they can complement one another, and how they can come into conflict.

AND THIS LITTLE BOTTLE WENT TO MARKET. 1974. 35mm filmstrip. 46 frames. Color. With phonotape, 6 minutes. January Productions, 13-00 Plaza Road, Post Office Box 244, Fair Lawn, New Jersey 07410.

Encourages the development of an awareness of the problems confronting consumers, such as budgeting, comparison shopping, and defective merchandise. Presents a story about a milk bottle and its journey from the milk bottling plant to the store. For primary grades. Part of the series Alice in Consumerland.

APPLYING FOR CREDIT. 1976. 35mm filmstrip. 84 frames. Color. With phonodisc or cassette, 12 minutes. Guidance Associates, 757 Third Avenue, New York, New York 10017.

Deals with problems encountered in applying for credit, various hazards in using credit, and how to go about obtaining a credit card or charge account. Includes a discussion guide. Part of the Consumer Skills Series.

ARE DRUGS THE ANSWER? 1970. 16mm film. Color. Sound. 20 minutes. General Services Administration, National Audiovisual Center, Washington, D.C. 20409.

A former disciple of Timothy Leary, Dr. Alan Cohen, crusades against drug abuse. He discusses the nature and harmful effects of various kinds of drugs, such as the psychedelics, speed, and marijuana.

THE BANK LOAN. 1969. 35mm filmstrip. 32 frames. Color. With phonodisc. Bailey Films. Released by BFA Educational Media, 2211 Michigan

Audiovisual Materials

Avenue, Santa Monica, California 90404.

A recent high school graduate learns about bank loans when she applies for a bank loan in order to purchase a used car. The banker instructs her in the process of financing a car through the bank. She learns the difference between add-on and discount interest, the meaning of simple interest and true annual interest, and other aspects of car loans.

BE A BETTER SHOPPER. 1977. Slide kit. 140 slides. Color. With leader's guide and participant guide. By Heinz B. Biesdorf, Mary Ellen Burris, and Josephone Swanson. Better Shopper, Cornell University, Box 191, Department LG-1-17, Ithaca, New York 14850.

Shows how to be a wise, efficient shopper in a supermarket and save as much as 15% on purchases.

BE CREDIT-WISE. 1970. 35mm filmstrip. 87 frames. Color. With phonodisc. Made by Betzer Productions. Household Finance Corporation, Money Management Institute, Prudential Plaza, Chicago, Illinois 60601.

Illustrates the various types and sources of consumer credit. Portrays the advantages and disadvantages of buying on credit and the responsibilities of the purchaser.

BEING A WISE SHOPPER - MORE MEAT FOR YOUR MONEY. 1974. 35mm filmstrip. 30 frames. Color. With phonodisc, 7 minutes. U.S. Department of Agriculture Cooperative Extension Service. Made and released by Double Sixteen Company, Post Office Box 1616, Wheaton, Illinois 60187.

Shows the importance of proper nutrition while watching the budget. Gives concerned shoppers pointers on selecting breads, produce, and meats. Part of a series on nutrition.

THE BIG BUY. 1975. 35mm filmstrip. 42 frames. Color. Visual Education Consultants, Incorporated, Box 52, Madison, Wisconsin 53701.

Examines some common buying and credit practices in the American marketplace. Helps young people understand and cope with money-handling problems in today's world. With captions.

BLUEPRINT FOR HOME BUYING. 1971. 16mm film. Color. Sound. 14 minutes. American Land Title Association, 1828 L Street, Northwest, Washington, D.C. 20036.

Explains the basic steps in selecting, financing, and closing the purchase of residential real estate. Apologizes somewhat for the costs of title searches. Makes a pitch for lenders' and owners' title insurance.

BRAND NAMES AND LABELING GAMES. 1973. 16mm film. Color. Sound. 9 minutes. National Educational Television. Released by Benchmark Films, 145 Scarborough Road, Briarcliff Manor, New York 10510.

Shows how brand names and advertising often contribute nothing more than a higher price to common household products and foods. Demonstrates the importance of comparison shopping, reading labels, and spot-checking government regulations.

BUBBLE, BUBBLE, TOYS, AND TROUBLE. 1975. 16mm film. Color. Sound. 10 minutes. U.S. Consumer Product Safety Commission. Made by Production House, Incorporated. Released by National Audiovisual Center, U.S. General Services Administration. Washington, D.C. 20409.

Evaluates good and bad qualities in children's toys by presenting a sketch about a witch who makes the world's worst toys. These toys have small parts, sharp points and edges, and toxic substances.

BUYER BEWARE. 1971. 35mm filmstrips. 6 filmstrips. Color. With 6 phonodiscs. Made by Joshua Tree Productions. Released by Westinghouse Learning Corporation, 100 Park Avenue, New York, New York 10017.

A consumer education program based on guidelines established by the President's Committee on Consumer Affairs. Explains consumer rights and responsibilities. Deals with the consumer as an individual and the consumer in society. Points out alternatives in the marketplace.

BUYER BEWISE SERIES. 1972. 35mm filmstrips. 6 filmstrips. Color. With 6 phonodiscs or cassettes, 30 minutes each. Current Affairs Films, 24 Danbury Road, Wilton, Connecticut 06897.

Covers six topics: consumer credit; food and clothing; cars and motorcycles; fraud and deceptions; advertising; and consumer power and social change. Produced in cooperation with the Council of Better Business Bureaus.

BUYING A HOUSE. 1971. 35mm filmstrip. 76 frames. Color. With phonodisc. CUNA International. Made by Gilbert Altschul Productions. Released by Journal Films, 909 West Diversey Parkway, Chicago, Illinois 60614.

Stresses the need for careful investigation and legal advice before purchasing a house. Explains the various points to consider, including the community, its services and resources, and the schools. Part of a consumer education program called Using Your Money.

BUYING CAREFULLY. 1969. 35mm filmstrip. 54 frames. Color. With learning manual. Educational Projections Corporation, 527 South Commerce Street, Jackson, Mississippi 39205.

Supplies information about making wise purchases. Includes advice about the checking of prices, taking advantage of yearly sales, and special pointers on buying food.

BUYING CLOTHING. 1971. 35mm filmstrip. 88 frames. Color. With phonodisc. CUNA International. Made by Gilbert Altschul Productions. Released by Journal Films, 909 West Diversey Parkway, Chicago, Illinois 60614.

Emphasizes the importance of wise advance planning so that the purchase of good practical clothing becomes a worthwhile long term investment. Explains how to plan a wardrobe, what to look for in terms of quality, how to determine the proper fit of a garment, and how to tell whether or not a sale is a bargain. Part of a consumer education program called Using Your Money.

BUYING ON THE INSTALLMENT PLAN. 1976. 35mm filmstrip. 89 frames. Color. With phonodisc or cassette, 15 minutes. Guidance Associates, 757 Third Avenue, New York, New York 10017.

Discusses skills needed for reading and understanding a retail installment contract. Explains credit terms and various provisions for installment purchases. Includes a discussion guide. Part of the Consumer Skills Series.

BUYING THE BASICS: FOOD AND CLOTHING. 1973. 35mm filmstrip. 97 frames. Color. With phonodisc, 18 minutes. Jacoby/Storm Productions. Released by Current Affairs Films, 24 Danbury Road, Wilton, Connecticut 06897.

Explains how to make wise purchases in order to eat and dress well. Points out how to compare prices, read labels, and compare brand names. Tells how to recognize deceptive practices and how to shop the ads. Part of the series Buyer beWise.

BUYING WISELY. 1971. 35mm filmstrip. 79 frames. Color. With phonodisc. Society for Visual Education, 1345 West Diversey Parkway, Chicago, Illinois 60614.

Explains the relationship between consumer purchasing and the national economic system. Portrays members of a middle-income family and shows how they demonstrate consumer skills as they purchase food, clothing, an appliance, and repair service.

BUYING WITH A TWISTED ARM. 1975. 16mm film. Color. Sound. 13 minutes. Gilbert Altschul Productions. Released by Journal Films, Incorporated, 909 West Diversey Parkway, Chicago, Illinois 60614.

Presents four vignettes in which buyers appear trapped into making purchases. Shows how the consumer can be affected by an emergency, pressure, emotions, or the flattery of a salesman.

CATCH A COMMERCIAL. 1974. 35mm filmstrip. 41 frames. Color. With phonotape, 6 minutes. Produced by Phyllis Dolgin. January Productions, 13-00 Plaza Road, Post Office Box 244, Fair Lawn, New Jersey 07410.

Presents a fantasy story about commercials on children's television. Encourages the development of an awareness of the problems confronting the consumer, such as budgeting, comparison shopping, and defective merchandise. For primary grades. Part of the series Alice in Consumerland.

Audiovisual Materials

CHOOSING WHAT TO BUY. 1974. 35mm filmstrip. 129 frames. Color. With phonodisc, 15 minutes. Centron Corporation. Released by Centron Educational Films, 1621 West Ninth Street, Lawrence, Kansas 66044.

Fosters an understanding of the ways in which money management and goal analysis can help consumers in deciding what to buy.

CLASSROOM MONEY MANAGEMENT KIT. 1973. A multi-media kit including 4 cassettes with 8 - 21 minute lessons on various aspects of consumer credit and printed materials. CUNA Mutual Insurance Society, Post Office Box 391, Madison, Wisconsin 53701.

Presents a mini course in consumer credit. Printed materials include: 15 copies of Everybody's Money; 30 copies of a 24-page booklet, Personal Money Manager; 30 reprints of "Smart Saving, Borrowing, Budgeting" from Scholastic Magazine; a board game, "Managing Your Money," 1 copy of Suggested Guidelines for Consumer Education, Grades K-12; a 4-page glossary; and a teacher's guide.

CONCERNING YOUNG CONSUMERS. 1975. 6 35mm filmstrips. With 6 phonodiscs, 10 minutes each. Association-Sterling Films. Released by Macmillan Publishing Company, 866 Third Avenue, New York, New York 10022.

Contents: 1. What's Behind the Price Tag? 72 frames. 2. Are You Getting the Message? 72 frames. 3. Does shopping mean buying? 70 frames. 4. How Do You Pay for It? 74 frames. 5. Do Consumers Have Rights? 81 frames. 6. When Does Value End? 64 frames. Consumer education filmstrips for primary grades.

THE CONSUMER AND CREDIT. 1973. 35mm filmstrip. 80 frames. Color. With phonodisc, 18 minutes. Jacoby/Storm Productions. Released by Current Affairs Films, 24 Danbury Road, Wilton, Connecticut 06897.

Describes various types of credit and tells of their use and misuse. Explains available legal protection for consumers, as well as legal recourses available to creditors. Part of the series Buyer beWise.

CONSUMER AT LARGE: BUDGET BLUES. 1972. 35mm filmstrip. 48 frames. Color. With phonodisc, 12 minutes. Coronet Instructional Media, 65 East South Water Street, Chicago, Illinois 60601.

Describes a budget and explains the necessity of having one in order to save money for a desired item.

CONSUMER AT LARGE: BUYING THE BIG ONES. 1972. 35mm filmstrip. 56 frames. Color. With phonodisc, 15 minutes. Coronet Instructional Media, 65 East South Water Street, Chicago, Illinois 60601.

Explains that the consumer needs special skills in selecting and purchasing items that are to be used over a long period of time.

CONSUMER AT LARGE: CASH OR CREDIT? 1972. 35mm filmstrip. 54 frames. Color. With phonodisc, 15 minutes. Coronet Instructional Media, 65 East South Water Street, Chicago, Illinois 60601.

Shows what credit is and how it works, tells some of the dangers in using credit, and explains alternatives available to the consumer when credit is needed to make a purchase.

CONSUMER AT LARGE: EVERYDAY SHOPPING SAVVY. 1972. 35mm filmstrip. 51 frames. Color. With phonodisc, 13 minutes. Coronet Instructional Media, 65 East South Water Street, Chicago, Illinois 60601.

Discusses the importance of comparison shopping when buying household necessities.

CONSUMER AT LARGE: NURTURING A NEST EGG. 1972. 35mm filmstrip. 56 frames. Color. With phonodisc, 14 minutes. Coronet Instructional Media, 65 East South Water Street, Chicago, Illinois 60601.

Shows the need for saving money and the importance of investing wisely.

CONSUMER AT LARGE: SHOPPING FOR SERVICES. 1972. 35mm filmstrip. 55 frames. Color. With phonodisc, 14 minutes. Coronet Instructional Media,

Audiovisual Materials

65 East South Water Street, Chicago, Illinois 60601.

Shows how to comparison shop for various services by checking reputation, quality, and price.

CONSUMER BE WARNED: FRAUDS AND DECEPTION. 1973. 35mm filmstrip. 84 frames. Color. With phonodisc, 18 minutes. Jacoby/Storm Productions. Released by Current Affairs Films, 24 Danbury Road, Wilton, Connecticut 06897.

Teaches the consumer how to recognize various frauds and deceptions and how to avoid being taken in by them. Part of the series Buyer beWise.

CONSUMER EDUCATION. 1973. 5 35mm filmstrips. Approximately 49 frames each. Color. With 5 cassettes of phonotape, approximately 14 minutes each. Interpretive Education, 2225 Winters Drive, Kalamazoo, Michigan 49002.

Designed for secondary special education students. Helps acquaint handicapped children with wise ways of shopping.

CONSUMER EDUCATION. 1973. 35mm filmstrip. 55 frames. Color. With phonodisc, 14 minutes. Teaching Resources Films, 2 Kisco Plaza, Mount Kisco, New York 10549.

Examines product promotion, the force of advertising, consumer demand, and the guidelines with which to appraise them. Part of the School Times Series.

CONSUMER EDUCATION. PART 2: MANAGING YOUR MONEY. 1974. 4 35mm filmstrips. Color. With 2 phonodiscs, 14 minutes each side. Teaching Resources Films, 2 Kisco Plaza, Mount Kisco, New York 10549.

Contents: 1. Living within your means, 51 frames. 2. Making your money work, 53 frames. 3. Planning your financial future, 51 frames. 4. Recognizing fraud, quackery, and deception, 57 frames. Juvenile filmstrips for elementary grades.

CONSUMER EDUCATION. PART 3: MAKING IT ON YOUR OWN. 1975. 4 35mm filmstrips. Color. With 4 phonodiscs, about 12 minutes each.

Teaching Resources Films, 2 Kisco Plaza, Mount Kisco, New York 10549.

Contents: 1. Understanding your paycheck, 47 frames. 2. How to select professional assistance, 57 frames. 3. Good maintenance makes sense, 74 frames. 4. Making the most of yourself, 71 frames.

CONSUMER EDUCATION I. 1971. 4 35mm filmstrips. Color. With 4 phonodiscs. Hanna-Barbera Productions, Incorporated, Educational Division, 3400 Cahuenga Boulevard, Hollywood, California 90068.

Stresses money management: easy come, easy go. Explains credit and contracts. Also deals with problems in selection of housing and food.

CONSUMER EDUCATION II. 1971. 4 35mm filmstrips. Color. With 4 phonodiscs, approximately 12 minutes each. Hanna-Barbera Productions, Incorporated, Educational Division, 3400 Cahuenga Boulevard, Hollywood, California 90068.

Contents: 1. Buying protection: health and life insurance. 2. Furniture and appliances. 3. Transportation. 4. Clothing.

CONSUMER EDUCATION: BUDGETING. 1969. 16mm film. Color. Sound. 12 minutes. Bailey-Film Associates. Released by BFA Educational Media, 2211 Michigan Avenue, Santa Monica, California 90404.

Emphasizes the importance of sound budget planning. Dramatizes the financial difficulties of two sisters who over-extend their credit purchasing.

CONSUMER EDUCATION: BUYER BE WISE. 1975. 4 35mm filmstrips. 225 frames. Color. With 4 phonodiscs, 80 minutes. Teaching Resources Films, 2 Kisco Plaza, Mount Kisco, New York 10549.

Contents: 1. Budgets, batteries, and bicycles. 2. Supershopper goes to market. 3. Health is a best buy. 4. And now, a word from our sponsor.

CONSUMER EDUCATION: BUYING AN AUTOMOBILE. 1974. 16mm film. Color. Sound.

14 minutes. Charles Cahill and Associates. Released by AIMS Instructional Media Services, Incorporated, 5420 Melrose Street, Hollywood, California 90028.

Offers advice for buying an automobile. Discusses financing, insurance, dealing with salesmen, and the purchase of used cars from private individuals.

CONSUMER EDUCATION: BUYING IN A SUPERMARKET. 1973. 16mm film. Color. Sound. 15 minutes. AIMS Instructional Media Services, Incorporated, 5420 Melrose Street, Hollywood, California 90028.

Gives hints on how to get the best value for money spent in a supermarket. Points out the psychological effect advertising has on the average consumer.

CONSUMER EDUCATION: HOW TO SHOP WISELY. 1973. 4 35mm filmstrips. 220 frames. Color. With 2 phonodiscs, 60 minutes. Teaching Resources Films, 2 Kisco Plaza, Mount Kisco, New York 10549.

Contents: 1. Becoming a responsible consumer. 2. Buying quality on a budget. 3. Finding a place to live. 4. Shopping for a car.

CONSUMER EDUCATION: INSTALLMENT BUYING. 1969. 16mm film. Color. Sound. 13 minutes. Bailey-Film Associates. Released by BFA Educational Media, 2211 Michigan Avenue, Santa Monica, California 90404.

Dramatizes the benefits and pitfalls of making purchases on an installment plan.

CONSUMER EDUCATION: MAINTAINING AN AUTOMOBILE. 1974. 16mm film. Color. Sound. 11 minutes. Charles Cahill and Associates. Released by AIMS Instructional Media Services, Incorporated, 5420 Melrose Street, Hollywood, California 90028.

Offers help in choosing a qualified mechanic and in purchasing accessories for maintaining an automobile. Shows how proper servicing can make owning a car a pleasure.

CONSUMER EDUCATION: RETAIL CREDIT BUYING. 1969. 16mm film. Color. Sound. 11 minutes. Bailey-Film Associates. Released by BFA Educational Media, 2211 Michigan Avenue, Santa Monica, California 90404.

Demonstrates correct methods of computing credit charges. Dramatizes the various facets of buying on credit.

CONSUMER EDUCATION: WHO NEEDS IT? 1972. 16mm film. Color. Sound. 15 minutes. Bill Crain and Richard Wallace. Released by Churchill Films, 622 North Robertson Boulevard, Los Angeles, California 90069.

Discusses advertising technique, how interest is computed, and the use of credit. Explains the need for consumer protection. Includes examples of such problem areas as food quality, pricing, labeling, and automobile sales, service, and safety.

CONSUMER EDUCATION SERIES. 1972. 6 35mm filmstrips. Color. With 6 phonodiscs. Doubleday Multimedia, 1371 Reynolds Avenue, Santa Ana, California 92705.

Contents: 1. Getting ahead of the game, 81 frames, 16 minutes. 2. Decisions, decisions, 55 frames, 13 minutes. 3. Your money: now you see it, now you don't, 72 frames, 15 minutes. 4. How to be a loser, 65 frames, 18 minutes. 5. The law and your pocketbook, 70 frames, 15 minutes. 6. The all-American consumer, 63 frames, 12 minutes.

THE CONSUMER GAME. 1973. 16mm film. Color. Sound. 20 minutes. Directions Unlimited Film Corporation. Released by Pyramid Films, Incorporated, Post Office Box 1048, Santa Monica, California 90406.

Helps consumers learn how to shop wisely through comparison shopping, unit pricing, and resistance to advertising pressures and ploys.

CONSUMER POWER: ADVERTISING. 1971. 16mm film. Color. Sound. 22 minutes. By J. Gary Mitchell. Released by BFA Educational Media, 2211 Michigan Avenue, Santa Monica, California 90404.

Consumer advocate Ralph Nader and advertising executive Ted Factor discuss the morality of advertising and the individual's power to affect advertising practices. They explain the role of private and public consumer protection agencies in preventing deceptive advertising.

CONSUMER POWER AND SOCIAL CHANGE. 1973. 35mm filmstrip. 81 frames. Color. With phonodisc, 18 minutes. Jacoby/Storm Productions. Released by Current Affairs Films, 24 Danbury Road, Wilton, Connecticut 06897.

Explains that consumer power is represented by government spokesmen, independent consumer groups, and organizations at the community and neighborhood levels. Tells of methods of consumer protection, including publicity, lobbying, boycotts, organized complaints, and consumer cooperatives. Produced in cooperation with the Better Business Bureau. Part of the series Buyer beWise.

CONSUMER POWER: CREDIT. 1973. 16mm film. Color. Sound. 21 minutes. By J. Gary Mitchell. Released by BFA Educational Media, 2211 Michigan Avenue, Santa Monica, California 90404.

Consumer advocate Ralph Nader, psychoanalyst Dr. Isidore Ziferstein, and bank executive J. Hynes present three differing points of view about Americans' use of credit. Defines the benefits and dangers of credit buying in interviews with these authorities, and in interviews with consumers.

CONSUMER POWER: WHISTLEBLOWING. 1973. 16mm film. Color. Sound. 23 minutes. By J. Gary Mitchell. Released by BFA Educational Media, 2211 Michigan Avenue, Santa Monica, California 90404.

Consumer advocate Ralph Nader and author Robert Townsend urge ethical whistleblowing as a form of individual action against public abuses by large corporations.

CONSUMER REPORTS FROM CONSUMERS UNION. 1974. 16mm films. Color. Sound. 26-week series of 2 films per week, each about 2 minutes. Consumers Union of United States, Incorporated, 256 Washington Street, Mount Vernon, New York 10550.

A film series based on material appearing in Consumer Reports magazine. Offered at cost to television stations throughout the United States for use on news or consumer affairs programs. Reports deal with the performance of automobiles, pet deaths in airline baggage compartments, deceptive advertising, ratings of products and services, and similar topics of interest to consumers.

CONSUMER SKILLS: BUDGETING YOUR MONEY. 1976. 16mm film. Color. Sound. 13 minutes. Coronet Instructional Media, 65 East South Water Street, Chicago, Illinois 60601.

Shows four young people in different financial situations discussing their budgeting problems. Their conversations lead to information on how budgets are made and carried out.

CONSUMER SKILLS: BUYING FOR IMMEDIATE USE. 1976. 16mm film. Color. Sound. 14 minutes. Coronet Instructional Media, 65 East South Water Street, Chicago, Illinois 60601.

Rates the consumer shopping skills of three young shoppers making typical purchases for immediate use. Illustrates judging quality, price, and service and determining which of these three factors are valuable in making these purchases.

CONSUMER SKILLS: BUYING FOR LONG-TERM USE. 1976. 16mm film. Color. Sound. 12 minutes. Coronet Instructional Media, 65 East South Water Street, Chicago, Illinois 60601.

Shows a panel of consumers turning back the clock a year and telling how accurate their predictions have been for major purchases made a year ago.

CONSUMER SKILLS: BUYING ON CREDIT. 1976. 16mm film. Color. Sound. 13 minutes. Coronet Instructional Media, 65 East South Water Street, Chicago, Illinois 60601.

Shows what credit is, how it works, and some of the dangers involved in using credit. Uses a conversation between three young men to introduce finance charges, bank loans, down payment, interest, and installment payments.

Audiovisual Materials

CONSUMER SKILLS: BUYING SERVICES. 1976. 16mm film. Color. Sound. 14 minutes. Coronet Instructional Media, 65 East South Water Street, Chicago, Illinois 60601.

Reveals the experiences of four young people with saving and investing programs. Shows what they've learned about credit unions, savings and loan companies, banks, and types of investment.

CONSUMER SKILLS: SAVINGS AND INVESTING. 1976. 16mm film. Color. Sound. 15 minutes. Coronet Instructional Media, 65 East South Water Street, Chicago, Illinois 60601.

Shows the need for savings and the importance of investing money wisely. Uses the experiences of a young man involved in an automobile accident to illustrate the importance of being financially prepared for an emergency.

CONSUMER STUDIES: BUYER BEWARE! 1972. 35mm filmstrip. 56 frames. Color. With phonodisc, 8 minutes. Guidance Associates of Pleasantville, Post Office Box 5, Pleasantville, New York 10570.

Probes a wide variety of fraud and misrepresentation commonly found in advertising, retail practices, and labeling. Provides specific guidelines for avoiding fraud in making ordinary and special purchases. A juvenile filmstrip for elementary grades.

CONSUMER STUDIES: MAKING ENDS MEET. 1972. 35mm filmstrip. 55 frames. Color. With phonodisc. Guidance Associates, Post Office Box 5, Pleasantville, New York 10570.

Presents a model family budget that emphasizes orderly allocation of money resources. Emphasizes the importance of setting limits and staying within them. Discusses flexibility in arranging priorities and in making purchases.

CONSUMER STUDIES: MONEY WELL SPENT. 1972. 35mm filmstrip. 71 frames. Color. With phonodisc, 8 minutes. Guidance Associates of Pleasantville, Post Office Box 5, Pleasantville, New York 10570.

Describes the vastness of the American economy. Discusses the relationship between the consumer and the seller and advertiser. Considers sales appeals that are based on insecurity or gullibility. Emphasizes the importance of gleaning hard information from advertisements and labels. A juvenile filmstrip for elementary grades.

CONSUMER STUDIES: THE PRICE OF CREDIT. 1972. 35mm filmstrip. 58 frames. Color. With phonodisc, 9 minutes. Guidance Associates of Pleasantville, Post Office Box 5, Pleasantville, New York 10570.

Simulates a used car "deal" to demonstrate deceptive sales lines. Underscores the importance of reading all sales documents and insisting that they be completed on the spot. Explores credit problems and suggests comparison shopping for the best credit terms.

CONSUMERISM. 1973. 35mm filmstrip. 132 frames. Color. With phonodisc, 11 minutes. Made by Audiovisual Department, Field Educational Publications, 2400 Hanover Street, Palo Alto, California 94304.

Describes the origin and development of the consumer society, pointing out its advantages and disadvantages and considering its future impact on people and the environment. Part of the series Quest for Liberty.

CONSUMERISM: LET THE SELLER BEWARE! 1975. 16mm film. Color. Sound. 21 minutes. Document Associates, Toronto, and Hobel-Leiterman Productions, Toronto. Released in the United States by ACI Films, Incorporated, 35 West 45th Street, New York, New York 10036.

Helps consumers to be aware of the need to enter the marketplace with caution. Shows how consumers can become active in combating the abuses of manufacturers and marketers. Part of the series Coping with Tomorrow.

CONSUMERLAND: HOW HIGH THE MOUNTAIN? 1972. 35mm filmstrip. 132 frames. Color. With phonodisc or cassette. Argus Communications, 7440 Natchez Avenue, Niles, Illinois 60648.

Uses a cartoon format to get across many aspects of "consumerism." No specific subject is covered in depth. Could be used as an introduction to consumer education.

Audiovisual Materials

CONSUMERS: POOR TODAY, POORER TOMORROW? 1975. 35mm filmstrip. 68 frames. Color. With phonodisc, 10 minutes. Crocus Productions. Released by Doubleday Multimedia, 1371 Reynolds Avenue, Santa Ana, California 92705.

Uses a science fiction episode to discuss the position of the consumer under contemporary and projected conditions of affluence. Poses alternative solutions to extremes of overabundance and scarcity based on consumer protection and consumer regulation. Part of the series Economics and the Future: The Consumer of Tomorrow.

CONSUMER'S WORLD - IT'S YOUR DECISION: BUYING A CAR. 1974. 35mm filmstrip. 107 frames. Color. With phonodisc, 13 minutes. Made by Richard Starkey Video Productions. Distributed by Globe Filmstrips, 65 East South Water Street, Chicago, Illinois 60601.

Presents a three-part inquiry into procedures involved in buying a used car.

CONSUMER'S WORLD - IT'S YOUR DECISION: BUYING CLOTHING. 1974. 35mm filmstrip. 98 frames. Color. With phonodisc, 12 minutes. Made by Richard Starkey Video Productions. Distributed by Globe Filmstrips, 65 East South Water Street, Chicago, Illinois 60601.

Presents three differing views on purchasing clothing.

CONSUMER'S WORLD - IT'S YOUR DECISION: BUYING FOOD. 1974. 35mm filmstrip. 107 frames. Color. With phonodisc, 11 minutes. Made by Richard Starkey Video Productions. Distributed by Globe Filmstrips, 65 East South Water Street, Chicago, Illinois 60601.

Three young men sharing an apartment have different systems for buying food on a budget.

CONSUMER'S WORLD - IT'S YOUR DECISION: BUYING HOME FURNISHINGS. 1974. 35mm filmstrip. 102 frames. Color. With phonodisc, 11 minutes. Made by Richard Starkey Video Productions. Distributed by Globe Filmstrips, 65 East South Water Street, Chicago, Illinois 60601.

Newlyweds face three dilemmas in furnishing their first apartment.

CONSUMER'S WORLD - IT'S YOUR DECISION: BUYING TROUBLE. 1974. 35mm filmstrip. 86 frames. Color. With phonodisc, 7 minutes. Made by Richard Starkey Video Productions. Distributed by Globe Filmstrips, 65 East South Water Street, Chicago, Illinois 60601.

Explores the pitfalls of signing a contract without checking some points first.

CONSUMER'S WORLD - IT'S YOUR DECISION: RENTING AN APARTMENT. 1974. 35mm filmstrip. 96 frames. Color. With phonodisc, 10 minutes. Made by Richard Starkey Video Productions. Distributed by Globe Filmstrips, 65 East South Water Street, Chicago, Illinois 60601.

A young man, his fiancée, and his sister debate the pros and cons of two apartments they are considering renting.

CONSUMERSHIP: GETTING MORE FOR YOUR MONEY. 1974. 35mm filmstrip. 115 frames. Color. With phonodisc, 15 minutes. Centron Corporation. Released by Centron Educational Films, 1621 West Ninth Street, Lawrence, Kansas 66044.

Shows how wise buying practices, such as the evaluation of goods on the basis of need, cost, and quality, can help save money. A juvenile filmstrip for primary grades. Part of the series Consumer Education for the Elementary Grades.

THE CONTEMPORARY CONSUMER SERIES. 1975. 8 35mm filmstrips. 60 frames each. Color. With 8 cassettes of phonotape, 30 minutes each. McGraw-Hill/University Films. Released by Gregg and Community College Division, McGraw-Hill Book Company, 1221 Avenue of the Americas, New York, New York 10020.

Discusses some of the common dilemmas facing young consumers today.

CREDIT CARDS. 1975. 35mm filmstrip. 64 frames. Color. With phonodisc. BFA Educational

Media in cooperation with TRW Credit Data. Released by BFA Educational Media, 2211 Michigan Avenue, Santa Monica, California 90404.

Teaches some important ideas about credit and how to apply these ideas to personal money management. Deals with the uses of credit cards. Tells ways to protect cards from theft or to prevent their use in the event of loss. Part of the series Consumer Credit and Money Management. Issued with a teaching guide, readings, and supplementary material.

CREDIT: THE BANK. 1975. 35mm filmstrip. 59 frames. Color. With phonodisc. BFA Educational Media in cooperation with TRW Credit Data. Released by BFA Educational Media, 2211 Michigan Avenue, Santa Monica, California 90404.

Teaches about interest rates, showing how to shop for the lowest rate. Explains how to convert interest rates to an annual percentage rate. Discusses what one should consider when preparing to buy a new car and other purchases. Part of the series Consumer Credit and Money Management. Issued with a teaching guide, readings, and supplementary material.

CREDIT: THE FINANCE COMPANY. 1975. 35mm filmstrip. 64 frames. Color. With phonodisc. BFA Educational Media in cooperation with TRW Credit Data. Released by BFA Educational Media, 2211 Michigan Avenue, Santa Monica, California 90404.

Teaches some important ideas about credit and financing loans. Part of the series Consumer Credit and Money Management. Issued with a teaching guide, readings, and supplementary material.

CREDIT: THE RETAIL STORE. 1975. 35mm filmstrip. 72 frames. Color. With phonodisc. BFA Educational Media in cooperation with TRW Credit Data. Released by BFA Educational Media, 2211 Michigan Avenue, Santa Monica, California 90404.

Teaches about buying and borrowing with a revolving charge account. Compares three types of retail store credit. Part of the series Consumer Credit and Money Management. Issued with a teaching guide, readings, and supplementary materials.

THE CRITICAL DECADES. 1965. 16mm film. Black and white. Sound. 30 minutes. Center for Mass Communication of Columbia University Press, 1125 Amsterdam Avenue, New York, New York 10025.

In order to emphasize the importance of various approaches to health problems, a small-town physician compares some of his active elderly patients with three complaining middle-aged patients.

DRUGS AND THE NERVOUS SYSTEM. 1967. 16mm film. Color. Sound. 16 minutes. Churchill Films, Incorporated, 662 North Robertson Boulevard, Los Angeles, California 90069.

Demonstrates the effects of drugs on body organs. Explains the serious disruption of the nervous system caused by airplane glue, stimulants, depressants, and hallucinogens.

FABLES AND LABELS. 1974. 35mm filmstrip. 41 frames. Color. With phonotape cassette, 6 minutes. January Productions, 13-00 Plaza Road, Post Office Box 244, Fair Lawn, New Jersey 07410.

Shows the kinds of things to look for on product labels. Encourages the development of an awareness of the problems confronting the consumer, such as budgeting, comparison shopping, and defective merchandise. A juvenile filmstrip for primary grades.

FOOD, FADS, & FALLACIES. 1976. 4 35mm filmstrips. Approximately 48 frames each. Color. With 4 cassettes, approximately 8 minutes each. Walt Disney Educational Media Company, 500 South Buena Vista Street, Burbank, California 91521.

Investigates the difference between food fallacies and good nutrition. Contents: 1. I Eat What I Like, Regardless. 2. Food Fads: You Bet Your Life! 3. Is "Natural" Healthy? 4. Is There a Perfect Diet?

FOOD: MORE FOR YOUR MONEY. 1974. 16mm film. Color. Sound. 14 minutes. Alfred Higgins Productions, 9100 Sunset Boulevard, Hollywood, California 90069.

Offers a number of hints on how to shop wisely for food. Shows how to look for good value in meats

Audiovisual Materials

and other sources of protein, how to look for bargains in store brands, how to use unit pricing to get the best value, and how to use other shopping techniques designed to get the most food for the food dollar.

FOOD PRICES UP AND DOWN. 1973. 35mm filmstrip. 42 frames. Color. With captions. Visual Education Consultants, Incorporated, Post Office Box 52, Madison, Wisconsin 53701.

Explains some of the reasons behind changes in food prices, and shows some of the ways the wise shopper can save in buying food.

GET YOUR MONEY'S WORTH. 1972. 35mm filmstrip. 35 frames. Color. With phonodisc, 10 minutes. Jo Butler and Elsa Barlett. Made and released by Urban Media Materials, 212 Mineola Avenue, Roslyn Heights, New York 11577.

Fosters a child's ability to weigh and evaluate advertising claims and other kinds of sales pressures. A juvenile filmstrip for elementary grades. Part of the series The Price Is Right, or Is It?

GETTING A BETTER BUY IN A USED CAR. 1976. 16mm film. Color. Sound. 25 minutes. For sale by Trikon Productions, Post Office Box 21, La Jolla, California 92038. For rent by Association-Sterling Films, 512 Burlington Avenue, La Grange, Illinois 60525.

Demonstrates, with an entertaining plot, how to buy a bargain or choose a lemon in selecting a used car. An instructive film for teenagers and adults.

THE GIFTS. 1970. 16mm film. Color. Sound. 28 minutes. Richten-McBride Production. Capital Films, 470 E Street, Southwest, Washington, D.C. 20024.

A documentary film stressing environmental problems - water pollution, erosion, chemical acids, etc.

THE GOOD, GOOD, GOOD, GOOD LIFE. 1975. 16mm film. Color. Sound. 10 minutes. Franciscan Communications Center, 1229 South Santee Street, Los Angeles, California 90015.

Uses a comical situation to encourage consumer consciousness. Tells of the struggle between the different value systems of a widower and his well-meaning family who believe he will never find a wife unless he has the gadgets, cosmetics, and styles of the good life.

GUARANTEES, WARRANTIES, AND SERVICES. 1971. 35mm filmstrip. 72 frames. Color. With phonodisc. CUNA International. Made by Gilbert Altschul Productions. Released by Journal Films, 909 West Diversey Parkway, Chicago, Illinois 60614.

Points out the importance of checking the exact wording on a guarantee or warranty before making a purchase. Uses as an example an incident about a family and its discovery that the guarantee on its new television set offers little protection against costly repairs.

A HALF MILLION TEENAGERS. 1969. 16mm film. Color. Sound. 16 minutes. Churchill Films, 662 North Robertson Boulevard, Los Angeles, California 90069.

Employs photography and animation to present the physiological aspects of venereal disease. Discusses gonorrhea and syphilis in detail, explaining how the organisms enter the body, how the diseases affect organs and tissues, and how the symptoms can be recognized. Emphasizes the need for early treatment in explaining how the diseases can be cured.

HOW TO BE A LOSER. 1972. 35mm filmstrip. 65 frames. Color. With phonodisc, 18 minutes. Doubleday Multimedia, 1371 Reynolds Avenue, Santa Ana, California 92705.

An unexpected gift of a two-hundred-dollar sewing machine results in some unwanted additional expenses as a woman is bilked by unscrupulous salesmen. Part of a Consumer Education Series.

HOW TO BUY A USED CAR. 1972. 35mm filmstrip. 85 frames. Color. With phonodisc. Made by Easy Klein. McGraw-Hill Book Company, Incorporated, 330 West 42nd Street, New York, New York 10036.

Provides guidelines for the consumer in purchasing

a used car. Part of a Consumer Education Series.

HOW TO BUY CLOTHES. 1972. 35mm filmstrip. 85 frames. Color. With phonodisc. Made by Easy Klein. McGraw-Hill Book Company, Incorporated, 330 West 42nd Street, New York, New York 10036.

Provides guidelines to aid the consumer in purchasing clothing. Part of a Consumer Education Series.

HOW TO BUY FOOD. 1972. 35mm filmstrip. 85 frames. Color. With phonodisc. Made by Easy Klein. McGraw-Hill Book Company, Incorporated, 330 West 42nd Street, New York, New York 10036.

Offers guidelines for the consumer in purchasing food. Part of a Consumer Education Series.

IF IT DOESN'T WORK...COMPLAIN. 1975. 16mm film. Color. Sound. 15 minutes. Gilbert Altschul Productions. Released by Journal Films, Incorporated, 909 West Diversey Parkway, Chicago, Illinois 60614.

Highlights the steps an individual consumer can take to recover the loss from the purchase of an unreliable product or service.

THE INDIVIDUAL AS CONSUMER. 1976. 4 unit multimedia kit. 35mm filmstrips. Audiotapes. Control Data Corporation, 8100 34th Avenue, South, Minneapolis, Minnesota 55440.

Contains units on credit, insurance, money management, and investments. Each unit includes student manuals, a resource file of student activities, and test questions, as well as filmstrips and audiotapes. Sequenced learning activities are keyed to instructional objectives and goals. The 60-hour series is suitable for class or individual instruction at the high school level.

INVITATIONS TO BURGLARY. 16mm film. Color. Sound. 24 minutes. PTOS Film Enterprises, 1419 North Poinsettia Place, Los Angeles, California 90046.

Raymond Burr explains the various locks and locking devices that can help homeowners and tenants protect themselves and their possessions against intruders.

IT'S NEW...IT'S NEAT...IT'S OBSOLETE. 1975. 16mm film. 15 minutes. Color. Sound. By Alec Lorimer and Jim Foster. Released by BFA Educational Media, 2211 Michigan Avenue, Santa Monica, California 90404.

Shows how to watch out for the marketplace gimmicks of quick obsolescence and fashionable gimmickry. Helps consumers determine the real value of a product aside from how fashionable it is.

JUST SIGN HERE. 1970. 16mm film. Color. Sound. 14 minutes. Better Business Bureau of Washington, D.C. Released by Macmillan Films, 866 Third Avenue, New York, New York 10022.

Dramatizes four different types of credit misrepresentation and explains how to recognize and avoid each type.

JUSTICE IN THE MARKETPLACE. 1974. 2 35mm filmstrips. Part 1, 93 frames; Part 2, 131 frames. Color. With 2 phonodiscs, 31 minutes. Made by Production Group, Changing Times Education Service, 1729 H Street, Northwest, Washington, D.C. 20006.

Presents five case studies in order to show young consumers how to use various agencies, including the government, a small claims court, and legal assistance, to obtain justice in the marketplace.

KICKING TIRES IS NOT ENOUGH! or How to Buy a Used Car. 1975. 16mm film. Color. Sound. 16 minutes. Made by Broadcast/Film Division. Consumers Union of the United States, Incorporated, 256 Washington Street, Mount Vernon, New York 10550.

An upbeat look at the basics of buying a good used car. Includes interviews with consumers who made bad purchases and advice from Consumer Reports' auto engineers.

THE LAW AND YOUR POCKETBOOK. 1972. 35mm filmstrip. 70 frames. Color. With phonodisc, 15 minutes. Doubleday Multimedia, 1371 Reynolds Avenue, Santa Ana, California 92705.

Explains a number of deceptive advertising and business practices such as the bait and switch scheme and "free" gifts. Also discusses various laws that protect consumers and what actions can be taken if a swindle is suspected. Part of a Consumer Education Series.

LEARNING ABOUT CONSUMER EDUCATION. 1971. 4 35mm filmstrips. 151 frames. Color. With 4 phonodiscs, 29 minutes. Aids Audiovisual Instructional Devices, 47-20 Bell Boulevard, Bayside, New York 11360.

Contents: 1. Mail order coupons. 2. Novelty buying. 3. Commercials on television. 4. Department store shopping. Juvenile filmstrips for teaching children in elementary grades how to manage money.

LEARNING TO BE A WISE CONSUMER. 1975. 4 35mm filmstrips. 69 to 80 frames each. Color. With 4 phonodiscs. Guidance Associates, 757 Third Avenue, New York, New York 10017.

Helps children understand some of the features of the marketplace, including the laws of supply and demand, the need to budget, comparison shopping, and product safety and responsibility. For elementary grades.

LET THE BUYER BEWARE. 1971. 35mm filmstrip. 65 frames. Color. With phonodisc. Society for Visual Education, 1345 West Diversey Parkway, Chicago, Illinois 60614.

Illustrates three basic types of consumer fraud: the bargain, misleading advertising, and excessive interest rates. Explains several practices the consumer can use to help avoid fraud and deception. Part of the series Getting Your Money's Worth.

MAKING CREDIT WORK FOR YOU. 1971. 35mm filmstrip. 72 frames. Color. With phonodisc. Society for Visual Education, 1345 West Diversey Parkway, Chicago, Illinois 60614.

Identifies the most common sources of consumer credit. Explains how credit is obtained and ways in which credit obligations are repaid. Examines the relationship between buying on credit and the national economy. Contrasts the difference in life styles between two young credit users in order to show the advantages and dangers of consumer credit and installment buying. Part of the filmstrip series called Getting Your Money's Worth.

MAKING THE BEST BUY IN FOODS. 1971. 35mm filmstrip. 74 frames. Color. With phonodisc. CUNA International. Made by Gilbert Altschul Productions. Released by Journal Films, 909 West Diversey Parkway, Chicago, Illinois 60614.

Presents pointers on how to get the best buy for each food dollar spent. Emphasizes the need for effective planning followed by careful selection. Explains the legal requirements for labeling of weight. Tells how to calculate the cost per unit of measure. Part of a Consumer Education Series entitled Using Your Money.

MARKETPLACE ETHICS. 1975. 5 35mm filmstrips. Approximately 65 frames each. Color. With 5 phonodiscs, approximately 11 minutes each. Prentice-Hall Media, Incorporated, 150 White Plains Road, Tarrytown, New York 10591.

Explores various aspects of ethical behavior, such as honesty, trust, responsible behavior, sense of morality, conduct, values. The series uses food and product prices, drug labeling, food additives, fabric flammability, "whistle blowers", and even Watergate as subjects for discussion of ethical issues.

MARRIAGE AND MONEY. 1974. 35mm filmstrip. 67 frames. Color. With phonodisc, 15 minutes. By Institute of Life Insurance. Released by Association-Sterling Films, 866 Third Avenue, New York, New York 10022.

Uses a case study about a young married couple learning to identify basic financial goals and make decisions. Illustrates how valid principles of money management are developed.

MATHMATTERS: MEASUREMENT - FROM CUBITS TO CENTIMETERS. 1975. 2 35mm filmstrips. Part 1, 59 frames; Part 2, 72 frames. Color. 2 phonodiscs: Part 1, 11 minutes; Part 2, 12 minutes. Guidance Associates, 757 Third Avenue,

Audiovisual Materials

New York, New York 10017.

Traces the history of money and the development of coinage and paper money. Discusses personal credit as a new form of money. Juvenile filmstrips for elementary grades.

MATHMATTERS: MONEY - FROM BARTER TO BANKING. 1975. 2 35mm filmstrips. Part 1, 59 frames; Part 2, 70 frames. Color. 2 phonodiscs: Part 1, 9 minutes; Part 2, 10 minutes. Guidance Associates, 757 Third Avenue, New York, New York 10017.

Traces the history of money and the development of coinage and paper money. Discusses personal credit as a new form of money. Juvenile filmstrips for elementary grades.

THE MEANING OF MONEY. 1976. 4 35mm filmstrips. Approximately 77 frames each. Color. With 4 phonodiscs or cassettes, approximately 10 minutes each. Newsweek, 444 Madison Avenue, New York, New York 10022.

Contents: 1. Money - Understanding It. 2. Earning It. 3. Spending It. 4. Making It Work. A multimedia kit including a teacher's guide, Resource Manual, and 7 duplicating masters.

MONEY AND LIFE STYLE. 1976. 2 35mm filmstrips. Approximately 122 frames each. Color. With 2 phonodiscs or cassettes, about 14 minutes each. Changing Times Education Service, 1729 H Street, Northwest, Washington, D.C. 20006.

Emphasizes intelligent money management and the choice of a life style fitting personal values. Deals with budgeting, determining resources available, and how to find help in managing finances.

MONEY FOR SALE. 1974. 16mm film. Color. Sound. 13 minutes. David Nulsen Enterprises. Released by AIMS Instructional Media Services, Incorporated, 5420 Melrose Street, Hollywood, California 90028.

An animated film uses the character of a kindly pawnbroker to show how to borrow money intelligently. Suggests sources for borrowed money, stressing the importance of shopping for a loan and restraint in borrowing. Also explains in detail federal truth in lending legislation.

MONEY: HOW ITS VALUE CHANGES. 1971. 16mm film. Color. Sound. 14 minutes. Coronet Instructional Films, 65 East South Water Street, Chicago, Illinois 60601.

Explains how changes in the value of money are related to the cost of living concept and other factors such as recession, depression, supply and demand, and inflation.

MONEY MANAGEMENT FILMSTRIPS. 35mm filmstrips. Color. With printed captions. Money Management Institute of Household Finance Corporation, Prudential Plaza, Chicago, Illinois 60601.

The filmstrips illustrate real life situations and show the importance of good financial management and how to practice it. Titles include: A New Look at Budgeting; Your Money's Worth in Shopping; Managing Your Clothing Dollars; Focus on Food Dollars; Your World and Money; Be Credit Wise; and others.

NOBODY'S VICTIM. 1972. 16mm film. Color. Sound. 20 minutes. Ramsgate Films, 704 Santa Monica Boulevard, Santa Monica, California 90401.

Instructs women in fundamental techniques of self-defense.

NOT SO EASY. 1973. 16mm film. Color. Sound. 17 minutes. FilmFair Communications, 10820 Ventura Boulevard, Studio City, California 91604.

Demonstrates essential safety rules for motorcycle riding on streets and highways. Presents instructions on wearing protective clothing and on safety checks for equipment. Points out the dangers of motorcycles. Emphasizes the advantages of motorcycles for safe transportation and pleasure riding when the proper precautions are observed. Features Evel Knievel. Narrated by Peter Fonda.

NUTRITION. 1976. 3 16mm films. Color. Sound. Barr Films, Post Office Box 5667, Pasadena, California 91107.

Audiovisual Materials

Contents: 1. The Consumer and the Supermarket (15 minutes) deals with various aspects of supermarket store layout, packaging, and labeling. 2. The All American Meal (11 minutes) discusses the "fast food" culture, the nutritional aspects of fast foods, and how we are losing touch with some of the real values of life. 3. You Are What You Eat (10 minutes) presents information on nutrition in an amusing animated film.

NUTRITIONAL QUACKERY. 1967. 16mm film. Color. Sound. 20 minutes. Associated Film Services. Released by AIMS Instructional Media Services, Post Office Box 1010, Hollywood, California 90028.

Stresses a balanced diet as the key to good health. Counteracts the claims of food faddists by exposing the myths on which food quacks thrive.

ON YOUR OWN. 1972. 16mm film. Color. Sound. 23 minutes. Film Fair Communications, 10820 Ventura Boulevard, Studio City, California 91604.

Describes subjects covered in high school consumer education classes. Includes information on comparison shopping, perpetual styles in clothing, home ownership versus renting, learning to bake bread at ten cents a loaf, using consumer pressure to improve retailing practices, fixing old furniture, operating child care centers on college campuses, running community research programs, credit and money management, and family relations. Part of a series Consumer Education.

OVER-THE-COUNTER PILLS AND PROMISES. 1977. 16mm film. Color. Sound. 16 1/2 minutes. Alfred Higgins Productions, Incorporated, 9100 Sunset Boulevard, Los Angeles, California 90069.

Points out that highly advertised over-the-counter medicines may not offer the best values. Explains that less expensive brands and "home remedies" are often as effective in treating ailments.

THE OWL WHO GAVE A HOOT. 1967. 16mm film. Color. Sound. 14 minutes. U.S. Office of Economic Opportunity. Released by National Audiovisual Center, U.S. General Services Administration, Washington, D.C. 20409.

Uses animation to describe the exploitation, connivance, and fraud in the consumer world of the ghetto. Shows what the community can do about it.

PEOPLE MAKE IT HAPPEN. 1976. 16mm film. Color. Sound. 23 minutes. Modern Talking Picture Service, 2323 New Hyde Park Road, New Hyde Park, New York 11040.

Uses animation, humorous skits, and songs to demonstrate the importance of the proper selection, maintenance, use, storage, and disposal of consumer products. A film for elementary grades sponsored by the U.S. Consumer Product Safety Commission.

PLAY IT SAFE. 1975. 16mm film. Color. Sound. 12 minutes. U.S. Consumer Product Safety Commission. Made by Amram Nowak Associates. Released by National Audiovisual Center, U.S. General Services Administration, Washington, D.C. 20409.

Reviews safety tips for using power lawnmowers and hedge trimmers.

THE POOR PAY MORE. 1967. 16mm film. Black and white. Sound. 60 minutes. National Educational Television & Radio Center, 10 Columbus Circle, New York, New York 10019.

Depicts the special hardships encountered by poor people in consumer purchasing. Examines the pricing practices of supermarket chains, techniques of food freezer salesmen, and shady methods used by furniture and appliance stores and finance companies. Officials from various government and private organizations present the problems and show what they are attempting to do to alleviate them.

PRODUCTS AND THE LAWSUIT EXPLOSION: WHO PAYS? 1976. 16mm film. Color. Sound. 18 1/2 minutes. Insurance Information Institute, 110 William Street, New York, New York 10038.

Explores the product liability problem and its impact on consumers, manufacturers, and the insurance industry. A representative of each group takes part in this talk show.

Audiovisual Materials

READ THE LABEL, SET A BETTER TABLE. 1974. 16mm film. Color. Sound. 14 minutes. By the Department of Health, Education, and Welfare's Food and Drug Administration. Modern Talking Picture Service, 2323 New Hyde Park Road, New Hyde Park, New York 11040.

Shows consumers how to use nutrition labels to get more value for their food dollars. Produced by the U.S. Food and Drug Administration to help consumers understand nutrition labels on food products. Features movie and television star Dick Van Dyke.

SHOPPING FOR HEALTH CARE. 1976. 2 35mm filmstrips. Approximately 100 frames each. With 2 phonodiscs or 2 cassettes, approximately 17 minutes each. Guidance Associates, 757 Third Avenue, New York, New York 10017.

Explains how to become a wise, well-informed consumer of health services. Deals with the need to make intelligent health care decisions. Includes a discussion guide. Part of the Consumer Skills Series.

THE SILENT GUARDIAN. 1976. 16mm film. Color. Sound. 27 minutes. Modern Talking Picture Service, Incorporated, 1212 Avenue of the Americas, New York, New York 10036.

Demonstrates the activities of Underwriters' Laboratories in testing and checking the safety of electrical appliances and other consumer products.

THE SIX BILLION $$$ SELL. 1976. 16mm film. Color. Sound. 15 minutes. Consumer Reports Films, 256 Washington Street, Mount Vernon, New York 10550.

Points out advertising techniques used in television commercials. Shows elementary and junior high school students how the commercials are designed to influence television viewers.

SMART SPENDING. 1971. 2 35mm filmstrips. Part 1, 25 frames; Part 2, 32 frames. Color. With phonodisc, 18 minutes each side. Olcott Forward, Incorporated. Released by Educational Audio Visual, Incorporated, Pleasantville, New York 10570.

Deals with consumer affairs. Teaches the student to become a responsible buyer and discusses various forms of credit.

SO YOU WANT TO USE CREDIT. 1972. 35mm filmstrip. 187 frames. Color. With phonodisc, 27 minutes. Made by Production Group, Changing Times Education Service, 1729 H Street, Northwest, Washington, D.C. 20006.

Outlines the methods used to obtain credit, and the responsibilities and dangers which accompany buying on credit.

SOME ARE MORE EQUAL THAN OTHERS. 1971. 16mm film. Black and white. Sound. 40 minutes. Carousel Films, Incorporated, 1501 Broadway, New York, New York 10036.

Deals with the legal treatment of ethnic minorities. Explains the inequities of the bail system, discriminatory practices in jury selection, and creditor/debtor civil actions. Shows how the system works mostly against the poor.

SOOPER GOOP. 1975. 16mm film. Color. Sound. 13 minutes. Churchill Films, 622 North Robertson Boulevard, Los Angeles, California 90069.

Uses an animated story about an actor and an advertising man and their deceptive television commercial for a cereal in order to present the problem of false advertising and the need for concern about buying habits. An American Film Festival award winning film. A juvenile film for elementary grades.

STANDARDS FOR EXCELLENCE. 1976. 16mm film. Color. Sound. 28 1/2 minutes. Association Films, Incorporated, 866 Third Avenue, New York, New York 10022.

Emphasizes the influence of standards and measurement on everyday life. Shows exciting scientific discoveries and their practical consequences. Released by the U.S. National Bureau of Standards.

STEERING CLEAR OF LEMONS. 1975. 16mm film. Color. Sound. 16 minutes. Consumers Union of the United States, Incorporated, 256

Washington Street, Mount Vernon, New York 10550.

A consumer education film, providing information on product evaluation, buying, product safety, and the role of government, as seen through seven specific reports on diet goods, fair trade laws, stereos, pain relievers, 10-speed bicycles, grade labeling of beef, and aerosols.

SUPER-SNOOPER. 1972. 35mm filmstrip. 35 frames. Color. With phonodisc, 10 minutes. Jo Butler and Elsa Barlett. Made and released by Urban Media Materials, 212 Mineola Avenue, Roslyn Heights, New York 11577.

Assists in developing sound purchasing standards in a child, and his ability to detect deceptive food merchandising. A juvenile filmstrip for elementary grades. Part of the series Price Is Right, or Is It?

THAT THE BEST WILL BE OURS. 1970. 16mm film. Color. Sound. 18 minutes. U.S. Department of Agriculture. Released by National Audiovisual Center, U.S. General Services Administration, Washington, D.C. 20409.

Covers the handling, processing, and labeling requirements that meat and poultry packers must heed in preparing their products. Shows the shopping, handling, storage, and preparation steps that consumers can take to get the best buys and to keep the foods safe.

THERE IS A LAW AGAINST IT. 1972. 16mm film. Color. Sound. 8 minutes. FilmFair Communications, 10820 Ventura Boulevard, Studio City, California 91604.

Explains four legal developments concerning consumer protection. Demonstrates how consumer laws can protect the consumer in cases involving garnishment of wages, unauthorized automobile repair work, payment demanded for a debt already paid, and pressure exerted by a salesman on a customer to sign a purchase contract. Part of a series Consumer Education.

THIS IS FRAUD! 1972. 16mm film. Color. Sound. 8 minutes. FilmFair Communications, 10820 Ventura Boulevard, Studio City, California 91604.

Describes common consumer frauds, and tells where to seek recourse, including trade association offices, small claims courts, and licensing bureaus. Part of a series Consumer Education.

THE TORTURE TESTERS. 1971. 16mm film. Color. Sound. 13 1/2 minutes. Modern Talking Picture Service. Underwriters' Laboratories, Incorporated, 207 East Ohio Street, Chicago, Illinois 60611.

Tells the story of how Underwriters' Laboratory investigates thousands of products for fire, accident, electrical shock, or casualty hazards. Tests involve building materials, electrical, marine, heating, refrigeration, air conditioning, and chemical items. Also deals with burglary prevention and signaling systems and devices.

TWO SIDES OF BORROWING. 1975. 35mm filmstrip. 81 frames. Color. With phonodisc. BFA Educational Media in cooperation with TRW Credit Data. Released by BFA Educational Media, 2211 Michigan Avenue, Santa Monica, California 90404.

Teaches some important ideas about credit and how to apply these ideas to personal money management. Shows a typical young couple and their financial problems which resulted because they never learned how to use credit. Part of the series Consumer Credit and Money Management. Issued with a teaching guide, readings, and supplementary materials.

TYPICAL GYPS AND FRAUDS. 1973. 35mm filmstrip. 200 frames. Color. With phonodisc, 28 minutes. Made by Production Group, Changing Times Education Service, 1729 H Street, Northwest, Washington, D.C. 20006.

Presents five real-life situations which help alert students to a variety of gyps and frauds in the marketplace.

USING MONEY WISELY. 1971. 16mm film. Color. Sound. 18 minutes. CUNA International. Made by Gilbert Altschul Productions. Released by Journal Films, 909 West Diversey Parkway, Chicago, Illinois 60614.

Introduces three families who represent a cross section

of economic levels. Shows how the families reach solutions to the money management problems they encounter. Part of the series Using Your Money.

USING SOMEONE ELSE'S MONEY. 1971. 35mm filmstrip. 61 frames. Color. With phonodisc. CUNA International. Made by Gilbert Altschul Productions. Released by Journal Films, 909 West Diversey Parkway, Chicago, Illinois 60614.

Emphasizes the importance of careful investigation when seeking a source from which to borrow money. Part of the series Using Your Money.

WHEN THERE IS A HOLE IN YOUR POCKET. 1974. 35mm filmstrip. 43 frames. Color. With phonotape, 7 minutes. Produced by Phyllis Dolgin. January Productions, 13-00 Plaza Road, Post Office Box 244, Fair Lawn, New Jersey 07410.

Introduces some of the techniques of budgeting. Encourages the development of an awareness of the problems confronting the consumer, such as budgeting, comparison shopping, and defective merchandise. For primary grades. Part of the series Alice in Consumerland.

WHEN THINGS DON'T WORK. 1974. 35mm filmstrip. 41 frames. Color. With phonotape, 6 minutes. Produced by Phyllis Dolgin. January Productions, 13-00 Plaza Road, Post Office Box 244, Fair Lawn, New Jersey 07410.

Shows what to do when things don't work properly. Encourages the development of an awareness of the problems confronting the consumer, such as budgeting, comparison shopping, and defective merchandise. For primary grades. Part of the series Alice in Consumerland.

WHEN YOU BUY A CAR. 1971. 35mm filmstrip. 81 frames. Color. With phonodisc. CUNA International. Made by Gilbert Altschul Productions. Released by Journal Films, 909 West Diversey Parkway, Chicago, Illinois 60614.

Stresses the importance of looking into one's motives when buying a car. Shows how to be sure that the car is worth its cost. Part of the series Using Your Money.

WHERE DOES YOUR ALLOWANCE GO? 1974. 35mm filmstrip. 53 frames. Color. With phonodisc, 9 minutes. Producer and writer, Mary H. Manoni. Society for Visual Education, 1345 West Diversey Parkway, Chicago, Illinois 60614.

Presents a series of vignettes, showing what influences consumer buying habits, particularly those of young people. A juvenile filmstrip for elementary grades. Part of the series You, the Consumer.

WHY DO YOU BUY? 1971. 16mm film. Color. Sound. 10 minutes. Made by Gilbert Altschul Productions. Released by Journal Films, 909 West Diversey Parkway, Chicago, Illinois 60614.

Uses a comical approach to focus on the emotional elements which influence buying decisions. Shows how advertising employs emotional appeals to sway purchasers.

WHY YOU NEED CONSUMER KNOW-HOW. 1971. 35mm filmstrip. 70 frames. Color. With phonodisc. Society for Visual Education, 1345 West Diversey Parkway, Chicago, Illinois 60614.

Illustrates the complexity of the marketplace and the difficulties involved in making intelligent consumer decisions. Identifies and explains the major factors which contribute to an intelligent consumer decision. Examines the basic relationship between the consumer and the national economy. Part of the series Getting Your Money's Worth.

WISE AND RESPONSIBLE CONSUMERSHIP. 1973. 16mm film. Color. Sound. 14 minutes. Centron Corporation. Released by Centron Educational Films, Suite 652, 1255 Port Street, San Francisco, California 94109.

Explains how to become a wise consumer. Deals with pitfalls of impulsive buying, describes various merchandising and promotional tactics used by retailers, and emphasizes the importance of reading labels and following other prudent buying practices.

YOUR CREDIT IS GOOD - A FILM ABOUT PAYING LATER. 1972. 16mm film. Color. Sound. 15 minutes. Gilbert Altschul Productions. Released by Journal Films, Incorporated, 909 West Diversey Parkway, Chicago, Illinois 60614.

Audiovisual Materials

Describes how installment buying works. Demonstrates that extended credit can hold many hazards for the unwary consumer.

YOUR MONEY: NOW YOU SEE IT, NOW YOU DON'T. 1972. 35mm filmstrip. 72 frames. Color. With phonodisc, 15 minutes. Doubleday Multimedia, 1371 Reynolds Avenue, Santa Ana, California 92705.

A young man's desire for a car leads him into a questionable loan agreement which teaches him about consumer credit practices and their hazards. Part of the Consumer Education Series.

SECTION VI

INDEXES

Three types of indexes are provided: Organization Index, Personnel Index, and Publication Index.

The Organization Index presents an alphabetical and keyword listing of the government organizations included in Section I, and the associations, centers, institutes, etc. included in Section II.

The Personnel Index includes company, media and organization personnel whose names are provided in Sections I-IV.

The Publication Index lists titles of publications included in Section V, and publications of the organizations described in Sections I and II.

Organization Index

A

AA (Addicts Anonymous)   136
AA (Alcoholics Anonymous)   137
AAA (American Automobile Association)   241
AAAM (American Association for Automotive Medicine)   180
AABR (Association for Advancement of Blind and Retarded)   144
AAEE (American Academy of Environmental Engineers)   121
AAHA (American Association of Homes for the Aging)   192
AAIA (Association on American Indian Affairs)   195
AAL (Aid Association for Lutherans)   240
AAMA (American Apparel Manufacturers Association)   241
AAO (American Association of Ophthalmology)   138
AAPCC (American Association of Poison Control Centers)   138
AAPCO (Association of American Pesticide Control Officials)   122
AAPSC (American Association of Psychiatric Services of Children)   138
AARP (American Association of Retired Persons)   192
AASE (American Academy of Safety Education)   180
AASK (Aid to Adoption of Special Kids)   192
AATCC (American Association of Textile Chemists and Colorists)   241
AATR (Association of Auto and Truck Recyclers)   246
AAWB (American Association of Workers for the Blind)   138
ABA (American Bankers Association)   242
ABA (American Bar Association)   231
ABC (Action for Brain-Handicapped Children)   136
ABC (Architectural Barriers Committee)   143
ABYC (American Boat and Yacht Council)   242
AC (Advertising Council)   240
Academy of Pharmaceutical Sciences (APS)   240
ACAP (American Council on Alcohol Problems)   139
ACAP (Aviation Consumer Action Project)   82
ACB (American Council of the Blind)   139
ACCH (Association for the Care of Children in Hospitals)   145
ACCI (American Council on Consumer Interests)   81
Accident Prevention Research Center   180
ACE (Active Corps of Executives)   28
ACE (American Council on the Environment)   121
ACF (American Culinary Federation)   242
ACLD (Association for Children with Learning Disabilities)   144
ACR (Americans for Childrens Relief)   194
A/CRMD (Association for Children with Retarded Mental Development)   144
ACS (American Cancer Society)   139

ACT (Action for Children's Television)   81
ACTION
    Office of Public Affairs   1
        Foster Grandparent Program (FGP)   1
        Mini-Grant Program   1
        National Student Volunteer Program (NSVP)   1
        Peace Corps   1
        Program for Local Service (PLS)   1
        Retired Senior Volunteer Program (RSVP)   1
        Senior Companion Program   1
        Special Volunteer Programs (SVP)   1
        University Year for Action (UYA)   1
        Volunteers in Service to America (VISTA)   1
        Youth Challenge Program (YCP)   1
Action for Brain-Handicapped Children (ABC)   136
Action for Child Transportation Safety (ACTS)   180
Action for Children's Television (ACT)   81
Action for Prevention of Burn Injuries to Children (APBIC)   136
Action on Smoking and Health (ASH)   136
Active Corps of Executives (ACE)   28
Actors' Fund of America   192
ACTS (Action for Child Transportation Safety)   180
ADA (American Dental Association)   242
ADA (American Dietetic Association)   139
ADA (Americans for Democratic Action)   81
ADAMHA (Alcohol, Drug Abuse and Mental Health Administration)   17
ADC (Aviation Development Council)   247
Addiction Research and Treatment Corporation   136
Addicts Anonymous (AA)   136
Administration on Aging (AoA)   15
ADPA (Alcohol and Drug Problems Association of North America)   137
Advertising Council (AC)   240
AEE (Alliance for Environmental Education)   121
AELE (Americans for Effective Law Enforcement)   231
AES (American Epilepsy Society)   139
AF (Arthritis Foundation)   144
AFA (Allergy Foundation of America)   137
AFB (American Foundation for the Blind)   140
AFCWBVH (American Federation of Catholic Workers for the Blind and Visually Handicapped)   140
AFDC (Aid to Families with Dependent Children)   18
AFDO (Association of Food and Drug Officials)   145
Affairs Division (Department of the Treasury)   32
AFFI (American Frozen Food Institute)   243
AGA (American Gas Association)   243
AGBA (Alexander Graham Bell Association for the Deaf)   137
AGE (American Aging Association)   138
Agricultural Marketing Service (AMS)   2
Agricultural Research Service (ARS)   2
Agriculture, Department of   1
AHA (American Heart Association)   140
AHAM (Association of Home Appliance Manufacturers)   246
AHEA (American Home Economics Association)   193
AHF (American Health Foundation)   140

Organization Index

AIA (American Insurance Association) 244
AIC (American Institute of Cooperation) 81
AIC (Automotive Information Council) 247
Aid Association for Lutherans (AAL) 240
Aid to Adoption of Special Kids (AASK) 192
Aid to Families with Dependent Children(AFDC) 18
AIO (Americans for Indian Opportunity) 194
AIPA (American Indian Press Association) 243
Air-Conditioning and Refrigeration Institute (ARI) 240
Air Moving and Conditioning Association (AMCA) 240
Air Pollution Control Association (APCA) 121
Air Transport Association of America (ATA) 241
AITC (American Institute of Timber Construction) 243
AJS (American Judicature Society) 231
ALAA (Association of Legal Aid Attorneys of the City of New York) 232
Al-Anon Family Group Headquarters 136
Alcohol and Drug Problems Association of North America (ADPA) 137
Alcoholics Anonymous (AA) 137
Alexander Graham Bell Association for the Deaf (AGBA) 137
Allergy Foundation of America (AFA) 137
Alliance for Environmental Education (AEE) 121
ALSAC - Saint Jude Children's Research Hospital 138
ALSC (American Lumber Standards Committee) 244
Alston Wilkes Society 192
AMA (American Medical Association) 141
AMC (American Movers Conference) 244
AMCA (Air Moving and Conditioning Association) 240
American Academy of Environmental Engineers (AAEE) 121
American Academy for Professional Law Enforcement 231
American Academy of Safety Education (AASE) 180
American Aging Association (AGE) 138
American Apparel Manufacturers Association (AAMA) 241
American Association for Automotive Medicine (AAAM) 180
American Association of Homes for the Aging (AAHA) 192
American Association of Ophthalmology (AAO) 138
American Association of Poison Control Centers (AAPCC) 138
American Association of Psychiatric Services for Children (AAPSC) 138
American Association of Retired Persons (AARP) 192
American Association of Textile Chemists and Colorists (AATCC) 241
American Association of Workers for the Blind (AAWB) 138
American Automobile Association (AAA) 241
American Bankers Association (ABA) 242

American Bar Association (ABA) 231
American Boat and Yacht Council (ABYC) 242
American Cancer Society (ACS) 139
American Council of the Blind (ACB) 139
American Council on Alcohol Problems (ACAP) 139
American Council on Consumer Interests (ACCI) 81
American Council on the Environment (ACE) 121
American Culinary Federation (ACF) 242
American Dental Association (ADA) 242
American Dietetic Association (ADA) 139
American Epilepsy Society (AES) 139
American Federation of Catholic Workers for the Blind and Visually Handicapped (AFCWBVH) 140
American Foundation for the Blind (AFB) 140
American Freedom from Hunger Foundation (FFH) 193
American Frozen Food Institute (AFFI) 243
American Gas Association (AGA) 243
American Health Foundation (AHF) 140
American Heart Association (AHA) 140
American Home Economics Association (AHEA) 193
American Indian Law Center 231
American Indian National Bank and Buy Indian Contracts) 22
American Indian Press Association (AIPA) 243
American Institute of Cooperation (AIC) 81
American Institute of Timber Construction (AITC) 243
American Insurance Association (AIA) 244
American Judicature Society (AJS) 231
American Ladder Institute 180
American Lumber Standards Committee (ALSC) 244
American Lung Association 140
American Meat Institute (AMI) 244
American Medical Association (AMA) 141
American Medical Students Association 141
American Movers Conference (AMC) 244
American Mutual Insurance Alliance (AMIA) 244
American National Red Cross (ARC) 193
American National Standards Institute (ANSI) 245
American Natural Hygiene Society (ANHS) 141
American Naturalized Citizen Welfare Association (ANCWA) 193
American Nurses' Association (ANA) 245
American Oceanic Organization (AOO) 121
American Optometric Association (AOA) 141
American Parkinson Disease Association 141
American Pharmaceutical Association (APhA) 142
American Physical Fitness Research Institute (APFRI) 142
American Printing House for the Blind (APH) 142
American Public Gas Association (APGA) 245
American Public Health Association (APHA) 142
American Rehabilitation Committee (ARC) 142
American Rehabilitation Foundation (ARF) 143
American Rescue Workers 194
American Rheumatism Association (ARA) 143
American Safety Belt Council (ASBC) 180
American Safety Council (ASC) 181

1524

Organization Index

American Society for Quality Control (ASQC) 245
American Society for Testing and Materials (ASTM) 246
American Society of Safety Engineers (ASSE) 181
American Society of Sanitary Engineering (ASSE) 143
American Society of Travel Agents (ASTA) 246
American Traffic Services Association (ATSA) 181
American Trucking Associations, Inc. (ATA) 246
American Women's Voluntary Services (AWVS) 194
Americans for Childrens Relief (ACR) 194
Americans for Democratic Action (ADA) 81
Americans for Effective Law Enforcement (AELE) 231
Americans for Indian Opportunity (AIO) 194
AMI (American Meat Institute) 244
AMIA (American Mutual Insurance Alliance) 244
Amputee Shoe and Glove Exchange 194
APFRI (American Physical Fitness Research Institute) 142
AMS (Agricultural Marketing Service) 2
AMSA (Association of Metropolitan Sewerage Agencies) 122
ANA (American Nurses' Association) 245
Anacostia Neighborhood Museum 29
Anamilo Club of Detroit 143
ANCWA (American Naturalized Citizen Welfare) 193
ANHS (American Natural Hygiene Society) 141
Animal and Plant Health Inspection Service (APHIS) 2
ANSI (American National Standards Institute) 245
Antitrust Division (Department of Justice) 24
AoA (Administration on Aging) 16
AOA (American Optometric Association) 141
AOO (American Oceanic Organization) 121
APA (Assistance Payments Administration) 18
APAA (Automotive Parts and Accessories Association) 247
APBIC (Action for Prevention of Burn Injuries to Children) 136
APCA (Air Pollution Control Association) 121
APGA (American Public Gas Association) 245
APH (American Printing House for the Blind) 142
APhA (American Pharmaceutical Association) 142
APHA (American Public Health Association) 142
APHIS (Animal and Plant Health Inspection Service) 2
APS (Academy of Pharmaceutical Sciences) 240
ARA (American Rheumatism Association) 143
ARC (American National Red Cross) 193
ARC (American Rehabilitation Committee) 142
Architectural Barriers Committee (ABC) 143
ARF (American Rehabilitation Foundation) 143
ARI (Air-Conditioning and Refrigeration Institute) 240
Army Relief Society (ARS) 194
Arrow, Incorporated 195
ARS (Agricultural Research Service) 2
ARS (Army Relief Society) 194
Arthritis Foundation (AF) 144

ASBC (American Safety Belt Council) 180
ASC (American Safety Council) 181
ASCA (Association for Sickle Cell Anemia) 145
ASCE (Association of Safety Council Executives) 181
ASH (Action on Smoking and Health) 136
ASMFC (Atlantic States Marine Fisheries Commission) 122
ASQC (American Society for Quality Control) 245
ASSE (American Society of Safety Engineers) 181
ASSE (American Society of Sanitary Engineering) 143
Assistance Payments Administration (APA) 18
Associated Blind 144
Association for Advancement of Blind and Retarded (AABR) 144
Association for Children with Learning Disabilities (ACLD) 144
Association for Children with Retarded Mental Development (A/CRMD) 144
Association for Sickle Cell Anemia (ASCA) 145
Association for the Care of Children in Hospitals (ACCH) 145
Association of American Pesticide Control Officials (AAPCO) 122
Association of Auto and Truck Recyclers (AATR) 246
Association of Food and Drug Officials (AFDO) 145
Association of Home Appliance Manufacturers (AHAM) 246
Association of Jewish Anti-Poverty Workers 195
Association of Legal Aid Attorneys of the City of New York (ALAA) 232
Association of Metropolitan Sewerage Agencies (AMSA) 122
Association of Rehabilitation Facilities 145
Association of Safety Council Executives (ASCE) 181
Association on American Indian Affairs (AAIA) 195
ASTA (American Society of Travel Agents) 246
ASTM (American Society for Testing and Materials) 246
ATA (Air Transport Association of America) 241
ATA (American Trucking Associations, Inc.) 246
Atlantic States Marine Fisheries Commission (SAMFC) 122
ATSA (American Traffic Services Association) 181
AUTOCAP (Automotive Consumer Action Program) 81
Automated Data and Telecommunications Service 13
Automobile Owners Action Council 82
Automotive Consumer Action Program (AUTOCAP) 81
Automotive Information Council (AIC) 247
Automotive Parts and Accessories Association (APAA) 247
Automotive Service Councils 247
Aviation Consumer Action Project (ACAP) 82

Organization Index

Aviation Development Council (ADC) 247
AWVS (American Women's Voluntary Services) 194

B

Baking Industry Sanitation Standards Committee 247
Bass Anglers for Clean Waters 122
BBA (Big Brothers of America) 195
BDFGA (Bio-Dynamic Farming and Gardening Association) 146
Beadle Bumble Fund 232
BERC (Black Economic Research Center) 195
Better Business Bureaus 82
Better Light Better Sight Bureau 247
Better Vision Institute (BVI) 146
Beverage Container Control Coalition (B3C) 122
BIA (Braille Institute of America) 146
Bicycle Manufacturers Association (BMA) 248
Big Brothers of America (BBA) 195
Big Sisters, Inc. 195
Bio-Dynamic Farming and Gardening Association (BDFGA) 146
Black Economic Research Center (BERC) 195
Black Lung Association 181
Blind Service Association (BSA) 146
Blinded Veterans Association (BVA) 146
BLS (Bureau of Labor Statistics) 25
Blue Card 196
BMA (Bicycle Manufacturers Association) 248
B'nai B'rith Career and Counseling Services 196
BNF (Brand Names Foundation) 248
BOCA (Building Officials and Code Administrators International) 248
Braille Institute of America (BIA) 146
Brand Names Foundation (BNF) 248
Brethren Volunteer Service (BVS) 196
Bridge 146
Brighten the Night Program 181
BSA (Blind Service Association) 146
B3C (Beverage Container Control Coalition) 122
Building Officials and Code Administrators International (BOCA) 248
Bureau of Alcohol Tobacco and Firearms 32
Bureau of Biologics 17
Bureau of Community Health Services 18
Bureau of Consumer Protection 12
Bureau of Drugs 17
Bureau of Economic Analysis 5
Bureau of Education for the Handicapped 17
Bureau of Epidemiology 17
Bureau of Foods 17
Bureau of Health Education 17
Bureau of Health Manpower 18
Bureau of Health Planning and Resources Development 18
Bureau of Indian Affairs 22
Bureau of Information and Education 6
Bureau of International Labor Affairs 25
Bureau of Labor Statistics 25
Bureau of Laboratories 17
Bureau of Land Management 23
Bureau of Medical Devices and Diagnostic Products 17
Bureau of Medical Services 18
Bureau of Mines 23
Bureau of Occupational and Adult Education 17
Bureau of Outdoor Recreation 23
Bureau of Postsecondary Education 17
Bureau of Prisons 24
Bureau of Quality Assurance 18
Bureau of Radiological Health 17
Bureau of School Systems 17
Bureau of Smallpox Eradication 17
Bureau of State Services 17
Bureau of the Census 5
Bureau of Training 17
Bureau of Tropical Diseases 17
Bureau of Veterinary Medicine 17
Buxom Belle, International 147
BVA (Blinded Veterans Association) 146
BVI (Better Vision Institute) 146
BVS (Brethren Volunteer Service) 196

C

CA (Checks Anonymous) 198
CAB (Civil Aeronautics Board) 4
CAG (citizen Action Group) 84
CAGE (Convicts Association for a Good Environment) 125
CAJ (Center for Administrative Justice) 232
California Tomorrow 122
California Traffic Safety Foundation (CTSF) 182
Call for Action (CFA) 196
CALM (Child Abuse Listening Mediation) 198
CAN (Citizens Against Noise) 123
CAN (Consumer Action Now) 125
Cancer Care, Inc. (CCI) 147
Candlelighters 147
Canned Salmon Institute (CSI) 248
Capital Formation 196
Car Care Council (CCC) 248
CARF (Commission on Accreditation of Rehabilitation Facilities) 149
CARIH (Children's Asthma Research Institute and Hospital at Denver) 147
Carnegie Hero Fund Commission 196
Carpet and Rug Industry Consumer Action Panel (CRICAP) 82
Carpet and Rug Institute 249
CAS (Council of Adult Stutterers) 151
CASE (Citizens Association for Sound Energy) 123
Catholic Big Brothers 197

Organization Index

Catholic Guardian Society   197
CBBB (Council of Better Business Bureaus)   86
CBC (Citizens for Better Care in Nursing Homes, Homes for the Aged and Other After-Care Facilities)   148
CBD (Children Before Dogs)   199
CCA-UWEX (Center for Consumer Affairs, University of Wisconsin Extension)   82
CCC (Car Care Council)   248
CCC (Center for Community Change)   197
CCC (Citizen's Committee for Children of New York)   199
CCC (Citizens Communication Center)   233
CCE (Crusade for a Cleaner Environment)   125
CCHD (Committee to Combat Huntington's Disease)   149
CCI (Cancer Care, Inc.)   147
CCR (Commission on Civil Rights)   6
CDC (Community Development Corporation)   19
CDF (Community Development Foundation)   200
CECF (Corrective Eye Care Foundation)   150
CEI (Committee for Environmental Information)   124
Center Bureau for the Jewish Aged   198
Center for Administrative Justice (CAJ)   232
Center for Auto Safety   182
Center for Community Change (CCC)   197
Center for Concerned Engineering   197
Center for Consumer Affairs, University of Wisconsin Extension (CCA-UWEX)   82
Center for Disease Control   17
Center for Growth Alternatives (CGA)   197
Center for Independent Action (CFIA)   197
Center for Law and Education   232
Center for Law and Social Policy   232
Center for Law in the Public Interest   233
Center for New Corporate Priorities (CNCP)   83
Center for Policy Research, Inc.   198
Center for Safety and Traffic Education   182
Center for Science in the Public Interest (CSPI)   83
Center for Study of Responsive Law   83
Center for the Visual Environment   123
Center on Social Welfare Policy and Law   233
Central Services Division (Library of Congress)   26
Centro Hispano Catolico   198
CEP (Council on Economic Priorities)   87, 201
CEP (Court Employment Project)   201
CEPA (Consumers Education and Protective Association International)   85
CEPCAD (Committee to Eliminate Premature Christmas Advertising and Display)   84
Cereal Institute   249
CES (Committee to Eradicate Syphilis)   149
CFA (Call for Action)   196
CFA (Consumer Federation of America)   84
CFIA (Center for Independent Action)   197
CGA (Center for Growth Alternatives)   197
CGS (Community Guidance Service)   149
Chamber of Commerce of the United States   83
Checks Anonymous (CA)   198

CHGC (Committee for Hand Gun Control)   182
Chief Postal Inspector   27
Child Abuse Listening Mediation (CALM)   198
Child Care Program   3
Child Neurology Program   147
Child Welfare League of America (CWLA)   199
Children Before Dogs (CBD)   199
Children's Asthma Research Institute and Hospital at Denver (CARIH)   147
Children's Blood Foundation   147
Children's Foundation   199
Choice   148
Christian Record Braille Foundation (CRBF)   148
CIC (Consumer Information Center)   13
Citizen Action Group (CAG)   84
Citizens Against Noise (CAN)   123
Citizens Association for Sound Energy (CASE)   123
Citizen's Committee for Children of New York (CCC)   199
Citizens Communication Center (CCC)   233
Citizens for a Quieter City (CQC)   123
Citizens for Better Care in Nursing Homes, Homes for the Aged and Other After-Care Facilities (CBC)   148
Citizens for Clean Waters   123
Citizens League Against the Sonic Boom (CLASB)   124
Citizens' Organization for a Sane World: Sane   222
City of Hope   148
Civil Aeronautics Board (CAB)
   Office of the Consumer Advocate   4
Civil Division (Department of Justice)   24
Civil Rights Division (Department of Justice)   24
Civil Service Commission (CSC)
   Office of Public Affairs   4
      Complaints Office   4
      Federal Job Information Center   4
      Retirement and Insurance Information Office   4
Clearing House for Professional Responsibility   84
CLASB (Citizens League Against the Sonic Boom)   124
CLEHA (Conference of Local Environmental Health Administrators)   150
Clinical Center   18
CLUSA (Cooperative League of the U.S.A.)   86
CNCP (Center for New Corporate Priorities)   83
COAC (Council on Adoptable Children)   201
Coalition Against the SST   124
Coalition on National Priorities and Military Policy   199
Coast Guard   30
CODE (Committee on Donor Enlistment)   149
Combined Apprenticeship and Journeyman Outreach Program   25
Commerce, Department of   5
Commission on Accreditation of Rehabilitation Facilities (CARF)   149

Organization Index

Commission on Civil Rights (CCR)
   Office of Public Affairs   6
      Complaints Unit   6
      Publications Management Division   6
Committee for Environmental Information (CEI)   124
Committee for Hand Gun Control (CHGC)   182
Committee for Social Responsibility in Engineering   200
Committee on Donor Enlistment (CODE)   149
Committee on Noise as a Public Health Hazard   124
Committee on Radioactive Waste Management (CRWM)   124
Committee to Combat Huntington's Disease (CCHD)   149
Committee to Eliminate Premature Christmas Advertising and Display (CEPCAD)   84
Committee to Eradicate Syphilis (CES)   149
Common Cause   84
Community Council of Greater New York   200
Community Development Corporation   19
Community Development Foundation (CDF)   200
Community Guidance Service (CGS)   149
Community Relations Service   24
Community Systems Foundation (CSF)   150
Complaints Office (Civil Service Commission)   4
Complaints Unit (Commission on Civil Rights)   6
Concern, Inc.   124
Concerned Citizens for Migrants   200
Conference of Local Environmental Health Administrators (CLEHA)   150
Conference of State Sanitary Engineers (CSSE)   150
Conference on Personal Finance Law   233
Consolidated Tenants League   200
Consortium of Regional Environmental Councils   125
Consumer Action Now (CAN)   125
Consumer Advocate (Postal Service)   27
Consumer Affairs Section (Department of Justice)   24
Consumer and Homemaking Education Program   16
Consumer Federation of America (CFA)   84
Consumer Information Center (General Services Administration)   13
Consumer Offices
   State, County, and City Government   34–66
Consumer Organizations
   State and Local Voluntary   95–120
Consumer Product Safety Commission (CPSC)
   Bureau of Information and Education   6
   Office of Public Affairs   6
      National Electronic Injury Surveillance System (NEISS)   6
Consumer Products and Technology Branch (Energy Research and Development Administration)   7
Consumer Protection Center   85
Consumer Research Center   85
Consumer Research Institute   85
Consumers Education and Protective Association International (CEPA)   85

Consumer's Research, Inc. (CR)   85
Consumers Union of the United States, Inc. (CU)   86
Continental Association of Funeral and Memorial Societies   249
Convicts Association for a Good Environment (CAGE)   125
Cooley's Anemia Blood and Research Foundation for Children   150
Cooperative League of the U.S.A. (CLUSA)   86
COPE (Council on Population and Environment)   125
Copyright Office (Library of Congress)   26
Corrective Eye Care Foundation (CECF)   150
Cosmetic, Toiletry and Fragrance Association, Inc. (CTFA)   249
Council for Health and Welfare Services, United Church of Christ   201
Council of Adult Stutterers (CAS)   151
Council of Better Business Bureaus (CBBB)   86
Council of Mutual Savings Institutions   249
Council of Presidents of Women's National Organizations   182
Council of Psychoanalytic Psychotherapists (CPP)   151
Council of the Southern Mountains (CSM)   201
Council on Adoptable Children (COAC)   201
Council on Children, Media and Merchandising   87
Council on Economic Priorities (CEP)   87, 201
Council on Population and Environment (COPE)   125
Court Employment Project (CEP)   201
CPP (Council of Psychoanalytic Psychotherapists)   151
CPSC (Consumer Product Safety Commission)   6
CQC (Citizens for a Quieter City)   123
CR (Consumer's Research, Inc.)   85
CRBF (Christian Record Braille Foundation)   148
Credit Union National Association (CUNA)   88
CRICAP (Carpet and Rug Industry Consumer Action Panel)   82
Criminal Division (Department of Justice)   24
Crusade for a Cleaner Environment (CCE)   125
CRWM (Committee on Radioactive Waste Management)   124
CSA (Public Services Administration)   18
CSC (Civil Service Commission)   4
CSF (Community Systems Foundation)   150
CSI (Canned Salmon Institute)   248
CSM (Council of the Southern Mountains)   201
CSPI (Center for Science in the Public Interest)   83
CSSE (Conference of State Sanitary Engineers)   150
CTFA (Cosmetic, Toiletry and Fragrance Association, Inc.)   249
CTSF (California Traffic Safety Foundation)   182
CU (Consumers Union of the United States, Inc.)   86
CUNA (Credit Union National Association)   88
Customer Information Branch Services Section (Government Printing Office)   14
Customs Service (Department of the Treasury)   32
CWC (National Committee for a Confrontation With Congress)   212

Organization Index

CWLA (Child Welfare League of America) 199
Cystic Fibrosis Foundation 151

D

Dairy and Food Industries Supply Association (DFISA) 250
DDO (Development Disabilities Office) 16
DEAN (Deputy Educators Against Narcotics) 151
Defense, Department of 7
Delta Ministry 202
Department of Agriculture (USDA)
    Agricultural Marketing Service (AMS) 2
    Agricultural Research Service (ARS) 2
    Animal and Plant Health Inspection Service (APHIS) 2
    Extension Service (ES) 2
    Farmers Home Administration (FmHA) 4
    Food and Nutrition Service (FNS) 2
        Child Care Program 3
        Food Stamp Program 3
        National School Lunch Program 3
        School Breakfast Program 3
        Special Milk Program for Children 3
        Special Supplemental Food Program for Women, Infants, and Children (WIC) 3
        Summer Food Service Program for Children 3
        Supplemental Foods for Health Program 3
    Food Safety and Quality Service (FSQS) 3
    Forest Service (FS) 3
    Office of the Secretary of Agriculture 1
    Rural Development Service (RDS) 3
    Rural Electrification Administration (REA) 4
Department of Commerce (USDC)
    National Bureau of Standards (NBS) 5
    National Fire Prevention and Control Administration (NFPCA) 5
    National Oceanic and Atmospheric Administration (NOAA) 5
        National Marine Fisheries Service (NMFS) 5
    Office of the Secretary 5
        Bureau of Economic Analysis 5
        Bureau of the Census 5
        Domestic and International Business Administration 5
        Economic Development Administration 5
        Maritime Administration 5
        National Technical Information Service 5
        Office of Minority Business Enterprise 5
        Office of Telecommunications 5
        United States Travel Service 5
    Patent and Trademark Office (PTO) 6
Department of Defense (DOD)
    Office of the Assistant Secretary of Defense (Public Affairs) 7
    (PX) Quality Assurance Program 7

Department of Health, Education, and Welfare (HEW)
    Education Division 16
        Office of Education (OE) 16
            Bureau of Education for the Handicapped 17
            Bureau of Occupational and Adult Education 17
            Bureau of Postsecondary Education 17
            Bureau of School Systems 17
            Consumer and Homemaking Education Program 16
            Office of Consumer Education 16
            Office of Indian Education 17
        Office of the Assistant Secretary for Education 16
            Fund for the Improvement of Postsecondary Education 16
            National Center for Education 16
    Office of Human Development (OHD) 15
        Administration on Aging (AoA) 15
            National Nutrition Program for the Elderly 15
        Development Disabilities Office (DDO) 16
        Office of Child Development (OCD) 16
            Head Start 16
            National Center on Child Abuse and Neglect 16
        Office of Native American Programs (ONAP) 16
        Office of Youth Development (OYD) 16
        Rehabilitation Services Administration (RSA) 16
    Office of the Secretary 15
        Office for Civil Rights 15
        Office of Consumer Affairs 15
    Public Health Service 17
        Alcohol, Drug Abuse and Mental Health Administration (ADAMHA) 17
            National Institute of Alcohol Abuse and Alcoholism 17
            National Institute of Mental Health 17
            National Institute on Drug Abuse 17
        Center for Disease Control 17
            Bureau of Epidemiology 17
            Bureau of Health Education 17
            Bureau of Laboratories 17
            Bureau of Smallpox Eradication 17
            Bureau of State Services 17
            Bureau of Training 17
            Bureau of Tropical Diseases 17
            National Institute for Occupational Safety and Health 17
        Food and Drug Administration (FDA) 17
            Bureau of Biologics 17
            Bureau of Drugs 17
            Bureau of Foods 17
            Bureau of Medical Devices and Diagnostic Products 17
            Bureau of Radiological Health 17
            Bureau of Veterinary Medicine 17
            National Center for Toxicological Research 17

Organization Index

Department of Health, Education and Welfare (HEW) (continued)
  Public Health Service
    Health Resources Administration (HRA) 18
      Bureau of Health Manpower 18
      Bureau of Health Planning and Resources Development 18
      National Center for Health Services Research 18
      National Center for Health Statistics 18
    Health Services Administration (HSA) 18
      Bureau of Community Health Services 18
      Bureau of Medical Services 18
      Bureau of Quality Assurance 18
      Indian Health Services 18
    National Institutes of Health (NIH) 18
      Clinical Center 18
      National Cancer Institute 18
      National Eye Institute 18
      National Heart and Lund Institute 18
      National Institute of Allergy and Infectious Diseases 18
      National Institute of Arthritis, Metabolism, and Digestive Diseases 18
      National Institute of Child Health and Human Development 18
      National Institute of Dental Research 18
      National Institute of Environmental Health Sciences 18
      National Institute of General Medical Sciences 18
      National Institute of Neurological and Communicative Disorders and Stroke 18
      National Institute on Aging 18
      National Library of Medicine 18
  Social and Rehabilitation Service (SRS) 18
    Assistance Payments Administration (APA) 18
      Aid to Families with Dependent Children (AFDC) 18
    Medical Services Administration (MSA) 19
      Early and Periodic Screening Diagnosis Treatment (EPSDT) 19
      Medicaid 19
    Public Services Administration (CSA) 18
  Social Security Administration 19
Department of Housing and Urban Development (HUD)
  Community Development Corporation (CDC) 19
  Federal Disaster Assistance Administration (FDAA) 20
    Disaster Relief Fund 20
  Federal Insurance Administration 20
    Federal Crime Insurance Program 20
    Riot Reinsurance Program 20
  Office of the Assistant Secretary for Community Planning and Development 20
  Office of the Assistant Secretary for Fair Housing and Equal Opportunity 20
  Office of the Assistant Secretary for Neighborhoods, Voluntary Associations, and Consumer Protection 21
    Interstate Land Sales Registration 21
    Mobile Homes Standards Division 21
      Interstate Land Sales Program 21
    Real Estate Settlement Procedures Program 21
  Office of the Secretary 19
    Office of Public Affairs 19
    Program Information Center 19
Department of Justice (USDJ)
  Office of Public Information 24
    Antitrust Division 24
    Bureau of Prisons 24
    Civil Division 24
    Civil Rights Division 24
    Community Relations Service 24
    Consumer Affairs Section 24
    Criminal Division 24
    Drug Enforcement Administration 24
    Federal Bureau of Investigation (FBI) 24
    Immigration and Naturalization Service 25
    Land and Natural Resources Division 24
    Law Enforcement Assistance Administration 24
    Tax Division 24
Department of Labor (DOL)
  Bureau of International Labor Affairs (ILAB) 25
  Bureau of Labor Statistics (BLS) 25
  Employment and Training Administration (ETA) 25
    Combined Apprenticeship and Journeyman Outreach Program 25
    Job Corps 25
    National Indian and Native American Program 25
    National Migrant Worker Program 25
    National Older Worker Program 25
    National On-the-Job Training Program 25
    Unemployment Insurance Service (UIS) 25
    Work Incentive Program (WIN) 25
  Employment Standards Administration (ESA) 25
  Labor-Management Services Administration (LMSA) 26
  Occupational Safety and Health Administration (OSHA) 26
  Office of the Secretary 25
Department of State
  Passport Office 29
  Public Affairs Office 29
Department of the Interior (USDI)
  Bureau of Indian Affairs 22
    American Indian National Bank and Buy Indian Contracts 22
    Employment Assistance Program 22
    Indian Action Teams 22
      Office of Indian Water Rights 22
  Bureau of Land Management 23
  Bureau of Mines 23
  Bureau of Outdoor Recreation 23
    Land and Water Conservation Fund 23

Organization Index

Department of the Interior (USDI) (continued)
    Bureau of Reclamation   23
    Fish and Wildlife Service   21
    Geological Survey   21
        Information Office   21
        National Cartographic Information Center   21
        Visual Services Branch   22
    National Park Service   22
    Office of the Secretary   21
Department of the Treasury (USDT)
    Bureau of Alcohol Tobacco and Firearms   32
    Customs Service   32
        Affairs Division   32
        General Information   32
        Mailed Packages Division   32
    Internal Revenue Service (IRS)   32
        Public Affairs Division   32
    Office of the Comptroller of the Currency   32
    Office of the Secretary   32
    Savings Bonds Division   33
Department of Transportation (DOT)
    Coast Guard   30
    Federal Aviation Administration (FAA)   30
        Office of Public Affairs   30
    Federal Highway Administration (FHWA)   30
    Federal Railroad Administration   31
    National Highway Traffic Safety Administration   31
    Office of the Secretary   30
        Office of Public Affairs   30
    Urban Mass Transportation Administration (UMTA)   31
Deputy Educators Against Narcotics (DEAN)   151
Development Disabilities Office   16
DFISA (Dairy and Food Industries Supply Association)   250
Dial-A-Museum   29
Dial-A-Phenomenon   29
Direct Mail/Marketing Association (DMMA)   88, 250
Direct Selling Association (DSA)   250
Division for the Blind and Physically Handicapped   26
Division of Consumer Affairs (Federal Reserve System)   12
Divorce Anonymous   202
DMMA (Direct Mail/Marketing Association)   88, 250
Do It Now Foundation   151
DOD (Department of Defense)   7
DOL (Department of Labor)   25
Domestic and International Business Administration   5
DOT (Department of Transportation)   30
Drug Abuse Council   152
Drug Enforcement Administration   24
DSA (Direct Selling Association)   250

E

EAC (Environmental Action Coalition)   127
EAE (Ecology Action East)   126
EAEI (Ecology Action Educational Institute)   126
EAF (Earth Awareness Foundation)   126
EAF (Environmental Action Foundation)   128
Early and Periodic Screening Diagnosis Treatment   19
Earth Awareness Foundation (EAF)   126
Easter Seal Home Service   152
EC (Ecology Center)   126
Ecology Action East (EAE)   126
Ecology Action Educational Institute (EAEI)   126
Ecology Center (EC)   126
Ecology Center of Louisiana   126
Ecology Forum, Inc.   126
Economic Development Administration   5
ECRI (Emergency Care Research Institute)   152
EDF (Environmental Defense Fund)   128
EDNA (Emergency Department Nurses Association)   152
Education Division (Department of Health, Education and Welfare)   16
EEOC (Equal Employment Opportunity Commission)   9
EFA (Epilepsy Foundation of America)   153
EIA (Electronic Industries Association)   250
Electronic Industries Association (EIA)   250
ELI (Environmental Law Institute)   233
EMA (Evaporated Milk Association)   250
Emergency Care Research Institute (ECRI)   152
Emergency Department Nurses Association (EDNA)   152
Emphysema Anonymous   152
Employment and Training Administration   25
Employment Assistance Program   22
Employment Standards Administration   25
ENACT (Environmental Action for Survival)   127
Energy Research and Development Administration (ERDA)
    Office of Public Affairs   7
        Consumer Products and Technology Branch   7
Environment Information Center, Inc.   127
Environmental Action Coalition (EAC)   127
Environmental Action for Survival (ENACT)   127
Environmental Action Foundation (EAF)   128
Environmental Action, Inc.   127
Environmental Defense Fund (EDF)   128
Environmental Law Institute (ELI)   233
Environmental Policy Center (EPC)   128
Environmental Protection Agency (EAP)
    Office of Air and Waste Management   8
    Office of the Administrator   8
        Office of Public Affairs   8
        Public Information Center   8
    Office of Water and Hazardous Materials   8

Organization Index

Environmental Technology Seminar 128
EPA (Environmental Protection Agency) 8
EPC (Environmental Policy Center) 128
Epilepsy Foundation of America (EFA) 153
EPSDT (Early and Periodic Screening Diagnosis Treatment) 19
Equal Employment Opportunity Commission (EEOC)
   Office of Public Affairs 9
ERDA (Energy Research and Development Administration) 7
ES (Extension Service) 2
ESA (Employment Standards Administration) 25
ETA (Employment and Training Administration) 25
Evaporated Milk Association (EMA) 250
Extension Service 2
Eye-Bank for Sight Restoration 153

F

FAA (Federal Aviation Administration) 30
Fair Chance, Inc. 202
Farm Credit Administration (FCA) 9
Farmers Home Administration 4
FBI (Federal Bureau of Investigation) 24
FCA (Farm Credit Administration) 9
FCC (Federal Communications Commission) 9
FCH (Foundation for Cooperative Housing) 88
FDA (Food and Drug Administration) 17
FDAA (Federal Disaster Assistance Administration) 20
FDIC (Federal Deposit Insurance Corporation) 10
FDIC (Fire Department Instructors Conference) 183
FEA (Federal Energy Administration) 10
Federal Aviation Administration 30
Federal Bureau of Investigation 24
Federal Communications Commission (FCC)
   Office of Public Information 9
Federal Crime Insurance Program 20
Federal Department of Energy
   Energy Research and Development Administration 7
   Federal Energy Administration 10
   Federal Power Commission 11
Federal Deposit Insurance Corporation (FDIC)
   Office of Bank Customer Affairs 10
      Information Office 10
Federal Disaster Assistance Administration (FDAA) 20
Federal Energy Administration (FEA)
   Office of Consumer Affairs and Special Impact 10
      National Energy Information Center (NEIC) 10
      Office of Communications and Public Affairs 10
Federal Fire Council (FFC) 183
Federal Highway Administration (FHWA) 30
Federal Home Loan Bank Board (FHLBB)
   Office of Housing and Urban Affairs 11
      Federal Home Loan Mortgage Corporation 11

Federal Savings and Loan Insurance Corporation (FSLIC) 111
   Office of Communications 11
Federal Information Centers (FIC) 13
Federal Insurance Administration) 20
Federal Job Information Center (Civil Service Commission) 4
Federal Maritime Commission (FMC)
   Office of Public Information 11
Federal Power Commission (FPC)
   Office of Public Information 11
Federal Preparedness Agency 13
Federal Railroad Administration 31
Federal Reserve System (FRS)
   Division of Consumer Affairs 12
Federal Savings and Loan Insurance Corporation 11
Federal Supply Service 13
Federal Trade Commission (FTC)
   Bureau of Consumer Protection 12
   Office of Public Information 12
Federal Water Quality Association 128
Federation Employment and Guidance Service (FEGS) 202
Federation of Homemakers 88
Federation of Jewish Philanthropies of New York (FJP) 202
Federation of Southern Cooperatives 88
FEGS (Federation Employment and Guidance Service) 202
Fertilizer Institute (TFI) 251
FFC (Federal Fire Council) 183
FFH (American Freedom from Hunger Foundation) 193
FGP (Foster Grandparent Program) 1
FHLBB (Federal Home Loan Bank Board) 11
FHWA (Federal Highway Administration) 30
FIC (Federal Information Centers) 13
FICAP (Furniture Industry Consumer Action Panel) 89
FIFC (Fur Information and Fashion Council) 251
Fine Arts and Portrait Galleries 29
Fire Department Instructors Conference (FDIC) 183
Fire Marshals Association of North America (FMANA) 183
Fire Retardant Chemicals Association (FRCA) 251
Fish and Wildlife Service 21
Fishermen's Clean Water Action Project 129
FJP (Federation of Jewish Philanthropies of New York) 202
Flight Safety Foundation (FSF) 183
FMANA (Fire Marshals Association of North America) 183
FMC (Federal Maritime Commission) 11
FmHA (Farmers Home Administration) 4
FNS (Food and Nutrition Service) 3
FNS (Frontier Nursing Service) 153
Food and Drug Administration 17
Food and Nutrition Service 3
Food Research and Action Center (FRAC) 202

1532

Organization Index

Food Safety and Quality Service   3
Food Service Executives' Association (FSEA)   251
Food Stamp Program   3
Forest Products Safety Conferences (FPSC)   183
Forest Service (FS)   3
Fortune Society   203
Forty Plus Club of New York   203
Foster Grandparent Program   1
Foundation for Cooperative Housing (FCH)   88
FPC (Federal Power Commission)   11
FPSC (Forest Products Safety Conference)   183
FRAC (food Research and Action Center)   202
Fran Lee Foundation, Inc.   89
FRCA (Fire Retardant Chemicals Association)   251
Freer Gallery of Art   29
Friendly Hand Foundation   153
Friends of the Earth   129
Friends of the Superior Court   203
Frontier Nursing Service (FNS)   153
FRS (Federal Reserve System)   12
FS (Forest Service)   3
FSEA (Food Service Executives' Association)   251
FSF (Flight Safety Foundation)   183
FSI (International Society of Fire Service Instructors)   185
FSLIC (Federal Savings and Loan Insurance Corporation)   11
FSQA (Food Safety and Quality Service)   3
FTC (Federal Trade Commission)   12
Full Circle Associates   203
Fund for the Improvement of Postsecondary Education   16
Fur Information and Fashion Council (FIFC)   251
Furniture Industry Consumer Action Panel (FICAP)   89
Futures for Children   203

G

GA (Gamblers Anonymous)   204
Gam-Anon   203
Gamblers Anonymous (GA)   204
GEB (Guiding Eyes for the Blind)   154
General Federation of Women's Clubs (GFWC)   204
General Information (Department of the Treasury)   32
General Reference and Bibliography Division (Library of Congress)   26
General Services Administration (GSA)
   National Audiovisual Center (NAC)   14
   Office of Information   12
      Automated Data and Telecommunications Service   13
      Federal Preparedness Agency   13
      Federal Supply Service   13
      National Archives and Records Service   13
      Public Buildings Service   13
   Office of the Administrator   13
      Consumer Information Center (CIC)   13
      Federal Information Centers (FIC)   13
Geological Survey   21
Get Oil Out (GOO!)   129
GFWC (General Federation of Women's Clubs)   204
GIA (Goodwill Industries of America)   154
Golden Ring Council of Senior Citizens Clubs   204
GOO! (Get Oil Out)   129
Good American Helping Hands   153
Goodwill Industries of America (GIA)   154
Government Offices
   Metropolitan Washington, D.C.   72-77
Government Printing Office (GPO)
   Superintendent of Documents   14
      Customer Information Branch Services Section   14
      Pueblo Distribution Center   14
GPO (Government Printing Office)   14
Gray Panthers   204
GSA (General Services Administration)   12
Guide Dog Foundation for the Blind   154
Guide Dogs for the Blind   154
Guiding Eyes for the Blind (GEB)   154

H

Harvard Environmental Law Society   234
Hay Fever Prevention Society   154
HDRF (Heart Disease Research Foundation)   155
Head Start   16
Health, Education and Welfare, Department of   16
Health Insurance Institute   154
Health Policy Advisory Center (HPAC)   154
Health Research Group   155
Health Resources Administration (HRA)   18
Health Services Administration (HSA)   18
HEART (Household Employment Association for Re-evaluation and Training)   204
Heart Disease Research Foundation (HDRF)   155
HELP (Homophile Effort for Legal Protection)   234
Help, Inc.   204
HERS (National Heart Education Research Society)   167
HEW (Department of Health, Education, and Welfare)   15
HFDA (Hospital Food Directors Association)   155
HGF (Human Growth Foundation)   156
Highway Users Federation for Safety and Mobility   184
Home Owners Warranty Corporation (HOWC)   251
Home Ventilating Institute (HVI)   251
Homophile Effort for Legal Protection (HELP)   234
Hospital Food Directors Association (HFDA)   155
Hospitalized Veterans Writing Project (HVWP)   155
Household Employment Association for Re-evaluation and Training (HEART)   204

1533

Organization Index

Housing and Urban Development, Department of 19
HOWC (Home Owners Warranty Corporation) 251
HPAC (Health Policy Advisory Center) 154
HRA (Health Resources Administration) 18
HRW (Human Rights for Women) 205
HSA (Health Services Administration) 18
HUD (Department of Housing and Urban Development) 19
Human Growth Foundation (HGF) 156
Human Rights for Women (HRW) 205
Hundred Club of Massachusetts 205
HVI (Home Ventilating Institute) 251
HVWP (Hospitalized Veterans Writing Project) 155

I

IAAI (International Association of Arson Investigators) 184
IAEI (International Association of Electrical Inspectors) 252
IAFC (International Association of Fire Chiefs) 184
IAHIC (International Association of Home Improvement Councils) 252
IAI (International Apple Institute) 252
IAL (International Association of Laryngectomees) 157
IAMFES (International Association of Milk, Food and Environmental Sanitarians) 252
IAPC (International Association for Pollution Control) 129
ICBO (Interracial Council for Business Opportunity) 207
ICC (Interstate Commerce Commission) 24
ICCA (International Consumer Credit Association) 253
ICD Rehabilitation and Research Center 156
ICSRI (Interfaith Committee on Social Responsibility in Investments) 206
IDAA (International Doctors in Alcoholics Anonymous) 157
IFCO (Interreligious Foundation for Community Organization) 207
IFI (International Fabricare Institute) 253
IFSTA (International Fire Service Training Associations) 184
IFTF (Inter-Faith Task Force) 206
IGE (International Guiding Eyes) 158
IHG (Industrial Health Foundation) 156
IIEC (Inter-Industry Emission Control Program) 129
IIHS (Insurance Institute for Highway Safety) 184
III (Insurance Information Institute) 252
ILAB (Bureau of International Labor Affairs) 25
ILI (Institute of Life Insurance) 252
IMBE (Institute for Minority Business Education) 205
Immigration and Naturalization Service 24
Independent Snowmobile Medical Research (ISMR) 184

IN-DEV-IL (Institute for the Development of Indian Law) 234
Indian Action Teams 22
Indian Health Services 18
Indian Rights Association (IRA) 205
Individual Retirement Accounts (IRA's) 27
Indoor Sports Club (ISC) 156
Industrial Health Foundation (IHG) 156
Information Division (Farm Credit Administration) 9
Information Office (Department of the Interior) 21
Information Office (Federal Deposit Insurance Corporation) 10
Information Office (Library of Congress) 26
INSPIRE (Institute for Public Interest Representation) 234
Institute for Advanced Study in Rational Psychotherapy 156
Institute for Minority Business Education (IMBE) 205
Institute for Public Interest Representation (INSPIRE) 234
Institute for Public Understanding (IPU) 206
Institute for the Development of Indian Law (IN-DEV-IL) 234
Institute of Life Insurance (ILI) 252
Insurance Information Institute (III) 252
Insurance Institute for Highway Safety (IIHS) 184
Inter-Faith Task Force (FTF) 206
Interfaith Committee on Social Responsibility in Investments (ICSRI) 206
Inter-Industry Emission Control Program (IIEC) 129
Interior, Department of 22
Internal Revenue Service (IRS) 32
International Apple Institute (IAI) 252
International Association for Medical Assistance to Travelers 157
International Association for Pollution Control) (IAPC) 129
International Association of Arson Investigators (IAAI) 184
International Association of Electrical Inspectors (IAEI) 252
International Association of Fire Chiefs (IAFC) 184
International Association of Home Improvement Councils (IAHIC) 252
International Association of Laryngectomees (IAL) 157
International Association of Milk, Food and Environmental Sanitarians (IAMFES) 252
International Consumer Credit Association (ICCA) 253
International Council for Infant Survival 157
International Council of Seamen's Agencies 207
International Doctors in Alcoholics Anonymous (IDAA) 157
International Fabricare Institute (IFI) 253
International Fire Service Training Associations (IFSTA) 184
International Food Research and Educational Center 157

Organization Index

International Guiding Eyes (IGE) 158
International Myopia Prevention Association (MPA) 158
International Parents' Organization (IPO) 158
International Rotary Engine Club (IREC) 253
International Safety Institute (ISI) 185
International Society of Fire Service Instructors (FSI) 185
International Tsunami Information Center (ITIC) 185
Interracial Council for Business Opportunity (ICBO) 207
Interreligious Foundation for Community Organization (IFCO) 207
Interstate Commerce Commission (ICC)
   Office of Public and Consumer Information 2
Interstate Land Sales Program 21
Interstate Land Sales Registration 21
Investors Service Bureau 89
IPO (International Parents' Organization) 158
IPU (Institute for Public Understanding) 206
IRA (Indian Rights Association) 205
IRA's (Individual Retirement Accounts) 27
IREC (International Rotary Engine Club) 253
IRS (Internal Revenue Service) 32
ISC (Indoor Sports Club) 156
ISI (International Safety Institute) 185
ISMR (Independent Snowmobile Medical Research) 184
ITIC (International Tsunami Information Center) 185
IWLA (Izaak Walton League of America) 130
Izaak Walton League of America (IWLA) 130

J

JACS (Joint Action in Community Service, Inc.) 208
JASA (Jewish Association for Services for the Aged) 207
Jesuit Volunteer Corps (JVC) 207
Jewish Association for Services for the Aged (JASA) 207
Jewish Guild for the Blind (JGB) 158
JGB (Jewish Guild for the Blind) 158
JOB (Just One Break) 208
Job Corps 25
John F. Kennedy Center for the Performing Arts 28
Joint Action in Community Service, Inc. (JACS) 208
Joseph H. Hirschhorn Museum and Sculpture Garden 29
Just One Break (JOB) 208
Justice, Department of 24
JVC (Jesuit Volunteer Corps) 207

K

KAB (Keep America Beautiful) 130
Keep America Beautiful (KAB) 130

L

Labor, Department of 25
Labor-Management Services Administration 26
Land and Natural Resources Division (Department of Justice) 24
Law Enforcement Assistance Administration 24
Law Students Civil Rights Research Council (LSCRRC) 234
Lawyers' Committee for Civil Rights Under Law 235
LC (Library of Congress) 26
LCV (League of Conservation Voters) 130
LDF (Legal Defense and Educational Fund, NAACP) 236
Leader Dogs for the Blind 158
League of Conservation Voters (LCV) 130
Legal Aid Warranty Fund 235
Legal Service for the Elderly Poor (LSEP) 235
Leukemia Society of America (LSA) 158
LI (Lions International) 208
Library of Congress (LC)
   Information Office 26
      Central Services Division 26
         Copyright Office 26
         Division for the Blind and Physically Handicapped 26
         General Reference and Bibliography Division 26
         National Referral Center for Science and Technology 26
Lions International (LI) 208
Little City Foundation 159
Little People of America (LPA) 208
LMSA (Labor-Management Services Administration) 26
LPA (Little People of America) 208
LSA (Leukemia Society of America) 158
LSCRRC (Law Students Civil Rights Research Council) 234
LSEP (Legal Service for the Elderly Poor) 235

Organization Index

M

MACAP (Major Appliance Consumer Action Panel) 89
Magazine Action Line 89
Magazine Publishers Association, Inc. 253
Mail Order Action Line, Mail Preference Service 89
Mailed Packages Division (Department of the Treasury) 32
Major Appliance Consumer Action Panel (MACAP) 89
Make Today Count (MTC) 159
MALDEF (Mexican American Legal Defense and Educational Fund) 235
Manhattan Bowery Project (MBP) 159
Manufactured Housing Institute 254
Manufacturing Chemists Association (MCA) 254
Marine Society of the City of New York 254
Maritime Administration 5
Mass Retailing Institute (MRI) 254
Maternity Center Association (MCA) 159
Mattachine Society of New York (MSNY) 208
MBP (Manhattan Bowery Project) 159
MCA (Manufacturing Chemists Association) 254
MCA (Maternity Center Association) 159
MCAP (Minority Contractors Assistance Project) 209
MCMA (Metal Cookware Manufacturers Association) 255
MDAA (Muscular Dystrophy Associations of America) 160
MDNA (Mobilehome Dealers National Association) 255
MDS (Mennonite Disaster Service) 209
Medicaid 19
Medical Liberation Front (MLF) 159
Medical Services Administration (MSA) 19
Mended Hearts, Inc. 160
Mennonite Disaster Service (MDS) 209
Men's Fashion Association of America (MFA) 254
Mental Health Law Project 235
Mental Research Institute (MRI) 160
Metal Cookware Manufacturers Association (MCMA) 255
Metal Ladder Manufacturers Association (MLMA) 185
Metropolitan Washington, D.C., Government Offices 72-77
Mexican American Legal Defense and Educational Fund (MALDEF) 235
MFA (Men's Fashion Association of America) 254
MFY (Mobilization for Youth) 209
MG (Myasthenia Gravis Foundation) 160
Michigan Pure Water Council 130
Mini-Grant Program 1

Minority Contractors Assistance Project (MCAP) 209
Minority Small Business (MSB) 28
MLF (Medical Liberation Front) 159
MLMA (Metal Ladder Manufacturers Association) 185
MM (Morality in Media) 90
Mobile Homes Standards Division 21
Mobilehome Dealers National Association (MDNA) 255
Mobilization for Youth (MFY) 209
Morality in Media (MM) 90
Mothers of Children with Down's Syndrome 160
Motion Picture and Television Fund (MP&TF) 209
Mountain Rescue Association (MRA) 185
Movement for Economic Justice 90
MP&TF (Motion Picture and Television Fund) 209
MPA (International Myopia Prevention Association) 158
MRA (Mountain Rescue Association) 185
MRI (Mass Retailing Institute) 254
MRI (Mental Research Institute) 160
MSA (Medical Services Administration) 19
MSB (Minority Small Business) 28
MSNY (Mattachine Society of New York) 208
MTC (Make Today Count) 159
Muscular Dystrophy Associations of America (MDAA) 160
Myasthenia Gravis Foundation (MG) 160

N

NAACP Legal Defense and Educational Fund (LDF) 236
NAAMIC (National Association of Automotive Mutual Insurance Companies) 255
NAB (National Alliance of Businessmen) 209
NABM (National Association of Black Manufacturers) 210
NAC (National Audiovisual Center) 14
NACC (National Air Conservation Commission) 130
NACWC (National Association of Colored Women's Clubs) 210
NADA (National Automobile Dealers Association) 257
Nader-related organizations
    Aviation Consumer Action Project (ACAP) 82
    Center for Concerned Engineering 197
    Center for Study of Responsive Law 83
    Citizen Action Group 84
    Clearing House for Professional Responsibility 84
    Health Research Group 18
    Public Action Coalition on Toys 92
    Public Citizen, Inc. 92
    Public Citizen Visitors Center 92
    Public Interest Research Group 93
    Tax Reform Research Group 94

Organization Index

NADS (National Association for Down's Syndrome) 161
NAF (National Amputation Foundation) 161
NAFED (National Association of Fire Equipment Distributors) 186
NAFM (National Association of Furniture Manufacturers) 255
NAHB (National Association of Home Builders of the United States) 256
NAHB (National Association of Homes for Boys) 210
NAHC (National Association of Housing Cooperatives) 90
NAHM (National Association of Hosiery Manufacturers) 256
NAHRO (National Association of Housing and Redevelopment Officials) 210
NAHSA (National Association for Hearing and Speech Action) 161
NAIA (North American Indian Association) 218
NAIL (Neurotics Anonymous Infernational Liaison) 170
NAISC (National American Indian Safety Council) 185
NALU (National Association of Life Underwriters) 256
NAMH (National Association for Mental Health, Inc.) 162
NANHC (National Association of Neighborhood Health Centers) 162
NAPAN (National Association for the Prevention of Addiction to Narcotics) 162
NAPH (National Association of the Physically Handicapped) 163
NAPHT (National Association of Patients on Hemodialysis and Transplantation) 163
NAPRA (National Association of Progressive Radio Announcers) 256
NARAL (National Abortion Rights Action League) 161
NARB (National Advertising Review Board) 255
NARC (National Association for Retarded Citizens) 162
Narcotic Educational Foundation of America (NEFA) 161
Narcotics Education 161
NAREB (National Association of Real Estate Brokers) 257
NARP (National Association of Railroad Passengers) 90
NASCO (North American Student Cooperative Organization) 91
NASFCA (National Automatic Sprinkler and Fire Control Association) 186
NATB (National Automobile Theft Bureau) 257
National Abortion Rights Action League (NARAL) 161
National Advertising Review Board (NARB) 255
National Air and Space Museum 29

National Air Conservation Commission (NACC) 130
National Alliance of Businessmen (NAB) 209
National American Indian Safety Council (NAISC) 185
National Amputation Foundation (NAF) 161
National Archives and Records Service 13
National Assistance League 210
National Association for Down's Syndrome (NADS) 161
National Association for Hearing and Speech Action (NAHSA) 161
National Association for Mental Health, Inc. (NAMH) 162
National Association for Retarded Citizens (NARC) 162
National Association for the Prevention of Addiction to Narcotics (NAPAN) 162
National Association of Accountants for the Public Interest 255
National Association of Automotive Mutual Insurance Companies (NAAMIC) 255
National Association of Black Manufacturers (NABM) 210
National Association of Colored Women's Clubs (NACWC) 210
National Association of Fire Equipment Distributors (NAFED) 186
National Association of Furniture Manufacturers (NAFM) 255
National Association of Home Builders of the United States (NAHB) 256
National Association of Homes for Boys (NAHB) 210
National Association of Hosiery Manufacturers (NAHM) 256
National Association of Housing and Redevelopment Officials (NAHRO) 210
National Association of Housing Cooperatives (NAHC) 90
National Association of Life Underwriters (NALU) 256
National Association of Negro Business and Professional Women's Clubs 211
National Association of Neighborhood Health Centers (NANHC) 162
National Association of Patients on Hemodialysis and Transplantation (NAPHT) 163
National Association of Progressive Radio Announcers (NAPRA) 256
National Association of Railroad Passengers (NARP) 90
National Association of Real Estate Brokers (NAREB) 257
National Association of Realtors 257
National Association of the Physically Handicapped (NAPH) 163
National Association of Women Highway Safety Leaders (NAWHSL) 186
National Ataxia Foundation 163

Organization Index

National Audiovisual Center (General Services Administration) 14
National Automatic Sprinkler and Fire Control Association (NASFCA) 186
National Automobile Dealers Association (NADA) 257
National Automobile Theft Bureau (NATB) 257
National Benevolent Association of the Christian Church (NBA) 211
National Braille Association (NBA) 163
National Braille Press (NBP) 164
National Bureau of Standards 5
National Businessmen's Council (NBMC) 257
National Cancer Foundation 164
National Cancer Institute 18
National Canners Association (NCA) 257
National Cartographic Information Center 21
National Catholic Disaster Relief Committee (NCDRC) 211
National/CEBO (National Council for Equal Business Opportunity) 213
National Center for Dispute Settlement of the American Arbitration Association (NCDS) 236
National Center for Education 16
National Center for Health Services Research 18
National Center for Health Statistics 18
National Center for Toxicological Research 17
National Center for Voluntary Action 211
National Center on Child Abuse and Neglect 16
National Child Safety Council (NCSC) 186
National Citizens Committee for Broadcasting (NCCB) 90
National Clergy Conference on Alcoholism 164
National Committee Against Discrimination in Housing (NCDH) 212
National Committee Against Fluoridation (NCAF) 130
National Committee for a Confrontation with Congress (CWC) 212
National Committee for Prevention of Child Abuse 212
National Committee for the Prevention of Alcoholism and Drug Dependency 164
National Committee on Films for Safety (NCFS) 186
National Committee on Household Employment (NCHE) 212
National Conference of Catholic Charities (NCCC) 212
National Conference of Shomrim Societies (NCSS) 186
National Congress for Community Economic Development (NCCED) 213
National Consumer Finance Association (NCFA) 258
National Consumer Law Center 236
National Consumers Committee for Research and Education 91
National Consumers Congress (NCC) 91

National Consumers League (NCL) 91
National Council Against Illegal Liquor (NCAIL) 258
National Council for Equal Business Opportunity (National/CEBO) 213
National Council for Homemaker-Home Health Aide Services 213
National Council for the Public Assessment of Technology (NC/PAT) 91
National Council of Adoptive Parents Organizations (NCAPO) 213
National Council of Catholic Laity (NCCL) 214
National Council of Churches of Christ in the U.S.A. (NCC) 91
National Council of La Raza 214
National Council of Obesity (NCO) 164
National Council of Puerto Rican Volunteers (NCPRV) 214
National Council of Senior Citizens (NCSC) 214
National Council of the Paper Industry for Air and Stream Improvement 131
National Council of Women of the United States (NCW) 214
National Council on Drug Abuse (NCDA) 165
National Council on Radiation Protection and Measurements (NCRP) 131
National Council on the Aging (NCOA) 215
National Credit Union Administration (NCUA) Office of the Administrator 27
National Dairy Council (NDC) 258
National Drivers Association for the Prevention of Traffic Accidents (NDAPTA) 187
National Easter Seal Society for Crippled Children and Adults 165
National Electronic Injury Surveillance System 6
National Electronic Service Dealers Association (NESDA) 258
National Employment Law Project 237
National Energy Information Center (NEIC) 10
National Environmental Development Association (NEDA) 131
National Environmental Health Association 165
National Eye Institute 18
National Eye Research Foundation 165
National Family Council on Drug Addiction 165
National Farm Worker Ministry (NFWM) 215
National Federation of Settlements and Neighborhood Centers (NFS&NC) 215
National Federation of Women's Exchanges 215
National Fire Prevention and Control Administration 5
National Fire Protection Association (NFPA) 187
National Forest Products Association (NFPA) 259
National Foundation for Asthmatic Children at Tucson (NFAC) 166
National Foundation for Conservation and Environmental Officers 215
National Foundation for Consumer Credit (NFCC) 259

Organization Index

National Foundation for Jewish Genetic Diseases 166
National Foundation for Sudden Infant Death 166
National Foundation for the Handicapped and Disabled (NFHD) 166
National Foundation - March of Dimes 166
National Gallery of Art 29
National Health Council (NHC) 167
National Health Federation (NHF) 167
National Heart and Lung Institute 18
National Heart Education Research Society (HERS) 167
National Hemophilia Foundation (NHF) 167
National Highway Traffic Safety Administration (NHTSA) 31
National Home Furnishings Association (NHFA) 259
National Home Study Council (NHSC) 259
National Housing Conference (NHC) 215
National Indian and Native American Program 25
National Industries for the Blind (NIB) 167
National Institute for Automotive Service Excellence (NIASE) 260
National Institute for Consumer Justice 237
National Institute for Occupational Safety and Health 17
National Institute of Alcohol Abuse and Alcoholism 17
National Institute of Allergy and Infectious Diseases 18
National Institute of Arthritis, Metabolism, and Digestive Diseases 18
National Institute of Child Health and Human Development 18
National Institute of Credit (NIC) 260
National Institute of Dental Research 18
National Institute of Environmental Health Sciences 18
National Institute of General Medical Sciences 18
National Institute of Mental Health 17
National Institute of Neurological and Communicative Disorders and Stroke 18
National Institute on Aging 18
National Institute on Drug Abuse 17
National Institutes of Health 18
National Interagency Council on Smoking and Health (NIC) 168
National Kidney Foundation 168
National Latin American Federation 216
National Lawyers Wives 237
National Legal Aid and Defender Association (NLADA) 237
National Library of Medicine 18
National Live Stock and Meat Board (NLSMB) 260
National Marine Fisheries Service 5
National Medical Association Foundation (NMAF) 168
National Migrant Worker Program 25
National Mine Rescue Association (NMRA) 187
National Mineral Wool Insulation Association (NMWIA) 260
National Multiple Sclerosis Society 168
National Museum of History and Technology 29
National Museum of National History 29
National Nutrition Program for the Elderly 15
National Oak Flooring Manufacturers Association (NOFMA) 260
National Oceanic and Atmospheric Administration 5
National Older Worker Program 25
National On-the-Job Training Program 25
National Organization to Insure a Sound-Controlled Environment (NOISE) 131
National Osteopathic Foundation (NOF) 168
National Paint and Coatings Association (NPCA) 261
National Paraplegia Foundation (NPF) 168
National Park Service 22
National Parkinson Foundation (NPF) 169
National Pest Control Association (NPCA) 261
National Progress Association for Economic Development (NPAED) 216
National Rare Blood Club (NRBC) 169
National Referral Center for Science and Technology 26
National Retail Merchants Association (NRMA) 261
National Retired Teachers Association (NRTA) 216
National Rural Housing Coalition (NRHC) 216
National Safe Boating Committee (NSBC) 187
National Safety Council 188
National Safety Council's Conference for Religious Leaders 188
National Sanitation Foundation (NSF) 169
National Save-A-Life League 169
National School Lunch Program 3
National Sharecroppers Fund (NFS) 216
National Sickle Cell Disease Research Foundation (NSCDRF) 169
National Social Conditioning Camps (NSCC) 216
National Society for Autistic Children (NSAC) 169
National Society for the Prevention of Blindness (NSPB) 170
National Student Volunteer Program 1
National Tay-Sachs and Allied Diseases Association (NTSAD) 170
National Technical Information Service 5
National Tenants Organization (NTO) 217
National Water Safety Congress (NWSC) 188
National Water Supply Improvement Association (NWSIA) 131
National Welfare Rights Organization (NWRO) 217
National Woodwork Manufacturers Association 261
National Yokefellow Prison Ministry 217
National Zoological Park 28
Natural Resources Defense Council (NRDC) 132, 237
Navy Relief Society 217
NAWHSL (National Association of Women Highway Safety Leaders) 186

1539

Organization Index

NBA (National Braille Association) 163
NBA (National Benevolent Association of the Christian Church) 211
NBMC (National Businessmen's Council) 257
NBP (National Braille Press) 164
NBS (National Bureau of Standards) 5
NCA (National Canners Association) 257
NCA (National Council on Alcoholism) 165
NCAF (National Committee Against Fluoridation) 130
NCAIL (National Council Against Illegal Liquor) 258
NCAPO (National Council of Adoptive Parents Organizations) 213
NCC (National Consumers Congress) 91
NCC (National Council of Churches of Christ in the U.S.A.) 91
NCCB (National Citizens Committee for Broadcasting) 90
NCCC (National Conference of Catholic Charities) 212
NCCED (National Congress for Community Economic Development) 213
NCCL (National Council of Catholic Laity) 214
NCDA (National Council on Drug Abuse) 165
NCDH (National Committee Against Discrimination in Housing) 212
NCDRC (National Catholic Disaster Relief Committee) 211
NCDS (National Center for Dispute Settlement of the American Arbitration Association) 236
NCFA (National Consumer Finance Association) 258
NCFS (National Committee on Films for Safety) 186
NCHE (National Committee on Household Employment) 212
NCL (National Consumers League) 91
NCO (National Council of Obesity) 164
NCOA (National Council on the Aging) 215
NC/PAT (National Council for the Public Assessment of Technology) 91
NCPRV (National Council of Puerto Rican Volunteers) 214
NCRP (National Council on Radiation Protection and Measurements) 131
NCSC (National Child Safety Council) 186
NCSC (National Council of Senior Citizens) 214
NCSS (National Conference of Shomrim Societies) 186
NCUA (National Credit Union Administration) 27
NCW (National Council of Women of the United States) 214
NDAPTA (National Drivers Association for the Prevention of Traffic Accidents) 187
NDC (National Dairy Council) 258
NEDA (National Environmental Development Association) 131
Needlework Guild of America (NGA) 217

NEFA (Narcotic Educational Foundation of America) 161
NEIC (National Energy Information Center) 10
NEISS (National Electronic Injury Surveillance System) 6
NEIWPCC (New England Interstate Water Pollution Control Commission) 132
NESDA (National Electronic Service Dealers Association) 258
Neurotics Anonymous International Liaison (NAIL) 170
New England Interstate Water Pollution Control Commission (NEIWPCC) 132
New Eyes for the Needy 170
New York Association for New Americans (NYANA) 218
New York Exchange for Women's Work 218
New York Society for the Deaf 171
NFAC (National Foundation for Asthmatic Children at Tucson) 166
NFCC (National Foundation for Consumer Credit) 259
NFHD (National Foundation for the Handicapped and Disabled) 166
NFPA (National Fire Protection Association) 187
NFPA (National Forest Products Association) 259
NFPCA (National Fire Prevention and Control Administration) 5
NFS&NC (National Federation of Settlements and Neighborhood Centers) 215
NFWM (National Farm Worker Ministry) 215
NGA (Needlework Guild of America) 217
NHC (National Health Council) 167
NHC (National Housing Conference) 215
NHF (National Health Federation) 167
NHF (National Hemophilia Foundation) 167
NHFA (National Home Furnishings Association) 259
NHSC (National Home Study Council) 259
NIASE (National Institute for Automotive Service Excellence) 260
NIB (National Industries for the Blind) 167
NIC (National Institute of Credit) 260
NIC (National Interagency Council on Smoking and Health) 168
NIH (National Institutes of Health) 18
NLADA (National Legal Aid and Defender Association) 237
NLSMB (National Live Stock and Meat Board) 260
NMAF (National Medical Association Foundation) 168
NMFS (National Marine Fisheries Service) 5
NMRA (National Mine Rescue Association) 187
NMWIA (National Mineral Wool Insulation Association) 260
NOAA (National Oceanic and Atmospheric Administration) 5
NOF (National Osteopathic Foundation) 168

Organization Index

NOFMA (National Oak Flooring Manufacturers Association) 260
NOISE (National Organization to Insure a Sound-Controlled Environment) 131
Nonsmokers Travel Club (NTC) 132
NOREC (Northern Environmental Council) 132
North American Indian Association (NAIA) 218
North American Student Cooperative Organization (NASCO) 91
Northern Environmental Council (NOREC) 132
NPAED (National Progress Association for Economic Development) 216
NPCA (National Paint and Coatings Association) 261
NPCA (National Pest Control Association) 261
NPF (National Paraplegia Foundation) 168
NPF (National Parkinson Foundation) 169
NRBC (National Rare Blood Club) 169
NRDC (Natural Resources Defense Council) 132, 237
NRHC (National Rural Housing Coalition) 216
NRMA (National Retail Merchants Association) 261
NRTA (National Retired Teachers Association) 216
NSAC (National Society for Autistic Children) 169
NSBC (National Safe Boating Committee) 187
NSCC (National Social Conditioning Camps) 216
NSCDRF (National Sickle Cell Disease Research Foundation) 169
NSF (National Sanitation Foundation) 169
NSF (National Sharecroppers Fund) 216
NSPB (National Society for the Prevention of Blindness) 170
NSVP (National Student Volunteer Program) 1
NTC (Nonsmokers Travel Club) 132
NTO (National Tenants Organization) 217
NTS (Nutrition Today Society) 171
NTSAD (National Tay-Sachs and Allied Diseases Association) 170
Nutrition Foundation, Inc. 171
Nutrition Today Society (NTS) 171
NWRO (National Welfare Rights Organization) 217
NWSC (National Water Safety Congress) 188
NWSIA (National Water Supply Improvement Association) 131
NYANA (New York Association for New Americans) 218

O

OA (Osborne Association) 219
OA (Overeaters Anonymous) 172
Occupational Health Institute (OHI) 171
Occupational Safety and Health Administration (OSHA) 26
OCD (Office of Child Development) 16
Odyssey Institute 171
OE (Office of Education) 16

Office for Civil Rights (Department of Health, Education and Welfare) 15
Office of Advocacy (Small Business Administration) 28
Office of Air and Waste Management (Environmental Protection Agency) 8
Office of Bank Customer Affairs (Federal Deposit Insurance Corporation) 10
Office of Child Development (OCD) 16
Office of Communications (Federal Home Loan Bank Board) 11
Office of Communications (Pension Benefit Guaranty Corporation) 27
Office of Communications and Public Affairs (Federal Energy Administration) 10
Office of Consumer Affairs (Department of Health, Education and Welfare) 15
Office of Consumer Affairs (Postal Service) 27
Office of Consumer Affairs (Securities and Exchange Commission) 28
Office of Consumer Affairs and Special Impact (Federal Energy Administration) 10
Office of Consumer Education 16
Office of Education (OE) 16
Office of Housing and Urban Affairs (Federal Home Loan Bank Board) 11
Office of Human Development (Department of Health, Education and Welfare) 15
Office of Indian Education 17
Office of Indian Water Rights 22
Office of Information (General Services Administration) 12
Office of International Concerns (Postal Service) 27
Office of Minority Business Enterprise 5
Office of Native American Programs 16
Office of Public Affairs (ACTION) 1
Office of Public Affairs (Civil Service Commission) 4
Office of Public Affairs (Commission on Civil Rights) 6
Office of Public Affairs (Consumer Product Safety Commission) 6
Office of Public Affairs (Energy Research and Development Administration) 7
Office of Public Affairs (Environmental Protection Agency) 8
Office of Public Affairs (Equal Employment Opportunity Commission) 9
Office of Public Affairs (Department of Housing and Urban Development) 19
Office of Public Affairs (Securities and Exchange Commission) 28
Office of Public Affairs (Smithsonian Institution) 28
Office of Public Affairs (Department of Transportation) 30
Office of Public and Consumer Information (Interstate Commerce Commission) 24
Office of Public Information (Department of Justice) 24
Office of Public Information (Federal Communications Commission) 9

Organization Index

Office of Public Information (Federal Maritime Commission) 11
Office of Public Information (Federal Power Commission) 11
Office of Public Information (Federal Trade Commission) 12
Office of Public Information (Securities and Exchange Commission) 28
Office of Public Information (Small Business Administration) 28
Office of Telecommunications 5
Office of the Administrator (Environmental Protection Agency) 8
Office of the Administrator (General Services Administration) 13
Office of the Administrator (National Credit Union Administration) 27
Office of the Assistant Secretary for Community Planning and Development 20
Office of the Assistant Secretary for Education 16
Office of the Assistant Secretary for Fair Housing and Equal Opportunity 20
Office of the Assistant Secretary for Neighborhoods, Voluntary Associations, and Consumer Protection 21
Office of the Assistant Secretary of Defense (Public Affairs) 7
Office of the Comptroller of the Currency (Department of the Treasury) 32
Office of the Consumer Advocate (Civil Aeronautics Board) 4
Office of the Secretary (Department of Commerce) 5
Office of the Secretary (Health, Education, and Welfare) 15
Office of the Secretary (Department of Housing and Urban Development) 19
Office of the Secretary (Department of the Interior) 21
Office of the Secretary (Department of Labor) 25
Office of the Secretary (Department of Transportation) 30
Office of the Secretary (Department of the Treasury) 32
Office of the Secretary of Agriculture 1
Office of Veterans Services (Veterans Administration) 33
Office of Water and Hazardous Materials (Environmental Protection Agency) 8
Office of Youth Development (OYD) 16
OHD (Office of Human Development) 15
OHI (Occupational Health Institute) 171
OICs/A (Opportunities Industrialization Centers of America) 218
OMICA (Organized Migrants in Community Action) 219
ONAP (Office of Native American Programs) 16
OPEI (Outdoor Power Equipment Institute) 261

Operation: Peace of Mind (POM) 218
Operation Venus 172
Opportunities Industrialization Centers of America (OICs/A) 218
Optimist International 218
Optimist Octagon Clubs 219
Organized Migrants in Community Action (OMICA) 219
Orphan Voyage 219
Osborne Association (OA) 219
OSHA (Occupational Safety and Health Administration) 26
Outdoor Power Equipment Institute (OPEI) 261
Overeaters Anonymous (OA) 172
OYD (Office of Youth Development) 16

P

PACT (Public Action Coalition on Toys) 92
Palm Beach Psychotherapy Training Center (PBPTC) 172
Parents Anonymous 219
PAS (Patients' Aid Society) 172
PAS (Physicians for Automotive Safety) 188
Passport Office (Department of State) 29
Patent and Trademark Office 6
Patients' Aid Society (PAS) 172
PBGC (Pension Benefit Guaranty Corporation) 27
PBPTC (Palm Beach Psychotherapy Training Center) 172
PCA (Portland Cement Association) 262
PCL (Planning and Conservation League) 133
Peace Corps 1
Pension Benefit Guaranty Corporation (PBGC)
   Office of Communications 27
      Individual Retirement Accounts (IRA's) 27
People's Law School (PLS) 238
People's Lobby 132
Pharmaceutical Manufacturers Association (PMA) 262
PHCIB (Plumbing-Heating-Cooling Information Bureau) 262
PHWA (Protestant Health and Welfare Assembly) 221
Physicians for Automotive Safety (PAS) 188
Physicians Forum 172
PIA (Pilots International Association) 262
Pilot Club International 220
Pilot Guide Dog Foundation 173
Pilots International Association (PIA) 262
Planning and Conservation League (PCL) 133
PLS (People's Law School) 238
PLS (Program for Local Service) 1
Plumbing-Heating-Cooling Information Bureau (PHCIB) 262
PMA (Pharmaceutical Manufacturers Association) 262
POCA (Psychiatric Outpatient Centers of America) 173

Organization Index

Policyholders Protective Association International 92
POM (Operation: Peace of Mind) 218
Portland Cement Association (PCA) 262
Postal Service (USPS)
    Consumer Advocate 27
        Chief Postal Inspector 27
        Office of Consumer Affairs 27
        Office of International Concerns 27
Potomac Institute 220
Power Tool Institute (PTI) 263
Price-Pottenger Nutrition Foundation 173
Profit Sharing Research Foundation (PSRF) 263
Program for Local Service 1
Program Information Center (Department of Housing and Urban Development) 19
Project Concern, Inc. 220
Project Outreach 220
Project Transition 220
Protect Your Environment (PYE) 133
Protestant Health and Welfare Assembly (PHWA) 221
PSRF (Profit Sharing Research Foundation) 263
PSA (Psychologists for Social Action) 221
Psychiatric Outpatient Centers of America (POCA) 173
Psychologists for Social Action (PSA) 221
PTI (Power Tool Institute) 263
PTO (Patent and Trademark Office) 6
Public Action Coalition on Toys (PACT) 92
Public Affairs Division (Internal Revenue Service) 32
Public Affairs Office (Department of State) 29
Public Buildings Service 13
Public Citizen, Inc. 92
Public Citizen Visitors Center 92
Public Defender Service 238
Public Health Service 17
Public Information Center (Environmental Protection Agency) 8
Public Interest Research Group (PIRG) 93
Public Services Administration 18
Public Utility Commissions, State 67-71
Publications Management Division (Commission on Civil Rights) 6
Pueblo Distribution Center (Government Printing Office) 14
Purchase Power, Inc. 93
Pure Water Association of America 133
(PX) Quality Assurance Program 7
PYE (Protect Your Environment) 133

R

Rachel Carson Trust for the Living Environment 133
Radiation Biology Laboratory 29
Radiation Research Society (RRS) 133
Railroad Advancement Through Information and Law Foundation 93

Rape Crisis Center (RCC) 221
RCC (Rape Crisis Center) 221
RDS (Rural Development Service) 3
REA (Rural Electrification Administration) 4
REACT 188
Real Estate Settlement Procedures Program 21
Real Great Society 221
Recording for the Blind (RFB) 173
Recovery, Inc. 173
Recycling Legislation Action Coalition (RLAC) 133
Recycling Revolution Cooperative 134
Registry of Interpreters for the Deaf (RID) 173
Rehabilitation Services Administration 16
Renwick Gallery 29
Rescue, Inc. (RI) 174
Retarded Infants Services (RIS) 174
Retired Senior Volunteer Program 1
Retirement and Insurance Information Office (Civil Service Commission) 4
Revitalization Corps 221
RFB (Recording for the Blind) 173
RHA (Rural Housing Alliance) 222
RI (Rescue, Inc.) 174
RID (Registry of Interpreters for the Deaf) 173
Riot Reinsurance Program 20
RIS (Retarded Infants Services) 174
RLAC (Recycling Legislation Action Coalition) 133
RMA (Rubber Manufacturers Association) 263
Roscoe Pound-American Trial Lawyers Foundation 238
RRS (Radiation Research Society) 133
RSA (Rehabilitation Services Administration) 16
RSVP (Retired Senior Volunteer Program) 1
Rubber Manufacturers Association (RMA) 263
Rubella Birth Defect Evaluation Project 174
Rubicon, Inc. 174
Rural Development Service 3
Rural Electrification Administration 4
Rural Housing Alliance (RHA) 222
Ruth Rubin Feldman National Odd Shoe Exchange 222

S

Safe Car Educational Institute 189
Safe Winter Driving League (SWDL) 189
Safety Center 189
Safety Helmet Council of America (SHCA) 189
SAI (Senior Advocates International) 223
Saint Joh's Guild - The Floating Hospital 174
Salt Institute 263
Salvation Army 222
Sane: Citizens' Organization for a Sane World 222
SAPhA (Student American Pharmaceutical Association) 177
SAPL (Seacoast Anti-Pollution League) 134

Organization Index

SASI (Society of Air Safety Investigators)   189
Savings and Loan Foundation (SLF)   263
Savings Bonds Division (Department of the Treasury)   33
SBA (Small Business Administration)   28
SBDC (Small Business Development Center)   224
School Breakfast Program   3
Sci-International Voluntary Service   222
Science for the Blind   175
Scientists' Committee for Public Information (SCPI)   134
Scientists' Institute for Public Information (SIPI)   134
SCLDF (Sierra Club Legal Defense Fund)   238
SCORE (Service Corps of Retired Executives)   28
SCPI (Scientists' Committee for Public Information)   134
SCSA (Soil Conservation Society of America)   135
SCWPH (Students Concerned with Public Health)   177
SDA (Soap and Detergent Association)   263
Seacoast Anti-Pollution League (SAPL)   134
SEC (Securities and Exchange Commission)   28
Securities and Exchange Commission (SEC)
   Office of Consumer Affairs   28
      Office of Public Affairs   28
      Office of Public Information   28
Seeing Eye   175
Seismological Society of America (SSA)   189
Self-Help Enterprises (SHE)   223
Senior Advocates International (SAI)   223
Senior Companion Program   1
SER (Service, Employment, Redevelopment)   223
Service Corps of Retired Executives (SCORE)   28
Service, Employment, Redevelopment (SER)   223
7th Step Foundation   223
SFMA (Southern Furniture Manufacturers Association)   264
Share, Inc.   223
SHCA (Safety Helmet Council of America)   189
SHE (Self-Help Enterprises)   223
SHSLB (Street and Highway Safety Lighting Bureau)   264
SI (Smithsonian Institution)   28
Sickle Cell Disease Foundation of Greater New York   175
SIPI (Scientists' Institute for Public Information)   134
Sierra Club Legal Defense Fund (SCLDF)   238
Singles in Service (SIS)   224
SIS (Singles in Service)   224
Sky Ranch for Boys   224
SLF (Savings and Loan Foundation)   263
Small Business Administration (SBA)
   Office of Advocacy   28
      Active Corps of Executives (ACE)   28
      Minority Small Business (MSB)   28
      Office of Public Information   28
      Service Corps of Retired Executives (SCORE)   28
Small Business Development Center (SBDC)   224

SMHA (Southern Mutual Help Association)   225
Smithsonian Institute (SI)
   Freer Gallery of Art   29
   Joseph H. Hirschhorn Museum and Sculpture Garden   29
   National Air and Space Museum   29
   National Gallery of Art   29
   National Museum of National History   29
   Office of Public Affairs
      Anacostia Neighborhood Museum   29
      Dial-A-Museum   29
      Dial-A-Phenomenon   29
      Fine Arts and Portrait Galleries   29
      John F. Kennedy Center for the Performing Arts   28
      National Museum of History and Technology   29
      National Zoological Park   28
      Radiation Biology Laboratory   29
         Renwick Gallery   29
      Visitor Information and Associates Reception Center   28
SNE (Society for Nutrition Education)   175
Soap and Detergent Association (SDA)   263
Social and Rehabilitation Service (SRS)   18
Social Psychiatry Research Institute   175
Social Security Administration   19
Society for Clinical Ecology   134
Society for Nutrition Education (SNE)   175
Society for Public Health Education (SOPHE)   176
Society for Social Responsibility in Science (SSRS)   224
Society for the Protection of the Unborn Through Nutrition (SPUN)   176
Society for the Rehabilitation of the Facially Disfigured   176
Society of Air Safety Investigators (SASI)   189
Society of Prospective Medicine (SPM)   176
Society of St. Vincent De Paul   224
Soil Conservation Society of America (SCSA)   135
SOPHE (Society for Public Health Education)   176
SOS (Special Organizational Services)   264
Source Catalog Collective   224
Southern Furniture Manufacturers Association (SFMA)   264
Southern Mutual Help Association (SMHA)   225
Special Milk Program for Children   3
Special Organizational Services (SOS)   264
Special Supplemental Food Program for Women, Infants, and Children   3
Special Volunteer Programs (SVP)   1
SPM (Society of Prospective Medicine)   176
SPUN (Society for the Protection of the Unborn Through Nutrition)   176
SRS (Social and Rehabilitation Service)   18
SSA (Seismological Society of America)   189
SSI (Supplementary Security Income Program)   19
SSRS (Society for Social Responsibility in Science)   224
SSS (System Safety Society)   190

Organization Index

STASH (Student Association for the Study of Hallucinogens) 177
State and Local Voluntary Consumer Organizations 95-120
State, County, and City Government Consumer Offices 34-66
State, Department of 29
State Public Utility Commissions 67-71
Street and Highway Safety Lighting Bureau (SHSLB) 264
Stroke Club of America 176
Student American Pharmaceutical Association (SAPhA) 177
Student Association for the Study of Hallucinogens (STASH) 177
Student Legal Action Organizations 93
Student Volunteers for American Indians 225
Students Concerned with Public Health (SCWPH) 177
Suicide Prevention Center of Los Angeles 177
Summer Food Service Program for Children 3
Superintendent of Documents (Government Printing Office) 14
Supplemental Foods for Health Program 3
Supplementary Security Income Program 19
SVP (Special Volunteer Programs) 1
SWDL (Safe Winter Driving League) 189
Synanon Foundation 178
System Safety Society (SSS) 190

T

TAISSA (Travelers Aid - International Social Service of America) 225
Tapes for the Blind 178
Tax Division (Department of Justice) 24
Tax Reform Research Group 94
TCA (Trailer Coach Association) 264
Telephone Pioneers of America (TPA) 225
Telephone Users Association (TUA) 94
Terra Society 135
TFI (Fertilizer Institute) 251
TI (Tippers International) 94
Tippers International (TI) 94
Tire Industry Safety Council 190
Tops Club (Take Off Pounds Sensibly) 178
Toy Manufacturers of America, Incorporated 264
TPA (Telephone Pioneers of America) 225
Trailer Coach Association (TCA) 264
Transportation, Department of 30
Travelers Aid - International Social Service of America (TAISSA) 225
Treasury, Department of 32
TUA (Telephone Users Association) 94

U

UCPA (United Cerebral Palsy Associations) 178
UFFVA (United Fresh Fruit and Vegetable Association) 264
UIS (Unemployment insurance Service) 25
UL (Underwriters Laboratories, Inc.) 190
ULI (Urban Law Institute of Antioch College) 238
UMBA (United Mortgage Bankers of America) 264
UMTA (Urban Mass Transportation Administration) 31
UNA (United Native Americans) 226
Underwriters Laboratories, Inc. (UL) 190
Unemployment Insurance Service (UIS) 25
Union Settlement Association (US) 226
United Cerebral Palsy Associations (UCPA) 178
United Fresh Fruit and Vegetable Association (UFFVA) 264
United Mortgage Bankers of America (UMBA) 264
United Native Americans (UNA) 226
United Ostomy Association 179
United Parkinson Foundation (UPF) 179
United Presbyterian Health, Education and Welfare Association (UPHEWA) 226
United Southeastern Tribes (USET) 226
United States League of Savings Associations 265
United States Travel Service 5
United Voluntary Services (UVS) 227
University Year for Action (UYA) 1, 227
UPF (United Parkinson Foundation) 179
UPHEWA (United Presbyterian Health, Education and Welfare Association) 226
Urban Law Institute of Antioch College (ULI) 238
Urban Mass Transportation Administration (UMTA) 31
US (Union Settlement Association) 226
USDA (Department of Agriculture) 1
USDC (Department of Commerce) 5
USDI (Department of the Interior) 21
USDJ (Department of Justice) 24
USDT (Department of the Treasury) 32
USET (United Southeastern Tribes) 226
USPS (Postal Service) 27
UVS (United Voluntary Services) 227
UYA (University Year for Action) 1

V

VA (Veterans Administration) 33
Vacations for the Aging and Senior Centers Association 227
Variety Clubs International (VCI) 227
VCI (Variety Clubs International) 227
Vehicle Equipment Safety Commission (VESC) 190

Organization Index

Vera Institute of Justice   238
VESC (Vehicle Equipment Safety Commission)   190
Vest   227
Veterans Administration (VA)
    Office of Veterans Services   33
Veterans of Safety (V of S)   190
VFI (Vocational Foundation, Inc.)   228
V for V (Volunteers for Vision)   179
VIP Division   227
Visitor Information and Associates Reception Center
    (Smithsonian Institution)   28
VISTA (Volunteers in Service to America)   1
Visual Services Branch (Department of the Interior)   22
Vocational Foundation, Inc. (VFI)   228
V of A (Volunteers of America)   228
V of S (Veterans of Safety)   190
Volunteer Prison League (VPL)   228
Volunteers for Vision (V for V)   179
Volunteers in Service to America   1
Volunteers of America (V of A)   228
VPL (Volunteer Prison League)   228

W

Waif   228
Wallcovering Manufacturers Association   265
Washington Center for the Study of Services   94
Washington Ecology Center   135
Water Facts Consortium (WFC)   135
Water Pollution Control Federation   135
Water Quality Research Council (WQRC)   265
WEIU (Women's Educational and Industrial Union)   229
Western Center on Law and Poverty   239
WFC (Water Facts Consortium)   135
Whistlestop Community Services   190
WIC (Special Supplemental Food Program for
    Women, Infants, and Children)   3
WICS (Women in Community Service)   228
WIN (Work Incentive Program)   25, 229
Women in Community Service (WICS)   228
Women in the Urban Crisis, Inc.   229
Women's Educational and Industrial Union (WEIU)   229
Women's Prison Association (WPA)   229
Work Incentive Program (WIN)   25, 229
WPA (Women's Prison Association)   229
WQRC (Water Quality Research Council)   265

Y

YCP (Youth Challenge Program)   1
Young Adult Institute and Workshop   179
Young World Development   229
Youth Challenge Program   1
Youth Highway Safety Advisory Committee   191
Youth Network Council of Chicago, Inc.   230

Personnel Index

A

Aandahl, Irma 299
Aanenson, Vernon O. 1031
Aaron, James E. 189
Aasen, Lawrence O. 146
Abbott, John W. 122
Abbott, Joseph C. 629
Abbott, Morton I. 971
Abel, De Forest W., Jr. 363
Abel, Vernon T. 576
Abels, Robert S. 1194
Abelson, Nat 716
Aberg, Charles P. 880
Abernathy, K.B. 463
Abernathy, U.B. 463
Abernethy, Julius W. 492
Abker, Tom 425
Ablah, George 1299
Ablove, Jacob C. 762
Abplanalp, Robert H. 1096
Abraham, Lee 385
Abrams, Allan 380
Abrams, Bernard 651
Abrams, Harry N. 323
Abrams, Richard E. 96
Abrams, Robert C. 547
Abrams, Sol 971
Abrams, Warren 1009
Abt, Walter H. 350
Abt, Walter L. 983
Abusamra, Mark 286
Accetta, Anthony T. 39
Achenbach, Gerald H. 1080
Acker, Arthur M. 1214
Ackerman, Arnold W. 527
Ackerman, L.C. 321
Acree, John T., III 898
Acworth, Brian B. 1203
Adair, Paul H. 1407
Adair, W.C. 826
Adam, Robert B. 326
Adams, Ann 275
Adams, Arthur R. 327
Adams, Ben R. 327
Adams, Charles R. 1149
Adams, Earl H. 290
Adams, Erwin 470
Adams, J. Cooper 703
Adams, Jack L. 596
Adams, James 291
Adams, John 273
Adams, John G. 327
Adams, John H. 132, 237
Adams, John P. 472

Adams, Joseph H. 326
Adams, Lane W. 139
Adams, Philip 326
Adams, Raymond C. 715
Adams, Vera E. 130
Adams, William E. 1149
Adamson, Sandy 117
Adduci, V.J. 250
Adelaar, Emil 328
Adelman, Burton 878
Adelman, Emanuel L. 1188
Adelman, Herbert A. 565
Adler, Frederick R. 816
Adler, Herbert 441
Adler, Robert P. 429
Aetzner, Mark 112
Affleck, James G. 352
Affolter, L.W. 1008
Affronti, Joseph A. 937
Agen, J.R., Jr. 496
Agueros, Jack 209
Aguigui, Cel 95
Ahern, James P. 1207
Ahern, John I. 939
Ahern, Richard 1143
Ahern, Richard I. 1357
Ahlstrom, Bjorn 1386
Ahrens, Paul 970
Ajmo, Louis V. 1162
Akchin, Don 275
Akers, James J. 951
Akers, Phyllis M. 302
Akin, Paul B. 874
Akoff, Samuel Z. 356
Alayon, Adolfo G. 110
Albert, Donald B. 837
Albert, Warren 141
Albertson, Frank O. 1229
Albright, Harry W., Jr. 598
Albright, James K. 1241
Alden, Harold 453
Alderson, George 124
Aldrich, Corenna 282
Aldridge, Mae 102
Alexander, Eric 782
Alexander, G. "Joe" 208
Alexander, Gary R. 46
Alexander, Glenn P. 389
Alexander, Herbert M. 1340
Alexander, Leon G. 1388
Alexander, Norman E. 1286
Alexander, Richard 99
Alexander, Willis W. 242
Alfaro, Ruben R. 200
Alfieri, Dan 23
Alfierie, Louis 964
Alfiero, Sal H. 931
Alfond, Harold 594
Alger, Shirl R. 340

Alibrandi, Joseph F. 1416
Alioto, John I. 1047
Alksne, Harold 162
Allard, Gerald R. 733
Allegretti, Albert J. 341
Allen, A.E. 1076
Allen, A. Edward, Jr. 1365
Allen, Albert A. 786
Allen, Ben 342
Allen, Boyd 341
Allen, Charles C. 1234
Allen, D.E., Jr. 341
Allen, Don L. 981
Allen, Douglas S. 104
Allen, Fred T. 1083
Allen, Harry 1008
Allen, John W. 341
Allen, June 117
Allen, Leo 1390
Allen, Michael 304
Allen, R.I. 1175
Allen, Ray 107
Allen, Thornton V., Jr. 341
Allen, Walter G., Jr. 341
Allenby, Clyde G. 626
Alley, Alvan R. 796
Alley, William J. 687
Allin, Kenn 211
Allina, Curtis J. 1074
Allison, Bob 120
Alperin, Irwin M. 122
Alperin, Melvin G. 492
Alsbrooks, Claude L. 555
Alter, Jerome 589
Alterman, Isidore 346
Altman, Donald M. 51
Altman, Murray 1318
Altman, R.G. 1002
Alton, Ann 49
Altshul, Harold M. 853
Amador, Victor 326
Ambrogi, W.P. 1395, 1415
Ambros, Dieter A. 396
Amerling, JoAnn 301
Ames, Arthur R. 363
Ames, B. Charles 1137
Ames, B.N. 1360
Amick, C. Harold 65
Amper, Moss 306
Amrein, Lewis 646
Analyan, William G. 1204
Ancell, Nathan S. 644
Ancellin, P.J. 866
Anderer, Joseph 908
Andersen, A.L. 693
Andersen, R.D. 1016
Anderson, Alan T. 440
Anderson, Barbara 66
Anderson, Carroll R. 69

Personnel Index

Anderson, Edwin 1443
Anderson, Eugene I. 383
Anderson, Frederick R. 233
Anderson, G.E. 1008
Anderson, G.S. 38
Anderson, Gene S. 65
Anderson, Gerald E. 1009
Anderson, Herbert H. 455
Anderson, J.D. 1249
Anderson, John S. 1333
Anderson, Judge F. 362
Anderson, L.S. 482
Anderson, Lawrence 68
Anderson, Lee C. 594
Anderson, M.J. 379
Anderson, Olof V. 369
Anderson, Peter 120
Anderson, R.L. 859
Anderson, Richard N. 367
Anderson, Robert 1156
Anderson, Robert J. 140
Anderson, Roger E. 546
Anderson, William C. 828
Anderson, William S. 995
Andes, Charles L. 687
Andrea, Frank A.D., Jr. 367
Andrek, George 128
Andreoli, Andre J. 1336
Andrews, Clifford H. 695
Andrews, Douglas J. 198
Andrews, J. Floyd 1047
Andrews, L.M., Jr. 357
Andros, Andrew A. 798
Angell, Paul M. 1012
Angelos, Arthur C. 632
Angstandt, Earle K., Jr. 945
Ankrum, L. Doyle 1235
Anku, Geoffrey B. 224
Annenberg, W.H. 1340
Annich, Virginia Long 51
Anonsen, Stanley H. 924
Anrig, R.M. 612
Ansbre, Mary 109
Anthony, Guy M. 370
Anthony, Mike 306
Anthony, Myron Philip 370
Antle, Robert V. 465
Antoine, Robert 737
Antokal, Howard M. 438
Anton, F.W., III 1067
Anton, Mark 1284
Aoki, Yunosuke 422
Appel, Harry M. 41
Appelbaum, Joseph 607
Appignani, Louis J. 406
Apple, L.E. 140
Apple, William S. 142
Applebaum, Hy 371

Applegate, Rick 107
Appleman, Stratton L. 1246
Applestein, Allan H. 725
Appleton, Arthur T. 372
Applewhite, Walter 1347
Aquilina, Joseph 1378
Aram, Nathan W. 1442
Aransky, David A. 503
Aransky, Peter P. 1415
Arbuckle, John W. 809
Arch, Charles E. 437
Archambault, Bennett 1276, 1321
Archambault, Paul S. 168
Archer, Robert M. 621
Archer, Thomas 1319
Archibald, Douglas C. 374
Archibald, Kenneth W. 794
Arditti, Leon A. 375
Areen, Gordon E. 518
Arena, Saverio 545
Arenas, Dolores 216
Aresty, Maurice J. 411
Ariens, Michae S. 376
Armanetti, Anthony L. 458
Armatys, Walter W. 264
Armour, Cathy 61
Armour, M.K. 605
Armstrong, Dewey 115
Armstrong, Frank, III 1001
Armstrong, G.R. 907
Armstrong, John J. 1041
Arnall, Ellis 528
Arnds, Burton N., Jr. 1251
Arndt, Michael T. 379
Arneson, Howard M. 379
Arnold, Duane 818
Arnold, James S. 65
Arnold, John R. 379
Arnold, Leslie B. 1236
Arnold, Pat 273
Arnold, Richard 789
Arnold, Tracy 379
Arnold, Willard M. 379
Arolussi, Wallace F. 391
Arps, F.B. 380
Arrigo, Barbara 282
Arrigoni, Louis 543
Arroll, Roy 598
Arsenof, Mary 13
Artabasy, R.J. 347
Arthur, John M. 614
Arvold, William V. 1398
Aschinper, C.J., Jr. 537
Ash, Mary Kay 937
Ash, William 813
Asher, Benjamin 383
Ashford, L. Jerome 162
Ashley, Harry R. 629
Ashton, Harris J. 706

Ashway, J.N. 665
Askenazi, Ely E. 1245
Asmuth, James E. 1426
Aspach, P.H. 437
Asscoff, Uriel 1031
Asthalter, Jach 937
Astle, Stephen R. 928
Aston, Cletus 291
Atcheson, William E. 1053
Atchison, Richard 1369
Atkins, Donald K. 1425
Atkins, Orin E. 384
Atkinson, B.E. 387
Atteberry, William D. 621
Attwood, William 1012
Atwater, Franklin S. 786
Atwell, W.L. 1071
Atwood, R.W. 616
Aubrey, Donald M. 390
Auerbach, Frederick F. 391
Auerbach, John 248
Auerbach, Minx M. 45
Auerswald, William H. 1346
Aughinbaugh, Richard 63
Aulenti, Mike 98
Ausnit, Steven 968
Austin, Dorothy M. 112
Austin, Howard K. 391
Austin, K.R. 641
Austin, M.L. 183
Austin, Roland 927
Austin, W.N. 697
Austin, William B., Jr. 56
Authement, Calvin J. 392
Autry, Aaron E. 501
Averett, Elliot 404
Averitte, Clint 62
Avery, Dennis S. 39
Avischious, R.G. 1221
Avner, Louis L. 1322
Avril, Arthur C. 1180
Awrey, Robert C. 395
Axelrad, Milton 1049
Ayala, G.F. 139
Aydelott, Gayle B. 591
Ayers, John G. 682
Ayers, Thomas G. 539
Aymond, Alphonse H. 545
Ayres, John 549
Azarnoff, Pat 145

B

Babkes, Jack 1244
Baccigaluppi, Roger J. 478
Baccus, Robert L. 322

1548

Personnel Index

Bach, Bronson L. 301
Bachman, E.R. 399
Bachman, Stanely N. 859
Bacon, H.W. 1257
Bacon, John A., Jr. 321
Badcock, Wogan S., Jr. 399
Bader, Nathan 1039
Baer, Alan 451
Baer, Harris E. 867
Baer, J.A., II 1276
Baer, W.B. 1419
Bagg, Edward P., III 1058
Bagley, Herbert P., II 1412
Bagley, Smith 1396
Bagnal, Garland 292
Baia, Phillip 400
Baile, Harold Scott 1094
Bailey, Donald O. 1143
Bailey, Eugene L. 1019
Bailey, H.W. 684
Bailey, J. Harold 141
Bailey, Joseph T. 1394
Bailey, Morris 728
Bailey, R.H. 123
Bailey, William D. 768
Baily, Richard O. 893
Bair, Harley 400
Bair, Roger I., Sr. 898
Bair, Ronald L. 172
Baird, H. Vernon 973
Baird, Henry H. 1199
Baker, A.L. 425
Baker, Bernard R. 39
Baker, Bert, Sr. 1344
Baker, DeWitt C. 400
Baker, Dudley L. 224
Baker, Eugene 210
Baker, John F. 767
Baker, John R. 360
Baker, Lawrence C., Jr. 376
Baker, Milton 923, 1135
Baker, Newell A. 1280
Baker, Robert C. 360
Baker, Robert F. 716
Baker, Ronald D. 1397
Baker, Russell L. 631
Baker, Ruth 37
Baker, Samuel 350
Baker, Sherman N. 1003
Baker, W.W. 844
Bakke, Lawrence C. 1284
Bakkensen, Joseph M. 406
Baldinger, Stuart 626
Baldridge, Julie 271
Baldridge, Malcolm 1199
Baldwin, Douglas 24
Baldwin, Everett E. 1394
Baldwin, Ralph B. 1034
Bales, Bruce B. 36

Balkam, Gilbert 515
Ball, Bill 283
Ball, Edward 675
Ball, John A. 1360
Balridge, Jerald T. 708
Banas, Stanley F. 560
Bancroft, Joseph C. 563
Baness, L.S. 1426
Bang, Thomas O. 542
Banko, Jo 295
Banks, H. 751
Banks, Russell 742
Bannister, Rosella 106
Banta, Merle H. 889
Bantle, Louis A. 1361
Banzhaf, John F., III 136
Baptiste, Philip M. 103
Barach, Philip G. 1361
Barancik, Charles 840
Barancik, Charles 945
Barbaris, E.H. 1334
Barbeau, Earlene 126
Barber, Dave 302
Barbera, Joseph R. 755
Barbour, William A. 515
Barchas, Rudy 42
Barclay, Lillian E. 195
Bard, Randolph O. 407
Bard, Robert E. 788
Barden, Bryce 407
Bardfeld, Gustave 711
Barg, Herbert 338
Barg, Herbert 1345
Barker, Charles F. 407
Barker, George 1256
Barker, Gilbert M. 766
Barker, Gregson 1351
Barker, Hugh A. 1107
Barker, James R. 983
Barker, Stephen 980
Barker, W.G. 986
Barkley, Peyton J. 634
Barkus, Jennie (Winch) 152
Barnard, Kurt 254
Barnes, B. Jack 798
Barnes, Hyland J. 940
Barnes, Leslie O. 1173
Barnes, Zane E. 1249
Barnett, Atheral A. 538
Barnett, Edward 408
Barnett, Frank E. 1355
Barnett, Harold C. 178
Barnett, James R. 58
Barnett, S. Meyer 1137
Barnhill, Howard E. 1018
Baron, Morton H. 1168
Baron, Robert Alex 123
Baroni, Geno 21
Barr, John J. 362

Barran, A.J. 708
Barrett, Ed 285
Barrett, Stephen 114
Barrett, William R., Sr. 811
Barrick, M.B. 970
Barrie, George 650
Barrileaux, Gladys 293
Barrow, Willie 101
Barry, Edwin W. 53
Barry, Herbert 1354
Barry, John S. 1388
Barsby, Steven L. 258
Barse, Josephine 1330
Bartlett, Earl P., Jr. 351
Bartlett, Edward E. 409
Bartlett, Robert A. 410
Bartnoff, S. 830
Bartol, G.E., III 430
Bartolotta, Anthony J. 1379
Barton, Carl P. 1009
Barton, D.J. 1165
Barton, De Witt A. 907, 1413
Barton, R.D. 190
Bartos, John 518
Bartz, Edward C. 434
Barum, Thomas F. 860
Barwell, Basil B. 648
Barwick, E.T. 410, 979
Basiliou, George 1139
Bass, Harry A. 489
Bassett, H.H. 667
Bassett, J.E., Sr. 411, 1098
Bassett, Raymond 1057
Bata, Thomas J. 411
Batchelor, Cal 1362
Bateman, J. Carroll 252
Bateman, William M., Jr. 42
Bates, Edward B. 542
Bates, James E. 263
Batkin, Helen 100
Batrel, George E. 962
Batson, Charles A. 555
Batson, Fred J. 860
Batt, Sam H. 915
Battiste, Josephine 59
Battle, William C. 663
Bauder, Frank E. 501
Baudhuin, Donald J. 604
Bauer, Carl 972
Bauer, Rodney E. 968
Bauer, W. Cecil 1246
Bauerle, James A. 1292
Baugh, Ken 304
Baum, S.M. 483
Baum, Selma 716
Bauman, H.A. 638
Baumgardner, John 1082
Baumgart, Guenther 246
Baumgartner, Ann 275

Personnel Index

Baver, T.R. 751
Baxt, Roland 202
Baxter, A.C.C. 934
Baxter, Lionel 431
Baxter, R.R. 474
Bay, J. Myron 977
Bayer, Jesse 1305
Bayer, Merwin 379
Bayne, William F. 616
Beach, Morrison H. 508
Beach, Morrison S. 1337
Beadel, Robert O. 1091
Beagle, Ralph G. 414
Beaham, Gordon T., Jr. 658
Beaird, Charles T. 414
Beales, James A.G. 1056
Beall, J.V. 386
Beaman, William H., Jr. 1329
Beamschutt, Jeeter 312
Bean, G. Clarke 376
Bean, M. Lamont 1062
Bear, Fred B. 414
Beard, C.R., Jr. 369
Beard, Samuel S. 196
Beattie, Paul R. 243
Beaty, Orren 90
Beaumont, Pamela 337
Beaver, H. Dennis 35
Beavers, Tom 287
Bechik, Anthony 416
Beck, Charles E. 348
Beck, Guenter J. 451
Beck, James H. 1096
Beck, John A., Jr. 1067
Beck, L. Gray 708
Beck, R.E. 645
Beck, Robert 633
Beck, Robert A. 1106
Beck, William M. 335
Becker, Charles L. 754
Becker, Clarence J. 786, 886
Becker, Hy 499
Becker, Lyle 290
Becker, Murray C. 1007
Becker, R.J. 513
Becker, Stonie, Jr. 819
Beckerman, David A. 1084
Beckett, John R. 1336
Beckleman, B.F. 1156
Beckman, Luke F. 969
Beckwith, A.E. 708
Bedford, Frederick T., III 1104
Bednarz, Edward J. 1081
Bedol, Alan P. 934
Beebe, W.T. 588
Beeler, Robert W. 671
Beeler, William C. 1382
Been, Vicki 98
Beeny, Glover W. 520

Beer, Evelyn 147
Beers, William O. 867
Beeson, Mike 298
Beeson, Richard C. 484
Begley, Robert J. 417
Behr, John H. 935, 1298
Behren, Gene 384
Behrendt, Peter 559
Behrent, David F. 383
Beich, William A. 418
Beinetti, George S. 1155
Belcher, Loren C. 856
Belinn, Clarence M. 906
Bell, C. Huston 1157
Bell, Colleen 46
Bell, Drummond C. 414, 1000
Bell, Fletcher 44
Bell, Gordon 304
Bell, J.A. 445
Bell, James A. 49
Bell, Louis C. 264
Bell, R. Winston 460
Bell, Richard S. 963
Bell, W. Douglas 756, 1269
Bellinger, J.D. 667
Bellows, H. Arthur, Jr. 1340
Bellwood, Wesley E. 1434
Belshaw, Thomas E. 421
Belzberg, Morris 465
Belzer, Charles H. 761
Bemis, Francis K. 421
Bemstein, Hyman 1165
Benbow, Dave 346
Bench, Leigh 1438
Bendavid-Val, Avrom 197
Bendixen, Harold A. 526
Benecke, O.F. 336
Benedict, Andrew B. 667
Benedict, R.H. 1376
Benesch, E.A. 692
Benetti, John G. 1065
Bengert, George W. 1022
Benham, T.A. 175
Benjamin, Thomas B. 104
Benkelman, William B. 476
Benner, Paul R. 1418
Bennett, Alvin S. 894
Bennett, Carl 478
Bennett, Marshall G. 49
Benning, Arthur E. 347
Benninger, Fred 957, 1406
Benoit, Constant, Jr. 1070
Benson, Audrey 107
Benson, D.F. 1298
Benson, David O. 67
Benson, Frank W. 654
Benson, John S. 1150
Benson, William H. 1414
Bent, Richard 100

Bent, Willard O. 700, 966
Bentis, Catherine E. 238
Bentley, Donald J. 423
Bentley, George A. 547
Benton, Oliver, Jr. 976
Benton, W.P. 679
Benua, L.P. 625
Benziger, J.B. 1056
Berdon, Sheldon 489, 1107
Bere, James F. 446
Beretta, David 1356
Berg, Eugene P. 465
Berg, Thomas 522, 691
Berger, Frank 709
Berger, Leslie 489
Berger, Max 1009
Berger, Murry P. 1203
Berger, S.S. 666
Bergerac, Michael C. 1142
Bergeron, V.J., III 1335
Berghoff, H. Lee 1114
Bergman, Burton 470
Bergman, Robert S. 424
Bergman, William S. 251
Bergmann, W.E. 1363
Bergstein, Frank D. 816
Bergstrom, D.W. 424
Berk, Jerome 1362
Berkeley, Norman, Jr. 511
Berkey, Benjamin 424
Berkley, Allen 424
Berkley, E. Bertram 1314
Berkman, Marshall L. 1173
Berkowitz, Abe W. 1244
Berkowitz, Benedict 425
Berkowitz, Paul 972
Berkowitz, Robert H. 501
Berland, Theodore 123
Berliant, Edward 540
Berlin, Arnold M. 514, 1017
Berlinsky, Elaine 130
Berman, Barbara 51
Berman, Josephine 163
Berman, Milton 840
Berman, Milton S. 677
Berman, Morton R. 394
Berman, Myron P. 1190, 1265
Berman, Philip I. 773
Berman, Sidney M. 552
Bernard, Emile N. 508
Bernard, Jules F. 425
Bernardin, A.L. 426
Bernat, Edward W. 700
Bernat, William A. 426
Berner, T. Ronald 570
Bernet, Robert G. 1432
Berns, Peter V. 114
Bernstein, Bernard 1158
Bernstein, David W. 350

1550

Personnel Index

Bernstein, Harvey 1256
Bernstein, Hyman 964
Bernstein, Milton 1003
Bernstein, Robert L. 1123
Bernstein, Samuel J. 981
Bernstein, Samuel M. 333
Bernth, Robert M. 279
Bernthal, Harold G. 355
Berol, E. Albert 426
Berreth, Donald A. 17
Berry, C. Martin 323
Berry, Frank 97
Berry, Mary 16
Berry, Sam M. 256
Berson, C.H. 1001
Bertrand, C.E. 1127
Bertsch, Frank H. 674
Bertschie, John 1159
Best, John C. 1091
Best, Lucius P. 559
Besthoff, S.J. 846
Betker, T.C. 559
Betten, David 1227
Betterton, Drew 208
Bettis, G.G. 1007
Bettman, Irvin, Jr. 937
Betz, Glenn W. 336
Bever, C.C., Sr. 396
Beyer, Ragnar 772, 1049
Bez, John P. 1072
Bezark, Richard S. 1293
Biaggini, B.F. 1248
Bialo, Walter 1375
Bianchi, F. 326
Bianchini, Neil L. 1418
Biane, Pierre 460
Biblowitz, Louis 876, 941
Bickel, Andy 305
Bickel, J.E. 449
Bickford, Jewelle 175
Bickley, Ervin F., Jr. 530
Biddinger, Frank J. 43
Biehle, George A. 1408
Bienenfeld, Marvin 427, 897
Bierbaum, J.A. 900
Bierer, W.E. 640
Biever, William, II 345
Bigelow, David C. 431
Bigelow, O. Reed 1119
Bigham, Bruce H. 384
Bilger, Nathan 1004
Billera, I. John 1360
Billik, Joseph 733
Billington, Thompson H. 614
Binder, Charles A. 261
Binder, Donald P. 179
Bindler, Leonard 555
Bindner, Harry L. 354
Bingay, James S. 993

Bingham, Barry 557
Bingham, Edward F. 432
Binns, James H. 378
Binswanger, Milton S., Jr. 432
Birckhead, Oliver W. 501
Bird, Dorothy A. 115
Birdsall, Ray 586
Birdsong, E.L. 1062
Birk, Merlin H. 347
Bisgrove, John 1131
Bishop, C.M., Jr. 1065
Bishop, Charles F. 455
Bishop, Herbert B. 1261
Bishop, Howard W. 423
Bishop, John 1302
Bishop, Louis S. 1215
Bishop, Robert J. 40
Bissell, J.M. 434
Bissell, Marshall P. 1011
Bistline, Dean 16
Bixler, Harris J. 930
Bizalion, Anne Catherine 225
Bizzarri, Anthony 370
Black, A.C., Jr. 620
Black, Carl L. 789
Black, Eli M. 1358
Black, L.K. 1311
Black, Leonard J. 721
Black, Louis E. 506
Black, Richard B. 929
Black, Theodore M. 435
Black, William 516
Blackburn, James 56
Blackford, Benjamin 1269
Blackstone, Henry 1211
Blackton, Mark 435
Blackwell, LeRoy G. 109
Bladen, Edwin M. 47
Bladh, E. Herbert 1025
Blair, Allen 1024
Blair, Beatrice 161
Blair, Claude M. 1000
Blair, H.A. 500
Blair, John J. 41
Blair, John L. 1010
Blair, Ronald 436
Blaisdell, George G. 1444
Blake, William Henry 253
Blakkan, Bruce 901
Blalock, W.S. 936
Blanc, Yale A. 1124
Bland, Barbara 744
Bland, John P. 1230
Blanker, William C. 642
Blasch, Bruce B. 138
Blase, Beverly 303
Blase, Ken 298
Blaser, E.G. 357
Blatmann, Gene 710

Blatz, Durand B. 811
Blaut, Stephan J. 1382
Blauvelt, Howard W. 547
Blayton, Zada 281
Bleicken, Gerhard D. 833
Blenko, W.H., Jr. 437
Bleyer, Alfred, Jr. 437
Blitzer, William F. 896
Bloch, E.S. 437
Bloch, Henry 747
Bloch, Stuart F. 437
Block, Frederick L. 437
Block, Henry 437
Block, Jay L. 437
Block, Leonard 437
Block, Walter W., Jr. 1112
Block, William 356
Blom-Jensec, J. 825
Blommer, Henry 438
Bloom, Herbert 577
Bloom, Joseph 1184
Bloom, Lewis 438
Bloomberg, Robert T. 1113
Bloomfield, Lionel N. 1440
Blough, B.F. 1411
Bluestein, Paul H. 641
Bluestein, Whitey 117
Bluestone, J. 424
Bluhdorn, Charles G. 744
Blum, Alan 111
Blum, M. 1198
Blum, William E. 378
Blumberg, Rena 305
Blumenthal, Bernhard S. 1393
Blumenthal, Isadore D. 1119
Blumenthal, Larry 672
Blumenthal, W. Michael 421
Blumstein, Stanley 910
Blunt, A.C., III 1216
Blythe, J.H. 528
Board, Fred C. 208
Board, Robert R. 683
Boatman, Bill 441
Bobley, Peter M. 922
Bochat, Robert E. 176
Bodden, Debbie 100
Bode, Barbara 199
Boe, Archie R. 344
Boehm, John F. 1369
Boeschenstein, William W. 1043
Bogdanovich, Joseph J. 1267
Boggs, William W. 426
Bogusz, Frank 864
Bohan, Mary 192
Bohde, Edward L. 48
Bohmbach, S.M. 1287
Bohnert, L.G. 809
Boies, Edward A. 282
Boise, Spencer 942

Personnel Index

Boitano, James 36
Bolander, Donald O. 489
Bolden, Darwin W. 207
Bolduc, Ernest J., Jr. 131
Boles, Donald R. 443
Boles, Wayland 1185
Bolin, Mathew G. 518
Bolinger, G. Noel 1261
Bolling, Cherri 96
Bolwell, Harry J. 962
Bolz, Robert M. 944, 1040
Bond, David G. 179
Bonfiglio, Lynn 143
Bong, Eugene R. 419
Bonham, Dwight D. 66
Bonner, Charles W. 445
Bonsack, Samuel E. 512
Bonsall, George 457
Boody, Irving R., Jr. 445
Booher, Edward E. 355
Booher, Edward E. 1003
Bookout, John F. 1216
Boornazian, S.T. 1063
Boorstein, Allen L. 1152
Booth, Darrell R. 843
Booth, Wallace 1357
Borchardt, Herbert H. 1128
Boreham, Roland S., Jr. 402
Borick, Louis L. 1292
Boriskin, Joel 97
Borman, Frank 622
Borman, Paul 447
Born, Ira B. 839, 933
Born, Jack 368
Borse, Anton G. 447
Borten, Richard A. 47
Bortin, Harry 273
Bortis, Linda 50
Bosca, M.E. 447
Bosch, H.G. 511
Bosell, Michael 1213
Bosman, Abraham 1112
Boss, Bradford R. 564
Bosse, William R. 306
Bossemeyer, Woode 438
Bost, Lloyd C. 447
Boston, Ernie 301
Bostrom, Glenn W. 135, 150
Boswell, Floyd C. 1311
Boucai, Solomon 1198
Boucher, T.O. 519
Boudreau, Donald 405
Bouldin, B.F. 366
Bourgeois, Jean 111
Boutros, Richard D. 975
Bowab, J. Alex 302
Bowback, James 285
Bowden, Burnham 468, 906

Bowen, D.J. 513
Bowen, Joseph 108
Bowen, Kenneth E. 500
Bowen, Richard 689
Bowen, Uvelia S.A. 204
Bowers, Frederick W. 1406
Bowers, Jean S. 112
Bowles, Ralph H. 709
Bowley, Gordon F. 37
Bowman, Robert G. 713
Bowser, P.C. 587
Boyce, Virginia S. 170
Boyd, George F., Sr. 1339
Boyd, William E. 1046
Boydston, Grover 170
Boyer, Charles 196
Boyer, Hugh M. 776
Boyer, Robert J. 450
Boyer, Welch H. 151
Boyle, Mona 678
Boyle, P.J. 1196
Boyle, Thomas K. 400
Bozich, A.T. 801
Bradbury, Beth 293
Braden, Joan R. 29
Bradford, F. Hayden 282
Bradley, Charles E. 1424
Bradley, Douglas H. 818
Bradley, G.F. 1368
Bradley, James W. 678
Bradley, Richard J. 1378
Brady, Frank L. 936
Braendel, F.W. 741
Braff, Jerome 681
Bragg, John M. 895
Braiman, Judy 110
Brain, David L. 852
Brainard, Alexander N. 543
Brainerd, Harry H. 190
Branaghan, Richard L. 149
Branch, C.B. 607
Brand, Abe 1041
Brand, Cobell 1282
Brand, Hyman 451
Brandell, Raymond E. 423
Brandon, Robert M. 94
Brandschutz, Walter 927
Brandt, James A. 1189
Brandt, Paul 451
Brangato, Leo J. 974
Branham, William T. 663
Brannan, Donald D. 374
Brannan, Robert R. 366
Bransted, William 283
Branstein, Edward 916
Brashear, Turner G. 1378
Brashears, Edwin L., Jr. 608
Brassell, J. Thomas 34
Braswell, Albert M., Jr. 452

Brauchli, Robert C. 34
Braun, Daniel C. 156
Braun, Dick 301
Braun, E.J. 729
Braun, Harvey A. 665
Braver, Thomas R. 781
Braverman, Melvin 319
Bray, J.W. 452
Brayton, Roswell 1430
Brazier, Geoffrey 50
Brazil, Eric C. 273
Breach, Theodore W. 777
Breakstone, M. 1134
Brearley, John 452
Brecher, Nicholas M. 1052, 1253
Brecher, Ronald 398
Brecker, Manfred 1013
Bregaw, George 18
Bregman, Benjamin B. 1344
Brehmer, Patricia 61
Breidegam, DeLight E., Jr. 622
Bremner, Edward G., Jr. 453
Bremner, Herbert 753
Brendza, Anna Lee 289
Brenin, Barnett E. 602
Brenn, Earl 796
Brenner, Murry J. 604
Brenner, Theodore E. 263
Brereton, Renee 98
Bresky, H.H. 1202
Bresler, Harry O. 454
Bresnahan, W.A. 246
Bressler, Simon M. 454
Bretzfelder, Robert K. 867
Breuer, Adam A. 454
Breuner, William R. 454
Brewer, Charles P. 419
Brewer, Wayne B. 550
Brewster, E. Billings 874
Brewster, William S. 1351
Brian, James H. 1235
Brice, Ed 293
Brick, Maurice J. 1010
Bricker, W.H. 596
Brickman, H. 646
Bridge, Arthur 450
Bridgford, Allan L. 455
Brier, Jack 861
Brierley, R.G. 1271
Briese, Franklin 969
Brigance, D.H. 455
Briggs, Shirley A. 133
Brigham, James R. 595
Bright, Catherine 291
Bright, Harvey R. 622
Bright, John H. 64
Bright, Willard M. 851
Bright, William T. 455
Brightman, Lehman L. 226

Personnel Index

Briley, Dean A. 68
Brilis, Michael N. 56
Brill, Leonard B. 456
Brimhall, W.S. 63
Brindis, Bernard 888
Brindle, A.W. 1394
Brine, William F., Jr. 1350
Brink, M.F. 258
Brinkman, Lloyd D. 714
Brinkmann, Klaus P. 456
Brisell, Robert 1439
Briskin, Bernard 1310
Bristow, E.K. 103
Brite, Alan D. 551
Britt, Rolland W. 708
Britton, Odette M. 57
Britz, Jeffrey E. 1046
Brizzolara, Marco A. 456
Broach, Evelyn 294
Broadhead, Daken K. 343
Broan, John L. 458
Brobeck, Stephen 112
Broberg, Jack M. 822
Brock, Glen P. 805
Brock, Paul K. 458
Brock, Pope F. 694
Brockey, Harold 1147
Brockman, J.H., Jr. 459
Brockmann, Robert J. 356
Brockway, George P. 1022
Brodkin, Sid 1171
Brodrick, M.H. 861
Brody, Arthur 723
Brody, Edward 648
Brody, Harry 458
Brody, Leo 1343
Brody, Martin 1141
Brog, J. Eugene 1254
Bromley, Richard N. 1112
Broner, Herbert J. 1353
Bronner, Maurice H. 696
Bronson, James D. 516
Bronstein, E.L., Jr. 639
Bronstein, Edward L., Sr. 1359
Brook, A.F. 1425
Brookfield, Dutton 1362
Brookhuis, J.G. 355
Brooking, El 565
Brooklyn, Donald F. Marsh 1345
Brooks, Almetta 220
Brooks, C. Robert 771
Brooks, Emmert F. 326
Brooks, Francis F. 419
Brooks, Glenn S. 925
Brooks, H.J. 551
Brooks, Joseph E. 906
Brooks, Owen 202
Brookshire, Bruce G. 460
Brookshire, Paul 275

Brose, C. Richard 1196
Brose, E.J. 789
Broughton, Carl L. 460
Broughton, Louis C. 1410
Brous, R.P. 1099
Brouse, J. Robert 250
Brower, Ned H. 415
Brown, Ann 99
Brown, Arthur J. 319
Brown, C. Terry 389
Brown, Charles H. 1241
Brown, Charles M. 514
Brown, Colon 1001
Brown, Douglas Owen 1043
Brown, Edward I. 1138
Brown, Galen 103
Brown, Gene W. 933
Brown, George 527
Brown, George A. 802
Brown, Herbert 284
Brown, Hugh C., Jr. 1322
Brown, I. Robert 1174
Brown, Ira D. 1189
Brown, James 1228
Brown, Kenneth H. 462
Brown, Leonard 963
Brown, Martin S. 576
Brown, Meade P. 159
Brown, R.E. 1247
Brown, Reeves 758
Brown, Richard J. 63
Brown, Richard R. 1239
Brown, Richard T. 1394
Brown, Robert W. 902
Brown, Roger 38
Brown, Samuel R. 721
Brown, Sandra J. 196
Brown, Theodore D. 667
Brown, W.E. 430
Brown, W.L. Lyons, Jr. 461
Brown, Walter H. 403
Brown, Werner C. 771
Browne, Helen E. 153
Browne, Robert S. 195
Browning, Frederick M. 462
Browning, J. Daniel 300
Broyhill, Paul 462
Brozman, Robert F. 500, 502
Brubaker, C. Harper 1364
Bruce, J.W., Jr. 849
Bruder, Thomas A., Jr. 463
Brueggemeier, Edwin 445
Bruenn, Adrienne 93
Brumberger, Louis 1153
Brumberger, Sidney 463
Bruna, Joseph 1336
Bruner, J.L. 463
Brunn, Gustave C. 403
Brunn, Herbert T. 1117

Brunner, Robert C. 831
Bruno, Andy 273
Bruno, Joseph 463
Bruno, Vincent 328
Brunskill, James B. 648
Bryan, J.F., III 808
Bryan, John H., Jr. 543
Bryan, Wheeler 42
Bryant, Edwin E. 1007
Bryant, Thomas E. 152
Brydon, J.B. 459
Brzeski, Alfons 366
Bubb, Harry G. 1047
Buchan, R.G. 492
Buchanan, Harry W. 1382
Buchanan, Lynn K. 185
Buchanan, Martin 1391
Buchling, Ramon 1270
Buchman, Alex 406
Buchsbaum, Chester W. 862
Buchwach, S. Bob 326, 385
Buck, Harold S. 118
Buck, J.R. 464
Bucker, Leroy M. 812
Buckle, J.R. 966
Buckler, Bruce 465
Buckley, Christopher H. 1150
Buckley, Irene G. 147, 164
Buckley, R.E. 1083
Buckreus, Allan J. 415
Buddig, Robert C. 465
Budke, George P. 1075
Budlong, Adrian E., Jr. 859
Budnitz, Mark 105, 236
Buege, Carl E. 689
Buehler, Albert C., Jr. 1378
Buehler, R.C. 1063
Buek, Charles W. 1361
Buenting, Robert E. 687
Buffing, H.C. 351
Buffington, A.L. 596, 1290
Buhl, Paul 1015
Buitoni, Marco 466
Bukaty, John, Jr. 44
Bulasky, Joseph 385
Bull, B.M. 1308
Bullock, H. Ridgely 1351
Bullock, Robert V. 44
Bumby, A.J. 916
Bumby, John E. 1150
Bundy, Stephen A. 671, 984
Bunker, John B. 784
Bunn, Wallace R. 1047
Bunting, George L., Jr. 1023
Bunting, John R. 668
Bunting, Ken 289
Burack, Alvin L. 879
Burd, Samuel I. 921
Burdett, Philip H. 1138

Personnel Index

Burdick, Karen 306
Burdorf, W.L. 566
Burgard, Peter W.H. 961
Burge, W. Lee 1141
Burger, Alex 381
Burger, Christine 291
Burgess, Carter 670
Burgess, Rob 104
Burget, William C. 433
Burgoyne, Joseph F., Jr. 467
Burish, Bennie C. 399
Burk, Arnold D. 1055
Burk, Richard J., Jr. 133
Burke, Dennis J. 1437
Burke, Halsey C. 467, 468
Burkenroad, W.B., Jr. 380
Burket, Carl E. 378
Burman, Joanne 111
Burnett, Albert 1186
Burnett, Harry A. 597
Burnett, Robert A. 955
Burnham, Joseph A. 750, 934
Burns, Dan 1187
Burns, John T. 1255
Burns, Robert M. 783
Burnside, Ralph W. 1031
Burnside, Robert F. 187
Burnworth, C.A. 469
Burow, Richard E. 869
Burr, Stuart C. 1371
Burrell, Berkeley G. 220
Burris, J. Wayne 469
Burritt, Stephen G. 1269
Burroughs, Charles F., Jr. 1170
Burrows, Fred W. 252
Burstein, Jerome E. 469
Burt, Wilma 114
Burten, Marvin F. 451
Burton, Florence 53
Busbee, Eugene C. 396
Busby, Jack K. 1067
Busby, Richard H. 357
Busch, August A., III 368
Busch, Fred 387
Buse, J. Barret 1030
Buse, Raymond L., Jr. 652
Bush, John 863
Bushnell, David P. 470
Buss, J. Gordon 1321
Bussey, C.W., Jr. 883
Bussey, Debbie 290
Bussmann, J.A. 947
Bussmann, Joseph A., Jr. 470
Busso, Tomaso 820
Butcher, Willard C. 509
Bute, John 470
Butkys, Adolph S. 114
Butler, Jim 280
Butler, Rhett W. 1356

Butnik, Bernard D. 477
Butt, Charles C. 471
Butt, Joseph L. 515
Butterbrodt, John E. 385
Butterfield, R.F. 480
Button, Daniel E. 144
Butts, Cathy 102
Butts, Joseph A. 459
Butz, J.T. 1378
Buxton, C.I., II 660
Buxton, Robert L. 471
Buyers, J.W.A. 709
Buzzard, Charles E. 297
Buzzard, J.A. 1417
Byer, Ellis M. 1038
Byler, William 195
Byrd, Russell A. 187
Byrne, Jane M. 43
Byrnes, D.J. 398
Byron, Nicholas G. 43

C

Cable, Austin 475
Cabot, Samuel 475, 1285
Cady, Sheldon H. 260
Caffey, Guy H., Jr. 433
Cahen, Edward B. 344
Cahn, Jean Camper 238
Cahn, William 151
Cain, Dee 274
Cain, Nancy 292
Cain, Robert H. 477
Calamia, Waldon 1157
Caldwell, Carlyle G. 1003
Caldwell, E.L., Jr. 1303
Caldwell, Guy L. 746
Caldwell, Lowell 893
Caldwell, R.J. 479
Caldwell, W.A., Jr. 921
Caldwell, William M. 1247
Caley, Richard J. 1018
Calhoun, Robert, Jr. 477
Callahan, Bill 115
Callahan, Frank C. 765
Callan, W.W. 500
Calliotte, Ms. Clyde 34
Calvo, Mary 1016
Camarota, Richard J. 321
Camas, Walter C. 572
Cameron, H.C. 1120
Cameron, Paul A. 1110
Camit, N.R. 591
Campbell, Carl N. 483
Campbell, Dick 175
Campbell, Donald B. 790

Campbell, Doris 108
Campbell, Edward A. 247
Campbell, F.L. 1429
Campbell, Frank G. 483
Campbell, Harold W. 691
Campbell, James L. 1249
Campbell, Mrs. Marion D. 388
Campbell, Norman L. 1001
Campbell, R. Craig 1402
Campbell, Robert D. 1012
Campbell, Robert G. 473
Campbell, Virgil 1164
Campbell, William M. 220
Campion, Mrs. Frank D. 182
Campion, Robert T. 886
Canavan, Richard J. 251
Candee, R.S. 849
Canepa, Joseph F. 110
Canfield, Patrick Lyle 35
Cangemi, Anthony 937
Canham, Robert A. 135
Cannon, John 752
Cannon, Rowland M. 1365
Cantisano, Ralph 1120
Cantor, Emanuel D. 486
Cantor, Sylvia 109
Cantrell, Janet 117
Capelouto, Victor 1091
Caplan, Marc 98
Capps, Clifton 479
Capps, William T. 487
Cappuccio, Joseph F. 473
Caprio, Ralph 69
Cardilli, Louis 670
Cardin, William 11
Cardon, Leon 1267
Carey, Charles J. 257
Carey, Dean L. 863
Carey, R.B. 352
Carlisle, M.E., Jr. 356
Carlisle, Tyler 490
Carlsen, Albert 803
Carlson, Chris 21
Carlton, Doyle E., Jr. 763
Carlton, Winslow 88
Carmack, Stan 312
Carmine, Samuel A., III 491
Carnegie, Dorothy 574
Carnes, Ron 300
Carney, Frank L. 1083
Carney, William T. 1025
Caro, Harold G. 1093
Caron, J.B. 536, 1337
Carothers, Stuart 173
Carpenter, Edward M. 1047
Carpenter, Monte C. 674
Carpenter, William C. 1315
Carpenter, William P. 1292
Carr, Hal N. 1019

Personnel Index

Carriere, Albert 180
Carrillo, Roberto 875
Carrington, Frank G. 231
Carroll, John L. 1020
Carroll, Katherine 280
Carroll, Matthew E. 1274
Carroll, Thomas S. 892
Carroll, Walter E. 709
Carrow, Milton M. 232
Carson, Charles 340
Carson, George 228
Carson, Johnny 494, 834
Carson, Nathan B. 550
Carson, W.L. 1238
Carter, Claude I. 540
Carter, Dickie S. 209
Carter, Edward W. 458
Carter, Francis C. 597
Carter, Gibert 117
Carter, H. LeRoy, Jr. 1141
Carter, J.S. 844
Carter, L.C., Sr. 1145
Carter, Leigh 1339
Carter, Lynn 1216
Carter, Robert D. 146
Carter, Robert E. 495
Carter, W.L. 1346
Cartwright, John R. 121
Carty, Lee 235
Caruso, Art 305
Caruso, Austin A. 1248
Caruso, Ignazio F. 745
Carvel, Thomas 495
Carver, Carleton G. 829
Carver, Donald S. 558
Cary, Frank T. 813
Cary, Victor L. 1432
Casey, Albert V. 349
Casey, E. Paul 946
Casey, Raymond J. 186
Casey, Thomas F. 1304
Cashel, William S., Jr. 419
Caskey, Dolores 290
Casper, Ronald 70
Cass, William F. 497
Cassador, Arnold 110
Cassell, Jane 279
Cassingham, James 105
Cassini, Oleg 1033
Caste, Jean 555
Castello, Albert P. 865
Castle, Jerome 1066
Caston, Alan D. 991
Caston, Douglas E. 117
Catain, Jack, Jr. 1172
Catalani, Arthur P. 454
Cate, R.M. 841
Catena, M.J. 511
Cater, John T. 1315

Catlett, E.T., Jr. 606
Cato, Frank 61
Cato, Wayland H., Jr. 498
Catt, Glen 1252
Cattaneo, Donald 1075
Cattani, Maurice A. 937
Caulfield, Tom 111
Cavanagh, Thomas M. 872
Cavanaugh, W.T. 246
Celauro, Frank 459
Center, Dave 1043
Cesarone, Lucille H. 228
Chadwick, Thomas W. 27
Chadwick, W.S. 1246
Chalk, Elmer W. 111
Chamberlain, Herbert J. 1155
Chamberlain, M.J. 1212
Chamberlain, W. James 715
Chamberlain, William E. 222
Chamblee, Leonard 271
Champlin, George S. 578
Chandler, Doris 275
Chandler, I.V. 1059
Chandler, Otis 907
Chandler, R. Carl 831
Chandley, Martha 62
Chang, James H. 38
Chapin, Roy D., Jr. 358
Chapman, Alva H. 862
Chapman, Douglas K. 324
Chapman, Hugh M. 521
Chapman, Mary Lou 39
Charles, Seymour 188
Charren, Peggy 81
Chase, Gordon W. 692
Chatham, Richard T. 509
Chauvin, Marvin 312
Chavkin, Judith B. 64
Chavkin, Wallace 429
Cheatham, J.M. 613
Chedekel, Paul N. 998
Cheek, Henry C. 589
Cheek, Thomas M., Jr. 398
Cheek, Thomas S. 1381
Cheiten, Marvin 1397
Chenoweth, Sherry 48
Chernoff, M.B. 997
Cherot, Dennis G. 52
Chesebro, R.E., Jr. 1417
Chester, Hyman 295
Chestnut, George W. 320
Chestnut, N.P. 1249
Chiappini, Gerry 114
Chickey, R.L. 870
Chiera, Elizabeth 96
Childerston, Ward 303
Childress, James D. 39
Childs, E.L. 635
Ching, Anthony B. 34

Ching, Hung Wo 345
Ching, Peter P.S. 193
Chipurnoi, Laurance Z. 516
Choate, Mrs. Edward 166
Choate, Robert B. 87
Chomeau, David D. 1137
Chomet, Charles 105, 148
Chreist, Louis R., Jr. 1246
Christel, Norbert R. 1275
Christensen, D. Kenneth 1021
Christensen, David A. 1125
Christensen, Delbert 673, 1395
Christensen, J.P. 708
Christensen, Wayne C. 181
Christian, John W., Jr. 1036
Christian, Miles 657
Christian, Richard 285
Christie, Claude 1299
Christie, George N. 260
Christie, John M. 1148
Christie, Soren L. 517
Christmas, William G. 1268
Christopher, R.L. 729
Christopherson, Weston R. 831
Christopoulos, George 89
Chrones, Anthony 1138
Chubb, Percy, II 659
Chubb, Percy, III 533
Chudnow, Paul 902
Chung, James L. 693
Chute, Mortimer H., Jr. 400
Cicone, Vincent 508
Cifers, E.C. 399
Civis, Jacob 113
Cizak, Robert 550
Clair, Joseph E. 1377
Clancy, James 721
Clapp, Nathaniel D. 1389
Clapp, Norton 1410
Clapp, R.H. 956
Clarey, Robert L. 54
Clark, Ashton R. 341
Clark, D.E. 1422
Clark, David O. 1247
Clark, Donald 108
Clark, Donald L. 426
Clark, Earl 1027
Clark, Edwin J. 617
Clark, Frank S. 736
Clark, H.R. 1189
Clark, John P. 1422
Clark, John W. 589
Clark, Julia 100
Clark, Julian L. 591
Clark, Mike 116
Clark, Robert B. 781
Clark, William J. 939
Clarke, Bernard J. 535
Clarke, Henry D., Jr. 340, 1331

1555

Personnel Index

Clarke, W.C., Jr.   606
Clary, John G.   327
Classen, Allan   101
Claster, Kermit G.   1029
Clausen, George E.   715
Claussen, Edward J.   524
Clawson, Charles H.   458
Clay, Betty Jean   293
Clay, Bob   84
Clay, William Henry, Jr.   471
Clayton, Charles L.   864
Clayton, William, Jr.   524
Claytor, W. Graham, Jr.   1248
Cleary, F.J.   589
Cleary, Russell G.   768
Clegg, Johnson Rosell   525
Clemen, Clarence W.   333
Clemence, Robert V.   798
Clements, W.W.   601
Clemmens, W.B.   790
Clerici, John   1335
Clews, Vincent   308
Clifford, Patrick J.   511
Clifford, Robert W.   333
Clift, J.B.   408, 1099
Cline, Alec   242
Cline, Neil M.   131
Clohesy, Stephanie J.   198
Close, H. William   1260
Cloud, William   189
Clouston, Ross   729
Clyde, Barbara C.   287
Coady, J.J.   1353
Coady, Leo J.   211
Coates, Norman J.   63
Coates, William P., Jr.   44
Cobourn, William R.   603
Cochran, Clay L.   222
Cochran, John M.   914
Cochrane, James R.   1207
Cochrane, T.E.   528
Cockrill, John L.   346
Cockroft, William C.   1358
Codekas, Tellis   479
Codrea, Raymond   889
Coe, Fred A., Jr.   469
Coe, Thomas D.   1389
Coey, J.S.   787
Cofer, H.J., Jr.   1202, 1204
Coffman, Margo   279
Coffman, Max   925
Cogan, David H.   1366
Cohen, Alan N.   919
Cohen, Arthur G.   377
Cohen, Boris   340
Cohen, Charles   1120
Cohen, Daniel   492
Cohen, Donald P.   1036, 1415
Cohen, Harold   863

Cohen, Isadore M.   530
Cohen, Joe   875
Cohen, Julius J.   1195
Cohen, Lawrence A.   408
Cohen, Melvin S.   530, 599
Cohen, Milton L.   896
Cohen, Morton R.   606
Cohen, Nathaniel   1211
Cohen, Oscar   1292
Cohen, Rebecca   249
Cohen, Richard W.   923
Cohen, Stanford   987
Cohen, Zvi R.   397, 1099
Cohn, Earl   1293
Cohn, Harold S., III   299
Cointreau, Jacques Mercier   530
Colasurdo, L.L.   1311
Colavecchio, John   487
Colbert, Robert B., Jr.   1399
Colborn, C. Page   502
Colburn, Philip W.   1039
Cole, F. Crunden   566
Cole, J. Owen   667
Cole, John W.   914
Cole, Joseph E.   531
Cole, Mary   100
Cole, Richard J.   876
Cole, Vera   95
Colehower, H. Howard   836
Coleman, Beatrice   922
Coleman, John J.   1381
Coleman, R.E.   1148
Coleman, Sheldon   531
Coleman, Tom   161
Coleman, Walter   99
Coles, Lawrence G.   869
Coll, Edward T.   221
Coll, Henry H.   517
Collett, John   770
Collette, W.R.   1026
Collier, David C.   466
Collier, Robert   134
Collier, Robert A.   917
Collings, John K., Jr.   372
Collins, Charles D.   1144
Collins, George F., Jr.   894
Collins, James A.   532
Collins, L.   429
Collins, Michael J.   663
Collins, Paul F.   1251
Collins, Rita   119
Collins, Robert H., Jr.   532
Collins, Steve   274
Collins, Wesley E.   426
Collins, William F.   1142
Colman, Alex   532
Colosimo, E. Thomas   195
Coltman, Bertram W., Jr.   1140
Combe, Ivan D.   537

Combs, Mary   280
Combs, Theodore   761
Comegys, C. Willcox, Sr.   1418
Comer, Donald, III   395
Comer, Monte   1077
Comer, T.W.   1396
Comet, John A.   1358
Comey, David   101
Conant, Howard R.   379, 634
Conaway, G.E.   860
Condon, Edward M.   1088
Condon, John P.   209
Conese, Eugene P.   819
Conklin, George T., Jr.   742
Conklin, T.R.   914
Conkling, Frank W.   335
Connell, P.G., Jr.   352
Conner, Collins   275
Conner, Fox B.   341
Conner, Roger   106
Connolly, Gerald E.   193, 229
Connolly, John S., Jr.   759
Connolly, Pat   173
Connor, Frank H.   668
Connor, Gordon R.   542
Connor, John T.   343
Connor, Raymond   1138
Connor, Wallace J.   542
Conrad, Leonard W.   768
Contogouris, Christos S.   374
Conway, Bruce B.   1313
Conway, Robert A.   839
Conway, William A.   973
Conway, William E.   998
Conzelmann, Paul A.   389
Cook, Carol   913
Cook, Denver   107
Cook, Donald   1029
Cook, Donald C.   501
Cook, Everett R.   548
Cook, George H., Jr.   1324
Cook, Herbert   441, 549
Cook, J. Lawson   415
Cook, S.R.   514
Cook, T.G.   1391
Cook, Willie, Jr.   99
Cook, Winifred I.   284
Cooke, M. Todd   1076
Cookenbach, T.   1133
Cookler, N.N.   715
Cooley, Richard P.   1403
Cooling, Robert O.   1327
Coombs, E.S., Jr.   1121
Coon, Charles C.   244
Cooney, Ida   292
Cooper, Arnold   1063
Cooper, E.   877
Cooper, E. Leon   168
Cooper, Elsie   824

1556

Personnel Index

Cooper, Evertt A.   1287
Cooper, G.G.   550
Cooper, George   1369
Cooper, Harold   1228
Cooper, Harold P.   119
Cooper, Harris   352, 814
Cooper, Herman   703
Cooper, Lucille   112
Cooper, Marvin   618
Cooper, Morton   550
Cooper, Robert E., Jr.   550
Cooper, Robert L.   1414
Cooper, Sol   1059
Coopersmith, Edward   1303
Coords, Henry H.   669
Coors, William K.   550
Copeland, Randall E.   1280
Copland, James P.   35
Copley, Helen K.   550
Copp, Earle M., Jr.   294
Coppenrath, Robert A.M.   332
Coppens, John H.   1020
Copps, Chandler V., II   551
Corbett, William H.   1368
Corbin, David C.   473
Corbman, Robert   328
Corcoran, Lawrence J.   212
Cordell, Joe B.   832
Corette, John E.   981
Corey, S.F.   404
Corley, John Jay   1004
Cornell, Harry H., Jr.   888
Cornet, Robert   553
Cornwell, A.M.   823
Corral, James J.   554
Correa, Henry A.   320
Corrigan, Fredrick H.   1063
Corrigan, J.H.   1118
Corrigan, Wilfred J.   652
Corson, Thomas H.   527, 1379
Corwin, Barbara   224
Corwin, David R.   801
Cory, David   424
Cosby, Eric L.H.   555
Cosby, John W., Jr.   776
Cosby, Lin   117
Coss, C.F.   638
Costa, G.   555
Costa, Gregory, Jr.   555
Costacos, Jerry A.   335
Costello, B.A.   475
Costello, Marilyn E.   1244
Costello, Reno   382
Cotsen, Lloyd E.   1008
Cott, John   556
Cotter, John M.   556
Cotton, Martha   282
Cotton, R. Gene   556

Counter, Ben F.   682
Courtney, Edwin Raleigh   1397
Covington, Dayton   647
Cowart, D.R.   985
Cowen, Robert I.   727
Cowen, T.A., Jr.   421
Cowie, William H., Jr.   1355
Cowles, Alfred E.   236
Cowles, Gary M.   324
Cowley, C. Frank   455
Cox, Bert G.   563, 837
Cox, C. Russell   367
Cox, Gilbert E.   321
Cox, Iris Pettiford   169
Cox, Leslie E.   750
Cox, Mary   312
Cox, Robert M.   1260
Cox, Robert N.   644
Coyman, Clifford H.   1068
Coyne, Robert T.   544
Crabb, Chuck   278
Craddock, J. Douglas   788
Cragg, E.E.   1396
Craig, Frank   551
Craig, Gordon   446
Craig, William E.   210
Craighill, Polly W.   46
Cram, Anne H.   229
Cramer, Helen M.   347
Crane, Bruce   560
Crane, Edward J.   1044
Crane, John F.   274
Crane, Keith   531
Crane, Neal D.   824
Cranford, Hugh H.   218
Cranshaw, Robert W.   1373
Crawford, Clyne   560
Crawford, James   59
Crawford, John J.   1010
Crawford, Morris D., Jr.   449
Crawford, R.C.   1433
Cray, Richard B.   946
Creager, Frank W.   1052, 1323
Creal, J.B.   241
Crean, John C.   673
Crecelius, Charles I.   167
Creech, John S.   1356
Creedon, David   1228
Creger, Bruce E.   469
Creighton, Albert M., Jr.   593
Creitz, W.M.   958
Cremona, Vince   298
Cretens, Nan   273
Crews, W.A.   1020
Crilly, William M.   449
Crippen, Mrs. John T.   204
Crisafulli, Stephen W.   1233
Crist, Frederic E.   469
Crist, Jacquie   306

Crist, Thomas D., Jr.   66
Croch, R.P.   529
Crocker, Jack J.   1291
Crohn, Norman   892
Cromenworth, C.D.   595
Cron, Theodore O.   12
Cronin, Robert P.   1270
Cronk, C. Robert   220
Cronstrom, Kenneth A.   564
Crook, William A.   564
Crosby, James F.   1436
Cross, Clinton   62
Cross, Wilson W.   854
Crossman, William W.   802
Crowe, Byron A.   565
Crowell, W.A.   1000
Crowley, Francis E.   565
Crowley, Jerome J.   693, 1027
Crowley, W.H.   1369
Crown, Lester   705
Crowther, Chester W.   399
Crudup, Gloria   108
Cruse, Edward A.   240
Crutchfield, Edward E., Jr.   668
Cuellar, Gilbert   630
Culbreath, Hugh L.   1304
Cullen, Stanley R.   1187
Culligan, J.W.   625
Cullman, Edgar M.   705
Cullum, Charles G.   532
Culpepper, J. Manning   450
Culver, J.E.   485
Cumming, J.L.   1206
Cummings, H. King   744
Cummings, Hugh   569
Cummings, John J., Jr.   810
Cummings, Nathan   385
Cunerd, Earl H.   178
Cunha, A.P.   390
Cunning, Jerry   302
Cunningham, Austin   1287
Cunningham, David A., Jr.   568
Cunningham, Gardner R.   1443
Cunningham, H.M.   518
Cunningham, Howard   68
Cunningham, John P.   164
Cuny, Gene   314
Cupp, Paul J.   325
Curran, Don B.   309
Currie, C.P.   525
Currier, John   681
Curry, Robert L.   568
Curtis, Andrew   95
Curtis, Arthur S.   94
Curtis, Ellwood F.   585
Curtis, Frank J.   570
Cushman, L. Arthur, Jr.   350
Cussins, Wayne   38
Cutcheon, Edward C.   1229

Personnel Index

Cutchins, C.A., III 1382
Cutler, Donald E. 1244
Cutler, Henry H. 571
Cutler, Mimi 82, 99
Cutler, Morris 552
Cutler, Timothy R. 970
Cutler, Virginia 116
Cutrone, John 1122
Cutter, David L. 571
Czapor, Edward P. 587

D

Dachman, Robert 159
Dadourian, Alexander A. 816
Dages, James F. 454
Dahl, C.R. 566
Dahl, Jack E. 743
Dahl, John C. 573
Dahl, John M. 1228
Dahlberg, Kenneth H. 573
Dahlberg, Truman 760
Dahlgren, Carl 114
Dalan, William A. 1417
Dale, Robert V. 935
Daley, C.L. 1426
Dalquist, H. David 1020
Dalsemer, Richard C. 128
Dalwin, Louis Arthur 373
Daly, Charles P. 950
Daly, Denis 847
Daly, Edward J. 1431
Daly, John H., Jr. 1075
Dalzell, David B., Sr. 683
D'Ambruoso, Dom S. 69
Damon, John K. 541
D'Amour, Gerald E. 431
D'Amour, R.A. 1398
Dancewicz, Joseph A. 1008
Danforth, Robert L. 105
D'Angelo, Carl 945
D'Angelo, Gene 314
Daniel, Richard I. 574
Daniel, V.J., Jr. 971
Daniels, W. Riley 978
Danielson, Robert W. 977
Danjczek, William E. 864
Danley, Mrs. J.C. 96
Dann, B.J., Jr. 770
Danner, Raymond 1219
D'Annunzio, Joseph 1311
Dantowitz, Samuel 336
Darby, William J. 171
Darcy, John F. 855
Darer, Norman A. 473
Darnell, W. Raleigh 578

Daroff, Joseph A. 578
Daroff, Michael 448
Darrell, Frank, Jr. 96
Dart, Justin 578
Dartland, Walter T. 41
Daubert, G.A. 579
Daughtery, A. Clark 924
Davant, James W. 1049
Davenport, A.L., Jr. 1048
Davenport, R.B., III 869
Davidson, Carl D. 615
Davidson, Harold P. 1342
Davidson, John A. 758
Davidson, Leroy 1349
Davidson, Sydney 579
Davidson, Tom 105
Davidson, William H. 742
Davies, David L. 140
Davies, E.R. 830
Davies, W.R., Jr. 912
Davies, William D., Jr. 986
Davis, Aliawatha 98
Davis, Anita O. 89, 1107
Davis, B.L. 1158
Davis, C.M. 663
Davis, Charles L. 328
Davis, D. Barry 1260
Davis, D.W. 1266
Davis, Donald A. 109
Davis, Edward W. 67
Davis, Finis E. 142
Davis, George A., Sr. 580
Davis, Georgean 156
Davis, J. Luther 1346
Davis, Jack 340, 572
Davis, Jack L. 64
Davis, Jame L. 580
Davis, James E. 360, 1044
Davis, Joel 580
Davis, John W. 468
Davis, Luke 795
Davis, O.C. 1068
Davis, Oscar 765
Davis, Paul J. 572
Davis, Ralph M. 1107
Davis, Rex R. 1301
Davis, Roger P. 166
Davis, S. Robert 1037
Davis, T.H. 1079
Davis, Tine W. 1424
Davis, Tyler B. 404
Davis, W.L. 395
Davis, William H. 1417
Davis, William J. 809
Davis, William L., Jr. 580
Davison, R.W. 1318
Davison, Sam 573
Davret, Martin 783
Dawson, D.E., Jr. 1248

Dawson, James H. 404
Dawson, Russell H. 21
Dawson, Thomas J. 710
Dax, Otto J. 1222
Day, H. Winston 513
Day, James M. 460
Day, John 1088
Day, Robert L. 488
Day, Timothy T. 568
Dayton, Bruce B. 581
Dayton, Douglas M. 981
Dean, Howard M., Jr. 583
Dean, J.C. 680
Dean, Jimmy 832
Dean, R. Hal 1122
Deane, Frederick C., Jr. 404
Deane, M.A. 638
Dearden, William E. 1133
DeArment, George S. 506
Dearmin, Carl A. 755
DeCarlo, R.G. 358
Decio, A.J. 1232
Dederich, Charles E. 178
DeDomenico, Paskey 725
DeDomenico, Paul 713
Dee, R.F. 1237
Dee, W. Stephen 1433
Deeley, William R. 345
DeFlorez, Suzanne 796
DeForest, Abel W., Jr. 363
DeFrancesco, Aldo 865, 997
DeGregory, John 1263
Deknatel, Charles 119
DeLancey, W.J. 1140
Delaney, Tom A. 744
Delaney, W.A., Jr. 890
DeLay, Robert 88, 250
Delchamps, A.F., Sr. 587
DeLeeuw, Bert 90
Delehanty, L.J. 1109
Deliso, Joseph 1329
Delman, Joseph 1256
DelNegro, Arthur L. 55
Deloria, P.S. 231
DeMers, Bruce E. 534
Demers, Normand 624
DeMicco, Stephan 109
Demmer, Richard A. 1089
DeMonenico, Paskey 971
DeMoss, Arthur S. 1001
DeMott, George 1414
Dempsey, George M. 67
Dempsey, Kenneth E. 745
Dempster, R.V. 946
Denerstein, Ezra J. 1440
Denham, Robert O. 987
Denmark, Bernhardt 429
Denne, Roger A. 1385
Denney, Corwin D. 393

Personnel Index

Dennis, John F. 590
Dennis, Louis S. 164
Densen-Gerber, Judianne 171
Dentan, Rene 359
Denton, Frederico Hernandez 61
DePalma, Robert E. 420
DePetrillo, Thomas L. 395
DePree, Hugh 966
DeRado, George 1309
Derethin, Bill 592
Derisco, G.H. 1424
Derleth, H.R. 1070
Derleth, Robert J. 987
DeRose, Robert A. 582
Dery, Arthur 575
de Saint Aubin, Ovide E. 976
DeSanti, Robert P. 36
Deschamps, Robert, III 50
de Schepper, Harry Y. 737
Deshler, William 1047
Desmarais, Lawrence P. 623
DeSmedt, A.T. 1106
Desmond, Mrs. Gordon B. 88
Desmond, William J. 585
de Tessan, Suzanne 521
Detjen, Gustav, Jr. 593
Detjens, John 1414
de Trey, Robert J. 591
Detrick, Ronald M. 34
Deutsch, George S. 349
Devanna, Jan 285
Devenow, Chester 1216
Devereux, Robert D. 1036
Devlin, Edward J. 717
Devon, Fred 594
DeVore, William D. 329
DeVos, Richard 1025
Dewberry, Glenn, Jr. 389
Dewberry, James W. 1000
DeWeese, Mary Ann 583
DeWitt, Frank P. 1219
DeWoskin, Irvin S. 421
Dial, Wendy 275
Diamant, Clara R. 517
Diamant, Fred J. 592
Diamond, Leo 1445
Diamond, Moe 204
Diaz, Carlos 103
Dick, Donald G. 732
Dickelman, Howard C. 1196
Dickerman, Lola 46
Dickert, William A. 115
Dickey, Charles D. 1199
Dickey, Robert III 608
Dickinson, Elmer N. 1004
Dickinson, John F. 540
Dickinson, Juliet P. 235
Dickinson, William E. 263
Dickson, Frederick S. 355

Dickson, George 1397
Dickson, J.L. 1246
Diedrich, Eugene F. 1043
Diehl, W.M. 585
Diekema, Willis A. 582
Dieppe, William A. 344
Diesbach, Frederick B. 868
Dietrich, H. Richard, Jr. 910
Dietz, Irving 604
Dietz, John S. 597
Dietz, Mark T. 606
Dietze, John H. 453
DiGiacomo, Jacob 444
Dillard, William 597
Diller, Barry 1054
Dillingham, Lowel S. 597
Dillon, George C. 470
Dillon, George S. 334
Dillon, R.E. 598
Dillon, Robert E. 597
Dillon, Susan 90
Dillon, W.M. 1022
Dillow, Frank 58
DiLoreto, Edward 1436
Dils, Pierre 1176
Dilschneider, J.M. 1360
DiLuco, Eugene 888
DiMaria, Charles C. 650
Dimas, George C. 165
DiMichael, Salvatore G. 156
Dimling, David S. 714
Disney, Dick M. 50
Disney, Roland C. 701
Distillator, Philip R. 824
Dix, Dennis C. 261
Dixon, George H. 668
Dixon, Michael 1199
Dixon, Wendell L. 561
Dixon, William J. 1406
Dixson, Carl E. 462
Dobbs, D.E. 1098
Dobos, Carl W. 743
Dockson, Robert R. 479
Dodd, Edward H., Jr. 601
Dodd, Edwin D. 1043
Dodd, J.P. 1000
Dodd, John F. 676
Dodds, Wayne S. 640
Dodson, James 755
Doelz, Paul R. 969
Doherty, Donald W. 1114
Doherty, George P. 419
Doherty, William A. 739
Dohrn, Wayne E. 602
Dolan, Beverly F. 1089
Dolan, Kay Frances 4
Dolan, Mary Ann 274
Dolbeare, Cushing N. 216
Dolin, Nate 857

Domin, Daniel J. 1301
Donahue, Martin J. 497
Donati, Enrico 790
Donegan, E. 938
Donehue, Gerald F. 657
Doner, Paul N. 48
Donley, Edward 334
Donnan, James R. 574
Donnell, Barry 1333
Donnell, Edward S. 981
Donnell, Fred L. 589
Donnelly, James F. 172
Donnelly, Joseph 52
Donner, Kenneth 407
Dooley, C.K. 272
Dooner, William J. 1199
Doran, Timonty P. 207
Dorf, Richard H. 1194
Dorfman, Henry S. 688
Dorfman, Jerry 1105
Dorfman, M. 1127
Dorman, Louis H. 605
Dorrance, G. Morris 1076
Dorsey, Patsy R. 387
Dosing, E.J. 697
Doty, John 271
Doty, Wendell E. 412
Douce, C. 1077
Doucette, Robert J. 680
Dougherty, Charles J. 1355
Dougherty, George G. 536
Douglas, Dwight 299
Douglas, Virginia 15
Doulton, Charles W. 634
Doumakes, John 606
Doup, George 1357
Douriet, Ernest F. 581
Douthat, Edward M. 903
Douthit, Loren B. 559
Dow, Anna 280
Dowling, Kenneth 121
Dowling, Maurice 519
Down, Paul L. 712
Downe, Edward R., Jr. 947
Downey, W.R. 605
Downing, L.M. 908
Downs, T. George 607
Doyle, Bernard 189
Doyle, Donald M. 588
Doyle, Harold D. 735
Doyon, Paul R. 155
Draddy, Vincent 579
Draguesku, O.J. 893, 1002
Draheim, E.J. 456
Drake, C.B., Jr. 1179
Drake, Francis E., Jr. 1155
Drake, William P. 1067
Drechsler, Arthur 571
Dreifalt, Lennart 756

Personnel Index

Dreifuss, F.E. 147
Drell, L.B. 589
Dremel, William E. 608
Dressler, Erik 54
Drexler, Lloyd 343
Dreyer, Stanley 86
Driscoll, Andy 105
Driscoll, Clarence V. 1415
Driver, William J. 254
Droege, John A. 632
Drohan, Thomas E. 680
Drumm, W.C. 957
Drury, Charles E. 764
Druth, Joseph S. 610
DuBain, Myron 355, 666
Dubbin, Daniel S. 484
Dubin, Hy 826
Dubin, Melvin 1233
Dublin, Norman M. 43
Duchowny, Jack 1139
Duckwall, A.L., Jr. 611
Duckwall, Richard F. 611
Duebel, Joanne 289
Duensing, D.L. 378
Duerr, Roger K. 932
Duffy, Charles W. 1122
Duffy, Edward W. 931, 1359
Duffy, James E. 351
Dugan, Richard T. 519
Dugdale, Richard T. 1035
Duggan, J. Roy 857
Duggan, Jerry T. 701
Duimet, Emil R. 395
Dunbar, Tad 108
Duncan, E.A. 1337
Duncan, Edwin, Sr. 909
Duncan, L. Earl 584
Duncan, William A. 852
Dunham, Jack 640
Dunitz, H.I. 721
Dunlap, Louise 128
Dunlop, Ann 106
Dunn, Adam G. 548
Dunn, Barbara 28
Dunn, Elwood 106
Dunn, Joseph M. 1072
Dunn, M. Joseph 1438
Dunn, Norman A. 613
Dunn, Norman S. 788
Dunn, Roy 1324
Dunne, Thomas P. 20
Dunnigan, Frank J. 1097
Dunoyer, Phillipe 1332
Duque, Roland 878
Durein, Douglas 353
Durell, Edward 1355
Durham, Stanley W. 387
Durkee, A. Bruce 616
Durland, Jack 477

Durot, Marcel C. 1071
Duryea, George 1309
Duryea, Rezenol 1066
Duval, Albert F. 752
Dwork, H.K. 1130
Dworkin, Sidney 1141
Dwyer, John W. 360
Dwyer, Lawrence P. 618
Dye, L.J. 1308
Dyer, Lloyd T. 759
Dyer, Ruth 169
Dyer, W.E. 988
Dyer, William F. 291
Dyke, F.J., Jr. 1000
Dystel, Oscar 405

E

Eagle, Manny 1117
Eagleson, William B., Jr. 716
Eames, Stanley B. 5
Early, Bert H. 231
Early, Carole A. 210
Early, Robert E. 656
Early, Steve 117
Eastham, William K. 834
Easton, John J., Jr. 63
Ebbinghausen, Frank 911
Ebeling, Henry O. 625
Eberline, John 276
Ebert, G. Donald 632
Ebert, Mrs. Robert A. 237
Ebstyne, Harold D. 374
Eckart, E. Albert, Jr. 1186
Eckels, Theodore W. 793
Eckerd, Jack M. 625
Eckert, Fred D. 334
Eckman, D. Richard 60
Eckman, J.W. 1161
Eckmann, Harold A. 500
Eckrich, Donald P. 625
Eckstein, Ernest 1177
Eddy, N.A. 748
Edel, Edwin E. 365, 1003
Edelson, Kenneth J. 708
Eden, Earl M. 1045
Eden, Harold E. 817
Edey, Marion 130
Edge, A.B., III 537
Edgerly, William S. 1269
Edison, Bernard A. 627
Edison, Robert G. 861
Edmiston, James H. 1298
Edmonston, Henry W. 49
Edmundson, Mrs. Lewis 186
Edson, Eugene H. 628

Edson, G. Londale 564
Edwards, Albert 283
Edwards, G. Fesler 1066
Edwards, J.A. 900
Edwards, Richard D. 1355
Edwards, Thomas C. 1309
Egan, Harold A., Jr. 1349
Egan, William C. 581, 1062
Eggers, E.R. 903
Eggleston, Warren N. 1395
Egozi, David 1284
Ehinger, C.D. 1361
Ehlers, Charles H. 594
Ehly, R.E. 578
Ehre, Victor T. 1365
Ehrlich, Robert 1334
Ehrman, Samuel K. 629
Eich, Henry 150
Eichlin, Diana 274
Eichholz, Arthur H. 501
Eichner, Albert D. 602
Einhorn, Aaron 1096
Einsenberg, George M. 1050
Eiseman, Jack B. 407
Eisenberg, Allan J. 303
Eisenberg, Jacob 1143
Eisenberg, Leonard 169
Eisenberg, Stanley 1288
Eisendrath, Joseph L. 405
Ekanem, Udo F. 216
Ekblom, H.E. 645
Eklund, Coy 640
Eland, S.S. 1114
Elbaugh, Irvin, Sr. 463
Elberson, Elwood L. 598
Elder, H. Vernon 894
Elder, R.D. 391
Elder, Thomas C. 631
Eldredge, Richard 261
Elesh, James N. 674
Elgood, D.L. 599
Elias, Charles 533
Elias, Fred 633
Elicker, Paul H. 1174
Elins, E.S. 628
Elion, Maurice 557
Eliopulos, Alex J. 71
Elkann, Jean Paul 493
Elkins, Jerry J. 634
Eller, Karl 537
Ellinghaus, William M. 1011
Elliot, Robert M. 892
Elliott, A. Naylor 1005
Elliott, Glendon M. 1144
Elliott, Harry L. 290
Elliott, Jack C. 973
Elliott, Jim 303
Ellis, Albert 156
Ellis, G.R. 792

Personnel Index

Ellis, Juanita 123
Ellis, R.F., Jr. 744
Ellis, William H. 655
Ellman, Lawrence 905, 1270
Ellrod, Fred E., Jr. 1113
Elsberg, Milton L. 610
Elsey, George M. 193
Elston, Lloyd W. 1072
Elston, Sidney 820
Embry, Robert C. 20
Emerick, Alan 735
Emerson, Eric 527
Emerson, William M. 613
Emery, J.C., Jr. 636
Emmerson, A.A. 1222
Enck, David P. 562
Endervelt, J.K. 963
Engebretsen, Ed 543
Engels, Lynn 22
England, Fay 103
Engle, Fred J., III 38
English, Alfred C. 447
English, James F., Jr. 542
English, N.C., III 493
Enloe, Cortez F., Jr. 171
Enoch, Charles J. 639
Ensminger, G.A. 337
Ensminger, J. Neal 292
Epstein, Arthur M. 640
Epstein, Donald M. 1341
Epstein, Donald R. 682
Epstein, Gerson 516
Epstein, Herbert S. 384
Epstein, Jerry 704
Epstein, John H. 735
Epstein, Louis 877
Erburn, Robert 1325
Erenberg, Victor 1292
Erenstein, Bernard J. 832
Erickson, C.L. 685
Erickson, Carl R. 581
Erickson, Hyland B. 446
Ericsson, William G. 358
Eriksen, Otto L. 802
Erlewine, Richard H. 707
Erlich, Alvin L. 1393
Erlinger, A.A. 1311
Ernst, D. Fritz 641
Ernst, Jerome 104
Ertegun, Ahmet M. 389
Ertel, William B. 915
Erteszek, Jan J. 1033
Ertl, Fred, Jr. 642
Esgro, Francis J. 642
Eshelman, H.R., Jr. 642
Esmond, Lawrence 1011
Essick, Robert L. 439
Estes, Elliot M. 707
Estes, Joseph F. 748, 1167

Estes, Vernon 643
Estwing, Norman E. 644
Etherington, Roger B. 358
Ethier, C. James 470
Eubanks, Richard L. 713
Evans, Carleton B. 251
Evans, Daniel F. 395
Evans, David B. 723
Evans, E.H. 616
Evans, F. 217
Evans, Harvey B. 645
Evans, Herbert W., Jr. 1430
Evans, Jack W. 1328
Evans, Katherine S. 126
Evans, M.K. 1409
Evans, Max H. 102
Evans, Nicholas M. 608
Evans, Oakley S. 1443
Evans, Ralph L., Jr. 1444
Evans, V.B. 847
Evans, William T. 63
Evans, William W. 653
Evatt, Parker 192
Everly, B.A. 326
Evers, Bernard, Jr. 351
Evinrude, Ralph S. 1042
Ewen, William H. 255
Ewing, Robert E. 1370

F

Faas, Leonard A., Sr. 857
Fabeck, J.E. 384, 784
Faber, Eberhard 625, 650
Faber, Horace B., Jr. 1265
Fabiani, Dante C. 560
Fabrick, Seymour C. 1385
Fachtman, Edmund L., Jr. 1172
Factor, Max 39
Faden, C.A. 1260
Fails, Penny 118
Fairbanks, J.M. 644
Fairbanks, Jane 201
Falk, Ferdie A. 673
Fallek, Fred S. 653
Fallon, Walter A. 623
Fan, J.C. 909
Fanell, Joseph P., Jr. 1139
Fanelli, Robert G. 379
Fanning, Robert P. 1190
Fansier, Richard 289
Fantle, S.W. 1068
Farah, Henry 908
Farah, William F. 655
Farber, Martin J. 664
Farberow, Norman L. 177

Farguhar, Robert C. 849
Farias, Alberto 394
Farish, Charles A. 169
Farish, John M. 991
Farkas, Alexander 338
Farkas, James 54
Farley, John C. 923
Farley, Joseph M. 336
Farley, T.A. 1110
Farmer, Jerome 359
Farmer, Roy L. 64
Farnell, Richard 37
Farr, R.W. 37
Farrar, Sally 292
Farrell, Charles F., Jr. 897, 911
Farrell, David C. 944
Farrell, Richard 289
Farrell, Thomas J. 767
Farrington, James F. 1036
Farwell, Frank L. 894
Farwell, Robert L. 173
Fass, Peter J. 1136
Fasse, Adrian L. 1239
Fassett, John D. 1358
Faulk, Charles 283
Faulkner, Joe P. 294
Fauntleroy, Mrs. Billie 45
Fautsch, Roger A. 618
Fawcett, Henry M. 978
Fawcett, Roger 658
Fayerman, Jeverin 402
Fazio, John 669
Fearnley, W.E. 1268
Feder, Allan A. 601
Feder, Jay 406
Feder, Leon A. 1207
Feder, William R. 180
Federbush, Alexander P. 357
Feen, Eugene 1056
Feig, Jerome H. 872
Feighner, J.W. 1329
Feinberg, David 620
Feinberg, George K. 612
Feinberg, Norman S. 448
Feinberg, Sydney S. 1360
Feingold, Audrey 51
Feingold, S. Norman 196
Feinson, Burton L. 352
Feit, Seymour 1286
Feitler, Robert 1410
Felber, Thomas L. 774
Feld, Irvin 1149
Feldberg, Stanley H. 1441
Feldman, A.L. 692
Feldman, Benjamin 114
Feldman, Howard S. 1192
Feldman, Mervin B. 565
Feldman, Ruth Rubin 222
Feldman, Samuel 1400

1561

Personnel Index

Feldmann, C. Russell 1080
Feldstein, Irving M. 796
Felice, G.A. 733
Fellendorf, George W. 137
Fellows, Olin B., Jr. 651
Felsher, Elaine 96
Femia, Charles 1154
Fenley, G. Ward 285
Fenn, Robert D. 1330
Fennell, Jerold V. 50
Fenske, Helen 8
Fenstermaker, John R. 401
Fenton, Frank M. 661
Fenton, Melissa 96
Ferguson, Crawford R. 661
Ferguson, Daniel C. 1011
Ferguson, Daniel C., Jr. 620
Ferguson, Francis E. 1021
Ferguson, Frank E. 447
Ferguson, James I. 706
Fergusson, Donald W. 1173
Fernandes, Joseph E. 661
Fernandez, A.S. 1030, 1317
Fernandez, Orlando 198
Ferrara, Charles T. 1216
Ferris, E.W. 1170
Ferris, Leonard 422
Ferris, Richard J. 1356
Ferris, W.C. 1002
Fery, John B. 442
Fesperman, James L. 1209
Feuer, Leo J. 494
Feur, Perry 1440
Fichtenbaum, George L. 246
Ficks, G.J., Jr. 663
Fiddelman, Donald 535
Fiebach, Ralph P. 844
Field, E.S., Jr. 421
Field, Elizabeth B. 106
Field, Marshall 514
Field, William 878
Field, William D. 544
Fields, David J. 612
Fields, Mrs. Howard R. 179
Fields, Judy 276
Fieldsteel, Robert J. 718
Fiene, Earl R. 447
Fierle, Edward J. 1198
Fife, Bernard 1264
Fife, H. Frank 51
Figgie, Harry E., Jr. 322
Finazzo, Paul J. 334
Finch, C.B. 980, 1094, 1405
Finch, Parker T. 796
Finch, Tom A. 1320
Finck, Marshall 639
Fine, David L. 448
Fine, Joseph 665
Fine, Paul 955

Fine, W.C. 1258
Fine, William M. 1393
Finegood, David 727
Fingerhut, Manny 666
Fink, Nathan 736
Fink, Peter R. 1222, 1337
Finkel, Albert 822
Finkel, Leonard E. 323
Finkelstein, Edward 918
Finkelstein, Elliot 666
Finkelstein, Melvin 791, 1348
Finkelstein, Seymour 719
Finnegan, Lawrence J. 448
Finoli, Vincent A. 789
Firestein, Chester 943
Firestone, R.B. 482
Fischberg, Maurice 806
Fischer, Herbert 825
Fischer, Louis C. 716
Fischer, Norman J. 1363
Fischer, Ray C. 819
Fischer, Stanley T. 34
Fischman, Harry 1127
Fish, Aaron M. 804
Fish, Kay 287
Fish, Lawrence 105
Fishell, Clair N. 522
Fisher, Benjamin R. 669
Fisher, Bob 99
Fisher, Bob 1064
Fisher, Daniel R. 620
Fisher, Donald E. 574
Fisher, Fred 669
Fisher, George 1340
Fisher, John E. 1004
Fisher, John W. 402
Fisher, Kay 299, 310
Fisher, Ken 669
Fisher, Kenneth R. 738
Fisher, Louis E. 802
Fisher, Paul C. 669
Fisher, W. Frank 1069
Fisher, Wayne H. 910
Fishman, Meyer H. 669
Fishwick, John P. 1016
Fiske, Phineas 288
Fitch, William C. 223
Fitzgerald, Albert J. 363
Fitzgerald, Donald F. 1244
Fitzgerald, Edward E. 445
Fives, Frank M. 634
Flachs, Arthur 906
Flachsenhaar, James 284
Flagg, John E. 523
Flaherty, Charles J. 670
Flake, J.C. 250
Flamberg, Morton 333
Flanders, Don H. 671
Flannery, J. Harold 232, 235

Flavin, Joseph B. 1229
Fleischmann, Isaac 6
Fleisher, Leonard T. 673
Fleishman, Jerome 1132
Fleming, Harold C. 220
Fleming, Ned N. 673
Fleming, Wes 845
Flenor, Henry C. 954
Fles, J. Herman 385
Fletcher, Robert D. 394
Flicker, Irving 785
Flinn, Donald D. 184
Flint, William A., Jr. 674
Flocker, Gilbert 1180
Foote, Guy M. 1402
Foote, Robert T. 1362
Florang, Clarence A. 468
Floreen, David A. 388
Flournoy, Rochelle 99
Flournoy, W.G. 64
Floweree, Robert E. 711
Flowers, Dave 293
Floyd, Frank W. 234
Foddrill, John A. 493
Foerstner, George C. 347
Fogarty, Robert S., Jr. 706
Foisie, Sue 118
Folck, Roy E., Jr. 343
Folger, Peter 678
Folin, Sam 101
Follett, Dwight W. 678
Folz, A. Lorch 906
Fonda, Avery H. 894
Foos, W.F. 662
Ford, Henry, II 679
Ford, Leslie A. 1215
Ford, T. Mitchell 636
Fore, William F. 91
Forish, Joseph J. 172
Forkey, Raymond J. 551
Forman, Maurice R. 681
Forman, William 594
Forman, William R. 520
Formanek, Peter 1290
Forney, Robert R. 897
Forrester, Frank 21
Forsley, Victor M. 47
Forst, Charles J. 682
Fort, Robert W. 951
Forti, Corinne A. 731
Fortugno, Alfred 1044
Foster, Bob 273
Foster, Dale 277
Foster, David 683
Foster, Howard S. 683
Foster, R.A. 1304
Foster, R. Jack 663
Foster, Thomas S. 683
Foster, W. Douglas 1180

Personnel Index

Foster, Willard A. 1382
Foster, Willett S. 627
Fought, Thomas E. 58, 112
Fowler, F.E., III 1247
Fowler, Glen C. 514
Fowler, William A. 259
Fox, Allen K. 362
Fox, Bernard 650
Fox, Charles J. 684
Fox, David 760, 761
Fox, Earl S. 899
Fox, Eldon E. 320
Fox, Jean A. 60, 114
Fox, John F. 684
Fox, Joseph P. 505
Fox, Louis 385
Fox, Milton 933
Fox, Robert 1350
Fox, Robert J. 203
Fox, Robert K. 879
Fox, Robert P. 355
Fox, Samuel 684
Fox, Samuel 846
Foy, Edward A. 685
Fraley, John L. 492
France, Rene 521
Francini, J.P. 1296
Francke, Robert W. 373
Frank, Richard N. 884
Frank, Samuel M., Jr. 686
Frank, Stanley 785
Frank, Wally 686
Frankel, Andrew J. 1001, 1364
Frankel, Arnold 1074
Frankenberger, Bertram 979
Frankenstein, Lester E. 959
Frankfort, Dick 603
Frankl, Sy 686
Franklin, Betty Gyneth T. 133
Franklin, Glenn 1362
Franklin, J.J. 174
Franks, George S. 51
Franzia, Joseph J. 687
Fraser, Calvin W. 681
Fraser, D.H. 434, 1281
Frazer, J. Howard 1387
Frazer, Robert E. 581
Frazier, Norridean 110
Frazier, Ruth 203
Frederick, Gerald B. 1021
Frederick, Philip 1294
Fredericks, Robert R. 613
Freedman, Ernest M. 389
Freedman, Gary 96
Freedman, Henry A. 233
Freedman, Kenneth 1091
Freeman, Mrs. B.H. 689
Freeman, E.E. 608
Freeman, Edward L. 846

Freeman, Elaine 59
Freeman, Ernest J. 1186
Freeman, George S. 661
Freeman, Richard L. 689
Freeman, Roger M., Jr. 342
Freese, V. Dean 693
Freirich, Jerry 689
Fremont, Robert S. 751
French, Exie 107
French, Glendon E., Jr. 379
French, Rae Ann 45
French, W.W., III 983
Freundlich, Richard L. 1218
Frey, A. 1184
Frey, William H. 1109
Frick, O. Guy 38
Frick, Paul H., Jr. 690
Fried, Cliff M. 1147
Fried, Jeffrey L. 1393
Fried, Jerome 979
Fried, Milton 1170
Friedberg, S.M. 651
Frieder, Leonard P., Jr. 710
Friedland, Alan 482
Friedman, Albert 1362
Friedman, Alvin 535
Friedman, G. 364
Friedman, Henry 831
Friedman, Herbert L. 580
Friedman, Jack N. 675
Friedman, Joseph 518
Friedman, Martin B. 681
Friedman, Myles F. 422
Friedman, Norman P. 346
Friedman, Percy 486
Friedman, R.Z. 646
Friedman, Ray 439
Friedman, Robert B. 710
Friedman, Sigmund 1128
Friel, S.E.W., Jr. 691
Friend, Hugo M., Jr. 798
Friep, Lucy 96
Frier, George 691
Fries, R.S. 491
Friesendorf, E.C. 754, 1178
Frigo, Peter 691
Frisbie, O.H. 390
Frisch, Walton 779
Frisvold, Peter M. 118
Fritsch, Albert 83
Fritz, Louis G. 838
Froehlich, Henry 865
Froelich, Jeffrey E. 57
Fromkes, Saul 522
Fromm, Alfred 692
Fronk, William J. 800
Frost, Frank L. 958
Frost, John J. 692
Fruhman, Leo 543

Fruin, John 916
Fruit, Roy H. 628
Fry, Charles L. 693
Fry, Hubert D., Sr. 776
Fry, Robert J. 662
Frye, Thomas C. 803
Fryer, Jerome M. 697
Fucci, Louis V. 154
Fuchs, Alfredo 802
Fucigna, Warren A. 1010
Fuerst, Walter E. 569
Fuhrman, Herbert S. 260
Fulenwider, Jack 41
Fulham, John N. 691
Fuller, Bernard 694
Fuller, James C.E. 378
Fuller, Richard 693
Fuller, Robert A. 1267
Fuller, S.B. 450
Fuller, T.R. 1319
Fulton, David H., Jr. 1084
Fulton, Paul M. 590
Fults, L.A. 1406
Funabashi, A. 963
Fundis, J.D. 1132
Funk, A.J. 694
Funk, Albert P., Jr. 875
Funk, Paul E. 153
Funk, Tim 116
Funke, Alfred H., Jr. 1151
Fuqua, J.B. 694
Furman, F. Foster 694
Furst, Frank E. 695
Furst, Mark J. 694
Furst, Melvin 351
Furuta, M. 823
Fusee, Fred G. 395
Futorian, Morris 695
Futter, Thomas M. 849

G

Gabor, Larry 55
Gabriel, Stephen 110
Gadau, Harry L. 1151
Gaebler, Edward F. 1091
Gage, George H. 708
Gagliano, V. 1178
Gahm, W. Dwight 860
Gainer, Joseph 216
Gaither, Howard 505
Gale, A.A., Jr. 1272
Gale, C.O. 1075
Galef, Andrew 1379
Gall, Gene E. 698
Gallagher, Edward A. 1408

Personnel Index

Gallagher, John P. 511
Gallagher, Joseph A. 810
Gallagher, Joy H. 282
Gallagher, Thomas 607
Gallagher, Virginia 54
Gallagher, Wes 385
Gallaher, W.W. 991
Galland, Richard I. 359
Galle, Virginia 65
Gallery, J.J. 616
Gallery, James 764
Galligan, Harry A., Jr. 67
Galligan, Thomas J. 447
Gallo, Julio 698
Gallup, John G. 1279
Galperson, Julian 409
Galvani, Albert J. 604
Gambino, John 1119
Gamble, Bertin C. 698
Gamel, Thomas W. 1325
Gammon, Joseph A. 1001
Gammons, Robert F. 1079
Gandrud, E.S. 699
Ganguzza, Philip 1368
Gannon, Thomas A., Jr. 980
Gant, Roger, Jr. 719
Gantt, John W. 667
Gantz, David M. 1422
Gantz, Jack 637
Ganz, Claude L. 618
Ganz, Jerry 702
Ganz, Victor W. 901
Gape, B.K. 413
Garber, J.F., Jr. 1065
Garcetti, Gill 35
Gardell, John P. 936
Gardner, Austin T. 588
Gardner, Edith L. 846
Gardner, Ellis B., Jr. 353
Gardner, Gene P. 907
Gardner, Grant 1403
Gardner, Howard 860
Gardner, James 57
Gardner, John C. 700
Gardner, Lawrence B. 276
Gardner, Otto 812
Garfield, Eugene K. 392
Garfinkle, William I. 1416
Garfunkel, Peter H. 668
Garibaldi, Vincent 662
Garkie, James B. 1183
Garland, Harry P. 1239
Garmon, William F. 346
Garnos, Gordon 292
Garrett, B.R. 812
Garrett, Julian B. 44
Garrett, L.J., Jr. 35
Garrett, R. 496

Garrett, Robert M. 181
Garrity, Paul G. 701
Garrity, W.L. 1192
Garrou, Louis W. 336
Garson, Dan 908
Gartenberg, Seymour L. 561
Gartenlaub, Morris 848
Garton, David 701
Garvey, R.F. 1065
Garvey, R.F., Jr. 966
Garvey, Thomas G. 701
Garza, David, Jr. 981
Gash, Russell 877
Gaskell, Jon M. 48
Gates, Charles C., Jr. 702
Gates, George M. 103
Gates, Harold W. 703
Gates, Jerome 701
Gates, Richard J. 1236
Gattas, Fred P., Sr. 138
Gaudrault, Robert J. 691
Gaugler, Newman R. 217
Gaul, Christopher R. 310
Gaul, R.W. 328
Gauntley, J.A. 791, 882
Gauthier, C.J. 1020
Gautieri, Emilio G., Jr. 1150
Gavin, John A. 568
Gavito, Joe, Jr. 635
Gaylord, Edward L. 702
Geary, John D. 962
Gebeaux, Howard 294
Geddes, Allan P. 738
Geddes, William W. 1421
Gehring, G. Gregory 703
Geiger, Harry A. 347
Geiman, Rodney T. 961
Geiselman, William J. 636
Geiser, Paul E. 1065
Geisler, David 50
Geisler, H.O. 704
Gelb, Richard L. 456
Gelb, Victor 1430
Gelbach, J.A. 501
Gelber, Roy C. 976
Gelfman, Max 869
Geller, Max A. 1438
Geller, Stanley 1035
Gelman, Mac 538
Gelsthorpe, Edward 787
Gelvin, Philip D. 532
Gemmel, William A. 1246
Gencher, Mary C. 893
Gendel, William 907
Geneen, Harold S. 801
Genovese, Leonard 710
Gentil, Kenneth G. 1042
Gentry, Grant C. 735
Geoffroy, Charles H. 715

Geoghegan, John J. 558
Geonie, Carmine F. 150
George, Charles 993
George, John 485
George, Thomas J. 712
George, W.H. Krome 347
George, William W. 902
Geraghty, James J. 595
Gerb, Irving 804
Gerber, Oscar L. 711
Gerbery, Martin P. 938
Gerchenson, Emile 347
Gerhard, Fred 383
Geringer, Leonard 712
Gerken, J.R., Jr. 1022
Gerlach, J.B. 879
Gerli, Francis M. 712
Germond, Henry S., III 1142
Gerrish, Hallis G. 1261
Gershman, Susan 174
Gerstein, David B. 1318
Gerstenberger, Donald J. 367
Gerstenmaier, John H. 728
Gerwin, Robert E. 838
Gessner, Charles H. 1036
Gestenberger, Donald J. 1146
Getty, J. Paul 712
Gettys, James E. 1264
Getz, Oscar 410
Geyer, William O. 1174
Ghent, Peer 1073
Gherra, William L. 1061
Giancola, Louis R. 141
Gibb, John R. 780
Gibble, William T. 211
Gibbons, C. Thomas 789
Gibbons, Edward F. 1430
Gibbons, Thomas J. 361
Gibbs, A.N. 329
Gibbs, Stephen 112
Gibian, Richard 351
Giblin, James P. 1432
Gibson, H.R., Sr. 600
Gibson, Kay 353
Gibson, Robert E. 259
Gibson, Robert L. 478
Gidding, Louis R. 714
Giddins, Robert 897
Gidwitz, Gerald 768
Giebel, Robert R. 1421
Giese, Jan 311
Gifford, Claude W. 1
Gifford, Nelson S. 590
Gilbert, Charles E., Sr. 519
Gilbert, Frank 525
Gilbert, Ivan 714
Gilbert, J.E., Jr. 509
Gilfillen, George C., Jr. 917
Gilgoff, Henry 286

Personnel Index

Gilgun, John J. 61
Gilkeson, Robert F. 1075
Gill, Harry R. 1001
Gill, Kenneth P. 1366
Gill, Robert E. 378
Gillaspy, John J. 278
Gillenson, Lewis W. 565
Gillespie, Theresa 173
Gillette, R.S. 1156
Gillette, Stanley C. 948
Gillford, Alfred T. 557
Gilliam, L.S., Jr. 715
Gillies, J.H. 960
Gillinder, William T. 715
Gilling, Earl A. 1412
Gilluly, J.W. 531
Gilman, Alan 1184
Gilman, Charles, Jr. 715
Gilman, Milton 363
Gilmer, Virginia 158
Gilmore, Robert L. 69
Gimbel, S. Stinor 1272
Gindoff, Martin 896
Gingher, Paul R. 537
Gingold, Eli 1080
Ginsberg, David 1009
Ginsberg, Lee 232
Ginsburg, Abe 824
Ginsburg, Robert S. 1243
Gioia, Anthony J. 716
Giordeno, Salvatore 1017
Gips, W.F., Jr. 745
Giragosian, Kegham 515
Girard, Theodore A. 960
Girves, Gus 461
Gislason, T. 530
Gisler, Albert C. 867
Gitles, Arlene 101
Gittleman, Benjamin 898
Giurlani, Louis A. 717
Given, H.W., Jr. 375
Givler, Donald N. 740
Glade, Dale P. 717
Gladner, Albert 48
Gladstone, Milton 375
Glaser, Jim 106
Glaser, Marcus 718
Glass, Anna 286
Glass, Arthur A. 595
Glass, Gerald 46
Glass, Ralph H. 1325
Glass, Richard L. 258
Glatfelter, P.H., III 718
Glatt, Herb 1316
Glatter, Hal 19
Glauberman, Abe 924
Glaubman, Milton M. 354
Glazer, Edward 595
Gleason, Francis J. 1192

Gleason, John S., Jr. 514
Gleason, M.L. 1133
Gleason, Thomas D. 1428
Glenn, Robert 624
Glick, Charles 101
Glick, Samuel 936
Glickman, Arthur 213
Glickman, Carl K. 1042
Glickman, Joe 930
Glines, Everett S. 814
Globus, Alfred R. 742
Glottstein, William 880
Glover, Monica 285
Glover, Walter 854
Glover, William D. 1433
Gluck, Hazel 52
Gluck, Stephen H. 806
Glump, Henry Leonard 1015
Gobin, Leo C. 441
Gobis, Harvey A. 1127
Goboney, M.W. 784
Gochenour, Warren 1431
Gochneaur, Roger V. 657
Goddard, Richard D. 1402
Godfrey, John A. 722
Godfrey, Peter 953, 1200
Goes, Charles B. 722
Goeschel, Arthur L. 478
Goething, Marsha 102
Geotsch, Jim 101
Goetze, R. Melvin, Jr. 722
Goff, Alan H. 1210
Goffstein, Albert A. 322
Goggin, Edward F. 927
Goglia, Mr. 110
Golann, Dwight 234
Golay, C.R. 517
Gold, Allen J. 997
Gold, Bernard 1139
Gold, Joel 659
Gold, Paula 46
Gold, Richard L. 325
Gold, Walter 1274
Goldberg, Bernard 352
Goldberg, George 704
Goldberg, Irving 18
Goldberg, J. 438
Goldberg, Morris J. 814
Goldberg, Sheldon 463
Goldberg, Stanley 32
Goldberger, Eugene 724
Goldberger, Irving L. 846
Goldberger, Irwin 988
Goldblatt, Maurice 724
Golden, Daniel 66
Golden, Joel H. 957
Golder, Morris T. 1310
Goldfeder, Howard 466
Goldhush, Alvin A. 1126

Goldin, Elaine 52
Goldinger, Shirley 35
Goldman, Carl 1035
Goldman, David 376
Goldman, Harold 818
Goldman, Henrietta 146
Goldman, Ilene 125
Goldman, Norman 1310
Goldman, Stanley 621
Goldring, Stephen 1190
Goldsmith, Alfred J. 726
Goldsmith, Carol 283
Goldstein, Benjamin 213
Goldstein, Jerome 1199
Goldstein, Leonard 429
Goldstein, Maxwell 660
Goldstein, Morris 522
Goldstein, S. 448
Goldstein, Steve 108
Golub, Leonard 457
Golub, William 726
Gomena, John E. 878
Gomes, Ruth 272
Gonzales, Peggy 273
Gonzales, Rudofo 98
Good, A. Jerry 1078
Good, Sidney S., Jr. 727
Good, Tom 1164
Goodale, William F., Jr. 427
Goodall, Jack 679
Goodier, E.J., Jr. 555
Goodman, Alan 105
Goodman, Andrew 424
Goodman, Clarence M. 929
Goodman, Frederick L. 150
Goodman, L. 448
Goodman, Leonard 728
Goodman, Paul 711
Goodman, Peter 577
Goodstein, Albert 728
Goodwin, E.L. 486
Goodwin, Edward 323
Goodwin, W. Richard 834
Goody, Sam 728
Gookin, R. Burt 768
Gordon, Barnett D. 916
Gordon, Charles O. 729
Gordon, Douglas 117, 118
Gordon, Harry B. 729
Gordon, Ira H. 1298
Gordon, James D. 112
Gordon, Melvin 1330
Gordon, Melvin J. 753, 925
Gordon, Melvin P. 685
Gordon, Melvin S. 1054
Gordon, Michael 866
Gordon, Rex B. 190
Gore, Jerome S. 761
Gorell, Frank 1205

1565

Personnel Index

Gorguze, Vincent T.   636
Gorham, Posey   287
Gorin, William   729
Gorman, Donald J.   541
Gorman, Edward M.   496
Gorman, Leon A.   414
Gormley, John F.   350
Gorseth, Royce P.   295
Goshorn, Lawrence A.   704
Goss, Howard J.   759
Gottesman, R.G.   1054
Gottlieb, Michael   894
Gottlieb, Robert   376, 863
Gottlieb, Sanford   222
Gottwald, Bruce C.   644
Gould, D.D.   933
Gould, Robert   461, 504
Gould, William   353
Gradinger, J. Gary   725
Graf, Robert   1315
Grafft, W.H.   684
Grafman, Howard   502
Gragg, Williford   1359
Graham, David   936
Graham, George   125
Graham, Katharine   1396
Graham, Robert   1082
Graham, Sidney G.   1003
Graham, Thomas C.   836
Grahner, Robert E.   1388
Grais, Edward   1170
Granick, Gordon   519
Granoff, Martin J.   543
Grant, Michael   282
Grant, Roberta   112
Grant, Thomas C.   693
Grantham, Don L.   703
Grass, Alex   1150
Gratz, Samuel   881
Gravely, H.C.   734
Graves, Herbert C.   1345
Graves, J.R.   521, 1087
Graves, Kristin K.   96
Graves, R.E.   1338
Gray, Beatrice Follett   153
Gray, Deane B.   1033
Gray, Howard P.   1385
Gray, James L.   103
Gray, Jesse   217
Gray, Robert   412
Gray, Weldon S.   626
Grayson, Lee H.   1007
Grayson, R.C.   1179
Graziano, Joseph S.   618
Greeley, Samuel S.   939
Green, A.G.   536
Green, Don L.   583
Green, Everett W.   69
Green, Frank W.   881

Green, Jack I.   1020
Green, James   633
Green, James E.   37
Green, Joshu, III   1068
Green, Kinsey B.   193
Green, Richard C.   972
Green, Walter   401
Green, William   987
Greenawalt, Don L.   473
Greenberg, Arnold C.   531
Greenberg, Fred P.   976
Greenberg, Harry H.   1168
Greenberg, Herbert   738
Greenberg, Jack   236
Greenberg, Richard   1000
Greenberg, Robert   758, 1206
Greenblatt, Carl J.   696
Greenblatt, Jay   955
Greene, Allen B.   465
Greene, George S.   1406
Greene, Kermit   878
Greene, Leonard M.   1177
Greene, Liz   285
Greene, Roger C.   534
Greenlee, James V.   1402
Greenman, Bernard   738
Greenman, T.P.   965
Greenough, Harry W.   722
Greenspon, Stuart   286
Greenwald, Manuel   737
Greenwalt, Robert R.   411
Greenwell, Martin D.   64
Greer, Betsey   125
Greer, Lionel W.   684
Gregg, Barbara B.   46
Gregg, John E.   92
Gregg, Walter E.   995
Gregg, Warren E.   399, 769
Gregory, Thorne   451
Gregory, Vincent L.   1158
Greif, Herbert   354
Greif, Norman L.   717
Greiner, Fred J.   250
Gress, K.   295
Grethel, Henry   926
Grevendick, Paul   1027
Grey, J.R.   513
Grey, Richard E.   1350
Griebel, Richard   1306
Grieco, Nicholas   739
Grief, Herbert   544
Griffin, B.E.   1189
Griffin, Ben Hill, III   739
Griffin, D.K.   855
Griffin, John H.   882
Griffin, John T.   739
Griffin, Robert E.   809
Griffin, William   44
Griffith, David L.   65

Griffith, Dean L.   740
Griffith, F.W.   818
Griffith, John E.   1148
Griffiths, G.F., Jr.   1015
Griggy, Kenneth J.   1421
Grimes, Joseph F.   455
Grimm, Bobbi   297
Grimmell, Lester   53
Grinberg, G.   1018
Grober, Jack E.   701
Grochla, Guenter   396
Grochow, Frances   304
Grodnick, William   40
Grogan, Carol J.   60
Grooms, J.W.   1435
Gropper, Edward   1362
Grosfeld, Albert   741
Gross, Albert   1069
Gross, Alex   337
Gross, H.N.   852
Gross, Herbert   107
Gross, Louis N.   451
Gross, Milton M.   741
Gross, Sanford   1215
Grossman, Barbara   106
Grossman, Jack J.   475
Grossman, James   51
Grossman, Peter   1024
Grossman, Sidney L.   53
Grossman, Steven   939
Grossman, William   741
Grosz, Zolten J.   602
Groupe, Leonard M.   277
Grover, Harry G., Jr.   1370
Grover, Robert L.   1238
Gruber, John L.   562
Grubstein, Joseph F.   356
Grumbacher, Joseph   742
Grunchacz, Robert S.   391
Grundfest, Dave, Sr.   1274
Grunewald, Claude J.   1392
Grunther, Nelson   405
Grupe, Henry W.   536
Gruver, William R.   51
Grymes, Douglas   866
Guardiani, F.   399
Gudefin, George M.   743
Gudnason, Harold   339
Guebert, Kenneth E.   405
Guendel, T.J.   496
Guerrant, David E.   1007
Guerry, Alex   509
Guest, James A.   63
Guffey, James V.   61
Guggenheimer, Elinor   55
Guihooley, John J.   1336
Guild, D.S.   764
Guillow, Gertrude H.   744
Guinzburg, Thomas H.   1380

Personnel Index

Guittar, Lee J. 593
Gullang, Marvin O. 633
Gulley, Wik 109
Gullickson, William D. 948
Gummere, Walter C. 1374
Gunsberg, Sheldon 1126
Gunson, Leo J. 546
Gunst, Henry, Sr. 1401
Gunter, Annie Laurie 34
Gunts, Robert F. 1395
Gurbst, H. 1138
Gurley, Diana 102
Gurman, Charles 746
Gurney, Ginsey 292
Gussack, M.P. 733
Gustafson, John G. 49
Gutmann, Max 631
Guttag, Jack 659
Gutterman, Harold M. 979
Gutting, Fred J. 997
Guttman, Zoltan 495
Guynn, Forrest D. 1018
Guyol, John T. 354
Gwinn, Robert P. 1287
Gwodz, Frank J. 253

H

Haas, Anne Jones 117
Haas, Howard G. 1204
Haas, Kenneth J. 480
Haas, Paul E. 540
Haas, Peter E. 1280
Haas, Richard 295
Haas, Ronald C. 1234
Haber, Richard L. 748
Habig, Thomas L. 827, 855
Hack, Sidney 1354
Hackl, A.J. 772
Haddad, Amram 319
Haddad, Frederick L. 767
Haddon, William, Jr. 184
Hadley, J.M. 461
Hadley, James E. 970
Hadley, Marlin L. 417
Hadley, Walter 477
Haehl, John G., Jr. 1012
Haft, Herbert H. 578
Haft, Howard 381
Hagan, John 38
Hagan, Ward S. 1316, 1394
Hagel, Herbert N. 1002
Hagel, Raymond C. 917
Hagel, Roger S. 413
Hageman, Fred L. 55
Hageman, Teri 289

Hagerty, Marilyn 288
Haggar, Joseph M., Jr. 748
Haggarty, John 1359
Haggerty, W.J. 748
Hagle, James L. 1432
Hahn, H.P. 834
Hahn, Lloyd C. 749
Haight, Henry H., IV 636
Haigler, J. Fred 818
Haigley, Harry 275
Hail, Joy 275
Haims, Joseph 524
Halberg, Carl J. 167
Hale, Katharine 108
Hale, Kenneth W. 55
Hale, Legare R. 536
Hale, William M. 1167
Haley, F.T. 460
Hall, Bob 109
Hall, Carlyle W., Jr. 233
Hall, Donald J. 750
Hall, E.V. 252
Hall, George P. 399
Hall, Harry A., III 871
Hall, J.L. 1294
Hall, Jack H. 176
Hall, John N. 1404
Hall, John T. 750
Hall, Joseph E. 504
Hall, R. 751
Hall, R.D. 750
Hall, Rowland F. 763
Hallaren, Mary A. 228
Hallberg, Owen K. 81
Hallman, A.P. 551
Hally, R.B. 1406
Halperin, Maurice A. 749
Halpern, Robert 402
Halpert, Edward 754
Halpert, Leonard S. 529
Halstead, Dorothy 119
Halstead, George C. 337
Halsted, Donald M., Jr. 388
Halverstadt, Robert D. 341
Hamawaki, Y. 846
Hamberger, David 751
Hamel, Dana A. 1065
Hamid, M. 1035
Hamilburg, Daniel M. 1087
Hamilton, C.D.P., III 752
Hamilton, Clarence O. 752
Hamilton, J.S. 1399
Hamilton, Richard P. 676
Hamley, J. David 752
Hamm, Frederick Werner 438
Hammack, L.D. 1307
Hammer, Armand 1027
Hammer, Kenneth F. 535
Hammod, Robert L. 725

Hammond, Charles E. 64
Hammond, Charles E. 1409
Hammond, John A. 962
Hammond, Joseph M. 904
Hammond, Stuart L. 753
Hammons, Dwain 753
Hamper, Francis W. 709
Hampshire, John F. 1173
Hampson, Edward R. 1158
Hampton, Colin C. 1355
Hamstra, John 753
Hanafin, J.W. 403
Hanania, David 1089
Hanback, Bernice Rutherford 1173
Hancock, Thomas 1335
Hancock, Tom 68
Handleman, David 754
Handler, Mark S. 403
Handler, Milton 780
Handley, Raymond G. 437
Handrich, Gordon 240
Handwerker, Murray 998
Hanelt, Frederic M. 35
Haner, Shirley 98
Hanes, Gordon 755
Haney, William E. 376
Hanifin, John W. 512
Hanley, John W. 980
Hanley, William 103
Hanna, George 41
Hanna, Jay S. 755
Hanna, Mark 292
Hanna, Thomas A. 652
Hannan, Rubin Morris 95
Hannigan, Judson 815
Hannon, John W., Jr. 405
Hannon, William M. 991
Hano, George 755
Hans, Merwin S. 229
Hansberger, William L. 1122
Hansbury, G. Donald 341
Hanscum, Art 66
Hanse, Frederick R. 414
Hanselman, Richard W. 1182
Hansen, David F. 1067
Hansen, Dorothy 116
Hansen, Elwood F. 609
Hansen, John A. 756
Hansen, Keld Rosager 577
Hansen, Kenneth W. 567
Hansen, Leroy C. 506
Hansen, W.B. 586
Hanson, Bruce A. 300
Hanson, Charles G. 1282
Hanson, John V. 1424
Hanson, Philip S. 756
Hanson, Richard A. 136
Hapgood, Edward T. 672
Hara, James E. 1230

1567

Personnel Index

Hara, Joe 1347
Harada, Akira 942, 1051
Harbin, John P. 750
Harbin, Virginia R. 100
Hardin, Hal S. 1006
Hardin, Harry T., III 45
Hardin, John A. 992
Harding, John C. 874
Hardwick, Frank T. 758
Harge, Solomon 112
Hargrave, Alexander D. 898
Harinschfeger, Henry 759
Harlen, Nigel 1261
Harman, Denham 138
Harmon, Harold C. 681
Harned, Malcolm S. 504
Harness, E.G. 508
Harnett, Daniel J. 331
Harnik, Peter 127
Harper, Barbara T. 62
Harper, Paul C., Jr. 1006
Harper, Robert 108
Harries, Brenton W. 1263
Harrigan, John F. 1047
Harrington, Doris 962
Harris, Albert P. 1355
Harris, Allan 759
Harris, Donald G. 456
Harris, E.N. 442
Harris, G.D., Jr. 759
Harris, Harold C., Jr. 759
Harris, J.C. 760
Harris, James 457
Harris, Murray 518
Harris, Philip B. 1022
Harris, S. Miller 621
Harris, Shearon 492
Harris, Stewart G. 773
Harris, Walter E., Jr. 613
Harris, William T. 760
Harrison, Ben F. 1359
Harrison, Robert D. 1393
Harriss, Lloyd J. 760
Harrowe, Elliot 892
Harsch, William 70
Harsh, Mary F. 798
Harshbarger, T.L. 1321
Hart, Edward B. 1061
Hart, F. Donald 243
Hart, James A. 16
Hart, Janet 12
Hart, John H. 385
Hart, Joy 293
Hart, L.J. 23
Hart, W.A. 1002
Harte, Houston H. 761
Hartford, Michael 151
Hartl, Albert V. 1041
Hartley, Fred L. 1355

Hartman, Clinton W. 475
Hartman, Grant W. 988
Hartman, I.H., Jr. 886
Hartman, Joseph H. 340
Hartman, Robert S. 383
Hartman, William R. 816
Hartmire, Wayne C., Jr. 215
Hartsig, Richard D. 390
Hartstock, James R. 907
Hartwell, Robert 761
Harty, William A., Jr. 649
Hartz, Paul F. 685
Harvard, L.B. 1289
Harvey, Frank W. 477
Harvey, Herschel A., Jr. 762
Harvey, I.L. 1029
Harvey, Irwin M. 697
Harvey, James A. 500
Harvey, Patricia 107
Harvey, Peter R. 403
Harvey, Robert D.H. 938
Harvin, Lucius H. 1163
Haselton, William R. 1179
Haskell, Edward N. 762
Haskell, Harry G., Jr. 323
Hasman, Karen 277
Haspel, Leo A. 763
Hassenfeld, Harold 637
Hassenfeld, Stephen 762
Hastings, Glenn A. 358
Hastings, Jack 284
Hastings, Richard C., Jr. 1266
Haswell, Anthony 93
Hatch, Edwin I. 711
Hatfield, Robert S. 546
Hathaway, H. Grant 641
Haubert, Carol 476
Haufler, George J. 503
Hauge, Gabriel 927
Haugh, Robert C. 1042
Haughton, Daniel J. 903
Haughton, James 212
Haulicek, Chuck 108
Hauser, Martin 967
Hauserman, William F. 763
Hausman, Arthur H. 364
Hausner, A.H. 570
Haverty, Rawson 763
Haviland, J.M. 763
Haviland, Theodore, II 763
Hawes, Howard 955
Hawkes, Thomas P. 1079
Hawkins, Carl 52
Hawkins, John 299
Hawkins, O.J. 460
Hawkins, S.O. 498
Hawkins, Wilton A. 511
Hawkinson, Robert W. 418
Hawley, Alexander 542

Hawley, Philip M. 494
Haworth, Howard H. 609
Haydanek, Patricia 54
Hayden, Eugene B. 249
Hayden, Keith 113
Hayes, Howard 764
Hayes, Joan 100
Hayes, Laura 307
Hayes, Thomas F. 1076
Hayman, C.M., Jr. 683
Haynes, H.J. 1264
Hazeltine, Sherman 667
Headlee, Richard H. 338
Heald, George, Sr. 471
Health, James W. 774
Hearin, Robert M. 1195
Heath, G.A. 925
Heath, John L. 766
Heaton, Berton W. 49
Heazlitt, Sherman 1052
Hebert, William R. 477
Hechinger, John W. 767
Hecht, George J. 1055
Hecht, Howard W. 946
Hecht, Irvin H. 251
Heckethorn, William R. 767
Hect, Joseph H. 610
Hedberg, Roy 1289
Hedden, Russell A. 848
Hedger, Steve 117
Hedglin, Daniel L. 1026
Hedrick, Frank E. 417
Hefner, Hugh H. 1085
Hegeman, Walter L. 1300
Hegg, Allan B. 502
Hegre, T.A. 428
Heide, Andrew H. 767
Heidrich, James K., Sr. 959
Heidt, George, Jr. 1170
Heilicher, Amos 1078
Heilman, Leonard 1376
Heilmann, John E. 1244
Heiman, Howard 1066
Heiman, Jordan 817
Heimann, Robert K. 350
Heimstra, Norman W. 180
Hein, Gary L. 898
Heineman, Albert P. 548
Heineman, Ben W. 1021
Heineman, Ralph 353
Heinkel, Fred V. 972
Heinz, Harro K. 1125
Heinze, Karl G. 1093
Heironimus, Robert A. 365
Heise, Kenan 277
Heiser, Arthur H. 1324
Heistein, B. John 1191
Heithaus, Harriet 290
Hekman, Edgar J. 768

Personnel Index

Hekman, John H. 1429
Helfer, Edward 952
Helgason, Sigurdur 802
Helland, R.E. 486
Heller, Henry R., Jr. 330, 758
Heller, L.H., Sr. 1020
Heller, W.G. 868
Hellman, Bernard A. 441
Hellman, Irving 1064
Helm, DeWitt F., Jr. 966
Helm, Jacquelyn V. 99
Helms, J. Ben 916
Helms, J.L. 1082
Heman, Richard D., Jr. 68
Hemingway, Stuart C. 1091
Heminway, Willard E., Jr. 769
Hemmerich, Alfred G. 425
Hemminger, Arthur J. 692
Henderson, Claude 704
Henderson, Judy 65
Henderson, Luther A. 1079
Hendon, Norris B. 388
Heneger, Jacob E. 1368
Hengstler, Heinz R. 767
Henke, Harold 783
Henke, Harry, III 1167
Henke, William G. 1408
Henkel, Mary M. 770
Henkin, Daniel J. 704
Henley, Carl 913
Henley, Henry H. 527
Henning, James L. 1084
Henning, John 333, 947
Henry, H.W., Jr. 732
Henry, Robert 481
Henry, William A. 1231
Henslee, Doris L. 210
Hensley, Stuart, K. 794, 1145
Henson, Luton 771
Henze, Calvin R. 953
Herbert, Charles J. 752
Herbert, Edward F. 258
Herbert, William D. 499
Herbst, John F. 771
Herleman, W.N. 1433
Herlihy, Sylvester 506
Herman, Bruce E. 474
Herman, I.M. 1139
Hermanson, Jerry 972
Hermenet, Eugene W. 1225
Hermes, Charles R. 617
Herr, Frank V. 947
Herrera, Frank E. 626
Herring, James P. 869
Herrmann, Raymond R., Jr. 948
Herron, F. Leon, Jr. 1198
Hersheway, Charles 1074
Hershner, John D. 1357
Herskovic, W. 520

Herter, Ann 110
Hertford, Robert 1382
Hertzberg, Ira 773
Hertzler, L.M. 776
Herzog, Lester W., Jr. 1000
Heslin, Mary M. 39
Hess, Charles W. 1253
Hess, M. Henry 935
Hesse, John R. 354
Hessey, Jay 109
Hesson, H. 368
Heth, Donald G. 895
Hetzek, Theodore B. 205
Hetzel, Roger H. 366
Heumann, Fred J. 1034
Hewlett, Augustus H. 137
Hewlett, William R. 774
Hexom, J. Gene 115
Heyer, Arthur J. 774
Heyl, Donald C. 1382
Heyman, Leonard J. 774
Heyman, Lyons J. 684
Heyman, Sol 995
Heywood, John 774
Heywood, John H. 902
Hiatt, Arnold 1094, 1281, 1400
Hibbert, Maurice E. 504
Hibschman, James R. 899
Hickey, Francis 68
Hickey, Walter B.D., Sr. 776
Hickman, Paula 307
Hickman, William P. 784
Higgins, Carlisle W., Jr. 1373
Higgins, Edgar T. 422
Higgins, James H. 952
High, Nancy 264
Highleyman, Samuel L. 1136
Hightower, William H., Jr. 1320
Higier, Julius A. 562
Hildebrand, Gordon F. 482
Hildreth, Gordon 858
Hilgendorf, Robert 52
Hilgert, Olive 441
Hill, Carrick A. 591
Hill, David L. 443, 1042
Hill, Dwight A. 530
Hill, Edwin H., Jr. 777
Hill, Francis F. 1021
Hill, Frederick B., III 970
Hill, J.M. 505, 1123
Hill, Morton A. 90
Hill, Richard D. 667
Hill, Richard K. 382
Hill, Thomas F. 409
Hillerich, John A. 778
Hilley, David B. 1429
Hillman, Zahn J. 512
Hills, Harold 993

Hills, Reuben W., III 778
Hillyard, R. Haskell 778
Hilsinger, A.R., Jr. 645
Hilton, Barron 778
Hilton, Charles M. 462
Himmel, Martin 829
Hinch, John B. 325
Hinckley, G.F. Steedman 1042
Hinds, C.C. 941
Hinds, Jackson C. 1358
Hine, George A. 1372
Hiner, Robert L. 359
Hinerfield, Norman M. 847
Hines, Andrew H., Jr. 675
Hines, Marshall A. 62
Hinkle, B.J. 816
Hinkley, D.R. 636
Hinman, Franklin R. 1397
Hintlian, Harry 591
Hintlian, James T. 886
Hipkens, J.P. 145
Hipp, Francis M. 894
Hipwell, Harry H. 779
Hirsch, Albert Linz 899
Hirsch, E. 617
Hirsch, Harry D. 989
Hirsch, Henry 1402
Hirsch, Ira 1048
Hirsch, Jack 574
Hirsch, Lewis A. 779, 1054
Hirsch, Murray B. 444
Hirschberg, Arthur A. 1385
Hirschfield, Erich 1421
Hirschhorn, Donald S. 780
Hite, J.T. 817
Hoak, D.R., Jr. 1405
Hobart, W.H., Jr. 780
Hobbs, Matthew S. 744
Hobbs, William D. 1143
Hobby, William P. 792
Hobe, Donald 780
Hobert, Jack R. 402
Hobson, Willis S. 1212
Hochberg, Irving 1280
Hochfelder, J. Gene 418
Hochstadter, Alex 1142
Hochstein, Bernard 941
Hock, Conrad, Jr. 1420
Hodges, Luther H. 1018
Hodges, Ralph D., Jr. 259
Hodgkins, Theodore R. 682
Hodgson, William M., Jr. 1264
Hodin, Jay 176
Hodin, Morris L. 713
Hoehne, Clifford D. 908
Hoel, Kjell S. 1304
Hofert, Alvin H. 781
Hoff, Stephen J. 538, 781
Hoffberger, C.B. 836

Personnel Index

Hoffberger, Jerold C. 999
Hoffer, Robert M. 1426
Hoffinger, Martin 526
Hoffman, Dennis J. 279
Hoffman, E.C. 1235
Hoffman, Edwin K. 1430
Hoffman, Herbert S. 432, 781
Hoffman, J.H. 927
Hoffman, James E. 1162
Hoffman, John D. 238
Hoffman, M.E. 781
Hoffman, R.L. 781
Hoffman, Richard E. 324
Hoffman, Robert J. 788
Hofstad, Ralph 879
Hogan, Ben 320
Hogan, C.F. 502
Hogan, Ernest L. 1068
Hogeman, George L. 394, 1061
Hogg, James G. 1087
Hogg, William J. 389
Hoglin, David 302
Hoglund, John W. 185
Hogue, Don F. 778
Hohner, Frank 782
Hoki, Murray M. 297
Hokom, Dee 276
Holas, Frank W. 446
Holberg, Bruce 301
Holck, Charles H. 426
Holcomb, Lindsay, Sr. 1081
Holden, Richard Y. 752
Holder, George H. 773
Holderness, H. Dail 492
Holderness, Howard 829
Holding, Lewis R. 667
Holding, Robert L. 89
Holeman, Frank 190
Hollaender, Sidney W. 646
Holland, Eugene R. 1146
Holland, John B. 1356
Holland, Richard F. 353
Hollander, Marshall, J. 825
Hollands, John H. 397
Holleb, Robert 783
Hollen, Sharron 284
Hollin, Harris N. 890
Hollingsworth, G.R. 974
Hollingsworth, Mark 784
Hollis, Raymond 735
Hollowell, Wayne E. 961
Holm, Melvin C. 494
Holman, D.V. 328
Holman, George 877
Holmes, David H. 823
Holmes, Howard S. 510
Holmes, John B. 567
Holmes, John R.H. 760
Holmes, Thomas A. 810

Holmes, Walter S., Jr. 474
Holmgren, Edward L. 212
Holsclaw, Charles H. 785
Holt, Ralph M., Jr. 785
Holterbosch, H.D. 785
Holton, I.J. 789
Holtzer, H.N. 524
Holzer, Julian 785
Holtzman, Samuel 403
Holtzworth, Charles W. 1002
Honig, O. Charles 336
Honigberg, Joel D. 934
Hood, Elizabeth 49
Hood, Robert C. 369
Hood, William 796
Hooffstetter, J.E. 809
Hook, August F. 787
Hooker, J. Clyde, Jr. 787
Hooper, Blake H. 984
Hooper, J.E., Jr. 788
Hooper, William K. 337
Hoopman, H.D. 928
Hoover, Charles M. 1161
Hoover, Robert R. 1152
Hopkin, Alfred W. 381
Hopkins, Brenda 115
Hopp, Philip 788
Hopper, C.C. 1250
Hopper, Lewis 302
Hopper, Richard N. 82, 249
Hoppock, David W. 464
Horan, John J. 954
Horan, Jules 52
Horan, Raymond E. 824
Horn, Carl, Jr. 612
Horn, Earl G. 716
Horn, James P. 353
Horn, Robert E. 321
Hornady, Harold P. 485
Horne, Frank L. 701
Horner, Richard E. 834
Horness, Joseph W. 462
Hornig, W. Walter 707
Horowitz, Abraham H. 789
Horowitz, Ben 148
Horowitz, I. Ronald 1367
Horowitz, Isadore 746
Horowitz, Jack 422
Horowitz, Robert 706
Horowitz, Stanley 635
Horrell, Maurice W. 1152
Horrigan, Edward A. 464
Horrocks, Mike 92
Horrocks, Wayne 117
Horsman, John G. 450
Horstman, Robert L. 1156
Horton, Harold L. 565
Horton, Jack K. 1247
Horward, Frank 289

Horwich, Edward I. 941
Horwitch, Joseph W. 935
Hosmer, Walker J. 966
Hostetler, John E. 579
Hostetter, Nelson 209
Hotchkiss, Bruce 274
Hotchkiss, Hilton D. 627
Hotchkiss, Ralf 197
Hough, John 790
Houghton, Malcolm 489
House, James T. 1331
Housen, Charles B. 642
Houser, Robert W. 1095
Housman, Edward L. 393
Houston, Walter A. 135
Howard, Edward L. 1000
Howard, Fred H. 160
Howard, Harry S., Jr. 351
Howard, Howard K. 1188
Howard, Howell 779
Howard, J.W. 951
Howard, Jasper S. 792
Howard, Morton 1340
Howard, Robert T. 999
Howard, William L. 688
Howarth, Frederick W. 749
Howden, Ted 52
Howe, Claudett 47
Howe, Wesley J., Jr. 416
Howell, A. Clewis 930
Howell, George B. 547
Howell, John S. 793
Howie, Jack 320
Howland, Lewis S. 1324
Howlett, J. Richard 462
Howlett, Joe R. 478
Howlett, William 1393
Hoye, Robert G. 837
Hoyer, Vincent E. 1010
Hoyos, Lillian 34
Hoyt, Charles L. 793
Hoyt, Joseph H. 1160
Hubbard, Paul H. 152
Hubbard, Robert L. 349
Hubbard, William 1364
Hubbell, Virginia 95
Hubley, Nathon C., Jr. 495
Hubley, Raymond C., Jr. 130
Huckaby, Loreta 288
Hudiburg, Everett 184
Hudson, Douglas F. 663
Hudson, Joseph L., Jr. 794
Huff, Henry P. 1336
Huff, Major 534
Huffman, Joseph E. 387
Huffman, Kenneth W. 323
Huffman, R.W. 1244
Hugel, Charles E. 1029
Huges, Robert M. 608

Personnel Index

Huggins, Charles N. 1206
Hughes, J. Lawrence 985
Hughes, Robert 1149
Hulan, G.H., Jr. 992
Hull, A.M. 1204
Hull, J. Brannon 795
Hull, Jerome W. 419, 1047
Hulse, Frank W. 1247
Hulseman, L.J. 1243
Hulsen, Robert B. 983
Hulsey, Billie 297
Humble, David R. 1209
Hummel, James A. 1185
Humphrey, Bruce 289
Humphrey, Clifford C. 126
Humphreys, Burnham L. 410
Humphries, D.M., Jr. 448
Hundt, Donald D. 1204
Huneeus, A. 940
Hungerford, John R. 1247
Hunt, Cathi 522
Hunt, Errol 115
Hunt, William D. 1437
Hunt, William J. 912
Hunter, Edward C. 909
Hunter, J. Robert 20
Hunter, Joseph 796
Hunting, Allen I. 1279
Huntington, Robert I. 796
Huntley, Fulton A. 1405
Huppert, Everett R. 686
Hurcomb, Thomas J. 501
Hurdlebrink, M.W. 936
Hurley, A.F. 1228
Hurlin, D.D. 727
Hurst, Archie S. 116
Hurth, John E. 47
Husonsky, Ivan S. 955
Hussey, Edward J. 894
Hustis, Joan 278
Huston, Michael 110
Hutchens, George W. 430, 679
Hutches, Clarence F., II 68
Hutchinson, James A., Jr. 455
Hutchinson, James F. 804
Hutchinson, R.L. 960
Hutchinson, Sue 291
Hutchinson, William Y. 547
Huth, John 289
Hutton, George N., Jr. 797
Hutton, Robert W. 404, 905
Hutton, William R. 214
Hutzler, Joel G.D. 798
Huwlett, Susan 118
Huws-Davies, James Y. 1044
Hvass, Kresten 990
Hyan, Jaishon 826
Hyde, C.F., Jr. 1040
Hyde, Cliff C. 751

Hyde, Edwin 965
Hyde, George T. 953
Hyde, Harry, Jr. 113
Hyde, K.C. Vander 743
Hyde, Richard L. 798
Hyer, Frank S. 1317

I

Iacocca, Lee 679
Iason, Girard 641
Idestone, Frank F. 1086
Ielmini, Mario 1060
Ignatius, Paul R. 241
Iida, Tetsutaro 1303
Iiwin, J. 985
Iizuka, K. 1361
Ikeda, Toro 428
Iler, J.C., III 561
Imig, Joanne 276
Imming, Bernard J. 264
Indelicato, Venerando J. 958
Ingerman, Ira 920
Ingersoll, Paul M. 1106
Ingram, Barbara 109
Ingram, Edger W., Jr. 1412
Ingram, John W. 514
Inman, Harold W. 1014
Intorre, Joseph V. 180
Invernizzi, Antonio 418
Ireland, Donald A. 693
Irmischer, Paul 818
Irmiter, Pete 299
Irving, Rebecca 286
Irwin, John 457
Irwin, Richard B. 683
Irwin, Samuel N. 1299
Isbell, Marion W. 1122
Israel, Joseph S. 687
Issackedes, Jordan 705
Issenberg, Daniel 898
Ito, Kichi 826
Itzkowitz, Murray 146
Ivans, W.S. 530
Ivie, Robert M. 744
Ivie, W.M. 874
Ix, Robert E. 476, 1197

J

Jack, Alec R. 797
Jackson, Brenda 115
Jackson, Jack B. 1066

Jackson, Kelly L. 50
Jackson, R. 1108
Jackson, Richard M. 1203
Jackson, Robert T. 1077
Jackson, S.W. 1402
Jackson, W.R. 525
Jacobi, Eileen M. 245
Jacobs, Charles R. 283
Jacobs, Herman 749, 784
Jacobs, Larry 298
Jacobs, Melvin 467
Jacobs, Phil 1075
Jacobs, Richard C. 831
Jacobsohn, Howard G. 632
Jacobson, Dan 665
Jacobson, Ira 530
Jacobson, Michael 83
Jacoff, Richard 736
Jaeger, Jack R. 967
Jaehnig, Adele 282
Jaffe, J. 1195
Jaffe, Leo 536
Jaffe, Sidney 691
Jaffee, Richard M. 1029
Jager, Frank P. 1355
Jaharis, Michael, Jr. 854
Jahn, Tom F. 651
Jaicks, W.A., Jr. 877
Jakaus, Delores D. 47
James, Forrest H., Jr. 600
James, Frank N. 533
James, Howard P. 1217
James, J.W. 999
James, John V. 609
James, Mike 272
James, W.H. 1011
Jamison, Edith 105
Jamison, G.O. 410
Jandecek, George W. 523
Janover, Robert G. 356, 390, 745
Jansey, Theodore T. 1341
Japp, Leonard, Sr. 828
Jaques, Jerald T. 632
Jarvis, Edwin H. 865
Jaus, William C. 434
Javin, Linda 115
Jeffers, Henry W., III 1390
Jeffrey, Balfour S. 844
Jeffries, James D. 66
Jellison, Fern 38
Jenkins, Charles H. 1107
Jenkins, George 779
Jenkins, Lonnie P. 612
Jenkins, R. Lee 1086
Jenkins, William M. 1205
Jenks, Downing B. 972
Jenks, James M. 338
Jenks, Marry Ellen 737

Personnel Index

Jenn, Louis J.   829
Jenner, Myron   829
Jennings, Edward J., Jr.   1289
Jennings, Gerald M.   646
Jennings, Joseph A.   1362
Jennings, Neal L.   1076
Jennings, W.H., Jr.   409
Jensen, J. Lowell   67
Jensen, R.V.   833
Jensen, Robert P.   705
Jensen, Ronald R.   1051
Jeppsson, George A.   883
Jersig, Harry D.   905
Jewell, David A.   30
Joanis, John W.   1209
Johansen, Paul E., Sr.   833
Johns, Ray A.   868
Johnson, A.Y.   1067
Johnson, Allan R.   1180
Johnson, Darrel   1004
Johnson, Donald M.   331
Johnson, E. Alan   767
Johnson, Ed L.   822
Johnson, Edna DeCoursey   104
Johnson, Edward R.   1341
Johnson, George E.   835
Johnson, Glendon E.   358
Johnson, Gregory H.   811
Johnson, H. Clay Evans   816
Johnson, H.L.   620
Johnson, Harry A.   1255
Johnson, Herbert H.   1427
Johnson, Howard B.   792
Johnson, J. Hilbert   776
Johnson, J. Phillips L.   569
Johnson, J.R.   1167
Johnson, Julius X.   45
Johnson, Katie Everette   229
Johnson, Langdon   648
Johnson, Leland H.   668
Johnson, Lesie D.   1054
Johnson, Martha C.   130
Johnson, Marucie D.S.   521
Johnson, Milton G.   881
Johnson, P.J.   181
Johnson, Philip L.   213
Johnson, Spencer A.   259
Johnson, Stephen I.   763
Johnson, Steve   113
Johnson, Susan L.   107
Johnson, V.S., Jr.   336
Johnson, W.W.   405
Johnson, Walter   1241
Johnson, Wesley R.   1429
Johnson, William R.   67
Johnston, Don   1320
Johnston, Gansey R.   938
Johnston, Gaston   701
Johnston, Kenneth H.   255

Johnston, Richard B.   352
Jolly, Elton   218
Jonas, Donald L.   406
Jonas, Dorothy   95
Jones, Bernice F.   271
Jones, Carl O.   963
Jones, Donald W.   327
Jones, Douglas A.   1154
Jones, E.C.   836
Jones, E.I.   1316
Jones, Edwin S.   667
Jones, Gilbert H.   1365
Jones, Harry D.   450
Jones, Harvey   837
Jones, Henry E.   1079
Jones, Horace   468
Jones, J.M., Jr.   292
Jones, Jack   113
Jones, Jerry J.   1182
Jones, Joseph F.   501
Jones, Judith   99
Jones, K.R.   737
Jones, Mary Gardiner   1409
Jones, Reginald H.   705
Jones, Kenneth E.   111
Jones, Richard   300
Jones, Roger W.   1205
Jones, Ronald W.   792
Jones, Roy H.   553
Jones, Sam   276
Jones, Saunders   388, 433
Jones, T. Lawrence   244
Jordan, Candice   194
Jordan, D.D.   792
Jordan, Ernest M., Jr.   70
Jordan, H. Dale   691
Jordan, J.H.   1389
Jordan, Jane B.   241
Jordan, John F.   402
Jorden, Betty   102
Joseph, Merwin J.   847
Joseph, Wilhelm H.   234
Josephs, C.R.   548
Jovanovich, William   757
Joy, Linda   47, 106
Juarez, Rodolfo   219
Juceam, Arthur D.   889
Judd, C.M.   453
Judge, Curtis H.   906
Judge, David H.   644
Juell, Bruce C.   736
Julian, Anthony C.   58
Jung, D.R.   1340
Junkunc, Allan B.   418
Jurist, Nathan   1442
Jurkops, Theodore F.   517
Jurutka, Peter J.   556
Juster, Leon   1262
Justin, Enid   1015

Justin, John S.   840
Juttner, Gordon J.   1156

K

Kabat, Herbert   1035
Kaehler, Leonard   748
Kaeser, H.E.   356
Kagan, Irving   1067
Kagan, Norman   1165
Kagen, Joseph   577
Kahn, E.A.   489
Kahn, Julius M.   579, 842
Kahn, Leo   1109
Kahn, Marvin   648
Kahn, Roger   98
Kahn, Walter   637
Kaiser, Albert F.   745
Kaiser, Edgar F.   842
Kaiser, John E.   918
Kaiser, Paul R.   1306
Kaitz, Ben B.   1050
Kalb, Mary   111
Kalinoski, Doris D.   113
Kalinski, Felix   1343
Kalkman, James R.   57
Kallman, Cynthia   274
Kalman, Bernard   533
Kalmonovitz, Paul   653
Kalov, Jerry   830
Kaltman, Jack   546
Kalwajtys, Raymond S.   707
Kaman, Charles H.   843
Kamins, Bernard F.   95
Kamins, R.L.   523
Kamins, Seymour   475
Kaminsky, H.R.   843
Kaminsky, Sol   161
Kammerman, O.   717
Kanabasch, C.T.   874
Kane, Alan   599
Kane, Dean   41
Kane, E.R.   614
Kane, Robert F.   980
Kanelos, George A.   367
Kanoff, Harry   1313
Kanter, Bernard   824
Kanter, James I.   343
Kantor, Sam   1344
Kantz, Norman J.   412
Kaplan, Alvin   1155
Kaplan, Charles A.   623
Kaplan, Harold M.   844
Kaplan, Ira   857
Kaplan, Leonard P.   381
Kaplan, Mandall   759

Personnel Index

Kaplan, Ronald 844
Kaplan, Sheldon 740
Kaplan, Simon 844
Kapp, M.L. 817
Kappe, Stanley E. 121
Karatsis, George 1160
Karelis, L. Howard 342
Karls, Ronald M. 1126
Karoll, I. 590
Karosen, Leon 1440
Karp, Herb 839
Karp, J.L. 845
Karp, J.M. 855
Karpatkin, Rhoda H. 86
Karpeles, John J. 198
Karpen, King 334
Karr, Norman 254
Karsnitz, George S. 615
Kashi, George M. 59
Kasin, Martin 1072
Kaskel, Edward 845
Kassan, Martin 151
Kasser, Raymond H. 845
Kasten, George F. 668
Kastin, Jack J. 886
Katayama, Y. 1014
Kather, E.N. 370
Kathol, Kay 303
Katsafanas, Kathryn 60
Katt, Shirley 51
Kattan, Arthur A. 1029
Kattel, Richard L. 521
Kattner, Patty 293
Katz, Ira R. 761
Katz, Joseph M. 885, 891, 1053
Katz, Mrs. Michael 147
Katzman, Lawrence 848
Kauffman, Ewing M. 931
Kauffman, John 289
Kauffman, Raymond R. 177
Kaufman, Earle B. 448
Kaufman, Howard 42
Kaufman, Howard C. 649
Kaufman, Jean 286
Kaufman, Lester G. 1008
Kaufman, Rolf 1403
Kaufmann, Lester M. 846
Kauth, Donald Z. 154
Kaveny, J. Gordon 1115
Kawamoto, I. 780
Kawashima, Hiroshi 1436
Kay, William M. 797
Kaye, Paul 373
Kaye, Tanya 311
Kayle, J.P. 1047
Keach, Margaret Sally 155
Kearney, Calvin 109
Kearney, John E. 806

Keating, Kerry 974
Keating, Robert J. 1058
Keating, Stephen F. 787
Keating, William J. 519
Keay, James 1140
Keays, John W. 378
Kech, Pauline 97
Keegan, William 699
Keeling, E.W. 1219
Keenan, Donald L. 808
Keenan, J.J. 1405
Keenan, R.L. 1393
Keeney, Irene 285
Keeney, Lafayette 1178
Kees, Wayne G. 1182
Keeter, James P. 797
Kehrl, H.H. 1033
Keim, Robert P. 240
Keimer, Ronald 771
Keirns, W. Jeff 265
Keisman, Daniel 1423
Keister, Charles R. 694
Keister, George 830
Kellam, Connie 285
Keller, Betty C. 45
Keller, Charles A. 849
Keller, George M. 948
Keller, H.A. 849
Keller, J. Harrison 1180
Keller, R. Davidson, Jr. 206
Kelley, Edward W., Jr. 849
Kelley, James H. 490
Kelley, Lawrence P. 1434
Kelley, Paul J. 1351
Kelley, Robb B. 637
Kelley, S.D. 581
Kelley, Susan 119
Kelley, W.E. 373
Kelley, Wendell 805
Kelley, William H. 722
Kellman, Alan 48
Kellman, Morrie 720
Kellner, Jack F. 711
Kelly, Bobbie 509
Kelly, Douglas, Jr. 1151
Kelly, Harold A. 429
Kelly, James J. 853
Kelly, Lloyd A. 1011
Kelly, Orville E. 159
Kelly, Paul 305
Kelly, Paul J., Jr. 113
Kelly, Phyllis 279
Kelly, R.M. 807
Kelly, Sam 62
Kelly, Stephen E. 253
Kelly, William J. 58
Kelly, William R. 850
Kemp, Margeret 37
Kemp, Nelson J. 758

Kemp, Robert D. 342
Kemp, T.P. 381
Kemp, William P., Jr. 850
Kemper, James S., Jr. 358, 850
Kendall, Chester 758
Kendall, Donald M. 1068
Kendall, James 265
Kendell, Harvey A. 1270
Kendrick, Marron 1193
Kendrick, Mary 287
Kendrick, Meade 1154
Kendrick, Warren R. 851
Kenna, Frank 932
Kennard, Byron 91
Kennard, Edward C. 476
Kennedy, D. Herman 1249
Kennedy, David O'D. 852
Kennedy, Donald S. 1030
Kennedy, J.B. 67
Kennedy, J.W. 1438
Kennedy, John P. 953
Kennedy, Maynard 218
Kennedy, Pegg 279
Kennedy, Robert J., III 67
Kennedy, Robert S. 1254
Kent, J.W. 513
Kent, Margaret M. 99
Keogh, Bernard T. 1405
Keough, Donald R. 528
Keppel, Robert F., Jr. 852
Kerans, John 312
Kerby, William F. 607
Kerenge, John F., Jr. 177
Kerley, James K. 34
Kern, Charles 852
Kern, Charles J. 1433
Kern, Irving J. 589
Kerr, H.S. 412
Kerr, James R. 494
Kerr, William 853
Kerrigan, James L. 739
Kersey, R.E. 356
Kersey, R.W. 591
Kerstaw, Andrew G. 1028
Kerzner, Alfred M. 1077
Kessler, Chester 853
Kessler, Siegfried 1442
Ketcham, F. Lee, Jr. 767
Ketner, Ralph W. 678
Ketner, Will T. 70
Kettenburg, Paul A. 853
Kettlewell, George 1015
Keyser, F. Ray, Jr. 1376
Keyworth, R. Allen 532
Kiam, Victor K. 423
Kibler, Frank M. 658
Kidd, Mrs. William R. 182
Kidder, R.E. 1413
Kiefer, Charles P. 433

1573

Personnel Index

Kiernan, R.L. 1311
Kiewel, Frank D. 732
Kill, B. Robert 1299
Kille, Jack 102
Killgallon, William C. 636, 674, 1029
Kilmer, J.E. 321
Kilpatrick, James J. 232
Kimball, Alberta S. 964
Kimsey, Edwin R. 767
Kincaid, J. Wade 856
King, David F. 1397
King, E. William 939
King, Edward J., Jr. 857
King, Edward L. 199
King, G.P. 756
King, Sharon 311
King, Thomas L. 527
King, Walter W. 569
King, William T. 1152
Kingsley, David G. 320
Kinkead, William S. 858
Kinnaird, W.H. 1215
Kinney, Samuel M., Jr. 1354
Kinsley, Samuel R. 731
Kinst, George F. 987
Kip, John H. 948
Kirbey, Russell W. 146
Kirby, Arthur F. 407
Kirby, Richard L. 525
Kirchoff, Charles L. 688
Kiriacon, Arthur J. 495
Kirk, Kenneth W. 387
Kirk, Roger M. 605
Kirkland, James G. 1288
Kirkley, Dorothy 42
Kirkorian, Kirk C., Jr. 901
Kirkpatrick, Oran G. 864
Kirkpatrick, Robert L. 122
Kirkwood, Clara 119
Kirsch, David A. 1014
Kirsch, John W. 859
Kirsch, Lee 859
Kirtland, Clifford M., Jr. 558
Kissenger, Walter B. 342
Kissling, A.C. 859
Kissner, J. 677
Kittinger, E.P. 1361
Kitzman, Oliver S. 63
Kives, Philip 841
Kivett, Jerome S. 1134
Kiviat, Harold 616
Kjellberg, Jonas C. 1175
Klassen, David R. 163
Klauber, Roger 860
Klehm, Howard G. 699
Kleiman, Lowell A. 1197
Kleiman, Murray 326
Klein, Alfred 1264

Klein, Edgar A. 861
Klein, Frank 492
Klein, George 410
Klein, Jonas B. 623
Klein, Joseph 1077
Klein, Justin 28
Klein, Michael S. 680
Klein, Murray 333
Klein, Thomas 1374
Klein, Walter C. 466
Kleinbart, Leon 676
Kleiner, Mark 644
Kleinert, Robert W. 1010
Kleinwald, Arthur 1371
Klemer, Robert W. 655
Klepper, Lawrence R. 580
Kleven, Paul I. 848, 861
Kley, John A. 557
Klimczak, Ernest J. 343
Kline, Sidney D. 350
Klinger, Richard E. 783
Klinghoffer, Albert 1164
Klingsberg, Cyrus 124
Klinsky, William B. 337
Klintrup, Helen 153
Klipsch, Paul W. 861
Klopp, Wayne C. 358
Kloss, Henry 330
Klothe, William M. 1064
Kluener, Robert G. 483
Kluge, John W. 958
Kluger, Samuel B. 621
Klumb, Richard A. 1405
Knapp, John 48
Kneibert, Douglas 284
Knenlein, Donald R. 13
Knerr, Richard P. 1410
Knight, D. Victor 1204
Knight, J.A. 766
Knight, John F. 1371
Knight, V.C. 327
Knoerzer, L. Peter, Jr. 505
Knope, Donald J. 862
Knopf, Allan J. 851
Knopf, L.A. 959
Knott, James 863
Knowles, Legh F., Jr. 415
Knowlton, Winthrop 759
Knox, Mitchell 863
Knudsen, S.E. 1413
Knudson, Barry P. 1391
Knutson, Lee T. 960
Knutson, Thelma 68
Kober, Helen 196
Koch, David A. 731
Koch, Robert L. 863
Koch, Roderic M. 1264
Koch, William C., Jr. 61
Kodaira, I. 1334

Koehler, Sherry 127
Koentopf, David 706
Koeppel, Donald A. 439
Koffler, Sol 357
Koffman, Burton I. 735
Kofoed, Jack F. 863
Kogelschatz, G.L. 536
Koger, Robert K. 69
Kohl, Herbert 864
Kohl, Richard W. 845
Kohler, Herbert V., Jr. 864
Kohler, Robert E. 1381
Kohn, Jacques 403
Kohn, Louis B., II 780
Kohne, Kenyon K. 37
Kohnstomm, Paul L. 864
Kohorn, Kurt S. 683
Koin, N.L. 634
Kojis, John J. 922
Koldyke, Martin J. 747
Kole, Richard L. 865
Kolin, Oscar 768
Kollegger, James G. 126
Koller, Edmund B. 1392
Koltnow, Peter G. 184
Koltun, Sanfred 869
Komessar, Saul 1123
Komfeld, Lewis 1120
Konheim, Carolyn S. 134
Konz, R.L. 865
Koons, J.F., Jr. 467
Koontz, Raymond 597
Kopald, G.E. 464, 573
Koplow, Jack 843
Koppel, Stanton R. 182
Koppelman, Theodore 874
Korn, Carl 619
Korn, Philip A. 467
Korn, William T. 340
Kornet, J.L. 1075
Korth, William H. 38
Kosier, Howard W. 1181
Kosmin, Louis 548
Koss, John C. 866
Kosta, Peter L. 824
Kostelni, James C. 711
Koster, Herbert 6
Kotelchuck, Ronda 154
Kothlow, Richard J. 391
Kotkins, Henry 1233
Kottler, Louis E. 858
Kotzin, Tobias 321
Koupal, Edwin A. 132
Koupal, Joyce 97
Koury, Joseph D. 867
Kovens, Michael 1363
Kovier, Everett 414
Kowalski, Stephen Z. 867
Koza, Joseph D. 446

Personnel Index

Kraines, Lawrence M. 867
Kramer, Albert H. 12
Kramer, Arnold, Sr. 1341
Kramer, Ben D. 1247
Kramer, Debora D. 138
Kramer, Fred K. 64
Kramer, L.D. 853
Kramer, Martin 1231
Kramer, Philip 349
Kramer, R.P. 731
Kramer, Victor H. 234
Krantzman, Merle M. 732
Krasl, George J. 887
Krasney, S.J. 539
Krassner, Matthew H. 530
Krause, Charles A. 868
Krause, Robert F. 1008, 1009
Krausman, Arthur H. 324
Krauthamer, Harold 104
Krebs, Walter O. 361
Kreer, Henry B. 188
Krehbiel, John H., Sr. 978
Kreider, Frank B. 450
Kreiss, Sidney J. 868
Kreizenbeck, Mrs. Frank P. 100
Krementz, Richard, Jr. 868
Kremer, Merle W. 696
Kremsdorf, J. 743
Krensky, Harold 660
Krenzler, Leo M. 357
Kretchmer, C.M. 357
Kretchmer, Walter 1064
Krewson, C.N. 709
Krey, John F. 868
Krieg, Anthony W. 571
Krier, Ray D. 868
Krihorian, Robert V. 1143
Krinsk, K. Arnold 783
Krisch, Joel 358
Kroenert, Randolph J. 408
Kronsberg, Auram 628
Kropf, R.T. 418
Kropp, Robert 542
Krueger, A.E. 538
Krueger, Alan E. 41
Krueger, Marilyn A. 49
Krughoff, Robert 94
Kruidenier, David 592
Krumm, Daniel J. 945
Krussman, Louis F. 1340
Krysiak, Joseph F. 388
Kubicek, Jan 63
Kuc, John 1364
Kuebler, Thomas L. 1354
Kuepper, George C. 869
Kugel, Julian E. 489
Kuhn, Anton J., Jr. 1064
Kuhn, Donald W. 774
Kuhn, Jack W. 870

Kuhn, Margaret 204
Kuhn, Robert A. 353
Kuhre, V.J. 1280
Kummel, Eugene H. 946
Kunkleman, Benjamin F. 451
Kunkler, J.E. 378
Kunnes, Richard 159
Kunsberg, Stanley H. 1011
Kuretsky, William H. 48
Kurie, E.J. 1163
Kurtz, Irving W., Jr. 439
Kurtz, Ralph 1439
Kurtz, Robert M., Jr. 870
Kurtzer, Robert 693
Kushner, Morris 1133
Kuss, Richard L. 444
Kutchins, Longin 1010
Kutner, David H. 731
Kutzin, Milton 1112
Kwasnick, Paul 858
Kwedar, Warren J. 744
Kydonieus, Agis 772
Kyger, Harry, Jr. 1192
Kyle, George 23

L

LaBalme, Guy 40
LaBarre, Carl 14
Labas, A. 281
Labby, Hans A. 489
Lachman, Lawrence 438
Lack, James J. 54
Ladany, William 1379
Ladd, Anthony J. 57
Ladley, R. Stanley 1438
LaDuke, Richard E. 343
LaFehr, L.E. 252
Lafetra, Mary E. 1120
Laffen, Mary 107
Lafferty, Ralph F. 1062, 1441
Lafferty, Ralph L. 463
Lagerroos, Dorothy 119
Laginestra, Rocco 1117
Laher, P.J. 882
Laher, T.J. 877
Lahr, Robert A. 321
Laird, L.W. 877
Laitin, Joseph 32
Lake, C. W., Jr. 604
Lake, Joanne 279
Lake, Thomas H. 897
Lake, Willett R., Jr. 922
LaLanne, Jack 873
LaLiberte, Clarence E. 571
Lama, Joseph H. 878

LaMantia, Robert S. 1430
Lamb, Darren K. 307
Lamberg, H. 1413
Lambert, Charles F. 524
Lambert, W.B. 878
Lamble, William E. 1248
Lamm, Harvey H. 1284
Lamm, Joseph H. 925
Lamour, Charles C. 878
Lamoureux, Helen P. 321
Lamoureux, Lucien 976
Lamoureux, Philip J. 1395
Lampe, Robert J. 627
Lancaster, Scott D. 164
Land, Edwin H. 1089
Landau, William 879
Landay, David L. 459
Landis, Clayton D. 735
Landis, J. Keaton 432
Landis, John E. 452
Landis, Richard G. 586
Landish, Joshua M. 50
Landsman, Jerome A. 1432
Lane, Edward M. 1055
Lane, Harold M., Jr. 891
Lane, L.W., Jr. 880
Lane, Stephen L. 923
Lane, William H. 1151
Lang, A.E. 1107
Lang, George A., Jr. 573
Lang, Jacob 1108
Lang, Jonathan 298
Langdon, Jervis, Jr. 1065
Lange, Arthur 1056
Lange, Robert B. 880
Lange, Steve J. 1043
Langenfeld, N.A. 1121
Langer, Jules 569
Langer, Sal 367
Langer, W. 647
Langley, E.L. 708
Langley, William S. 385
Langman, David 487
Langsam, Alexander E. 621
Langston, Clevel 1161
Lanier, Joseph L., Jr. 1405
Lankerster, W.G.F. 782
Lanners, Fred T. 626
Lansing, John Y. 1047
Lansky, David R. 1226
Lanvin, David J. 1285
Lapedes, Clarence 900
Lapetina, Robert A. 628
Lapham, Robert J. 541
Laporte, William F. 355
Largay, Redmond J. 726
Larkin, Arthur E., Jr. 848
Larkin, Daniel C., Jr. 562
Larkin, Frederick G., Jr. 1206

1575

Personnel Index

Larmer, E.P.   1103
LaRocque, Daniel   66
Larsen, Benny O.   154
Larsen, Carl W.   28
Larsen, Gorm   576
Larson, Charles O.   882
Larson, Edward C.   367
Larson, Louis C.   882
Lasater, Donald E.   954
Lasher, W.K.   360
Lasken, J.   1409
Lasky, Mrs. R. Glaser   1142
Latchaw, Frederic K.   65
Lattimore, B.E.   56
Lau, David C.   391
Laub, W.M.   1249
Lauder, Estee   643
Lauenstein, Gertrude   284
Lauffer, H.E.   883
Laughlin, Leo L.   205
Laughlin, Theron L.   883
Laurence, Robert   391
Lauter, Aaron Robert   559
Lauterbach, Henry S.   1261
Lauterbach, R.E.   835
Lavalee, Art   325
Lavalee, John A.   883
Lavery, R.E.   1414
Laverty, Robert E.   1322
Lavezzorio, Leonard M.   526
Lavietes, Robert A.   601
Lavin, Herman K.   728
Lavin, Leonard H.   337
Law, Bob   305
Lawler, Joe   50
Lawrence, George A.   1308
Lawrence, Major   884
Lawry, Sylvia   168
Laws, Donald P.   460
Laws, Robert E.   802
Lawson, William L., Jr.   1415
Layden, Joseph   283
Lazar, Donald   539
Lazarus, Charles Y.   885
Lazarus, James J.   872
Lazio, Tom   885
Lazrus, Julian   449
Lazzara, Vincent S.   745
Leach, Ed   293
Leach, Robert M.   1289
Leach, Robert M., II   719
Leads, Laurence C., Jr.   926
Leahy, Edward J.   423
Leake, James A.   447
Lear, Chuck   107
Leary, James E.   399
Leary, Leo F.   679
Leary, Ryan   101
Leatherman, S.R., Jr.   953

Leavitt, Arnold   543
Lebow, Harry   887
Lebow, Morton A.   18
Lebowitz, David K.   1041
Le Brecht, Robert T.   1233
Lechman, Howard M.   491
Lechman, Louis N.   643
Le Claire, Harry W.   1302
Le Comte, Douglas K.   885
Ledder, Edward J.   323
Ledgard, W. Kenneth, Jr.   359
Ledlow, Fred G.   1263
Lee, Bob   305
Lee, Bonnie L.   116
Lee, Burt   1053
Lee, Dennis Earl   301
Lee, E. Desmond   887
Lee, Fran   89, 199
Lee, Henry L., Jr.   887
Lee, Howard   116
Lee, James G.   392
Lee, John A.   1129
Lee, John L.   1130
Lee, M.O.   1366, 1371
Lee, Marvin   785
Lee, Monroe A.   912
Lee, Myrtle   819
Lee, R.E.   888
Lee, Richard E.   1224
Lee, Thomas M.   69
Lee, W.L.   388
Lee, William E.   1221
Leek, John E., Jr.   1046
Leeker, A. Elmer   1240
Leenhouts, Keith J.   227
Leet, Glen   200
Leff, Joseph   1003
Lefton, George L.   888
Lehan, Jonathan   36
Lehman, Mildred K.   17
Lehner, Bernard H.   1365
Lehren, James L.   1428
Lehrman, David   818
Lekashman, Lawrence L.   1034
Lengfeld, Helen F.   227
Lenke, George, Jr.   572
Lenna, Reginald A.   435
Lenon, Richard A.   815
Lentz, Charles W.   536
Lenz, Dorie   314
Leonard, Edward   52
Leonard, Thomas M.   1175
Leone, W.C.   1143
Lepore, Donald   334
Lerner, Allan S.   1291
Lerner, Marvin   442
Lerner, Robert   681
Lerner, Stephen M.   143
Lesh, C.P.   782

Lesher, Richard L.   83
Lesley, Jason R.   288
Leslie, Elizabeth A.   106
Leslie, John W.   25
Leslie, Loren R.   143
Lester, James V.   801
Lester, W.J.   875
Letton, H.P., Jr.   1247
Leupold, Norbert   892
Levenstein, Robert   1076
Levey, Jeanne   169
Levey, Lionel M.   661
Levi, Renato   574
Levin, Ezra   1381
Levin, Irving J.   1241
Levin, Ralph   1009
Levin, Richard M.   827
Levin, Thomas   1286
Levine, Abner   257
Levine, Alan R.   407
Levine, Benjamin   1086
Levine, Irving   904
Levine, Joseph E.   394
Levine, Leon   653
Levine, Marjory Stone   40
Levine, Nathan C.   475, 900
Levine, Noel   799
Levine, Rita   299
Levine, Robert   989
Levinson, Charles   108
Levinson, Gerald   655
Levinson, Marshall E.   1338
Levinson, Robert E.   1271
Leviton, Harold   892
Levitt, D.J.   1093
Levitt, Dana G.   914
Levitt, David M.   572
Levoff, Philip   223
Levy, Barnett   53
Levy, Benjamin   923
Levy, Harold   1358
Levy, Herbert S.   772, 893
Levy, Irving W.   730
Levy, Lazare, Jr.   590
Levy, Morton   255
Levy, Norman F.   564
Levy, Sol G.   539
Levy, Theodore   457
Levy, Willard L.   368
Lewarne, R.F.   910
Lewis, Arthur   652
Lewis, Cathy   304
Lewis, Celian M.   893
Lewis, Charles H.   53
Lewis, David   643
Lewis, E.F.   1384
Lewis, Eleanor J.   51
Lewis, Elvirita   1007, 1014
Lewis, Frederick D., Jr.   231

Personnel Index

Lewis, George W. 1159
Lewis, Lloyd 294
Lewis, M. Leonard 389
Lewis, Martin M. 549
Lewis, Martin R. 1419
Lewis, R.T. 1170
Lewis, Richard S. 893
Liberman, A. 1303, 1368
Licht, Robert P. 370
Lichtenstein, David B. 894
Lichtig, Edwin L., Jr. 690
Lico, Fred A. 1183
Liddell, Alice 1353
Lidz, Edward 895
Lieberman, A.R. 643
Lieberman, Irving 141
Lieberman, Jack 740
Lieberman, Trudy 282
Liebl, Robert H. 1215
Lieblich, Daniel Parke 1338
Liebscher, G.F. 1212
Liedtke, William C., Jr. 1067
Lievow, Patricia 172
Lifgren, Derwood K. 386
Lifka, W.J. 793
Lighbum, James B. 189
Light, Frank R. 1288
Light, R.F. 1287
Light, T.G. 857
Ligon, Robert 394
Liles, Woodie A. 41
Lilley, Harold R. 691
Lillie, John M. 892
Lincoln, Robert 992
Lindberg, Ralph D. 479
Linden, Benjamin 881
Linden, Sidney 899
Linder, O.D. 684
Linderoth, Robert S. 363
Lindgren, Richard J. 864
Lindgren, Richard W. 42
Lindholm, William L. 361
Lindner, Carl H. 353
Lindsey, Franklin A. 820
Lindstrom, Robert J. 1275, 1442
Lineberger, Walter 1383
Link, Henry T. 600, 899
Linker, Betty B. 60
Linn, Milman H., Jr. 1441
Linsenmeyer, F.X. 1164
Linton, Phillip C. 63
Lioi, Michael A. 505
Lipic, Joseph 338
Lipic, Leonard 900
Lippert, Albert 1401
Lippert, Ralph L. 752
Lippincott, J.W. 900
Lippmann, G. James 242
Lipscomb, John D. 1333

Lipsey, E. 693
Lipshie, Joseph 1180
Lipsitz, Robert J. 843
Lipson, Gerald R. 789
Lissauer, Franz A. 385
List, Christine 59
Litner, W. 813
Little, Charles 587
Little, Matt 1113
Little, Royal 365
Little, Vincent R. 1165
Little, Walter 59
Littlejohn, Broadus R., Sr. 539
Littman, Samuel 358
Livesey, Robert E. 554
Llaneza, Frank 1380
Llewellyn, William A. 955
Lloyd, John A. 1355
Lloyd, John H. 513, 1315
Loar, Robert F. 742
Lockman, Richard 828
Lockridge, Robert S. 558
Lockshin, Samuel D. 1098
Lockwood, H.A. 609
Lockwood, Linda 281
Lodato, Paul 28
LoDico, Maggie M. 47
Loecher, Gerald S. 592
Loehmann, Charles C. 903
Loemker, Thomas R. 979
Lofgren, Charles W. 1184
Loft, Bernard I. 182
Loftin, Gordon 959
Logan, J.L. 698
Logan, Romona 102
Logowitz, Kenneth 1042
Loitz, Robert 112
Lombard, Howard 1316
Lombard, Mary T. 710
Lombardo, Philip J. 552
London, Alvin 1409
London, Norman 1395
Long, Alvin W. 514
Long, Frank T. 283
Long, Henry F., Jr. 1000
Long, Howard C. 142
Long, Joseph M. 905
Long, Mildred B. 1281
Long, Virginia 304
Longden, Jerry 256
Longreen, Mogens 756
Lonnecker, P.L. 1320
Lonning, J.E. 849
Loomis, Bernard 851
Loomis, Worth 594
Looney, John 112
Loos, Augus W. 906
Lopapas, J. Richard 375
Lopata, Stanely L. 488

Lopez, B.H. 352
Lorberbaum, Donald 884
Lorentzsen, Norman M. 397
Lorenz, M. James 37
Lorenzo, Francisco A. 1316
Lorenzotti, Guido 1034
Loring, Richard 173
Lothrop, F.B., Jr. 602
Lotito, Ernest 5
Lotter, John G.H. 1269
Lourie, Marvin H. 335
Love, Carl F. 479
Love, Howard 95
Love, Howard M. 1004
Love, J.B. 361
Love, James 95
Love, Richard A. 755
Love, Stanley 908
Lovegren, James P. 176
Lovell, James C. 954
Lovett, W.R. 1079
Lovette, Fred 784
Low, Robert K. 1189
Low, Stuart M. 673
Lowe, Webster 444
Lowell, Malcolm R., Jr. 263
Lowenbaum, Ralph 908
Lowenfels, Fred C. 790
Lowenthal, Harvey L. 922
Lowery, James C. 83
Lowrance, Darrel 909
Lowry, E.J. 1369
Lowry, Walter R. 847
Loxier, Allan 354
Loy, Percy W. 869
Loynd, Richard B. 635
Lozyniak, Andrew 618
Lrohman, Robert T. 690
Luber, Diane 102
Lubetkin, Alvin N. 1040
Lubic, Ruth W. 159
Lubin, Marvin 390
Lucas, R.J. 378
Lucchesi, L. 1363
Luce, Charles F. 543
Lucht, Allan P. 1211
Lucier, Francis P. 434
Luckie, Robert G. 453
Ludington, Francis H., Jr. 508
Ludington, J.S. 607
Ludwig, Harvey 1313
Ludwig, William F., Jr. 910
Luevano, Daniel M. 239
Luger, R.J. 911
Luhrs, H.R. 418
Lukash, Alvin 775
Luke, David L., III 1410
Lumpkin, John H. 1246
Lund, Gordon H. 911

Personnel Index

Lundberg, K.F. 332
Lundberg, Rex W. 50
Lundell, Vernon J. 912
Lundstrom, Leif 666
Lunenburg, Frederick W. 254
Lunn, James F. 885
Lunt, Denham C., Jr. 1158
Luntley, Eugene H. 459
Lupfer, Robert N. 1259
Lurie, Jerry 675
Lurton, H. William 837
Lusby, R. Newell 598
Lussky, William 1104
Lutkin, D.C. 971
Lutz, Rowena 101
Lutz, Theodore 285
Luviano, John J. 565
Lyet, J.P. 1255
Lyle, Dorothy S. 253
Lynch, C.J. 319
Lynch, Donna 280
Lynch, Francis 15
Lynch, John E. 1098
Lynch, Tom J. 305
Lyng, Richard 244
Lynott, Thomas L. 1136
Lyon, C.M. 936
Lyons, Mrs. H.R. 170
Lyons, Jerome D. 784
Lyons, Richard B. 335

M

Mabie, Kathie 38
McAlvay, J.C. 1401
MacArthur, John D. 405
McAshan, S.M., Jr. 367
MacAvoy, Thomas C. 553
McBeath, William H. 142
McBee, Walter 814
MacBeth, W.E. 1309
McBride, Robert D. 733
McCaffery, Francis X. 539
McCaffrey, James P. 907
McCaffrey, John T. 1285
McCall, Roy C., Jr. 1268
McCarroll, Berton S. 693
McCarthy, Donald W. 1020
McCarthy, J.D. 364
McCarthy, John J. 1370
McCarthy, Paul 325
McCarty, Charles I. 461
McChesney, Russell J. 432
McClain, B.H. 1106
McClanan, J.N. 64
McClarran, Arlene 290
McClellan, James E. 351

McClendon, Zach, Jr. 979
McClenic, Patricia L. 305
McCloskey Evans, Hugh 785
McCloskey, J.E. 1430
McClure, Clara 274
McClurkin, Johnson T. 257
McCollam, William Jr. 1010
McCollough, Roy C. 938
McCollough, William A. 366
McColough, C. Peter 1435
McConachie, Charles R. 24
McConnor, W.S. 1355
MacCormick, Austin H. 219
McCormick, Brooks 814
McCormick, Joseph R. 761
McCormick, Robert 271
McCormick, William W. 837
McCoy, Arthur H. 298
McCoy, Calvin 116
McCoy, Nelson 946
McCracken, Robert C. 594
McCrady, Kenneth A. 639
McCrae, Charles A. 572
McCraith, Libby 39
McCreary, Harry C. 946
McCreight, Harold W. 1111
McCrummer, J.B. 118
McCullen, Patrice 294
McCullough, Donald F. 532
McCullough, Jack 106
McCurdy, Gilbert J.C. 946
McCurry, Dan 101
McCurry, R.B. 602
McDaniel, Durward K. 139
McDaniel, L.H., Jr. 1269
McDavid, O.C. 283
McDermott, J.R. 927
McDermott, Marno 1441
McDevitt, Joan 291
MacDonald, Alan 1021
McDonald, Barry 273
McDonald, David J. 996
McDonald, E.R. 899
McDonald, F.J. 513
MacDonald, G.R. 300
MacDonald, Gordon 1087
McDonald, Howard C. 1027
McDonald, Jack 1044
MacDonald, James 194
McDonald, John V. 516
McDonald, Marshall 675
MacDonald, Ray W. 469
McDonald, Robert 367
McDonald, Roderick N. 974
McDonald, Stanley B. 1101
McDonnell, John T. 1395
MacDougall, Roderick M. 1009
MacDowell, William D. 469
Macedo, Joseph 599

McElhinny, Wilson D. 999
McElnea, William H., Jr. 476
McElroy, Randolph W. 666
McEwen, Owen C. 1271
McEwen, Robert J. 105
McFall, H.P. 649
McFarland, James P. 707
MacFarlane, John C. 783, 1439
McFarlane, Willis M. 385
McGannon, Donald H. 803, 1409
McGarry, Bart 7
McGarvey, Robert M., Jr. 947
McGee, Kay 161
McGee, Norman A. 1249
McGhan, William F. 240
McGhee, R.E. 717
McGill, Mrs. M.F. 1432
McGill, William 100
McGinley, James K. 615
McGinnity, James R. 974
McGivney, James E. 51
McGough, G. 1408
McGovern, R.G. 1068
McGowan, Alan 134
Macgowan, Clifford 917
McGowan, Harold P. 638
McGowan, John M. 1353
McGowan, John S. 466
McGowan, Richard 32
McGrath, Kenneth G. 1196
McGraw, Harold W. 947
McGraw, Harold W., Jr. 947
Macgregor, Dugald 500
McGrew, David 135
McGrory, John J. 766
McGrummer, Warren 363
McGruther, G. Raymond 616
McGuire, Chester C. 20
McGuire, Frank 203
McGuire, Rosalie 211
McGuirk, Tom 1271
McHale, Thomas A. 608
MacHarg, L.P. 1420
McIlhenny, Walter S. 948
McIntosh, Thomas 60
McIntyre, Charles S., III 980
Macioce, Thomas M. 344
Mack, Alan R. 917
Mack, Charlene 97
Mack, John Wilbur 917
McKay, Don A. 732
MacKay, Gordon D. 1009
McKay, Robert L. 1302
McKay, Sue 105
McKee, F.L., Sr. 1004
McKee, James W. 475
McKee, Joseph V. 1004
McKee, Joseph V., Jr. 644
McKee, O.D. 948

Personnel Index

McKenna, Alex G. 851
McKenna, William 1309
McKenna, William J. 887
MacKenzie, Howard J. 1264
Mackenzie, Joseph W. 663
McKinley, John K. 1315
McKinney, John R. 999
Mackle, Frank E., Jr. 589
McKool, M.G. 901
McKoy, A.C. 939
MacLachlan, Robert H. **796**, 1236
McLaughlin, David T. 1331
MacLaughlin, Donald C. 376
McLaughlin, Frank 15
McLaughlin, Joe, Jr. 281
McLaughlin, Robert J. 663
McLaughlin, Terrance 1343
McLauglin, James 1358
McLaurin, R.T. 1018
MacLean, Barry L. 917
MacLean, R.B. 1157
MacLean, Robert D. 262
McLean, Robert W. 990
McLennaghm, Robert 898
McLeod, John 765
MacLeod, William B. 1101
MacMahon, Donald A. 1167
McMahon, John F. 228
McMahon, Nelson 673
McMaster, Thomas 344
McMillan, Edward L., Jr. 367
MacMillan, Jackie 221
MacMillan, Whitney 490
McMillen, Dale W., Jr. 501
McMoran, George A. 512
McMorris, Donald L. 1437
McMullin, Margery D. 152
McMurray, M.T. 567
McMurtney, Wayne A. 870
McNair, Evans 1228
McNally, Andrew, III 1122
McNamee, J.O. 603
MacNaughton, Malcolm 497
McNeal, James H., Jr. 465
McNeely, E.L. 1416
McNeely, Joseph 104
McNeer, Charles S. 1426
MacNeille, R.A. 1178
McNitt, James R. 802
McNutt, James W. 863
Macomber, John D. 499
McPartlin, John E. 348
McPhee, D. 1396
MacPherson, Robert W. 481, 494
MacPherson, Rod 814
McQueen, James R., Jr. 1343
McQueeney, William A. 39
McQuilkin, W.W. **412**

McQuinn, William P. 929
Macrae, John, Jr. 617
McRobbie, J.J. 872
McSwine, T.L. 542
McSwiney, James W. 948
Mactier, J.A. 981
McTyeire, William W., III 433
McVicar, Robert L. 806
MacWilliams, John, Jr. 533
Madama, John 134
Madden, Richard B. 1093
Madden, Roberta, M. 45
Maddox, Dan 1321
Madison, Samuel R. 69
Madway, Hillard 1147
Maer, Stanley 388
Maffin, Robert W. 210
Magee, James A. 919
Magee, John F. 191
Magenau, John M., Jr. 641
Magers, Jane 101
Maggio, William 591
Magliocco, A. 1064
Magoon, John H., Jr. 763
Maguire, Samuel F. 665
Maharam, Donald H. 922
Maher, M. 1318
Mahery, C.C., Jr. 387
Mahoney, David J. 1022
Mahoney, E.L. 537
Maier, M.J. 924, 979
Mainegra, C.M. 600
Mainzer, Alfred 923
Mair, Alex C. 1091
Maisano, John F. 888
Maisel, Saul 915
Maitland, George B. 1383
Maitland, Joanna C. 1255
Major, J.N., Jr. 1033
Makeover, Sylvan A. 1219
Malik, Russell R. 1286
Malizia, A.A. 947
Mallach, Aubrey 158
Mallard, Karl 924
Mallen, James R. 1334
Mallet, Dorothy M. 924
Maloney, Celia A. 42
Malott, Robert H. 650
Maloy, Margaret 5
Malsin, Arthur 558, 880
Maltese, I. Charles 181
Malzahn, Ed 507
Manchester, C.H. 334
Mancuso, Henry 782
Mancuso, Richard M. 53
Mand, Emery M. 925
Mandell, Alyce 559
Manfred, Roger L. 1338
Mangels, Roger N. 926

Mahold, Earl K., Jr. 1133
Manier, Alex F. 1069
Manischewitz, Bernard 926
Mankoff, F.J. 1388
Manley, Charles G. 926
Mann, Gary I. 926
Mann, Jerome S. 480
Mann, L.K. 438
Mann, Milton 879
Mann, Roy W. 427
Mann, Seymour 324
Mann, W.A. 498
Mann, William H. 890
Mannhaupt, John F. 343
Manning, William S. 429
Manoogian, Alex 938
Manos, Steven S. 159
Mansfield, Charles F. 931
Manz, Esther S. 178
Mapstone, Herbert W. 564
Marcalus, Robert L. 929
Marcello, David 103
Marcheschi, Henry 361
Marcus, Alex 751
Marcus, Ben S. 610
Marcus, Bernard 754
Marcus, Richard C. 1006
Marding, Sheryl 116
Marek, Edward R. 511
Marescot, Henri G. 333
Margolies, Louis 556
Margolis, C.R. 1349
Mariani, Robert 325
Marin, G. 393
Marino, J.A. 452
Marino, Vince 281
Marion, Samuel 432
Mark, Joan 56
Markewitz, Fred 780
Markham, G.J. 374
Markham, Walter J. 495
Markin, David 510
Markley, H.E. 1325
Marko, James A. 1304
Markowitz, David 683
Markowitz, Marty 110
Marks, Alvin 1402
Marks, Jesse James 45
Marks, R.H. 1313
Marks, Sidney 915
Marlas, James C. 960
Marlette, C. Alan 81, 257
Marlin, Alice Tepper 87, 201
Marlowe, Murray 522
Marolf, Fred, Jr. 557
Marona, Nicholas R. 1104
Marq, Michel 1391
Marquard, William A. 361
Marquardt, W.G. 1315

Personnel Index

Marquis, Bill 62
Marran, C. Charles 1254
Marran, Frank L. 765
Marriott, J. Willard, Jr. 933
Marschalk, H. Robert 1146
Marsh, Brooklyn, Donald F. 1345
Marsh, Estel V. 934
Marsh, Ford A. 615
Marshall, Alfred 934
Marshall, David Cameron 496
Marshall, James H. 478
Marshall, Joseph 31
Marshall, M.S. 716
Marshall, Richard P. 423
Marshall, Robert 223
Marston, Frederick T. 846
Marten, Henry H. 1363
Marth, Martha 275
Martin, Ernest P. 712
Martin, Frank H. 935
Martin, George 971
Martin, John H. 902
Martin, John M. 254
Martin, Paul E. 1029
Martin, R. Gordon 1127
Martin, Ruth 280
Martin, Sandy 303
Martin, W.F. 1076
Martin, W.H., Jr. 936
Martin, William H., III 857
Martin, William R., Jr. 241
Martindale, Robert H. 936
Martinelli, David E. 379
Martinez, Vilma S. 235
Martino, Frank M. 1172
Marvin, Roger A. 519
Maschke, Alfred B. 996
Mascuch, Joseph J. 453
Mash, George T. 967
Masland, William S. 939
Maslyn, Theodore C. 528
Mason, Austin B. 910
Mason, J. Owen 939
Mason, Ralph E. 939
Mason, Robert P. 939
Mason, Thomas L. 1044
Mason, William 109
Massaroni, D.A. 56
Massey, A. Elmer, Jr. 710
Massey, H.C. 116
Massie, Burton S. 625
Masteller, Harold W. 1415
Masters, L.N. 1408
Masterson, Mike 272
Matcalf, Arthur G.B. 632
Matestic, Fred 66
Mather, James A. 973
Mather, Roland D. 43
Mather, Terry 379

Matheson, Franklin B. 362
Mathiew, Bernard W. 1249
Mathis, Louie 15
Mathues, T.O. 811
Matson, William F. 114
Matt, Walter J. 1405
Mattes, Joe 279
Matthaci, Charles W.H. 1160
Matthews, R.J. 458
Matthews, W.C. 419
Matthey, Louis W. 841
Mattoon, John 21
Mattutat, F.H. 1421
Matz, David A. 119
Matz, Edward, Jr. 870
Mauer, Mary Jane 98
Maull, Louis T. 942
Mavel, Thomas J. 1106
Maxted, J.F., Jr. 767
Maxwell, Gregory W. 641
Maxwell, Philip K. 62
May, Frank 944
May, J.Y. 389
May, R.E. 184
May, R.L. 1412
Mayer, Ernst 1096
Mayer, J. Gerald 717, 1062
Mayer, Jack F. 1316
Mayhew, Thomas M. 1407
Maynard, Victor A. 665
Mayo, E. 382
Mays, John C. 41
Maytag, Lewis B. 998
Mazer, A. Lincoln 945
Mazer, William 794
Mazerland, Max 1142
Maziar, H. 1442
Mead, Bill O. 483
Mead, George W., II 544
Meadows, J.E. 1107
Meagher, J.L. 1279
Mealey, Margaret 214
Meals, J.T. 1307
Mears, Willard A. 306
Meath, Thomas E. 665
Mechem, Charles S., Jr. 1303
Medberry, C.J. 405
Medina, Antonio 226
Medina, Pablo 994
Medlin, John G., Jr. 1388
Medwick, Maury P. 328
Meehan, John E. 1132
Meeker, David B. 780, 860
Meenach, Durward H. 1292
Meer, George, Jr. 951
Meese, William G. 593
Meeske, Paul 1223
Megerle, Eugen 1403
Mehken, R.C. 1348

Meijer, Frederick 951
Meindl, Leo 286
Melcher, LeRoy, Sr. 652
Meldahl, Philip M. 1335
Mellen, Amory, Jr. 948
Mellinger, Frederick N. 688
Mellish, Richard E. 1150
Mello, Kerry 281
Melnikoff, H. 1084
Melott, Ronald K. 183
Melton, Linwood E. 1394
Meltzer, Charles 932
Meltzer, Donald R. 516
Meltzer, Henry 940
Melville, Ward 953
Mendelson, William J. 778
Mendillo, V.F. 1204
Menk, Louis W. 468, 1257
Mennel, Donald M. 953
Menon, Bhasker 487
Menson, J.L. 596
Mentzer, John F. 640
Menuto, Angelo T. 641
Menzies, J.M. 1058
Mercer, R.E. 850
Mercer, Walter C. 1029
Mercer, William C. 1009
Merians, Melvin L. 1044
Mericle, Dean 97
Merino, Denise T. 722
Merkel, Daniel 470
Merkowitz, Lucille 304
Merle, Andrew W., Jr. 1263
Merna, Thomas F. 630
Merriam, James 1229
Merrill, Wanda 58
Merritt, James H. 249
Merry, A.D. 225
Merszei, Zoltan 607
Merta, Leonard C. 977
Merwin, George W. "Bud", III 247
Mesnick, Samuel H. 35
Mester, Hyman J. 534
Metcalfe, F.M. 1322
Metrailer, Francis M. 860
Mettler, Ole R. 622
Mettler, R.F. 1301
Metzen, Charles A. 1274
Metzger, B.L. 263
Metzger, R. William 1365
Meyer, C.F.G., III 958
Meyer, Frank 958
Meyer, Fred G. 958
Meyer, Gay H. 953
Meyer, H. Harold 959
Meyer, Helen 587
Meyer, John 834
Meyer, Louis 114

Personnel Index

Meyer, Louis C. 990
Meyer, R.L. 531
Meyer, Randall 649
Meyer, Richard E. 837
Meyer, Roy 104
Meyerherm, Charles H. 38
Meyers, E. Don 568
Meyers, Edgar W. 1341
Meyers, Edwin W. 476
Meyers, Phillip M. 656
Meyers, William 1214
Michaels, Edmund 334
Michaels, Robert L. 959
Michell, Jerome N. 402
Michener, Mildred N. 217
Michener, Robert E. 934
Michie, Billy E. 1013
Michlin, Robert R. 1057
Middleton, H.H., Jr. 962
Middleton, Julie Barker 389
Mierzwa, Henry 67
Miesemer, Robert 329
Mikita, Betsey G. 60
Mikkelson, Gordon A. 302
Milckelson, William L. 1237
Mildred, Peter 1398
Miles, A. Stevens 667
Miles, Stanley J. 1117
Miles, T.R. 1266
Miley, Rod 1332
Milgram, Lester 964
Miller, Arnold 181
Miller, Ben A. 946
Miller, Bob 289
Miller, Charles 117
Miller, Charles 665
Miller, Charles D. 394
Miller, Charles D. 1315
Miller, D.J. 740
Miller, Earl A. 966
Miller, Edward A., Jr. 514
Miller, Edward B. 1130
Miller, Elizabeth 966
Miller, Eugene 1379
Miller, Fred 966
Miller, G. William 1316
Miller, Gaylord R. 185
Miller, Harold A. 680
Miller, Harold J. 387
Miller, Harold T. 790
Miller, Harvey Y. 1114
Miller, Henry C. 1187
Miller, Howard 272
Miller, Howard C. 485
Miller, I.H. 1151
Miller, J. Carter 494
Miller, Jack 705
Miller, Jack Brown 966
Miller, James C. 813

Miller, Jimmy 1263
Miller, John R. 766
Miller, Martin 70
Miller, Max M. 673
Miller, Mitchel 961
Miller, Norman 301
Miller, Ora E. 1411
Miller, Orie O. 966
Miller, Paul 699
Miller, Paul A. 624
Miller, Paul G. 538
Miller, Richard G. 633
Miller, Robert A. 567
Miller, Sarah J. 124
Miller, Steffne 1359
Miller, Victor A. 1366
Miller, Walter H. 857
Miller, William A. 616
Millhiser, Ross R. 1076
Milligan, Bruce L. 861
Milligan, Karen 160
Millikan, Steve 49
Milliken, Frank R. 851
Milliken, Roger 585
Millis, James H. 327
Mills, Harry C. 370
Mills, Osborne 967
Mills, R. Edwin 657
Mills, Ralph 562
Millspaugh, Samuel Kirk 859
Milner, Gene W. 881
Milone, Kathie 313
Milson, Robert C. 1083
Mindel, Seymour 1032
Miner, Jean M. 53
Minetti, A. Perelli 480
Mingle, Frank A. 987
Minnich, C.R. 617
Minnig, Max A. 446
Minnigerode, Donald 789
Minor, Henry H., Jr. 969
Minsky, Stuart A. 382
Minton, Dwight C. 519
Minton, Walter J. 1110
Mintzer, Jack 951
Miori, Nilo M. 482
Mirgain, Co 278
Mishkin, E. Archie 413
Mishkin, Ralph 784
Mitchell, Don 777
Mitchell, Edward A. 773
Mitchell, Frank 974
Mitchell, G.B. 575
Mitchell, Helen 292, 294
Mitchell, J.E. 940
Mitchell, John H. 1200
Mitchell, Mark H. 882
Mitchell, Parker, Jr. 974
Mitchell, Rege 96

Mitchell, Richard T. 799
Mitchell, Robert E. 1360
Mitchell, Vernon C. 149
Mitchell, W.S. 1177
Mitchell, W.W. 667
Mitchell, William G. 623
Mitnick, J.G. 1330
Mitrani, Marco 964
Mitros, George N. 1306
Mitzner, Jay M. 106
Mize, H. Richard 437
Mizuki, Tai 820
Mockler, Colman M., Jr. 715
Modell, William 976
Moe, Courtney 1292
Moede, Gustave H., Jr. 1426
Moffat, John 295
Mohler, H.S. 773
Mohney, F.W. 824
Mohrman, Harry L. 411
Moll, Curtis E. 916
Molla, Otto W. 978
Moller, T.F. 37
Molloy, James 1422
Monaco, Grace Powers 147
Monaghan, Joseph P. 993
Monasee, C.A. 351
Monfort, Kenneth W. 979
Monge, D. 334
Monnig, Oscar E. 980
Monosson, Fred 555
Monroe, Frank A., Jr. 1142
Monroe, J.D. 642
Monroe, Jay 1314
Monroe, John D. 1420
Monson, Karl W. 341
Montague, Katherine 110
Montant, Bernard 855
Montgomery, Charles R. 960
Montgomery, James F. 736
Montgomery, Mary 103
Montgomery, Parker G. 550
Montgomery, Robert 550, 1255
Montmarin, Pierce de 1074
Moody, Barbara 285
Moody, Braxton I., III 508
Moody, Dick 295
Moody, Robert 36
Moody, William E. 62
Moog, Hubert C. 982
Moon, J.S. 1161
Mooney, Paul 1115
Moore, Arthur S. 1337
Moore, Clarence C. 566
Moore, Edwin R. 982
Moore, Florence 213
Moore, H. Edward 932
Moore, Ken 879
Moore, M.E. 1301

Personnel Index

Moore, Robert F. 764
Moore, Sam 1007
Moore, Scott 983
Moore, T. Justin, Jr. 1382
Moore, Thomas F., Jr. 982
Moore, Walter L. 1354
Moore, Wayne R. 983
Moore, William E. 850
Moore, William J. 188
Moore, William W. 140
Moot, John R. 553
Moran, James D. 674
Morando, E.D. 1114
Mordoff, John D. 958
Morelli, J. 609
Morello, John B. 969
Moreno, Luis 62
Morgan, Alfred Y. 1414
Morgan, C.E. 136
Morgan, C.G. 1018
Morgan, Charles S. 187
Morgan, E.L. 1147
Morgan, Ivan H. 984
Morgan, John T. 442
Morgan, Lee L. 498
Morgan, Noel M. 57
Morgan, Paul S. 984
Morgan, Robert 322
Morgan, Robert 1421
Morgan, Robert F. 984
Morgan, Stephen 105
Morgan, William 580
Morikawa, Jiro 945
Morley, H.B. 1270
Moroney, Richard D. 1317
Morpurgo, Mario 599
Morrell, Warren 272
Morris, Andrew R., Jr. 392
Morris, Arthur A., Jr. 842
Morris, Curtis T. 570
Morris, J. Liwin 985
Morris, J.M. 1013
Morris, J. Roy 571
Morris, James 711
Morris, Joseph J. 505
Morris, Julian C. 247
Morris, Lewis S. 541
Morris, Melvin 1367
Morris, Norman A. 896
Morris, Norman M. 985, 1035
Morris, Robert E. 1326
Morris, Robert M. 1374
Morris, W.M. 417
Morris, W.T. 1430
Morris, William 895
Morrison, Edward W., Jr. 985
Morrison, Orville C. 1289
Morrison, Richard S. 978
Morrison, William W. 680

Morrissette, H. Taylor 533
Morrow, George L. 1019
Morrow, M.L. 1079
Morrow, R.G., Jr. 902
Morrow, Seymour A. 762
Morrow, Winston V., Jr. 394
Morse, Alfred L. 985
Morse, Melvin S. 1098
Morse, Philip S. 985
Morseth, Gordon 1092
Mortel, Donald 985
Mortensen, C.B. 871
Mortimer, Harold 115
Morton, James C. 982
Mosenkis, Robert 152
Moser, C.H. 603
Moser, C.R. 291
Moskowitz, Edward 627
Mosler, John 785
Mosling, John P. 1040
Moss, Cruse W. 321
Moss, George F. 1408
Moss, Jerome 319
Moss, Louis B. 362
Moss, Luis B. 928, 941
Mossberg, Alan 986
Mounger, Larry, Jr. 1048
Moulton, Ralph E. 392
Mourcott, Charles 911
Mous, Elwood R. 461
Mover, Eliot S. 467
Mower, H.W. 911
Mrdeze, George E. 986
Mueller, Paul 989
Muenze, Arthur K. 1417
Mufson, Harry 829
Muftic, Felicia 39
Mugar, John M. 1268
Muhlsteff, Herman A. 534
Mulcahey, James A. 613
Mulholland, James S., Jr. 764
Mulholland, Robert J. 490
Mullan, Cathal 818
Mullaney, Thomas P. 1422
Muller, John H., Jr. 706
Muller, Leonard A. 1281
Mullican, E.W. 634, 1333
Mulligan, Edward E. 997
Mulligan, Raymond J. 896
Mullikin, Harry 1407
Mullin, Lewis O. 1235
Mulready, Paul A. 835
Mulvaney, James F. 1360
Mumma, Bob 101
Mummert, J.R. 320
Mundt, Ray B. 337
Munford, Dillard 990
Munger, G.R. 240
Munns, M.W. 143

Munro, R. 106
Munsell, A.L. 1221
Munsell, Warren P. 192
Munson, Lawrence 46
Munzer, I. Walter 509
Murdock, F.M. 366
Murdock, Harold G., Jr. 990
Murdock, Robert M. 527
Murphree, Gayle 271
Murphy, Charles E. 1012
Murphy, Charles W. 397
Murphy, Colleen 97
Murphy, Edward J. 197
Murphy, Edward L., Jr. 991
Murphy, F.X. 991
Murphy, Gerald D. 622
Murphy, J.J. 428
Murphy, John A. 702, 965
Murphy, John D. 1426
Murphy, John T. 394
Murphy, Kenneth B. 174
Murphy, Michael J. 257
Murphy, Murlan J., Sr. 991
Murphy, Thomas S. 486
Murphy, W.R. 949, 1150
Murphy, William J. 740
Murphy, William T. 719
Murray, Charles C. 410
Murray, Don 224
Murray, Ian W. 1174
Murray, James 342
Murray, Leonard H. 1245
Murray, Mike 425
Murray, William F. 760
Muscio, U.V. 993
Muse, M. Lamar 1249
Musgrave, Gloria 297
Musicus, Raphael 1034
Musiel, H.J. 1410
Mustokoff, Michael M. 60
Mutchow, Paul J. 893
Myerholtz, Earl F. 933
Myers, C. Paul 841
Myers, Charles V. 1391
Myers, Jerome B. 1161
Myers, Jonathan 904
Myers, M.F. 427
Myers, Malcolm C. 491
Mynsberge, Richard C. 979

N

Naboicheck, N. Aaron 1264
Nachman, Jack 976
Nadel, Sylvia 1389
Nader, Ralph 83, 93

Personnel Index

Nadler, Murray 604
Nagatake, Yoshihiro 1332
Nagel, Margaret A. 996
Nagel, Walter A. 756
Nagle, Allan R. 1053
Nahmad, Albert H. 1398
Nahrgang, William L. 835
Naify, Robert A. 1356
Nakagawa, Roy Y. 460
Nakamichi, Tadao 846
Nakamura, H. 355
Nalen, Craig A. 1175
Nalle, George S. 996
Nania, Jake 454
Nania, Vincent, Jr. 996
Nanula, Savino P. 1012
Narens, Leonard L. 335
Narva, Louis 986
Nash, Bernard E. 192, 216
Nash, Joseph 703
Nash, Merrill L. 461, 1292
Nash, Monroe 1158
Nason, Fred, Sr. 429
Nasser, Morris 703
Nassimbene, Charles J. 1185
Naughton, Edward M. 1365
Naumoff, Charles P. 565
Nave, H.J. 917
Navis, Maida J. 206
Navropoulis, Elizabeth 70
Nay, Edward N. 1439
Naylor, Alexander L. 651
Nazzaro, Armand L. 322
Neal, Dan 985
Neal, Julian S. 663
Necly, Robert P. 793
Nee, George 115
Nee, Joseph F. 166
Neeb, Lou 1270
Needham, James J. 1011
Neely, R.C., Jr. 348
Neff, Harold L. 1006
Nehrez, William L. 1353
Neider, Bailey H. 505
Neidhardt, Paul W. 720
Neighbors, James E., Jr. 659, 1192
Nein, Lawrence F. 719
Neisewander, Ray H. 1126
Nellen, Arthur H., Jr. 248
Nelson, Brian 44
Nelson, C.S. 962
Nelson, Calvin L. 1007
Nelson, E.S. 377
Nelson, Edwin W., Jr. 1385
Nelson, Frank C. 650
Nelson, Glen, Jr. 1039
Nelson, H.D. 1124
Nelson, Helen E. 82, 119

Nelson, Irving 1425
Nelson, Jeff 278
Nelson, John 724
Nelson, Oliver D. 810
Nelson, Paul B. 912
Nelson, R.E. 354
Nemec, Frank A. 1439
Nemeth, Julius K. 444
Neptune, Kenneth E. 1226
Nero, Frank R., Jr. 1410
Nerret, Arthur 1116
Nesbit, Ralph 1355
Nesbitt, Arthur W. 997
Nester, Jack 1070
Nestler, Arthur A. 1273
Nethercutt, Robert 955, 1017
Neubauer, J.A. 1045
Neuber, Arno R. 393
Neuhoff, Henry, III 1008
Neuman, Guy W. 1117
Neumann, Vera 1191
Neumann, Walter 476
Neustadt, Jean 647
Neves, T.E. 452
Neville, Robert J. 1018
Nevin, Robert L. 523
Newberg, John T. 278
Newburg, Mort 932
Newcomb, D.R. 465
Newell, Robert L. 761
Newhaus, T.H. 668
Newman, R.O. 1107
Newman, Richard J. 392
Newman, Samual O. 793
Newman, Sarah 99
Newman, Shelley 96
Newton, Annette 104
Newton, Blake T., Jr. 252
Newton, James 289
Newton, Philip T. 600
Newton, Whitney G. 357
Ney, W. Roger 131
Nicastro, Louis J. 1206
Nicholas, Arthur S. 370
Nicholas, J. Roy 1167
Nicholas, Robert 59
Nichols, George A. 583
Nichols, Jim 288
Nichols, Robert P. 1334
Nichols, Russ 311
Nichols, Sherry 271
Nichols, Wolfe R. 1379
Nickell, Judy 285
Nickels, William C. 1140
Nickoley, Keith D. 1153
Nickow, Hy 706
Nicolette, Louis O. 55
Niederman, Howard I. 792
Nielsen, E.H. 399

Nielsen, Vincent W. 965
Nieman, Harold F. 686
Niemi, William F., Jr. 626
Niglio, Richard A. 972
Nikitas, John 1121
Nilsson, Mat G.E. 386
Nims, Lucius 878
Nishada, Shunkichi 975
Nishimura, Glenn 95
Nissen, George P. 1014
Nixon, C.W. 124
Nixon, James W. 1415
Nizamian, Harold 574
Noble, Alexander R. 446
Noble, Donald 1170
Nodtvedt, Magnus 1001
Noffsinger, Donald A. 1395
Noha, Edward J. 351, 546
Nolan, Robert C. 668
Nolan, Robert V. 325
Nolde, Edward P. 64
Nolde, George F., Jr. 1015
Noll, Sanford B. 569
Noojin, A.Y., Jr. 1259
Noonan, Edward T. 95
Noone, T. Francis 1015
Nophlin, Calvin 15
Nord, Alldor M. 1355
Nordham, Richard C. 1021
Nordlund, Donald E. 1262
Nordman, Karlfried 954
Nordstrom, John A. 1016
Nordstrom, Manfred A. 516
Norman, Wilfred H. 1040
Norris, Doris 294
Norris, H. Coleman 536
Norris, H.N. 1372
Norris, Kenneth T., Jr. 1017
Norris, Robert F. 674
Norris, William C. 547
Norsworthy, George H. 1195
North, Louise 19
North, William C. 568
Northrop, John L.S. 291
Northrop, Stuart J. 795
Norton, Joe 70
Noskin, Mary D. 313
Noveau, Barbara B. 243
Novogrod, Leonard J. 1234
Noyes, Pierrepont T. 1036
Noymer, Fritz S. 1023
Noznesky, Harry J. 704
Nunnally, Moses D., Jr. 786
Nurnberger, Thomas S. 1021
Nurse, David W. 766
Nye, Thomas R. 853
Nylen, L.A. 505
Nyrop, Donald W. 1021
Nyssen, M.P. 786

1583

Personnel Index

Nyssen, R.H. 833

O

Oakes, Herbert L. 509
Oakes, Lonnie 856
Oberg, James L. 1235
Oberhamer, Douglas R. 265
Oberlin, Abe 333
Obermeyer, Klaus F. 1257
Oberto, Edwin L. 467
O'Brien, D.W. 928
O'Brien, John H. 1398
O'Brien, Raymond F. 543
O'Brien, William J. 1161
O'Bryan, Michael L. 1027
Ochman, Samuel 502
O'Connell, Brian 162
O'Connell, R.G. 1332
O'Conner, Neal W. 395
O'Connor, Robert W. 183
O'Crowley, James 702
O'Daniel, Finis A. 1082
Odlum, G. McNaught 616
O'Donnell, H.R. 1155
O'Donnell, James M. 954
O'Donnell, Joseph C. 1354
O'Donnell, Thomas A. 360
Oelsner, Edward, Jr. 1360
Office, Gerald S., Jr. 1091
Offit, Julius 331
Ogburn, William H. 588
Ogden, Hub 284
Ogg, Robert D. 576
Ogle, Milton 119
Oglesby, Joseph E. 4
Ogosh, Yoshio 780
O'Hara, Edward H. 1022
O'Hara, William F. 60
O'Hare, Delmar T. 467
O'Keefe, Frank 1057
O'Keefe, G.J. 917
O'Kelley, H.E. 578
Okin, Eugene C. 1393
Okonski, Ray 960
O'Konski, Robert 908
Olcott, Charles C. 1298
Olderman, David J. 602
Oldershaw, Louis F. 999
Olgiati, Ennis J. 201
Olinger, Glenn S. 1254
Oliver, David B. 196
Olmsted, D.J. 333
Olney, Steve B. 507
Olsen, Harold S. 918
Olsen, Kenneth H. 597

Olsen, Paul J.J. 1133
Olseth, Dale R. 1329
Olson, B.T. 1048
Olson, Carl O. 1189
Olson, Charles B. 829
Olson, James E. 804
Olson, Martha 116
Olson, Oscar L. 1034
Olson, Richard H. 1042
Olson, Roland 9
Olsten, William 1034
O'Malley, Rory M. 62
O'Malley, Todd 59
Oman, Clifford E. 1359
Onasch, Donald C. 894
O'Neal, David T., Jr. 1187
O'Neal, J.C., Jr. 531
O'Neil, A.J. 985
O'Neil, Erma 108
O'Neil, Jim 1036
O'Neill, D.F. 1053
O'Neill, Donald E. 1056
O'Neill, James P. 197
O'Neill, Thomas F. 709
O'Nell, E.M. 706
O'Nell, Thomas C. 10
Onek, Joseph 232
Onesty, Mary Miller 614
Opitz, William 69
Opler, Edmond 548, 1431
Oppenheimer, E.G. 1391
Orchard, Robert H. 1038
Orear, Richard H. 539
O'Regan, Gerard W. 174
O'Reilly, J., Jr. 538
O'Reilly, Lawrence P. 1223
O'Reilly, Richard J. 342
Orentzel, J. 362
Orloff, Monford A. 645
Ormandy, Les 282
Orme, Keith M. 543, 718
Ornitz, Lawrence 603
Orr, G.W. 1041
Ortiz, Alfonso 225
Ortiz, Sonia 114
Ortmeyer, C.J. 1311
Ortner, Samuel 671
Osborn, Prime F. 907
Osborne, J. Russell 496
Oscherwitz, Harry 427
Oshei, R.C. 663
Oshei, R.J. 1340
Osher, Benjamin 861
Osrow, Harold 1040
Osrow, Leonard 1026
Ossian, Scott Hunter 564
Ossofsky, Jack 215
Ostwald, Venice V. 224
Oswald, Gilbert L. 1228

Otero, Jack A. 37
Otis, Jeannie 278
O'Toole, Patrick J. 1002
Ott, Luis J. 927
Ott, Robert C. 460
Otten, Eric 876
Otto, Carl J. 972
Otto, R.A. 558
Ottobrini, Harold 957
Overby, Chris 118
Overcash, Reece A., Jr. 386
Overholser, Ed 69
Overton, Frank W. 1043
Owen, Alex 525
Owen, Stephen C., Jr. 739
Owens, Luke 57
Oxman, Bennett N. 343
Ozmun, D.B. 562

P

Pabis, Frank D. 417
Pace, Warren M. 895
Pacek, Benjamin M. 1431
Pacheco, Raymond 112
Pacht, Harold 1102
Pachtner, Kay 96
Packer, Richard W. 597
Packer, Ronald O. 1048
Paddock, Benjamin H., III 521
Padek, Saul 1320
Padgett, Michael 271
Padovano, Robert 1268
Page, Henry, Jr. 1049
Page, J.F., Jr. 550
Page, Jack L. 842
Page, Jim C. 1049
Page, John H. 815
Page, Walter H. 984
Paine, John G. 812
Paley, William S. 473
Palmer, Arnold 379
Palmer, Curtis H. 375
Palmer, Edward C. 1050
Palmer, Richard M. 1050
Palmer, Robert J. 126
Palombo, Arthur J. 462
Palton, Leon D. 1132
Palumbo, Edwin P. 61
Palumbo, Norm 311
Panasci, Henry A., Jr. 658
Pantalone, Frank S. 53
Papas, Dean C. 1053
Papay, Michael P. 1003
Parham, Rick 276
Paris, Al 1374

Personnel Index

Paris, David 135
Parish, Charles E. 881
Parish, Richard L., Jr. 354
Park, John R. 361
Park, John W. 820
Parke, H.G. 474
Parker, Edward P. 1056
Parker, George 1057
Parker, Irvin D. 61
Parker, J.R. 1236
Parker, John T. 539
Parker, Norman F. 1372
Parkin, Alvin 589
Parkinson, Bruce S. 1251
Parkinson, Chauncey J. 336
Parkman, Earl 1400
Parks, Henry G., Jr. 1057
Parks, James J. 669
Parks, Richard 528
Parks, Robert M. 1057
Parmeter, O. 881
Parr, Charles R. 999
Parrill, I. Benjamin 965
Parris, Dale 271
Parron, Manuel 111
Parvis, Byron 279
Pasarow, Robert 474, 749
Pascoe, W.T., III 349
Pascucci, Vito 887
Pasin, M.A. 1120
Pate, Gale 840
Paton, Jean M. 219
Patrick, C.K. 305
Patten, Ann 312
Patterson, Charles 765
Patterson, O.F., Jr. 1060
Pauker, Richard H. 858
Paul, Bernard 706
Paul, Elias 984
Paul, Ernest 987
Paul, Gene 531
Paul, Lloyd 1444
Paul, Walter 70
Paulick, R.H. 583
Pauls, Robert Alan 106
Paulsel, Lee 952
Paulson, Harvey 1197
Paulson, Richard N. 814
Pawlak, Vic 151
Pawley, J.G. 335
Pawlicki, C.D. "Doc" 897
Paxson, James M. 1263
Payne, Ancil 856
Payne, B.S., Jr. 1318
Peak, B.L. 1249
Pearce, Robert 342
Pearcy, Glen 97
Pearlman, Edmond 1296
Pearlman, Leonard D. 876

Pearlstein, Irving 1300
Pearson, Chris 119
Pearson, Evelyn 646
Pearson, G.L. 1254
Pearson, H.F. 542
Pearson, John E. 1022
Pease, James L., Jr. 1062
Peck, Ben 1427
Peck, Donald D. 672
Peck, Ralph C. 730
Peck, Robert A. 295
Peck, Robert G. 108
Pecker, J. Howard 1231
Peckman, Paul 538
Peckoff, Kascal 1074
Pederson, Robert K. 1038
Pedone, Stefano J. 55
Peeks, Edward 295
Peet, Millis L. 1064
Peet, William J. 320
Peirce, David L. 590
Peirson, W.R. 364
Pelavin, Joseph Y. 881
Pell, Ronald 1084
Pellegrini, A.J. 450
Pellegrini, Louis 438
Pellegrino, Joseph A. 47
Pellegrino, Joseph P. 1101
Pelletier, George A. 535
Peloquin, Alfred E. 132
Pels, Donald A. 897
Pelzman, Frederick 30
Pena, Viola 52
Pendergast, Howard E. 994
Penick, James D. 1062
Penn, Edgar V. 703
Penn, Franklin E. 362
Penno, Jerry 10
Pennock, Robert L., Jr. 787
Penny, Paula 22
Pensmith, Alice 46
Pentony, Lynn 293
Penza, James 623
Peoples, Clara 113
Pepper, Lawrence 1374
Peraini, Roy T. 546
Percelay, Earl 1009
Percinal, Charles, Jr. 1105
Percy, Steve 103
Perelli, Sheri 48
Perelman, Raymond G. 420
Perera, Guido R. 458
Pergola, C.A. 1016
Perin, Monica Wilch 276, 277, 278
Perin, Robert W. 202
Perine, H. Ford 248
Perkins, Donald A. 1173
Perkins, Frederick G., III 963

Perkins, Harold 1031
Perkins, Homer G. 1266
Perkins, Ivan 607
Perkins, J. Stuart 1386
Perkins, L.H. 1040
Perkins, Reimer A. 949
Perkins, Wayne W. 342
Perlman, Alfred E. 1408
Perlmutter, Milton 1293
Perry, Allen E. 522
Perry, Arnold P. 442
Perry, Berard T. 603
Perry, Edgar, III 1071
Perry, M.L. 107
Perry, William H. 489
Persinger, Laverne O. 430
Person, Ann 1280
Person, E.A. 1324
Person, Robert T. 1107
Pertz, John 1406
Pessin, Norman E. 765
Pester, Jack 1071
Peters, Anthony J. 570
Peters, C. Wilbur 969
Peters, George 118
Peters, Melvin S. 1127
Peters, Robert 155
Petersen, Christian 1073
Petersen, H. William 1208
Petersen, Walter R. 505
Peterson, Aaron J. 1443
Peterson, D.A. 682
Peterson, Darrel E. 1198
Peterson, David D. 654
Peterson, Henry G. 1164
Peterson, Howard C. 663
Peterson, James R. 1080
Peterson, Jean 144
Peterson, John E., Jr. 1397
Peterson, Karen 133
Peterson, Leland J. 1063
Peterson, O. Eric 993
Peterson, W. 553
Peterson, W.C. 597
Petko, Edward A. 632
Petley, William G. 417, 1384
Petrocelli, Americo W. 1437
Pettengill, Lloyd R. 428
Petterson, Marilyn 279
Petty, Mari 272
Petzel, Stanley G. 372
Pew, Robert C. 1271
Peyser, Frederick M., Jr. 742
Peyton, Donald L. 245
Pfeffer, J.L. 1282
Pfeiffenberger, John 274
Pfeiffer, John P. 1425
Phelan, John D. 361

1585

Personnel Index

Phelps, E.R. 1062
Phelps, Richard J. 1293
Phifer, Reese 1075
Philips, Joel M. 329
Phillips, Anita 102
Phillips, Bradford E. 1332
Phillips, Charles D. 221
Phillips, Charles E. 335
Phillips, Dean 154
Phillips, Donelan J. 200
Phillips, Fred 1276
Phillips, Lewis 1006
Phillips, R.D. 1377
Phillips, Seymour J. 1077
Phillips, Sid M. 1393
Phillips, Thomas L. 1126
Philpott, J. Robert 468
Piane, John M., Jr. 578
Picariello, Pat 1341
Piciullo, Edna B. 1266
Pick, Albert, Jr. 1078
Pickard, Henry A., Jr. 1078
Pickard, J.D. 1079
Picken, James E. 54
Picken, Robert 1064
Picker, Samuel 154
Pickett, Lynn 280
Picone, Joseph 645
Piechota, F.A. 581
Pierce, James M. 216
Pierce, W.G., Jr. 1079
Pierihg, Pam 118
Pierson, J.W. 460
Pihringer, Charles R. 517
Pike, Allen W. 344
Pike, Bruce O. 1003
Pike, Charles 575
Pike, Enid L. 198
Pike, Sidney 311
Pilgrim, Raymond W. 677
Pilling, Neville 1444
Pincus, Bernard E. 795
Pincus, Irwin Nat 1081
Pine, Leon L. 1123
Pines, Leonard 766
Pinola, Joseph J. 1357
Pinon, Fernando 293
Pinsker, Casper, Jr. 604
Pipal, Donald L. 987
Pistilli, F.M. 1255
Piszek, E.J. 974
Pitman, Lolett 1083
Pitts, Roy E. 905
Pitts, T.R. 994
Pizza, Anthony J. 1083
Place, Don 724
Place, John B.M. 365
Plank, Raymond 370
Plath, Neil W. 1222

Platt, Henry B. 1324
Platt, James B., Jr. 1277
Platt, Paul 1085
Platts, Harvey N. 1407
Platts, John 1411
Plaxe, Rena 52
Pleskow, Eric R. 1356
Pletschet, Clifford 273
Pliskin, Robert 905
Plock, John L., Jr. 1216
Plumb, D. Rumsey 1087
Pocapalia, Dan 860
Pocklington, Harold L. 158
Pofen, Laurence 421
Pohlit, Nicholas 165
Polachek, Isabelle 1137
Poland, Ted 902
Polaner, Leonard S. 1088
Polikoff, Alexander L. 100
Polite, L. John, Jr. 643
Polk, Louis F., Jr. 889
Pollack, H. William 1089
Pollack, Herbert J. 566
Pollack, Kenneth W. 854
Pollack, Larry 432
Pollack, Ronald F. 202
Pollak, Henry 1089
Pollinow, F.J., Jr. 1377
Polon, Matthew 1118
Polos, C. Dan 1049
Polster, Lewis H. 837
Polychron, John P. 588
Pomasko, Walentyna 281
Pomerance, Lenore 99
Pomerantz, John 892
Pomeroy, Walter 132
Pomeroy, William T. 1273
Pond, Cecil 1411
Ponticelli, Francis 1328
Pontius, H. Jackson 257
Ponzi, Nancy 113
Poole, James E. 933
Poole, James I. 501
Pooler, Rosemary 52
Poor, John B. 1118
Pope, Gene 299
Popeil, Ronald M. 1160
Popp, H. Leslie 1069
Poppe, Martin C. 1351
Porco, Daniel A. 376, 816
Porter, Donald E. 424
Porter, H.G. 418
Porter, Harold H. 1268
Porter, Henry K. 1092
Porter, Robert 625
Portillo, Ernesto V. 297
Portway, Patrick 118
Posey, Lee 1132
Poskas, Lawrence D. 980

Posner, Victor 1003, 1214
Posnick, Adolph 662
Post, Mildred A. 132
Post, Robert S. 149
Post, Russell H. 1385
Pothier, Dick 291
Pothtar, Harold 1332
Potier, J.C. 689
Potter, J.T. 1094
Potter, Theodore P. 696
Potvin, Richard J., Jr. 419
Poulos, Michael S. 480
Poulter, Steve 282
Powell, E. Angus 885
Powell, Hampton O. 880
Powell, Jack B. 721, 736
Powell, Lewis F., Jr. 533
Powell, William A. 961
Power, Vernon C. 551
Powers, David B. 1232
Powers, Frederic B., Jr. 1125
Powers, J. Carl 816
Powers, Ralph A., Jr. 1154
Powers, Richard J. 809
Powers, Robert A. 1235
Powers, Robert T. 996
Powers, Roger W. 130
Powers, W.J. 1146
Pownell, Charlotte 38
Pozez, Louis 1386
Prairie, Eden 624
Prall, Ingrid E. 112
Prange, Henry C. 1095
Prashker, Robert M. 826
Pratt, D.M. 1000
Pratt, Edmund T., Jr. 1074
Pratt, Leonard C. 1095
Pratt, Ronald E. 622
Prejean, Charles O. 95
Prendergast, Thomas A. 432
Preonas, Demetri 439
Press, William 133
Pressman, Edward 1097
Pressman, Fred 408
Price, Andrew, Jr. 999
Price, Forrest W. 603, 751
Price, George E. 1099
Price, Noel B. 167
Price, R. 1123
Price, Randolph H. 503
Price, Robert 659
Price, W.J. 1265
Price, William 631
Prigmore, William H. 1307
Prigozen, Larry 768
Primavera, Victor 576
Primm, Beny 136
Prince, Frank J. 900
Prince, L.L. 450

1586

Personnel Index

Prindle, R.L. 627
Prinster, Frank, Jr. 521
Pritchard, Albert H. 656
Pritchard, H. Wayne 135
Pritchard, Peter C. 390
Procknow, Donald E. 1407
Proctor, A. Neville 613
Proctor, J.D. 891
Proctor, Richard 1002
Proctor, Roy V. 58
Proksch, William W., Jr. 69
Prorok, Stanley L. 141
Proudfoot, A.W. 570
Provo, Larry S. 513
Prudent, Mark R. 932
Pruyn, W.J. 447
Pulitzer, Sidney 1404
Purcell, Walter 186
Purmort, F.W., Jr. 500
Purnell, Hugh 1109
Purnell, James 262
Purner, Thomas F., Jr. 942
Purviance, Don A. 923
Putman, Dale C. 958
Putman, Paul 1114
Putterman, Milton 1436
Putterman, Saul 967
Pyatt, Richard 304, 313
Pyle, James T. 247
Pyle, Owen 858

Q

Quaritas, Jack H. 1065
Quayle, Vincent P. 104
Quigg, Catherine 101
Quinn, John E. 46
Quinn, John Q., Jr. 403
Quinn, Louis S. 68
Quirk, E. James 451
Quirk, Joseph 888
Quittmeyer, Robert T. 365

R

Raab, Hilary A. 622
Rabb, Sidney R. 1278
Rabin, Hy 1406
Rachelson, Charles 549
Rackoff, S.R. 360
Raczynski, Stanley F. 514
Rader, I.A. 341
Radford, George A. 450

Radnay, John P. 636
Radulovic, Peter 764
Radutzky, Alex 838
Rael, S. 1134
Raff, Gilbert 902
Raffel, Leroy B. 374
Ragan, Amos H., Jr. 1120
Ragan, Bradley E. 1120
Ragland, James B. 1120
Rague, John R. 137
Rahdert, Frederick C. 708
Raines, Earl 97
Raitzin, Samuel 1346
Raizen, Roy R. 628
Ralph, L.S. 564
Ramage, David, Jr. 197
Ramos, B.G. 992
Ramsay, David 851
Ramsey, Chaplain Elling E. 97
Ramsey, Claude S. 335
Randall, Harris 542
Randall, James R. 374
Rankin, David H. 625
Rankin, James L. 1255
Ranney, Jack L. 157
Ransbottom, J.A. 1155
Ransburg, David P. 1006
Ransom, Daniel G. 770
Ranzoni, Emanuele, Jr. 1160
Rapaport, Robert M. 1284
Rappaport, David 575
Rappaport, Earl 584
Rappaport, Ida 144
Rappaport, M. 386
Rashbaum, Phillip 686
Raskin, Rubin 583
Rasmus, Henrietta C. 112
Rasmussen, Bent 1191
Rasmussen, Wallace N. 415
Rasnick, Elmer 201
Rast, L. Edmund 1247
Rastelli, Raymond P. 439
Rasteter, J.E. 884
Ratcliff, Richard 107
Rathbun, A.F. 349
Rathe, Jan 113, 306
Rathke, Kenneth E. 898
Rathke, Wade 95
Rathman, I. 1311
Ratner, Abraham 1124
Ratner, Milton D. 962
Ratowsky, Moses 1320
Ratsey, Colin E. 1124
Rattner, George S. 1054
Raus, Heyman L. 708
Rautenberg, Leonard J. 577
Ravarino, A.J. 1125
Rawls, Joseph Leonard, Jr. 757
Ray, Rowe 294

Rayburn, B.J. 483
Raymond, Eugene B. 1342
Rayner, Merwin I. 627
Raynor, Robert D. 534
Raznick, Arthur S. 50
Rea, Clyde W. 934
Read, Robert J. 357
Reade, L.P. 195
Reagan, R.J. 549
Reardon, John D. 737
Reardon, Robert W. 594
Reasor, William S. 1128
Rebmann, Andrew J. 1373
Rector, Peter W. 1012
Reddig, Edward S. 1412
Reddington, Eileen 615
Reece, T.S. 547
Reed, A. Byron 990, 1372
Reed, D. Roger 65
Reed, George A. 1015
Reed, John 115
Reed, John S. 387
Reed, L.K. 157
Reed, Peter D. 1133
Reed, Roymond S. 1197
Reeder, D.L. 1426
Reef, Albert H. 113
Reehling, Stanley 684, 1400
Rees, George H. 1044
Rees, Janet 111
Reese, Gertrude P. 1197
Reeve, J.P. 372
Reeves, J.E., Jr. 1133
Reeves, Tom 671
Regan, Donald T. 956
Regenery, Henry 1136
Regier, Harold M. 466
Rehm, Donald S. 158
Reich, Don 297
Reich, Jack E. 362
Reich, James M. 920
Reich, Steve 508
Reich, Walter C., Jr. 343
Reichardt, Paul E. 1396
Reichert, J.F. 954
Reid, Elizabeth 123
Reid, James S., Jr. 1265
Reid, Joseph 199
Reidbord, Murray S. 1136
Reif, Louis R. 818
Reigle, James D. 1135
Reilly, Frances C. 1118
Reilly, Frank T. 459
Reilly, James T. 465
Reilly, W.P. 377
Reily, William B., III 1136
Reiman, Robert E. 677
Rein, William F. 1002
Reinhardt, Thomas M. 815

Personnel Index

Reis, Arthur, Jr. 1137
Reis, Robert S. 344
Reiss, Irving 485
Reiss, Victoria 92
Reiter, Victor 884
Reith, Carl J. 1043
Reitze, J.A. 708
Reitzin, Jason A. 1339
Remy, L. Guy 1264
Rena, Michael 449
Rendell, S.E. 713
Renkes, Dick 303
Renzi, Verginio 1139
Repass, Robert T. 500
Replogle, David 1095
Reter, Raymond R. 1141
Reuss, Robert P. 501
Reuther, C.G., Sr. 1141
Reveal, E.I. 689, 1417
Reynertson, J.L. 412
Reynolds, C.L. 277
Reynolds, J. Louis 642
Reynolds, James R., Jr. 1432
Reynolds, R. 515
Reynolds, R.T. 465
Reynolds, Richard S., Jr. 1143
Rheingans, Jake 714
Rhine, Julian D. 37
Rhodes, I.L. 1298
Rhodes, Kent 1126
Rhodes, M.H., Jr. 1144
Riboud, Jean 1194
Riccardo, Leonard T. 1187
Ricci, William S. 481
Ricciardi, Franc M. 553
Rice, E.B. 436
Rice, Florence M. 110
Rice, M.A. 1312
Rice, Raymond R. 1382
Rice, Robert L. 1090
Rice, Robert W. 666
Rice, W. Thomas 1202
Rich, John W. 1127
Rich, Mel 491
Rich, Robert E. 529, 1145
Richards, Deborah 180
Richards, H. Lee 799
Richards, Joseph, Jr. 1284
Richards, Paul G. 1426
Richards, Robert 1425
Richards, Thomas H., Jr. 1176
Richards, William C., Jr. 420
Richardson, Archie G., Jr. 82
Richardson, C.E. 295
Richardson, Colin E. 1108
Richardson, Dean E. 927
Richardson, Frank E. 690
Richardson, Jerome Johnson 1252
Richardson, John 1118

Richardson, Lee 103
Richardson, Meredith 88
Richardson, Paul F. 1201
Richardson, Thomas F. 1355
Richardson, Walter 35
Richter, Herman U. 533
Richter, Kurt G. 1147
Richter, Marvin 1215
Rick, James, III 570
Rickel, E.J. 1147
Ricker, John B., Jr. 448
Ricketts, J.M. 750
Ridenour, Dean F. 168
Ridings, D.A.A. 1059
Ridley, R.L. 1403
Rie, John L. 562
Riebel, R.E. 680
Riebman, Leon 353
Riedel, Paul 1381
Riedl, R.J. 1016
Riegel, Kurt 7
Rieger, C.C. 850
Kieger, Kenneth 289
Rieke, M.E. 1148
Riekes, Max 1148
Rifkin, Irwin 589
Rikhoff, James C. 215
Riklis, Meshulam 946, 1124
Riley, Alreda 105
Riley, D.C. 799
Riley, Joseph V. 43
Riley, Richard A. 666
Riley, Thomas A. 998
Rimland, Marvin 321
Rinard, Bradford G. 104
Rinckenberger, Albert E. 788
Ringer, Walter M., Jr. 677
Ripley, F. Fuller 1344
Riser, Frederick F. 432
Risk, J. Fred 809
Riskin, Jules 160
Ritchie, Reeves E. 377
Ritter, Floyd O. 1135
Ritter, Gerald 406
Ritter, William R. 355
Ritts, Herbert 1151
Rivasi, C.A. 1296
Rivers, W.K. 561
Rixman, D.F. 547
Rizek, Alejandro Asmar 85
Roads, Lee A. 1235
Roark, Barbara 124
Robbie, Walter J. 729
Robbins, Jack E. 1088
Robbins, Jerome W. 747
Robbins, Ray C. 890
Robbins, W.A. 437
Robert, Walter 633
Roberts, A. Addison 1138

Roberts, Alfred 1081, 1242
Roberts, Avis 281
Roberts, Donald 1153
Roberts, Henry R. 542
Roberts, John J. 356
Roberts, John M., IV 358
Roberts, Richard J. 887
Roberts, T.S., Jr. 982
Roberts, Thomas H. 586
Robertson, A. Richard 309
Robertson, C. Stuart 1154
Robertson, Donn J. 217
Robertson, John M. 908
Robertson, W.O. 138
Robillard, Harold 287
Robinson, A.L. 762
Robinson, Dorothy 112
Robinson, E.A. 532
Robinson, E.W. 68
Robinson, Edward A. 750
Robinson, H. Delmer, Jr. 1216
Robinson, H.R. 1155
Robinson, Jack A. 325
Robinson, James 353
Robinson, James W., Sr. 361
Robinson, John 281
Robinson, John W. 1155
Robinson, Ralph 968, 1373
Robinson, S. Warne 991
Roboz, Thomas 504, 1265
Roby, Frank M. 1242
Roche, Burke B. 432
Rocheleau, Donald 390
Roddenbery, J.B., Sr. 1157
Roddick, Jan 273
Rode, Betty 59
Rodemacher, W.D. 500
Rodenberg, Harry 1229
Rodgers, Robert 563
Rodgers, W. 1392
Rodin, Arnold W. 251
Rodin, Sidney H. 1157
Rodormer, E. Winston 628
Rodrigue, E.G. 907
Roe, Willard E. 571
Roeber, Karl 65
Roeckers, Eugene C. 262
Roegelein, William, Jr. 1157
Roesch, John A. 741
Rogel, Marty 99
Rogers, Barbara 288
Rogers, C.R. 778
Rogers, Donald L. 467
Rogers, Joe W., Jr. 1388
Rogers, John P. 1266
Rogers, Lewis H. 121
Rogers, Nat S. 667
Rogers, Paul 788
Rogers, Paul W. 365

Personnel Index

Rogers, Richard 1300
Rogers, Robert E. 832
Rogers, S.H., Jr. 1418
Rogers, W.F. 566
Rogg, Nathaniel 256
Rogoff, Solomon 1386
Rohe, F.W. 1221
Rohl, Patricia K. 303
Rokaw, Daniel R. 384
Roland, Robert A. 261
Rolfs, Thomas J. 364
Roller, William G. 696
Rollins, O. Wayne 1159
Rolly, John W. 63
Roloff, Harold W. 1159
Romberg, C.J. 521
Rome, Jay 930
Romeo, Andrew A. 397
Romero, Max A. 1129
Romick, M.M. 606
Romig, G.C. 349
Romweber, Anthony A. 354
Ronan, Phil 117
Ronan, William T. 958
Ronchetti, C. Vittorio 339
Rooke, Vernon W., Jr. 549
Roos, Phillip 162
Roosevelt, W. Emlen 1003
Rose, Clara 1341
Rose, Diane 279
Rose, J. Sanford 1144
Rose, Marshall 866, 1252
Rosemond, Leland E. 1041
Rosen, Barbara 54
Rosen, Carl 1109
Rosen, Jules 1052
Rosen, Martha 144
Rosen, S. Elly 195
Rosenau, Robert J. 997
Rosenbaum, Harold 856
Rosenberg, A. Richard 431
Rosenberg, Abraham 1048
Rosenberg, G.J. 1428
Rosenberg, Harold 1422
Rosenberg, Henry A., Jr. 565
Rosenberg, Leslie D. 1402
Rosenberg, Marvin 482
Rosenberg, Paul H. 1143
Rosenberg, Peter 511
Rosenberg, Philip I. 1306
Rosenberg, Robert 613
Rosenberger, Robert L. 389
Rosenblatt, Emanuel G. 940
Rosenblatt, Justin L., Sr. 1162
Rosenbloom, Bertram H. 891
Rosenbloom, David B. 925
Rosenfeld, G.P. 429
Rosenfeld, Jesse S., Jr. 583
Rosenfeld, Nathan 824

Rosenfeld, S. James 28
Rosenfield, Gerald 1125
Rosengarten, Martin 1219
Rosenhaus, M.B. 1420
Rosenkranz, L.J. 1004
Rosenow, T.L. 687
Rosenstein, Arthur 851
Rosenstock, Edward 455
Rosenthal, Andrew H. 1219
Rosenthal, Gary 1275
Rosenthal, Warren W. 830
Rosewall, Arthur A. 467
Rosin, Stephen V. 40
Rosko, T.A. 392
Rosner, Judy 179
Rosner, Richard 718
Rosoff, Saul R. 16
Ross, Clarence H. 1246, 1382
Ross, Edward W. 1004
Ross, G.M. 354, 1163
Ross, Harry 483
Ross, Henry L., Jr. 556
Ross, Howard B. 791
Ross, June 116
Ross, Kenneth 839
Ross, Louis R. 680
Ross, Melvin 1130
Ross, Nat 1244
Ross, Robert 160
Ross, Sherwood B. 504
Ross, Steven J. 1394
Rosset, Barney 741
Rossi, Anthony T. 1344
Rossi, Donald 1163
Rosskam, Lester G., Jr. 1112
Rosskamm, Martin 651
Rosso, Jean Pierre 1163
Rosson, William M. 548
Rostan, John P., Jr. 1390
Roston, Louis 1375
Roth, A. 1238
Roth, Edward 1307
Roth, George E. 1256
Roth, H. 1164
Roth, Harold 741
Roth, Harry 870
Roth, Herbert, Jr. 872
Roth, Herbert L. 1215
Roth, Joseph R. 691
Roth, Robert 826
Rothenberg, Al 247
Rothenberg, David 203
Rothenberg, Don 96
Rothenberg, Irving 568
Rothenberg, Jack 444, 838
Rothert, Matthew H., Sr. 481
Rothman, Andrew L. 28
Rothman, Irving 819
Rothman, Morton 1164

Rothschild, Donald 85, 99
Rothschild, Robert S. 804
Rothwell, W.R. 704
Roudebush, Helen Lee 163
Rouse, A.E. 1311
Rouselle, Charles R. 238
Roush, David P. 1026
Rousso, Louis E. 1172
Rovegno, John 1071
Rowan, John G. 631
Rowan, Robert D. 692
Rowe, D.E., Jr. 1165
Rowe, J.F. 969
Rowell, Theodore H., Jr. 1165
Rowen, Edward J., Jr. 1295
Rowley, Edward R. 995
Rowse, David R. 1008
Royce, A.J. 1170
Royce, John 701
Rubenstein, Albert 687
Rubenstein, M.D. 1170
Rubin, Allen 357
Rubin, Bennett S. 485
Rubin, Leon 387
Rubin, Samuel 893
Rubin, W.S. 837
Rubinstein, Sam 1415
Ruble, R.R. 1101
Ruby, Burton B. 828
Ruch, Edward T. 140
Rucker, Adin H. 1277
Rucker, Ellie 293
Rucker, Johnny B. 1171
Rudd, Eugene 1171
Rude, J. Arthur 182
Rudin, Leo B. 1340
Rudofker, Samuel 332
Rudolph, Frank A. 1150
Rudolph, Karl H. 525
Ruegger, Herman 1256
Ruesch, Carl 835
Ruger, William B. 1283
Rugg, Allen D. 1171
Rugger, Gerald K. 786
Rugland, Walter L. 333
Rule, Elton H. 351
Ruliffson, H.L. 1064
Rummel, H.E. 40
Runde, O.F. 659
Runke, Darrell M. 815
Runnstrom, W.C. 1202
Rupple, Brenton H. 400
Rushing, Delmas 723
Rusie, Albert E. 331
Russakov, Irwin J. 326
Russek, Louis 765
Russell, B.P. 1359
Russell, Barton D. 64
Russell, Bobby P. 1019

1589

Russell, Charles J. 1172
Russell, E.W. 566
Russell, J.P. 1111
Russell, John L. 45
Russell, L.E. 1310
Russell, Penrose 776
Russinof, Milton R. 409
Rust, Edward B. 1269
Rust, Maurice A. 1173
Ruth, Alpheus L. 889
Ruth, John N. 46
Ruth, William L. 889
Rutherford, James J. 469
Ruttenberg, Harold J. 322
Ruttenstein, Calman 445
Ruvance, Joseph J., Jr. 1038
Ruza, Stanley 633
Ryan, Alan R. 469
Ryan, Ferrell S. 1136
Ryan, Frank 842
Ryan, John P. 952
Ryan, Patrick C. 58
Ryan, T.J. 264
Ryan, Vincent J., Jr. 601
Rydberg, V.A. 815, 947
Ryles, Tim C. 42
Rymer, S.B., Jr. 920
Rynyan, William P. 1330
Ryon, John L. 815

S

Saad, Charles 274
Saad, Theodore 1178
Saalfield, Henry R. 1175
Sachs, Daniel E. 1123
Sachs, George 555
Sachs, Irving H. 510
Sachs, Richard C. 1176
Sackett, Ross D. 638
Sadacca, Albert V. 1015
Sadinoff, Seymour S. 414
Sadja, Elliott D. 513
Sadock, Sam W. 875
Sadow, Saul 1333
Saegi, Susumu 1017
Safran, Benjamin P. 1177
Safran, Charles 951
Sage, George 444
Sagner, Arnold 1178
Saidleman, Norton 1367
Saigol, M. Rafique 1049
Saint John, Michael 520
St. Thomas, James W. 1179
Saitoh, K. 1214
Saker, Joseph J. 679

Sakuma, Kenji 1437
Saldino, Michael D. 43
Saligman, Harvey 1114
Salik, David 643
Salisbury, Dallas 27
Salisbury, William H. 1181
Salmanson, Donald 326
Salmon, Charles R. 330
Salsbury, Sherrod 1212
Saltenstall, Robert, Jr. 1028
Salter, Sallye 276
Salton, Lewis L. 1181
Saltzman, Alan 234
Saltzman, Henry 199
Slaverda, Roy 1239
Salwen, Jesse L. 861
Salzbank, Jules 356
Samford, Frank P. 894
Sampson, H.M. 1020
Sampson, Harvey E., Jr. 762
Sampson, R.M. 406
Sams, Herbert W. 1200
Samsen, Joan 166
Samuel, T.R. 298
Samuelenas, Paul J. 1349
Samuels, Abe 1254
Samuels, Arthur 726
Samuels, Edward R. 1182
Samuels, Ronald 43
Samuels, T. William 1267
Sandau, Paul 281
Sandborn, Constance N. 928
Sandel, H.E. 37
Sander, Sterling 881
Sanders, Albert Jerry, Sr. 153
Sanders, Charles B. 597
Sanders, Frank X., Jr. 401
Sanders, J.V. 1143
Sanders, Richard 493
Sanders, Robert V. 526
Sanders, S. 1126
Sanderson, D.R., Sr. 1183
Sanderson, George N. 422
Sanderson, Richard L. 248
Sandler, Martin N. 641
Sands, Frank E., II 1184
Sands, Frank E., III 961
Sands, Marvin 484
Sands, Walter H. 371
Sandstrom, Dale V. 56
Sandvik, Richard M. 58
Sanford, Edward 1101
Sanford, Harvey 679, 1327
Sann, Joan 958
Sanna, F.L. 1185
Sanow, Robert 527
San Soucie, R.L. 1294
Sant, J.W. 1363
Santiestavan, Henry 214

Santini, Godfrey F. 1186
Santoro, Alfred 55
Saper, Lawrence 578
Sappie, Paul R. 738
Sappington, A.D. 915
Sargent, John T. 606, 901
Sargent, P. 282
Sarli, Ralph 350
Sas, Norman A. 1346
Sasser, Phil 379
Sassower, Philip S. 411
Satre, Wendell J. 1396
Satter, Marsha 120
Sattler, Elliot A. 51
Sauer, John C. 824
Sauey, William R. 671
Saul, David 1188
Sauler, Gerald 1309, 1346
Saulter, Leonard G. 763
Saunders, Richard D. 1009
Saunooke, Osley B. 226
Sauter, Janet 69
Sauvage, Jean Marie 1351
Savada, Morton J. 1189
Savage, Donald F. 54
Savage, John J. 1358
Savarick, Martin 414
Savinelli, Emilio A. 609
Sawvel, Milo C. 164
Sawyer, Dannis 1224
Sax, Frank 322
Sax, Herbert 459, 1014
Saypol, Ronald D. 900
Scalamandre, Franco 1191
Scarlet, Ted 807
Scerbo, Albert 1191
Schacht, Henry B. 568
Schacht, William 1192
Schadt, James P. 980
Schaeberle, Robert M. 995
Schaefer, Charles V., Jr. 331
Schafer, George M. 43
Schafer, Harold L. 723
Schaffer, Paul 426
Schaffer, Samuel 1192
Schaible, John F. 1192
Schaikowsky, Jan 101
Schaller, Maurice 892
Schalon, Edward I. 1204
Schankman, Milton 1262
Schardt, Artie 128
Scharf, Joel S. 605
Scharff, Kurt H. 881
Scharffenberger, George T. 521
Schattenstein, Alvin E. 1195
Schattinger, James H. 1082
Schatz, James L. 360
Schaub, Harold A. 483
Schaub, Walter R. 1197

Personnel Index

Schear, Hyman 894
Schechter, Sol 753
Schecter, Abraham 606
Scheffler, Leo 587
Scheib, Earl 1192
Scheiber, Ted 1229
Schein, Harvey L. 1244
Schein, John E. 94
Schenck, E.G. 427
Schenk, Boyd 1072
Scher, Joseph S. 639
Schere, Jordan 165
Scherer, Otto S. 437
Scherger, Louis C. 588
Scherr, Harold M. 1186
Schey, Ralph 1198
Schey, William B. 890
Scheyer, Stuart R. 541
Schieffelin, William J., III 1193
Schierl, Paul J. 682
Schiff, Herbert H. 1174, 1197
Schiffer, C.E. 480
Schirmer, Rudolph E. 1193
Schirmer, Walter E. 523
Schisano, Robert 595
Schlager, Walter L., Jr. 905
Schlanger, Robert S. 1088
Schlegel, Robert P. 363
Schleicher, Scott R. 802
Schlenker, Roy F. 785
Schlesinger, M. 1330
Schlink, F.J. 85
Schlomm, Boris 363
Schloss, Milton J. 842
Schlossberg, Louis 593
Schlueter, C.F. 637
Schlueter, Walter J. 1194
Schmid, Carl F. 1348
Schmid, Paul A. 1194
Schmidt, A.D. 1022
Schmidt, Bernard 486
Schmidt, Charles W. 1395
Schmidt, Chauncey E. 404, 667
Schmidt, Harry D. 507
Schmidt, N.G. 380
Schmidt, Robert A. 1034
Schmidt, Roger W. 168
Schmitz, L.H. 208
Schmitz, William F. 689
Schmlikler, Joseph 727
Schnadig, Lawrence K. 1194
Schnall, Herbert K. 1008
Schnapp, Sidney 1346
Schneider, Michael 62
Schneider, R.A. 1266
Schneider, Sidney 515
Schneider, Warren A. 623
Schneider, Yehochai 319
Schnitt, Albert 976
Schnitzler, Fred A. 1026

Schnuck, Donald O. 1194
Schnurr, Robert 1170
Schoditsch, Fred W. 461
Schoefer, Winnie 148
Schoelhorn, R.A. 887
Schoen, Herbert P. 761
Schoen, William J. 1192
Schoenbrun, Ernest J. 1188
Schoenfeld, Walter R. 712
Schoenhofen, Leo H. 929
Schoenly, Harry M. 500
Scholl, William H. 1195
Schollmaier, Edgar H. 337
Schottenfeld, Milton 583
Schottland, S.A. 350
Schrade, William A. 525, 1378
Schrader, Abe 1195
Schrader, Bill 278
Schramm, Arthur T. 678
Schramm, Leslie B. 1195
Schreiber, G.A. 1107
Schreiber, Martin J. 65
Schreiber, Toby 1253
Schreiner, Robert G. 581
Schreter, Sidney H. 1196
Schroeder, Bruce E. 66
Schroeder, C. Frederic 1086
Schroeder, John H. 562
Schubel, Adam J. 1215
Schubert, J.R. 1196
Schuch, Marge 277
Schuchman, F.E., Jr. 786
Schuchter, Maude F. 927
Schuette, Earl 1398
Schuette, John H. 817
Schuler, M.C. 447
Schuler, William C. 1196
Schultz, C.H. 1196
Schultz, Donald H. 1364
Schultz, Otto 350
Schultz, R.L. 1092
Schultz, Robert 947
Schultz, William D. 1225
Schulz, Donald A. 1174
Schulz, Howard N. 171
Schulz, Richard L. 1211
Schumacher, Edward W. 720
Schuman, Adolph P. 897
Schuman, Elaine 52
Schurgot, Paul D., Jr. 999
Schurter, G.T. 1417
Schuster, K.C. 830
Schutz, Bernard R. 665
Schutz, J.G. 1140
Schwaber, Joseph, Jr. 979
Schwager, Kurt 1299
Schwartz, Arthur R. 1196
Schwartz, Bernard 862, 1426
Schwartz, Carol H. 111

Schwartz, Edward 1150
Schwartz, Eugene P. 231
Schwartz, Harlan A. 1197
Schwartz, Henry E. 1428
Schwartz, Herman 1353
Schwartz, Ira 1316
Schwartz, Jerome 1308
Schwartz, Milton 403
Schwartz, Morris 842
Schwartz, Nathan R. 1299
Schwartz, Richard J. 836
Schwartz, Sanford 143
Schwartz, Shepard 944
Schweich, Anderson M. 514
Schwier, Fred W. 331
Schweiger, J.R. 1197
Schweitzer, M. Peter 1405
Schwinn, Frank V. 1197
Schwob, Mrs. Simon 1197
Sconyers, Hal W. 1408
Scott, Bill B. 888
Scott, Bob F. 856
Scott, David C. 344
Scott, Frank 66
Scott, Fred B. 1400
Scott, George G., Jr. 424
Scott, Glenn E. 1428
Scott, Joe M. 623, 1187
Scott, John G. 988
Scott, John W. 288
Scott, Marty 106
Scott, Norman 359
Scott, Paul 1280
Scott, Phil 300
Scott, William 115
Scotti, Salvatore G. 1198
Scribner, Charles, Jr. 1200
Scully, Frank 694
Scully, Michael 146
Seaberg, Robert 512
Seabrook, James M. 1203
Seagraves, Wayne 959
Seaman, Alfred J. 1175
Seaman, Edwin 1336
Searles, T.D. 244
Searles, T.M. 660
Seaton, Jay 314
Seawall, Donald R. 591
Seawell, William T. 1051
Seay, William H. 1250
Sebastian, J.R. 1320
Sebastian, Richard 59
Sebell, Adolph 1300
Seddon, Melvin E. 374
Seder, Herschel L. 968
Seeger, John R. 647
Seekon, Robert C. 692
Sefton, Thomas W. 1183
Segal, Herb 1080

Personnel Index

Segal, Philip L.   360
Segal, William   739
Segell, Jack   1003
Segil, Arthur W.   911
Seib, Charles   274
Seibel, Morris H.   902
Seidenberg, Paul   441
Seifert, William J.   1207
Seiff, Joel   1268
Seifried, Dean B.   1037
Seiler, Lewis P.   384
Seitz, Earl   1136
Seitz, Ernestine   473
Sekimoto, Masahiro   1207
Selby, John R., Sr.   1265
Seldin, Marc A.   1207
Selig, Robert J.   875
Selis, Irving M.   144
Sell, Larry J.   184
Sellars, Robert L.   41
Sellers, Harvey A., Jr.   775
Sellew, Carol A.   1361
Selnau, Edward W.   380
Selonick, Edward H.   1218
Seltzer, Ronald   918
Seltzer, Samuel M.   344
Selver, Rene T.   617
Selzer, William H.   558
Semenza, Joan   55
Semler, Susan L.   48
Semmler, Ray E.   1067
Sengbusch, Frederick G.   1209
Senior, Latimer   53
Sepinuck, Nathan   414
Serbin, Lewis I.   1210
Seretean, M.B.   554
Serlen, Michael   204
Serman, Michael   1210
Serpa, T.P.   1163
Serra, Javier, Jr.   575
Sethness, Charles H., Jr.   1211
Seton, Fenmore R.   1211
Settimi, Joseph C.   1138
Seubert, Helen   290
Sevier, Helen   122
Seward, Harold A.   185
Sewell, James H.   469
Sexton, Floyd   95
Sexton, M.   1212
Seyer, Frank H.   1193
Seymour, Edward H.   1212
Seymour, J.M.   207
Sforza, Alfred T.   1193
Shaer, David L.   994, 1213
Shaffer, A.M.   187
Shaffer, Burton   752
Shaffer, C. Elwood   1290
Shaffer, Don   273
Shaffer, R.W.   708
Shaheen, S.   1431

Shainberg, Herbert   1213
Shalhoub, Susan C.   105
Shalley, Thelma   60
Shames, Sidney J.   952
Shane, Sidney A.   1214
Shaner, Shirley   118
Shankman, Sam   886
Shannon, Gerald T.   898, 899
Shansby, J. Gary   1213
Shaper, Harry B.   637
Shaper, Lloyd S.   1109
Shapero, Ray A.   569
Shapira, George   766
Shapiro, Arthur H.   938
Shapiro, Carl   847
Shapiro, Esther K.   48
Shapiro, Gordon G.   729
Shapiro, Henry   1021
Shapiro, I.D.   924
Shapiro, Jay B.   366
Shapiro, Samuel   1297
Shapiro, Seymour   998, 1210
Shapoff, Lloyd M.   1132
Shapren, William   1077
Sharbaugh, H. Robert   1287
Sharkey, Samuel   9
Sharp, Merle R.   738
Sharpe, Henry D., Jr.   461
Sharpe, Ruel Yount   1080
Shaughnessy, Daniel R.   987
Shaver, Jesse M.   349
Shaw, Edward T.   70
Shaw, James J.   1001
Shaw, John S., Jr.   1248
Shaw, Leslie   656
Shaw, M.T., Jr.   1214
Shaw, Milton M.   1011
Shaw, Morris   1214
Shaw, Robert A.   633
Shaw, W.D.   1084
Shaw, William H.   1062
Shea, James J., Jr.   967, 1086
Shearman, Robert W.   245
Sheehan, J.C.   1318
Sheeline, Paul C.   812
Sheerin, Harry J.   856
Sheet, Grant M.   354
Sheffield, Peter Kyle   1215
Sheib, Simon   394, 457
Sheinberg, S.J.   915
Sheldon, A.L.   1215
Sheldon, Edward E.   883
Shelton, Catherine   288
Shelton, Henry   115
Shephard, Robert J.   121
Shepherd, Bill   108
Shepherd, John S.   477
Shepley, James R.   1325
Sheppard, Donna L.   1362

Sheridan, Thomas   277
Sherman, Daniel A.   1141
Sherman, E.   723
Sherman, Harold A.   183
Sherman, Jack   554
Sherman, William S.   578
Sherrow, James W.   583
Sherry, Frank   287
Sheskey, William   847
Shetterly, Robert B.   526
Shevell, D.E.   385
Shevell, Myron P.   623
Shick, Victor   810
Shields, Currin   95
Shiely, Vincent R.   455
Shimanoff, M.S.   36
Shinbach, Violet S.   458
Shinn, Richard R.   958
Shirey, David   1218
Shirk, Russell   417
Shlansky, Milton   1219
Shlora, Raymond B.   462
Shmueli, Kalman   715
Shockley, Nancy E.   98
Shoemaker, Dick E.   992
Shoemaker, John W.   261
Shoemaker, Richard W.   461
Sholtens, C.   986
Shomette, Bill   314
Shook, Eugene   1344
Shoop, Samuel G.   807
Shore, Harry M.   1293
Shorell, Irma   818
Shorin, Joel J.   1331
Short, Jeffrey R., Jr.   1220
Short, Richard A.   192
Short, Winthrop A.   862
Shover, Jayne   165
Shrifte, Evelyn   1371
Shriver, Thomas H.   1411
Shroyer, Lawton W.   1213
Shufelt, Max W.   765
Shuford, Harley F., Jr.   502
Shuford, Harley F., Sr.   1220
Shuford, Harry A.   667
Shugars, James E.   768
Shulga, John A.   997
Shulman, Daniel   1291
Shulman, M.L.   945
Shulman, Michael   96
Shull, Leon   81
Shumate, J.B., Jr.   531
Shumate, Marion   305
Shurcliff, William A.   124
Shure, Myron B.   1281
Shure, S.N.   1221
Shurtleff, Hugh   1149
Shurtz, Mary Ann   64
Shute, E. Clement   35

Personnel Index

Shuttleworth, Herbert L., II 977
Shvetz, Alexander E. 349
Sias, John B. 652
Sibley, Gerald 531
Sibley, Shermer L. 1047
Sidenberg, Ellen 129
Sidman, Louis E. 721
Sidore, Saul O. 460
Siebert, Dorothy A. 1163
Siegal, Eli J. 1385
Siegel, Benjamin M. 464
Siegel, Herbert B. 817
Siegel, Herbert J. 517
Siegel, Jesse 1222
Siegel, Lester, Jr. 762
Siegel, Sylvia 97
Siegenfeld, Morton 687
Sieh, A.B. 166
Siem, Martin 1325
Siems, Werner A. 30
Sierra, Pierre G. 1082
Siff, Harry S. 398
Sigler, Andrew C. 505
Signorelli, Richard 772
Sikes, James W. 1223
Silberstein, Charles K. 538
Silberstein, Robert J. 358
Silliman, Frederick B. 455
Sillin, L.F., Jr. 542, 1407
Sills, Stanley S. 1182
Silton, Fred 1224
Silva, R. Anthony 301
Silver, C. Hal 846
Silver, Nathan 53
Silver, R.E. 248
Silver, Robert 1225
Silverang, S. 1097
Silverberg, Mark B. 758, 828
Silverburg, M. 1166
Silverman, Albert A. 1380
Silverman, Alfred 432
Silverman, Jack 976
Silverman, Leonard 1057
Silverman, Richard T. 1247
Silverman, Samuel 1073
Silverman, Victor 320, 332
Silverstein, F.S. 1005
Silverstein, Robert 631
Silverstein, Wilbur 664
Silverstone, David 39
Simkalo, Richard B. 1304
Simmon, Fred 1227
Simmons, Charles A., III 1227
Simmons, Herbert 99
Simmons, Louise 98
Simmons, Mark 632
Simmons, R.M., Jr. 354
Simmons, Richard D. 612, 982
Simon, Betty Ann 306

Simon, Franklin 664
Simon, Philip 847
Simon, Sidney 594
Simon, Thomas B. 584
Simons, Dolph 1227
Simons, Lawrence B. 20
Simonsen, Henry 366
Simpson, Adele 328
Simpson, John W., Jr. 1129
Simpson, R.J. 698
Simpson, William S. 1125
Simpson, William S. 1228
Simson, Walter H. 374
Sinclair, Robert J. 1386
Sinda, Henry D. 43
Sindelar, J.C. 1400
Singal, Bruce A. 47
Singer, Albert E. 490
Singer, Leo 970
Singer, Phyllis 279
Singleton, Henry E. 1311
Sitter, Albert 271
Six, Robert F. 545
Skaer, P.F. 1197
Skaggs, Alice C. 41
Skaggs, L.S. 1230
Skalka, Stanley 1378
Skelton, J.F. 1316
Skilliter, Robert T., Jr. 325
Sklarsky, Sam 1353
Skolnick, David 693
Skutt, V.J. 993
Slade, G.J. 1408
Slais, Louis J. 1083
Slater, Herbert A. 1233
Slater, Louis 506
Slater, Stanley 118
Slater, Winston G. 795
Slatter, Jack 533
Slavin, Alberta 107
Slayden, James 1155
Slaymaker, Samuel C. 1233
Sledge, James T. 446
Sleep, Robin 118
Sleith, William S. 818
Slessman, Donald B. 689
Slikas, M. John 1303
Slikkers, Leon R. 1233
Slivko, Sharon A. 302, 312
Sloan, A.F. 879
Sloan, Charles T. 1234
Sloan, Edith B. 212
Sloan, Kitty 272
Sloate, Morton 1310
Slocum, H. Turner 1206
Sloiter, Robert J. 474
Slonecker, Howard L., Jr. 1029
Sloss, Richard A. 1110
Slotnick, Herbert N. 494

Smale, John G. 1103
Small, Philip 529
Small, Robert S. 575
Small, Willard A. 1057
Smalley, R.L. 131
Smallridge, John D. 1109
Smargon, Kenneth J. 816
Smart, John 642
Smart, Walter L. 215
Smerling, L.R. 669
Smetts, D.M. 525
Smiley, Dianne 116
Smiley, Donald B. 918
Smilow, Joel E. 815
Smith, A.M. 579
Smith, A.M. 668
Smith, C. Carney 256
Smith, Cecil W. 981
Smith, Charles A., Jr. 1379
Smith, Chester 515, 1236
Smith, Clayton E. 1236
Smith, D.M. 739
Smith, Daniel R. 36
Smith, Denton H. 980
Smith, Doug 101
Smith, Dudley 634
Smith, E. 386
Smith, Edward D. 667
Smith, Edward S. 1035
Smith, Edwin E. 1236
Smith, Floyd R. 745
Smith, Frank G., Jr. 377
Smith, Gary K. 362
Smith, George Blackwell 965
Smith, George G. 481
Smith, George J. 779
Smith, George M. 913
Smith, Goff 365
Smith, H. Arthur, III 285
Smith, Harlan W. 384
Smith, Harold Byron, Jr. 805
Smith, Howard 1382
Smith, Howard A. 409
Smith, Irene M. 104
Smith, Irving L. 580, 870
Smith, J.E. 419
Smith, J.F. 1067
Smith, J.L. 528
Smith, J.R. 1001
Smith, J.V. 1200
Smith, J. Morse 400
Smith, Joe 1394
Smith, John Burnside 330
Smith, John L. 139
Smith, Josephine 113
Smith, Joyce 271
Smith, K.B. 1438
Smith, K.D. 67
Smith, Kenneth B., Jr. 1429

Personnel Index

Smith, L. Chandler 541
Smith, L. Richard 1236
Smith, Leonard C. 957
Smith, Loren 1385
Smith, M.L. 352
Smith, Monroe G. 595
Smith, Muriel Mitchell 42
Smith, Okla Bennett 1030
Smith, Paul C. 1281
Smith, Peter W. 1407
Smith, R.R. 1237
Smith, R.W. 336
Smith, Ray Mace 97
Smith, Regina 286, 287
Smith, Richard A. 705
Smith, Richard S., Jr. 1149
Smith, Richey 1287
Smith, Robert C. 442
Smith, Robert E. 415
Smith, Robert I. 1107
Smith, Robert P. 974
Smith, S. Grover, Jr. 70
Smith, S. Kreis 707
Smith, Thomas J. 656
Smith, Warren B. 874
Smith, William H. 456
Smith, William L. 771
Smith, William S. 1143
Smith, Winton E. 823
Smith, Worthington L. 514
Smith, Wrede 359
Smittcamp, Robert E. 914
Smoke, Al 111
Smoler, Hy 1237
Smoler, Jerry 1238
Smolian, Robert 906
Smucker, Paul H. 1238
Smulowitz, William J. 899
Smylie, C.A. 1436
Smylie, Thomas M. 487
Smyser, Mary 292
Smyth, Raymond 1401
Snavely, Frank L. 544
Sneath, William S., Jr. 1354
Snedaker, R.H., Jr. 1361
Snediker, Robert R. 514
Snelham, Thomas 406, 727
Snelling, Richard A. 1215
Snelling, Robert O. 1238
Snider, R. Larry 1273
Snow, John A. 1217
Snow, John M. 255
Snyder, Arthur F.F. 404
Snyder, Harry W. 1240
Snyder, Paul L. 689
Snyder, Richard E. 1227
Sofro, David I. 791
Sohmer, Harry J., Jr. 1242
Sohngen, Neil L., II 882

Soifer, Herman 459
Sokol, Aaron 929
Solari, Joseph G. 735
Solender, Sanford 202
Soler, James 226
Sollenbarger, Lee R. 1336
Solley, Douglas A. 1141
Solmson, H.B. 944
Solof, Robert 649, 1286
Soloman, Howard 1219
Solomon, Arthur K. 1127
Solomon, Dudley 147
Solomon, Edward 761, 845
Solomon, Jack, Jr. 383
Solomon, Leonard 825
Solomon, Peter H. 772
Solomon, Seymour 1371
Solomonson, C.D. 440
Solon, Judy Smith 57
Somers, Lewis S., III 649
Sommer, Martin H. 1262
Sommez, John R. 854
Sondik, Leon 781
Sonn, Werner 1274
Sonnabend, Roger P. 1244
Sonneborn, Bill 272
Sonneborn, Richard F. 978
Sonners, Harold 1017, 1416
Sonnier, Sam 280
Soper, LaVern G. 1002
Sorenson, Bill W. 321
Soric, Peggy 284
Sorrentino, Stanley 1353
Soskis, Philip 218
Sostrin, Morey 1440
Souaid, George 436
Souhan, F.J. 1209
Southworth, John H. 1250
Souvall, Sam W. 346
Souweine, Jonathan Z. 105
Sovereign, W.F. 336
Sowden, A. James 1009
Sowers, Steve 283
Spack, Aloys P., Jr. 422
Spaet, Jon 304
Spahr, Charles E. 1265
Spain, John 311
Spangler, Harlan G. 1251
Spangler, William C. 593
Spaniel, Frank J. 1065
Speaker, John A. 1252
Speakman, Willard A., III 1252
Spears, B.M. 910
Spears, Lynn H. 1424
Spector, Edward 377
Spector, Raymond 859
Speed, J.B. 377
Speed, J.J. 495
Speer, Edgar 1361

Speer, Raymond G. 1254
Spellens, Melvin 1002
Spencer, Gordon W. 497, 1254
Spencer, W.H. 342
Spencer, W.O. 1217
Spencer, William I. 668
Sperry, Allen M. 1348
Spertus, Philip 813
Speyer, Lester D. 963
Spickerman, John F. 1314
Spiegel, Alan 593
Spiegel, Richard G. 873
Spiegelman, Edmond 707
Spiekermann, Otto 1388
Spielman, Sidney 325
Spier, Jill 39, 97
Spiewak, Gerald 1255
Spillane, Frank J. 120
Spillman, F.J. 1083
Spink, S.C. 1026
Spira, Joel S. 912
Sporck, Charles E. 1003, 1023
Spound, Albert M. 508
Sprague, W.W., Jr. 1189
Spreen, A.R. 1284
Sprigg, J.C., Jr. 1237
Spruce, George Blue 16
Spurway, Harold R. 494
Squier, Edward A. 426
Staal, Ben J. 810
Stabler, Griffin M. 1415
Stabler, William J. 1261
Stacey, John T. 464, 594
Stadelhofer, Fred 424
Stadl, Suzanne M. 113
Staggs, Jack E. 209
Stahl, Kate 8
Stahl, Milton 1394
Stainaker, Armand C. 704
Stall, James L. 1250
Stallings, Jesse F. 487
Stambaugh, John W. 346
Stamboni, Nance J. 46
Stamm, John C. 862
Stanback, T.M. 1263
Stanberry, William B. 798
Standish, Leigh M. 1266
Stanfill, Dennis 1348
Stanford, R.A. 848
Stangeland, Roger E. 527
Stanghellini, John 909
Stanko, John J. 606
Stanley, Edward L. 1106
Stanley, Joan 834
Stanton, David M. 353
Stanton, Gideon 103
Stanton, J.P. 691
Stanton, Stanley E. 687

1594

Personnel Index

Stanton, Thomas J., Jr. 667
Stapsy, Irving S. 466
Stark, Wilbur H. 59
Stark, William 1268
Starker, Abe 720
Starr, Leo 979
Starr, Leon D. 1090
Starrett, Douglas R. 1269
Stata, Ray 365
Statton, Philip B. 1270
Stauber, John C. 119
Stauffer, Thomas G. 1278
Stavin, Robert 749
Steacy, Kevin B. 310
Steakley, Elwood 711
Stebbins, Bryon 450
Stebins, Janet 110
Stecker, Herbert C. 1271
Stedman, W.D. 1271
Steeh, George 48
Steele, Allen M. 895
Steele, Edward C. 1131
Steele, George 332
Steele, Louis D. 49
Steele, Richard 1180
Steele, Richard A. 521
Steele, Vermon H. 658
Steere, David D. 343
Steiger, Albert E. 1271
Stein, Berard A. 778
Stein, Edward B. 1271
Stein, Harry 654
Stein, Julie R. 194
Stein, Karen 81
Stein, Sol 1271
Stein, Walter 1055
Steinberg, Irwin H. 955
Steinberg, Morton 1267
Steiner, Albert 590, 733
Steiner, John M. 1204
Steinhilb, K.E. 1163
Steinman, Helen 946
Steketee, Frank 1217
Steller, Philip 1272
Stelzer, Robert M. 330
Stemcosky, Norbert 55
Stenzel, Edwin L. 607
Stepelton, Norman A. 1001
Stephan, Richard W. 1273
Stephano, Stephen C.S. 1273
Stephens, L.C., Jr. 1080
Stephens, Theodore 1273
Stephenson, Betty 293
Stephenson, Thomas J., Jr. 863
Sterling, Guy 294
Sterling, J.H. 62
Sterling, Sandra DeMent 84
Stern, Charles 711
Stern, E.M., Jr. 1274

Stern, Edward L. 868
Stern, G.H., Jr. 778
Stern, Jack 1420
Stern, Lawrence J. 1274
Stern, Max 761
Stern, Richard 385
Sternberg, Irving 785
Sternberg, Paul C. 634
Sterne, A.H. 1345
Sterner, James 283
Sterzing, Carl B., Jr. 586
Stetler, C. Joseph 262
Stetson, John C. 596
Stetzelberger, W.P. 658
Steury, Norman 584
Stevens, Angus 1275
Stevens, Benjamin 1275
Stevens, D.G. 1383
Stevens, Emery W. 281
Stevens, George M. 1432
Stevens, John B. 923
Stevens, L.B., Jr. 734
Stevens, R.B. 1275
Stevens, Raymond D., Jr. 1095
Stevens, Ronald 1153
Stevens, Roy W. 779
Stevens, Whitney 1275
Stevenson, Michael C. 263
Stewart, A.K. 1311
Stewart, C. Jim 1275
Stewart, Donald R. 1276
Stewart, George 490
Stewart, Jefferson D., Jr. 659
Stewart, R.R., Jr. 1363
Stewart, R.W. 1344
Stewart, Robert, Jr. 404
Stiefel, Werner K. 1276
Stieff, Rodney G. 1276
Stiefvater, G.W. 547
Stier, Robert 1047
Still, Harold F., Jr. 501
Still, J.H. 70
Stillbolt, Hans P. 1359
Stillman, W. Paul 668, 992
Stilwell, Michael 118
Stinson, Charles B. 1276
Stinson, Jack 181
Stinson, Ralph E. 428
Stinson, Stephanie 309
Stitgen, Stanley F. 1146
Stockmeyer, C. Boyd 593
Stockton, Rodney M. 345
Stocktos, Mrs. W.V. 215
Stoddard, Stanford C. 960
Stoddart, Kenneth R. 428
Stokely, Alfred J. 1277
Stoll, Gladys H. 1108
Stoll, Robert A. 560
Stone, Donna J. 212

Stone, Eugene E., III 1277
Stone, F.T. 474
Stone, Harvey 1277
Stone, Henry S. 539
Stone, Irving I. 355
Stone, J. McWilliams, Jr. 612
Stone, Milton J. 805
Stone, Myron 592
Stone, Robert L. 773
Stone, Sam J. 454
Stone, Stephen A. 548
Stone, W. Clement 537
Storch, Adolph D. 1109
Storer, Peter 1278
Storey, Leo M., Jr. 1308
Stossel, John 313
Stoumen, Bernard 453
Stovall, Chester E. 107
Stover, Judy 59
Straight, J.J. 119
Strain, Robert C. 986
Stranaham, Robert A., Jr. 506
Strand, Curt T. 778
Strasma, Edward J. 908
Strassberg, Gerson 368
Straub, John W. 1280
Straubel, Louis A. 1280
Straus, L.H. 1322
Straus, Roger W., Jr. 656
Straus, S.C. 551
Strauss, Curt L. 756, 1077
Strauss, David 1055, 1439
Strauss, Donald B. 125
Strauss, Fred S. 761
Strauss, J.F. 348
Strauss, J.R. 526
Strauss, Jean 129
Strauss, L. 413
Strauss, L.S. 1280
Strauss, Leonard P. 1035
Strauss, Maurice L. 1058
Strauss, Willis A. 1020
Strawbridge, Herbert E. 776
Strawbridge, Nelson 534
Streim, Harry 409
Strichman, George A. 535
Strickland, Sanford E. 996
Stringer, Don 280
Stritt, Jack D. 581
Stroehmann, Harold J. 1281
Stroh, Peter W. 1281
Strombeck, Frederick K. 1281
Strother, R.G. 921
Stroud, David H. 260
Struchen, J. Maurice 1241
Stuckey, Williamson S. 1282
Strugatz, Arthur 392
Strum, Michael R. 907
Stuart, Benjamin F. 1312

1595

Personnel Index

Stuart, D.G. 901
Stuart, Dwight L. 491
Stuart, Michael 1356
Stuart, R.R., Jr. 428
Stuart, Robert 999
Stuart, Robert B. 1066
Stuart, Robert D., Jr. 1112
Stubbs, Alice C. 85
Stubbs, H.F. 388
Stuhler, F.R. 642
Stull, James 1333
Stults, Allen P. 769
Sulzberger, Arthur Ochs 1011
Sturm, Omer 827
Sturz, Herbert 238
Stutz, Rolf 390
Suerth, John C. 711
Sufana, Raymond C. 43
Sullivan, Charles L. 1181
Sullivan, Eugene J. 446
Sullivan, Fred R. 854
Sullivan, James 83
Sullivan, James 510
Sullivan, John W. 1231
Sullivan, Paul 297
Sullivan, R.P. 708
Sumas, Nicholas 1380
Sundberg, Edgar L. 584
Sundberg, Paul J., Jr. 1169
Sundmacher, Herbert C. 446
Sundquist, Ralph 1288
Sunnen, Robert 636
Sunshine, Morton 227
Supple, Edward T. 1294
Supranovich, John 104
Surdam, John L. 1040
Surdam, Robert M. 999
Surface, R.E. 1328
Surguy, Grace 218
Surloff, Bob 1294
Suslow, Robert J. 654
Sussberg, Darwin 898, 1062
Sussman, Harry 1310
Sutphin, Henrietta F. 136
Sutton, Berrien D. 604
Sutton, Thomas C. 606
Suzuki, S. 855
Svahn, John A. 18
Swain, Harlan 891
Swain, O. Everett 867
Swan, Ralph J. 423
Swanson, Alice Q. 177
Swanson, Bob 122
Swanson, Dwight H. 818
Swanstrom, K. Arent 1066
Swartz, Jane 288
Swartz, Thomas J. 1320
Swarzentruber, Arthur D. 1379
Swayne, Amos 496

Sweany, Gordon H. 706, 1177
Swearingen, John E. 1265
Swedlin, Jack 1430
Swee, Eugene A. 968
Sweeney, Alfred L. 9
Sweeney, James D. 1393
Sweeney, Robert J. 991
Sweet, James W. 1199
Sweet, Sidney E. 1313
Sweitzer, R.J. 1119
Swennarton, R.O. 23
Swenson, Harvey S. 1296
Swenson, Lowell 375
Swensson, Stuart J., Jr. 1427
Swett, Earl W. 932
Swett, H. 856
Swift, Humphrey H. 1298
Swift, Lamar 1175
Swig, Benjamin H. 652
Swiggett, Robert L. 865
Swindell, Elizabeth 287
Swindells, William, Jr. 460
Swisher, Randy 99
Switzer, Robert C. 581
Switzer, Russell M. 1299
Sylvester, Harcourt M., Jr. 656
Symmons, Paul C. 1300
Sympson, Claud F. 1056
Synder, Charles J. 324
Syvrud, Duane R. 534
Szal, Bruce 104
Szczygiel, Anthony 111

T

Tabacchi, Fred L. 788
Tabar, William J. 321
Tabat, E. Lawrence 597
Taber, James M. 306
Tack, Preston B. 122
Tackett, R.D. 1074
Taft, Caleb S. 714
Tague, Irving T. 795
Tait, Bob 37
Tait, J.M. 421, 521
Takata, M.R. 861
Takei, Taketsugu 35
Talbert, Lawrence J. 396
Talbot, James L. 70
Talbot, Mildred A. 214
Talge, H. Stephen 581
Tallent, Otto 273
Talley, Frank G. 1303
Tallman, J.W. 1016
Tallman, William C. 1107
Talpis, Stanley 742

Tampone, Dominic 752
Tanaka, Yasuo 387
Tanger, S.K. 561, 1304
Tankersley, James I. 1425
Tankersley, William H. 86
Tannenbaum, Fred F. 486
Tanner, J.C. 352
Tanner, James 71
Tanner, James T. 1305
Tanner, William G. 1354
Tanney, O. Morley 728
Tanselle, Donald W. 954
Taper, S. Mark 360
Tapp, Charles W. 45
Tapp, Patricia A. 109
Tappan, W. Richard 1305
Tarbox, Frank F. 1066
Tarlow, Isidor 338
Tarlow, Richard N. 458
Tarlton, W.D. 1071
Tarzian, Sarkes 1187
Tassie, Debbie 98
Tassie, John M. 890
Tate, Cassandra 276
Tate, James F. 653
Tatum, Donn B. 1392
Taub, Donald 407, 998
Taub, Stephen R. 54
Tauffer, Carl B. 1005
Taussip, Joseph K., Jr. 129
Taw, Dudley J. 622
Taylor, Claude E. 1302
Taylor, David G. 43
Taylor, Dean R., Jr. 388
Taylor, Frances 117
Taylor, Frankie 1308
Taylor, Harold N. 748
Taylor, Jack 519
Taylor, John A. 1436
Taylor, John D. 255
Taylor, Lloyd F. 496
Taylor, Lloyd S. 675
Taylor, Robert R. 969
Taylor, Mrs. Theodore 118
Taylor, Thomas E. 374
Taylor, Willard H. 1308
Taylor, William A., Jr. 1308
Taylor, William M. 225
Teater, Dorothy S. 57
Teets, John 739
Teich, William M. 762
Tell, Leon 744
Tellier, Jarold J. 348
Tellis, Jeffrey N. 298
Templeton, Bruce R. 61
Tenny, Morton 1355
Tennyson, Arlen 1259
Tennyson, Rod 100
Terlato, Anthony 1060

Personnel Index

Terner, Emanuel M. 962
Terra, Daniel J. 884
Terry, Charles P. 644
Terry, Clifton D. 404
Terry, S.L. 518
Tescher, Maynard K. 870
Testa, Joseph E. 952
Teters, H. Tiffin 1315
Tettlebaum, Harvey M. 49
Teweles, Robert L. 1315
Thacher, Carter P. 1417
Thalheimer, Ross 149
Thalhimer, William B., Jr. 1317
Thalhofer, Robert L. 720
Tharp, Charlotte S. 300
Thau, Morris 993
Thayer, Jack G. 999
Thayer, W. Paul 872
Theiling, Jane 65
Theis, Catherine 1317
Theis, R.E. 944
Theis, Robert J. 1300
Theiss, George B. 382
Theobald, George J., Jr. 167
Theobald, Harry 1317
Thiele, Joseph S. 730
Thies, J.M. 1319
Thomas, B.L. 386, 1424
Thomas, Bill 306
Thomas, Carol M. 12
Thomas, Douglas M. 535
Thomas, F.G 148
Thomas, J.R. 581
Thomas, John L. 1354
Thomas, Karen A. 96
Thomas, Michael H. 495
Thomas, O. Pendleton 728
Thomas, Ralph S. 1154
Thomas, Tedd 1162
Thomas, V.T. 1329
Thomas, William, Jr. 1099
Thompson, C. Hugh 128
Thompson, Carson R. 1315
Thompson, D.E. 658
Thompson, Edward A. 1320
Thompson, Emmet B. 1324
Thompson, James 719
Thompson, Jere W. 1249
Thompson, John A. 794
Thompson, John E. 1320
Thompson, Kenneth F. 1010, 1255
Thompson, Lea 310
Thompson, Mildred 116
Thompson, Morris 168
Thompson, Roger K. 851
Thompson, W.H., Jr. 1223
Thompson, W.J. 841
Thompson, W. Reid 1094

Thompson, William H. 726
Thompson, William I. 1044
Thompson, William N. 1146
Thompson, William T. 1320
Thomson, Donald 1363
Thomson, John B. 1321
Thorkilsen, Harold 1027
Thorne, Denton 654
Thornhill, Arthur H., Jr. 901
Thornton, James 273
Thorpe, James A. 1396
Thrasher, Jim 335
Thurlow, Annette L. 102
Thurlow, Elwin W. 500
Thurman, Donald J. 1394
Thurston, Doc J., Jr. 1323
Thurston, Lester R., Jr. 989
Tibbetts, H.M. 900
Tichenor, James H. 1359
Tichnor, Robert M. 1323
Tidmore, Wallace 67
Tieken, Theodore 398
Tiernan, William L. 97
Tierney, Richard 888
Tiger, John 234
Tilden, Robbins 1019
Tillinghast, Charles C., Jr. 1336
Tillou, William R. 438
Timberlake, T. Howard 1319
Timlin, Ronald G. 802
Timmons, Donald 868
Timothy, R.K. 988
Timpe, A. Dale 764
Tincher, W.R. 1109
Tindal, Mack D. 668
Tisch, Laurence A. 474, 909
Tiscorina, L.C. 392
Titelman, J. Richard 1142
Tobelmann, Paul A. 1297
Tober, Harold E. 1327
Tobey, Henry M. 1314
Tobias, C. Ellsworth 1207
Tobin, Bruce C. 60
Tobin, James E. 1199
Tochen, David 99
Todd, Zane G. 809
Tofany, Vincent L. 188
Tolbert, Rudolph 114
Tolk, Roy 1250
Tolkin, Morvin 574
Tollefson, Robert M. 1328
Tolson, Jay H. 668
Toman, Ludmilla 136
Tomlinson, William A. 1329
Tommasi, Guy J. 40
Tonemah, Orin J. 185
Tongren, Robert S. 57
Tongue, Ben H. 438
Topp, Louis 1331

Toppel, Alan H. 149
Toppel, George 1107
Torok, Lou 223
Torstenson, John A. 657
Touchoff, John L. 941
Toulmin, Virginia B. 501
Toussaint, Donald E. 1428
Toussaint, Wayne E. 1370
Towey, James F. 1033
Town, George F. 143
Townes, M. Halsey 724
Townsend, Don 1303
Townsend, Wilbur L. 414
Tracy, David M. 663
Tranter, W. Parke 1337
Trappey, William J. 1337
Trask, J.F. 572
Trauner, Richard 1444
Trautman, Gerald H. 739
Trautwein, Eleanor C. 915
Traver, David M. 622
Travis, Arthur R. 508
Travis, Dempsey J. 264
Travis, Roger E. 950
Trayhern, James 304
Trbovich, Robert G. 990
Tremaine, B.G., Jr. 966
Trenkle, Fred W. 1060
Trenkmann, Richard J. 705
Trewhella, S.W. 536, 1213
Trexler, Terry E. 1015
Tribuno, John L. 1340
Trieman, Rollyn C. 530
Trigg, D. Thomas 1215
Triplett, W.T., Jr. 413
Triplett, William R. 1342
Trippeer, Richard A., Jr. 1355
Troche, Carlos 221
Trogdon, George C. 1343
Trombley, James H. 665, 696
Troup, Prentice M. 1097
Trow, Robert C. 857
Truax, Richard 156
Trubek, Louise G. 119
Trueschler, Bernard C. 403
Truitt, Robert H. 833
Trullinger, Fred C. 897
Trumble, Alex D. 1012
Trussell, Albert C. 659
Trussell, Charles E. 947
Truxwell, Robert 696
Tsakanikas, Thomas, Jr. 799
Tsosie, Wilbert 110
Tuchfarber, W.C. 791
Tucker, Frank L. 702
Tucker, Irving 823
Tucker, James D. 1014
Tucker, John M. 1104
Tucker, Max W. 68

Personnel Index

Tucker, Sharon 275
Tucker, Sterling W. 678
Tucker, Tommy 1129
Tucker, W.R. 1084
Tuholski, James M. 949
Tulin, Marshall 1296
Tullis, Robert H. 786
Tuma, Quincy V. 190
Tumminello, Stephen C. 1018
Tunkel, Ray 1126
Tuohy, John J. 905
Turek, R.J. 1151
Turin, A. 630
Turmail, G.A., Sr. 441
Turnbull, James 284
Turner, Fred L. 947
Turner, George M. 1045
Turner, John E. 831
Turner, L.S., Jr. 575
Turner, Molly 310
Turner, R.E. 653
Turner, Richard L. 1193
Turner, Sonnie L. 528
Turner, W.L. 1360
Turrentine, Robert 325
Tushinsky, Joseph S. 1293
Tuttle, Gedney 703
Tuttle, Hope 307, 315
Twiggs, J.B. 1318
Twinem, Linn K. 233
Twiss, Chester K. 552
Twyford, R.H. 949
Tyler, Carol 43
Tyler, Dan 307
Tyler, Robert P., Jr. 1227
Tyo, Robert C. 599
Tyrone, Anthony R. 831
Tyrrell, John I. 620
Tyson, Don 1350
Tyson, Michael 113

U

Uccello, Ann 30
Uccello, Sam 41
Uecker, William F. 833
Uhlmann, R. Hugh 1264
Uihlein, Robert A., Jr. 1194
Ulinski, Susan 155
Ullrich, Helen D. 175
Umans, A.R. 1134
Umansky, David J. 31
Unanue, P. 730
Underkofler, James R. 1426
Underwood, George 344

Underwood, Robert K. 980
Unger, Daniel D. 1129
Unger, J.B. 499
Unger, Leo 354
Unger, Sidney 866
Unruh, Henry C. 1106
Upham, Roy W. 145
Upson, James J. 1364
Upthgrove, William 741
Usen, Irving 1028
Utke, Roy 1288
Utley, George R. 460, 819
Utter, Charles W. 291

V

Vachon, Frank E. 531
Vahlsing, F.H., Jr. 1367
Vai, Madalyn A. 568
Valade, Robert C. 490
Valdes, Petra G. 214
Valdes, Richard V. 536
Valdez, Luis 96
Valentine, G.H., Jr. 1203
Valenty, Thomas G. 1035
Valliant, S.S. 792
VanAndel, Jay 365
Van Baalen, Henry W. 376
Van Beckum, William G. 803
Van Browning, John 462
Van Brunt, Deborah 111
Vance, Julia 293
Van Dam, John 1369
Van der Eb, Henry G. 545
Vanderhorst, Thomas A. 1370
van der Orliandini, S. 841
Vandeventer, David R. 45
Vandivier, Kermit 290
Van Dyke, William 113
Van Ekris, Anthonie C. 847
Van Holten, E. Jerry 1370
Van Hoof, Gerard H. 1048
Van Hook, R.W. 524
Van Hook, Warren K. 205
Van Horne, R. Richard 365
Van Loan, William F. 1018
Van Meter, Dave 1156
van Munching, L. 1370
Van Ness, Edward H. 167
Van Ness, Stanley 51
Van Raalte, Thomas Z. 1405
VanRoden, D. 1236
Van Sinderen, Alfred W. 1248
Van Steenberg, Frank 401
Van Steenberg, Virginia 62
Van Tol, Arie 783

Van Tuyle, Robert 429
Van Vleck, James 1266
Van Vlett, Wayne L. 1341
Van Vranken, John A. 98
Van Wye, A.I. 1371
Van Zelst, Theodore W. 1242
Van Zetta, James A. 54
Varian, Janet S. 909
Varkonyi, Charlyne 290
Varner, Howard E. 790
Vaughan, Gager T. 1373
Vaughan, Howard A., Jr. 1372
Vaughan, J.R. 863
Vaughan, Stephen M. 116
Vaughn, Dorris W. 1248
Vaughn, Ernest 280
Vawter, Richard Q. 12
Velasquez, Emily 109
Veneman, Gerard E. 1006
Verde, J. 1065
Vereeke, Edwin W. 768
Vereen, William C., Jr. 1151
Verity, C. William, Jr. 378
Vernicos-Eugenides, Nicos 786
Vernon, William S. 482
Vesely, Eugene L. 1377
Vettel, Joseph, Jr. 592
Viehman, Russ 746
Vieser, Richard W. 1389
Viggiano, Victor 1030
Villegos, Beatriz 39
Villwoch, G. 1258
Vincent, B.J. 487
Vincent, Charles H. 63
Vincent, J. Ross 126
Vining, Rodney M. 731
Vink, Pieter C. 921, 1018
Virch, Kenneth 249
Visconti, Vincent S. 425
Vise, Harry 1315
Vitale, Pietro 1029
Vittone, A. 728
Vittori, Guido 339
Viviano, Joseph P. 1183
Viviano, Peter R. 724
Vogel, John H. 999
Vogl, Alex J. 1422
Voight, Howard 59
Volk, Harry J. 1354
Volkman, Florence 221
Vollbrecht, J.H. 331
Vollrath, Richard J. 1088
Volpe, Genevieve 313
von Berg, William G. 1299
Von Blomberg, Betty 297
von Czoernig, Carl E. 1194
Von der Ahe, Charles T. 1386
von Schlegell, Victor 683
von Schrader, Francis 1386

Personnel Index

Vorenberg, F. Frank 714
Voss, F.W. 1282
Voss, James M. 480
Vredenburg, Dwight C. 798
Vrsalovich, LaVora 203

W

Wachenfeld, R.B. 501
Wachter, William C. 617
Waddell, Dean T. 1388
Wade, L. James, Jr. 707
Wade, R.G. 652
Wagar, Ivan J. 189
Waggoner, W. Harlow 1185
Wagner, C. Allen, Jr. 1279
Wagner, E.P. 1389
Wagner, Ed 110
Wagner, Garfield 947
Wagner, Robert S. 1389
Wahl, W.P. 1389
Wahlert, R.C. 611
Wahlin, Fred W. 1258
Waidelich, Charles J. 520
Wainerdi, Richard E. 194
Waingrow, F.R. 1073
Waldbaum, Eric 737
Walden, Donald 100
Walden, Penny 100
Walden, Sol 684
Waldes, George 1390
Waldo, Laird D. 793
Waldron, Dave 111
Walgreen, C.R., III 1390
Walker, A.L. 868
Walker, Delmar D. 694
Walker, E.C. 107
Walker, Frank D. 1284
Walker, Henry A. 363
Walker, J.C. 1124
Walker, J.W. 264
Walker, James 109
Walker, John N. 988
Walker, Lucius, Jr. 207
Walker, Mary 276
Walker, Shaw 1214
Walker, T.C. 666
Walker, Mrs. Whitehouse 227
Walker, William E. 1391
Walkup, William E. 1223
Wall, Burton 502
Wall, C.I. 1082
Wall, Fred G. 1153
Wall, John B. 1391
Wall, John E. 589
Wall, Marvin D. 24

Wall, Robert E. 1391
Walla, Walter S. 898
Wallace, Bette 36
Wallace, David W. 404
Wallace, Edward M. 1391
Wallace, Herbert 53
Wallace, Mervin A. 559
Wallace, Miss Mickey 300
Wallace, Paul 272
Wallace, Robert J. 964
Wallach, S. 1389
Walley, Dewey E. 1392
Wallis, Gordon T. 819
Walpole, W.E. 1389
Walsh, E.F. 197
Walsh, James A. 379, 443
Walsh, M.E. 1004
Walsh, Walter J. 405
Walt, Thatcher 42
Walter, Edwin G. 750
Walter, Raymond J. 247
Walter, Stephen 1392
Walters, Jack 111
Walters, Richard J. 595
Walther, John H. 1010
Walther, Sally 99
Walton, Sam M. 1389
Wanderminden, Henry J.W., III 1311
Wang, An 1393
Wanish, Charles K. 554
Wantland, Earl 1310
Wanvig, Chester O., Jr. 720
Wappner, Charles L. 1029
Warach, Bernard 207
Ward, Charles D. 1394
Ward, Elmer L., Jr. 1050
Ward, Lee C., Jr. 1344
Ward, Louis L. 1172
Ward, Margaret 89
Ward, Max F. 928
Ward, Milton H. 615
Ward, R.A. 1312
Ward, R.E. 1338
Wardlow, Ervine 868
Wardwell, Michael P. 455
Ware, Caroline 91
Ware, Gordon K. 514
Warehime, Alan R. 755
Warn, T.L. 1394
Warner, Charles 300
Warner, Charles A. 741
Warner, Edward 535
Warner, F.P. 1395
Warner, Gill 384
Warner, Jack W. 745
Warner, James E. 412
Warner, Rawleigh, Jr. 975
Warner, Robert S. 1380

Warnken, Howard J. 1409
Warnock, William K. 866
Warren, Dean 58
Warren, Frank M. 1092
Warren, Harry M. 169
Warren, John A. 492
Warren, Paul B. 1352
Warren, Spence H. 686
Warren, Tom 116
Warshaw, Saul 388
Wartels, Nat 566
Wasch, Sidney G. 1351
Washburn, J.H. 331
Washburn, Kenneth W. 1356
Washington, Val 111
Wasiele, Harry, Jr. 451
Wasowicz, Frank 68
Wasserberger, Edward 931
Wasserman, Leonard 900
Wasserman, Milton 794
Wassner, I. Robert 379
Wassong, Dan 586, 1055
Waterhouse, Harry 303
Waterman, Nan F. 84
Waters, Lee 418
Waters, Robert A. 1397
Watkins, A. Rush 775
Watkins, C. Curtis 651
Watkins, Frederick D. 331
Watkins, Hay T. 513
Watkins, Ted 97
Watral, Henry J. 383
Watson, C. Gordon 242
Watson, Charles D. 161
Watson, Chenoweth J. 201
Watson, Gilbert 31
Watson, J.D. 768
Watson, J.J. 1097
Watson, James A. 1004
Watson, John 1327
Watson, Robert L. 44
Watson, Stuart D. 774
Watson, Thomas A. 898
Watt, Sidney 291
Watte, John E., Jr. 497
Watters, Thomas 219
Watterworth, S.E. 535, 963
Wattles, Gurdon B. 357
Wave, Charles 276
Waxelbaum, T.L. 931
Waxer, Sanford 106
Waxman, E. 697
Waxman, Louis E. 533
Wayland, Jeanne 313
Wayne, Stephen D. 1282
Weamer, Paul E. 1165
Wearden, Joseph E. 740
Weatherby, Roy E. 1399
Weatherford, Kline 986

1599

Personnel Index

Weatherly, Jack   271
Weaver, Donald K., Jr.   562
Weaver, Ralph L.   631
Weaver, Robert P.   112
Weaver, Ron E.   1211
Weaver, Victor F.   1399
Webb, Hal J.   940
Webb, William L.   11
Webbe, Scotson   754
Weber, A.C.   1400
Weber, Joseph A., Jr.   1400
Weber, William H.   1265
Webster, Dean K.   1400
Webster, Harry   113
Webster, Henry C.   460
Webster, Holt W.   334
Webster, Jerome R.   44
Webster, R.T.   1056
Webster, Robert B.   970
Webster, Ward A.   784
Wechsler, Norman V.   921
Wedel, Cynthia   188
Weekley, Nell   45
Weeks, Sinclair, Jr.   1132
Wegman, E.H.   787
Wegner, Herb   88
Wehle, John L.   709
Weibel, Fred E.   1401
Weidman, Allen E.   394
Weidmann, Walter E.   420
Weidner, Charles J.   1080
Weigel, Raymond A.   871
Weiger, Ralph J.   961
Weigl, Henry   1263
Weihe, D.L.   751
Weikel, M. Keith   19
Weil, John   621
Weil, Myron F.   1006
Weil, William   656
Weimer, John W.   1209
Wein, Irving L.   526
Weinberg, Harold   870
Weinberg, Max   356, 687
Weinberger, Jerome A.   734
Weinberger, William S.   476
Weiner, Harry   708
Weiner, Jay   335
Weiner, Max   85, 114
Weingarten, Bernard   1402
Weinik, G.J.   650
Weinman, J.K.   1022
Weinreich, Richard E.   936
Weins, Leo M.   1421
Weinstein, A.   1195
Weinstein, Fred D.   1402
Weinstein, Harvey   1405
Weinstein, Jerome J.   371
Weintraub, Donald   674
Weintraub, Lionel   804

Weir, Charles R.   539
Weir, D.W.   377
Weir, Davis   353
Weir, M. Brock   525
Weis, Edward   1268
Weis, K.M.   975
Weisberg, Joel   58
Weisberg, L.   817
Weisberger, Samuel   1053
Weisbrod, John H.   1201
Weisen, John J.   107
Weisenfeld, Mort   529
Weiser, Louis   187
Weiskopf, Robert C.   525
Weisman, Lawrence I.   1033
Weiss, Aaron   1340
Weiss, Edward   436
Weiss, Edwin T.   1283
Weiss, Fred F.   658
Weiss, Harold J.   883
Weiss, Jack   745
Weiss, Jonathan A.   235
Weissenborn, O.A.   707
Weissman, Abraham J.   54
Weissman, Joan   56
Weisz, William J.   987
Weitnauer, John   1147
Welch, Edward V.   1149
Welch, James O., Jr.   995
Welch, K.B.   851
Welch, Paul, Jr.   38
Welch, T.C.   756
Welch, Wilbur S.   1070
Weldon, Henry H.   336
Welge, Donald E.   716
Wellehan, Daniel J.   1205
Weller, H.D.   1350
Weller, Ralph A.   1041
Wellerkoff, J.   521
Wellington, Richard C.   1403
Wellman, W.A.   366
Wellner, George   1333
Wellott, Harry M., Jr.   1358
Wells, Ben H.   1212
Wells, Charles Wesley   1201
Wells, Douglas B.   894
Wells, Frank   1394
Wells, Harry K.   946
Wells, K.G.   1259
Wells, R.   657
Wells, Walter E.   1196
Wells, William T.   724
Welsch, Larry A.   569
Welsh, Albert D., Jr.   1403
Weltz, Nathan   359
Wemyss, C.C.   1371
Wemyss, James C., Jr.   742
Wenczel, Chester L.   1404
Wendel, William H.   489

Wendland, William E.   186
Wendling, Robert L.   555
Wendorff, H. Thomas   710
Wendrow, Benjamin R.   1361
Wendt, Henry   395
Wente, Karl L.   1404
Wentworth, Nathan H.   546, 666
Wenzel, Fred W.   849
Wenzel, John   803
Wenzel, William   1404
Werner, Herman S.   925
Werner, Jesse   696
Werner, L.L.   1404
Werner, Larry   280
Werner, R.L.   185
Wernham, S.C.   947
Werntz, George, Jr.   175
Werntz, Ted   200
Werthheimer, Alain   506
Wescoe, W. Clark   1273
Wesley, C.S.   1332
Wesley, Don   108
Wesley, Newton K.   165
Wessel, Harry N., Jr.   893
Wesson, W.S.   1198
West, C.O.   1405
West, Felicia E.   125
West, Frances M.   40
West, Frank D.   791
West, Fred   108
West, Fred W., Jr.   428
West, J.A.   483
West, Richard E.   947
Westberg, V. Luther   1406
Westerman, G.H.   488
Westerman, S.L.   1182
Weston, Joan   47
Weston, W. Galen   903
Westover, R.C., Jr.   1039, 1125
Wexelbaum, Joseph   335, 1131
Wexler, Herbert I.   1356
Wexler, Robert H.   1208
Wexner, Leslie H.   897
Weyerhaeuser, Frederick T.   548
Whalen, Kenneth J.   960
Whalen, Larry   425
Whaley, W.B.   735
Whatmore, Marvin C.   558
Whattam, G.F.   799
Wheatley, Charles F., Jr.   245
Wheaton, E.S.   1411
Wheaton, Frank H., Jr.   1266, 1411
Wheeler, Edwin M.   251
Wheeler, Halsted W.   829
Wheeler, Raymond G.   953
Wheeler, Roger   1311
Whelan, F.X.   361
Whitaker, Gaylord C.   731

Personnel Index

Whitby, James M. 96
White, Frank P. 206
White, Harlan A. 989
White, Harvey 804
White, John R. 1029
White, Kenneth G., Sr. 1415
White, Knowlton H. 1320
White, Leo L. 862
White, Ron 294
White, Ronald L. 1169
White, Stephen A. 1413
Thite, Thomas E. 119
White, W.S., Jr. 371
White, William J. 19
White, William V. 6
White, William W. 388
Whitehead, D.F. 1265
Whitehead, Frederick B. 727
Whitehead, Graham W. 457
Whitehead, J.F., Jr. 1134
Whitehorn, William V. 17
Whitehouse, Harvey B. 588
Whiteley, Les 280
Whiteman, Michael 364
Whiting, Richard R. 448
Whiting, Steve 57
Whitman, Mrs. David A. 229
Whitmire, H.E. 1415
Whitmore, Charles H. 818
Whitney, C. Roberts 1166
Whitney, Christine 118
Whitney, E.L. 1193
Whitney, John O. 1060
Whitney, R.E. 424
Wick, John F. 1335
Wickmertz, Peter 1184
Wickstra, H.E. 1217
Widerkehr, W.E. 359
Wiebusch, Richard V. 51
Wiecking, Fritz 101
Wiedenmayer, C.M. 650
Wiegand, Glenn W. 760
Wieler, W.H. 431
Wieloszynski, Roberta B. 56
Wien, Sigurd 1417
Wiener, Benjamin 1442
Wiener, Jerome 729
Wiener, Lester J. 1417
Wiener, N. Sidney 1417
Wigbels, Lawrence G. 1361
Wigen, J.O. 56
Wiggins, W. Frank 805
Wiggington, Linda 119
Wilber, George E., Jr. 555
Wilborg, James H. 1362
Wilbur, W.M. 1180
Wilcove, Ralph H. 1188
Wilcox, Ross G. 189
Wild, Carter W. 1002

Wild, Walter 489
Wild, William 289
Wilder, C.M.G. 523
Wilder, W.D. 1420
Wilder, William A., Jr. 56
Wildman, Frederick S. 1418
Wiley, M.O. 499
Wiley, W. Bradford 1418
Wilger, Eugene B. 802
Wilhem, Robert G. 637
Wilhite, Andrew H. 410
Wilke, Charles S. 711
Wilken, Robert 752
Wilkie, Leighton A. 547
Wilkie, Michael L. 601
Wilkins, Harold H. 713
Wilkins, Ralph R. 1418
Wilkinson, Howard R. 186
Willcox, Roger 90
Wille, James 852
Wille, James H. 679, 841
Willert, A.W., Jr. 819
Willet, E. Crosby 1419
William, Robert 1407
Williams, Arthur 927
Williams, Arthur M. 1246
Williams, Bill 288
Williams, Bob 283
Williams, Carl H. 764
Williams, Clarence E. 411
Williams, Cohen T. 1413
Williams, Dick 1420
Williams, Duane H. 1123
Williams, E.J. 947
Williams, Gonzella 114
Williams, H.L. 807
Williams, H. Neal 1106
Williams, Harmon G. 462
Williams, Harry V. 761
Williams, Hazel Pearson 765
Williams, Jack N. 44
Williams, James R. 154
Williams, John D. 381
Williams, John H. 1420
Williams, John R. 922
Williams, Jonathan 47
Williams, Langdon T. 687
Williams, Lawrence D. 561
Williams, Marshall R. 1390
Williams, Matthew E. 1275
Williams, Preston C., Jr. 1248
Williams, Robert 849
Williams, Robert D. 1419
Williams, Robert J. 476
Williams, Susan A. 301
Williams, Thelma 116
Williams, W.D. 1010
Williamson, Arthur 150
Williamson, C. Dickie 995

Williamson, Ellis 176
Williamson, Eve M. 272
Williamson, J. Don 1420
Williamson, John P. 1328
Williamson, Robert A. 795
Williford, J.H. 1351
Willinger, Harding W. 956
Willins, Henry H. 260
Willis, Clifford E. 587
Willis, George 898
Willner, Leonard 344
Willoughby, Russel 694
Wilmouth, Robert K. 563
Wilson, Al 302
Wilson, A.L. 321
Wilson, Bob A. 985
Wilson, Bruce A. 1269
Wilson, Charles E. 41
Wilson, Craig 288
Wilson, Donald H., Jr. 982
Wilson, Earl S. 1131
Wilson, Grant R. 57
Wilson, H. Clifton 500
Wilson, J. Tylee 1118
Wilson, Jackson 62
Wilson, James E. 203
Wilson, James H., Jr. 1180
Wilson, John A. 1304
Wilson, John R., Jr. 1155
Wilson, Kemmons 782
Wilson, Kermit H. 1221
Wilson, Lawrence 102
Wilson, Leonard W., Jr. 497
Wilson, N.E. 1109
Wilson, N.E., Jr. 1262
Wilson, Nan L. 50
Wilson, Paul L., Jr. 702
Wilson, Robert C. 532
Wilson, Robert F. 1391
Wilson, S. Shephard 901
Wilson, W.L. 208
Wilson, W.W. 1225
Wilson, William J. 701
Wilson, William L. 1114
Wilt, James P. 461
Wilton, Norman 1422
Wimberly, Richard D. 133
Wimer, Walter 817
Winard, Harold B. 360
Winarick, Jules 911, 1422
Winchell, Verne H. 590
Windham, James C. 1046
Winegard, John 1423
Winemaster, W.D. 1070
Winer, Louis 1424
Winfield, John A. 458
Winger, Maurice H., Jr. 353
Wingerter, Robert G. 894
Winig, Norbert 1424

Personnel Index

Winkel, Robert B. 1048
Winkelman, Stanley J. 1424
Winkler, Edward K. 1097
Winlack, Laurine A. 215
Winne, Judith 284
Winograd, Milton M. 957
Winship, H. Dillon, Jr. 711
Winship, William M., III 508
Winslow, Joseph C. 993
Winston, Bernard B. 362
Winston, James 1054
Winter, Elmer L. 927
Winter, Jack A. 823, 1425
Winters, Everett 1126
Wirtanen, Donald G. 829
Wirth, George P., Jr. 392
Wise, Paul S. 244, 255
Wise, Walter L., Jr. 1320
Wishnick, William 1427
Withington, Bill 103
Witsken, Clarence 624
Witt, C. 368
Wittcoff, H.B. 1428
Witter, William M. 1427
Wittlake, J.C. 470
Wobst, Frank 797
Woehr, H.C. 874
Woessner, Robert 295
Wohlfeil, Robert E. 302
Wohlstetter, Charles 547
Wojta, G.C. 1076
Wolberg, Gerald M. 647
Wolcott, Arthur 1208
Wold, Duane R. 1260
Wolf, Arnold 822
Wolf, Emanuel L. 343, 843
Wolf, Harold H. 660
Wolf, Howard B. 1427
Wolf, Robert 820
Wolfe, Harold 59
Wolff, Richard C. 699
Wolfgang, Michael G. 53
Wolfsohn, Venlo 246
Wolfson, David 546
Wolfson, Harold 1217
Wolfson, Mitchel 1428
Wolfson, Morey 98
Wolpert, Robert L. 521
Woltz, John E. 1113
Womack, Tom 283
Wong, Alan S. 97
Woo, Lillian C. 109
Wood, Alden 358
Wood, Arthur M. 1204
Wood, Duke 277
Wood, James 733
Wood, James R. 290
Wood, Joe C., Jr. 413

Wood, L. Delmer 904
Wood, M.K. 30
Wood, Marie V. 227
Wood, N.P. 528
Wood, Q.E. 1112
Woodfin, Gene M. 928
Woodford, Rex 295
Woodrow, Robert H., Jr. 667
Woods, David F. 281
Woods, Jonathan K. 438
Woods, Robert W., Sr. 1430
Woods, Thomas C., Jr. 898
Woodson, Benjamin N. 354
Woodward, M. Cambell, Jr. 801
Woodward, Richard 326
Woodworth, Leslie R. 1424
Woody, Ben D. 879
Woody, Robert W. 1007
Woodyard, Bill 34
Woolworth, Chester M. 1430
Wooster, June G. 218
Wopat, Robert M. 708, 1020
Workman, Gale 275
Workman, M.C. 422
Workman, Ross 479
Worley, Bland W. 352
Worley, Charles W. 398
Wormington, Bob 312
Worth, Robert 1431
Wozniak, Robert 459
Wraight, Duane 54
Wrenn, John P. 386
Wright, Douglas S. 44
Wright, Earl O. 252
Wright, Helen 110
Wright, Joe 1315
Wright, John R. 104
Wright, Paul H. 1158
Wright, William H. 414
Wrigley, William 1433
Wrobble, Richard E. 471
Wulff, P.F.A. 1361
Wulsin, Lucien 402
Wunderle, J. Mackie 1433
Wunderlich, Carle R. 338
Wurtele, C.A. 1368
Wurtzel, Alan 1394
Wustrow, Robert J. 794
Wyatt, Jane 58
Wyler, Victor A. 1433
Wyman, Henry W. 1052
Wynn, Al 307

Y

Yadamee, Virginia 292
Yadley, Barbara 310
Yamashiro, Walter T. 42
Yanow, J.L. 1372
Yarbrough, Kenneth F. 466
Yarrington, B.J. 358
Yaspan, Robert 683
Yates, Jane H. 1071
Yazel, Richard 104
Yeager, B. John 519
Yeager, C. Robert 402
Yeager, Dennis R. 237
Yeager, S.L. 939
Yeatman, C. James 992
Yedlin, Sidney 861
Yeoman, Robert I. 1084
Yetnikoff, Walter R. 473
Yianilos, Nicholas P. 1122
Ylvisaker, William T. 730
Yoder, Douglas O. 1438
Yoder, John B. 470
Yogman, Jack 1203
Yohe, Jack 4
York, Colon W. 1232
Yoshikawa, Tak 864
Yost, D.M. 1245
Yost, Frank A. 788
Yost, Lyle E. 773
Young, Conrad S. 1357
Young, Frank L. 353
Young, Fred M. 1439
Young, Jack 770
Young, Louise 120
Young, Norman 801
Young, R. Dwight 827
Young, Ray H. 46
Young, Raymond A. 1301
Young, Richard B. 326
Young, Robert F. 653
Young, Sally Fenelon 1439
Young, Shelby 343
Young, Sumner S. 882
Young, T.A. 131
Young, Vaile G. 466
Young, W.J. 889
Young, William R. 663
Younger, K.G. 770, 1253
Youngs, Sue 134
Yount, Robert M. 1012
Yuen, LeRoy 67
Yung, D.C. 481

Personnel Index

Z

Zabarsky, Martin N.   1179
Zabell, Emil M.   171
Zaccarelli, Herman E.   157
Zachowski, Walter A.   439
Zacks, Joseph   745
Zagor, Howard S.   1055
Zahn, J. Hillman   512
Zaleski, Jack   288
Zalusky, Lawrence   941
Zambetti, Felice   1272
Zapapas, J. Richard   633
Zausner, Sam   424
Zausner, Sol   1441
Zawel, Ellen   91
Zazueta, Ricardo   223
Zealand, David   712
Zechel, W.W.   1166
Zeder, Fred M., II   799
Zehnder, D.H.   486
Zehner, Robert C.   1441
Zeigler, B.E.   1107
Zelinkoff, Milton A.   1442
Zeller, Robert C., Jr.   1442
Zellers, E.G.   1442
Zempel, Clara   139
Zepernick, Fred   104
Zepht, Fritz H., Jr.   896
Zeratsky, John A.   1213
Zeysing, James J.   204
Zieglar, William, III   357
Ziegler, R.D.   551
Ziegler, William, III   1195
Ziemer, C.W.   970
Ziemer, P.D.   1426
Zierler, Harold   160
Ziff, Stephen J.   1245
Ziff, William   1443
Zimmer, Paul H.   1443
Zimmer, W.L., III   1154
Zimmer, Warren A.   600
Zimmerman, Raymond   1210
Zimmerman, Robert K.   844
Zimmerman, Stanley B.   1325
Zimmerman, William R.   980
Zimonick, Frank   737
Zinman, Noel   982
Zippert, John   95
Zipt, George G.   398
Zitlau, Walter A.   1183
Zolezzi, Walter   1027
Zorn, Miltorn J.   1383
Zrike, Raymond   1169
Zubler, Gayle   279

Zucker, Nathan S.   165
Zupan, Lawrence A.   138
Zupert, A.J.   1154
Zurek, Francis J.   1422
Zurn, Frank W.   1444
Zuver, David J.   534, 639
Zwecker, Irving   1092, 1278
Zwick, David R.   129
Zwieg, Robert M.   509
Zychick, Eugene   816

Publication Index

A

AA Comes of Age   137
AA Grapevine   137
AAA Maps and Tour Books   241
AAAM Quarterly   180
ABA Official Lists   242
ABC's of Borrowing   28
ABYC News   242
Academy Reporter   240
Accepted Dental Therapeutics   243
Access   5
Accident Control Reports   21
Accident Facts   188
Accident Prevention Bulletin   183
Accountability in Health Facilities   198
Accredited Home Study Courses for Industry Training   259
A/CRMD on the Record   145
Action Faction   1488
Action for a Change: A Student's Manual for Public Interest Organizing   93
Action for Outdoor Recreation for America   23
Action Handbook   193
Action Line   264
Action Report   82
ACTS Actions   180
Acts of Congress   12
ADA World   81
Adelante SER   223
Administration of Building Regulations   248
Adopted Break Silence   219
Advertising Forum   258
Advocate   1488
Advocates Handbook   233
Affirmative Action and Equal Employment: A Guidebook for Employers   9
AGA Monthly   243
AGA Rate Service   243
Aging   15
Agricultural Banker   242
Agricultural Digest   263
Agricultural Economic Reports   1
Agricultural Research   2
Agriculture Handbooks   1
Agriculture Information Bulletins   1, 1496
Agriculture Yearbooks   1496
AHEA Action   193
Aids from ABA   242
Aids to Navigation Bulletins   30
Air and Water News   1488
Air Carrier Financial Statistics   4
Air Carrier Traffic Statistics   4
Air Pollution Abstracts   8
Air Pollution Notes   1488

Air Quality Control Digest   1488
Air Travel Bargains; How to Get the Lowest Fares on all Airlines World Wide & U.S.A.   1457
Air Travelers' Fly-Rights   4
Airline Industry Economic Report   4
Airman   7
Airman's Information Manual   30
Airport Activity Statistics   30
Airport Ground Safety Bulletin   183
Al-Anon Family Group Forum   137
Alateen Talk   137
Alcohol and Tobacco Summary Statistics   32
Alcohol, Tobacco and Firearms Bulletin   32
Alcoholics Anonymous   137
ALERT Newsletter   232
All About Actions   1457
All Around You - An Environmental Study Guide   23
All Hands   7
Alliance News   210
Alliance Review   210
America the Beautiful; A Modern Guide to Sex, Security, and the Soft Buck   1457
American Bar Association Journal   231
American Bar News   231
American Consumer; Issues and Decisions   1457
American Cooperation   81
American Council on Consumer Interests Newsletter   1488
American Education   17
American Food Scandal; Why You Can't Eat Well on What You Earn   1457
American Health Empire: Prestige, Profits and Politics   155
American Heart   140
American Heart Association Cookbook   140
American Indian Calendar   22
American Indian Law Newsletter   231
American Indian Media Directory   243
American Issue   139
American Journal of Disease of Children   141
American Journal of Nursing   245
American Journal of Public Health   142
American Manpower   25
American Medical News   141
American Nurse   245
American Red Cross Youth News   193
American Rehabilitation   16
American Review of Respiratory Diseases   141
American Woods Series   3
Amp   161
AMS Food Purchases   2
Analysis of Employment Agency Practices in Montgomery and Prince George's Counties, Maryland; A MaryPIRG Report   1457
Analysis of Housing Markets   20
Angry Buyer's Complaint Directory   1449
Annual Directories of Certified Appliances   247
Annual Report on Project Head Start   16
Annual Voting Record of U.S. Congress   85

Publication Index

Answers 192
Answers to Your Everyday Money Questions 1457
Answers to Your Questions about American Indians 22
Anti-Swine Flu 89
APhA News 177
APHIS Series 2
Apparel Economic Summary 241
Apparel Industry Economic Profile (Focus) 241
Apparel Sales Compensation Survey 241
Applied Mathematics Series 5
Appraisals Journal 257
Approved Fire Resistance Ratings 248
AQUA News 132
Architect's Specification Manual 260
Archives of Clinical Ecology 135
Archives of Dermatology 141
Archives of Environmental Health 141
Archives of General Psychiatry 141
Archives of Internal Medicine 141
Archives of Neurology 141
Archives of Ophthalmology 141
Archives of Otolaryngology 141
Archives of Pathology 141
Archives of Survery 141
Area Trends in Employment and Unemployment 25
Arranging Transportation for Small Shipments 24
Arrow 195
Arthritis & Rheumatism 143, 144
As Bill Sees It 137
Asbestos and You 83
Aspects of Aging 198
Asset and Liability Trends 11
ASTA Travel News 246
Astanotes 246
Audit of Returns, Appeal Rights, and Claims for Refund 32
Auto Repair Frauds; How to Prevent Your Car From Driving You to the Poorhouse 1457
Automobile Guidelines 11
Automotive Recycler and Merchandiser 246
Auxiliary Advice 154
Aviation Mechanics Bulletin 183
Aviation Education Series 30

B

Back-County Travel in the National Park System 22
Balance 131
Bank Protection Bulletin 242
Banking 242
Banks for Cooperatives 9
Banned Products 7
Bar Guides 30
Bargain Hucksters 1457
Barker 227

Basic Building Code 248
Basic Facts About Military Life 7
Basic Fire Prevention Code 248
Basic Housing-Property Maintenance Code 248
Basic Mechanical Code 248
Basic Plumbing Code 248
Basic Produce Department Operations Manual 264
Basic Rights of the Mentally Handicapped 235
Batting the Breeze 153
BBB Standards for Charitable Solicitations 86
Be a Smart Shopper 1458
Beacon Newsletter 165
Benefits for Veterans and Service Personnel With Service Since January 31, 1955, and Their Dependents 33
Best 1458
Better Times 1458
Bibliography: Corporate Responsibility for Social Problems 1449
Bibliography of Child Abuse Literature 212
Bibliography of Gay Lib Books and Monography 209
Bibliography of Motor Freight Transportation 246
Bibliography of Publications and Audio-Visual Aids 258
Bibliography of Research on Consumer and Homemaking Education 1449
Bicycling for Recreation and Commuting 23
Biennial HUD Awards for Design Excellence 19
Big Brothers' Ambassador 195
Billion $ Swindle, Frauds Against the Elderly 1458
Bio-Dynamics 146
Birds of Our Lives 21
Birds of Town and City 21
Blindness 138
Boating Safety Newsletter 30
Boating Statistics 30
Book of ASTM Standards 246
Boom in Bikeways 248
Boom in Going Bust 1458
Braille Bible in King James Version 146
Braille Book Bank Catalog 163
Braille Calendar 146
Braille Forum 139
Braille Mirror 146
Break the Banks: A Shopper's Guide to Banking Services 1458
Bride's: Buyers' Guide for Young Homemakers 1458
Brief Guide to the National Gallery of Art 29
Brief Guide to the Smithsonian 29
Briefcase 237
Broadcast Services 10
Building Official and Code Administrator 248
Building Science Series 5
Bulletin on Rheumatic Diseases 144
Bureau of Land Management State Recreation Maps 23
Bureau of Mines Research Summary 23

Publication Index

Business and Consumer Education Case Studies 1458
Business and the Consumer; The Creative Interface 1459
Buxom Belle Courier 147
Buy It Right; A Shoppers Guide to Home Furnishings 1459
Buy It Right! An Introduction to Consumerism 1459
Buy Now, Pay Later 1459
Buyer Beware! 1965 1459
Buyer Beware! A Report on Product Safety and the Cost of Credit in the Retail Industry 1459
Buyer's Guide Annual; Consumer Discount Price Guide 1488
Buyer's Guide to Environmental Media; A Directory of Books, Magazines, Films, and Information Sources 1449
Buyer's Guides 12
Buying Government Surplus Personal Property 13
Buying Lots From Developers 21, 1459
Buying Solar 10
Buying Your Home 231

C

CA - A Cancer Journal for Clinicians 139
CA Monthly 198
CA Note 198
Cabin Crew Safety Exchange 183
Cable Television 10
California Today 133
California Tomorrow Plan 123
Call for Action; A Survival Kit for New Yorkers 1449
Call for Action Newsletter 196
Camping in the National Park System 22
Campus Co-ops in North America 92
Can You Afford Delivery Service? 28
Can You Be Sure of Your Experts? A Complete Manual on How to Choose and Use Doctors, Lawyers, Brokers - and all the Other Experts in Your Life 1459
Cancer Facts and Figures 139
Cancer News 139
Canned Food Pack Statistics 258
Capital 242
Capital Commentary 245
Capital Contacts in Consumerism 1449
Capital Information 196
Captains of Consciousness; Advertising and the Social Roots of the Consumer Culture 1460
Career Counseling for Women in the Federal Government 4
Careers for Women in the 70's 26
Carload Waybill Statistics 31
Carpet Specifers Handbook 249

Case for/against Nuclear Power Plant Safety 133
Cash and Credit 1460
Catalog of Research Projects 21
Catalog of Standards 245
Caveat Emptor! An Introductory Analysis of Consumer Problems 1460
CBBB In-Sight 86
Center for Science in the Public Interest Newsletter 1488
Certified Potato Seed Reports 264
Challenge of Consumerism; A Symposium 1460
Champagne Living on a Beer Budget; How to Buy the Best for Less 1460
Changing Times 1488
Charities USA 212
ChemEcology 254
Chemical Additives in Booze 1460
Chemical Feast; Nader Task Force Report on the Food and Drug Administration 1460
Chicago Chef 242
Child Welfare 199
Children Before Dogs 199
Children in Autos 184
Children's Friend (Braille) 148
Christian Record (Braille) 148
Christian Record Talking Magazine (Braille and Records) 148
Chronicle 171
Church and Safety 188
Ciencias Comerciales 85
Circulation 140
Circulation Research 140
Citizen Nader 1460
Citizens, Consumers and Communications 254
Citizens Network 91
Civil Rights Digest 6
Civil Service and the Nation's Progress 4
Civil Service Commission Today 4
Civil Service Journal 4
Claims Game 1460
Classified Index of Traffic Control, Safety and Health Equipment 181
Clean Air: The Breath of Life 8
Clean Air and Your Car 8
Clean Air Research 129
CLUSAgram 86
CNCP Newsletter 83
Coal - The Abundant Energy 10
Coalition 200
Coatings 261
Codes and Code Administration 248
Collection Process (Income Tax Accounts) 32
Commanders' Digest 7
Commerce America 5
Commerce Publications Catalog and Index 5
Commitment 18
Common Sense 91
Commonsense Guide to Doctors, Hospitals and Medical Care 1460

1606

Publication Index

Communicator   175, 195
Community Crime Control   198
Community Development Evaluation Series   19
Compensation in Mass Retailing   254
Compilation of Water Quality Data   8
Complaint Directory for Consumers, 1977   1449
Complete Food Handbook   1461
Comprehensive Guide to the English Literature on Cannabis   177
Computers in Medicine   141
Concern   192
Condition of Farmworkers and Small Farmers   216
Condominium Buyer's Guide and Home Buyer's Guide   256
Congressional Action   84
Conservation Bulletins   21
Conservation Directory, 1976; A List of Organizations, Agencies, and Officials Concerned With Natural Resource Use and Management   1449
Conservation Foundation Letter   1488
Conservation Yearbooks   21
Conservationist   1489
Consumer   1461
Consumer Action's Auto Insurance Guide   1450
Consumer Advocate Versus the Consumer   1461
Consumer Aid Series   31, 1496
Consumer Alert   1489
Consumer and Corporate Accountability   1461
Consumer and His Dollars   1461
Consumer - At the Bottom of the Totem Pole   1489
Consumer Beware! Your Food and What's Been Done to It   1461
Consumer Bibliography   1450
Consumer Book of Hints & Tips   1461
Consumer Bulletin   1489
  Changed to Consumer's Research Magazine
Consumer Bulletins   12, 1496
Consumer Buying for Better Living   1461
Consumer Choice: The Economics of Personal Living   1461
Consumer Choice in the American Economy   1461
Consumer Close-Ups   1489
Consumer Complaint Action Guide   1450
Consumer Complaint Directory   1462
Con$umer Complaint Guide, 1977   1450
Consumer Credit Reform   1462
Consumer Economic Problems   1462
Consumer Economics   1462
Consumer Education Bibliography   1450
Consumer Education Catalog   1450
Consumer Education Forum   1489
Consumer Facts on Air Fares   4
Consumer Federation of America News   1489
Consumer Finance   1462
Consumer Finance: A Case History in American Business   1462
Consumer Finance Law Bulletin   258
Consumer Fraud: An Annotated Bibliography   24
Consumer Fraud: Tips for Consumers   24

Consumer Fraud: What to Watch For   24
Consumer Guide: 1974 Best Buys & Discount Prices   1450
Consumer Guide to Audio Products Safety   250
Consumer Guide to International Air Travel   4
Consumer Guide to Product Information   1462
Consumer Guide to Used and Surplus Home Appliances and Furnishings   1462
Consumer Guides   1496
Consumer Health: Products and Services   1463
Consumer in American Society: Additional Dimensions   1463
Consumer Information; An Index of Selected Federal Publications of Consumer Interest   1451
Consumer Information Catalog   13
Consumer Information Handbook: Europe and North America   1463
Consumer Information Series   31, 1496, 1497
Consumer Information Systems & Consumer Policy   1463
Consumer Memos   1497
Consumer News   15, 1489
Con$umer New$weekly   1489
Consumer Price Index   25
Consumer Problems and Marketing Patterns in Low-Income Neighborhoods: An Exploratory Study   1463
Consumer Problems Textbook   85
Consumer Product Hazard Index   7
Consumer Protection; A Symposium   1463
Consumer Protection Directory; A Comprehensive Guide to Consumer Protection Organizations in the United States and Canada   1451
Consumer Protection Guide, 1977   1451
Consumer Protection in the States   1463
Consumer Protection Labs   1464
Consumer Protection News   1490
Consumer Protection Newsletter   1490
Consumer Protection Reporting Service   85, 1464
Consumer Reports   86, 1490
Consumer Services and How You Benefit   1
Consumer Skills   1464
Consumer Survival Book; How to Fight Inflation   1464
Consumer Survival Kit   1464, 1497
Consumer Swindlers and How to Avoid Them   1464
Consumer Tips   1490, 1497
Consumer Trends   253, 1490
Consumer Views   1490
Consumer Voice   85
Consumerism: The Eternal Triangle; Business, Government, and Consumers   1465
Consumerism: A New and Growing Force in the Marketplace   1464
Consumerism; A New Force in Society   1464
Consumerism: Search for the Consumer Interest   1464
Consumerism; Viewpoints from Business, Government, and the Public Interest   1465
Consumers All: The Yearbook of Agriculture   1465

Publication Index

Consumers Almanac 91
Consumers Almanac & Calendar 1465
Consumer's Arsenal 1465
Consumer's Buying Guide; How to Get Your Money's Worth 1465
Consumer's Catalog of Economy & Ecology 1465
Consumers Dental Bible - Tooth or Consequences 1465
Consumer's Dictionary of Cosmetic Ingredients 1451
Consumers Digest 1490
Consumers Directory, 1973-1974 1451
Consumer's Directory of Prince George's County Doctors 1451
Consumer's Guide to Bankruptcy 1466
Consumer's Guide to Banks 1466
Consumer's Guide to Better Buying 1466
Consumers Guide to Federal Publications 15
Consumer's Guide to Fighting Back 1466
Consumer's Guide to Insurance Buying 1466
Consumers Guide to Postal Services and Products 27
Consumers' Guide to Prescription Prices 1466
Consumer's Guide to Product Safety 1466
Consumer's Guide to Queens Doctors 1451
Consumer's Handbook 1466
Consumer's Handbook; 100 Ways to Get More Value for Your Dollars 1466
Consumers in Action 82
Consumers in Trouble; A Study of Debtors in Default 1467
Consumers Index to Product Evaluations and Information Sources 1452
Consumers Information Guide to Metal Cookware and Ovenware 255
Consumers' Research Magazine 86, 1490
Consumers Union News Digest 1452
Consumers Union Report on Life Insurance: A Guide to Planning and Buying the Protection You Need 1467
Consumers Voice 1490
Consumer's World: Buying, Money Management, and Issues 1467
Consuming Public 1467
Contacto 165
Cooperative Housing Directory 90
Cooperative Housing Journal 90
Cooperative News Service 86
Cornucopia 155
Corporate Examiner 206
Cost of Dying; And What You Can Do About It 1467
Counsel for the Deceived; Case Studies in Consumer Fraud 1467
Counselor's Information Service 196
Credit 258
Credit Jungle 1467
Credit Union Executive 88
Credit Union Magazine 88
Credit Union Statistics 27

Credit Union Yearbook 88
Credit World 253
Critical Water Problems Facing the Eleven Western States 24
Crop Protection Newsletter 258
Cross-Examiner 235
Crossing 147
Crusade for Honest Insurance Dealings 92
Cry California 123
CTFA Cosmetic Journal 249
CTFA Ingredient Dictionary 249
Culinarian 242
Culinary Review 242
Current Consumer; The Continuing Guide to Consumer Education 1490
Current Literature on Aging 215
Current Policy Statements 29
Current Wage Developments 25
Customs Bulletin 32
Customs Regulations of United States 32
Cycle 127

D

Dairy Council Digest 258
Dairy Councilor 258
Dairy Herd Improvement Letters 2
Dark Side of the Marketplace: The Plight of the American Consumer 1467
Day Care Series 16
Day the Pigs Refused to be Driven to Market; Advertising and the Consumer Revolution 1467
Deaf American 174
Dental Abstracts 242
Department of State Bulletin 29
Department of State Newsletter 29
Developing a Resource Center in Consumer Education: An Annotated Bibliography 1452
Dimensions/NBS 5
Diplomate 121
Direct Mail/Marketing Manual 250
Direct Marketing Magazine 250
Direct Selling World Directory 250
Directory and Resource Book 121
Directory of Accredited Private Home Study Schools 259
Directory of Agencies Serving the Visually Handicapped in the United States 140
Directory of Alcoholism Treatment Facilities 137
Directory of Child Life and Play Programs 145
Directory of Consumer Organizations 15
Directory of Criminal Justice Information Sources 24
Directory of Diocesan Agencies of Catholic Charities in the U.S., Puerto Rico and Canada 212

Directory of Direct Selling Purchasing Agents and Premium Buyers 250
Directory of Drug Information Groups 177
Directory of Executives (Goodwill Industries of America) 154
Directory of Federal, State, County, and City Government Consumer Offices 15, 1452
Directory of Government Agencies Safeguarding Consumer and Environment 1452
Directory of Governmental Air Pollution Agencies 121
Directory of Hemophilia Treatment Centers 167
Directory of Housing, Redevelopment and Codes Agencies 211
Directory of Legal Aid and Defender Services 237
Directory of Medicare Providers 19
Directory of Movers 244
Directory of Nonprofit Homes for the Aged - Social Components of Care 192
Directory of On-Going Research in Smoking and Health 17
Directory of Organizations Concerned With Learning Disabilities 144
Directory of Post Offices 27
Directory of Presbyterian Related Agencies 226
Directory of State and Local Government and Non-Government Consumer Organizations 85
Directory of State and Metropolitan Health Career Councils 167
Directory of State Government Energy-Related Agencies 10
Directory of U.S. Government Audiovisual Personnel 14
Directory of Venereal Disease Clinics 172
Directory of Voluntary Consumer Organizations; A Selected Listing of Nongovernmental Organizations at the Local, State, and National Level 1452
Disadvantaged Consumer 1468
Document Locator 32
Document Retrieval Index 24
Document Sales Information Sheet 15
Documents from America's Past 13
Dollar Squeeze and How to Beat It 1468
Dollars and Sense; The Teen-Age Consumer's Guide 1468
$$$ and Sense; Your Complete Guide to Wise Buying 1468
Domestic Postage Rates and Fees 27
Domestic Programs Fact Book 1
Domiciliary Houses and State and Provincial Alcoholism Programs 137
Donation of Federal Surplus Property 13
Don't Be Fuelish 10
Don't Risk Your Child's Life 188
Do's and Don'ts in Advertising Copy 86
Downs Syndrome 161
Ducks at a Distance 21

E

EAI Story 153
Earth Foods 1468
Earthquake Information Bulletin 22
Earthquake Notes 189
Earthworm News 134
Easter Seal Communicator 165
Eat Your Heart Out: Food Profiteering in America 1468
Eater's Digest; The Consumer's Factbook of Food Additives 1452
Eating Right for Less; Consumers Union's Practical Guide to Food and Nutrition for Older People 1468
Eco-News 127
Eco-Tips Series 125, 1497
Ecology and Your Career 25
Economics for Consumers 1468
Edors (Economic Development of the Rural South) 88
Education Around the World 17
Education Directory 17
Education Journal 234
Educational Pamphlets 1497
Educational Radio 10
Educational Television 10
EEOC at a Glance 9
Effluent Charges on Air and Water Pollution 234
$8 Billion Hospital Bed Overrun 155
El Grito de Guerra 222
Electric Power Statistics 12
Electronic Market Data Book 250
Electronic Market Trends 250
Electronic Service Industry Yearbooks 259
Electronics 1985 Proceedings 250
Employment and Earnings 25
Employment and Training Report of the President 25
Employment Standards Digest 26
Encounter (records) 148
Energy Conservation: Gaslights 10
Energy Conservation With Landscaping 10
Energy Conservation With Windows 10
Energy Directory 127
Energy Directory Update 127
Energy Directory Update Service 127
Energy Films Catalog 8
Energy In Focus 10
Energy Index 127, 1453
Energy Information Abstracts 127, 1453
Energy Regulation Update 127
Energy Regulation Update Service 127
Enforcement 83
Enforcing Air Pollution Controls 198
Enough! The Revolt of the American Consumer 1469

Publication Index

Envirofiche Micropublishing   127
Environment   134, 1491
Environment Abstracts   127, 1453
Environment Action Bulletin   1491
Environment and Behavior   1491
Environment Film Review   8
Environment Index   127
Environment Media Guide   127
Environment Midwest   8
Environment Regulation Handbook   127
Environment Report   1491
Environment Reporter   1491
Environment, U.S.A.; A Guide to Agencies, People, and Resources   1453
Environmental Action   127, 1491
Environmental Affairs   1491
Environmental Affairs Newsletter   258
Environmental Exchange   8
Environmental Facts   8
Environmental Law for Non-Lawyers   129
Environmental Law Reporter   234
Environmental Protection Directory   1453
Environmental Quality Abstracts   1453
Environmental Quality Magazine   1491
Environmental Science & Technology   1492
Environmental Values, 1860-1972; A Guide to Information Sources   1453
Environmentalist   128
E.P. - The New Conservation   130
EPA Journal   8
EPA Reports Bibliography Quarterly   8
Epilepsia   139
Equal Credit Opportunity Act   12
ERDA Energy Research Abstracts   7
Escape from the Money Trap   1469
ET Handbooks   25
ETA Interchange   25
ETA Publications   25
Evaluations of Drug Interactions (1973)   142
Evaluative Studies   1497
Everybody Can Help Somebody   211
Everybody's Money; The Credit Union Magazine for Consumers   88, 1492
Exchange Revue   218
Expectations   136
Expert Consumer: A Complete Handbook   1469
Extension Service Review   2
Eye on Environment   133

F

FAA Aviation News   30
FAA Statistical Handbook of Aviation   30
Fabricare News   253
Face-to-Face   225
Fact Sheets on Solar Energy   10
Factors Affecting Fuel Economy   8
Facts About Merchandise   1469
Facts About Nursing   245
Facts About the Pentagon   7
Facts About United States Money   32
Facts and Figures About Air Transportation   241
Facts and Figures on Older Americans   15
Facts and Pointers on Fresh Fruits and Vegetables   264
Fair Credit Billing   12
Family as Consumers   1469
Family Economics Review   2
Family Guide to Better Food and Better Health   1469
Family Guide to Children's Television   81
Family Guide to Successful Moving   1469
Family Health   1492
Family Management   161
Family Process   160
Family Safety   188, 1492
Family Talk   211
Famous Indians   22
Farm Credit System   9
Farm Workers Pesticide Safety   8
Farmers Bulletins   1, 1498
Farmers Tax Guide   32
Fast Food Packet   123
Fatal and Injury Accident Rates   31
Fatty Acid News Digest   263
FDA Clinical Experience Abstracts   17
FDA Consumer   17, 1492
FDA Consumer Index, 1967-1975   17
FDA Consumer Memos   1498
FDA Consumer Reprints   1498
FDA Drug Bulletin   17
FDA Public Surveys   1498
Feathered Shaft   227
Fed Facts Series   4
Federal Aircraft Noise Abatement Program   30
Federal and Indian Land   234
Federal and State Legislative Bulletins   254
Federal Benefits for Veterans and Dependents   33
Federal Consumer Focus   13
Federal Credit Unions   27
Federal Environmental Law   234
Federal Information Processing Standards Publications   5
Federal Land Banks   9
Federal Milk Order Statistics   2
Federal Power Commission - What It Is and What It Does   12
Federal Reserve System - Purposes and Functions   12
Federal Trade Commission Decisions   12
Federal Wage-Hour Laws: What's in Them for You?   26
Federation Reporter   184
Fees Charged by Foreign Countries for the Visa of United States Passports   29
Fertilizer Financial Facts   251

Publication Index

Fertilizer Index 251
Fertilizer Progress 251
FHA Homes 20
15 Years of Progress in Parkinsonism - 1957-1972 169
Fifty Homes for Birds 21
Figure Finaglers 1469
Finance Fact 258
Finance Facts Yearbook 258
Financial Facts About the Meat Packing Industry 244
Financial Forum 258
Financial Guide for the Self-Employed 1469
Financial Self-Defense 1469
Fire and Arson Investigator 184
Fire Command 187
Fire Department Instructors Conference Proceedings 185
Fire Journal 187
Fire Management 3
Fire Marshal's Association Directory 183
Fire Marshal's Bulletin 183
Fire News 187
Fire Protection Handbook 187
Fire Technology 187
Firewatch 186
Fireword 5
First Indictment of the Health Insurance Industry 92
First Line 4
First Offender 228
First Year 89
Fish Disease Leaflets 21
Fishery Bulletin 6
Fishery Information Bulletin 258
Fishing in the National Park System 22
Fishstrips 207
Fixing Up Your Home 19
Flammable Fabrics 17
Flight Safety Facts and Analysis 183
Flood-Prone Areas 22
Flood Insurance Studies 20
Floral Facts Booklets 264
FNS Handbooks 3
Food and Nutrition 3
Food and Nutrition News 260
Food and the Consumer 1470
Food Buying; Marketing Information for Consumers 1470
Food Chemical News 1492
Food Colors 1470
Food Co-op for Small Groups 1470
Food Co-op Handbook; How to Bypass Supermarkets to Control the Quality and Price of Your Food 1470
Food Co-ops; An Alternative to Shopping in Supermarkets 1470
Food Executive Magazine 251
Food Marketing Alert 2

For the People; A Consumer Action Handbook 1470
Foreign Languages and Your Career 25
Forest Industries Newsletter 259
Forest Resource Reports 1
Farming Consumer Organizations 1470
Forty Plus Club Newsletter 203
Forty-plus Ways to Cut Your Bill 94
Forum 129
FPC News 12
Frauds, Swindles, and Rackets; A Red Alert for Today's Consumers 1470
Freedom of Information Index 4
Fresh Forum 264
Friday Letter 165
Frontier Nursing Service Quarterly Bulletin 153
Frontiers in Adoption 201
Frontline 1492
FSLIC = Safety 11
FTC Buyer's Guides 1498
Full Circle Anthologies 203

G

Gam-Anews 203
Gas Data Book 243
Gas Facts 243
Gear 260
Gems in the Smithsonian Institution 29
General Information Concerning Patents 6
General Information Concerning Trademarks 6
Generations 163
Get Off (public service phonograph albums) 256
Getting the Most for Your Money; How to Beat the High Cost of Living 1471
Getting Your Share 1471
GFWC Clubwomen 204
Ghetto Marketplace 1471
Going Broke and How to Avoid It 1471
Good Neighbor 193
Government Affairs Report 250
Government Industry Relations Bulletin 258
Grassroots 177
Great American Food Hoax 1471
Grow It Safely! 155
Growin' Up Country 201
Growth Leaders on the Big Board 89
Guide Dog News 154
Guide for Airline Charters 4
Guide for the Responsible Consumer 1471
Guide Lines 154
Guide to Abortion Services in the Delaware Valley 148
Guide to Consumer Services; Consumers Union's Advice on Selected Financial and Professional Services 1471
Guide to Dental Materials and Devices 243

1611

Publication Index

Guide to Federal Consumer Services 15, 1454
Guide to Federal Power Commission Public Information 12
Guide to Films About Development 229
Guide to Neighborhood Ecology 123
Guide to Oak Floors 260
Guide to Personal Finance; A Lifetime Program of Money Management 1471
Guide to Shippers' Rights 4
Guide to Sources of Consumer Information 1454
Guide to Specifications and Standards of the Federal Government 13
Guide to Starting a Local Consumer Service Magazine 94
Guide to the U.S. Capitol 92
Guide to Traffic Safety Literature 188
Guidelines for Shippers 11
Guides of Profit Planning 28
Guides to Getting Things Done in the Visual Environment Series 123, 1498

H

Handbook for Automobile Maintenace 247
Handbook for the Home - 1973 Yearbook of Agriculture 1471
Handbook for the Informed Consumer 89
Handbook of Life Insurance 252
Handbook of Non-Prescription Drugs 142
Handbook of System and Product Safety 1471
Handling Your Money 1472
Hardwood Flooring Handbook 260
Hazard Prevention 190
HD Handbook for Health Professionals 149
Health: A Consumer's Dilemma 1472
Health Aspects of Pesticides Abstract Bulletin 8
Health Care Politics 198
Health Consequences of Smoking 17
Health Devices 152
Health Education Monography 176
Health Foods: Facts and Fakes 1472
Health Hucksters 1472
Health Information Series 1499
Health Insurance for the Aged 19
Health Insurance Racket and How to Beat It 92
Health Laboratory Science 142
Health Manpower Exchange 167
Health, Quackery & the Consumer 1472
Health Resources Studies 18
Health Robbers 1472
Healthways Advisor 141
Hearing and Speech Action 162
Heart Research Newsletter 140
Helicopter Safety Bulletin 183
Help: The Useful Almanac 1472
Hemodialysis for Transient Patient 163

Hemofax 167
Here's HOW 251
Heroin Supply and Urban Crime 152
HEW Consumer Information Series 1499
HGF Ink 156
Hidden Assassins 1472
Highlights 135
Highlights of Operations, FDIC 10
Highway Beauty Awards Competition 31
Highway Digest 263
Highway Focus 31
Highway Safety Literature 31
Highway Safety Literature Index 31
Highway Statistics 31
Highway Transportation 31
Highway User 184
Historic American Buildings Survey 22
Historical Handbook Series 22
Historical Vignettes 21
Hit & Run; The Rise - and Fall? - of Ralph Nader 1473
Home and Garden Bulletins 1, 1499
Home Buyer's Information Kit 19
Home Buyer's Guide 1473
Home Economics Research Abstracts 193
Home Economics Research Journal 193
Hope Through Research 179
Hot War on the Consumer 1473
Household Decision-Making 1473
Household Pest Control 155
Housekeeping Careers - A New Frontier 205
Housing and Planning References 19
Housing and Urban Development Trends 19
Housing Yearbook 216
HOW Consumer Information Booklet 251
How State and Local Governments May Purchase Surplus Property from the Federal Government 13
How They Do It, Illustrations of Practice in the Administration of AFDC 18
How to Address Mail 27
How to Avoid a Real Estate Agent 1473
How to Avoid Ponzi and Pyramid Schemes 28
How to Beat Inflation by Using It 1473
How to Buy a Used Car, 1967 1473
How to Buy a Used Car, 1975 1473
How to Buy at Auction 1473
How to Buy Furniture 1474
How to Buy Major Appliances 1474
How to Cut Losses from Flood and Water Damage 245
How to Deal With Motor Vehicle Emergencies 31
How to Fly 241
How to Get a Dollar's Value for a Dollar Spent 1474
How to Get More for Your Money in Running Your Home 1474
How to Get $100,000 Worth of Services Free, Each Year, from the U.S. Government 1474

Publication Index

How to Get Out of Debt and Stay Out of Debt 1474
How to Get 20 to 90% Off on Everything You Buy 1474
How to Hold Down Your Auto Insurance Premium Costs 245
How to Invest in Beautiful Things Without Being a Millionaire; How the Clever Consumer Can Outthink the Tastemakers 1474
How to Live Better on Less: A Guide for Waste Watchers 1475
How to Live Cheap But Good 1475
How to Live on Nothing 1475
How to Make the Most of Your Energy Dollars 10
How to Manage Your Money 1475
How to Paint Your Wood House 259
How to Pay Lots Less for Life Insurance...And Be Covered for as Much and as Long as You Want 1475
How to Reduce Your Medical Bills 1475
How to Save Money When You Buy and Drive Your Car 1475
How to Secure Help, A Guide to Social and Health Services in New York City 200
How to Set Up a Health Services Information Center 1475
How to Shake the Money Tree 1475
How to Start a Venereal Disease Hot-Line 172
How to Start Your Own Food Co-op (With a Little Help from Your Friends) 1476
How to Write a Job Description 28
How You Can Beat Inflation 1476
How Your Congressman Voted on Critical Environmental Issues 130
How Your Senator Voted on Critical Environmental Issues 130
HUD Challenge 19
HUD Newsletter 19
HUD Statistical Yearbook 19
Huff 'N Puff 139
Human Factors Bulletin 183
Human Relations in Small Business 28
Human Relations Tips and Trends 258
Hunting Regulations 21
Hurricanes 6

I

IAL News 157
Iditarod Gold Rush Trail, Seward-Nome 23
If It Doesn't Work, Read the Instructions 1476
If You Borrow to Buy Stock 12
IFSTA Proceedings 185
Illustrated Pamphlet Series 1499
Impact 182
Import Digest 241

In Common 1492
In Our Time 1476
In Productive Harmony 8
In the Bank...Or Up the Chimney 19, 1476
In the Marketplace; Consumerism in America 1476
Income Leaders on the Big Board 89
Independent Contractor in Direct Selling: A Guide to Formulating Company Policy 250
Index-Catalogue of Medical and Veterinary Zoology 2
Index of Patents 6
Index of Rheumatology 143, 144
Index of Trademarks 6
Index to Dental Literature 243
Indian Affairs Newsletter 195
Indian Land Areas 22
Indian Truth 205
Indians, Eskimos, and Aleuts of Alaska 22
Indians of Arizona 22
Indians of the Dakotas 22
Indians of the Great Lakes 22
Indians of the Gulf Coast 22
Industrial Hygiene Digest 156
Inequality in Education 232
Information and Travel Tips 29
Information for Everyday Survival; What You Need and Where to Find It 1454
Information Seekers; An International Study of Consumer Information and Advertising Image 1476
Infusion 141
Innocent Consumer vs. the Exploiters 1476
Inside News from CTFA 249
Inside NIB 168
Insider 133
Instant Exchange 121
Intelligent Buyer and the Telltale Seller 1477
Intelligent Consumer 1477
Intelligent Consumer; How Not to Be a "Connedsumer" 1477
InterACTION 1
Interchange 213
Interest Rates and Terms on Conventional Home Mortgages 11
Inter-Faith Task Force 206
Internal Revenue Bulletin 32
International Apparel Digest 241
International Coal Trade 23
International Directory of Genetic Services 166
International Directory of Neurotics Anonymous Groups 170
International Mail 27
International, Northern California, Southern California, Meeting Directories (Overeaters Anonymous) 172
International Notices to Airmen 30
International Petroleum Annual 23
International Stroke Club Bulletin 176

Publication Index

Introduction to the Federal Incentive Awards Program 4
Inventory of Revironmental Improvement Programs in the United States 130
Investigate Before You Invest 28
Investigation of Ralph Nader; General Motors vs. One Determined Man 1477
Investigations in Fish Control 21
Investor's Guide to Farm Credit Securities 9
Investors Service Bureau Directory 89
Is Your Drinking Water Safe? 8

J

JOB Aids 208
Job Discrimination Handbook 205
Job Health Hazards Series 26
Job Safety and Health 26
Jobs for Veterans Report 210
Joint Action in Community Service Volunteer 1492
Journal of ADA 139
Journal of American Insurance 245
Journal of Big Brothers Practice 195
Journal of Consumer Affairs 1493
Journal of Consumer Credit Management 253
Journal of Dental Research 243
Journal of Emergency Nursing 152
Journal of Endodontics 242
Journal of Environmental Health 165
Journal of Environmental Quality 1493
Journal of Forensic Sciences 246
Journal of Home Economics 193, 1493
Journal of Housing 211
Journal of Insurance Information 252
Journal of Mental Health 170
Journal of Milk and Food Technology 253
Journal of Nutrition Education 175
Journal of Oral Surgery 242
Journal of Pharmaceutical Sciences 142
Journal of Products Liability 1493
Journal of Property Management 257
Journal of Psychedelic Drugs 177
Journal of Quality Technology 245
Journal of Research 22
Journal of Safety Research 188
Journal of Soil and Water Conservation 135
Journal of Testing and Evaluation 246
Journal of the ADA 242
Journal of the Air Pollution Control Association 121
Journal of the AMA 141
Journal of the American Pharmaceutical Association 142
Journal of the AOA 141
Journal of the FHLBB 11
Journal of WPFC 135

Judicature 231

K

Keeping up With CALM 199
Key 136, 210
Kidney 168
Know HOW 251
Know Your Merchandise 1477
Koldfax 240
Konsum 86, 1493

L

Labor Law Series 26
Labor-Management Alcoholism Newsletter 165
Lamp 147
Land Planning Bulletin 20
Land Use Planning Abstracts 127
Law and the Consumer 1477
Law Enforcement Legal Defense Manual 232
Law Enforcement Legal Liability Reporter 232
Laws and Rules You Should Know 9
Lawsuits Without Lawyers 1477
League - Letter 210
Learning Opportunities for Schools 29
Leasing and Management of Energy Resources on the Outer Continental Shelf 23
Legal Analysis of the National Environmental Policy Act 234
Legal Protection for the Consumer 1477
Legislative 200
Legislative Alert Bulletin 258
Legislative Handbook for Direct Sellers 250
Legislative Lookout 1493
Legislative Newsletter 81
Legislative Review 234
Let the Seller Beware 1477
Let's Dump the Dump 8
Let's Talk 143
Let's Talk About Money 252
Levels of Care Facilities in Massachusetts 229
Library of Congress Information Bulletin 27
Library of Congress Publications in Print 27
Life and Health (Braille and Recorded) 148, 1493
Life Association News 256
Life Insurance Fact Book 252
Life Lines 240
Lifeline 172
Lifeline Bulletin 204
Lifestyle Index 83
Light Lists 30

Publication Index

Lion Magazine 208
List of Available Publications of the U.S. Department of Agriculture 1
List of Directories of Minority Business 206
List of FSLIC-Insured Member S & LA's 11
List of Treasury Publications 32
List of Worthwhile Life and Health Insurance Books 252
Listen 161
Listing: Food Service Equipment 169
Listing: Plastics for Potable Water & Drain, Waste & Vent 169
Listing: Swimming Pool Equipment 169
Litter Bits of News and Facts 125
Little City Lifeline 159
Living on Less and Liking It More 1477
Living With Renal Failure 163
Local Minority Business Directory 216
Log 219
Look You Like 141
Looking into Volunteering 211
Lost or Damaged Household Goods 24

M

MACAP Report to Consumers 89
Mail Fraud Laws Protecting: Consumers, Investors, Businessmen, Patients, Students 1477
Mail Order USA: A Consumer's Guide to over 1,500 Top Mail Order Catalogs in the United States and Canada 1454
Mailing Permits 27
Make the Most of Your Income 1478
Making It; The Encyclopedia of How to Do It for Less 1478
Man and Food 1478
Manage Your Money and Live Better; Get the Most from Your Dwindling Dollars 1478
Mandate 145
Manifest 254
Manpower Research and Development Projects 25
Manual for Lemon Owners 182
Manual for the Organization and Management of a Neighborhood Recycling Program 127
Manual of Classification 6
Manual of Death Education and Simple Burial 249
Maritime Safety Digest 26
Marketing Facts 2
Mass Merchandisers' Guide to Sales and Expense Reporting 254
Mass Retailers' Merchandising Report 254
MD News 160
Meat and Poultry Inspection Regulations 2
Meat Production Report 244
Medical and Dental X-rays: A Consumer's Guide to Avoiding Unnecessary Radiation Exposure 155

Medical Messiahs 1478
Medical News Report 168
Medical Socio-economic Research Resources 141
Medicine Show; Consumers Union's Practical Guide to Some Everyday Health Problems and Health Products 1478
Member Societies of the Continental Association 249
Mental Health Legislative Guide 235
Mental Health Services for the Vulnerable Child 138
Mental Hygiene 162
Mental Retardation News 162
Merchant and the Poor: A Selected Bibliography 1454
Merchant Vessels of United States 30
Messages from Heads of State 200
MHLP Summary of Activities 235
Michigan Water Cry Bulletin 130
Mind Your Money 1499
Mineral Trade Notes 23
Minerals and Materials, A Monthly Survey 23
Minerals Yearbook 23
Mobile Homes, The Low-Cost Housing Hoax 182, 1478
Model of Consumer Action Series 1499
Modern Concepts of Cardiovascular Disease 140
Modern Maturity 193, 1493
Monday Morning Hotline 255
Money Management Series 1499
Money Manager 252
Moneysworth 1494
Monitor 197
Monopoly Makers; Ralph Nader's Study Group Report on Regulation and Competition 1479
Monthly Catalog of U.S. Government Publications 15
Monthly Labor Review 25
Monthly News of Co-op Communities 92
Morbidity and Mortality Weekly Report 17
More Equality 198
Mother to Mother 161
Motor Vehicle Safety Defect Recall Campaigns 31
Motorcycles: A Buyer's and Rider's Guide 1478
Mountain Life and Work 201
Movers Journal 244
Moving: A Commonsense Guide to Relocating Your Family 1479
Moving Ahead With Group Action; The Buying Club 1479
MS Briefs 168
MS Messenger 168
MS Patient Service Newsletter 168
Musings on Money; How to Make Dollars Out of Sen$e 1479
Mutual Savings Reporter 249
Myopia News 158

Publication Index

N

NAHB Journal-Scope 256
NAHB's Scope on HOW 251
Narcotics and Youth 166
NAREB Report 257
National Adoptalk 214
National Audiovisual Center Services to the Public 14
National Cartographic Information Center Newsletter 22
National Consumers League Bulletin 1494
National Directory of Child Abuse Services and Information 212
National Directory of Educational Programs in Gerontology 15
National Directory of Services and Programs for Autistic Children 170
National Fire Codes 187
National Golfer 227
National Highway Institute Bulletins 31
National Hookup 156
National Institute of Industrial Gerontology Journal 215
National Lakeshore 22
National Mail Order Catalog Directory 1454
National Methadone Treatment Conference Proceedings 162
National Park Guide for the Handicapped 22
National Parks 22
National Pharmaceutical News 262
National REACTer 189
National Recreation Areas 22
National Rivers 22
National Roster of Realtors 257
National Safety News 188
National Scenic and Recreational Trails 23
National Scenic Trails 22
National Seashores 22
National Spokesman 153
National Transportation Reports 30
National Yokefellow Prison Ministry Directory 217
National Yokefellow Prison Ministry Journal 217
National Zip Code Directory 27
Nation's Business 84
Nation's Health 142
Native American Arts Series 21
Natural History Series 22
Natural Hygiene Educator 141
Natural Hygienews 141
NBS Bibliographic Subscription Services 5
NBS Consumer Information Series 5, 1500
NBS Interagency Reports 5
NBS Journal of Research - Mathematical Sciences 5
NBS Journal of Research - Physics and Chemistry 5
NCFA Office Manual 258
NCUA Publications List 27
NCUA Quarterly 27
Needed: Clean Air 8
Needed: Clean Water 8
Negro in the Field of Business 206
NEISS News 7
NEPA in the Courts 234
Network 204
New Consumerism: Selected Readings 1479
New Directions in Bike Safety 248
New Handbook of Prescription Drugs: Official Names, Prices, and Sources for Patient and Doctor 1479
New Harbinger: A Journal of the Cooperative Movement 92
New Hazards for Firefighters, Vinyl Chloride, Mercury, Carbon Monoxide, Carcinogens, and Lead 26
New Outlook for the Blind 140
New Physician 141
New York Mattachine Times 209
News and Features from NIH 18
News and Views 86, 138
News Briefs 89
News from TCA 264
News from the Home Front 147
Newsletter on American Indians 203
Newsletter on Colombia 203
NFS News 215
N.H.F. Bulletin 167
NHFA Reports 259
NIH Almanac 18
1977 Gas Mileage Guide 10
1977 Gas Mileage Guide for New Car Buyers 8
1973-1974 Bibliography on the Appalachian South 201
NISC Memo 215
No Smoking - Lungs at Work 141
NOAA Publications Announcements 6
NOAA Quarterly 6
NOAA Story 6
NOAA, The Marine Environment and Oceanic Life 6
Noise and You 8
Noise at Work 8
Noise on Wheels 8
North American Fauna Series 21
Nosiery Newsletter 256
Not Man Apart 129, 1494
Noticiero (in Spanish) 89
Nutrition Action 83, 1494
Nutrition News 258
Nutrition Notes 264
Nutrition Program News 2
Nutrition Scorecard: Your Guide to Better Eating 1479
Nutrition Today 171, 1494

Publication Index

O

Occupational Cancer 26
Occupational Outlook Quarterly 25, 1494
Oceanographic Reports 30
October Handbook of Buying Issue 86
Odyssey Newsletter 172
Of Strip Mining Laws 83
Off-Road Vehicle Use on Federal Lands 23
Official Directory of Optimist International 219
Official Gazette - Patents 6
Official Gazette - Trademarks 6
Older Worker Specialist 215
On Scene 30
One and Two Family Dwelling Code 248
Open Reality; The Way Out of Mimicking Happiness 1479
Operating Results of Self-Service Discount Department Stores 254
Operation ADEPT: Apartment Dwellers Emergency Preparedness Training 245
Operation EDITH: Exit Drills in the Home 245
Ophthalmologists 138
Opinions of Attorney General 24
Opportunities Abroad for Teachers 17
Optimist Magazine 219
Oral Research Abstracts 243
Organizing a Federal Credit Union 27
Organizing a Minority Trade Association 206
Organizing for Health Care: A Tool for Change 1480
Orphan Voyage 219
Ostomy Quarterly 179
Ostomy Review 179
OT Bulletins 5
OT Reports 5
OT Special Publications 5
Our Endangered World 8
Our Public Lands 23
Our Special (all in Braille) 164
Outcry 157
Outdoor America 130
Outdoor Recreation Action 23
Outlook 264
Outlook Newswire 264
Ozanam News 224

P

Paper Nutrition 89
Partners in Progress 13
Patents and Inventions - An Information Aid for Inventors 6
Patterns for Progress in Aging 15
Paying Through the Ear: A Report on Hearing Health Care Problems 1480
PBGB Fact Sheets 27
Peace Corps Bibliographies on Africa, Latin America, East Asia & Pacific 1
Peace Corps Handbook 1
Peace Corps Partnership Program 1
Pen-Point Magazine 198
People & Energy 83, 1494
People & Taxes 94
People on the Farm Series 1
People Power for Auto Owners 82
People's Yellow Pages 1454
People's Yellow Pages of America 1454
Personal Economics 1480
Personal Finance and Consumer Economics 1480
Personal Money Management 1480
Personal Selling Today 250
Perspective on Aging 215
Pesticide Compendium 122
Pesticides Monitoring Journal 8
Petroleum Products Surveys 23
Pfeiffer Garden Book 146
Pharmaceutical Directory 142
Physicians' Pamphlet 149
PIA/Checkout in Plane and Pilot Magazine 262
Pilot Log 220
Pilots Safety Exchange 183
Plain Talk About Your Life Insurance Policy 252
Planning for Retirement 252
Plant Disease Reporter 2
Plant Inventory 2
Plea 235
Plot to Make You Buy 1480
Poison Control Statistics 17
Policyholders' Guidebook of Health Insurance Buying and Collecting 92
Politics of Consumer Protection 1480
Pollution Abstracts 1455
Pollution and Your Health 8
Pollution Control in Marine Industries 129
Poor Pay More; Consumer Practices of Low-Income Families 1480
Popular Publications for the Farmer, Suburbanite, Homemaker, Consumer 1
Popular Publications of the United States Geological Survey 22
Population, Environment, and People (1971) 125
Postal Laws 27
Postal Life 27
Pot Luck in Texas: Changing a Marijuana Law, Drugs and Youth 152
Potentially Hazardous Materials 241
Power Unlimited 126
PR News 255
Practical Driving Tips 246
Pre-Employment Inquiries 9
Preliminary Determination of Epicenters 22

Publication Index

Premium Payer Be Damned   92
President's Committee on Consumer Interests and Office of Consumer Affairs: 1969-1977   15
Pretenders to the Throne   1480
Preventing Embezzlement   28
Prevention of Acquired Myopia   158
Preventive Medicine   140
Price Lists   15
Primer on Rheumatic Diseases   143
Primer on Wastewater Treatment   8
Prism   141
Private Assistance in Outdoor Recreation   23
Product Performance and Servicing; An Examination of Consumer Problems and Business Responses   1481
Product Quality, Performance, and Cost   1481
Product Safety in Household Goods   1481
Production Credit Associations   9
Professional Safety   181
Program Aids   1500
Program for Americans   81
Progressive Transmitter   256
Proposal for 1977: A National Foundation for Consumer Education   15
Proposals for Legislative Reforms Aiding the Consumer of Funeral Industry Products and Services   249
Protecting Consumer Interests; Private Initiative and Public Response   1481
Protecting Your Housing Investment   1481
Proudly We Hail: Profiles of Public Citizens in Action   1481
Psychology and Consumer Affairs   1481
Psychology Newsletter   204
Public Advisory Series   1500
Public Affairs Pamphlets   1500
Public Citizen's Action Manual   1481
Public Defender Service   238
Public Health Reports   18
Public Interest   1494
Public Relations Tips   211
Public Roads   31
Public Service Advertising Bulletin   240
Publications in Archeology Series   22
Publications of the Archives and Records Service   13

Q

Quarterly Journal of Library of Congress   27
Quarterly Merchandising Performance Record   254
Quarterly Review of Airline Traffic and Financial Data   241
Questions and Answers About Nuclear Power Plants   8

R

Radiation Data and Reports   8
Radiation Research   133
Radical Consumer's Handbook   1482
Radio Station and Other Lists   10
Rating the Diets   1482
Rational Living   157
R&D Monographs   25
REACT Team Directory   189
Real Estate Today   257
Real Great Society Newsletter   221
Realtist Flyer   257
Realtist Magazine   257
Realtor Headlines   257
Reclaiming Surface-Mined Lands for Outdoor Recreation   23
Recovery Reporter   173
Reducing Shoplifting Losses   28
Reference Information Catalog   8
Reference Guide for Consumers   1455
Refuge Leaflets   21
Register of Federal Employee Unions   26
Regulated Consumer   1482
Rehabilitation Literature   165
Rekindle   185
Report from Washington   84
Report UMTA Series   31
Reports and Resolutions of the First National Congress Optimum Population   125
Reported Tuberculosis Data   17
Rescue Herald   194
Research Grants Index   18
Research Relating to Children Bulletins   17
Resource and News Bulletin   148
Resource Directory of Selected Consumer Education Materials for Grades K-8   1455
Resource Recovery and You   8
Resources for Health R&D Reports   18
Responsibility   211
Retail Prices and Indexes   25
Retarded Infants Services News   174
Retirement Living   1494
Review of Black Political Economy   195
Revocation of Acceptance and the Auto Consumer   82
Rheumatism Review   143
Rhyme, Reason and Responsibility   205
Right to Read   17
River Basins of United States   22
River Currents   30
Roadrunner   152
Roots   126
Rubber Highlights   263
Rubicon Current   174

Publication Index

Rural Advance   216
Rural Housing   216

S

Safe Pesticides Use Around the Home   8
Safe Work Practices Series   26
Safety and Special Radio Services   10
Safety in Mineral Industries   23
Safety in the Marketplace; A Program for the Improvement of Consumer Product Safety   1482
Safety Standards for Small Craft   242
Sales Planning Guide for Manufacturers   256
Sane World   222
Save Gas and Save Money   247
Save Your Health and Your Money: A Doctor's Answers to Today's High Health Costs   1482
Savings and Home Financing Source Book   11
Savings and Loan Fact Book   265
Savings and Loan News   265
SBA Economic Review   28
Scientific Directory and Annual Bibliography   18
Scientific Monograph Series   22, 155
Screwing of the Average Man   1482
SEC Docket   28
Seeing Eye Guide   175
Selected and Annotated Bibliography of Reference Material in Consumer Credit   1455
Selected Bibliography for Arson Investigators   184
Selected Guide to Make-It, Fix-It, Do-It-Yourself Books   1455
Selected Industry Profiles for Minority Business Opportunity   206
Selected U.S. Government Publications   15, 1455
Senior Advocate   223
Senior Citizens News   214
Senior Citizens Reporter   204
ene With Dollars   1482
Series for Economic Education   1500
Service Shop   259
Service Society and the Consumer Vanguard   1482
Service, USDA's Report to Consumers   1
Services to AFDC Families   19
Settlement Costs: A HUD Guide   21
Shop Notes   247
Shopper's Guide   1483
Shopper's Guide to Lawyers   1483
Shopper's Guidebook to Life Insurance, Health Insurance, Auto Insurance, Homeowner's Insurance, Doctors, Dentists, Lawyers, Pensions, etc.   1483
Sight-Saving Review   170, 1494
Signs and Your Business   28
Sky Ranch Log   224
Small Business Administration Publications List   28
Small Business Bibliographies   28

Small on Safety: The Designed-In Dangers of the Volkswagen   182
Smart Shopper's Guide   1483
Smithsonian Collection of Automobiles and Motorcycles   29
Smithsonian Magazine   29
Smithsonian Research Reports   29
Smithsonian Year   29
Smog, Health, and You   8
Smog Kills, Industrial Air Pollution in Los Angeles   133
Smoke Signals   161
Smoking and Health Bulletins   17
Smoking and Health Newsletter   168
So You Want to Buy a House   1483
So You Want to Buy a Mobile Home   1483
So You'd Like to Adopt a Wild Horse   23
Social Action   221
Social Issues of Marketing in the American Economy   1483
Social Psychiatry Newsletter   175
Social Security Bulletin   19
Social Thought   212
Soldiers   7
S.O.S. - Save on Shopping! Shopper Recommended Good Buys for 1975
Source Book of Health Insurance Data   154
Source Catalog: Communications   1455
Source Catalog: Communities/Housing   1456
Southern Cooperator   88
Sowing the Wind; A Report from Ralph Nader's Center for Study of Responsive Law on Food Safety and the Chemical Harvest   1483
Space Environmental Vantage Point   6
Spark   200
Sparky News   187
Speaking of Everything - About Health and Welfare   201
SPEED: The Current Index to Drug Abuse Literature   177
Spenders   1484
Sport Fishery Abstract   21
Sport Fishery and Wildlife Research   21
Sport Fishing U.S.A.   21
Sportmanlike Driving   241
Squeaky Wheel   169
Standard Action   245
Standardization News   246
Standards and Recommended Practices   242
Standards Manual for Rehabilitation Facilities   149
Standards of Emergency Nursing Practice   152
Starting and Managing Series   28
STASH Capsules   177
States and Their Indian Citizens   22
Statutes and Court Decisions   12
Strategy for Personal Finance   1484
Street Drug Survival   151
Stroke - A Journal of Cerebral Circulation   140
Stroke Memo   176

Publication Index

Student (Braille and Recorded) 148
Students Speak on Drugs 152
Study in Neglect: A Report on Women Prisoners 229
Study of the Climate for Learning from Media 254
Subscription TV 10
Summary of Accidents Reported by Railroad Companies 31
Summary of Benefits for Veterans With Military Service Before February 1, 1955 and Their Dependents 33
Summary of Information for Shippers of Household Goods 24
Summary of Savings Accounts, FSLIC-Insured S & LA's 11
Summer in the City 203
Super Discount Shopping Guide 93
Super Threats; How to Sound Like a Lawyer & Get Your Rights on Your Own 1484
Superior Polluter 132
Supermarket Counter Power 1484
Supermarket Handbook: Access to Whole Foods 1484
Supermarket Trap; The Consumer and the Food Industry 1484
Supershopper; A Guide to Spending and Saving 1484
Sylvia Porter's Money Book; How to Earn It, Spend It, Save It, Invest It, Borrow It - and Use It to Better Your Life 1484

T

Take Care of Yourself; A Consumer's Guide to Medical Care 1484
Taking Charge, A New Look at Public Power 128
Taking the Pain Out of Finding a Good Dentist 155
Tax Guide for Small Business 32
Tax Politics 94
Teaching Guide to Listen Magazine 161
Teaching Tools for Consumer Reports 86
Techni-Tips 259
Technical Assistance Aids 25
Technical Assistance Bulletin 23
Technical Fact Sheets 1500
Technical Notes 5
Technometrics 245
Telecommunications Research Series 5
Telephone Pioneer 225
Telephone Tips 94
Telescope 152
Television Safety Tips 250
Tempest 186
10 Commandments of Safe Driving 181

Ten Questions to Ask Before You Buy Stocks 89
Tenants Outlook 217
Tenth Worst Killer Journal 174
Terra Abstract Bulletin 135
TERRA Geographic 126
Textile Chemist and Colorist 241
This is WICS 228
This is Your Federation 202
Through the Mental Health Maze: A Consumer's Guide to Finding a Psychotherapist 155
Thumb on the Scale; Or the Supermarket Shell Game 1485
Thursday's People on the Move 205
Tips for Energy Savers 10
Tire Science and Technology 246
Today's Health 141
    Changed to Family Health
TOPS News 178
Tornadoes 6
Toward Cleaner Water 8
Toy Buying Guide 92
Trade Directory 250
Trade Names Dictionary 1456
Trade Practice Rules 12
Trade Regulations Rules 12
Trademark Bulletin 249
Trademarks Listed With PMA 262
Traffic Facts 182
Traffic Safety 188
Training Household Technicians 205
Transplant Kidneys Don't Bury Them 163
Transport Topics 246
Transportation USA 30
Treasury Bulletins 32
Trends in Housing 212
Trends in Pollution Control 127
Trust Assets of Insured Commercial Banks 10
Twelve Steps and Twelve Traditions 137
Two Decades of Cooperative Development 89
200,000,000 Guinea Pigs; New Dangers in Everyday Foods, Drugs, and Cosmetics 1485

U

UCP Crusader 179
Unemployment Insurance 25
United Spudlight 264
U.S. Consumer 1494
    Changed to Con$umer New$weekly
U.S. Currency 12
United States Department of Justice Legal Activities 24
U.S. Journal of Drug and Alcohol Dependence 1494
Update 141

Publication Index

Urban Ecology Series 22
Used Car Game: A Sociology of the Bargain 1485
Utility Conservation Now (UCAN) 10

V

Vega Engine Failures 82
Veterans Education Newsletter 33
Veterans' Reemployment Rights Handbook 26
Veterans' Voices 156
Vincenpaul 224
VIP Examiner 228
Vocational Education Information Series 17
Vocational Training in New York City...Where to Find It 228
Voice for Children 1494
Volta Review 137
Voluntary Action Leadership 211
Voluntary Action News 211
Voluntary Product Standards 5
Volunteer 196, 208, 228
Volunteer Professional: What You Need to Know 196
Volunteers in ACTION 1
Vulnerable Americans 1485

W

Wake Up - Smoke Detectors Can Save Your Life 5
Wanted: Senior Volunteers 211
War Cry 222
Warpath 226
Warranties and the Consumer 89
Washington/A Cooperative Slant 86
Washington Consumers' Checkbook 94, 1494
Washington Ecotactics Guide 135
Washington Information Directory 1456
Washington Memo 237
Washington Notes 265
Washington Report 84, 192, 257
Washington Sounds 162
Waste Makers 1485
Water in the News 263
Water & Land Resource Accomplishments 24
Water Resources Investigations 22
Water Resources Research Catalog 21
We Bear This Cross 169
We Want You to Know About... 1501
Weights and Measures and the Consumer; Third National Survey of State Weights and Measures Legislation, Administration, and Enforcement 1485

Welfare Fighter 217
What Is a Day's Work 205
What To Do With Your Bad Car: An Action Manual for Lemon Owners 1485
What Truth in Lending Means to You 12
What We Eat Today; The Food Manipulators vs. the People 1485
What You Should Know Before You Buy a Car 1486
What You Should Know Before You Have Your Car Repaired 1486
What's Ecology? 126
What's What in Safety 190
Wheelhorse Newsletter 256
When Injured at Work 26
Where There's Smoke 139
Where to Find Certified Mechanics for Your Car 260
Whistle Blowing; The Report of the Conference on Professional Responsibility 1486
Who Put the Con in Consumer? 1486
Whole Truth About Economy Driving 1486
Whole Washington Handbook; Where to Go and What to Know in the Metropolitan Area 1456
Wholesale Prices and Price Indexes 25
Who's Who 240
Who's Who in Consumer Credit 253
Who's Who in Electronics Service 259
Wild and Scenic Rivers 23
Wildfire Statistics 3
Wildlife Leaflets 21
Wildlife Portrait Series 21
Wildlife Review 21
Winner 161
Winning at the Occupational Safety and Health Review Commission 155
Winter Activities in the National Park System 22
Winter Fire Safety Tips for the Home 5
Wise Home Buying 19, 1486
Wise Owl News 170
Women's Equity Action League Washington Report 1494
Word from Washington 179
Work of the Securities and Exchange Commission 28
Working for the U.S.A. 4
Worklife Magazine 25
World Directory Al-Anon Family Groups and Alateens 137
World Traveler 137

Y

Yearbook of American and Canadian Churches 91
Yellow-Book Road: The Failure of America's Roadside Safety Program 182
Yes 240

You and Your Money   1486
You and Your Passport   29
You Are a Consumer – of Clothing   1486
Young Soldier   222
Your Federal Income Tax   32
Your Home Furnishings Dollar   1487
Your Housing Investment   19
Your Insured Deposit   10
Your Insured Funds   27
Your Market   250
Youth Activities Newsletter   191
Youth Happiness (Braille and Large Print)   148

Z

Zoogoer   29

R 343.706 C758
Consumer sourcebook : a direct

0 1901 0065001 8
Carson Library, Lees-McRae College